Italian Art

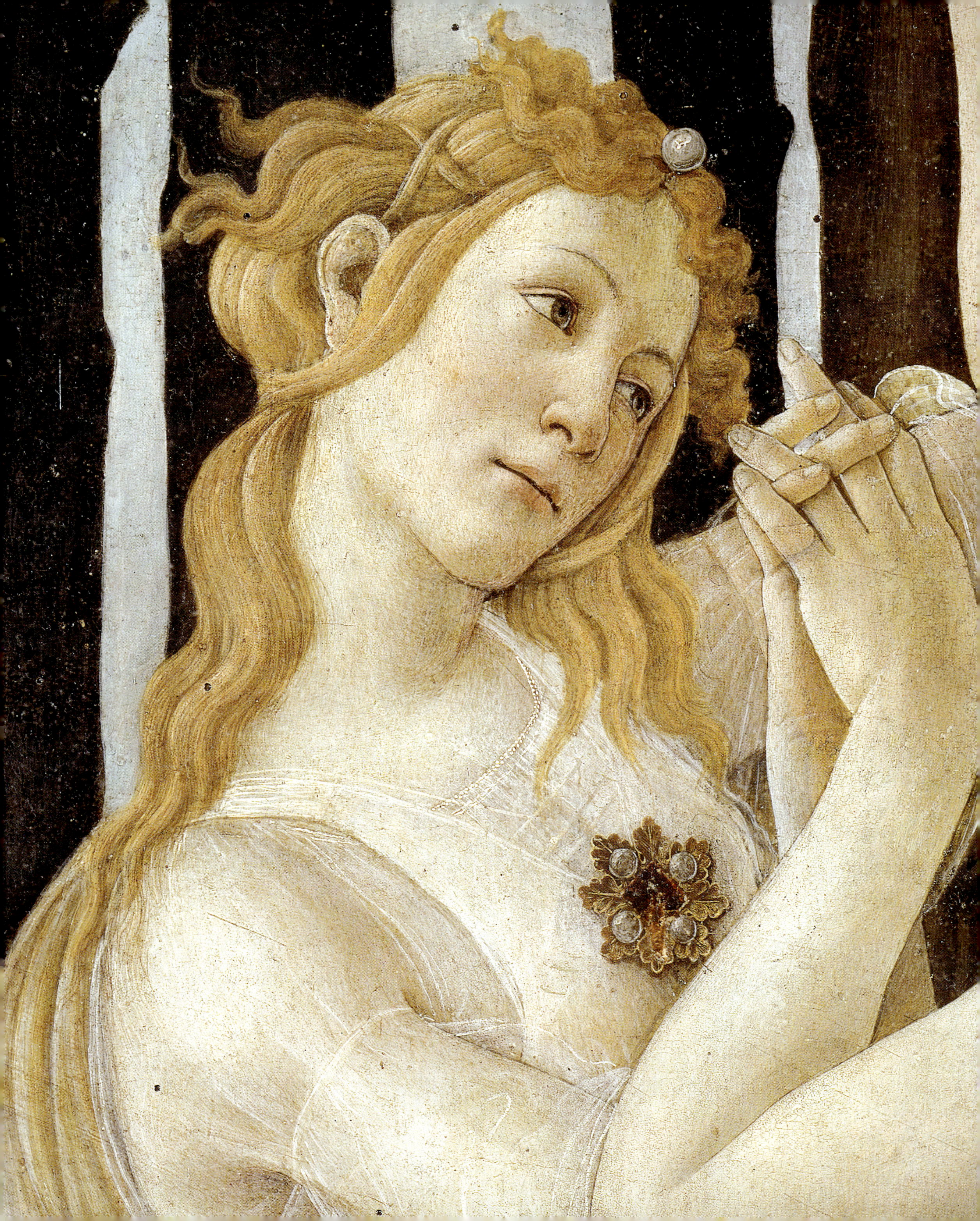

Italian Art

Painting, Sculpture, Architecture
from the Origins to the Present Day

Edited by GLORIA FOSSI

Texts by
Mattia Reiche
Gloria Fossi
Marco Bussagli

GIUNTI

Texts by:
Gloria Fossi (The Middle Ages and the XV Century)
Marco Bussagli (The XVI and XVII Centuries)
Mattia Reiche (The XVIII, XIX and XX Centuries)

Translation:
Catherine Frost (Texts)
Jeremy Carden for Lexis, Florence (Glossary and chronological tables)

Graphic design: Franco Bulletti

Special thanks for his precious advice to Michele Dantini.
We also would like to thank for their kind cooperation: Enrico Albisetti, Giovanni Bartoli, Rolando Bussi, Stefania Canta - Renzo Piano Building Workshop (Genoa), Maurizia Cicconi, Massimo Listri, Gianfranco Malafarina, Maddalena Torricelli.

www.giunti.it

Reprint	Year
6 5 4 3 2 1 0	2009 2008 2007 2006

Printed by Giunti Industrie Grafiche S.p.A. – Prato

Contents

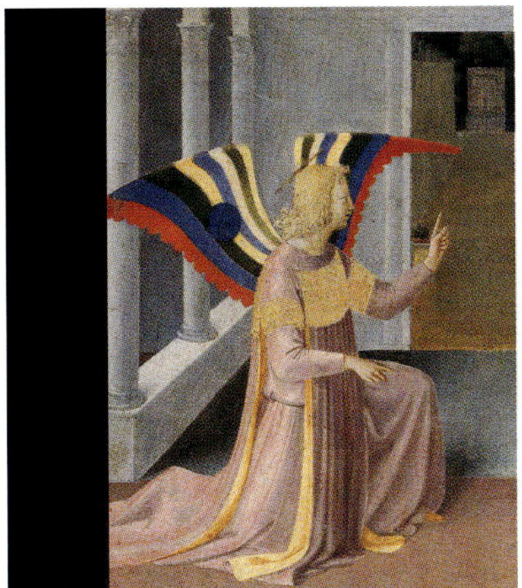

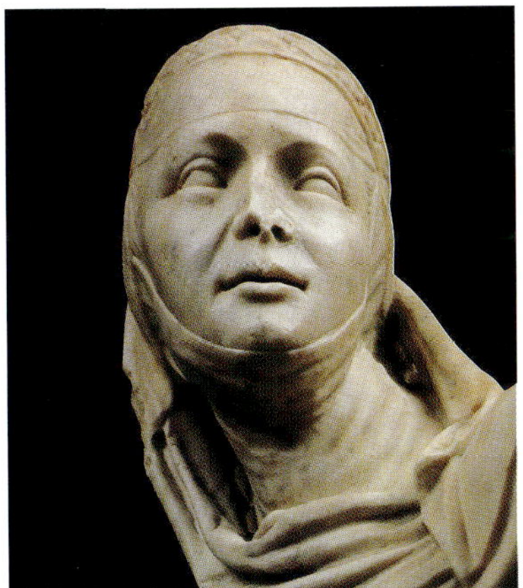

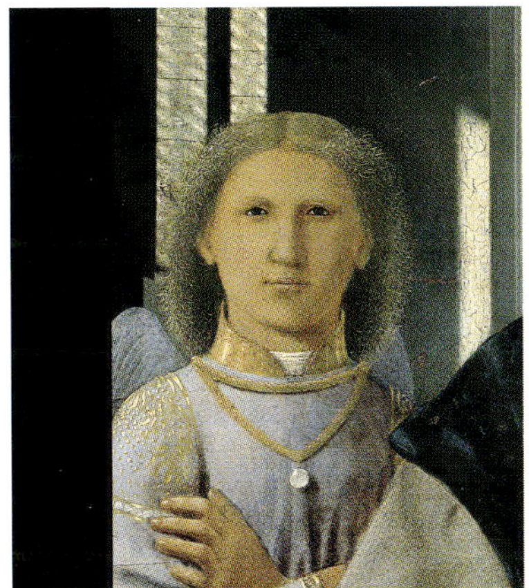

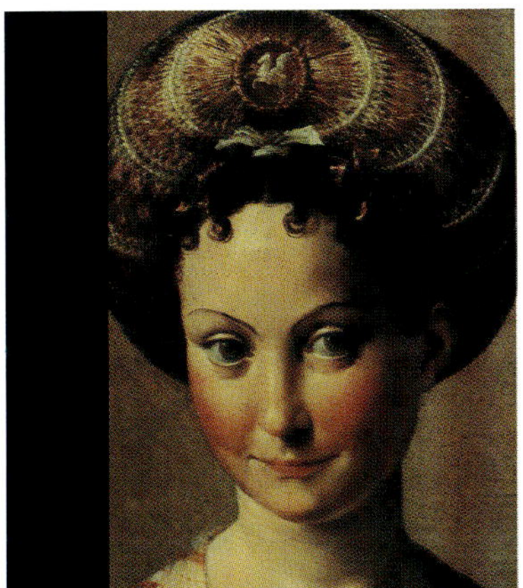

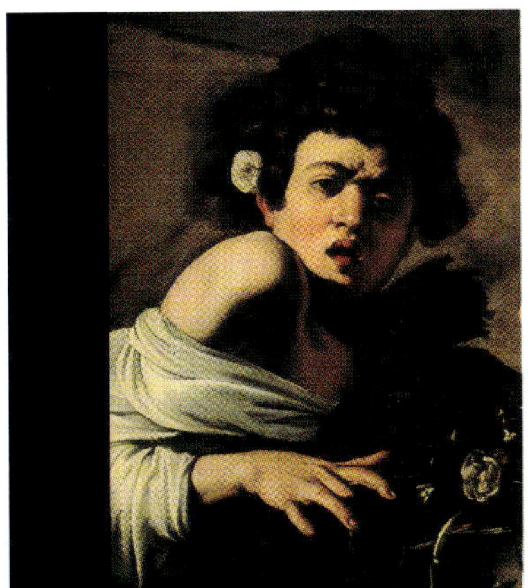

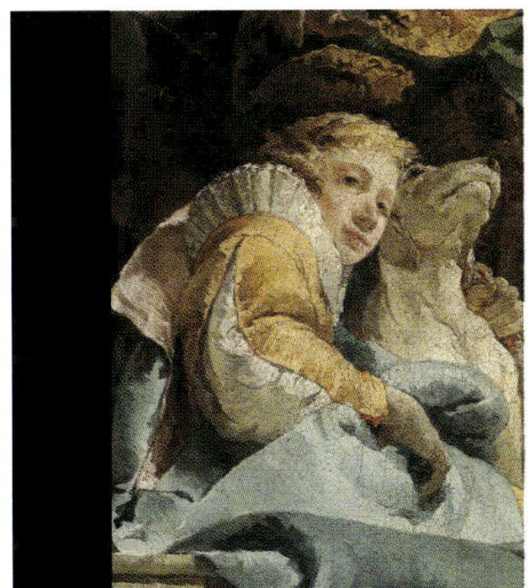

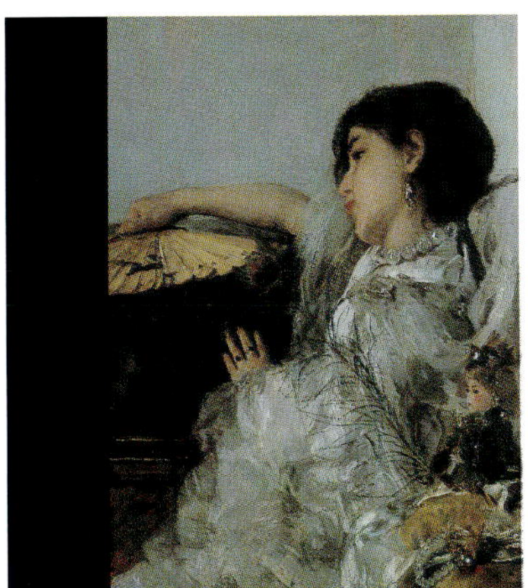

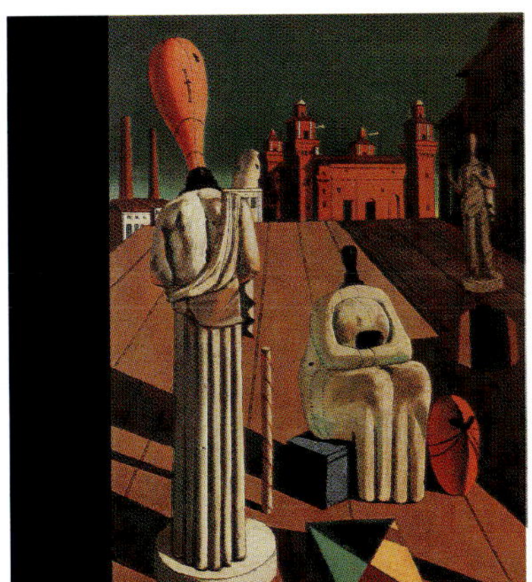

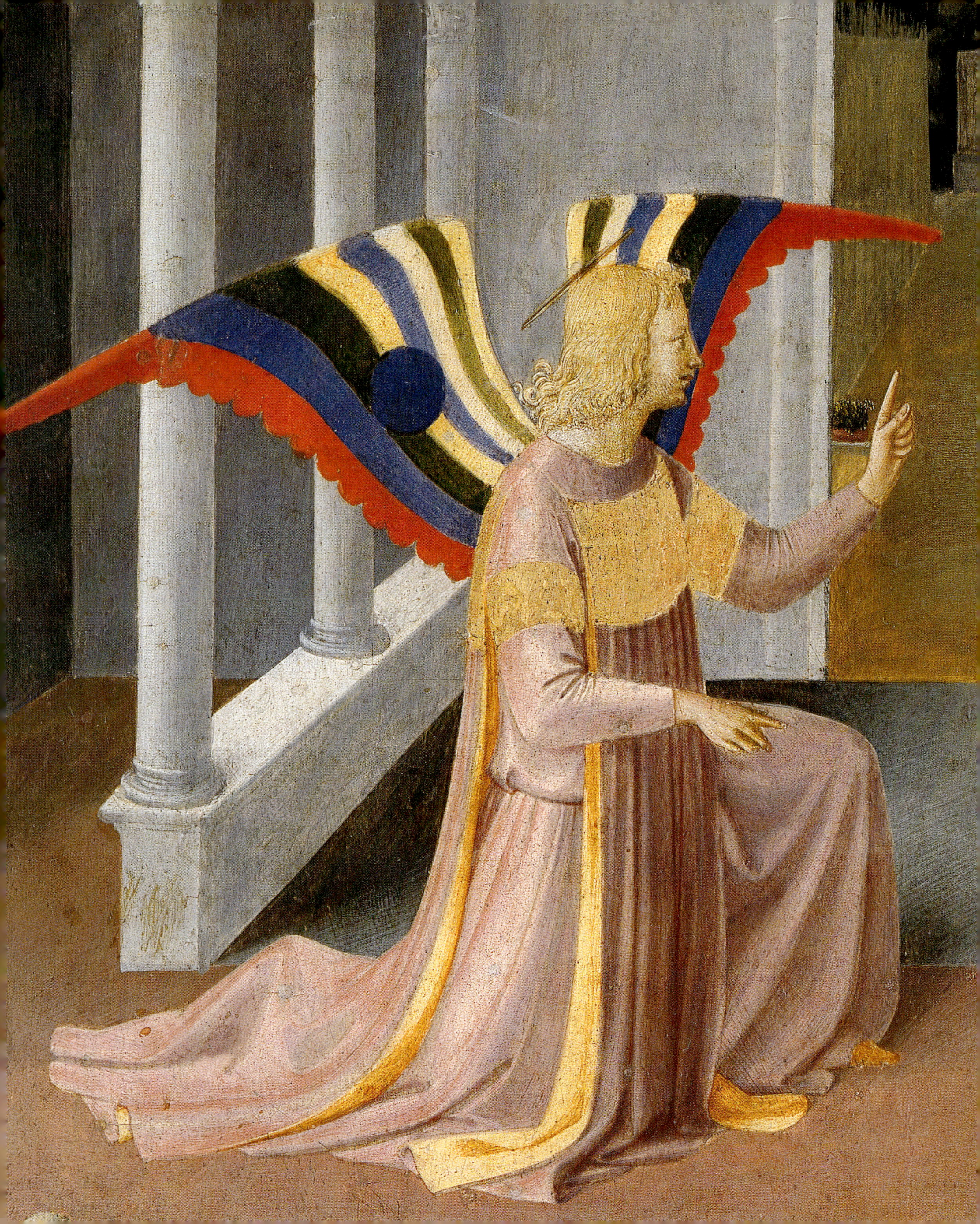

There really is no such thing as Art.
There are only artists.
ERNST H. GOMBRICH

THIS BOOK has been created with the aim of illustrating and describing Italian art to a vast public, we hope as vast as possible: illustrating it, primarily, with a good repertoire of images and describing it with simplicity and authority, but also from a particular approach, which will be apparent from the very first pages. It is neither a manual nor a compendium, since works of this kind, some of them inimitable, have existed already for years. Nor could it be called a dictionary, since it makes no claim to completeness, due to the inevitably limited number of pages for the many artists and the multitude of works produced, in Italy and abroad, in the course of ten centuries. It has instead been conceived as a kind of atlas, which takes account of the "geography" of Italian art and the chronology of its masters. Each artist is documented by a brief biography, illustrated with his portrait or self-portrait (when it exists, as in most cases) according to a tradition already dear to Giorgio Vasari, author of the first imposing collection of artists' biographies (*The Lives of the Most Excellent Painters, Sculptors and Architects*, an edition printed by the typographer Giunti in 1568, after a first version published in 1550). The activity of each master is then illustrated by one or more works, with brief commentaries concerning not only style but a variety of aspects: the historical and social context, the influence of other cultures, the significance of the work, and the discoveries that have emerged through restoration.

Beato Angelico, *Annunciation*, detail of the *Silver Cabinet*, c. 1450-52. Florence, San Marco Museum.

The reasons for an approach of this kind are soon stated. The heritage of Italian art is unanimously acknowledged to be one of the richest in the world, perhaps the richest of all. It consists not only of monuments, paintings and sculptures still in Italy but also of thousands of works now in the museums and collections of every continent. Such an enormous body of "material", so many buildings, masterpieces, movements, techniques and styles, may seem daunting to the neophyte. Ernst Gombrich, a great art historian and superb popularizer, has recently commented on the difficulty of teaching beginners, children in particular, for whom *art history does not exist.* Frequently art appears boring and incomprehensible, explained by trite formulas which not even visits to museums can make attractive. Moreover, art historians rarely attempt to act as serious educators, almost as if this were a profession of lesser rank. Two different schools thus exist, particularly in Italy: that of the experts, who address only their peers, but who have nonetheless made discoveries and formulated interpretations that would be interesting to any reader; and that of the compilers, not always possessing the updated knowledge of those who have specifically studied this discipline, which is moreover far from being an exact science. Yet foreign scholars such as Gombrich and Chastel have written magnificent art histories, accessible to all and enormously successful. In Italy only Roberto Longhi, a fine writer as well as art critic, produced in his youth a manual (which was also the parody of a manual) addressed mainly to the young and inexpert: the *Brief but True*

View of the Siena Duomo.

Ambrogio Lorenzetti, *Presentation of Jesus in the Temple*, detail, signed and dated 1342. Florence, Uffizi Gallery.

History of Italian Painting, based on lessons he gave in a Roman high school in long-ago 1914. More recently we have had only the rare lessons, or rather "conversations", almost extemporaneous and very clear, of Federico Zeri, known the world over as one of the greatest art historians of the 20th century. From these conversations, held in Milan for a single week in a hall packed with persons of every social and cultural level, listening in dead silence, emerged a fascinating book published in 1987, *Behind the Image*, offering a wealth of "eccentric and irregular" suggestions in place of the trite concept of "masterpieces by great painters". Zeri has taught us, often amid fierce controversy, that Italian art does not consist merely of masterpieces by famous artists but also of "pictures without a name and names without

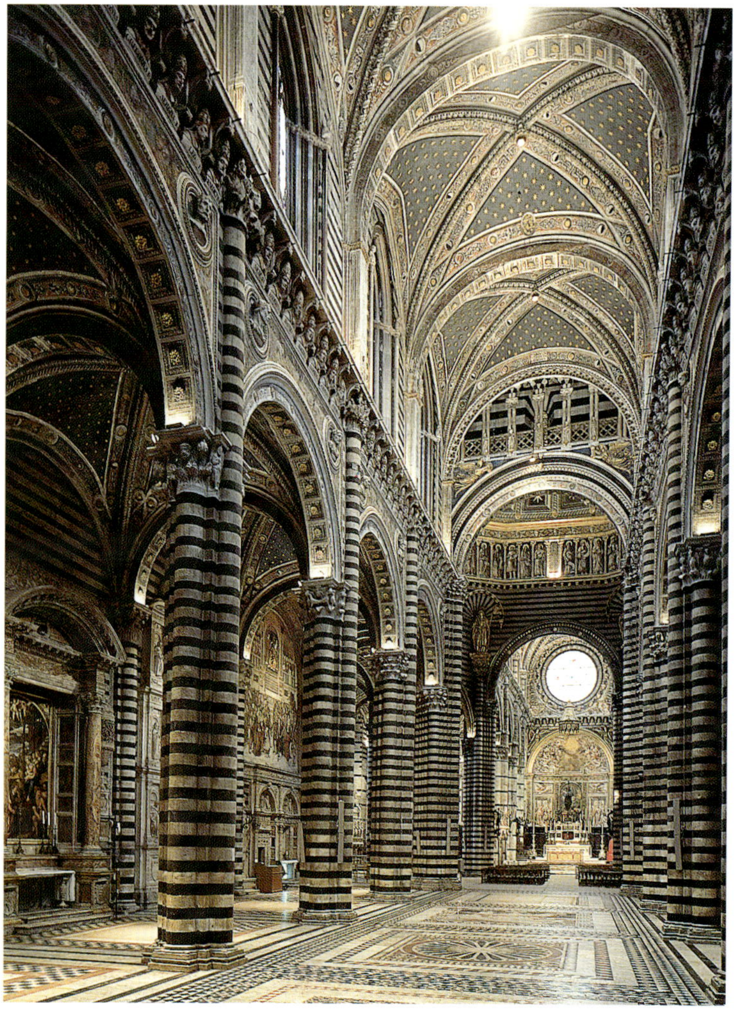

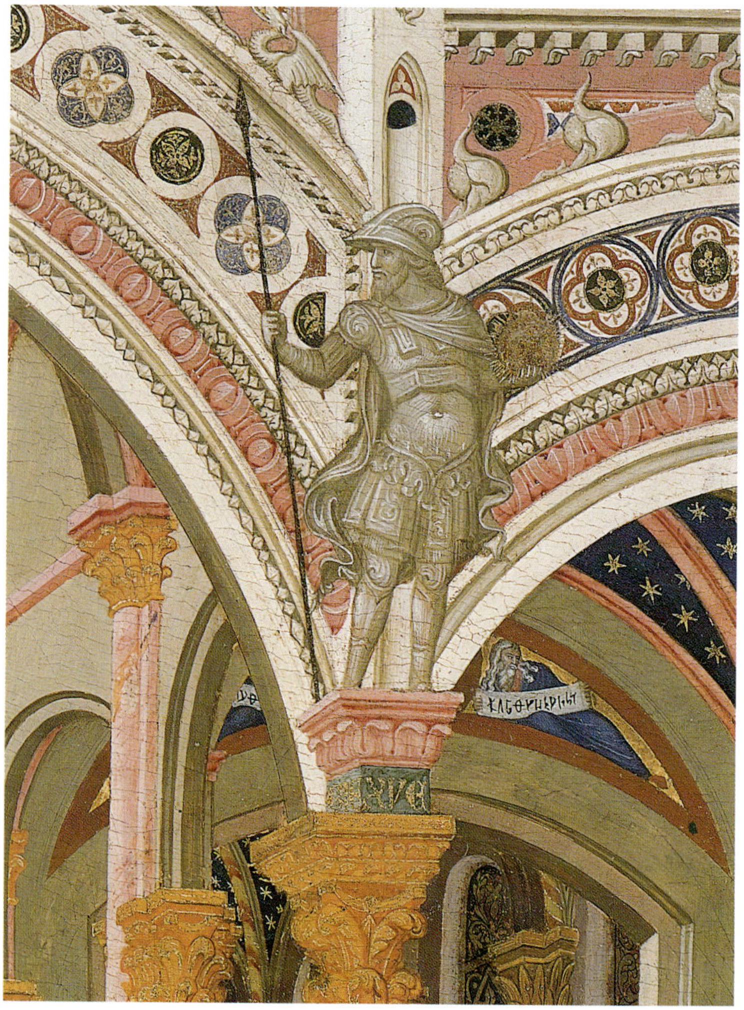

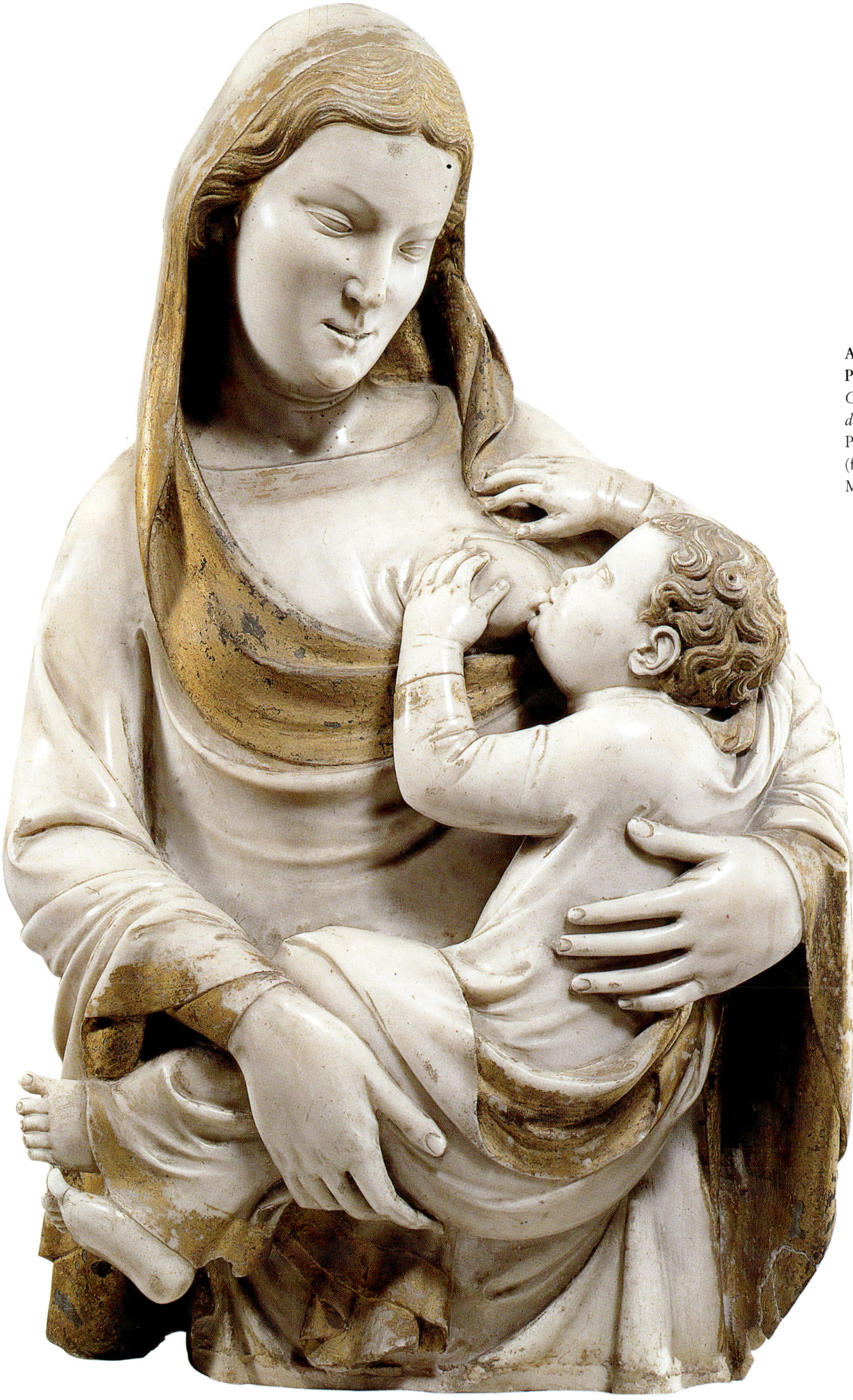

Andrea and Nino Pisano, *Madonna with Child* known as *Madonna del Latte*, c. 1350. Pisa, Museo di San Matteo (from the Church of Santa Maria della Spina).

Piero della Francesca, *Madonna del Parto*, c. 1455. Monterchi, Chapel of the Cemetery.

Francesco del Cossa, *Triumph of Venus*, detail of the month of *April*, c. 1469-70. Ferrara, Palazzo Schifanoia, Hall of the Months.

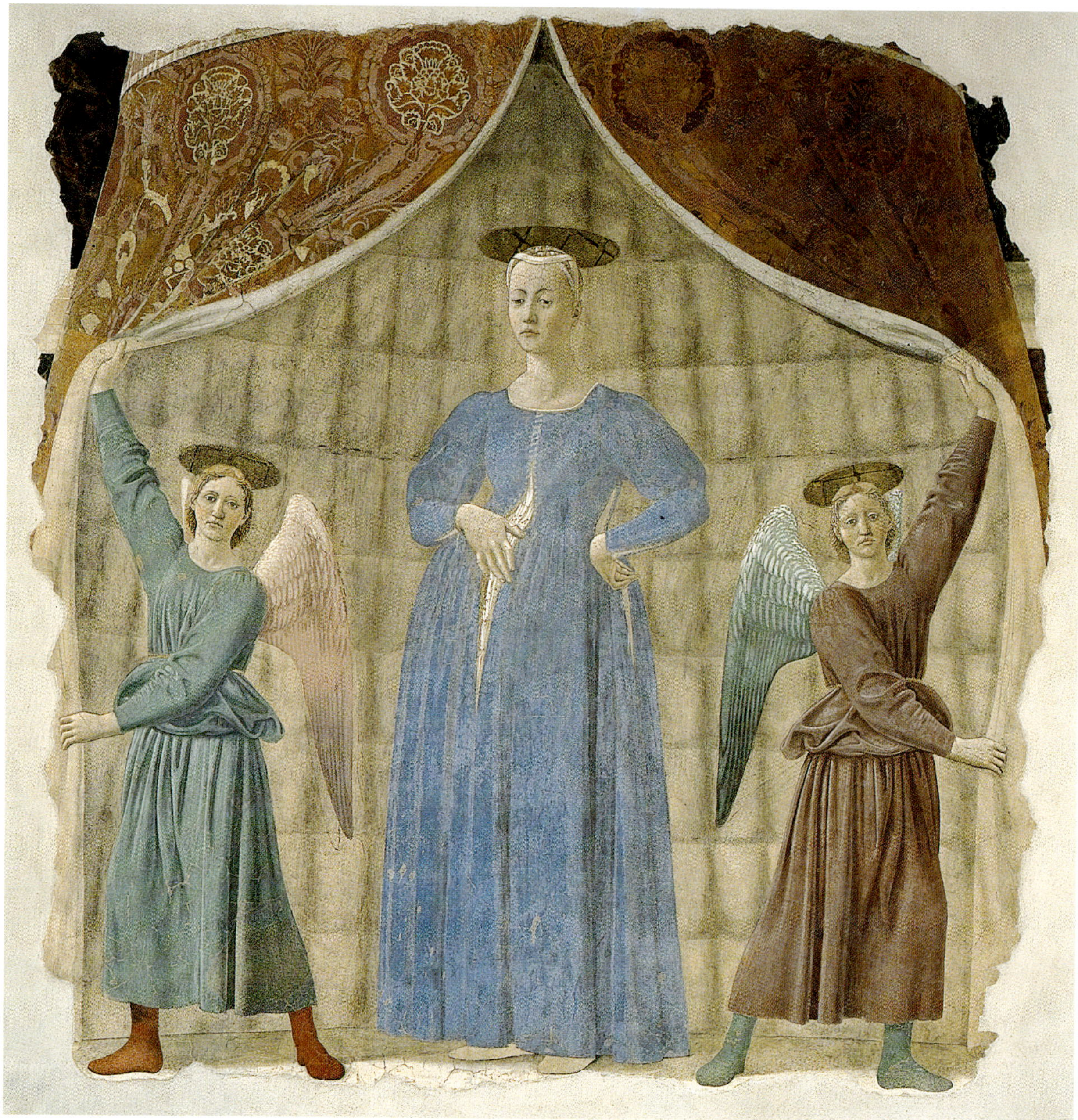

pictures", and of schools, branching out all over Italy, which it would be restrictive to call minor and which make the geography of Italian art diversified, rich in exchange, fascinating and complex like that of no other civilization. Inevitably, however, in the great cities of art, many visitors pause for only a moment before the most stereotyped monuments, probably already memorized from a postcard: "Well, now I've been here, I've seen it at last, let's go on". And in museums and churches as well tourists pause for a few seconds in front of the "masterpiece", read the caption and continue: "There, I've seen it, let's go on". Although they have indeed seen it, they have not really looked at it, have not assimilated any image. At the end of the day nothing remains but the illusion of cultural enrichment - and a splitting headache. Better a selection, then, no matter how difficult, better a few works and reliable, pertinent facts: information about the artist's personality, his patrons, a glance at a revealing detail. In Paris and Florence only a few of the brave avoid the endless queues that must be endured to view works which,

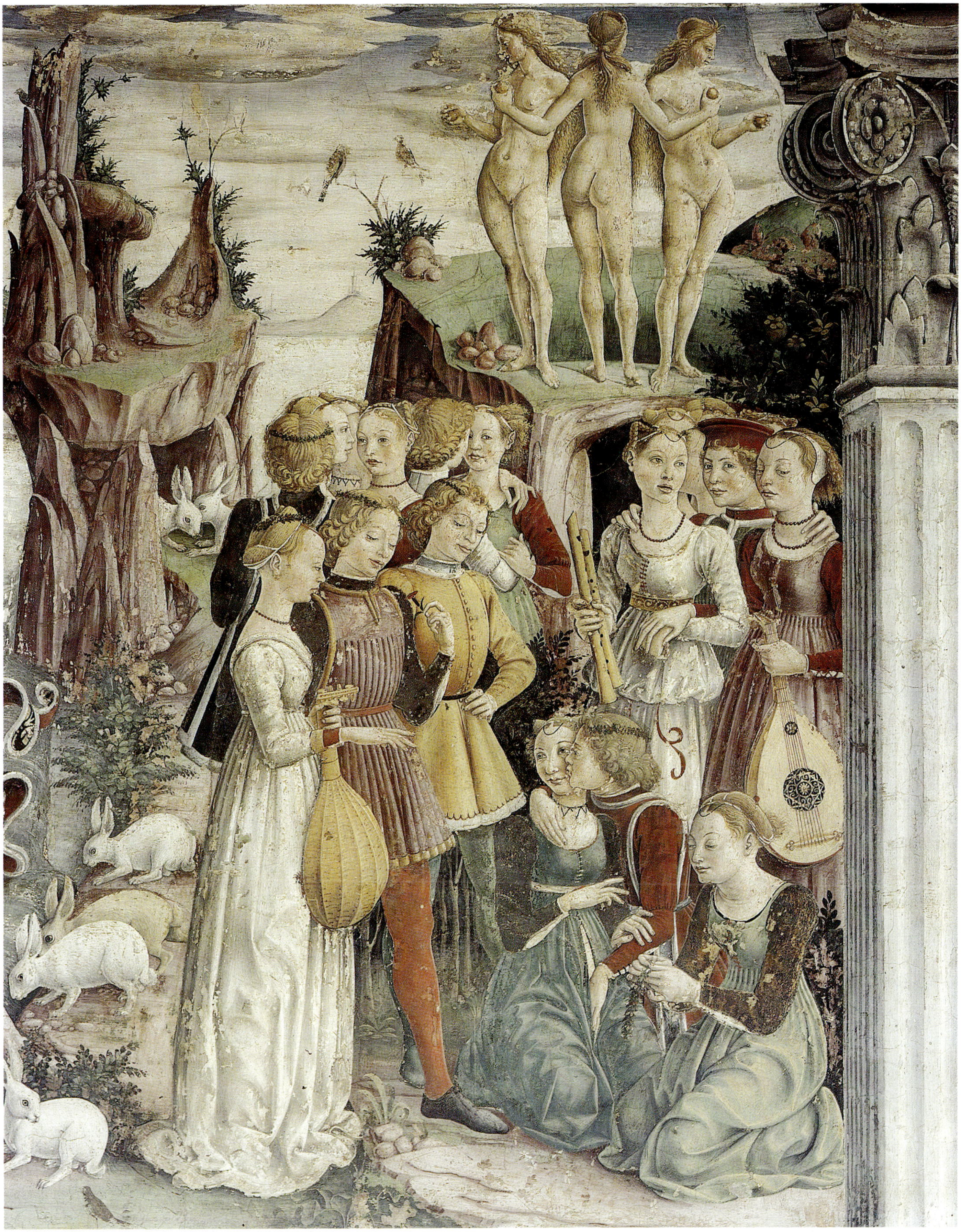

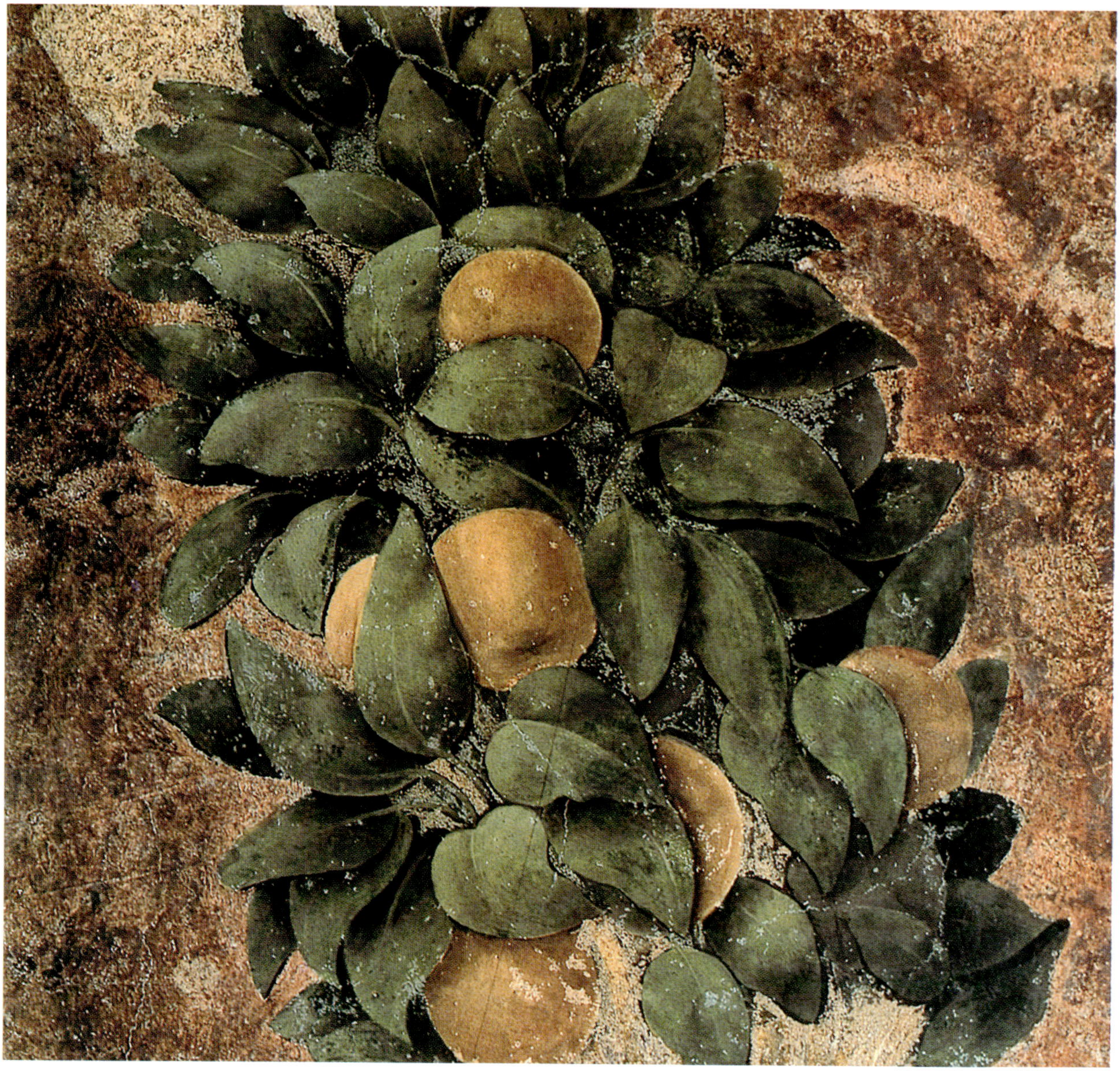

Leonardo da Vinci,
Garland, detail of the left lunette above the *Last Supper*, 1495-98. Milan, Refectory of Santa Maria delle Grazie.

Gianlorenzo Bernini,
Cornaro (or *St Teresa of Avila*) *Chapel*, 1647-51. Rome, Santa Maria della Vittoria.

though truly exceptional, have been over-inflated by the media: the *Mona Lisa*, the *Primavera* and the *David*, for instance. They appear in this book as well, with due importance assigned them, but along with such celebrities we also suggest unusual details and less famous names. Everyone goes to see how far the Tower of Pisa leans, ignoring the fact that the real masterpiece of the Piazza is the Duomo, and Buscheto is its great artificer; and although his contemporaries placed his tomb on the facade and compared him to the mythical Dedalus, the great architect has now been forgotten (and perhaps the reader will be curious to know more). In Florence, we maintain, it is more rewarding not to stop before the facade of Santa Croce, dating from the 19th century rather than the Middle Ages as is commonly thought, but to prefer instead the calm of the Rinuccini Chapel in the Sacristy with its 14th century frescoes by Giovanni da Milano. It is equally rewarding to pause before the stupendous predellas of Gentile da Fabriano in the Vatican and in Washington, or the work of Sassetta and the enigmatic Master of the Osservanza in the New York Metropolitan Museum, which the tourist in Siena can admire by walking from Piazza del Campo to the Chigi Saracini Collection; or to meditate on the symbolic evocations of Wili-

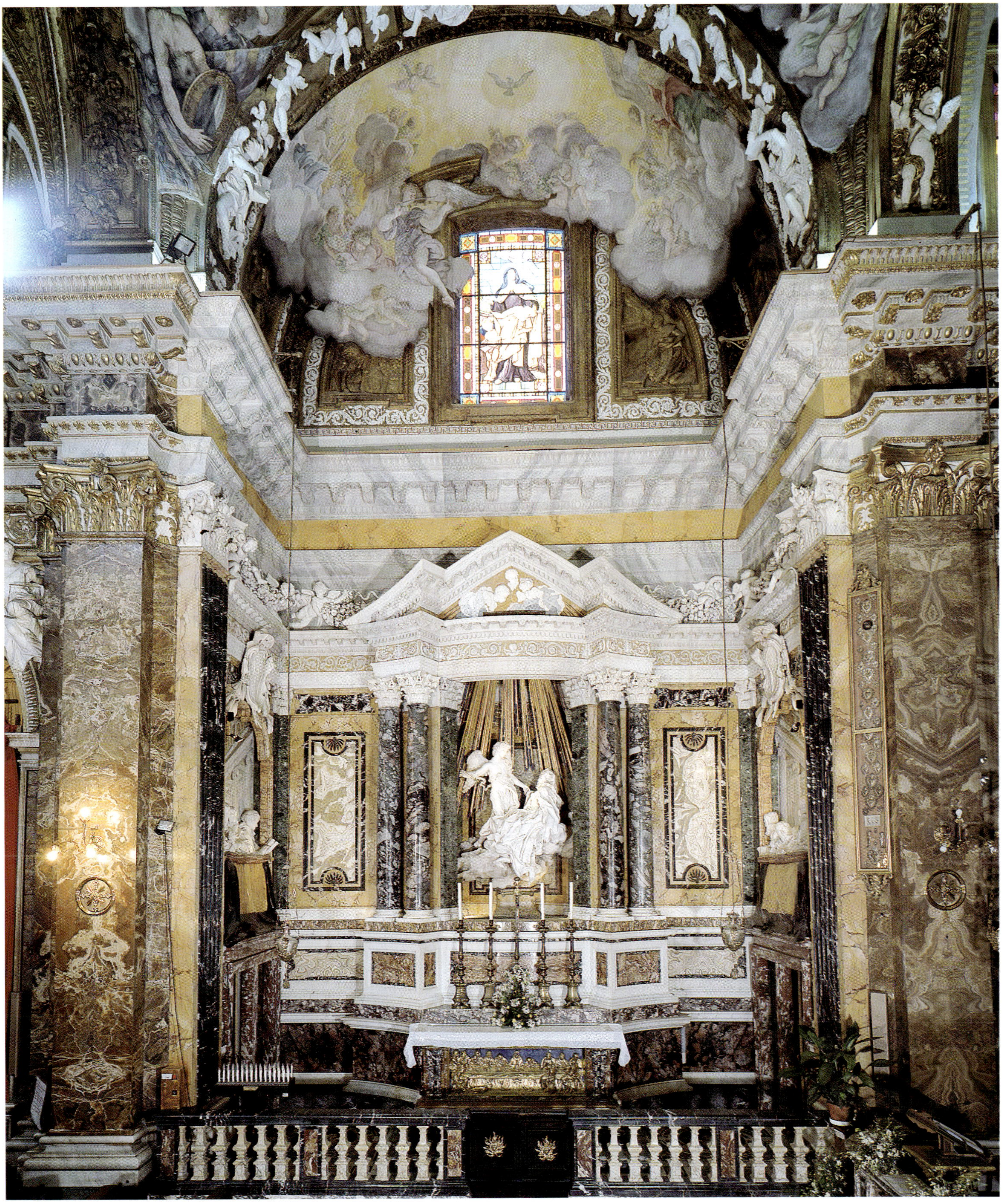

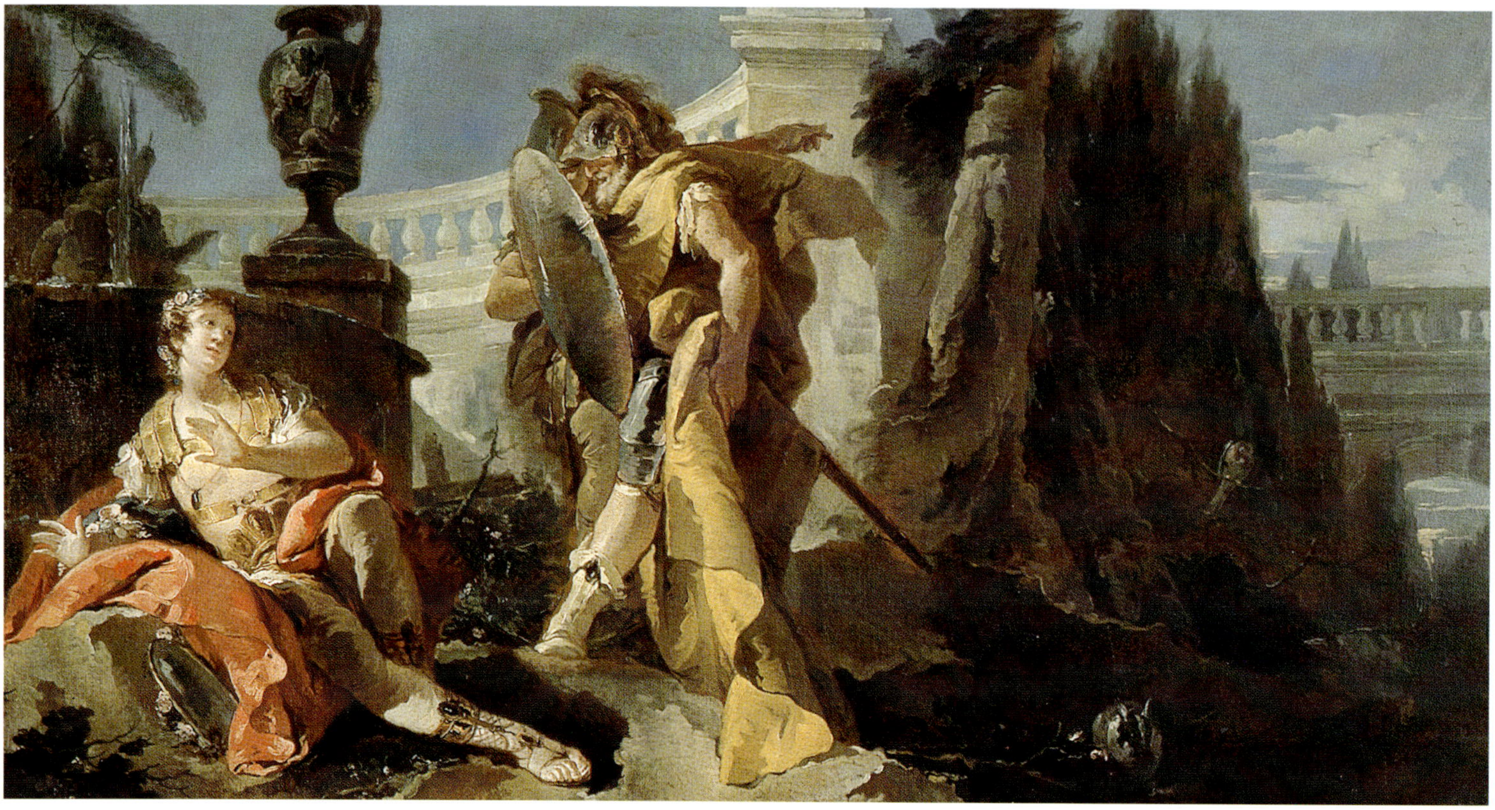

Giambattista Tiepolo, *Rinaldo Mirrors Himself in Ubaldo's Shield*, c. 1755. Florence, Uffizi Gallery.

Canaletto, *The Basilica of St. Mark's and the Ducal Palace*, detail, c. 1735. Washington, National Gallery.

gelmo and the expressionism of the Bolognese Vitale. We believe it important to know Modigliani and De Chirico, but also to be aware of the tendencies of the new generations, already appreciated in France and the United States. We find reassuring the statement with which the enormously successful *Story of Art told by Ernst Gombrich* begins: "There really is no such thing as Art. There are only artists. Once these were men who took colored earth and roughed out the forms of a bison on the wall of a cave; today some buy their paints, and design posters for billboards; they did and do many other things. There is no harm in calling all these activities art as long as we keep in mind that such a word may mean very different things in different times and places, and as long as we realize that Art with a capital A has no existence. For Art with a capital A has come to be something of a bogey and a fetish."

In conclusion, this book was born of the strong conviction of the publisher, for years committed not only to producing works of highest scientific content but also to a wider diffusion of culture; and of the ardent interest of the editor and the authors of the texts, for whom the study of art, including its social and anthropological implications, has long been a daily exercise. With enthusiasm and humility we therefore publish this book. If it gives the reader even a small part of the pleasure it has given us, we will already have attained the first of our objectives.

g. f.

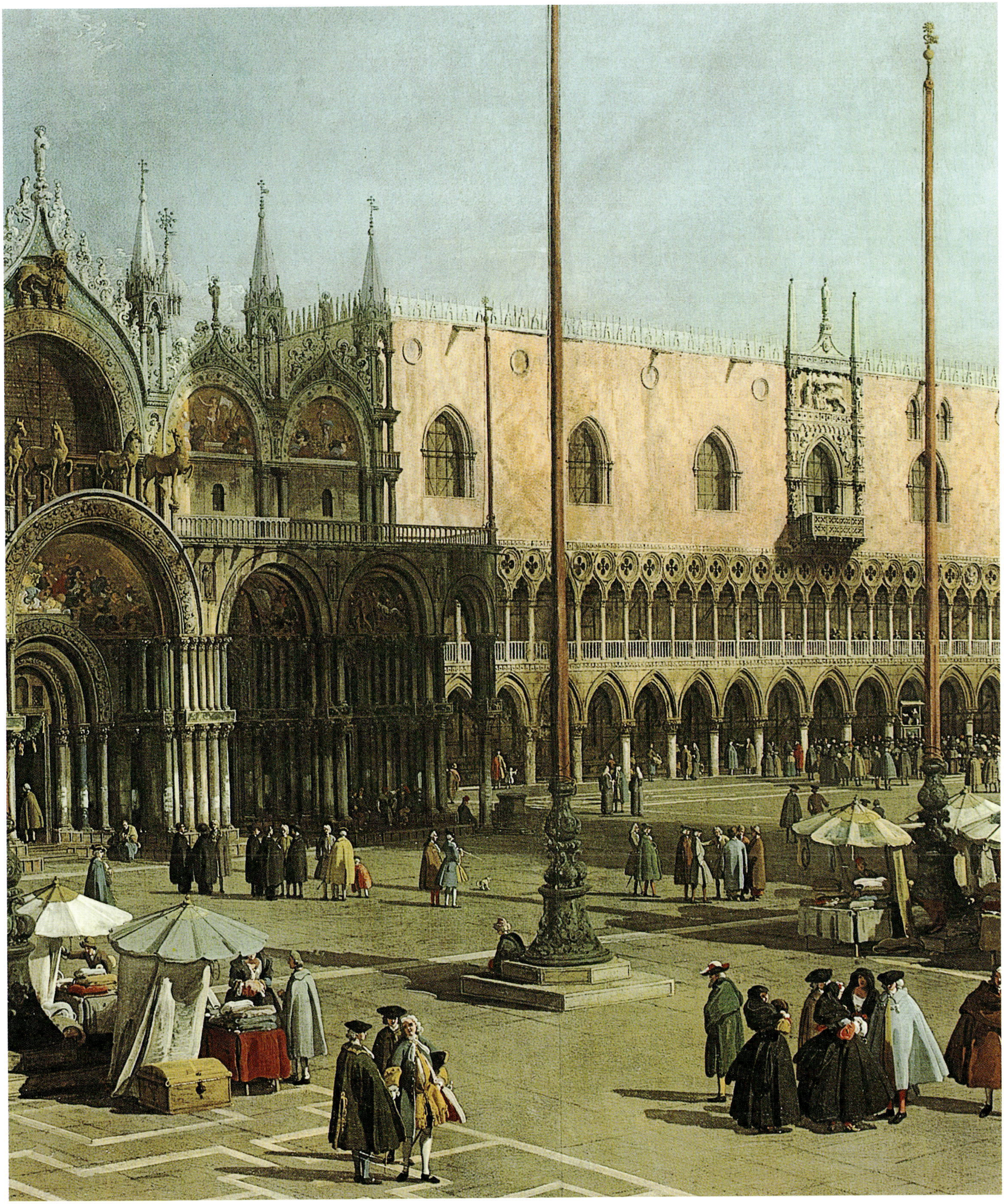

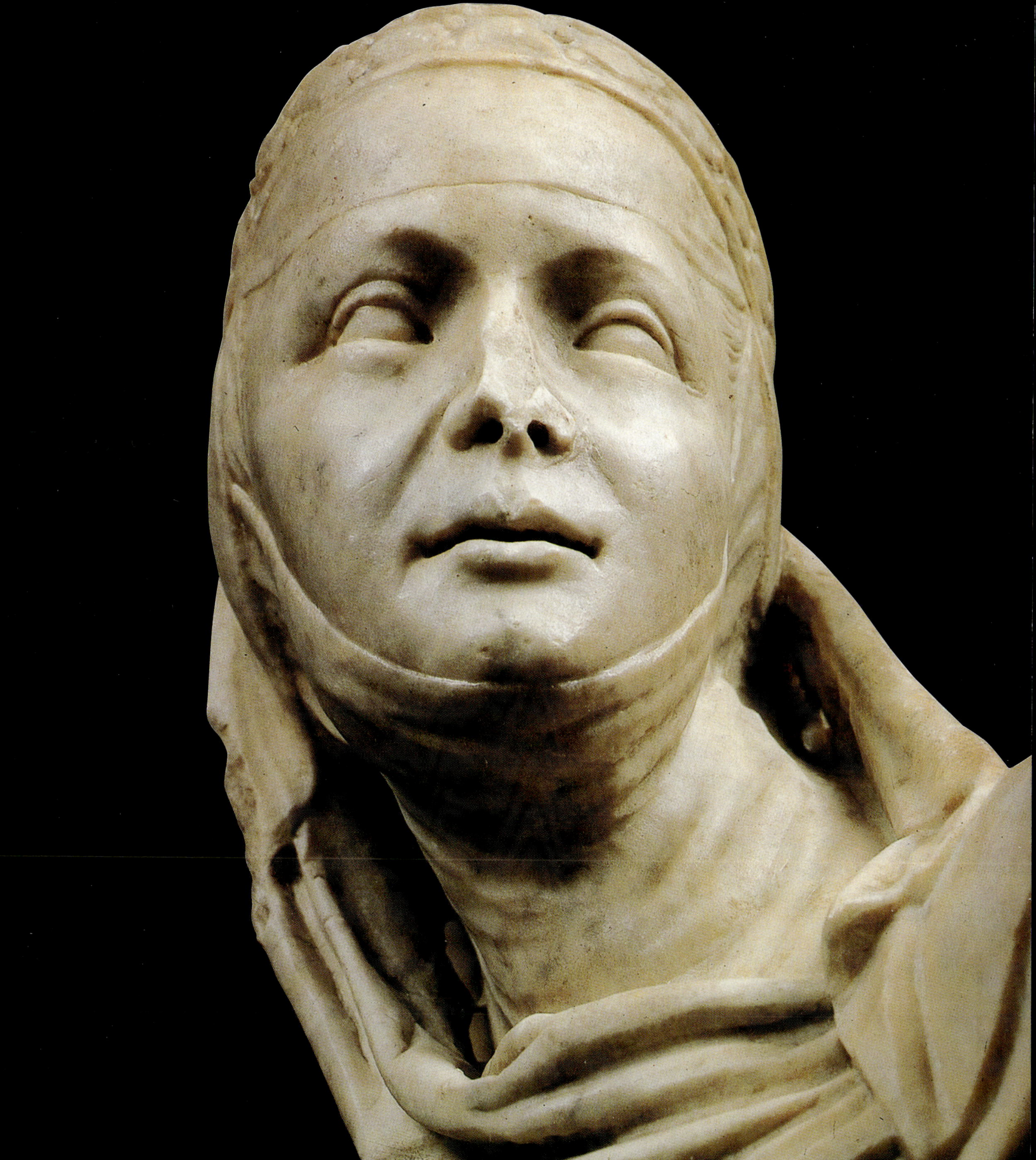

THE MIDDLE AGES

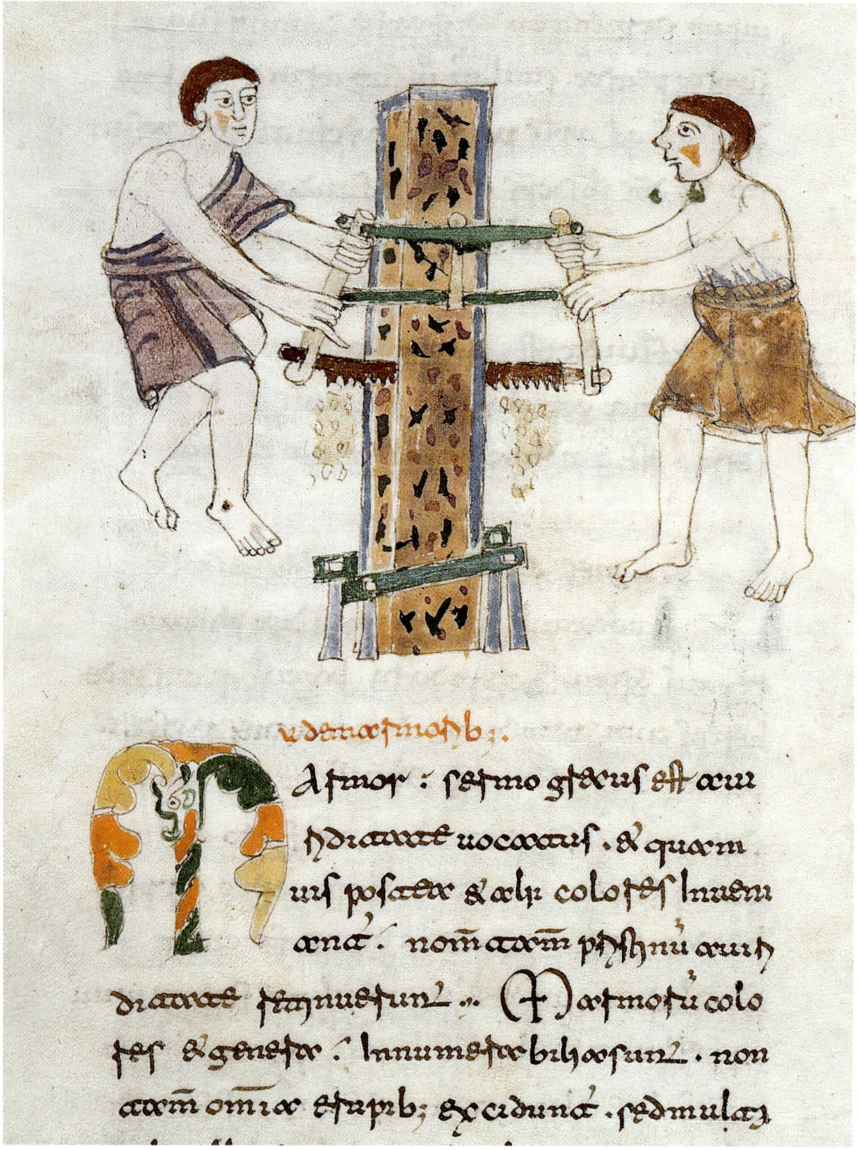

Southern Italian artist, *Carpenters at work,* illuminated page in the Cassino Codex of *De Universo* (9th century) by Hrabanus Maurus, Abbot of Fulda, c. 1022-1035. Montecassino, Abbey Archives, ms. 132.

Preceding page: **Giovanni Pisano,** *Elevatio animae (Ascension of the soul held up by angels) of Queen Margphareth of Brabante,* detail, c. 1313. Genoa, Museo di Sant'Agostino.

Around the year one thousand a sort of cosmic chaos seemed to shake all of Europe with a series of portents and catastrophic events: comets, eclipses, earthquakes, conflagrations, famines, even episodes of cannibalism. The order of the world, as has been noted by Georges Duby, "appeared overturned by various perturbations [...] which all proceeded from the same deep malaise". By now the hypothesis that the fear pervading those years sprang exclusively from the apocalyptic millenarian theories on the end of the world has been refuted. Rather it could be said that common man, crushed by a sense of inferiority to the forces of nature and still far from placing himself at the center of the cosmos, was constantly aware in those days of the precariousness of existence, which kept him in a perpetual state of uncertainty. Overwhelmed by nature, man's only chance of salvation lay in divine protection. Accordingly, while daily work measured his time in the slow rhythms of liturgy, every aspect of life was conditioned by eschatological values – the concept of sin staining the origins of man, punishment and atonement through work, fatigue and suffering. Not by chance did the Medieval imagination, and thus also the figurative arts, lay the foundations, more than at any other period in Western civilization, of a complex system of symbols where numbers, colors and musical tones were mystically linked to the harmony (or chaos) of the universe. A deeply fascinating language – whose apparent involution has intrigued 20th century artists such as Chagall, Picasso and Klee – united at least up to the 12th century, albeit with different styles and techniques, almost all of the figurative manifestations of the Christian West, in spite of its dissimilar political situations. In his *Histories*, tracing the story of the known world from the year 900 to 1044, the Bourgogne monk Radulfus Glaber describes the apparition in 1014 of a comet like an enormous sword, and comments that "Whenever men see a portent of this kind, it always happens that soon afterward some extraordinary and terrible event befalls them". Accordingly, a fire destroys the Church of Mont-Saint-Michel in Normandy, and in Italy (divided among Imperial, Pontificial and Byzantine rule), violent confla-

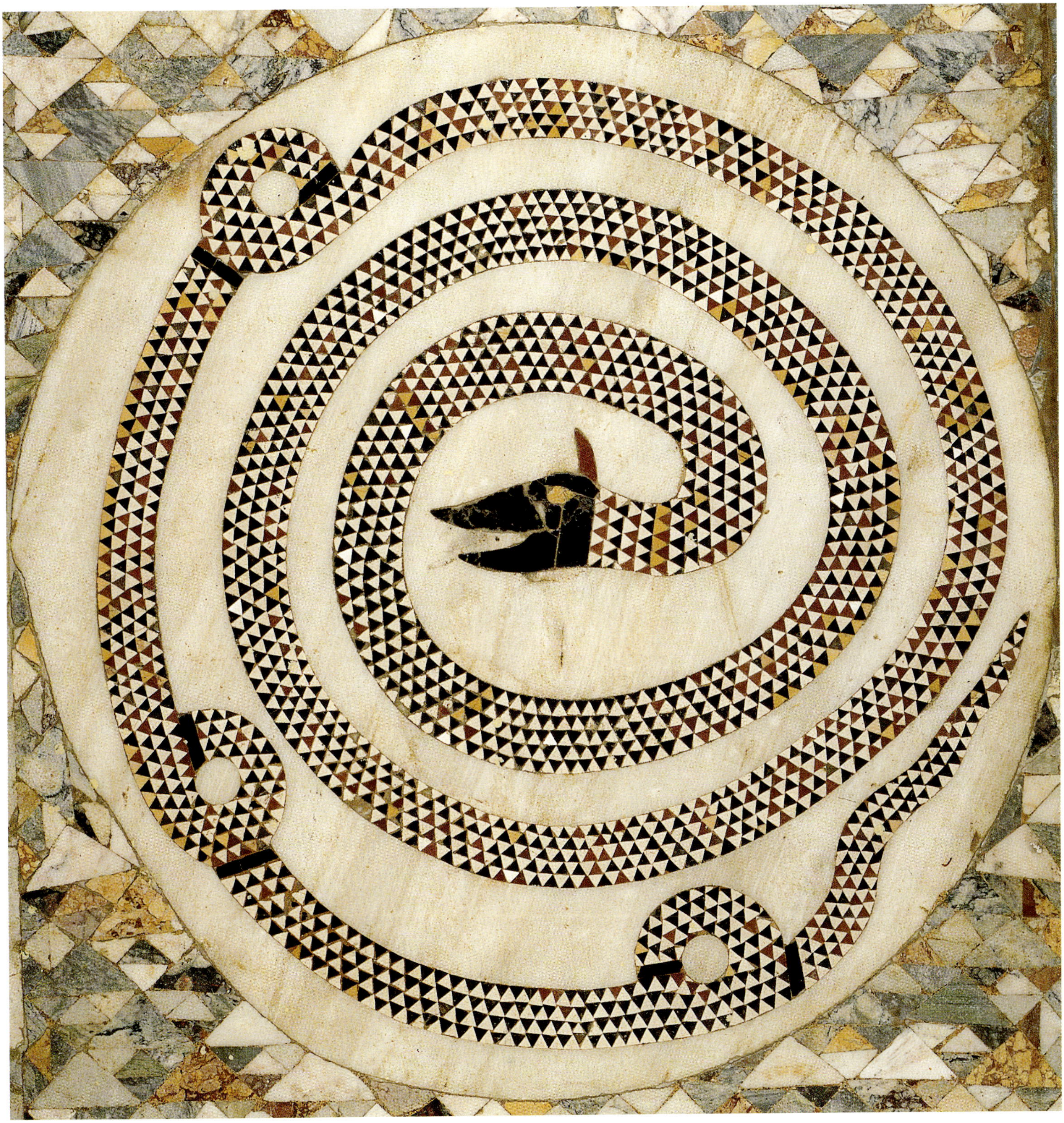

grations devastate cities, castles and monasteries. Even earlier, at the dawn of the year 1000, a comet "with a blazing tail" had appeared. It is recorded not by a direct witness, but by a chronicler in the 12th century.

What is most striking in his report, and what ushers us into the atmosphere charged with symbols of Medieval art, is that the enormous meteorite is said to have traced in the sky the image of a serpent. Undoubtedly, to the amazed

Southern Italian mosaic artist, *Serpent*, late 11th-early 12th century. San Demetrio Corone, Cosenza, detail of the *opus sectile* flooring.

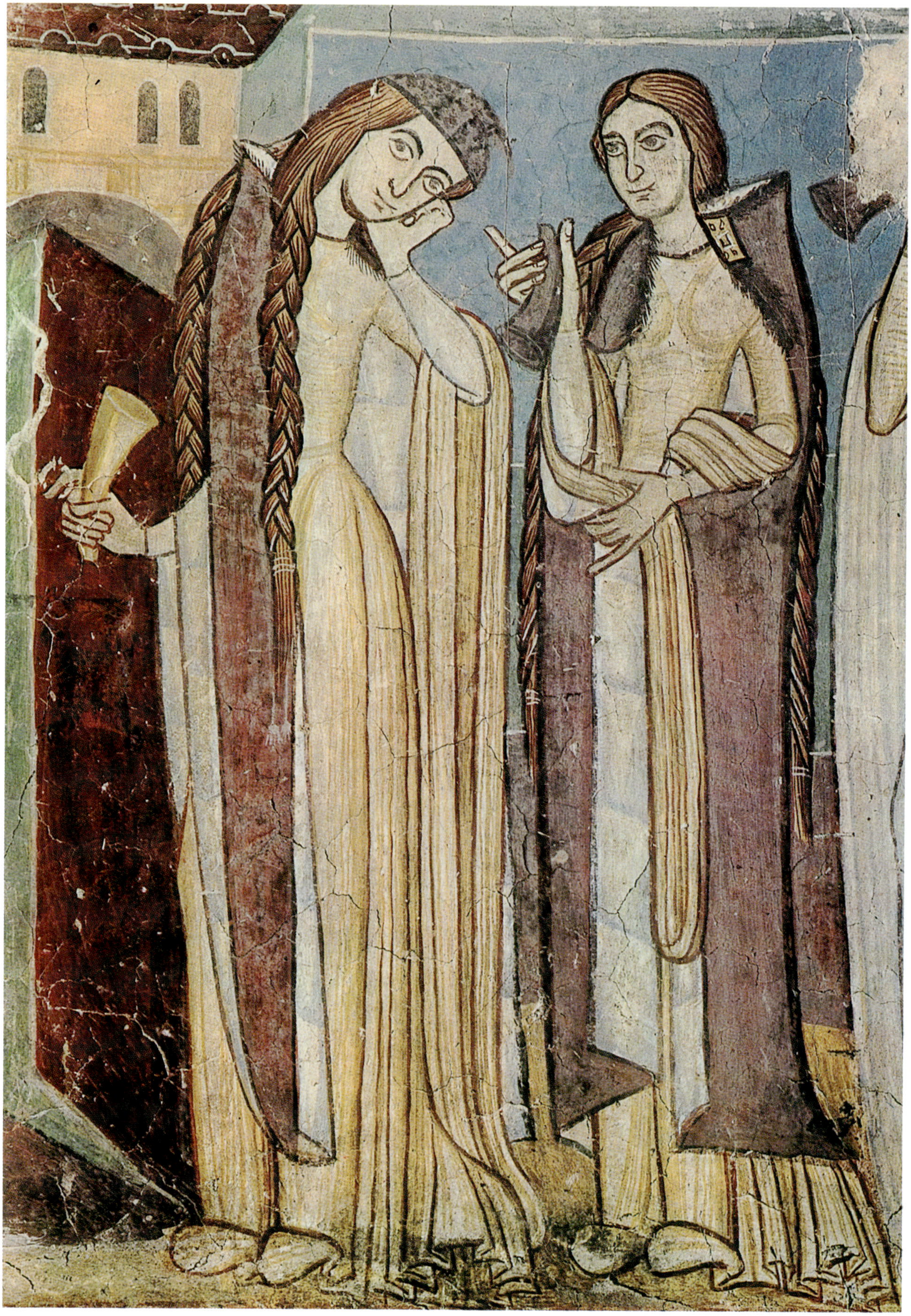

Master from Alto Adige, *Foolish Virgins*, end of 12th century, detail of the partially preserved frescoes with the parable of the *Wise and Foolish Virgins*. Castellappiano (Bolzano), Chapel of the Castle.

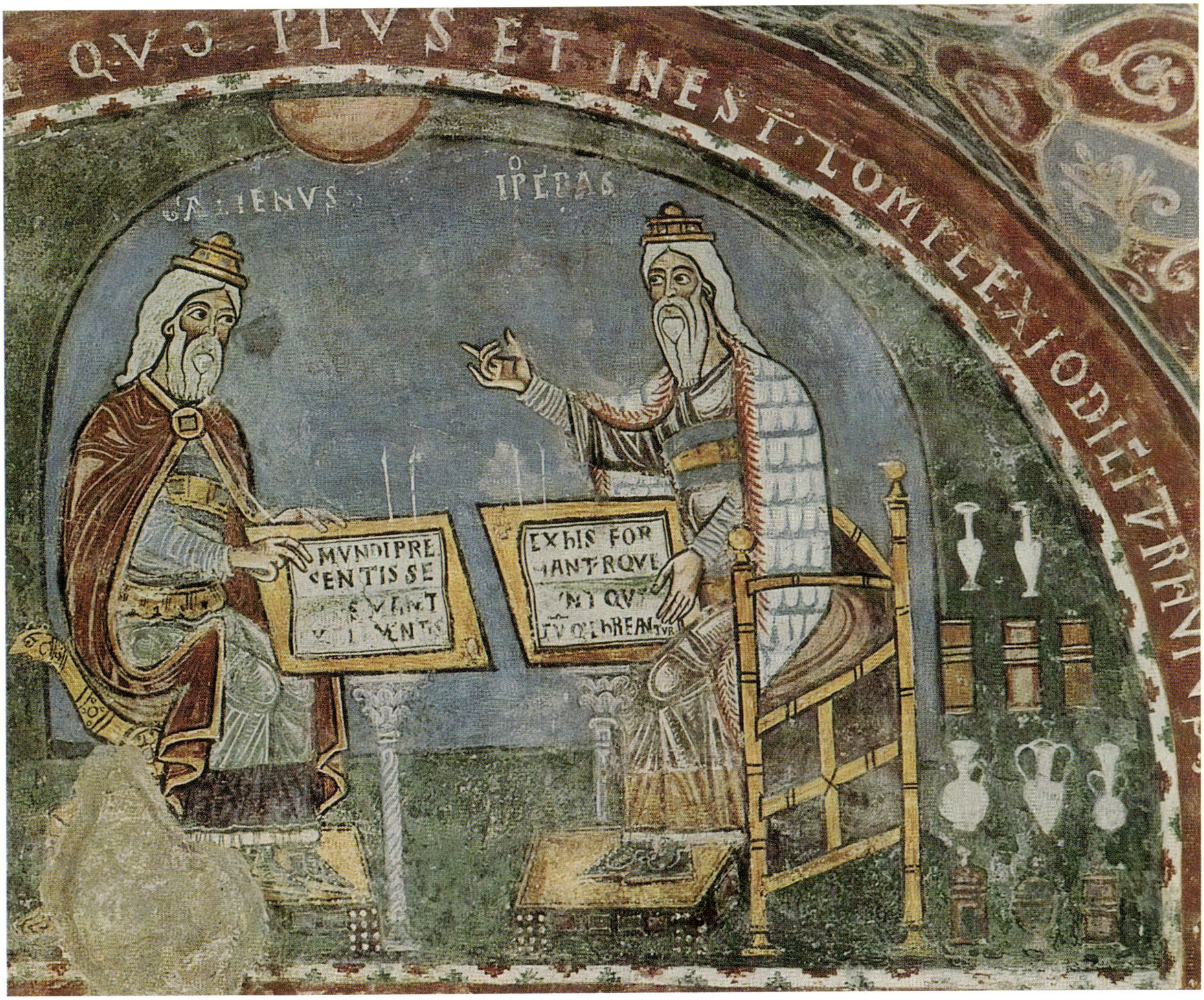

Artist from Lazio,
Hippocrates pronounces to Galenus the aphorism on the formation of the world, detail from the frescoed lunette, second quarter of the 13th century. Anagni (Frosinone), crypt of the Duomo.

eyes of the onlookers the comet seemed a sinister announcement; but even more significant is the fact that a century later the collective imagination still retained the vision, certainly more symbolical than real, of a serpent of light. Light is a sign from the heavens, but the serpent, ambiguous expression of the incomprehensible and the mysterious, incarnates negative aspects. The serpent is the seductive beast, often depicted with the face of a woman, who tricks Eve and is condemned for this to crawl upon the earth, and it is also the cosmic dragon of the Apocalypse. Satan, the Devil, the serpent, originally endowed with wisdom, thus becomes a metaphor for evil knowledge, the cause of the vices that lead to death.

Medieval thought, literature, and art used clearly metaphoric expressions. And it is with the apt metaphor of the "white mantle of churches" that Radulfus Glaber describes the artistic and decorative reawakening that occurred around the year One Thousand. "At the approach of the third year after the Millennium, over almost all of the earth, but especially in Italy and in Gaul, churches were being restored and renovated; although most of them were well-

Anonymous mosaic artist, *The City of Bethlehem*, detail of the apsidal mosaic, 12th century. Rome, San Clemente.

built and had no need of restoration, a true spirit of emulation urged every Christian community to have one more sumptuous than those of its neighbors. It might be said that the world itself was quivering to shake off the skin of old age, and to don again, everywhere, the white mantle of churches. Then almost all of the churches of the Episcopal seats, those of monasteries consecrated to all manner of saints and even little village oratories were rebuilt more beautiful than before by the faithful".

Thousands of churches and monasteries, renewed also in their decoration, were to cover again, in the course of the 11th and 12th centuries, Italy, France, Germany, and Christian Spain. And still we wonder at how it was possible that, despite material difficulties, a civilization managed to produce not only buildings and works of art in such great number but also, in many cases, extremely refined and daring structures, almost as if to emulate the grandiose edifices of the Roman Empire.

Although borrowing from other cultures as well, such as the Byzantine, the Arab and later,

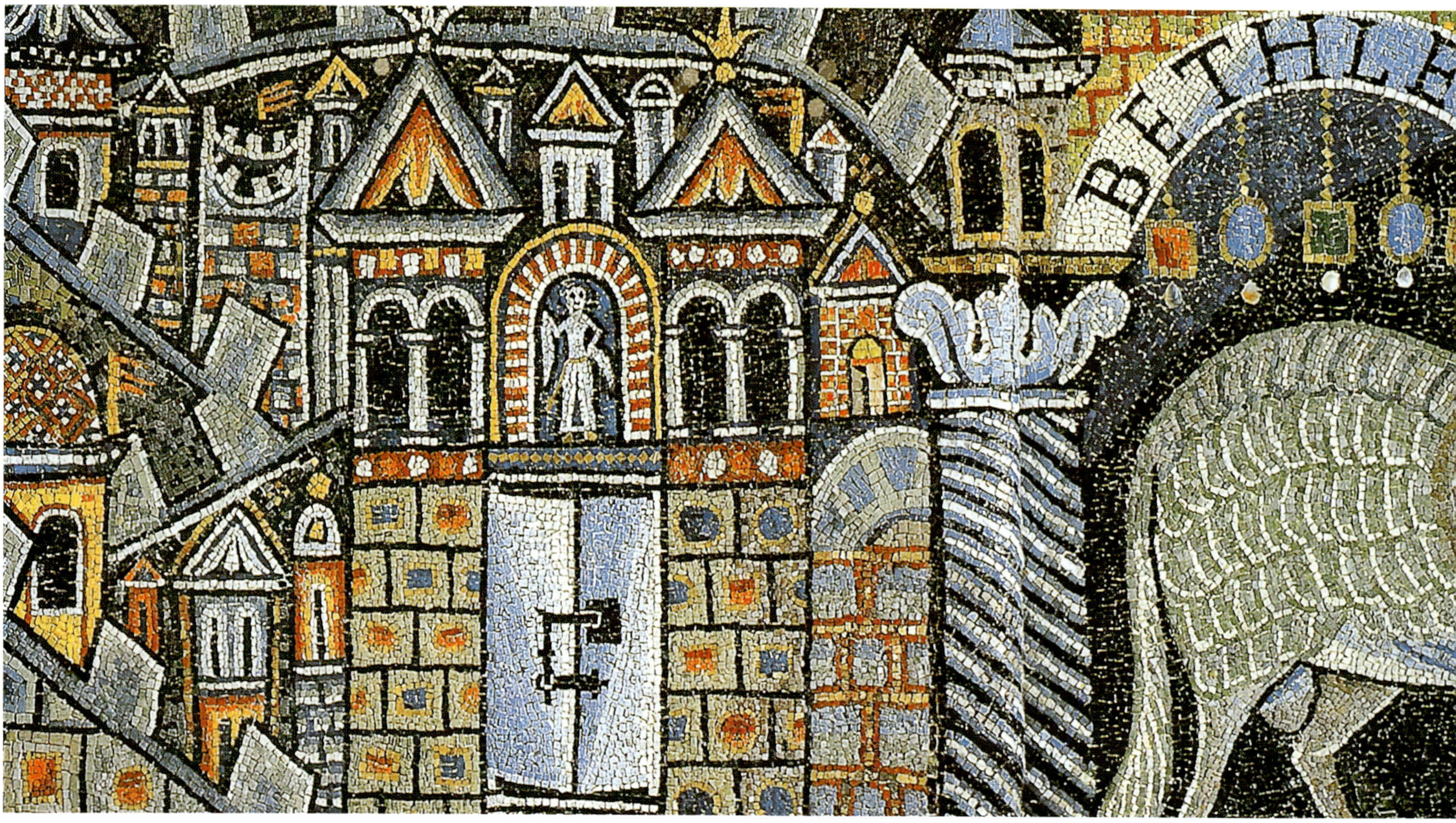

in the Kingdom of Sicily, the Norman, Italy built monuments of autonomous characteristics (one of these was the bell tower standing beside the church, rather than incorporated in its structure). Como, Milan, Pavia, Florence, Venice, Pisa, Modena, Bari, and Palermo, to name only the most ancient urban centers, saw imposing cathedrals and basilicas arise, some of them so harmonious as to arouse the later admiration of humanist architects such as Leon Battista Alberti, who in completing the façade of Santa Maria Novella in Florence purposely emulated the neo-platonic harmony of the marble inlays in the Basilica of San Miniato al Monte.

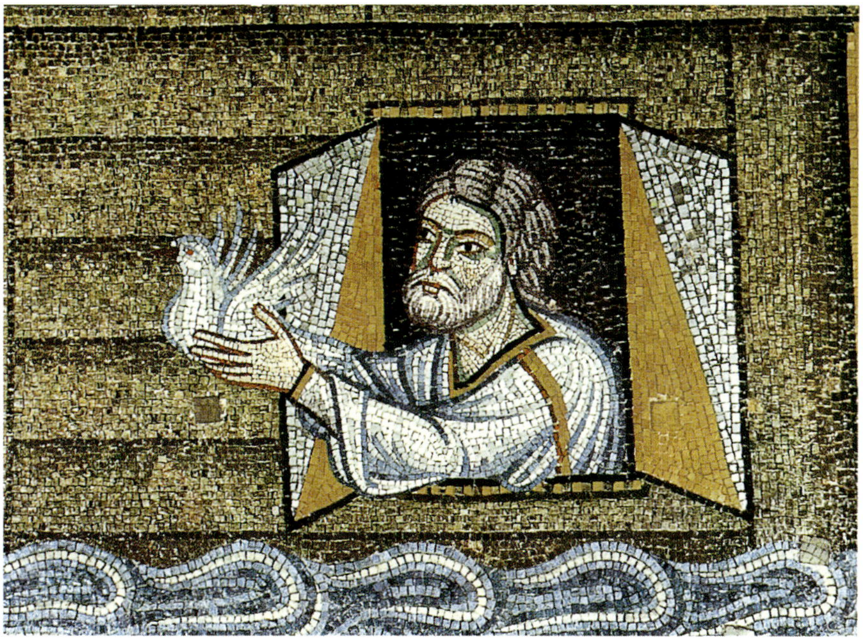

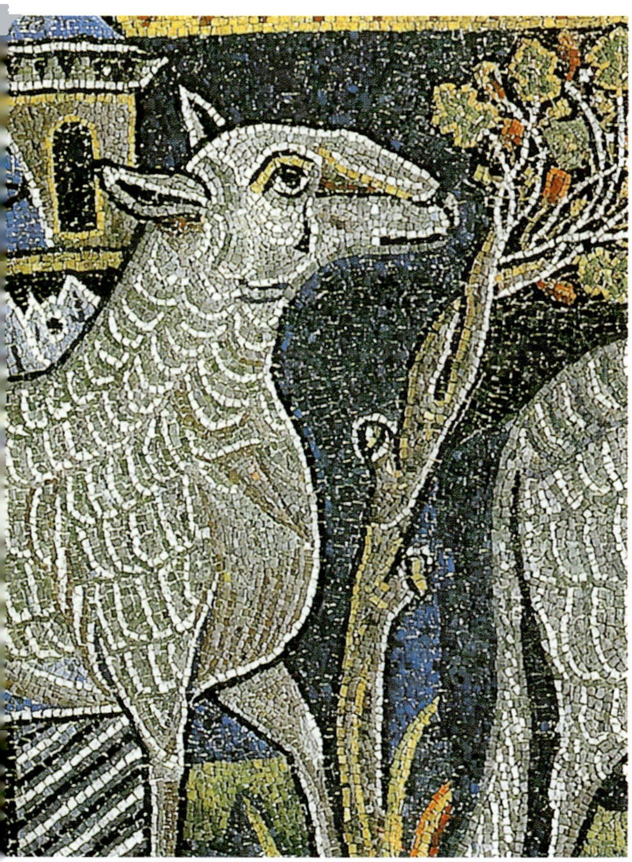

Anonymous mosaic artist, *Noah sends a raven and a dove out of the Arc,* detail from wall decoration in the atrium, c. 1210. Venice, St Mark's Basilica.

In a kind of *horror vacui* each church, from the smallest country parish to the great cathedral, covered itself with decorations. Mosaics, bas-reliefs, richly carved capitals, pulpits, baptismal fonts, wooden sculptural groups, and frescoes were created according to specific iconographic programs, to show the faithful, with obvious educational and sometimes propitiatory intentions, the path to salvation. Dozens, perhaps hundreds of architects, sculptors, stoneworkers, marble-cutters, foundrymen, goldsmiths, have remained anonymous. Very few instead, are the artificers (and among these no painter and no woman) who prior to the 13th century have left their names: Niccolò in Verona, Ferrara and Piacenza, Wiligelmo and Lanfranco in Modena, Antelami in Parma, Bonanno, Buscheto, Rainaldo, and Deotisalvi in Pisa, Biduino in Lucca, Barisano in Trani, Oderisi in Benevento. But the "legend of the artist" was a concept foreign to the times, and nothing is known of the cultural background of these talented personages, apart from a name either signed by them or handed down in eulogies expressed by their contemporaries.

Certain it is that their style soon led to the de-

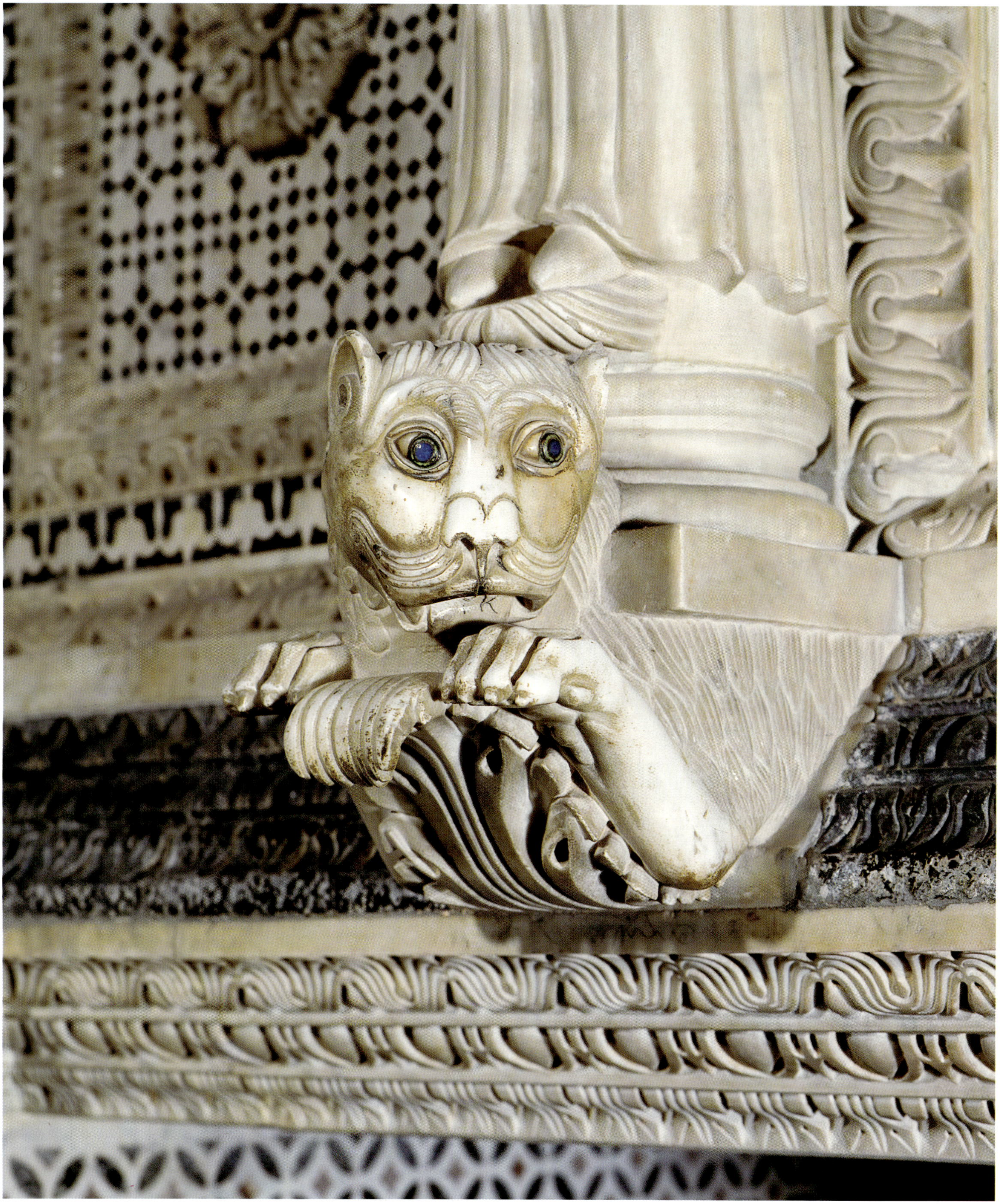

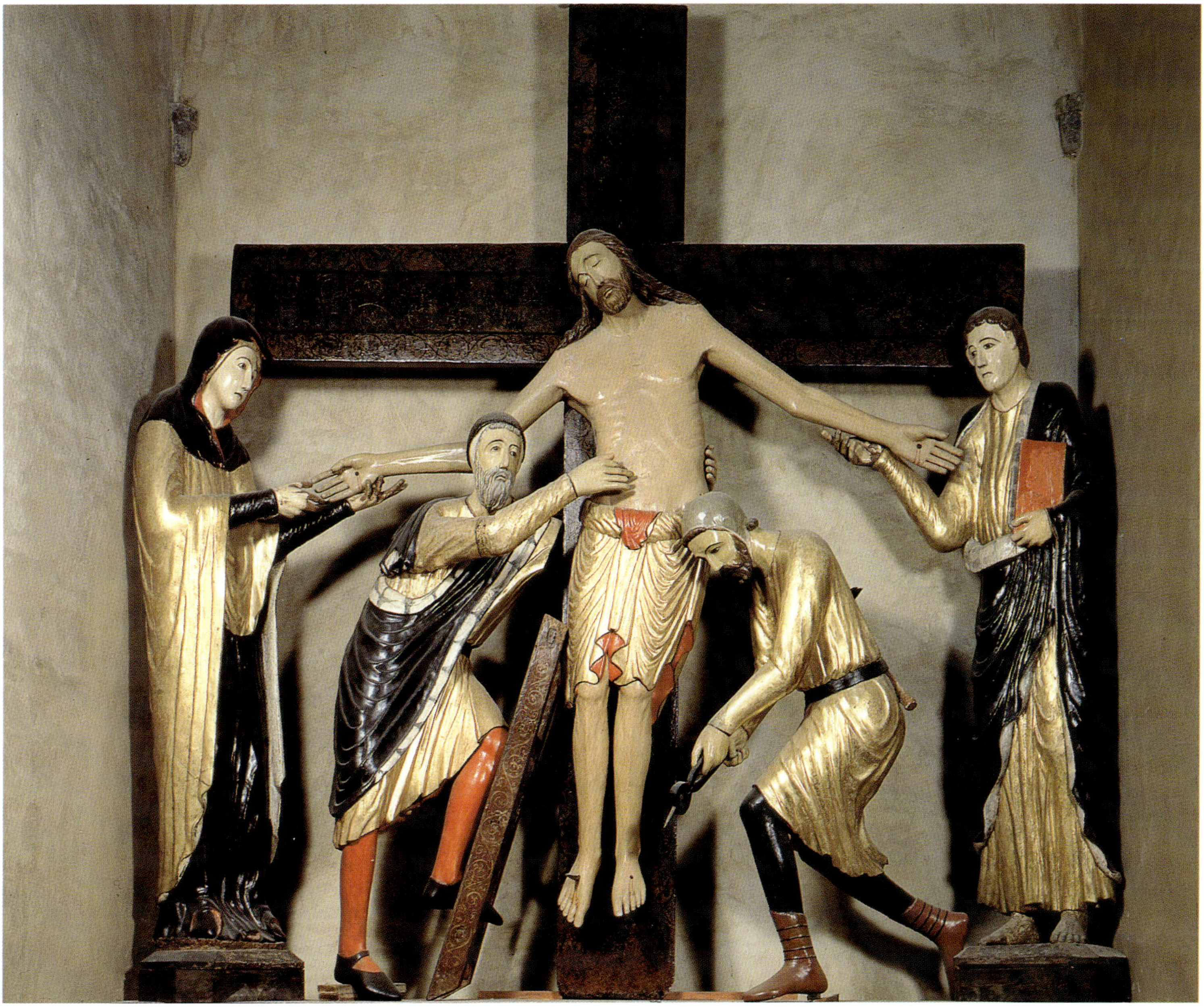

velopment of different schools over the Italian territory. That ideas, styles, and techniques were circulating in those days, in spite of the hazards and precarious nature of existence, is not surprising. Already for years pilgrimages to holy places, made sacred by the presence of important relicts, and the wide-spread diffusion of monasteries had contributed to an extraordinary mobility of men and materials. In Italy pilgrims were drawn especially to the Sanctuary of San Michele on the Gargano peninsula and to the tombs of the Apostles in Rome.

And Rome was the place that, despite its undeniable decline and its crumbling ancient monuments, still held the fascination of the Eternal City. "Although you now lie in ruins, o Rome, nothing is your equal", declared Hildebertus from Lavardin in a heart-felt eulogy expressed in around 1166. *Roma caput mundi*, Rome the honor of the world, the resplendent crown, says Amato, a monk from Montecassino.

And so classicism could be salvaged, through the desire for emulation of ancient splendor, through the skillful use of old columns, sarcophagi, and ancient fragments. Moreover, the great teachings of antiquity had not been lost: in

Anonymous sculptor, *Deposition*, c. 1228. Volterra, Duomo.

At left:
Anonymous sculptor, *Lion Cub*, detail from the pulpit, early 13th century. Florence, Basilica of San Miniato al Monte.

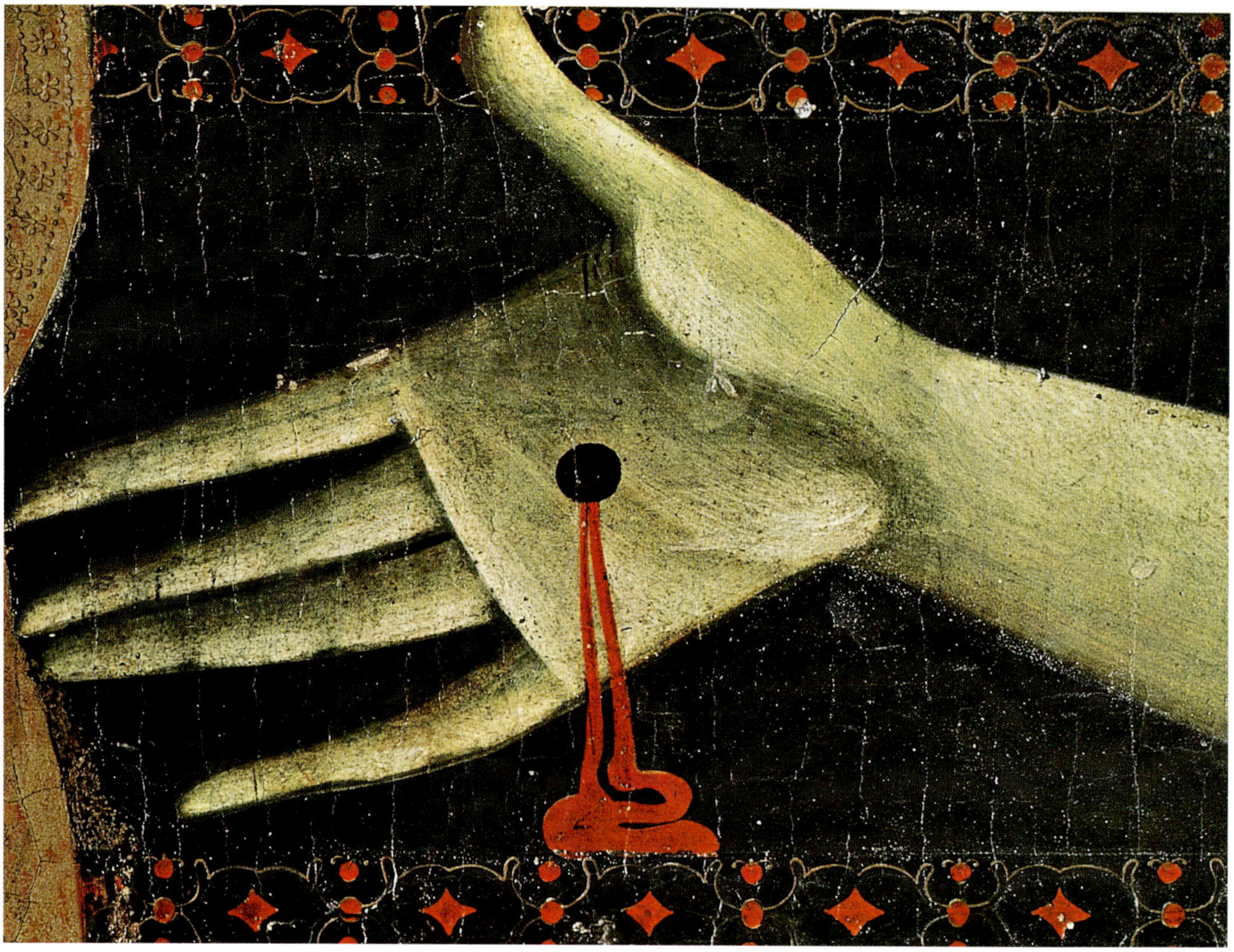

Cimabue, *Christ Crucified*, detail, c. 1270. Arezzo, San Domenico.

the *scriptoria* of the monasteries, vigorous centers of culture as well as of prayer, scribes and miniators were transcribing and illustrating not only sacred texts but also the classics such as Virgil, Ovid, Plautus and Terentius. It is thanks to them that the 15th century knew of the Greek treatises of scientists such as Hippocrates and Galenus and the great encyclopedic *summae* of Isidorus of Seville and Hrabanus Maurus, compiled at the time of the barbarian invasions with the contribution of the most advanced scientific culture, such as that of the Arabs. Illustrations rich in imagination distinguish the miniature schools of the Italian monasteries – Nonantola, Calci, Subiaco, Santa Cecilia and San Gregorio al Celio in Rome, Montecassino and Cava dei Tirreni. Already secular in nature by the 13th century were the vivacious Neapolitan shops from which came the illustrations of naturalistic codexes such as those on the baths of Pozzuoli (*De balneis,* now in the Biblioteca Angelica in Rome), or on hunting, compiled in Puglia by the Emperor Frederick II (*De arte venandi*, now in the Biblioteca Apostolica Vaticana).

The Kingdom of Sicily, first dominated by the Arabs, then by the Normans and the Suevians, was the cradle of renewed culture, open to so many influences that is still debatable whether the mosaics in the sumptuous monuments of Palermo were produced by local or Byzantine masters, and whether these worked first in Florence or in Venice, which, although independent for years, still retained close relations with Byzantium. With the decline of Islam's control of the seas, Genoa and Pisa too began to consolidate their power. New horizons were thus opened out to pilgrims and merchants, and new overland itineraries were added to the ancient network of roadways.

Now on the threshold of the 13th century, cul-

At right:
Pietro Lorenzetti, *Crucifixion*, detail of a soldier and a lady under the Cross, c. 1318. Assisi, Basilica of San Francesco, transept of the Lower Church, cycle of frescoes with *Stories of the Passion*.

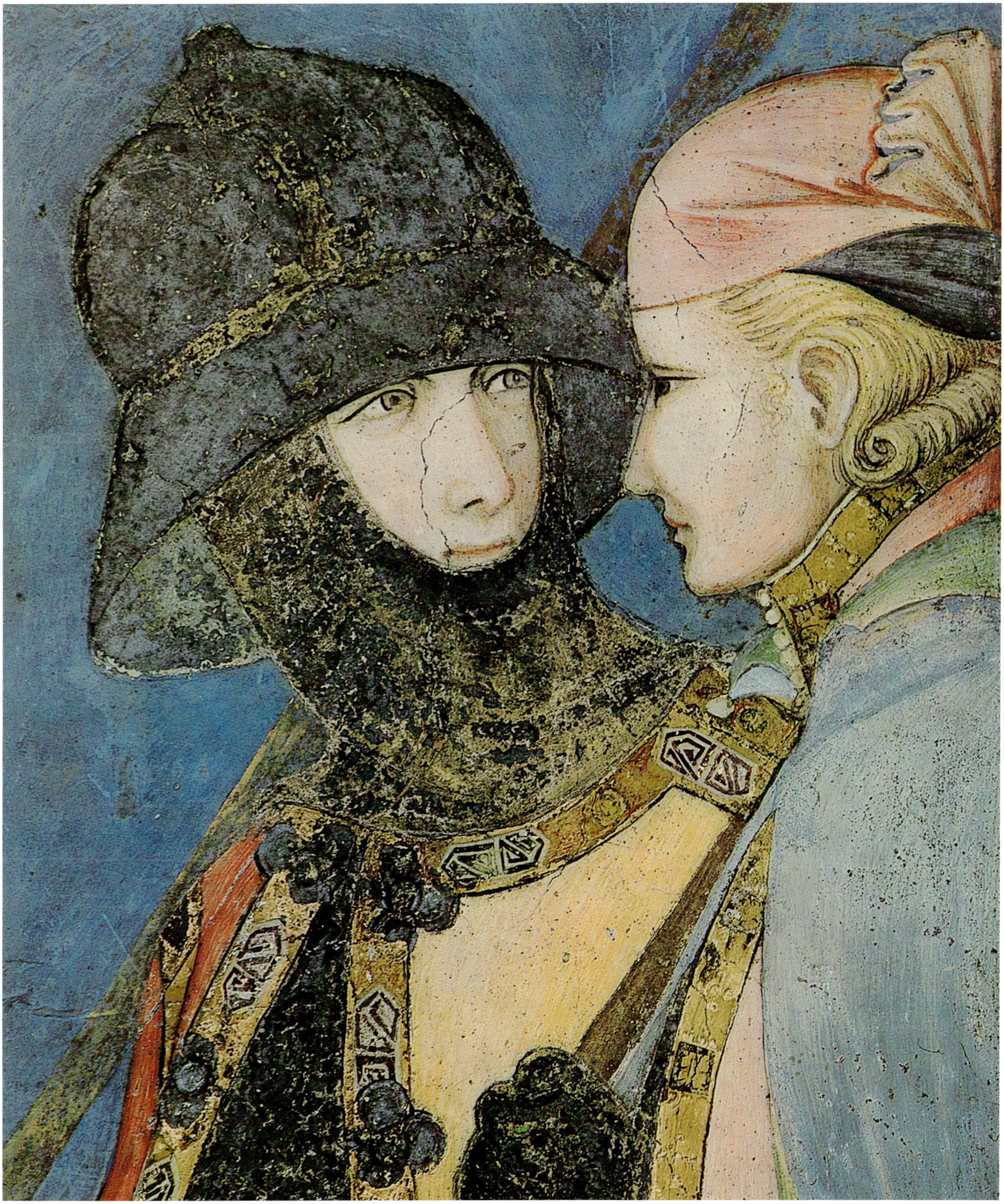

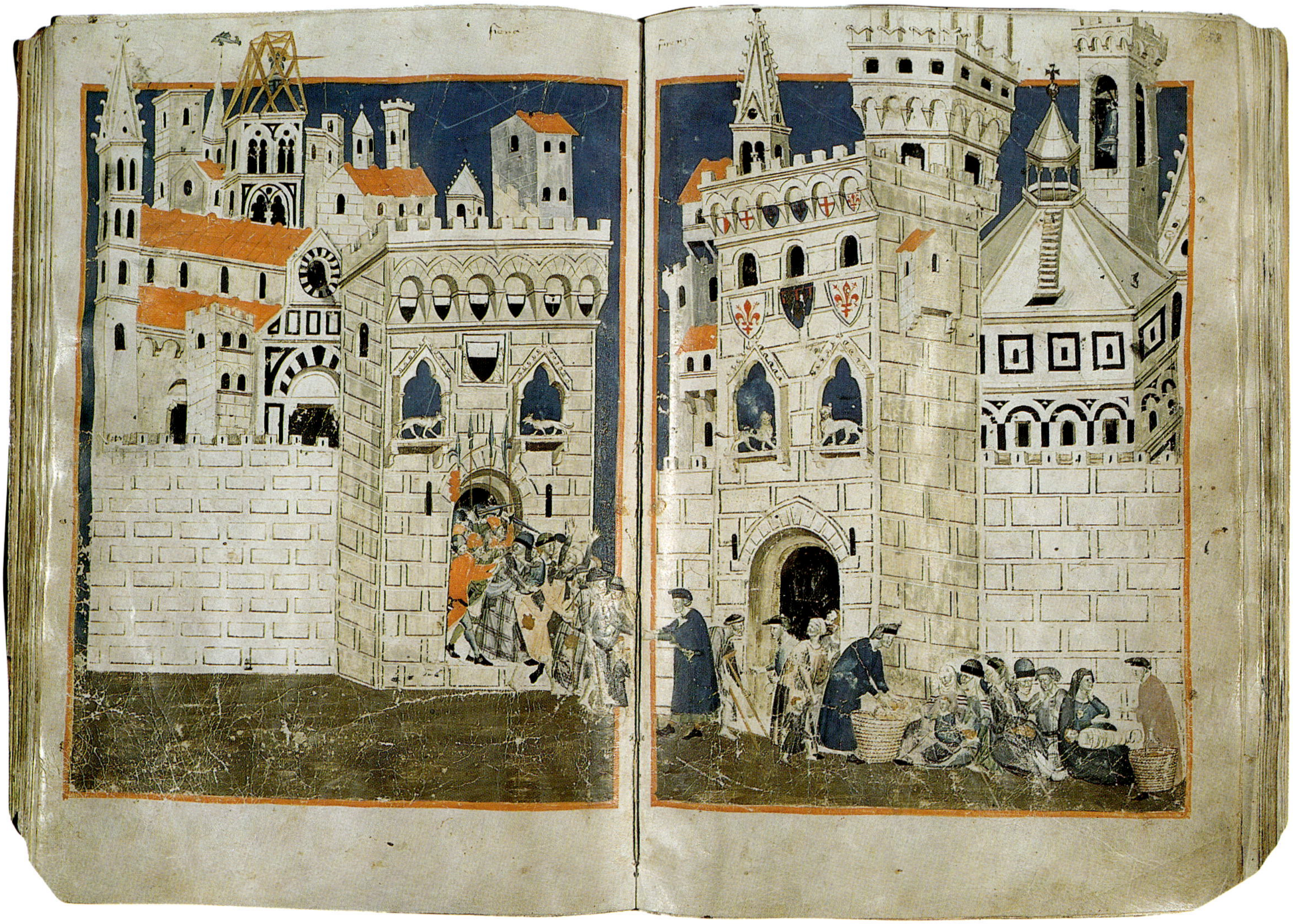

Master of Biadaiolo, *The poor driven out of Siena during the famine of 1328-30 are taken in at Florence*, first half of the 14th century. Florence, Biblioteca Medicea Laurenziana, Laur. Tempi 3, cc. 57 v-58 r.

ture was renewed with the urban universities and theological schools, while the Cistercian reform and the spread of the mendicant orders led to new artistic developments. Urban life took on new vigor and many Italian cities – Venice, Genoa, Pisa, Lucca, Rome, Florence, and Siena – assumed increasingly distinctive aspects which were also reflected in the development of their schools of art, while in Puglia, Campania and Sicily, Suevian domination renewed the Imperial dream, favoring a culture rich in classicizing traits which were to irradiate throughout Central Italy.

It is only on the basis of these premises, albeit highly summarized, that we can understand the transformations occurring in the 13th and 14th centuries in art, urban planning, the social organization of cities, the development of financial activity, and lastly the development of secular political organizations and the emergence of new social classes which, along with Ecclesiastical power, became increasingly important in commissioning monuments and works of art of all kinds. The 13th century closes with sculptural works that are highly innovative, as regards both "architectural" aspects (as in pulpits, fountains, and funerary monuments) and stylistic elements. The solemn classicism of the all-round statues and reliefs of Arnolfo and Giovanni Pisano, capable also of potent realism, determined a crucial transformation in the Medieval plastic tradition. It is through masters such as Tino di Camaino and Giovanni di Balduccio, heirs of the artistic legacy of Giovanni Pisano,

Ambrogio Lorenzetti,
View of Siena, detail,
1337-40. Siena, Palazzo
Pubblico, Hall of the
Nine, Cycle of frescoes
with *The effects of good
government in the
city and the countryside.*

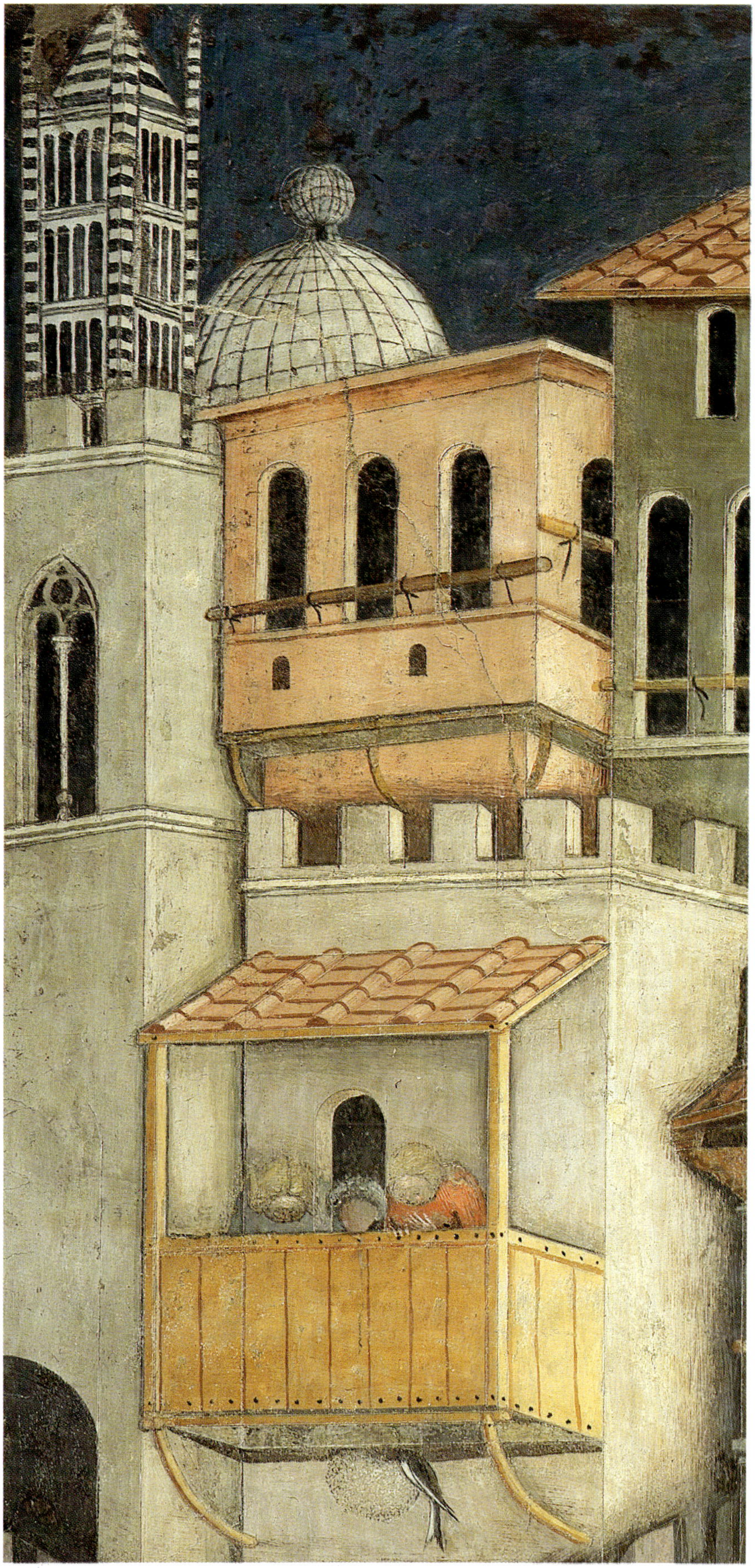

that sculpture of classicizing trend was to spread as far as the Italian South and the Northern region of Lombardy.

In painting, at Rome, in Umbria and Tuscany, artists such as Pietro Cavallini, Duccio, and Cimabue were progressively freeing themselves from Byzantine tradition, dominant up to the middle of the 13th century. It was to be Giotto, with the Sienese Simone Martini and the Lorenzetti brothers, to take the first decisive steps toward a new conception of man and of space.

The 14th century, which boasts among its other splendors a formidable literary triad – Dante, Petrarch, and Boccaccio – was however a century of unrest as well as of profound transformations, rocked by natural catastrophes such as the flood of 1333 in Florence, the Black Plague of 1348, and famine, undermined by the struggle between Pope and Emperor and by contrasts within the Church. While the economic conquests of the "new men" suddenly enriched through commerce and banking were striking, the bankruptcy and decline of entire families was equally abrupt. A gilded world of precious fabrics and magnificent (and priceless) works of art was still counterpoised to the violence of everyday life, always threatened by the terror of death. All of this can be read, by an attentive viewer, in the art of these great masters, who for the first time forcefully and decidedly emerged from the shadows of anonymity.

Wiligelmo

(active in Modena from c. 1099 to 1110)

Of Wiligelmo (or rather Vuiligelmo or Guiligelmo, as suggested by epigraphists and archaeologists), neither the date nor the place of birth is known. Thanks to the commemorative inscription on the façade of the Modena Cathedral it is however certain that he worked in the Modena site in the late 11th and early 12th centuries. "How much honor you deserve among sculptors, Vuiligelmo, is now clearly shown by your sculpture" *(Inter scultores quanto sis dignus onore claret scultura nunc Vuiligelme tua)*: these words can still be read in the last lines of the epigraph, held up by the patriarchs Enoch and Elijah, that commemorates the foundation of the Cathedral. Among the sculptors of his age Wiligelmo thus received from his contemporaries rare and very high praise. His feeling for the art of antiquity studied on Roman sarcophagi and reinterpreted with Christian significance in the winged cherubs on the façade was accompanied by an incomparable sense of the drama and pathos of the story told in Genesis. Unconvincing, instead, is the recent attribution to Wiligelmo of the enigmatic figures of hermaphrodites and jugglers that once adorned the buttresses of the cathedral (now in the Modena lapidary museum).

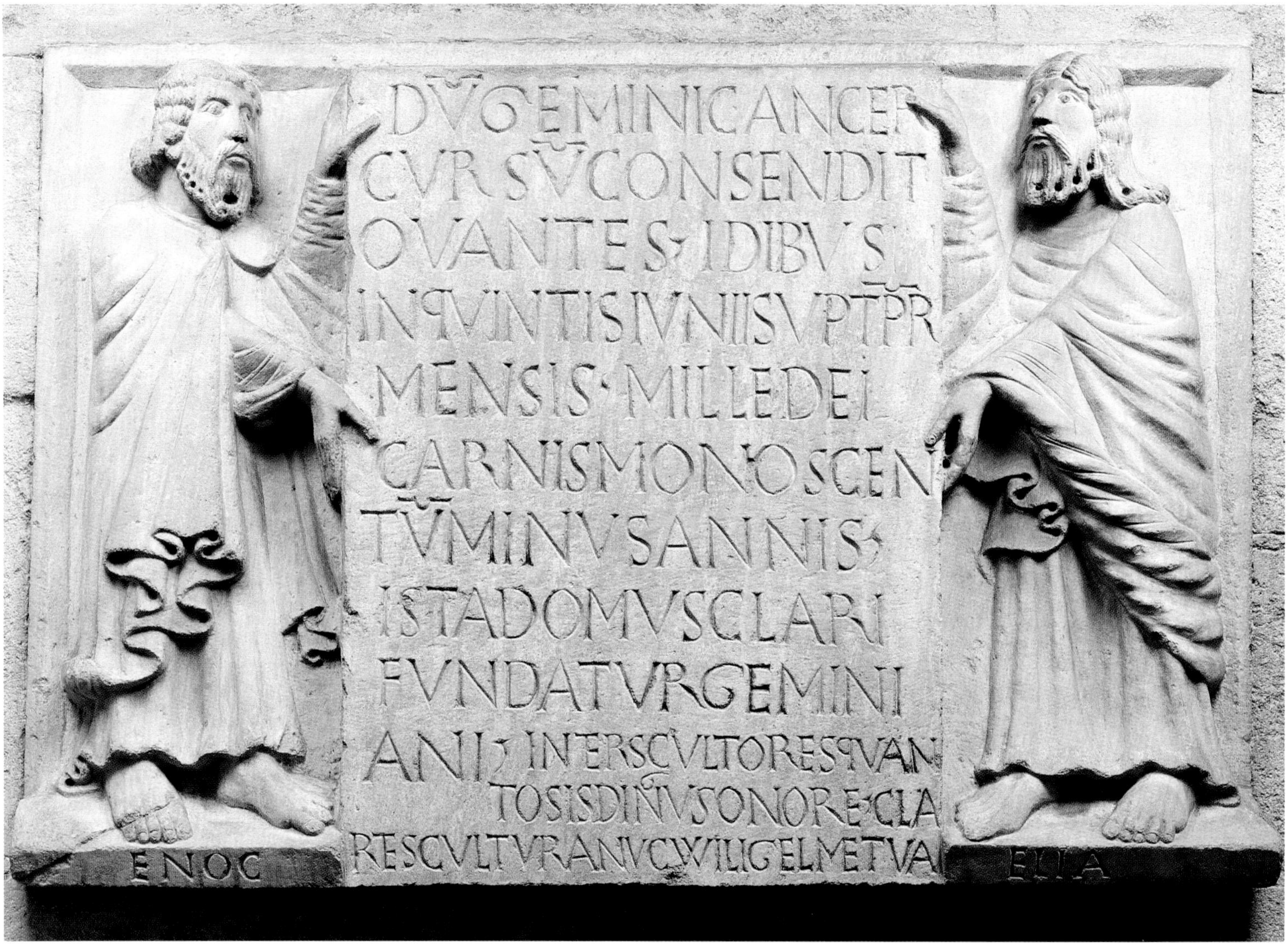

Wiligelmo
Stone slab held up by Enoch and Elijah with epigraph commemorating the foundation of the Modena Cathedral

c. 1099-1106
medium-grain marble
Modena, façade of the Cathedral.

The two patriarchs holding up the stone slab with its inscription are undoubtedly the work of Wiligelmo, who also carved the reliefs with stories from Genesis on the façade, entirely similar in style. Evidently the sculptor had prepared the slab on which others inscribed the date when the church was founded and, perhaps at a later time, the eulogy to the sculptor. Compositions of this type were inspired by Roman sarcophagi, where two funerary cherubs holding a plaque are usually found in place of the Enoch and Elijah portrayed here. The two patriarchs, who were taken up into heaven without undergoing death, symbolically confer immortality on the grandiose Modena church and its rich sculptural decoration.

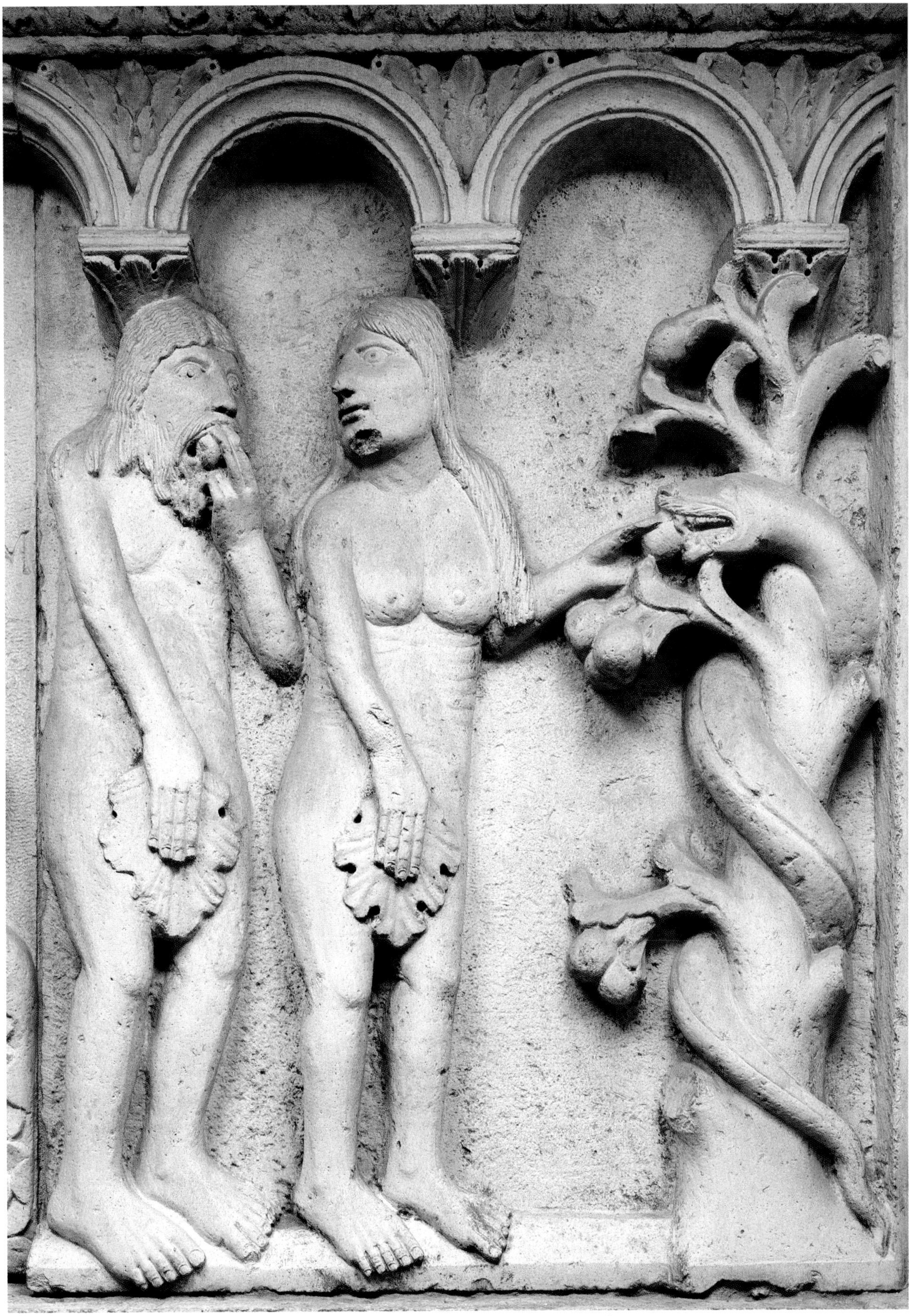

Wiligelmo
Adam and Eve and the Tree of Evil
c. 1099-1106
Vicenza soft stone
Modena, façade of the Cathedral.

Following the Biblical story told in the Book of Genesis, Wiligelmo narrates with urgent immediacy the story of Adam and Eve from the creation to the curse laid on them after their sin. He then continues with the fratricide of Abel and the death of Cain up to the episode of Noah's Arc. To portray sin the artist synthesizes several episodes in a single scene in highly original manner: Eve takes from the evil serpent's fangs the forbidden fruit that Adam is already eating, greedily but fearfully. At the same time the first parents, aware of sin and their nudity, cover themselves with large fig leaves. Eve, who in the preceding scene, as confirmation of her original innocence, is entirely devoid of sensuality, now displays an ample bosom. Her body, like that of Adam, is instead shapeless and covered by heavy garments in the scene portraying them atoning for their sin by hard work in the fields.

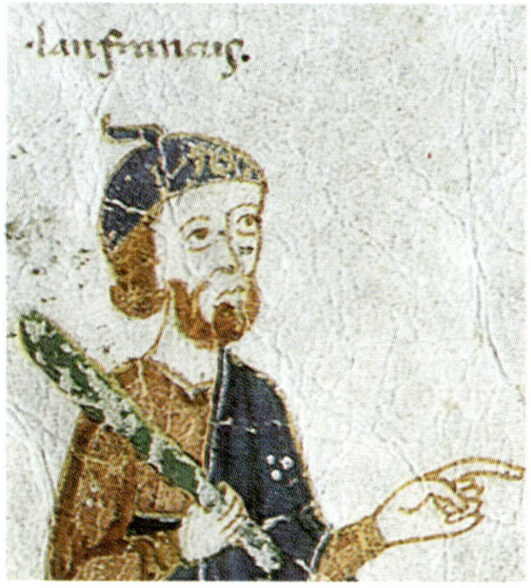

Lanfranco

(active in Modena from c. 1099 to 1110)

"Mirabilis artifex, mirificus edificator". The architect of the Modena Cathedral Lanfranco, whose birthplace is unknown, is described by these words in the illuminated manuscript on this page. It was considered providential to have found a highly talented designer for "such a great work". "Principal and supreme artificer of such an arduous undertaking", he was to have the honor, in 1106, of discovering, with Bonsignore, the Bishop of Reggio, the venerated urn containing the relicts of St Geminianus to be placed in the new crypt. The importance acknowledged Lanfranco in Medieval documents not only as designer and architect but also as director of works is confirmed by an apsidal epigraph in Latin which calls him "famous for ingenuity, knowledgeable and competent director of works, governor and master".

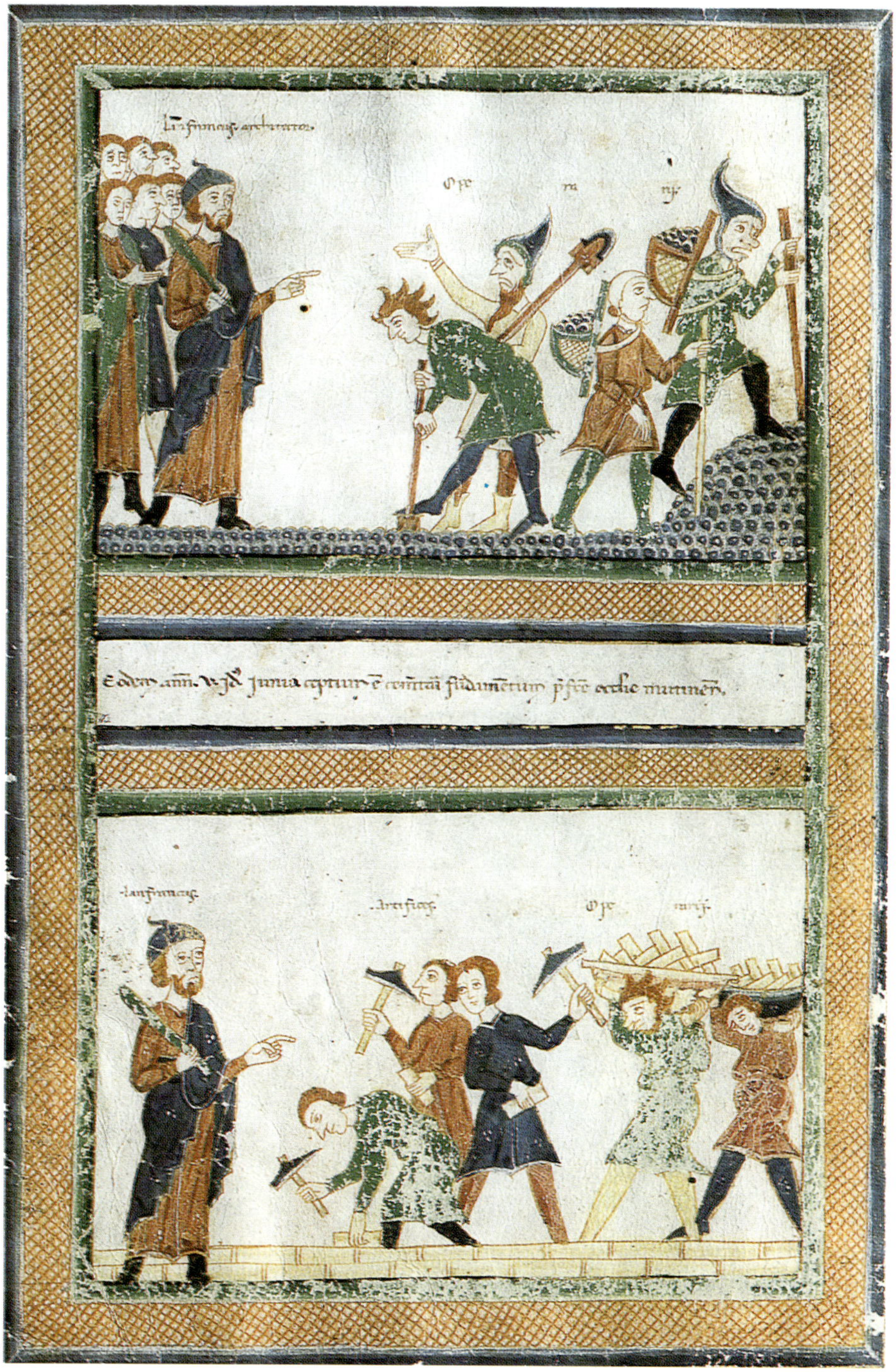

Modenese school
The architect Lanfranco directs work on the Modena Cathedral
early 13th century
illuminated page in the *Relatio de innovatione ecclesie sancti Geminiani, ac de translatione eius beatissimi corporis*
Modena, Chapter Archives, Ms. O.II.11, c. 1 v.

This illuminated page bears precious testimony to the construction activity carried out on the worksite for the Modena Duomo. Standing out among the personages, tallest among them, is the bearded figure of Lanfranco, wearing a sumptuous gown and headdress, and isolated from the others in both of the scenes. Like the angel of the Apocalypse who with his rod measures and constructs the heavenly Jerusalem, the architect, holding a *virga*, instrument of command and measurement, directs the workers and builders (*operarii e artifices*). The two scenes illustrate different stages in the construction of the building; above, diggers are excavating for the foundations; below, the walls are rising, constructed with blocks of stone transported by laborers.

Lanfranco
Modena Cathedral
begun on May 23, 1099; consecration of the altar to the Saint, October 8, 1106.

Symbol of the civic pride of Modena's inhabitants, who with this innovative marble-faced building aspired at the close of the 11th century to erect a church that would rival the Pisa Cathedral and the Florence Baptistery, the Modena Duomo is one of the finest examples of European Romanesque architecture. Its present-day appearance is the result of various reconstruction initiatives carried out later, on the northern side in particular. On the façade the rose window and the side doors are subsequent additions; to construct the latter, some of Wiligelmo's reliefs had to be raised. Despite these changes it is still clearly evident that the church's first architect designed a complex building, whose exterior and interior structures are closely related. To the rhythm of a system of arcades that continue from the apse, the first part to be built, along the sides and onto the façade, Lanfranco's church rises on the site of the original cathedral. As compared to the latter, it is longer, the interior has three naves instead of five, and the urban setting is different.

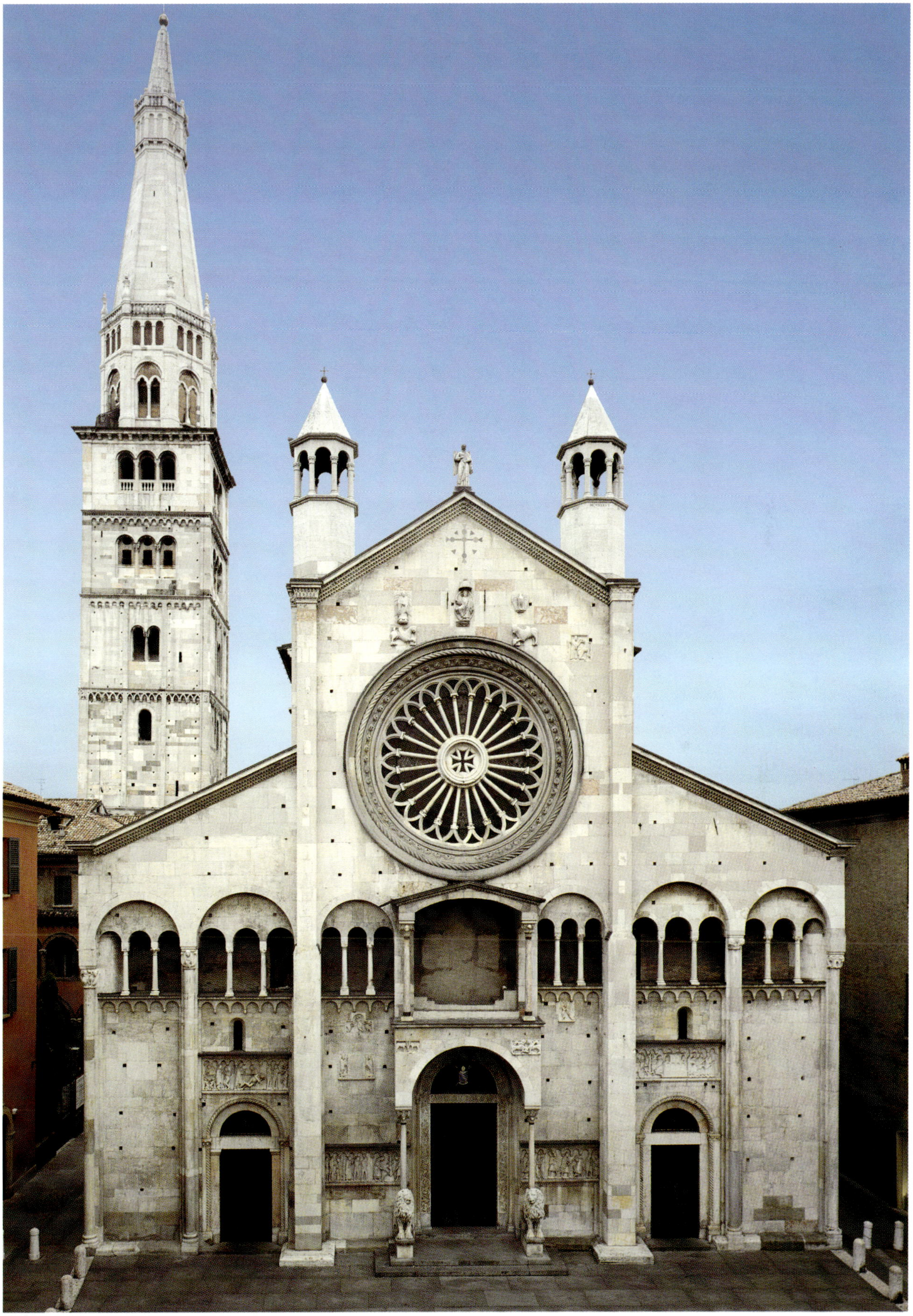

Buscheto

(information from 1063 – Pisa, c. 1110)

Buscheto, "astute as Ulysses, ingenious as Dedalus", was buried with high honors in the façade of the Pisa Duomo. Architect of the building made all of marble (*niveo de marmore templum*), he was the first to have his name acclaimed by contemporaries. As stated in the epigraph on his tomb, an ancient sarcophagus, he invented machines so ingenious as to allow ten boys to lift monolithic columns that could only be moved by a thousand oxen. Buscheto was renowned in Rome too for a machine operated by ten girls to lift the Vatican obelisk. Legends apart, the ambitious project for the Pisa Duomo emerged from a vast cultural background which presupposes, for the dome and its decorations, a knowledge of buildings located in different regions of the Mediterranean basin. The basilical design, enriched with marble from ancient buildings, shows a desire to emulate the architecture of Imperial and Early Christian Rome.

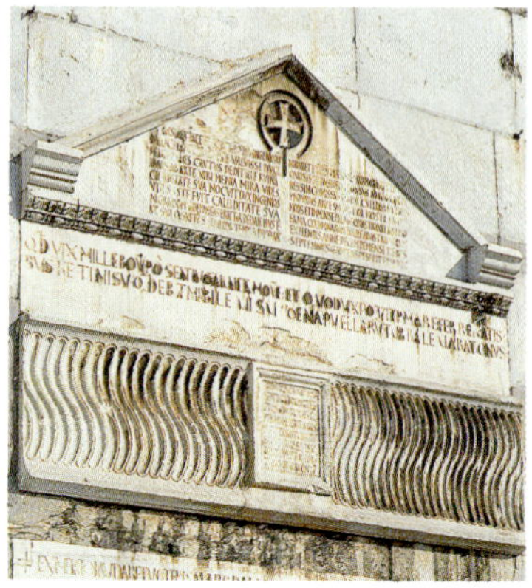

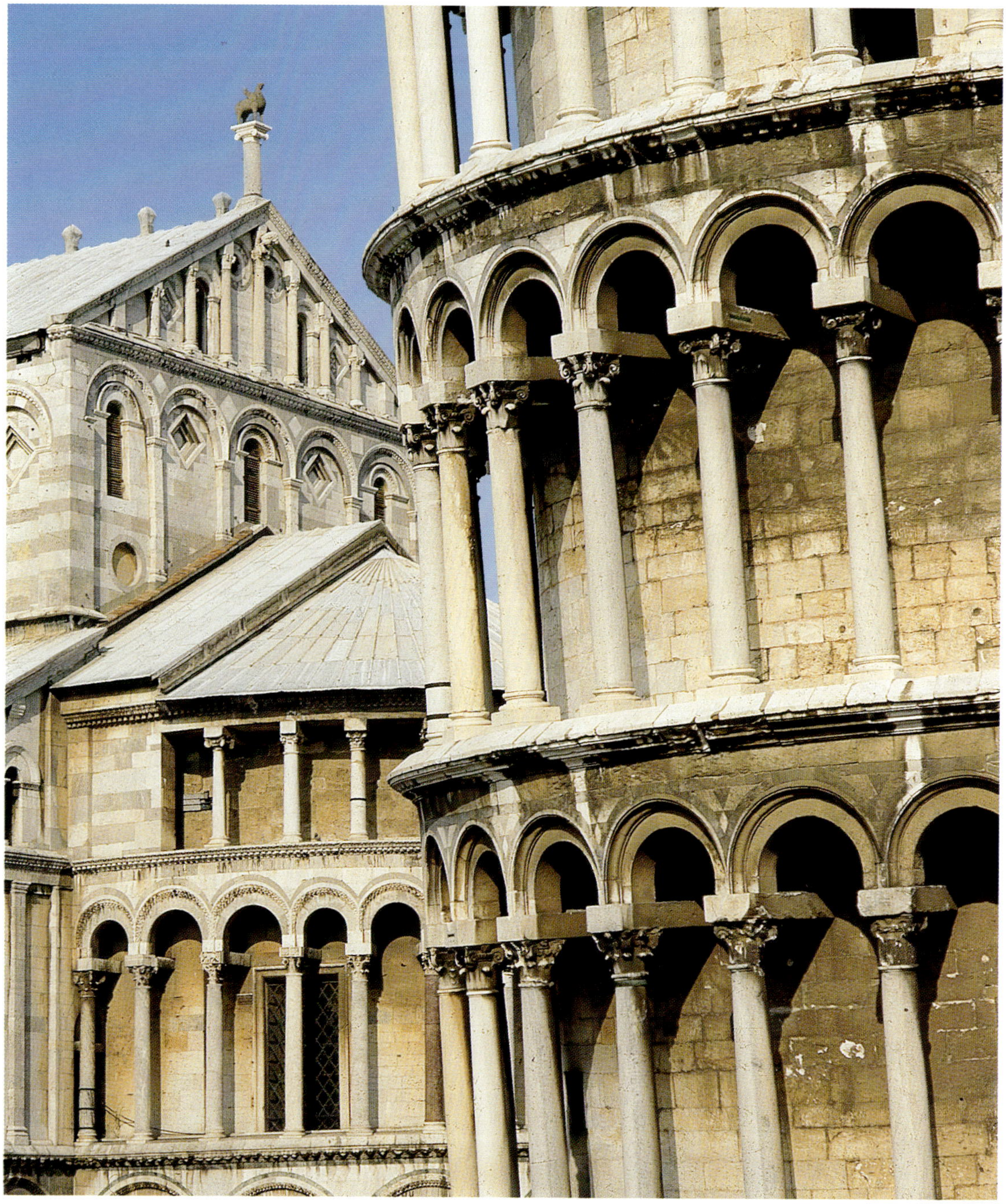

View of the Apse of the Pisa Duomo and the Bell Tower
end of 11th century

The Pisa Duomo, begun in 1063 after the great victory over the Saracens at Palermo and consecrated in 1118, is a construction virtually unrivalled for its height, its grandiose spaces and its imposing interior colonnade. Neither in Italy nor beyond the Alps had such a colossal monument yet been conceived (the dome is 48 meters high), as well-articulated as harmonious in its proportions. Not even the Basilica of St Mark's in Venice, more or less coeval, hurls such a magnificent challenge to antiquity. Although influenced by Islamic monuments and the Churches of Asia Minor, the Pisa Duomo, with five naves and an elliptical dome over the crossing of the three-naved transept, possesses autonomous characteristics, unique in the architecture of the times. It was soon to become the prototype for many Romanesque churches in the Pisan territory, erected in Lucca, Pistoia and even Sardinia, then under the domination of Pisa.

At left:
Tomb of the Architect Buscheto with commemorative inscription, end of 11th century. Pisa, Duomo, façade, first arch in the lower tier.

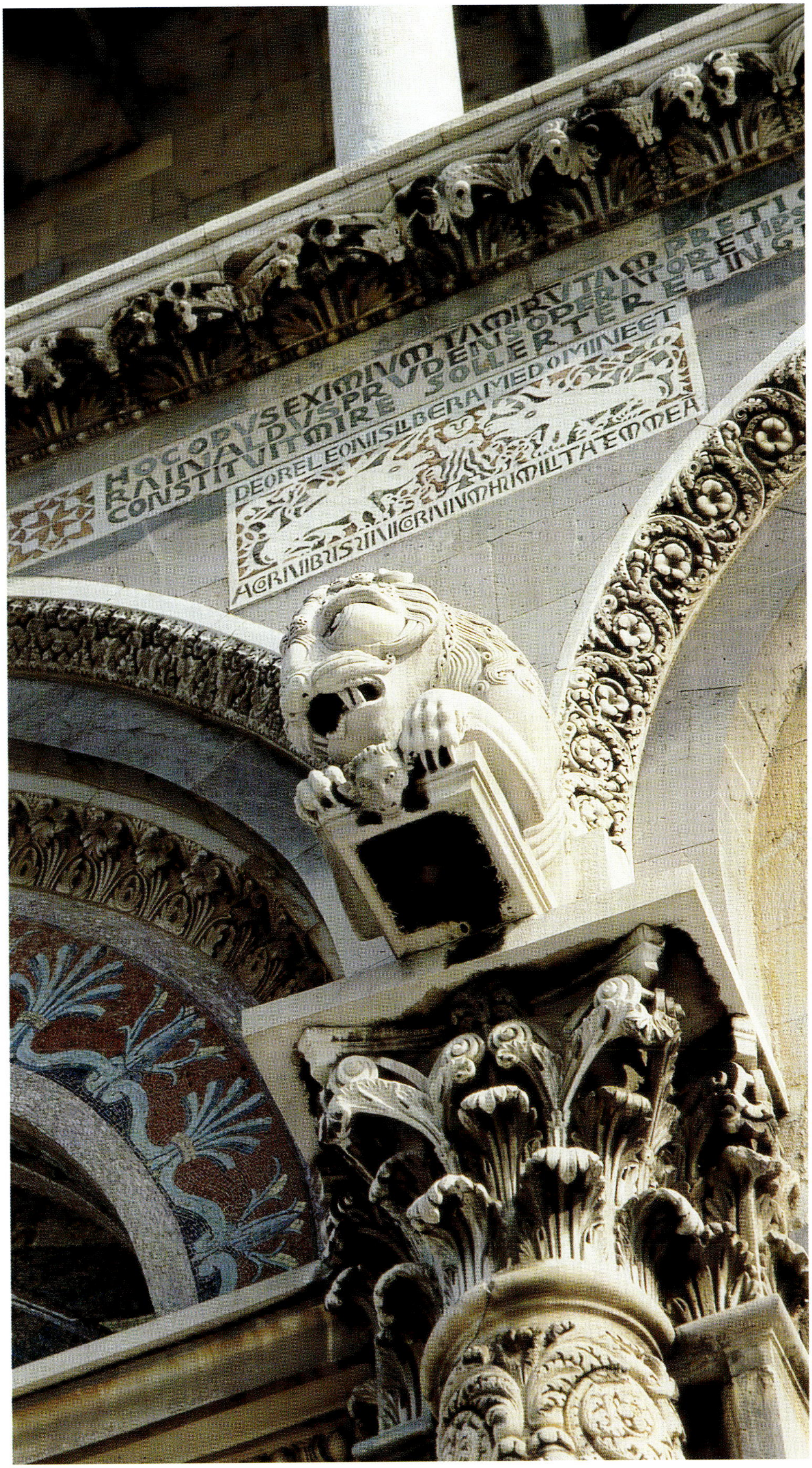

Commemorative inscription to Rainaldo
end of 11th century
polychrome marble
Pisa, Duomo, façade.

The inscription on the inlaid colored marble panel beside the lunette over the central portal praises Rainaldo who, after the death of Buscheto, continued work on the Duomo.

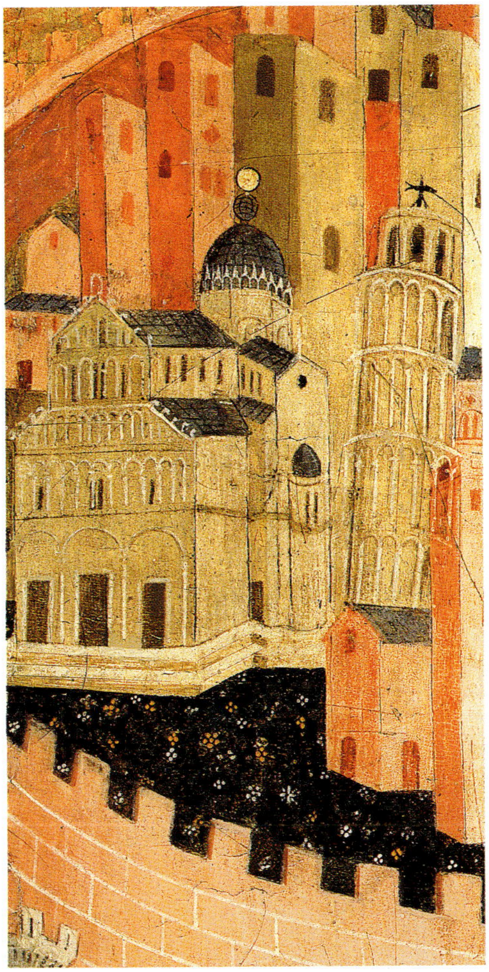

Anonymous artist
View of the Pisa Duomo
14th century
panel, detail of
San Nicola da Tolentino
Pisa, San Nicola.

This is one of the first representation of the Pisa Duomo and of the famous bell tower, it too marked by the rhythm of arches and loggias. The tower is shown already leaning. As the ground under it continued to yield, its construction became increasingly difficult, lasting from 1173 to the first half of the 14th century.

Bonanno Pisano

(Pisa, information between c. 1180 and 1186)

In 1595 a fire at Pisa destroyed the bronze frames of the central door to the Duomo. On this occasion the epigraph in which *Bonannus Pisanus* declares that he has completed the work in only one year, fortunately handed down to us by Vasari, was lost. This was the first testimony left by the artist, once considered, without valid grounds, to be the architect of the Tower of Pisa. In 1186, with evident civic pride, Bonanno signs himself again *civis pisanus* on the bronze door cast in only six months, probably at Pisa, and sent to Palermo for the Duomo of Monreale, where it remains today. The Pisan master was not the only expert in the art of casting bronze doors to leave his name. Barisano, for instance, signed his name on the door frames of the Trani Duomo (1175) and those of Ravello (1179). It was Bonanno however who renewed the Italian-Byzantine tradition in this field.

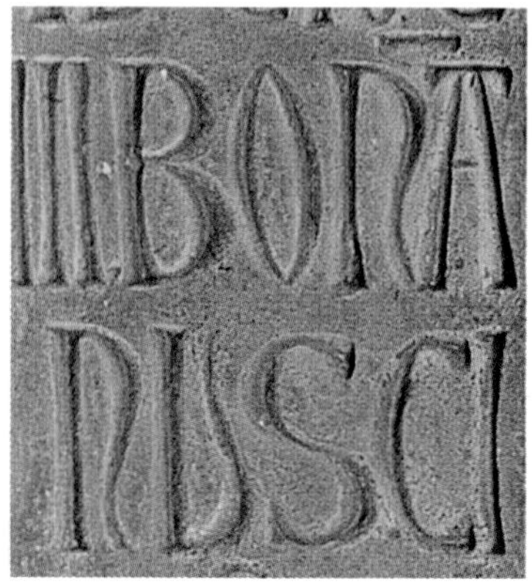

Bonanno Pisano,
Epigraph, detail with signature, 1185 (signed and dated 1186 according to the Pisan calendar). Monreale (Palermo), Duomo, left leaf of the main door.

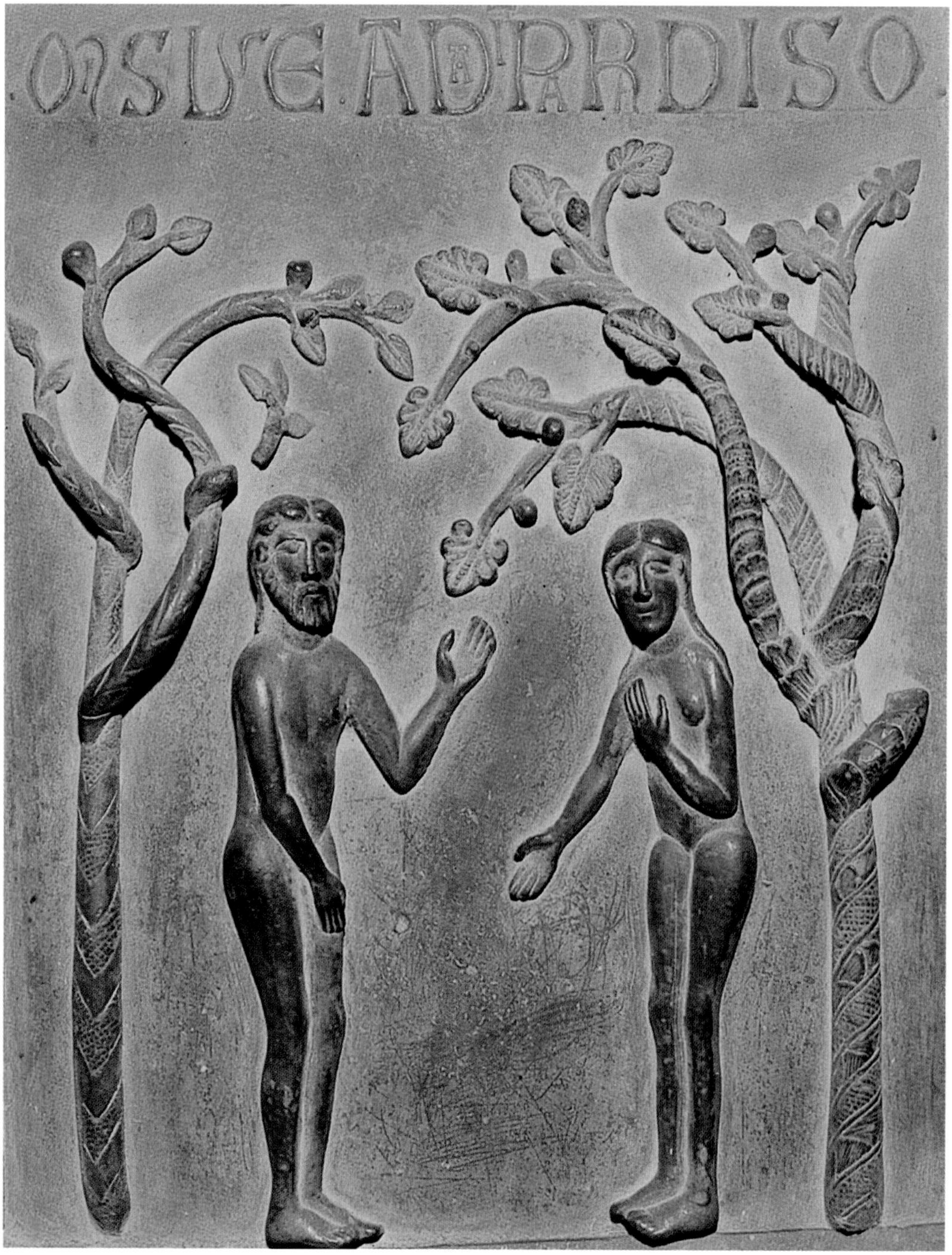

Bonanno Pisano
Adam and Eve in the Garden of Eden
1185 (signed and dated 1186 according to the Pisan calendar)
bronze, detail of the main door
Monreale (Palermo), Duomo.

The "royal" door of the Pisa Duomo having been destroyed by fire, two masterpieces by Bonanno remain: St Ranier's Door in the transept of the cathedral, with evangelical stories in twenty panels, and the main door of the Monreale Duomo, with forty scenes from the Old and New Testaments. Great skill is evident in the technique of casting and cold reworking of the reliefs modelled by Bonanno, whose workshop may have been located in the vicinity of the Pisa Duomo. The doors rest on a wooden base and the panels, cast one by one, are retained at the back by a metal frame fixed to the wood by nails whose heads are decorated with rosettes. The master's innovations were soon recognised. In 1329 a Florentine was commissioned to copy the Pisan doors as model for the one designed by Andrea Pisano for the Florence Baptistery.

Guglielmo

(active in Pisa, second half of the 12th century)

"Excellent in art", according to an inscription now lost, Guglielmo is considered the forerunner of Pisa's great Medieval sculpture. He is buried in and commemorated on the façade of the Cathedral along with Buscheto and Rainaldo, the designers of the building. The memorial stone cites *Guillelmus* as artificer of the pulpit of Saint Mary, that is, the Pisa Duomo, dedicated to the Virgin. In addition to the work shown here, later transferred to Cagliari, he is attributed with several capitals still in the Pisa Duomo and some plaques for the choir stall, later dismembered, pierced with open-work like fine embroidery. The *Holy Water Stoup of St Ranier* (New York, The Cloisters) also seems close to his style, which re-elaborates Classical and Middle Eastern themes with originality. His talent emerges in all-round sculpture, showing him to be an early forerunner of Nicola and Giovanni Pisano.

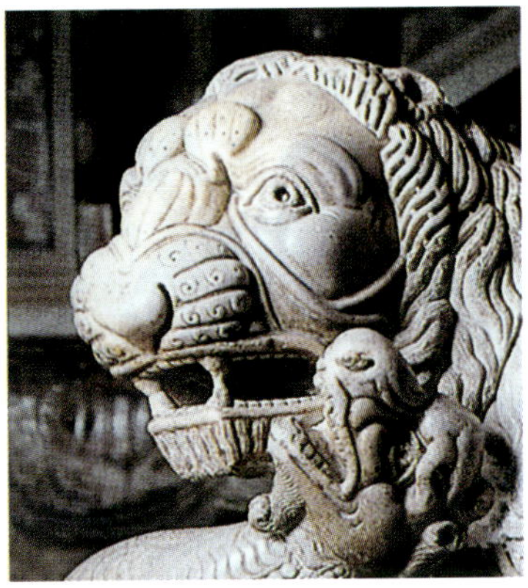

Guglielmo, *Lion with Dragon*, c. 1159-62. Cagliari, Duomo.

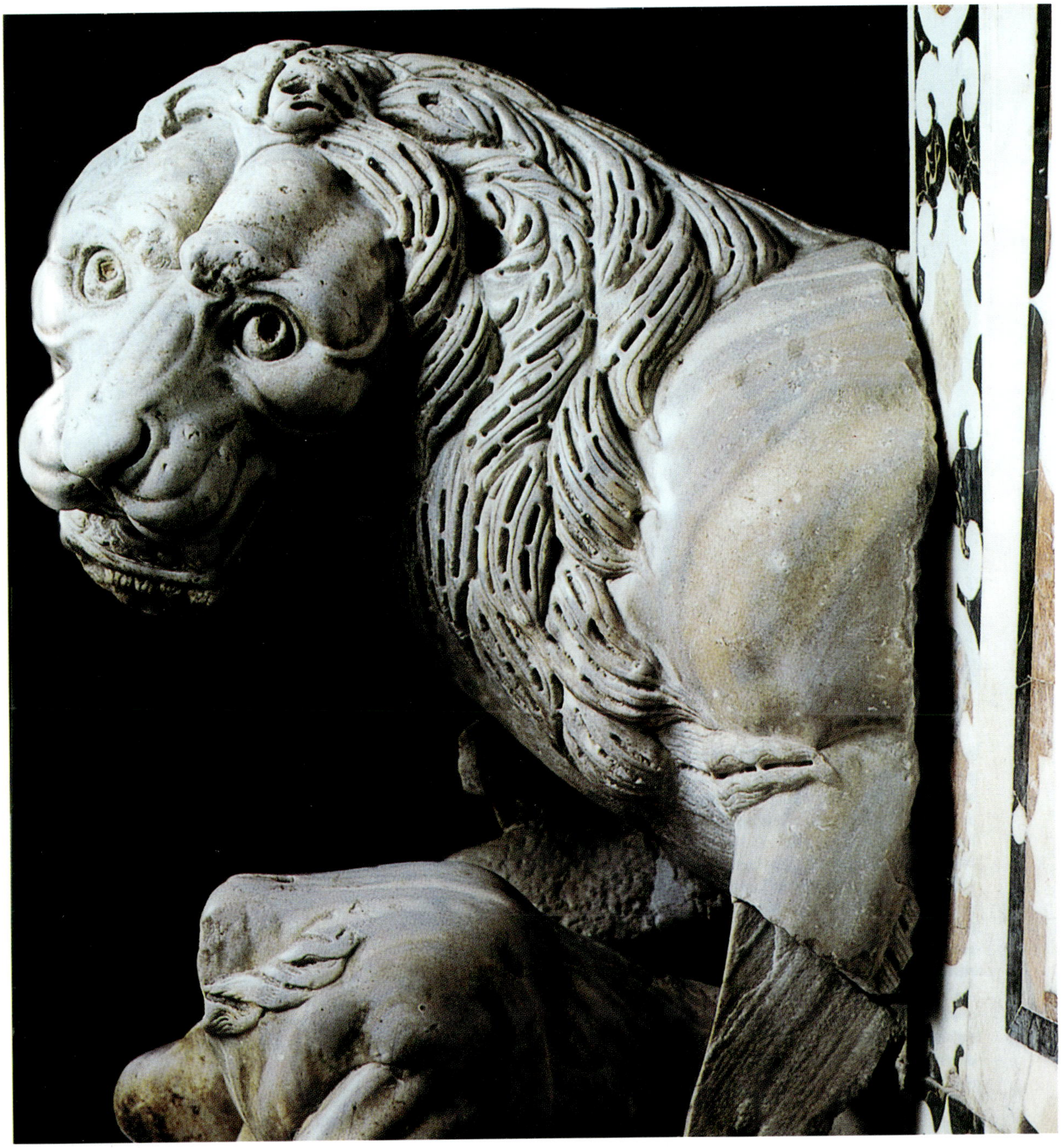

Guglielmo
Leon bringing down an Ox
marble
c. 1159-62
Cagliari, Duomo.

In 1312 a Pisan galley disembarked at Cagliari an ambo supported by sculptured lions. This work, which had been replaced in the Pisa Duomo by Giovanni Pisano's new pulpit, found a place in the Cathedral of Santa Maria di Castello, on the rock where the conquerors of Sardinia had erected one of the strongest medieval fortresses. A change in taste had occurred, and the Pisans must be credited for not having destroyed one of the highest examples of Romanesque sculpture. Such an unusual work may even have reinforced the image of the conquerors, who aspired to the title of heirs to ancient Rome and lords of the sea. It is thus unsurprising to find, in Guglielmo's lions, Syrian origins, classic plasticity and naturalistic details drilled in the marble.

Benedetto Antelami

(active in Parma and in Northern Italy between 1178 and 1230)

Enigma and controversial hypotheses still surround the cultural background and artistic career of Benedetto Antelami, the great master who worked at Parma and Borgo San Donnino, near Fidenza. His origin, first of all, is debatable. *Antelamus* (or *Intelvi*) is a Medieval place-name that indicates a valley near Lake Como, which may mean that a corporation of master builders emigrated from there to Liguria in the middle of the 12th century. While several generations of *magistri Antelami* worked in Genoa starting in 1157, no proof exists that Benedetto came from Liguria. His role as architect as well as sculptor is also uncertain, since Benedetto signs himself only *sculptor* in the Parma *Deposition*. His responsibility for the architectural project and for many of the reliefs in the interior and exterior of the Baptistery now seems convincing.

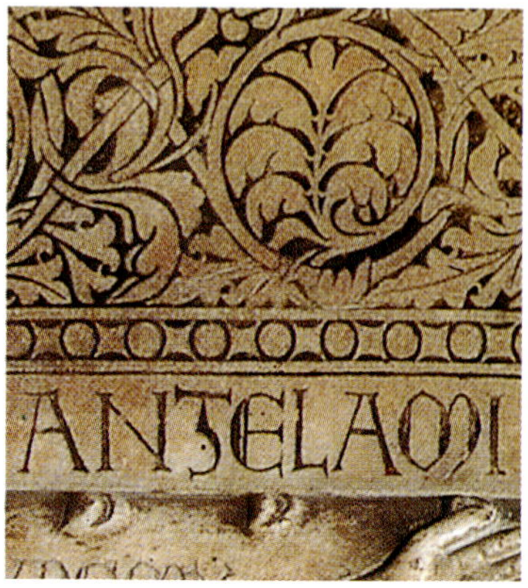

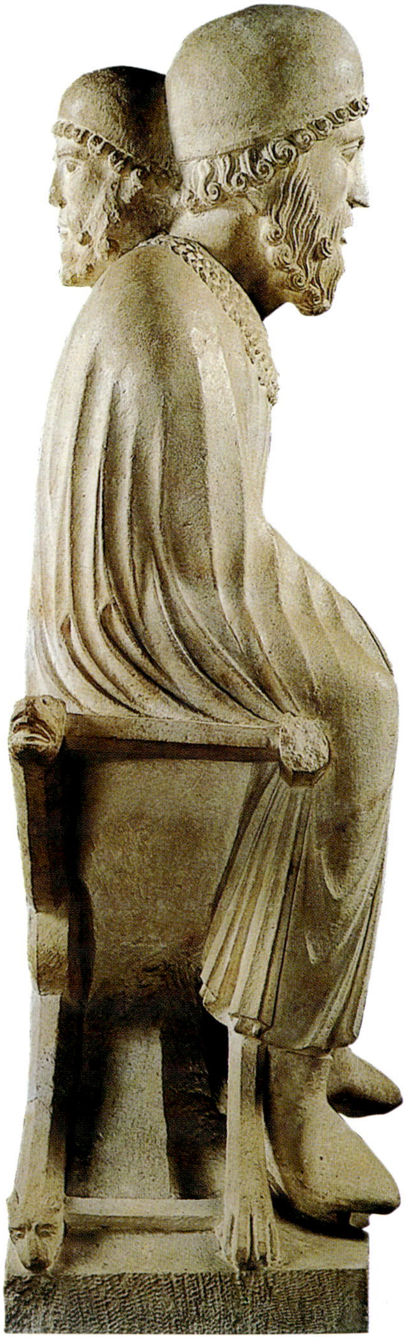

Benedetto Antelami
January and *September*
early 13th century
stone
Parma, Baptistery.

January, symbolised by the mythical two-fronted Janus seated on a scranno, and *September*, with a peasant harvesting grapes and the personification of Libra, form part of the famous cycle of *Months*, *Seasons* and the *Zodiac*, originally placed high inside the Baptistery, under the dome.
The sculptures formed a cycle of sixteen reliefs corresponding to the sixteen sectors into which the interior of the building is divided.
The whole plastic decoration seems inspired by an unitary, precise iconographic program.
Starting from the external reliefs on the lunettes above the three doors, which allude to the arduous journey of human life, it continues on the inside with reliefs and sculptures offering a reassuring message: danger and difficulty can be overcome through baptism which frees mankind of original sin.
Within this context the fascinating sculptures of the *Months* and the *Seasons*, represented for the first time in such complex, conspicuous manner, refer to the work of man, who through hard fatigue atones for the Biblical malediction. The harmonious combination of sculpture and architecture in the Parma Baptistery, whose project was begun by Antelami in about 1196, after the construction of the Duomo, has often been compared to that achieved during those same years in some Romanesque churches in France, Provence in particular, a region which the artist may have visited.

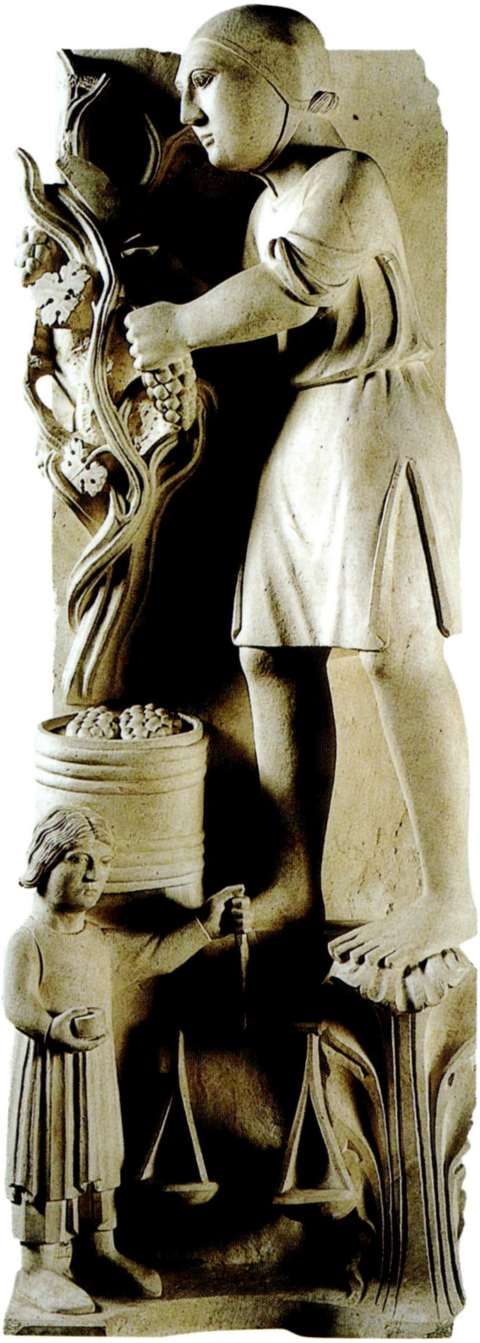

At left:
Benedetto Antelami, *Deposition*, detail with the sculptor's signature, 1178.
Parma, Duomo.

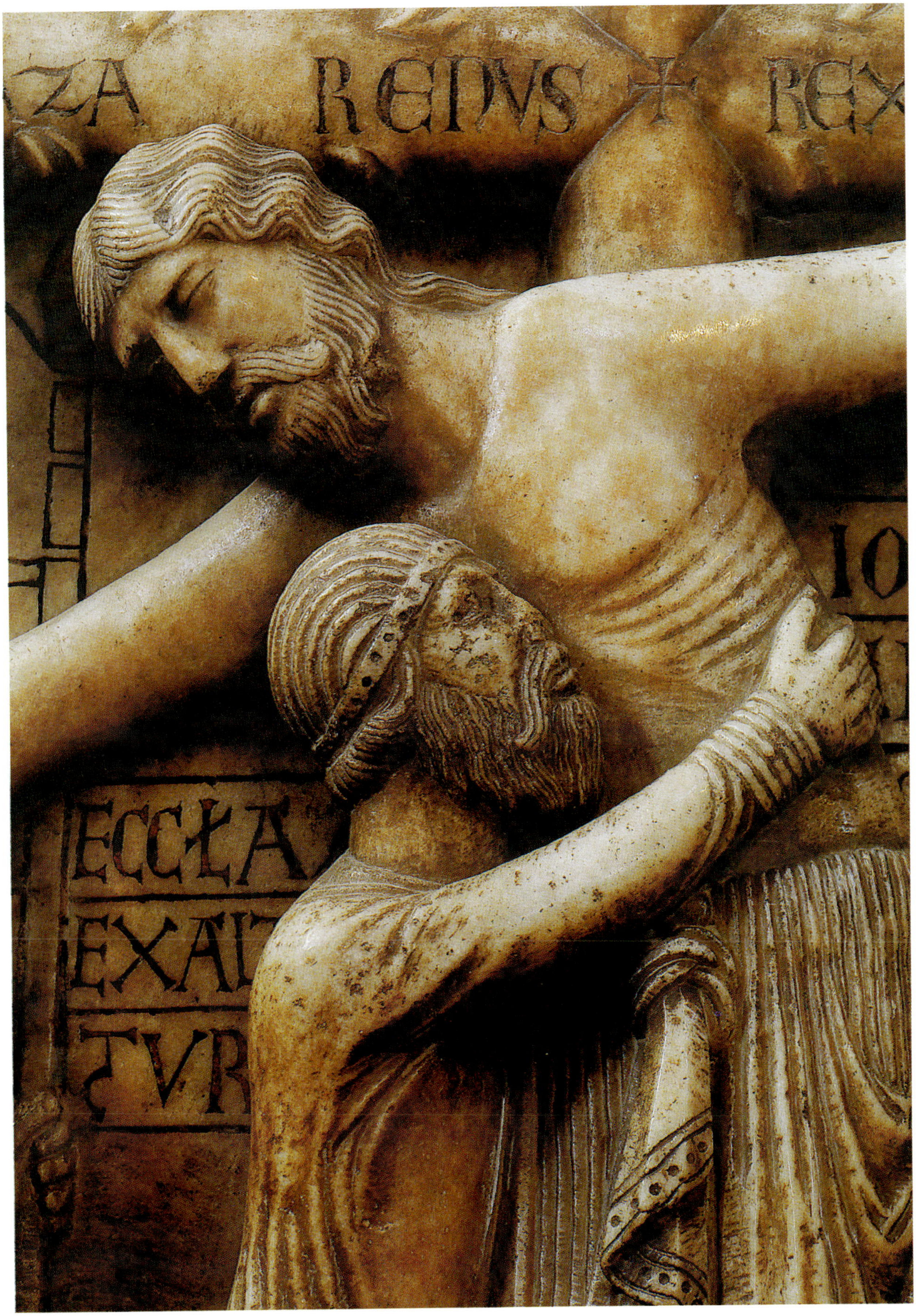

Benedetto Antelami
Deposition
1178
marble, detail of
Christ deposed by Joseph of Arimathea
Parma, Duomo.

Almost certainly part of a pulpit from which the Gospels were read, the *Deposition* is one of the most important works of the 12th century, both for its refined technique and for the equilibrium achieved between spiritual message and dramatic narration. On the entire slab, 230 centimetres long, events linked to Christ's Passion are presented simultaneously: at the left of the deposed Christ, Mary, accompanied by the pious women, lifts her son's hand to her cheek; on the right some soldiers are throwing dice, others are holding Christ's tunic, while Nicodemus on the ladder removes a nail from the Cross. While the influence of the Provençal style seems clear in some details, the *Deposition* as a whole remains a masterpiece without precedent, rich as never before in inscriptions serving as captions which contribute to creating an effect of deep, naturalistic space.

Bonaventura Berlinghieri

(Lucca, documented from 1228 to 1274)

A child of art, Bonaventura Berlinghieri was the most talented member of a large family of painters – his father Berlinghiero di Melanese da Volterra (died in about 1236), his brothers Barone and Marco (documented from 1232 to 1255), and lastly his stepson Lupardo di Benincasa (died in 1258), trained in the art by his stepfather Berlinghieri. Despite the slender list of works attributed to him with certainty, the life of Bonaventura is well documented, starting in 1228 when his name appears among the signers, along with his father and his brother Barone, of the appeal for peace between Lucca and Pisa. His reputation as painter is linked mainly to the Pescia Altarpiece, while the frescoes with birds and various ornamental elements in the Archdeacon's Chamber in the Lucca Duomo, painted in 1244 in collaboration with a certain Paolo da Lucca, have disappeared.

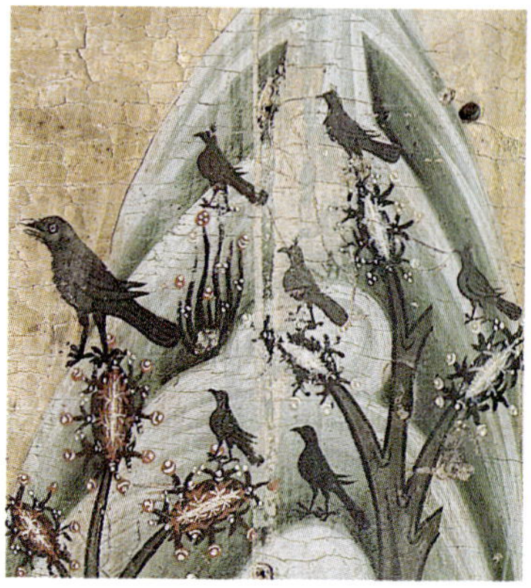

Bonaventura Berlinghieri, *Preaching to the Birds*, 1235, detail of the *Altarpiece with St Francis and Stories of his Life*. Pescia (Pistoia), San Francesco.

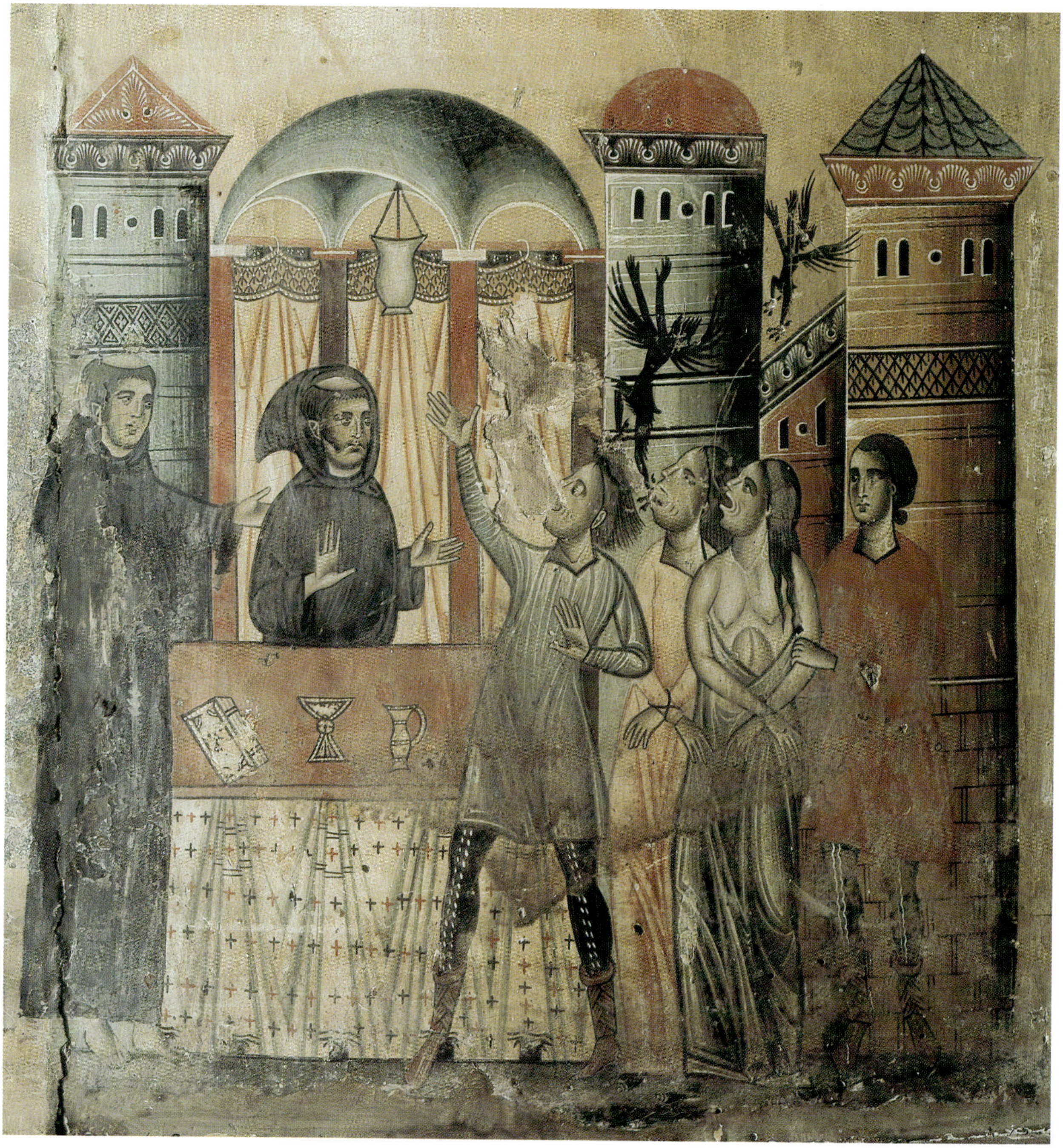

Bonaventura Berlinghieri
The Healing of the One Possessed
signed and dated 1235 panel, detail of the *Altarpiece with St Francis and Stories of his Life.*

The work has been known in its integrity only since 1851, when it was cleaned of a layer that had been totally repainted. The entire composition, dominated by the figure of St Francis, fixed and hieratic as an icon, is enlivened by six small scenes, marked by a timid attempt at life-like corporeality in the figures. The Franciscan iconography, prior to the *Treatise on Miracles* by Tommaso da Celano (c. 1250), probably derives from an altar frontal of slightly earlier date (Pisa, Museum of San Matteo) attributed to another great master of the times, Giunta Pisano, who also worked in Rome and Assisi. This is a confirmation of the primary role held at the time by Pisa and Lucca.

Southern Italian Miniator

(active in the middle of the 13th c.)

The Kingdom of Sicily, governed by Frederick II of Swabia (1194-1250) and later by his son Manfredi (crowned in1258) possessed cultural traits so original as to figure among the most significant in the western world in Medieval times. The opening to architecture and the figurative arts, sculpture in particular, took place under the sign of an ideological return to Roman classicism (within the sphere of the Imperial *renovatio*, the sculptor Nicola Pisano also trained in Puglia). In illuminated manuscripts, several artists, although anonymous, are worthy of attention. This is the case of the illustrator of the treatise on birds by Frederick II, known in its oldest illustrated version through a copy made for Manfredi. The anonymous illustrator, perhaps Neapolitan, is distinguished by a sensitivity for nature and the vivacious style of his miniatures.

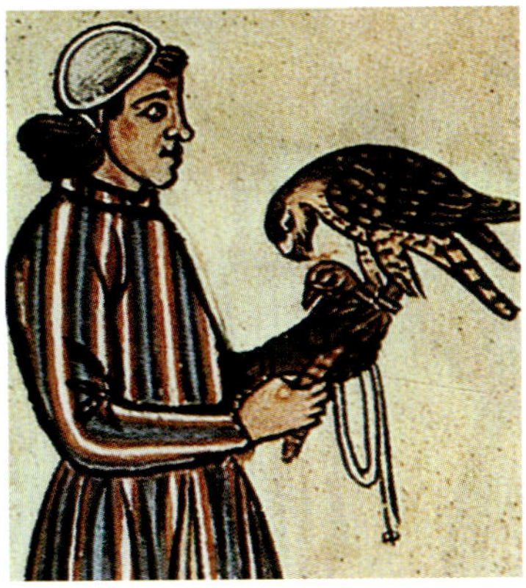

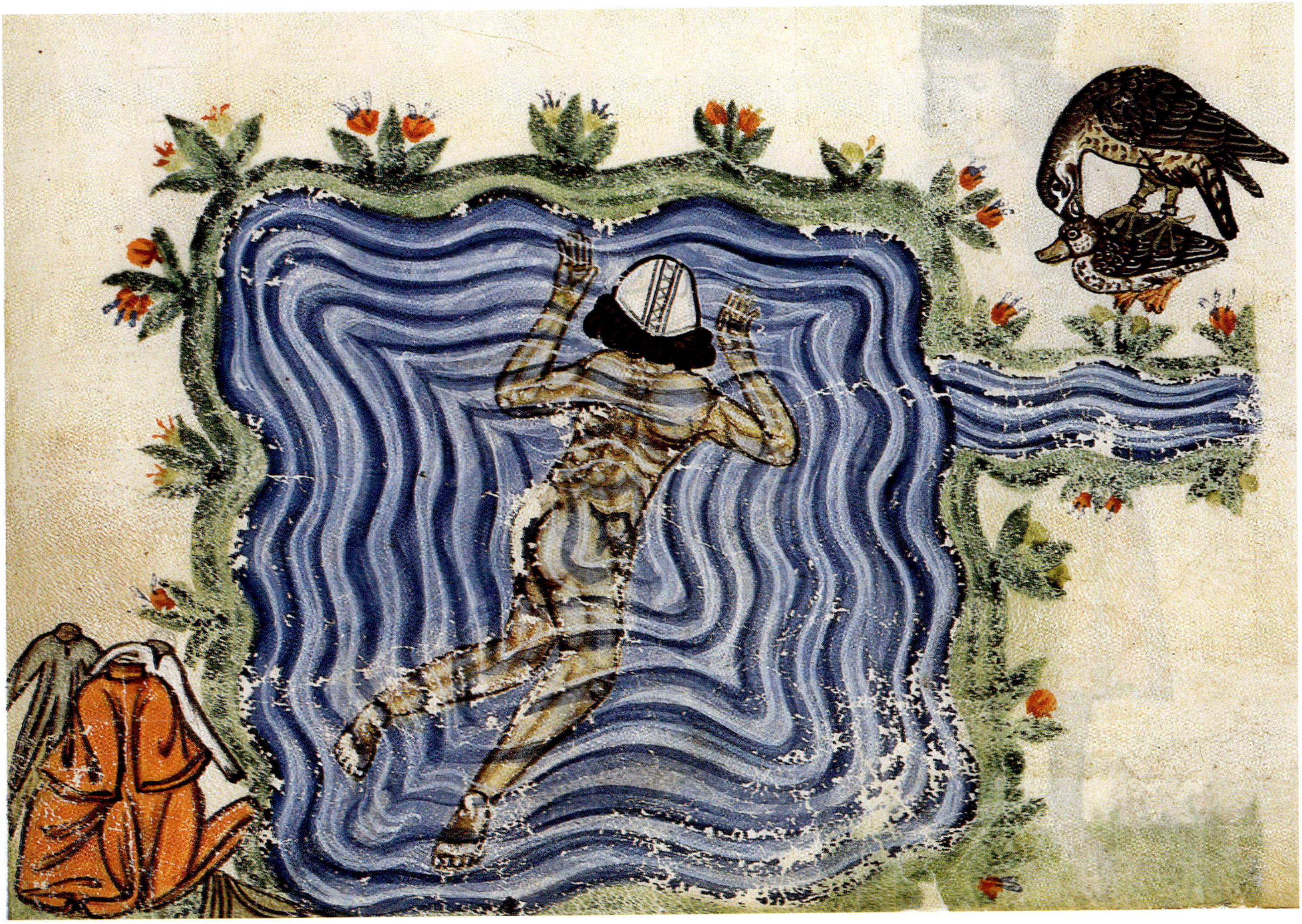

Southern Italian Miniator
The Falcon Hunter in the Lake
before 1258
parchment
Rome, Biblioteca Apostolica Vaticana, Pal. Lat. 1071, c. 69 r.

The first treatises on falconry in the western world date from the 10th century; but that of Frederick II of Swabia, who loved hunting in his Apulian estates, is by far the most complete, held in high consideration by naturalists even today. Compiled after thirty years of study even on Arabic texts and those of Aristotle, and consultation with experts called from afar, the original manuscript had disappeared already by 1248. One of its most precious copies is that of the Vatican, commissioned by Manfredi before his coronation (a French variation exists in Paris, National Library, Lat. 12400). The anonymous author of the brightly coloured illustrations manages to follow the text of *De arte venandi cum avibus* faithfully and effectively. In the lake scene, Federico comments that the falcon-hunter must be a good swimmer to reach his falcon.

Southern Italian Miniator, *The Falcon Hunter*, detail from *De arte venandi cum avibus* (*The Art of Hunting with Birds*), before 1258. Rome, Biblioteca Apostolica Vaticana, Pal. Lat. 1071, c. 81 r.

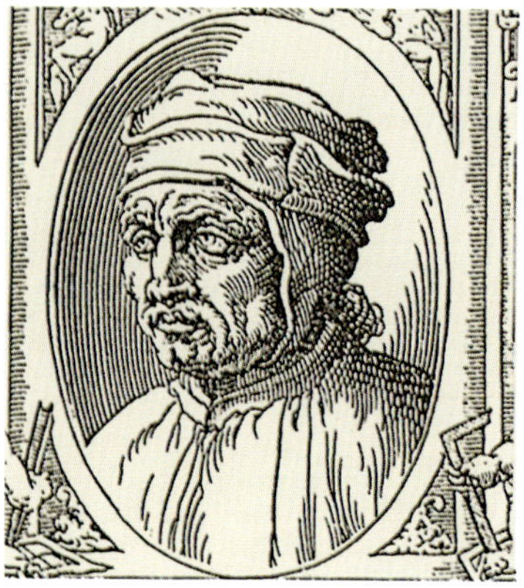

Arnolfo di Cambio

(Colle Val d'Elsa c. 1245 – Florence 1302)

A disciple of Nicola Pisano, Arnolfo *subtilissimus et ingeniosus magister*, as he was called by the Perugians in 1277, owes his immense fame to his work as architect rather than as sculptor. Up to the 19th century his statues, refined baldachins, tombs, and fountains were considered secondary, if not negligible, as compared to his religious and civil architectural projects (in Florence, Santa Croce, the Cathedral and Palazzo Vecchio). Moreover, on the *Tomb of Boniface VIII* the artist called himself *architectus*, referring also however to his funerary monuments, whose complex and "humanized" structures marked a turning point in this field, almost anticipating the humanistic formula of the early 15th century. Today, his sculptures reveal above all that 'dolce stil novo' which conferred on Arnolfo a dignity equal to that of Giotto and Dante.

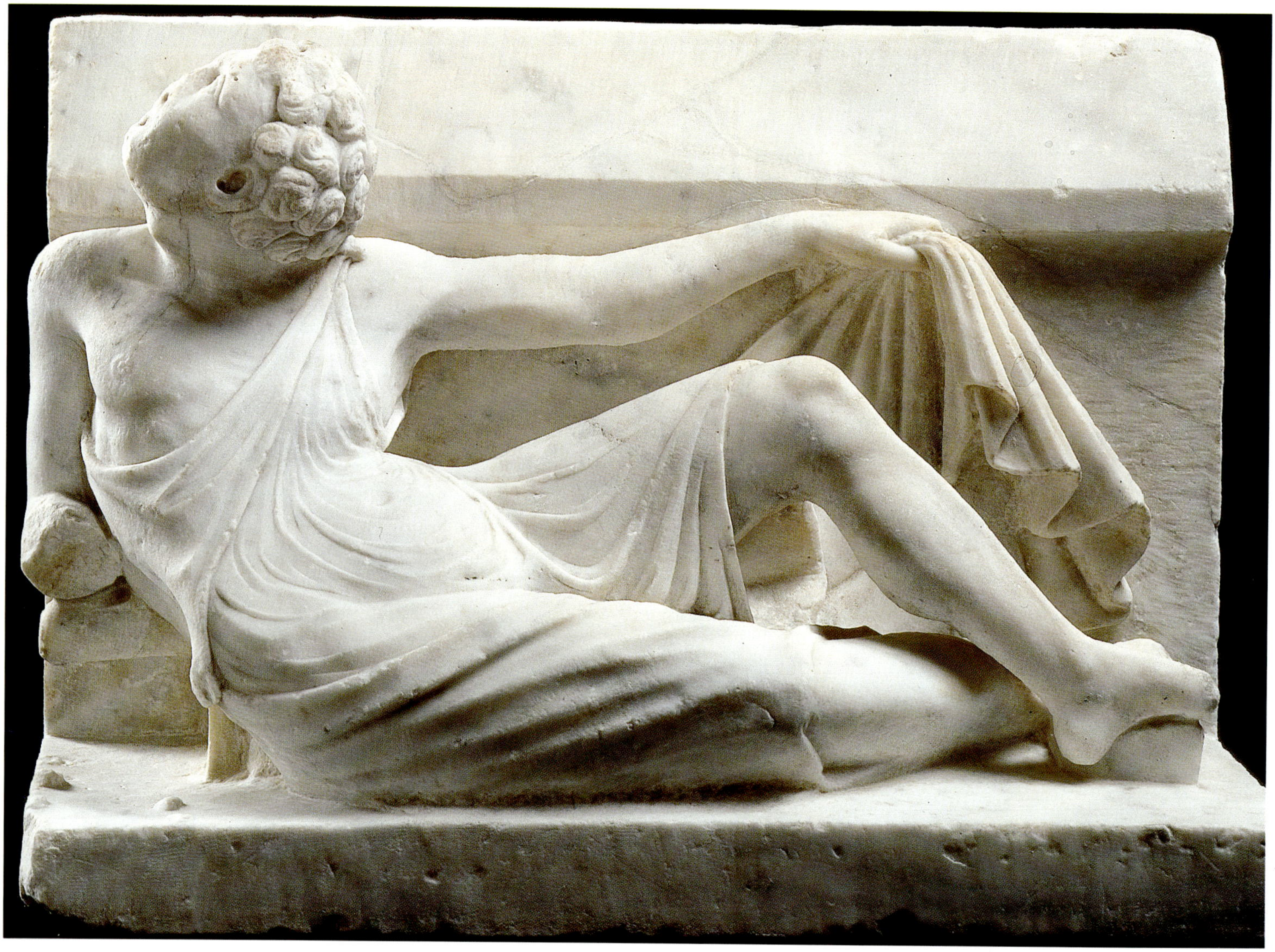

Giorgio Vasari, *Portrait of Arnolfo di Cambio*, from the *Lives*, Florence, Giunti, 1568.

Arnolfo di Cambio
The Thirsty Cripple
c. 1281
marble
Perugia, National Gallery of Umbria.

In 1277 Arnolfo was at the service of Charles of Anjou, lord of Naples, who allowed him to go to Perugia to direct work on the Fontana Maggiore, the great fountain which then, for unknown reasons, was to be constructed by Nicola Pisano and his son Giovanni. Only in 1281 was Arnolfo to work in Perugia on a smaller fountain, at the end of the Piazza del Comune. Of this structure, removed twenty years later, some fascinating fragments remain, among them the cripple who draws near to quench his thirst.

Conceived with sensitivity to the drama of human life, the statue seems to evoke antiquity in the realistic plastic representation of the distorted limbs.

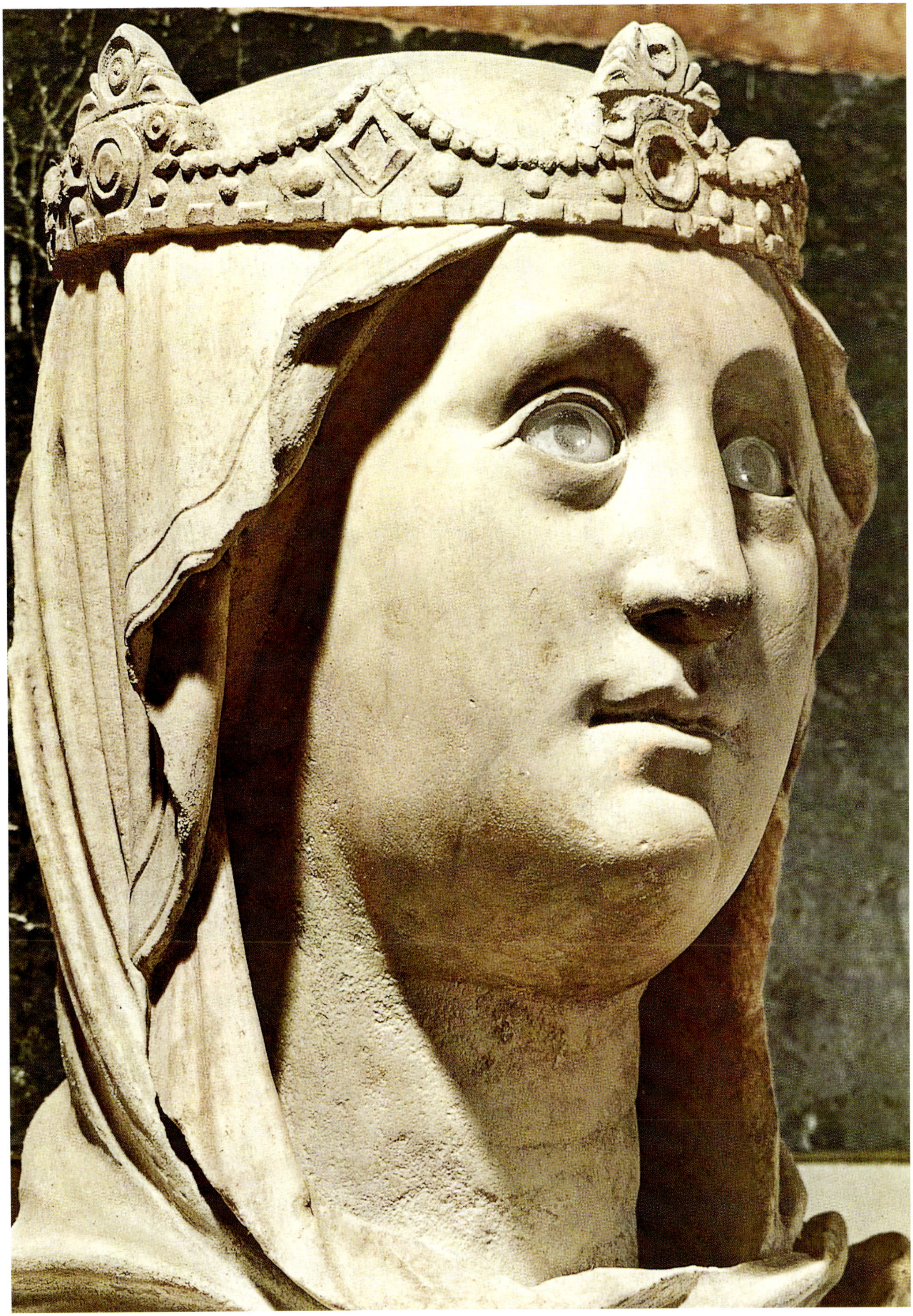

Arnolfo di Cambio
Madonna with Child
c. 1296
marble and glass paste, detail
Florence, Museo dell'Opera del Duomo.

Around 1294 Arnolfo was appointed architect of the Florence Duomo. Although now a successful artist, contended of the Anjou sovereigns by the Perugians, and active as sculptor in Rome and Orvieto, he was never mentioned by contemporaries such as Dante, Boccaccio and Sacchetti. The façade of the Duomo designed by him (destroyed in 1587) was described only in 1400 in Gregorio Dati's *Istoria*: "all of white marble and porphyry, with inlaid figures of marvelous beauty". Among the surviving statues, the *Madonna with Child Enthroned* comes from "a lovely, charming niche" above the central door. Here the statue was framed by a marble pavilion, emulating a curtain held open by two angels. The statue with its shining, almost ecstatic eyes, is reminiscent of the gentle *Madonna of San Giorgio alla Costa* by Giotto.

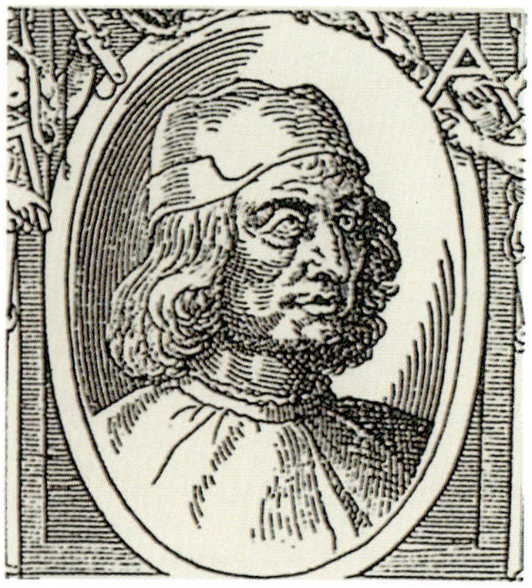

Nicola and Giovanni Pisano

(Nicola, c. 1215 – 1278/84; Giovanni, c. 1245 – after 1317)

Nicola and Giovanni, father and son, were among the first to study antiquity with eyes attentive to the proportions of the human body. Nicola, whom a document from 1265 mentions as living in Pisa with his son, trained in the Campano-Pugliese classicizing milieu, influenced by the refined, sophisticated court of Frederick II. His main works are found in Pisa and Siena, where he collaborated with Arnolfo and with his son Giovanni. The famous Fontana Maggiore at Perugia, with its rich bas-reliefs, completed in 1278, is also the fruit of close collaboration with Giovanni. The latter, almost certainly born in Pisa, was Master Builder of the Siena Cathedral in 1297, having lived in that city since 1285. Among his works are the Pistoia pulpit (c. 1301), that of the Pisa Duomo (c. 1310) and the *Tomb of Marghareth of Brabante* (Genoa, c. 1313).

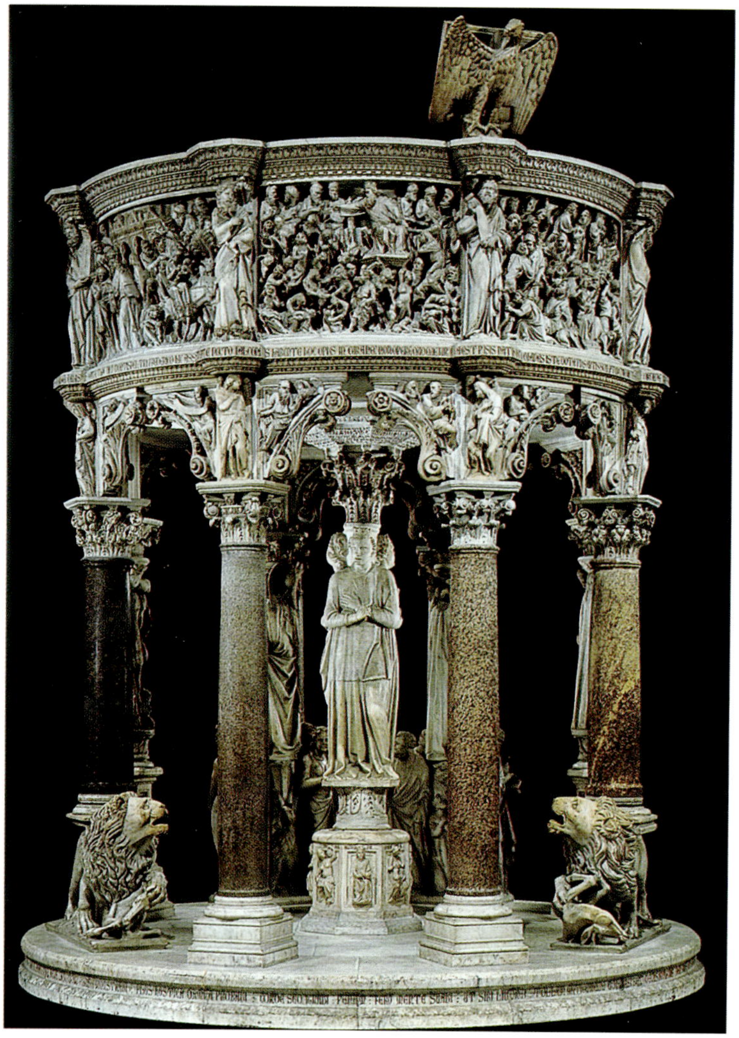

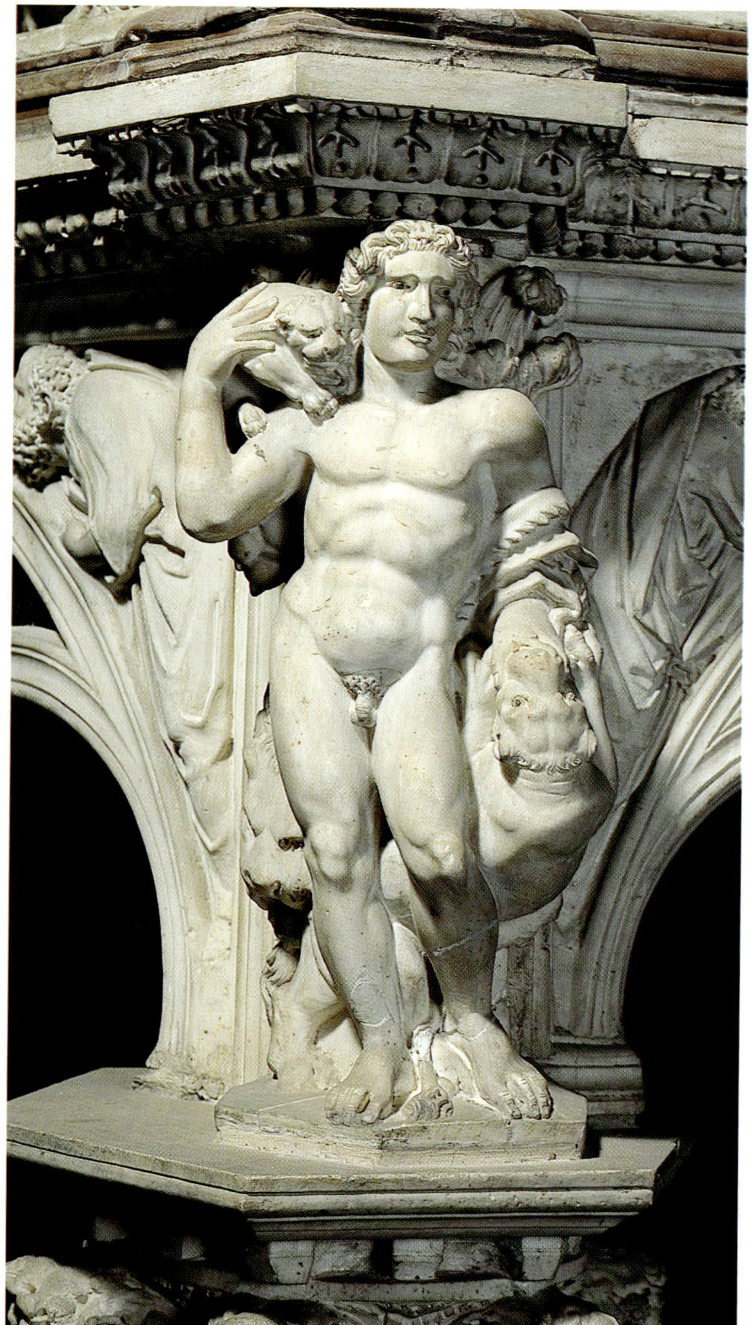

Giovanni Pisano
Pulpit
c. 1310
Carrara marble
Pisa, Duomo.

The talent of Giovanni, who praises himself in a long inscription on the base, emerges in all its mature complexity in the octagonal structure of the Pisa pulpit, one of the highest achievements of Gothic sculpture. In the lower part the plastic force of the column-bearing lions and the allegorical figures also serving as support is striking. Above, nine panels decorated with historical scenes, slightly convex, appear to form an elegantly decorated crown.

Above left:
Giorgio Vasari,
Portrait of Nicola Pisano,
from the *Lives*,
Florence, Giunti, 1568.

Lower left:
Nicola Pisano
Hercules
1260
marble, detail of
pulpit
Pisa, Baptistery.

Nicola Pisano, heedless of Medieval legends that attributed to sculpture the ancient significance of idolatry, was inspired for his Hercules by a figure on a Roman sarcophagus. In an all-round sculpture he created the first idealized nude hero in keeping with classical canons.

Right:
Giovanni Pisano
Fortitude and Temperance
c. 1310
marble, detail
of pulpit
Pisa, Duomo.

In the pulpit of the Cathedral Giovanni Pisano immortalized some of the most eloquent Medieval portrayals of women, including an all-round nude, extremely rare for the times. If the fully clothed woman probably symbolizes Fortitude, considering that she is holding a lion cub by the paw, the nude woman may represent Temperance. Evidently Giovanni was inspired here by the ancient model of the *Venus pudica*, which he had perhaps studied in the example discovered at Siena in those years and then lost, described as a "marvelous work" by the sculptor Lorenzo Ghiberti in his *Commentaries*.

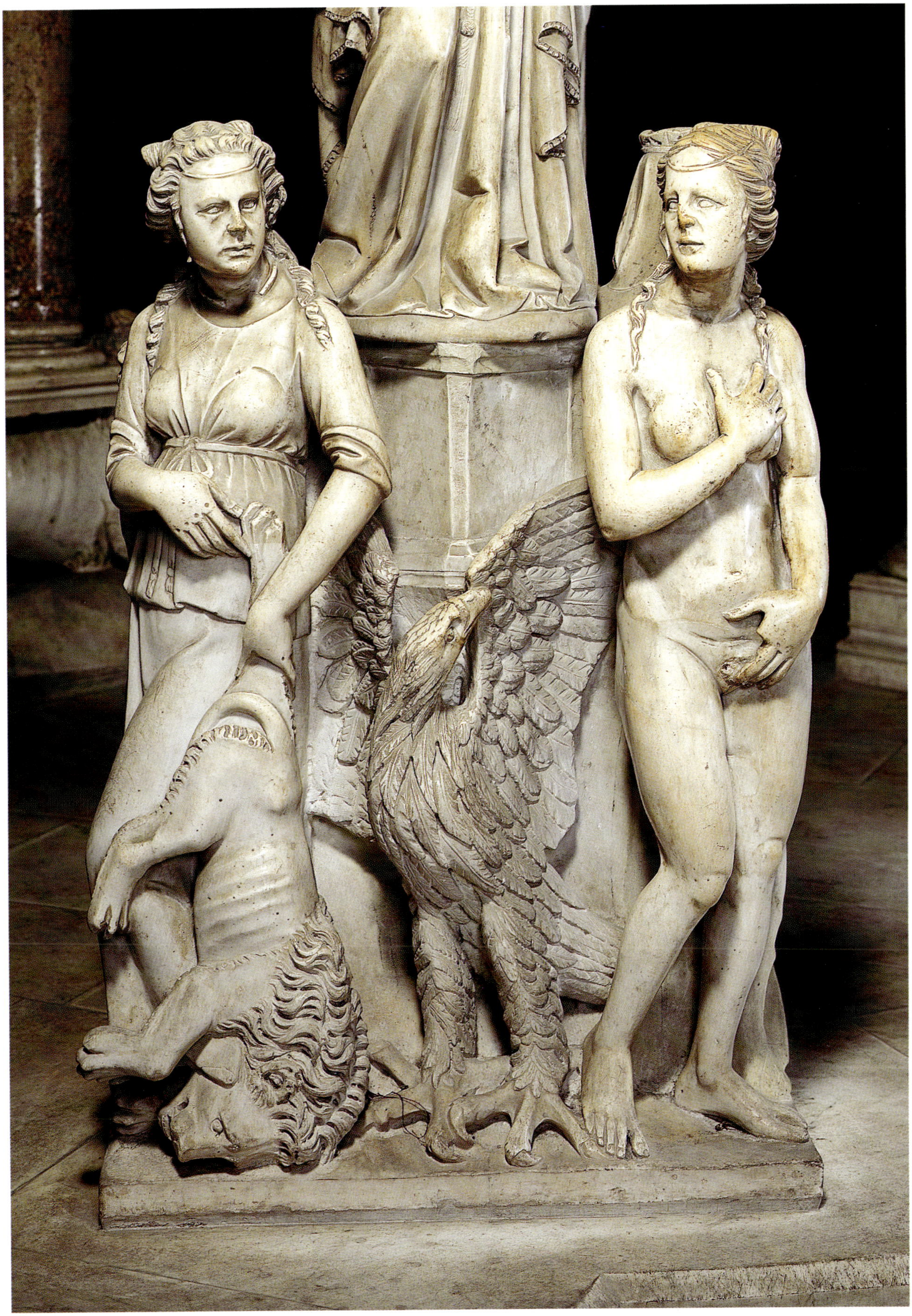

Pietro Cavallini

(active in Rome and Naples between 1273 and 1321)

Thanks to the strengthening of papal power and the sophisticated openness of the cosmopolitan court of Naples, the art of Central/Southern Italy was enlivened in the 13th and 14th centuries by patrons who encouraged experimentation crucial to the development of the Italian figurative civilization. While Iacopo Torrito and Filippo Rusuti in Rome showed their skill in various pictorial and sculptural initiatives, outstanding among them all was Pietro Cavallini. Although nothing is known of this early training, his hand is certain in the mosaics and frescoes of several Roman churches, whose decoration testifies to a new feeling for classical art and for the problems of representing space. Perhaps in contact with Arnolfo di Cambio, at the time when both artists were working in Santa Cecilia in Trastevere, he was called to Naples by Robert of Anjou in 1308, and richly compensated for his work.

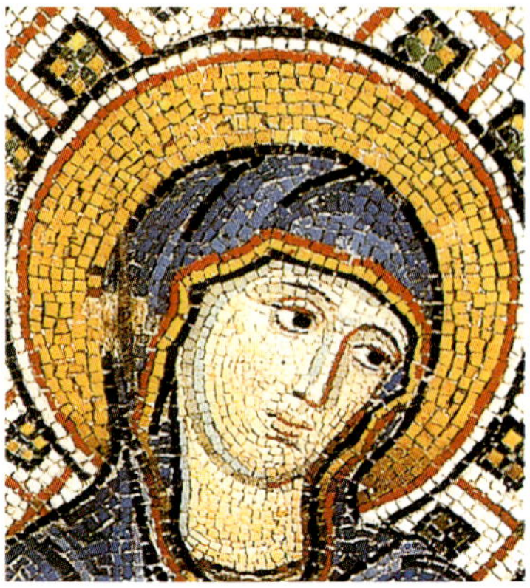

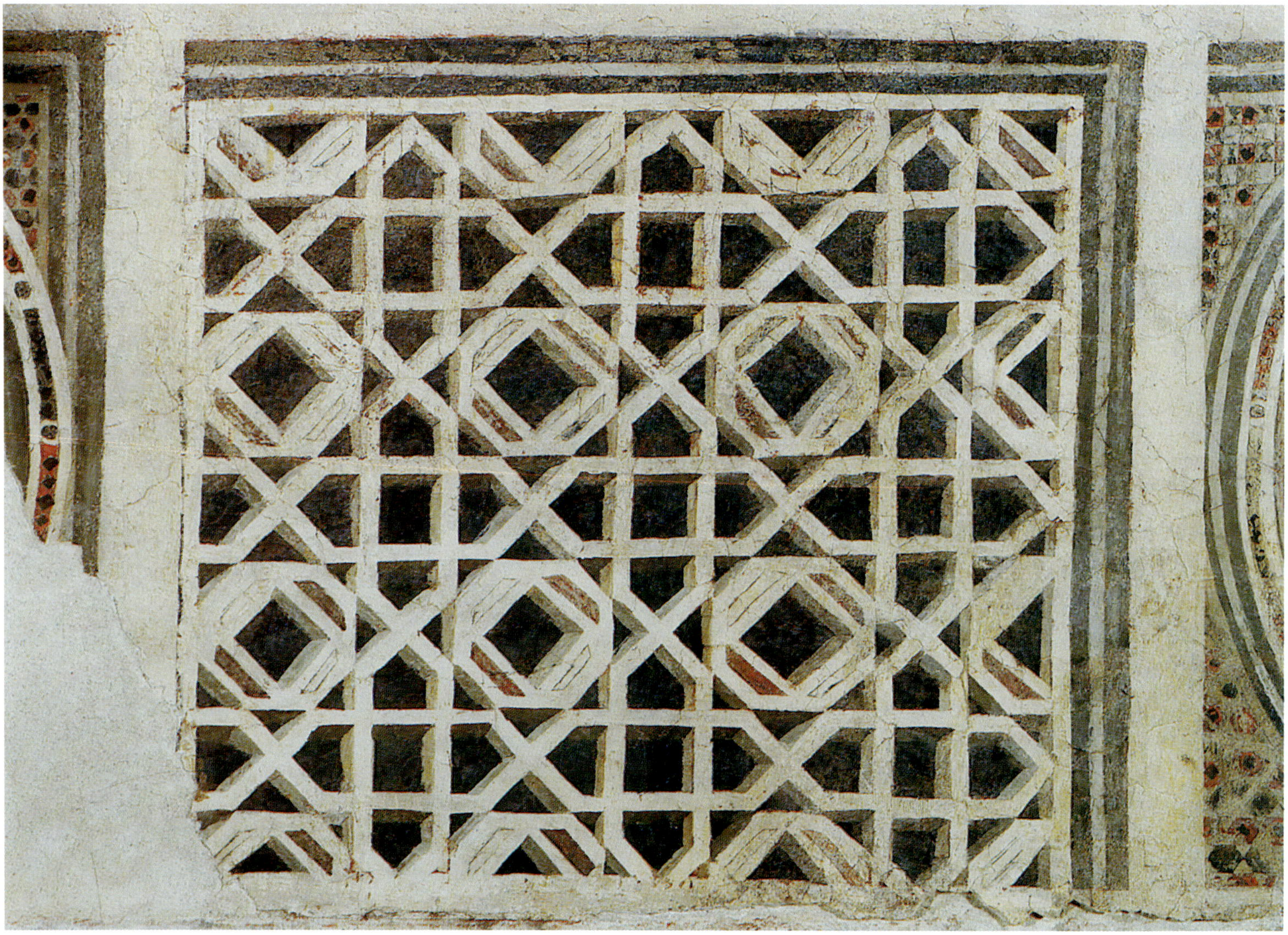

Pietro Cavallini (attr.)
Compartment with false screen in stucco
c. 1310
fresco, detail
Naples, Duomo,
St Aspreno Chapel.

Cavallini's activity in Naples, documented by his invitation to court in 1308, is not backed up by sources that specify the works accomplished. Presumably the master, assisted by several pupils, participated in the most important monumental building complexes, and certainly he was responsible for the decorative scheme in Santa Maria Donnaregina (1310-20). Not entirely certain instead is his role in the cathedral, where outstanding among the surviving frescoes for its masterful illusionist effect is the false screen depicted in perspective in the St Aspreno Chapel.

At left:
Pietro Cavallini,
Saint Anne, detail of apsidal mosaic with the *Birth of the Virgin*, last decade of the 13th century. Rome, Santa Maria in Trastevere.

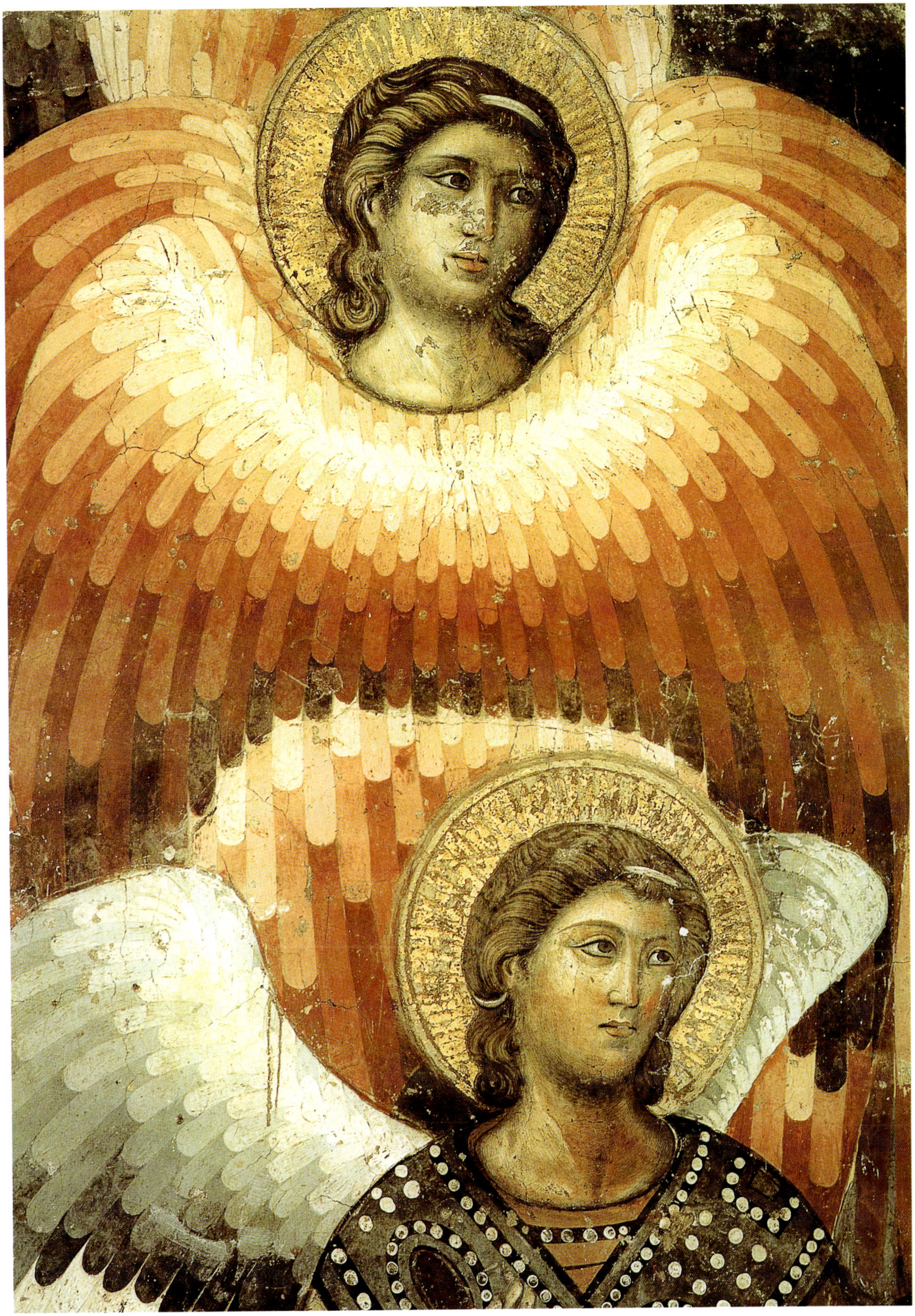

Pietro Cavallini
Seraphims
c. 1293
fresco, detail of the *Last Judgement*
Rome, Santa Cecilia in Trastevere.

Due to numerous modifications made in the interior of the Church of Santa Cecilia in Trastevere, Pietro Cavallini's masterpiece is now located in the choir of the cloistered nuns, which can be reached only by passing through some rooms in the convent. Discovered in 1900 in fragmentary conditions the surviving frescoes, restored in the past and already highly praised by Lorenzo Ghiberti in the 15th century, cover three walls with an extraordinary *Last Judgement*, an *Annunciation* and some episodes from the Bible. The artist's talent leaps to the eye for the richness of his palette still evident in the gaily coloured wings of the seraphim, for the firm modeling of the faces, and for the individualization and exceptional plastic power of the figures. Although almost illegible today, some of the damned, portrayed with realistic anatomical details, are among the most powerful nude figures of the times.

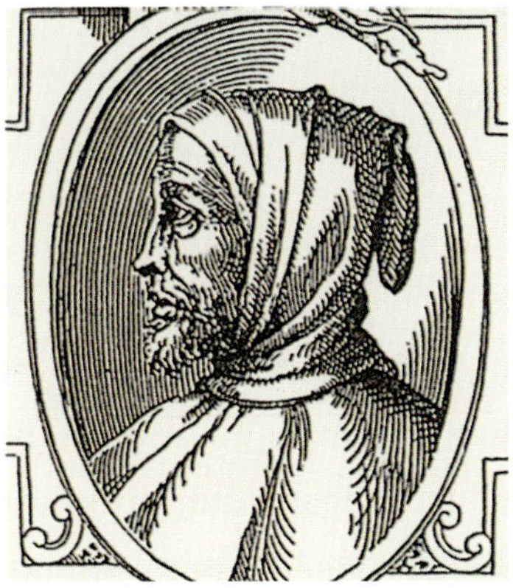

Cimabue

(Cenni di Pepe, or Pepo, Florence 1240? – 1302)

For its expressive power and the intense colors that heighten the plastic effect of the bodies, Cimabue's painting marks a progressive detachment from Byzantine flatness toward an independent figurative language that was at last Occidental, already partially launched in Florence by another highly original master, Coppo di Marcovaldo, who died in 1280. The fortune of Cimabue, overshadowed by the rising star of Giotto according to the platitude reported by Dante, is however clouded first by a lack of documents and then by recent disasters which have severely damaged some of his masterpieces: the *Crucifix* of Santa Croce in Florence (c. 1275), irreparably spoiled by the flood of 1966 (ironically enough, it had been safe in the Uffizi Gallery until a short time before); and the *Ceiling of the Evangelists* in Assisi, some extraordinary details of which were destroyed by an earthquake in 1998. Of his ac-

Giorgio Vasari, *Portrait of Cimabue*, from the *Lives*, Florence, Giunti, 1568.

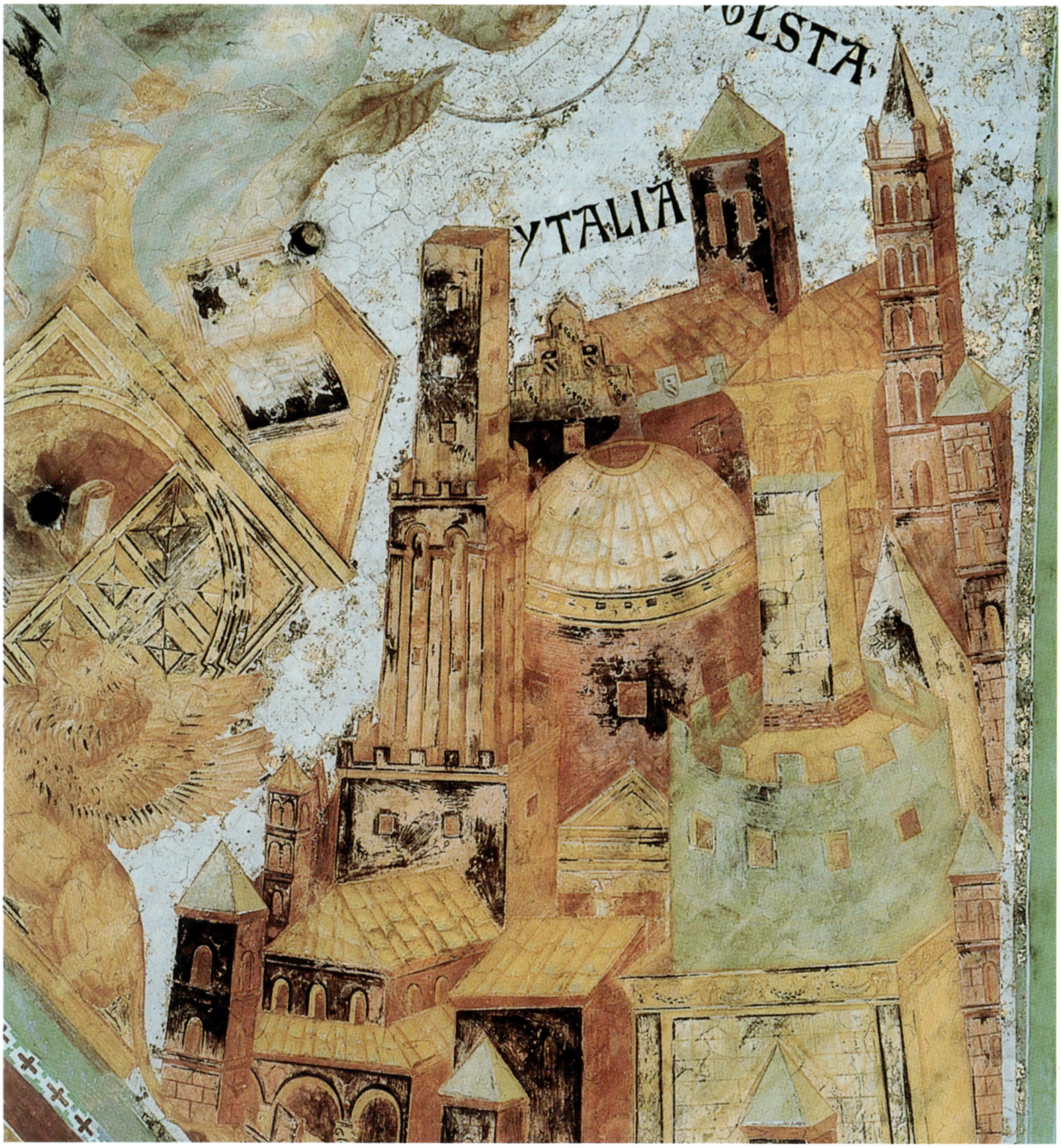

Cimabue
Ytalia
1277-80
fresco, detail of the vaulting cell with *St Mark the Evangelist*
Assisi, Basilica of St Francis, Upper Church, Evangelists' Ceiling.

Ytalia: for the first time this name appears in clear letters in a figurative context. The allegorical image, with a rare old view of Medieval Rome, adorns one of the four vaulting cells of the ceiling at the transept crossing, dedicated to the Evangelists and the countries christianized by them: John for Asia with Ephesus, Luke for Greece with Corinth, Matthew for Judea with Jerusalem. In the cell dedicated to Mark, along with the name Italy appear the emblematic monuments of Rome: the Pantheon, the Senatorial Palace, the façade of St Peter's and Castel Sant'Angelo. The frescoes were painted at the desire of Niccolò III, to proclaim the universality of Christianity and the central power of the Papacy.

tivity as artist, only two dates are certain: in 1272 he was in Rome, and between 1301 and 1302, the year of his death, in Pisa. Surviving in addition to the Assisi works, and to some drawings for mosaics in the Pisa Cathedral and the Florence Baptistery, are panel paintings of some of the most intense Crucifixes and Virgins in Medieval Art.

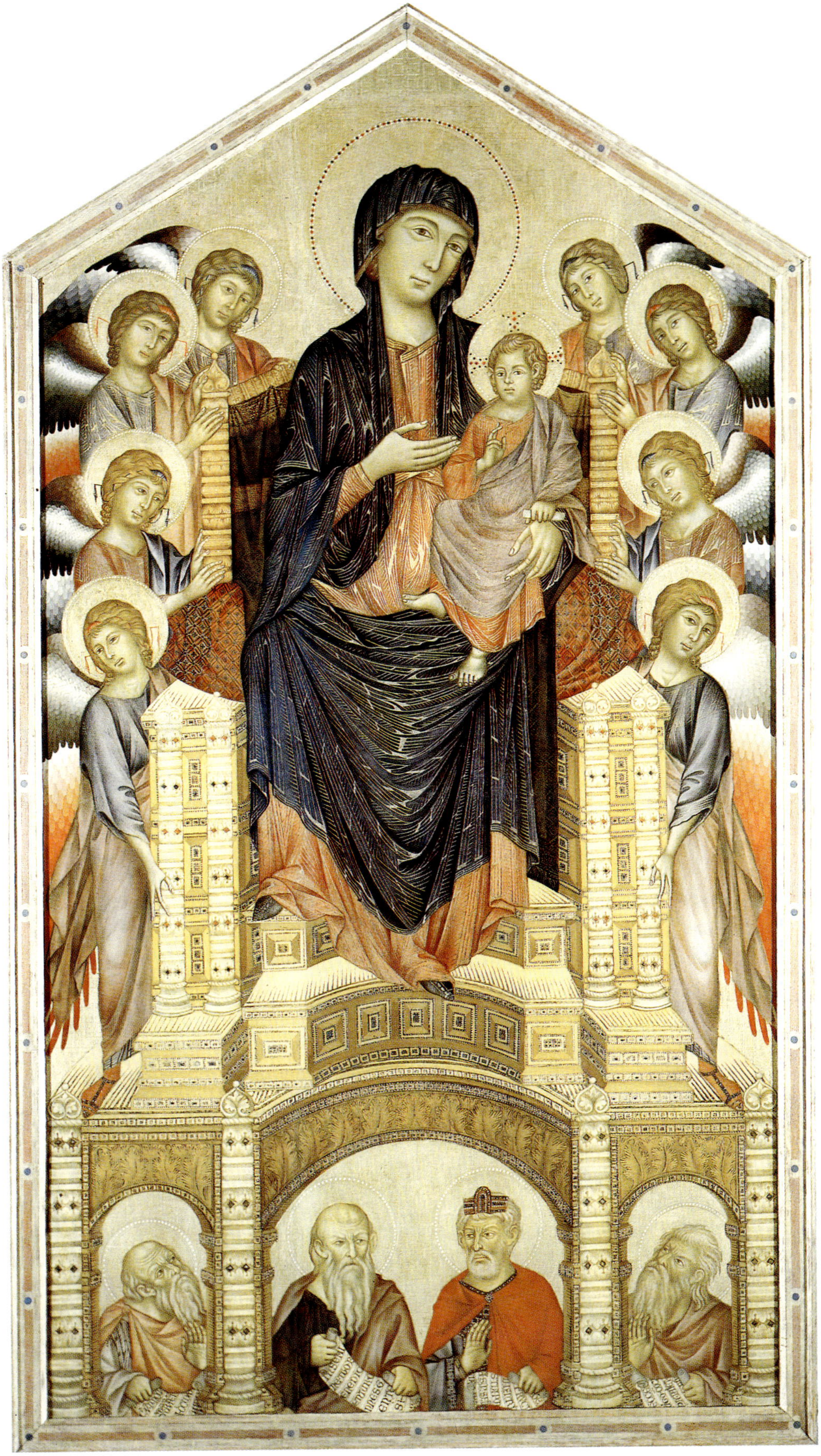

Cimabue
Santa Trinita Maestà
datable between 1280 and 1290
panel
Florence, Uffizi Gallery.

To fully comprehend the imposing power of this altarpiece it must be imagined in its original place. With its frame, now lost, it stood 465 centimeters high above the altar of the Church of Santa Trinita at Florence, as was calculated during restoration completed in 1993. The most striking innovation of the composition, a precursor of Giotto's three-dimensional experimentation, is the flared recess of the throne, where four prophets are portrayed with precise symbolic meanings. At the far ends Jeremiah and Isaiah gaze upward toward the Christ Child to confirm the prophecies inscribed on the scrolls, concerning the virgin birth of Jesus. The central position of Abraham and David, immediately below the throne, seems instead to refer to the birth of the Saviour, descended from their house.

Duccio di Buoninsegna

(Siena c. 1260 – 1318)

The prolific career of the Sienese artist is variously documented. In 1278 the municipal Ufficio della Biccherna paid him to paint chests for documents; later he was commissioned to paint, according to a typically Sienese custom, small panels (now lost) to decorate ledgers. The Altarpiece of Santa Maria Novella for the Brotherhood of the Laudesi dates from 1285, and the great stained-glass window for the Siena Duomo from 1285-88. Although the *Maestà* for the Chapel of the Nine in Palazzo Pubblico (1302) is lost, the great *Maestà* of the Duomo can still be admired in the Museum of Cathedral Works. A complex painting on which Duccio worked for three years, it portrays the Virgin enthroned surrounded by angels in strictly symmetrical order on the front panel. Now Duccio is appreciated for his early attention to the three-dimensional experimentation of the young Giotto.

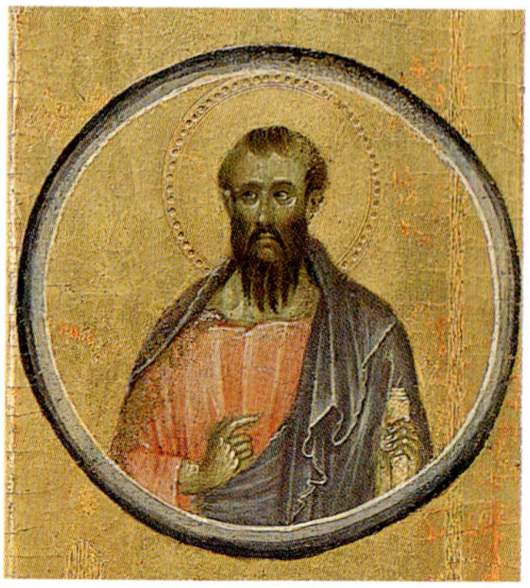

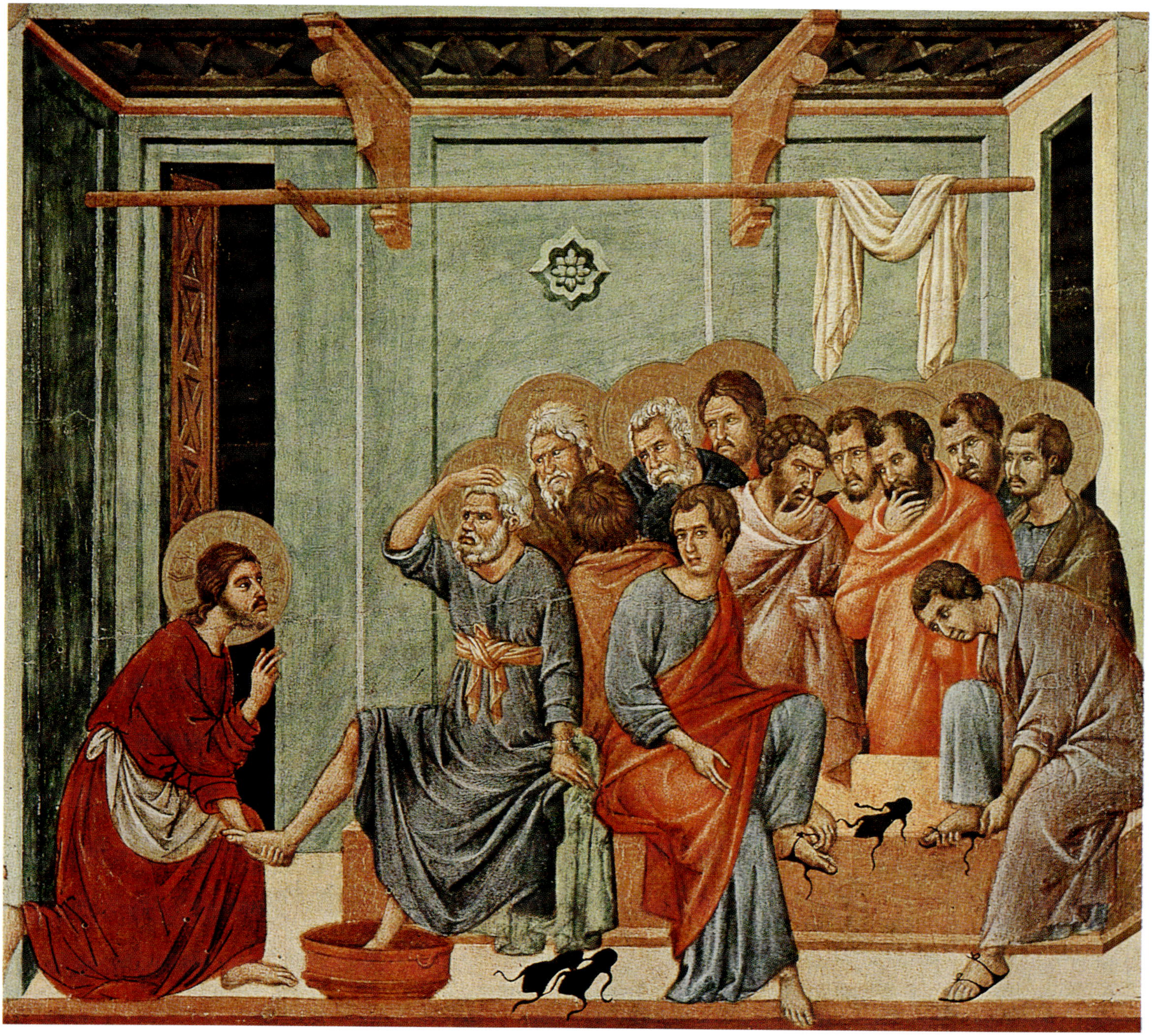

Duccio di Buoninsegna
The Washing of the Feet
1308-11
panel, detail from back of the *Maestà*
Siena, Museo dell'Opera del Duomo.

On the back of the *Maestà*, painted to adorn the high altar of the Siena Duomo, Duccio painted twenty-six scenes of Christ's Passion, expressing his highest talent as illustrator. Among the memorable details are the cloth hanging overhead and the Apostle's dark sandals.

Duccio di Buoninsegna
The Laudesi Maestà
1285
panel, entire (*at right*) and detail (*at upper left*) of the frame with medallion of a saint
Florence, Uffizi Gallery.

Painted for the chapel of the Brotherhood of the Laudesi in the Basilica of Santa Maria Novella at Florence, as stated in the contract dated April 15, 1285, this is the Sienese painter's first known masterpiece. Six angels symmetrically surround the colossal figure of the Madonna enthroned, her face still as vaguely enigmatic as an icon but already softened by the hint of a smile. Even the moulded frame has a fundamental role in the composition. The 1989 restoration has revived the luminous glow of the thirty medallions depicting Biblical figures and saints (among them St Peter Martyr, founder of the Laudesi Brotherhood) characterized, even in their reduced size, by individual features.

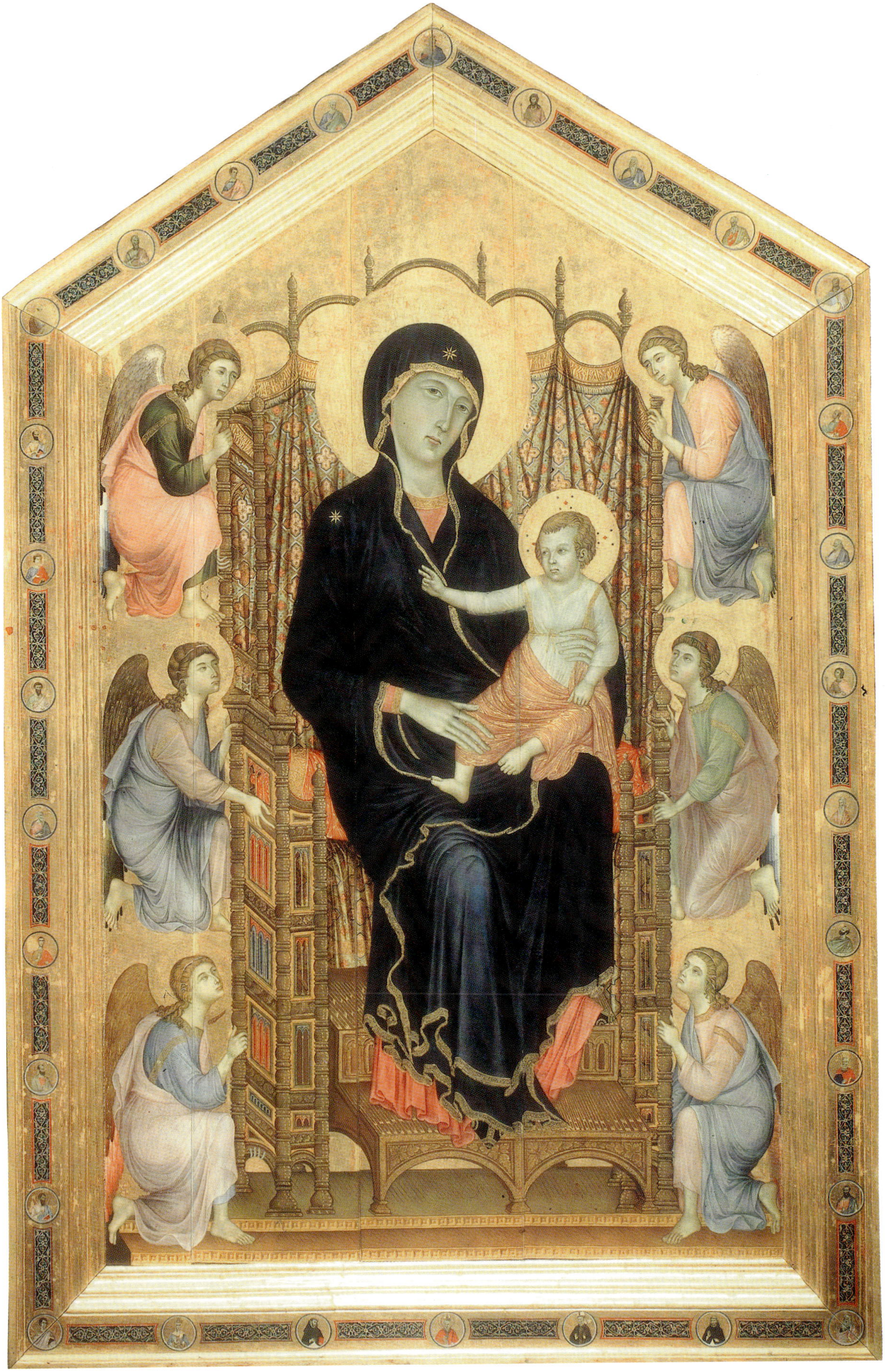

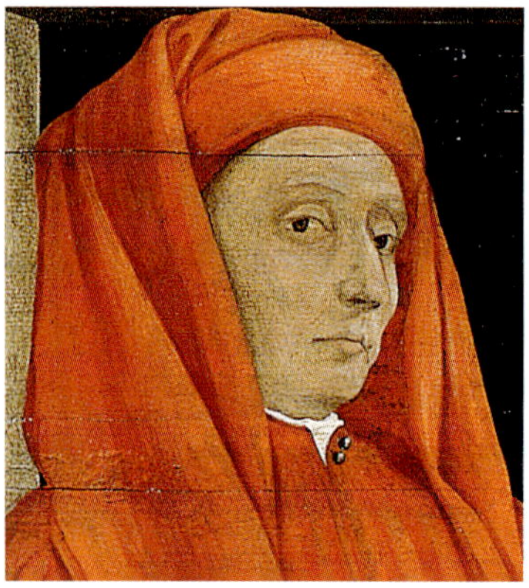

Giotto

(Agnolo di Bondone, Colle di Vespignano c. 1266 – Florence 1337)

Representing a crucial turning point in Medieval painting, Giotto is by unanimous consensus the most genial, versatile artist of his age. His contemporaries already compared him to the great masters of antiquity, even declaring him superior for his rare talent, his unrivaled skill in depicting the passions. More than any other Giotto was to "transmute art from Greek to Latin", as the theorist Cennino Cennini was to write of him at the end of the 14th century. This statement alone suffices to reveal how Giotto's contemporaries were already aware of the revolutionary nature of his painting. From the "Greek" language, the Byzantine modes handed down over the centuries, through him a new style, "modern and natural", was to emerge. Giotto renewed the conception of pictorial space, which appears three-dimensional in his paintings. Equally innovative was his representation of figures – solid,

Paolo Uccello (attr.), *Giotto*, detail of the *Portrait of Five Illustrious Men*, c. 1450, Paris, Louvre.

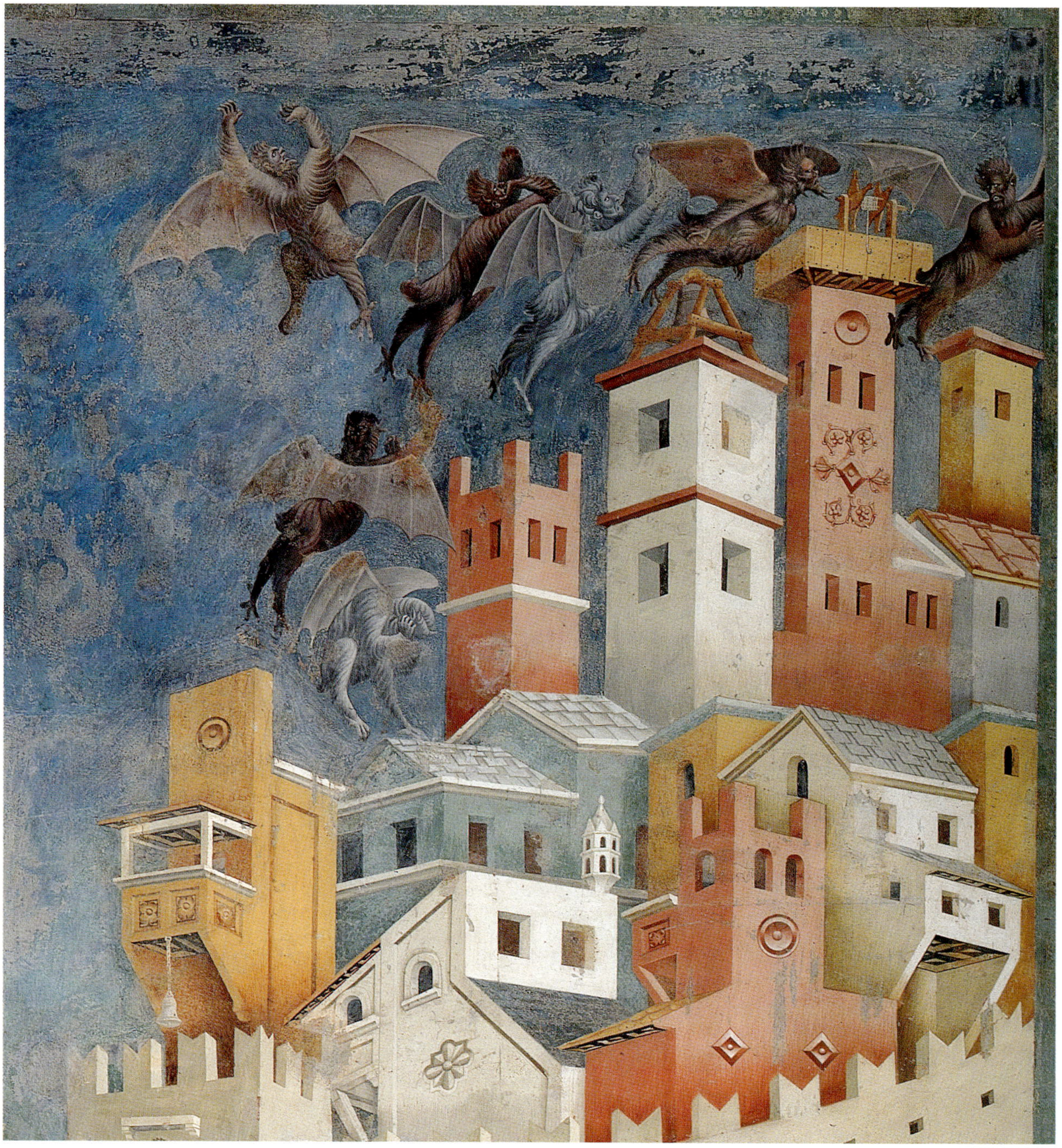

Giotto
Expulsion of the Devils from Arezzo
1296-1304
fresco, detail
Assisi, San Francesco, Upper Church.

In twenty-eight scenes the *Stories of St Francis* cover the walls of the nave in the Upper Church, dedicated to the founder of the Franciscan order. The iconography follows the *Legenda Maior*, compiled by St Bonaventura (c. 1260). The episode of the expulsion of the devils from Arezzo, the tenth scene in the cycle, is particularly striking for the bold angles of the towered city, where some houses have typical Medieval jetties.
The winged demons with falcons' feet are fleeing in exasperation, and the pathos is emphasized by the embittered features of the bearded, anthropomorphic faces. Giotto's authorship of the cycle has been often questioned due to stylistic differences from the Padua frescoes, and is still denied by some experts, although unconvincingly.

volumetric, no longer ethereal bodies fluctuating in an improbable space devoid of perspective but flesh-and-blood personages with realistic features. Like his artistic nature, Giotto's human character was marked by a strong practical sense and a certainty of his own gifts which allowed him to maintain excellent relations with clients and a perfect entrepreneurial organization. It seems probable that he was apprenticed in Florence to Cimabue, who according to tradition, mentioned also by Dante, was to be outstripped by his pupil ("Cimabue thought himself master in painting/and now the cry is Giotto", Purg. XI, 94-95). Between 1290 and 1304 it is believed, in a hypothesis subject to debate, that Giotto frescoed the *Stories of St Francis* in the Upper Basilica of Assisi. Before the end of the century he stayed in Rome and Rimini. By 1305 he had completed the Arena Chapel for Enrico Scrovegni in Padua. Returning to Florence, now famous and highly esteemed (and very well paid), he worked in Santa Croce for wealthy clients such as the Bardi and Peruzzi families. At Naples in 1329 at the court of Robert of Anjou with his pupil Maso di Banco, he was now "principle master and painter". He died at Florence where in the meantime he had also been appointed superintendent of fortifications and master builder of the Duomo.

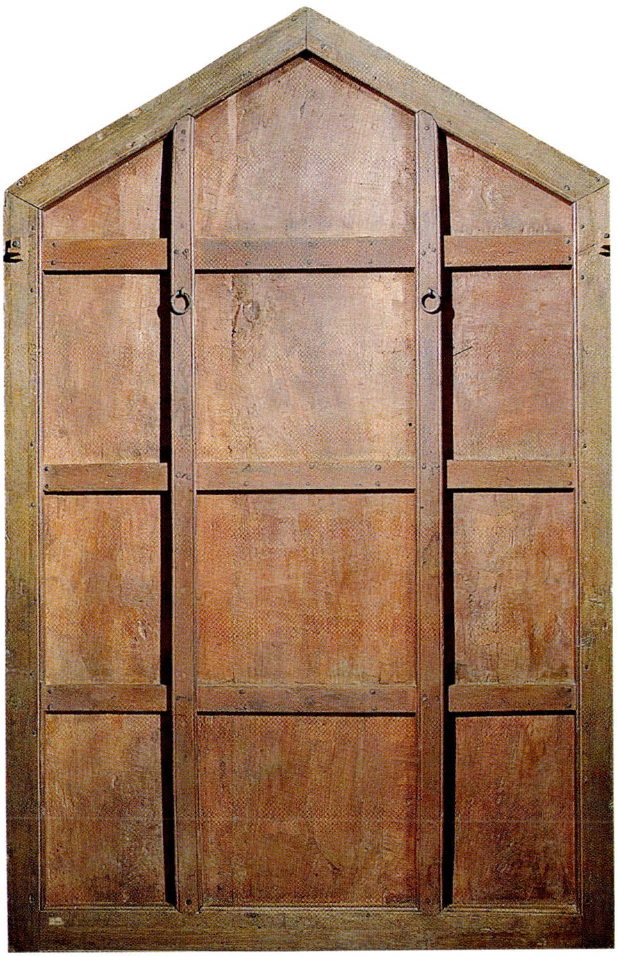

Back of Giotto's Ognissanti Madonna
c. 1310
poplar wood
Florence, Uffizi Gallery.

A true masterpiece of carpentry, documented by recent restoration.

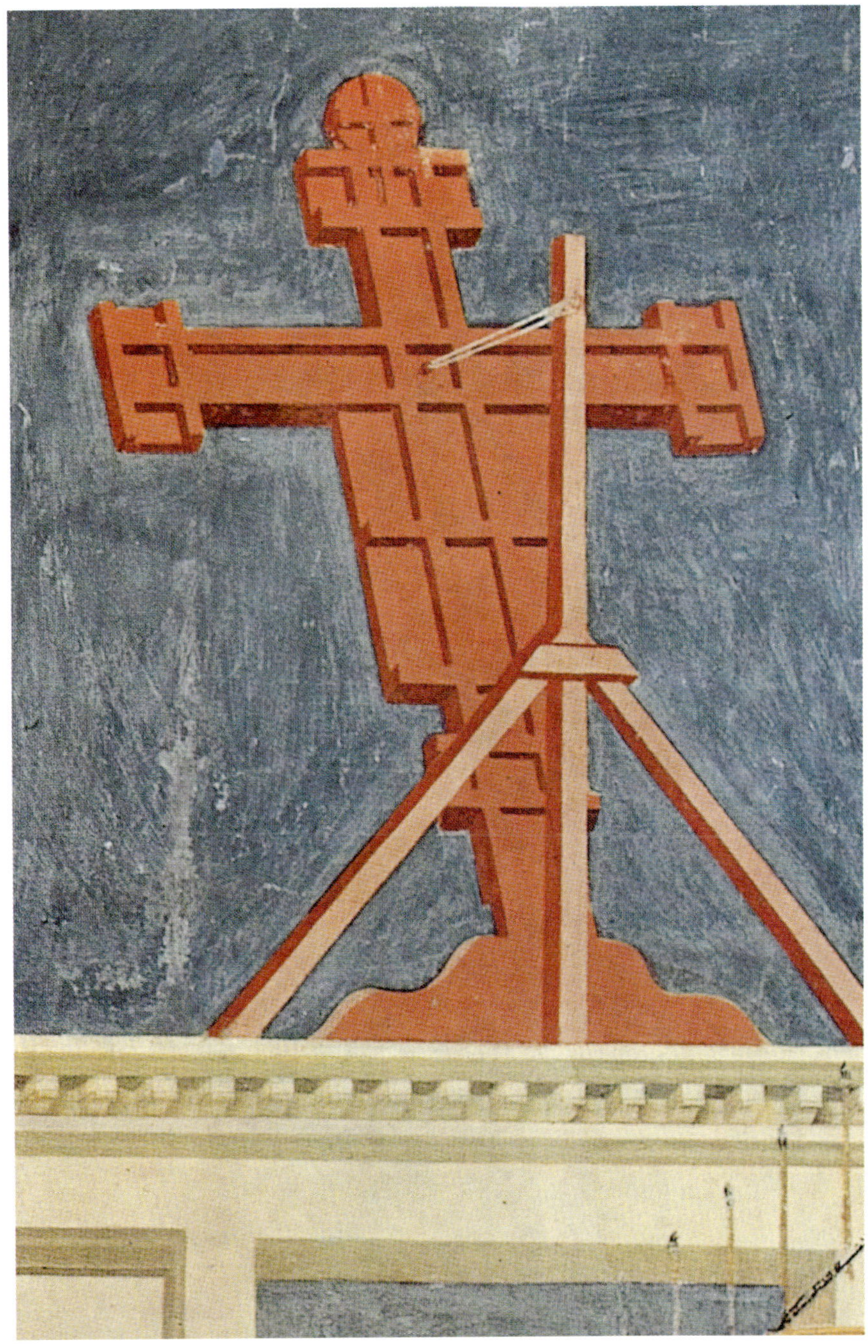

Giotto and Assistance
The Greccio Crèche
1296-1304
fresco, detail
Assisi, San Francesco, Upper Basilica.

The skill of the woodworkers in dealing with heavy works to be hung with campanas is clearly evident here.

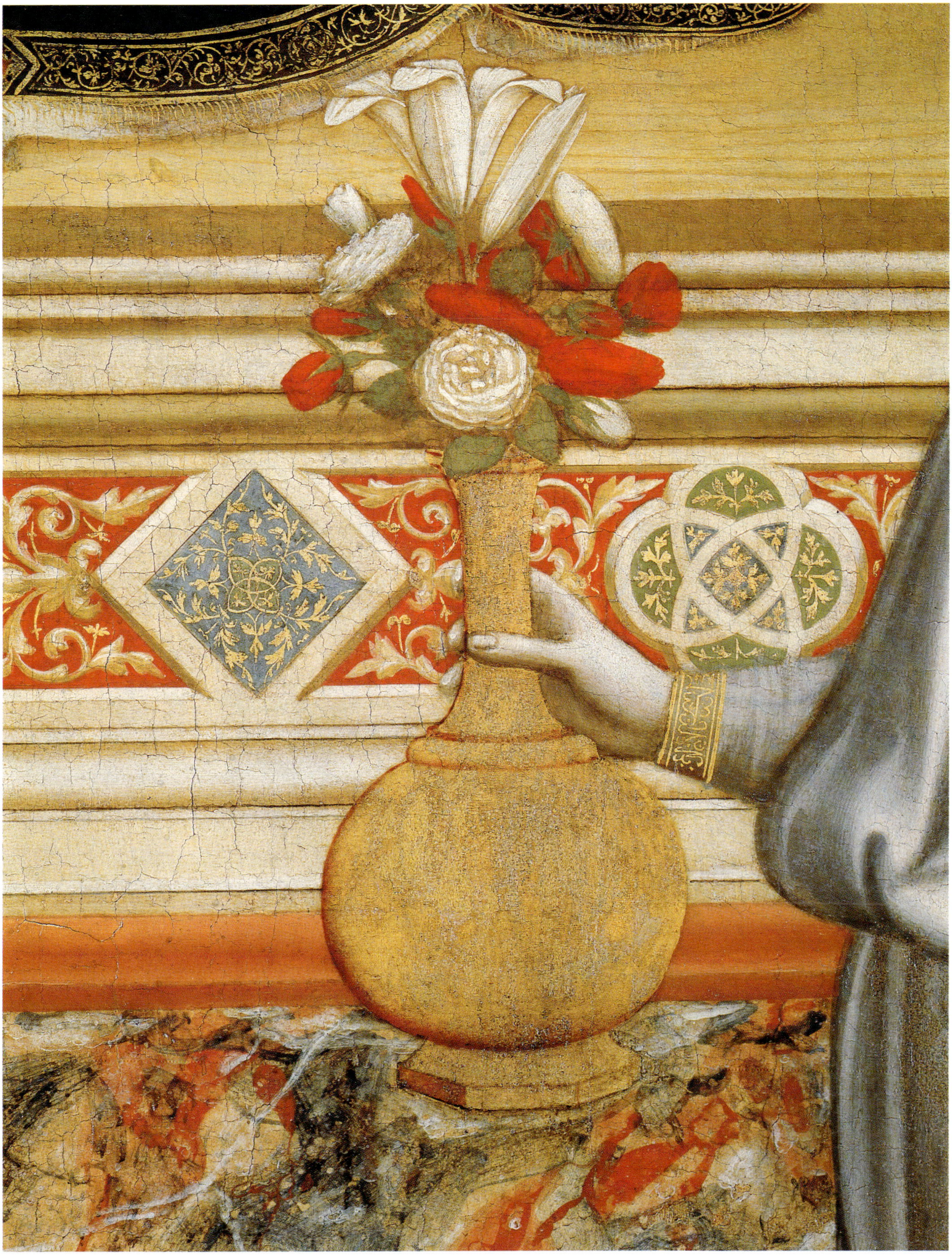

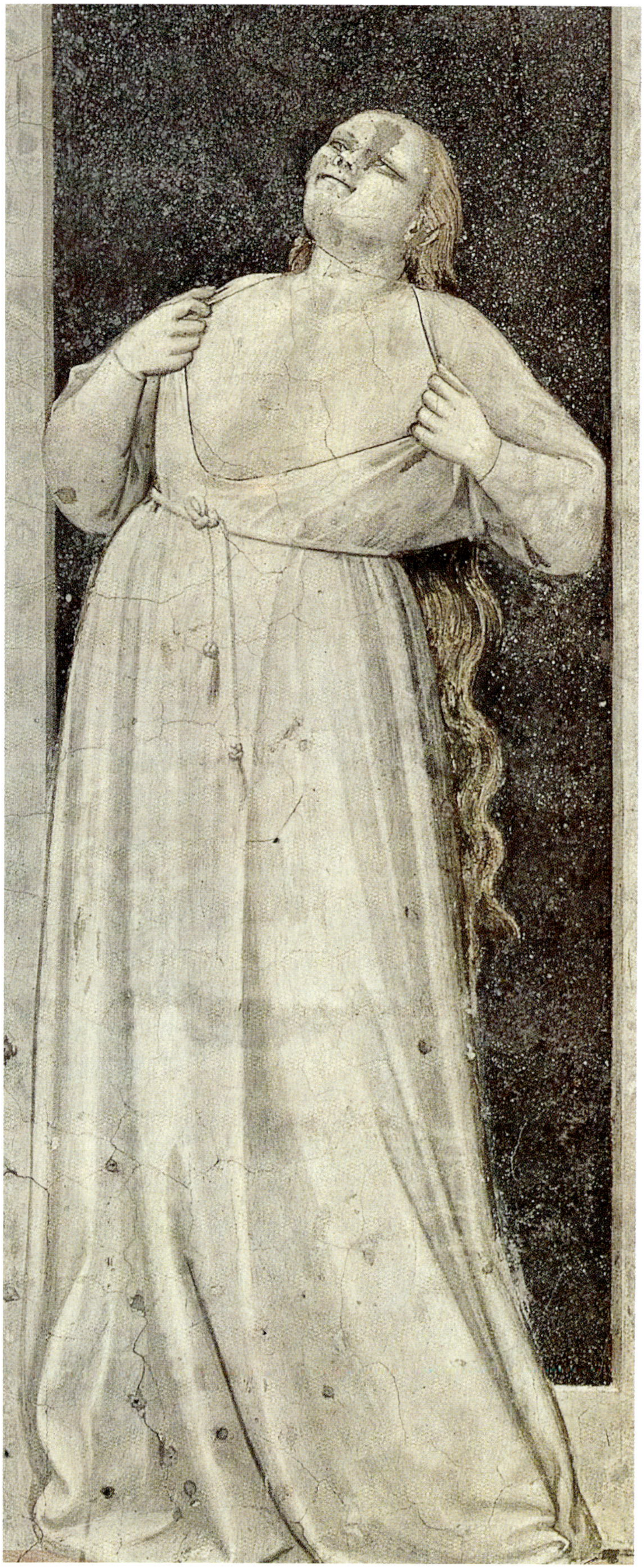

Giotto
Ire
1303-1305
fresco, from the cycle on the moulding with *Allegories and Vices*
Padua, Arena (or Scrovegni) Chapel.

The lower tier of the Padua chapel is painted like a false moulding with marble panels alternating with figured ones. Here Giotto evokes a sense of reality and space by having emerge from the background, almost like sculptures, the personifications of the Virtues and Vices portrayed in monochrome. In this forerunner of the cycle of *Illustrious Men* frescoed over a century later by Andrea del Castagno (now in the Uffizi) the 14th century artist reveals himself a keen observer of the human soul.

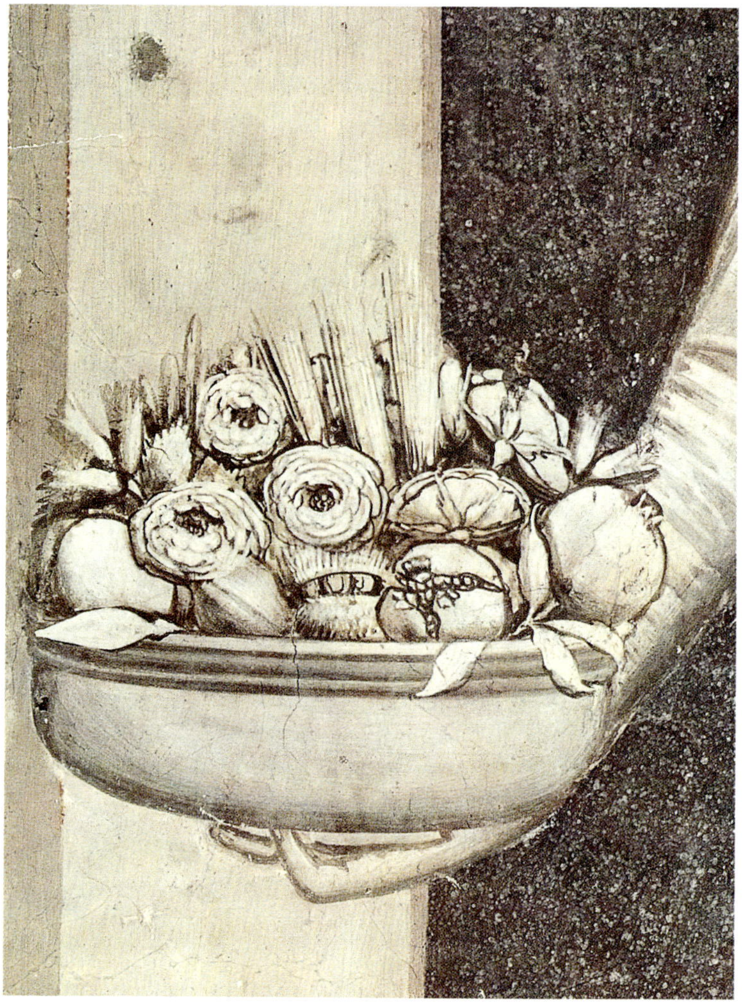

Giotto
Bowl with Flowers and Fruit
1303-1305
fresco, detail of *Charity*, from the cycle of *Allegories and Vices*
Padua, Arena (or Scrovegni) Chapel

The allegories of Virtues and Vices are a continuation of the iconographic program of the Paduan cycle. The frescoes along the walls of the chapel, culminating in the grandiose *Judgement* on the inner façade, allude to mankind's Christian journey of salvation, and were dictated by the need of the client Enrico Scrovegni to atone for the sins of his family, stained by the offense of usury. In the personages painted in monochrome Giotto emphasizes the gestures, indulges on the symbolic attributes of the allegories, and offers us incomparably fine details, such as the still life with roses, pomegranates and chestnut husks resting lightly and gracefully on the fingers of *Charity*: a detail that was to strike the imagination of Proust on his journey to Italy in 1900.

Giotto
Two Women
1303-1305
fresco, detail of the
Birth of Mary
from the cycle of
Stories of the Virgin
Padua, Arena
(or Scrovegni) Chapel.

Within a theatrical set that is bare and essential but always endowed with some element of striking impact on the spectator, Giotto's figures are delineated by simple, clear borders, which nonetheless reveal the physical nature of their bodies. A few traits, a few gestures, are enough to render the atmosphere of a fleeting moment, as in the case of the urgent, anxious exchange of a bundle between two women who meet at the entrance to the house where Mary has just been born. The eye moves from the face of the younger woman to the masterly play of hands – hands that offer and hands that grasp – up to the wrinkled face of the old woman emerging from the darkened doorway.

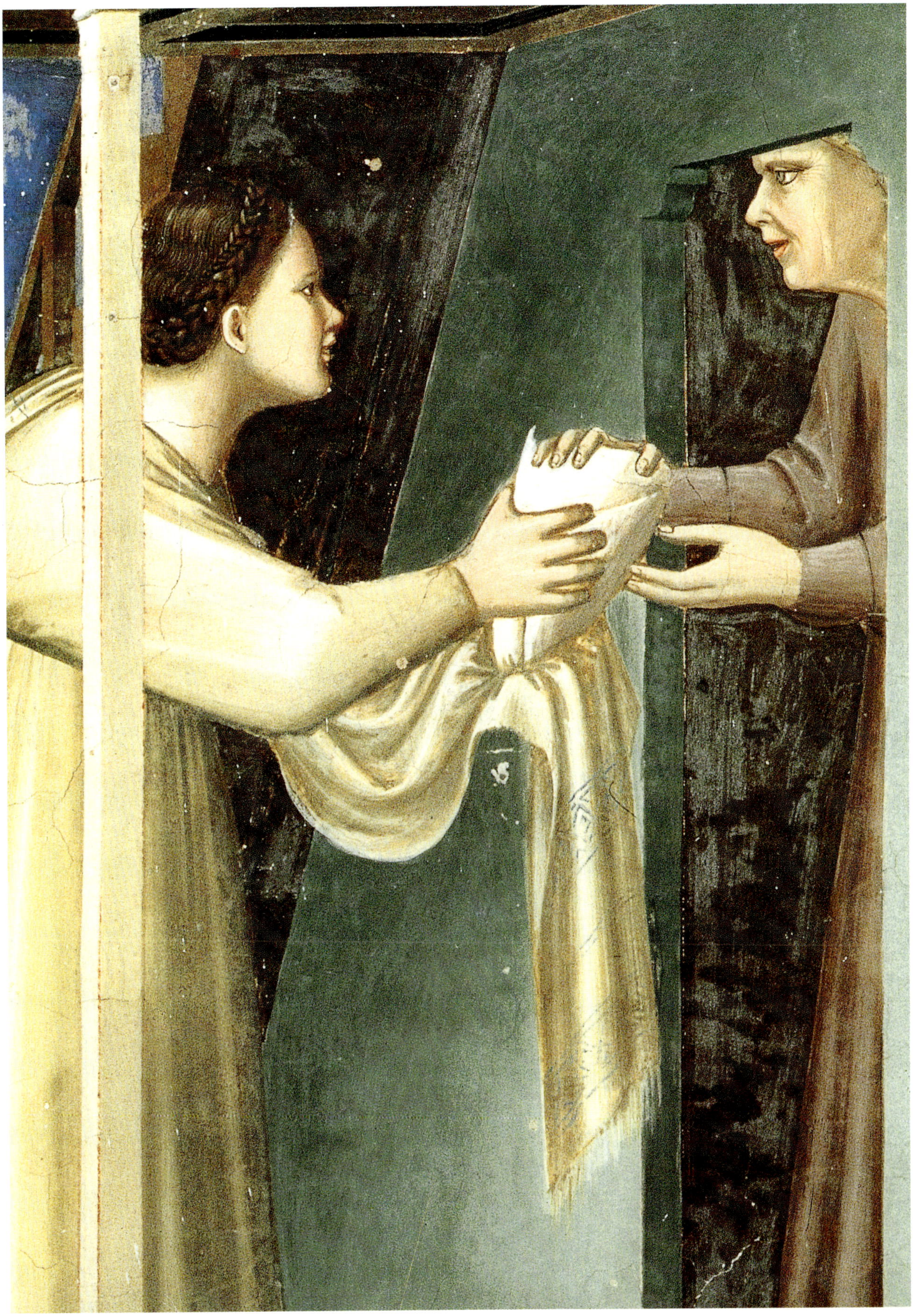

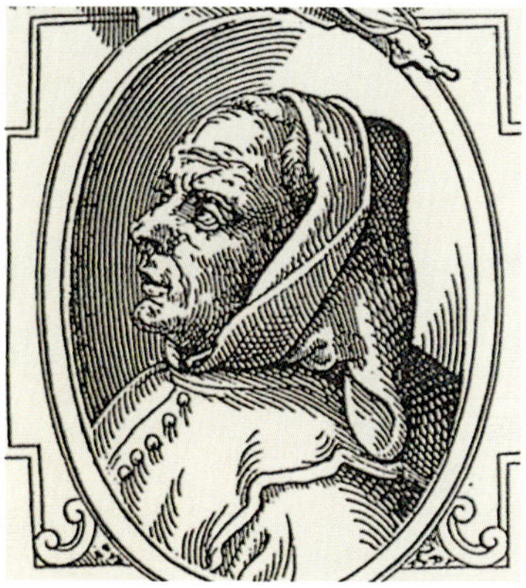

The Lorenzetti Brothers

Pietro
(Siena 1280 ca. – 1348?)

Ambrogio
(Siena, documented from 1319 to 1348)

The fame of the two Sienese brothers spread beyond the boundaries of their city to arrive as far as Florence, where Ambrogio painted his first datable work: the beautiful, strange *Madonna of Vico l'Abate* (1319, Florence, Diocesan Museum). Ambrogio, enrolled in 1327 in the Florentine Guild of the Physicians and Apothecaries, was to be esteemed by Ghiberti "most singular master", "most noble draftsman", "more learned than any other". Of Pietro's work, the frescoes for the Scala Hospital (1335) have been lost but many panels and the Assisi cycle of *Stories of the Passion* remain. By Ambrogio, who after Simone's departure for France became the official painter of the Republic, there remain at Siena a famous fresco in the Hall of the Nine in Palazzo Pubblico.

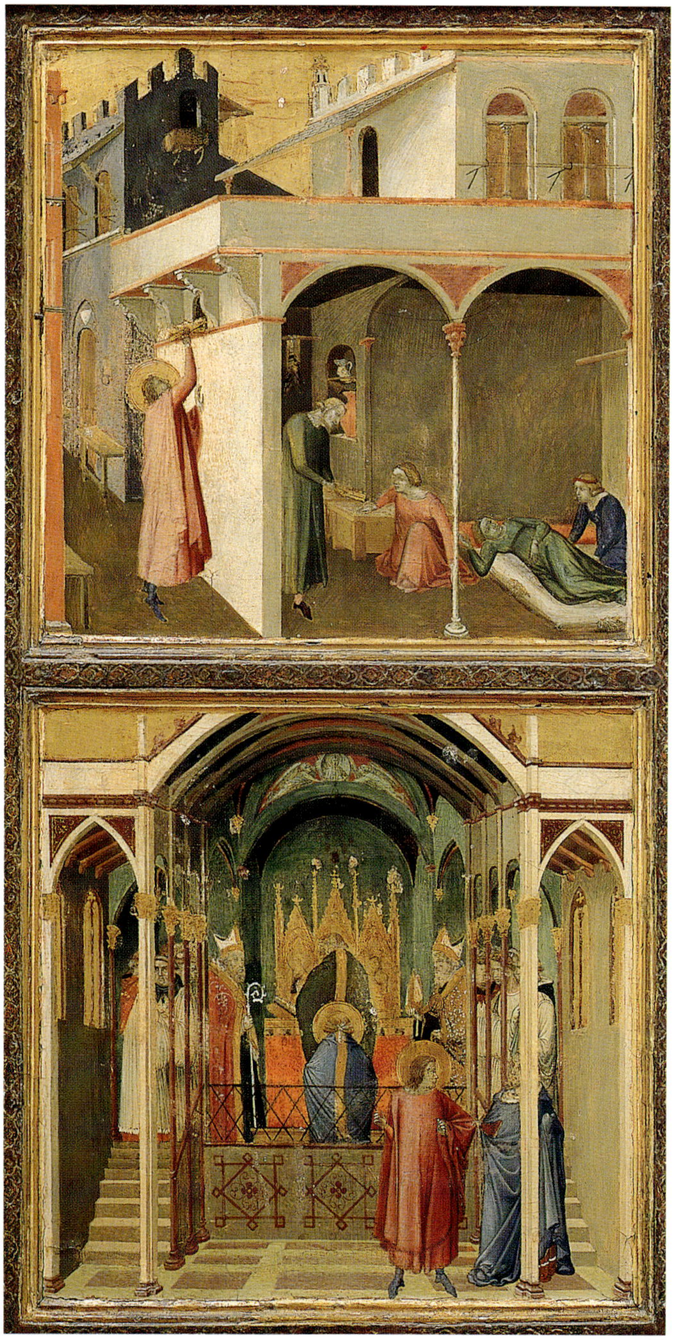

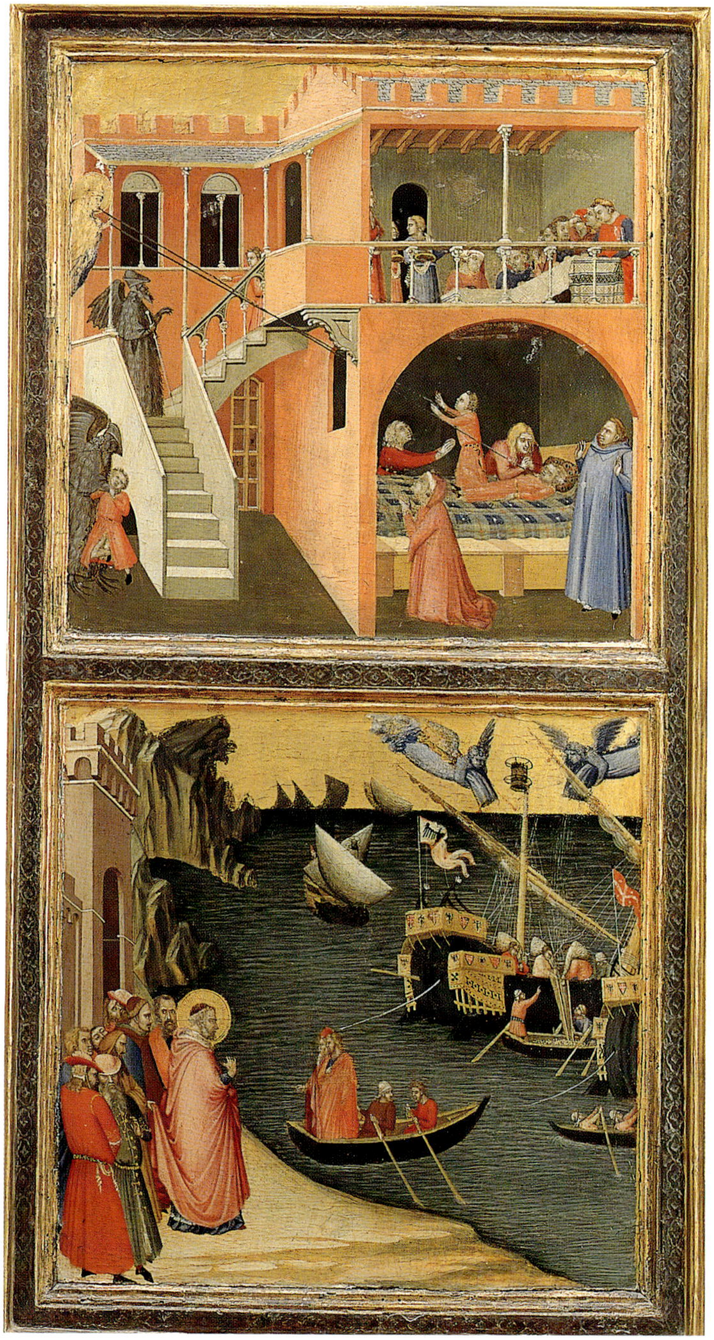

At left:
Giorgio Vasari,
Portrait of Ambrogio Lorenzetti, from the *Lives*,
Florence, Giunti, 1568.

Ambrogio Lorenzetti
Four Stories from the Life of St Nicholas of Bari
c. 1332
panel
Florence, Uffizi Gallery.

Painted for the Florentine church of San Procolo, as stated by the sources, the four scenes probably formed part of a lost altar frontal or tabernacle. Ambrogio's highest gifts as analytic narrator and experimenter in perspective are displayed here. He pauses with naturalness on details of daily life, ventures to depict figures turning their backs or emerging between the columns of a church, challenges the eye in a daring herring-bone perspective in a marine landscape where the horizon is broken by the profile of sails in the wind. And it is entirely credible that for this work, as Vasari was to report, the Sienese artist immediately received "infinite reputation" among the Florentines, accustomed to the essential lines of Giotto's compositions.

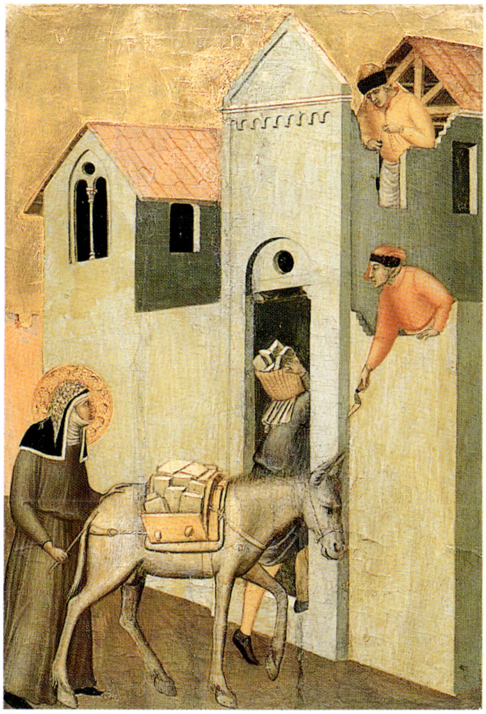

Pietro Lorenzetti
The Beata Umiltà bringing Bricks to the Monastery
c. 1340
panel, detail of the
Beata Umiltà Altarpiece
Florence, Uffizi Gallery.

The altarpiece, some of its parts missing, is dominated by the standing figure of the Blessed Rosanese dei Negusanti, who died in 1310. The surviving panels are rich in many scenes of daily life.

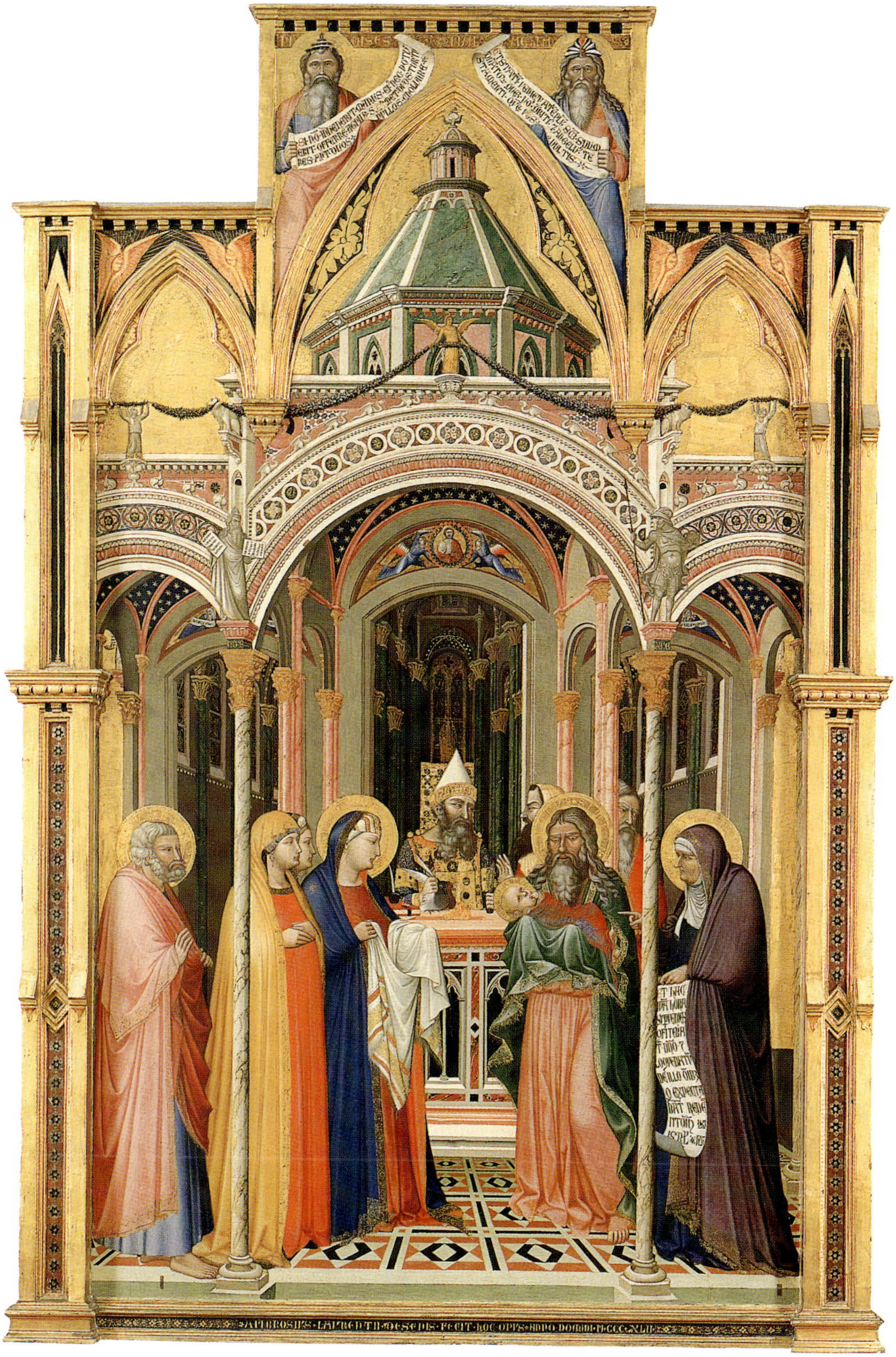

Ambrogio Lorenzetti
Presentation of Jesus in the Temple
signed and dated 1342
panel
Florence, Uffizi Gallery.

A few years before his death Ambrogio painted for the altar of San Crescenzio in the Siena Duomo one of the masterpieces of 14th century art. The composition (originally accompanied by two side panels) is arranged around a single vanishing point which from the richly inlaid polychrome flooring in the foreground slopes toward the apse of a magnificent church. Even the marble of the columns changes color according to the depth of the space. The false statues standing on the columns to protect the temple call to mind the ideals of heroic classicism.

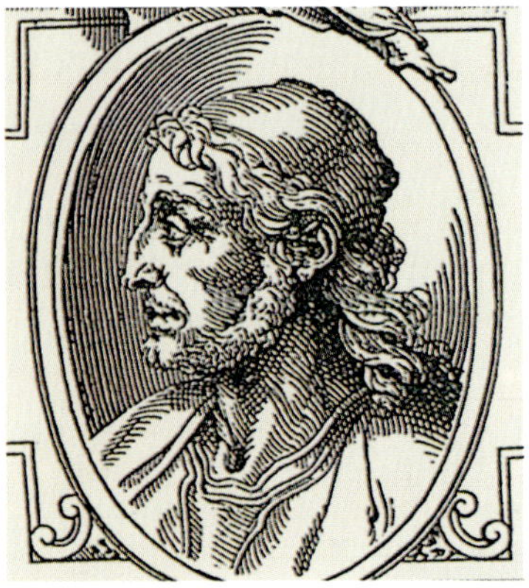

Simone Martini

(Siena c. 1284 – Avignone 1344)

In a sonnet by Francesco Petrarch, Simone flies up to Paradise to paint the "lovely face" of the mythical Laura beloved by the poet. Nothing is known of that portrait on parchment, which would be the first example of portrait painting in the history of the western world. Certainly, the friendship of Petrarch contributed significantly to the immediate fame of the refined Sienese artist. For the poet Simone also illustrated an erudite *Virgilian Allegory* in the frontispiece of a codex now at the Biblioteca Ambrosiana in Milan. Expert in both large and small formats, Simone, who with several "chompagni" had a shop in Siena, worked also in Pisa, Orvieto, Assisi and the Angevin court of Naples. While in the Assisi frescoes he almost seems willing to compete with Giotto, more often he remained faithful to a personal, aristocratic language, where color plays a primary role in conferring luminosity and depth.

Giorgio Vasari, *Portrait of Simone Martini*, from the *Lives*, Florence, Giunti, 1568.

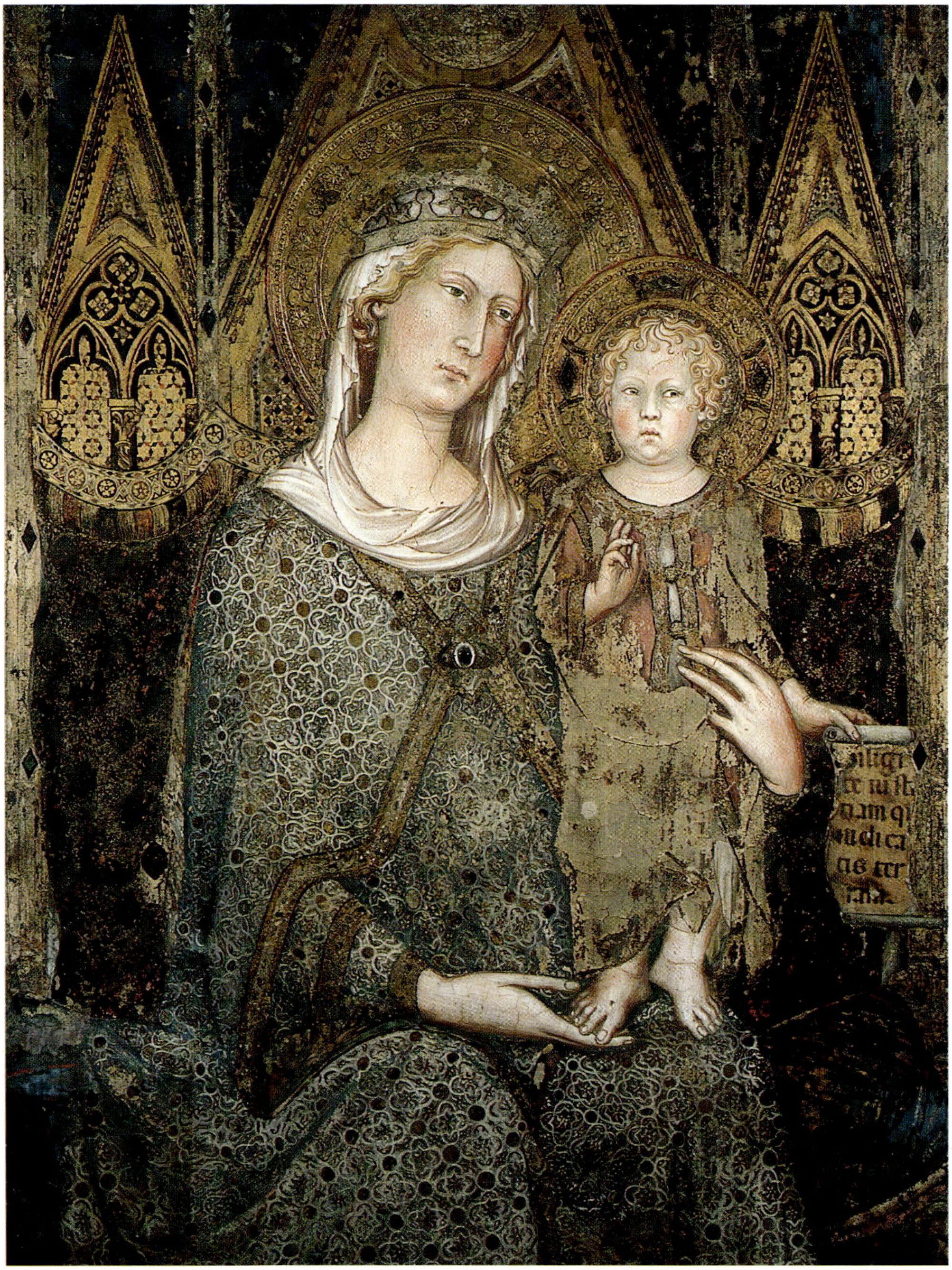

Simone Martini
Virgin with Child
signed and dated 1315
fresco, detail of the *Maestà*
Siena, Palazzo Pubblico, Hall of the Mappamondo.

Restored in 1994, the fresco is dominated by the Madonna with angels and saints. The first patron saint of Siena sits on a golden throne, wearing a queenly crown, under a baldachin of rich fabric. Restoration has been unable to salvage the precious colours of the clothing, applied "dry", which have been almost entirely lost. The first known work undoubtedly by Simone, it displays a complex iconography along with the composed detachment of Byzantine modes. The entire composition, over seven meters high and almost fifteen wide, remains the most grandiose fresco of the age, covering an entire wall of the hall where the General Council of the Republic met. The scroll held by the Child Jesus exhorts governors to love justice: "*Diligite iustitiam qui indicatis terram*".

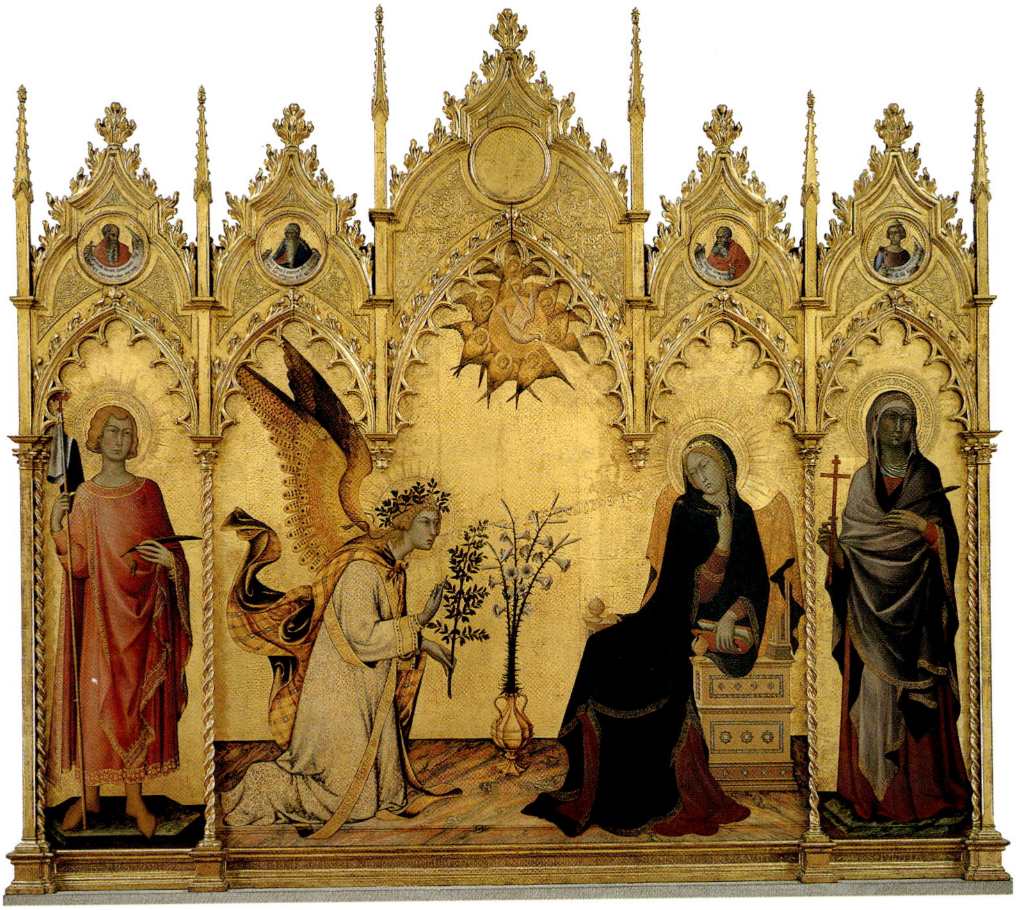

Simone Martini and Lippo Memmi
Annunciation
signed and dated 1333
panel
Florence, Uffizi Gallery.

The result of the combined efforts of Simone and his brother-in-law Lippo Memmi, the altarpiece comes from the Siena Duomo. Typically Sienese in the linear borders, precious in the details standing out against the dazzling gold-leaf background, the composition has a strong theatrical accent. The Virgin, timid and frightened, draws back from the angel, whose announcement is printed on the panel like a balloon in an *ante litteram* comic strip.

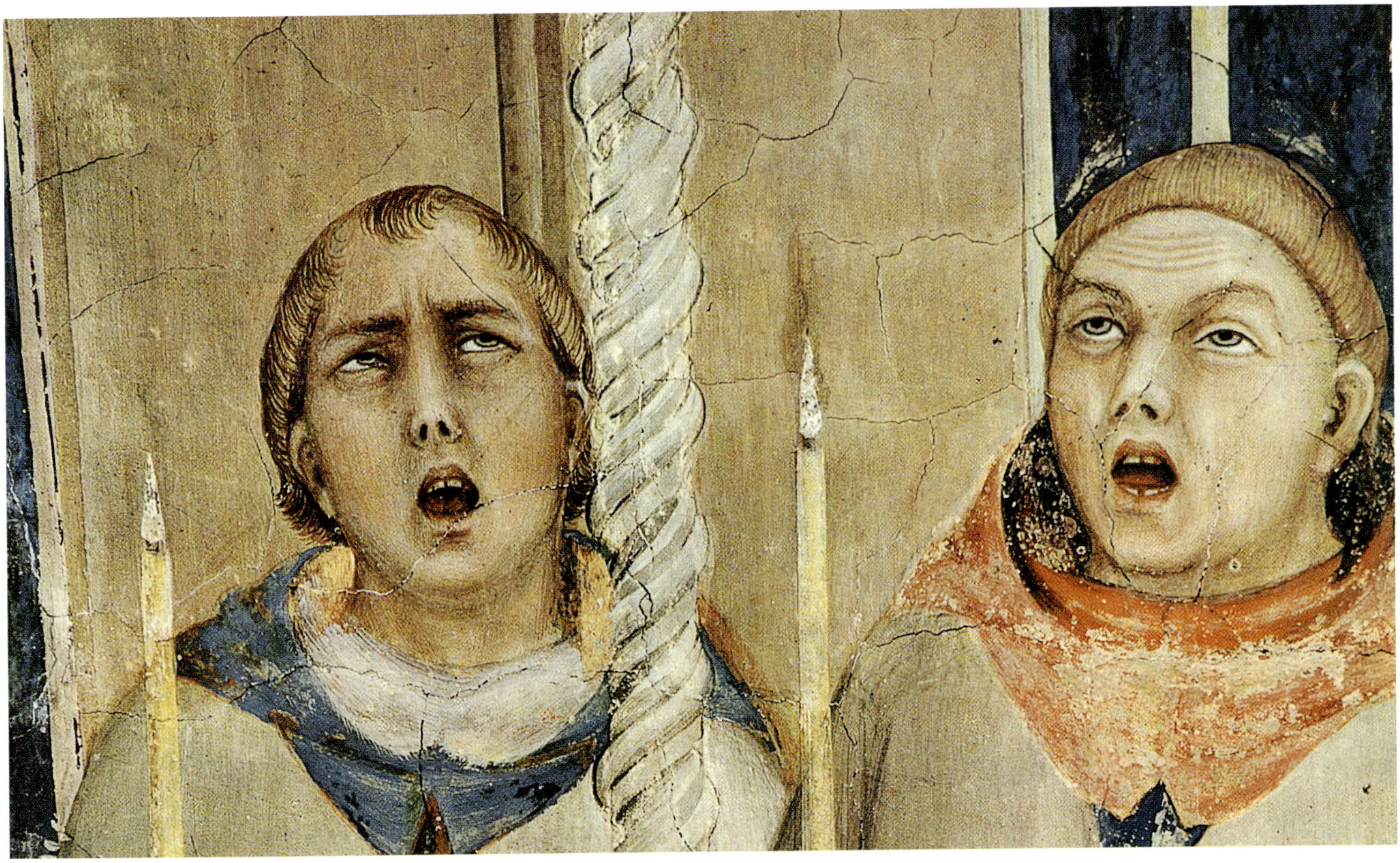

Simone Martini
Two Singing Choir-boys
1315-18
fresco, detail of the *Funeral*, from the cycle of *Stories of St Martin*
Assisi, Basilica of San Francesco, Lower Church, Chapel of St Martin.

While an echo of Giotto can be felt in the foreshortened faces and the architectural setting divided by spiral columns, the overall effect is that of an enchanted, courtly world. In the Chapel of St Martin, like a jewel casket dominated by the blue of lapis lazuli, Simone narrates with lyrical detachment the life of the chivalrous saint born in Pannonia in the 4th century.

Vitale da Bologna

(Vitale degli Equi, c. 1308 – died between 1359 and 1361)

Displaying pungent realism and acute expressiveness, an excellent talent for composition and soft, precious, at times brilliant colours, Vitale (or Vitalino) di Aymo de Equis worked in the university town of Bologna, as important as Paris at the time and highly stimulating culturally and artistically. Documented in 1330 for the decoration in the Church of San Francesco, he continued his frenetic activity in Ferrara, Udine and Pomposa as fresco artist, panel painter and perhaps even sculptor, assisted by a well-organized shop.

Giovanni da Milano

(Caversaccio, Como, c. 1320 – at Florence and Rome from 1346 to 1369)

Along with Taddeo Gaddi, Giovanni da Milano, painter of frescoes and panel paintings now dispersed throughout the world, is the most interesting of all the painters active in Florence in the mid-14th century. The artist came there from Lombardy in about 1346, and later went to Rome, called to the Vatican. His style, typical of the Po Valley artists in its pleasantly worldly scenes, is enhanced by spatial solutions which reveal an understanding of Giotto's highest achievements.

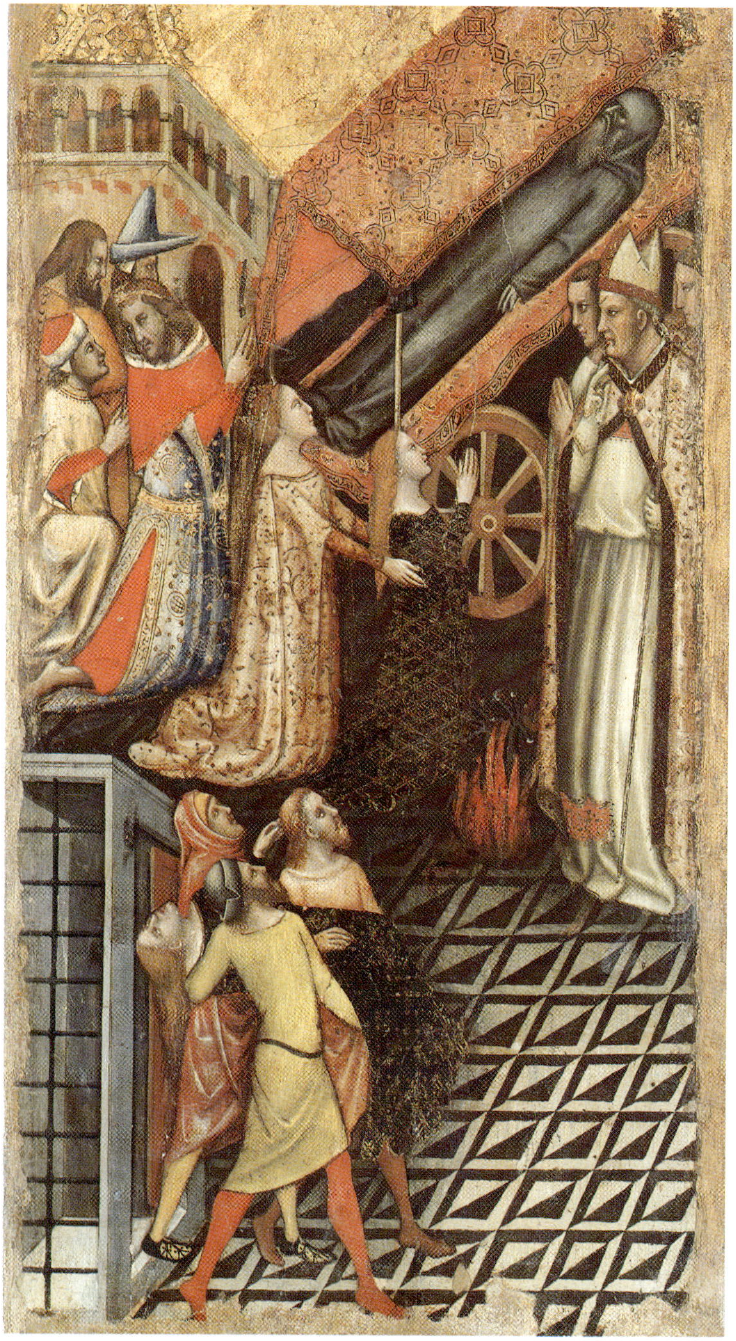

Vitale da Bologna
A Story of St Anthony Abbot
c. 1340-45
panel
Bologna, Pinacoteca Nazionale.

The vertical lines are emphasized by the steep slant of the flooring.

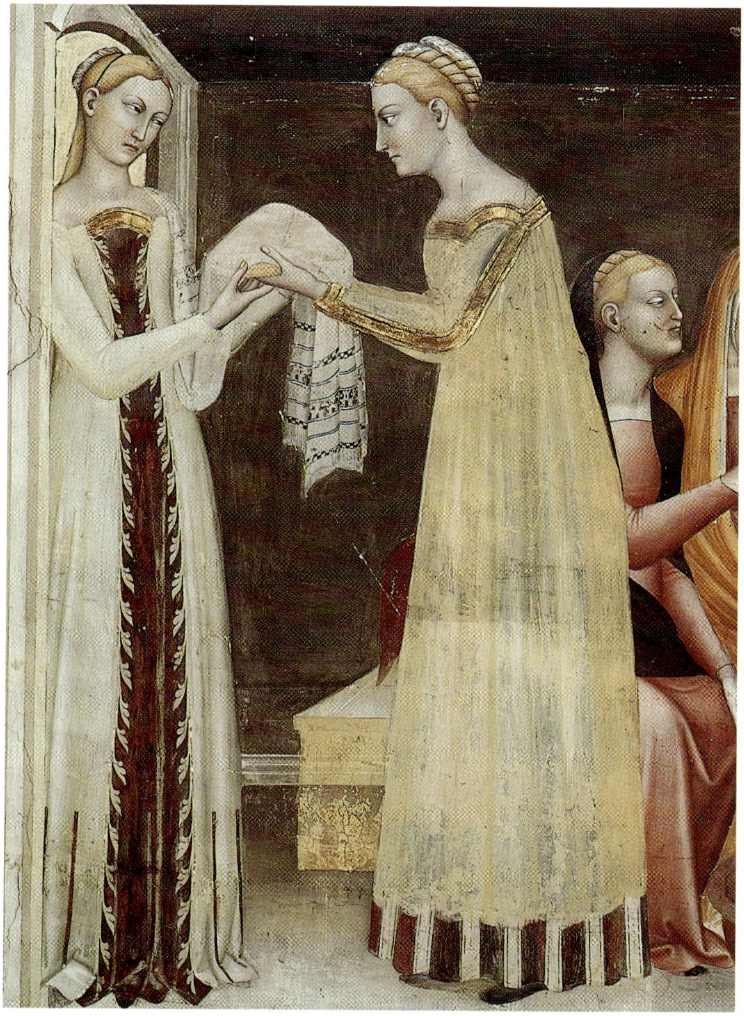

Giovanni da Milano
Two Women
c. 1365
fresco, detail from the cycle of the *Stories of Mary Magdalene and the Virgin*
Florence, Basilica of Santa Croce, Rinuccini (formerly Guidalotti) Chapel.

Commissioned of "*Johannes pictor de Kaverzaio*", the frescoes were believed to be by Taddeo Gaddi by Vasari: although mistaken in his attribution, he praises the figures and the "clothing of that time, beautiful and extravagant".

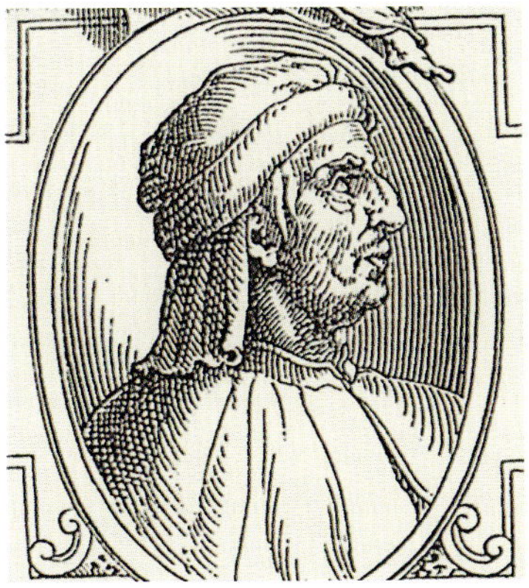

Giorgio Vasari, *Portrait of Buffalmacco*, from the *Lives*, Florence, Giunti, 1568.

Buonamico Buffalmacco

(documented from 1315 to 1340)

"Buonamico Buffalmacco, Florentine painter, who was a disciple of Andrea Tafi and, as a droll man, celebrated by Messer Boccaccio, was known to be a very dear friend of Bruno and Calandrino, jovial and pleasant painters themselves; and, as can be seen in his works scattered all over Tuscany, a man of very good judgement in his art of painting". So Vasari recalls Buffalmacco, already praised as outstanding artist by Boccaccio and Franco Sacchetti. The inventor of outlandish practical jokes, Buffalmacco incarnates in the *Decameron* and the *Trecentonovelle* one of the first portraits of the skillful, ingenious artist. In the workshop of Andrea Ricchi known as Tafo in 1320, he was among the first enrolled in the list of Florentine painters. While much is known of his personality and his reputation as excellent master, the certain works in his career are instead few.

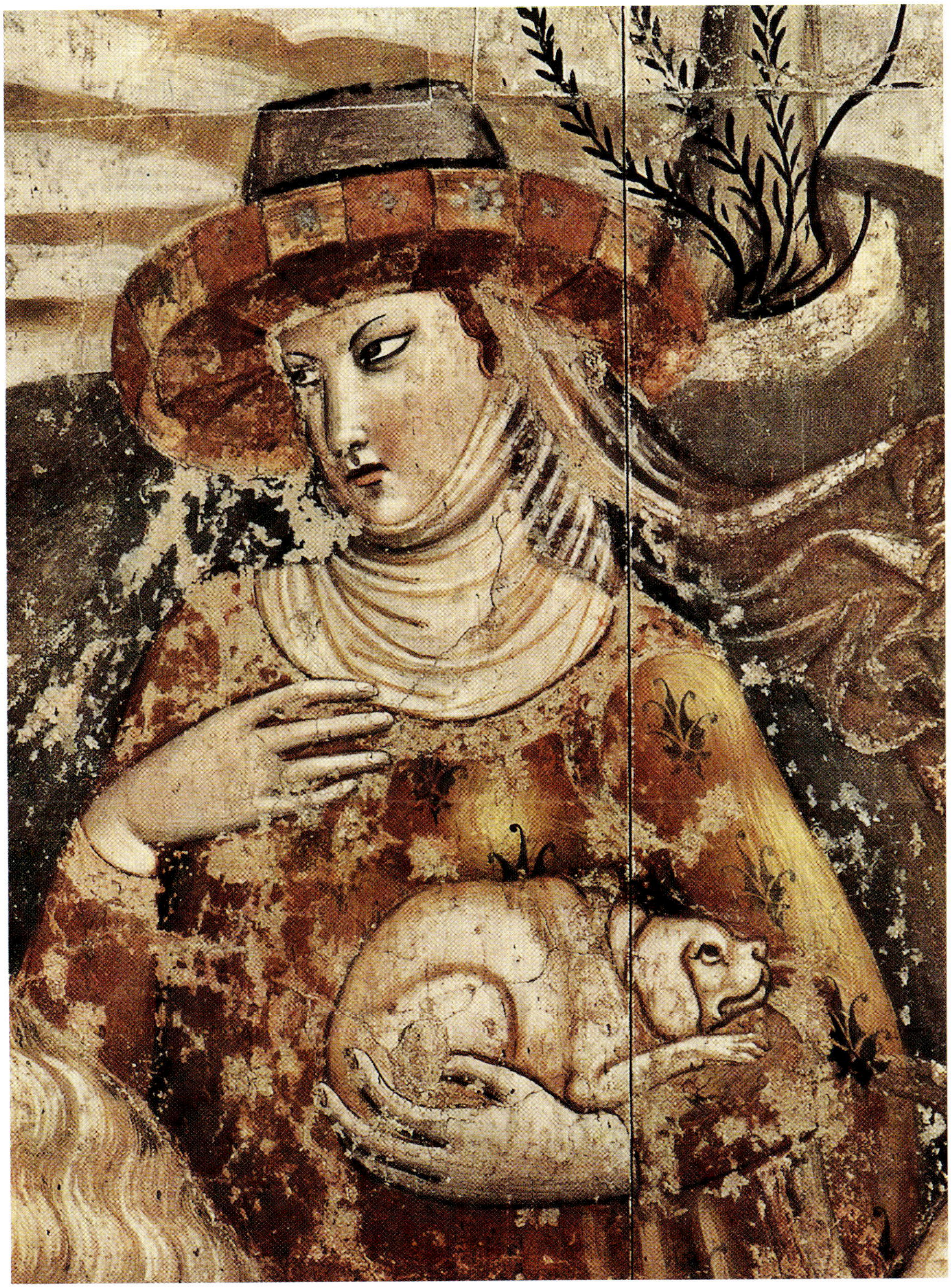

Buffalmacco
Young Woman with a Dog
c. 1340
fresco, detail of the *Triumph of Death*
Pisa, Camposanto.

Formerly attributed to the so-called Master of the Triumph of Death, the cycle of frescoes in the Pisa Camposanto, although fragmentary and in poor condition, is now considered to be Buffalmacco's masterpiece. Three vast scenes depicting the *Triumph of Death*, the *Judgement with Inferno* and the *Thebaide* (or *Stories of the Holy Fathers*) cover the eastern and southern walls of the monumental complex. Buffalmacco, perhaps assisted in the undertaking, expresses himself in an original language, varied and syncopated, emphasizing facial features and showing himself to be a keen observer of botanical species and animals. An artist who can be seen as "in opposition" to the Florentines of the Giottesque school, he was closer to the expressionism of Emilian painting of the times, and to the style of important painters and miniaturists.

Paolo Veneziano

(Venice, c. 1290 – c. 1362)

The chief painter of Venice in the early 14th century, Paolo is also the first name identifiable in Venetian painting. In a document dated March 30, 1341, he signs himself "Paulus pictor" and states that he lives in the San Luca quarter. Even earlier, in 1335, the Treviso notary Oliviero Forzetta mentions as being near the Frari Church the workshop of "Paolo da Venezia" and his brother Marco, also a painter, who specialized in stained glass windows and embroidery. The notary, it seems, wished to buy from Paolo some cartoons of *The Death of St Francis and of the Virgin*, painted "ad modo Theotenicum in pano" (painted on cloth in the Teutonic, or northern European, manner). This would seem valid proof, in the eyes of such an astute contemporary as Forzetta, of the artist's tendency to paint in the "Gothic", Occidental manner. Although not entirely abandoning the traditional Byzantine orientation of Venetian art, Paolo was the first to show, even in youthful works such as the *Palione* in Santa Maria e Donato at Murano (1310) vivacity and a strong naturalist sense clearly inspired by Giotto. Still closely linked to the Byzantine manner are the panels of the *Pala Feriale* (St Mark), painted with his sons Luca and Giovanni, who continued to paint after his death.

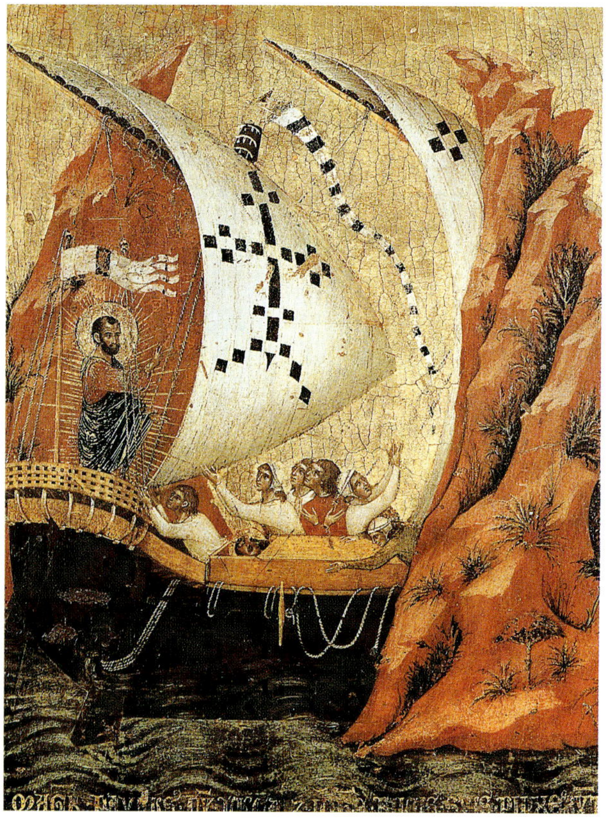

Paolo Veneziano and Assistance
Translation of the Body of St Mark
1345
panel, detail of the *Pala Feriale*
Venice, St Mark's Museum.

At the time of the Doge Andrea Dandolo, a learned humanist, these panels were painted to cover the famous *Pala d'Oro*, masterpiece of Italian Byzantine goldwork, on week-days.

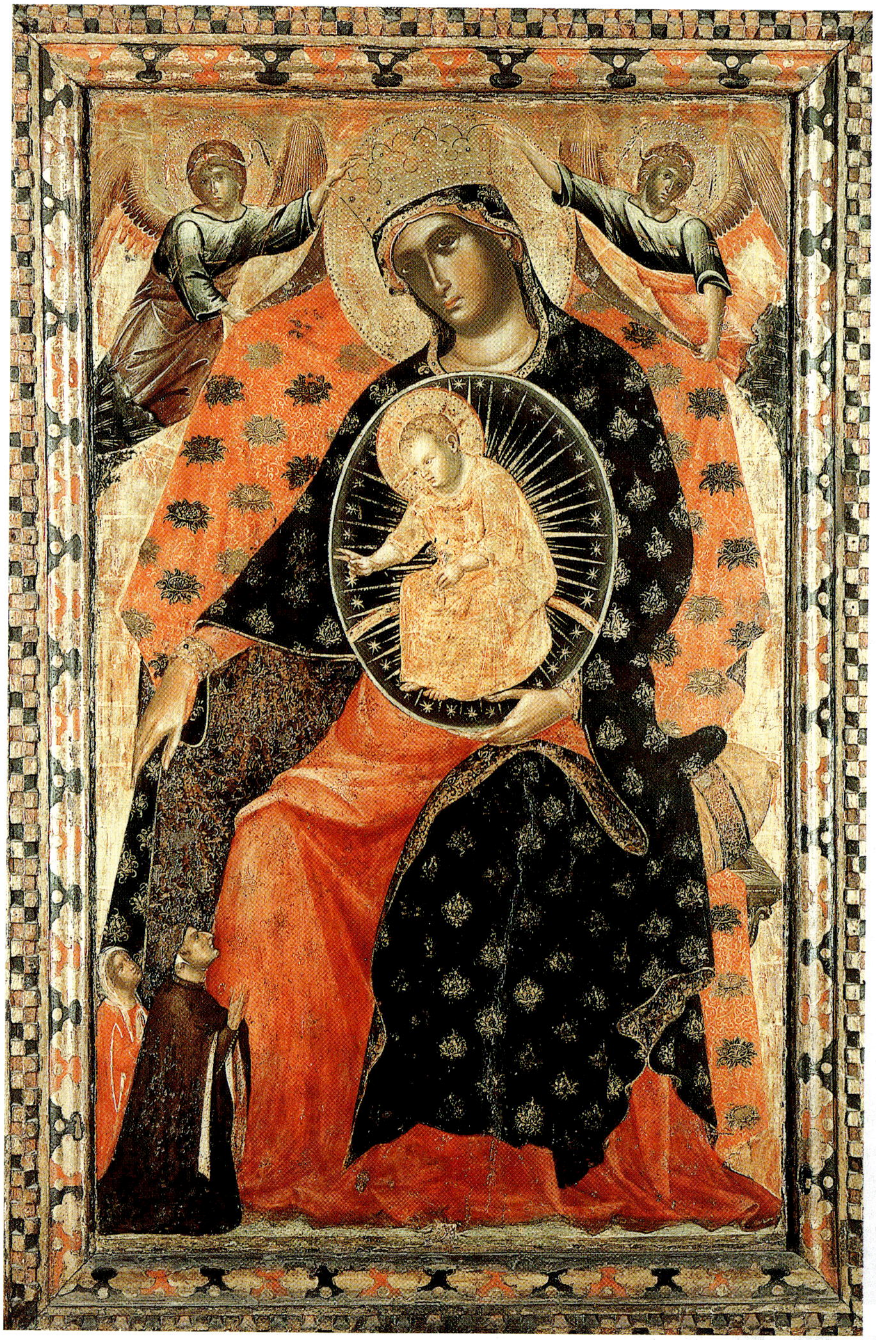

Paolo Veneziano
Madonna with Child and Two Donors
c. 1325
panel
Venice, Gallerie dell'Accademia.

The panel, still in its original frame, shows Syrian influence in the oval surrounding the Child. The "humanized" portraits of the donors are instead inspired by the Giotto of the Scrovegni.

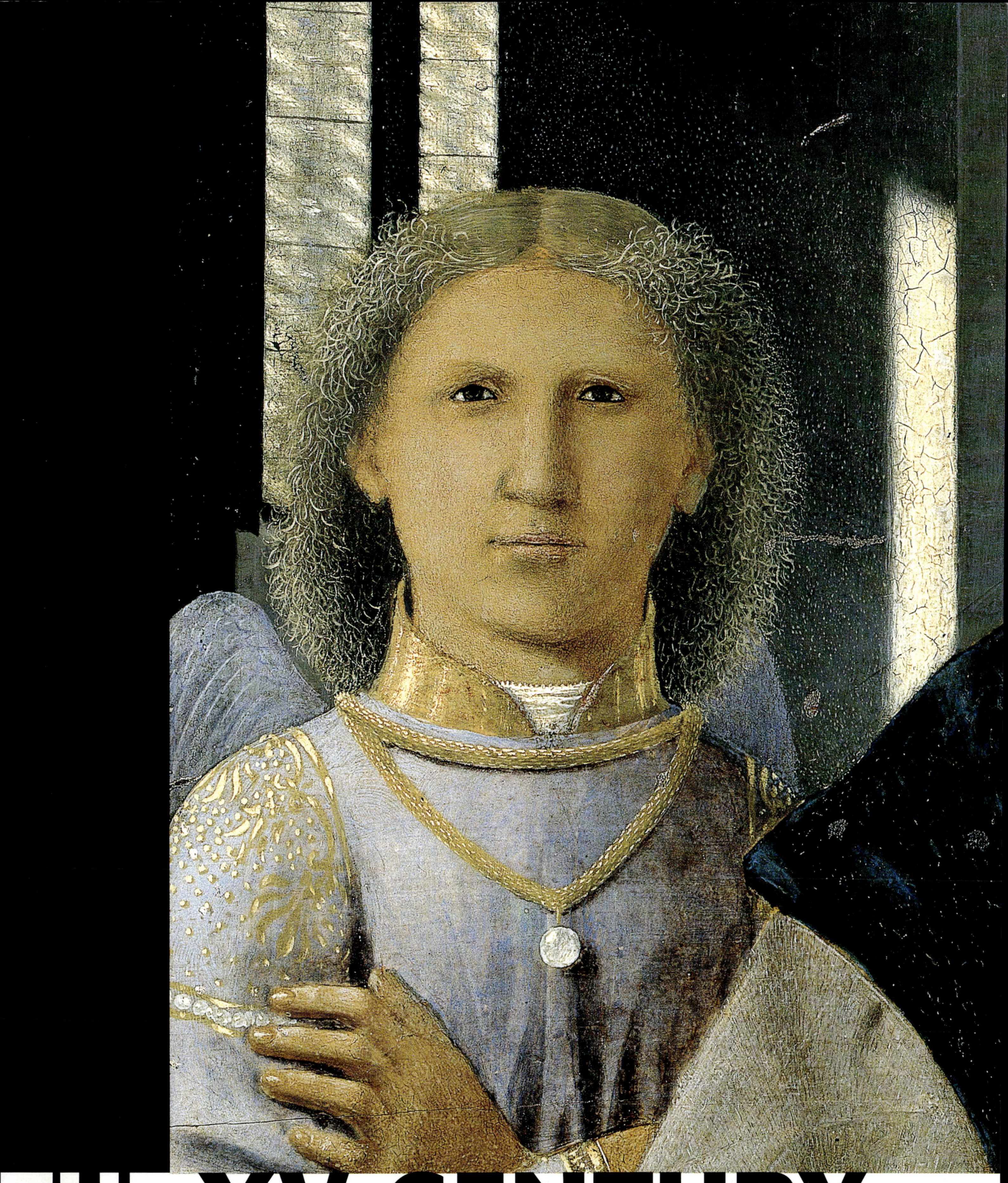

THE XV CENTURY

Giotto
Maestà
(Ognissanti
Madonna)
c. 1310
panel, whole and detail
Florence, Uffizi
Gallery.

In the great pentagonal altarpiece painted for the Umiliati altar in the Church of Ognissanti at Florence, the throne on which the Madonna with Child sits seems almost an open triptych, or rather a canopy, decorated in the Gothic manner with refined marble overlay. The space is rendered lifelike by a three-dimensional architectural structure, heightening the effect of the typical "perspective box" used by Giotto, who still retains, however, the traditional gold-leaf background. The obvious disproportion between the Virgin and the other figures may be due to the need to show to the greatest possible number of faithful an image of the majestic Virgin, who like that of Duccio formerly in Santa Maria Novella is designed to be seen from an off-center point of view. The ampulla with roses and lilies, both Marian symbols, are among the first Medieval examples of still life.

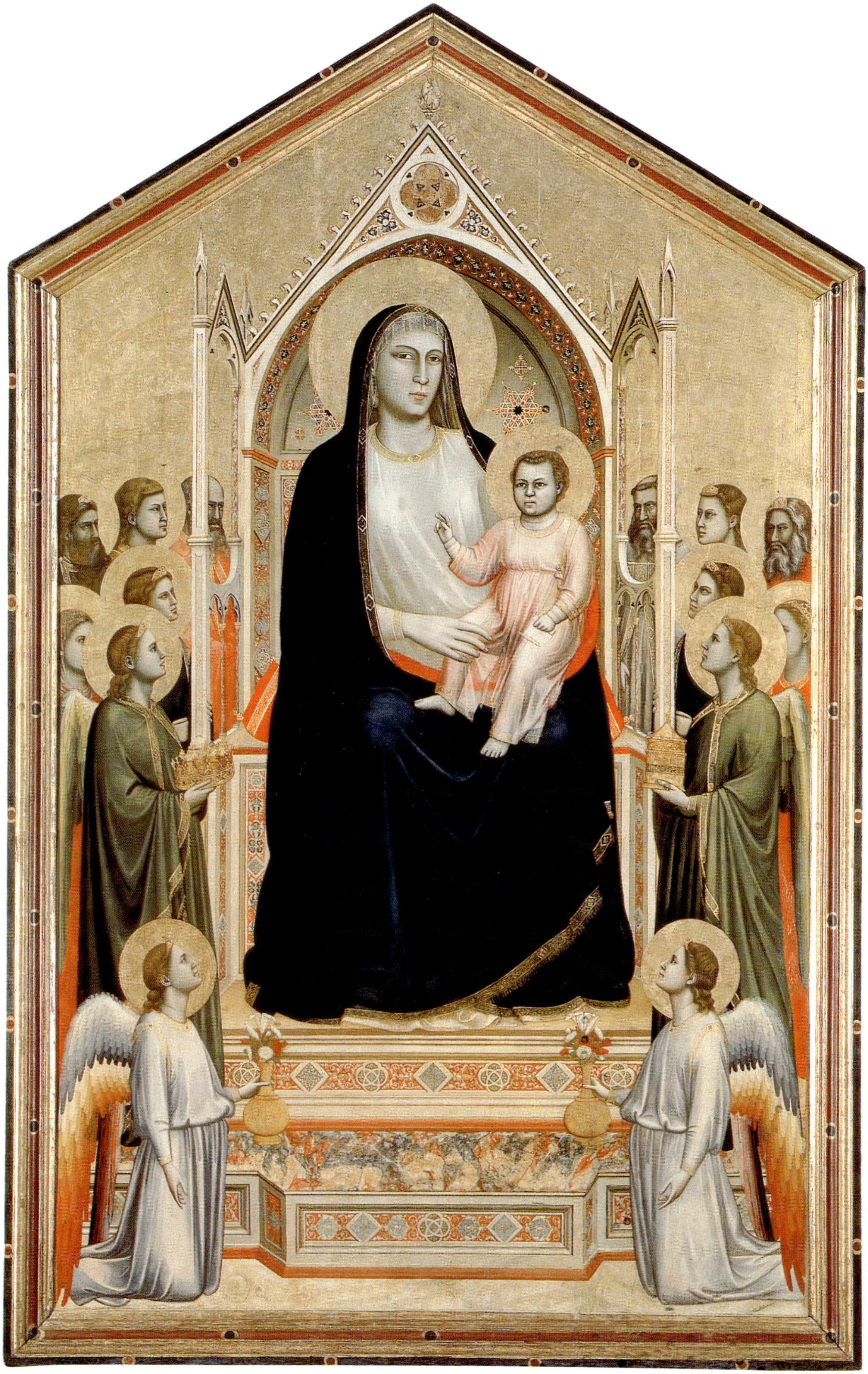

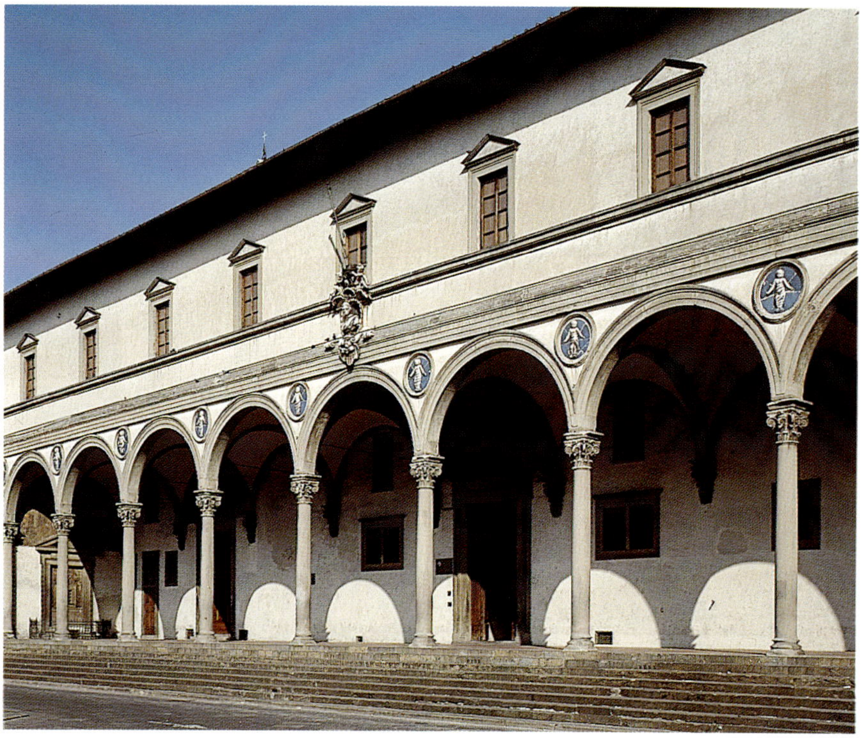

Far from his homeland – in years marked by political instability in all of the Italian cities – the young Leon Battista Alberti, Florentine by descent but born in Genoa in 1406 while his father was in exile, repeatedly wondered that "such excellent and divine arts and sciences", once so abundant, "were now so lacking and almost wholly lost". And he grieved that

Filippo Brunelleschi, *Portico of the Spedale degli Innocenti,* begun in 1419. Florence, Piazza della Santissima Annunziata.

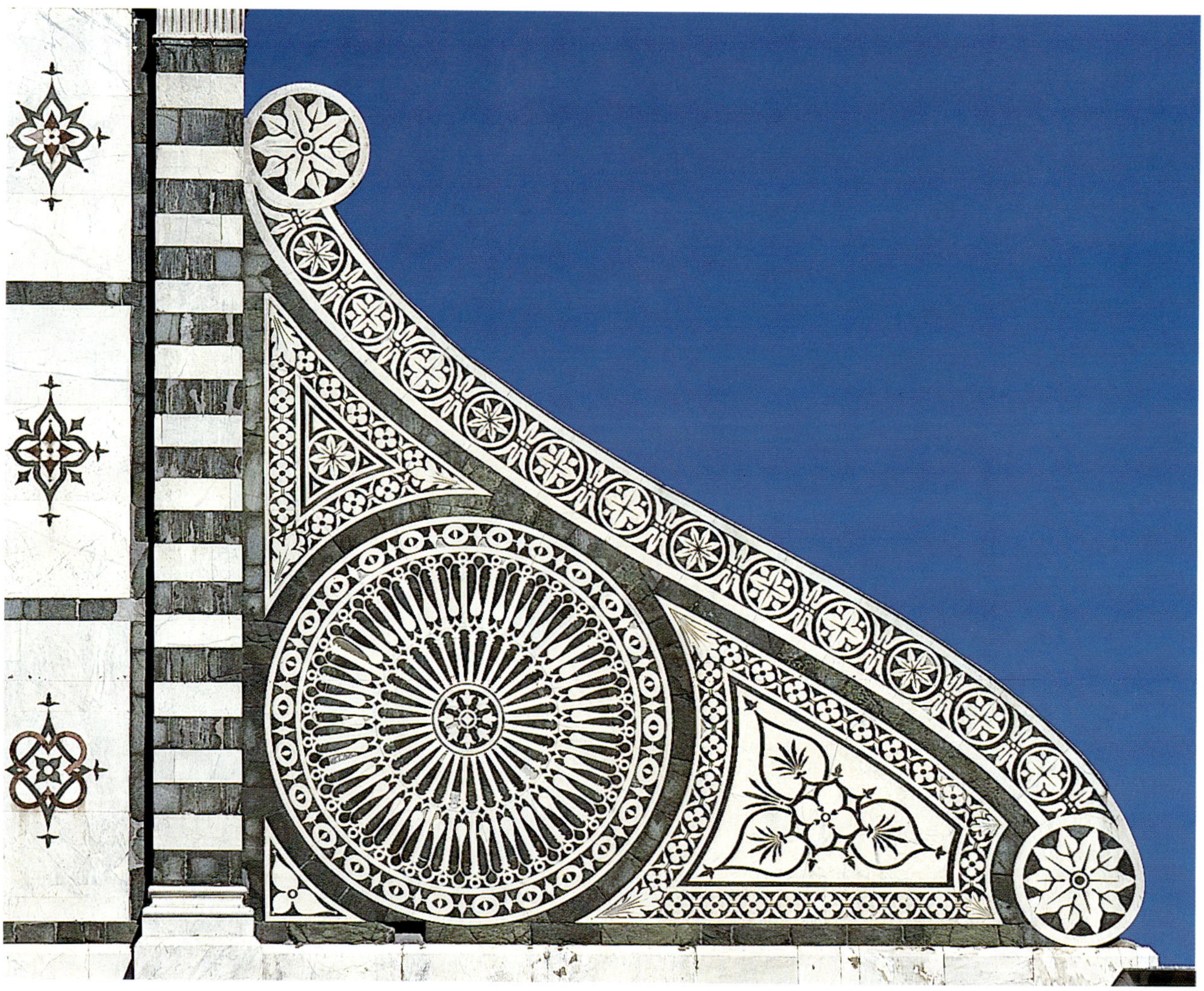

Leon Battista Alberti, *Detail of the façade of Santa Maria Novella,* commissioned between 1439 and 1442, finished in 1470. Florence.

Preceding page:
Piero della Francesca, *Senigallia Madonna,* detail, c. 1474. Urbino, Galleria Nazionale delle Marche.

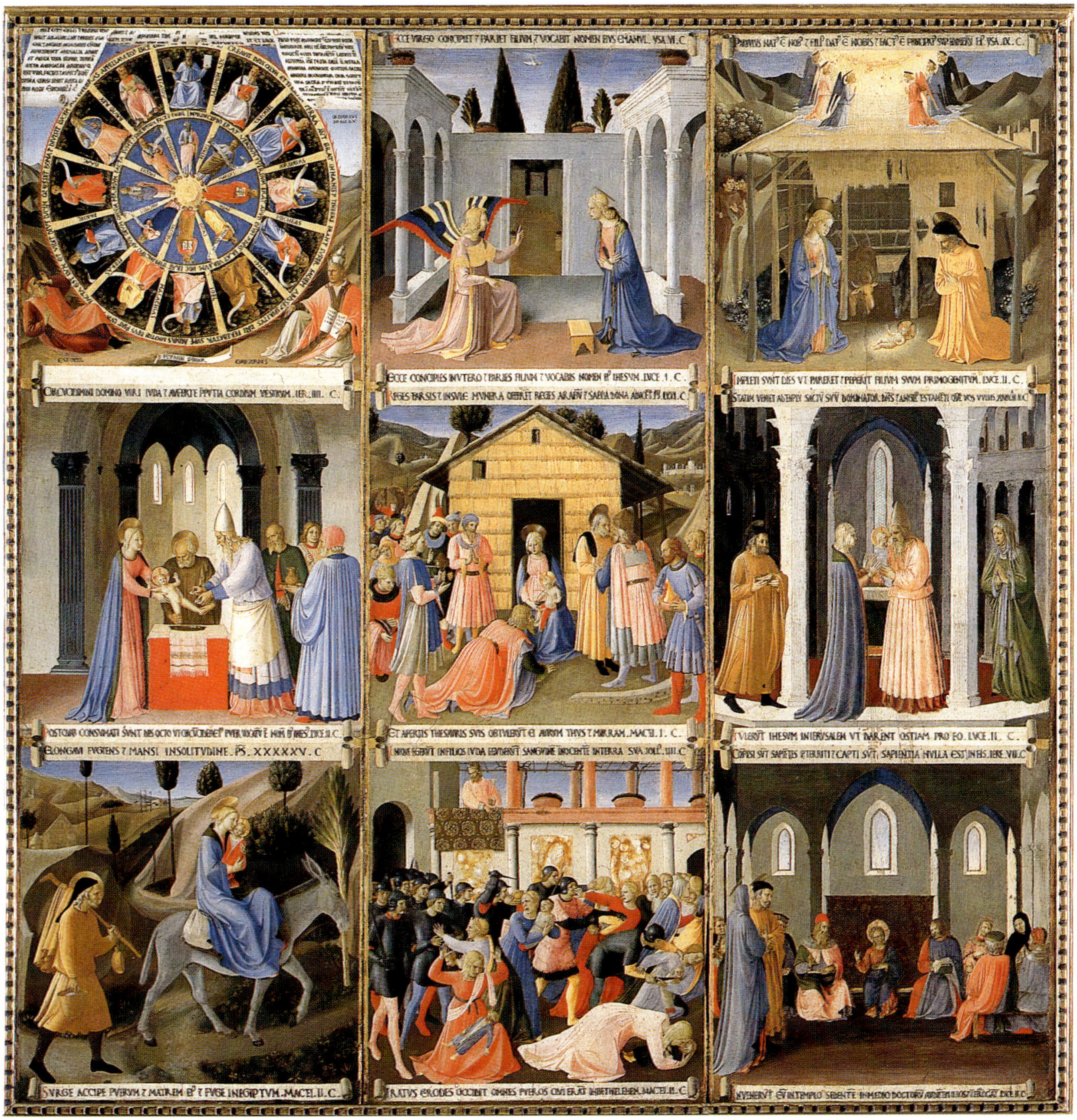

Beato Angelico,
Silver Cabinet, detail of the first nine stories, depicting, from upper left: *Mystic Wheel with the Vision of Ezechiel, Annunciation, Nativity, Circumcision, Adoration of the Magi, Presentation in the Temple, Flight into Egypt, Slaughter of the Innocents, Jesus Disputing with the Doctors*, 1450-52. Florence, San Marco Museum.

there now existed "neither giants nor geniuses". His pessimistic view was to change radically when he finally came to know his own city. In 1434 Alberti discovered Florence dominated by Brunelleschi's dome then being constructed, "a structure so great, rising above the heavens, so ample as to cast its shadow over all of the Tuscan peoples". And he was to see in Donatello, Ghiberti, Luca della Robbia and Masaccio, and above all Brunelleschi, a genius not inferior to any from antiquity. It was no coincidence that he dedicated to "Pippo", the great architect, his treatise on painting (1436), an imposing theoretical structure of primary importance for the whole century, up to the time of Leonardo.

It is unsurprising that Alberti, a sensitive adolescent living in exile, felt the decadence of civilization. He was not the first to feel it. Pessimism had dominated for years, even in Florence, as exemplified by the poet Franco Sacchetti bidding farewell to his century in 1399: "I see the universe with such evil signs of decline, that I believe that the divine trumpet will assign each to that valley from which, once having entered,

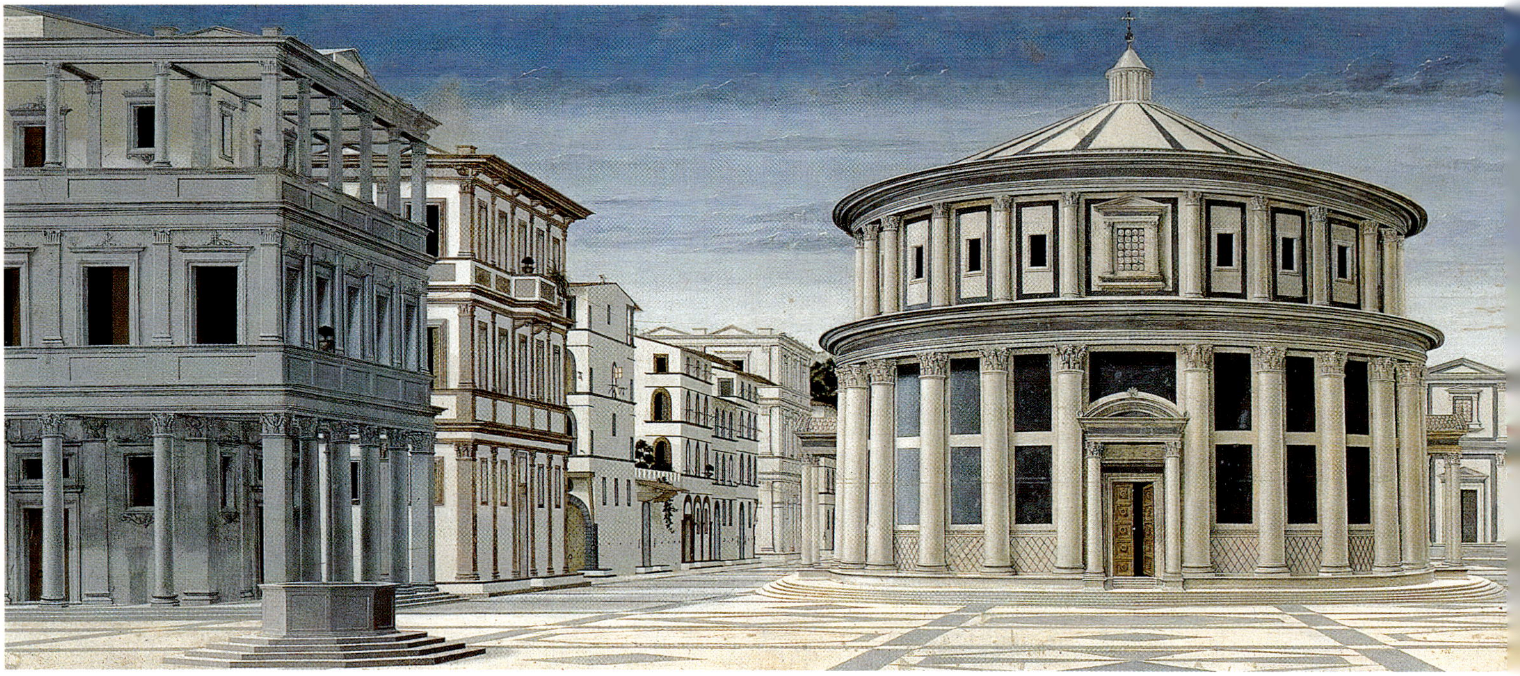

Anonymous artist (attr. also to Piero della Francesca, Giuliano da Sangallo, Sandro Botticelli), *Ideal City*, c. 1460-80. Urbino, Galleria Nazionale delle Marche.

Pisanello's circle, *Bacchic Scene*, copied in part from the Sarcophagus of Dionysias in the Vatican, detail, c. 1431-32. Milan, Biblioteca Ambrosiana, ms. F. 214 inf. 13.

Andrea Mantegna, *St George*, c. 1460-70. Venice, Gallerie dell'Accademia.

there is no return". This apocalyptic vision is reflected also in the artistic climate of the mature 14th century. In one of his novellas Sacchetti has Taddeo Gaddi, Giotto's last great follower, express an opinion shared by many after the Black Plague of 1348: the "worthy painters" no longer existed; art had vanished and was "lacking all the day". But even amid such crisis and latent disquiet Florence, like other cities, had in reality

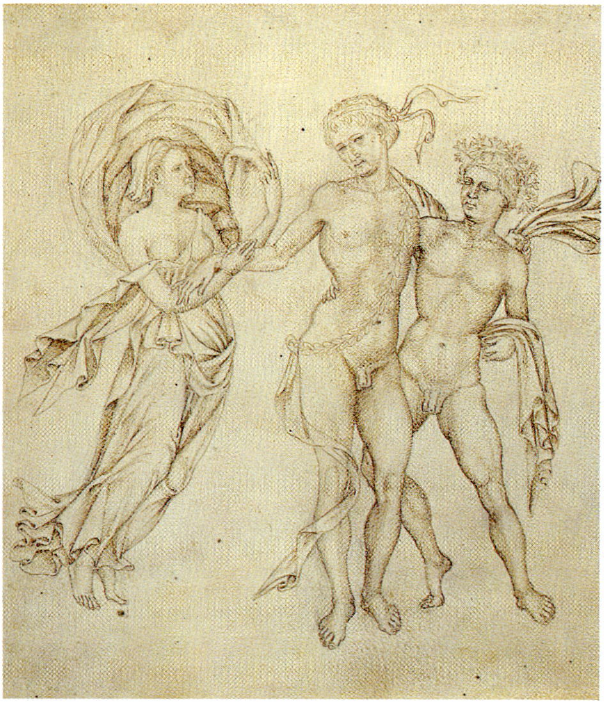

carried out initiatives of great civic value such as the Loggia dei Lanzi and Orsanmichele, the symbolic church of the city's guilds; while in painting, the tradition of Andrea Orcagna (member of the commission for the cathedral left unfinished by Arnolfo) was enriched by new stylistic traits, like those introduced by Lorenzo Monaco. In the North, which had boasted such original painters as Altichiero and Giusto de' Menabuoi, civic monuments were being erected under the sign of a growing urban vitality. In the Venice of Andrea Dandolo (Doge since 1343, waging war against Genoa and the Turks), construction was continuing on Palazzo Ducale, symbol of the concentration of power. The Lombardy of Giangaleazzo Visconti (Duke since 1395) held the grandiose international worksite of the Milan Duomo, where even French and German architects worked, and that of the Certosa at Pavia. This was the atmosphere surrounding Michelino da Besozzo and Pisanello, attentive to nature and also, in the case of the latter, to antiquity. Already as the 14th century came to an end, in Tuscany and in Veneto interest in antiquity, never entirely extinguished as has been seen with the Pisan sculptors, was flourishing. Now this interest was incremented

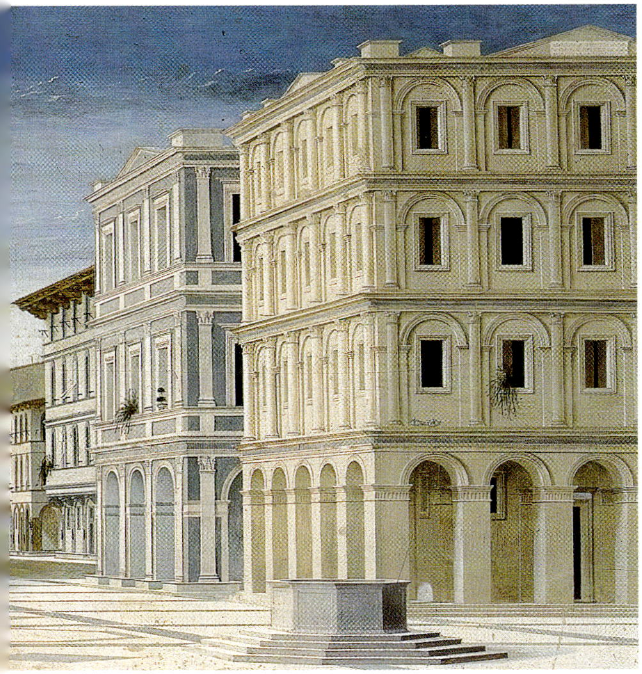

by humanists such as the Florentine Niccolò Niccoli, a collector of ancient gemstones and codexes, and the Chioggian Giovanni Dondi, who at Rome in 1375 transcribed epigraphs and measured ancient monuments (opening the way to the tradition within which Rome was to be visited by Donatello and Brunelleschi, among the first in the new century); or like the Carrara family, whose house in Padua was decorated with medallions imitating Roman Imperial coins, collected with fervent enthusiasm (in this tradition of historical and heroic re-evocation of the antique Mantegna was to attain the highest level, in full Quattrocento times).

With the new century, antiquity was increasingly regarded as a culture to be "revived"; and even more, to be studied, in the case of art, for its similitude, harmony and proportions. The study of sculptures, fragments of architecture and monuments became a constant pursuit among artists, even in their different approaches, conventionally summarized under three headings: the "archaeological" Humanism of Padua, the "philosophical and philological" one of Florence and the "mathematical" one of Urbino. It is interesting to note that the use of the term "rinascita" (rebirth) of Greek and Roman

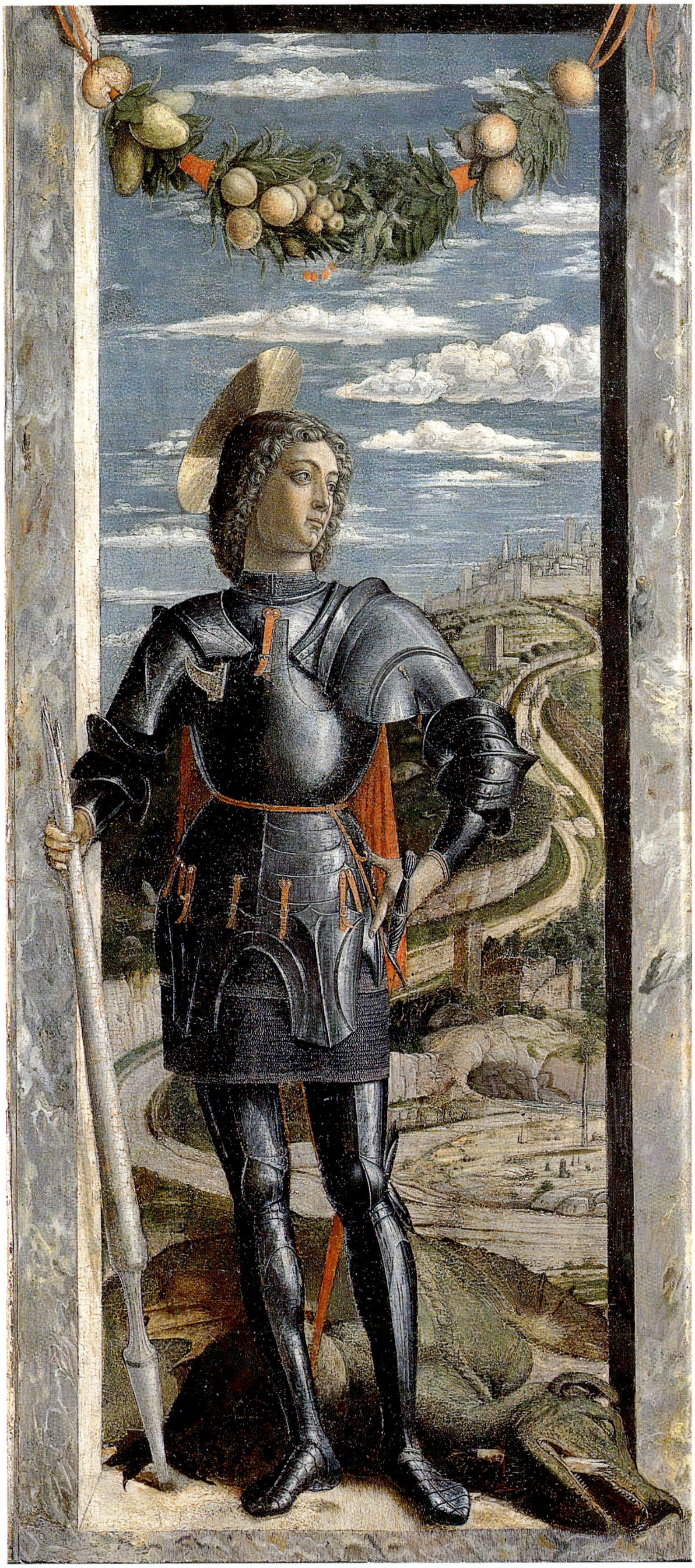

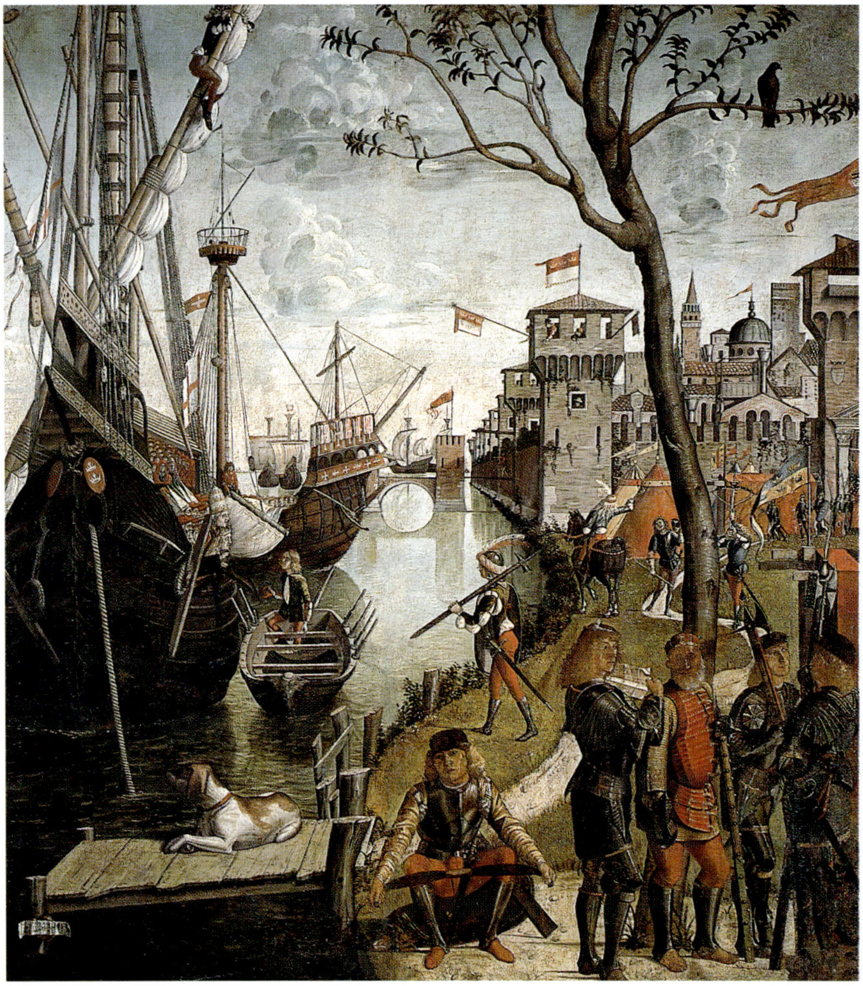

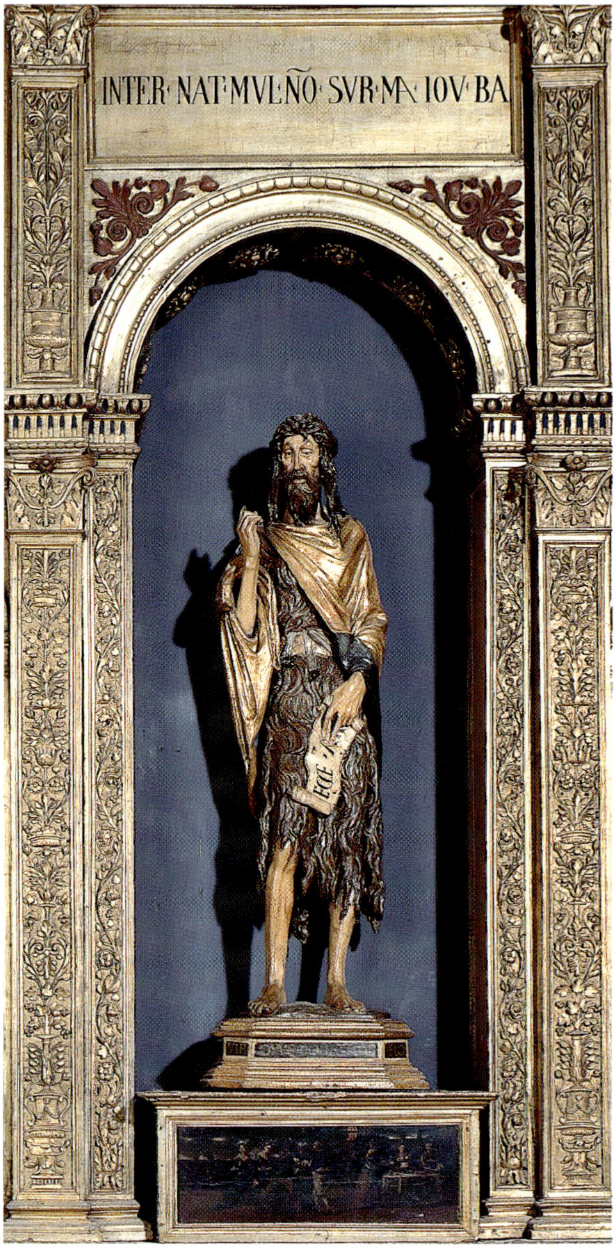

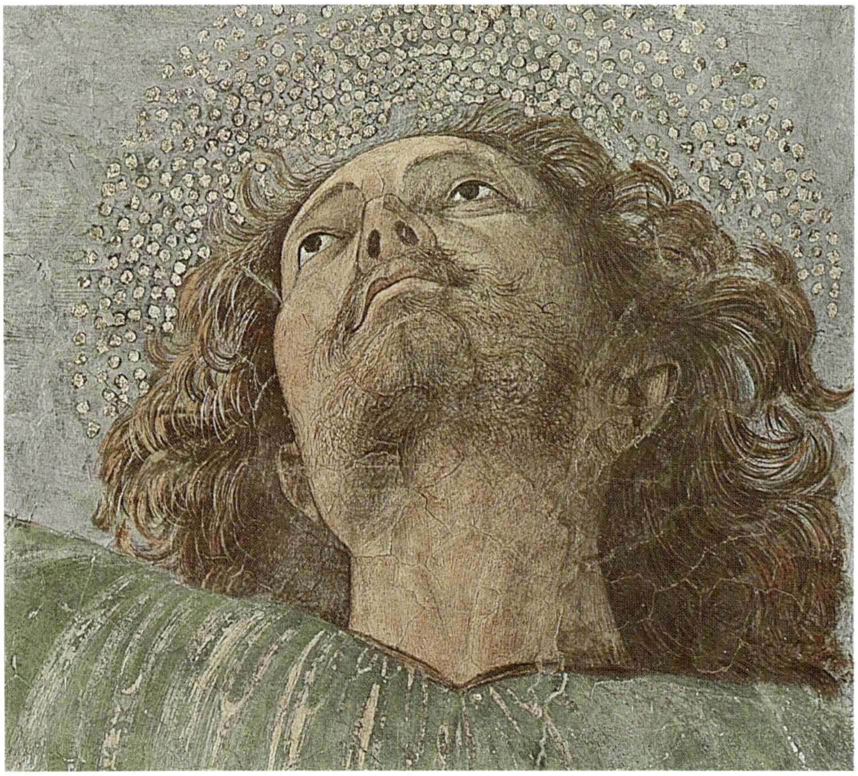

arts and culture is the only one, from among those conventionally used in historical classification, to date more or less from the same epoch to which it refers today.

But antiquity was not the only new reference point. A different conception of the relations between men, and between mankind and God, predominated in the 15th century. Finally occupying the center of the universe, no longer subjugated to divine forces, *homo faber* emerged, the artificer of himself, capable of emulating and even challenging the past with his own culture and techniques. Man was capable at last of attaining

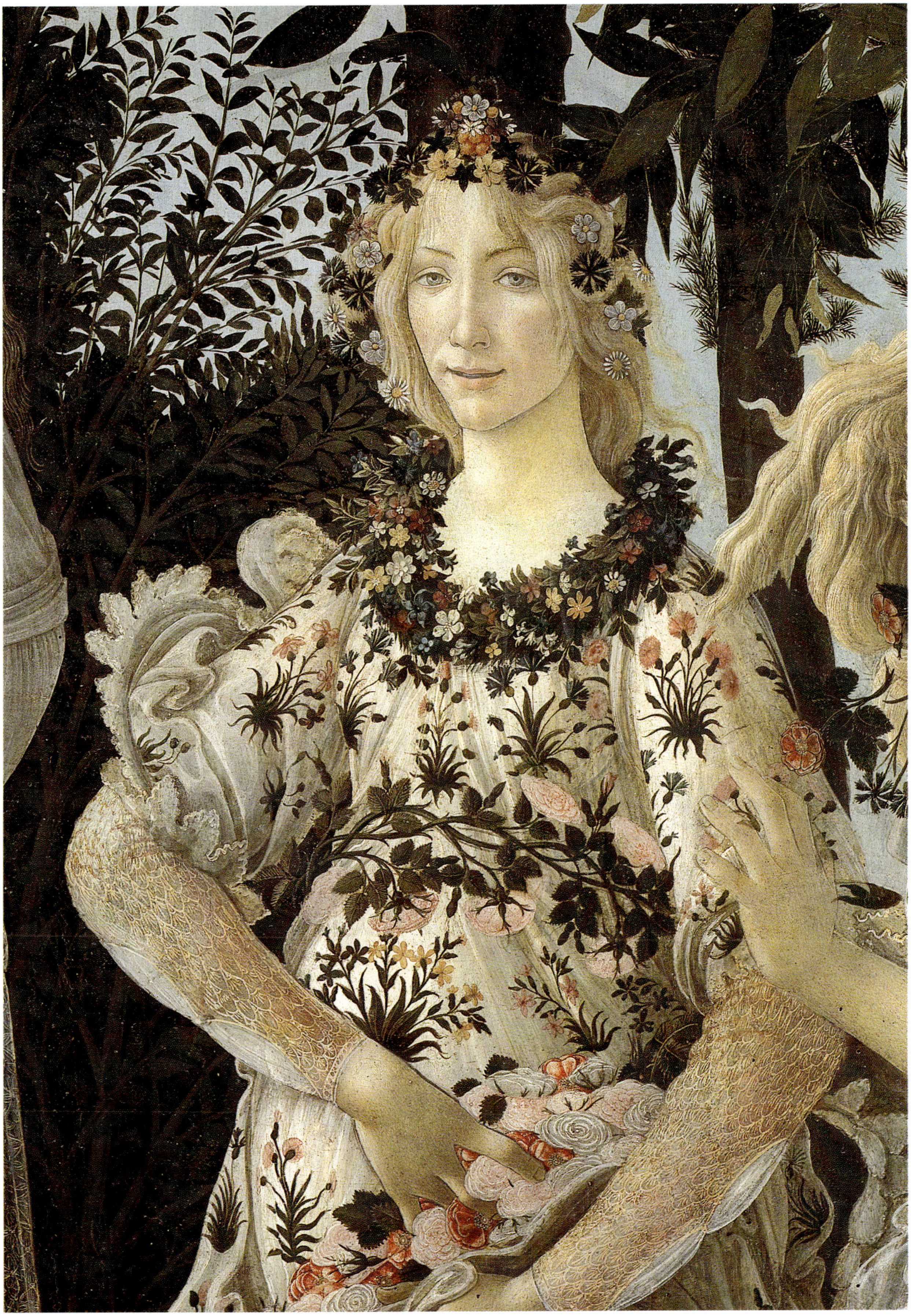

Preceding page:
Vittore Carpaccio,
Arrival at Cologne,
first work in the cycle
of the *Stories of St Orsola*,
signed and dated 1490.
Venice, Gallerie
dell'Accademia.

Melozzo da Forlì,
Head of an Apostle,
fragment of the apsidal
frescoes in the Basilica
of the Holy Apostles
in Rome, 1472-74.
Rome, Pinacoteca
Vaticana.

Donatello, *St John the Baptist*, 1438. Venice,
Santa Maria Gloriosa
dei Frari, Chapel of the
Florentine Brotherhood.

Sandro Botticelli,
Primavera, detail,
c. 1492. Florence,
Uffizi Gallery.

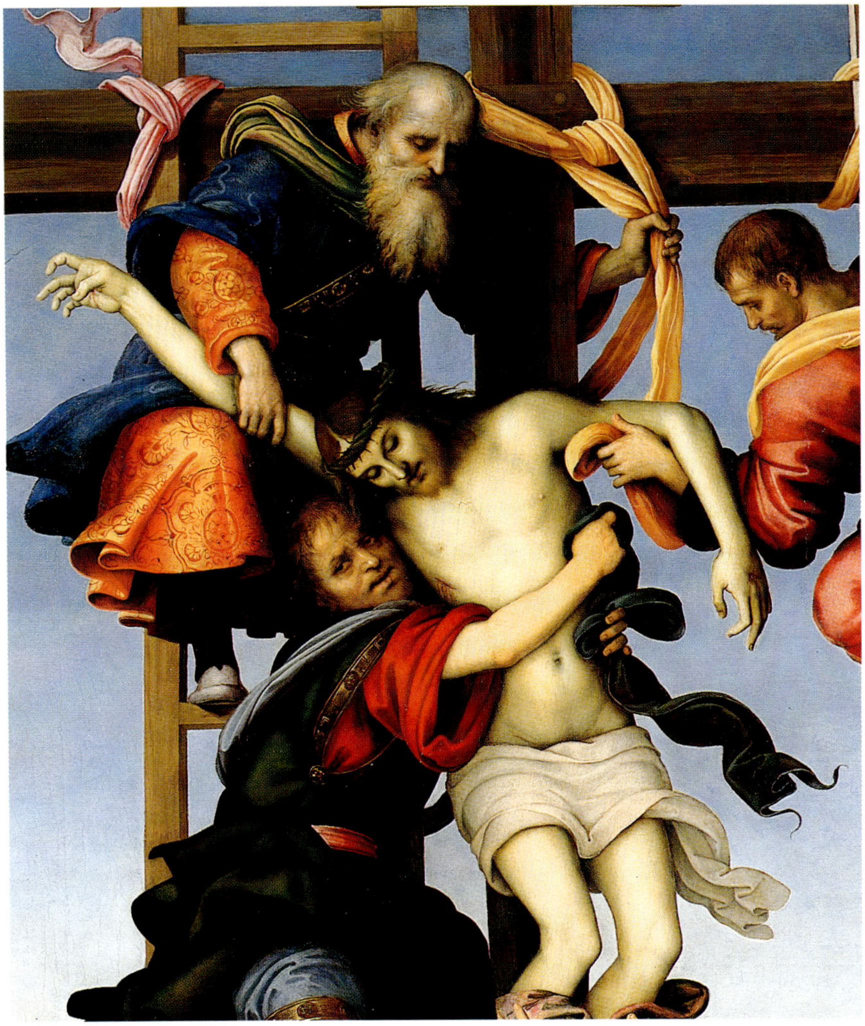

Filippino Lippi and **Pietro Perugino**, *Deposition from the Cross*, detail, 1504-1507. Florence, Accademia Gallery.

Giuliano da Sangallo, *Santa Maria delle Carceri*, begun in 1485. Prato.

in art "a spatial clarity, a psychological truth" which could explain him to himself, "helping him to understand his essence, to free himself from metaphysical myths and social conventions", as Zeri has noted in relation to Masaccio and Donatello. Thanks to these artists, and to the mathematical genius of Brunelleschi, the new experimentation had begun. Brunelleschi "had found this law", explains his biographer Antonio Manetti: a point of view is fixed, in relation to which the proportions and dimensions of the figures represented, and the distances between them, are established geometrically and precisely. The problem of representing depth in space was not really a new one (Giotto and the Lorenzetti brothers had already confronted it), nor was Brunelleschi's law the only method accepted in the 15th century, since variations quickly appeared: first in Florence, then in Venice, Padua, Mantua, Urbino, Perugia, Rome, Naples and as far as Sicily. Artists moreover, who were still artisans above all, often expert in many disciplines, were called increasingly often from one city to another, from one patron to another, in spite of the different political and social situations pertaining in the colorful mosaic of the Italian states.

Cultural exchange and enrichment was favored by the mobility of the masters, foreign ones as well, and the refined, eclectic taste of many patrons (private citizens, secular and religious institutions, princes and dukes). This is clearly shown by the interest in Flemish art, whose analytical description of reality was first

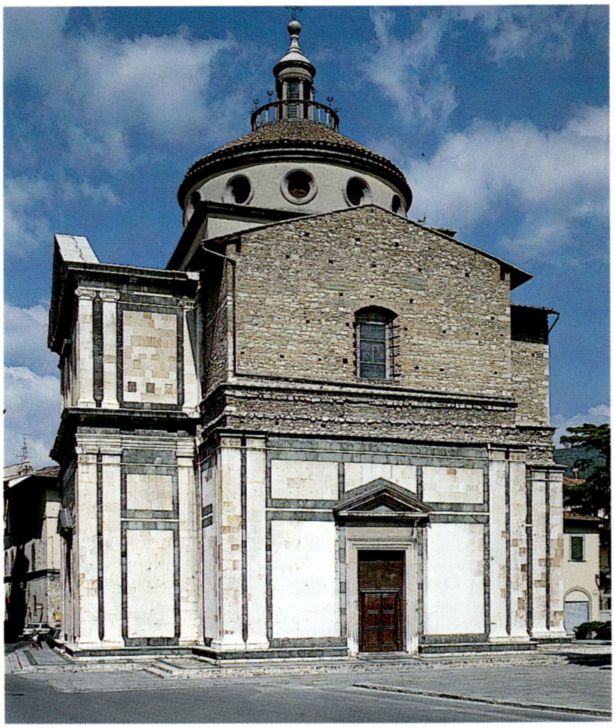

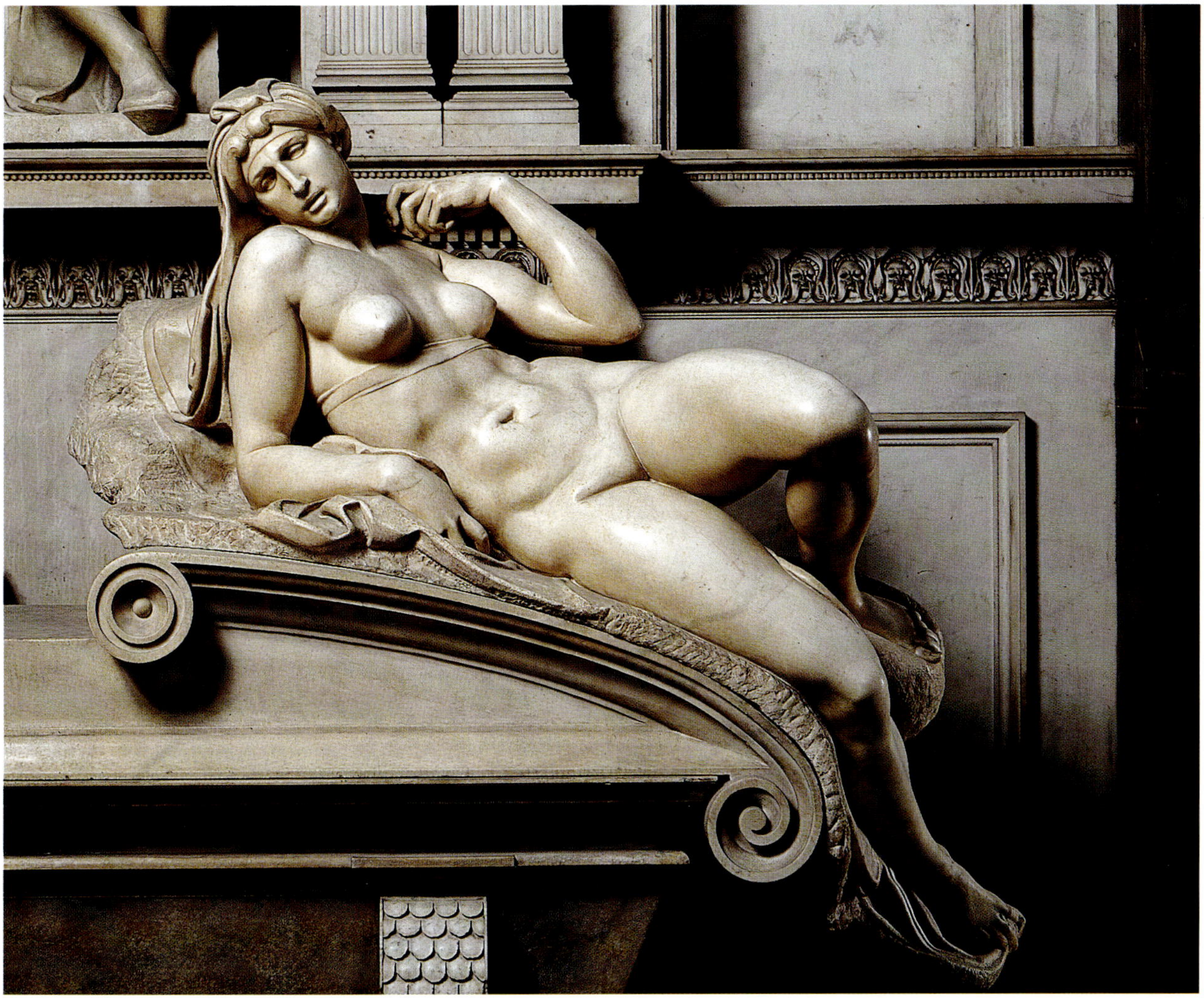

Michelangelo, *Dawn*, 1524. Florence, Medici Chapels.

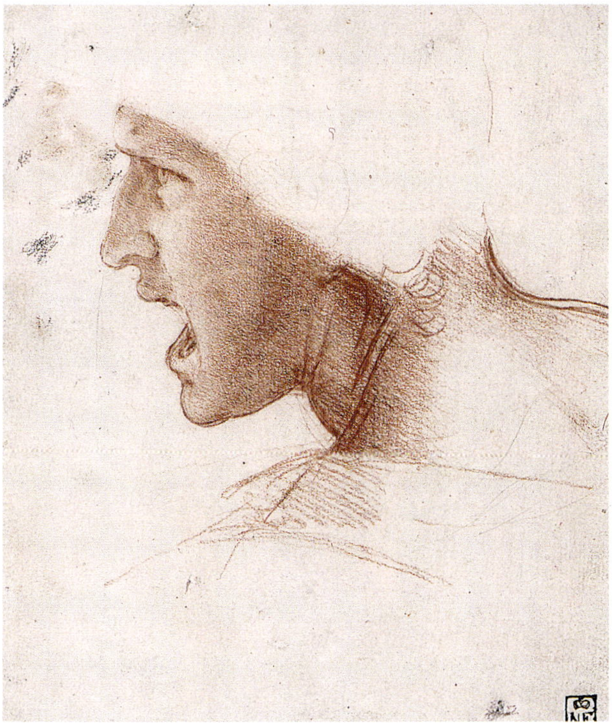

Leonardo da Vinci, *Study of a Head for the Battle of Anghiari*, c. 1504. Budapest, Szépmüvészeti Múzeum, inv. no. 1774 r.

admired by humanists such as the Neapolitan Facio, by great lords like the Medici, and by the artists they favored, Antonello da Messina and Filippo Lippo among others.

But the element which played the unifying role, "symbolic" of 15th century aspirations, was perspective: the urge to find a rational system for the world, to achieve harmony and proportion. It was only later, with the speculative mind of Leonardo, that a different conception of art and the world was to emerge; perspective was then to become the "daughter and not the mother of painting". With Leonardo's multi-faceted genius and the new manner of producing art, of being an artist, exemplified by Raphael and Michelangelo, masters who were already largely "16th century", a century so productive as to appear, paradoxically, longer than the others comes to a close.

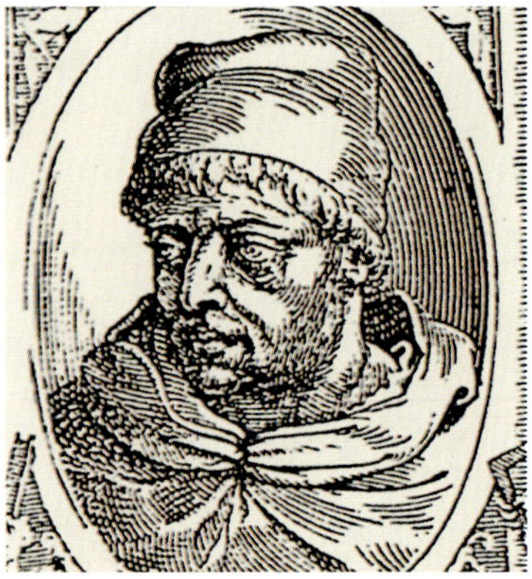

Lorenzo Monaco

(in the world Piero di Giovanni, Siena? c. 1370 – Florence c. 1425)

Don Lorenzo, a Camaldolensian monk, painter and miniator, is one of the outstanding figures in the transition between late Gothic and early Renaissance art, characterized in Florence by studies on the motion of bodies and precious colors, in his case gelid, almost metallic. Perhaps Sienese (a document calls him "dipintore de Siene"), he was a novitate in the Florentine Santa Maria degli Angeli Monastery in 1390, becoming a deacon six years later. Here he worked as miniator (his intense images of prophets decorate choir-books now in the Biblioteca Laurenziana). His *corpus* of panel paintings includes works of various formats now in museums all over the world. The largest core, documenting his activity from the beginning, is in the Florence Accademia Gallery, while two more recently restored masterpieces, the *Adoration* illustrated here and a grandiose *Coronation of the Virgin*, are in the Uffizi.

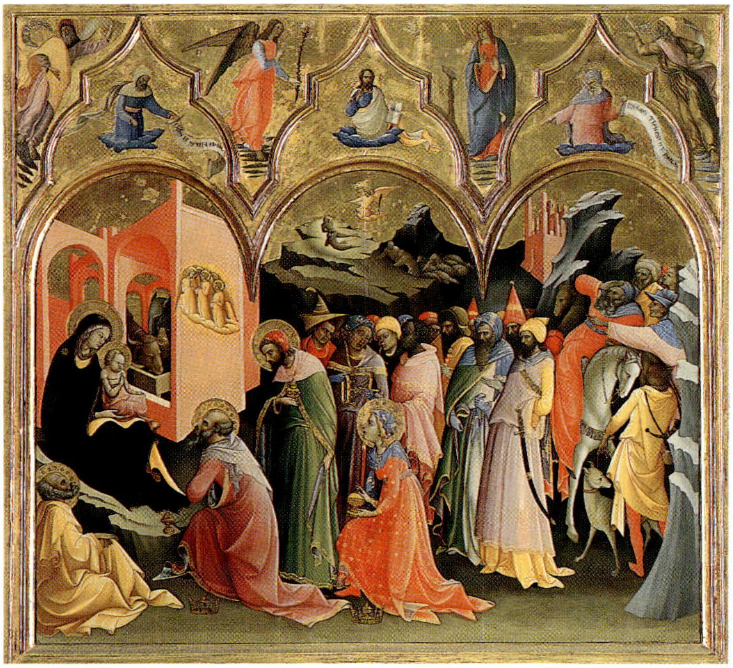

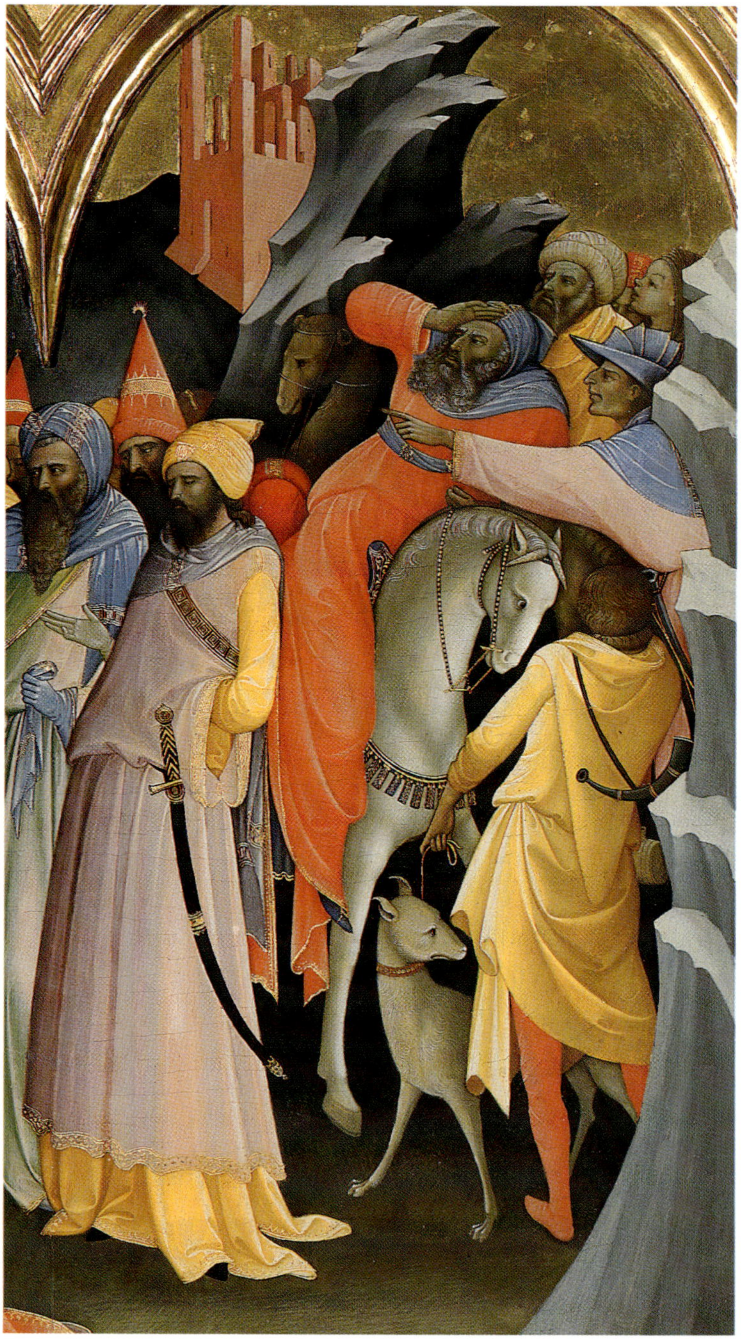

Giorgio Vasari, *Portrait of Lorenzo Monaco*, from the *Lives*, Florence, Giunti, 1568.

Lorenzo Monaco
(with subsequent intervention by Cosimo Rosselli)
Adoration of the Magi
c. 1420-22
panel, entire and detail
Florence, Uffizi Gallery.

The altarpiece, its colors enhanced by enamel and lapis lazuli, probably comes from the high altar of the Florentine Church of Sant'Egidio, reconsecrated by Martin V in 1419. Like the *Coronation*, also in the Uffizi (signed and dated 1414), the work confirms Don Lorenzo as an original artist, already sensitive to Ghiberti's innovations in sculpture. His stylistic "reform", based on the mature achievements of Giotto's school (later followers such as Orcagna and Agnolo Gaddi in particular), can be seen in the extenuated elongation of the bodies, whose movements involve every limb. Exotic details appear, such as the pseudosufic (ancient Arabic) characters embroidered on some of the mantles. The panel also testifies to the alterations frequently made in paintings due to a change in taste. In the second half of the 15th century, between the three pinnacles depicting Christ bestowing blessings and two prophets, Cosimo Rosselli added two more prophets and the two figures of the Annunciation, transforming the tricuspid altarpiece into a rectangular one, more consonant with Renaissance style.

Michelino da Besozzo

(Michelino Mulinari, Besozzo, Varese, information from 1388 to 1450)

Called by his contemporaries "supreme painter", "most illustrious among those of his age", "stupendous in painting animals", Michelino at the end of the 14th century was in Pavia, then a European art center, later in Venice and the Milan of the Visconti. Little is known of the early training of this eclectic artist who excelled in drawing, miniatures, frescoes, panels, gonfaloni, chests, many now lost. Praised by the Humanist Uberto Decembrio and his son Pier Candido, Michelino suffered a *damnatio memoriae* starting with Vasari, who erroneously thought him Agnolo Gaddi's pupil. In the 20th century Pietro Toesca and Roberto Longhi reevaluated him as master of the "tender style" in which he was "unrivaled", writes Longhi, even by great contemporary artists such as Lorenzo Monaco and the Cologne school painters.

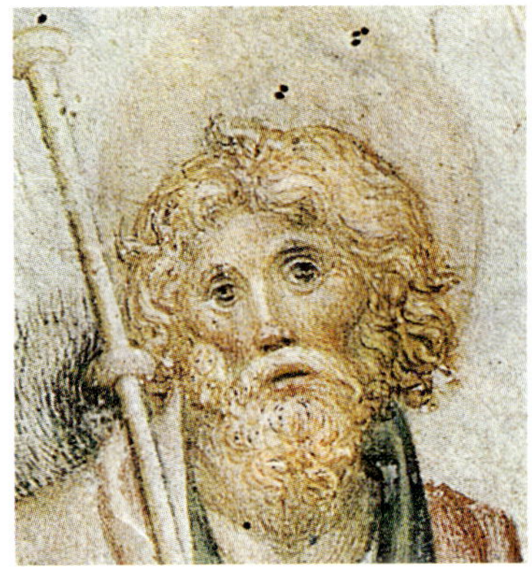

Michelino da Besozzo, *St James*, detail, early 15th century, Paris, Louvre.

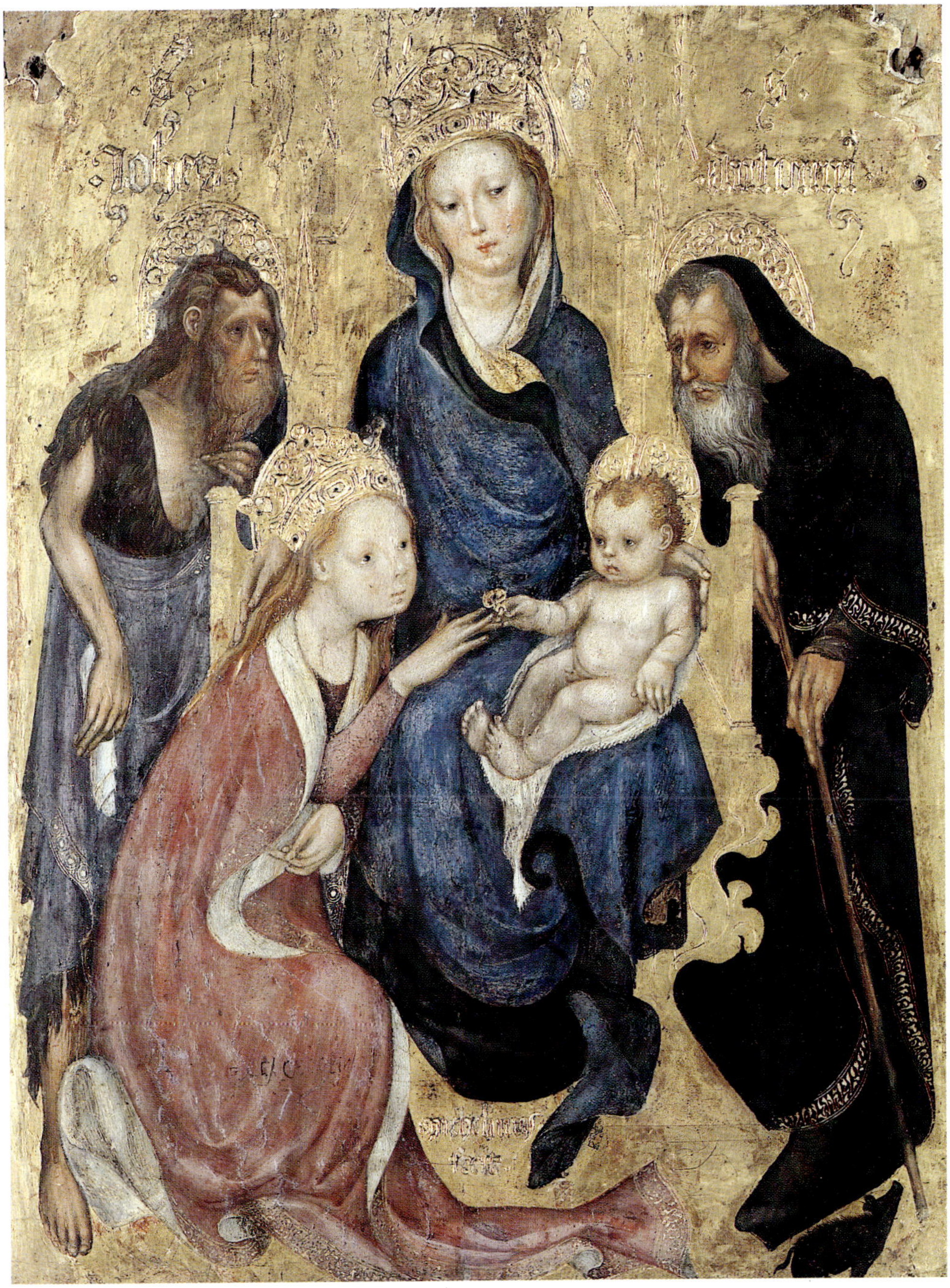

Michelino da Besozzo
The Marriage of St Catherine
c. 1420
panel
Siena, Pinacoteca Nazionale.

The only work signed by Michelino, and the only certain testimony, along with the *Marriage of the Virgin* in the New York Metropolitan Museum, of the artist's production of panel paintings, this gold-leaf work painting the signature *Michelinus fecit*, in gilded pastille like the haloes of the personages and the relief wording with the names of John the Baptist and Anthony Abbot, saints who act as witnesses to the mystic marriage of Catherine of Alexandria. Spatial effects are almost non-existent, only vaguely hinted at in the profile of the throne on which sits the Virgin with Child. Michelino focuses instead on a fairy-tale atmosphere, suspended in time. The two saints, almost bewildered, seem to witness with detachment the marriage of the child saint with her delicate features.

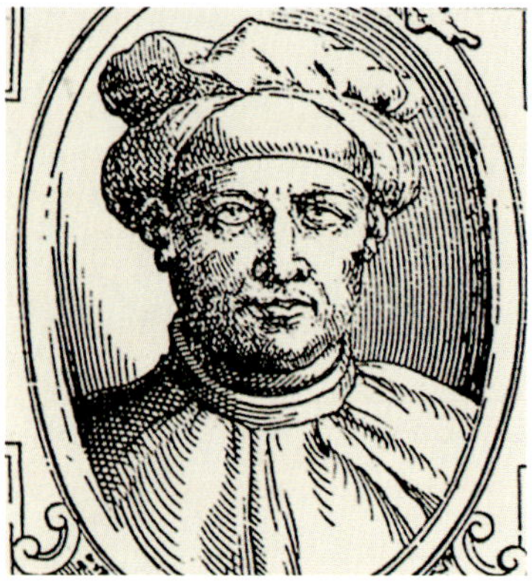

Giorgio Vasari, *Portrait of Gentile da Fabriano*, from the *Lives*, Florence, Giunti, 1568.

Gentile da Fabriano

(Fabriano c. 1370 – Rome 1427)

"In painting his hand was like his name", said Michelangelo of the restless, wandering artist from the Marches. As a youth he left Fabriano for Orvieto, "exquisite workshop of enamels and stained glass", as Roberto Longhi supposes, or perhaps for Lombardy, as may be indicated by his first known signed work, the *Madonna* of the Berlin Museums. In 1408 he was in Venice, paid the double of the local artist Niccolò di Pietro, where he painted a fresco finished by Pisanello in the Great Council Hall. In 1414 he worked for Pandolfo III Malatesta in Brescia. Returning to Fabriano, he then moved to Siena, Orvieto, Florence, where he painted the *Adoration* assisted by other artists: Arcangelo di Cola da Camerino, Giovanni da Imola, Michele d'Ungheria. In 1427 he was in Rome, where he painted frescoes in San Giovanni in Laterano, also finished by Pisanello, later destroyed.

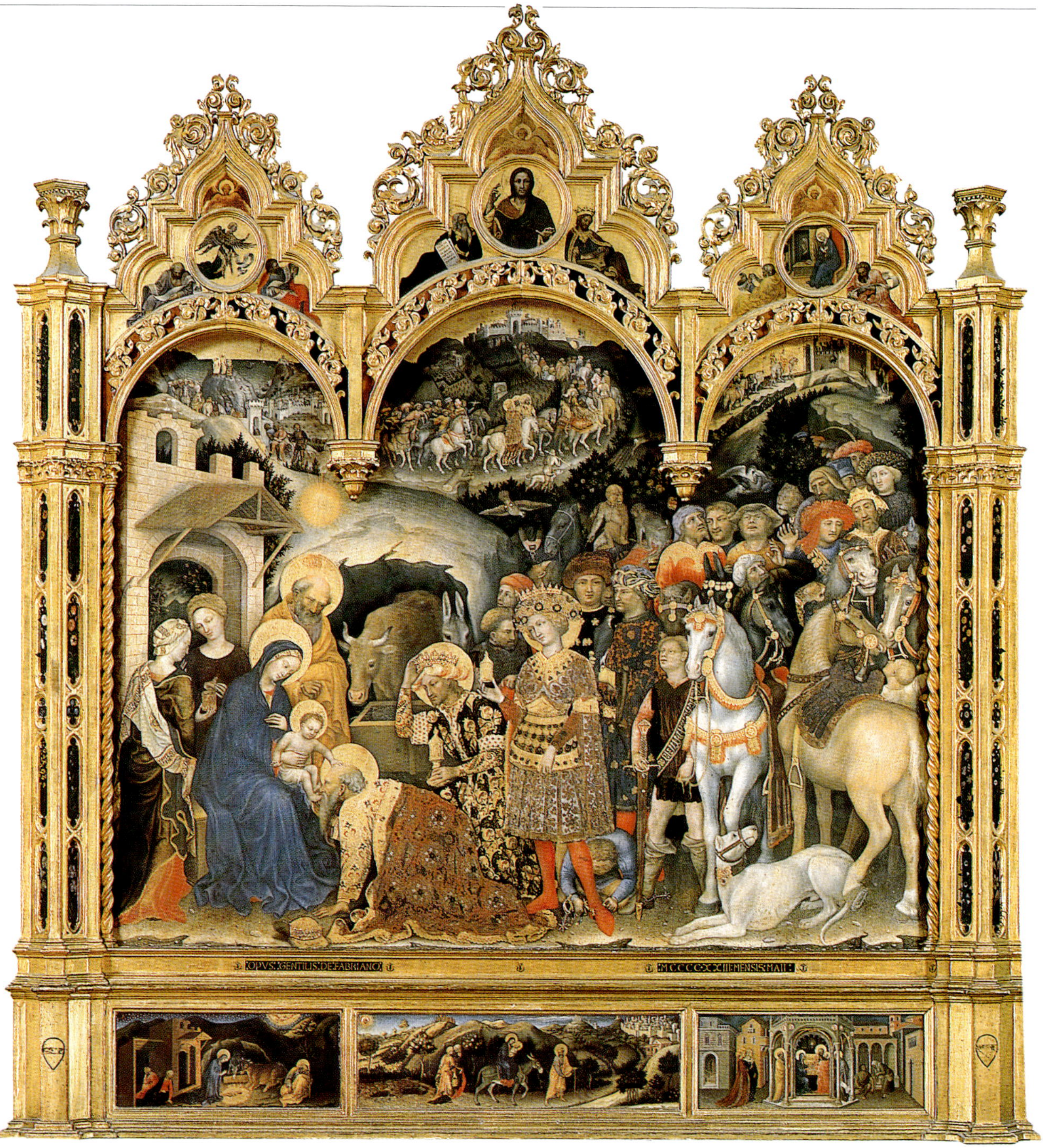

Gentile da Fabriano
Adoration of the Magi
signed and dated 1423
panel
Florence, Uffizi Gallery.

The altarpiece was painted for the chapel of the wealthy Palla Strozzi in Santa Trinita, then being built by Ghiberti. Palla, a rival of the Medici once exiled to Padua, steeped in Greek culture, was "soft and gentle", "more fitted to the delicacy of banquets and the leisure of his chambers than to the care of armies", commented the historian Giovanni Cavalcanti in about 1400. The *Adoration* was a demanding work. Completed after three years, in May of 1423, embellished by gold applied also in relief, it was a public manifesto of the erudition and wealth of Palla, the richest Florentine according to the census of 1427. A fairy-tale cavalcade, illuminated in the night by a comet, culminates in the foreground in a scene of sumptuous fabrics, elegant trappings and minute details.

Gentile da Fabriano
The Miraculous Tomb of St Nicholas
signed and dated May 1425
panel, from the predella of the *Quaratesi Polyptych*
Washington, National Gallery.

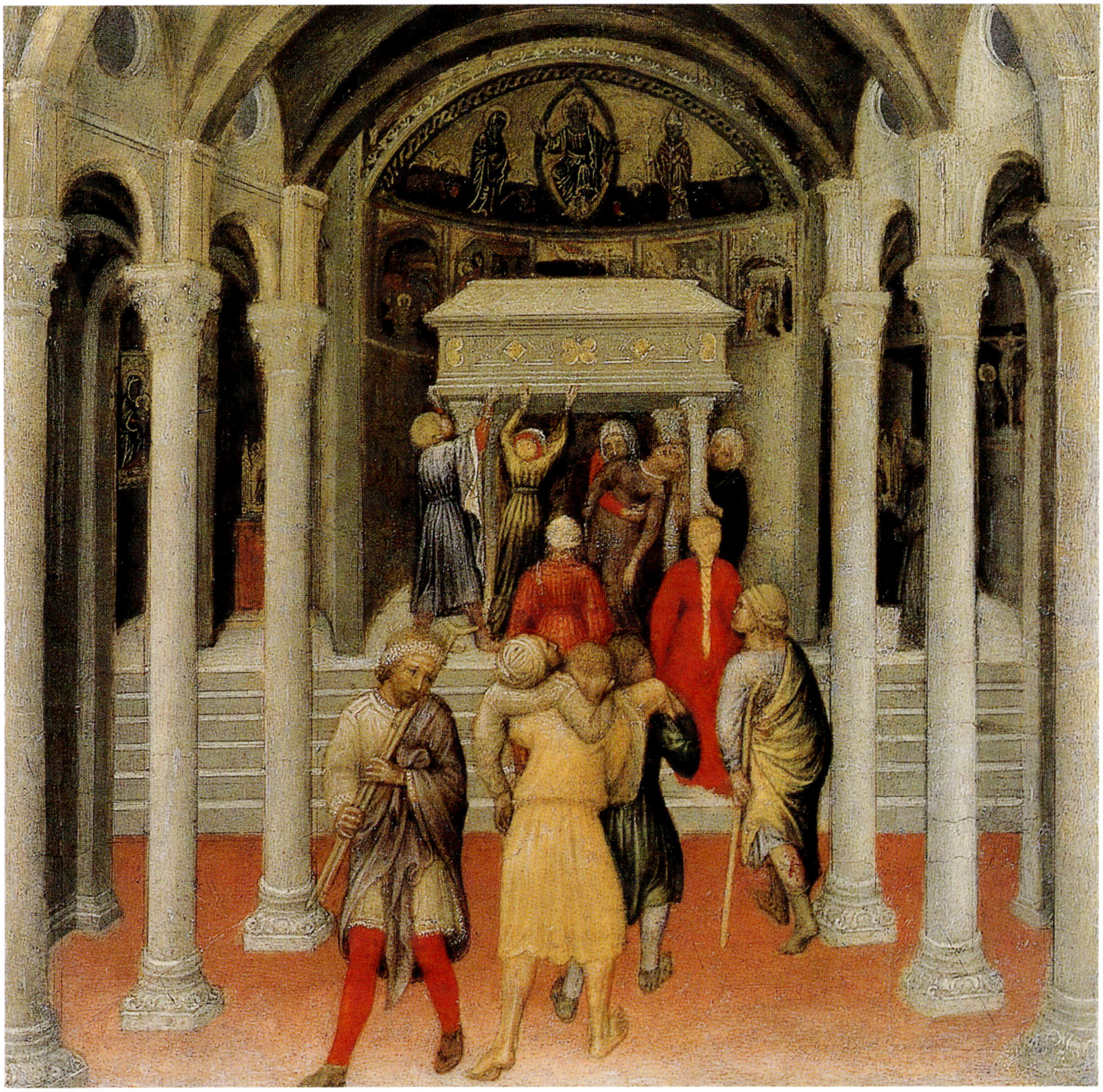

Arriving at Florence in 1420, Gentile remained there for several years. In 1421 he was enrolled in the Physicians and Apothecaries Guild, in which the painters of the times were registered, and in 1425 he signed the polyptych painted for the Quaratesi family which once decorated the altar of the high chapel in San Niccolò sopr'Arno. Composed of five pinnacled panels with the Madonna and Child at center flanked by five saints, it is completed by a predella with five stories of St Nicholas. Dismembered already in 1836, the polyptych is now dispersed between the Uffizi, Hampton Court, the National Gallery of Washington and the Pinacoteca Vaticana. In the detail shown here, originally the right-hand element of the predella, the pilgrims and invalids who venerate the tomb of St Nicholas are vivaciously portrayed. In the apsidal mosaic, under the effigy of the saint, Gentile has reproduced an exceptional painting within a painting : the same predellas as those of the painting, including this one, appear.

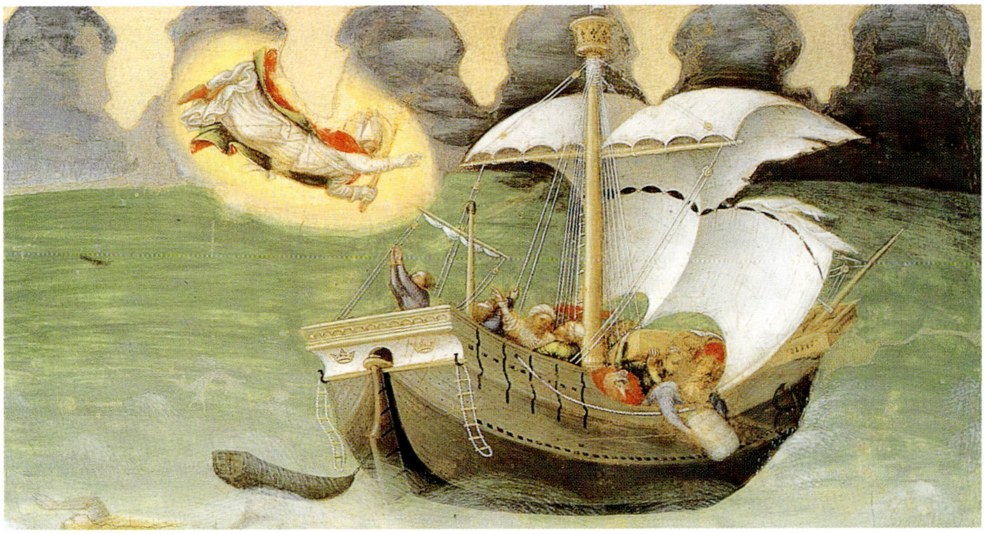

Gentile da Fabriano
The Miracle of St Nicholas
signed and dated May 1425
panel, from the predella of the *Quaratesi Polyptych*
Rome, Pinacoteca Vaticana.

Originally the central part of the predella, this delightful scene can be recognized also at the center of the apsidal mosaic painted by Gentile in the episode of the miraculous tomb of St Nicholas.

Pisanello

(Antonio di Puccio, Pisa c. 1390 – Mantova? c. 1455)

Among the masters of the early Quattrocento, Pisanello was praised by contemporaries such as Bartolomeo Facio, who in 1456 placed him on the same level as Gentile da Fabriano and the Flemish van Eyk and van der Weyden. A magnificent draftsman, he studied nature in line with the experimentation conducted in the 14th and 15th centuries by the Lombards Giovannino de' Grassi and Michelino da Besozzo, and by Gentile da Fabriano, some of whose frescoes he was to complete, at Venice in 1415 and Rome after 1427. Born in Pisa, the young man moved at his father's death to Verona, his mother's city, where the chief artistic model was still Altichiero, who worked until 1384 for the Scaligeri and in Sant'Anastasia. Working at different times for the Gonzaga in Mantua and for Lionello d'Este, Pisanello reflects in his portraits his skill as the finest medallion maker of the 15th century.

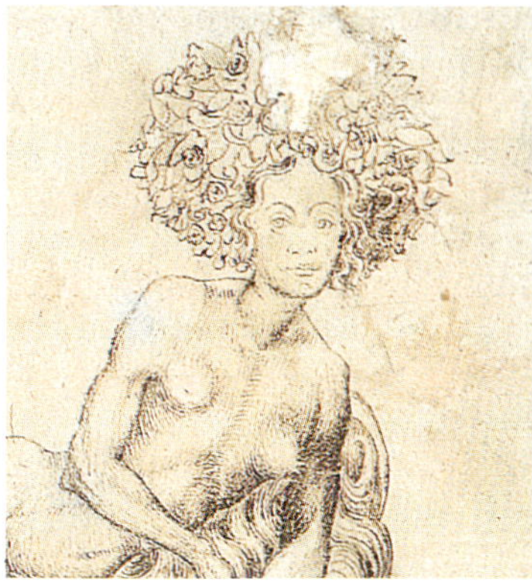

Pisanello, *Lust*, detail, c. 1420-30. Vienna, Graphische Sammlung Albertina.

Pisanello
The Hanged Men
1433-38
fresco, detail of
St George and the Princess
Verona, Sant'Anastasia.

For five years, starting in 1433, Pisanello stayed in Verona, where his family lived. To that period date the frescoes in the Dominican Church of Sant'Anastasia, above the entrance arch to the Pellegrini Chapel. In this highly deteriorated work the figures of St George, the Princess and the dragon have survived. Of the Pellegrini family, patrons of the chapel and commissioner of the frescoes, there also remains a beautiful "speaking" coat-of-arms, with one of the century's most expressive images of a pilgrim. Many drawings now in the Louvre document the artist's studies from life for the numerous animals appearing in the main scene. The preparatory sheet for the two hanged men swinging from the gibbet in the background is now in New York (Frick Collection).

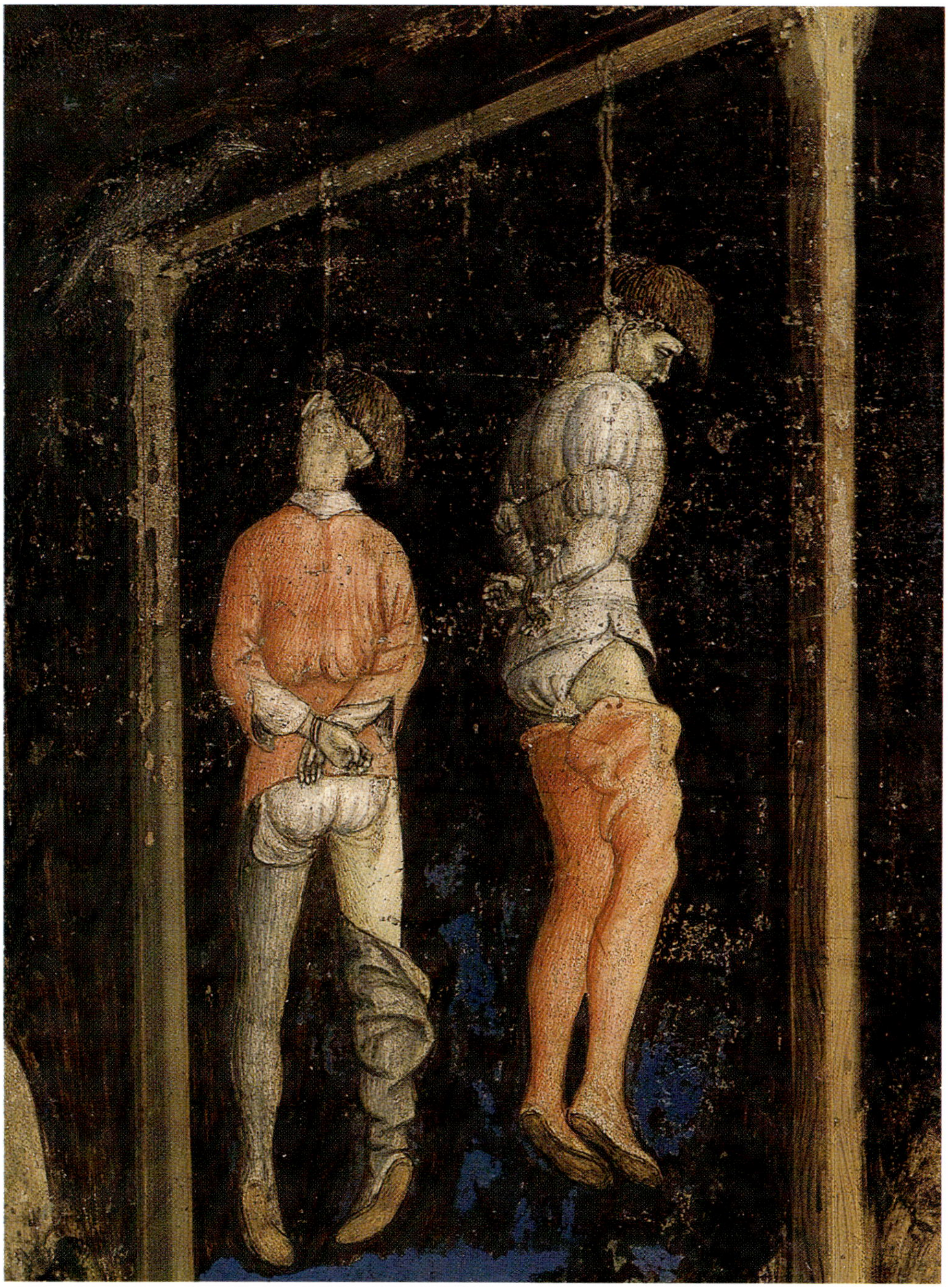

Pisanello
St George
1433-38
fresco, detail of
St George and the Princess
Verona, Sant'Anastasia.

Against the background of the Libyan city of Silena with its high towers, half Gothic, half Oriental in style, rising on the hillside, Pisanello portrays a St George inspired by the *Golden Legend* narrated by Jacopo da Varagine in about 1260, at the moment when the saintly knight is about to confront the dragon in defense of the princess. The painting reveals the maturity achieved by the artist, whose passion for the antique, demonstrated by numerous studies of sarcophagi, is re-elaborated in the key of fine chivalric poetry.

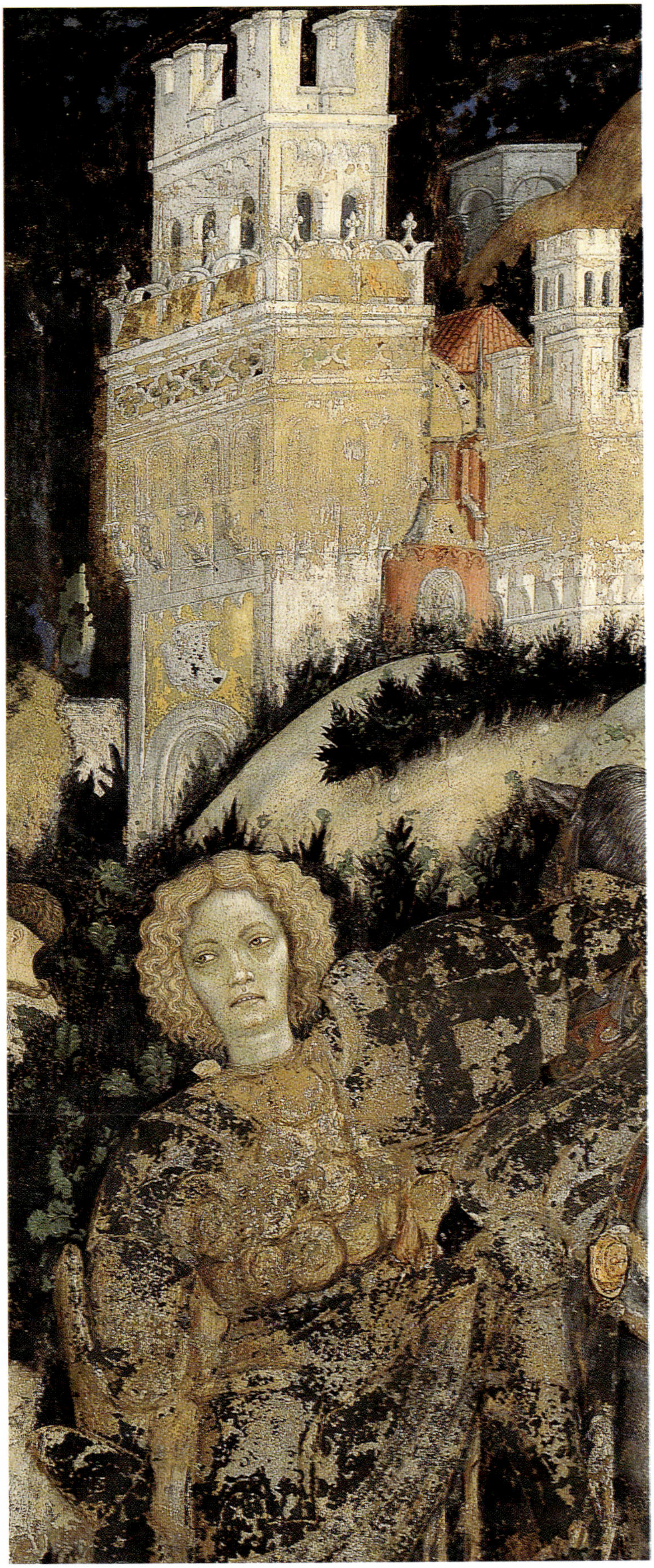

Pisanello
Temptation of St Anthony Abbot
signed, variously dated between 1430 and 1450
panel
London, National Gallery.

The origins and patron of this panel, the only one signed from among the few attributed with certainty to Pisanello, are unknown. The dating too is uncertain. According to one of the various hypotheses, this is the *Madonna* mentioned in a letter by Lionello d'Este, Lord of Ferrara, in 1432, promised to him by Pisanello upon his return from Rome. Even the iconography is singular and obscure : the Madonna with Child, surrounded by a luminous halo, looks down from heaven at St Anthony Abbot, accompanied by his usual attributes – a stick, a bell and a pig. The saint almost seems to threaten the young man dressed in refined armor and wearing a wide-brimmed straw hat who grasps his sword as the dragon twines about his legs. It is thought that the youth represents Lionello d'Este, or perhaps Ludovico Gonzaga, a devotee of St George.

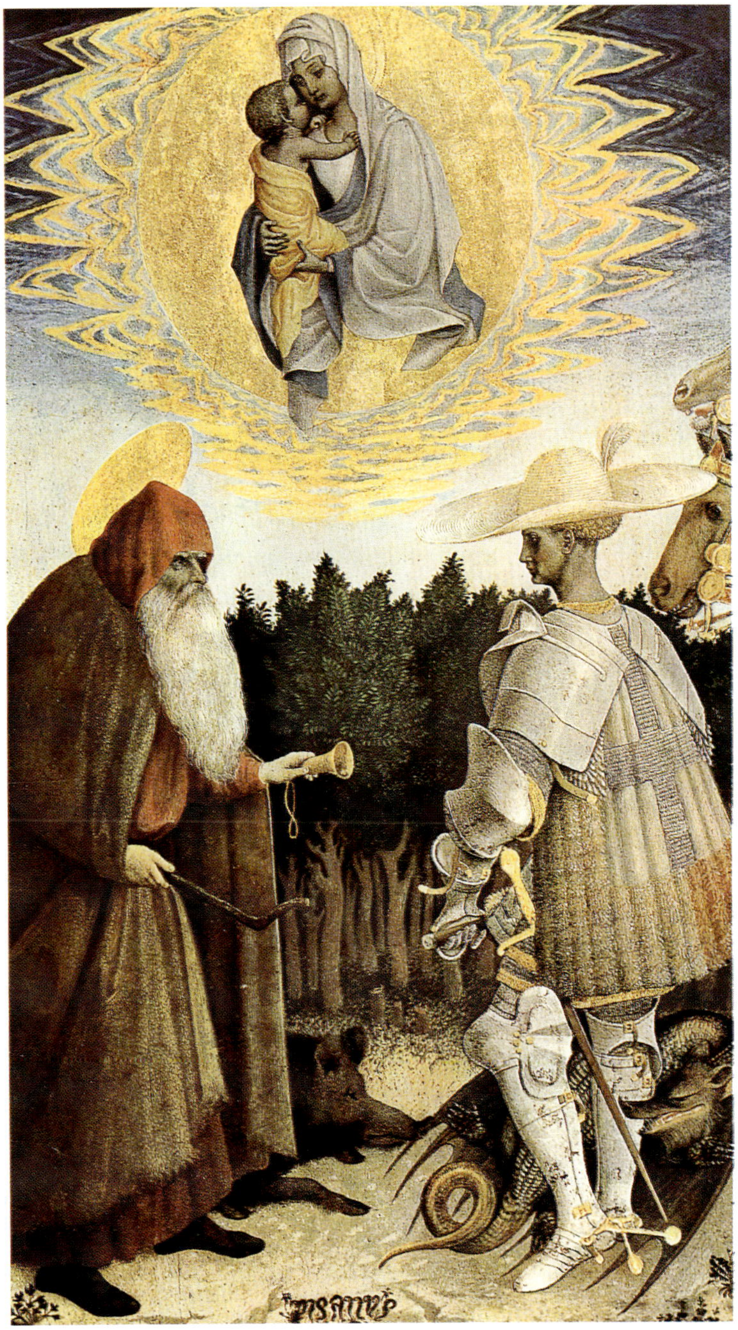

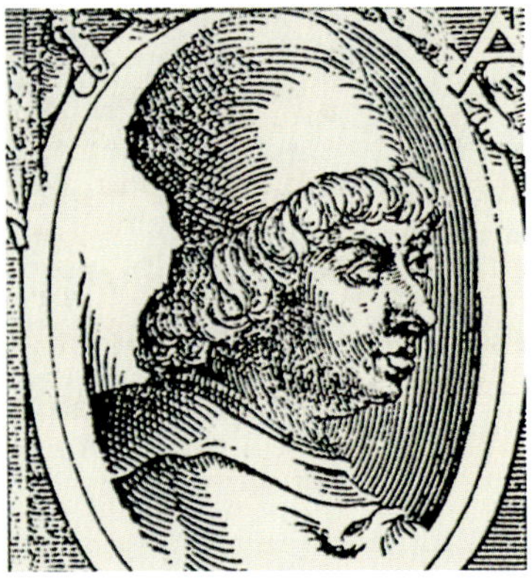

Jacopo della Quercia

(Siena c. 1371 – 1438)

Son of the Sienese goldsmith Piero di Angelo, Jacopo moved to Lucca with his father in 1391. After sculpting statues in wood he produced a superb masterpiece in 1406, the famous funerary monument to Ilaria del Carretto, where he re-elaborated in the classical sense the traditional sepulchral typology, with a refined antique-style sarcophagus embellished by a relief frieze of cherubs bearing garlands. After a stay in Ferrara he went to Siena where in 1409 he created another work of exceptional beauty and complexity, the Gaia Fountain for Piazza del Campo, at which he worked in several stages (his slowness to finish his works was proverbial) up to 1419 (the original fragments are now in the upper loggia of Palazzo Pubblico). Another of his masterpieces is the bronze portal of San Petronio in Bologna, begun in 1425 and left unfinished.

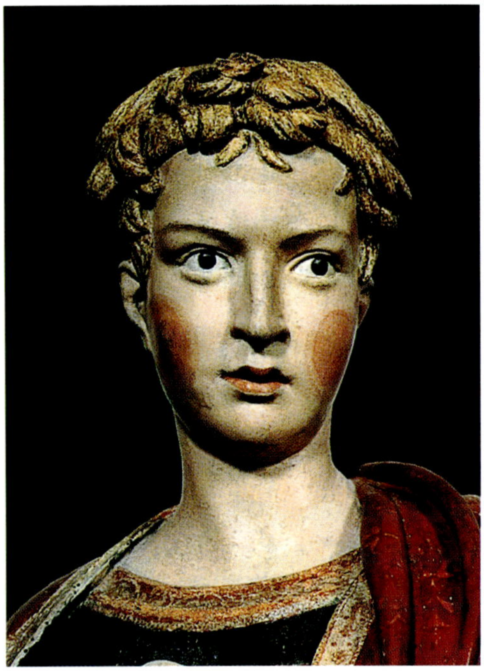

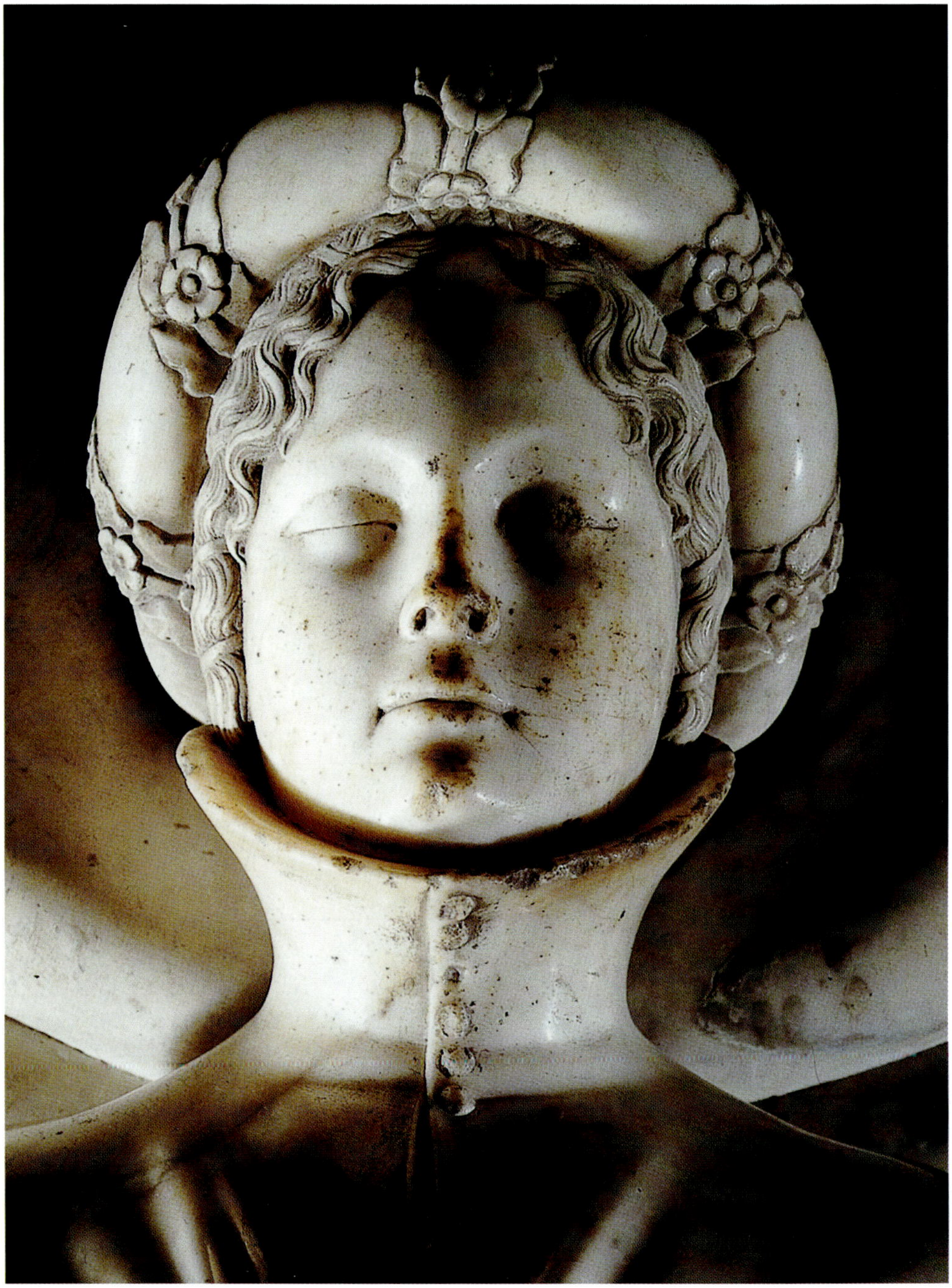

Giorgio Vasari, *Portrait of Jacopo della Quercia*, from the *Lives*, Florence, Giunti, 1568.

Jacopo della Quercia
Announcing Angel
signed, c. 1421-26
inlaid and colored wood
detail
San Gimignano, Collegiate.

The life-size angel comes from an *Annunciation* of which the *Madonna* has also survived. The coloring of the two sculptures is the work of another artist, Martino di Bartolommeo.

Jacopo della Quercia
Ilaria del Carretto
1496
marble, detail of the funerary monument
Lucca, Duomo.

The strikingly gentle effigy of Ilaria del Carretto, the wife of Paolo Guinigi, lord of Lucca, who died in childbirth on December 8, 1405, has entered the collective imagination as the most moving funerary monument of the 15th century.

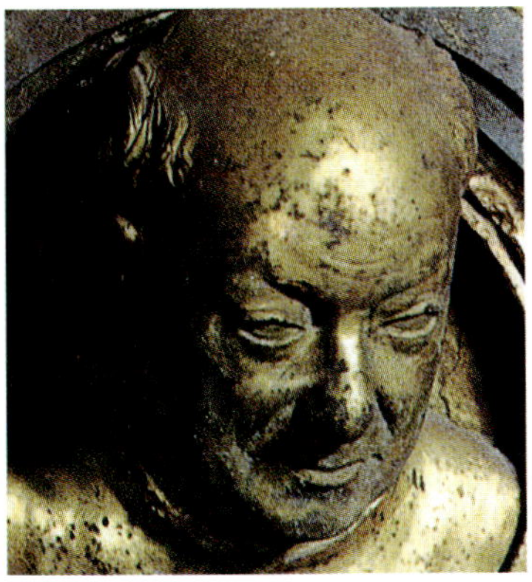

Lorenzo Ghiberti

(Florence 1378 – 1455)

Sculptor, goldsmith, architect, and man of learning, Ghiberti fully incarnates the image of the artist and theoretician of the early 15th century: student of antiquity, curious, investigative and ambitious. His reputation as sculptor was confirmed in 1402 when he won the contest for the second door of the Baptistery. Leaving the worksite of the Cathedral dome, where he had collaborated and quarreled with Brunelleschi, he organized an efficient shop (in which the young Donatello was also to work), assigned commissions for major projects, including the statues for Orsanmichele and the Doors of Paradise (1452). His *Commentaries* (1447-55), containing judgments on the great contemporary and 14th century masters as well as ancient texts and scientific theories on optics, anatomy, proportions, exemplify his artistic and literary experimentation in those years.

Lorenzo Ghiberti, *Self-portrait*, detail from the left leaf of the door, 1425-52. Florence, Baptistery, Doors of Paradise.

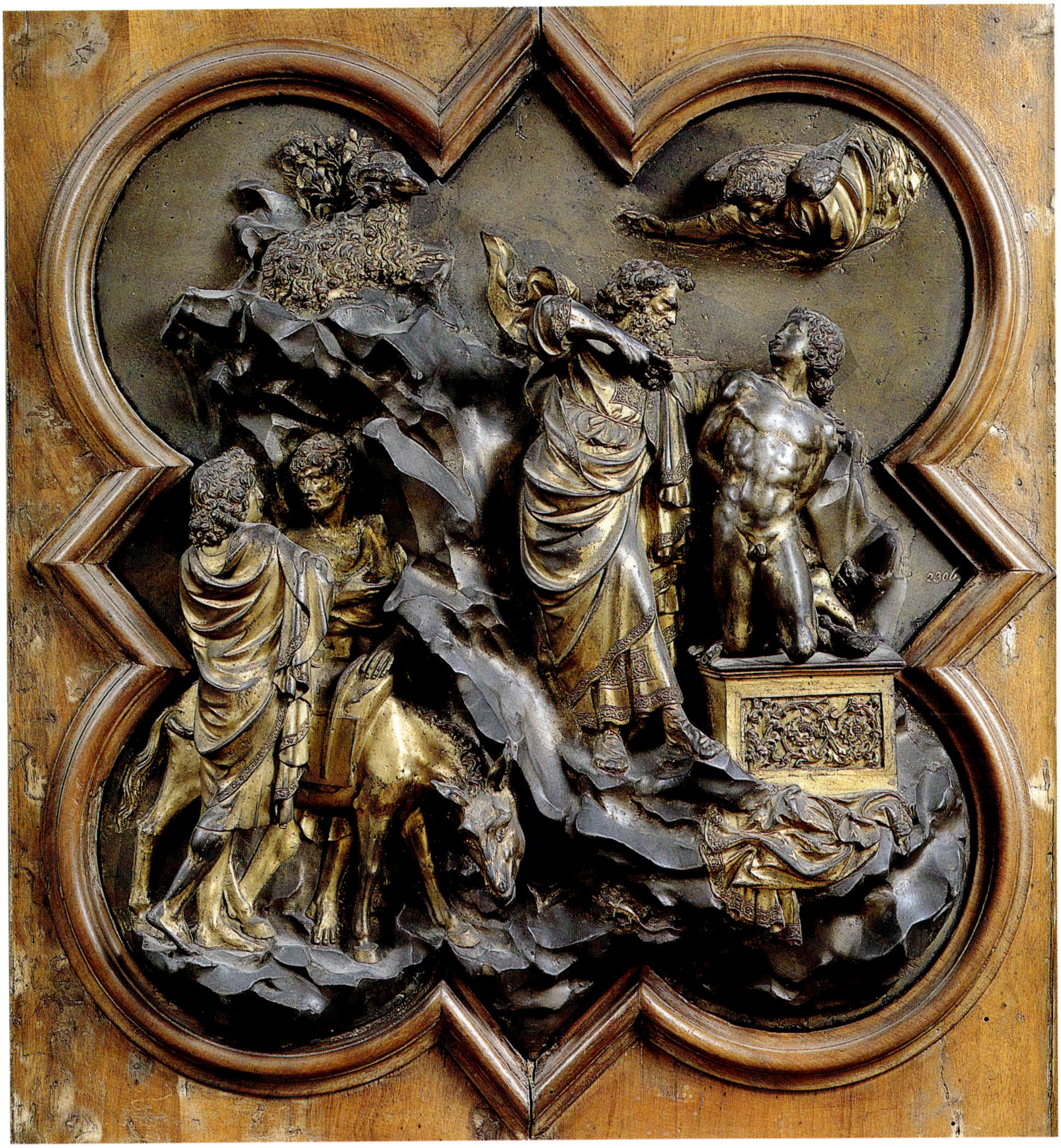

Lorenzo Ghiberti
Sacrifice of Isaac
1402
gilded bronze
Florence, Bargello Museum.

In 1401 the Arte di Calimala announced a contest for the second door of the Baptistery (the first, on the south side, has been completed by Andrea Pisano in 1336). Among the other competitors, in addition to Ghiberti, were Jacopo della Quercia and Brunelleschi. The subject was to be the same for all: a bronze plaque depicting the *Sacrifice of Isaac*. With the work now in the Bargello Ghiberti was declared winner. He proudly reports that the judges, "men highly expert in painting and sculpture", had felt no doubt: "I was granted the palm of victory by all of the experts". And probably this was really the case: his balanced composition fully satisfied the standard requisites of the time.

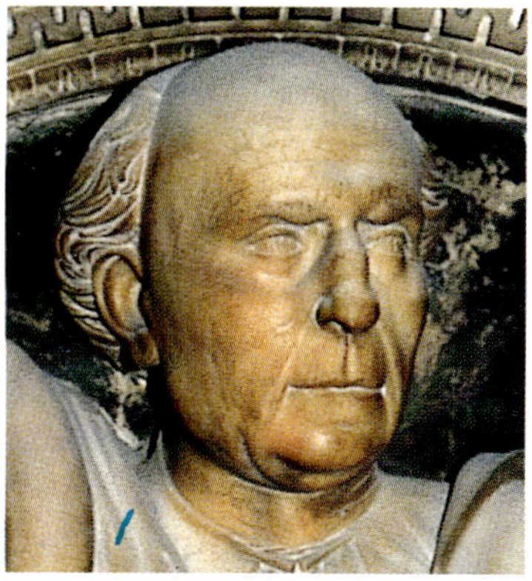

Filippo Brunelleschi

(Florence 1377 – 1446)

Goldsmith, sculptor and architect, "Pippo" as Leon Battista Alberti called him, is the dominant figure in early 15th century Florentine art. "He himself", wrote his biographer Manetti, "put in act what the painters now call perspective and from him was born the rule and those who could have taught it to him have been dead for centuries". Thanks also to his friendship with the scientist Paolo dal Pozzo Toscanelli, he progressed from intuitive experimentation to a scientific system of measuring space, first applied in two perspective panels of piazza Signoria and piazza Duomo. In addition to the Cathedral dome he designed harmonious structures such as the Portico of the Spedale degli Innocenti, the Churches of San Lorenzo and Santo Spirito and the Pazzi Chapel in Santa Croce. His sculptures include figures for the altar of San Jacopo in Pistoia and the Santa Maria Novella *Crucifix*.

Andrea di Lazzaro Cavalcanti, *Filippo Brunelleschi*, detail, 1446. Florence, Duomo.

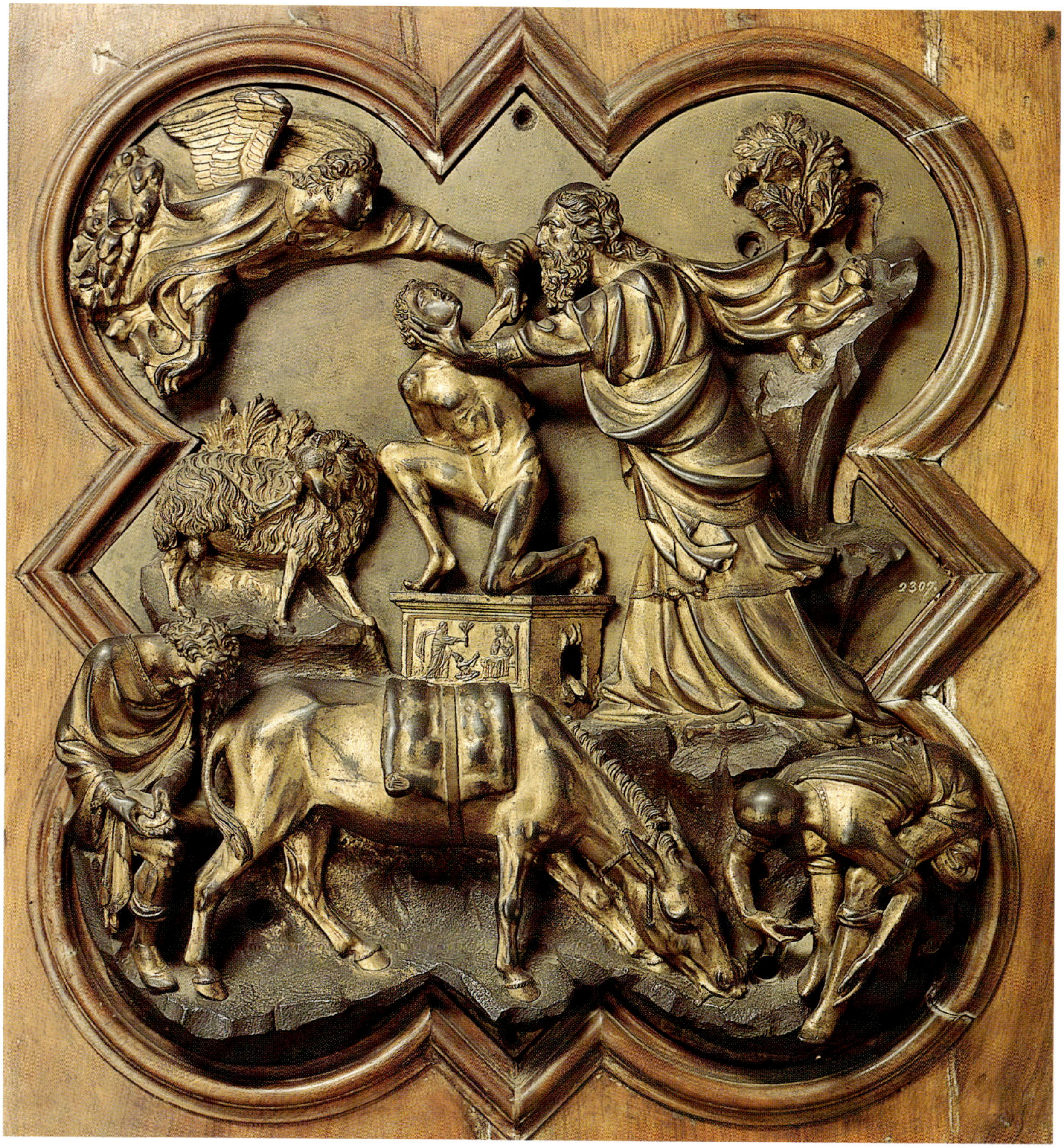

Filippo Brunelleschi
Sacrifice of Isaac
1402
gilded bronze
Florence, Bargello Museum.

The great loser in the contest for the Baptistery doors, Brunelleschi realized a composition even too innovative for the times. The drama of the event is emphasized by the excited gestures of the angel and of Isaac, whose scream can almost be seen to issue from his open mouth. By contrast, in the foreground dominated by the placid mule, the silence of the figures at either end, heedless of the tragic episode, seems almost tangible. The boy on the left, bending over, emulates the posture of the ancient sculpture of the *Boy Removing a Thorn from his Foot* (*Spinario*), confirming the artist's early interest in antiquity.

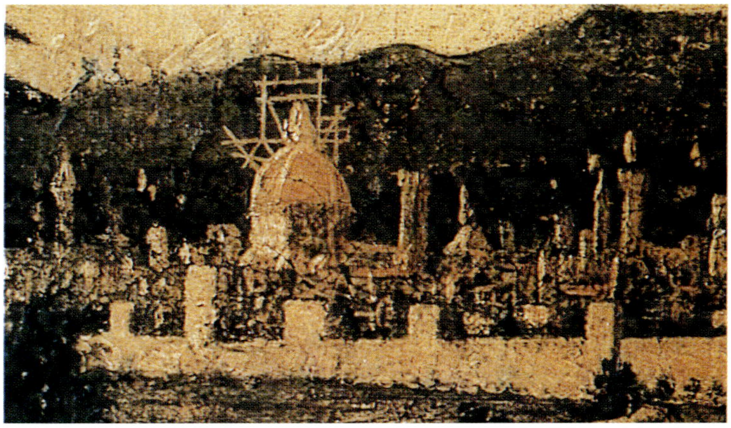

Biagio di Antonio
Tobias and the Archangels
c. 1470
canvas, detail
Florence, Bartolini Salimbeni Collection.

The Cathedral dome was now complete, except for the immense copper ball produced by Verrocchio's shop, hoisted to the top on the scaffolding visible around the lantern.

Filippo Brunelleschi
Dome of Santa Maria del Fiore
1423-38.
Florence, Duomo.

In 1418 a contest was proclaimed for the model of the dome, the first projects for which dated from a century before, but no winner was declared. Brunelleschi, who had journeyed to Rome with his friend Donatello to study ancient monuments, intensified his travels in the search for techniques that would allow him to "vault" a dome of great size without external reinforcement. Appointed superintendent together with Ghiberti in 1420, Filippo was now sure of his technical superiority to his rival, who became the object of his derision. The herring-bone system he designed, in part inspired by Roman building techniques, allowed the dome to stand alone as the work gradually progressed, supported by the counter-thrust of the ribbing. He continued the work on his own, designing devices to hoist the materials and scaffolding to build the lantern, completed after his death.

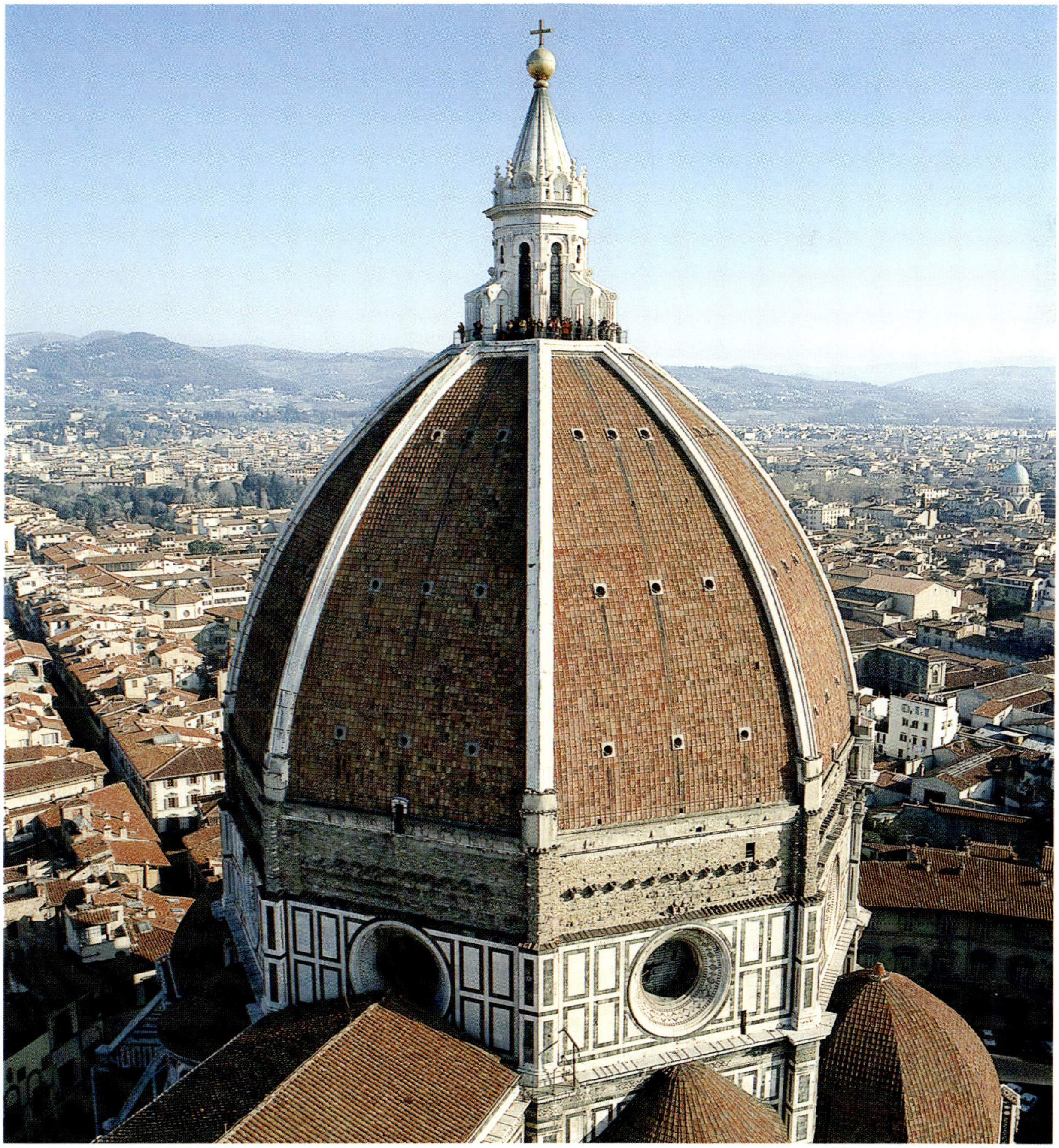

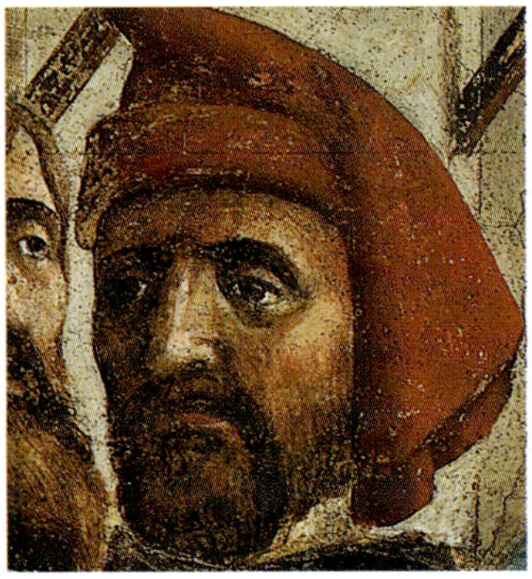

Masolino da Panicale

(Tommaso di Cristoforo Fini, Panicale in Valdarno 1383 – Florence 1440)

The critical neglect of this fine master, only in part linked to late Gothic tradition as has often been thought, stems from the fact that after beginning with Ghiberti and Starnina he collaborated with the younger, revolutionary Masaccio, working with him in Florence on one of the most important cycles of the early 15th century, the Brancacci Chapel in the Carmine. Still memorable is a passage by Roberto Longhi, who imagines Masaccio tearing the brush from the hand of the older artist to show him how one of his scenes should be painted. Masolino was in reality an artist of great sensitivity, highly esteemed by Cardinal Branda, in whose entourage he journeyed to Hungary (1425), Rome (1428), and Castiglione Olona in 1435, where he painted luminous, dramatic frescoes for his chapel.

Masaccio, *Presumed Portrait of Masolino*, detail of *St Peter Healing the Ill with his Shadow*, c. 1425. Florence, Santa Maria del Carmine, Brancacci Chapel.

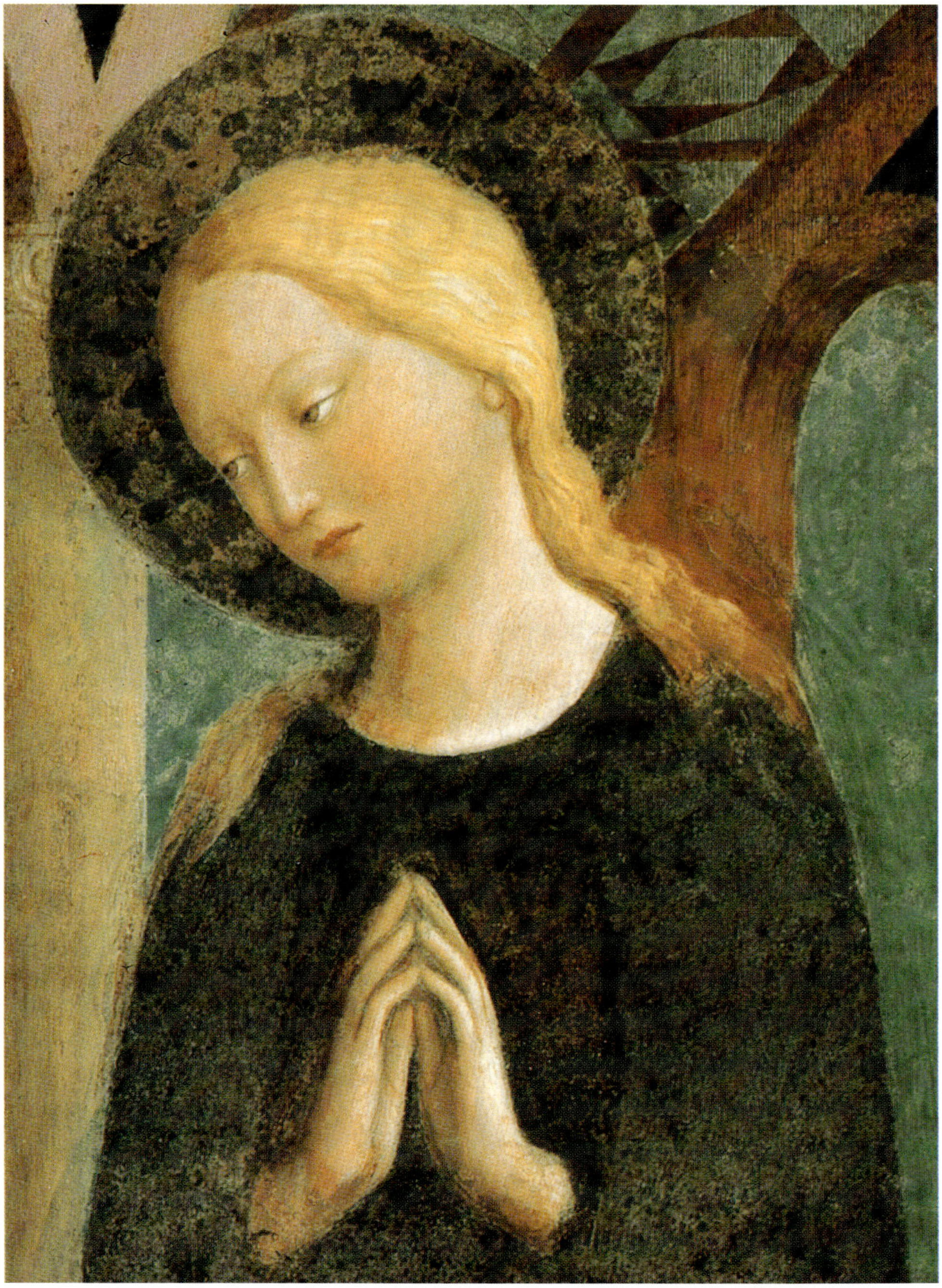

Masolino da Panicale
Our Lady of the Annunciation
1428-31
fresco, detail
Rome, San Clemente, Branda Chapel.

In decorating Cardinal Branda's chapel in San Clemente in Rome, Masolino expressed himself with impeccable elegance in fine facial expressions.

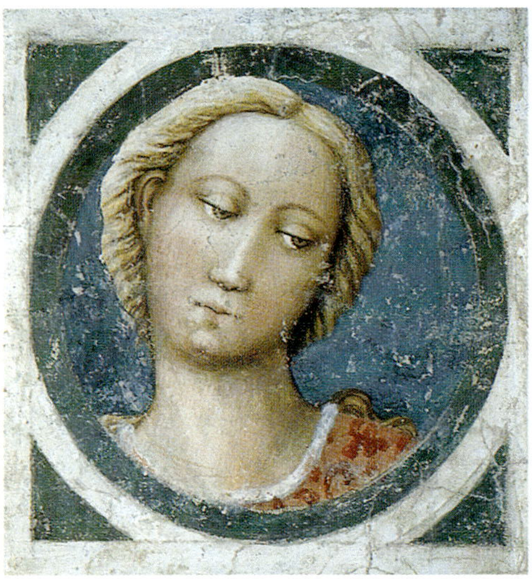

Masolino da Panicale
Head of a Woman
1424-25
fresco, detail
Florence, Santa Maria del Carmine, Brancacci Chapel.

Among the recent attributions to Masolino, after the restoration of the chapel, is the delicate face of a young woman appearing in one of the medallions on the friezes decorated with plant motifs, unfortunately badly damaged.

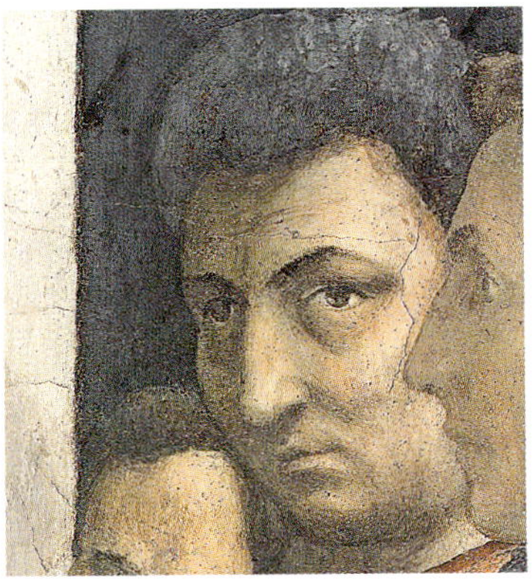

Masaccio

(Tommaso di Giovanni Cassai, San Giovanni Valdarno 1401 – Rome 1428)

"We have had a very great loss", declared Brunelleschi upon hearing that Masaccio had died in Rome at the age of twenty-six in mysterious circumstances, after having followed Masolino there. "Pure without ornament", perceptively noted Cristoforo Landino in 1481 in regard to the artist, reflecting Vitruvius' definition of the Doric column (*sine ornatu, nudam speciem*). Still debated is the chronology of the rare surviving works by this revolutionary artist, called "Giotto reborn" for the plastic solidity of his figures, an ideal reflection of the great 14th century painter. Extraordinary also for having immediately assimilated the experimentation of Brunelleschi, Masaccio was the first to translate into painting the new rules on perspective, with a rigorous construction of space always dominated by the human presence.

Masaccio, *Self-portrait*, detail of *St Peter in his Chair*, c. 1424-25. Florence, Santa Maria del Carmine, Brancacci Chapel.

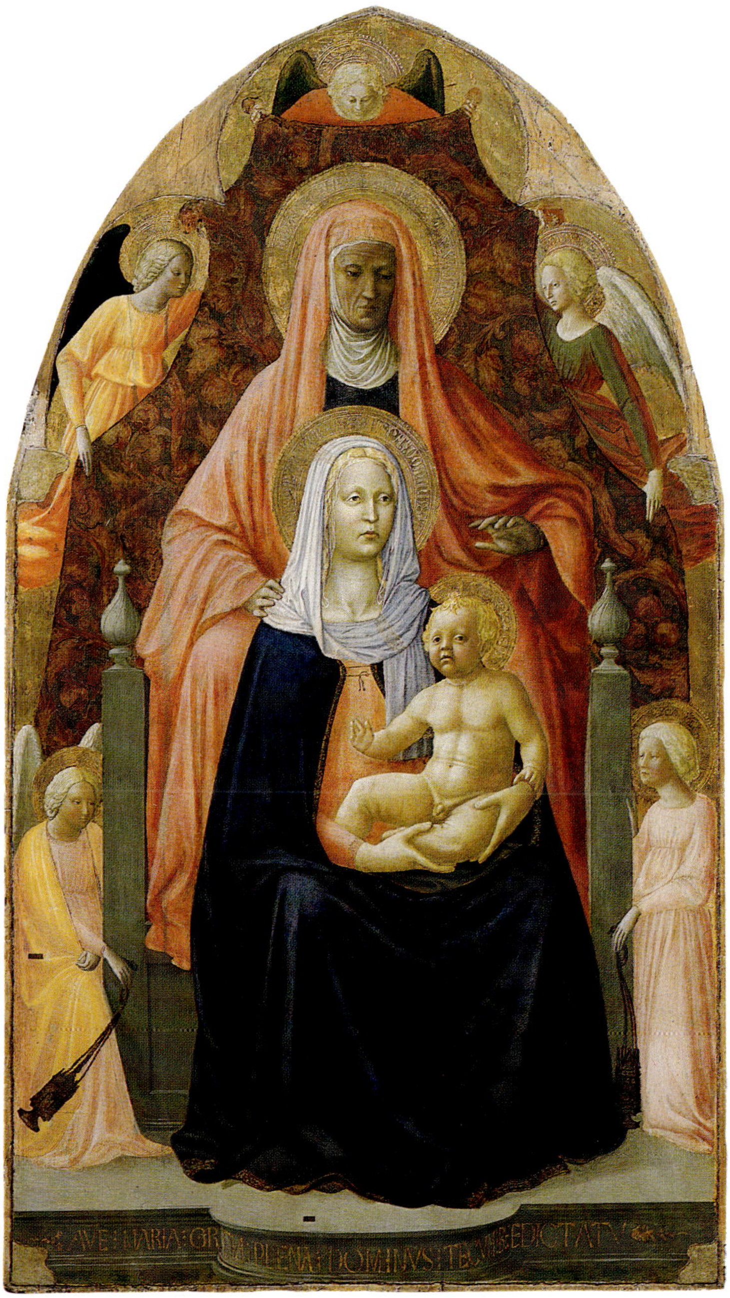

Masaccio and Masolino
St Anne Metterza
c. 1424
panel
Florence, Uffizi Gallery.

Painted in collaboration with Masolino, this work was fundamental to the development of early Renaissance art. It portrays the mother of the Virgin holding Maria and the Child on her lap. The angel at the upper right and the group of the Virgin with Child have generally been attributed to Masaccio. In the singular, apparently static composition, the three solid figures seem superimposed on the same axis. Dominating all is St Anne who protects her daughter and grandson with a reassuring gesture.

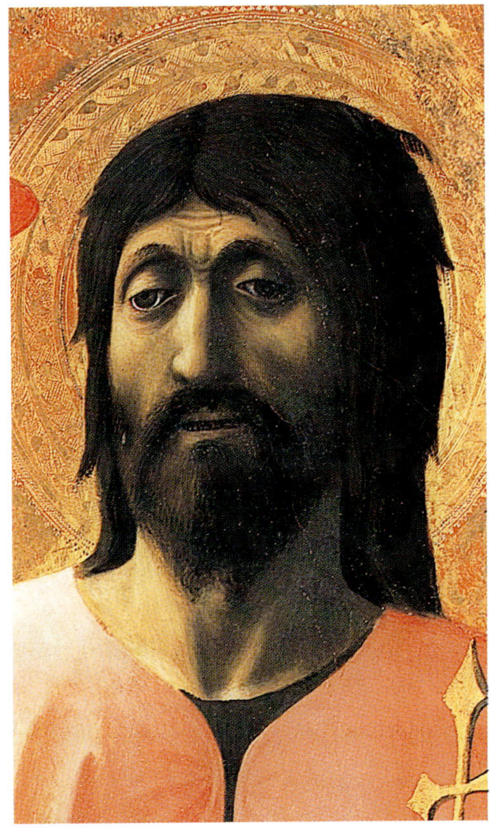

Masaccio
St John the Baptist
1428
panel, detail of one of the panels in the *Triptych of the Snow*
London, National Gallery.

Masaccio painted a suffering, pathetic face, it features emerging in intense chiaroscuro, for the *Triptych of the Snow* in Santa Maria Maggiore (now dispersed between London and Naples). On this work too, commissioned by Pope Martin V, the artist collaborated with Masolino, who painted a large part of the composition.

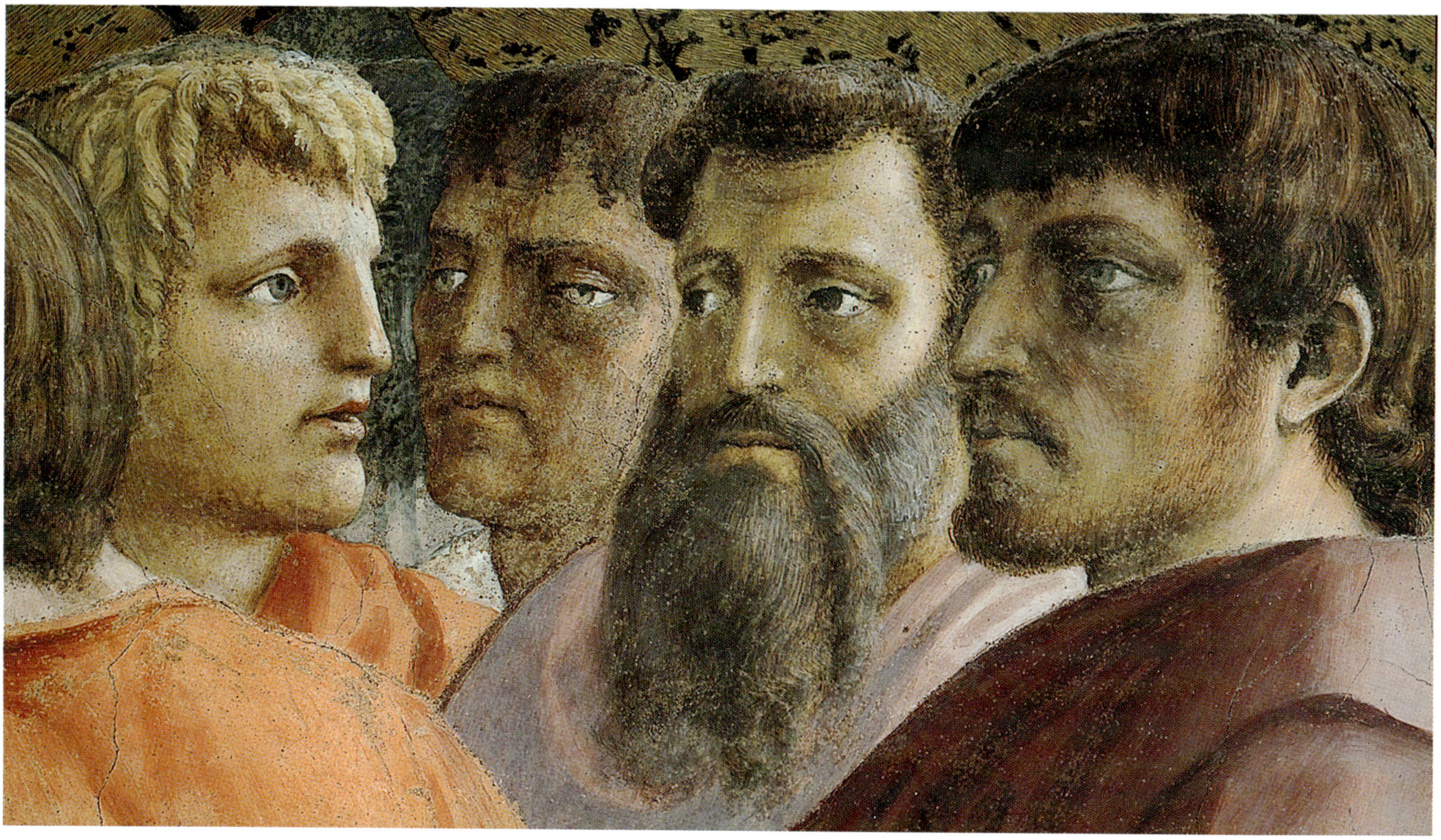

Masaccio
St Peter Paying Tribute
c. 1424-25
fresco, detail
Florence, Santa Maria del Carmine, Brancacci Chapel.

Profiles like ancient Roman medallions and individualist features, even in their synthetic plasticity: these are the faces of the Apostles, depicted by Masaccio in the Evangelical episode narrated by Matthew (17, 24-27). At Capernaum Jesus tells Peter to look for a coin, in the mouth of the first fish he catches, that will serve to pay the tribute demanded for the temple. Masaccio represents the scene with "a close circle of weighty men accented by a stormy light" (Longhi).

Masolino da Panicale, Masaccio, Filippino Lippi
View of the left wall of the Brancacci Chapel
c. 1424-25 and c. 1485
fresco
Florence, Santa Maria del Carmine.

The decoration of the chapel, commissioned of Masolino and Masaccio who left it unfinished, was requested by Felice Brancacci. A politician, diplomat, enterprising merchant and father-in-law of the wealthy Palla Strozzi, Felice fell into disgrace in 1436, was exiled and declared a rebel. For this reason all of the portraits of his family members were deleted. Only in about 1485 were the frescoes completed by Filippino Lippi.

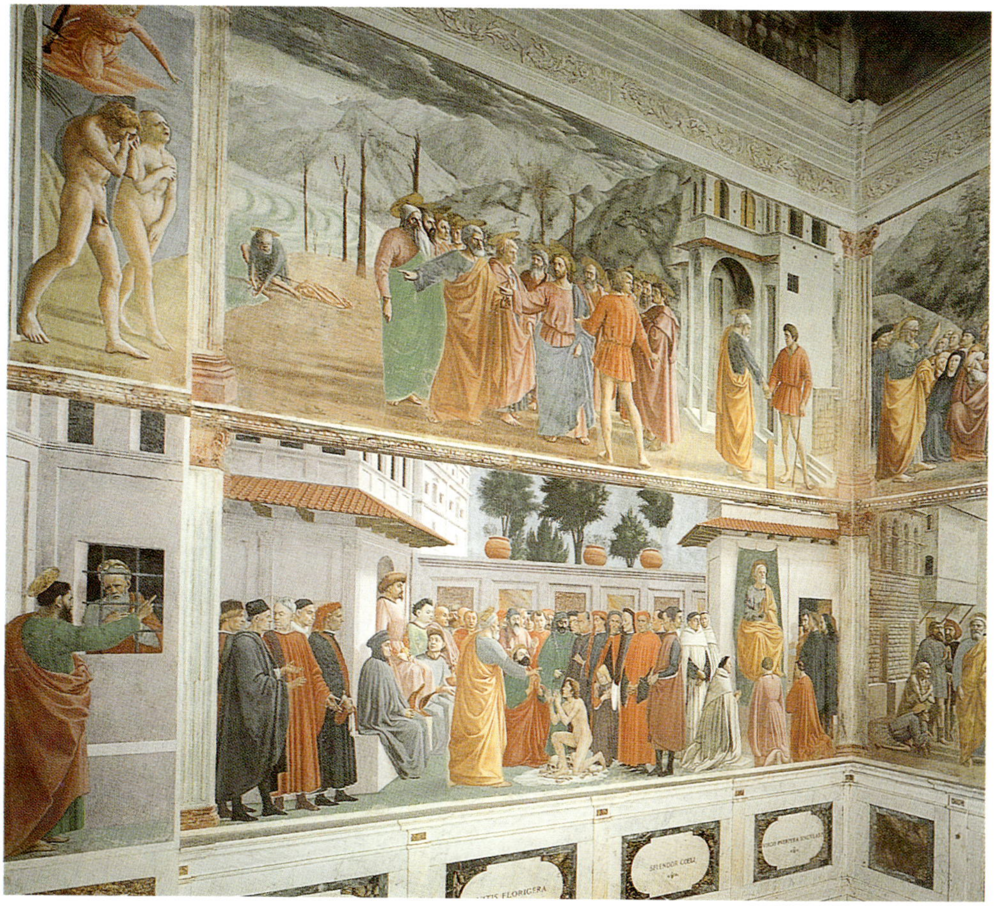

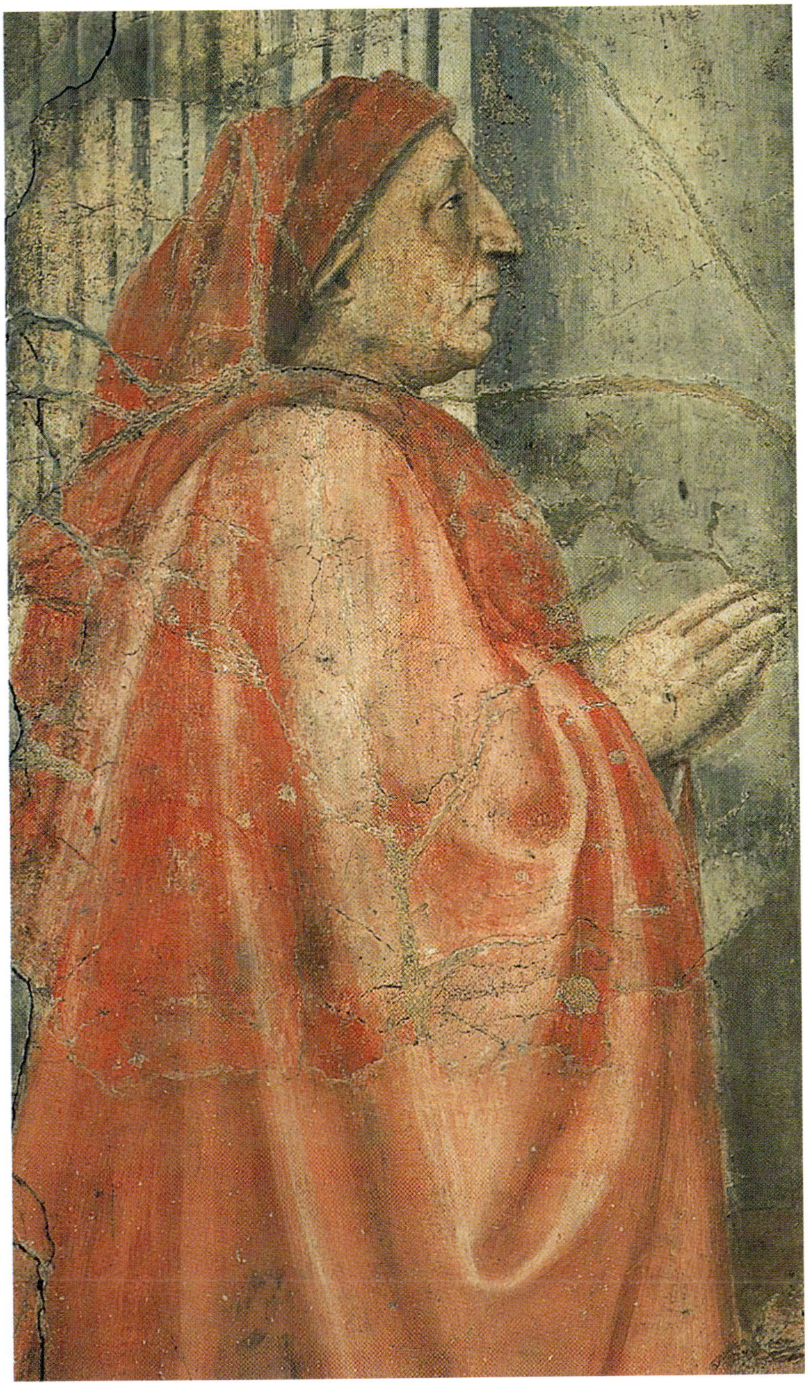

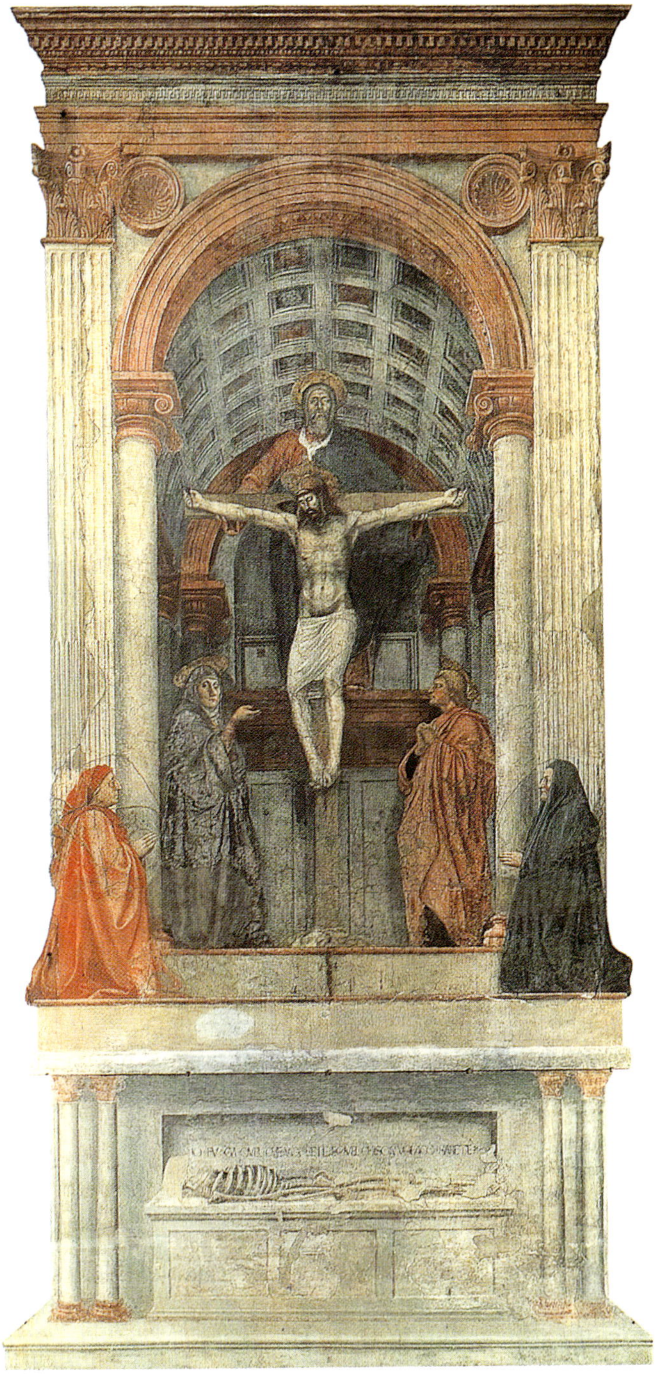

Masaccio
The Trinity
c. 1426-27
fresco, whole and detail
Florence, Santa Maria Novella.

Almost theatrical in its dramatic setting, the *Trinity* was frescoed by Masaccio perhaps at the request of Fra Lorenzo Cardoni, Prior of Santa Maria Novella from 1423 to early 1426; and perhaps also for the Gonfaloniere Domenico Lensi, who may be the man shown kneeling in prayer with his wife. Below is a powerful *memento mori* with a crudely realistic skeleton lying in the tomb. It has also been suggested that the fresco may have been painted for the erudite Alessio Strozzi, adviser of Ghiberti and Brunelleschi, who was named successor to Fra Cardoni but refused this position. Brunelleschi's perspective laws are manifested in painting for the first time, as a harmonious classicizing architectural ideal is re-evoked within a strict geometric scheme. The depth of space is rendered so effectively that the chapel seems real, painted in *trompe-l'oeil*.

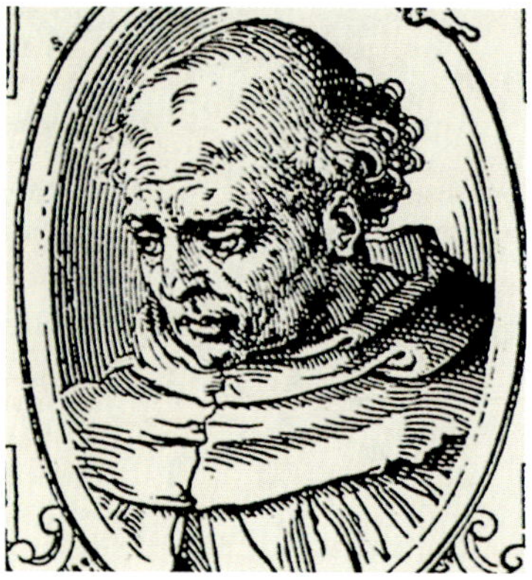

Beato Angelico

(Guido di Piero, Vicchio di Mugello, late 14th century – Rome 1455)

"Beato" since 1982, the painter received his popular pseudonym much earlier. Known to the English-speaking world as Fra Angelico, he entered history with this attribute in 1469, thanks to Fra Domenico di Giovanni da Corella, who called him *angelicus pictor*, divine painter. "Divine and affected" in Cristoforo Landino's *Comment* (1481), Guido di Piero (Fra Giovanni after taking Dominican vows) was according to Vasari "a truly divine father", "no less supreme painter and miniator than excellent monk", "most humble and modest", "in his painting easy and devote". This misleading label has persisted up to recent critical examination, which now assigns him a preeminent role in early 15th century painting. Active also in Cortona, Orvieto, Perugia and the Rome of Niccolò V, he was a cultured, refined interpreter of Masaccio's heritage, endowed with a strongly evocative language.

Giorgio Vasari, *Portrait of Beato Angelico,* from the *Lives*, Florence, Giunti, 1568.

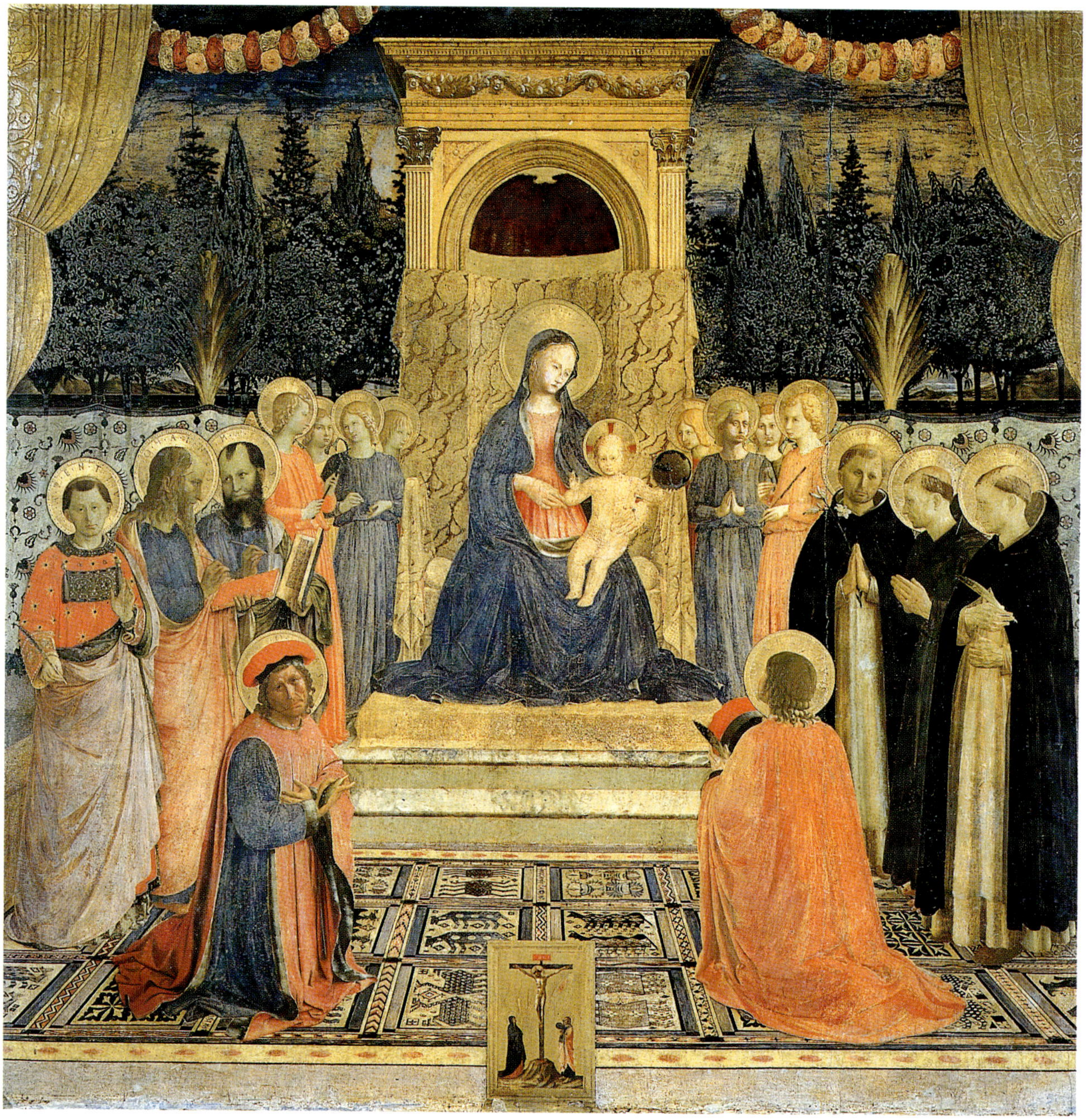

Beato Angelico
Madonna with Child and Saints (San Marco Altarpiece)
1438-43
panel
Florence, San Marco Museum.

In poor condition due to past restoration, this work comes from the high altar of the Dominican church where the painter-monk lived and worked for years. Turning toward the spectator is Cosmas, the saint for whom Cosimo de' Medici was named. Cosimo had planned an ambitious project, secretly self-laudatory, that of rebuilding the church and monastery to which he often retired, where his trusted architect Michelozzo had designed a harmonious library containing a wealth of ancient codexes. Striking elements in this ordered composition are the analytic description of the carpet, on which rests a *trompe-l'oeil panel* of the *Crucifixion*, confirmation of this attentive artist's early interest in Flemish art.

Beato Angelico and Assistance
Christ in Limbo
c. 1438-50
fresco
Florence, San Marco Museum, monastery, cell 31.

Two terrified devils watch the end of another, crushed by the door falling before Christ. This is one of the famous frescoes, painted for the contemplation of the monks, which decorate the cells in the monastery rebuilt in Renaissance style by Michelozzo.

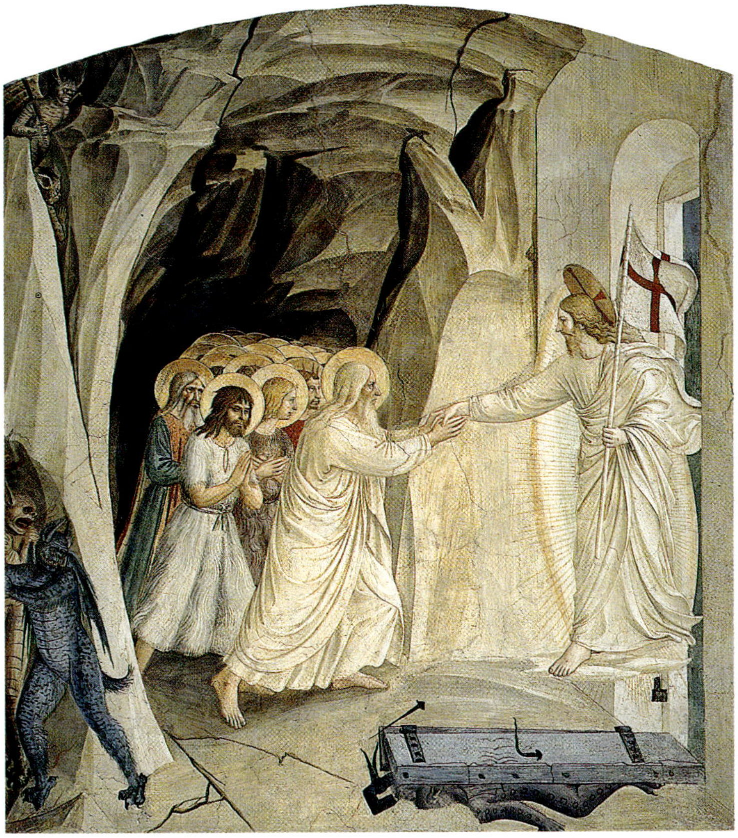

Beato Angelico
Martyrdom of St Mark
1433
panel, detail from the predella of the *Linaiuoli Tabernacle*
Florence, San Marco Museum.

This vivid little scene appears in the predella of the tabernacle commissioned by the Wool Merchants and Weavers Guild for their headquarters near the Old Market. The importance of the commission and the collaboration between various shops is confirmed by the fact that the marble frame is by Ghiberti, while the woodwork is by "Papero di Piero", whose name has luckily survived from among those of many skillful artisans now lost to memory.

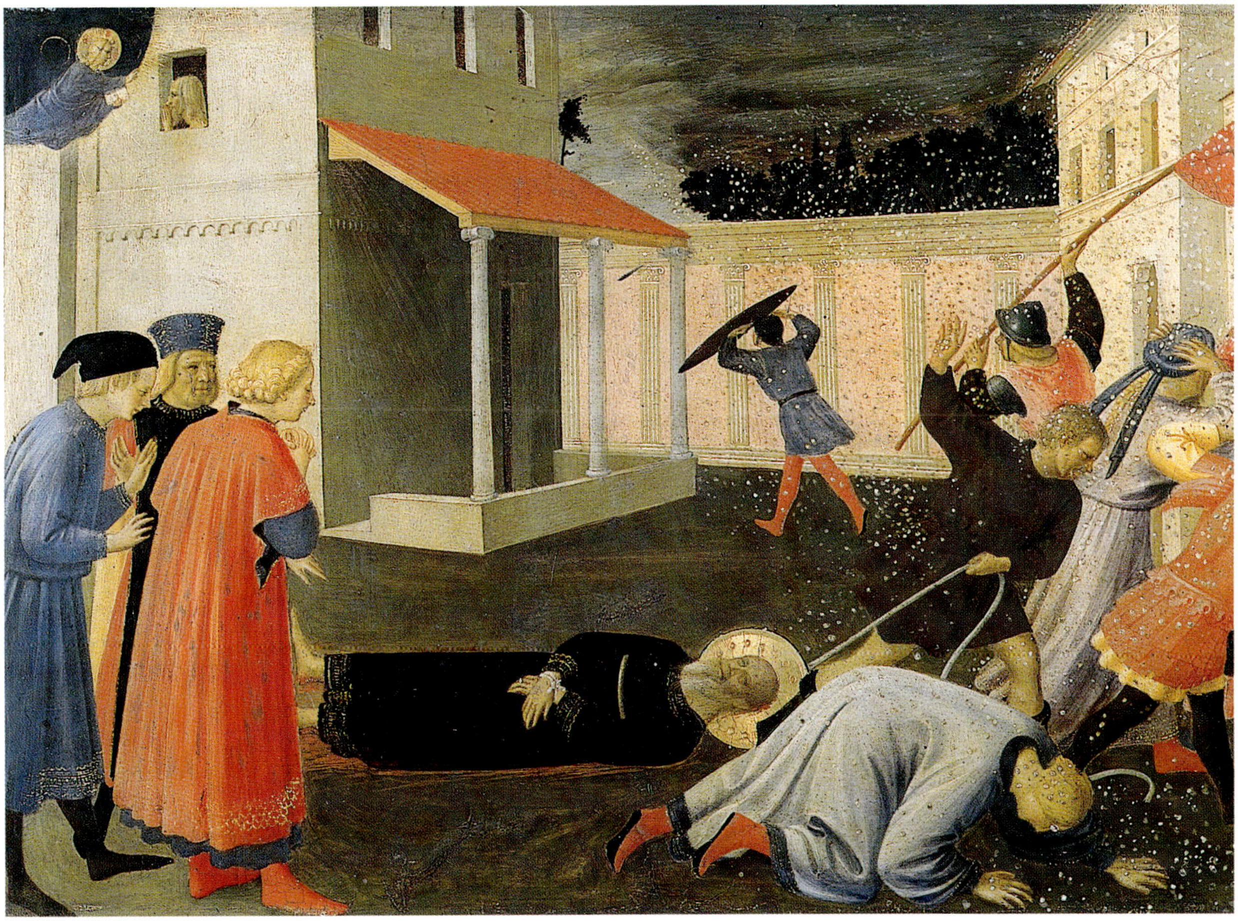

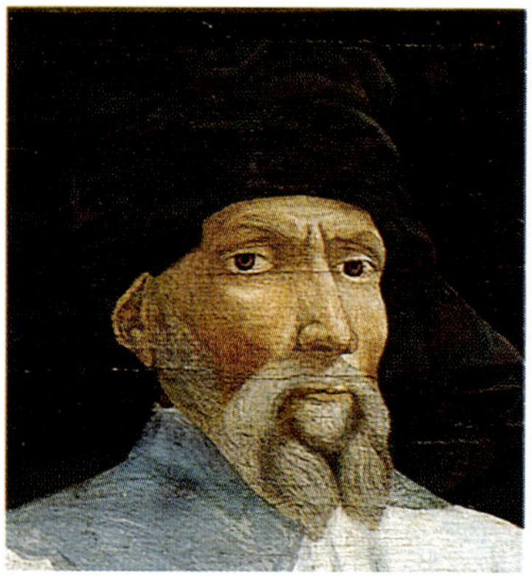

Donatello

(Donato di Niccolò di Betto Bardi, Florence 1386 – 1466)

Already praised by Alberti in 1436, today deemed the greatest sculptor of the century, Donatello had a long career marked by incessant activity which saw him still working when almost eighty, the tireless sculptor of the *Judith* and the bronze pulpits in San Lorenzo. A friend of Brunelleschi which whom he journeyed to Rome several times between 1402 and 1404 to study antiquity, he produced his first independent work in 1416, the *St George* for a niche in Orsanmichele (Florence, Bargello), whose bas-relief, executed "a stiacciato" and with the first "atmospheric" sky with clouds in the background and trees moving in the breeze, represents the first translation into sculpture of Brunelleschi's laws on perspective. He also worked "in company" with Michelozzo (1425-34), and was active in Pisa, Prato, Siena, Venice and Padua, where the high altar in the Basilica is one of his masterpieces.

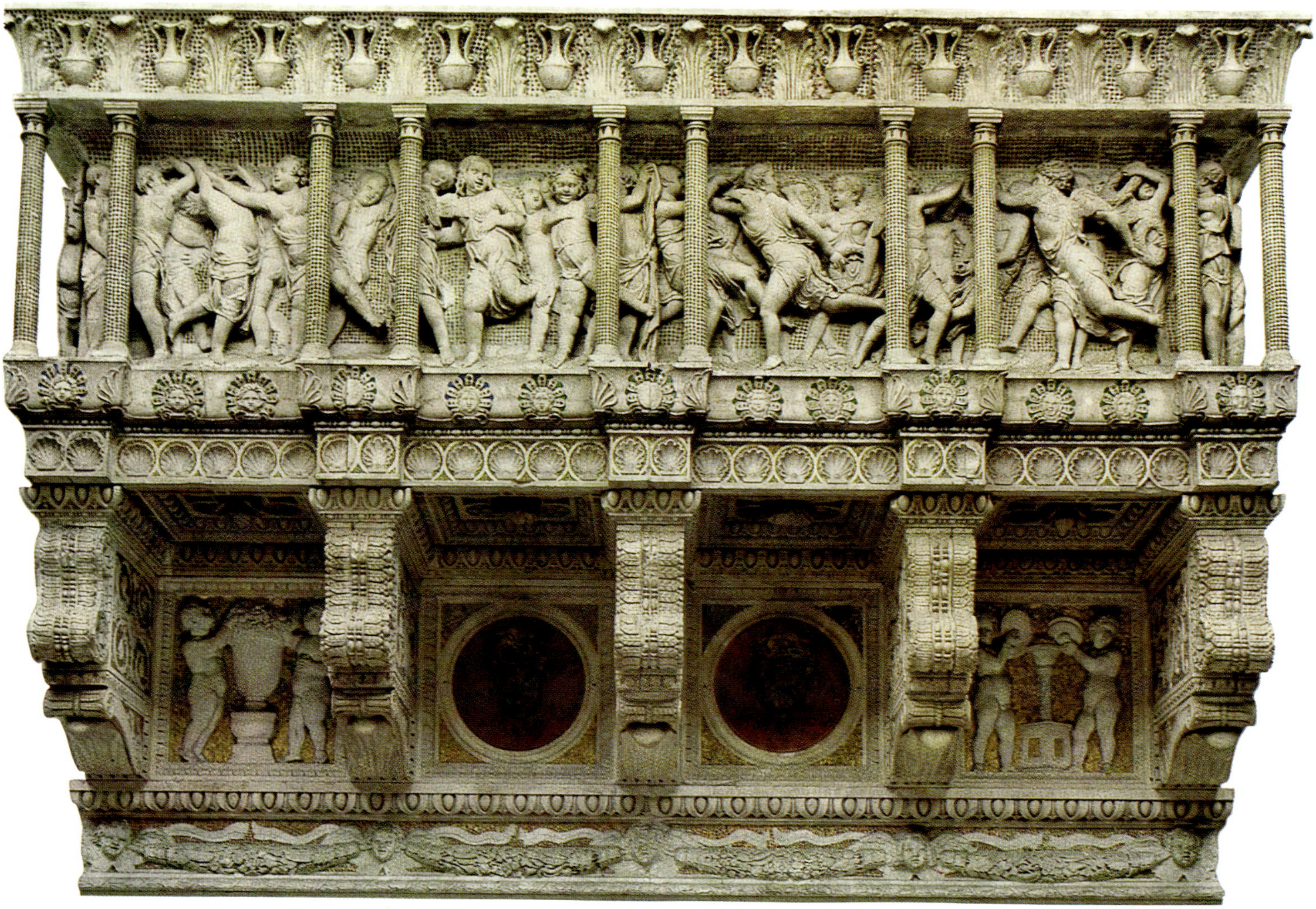

Paolo Uccello (attr.), *Donatello*, detail of *Portrait of Five Illustrious Men*, c. 1450. Paris, Louvre.

Donatello
Choir
1433-39
marble, detail
Florence, Museo dell'Opera del Duomo.

Sculpted by Donatello for the Santa Maria del Fiore Cathedral, contemporaneous with Luca della Robbia's *Choir*, the work is a clear manifesto of Donatello's love of antiquity, which however he re-elaborates with imagination and highest pictorial and decorative skill. In the continuous frieze behind the little columns, where even the color of the marble encrustation has a significant role, the convulsive dance of cherubs recalls a Dionysiac festival.

Although his passion for antiquity makes Donatello one of the champions of the humanistic rebirth of the arts, his interpretation of the antique is absolutely subjective. Today Reymond's comment (1898) that the sculpture of Donatello "whether he wished it or not, represents the most energetic protest ever made by an artist against the doctrines of antiquity" may seem no longer paradoxical.

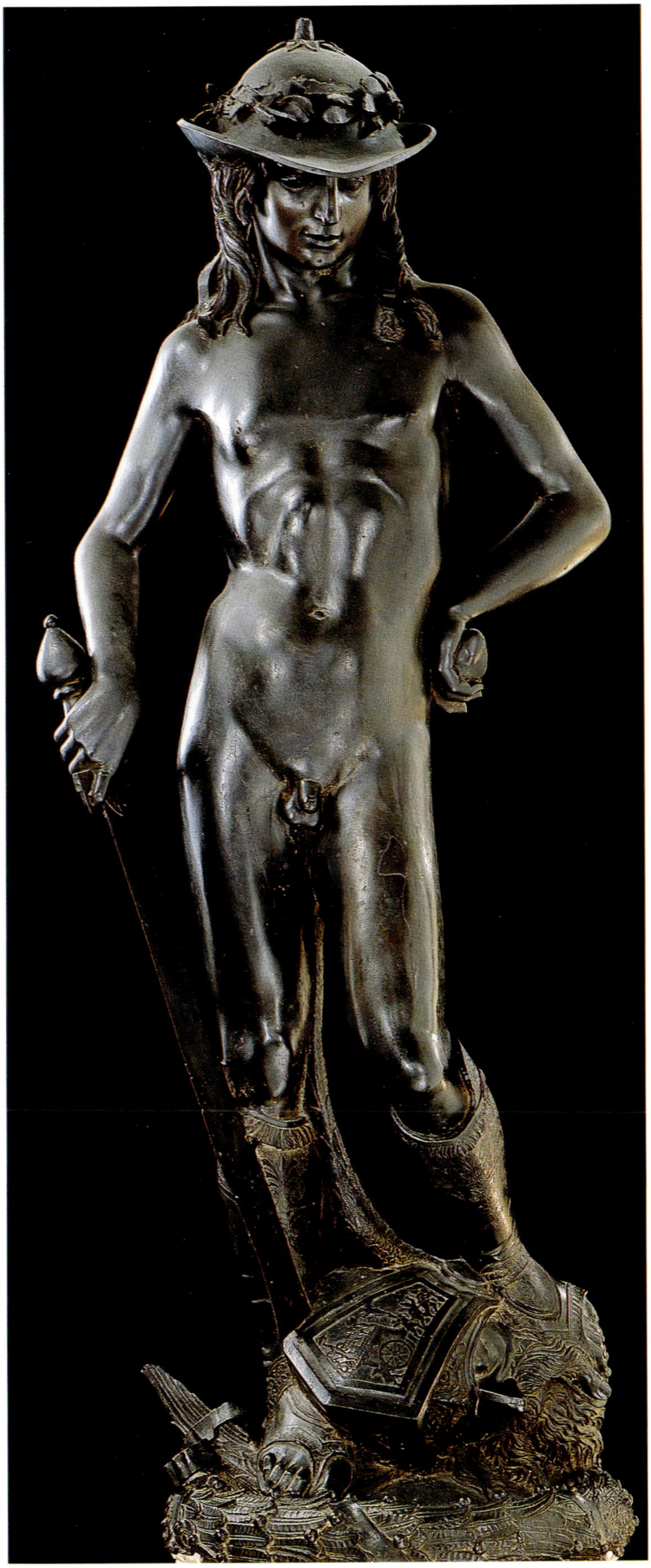

Donatello
David-Mercury
c. 1440-50
bronze
Florence, Bargello Museum.

Life-size, originally placed on a column at the center of the courtyard in Palazzo Medici, where it was mentioned in 1469, the statue was taken from the Medici family in 1494 at the time of their expulsion from Florence and brought to Palazzo Vecchio, perhaps to symbolize republican freedom. Its dating is still controversial, and the traditional identification of the hero as David has recently changed in the mythological direction: the statue probably represents Mercury.

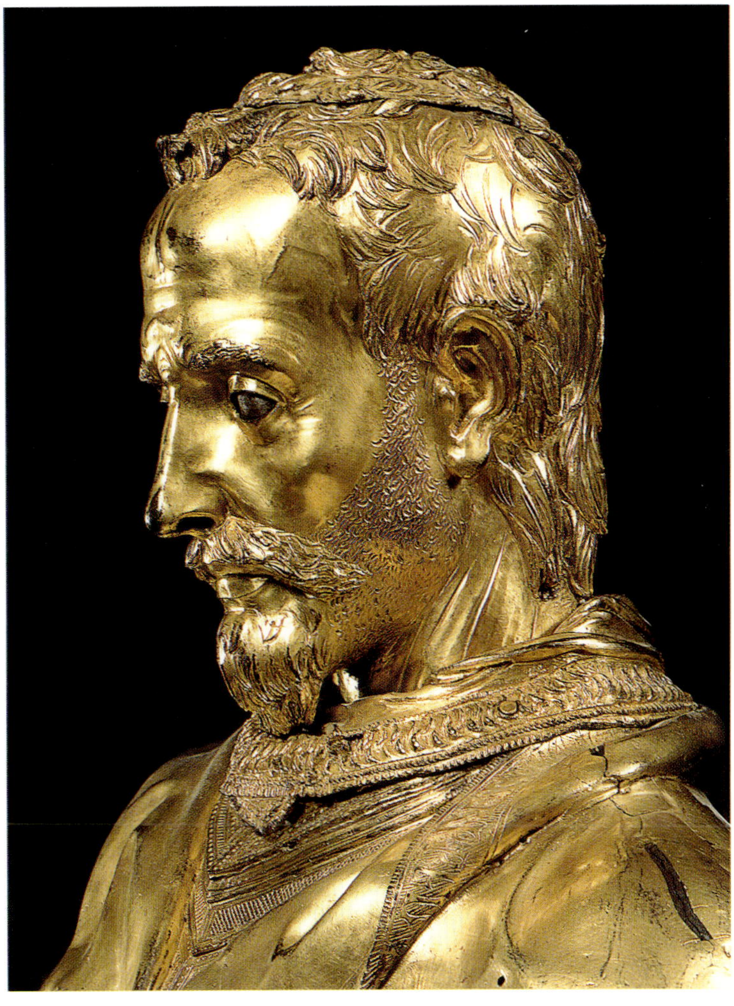

Donatello
San Lussorio
1425-27
bronze, partially gilded
Pisa, Museo Nazionale di San Matteo.

This is the only known representation of the Roman soldier beheaded in Sardinia under the Emperor Diocletian, venerated also in the territory of Pisa where he is popularly known as San Rossore. Donatello sculpted the bronze, which assumes the aspect of a real portrait, for the reliquary that was to contain the head of the saint, transferred to the Ognissanti Monastery in Florence in 1422. The bronze was cast by Giovanni di Jacopo in five pieces joined by screws.

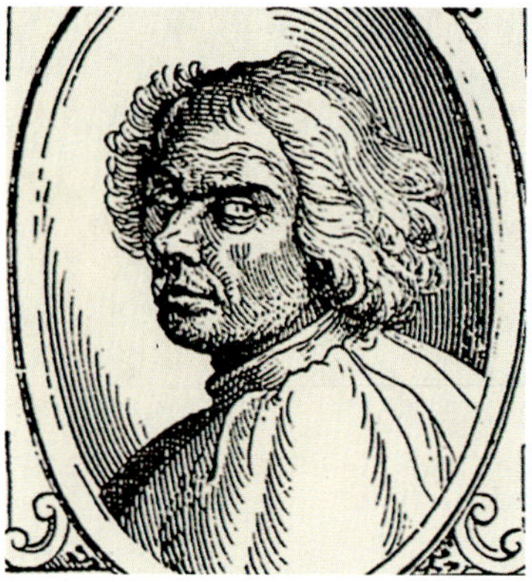

Andrea del Castagno

(Andrea di Bartolo, Castagno, Mugello, c. 1421 – Florence 1457)

"Andreino of the hanged men", he was called by the Florentines for having accepted an unrewarding task in 1440: that of painting the rebellious exiles led by Ormanno degli Albizzi hanging head down in the Podestà Palace. The "infamous paintings", with bodies swinging in dynamic poses amid twisting drapery, was an excellent exercise for the young artist, who was to repeat the experiment in the angels of the *Pazzi Madonna* (Florence, Uffizi). Sensitive to the plasticity of figures and with intense, original psychological realism, Andrea frescoed for the Carducci family a "magnificent" loggia as reported by Francesco Albertini in 1510, whose fragments, salvaged in 1847, show almost sculptural personages projecting from false frames simulating compartments in the wall, an experiment recognizable also in the *Last Supper*, his masterpiece.

Giorgio Vasari, *Portrait of Andrea del Castagno*, from the *Lives*, Florence, Giunti, 1568.

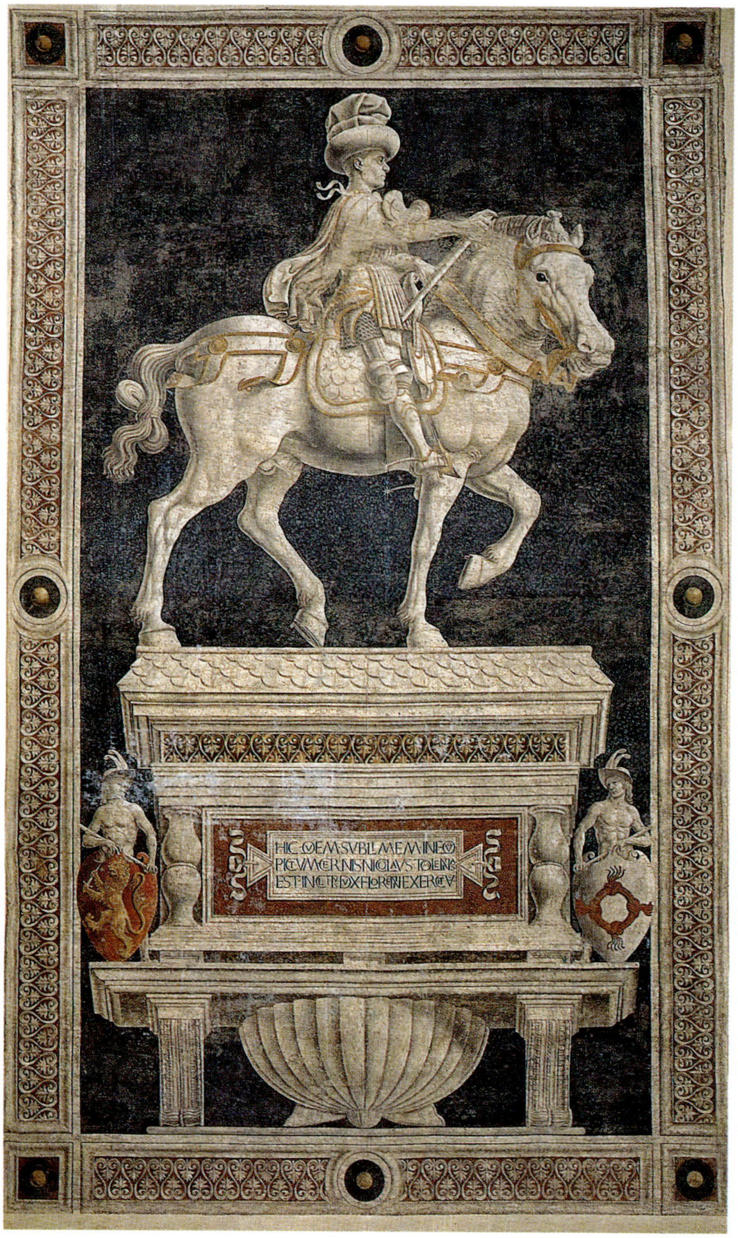

Andrea del Castagno
Niccolò da Tolentino
1456
fresco
Florence, Duomo.

In the humanistic atmosphere of 15th century Florence man, now viewed as defender of the city without the aid of any supernatural power, was glorified for his earthly virtues. Along with the renewed interest of biographies in illustrious men, condottieri and politicians who had contributed to the republican values of the city, the Florentine art of the times also celebrated its great historical figures. For the Duomo Andrea portrayed Niccolò da Tolentino, who led the Florentines to victory against the Sienese in the Battle of San Romano in 1432. In place of the initial marble project, this fresco of the knight posing proudly on his charger above an antique-style structure became the companion piece of Paolo Uccello's *Giovanni Acuto.*

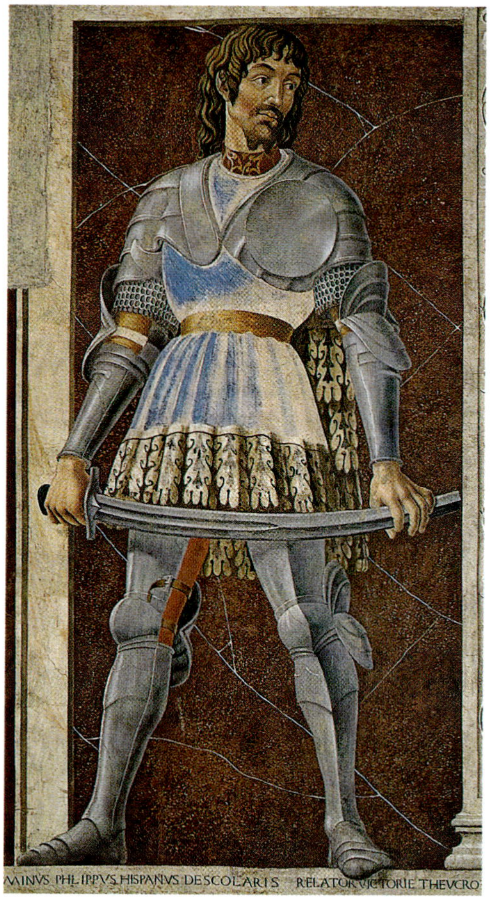

Andrea del Castagno
Pippo Spano
c. 1449-50
detached fresco
Florence, Uffizi Gallery.

For the villa of the Gonfaloniere Carducci at Legnaia, near Florence, Andrea frescoed a loggia with a cycle depicting personages from Florentine history, along with heroic figures from the Bible and antiquity. Pippo Spano, whose real name was Filippo Scolari, was a Hungarian of Florentine origin who died in 1426, a courageous captain at arms against the Bosnians and skillful diplomat of Sigismund of Bohemia, who appointed him Governor of Bosnia.

Andrea del Castagno
Last Supper
c. 1445-50
fresco, detail
Florence, Museo del Cenacolo di Sant'Apollonia.

Just opened to the public after long restoration (March 2000), the grandiose fresco with its foreshortened perspective, the first Last Supper of Renaissance stamp, displays all of the finest traits of Andrea's art, and in particular the almost cutting sharpness of the faces and the fabrics, the care dedicated to depicting the multi-colored false marbles and the winged sphinxes at the sides of the bench, draped in a woven flower-patterned cloth, as further confirmation of the artist's refined taste for precious details.

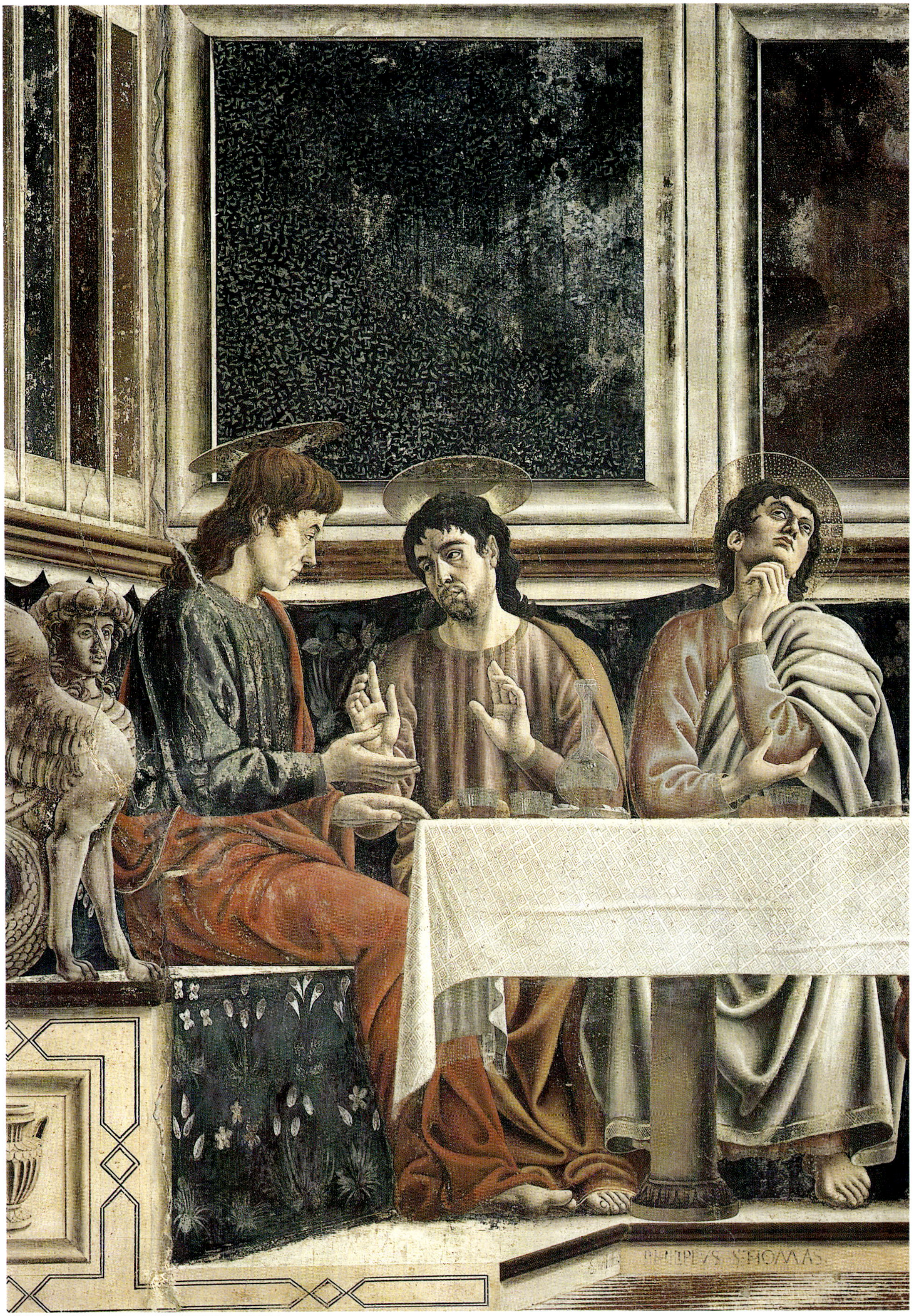

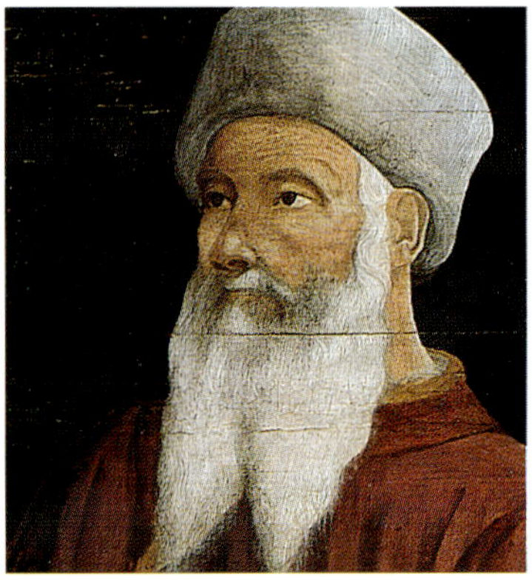

Paolo Uccello

(Paolo di Dono, Pratovecchio 1397 – Florence 1475)

"What a sweet thing is this perspective" Paolo Uccello answered his wife who was calling him to bed. The anecdote is reported by Vasari, who saw this great artist as a "subtle, sophisticated genius" who "delighted only in investigating some difficult, impossible matters of perspective". Even Donatello his friend admonished him: "Oh, Paulo, this perspective of yours will make you leave the certain for the uncertain". The painter of the famous lunettes in the Green Cloister of Santa Maria Novella and the *Battles* for Palazzo Medici, Paolo carried to exasperation the space "rationalized" by Masaccio, accentuating the figures in the foreground, falsifying the perception of distance through strong illusionist effects. Active also in Prato, Venice and Urbino, where he worked for Federico da Montefeltro, he died at the age of eighty, poverty-stricken and forgotten.

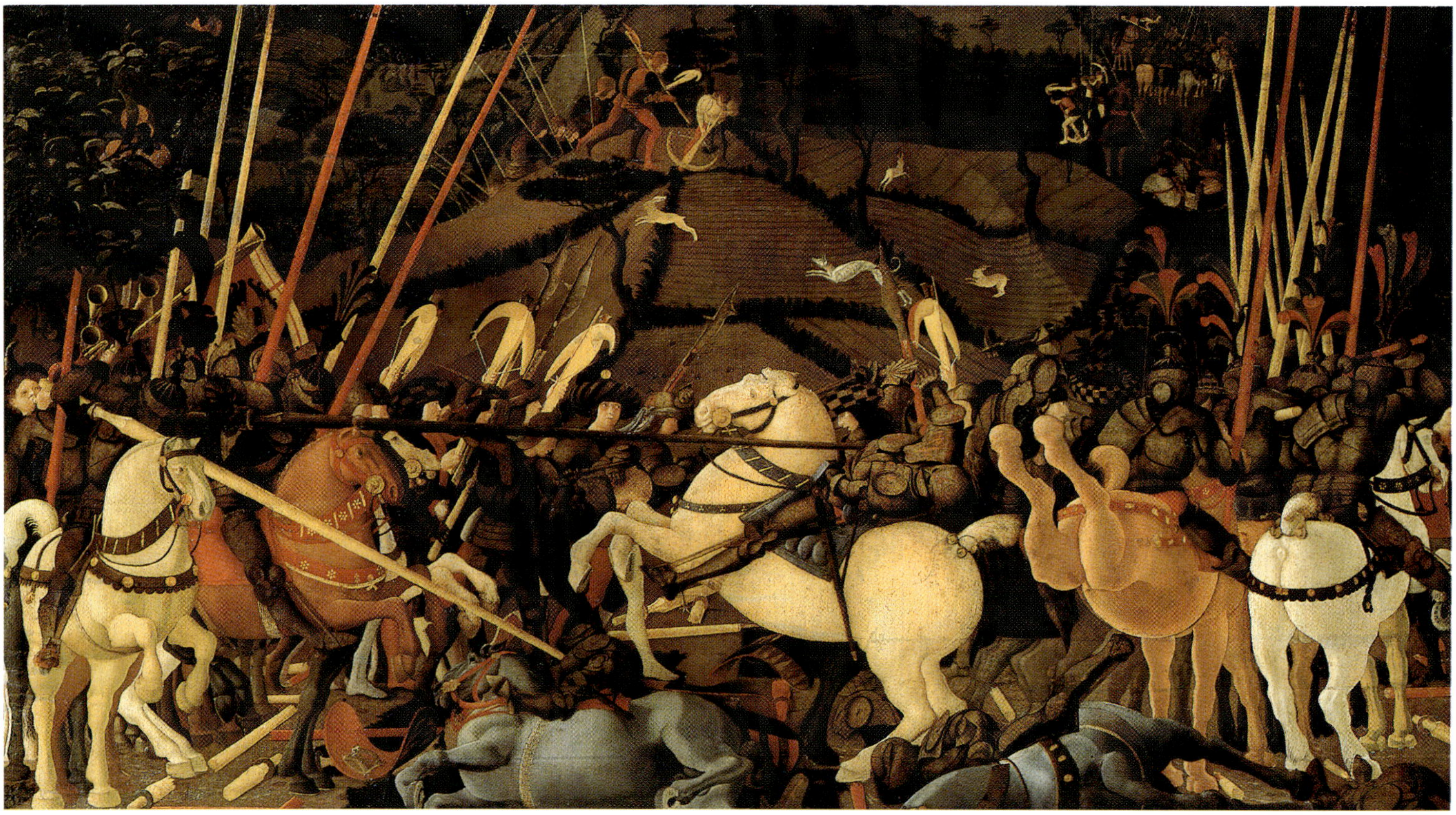

Paolo Uccello (attr.), *Self-portrait*, detail of the *Portrait of Five Illustrious Men*, c. 1450. Paris, Louvre.

Paolo Uccello
Battle of San Romano
variously dated 1435-38 and 1456-60
panel
Florence, Uffizi Gallery.

Still dubious is the dating of this work, which hung in the Lorenzo the Magnificent's bedroom in Palazzo Medici in 1492, along with three lost panels and another two paintings (now in London, National Gallery, and Paris, Louvre) depicting stages of the Battle of San Romano (fought in 1432 in Valdelsa, with the defeat of the Duke of Milan, ally of Siena, by the Florentines). It could thus be a commemoration painted soon after that victory, which owed much to the Captains Niccolò da Tolentino and Micheletto da Cotignola, financed by Cosimo de' Medici. Or it could date from 1460, after the Medici left their first residence for the new palace designed for Cosimo by the architect Michelozzo. In any case it remains a sophisticated, fascinating exercise in perspective, centered around the episode of the unhorsing of Bernardino della Ciarda, condottiere of the enemy troops.

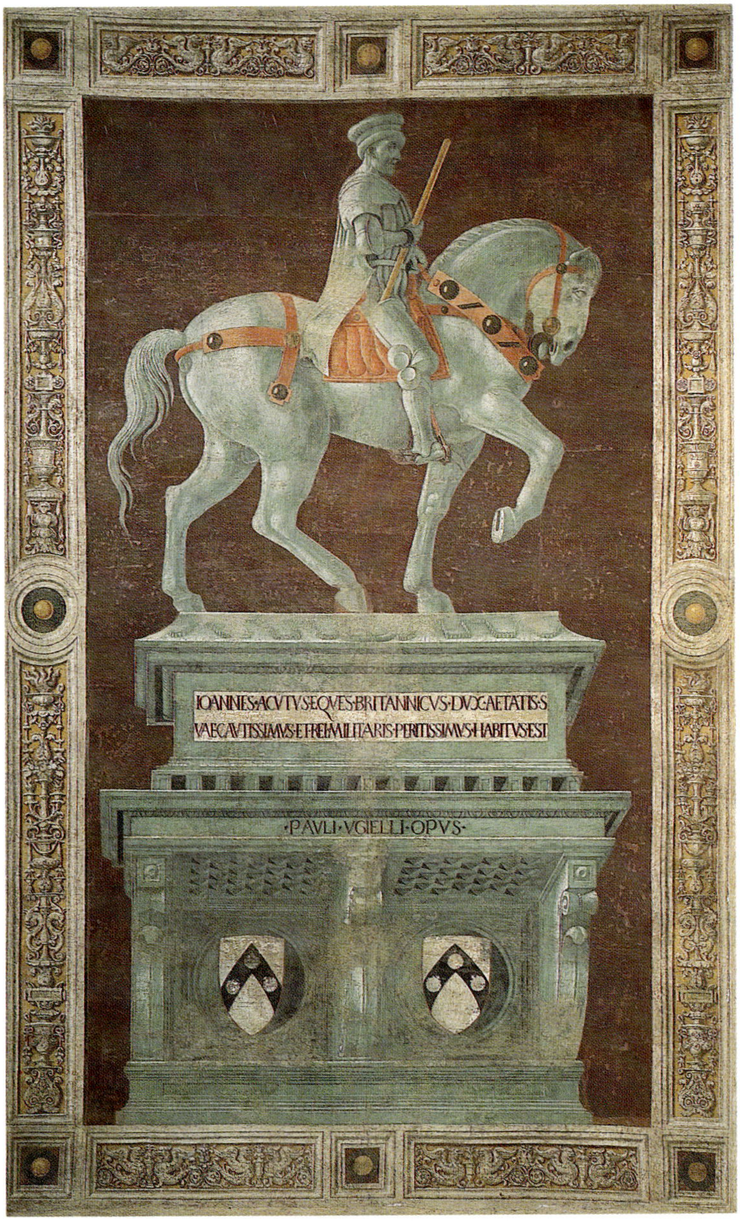

Paolo Uccello
Giovanni Acuto
signed 1436
fresco
Florence, Duomo.

A cenotaph to the Englishman Sir John Hawkwood, at the service of the Florentine Republic, who died in 1394, was planned already before the death of this condottiero, but the monument was to be executed only later. Requested of Paolo Uccello in "green clay", imitating bronze, the fresco was not accepted by the Workers of the Fabric of the Duomo, and Paolo was obliged to paint another one. Having completed the work, he also had to change the inscription, now of evident humanistic concept.

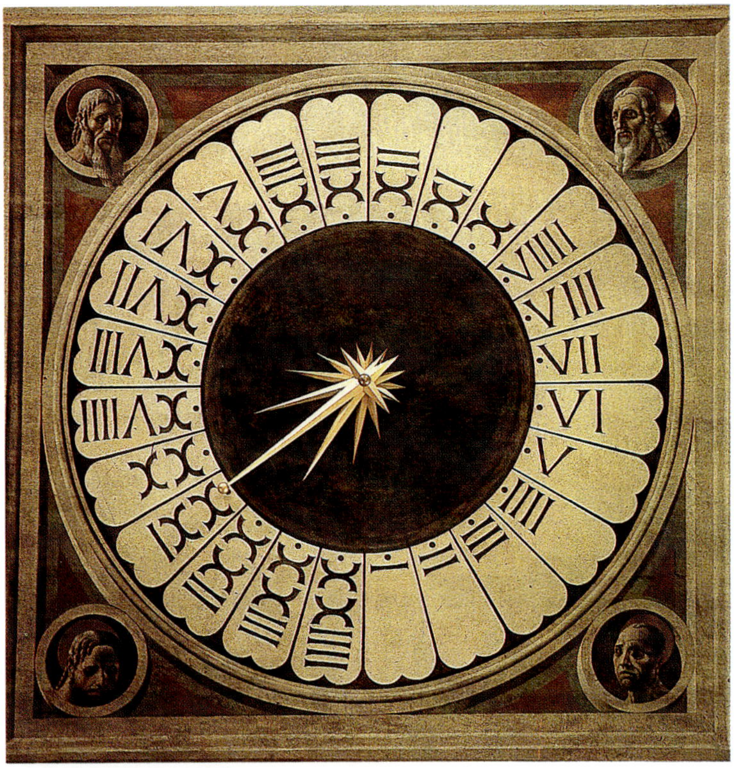

Paolo Uccello
Miracle of the Profaned Host
1467-68
panel, detail
Urbino, Galleria Nazionale delle Marche.

The predella shows the episode of the hanging of a Christina woman in Paris who in 1291 had sold a consecrated wafer to a Jewish merchant.

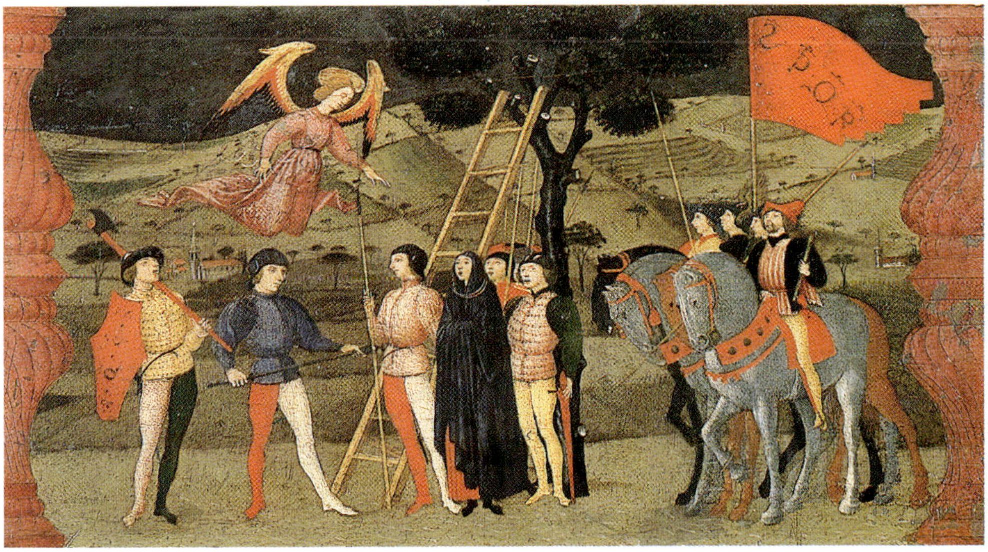

Paolo Uccello
Clock
1443
fresco, detail
Florence, Duomo.

For the inner façade of the Duomo Paolo frescoed the magnificent dial of a clock, surrounded by medallions enclosing extraordinary foreshortened heads. The work dates more or less to the period in which the artist was preparing the cartoons for three stained-glass windows in the lantern on the dome.

Sassetta and the Master of the Osservanza

(Stefano di Giovanni, active from 1423 – Siena 1450; Master of the Osservanza, active between 1425 and 1450)

Of these two artists, similar in style and recently reassessed by critics, attributions and chronology have been confused in the past. Several documentary sources mention Sassetta, an autonomous, highly original artist working in the second quarter of the 15th century, innovator of what has been called "the most radical experiment in realistic painting of those years". Nothing is known instead of the latter, no less able painter, still one of the most enigmatic anonymous masters in Italian art, whose pseudonym comes from a triptych in the Church of the Osservanza in Siena. He has been tentatively identified as a certain Vico di Luca, who collaborated with Sassetta on the standards in the Siena Duomo.

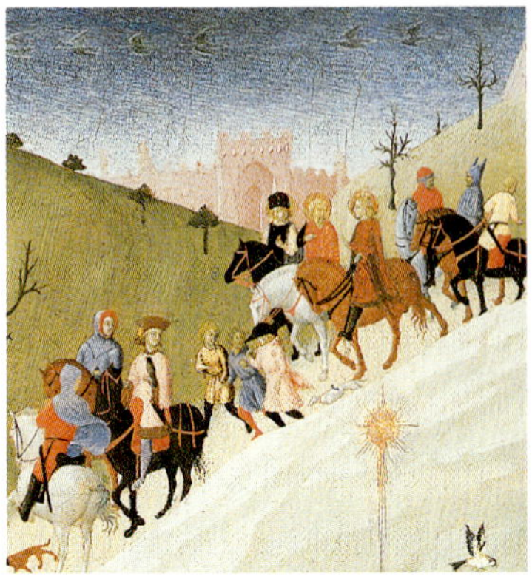

Sassetta, *The Journey of the Magi*, 1432-36. New York, The Metropolitan Museum of Art.

At right: **Domenico Veneziano**, *St John the Baptist*, detail of *Altarpiece of Santa Lucia dei Magnoli*, c. 1445. Florence, Uffizi Gallery.

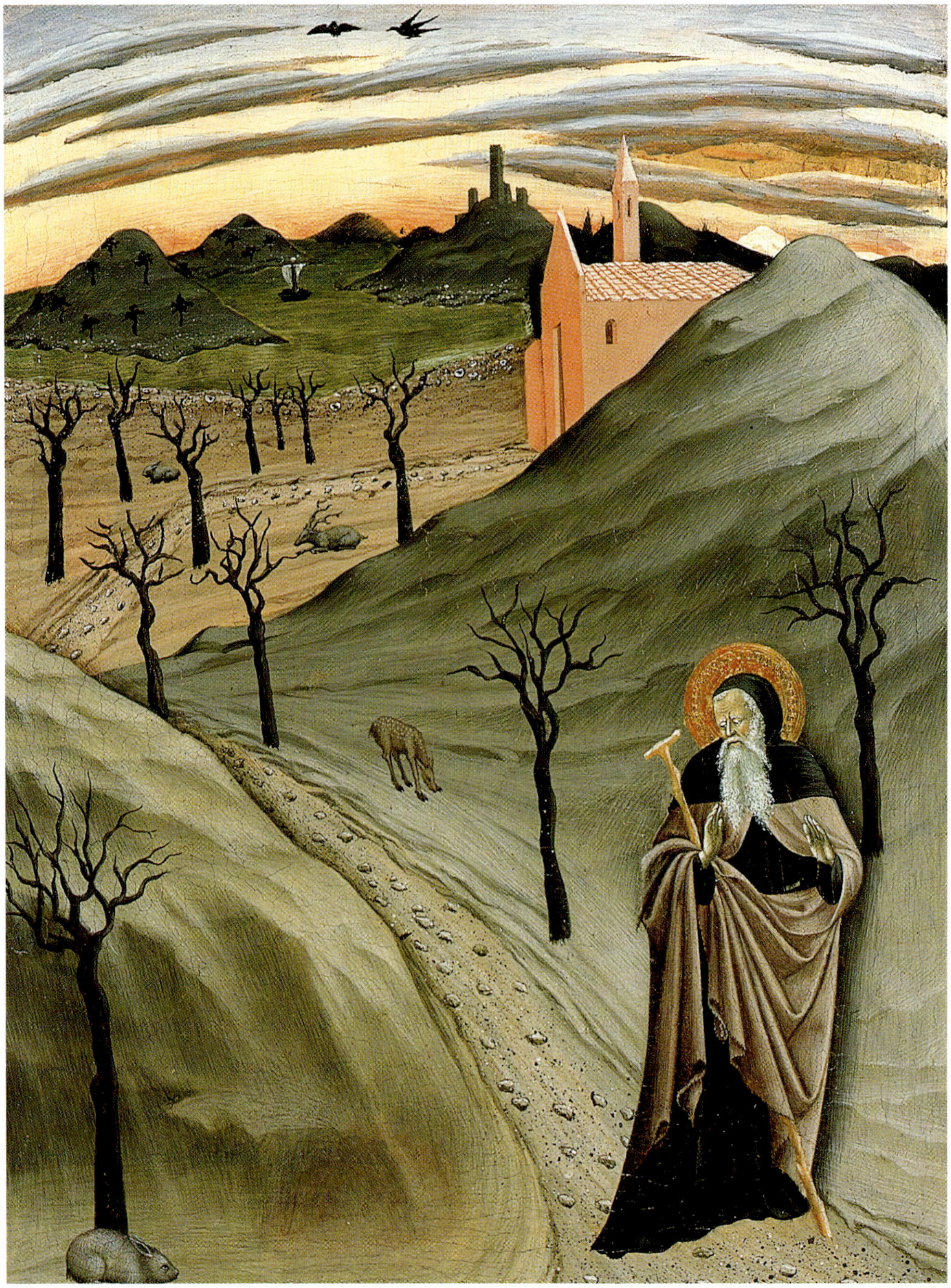

Master of the Osservanza
St Anthony Tempted by a Heap of Gold
c. 1440
panel
New York, The Metropolitan Museum of Art.

The reddish glow of sunset, two birds streaking across the sky, strategically viewed one head-on, the other from the side, a desolate, arid landscape which is nonetheless intriguing for a series of enchanted details, appearing motionless in the distance: the boat and a hill crowned with towers, a pink chapel, a rabbit, a deer. Even the saint, who according to legend had to flee from devils who were tempting him, stands fixed, almost unreal. The little panel forms part of a series of eight scenes of the life of St Anthony now dispersed among the Berlin Museums, the National Gallery of Washington, the Yale University Art Gallery and the Metropolitan Museum of New York.

Domenico Veneziano
St John in the Desert
c. 1445
panel
Washington, National Gallery of Art.

Spiky, bare mountains, a harsh landscape brightened by a few touches of green and a thicket of trees on the banks of the river, a blue sky streaked by clouds ; in this luminous panel Domenico Veneziano portrays his John the Baptist: nude, a camel skin thrown over his shoulder, as he abandons on the ground the red robe that alludes to martyrdom.

Domenico Veneziano

(Domenico di Bartolomeo, Venice c. 1410 – Florence 1461)

His name is shadowed by the legend, highly unreliable, that he was killed by his pupil Andrea del Castagno, as reported by Vasari. In reality Domenico died in 1461, after the death of Andrea, as recorded in the "book of the dead" of the Church of San Pier Gattolino. Venetian by birth, Domenico worked in Florence while still very young, perhaps with some assistants of Gentile da Fabriano. In 1438 he went to Perugia, from where he wrote Piero de' Medici asking for work. Back in Florence, he frescoed the choir of the Church of Sant'Egidio, working beside the young Piero della Francesca. With the latter he went to the Marches, where he left unfinished the cycle for the Church of the Madonna of Loreto. Although the delicate luminism of his painting exerted a strong influence in those years, and not in Florence alone, he was to die in poverty.

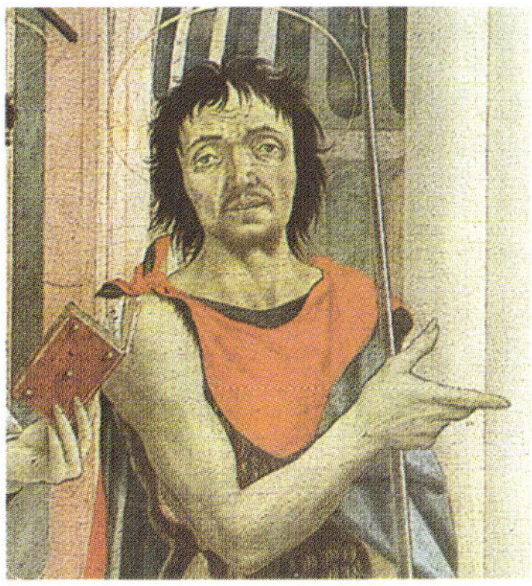

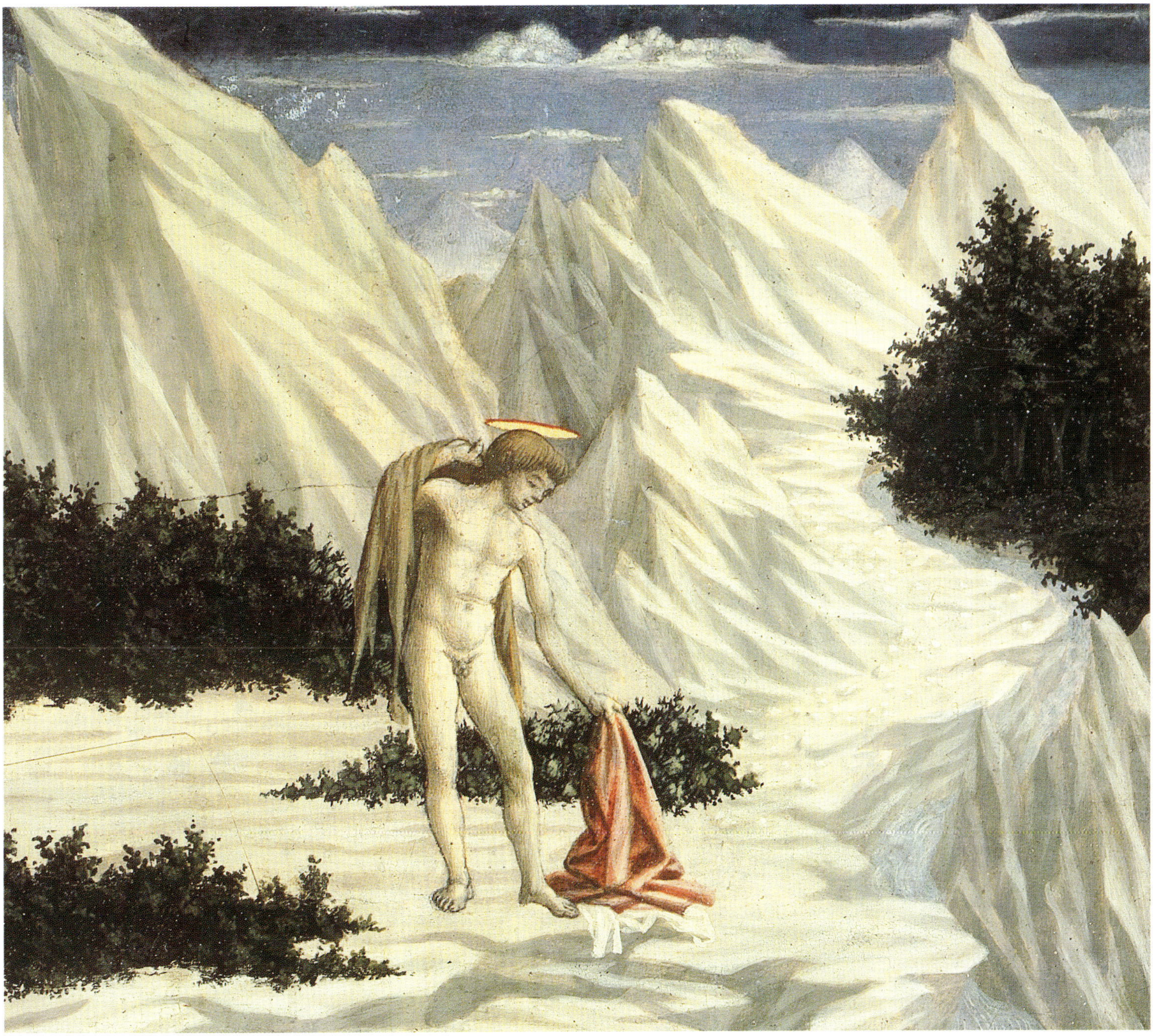

Piero della Francesca

(Pietro di Benedetto dei Franceschi, Sansepolcro c. 1411 – 1492)

Piero was not only an extremely talented painter but also a theoretician and mathematician, author of treatises on perspective and geometry. Born at Sansepolcro near Arezzo, he trained with Domenico Veneziano in Florence, with whom he worked in 1439 on the lost frescoes of Sant'Egidio, his only work accomplished in Florence. The chronology of his paintings, charged with still obscure symbolic meanings, is debatable where no certain documents exist. From his work in Ferrara nothing has survived, while in Rimini he signed the fresco of *Sigismondo Malatesta* in the Tempio Malatestiano in 1451. Starting in 1452 he painted one of the greatest cycles of the Renaissance, the *Legend of the True Cross* in the choir of San Francesco in Arezzo, whose restoration, revealing all of the luminosity of the frescoes, has just been completed.

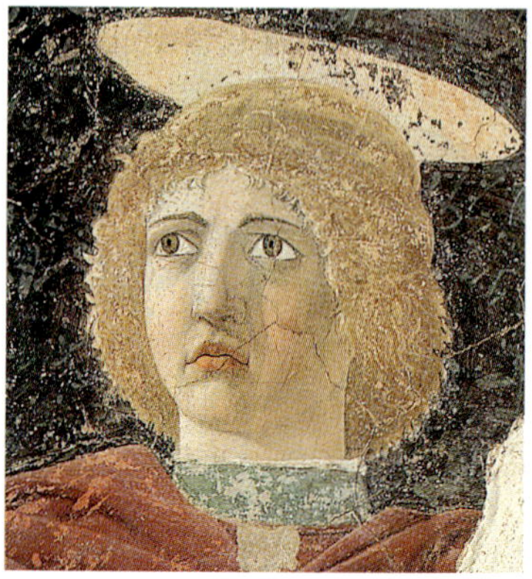

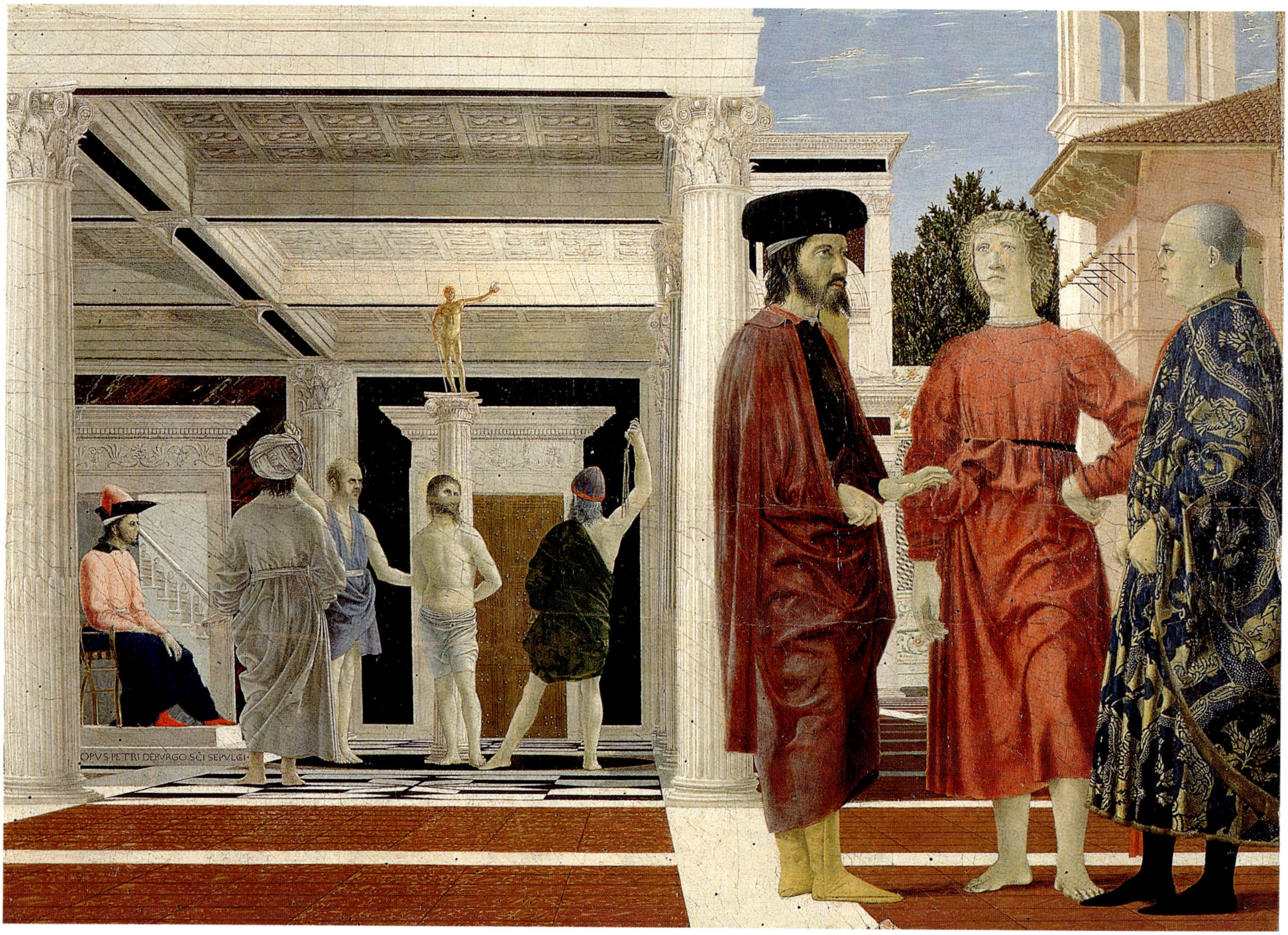

Piero della Francesca
The Flagellation of Christ
signed, after 1459?
panel
Urbino, Galleria Nazionale delle Marche.

This work, one of the most enigmatic of the Quattrocento, is signed by Piero on the base of the throne where Pilate sits. It is improbable that the personages on the right are Federico da Montefeltro, his son Guidobaldo, and Oddantonio, Federico's half-brother, as was thought in the past. Nor is it certain that Pilate, who watches the flagellation of Christ under a solemnly classic loggia inspired by Alberti, can be identified with the Emperor of the East John VIII Paleologus, nor the bearded man in the foreground with his brother Tommaso Paleologus, who may be meditating on the sad fate of Constantinople. The painting may allude to the plan for a crusade against the Turks proposed in 1459 by Pope Pius II Piccolomini, and in this case the blond youth gazing into the distance would be the Hungarian King Matthias Corvinus, among the few to adhere to the project.

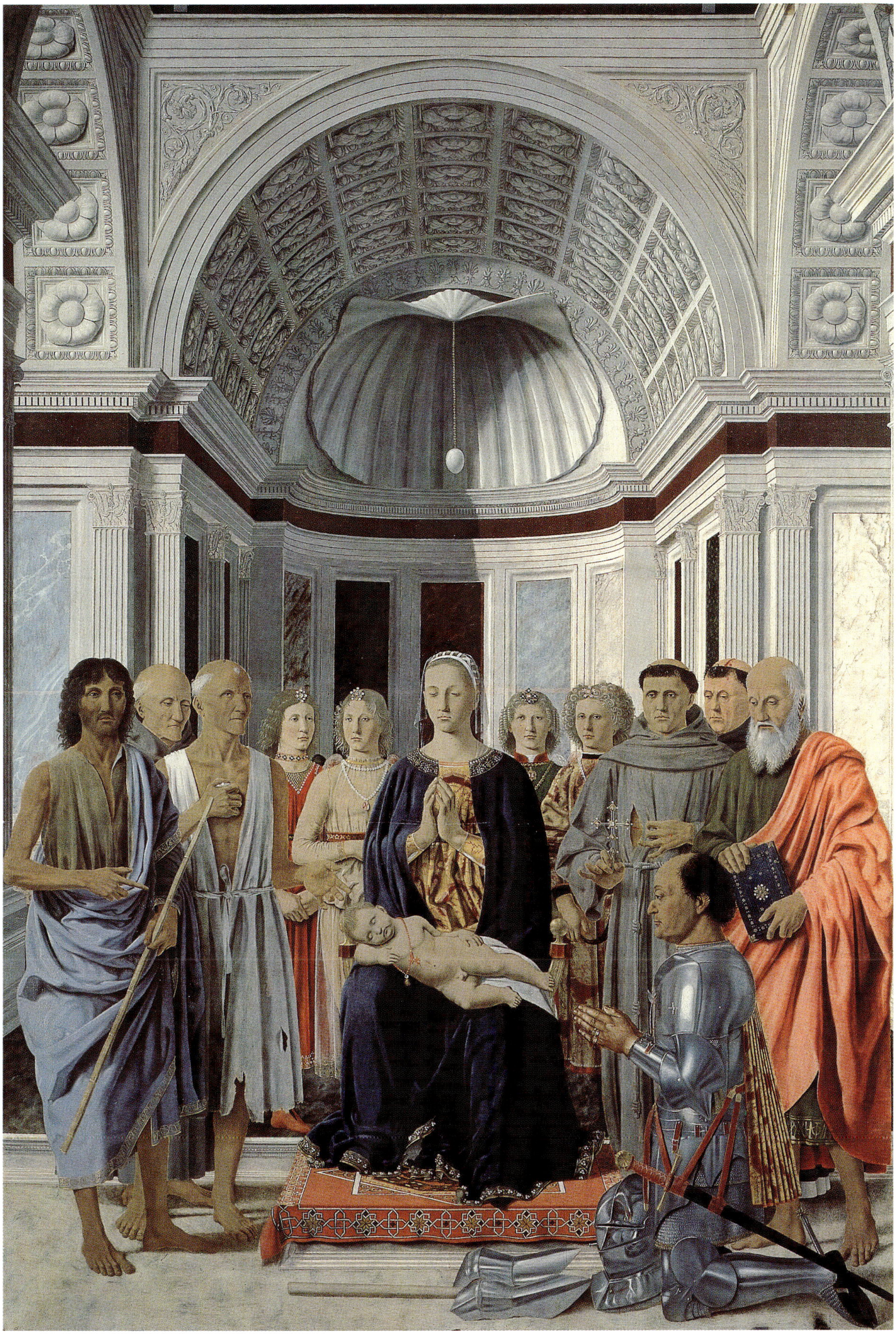

At left:
Piero della Francesca,
St Julian, detail,
c. 1450. Sansepolcro,
Museo Civico.

Piero della Francesca
Montefeltro Altarpiece
1472-74
panel
Milan, Pinacoteca di Brera.

This altarpiece was painted for Federico da Montefeltro at about the time when his wife, Battista Sforza, died in childbirth. It thus assumes a dual symbolic significance: the Duke's thanksgiving for the birth of his long-awaited heir Guidobaldo, and a commemoration of the mother who has died; and also, perhaps, glorification of the Montefeltro family, who had conquered Volterra in 1472 (not by chance, the kneeling Duke is dressed in splendid armor). The egg hanging from the shell symbolizes birth and eternal life. The Duchess' name is evoked by the figure of John the Baptist on the left. Federico's hands were not painted by Piero who, it seems, used the cartoon of the Montefeltro diptych now in the Uffizi for the Duke's portrait. This may be an indication of the artist's poor state of health reported by Vasari (who mentions blindness, not confirmed by the sources).

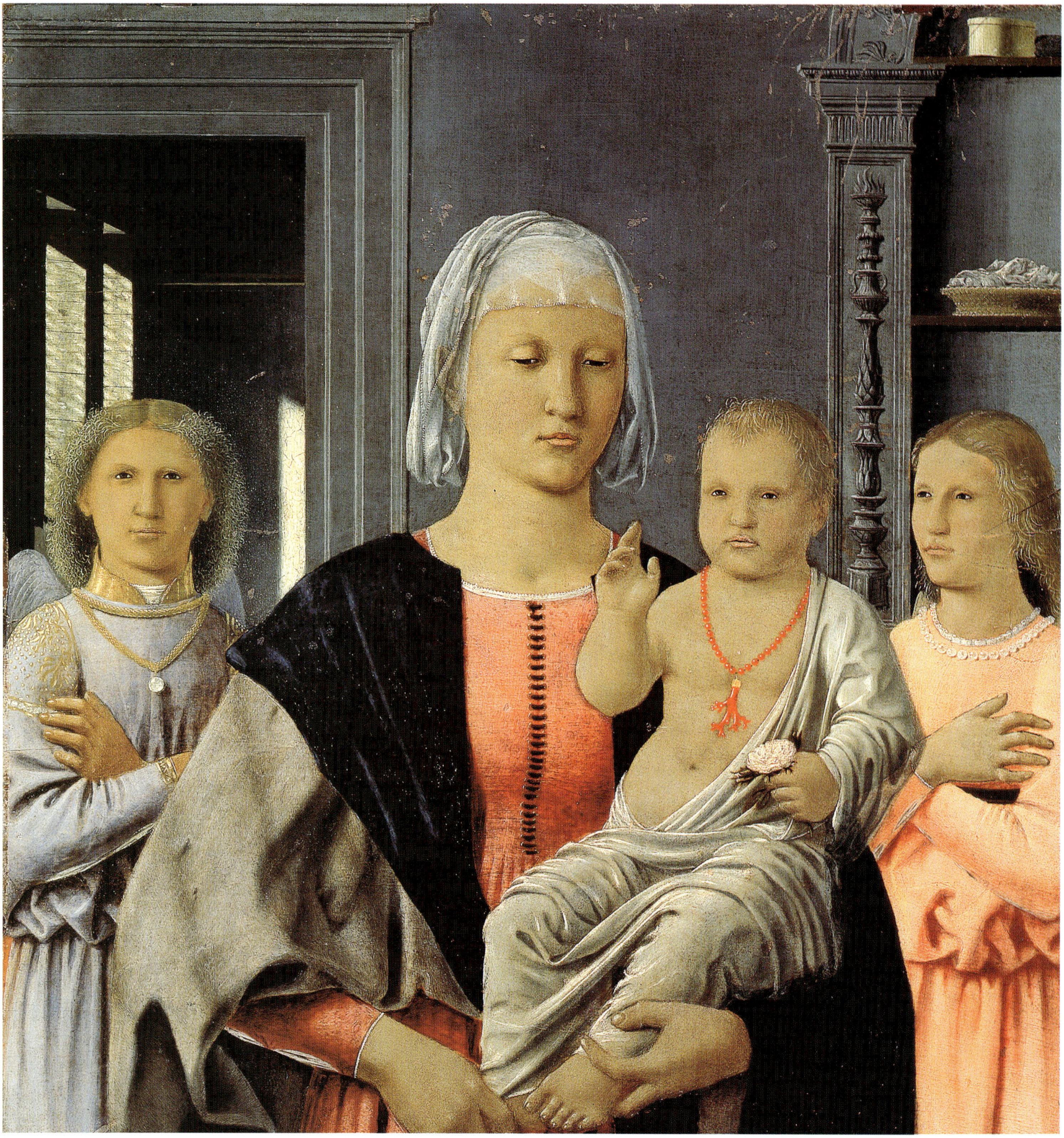

Piero della Francesca
Senigallia Madonna
c. 1474
panel

Urbino, Galleria Nazionale delle Marche.

Once again a luminous painting, balanced between its harmonic composition, set in a typically Renaissance interior, and the description, inspired by Flemish art, of each tiny detail : the box with the holy wafers, the wicker basket with the pieces of linen, the coral and glowing pearls of the jewelry. The painting is rife with symbolic allusions. The Christ Child holds a wild rose, symbol of divine love and of the rosary. On the shelf the box containing the host refers to the Eucharistic sacrifice. Lastly, the light passing through the windowpanes alludes to the spiritual conception of Mary.

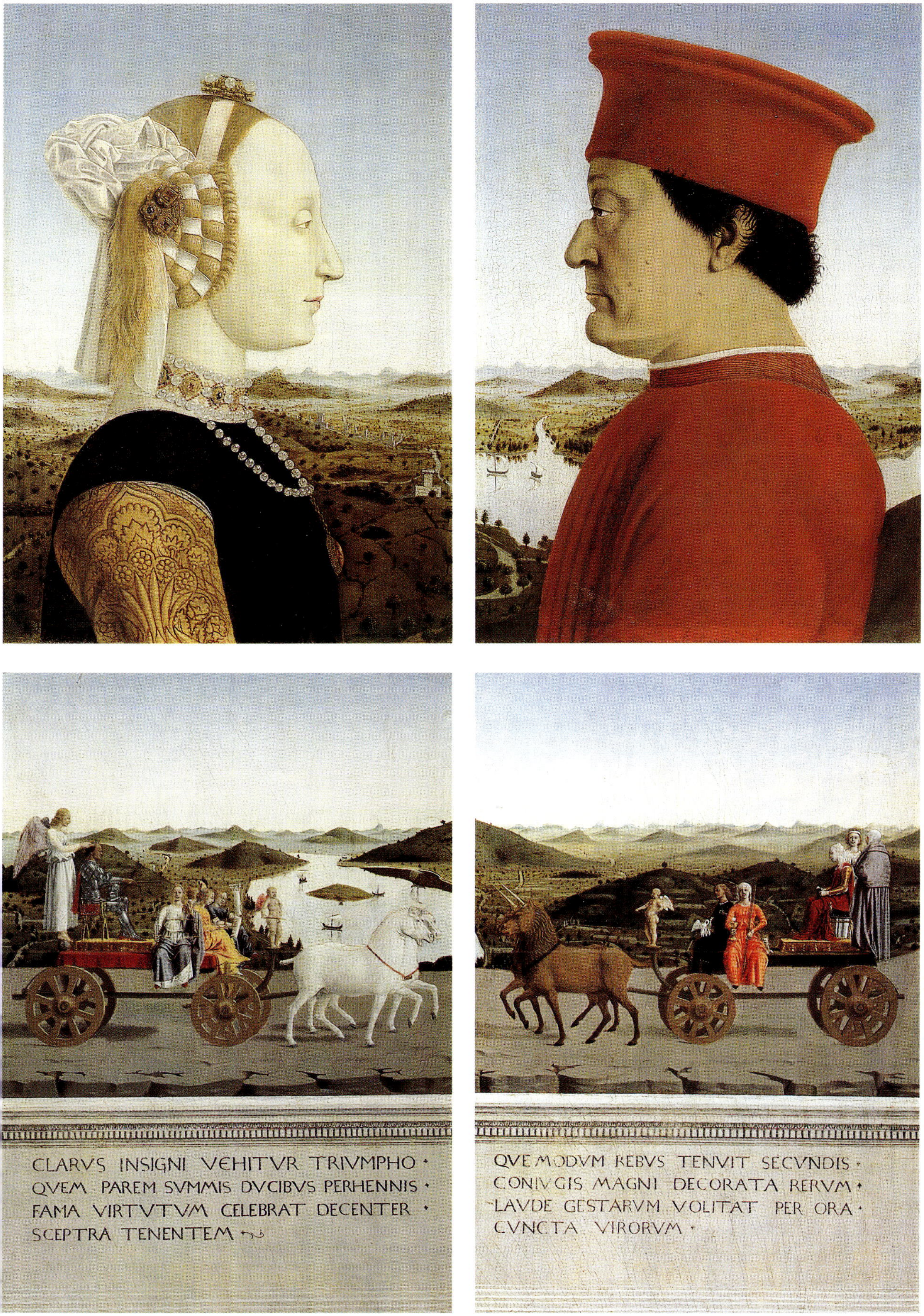

Piero della Francesca
Diptych of the Duke and Duchess of Urbino
c. 1467-72
panel
Florence, Uffizi Gallery.

Painted on both sides, originally hinged to open like a book, the diptych portrays on the inside the Duke and Duchess facing each other in solemn profile like classical medallions. The precise physiognomy, indulging in realistic details like Federico's nose, broken in a tournament, reveals Piero to be one of the most sensitive interpreters of Northern art. The crystal-clear landscape in the background, painted with an almost miniaturist technique, slopes back to distant hills on the horizon and continues even on the back. The magnificent birds' eye view unites the two panels in perspective without the customary expedient of a curtain or a window. On the back, the Virtues accompanying the triumphant chariots of Battista and Federico allude to their moral values.

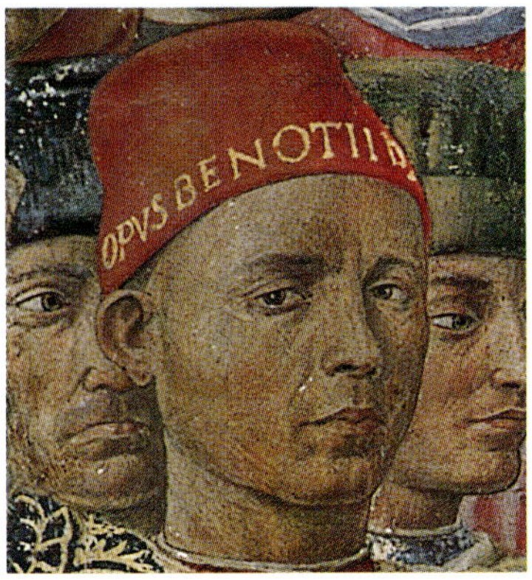

Benozzo Gozzoli

(Benozzo di Lese di Sandro, Florence c. 1421 – Pistoia 1497)

Benozzo, called Gozzoli only by Vasari, is known mainly for the decoration of the Medici's private chapel on the first floor of the palace in Via Larga. In this cycle of frescoes commissioned for commemorative purposes in 1458 by Piero, son of Cosimo, an enchanted cavalcade, embellished by exotic details and filled with contemporary portraits, parades majestically across the wall. Admired already in 1459 by Giangaleazzo Sforza, the chapel was an important element of representation for the Medici, manifesting the virtues of their house. Although Vasari considered Benozzo excellent at perspective, landscapes and animals, he nonetheless relegated him to a minor role, that of decorative and descriptive artist. Collaborating with Fra Angelico on various initiatives in Rome and Orvieto, Benozzo achieved his finest results in the churches of Montefalco.

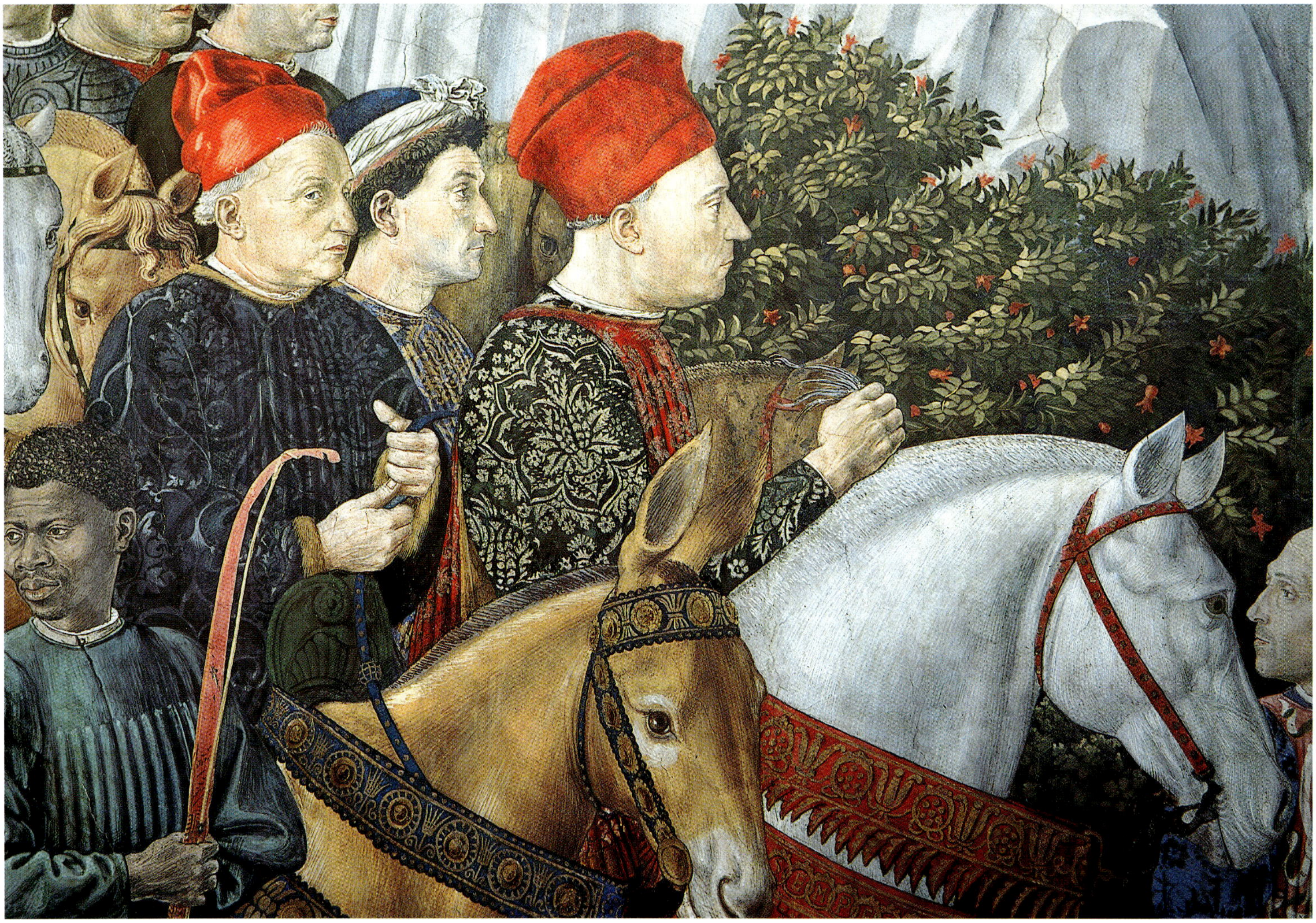

Benozzo Gozzoli, *Self-portrait with Signature on his Cap*, detail of the *Cavalcade of the Magi*, 1459. Florence, Palazzo Medici Riccardi, Chapel of the Magi.

Benozzo Gozzoli
Cavalcade of the Magi
1459
fresco, detail
Florence, Palazzo Medici Riccardi, Chapel of the Magi.

Among the numerous members of the Medici family portrayed by Benozzo in the sumptuous cavalcade of the Magi, Piero de' Medici (1416-69) is generally identified as the cavalier grasping his horse's mane, and his father Cosimo il Vecchio (1389-1464) as the older man holding the reins, to symbolize, in a fitting interpretation, the different roles held by the father and son in family life and above all in the political sphere.

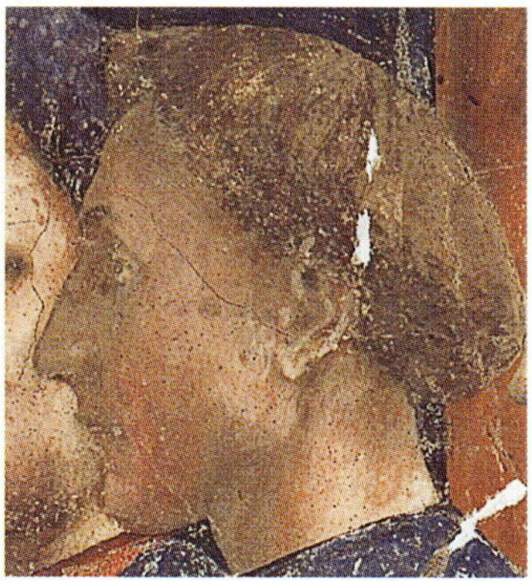

Leon Battista Alberti

(Genoa 1406 – Rome 1472)

For the events that brought the Albizzi to power in Florence the wealthy Alberti family were in exile when Leon Battista was born. He was to see his city only in 1434, after studying in Bologna and Rome. In Florence, while he completed the façade of Santa Maria Novella, he wrote some fundamental works, *Della Famiglia* and *De Pictura*, dedicated to Brunelleschi. He worked in Florence, Bologna, Ferrara and Rome where in 1452 he dedicated to the Pope a copy of *De Re Aedificatoria,* structured like Vitruvius' text. In 1447 he began the Tempio Malatestiano in Rimini. In 1459 he was in Mantua, returning several times for Sant'Andrea. In Rome in 1471 he accompanied Lorenzo de' Medici and Bernardo Rucellai to visit antiquities. A gifted intellectual, he studied optics, mathematics, history; a perceptive writer, he interpreted classicism with an antiquarian's taste.

Masaccio, *Presumed Portrait of Leon Battista Alberti*, detail of *St Peter in his Chair*, c. 1424-25. Florence, Santa Maria del Carmine, Brancacci Chapel.

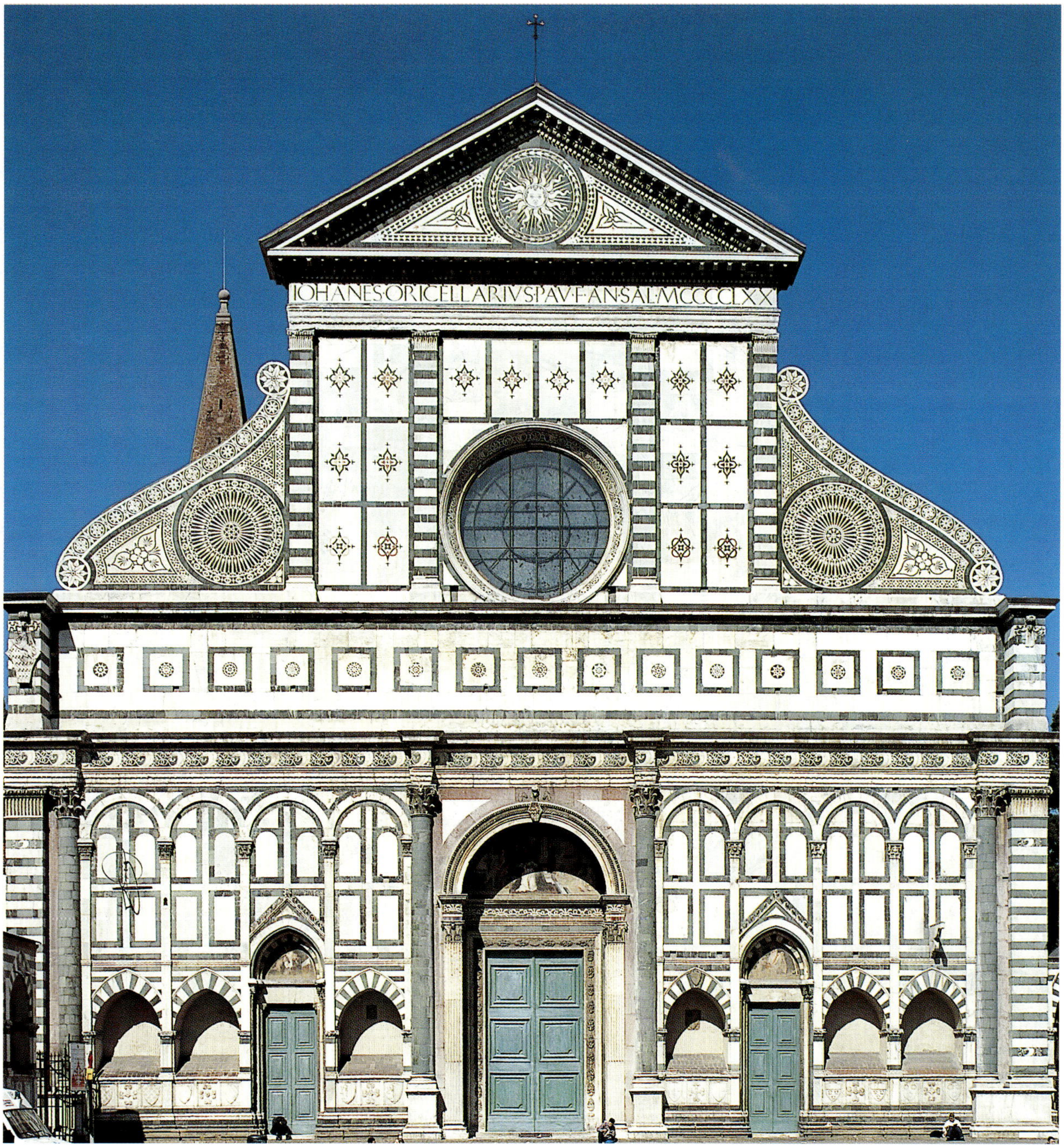

Leon Battista Alberti
Façade of Santa Maria Novella
commissioned between 1439 and 1442, completed in 1470
Florence.

The building plans of the rich, erudite Giovanni Rucellai were influenced by his knowledge of antiquity and Alberti's theories. For him Alberti designed the palace in Via della Vigna, the loggia facing it asymmetrically, and the marble-encrusted family templet in San Pancrazio, which imitates the Holy Sepulcher in Jerusalem. With his financing Alberti completed the façade of Santa Maria Novella, integrating it with the medieval part. The tympanum, with its sun in white and green inlaid marble, became the manifesto of the neoplatonic ideas diffused by Marsilio Ficino, author of *De Sole*, "the greatest of the celestial gods and the father of all things".

Cosmè Tura

(Ferrara c. 1430–1495)

Among the most original, autonomous artists of the Italian Quattrocento, Cosmè Tura represents, with his sharp, haunting images, the most advanced stage of the "Ferrara workshop" of which he was the leader. Born in the Emilian city, he was to work almost exclusively in his native town apart from a trip to Padua in the 1450s, where he encountered the antiquarian culture of an eccentric painter and collector of "anticaglie", Francesco Squarcione (1397-1468), with whom the young Mantegna was training. Returning to Ferrara, he worked at the vivacious, eclectic court of Ercole and Borso d'Este. In addition to many paintings now dispersed in museums all over the world, he supervised the decoration of the d'Este residences, including the Hall of Months in Palazzo Schifanoia, in which another great Ferrarese master his contemporary, Francesco del Cossa (c. 1436-c. 1478), also participated.

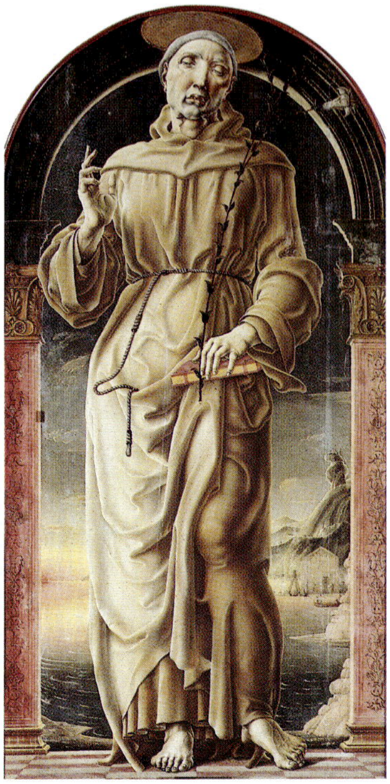

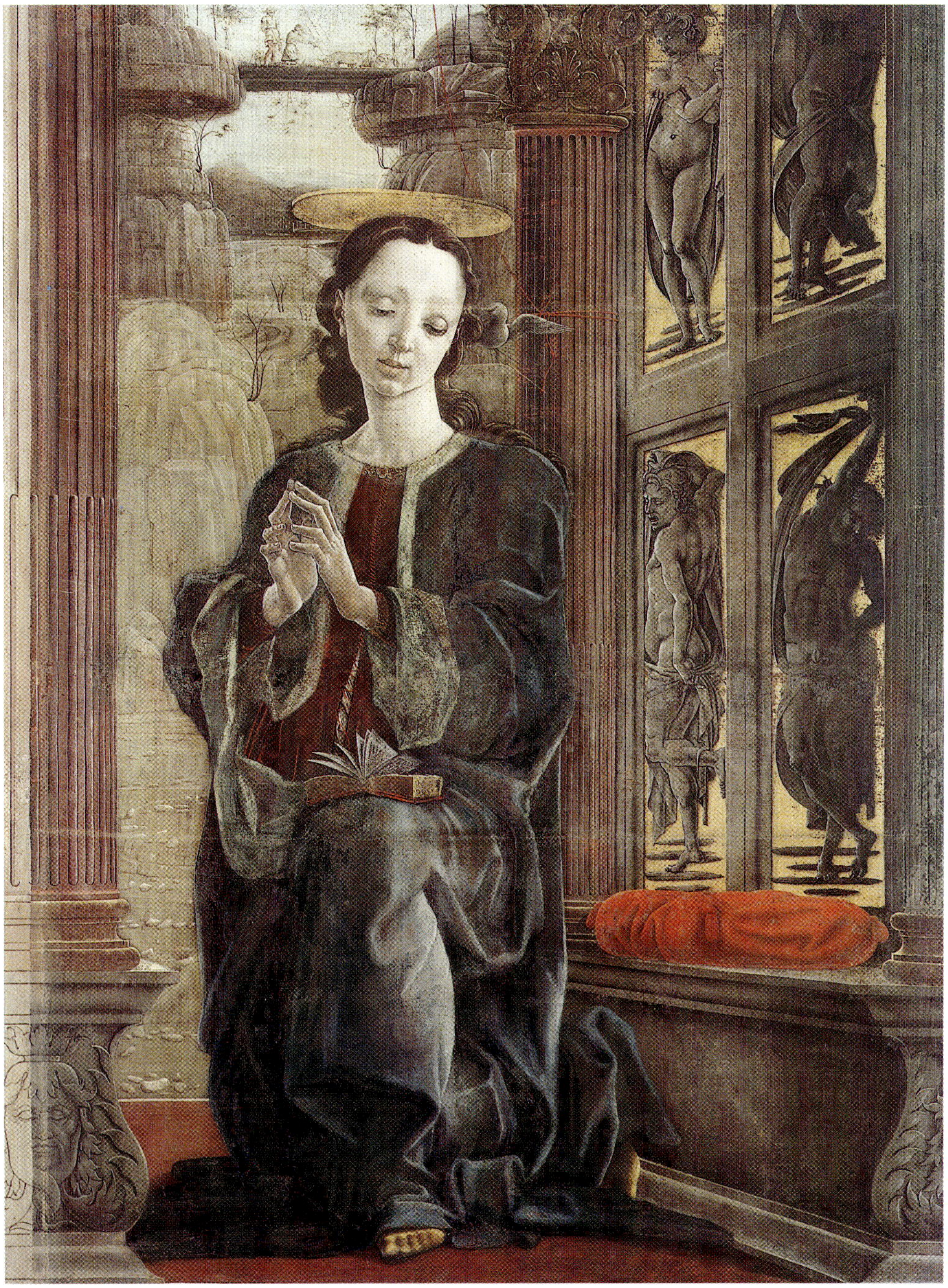

Cosmè Tura
Annunciation
1469
panel, detail
Ferrara, Museo dell'Opera del Duomo.

In 1469 Cosmè painted the doors of the organ in the Ferrara Cathedral with the *Stories of St George and the Dragon* on the outside and the *Annunciation* on the inside, of which recent iconographic analysis has revealed complex esoteric meanings.
The *Annunciation* is set in a Mantegna-like architecture with a harsh landscape in the background. While the Madonna's composed attitude contrasts with the usual convulsive action of Cosmè's figures, the classicizing bas-reliefs on the walls contain sculptured, almost real figures, animated by such delirious motion that they seem about to step out of the painting.

Cosmè Tura
St Anthony of Padua
c. 1490
panel
Modena, Galleria Estense.

An emaciated, contorted face, the metallic folds of his gown emphasizing a nervous leg; a tall figure, rising imposingly, boldly foreshortened, against an arcade of refined colors. In the background appears a seascape at sunset. "Have no fear of meeting Cosmè's individuals and you will be able to admire them !" wrote Roberto Longhi, the first perceptive critic of the Ferrara painter "to admire these bodies hurled in iron and jointed in diamond".

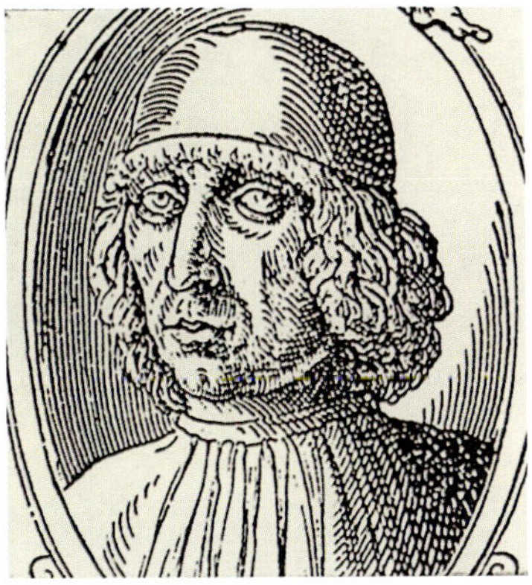

Ercole de' Roberti

(Ferrara c. 1450 – 1496)

After Cosmè Tura and Francesco del Cossa, Ercole is the third of the great 15th century Ferrarese masters, influenced by the first two. Still very young he collaborated on the frescoes in the Hall of Months in Palazzo Schifanoia, precociously revealing his talent in the *Month of September*, where he seems to emulate the fantastic visions of Cosmè, especially in the animated *Vulcan's Forge*. Following Cossa to Bologna, he collaborated with him on the *San Lazzaro Altarpiece*, destroyed in Berlin during World War II. For the *Griffoni Polyptych* in San Petronio he painted the predella with the *Miracles of San Vincenzo Ferrer*, displaying all his originality and imagination. In the grandiose *Santa Maria in Porto Altarpiece* (1481, Milan, Brera) he approached the modes of Antonello da Messina and Giovanni Bellini. Despite his early death, he left many works now dispersed throughout the world.

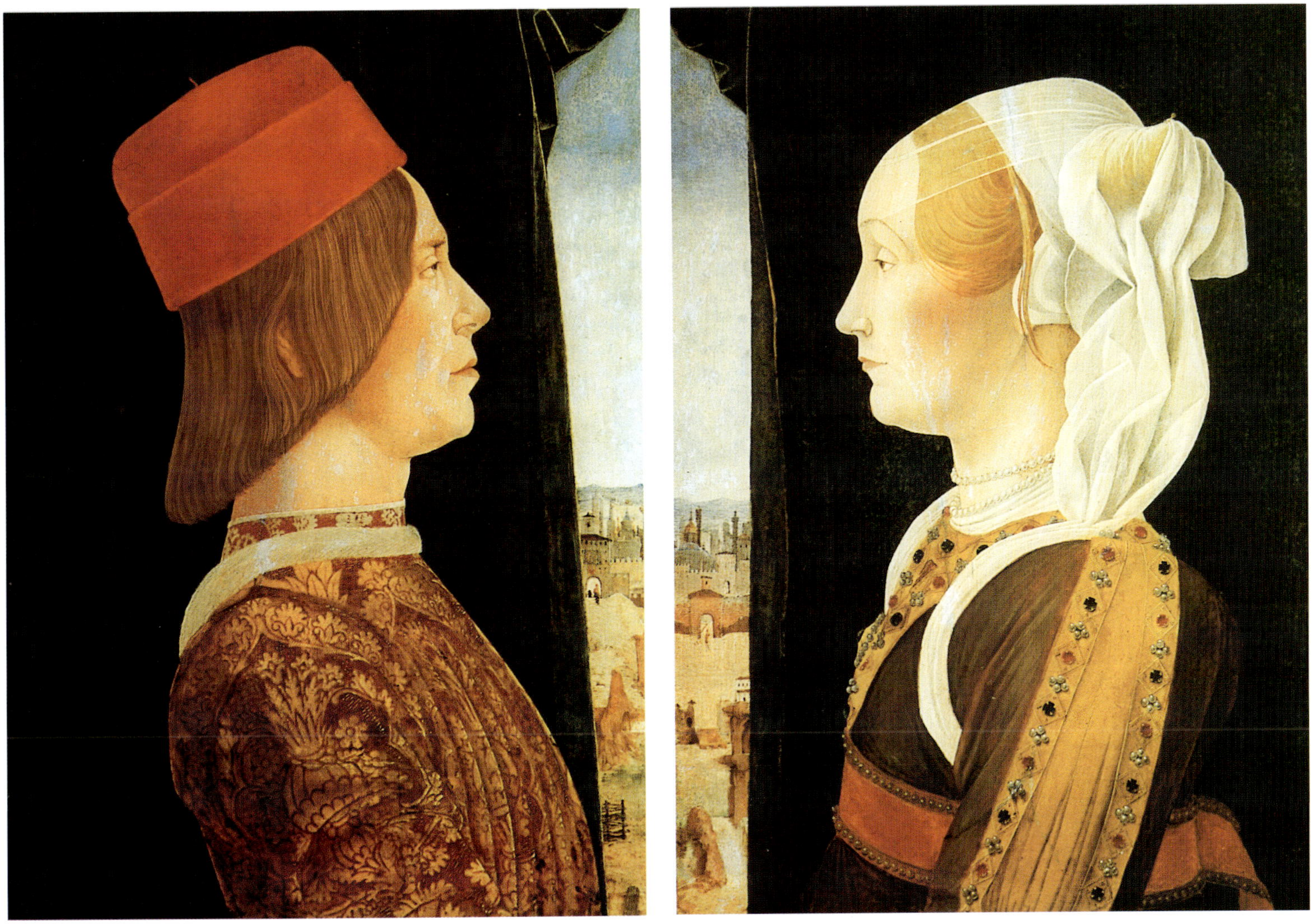

Giorgio Vasari, *Portrait of Ercole Ferrarese*, from the *Lives*, Florence, Giunti, 1568.

Ercole de' Roberti
Portrait of Giovanni II Bentivoglio and Ginevra Sforza
c. 1475
panel
Washington, National Gallery.

This double portrait depicts Giovanni II Bentivoglio and his wife Ginevra, the sister of Battista Sforza, wife of Federico da Montefeltro. It may be that the couple had seen the diptych of the Duke and Duchess painted by Piero della Francesca slightly earlier (Florence, Uffizi). The Ferrarese master was inspired by this prototype as model for the two idealized, commemorative profiles, abandoning it however in the composition of the background, where a landscape with a distant city on the horizon is revealed through the expedient of a half-open curtain.

Carlo Crivelli

(Venice c. 1430 – Fabriano c. 1495)

Admired by the English Pre-Raphaelites for his technical virtuosity, enthusiastically collected abroad, perhaps more for the curious details than for his particular features of totally unique artist in the panorama of the mature 15th century, Crivelli has recently been the subject of attentive critical review. After training in the school of the Venetian Vivarini and then at Padua, he left Venice for Zara in 1459 under the threat of a penal sentence for living with a seaman's wife whom he kept secluded, Crivelli moved in 1468 to the Marches, along the routes frequented at the time by slave merchants and Albanians. Here he was to remain until his death, finding good possibilities for work through wealthy families and ecclesiastical commissions. In Ascoli in 1473, now a successful artist, he painted one of his most famous works, the splendid, opulent *Polyptych* for the Duomo.

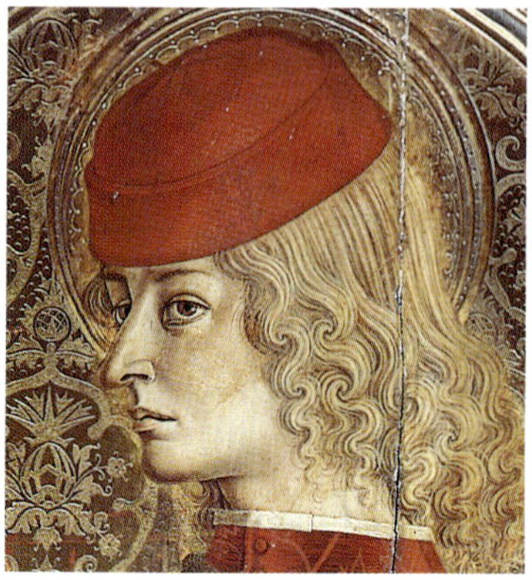

Carlo Crivelli, *St George*, detail of the *Ascoli Polyptych*, 1473. Ascoli, Duomo.

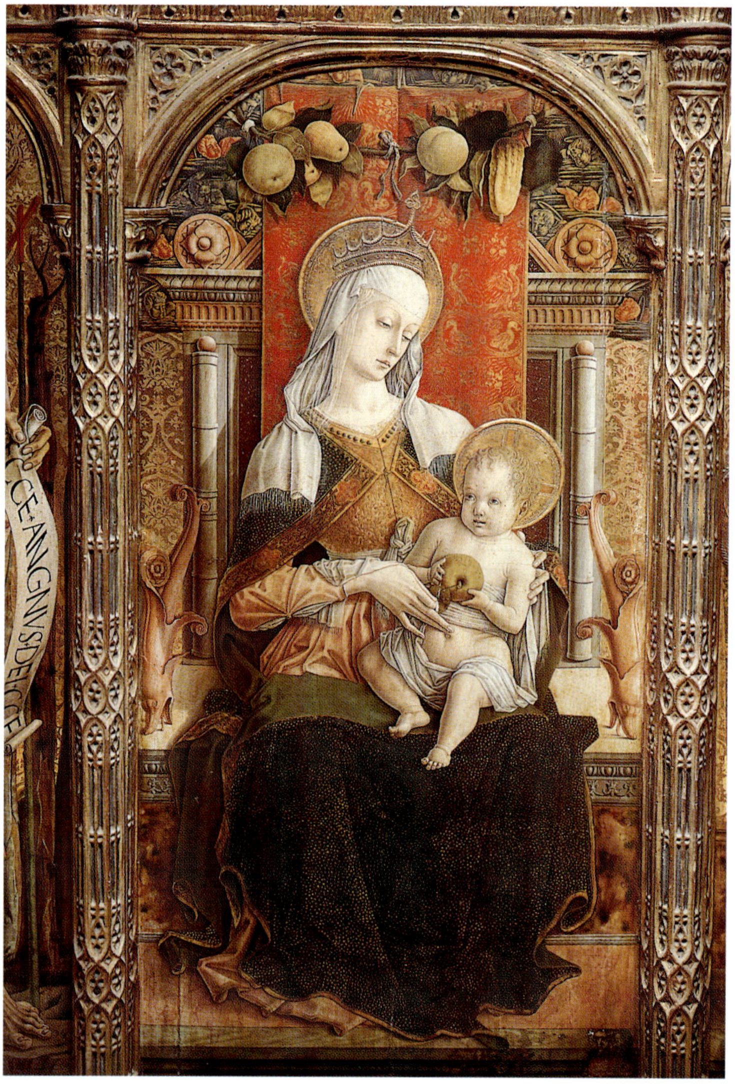

Carlo Crivelli
Madonna with Child
signed, 1473
panel, detail of the *Ascoli Polyptych*
Ascoli, Duomo.

At the center of the polyptych sits the Virgin with Child, her throne encrusted with precious marble and porphyry, the arms shaped like two fantastic dolphins. Above is a garland of fruit, whose brilliant yellows and greens stand out against the red of damask fabric. A striking figure among the saints is the blond, dandy-like St George wearing a red cap and dressed in the latest fashion.

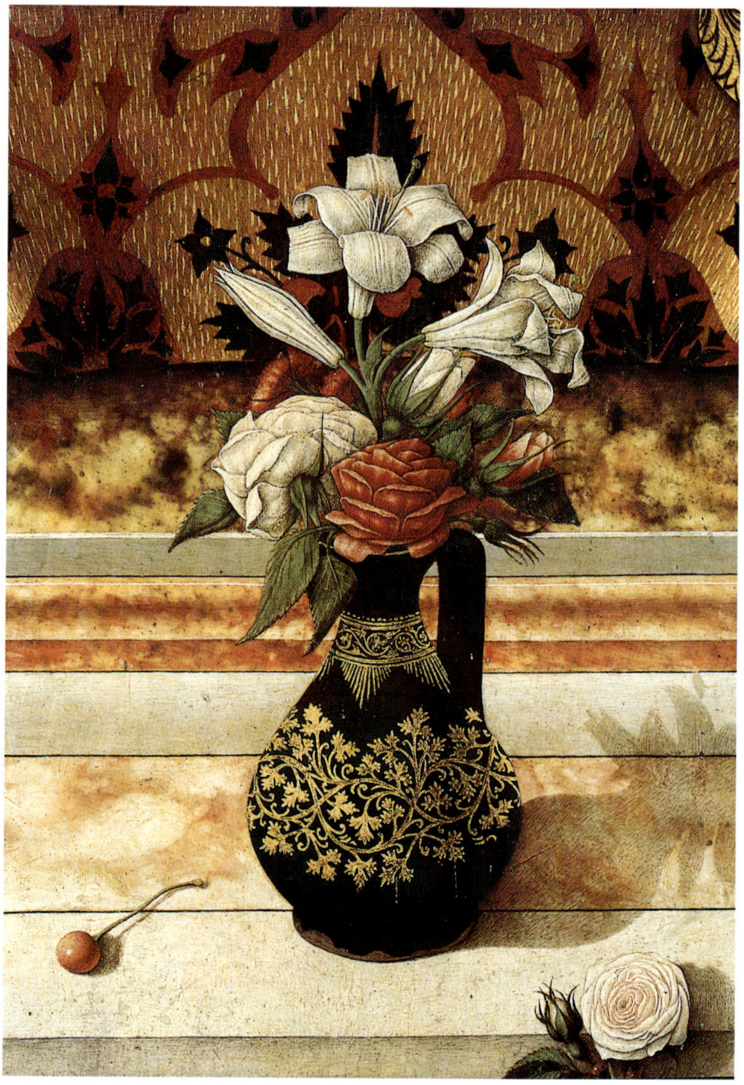

Carlo Crivelli
Vase with Flowers
signed, c. 1490
panel, detail of the *Madonna of the Candle*
Milan, Pinacoteca di Brera.

A splendid still life rests at the foot of the variegated marble throne on which the Virgin sits. The lilies and roses are typical Marian symbols of purity.

Vincenzo Foppa

(Orzinuovi, Brescia, 1427/30 – Brescia 1515/16)

An outstanding personality in the panorama of 15th century Lombard painting is the Brescian Foppa, a delicate, sensitive artist who, starting from the same Paduan bases as the youthful Mantegna, independently re-elaborated a style of his own distinguished by a skillful modulation of light, misty distances, and a sweetness that is never cloying. His first documented work is the Bergamo *Crucifixion*, which he signed *Vincencius Brixiensis* and dated 1456, month of April. His youthful works include the *Madonna of the Angels* in the Berenson Collection (Settignano). From 1458 Foppa lived in Pavia. From here he journeyed to Genoa and Milan, where in about 1468 he frescoed the Portinari Chapel in Sant'Eustorgio. Returning to his native city in 1490, he was granted a pension in return for teaching young artists.

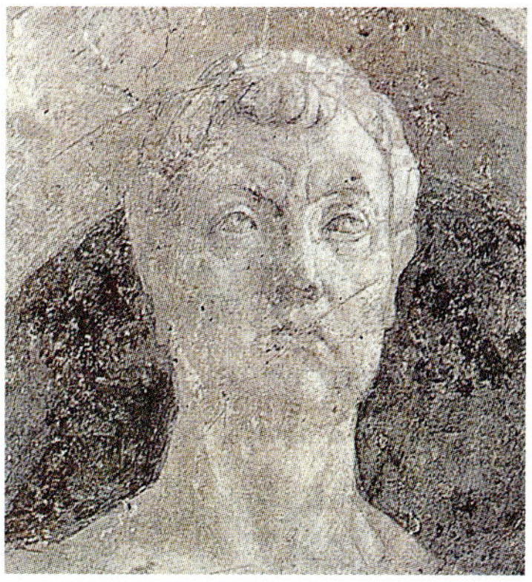

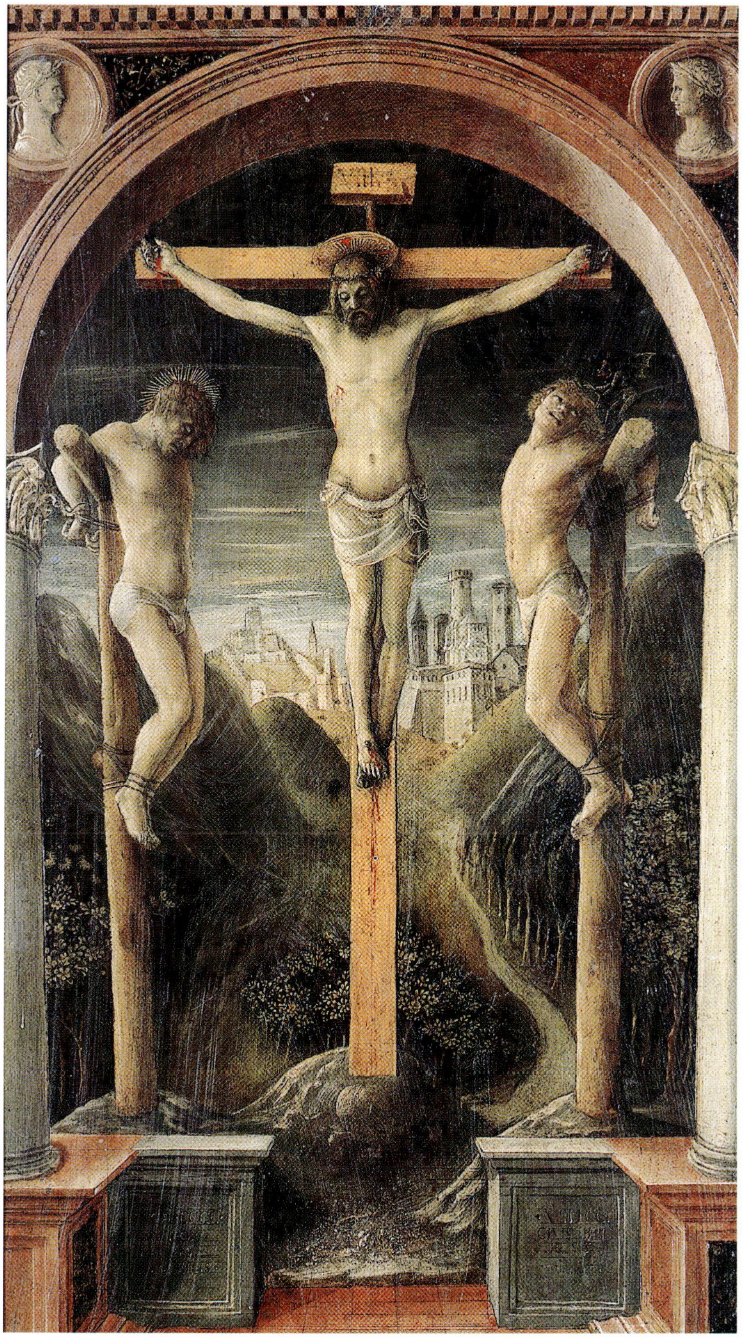

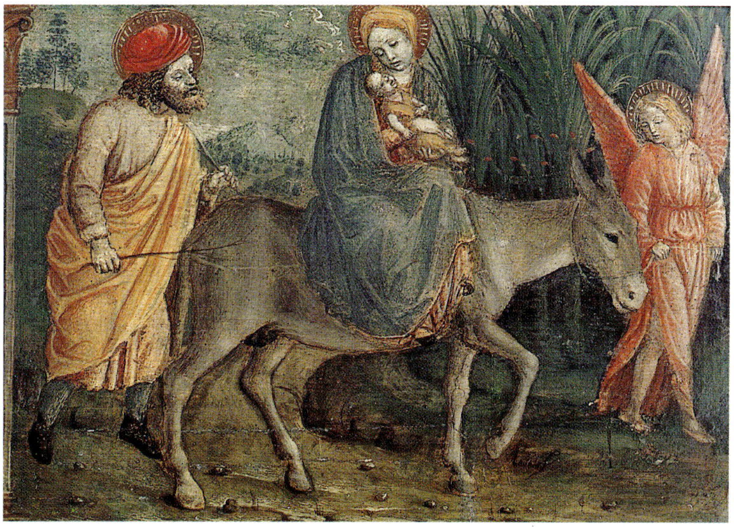

Vincenzo Foppa
Crucifixion
signed and dated 1456
panel
Bergamo, Accademia Carrara.

The three crucifixes are framed by a arch of evident classical style, not unlike the architecture of Mantegna, with two profiles in the upper medallions inspired by antiquity. But the drama of the event is tempered by the beautiful, serene landscape, where the tree-lined country road that guides the eye to the distant towers seems almost the setting for a fairy tale.

Vincenzo Foppa
Flight into Egypt
1476
panel, detail of the predella of the *Brera Polyptych*,
Milan, Pinacoteca di Brera.

Foppa's grace and delicacy appear at their finest in the *Brera Polyptych*, from the Church of the Grazie in Bergamo. Here the quiet gestures and looks of Joseph, Mary and the Angel all seem focused on protecting the newborn child from the fatigue of traveling.

Vincenzo Foppa,
Male Figure within a Medallion, detail, 1468.
Milan, Sant'Eustorgio, Portinari Chapel.

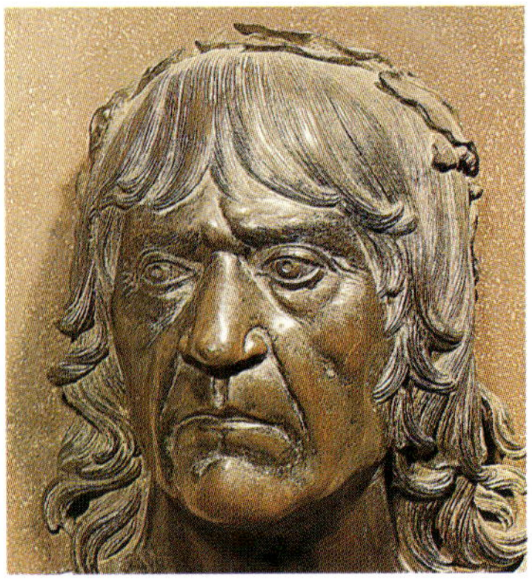

Andrea Mantegna

(Isola di Carturo, Padua, 1431 – Mantua 1506)

When in about 1470 Raphael's father Giovanni Santi listed the finest artists of the times at the court of Urbino, he placed Mantegna before Leonardo, confirming the great fame accorded this artist in his lifetime. Apprenticed to the shop of Francesco Squarcione in Padua, filled with antiquities, in 1448 he frescoed the Ovetari Chapel in Padua (destroyed during the war), where his mastery of perspective was already striking. A genial innovator of perspective foreshortening, which was to be determinant for Correggio, Mantegna revived antiquity in the heroic sense: his allegories, unlike those of other artists who modernized their compositions, were set in the past.

Gianmarco Cavalli, *Portrait of Andrea Mantegna in Bronze,* detail, c. 1480. Mantua, Sant'Andrea.

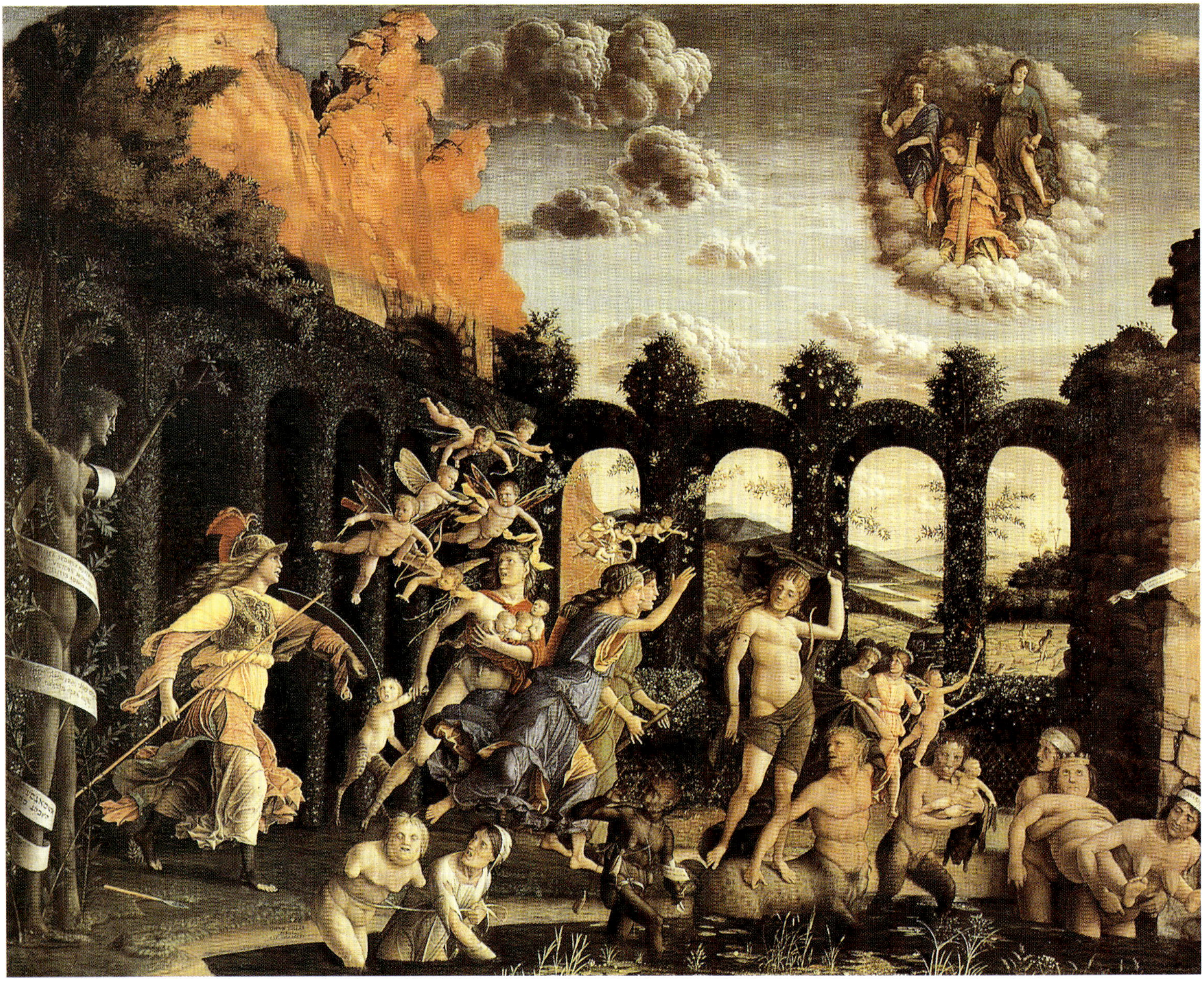

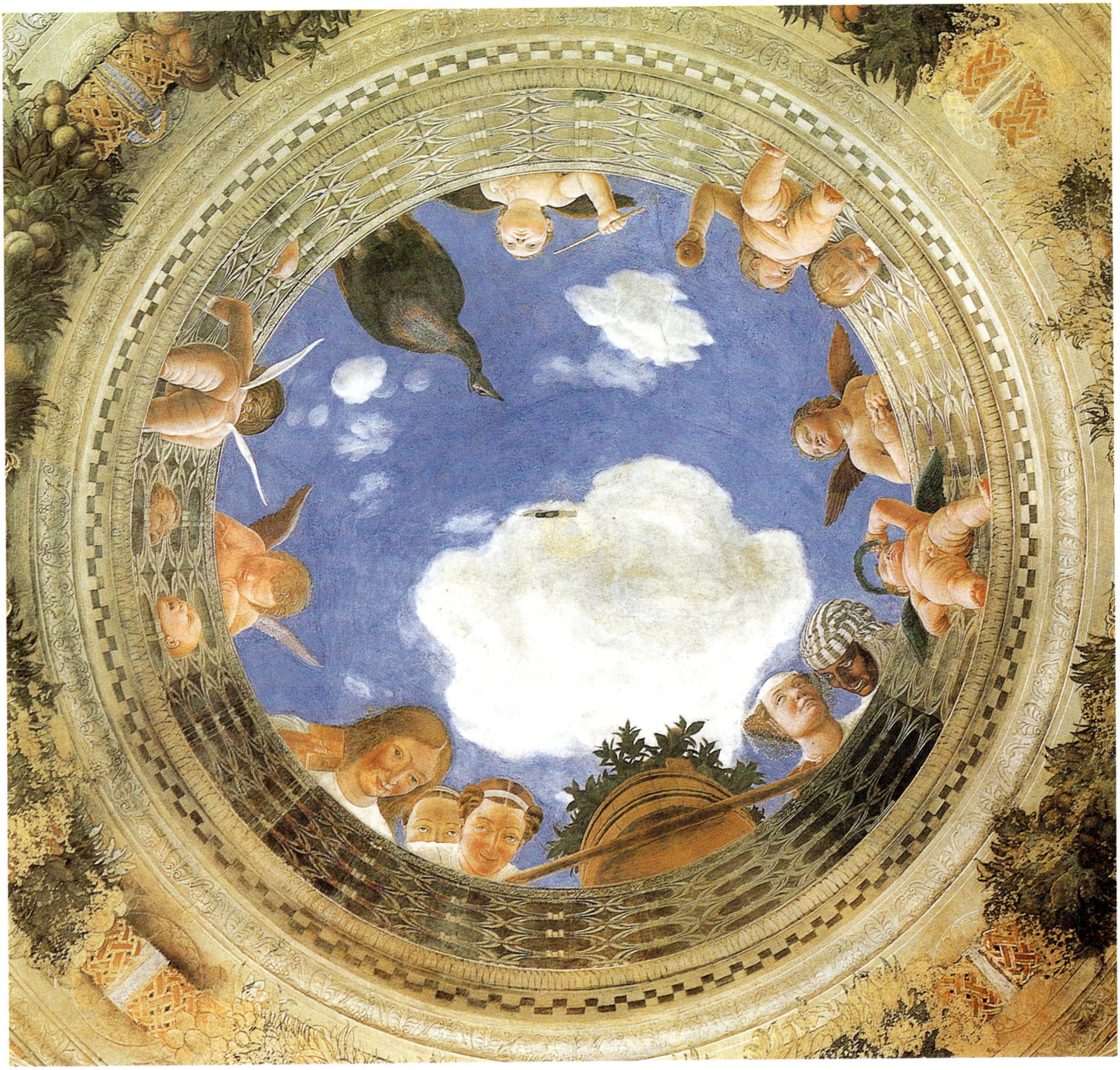

Andrea Mantegna
Pallas Drives the Vices from the Garden of Virtues
c. 1499-1502
canvas
Paris, Louvre.

The second of two paintings (the other is the *Parnassus*, also in the Louvre) for Isabella d'Este's Studiolo in the San Giorgio Castle illustrates with a wealth of figures a *fabula antica*, whose symbology is explained in writing on scrolls (the first appears at the left, wound around a Virtue transformed into a laurel tree). The four cardinal Virtues have abandoned the garden when Minerva bursts in threatening the Vices who have occupied it. They flee into a swamp, led by Avarice, Ingratitude and Ignorance.

Andrea Mantegna
Oculus with Cherubs and Ladies Looking Down
1465-74
fresco, detail of the oculus in the ceiling
Mantua, Palazzo Ducale, The Bridal Chamber.

Starting in 1460 Mantegna was at the Mantuan court of Ludovico Gonzaga, whose archaeological and antiquarian interests he shared. For him he frescoed the Bridal Chamber, celebrating the numerous Gonzaga family with various symbolic allusions and many portraits of contemporaries.

Painted as if it were really an opening in the ceiling, the oculus represents the first bold experiment by an Italian artist in foreshortened illusionist perspective viewed from below.

Andrea Mantegna
San Zeno Altarpiece
1456-59
panel, detail
Verona, San Zeno.

It was in Padua that Mantegna painted for the protonotary Gregorio Correr, Abbot of San Zeno, the great altarpiece for the choir of the Verona church. The work engaged him at length, and in the meantime Lodovico Gonzaga was sending numerous missives summoning him to the Mantuan court. The frame, strictly functional to the painting, was also designed by Mantegna. Its four half-columns at the front only apparently divide the composition like a traditional triptych. In reality they function as the architectural supports of a loggia, opening out into the magnificent unitary setting of the sacred scene. This is the first, majestic example of this kind in the figurative panorama of Northern Italian art.

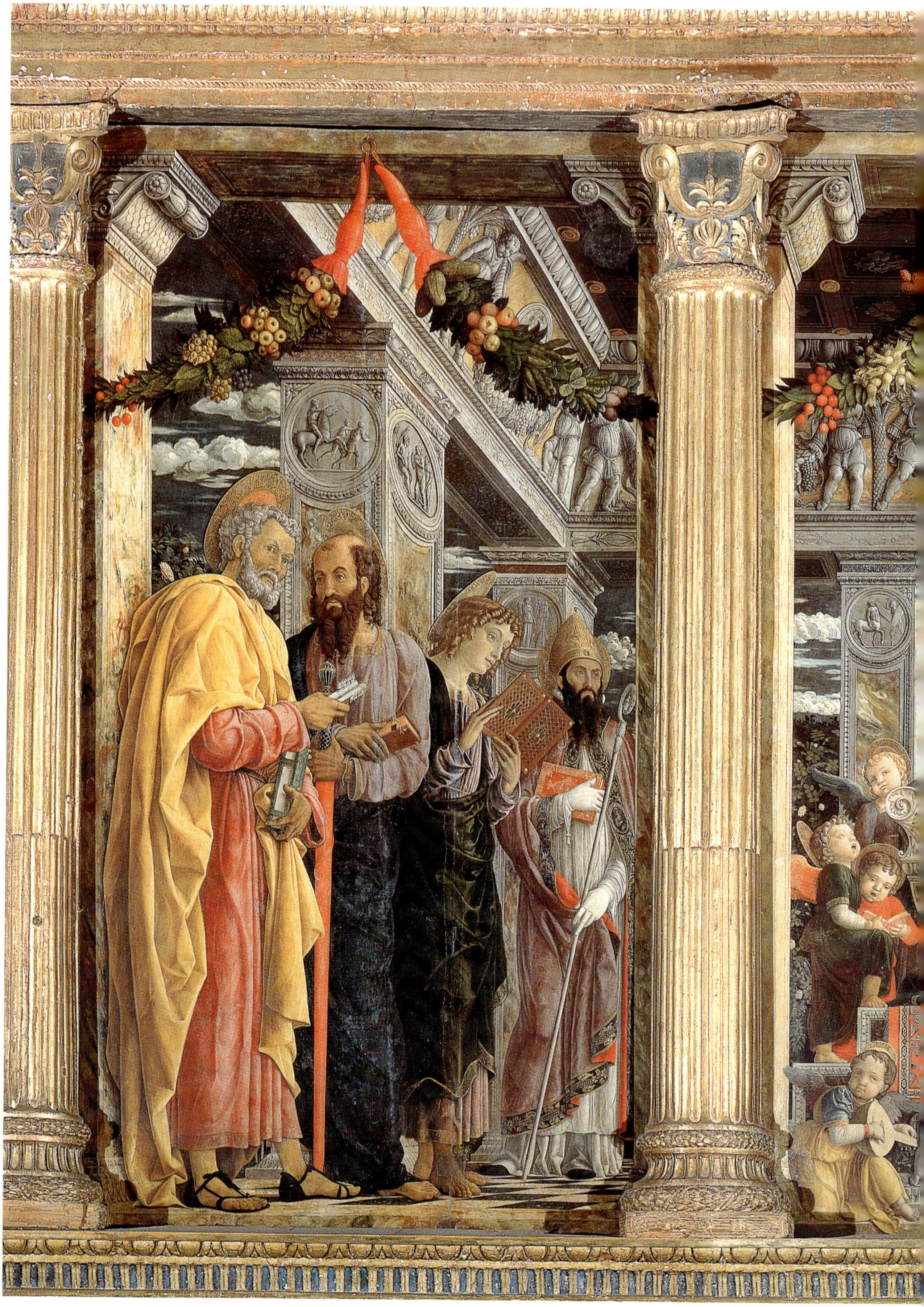

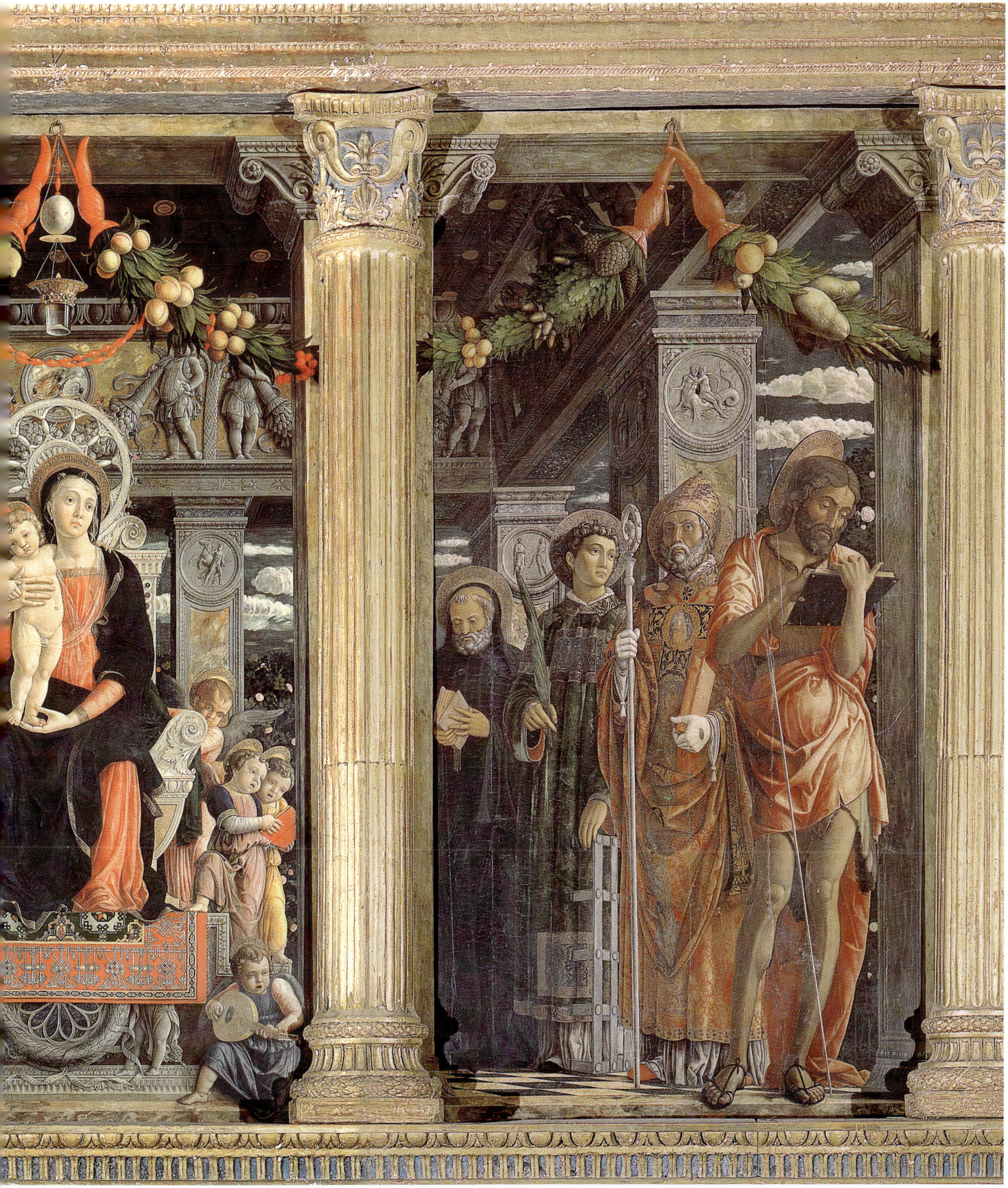

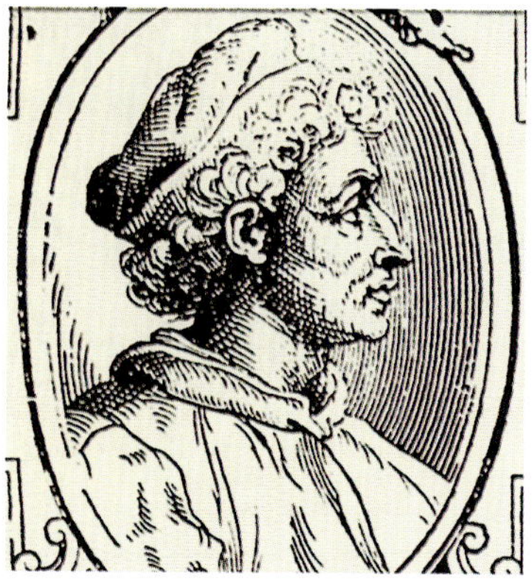

Giorgio Vasari, *Portrait of Antonello da Messina*, from the *Lives*, Florence, Giunti, 1568.

Antonello da Messina

(Messina c. 1430 – 1479)

An artist apparently at a disadvantage due to having been born in a relatively isolated area far from the great Italian art centers of the 15th century, Antonello was in reality highly stimulated by the vivacious, international atmosphere of Naples at mid-century. It is here that he probably encountered Flemish art, of which the Neapolitan Bartolomeo Facio was also a passionate admirer. Excelling also at portraiture, Antonello made a crucially important journey to Venice in about 1475, from where he went on to Milan. His *San Cassiano Altarpiece* (fragments in Vienna, Kunsthistorisches Museum) was to be a fundamental reference point for Veneto artists.

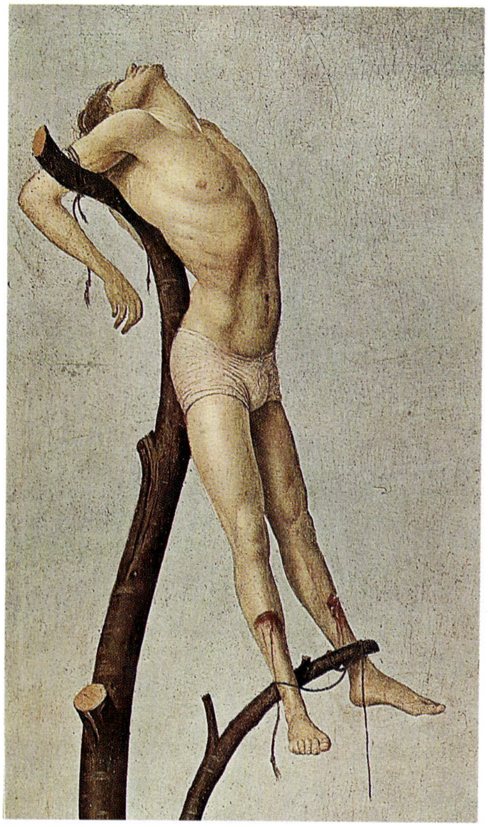

Antonello da Messina
Crucifixion
c. 1475-76
panel, detail
Antwerp, Musée des Beaux Arts.

A body tensely contracted in the last moment of suffering before death is rendered even more dramatic by the harsh, bare tree trunk.

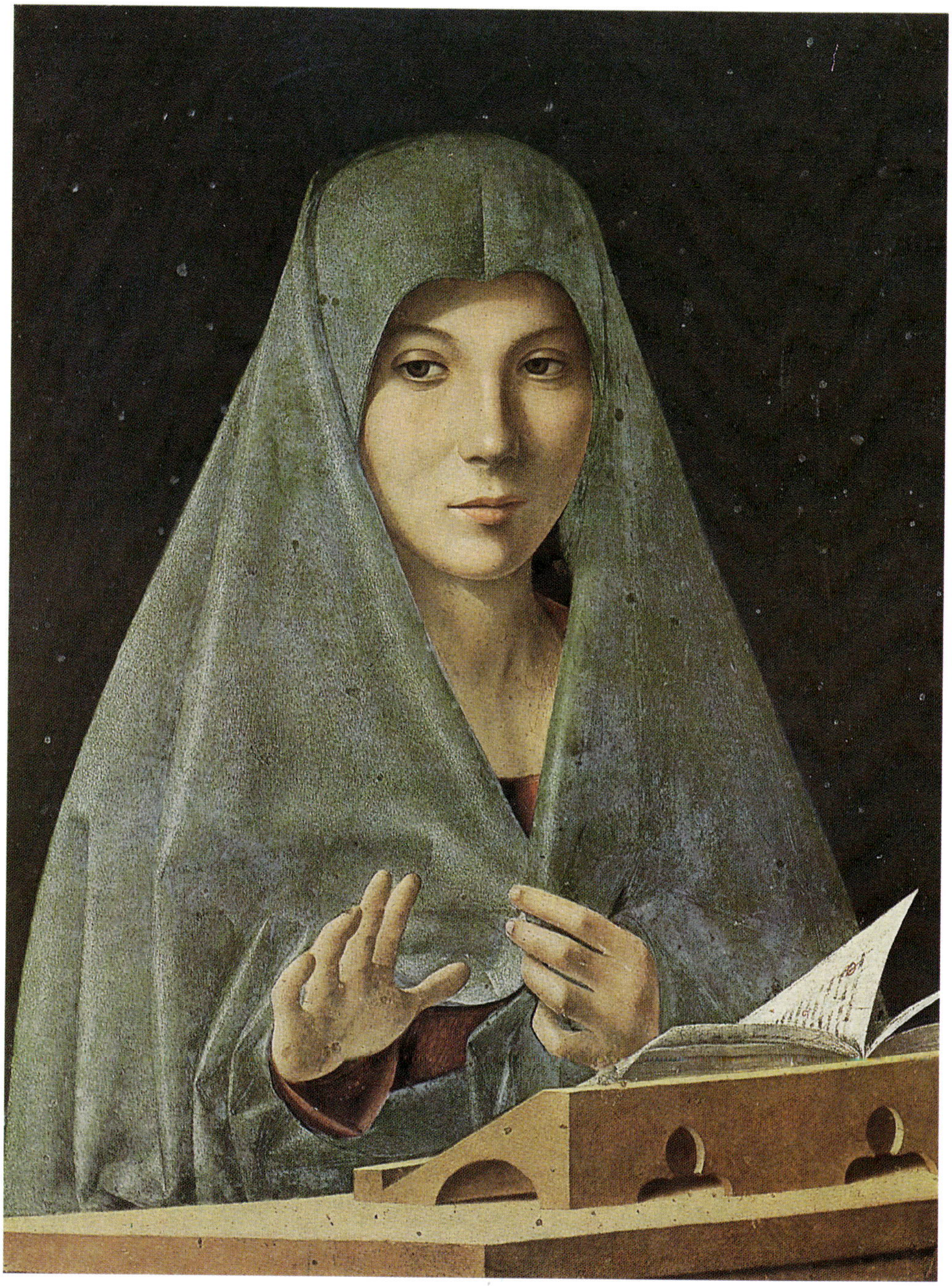

Antonello da Messina
Our Lady of the Annunciation
1474
panel
Palermo, Galleria Nazionale della Sicilia.

The striking innovation of the most singular and fascinating 15th century representation of the Madonna lies all in that hand stretched out toward the spectator.

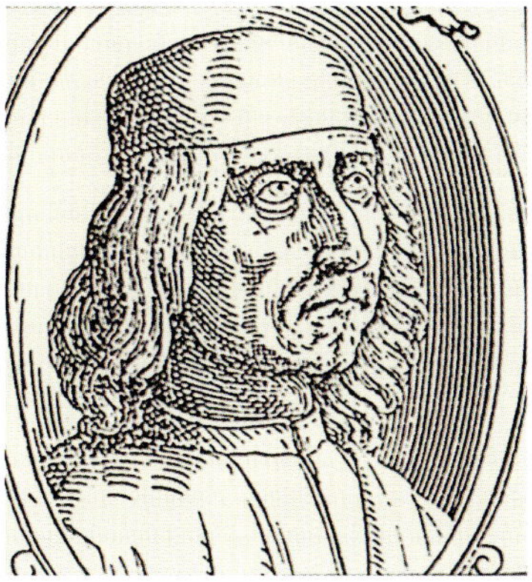

Giovanni Bellini
(Venice 1430 – 1516)

Bellini's long career was to form the backbone of Venetian Renaissance painting. The brother of Gentile (c. 1429-1507), also a painter, he learned the first rudiments from his father Jacopo, head of a prolific workshop. Giovanni was the first of the Venetians to make color and light the atmospheric essence of painting, which was to become distinctive of the Venetian school, traditionally opposed to that of Tuscany and Central Italy, based on linear drawing. Considered by Vasari the greatest Venetian artist of his day, from the 1490s he had a successful shop producing great altarpieces as well as portraits and allegories. His early style was influenced by his brother-in-law Mantegna and by the arrival of Antonello in Venice. From the latter he was inspired to turn from tempera to oil and toward a softer sfumato. He was to be innovative to the end, as proven by the *San Zaccaria Altarpiece* (1505).

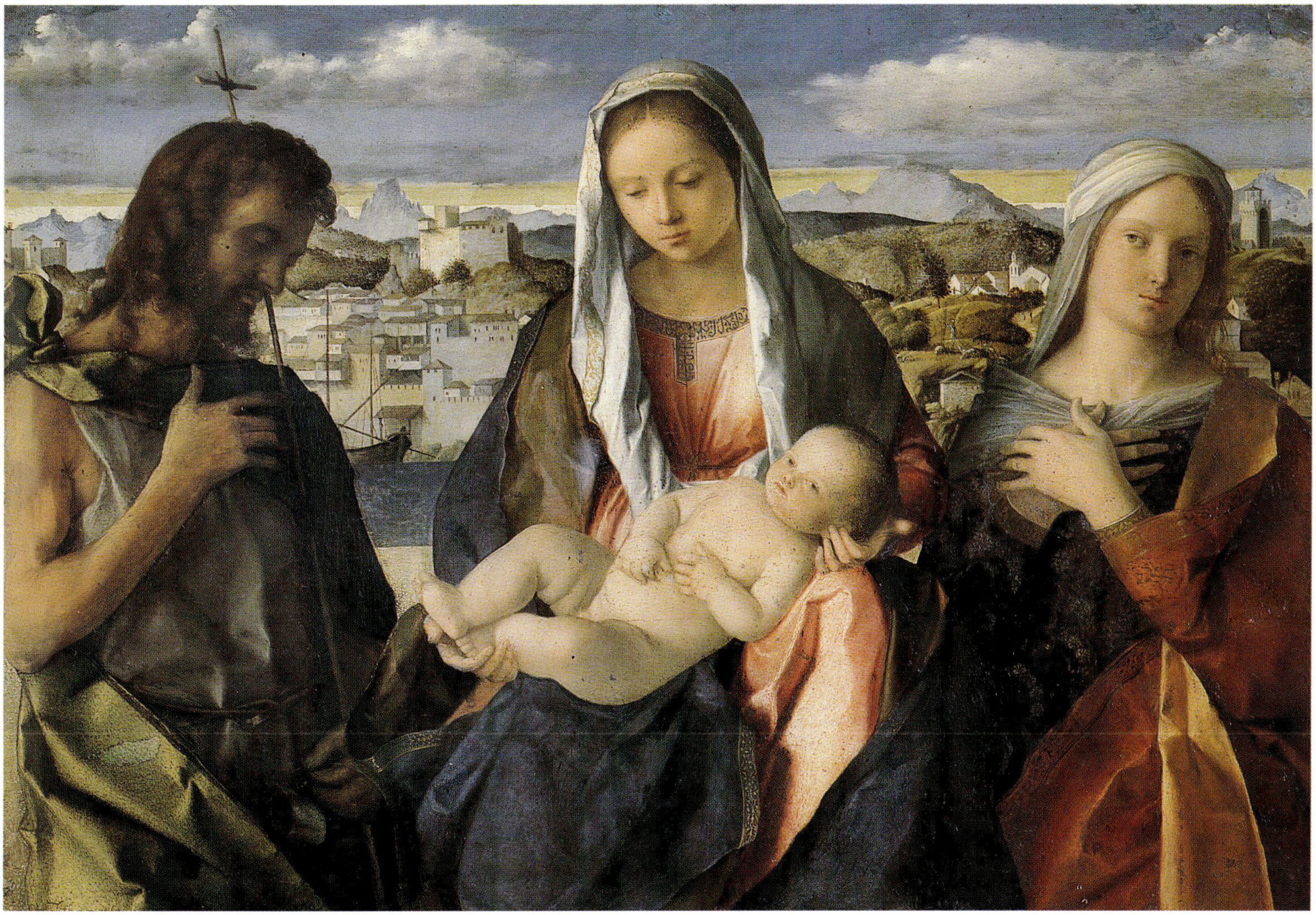

Giorgio Vasari, *Portrait of Giovanni Bellini*, from the *Lives*, Florence, Giunti, 1568.

Giovanni Bellini
The Giovanelli Holy Conversation
signed, c. 1504
panel
Venice, Gallerie dell'Accademia.

This work from the artist's last stage (painted when he was over seventy) demonstrates his enduring vitality and capacity for renewal. A striking background to the three monumental figures is provided by a stupendous landscape with a city overlooking the sea at left and distant mountains painted in bluish, lighter tones, almost as if the painter were applying the indications given by Leonardo in his *Book of Painting*. The painting takes its name from Prince Giovanelli, its last owner.

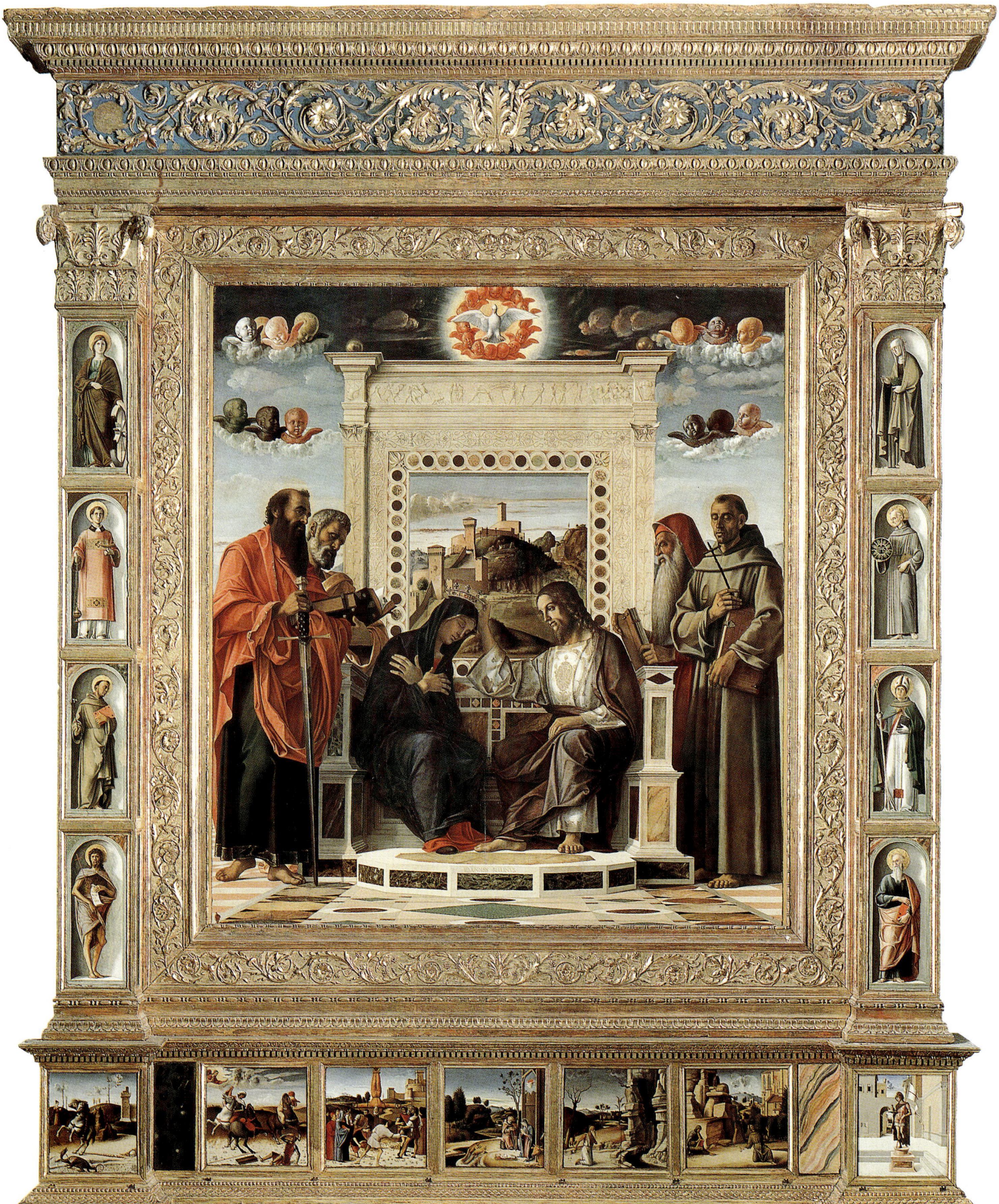

At left:
Giovanni Bellini
Coronation of the Virgin (Pesaro Altarpiece)
signed, c. 1474
panel, reconstruction
Pesaro, Museo Civico.

Highly controversial is the dating of this famous altarpiece, which belongs in any case to the central period of the Venetian master's career. Note that only the central panel and pilasters now in the Pesaro Civic Museum are original, while the predellas are a reconstruction (the authentic ones are now in the Pinacoteca Vaticana). Painted with the oil technique for the high altar of the Church of San Francesco in Pesaro, the work is extraordinarily beautiful. The elaborate frame encloses a painting within a painting, the sacred representation, which in turn, delimited by splendid architecture, frames the landscape in the background, another masterly painting within a painting.

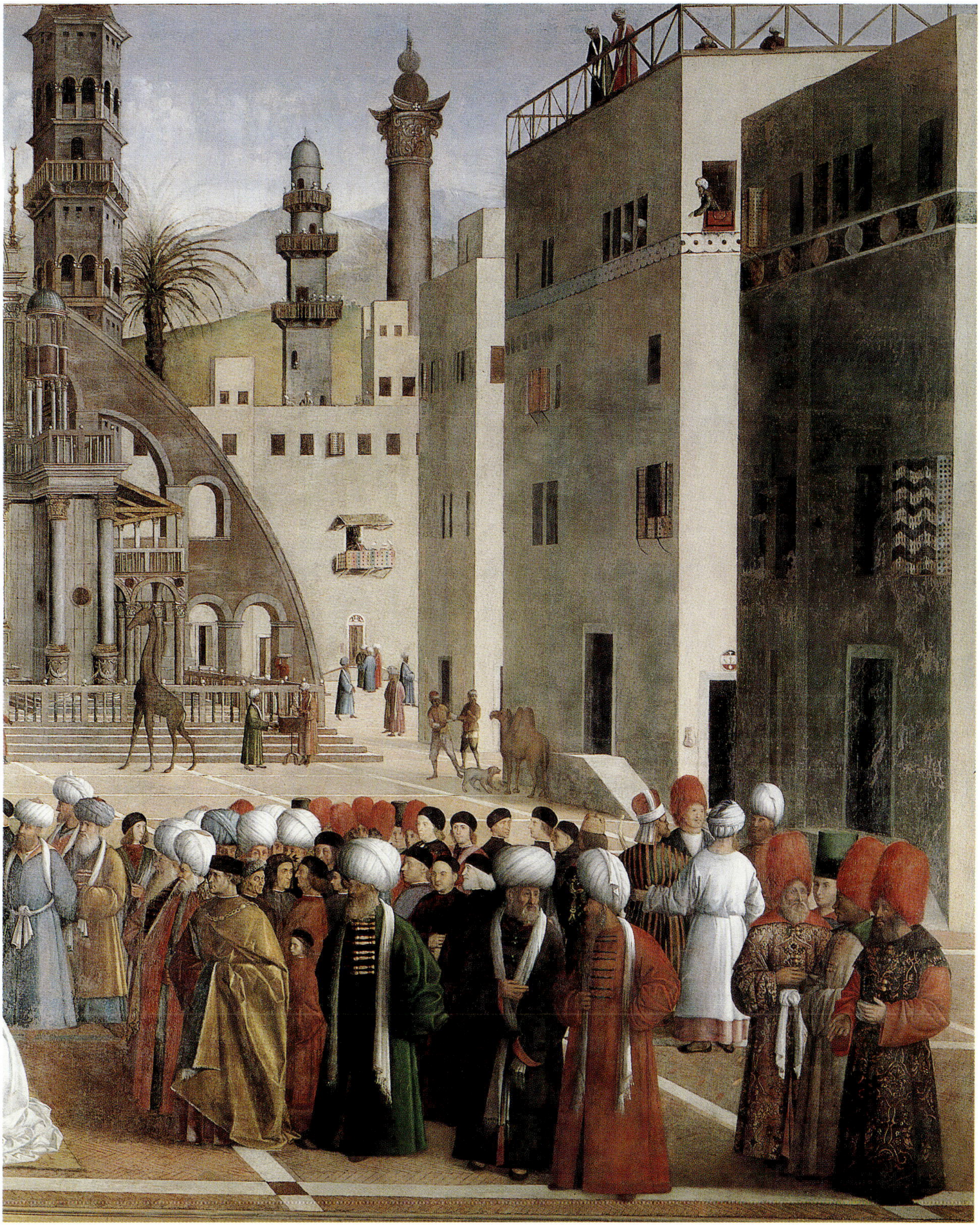

Gentile and Giovanni Bellini
Preaching of St Mark in Alexandria
1507
canvas, detail
Milan, Pinacoteca di Brera.

This great canvas, painted for the Scuola Grande di San Marco in Venice, is the work of both Giovanni (or rather "Zuan" as he was called by the Venetians in documents) and his brother Gentile, of whom it was originally commissioned but who died before completing it. A wealth of exotic details enliven the grandiose theatrical setting.

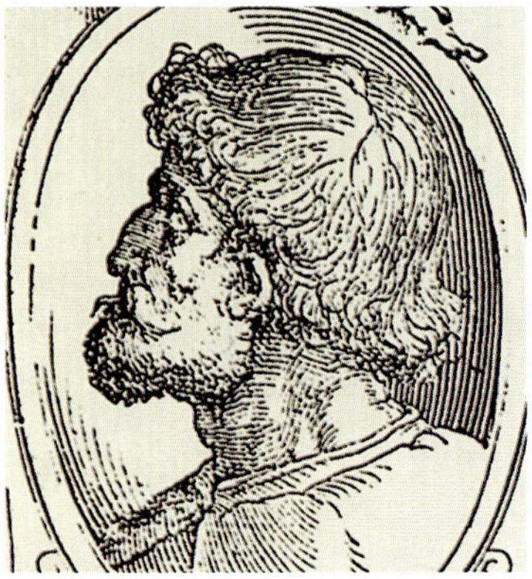

Vittore Carpaccio

(Venice c. 1460 – c. 1525)

The career of "Vetor Scarpaza de la Zudecha", as he was called by the Venetians, unfolded mainly in Venice, where he set up his own shop. He is famed chiefly for his talent as perceptive narrator in four important Venetian cycles, the so-called "teleri": the *Stories of St Orsola* (1490-96) for the brotherhood of the same name; the *Stories of Christ and the Dalmatian Saints* for the Scuola di San Giorgio degli Schiavoni (1502-07); the *Cycle of the Scuola degli Albanesi* (1504); the *Stories of St Stephen* for the Scuola dei Lanieri (1511-20). His magical spirit of observation, which Ruskin was one of the first to admire, is expressed in intense portraits, altarpieces, and profane subjects such as the enigmatic *Young Cavalier* (1510), Madrid, Thyssen Foundation) and the so-called *Courtesans* (Venice, Correr Museum), once united to the *Hunt in the Lagoon* (Malibu, Paul Getty Museum).

Giorgio Vasari, *Portrait of Vittore Scarpaccia,* from the *Lives*, Florence, Giunti, 1568.

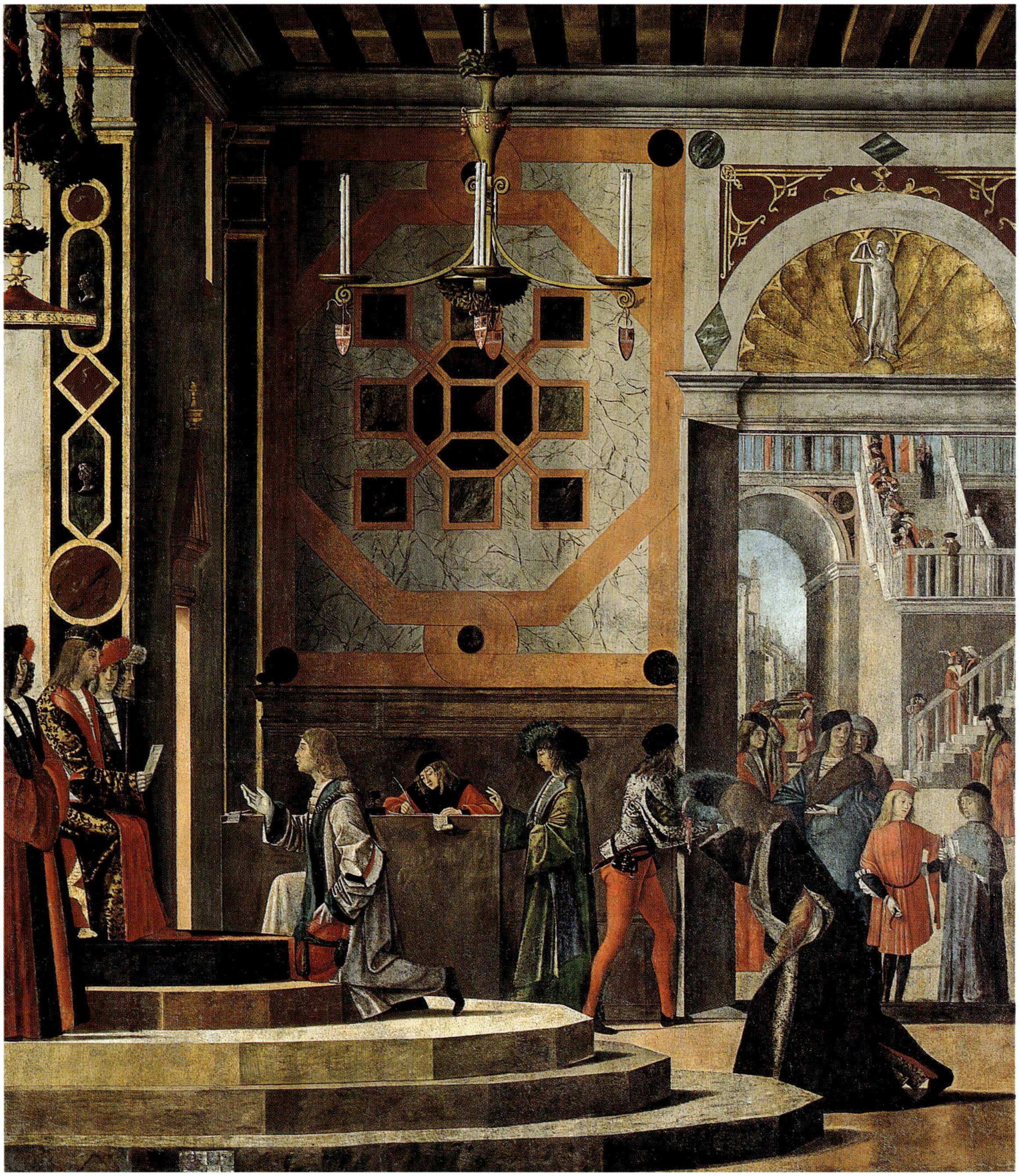

Carpaccio
Departure of the English Emissaries
signed, 1495-96
canvas
Venice, Galleria dell'Accademia.

The traditional narrative tendency of Venetian art, tracing back to the Byzantine mosaics in St Mark's Basilica, reached its culmination in the late 15th century with the *teleri*: vast mural cycles painted on canvas (from the Venetian *telèr*, or canvas). Carpaccio (like the Bellini brothers) evokes an imaginative Venice, swarming with life in sumptuous architectural scenarios. The cycle for the Brotherhood of St Orsola is the first of those painted by him, still very young but already expert in this field, perhaps having collaborated with the older Bellinis. The *Departure* illustrates the outcome of diplomatic negotiations in Brittany for the marriage of the English King's son, Ereus, to Orsola, Princess of Brittany.

Carpaccio
Return of the English Emissaries
signed, c. 1493-95
canvas
Venice, Galleria dell'Accademia.

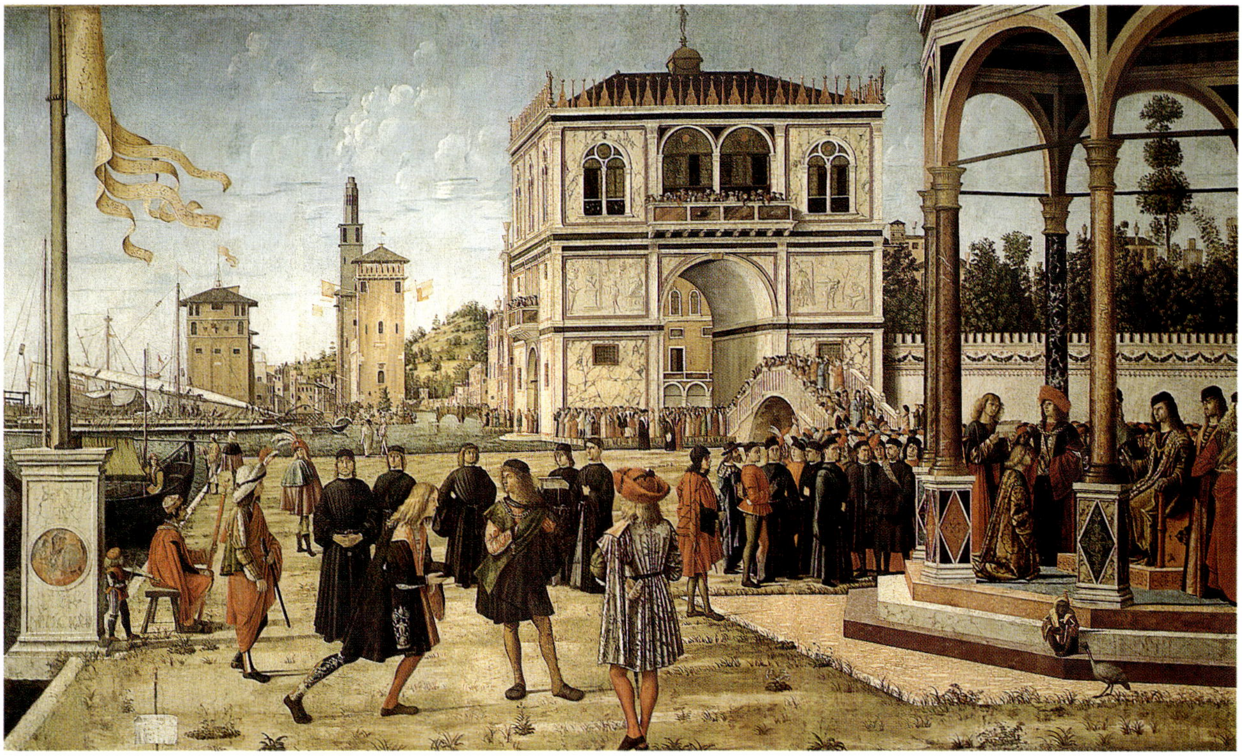

For her heroic devotion the martyr Orsola has always captured the popular fantasy. Requested as bride for the pagan son of the powerful King of England, she asked for three years of time to make a pilgrimage to Rome with her companions. But on the return voyage she disembarked at Cologne with Pope Cyriac and was martyred by King Maurus. Carpaccio, for what reason is unknown, painted over a period of time seven "teleri" without following any sequential order of events (the *Arrival at Cologne*, here illustrated on page 70, is the first of the series, bearing the date 1490 inscribed by Carpaccio himself). The *Return of the English Emissaries* to the court of the King of England is set in a fully Venetian scenario: on the left, accompanied by a page sounding a trumpet, is seated the "scalco", whose role in Venice was that of introducing ambassadors to the Doge.

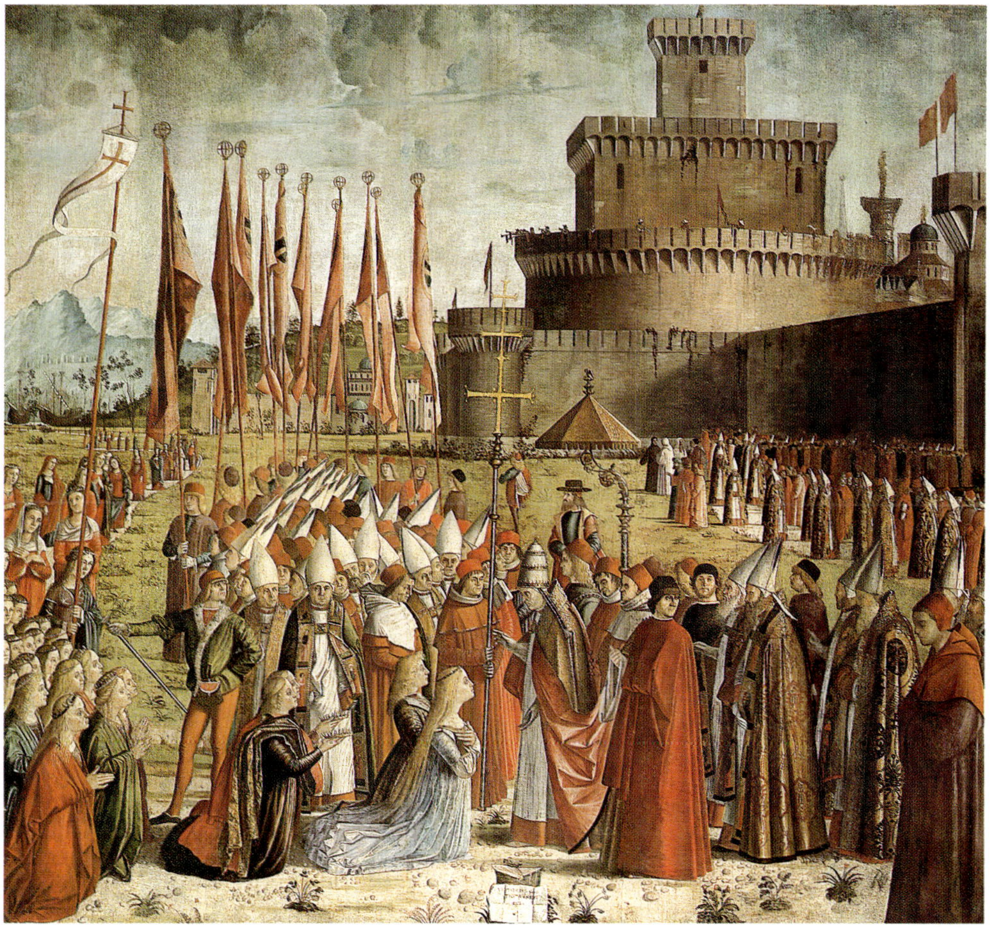

Carpaccio
Meeting of the Pilgrims with the Pope
signed, after 1493
canvas
Venice, Galleria dell'Accademia.

The episode, which takes place against the background of Castel Sant'Angelo, is enriched by contemporary portraits such as that of the Humanist philosopher Ermolao Barbaro who died in Rome in 1493, depicted standing behind the Pope. Invaluable testimony of a typical scene of Roman pilgrimage, the canvas suggests that the Venetian artist may also have journeyed to the great city. As in other "teleri" of the series, the composition is marked by a strong theatrical note.

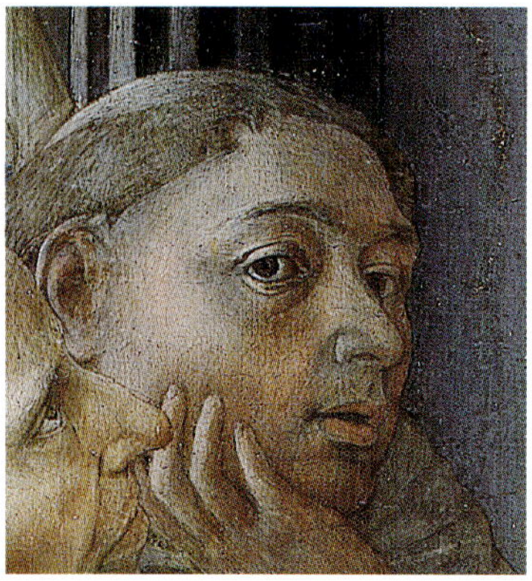

Filippo Lippi

(Florence c. 1406 – Spoleto 1469)

Known for his liaison with Lucrezia Buti, who gave birth to their son Filippino, the artist trained as novice in the Carmine Monastery where he copied Masaccio's frescoes, more interested in them than in studying (running away from the monastery, he was imprisoned by the Moors, whom he enchanted with his portraits). Cosimo il Vecchio, his patron, pardoned his transgression with this justification: "Great minds are heavenly forms and not dray-horses for hire". These anecdotes have appealed to romantic authors, but Filippo's role in the transition of art to the mature Renaissance stage is complex and important. Among the first to be influenced by Flemish painting (as shown by the youthful *Madonna of Corneto Tarquinia*, Rome, Palazzo Venezia Museum), he created novel, inventive compositions in imposing altarpieces, many painted for the Medicis. He also worked in Prato and Spoleto, where he died.

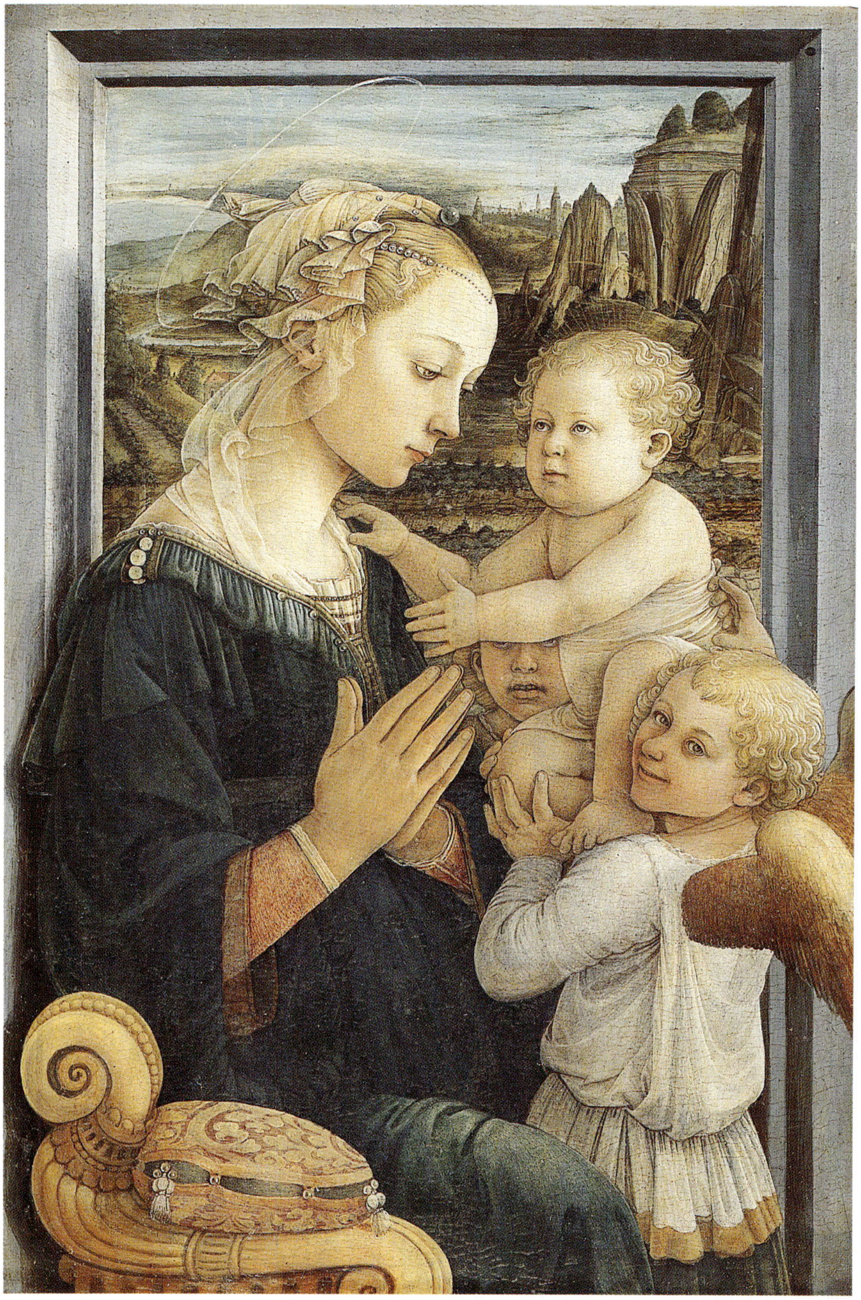

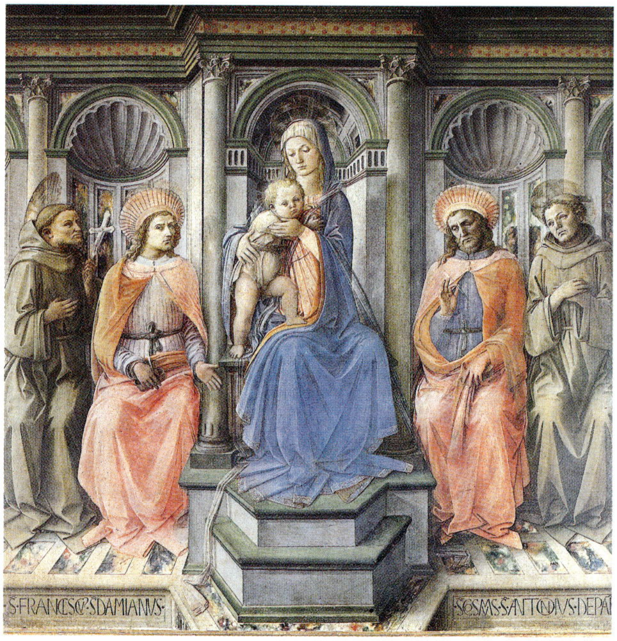

Filippo Lippi
Madonna with Child and Two Angels
c. 1465
panel
Florence, Uffizi Gallery.

The profile of the Madonna, her hair entwined with precious pearls, may be that of Lucrezia Buti, the nun beloved by the painter. The group stands out from the frame with a delicacy reminiscent of the classical-style reliefs of Donatello and Luca della Robbia (here the angel in the foreground derives from the cherub on an ancient sarcophagus). The background, a painting-within-a-painting, anticipates the expansive landscapes of Leonardo.

Filippo Lippi
The Novitiate Altarpiece
c. 1445
panel
Florence, Uffizi Gallery.

The classic-style altarpiece, painted at the request of Cosimo il Vecchio for the Novitiate Chapel in Santa Croce, harmonizes with Michelozzi's architecture in which it was to be placed. Filippo enlivens the composition with multi-colored false marble and the red Medici emblems on the top of the frieze.

Above:
Filippo Lippi, *Self-portrait*, detail of the *Coronation of the Virgin*, c. 1439-47. Florence, Uffizi Gallery.

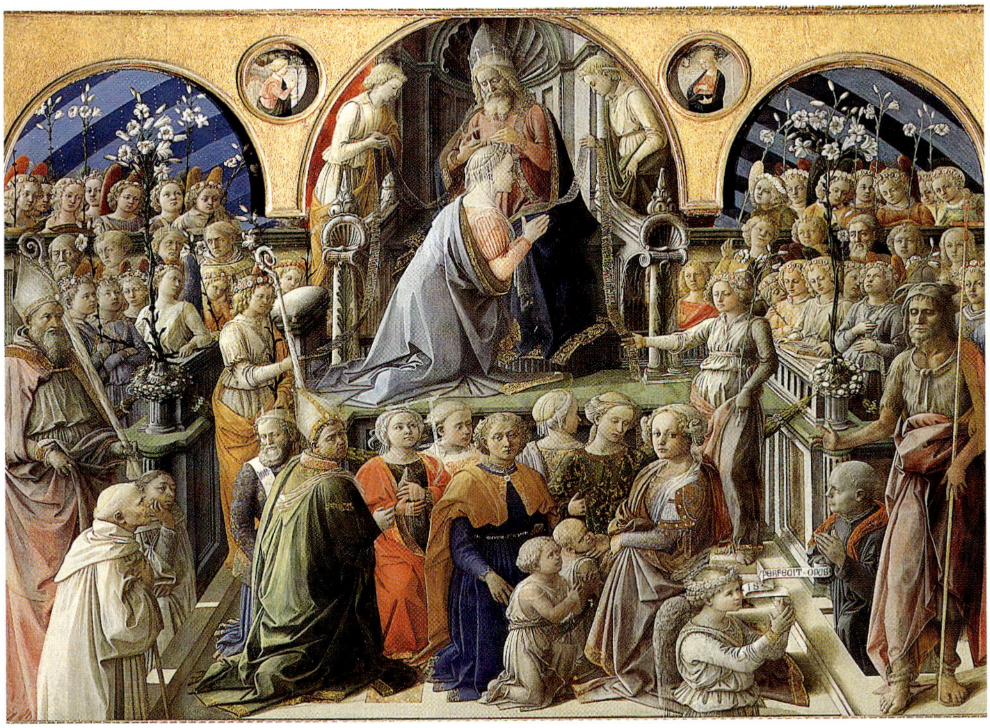

Filippo Lippi and Assistance
Coronation of the Virgin
signed, c. 1439-47
panel, entire and details,
Florence, Uffizi Gallery.

A number of "dipintori" and at least two skilled carpenters are documented as having participated in this work. The original frame has been dispersed and a part of the predella is in the Berlin Museums. In 1446 the altarpiece was moved from the painter's home to the Sant'Apollonia Monastery, where the blue pigment used to complete it was kept. A year later it finally reached the high altar of Sant'Ambrogio. Admiring awe must have been aroused by the crowded scene of Mary's coronation upon her arrival in heaven, perhaps alluded to by the intense blue and azure diagonal stripes. Standing at the far left is St Ambrose; kneeling below him is a self-portrait of the monk, gazing idly at the spectator. In the center is St Eustachius with his two children and his wife Theophista; at right the donor, Prior Francesco Maringhi, beside the words "Is perfecit opus".

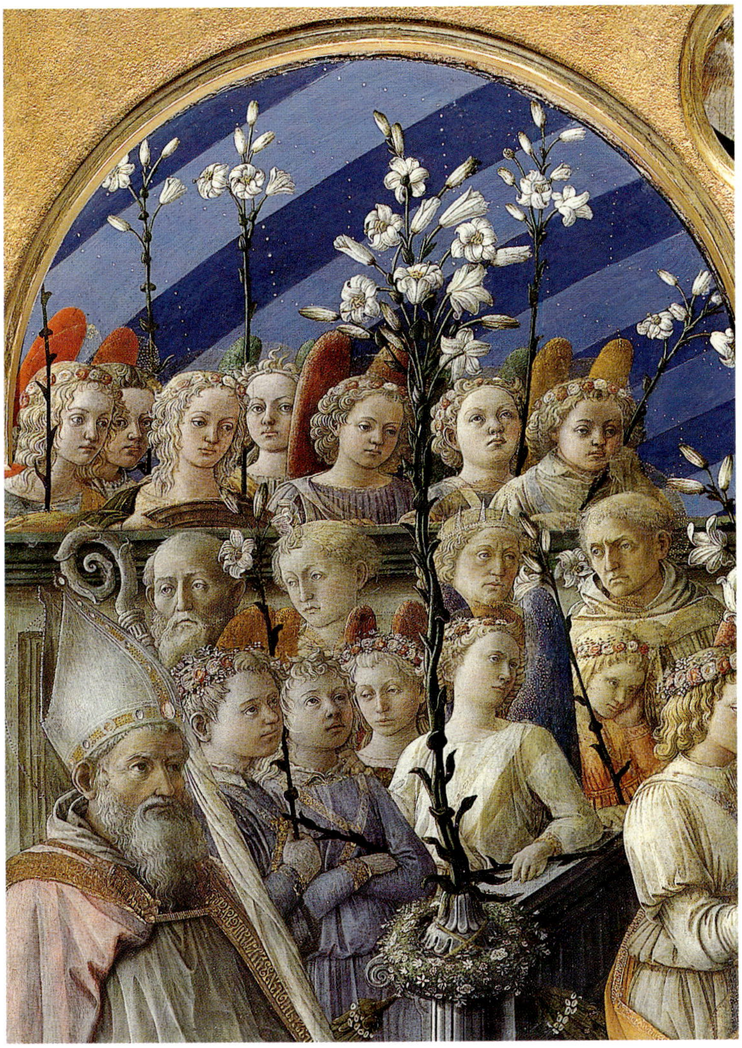

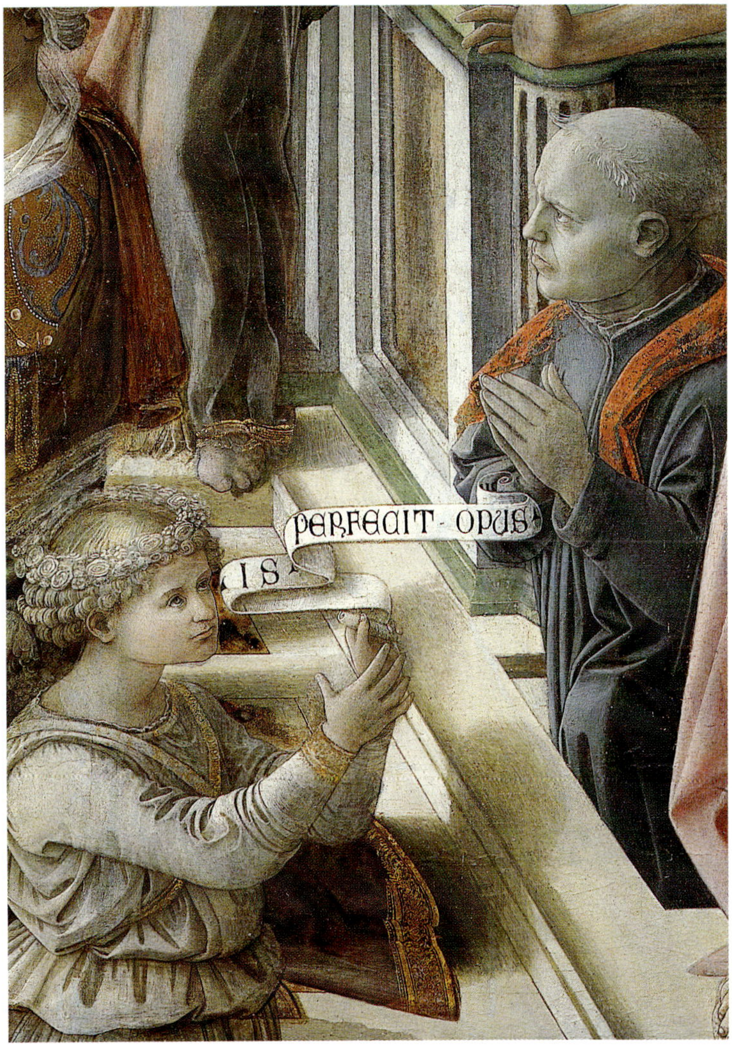

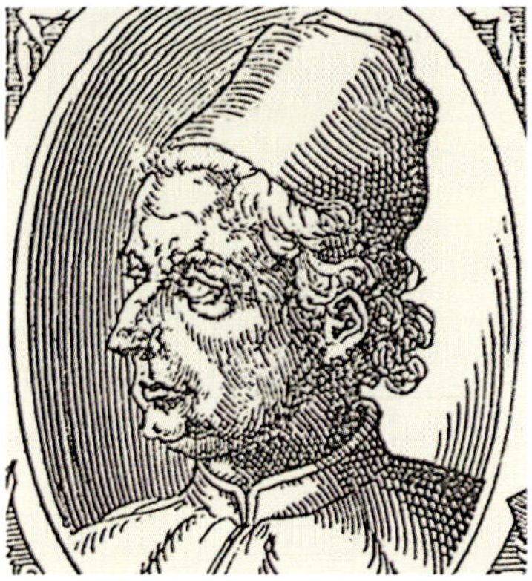

Antonio and Piero del Pollaiolo

(Antonio Benci, Florence c. 1435 – Rome 1498; Piero Benci, Florence c. 1441 – Rome 1496)

In the Florence of the late 15th century the two brothers, sons of a poultry vendor (the origin of their pseudonym), ran a prolific, versatile shop, expert in every artistic technique. In addition to paintings it produced drawings for other painters, sculptors and goldsmiths, as reported by Benvenuto Cellini, and created jewels, fabrics, embroidery, goldwork, bronzes, terracottas and engravings. The brothers' mastery of the use of such varied materials procured them public commissions not only in Florence – where among other things Piero painted the *Virtues* for the Merchants' Guild (1469, Uffizi) and Antonio, a superb goldsmith, executed works in silver for the Opera del Duomo and embroidery patterns for the Baptistery vestments – but also in Rome, where they both collaborated on the Papal tombs of Sixtus IV and Innocent VIII.

Giorgio Vasari, *Portrait of Antonio del Pollaiolo*, from the *Lives*, Florence, Giunti, 1568.

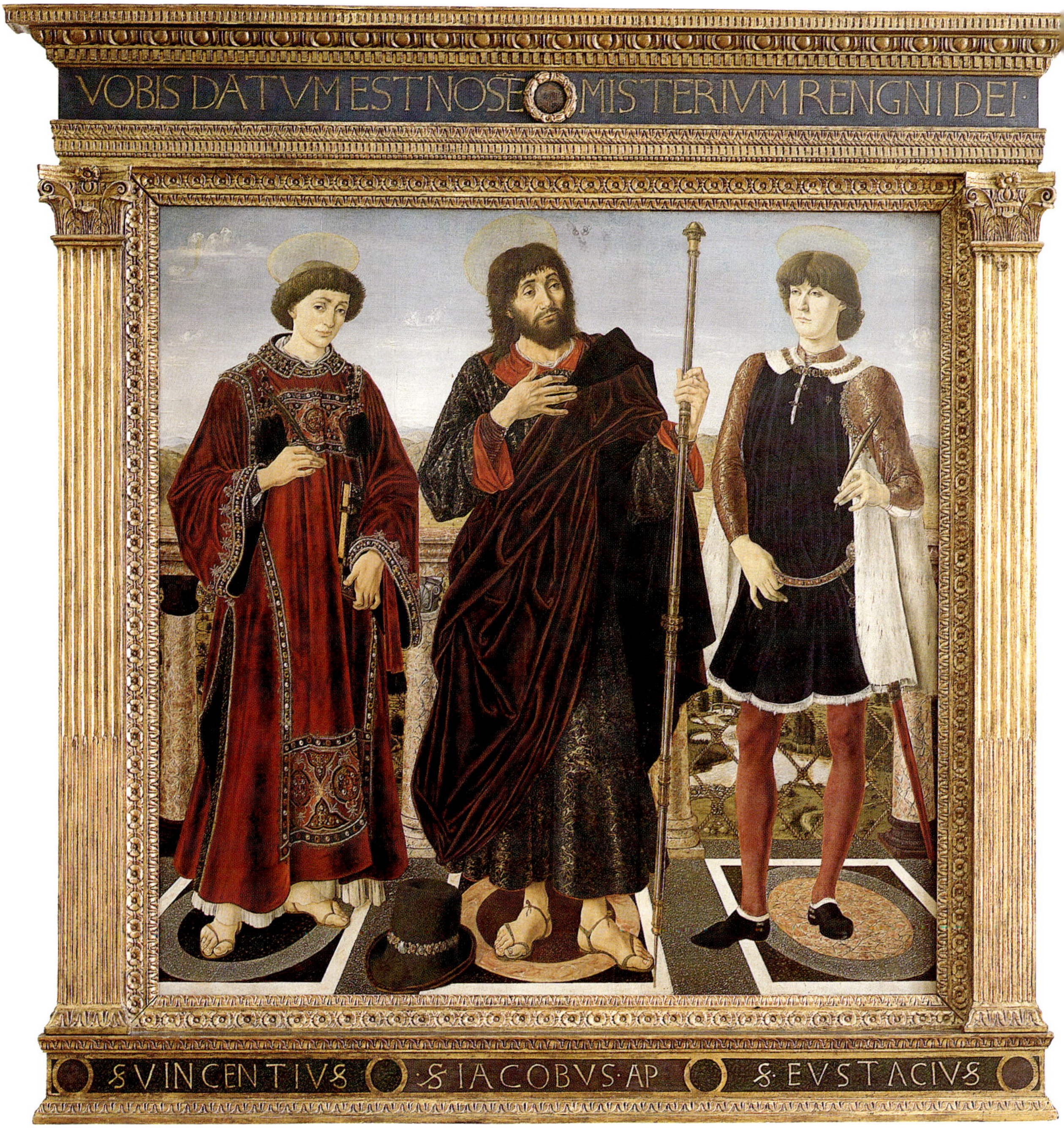

Antonio and Piero del Pollaiolo
Cardinal of Portugal's Altarpiece
1466-68
panel
Florence, Uffizi Gallery.

In 1459 the Cardinal of Lisbon Jacopo di Lusitania died in Florence. A chapel in San Miniato al Monte was dedicated to him, to be decorated by the finest artists of the times – Luca della Robbia, Alesso Baldovinetti, and Antonio Rossellino. The Pollaiolo altarpiece displays a tendency toward richly varied composition and refined details, as in the garments studded with jewels and the lovely Flemish-style landscape. On the hat at the feet of St James of Compostela, for whom the deceased Cardinal was named, is a shell, the saint's attribute and emblem of the pilgrims of whom he is the patron. Restoration has revealed that the Cardinal's coat-of-arms appearing at the center of the frame, gilded and inlaid by Giuliano da Maiano, is a real jewel in enameled bronze.

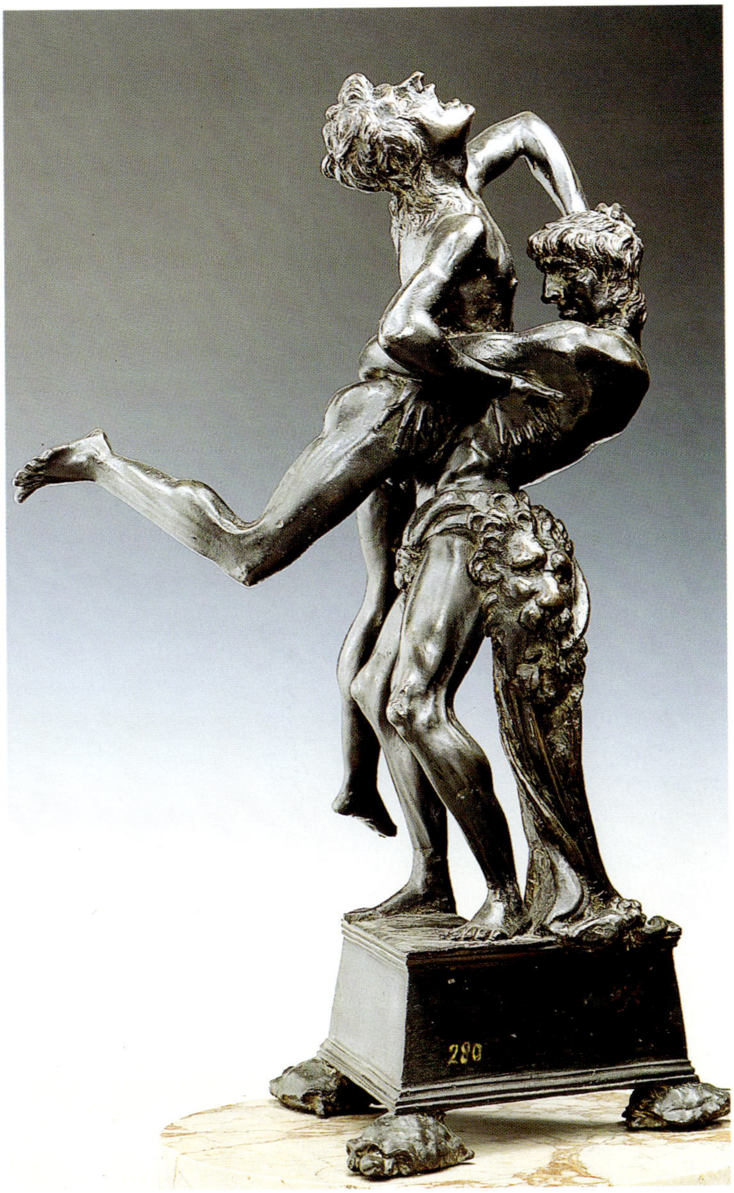

Antonio del Pollaiolo
Hercules and Anteus
c. 1478
bronze
Florence, Bargello National Museum.

The dynamic impulse of Anteus' muscular body is opposed to the tension of his rival's muscles, equally powerful and nervous. This famous small bronze is exemplary of Antonio's experimentation with the jointing of limbs and the movement of bodies. Vasari reports that Antonio "had a more modern understanding of nudes than any other before him, and dissected many bodies to see the underlying anatomy". The study of cadavers was to become frequent with Leonardo and Pontormo.

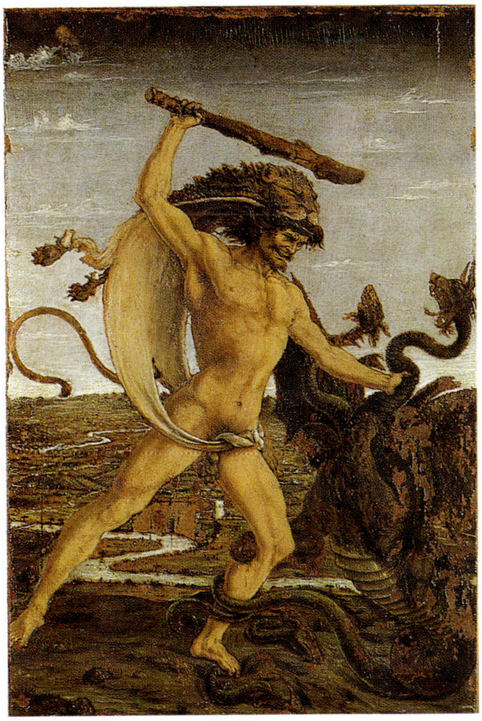

Antonio del Pollaiolo
Hercules and the Hydra
c. 1475
panel
Florence, Uffizi Gallery.

Along with another small panel also in the Uffizi and a third in a private collection, this work replicates in reduced format the cycle of the *Labors of Hercules* painted by Antonio for the Medici Palace in Via Larga.

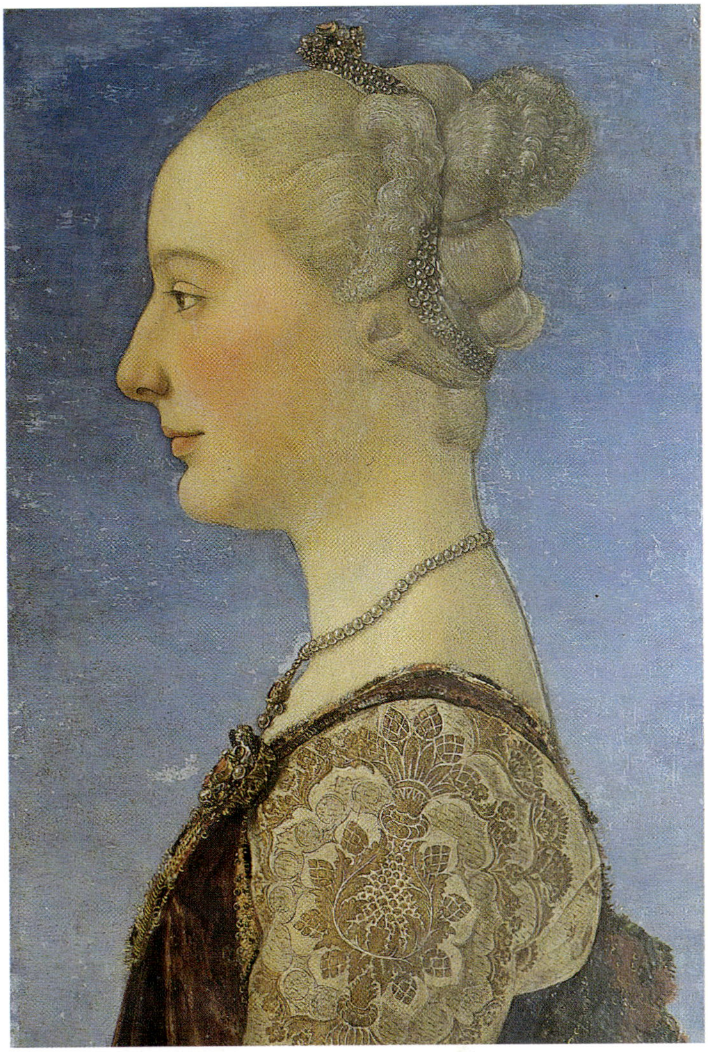

Piero del Pollaiolo
Portrait of a Woman
c. 1475
panel,
Florence, Uffizi Gallery.

Against a precious lapis lazuli background the woman is heraldically portrayed in profile, while Botticelli's portraits painted in those same years were already turning to face the spectator. A fine veil covers the woman's ears and elaborate coiffure. The jewel and the embroidered fabric may be inspired by products from the shop of the Pollaiolo brothers themselves, skilled goldsmiths and embroiderers.

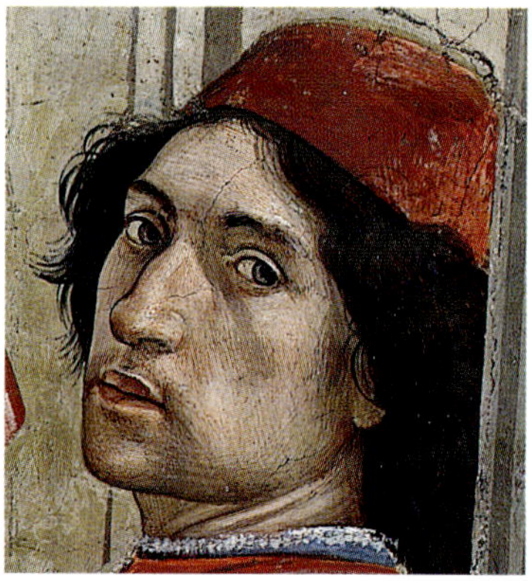

Domenico Ghirlandaio

(Domenico Bigordi, Florence 1449 – 1494)

Apprenticed to Alesso Baldovinetti (1426-1499) but influenced from the start by Domenico Veneziano, Andrea del Castagno and Verrocchio, Ghirlandaio was an independent artist by 1470, a skillful portraitist and successful fresco painter. The last great narrator among those attentive to Flemish art, his inspiration for landscapes and decorative touches, he interpreted his stories with details from daily life and contemporary portraits. Vasari, who praised the Archangel Michael's armor in the St Justus altarpiece, credited Ghirlandaio with having invented a technique for representing the shine of precious metals not by gilding but by color alone. From 1475 Ghirlandaio headed a shop where his brothers Davide and Benedetto also worked. His most famous cycles are in Santa Maria Novella and Santa Trinita (Florence), in San Gimignano and in the Sistine Chapel.

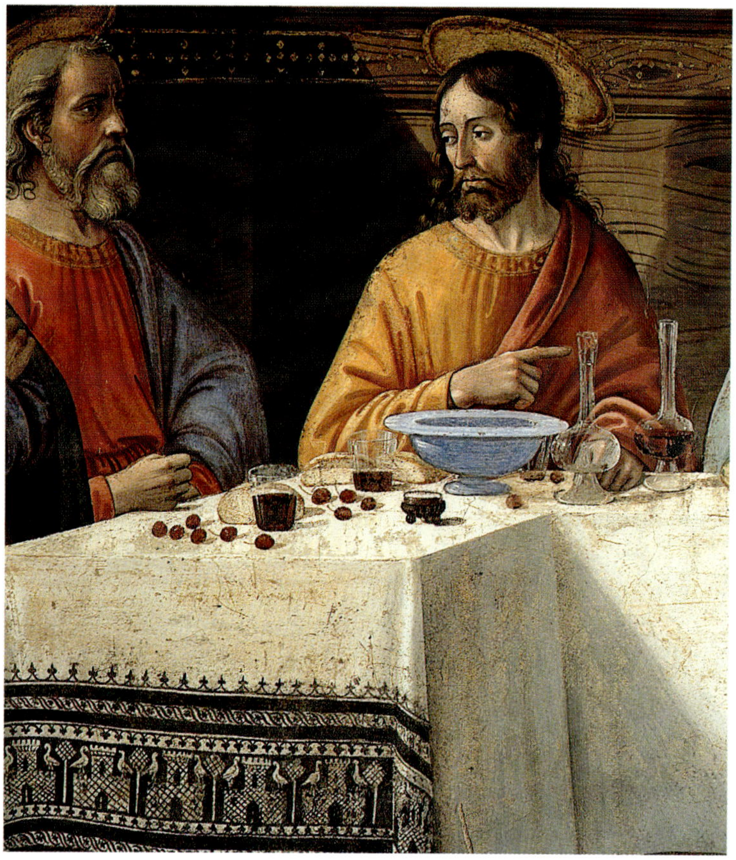

Domenico Ghirlandaio, *Self-portrait*, detail of the *Miracle of the Revived Boy*, c. 1483. Florence, Santa Trinita, Sassetti Chapel.

Domenico Ghirlandaio
Last Supper
1477-80
fresco, detail
Florence, Monastery of San Marco, small refectory.

Ghirlandaio shows himself a keen observer of reality in his accurate representation of the table-cloth and the objects on the table.

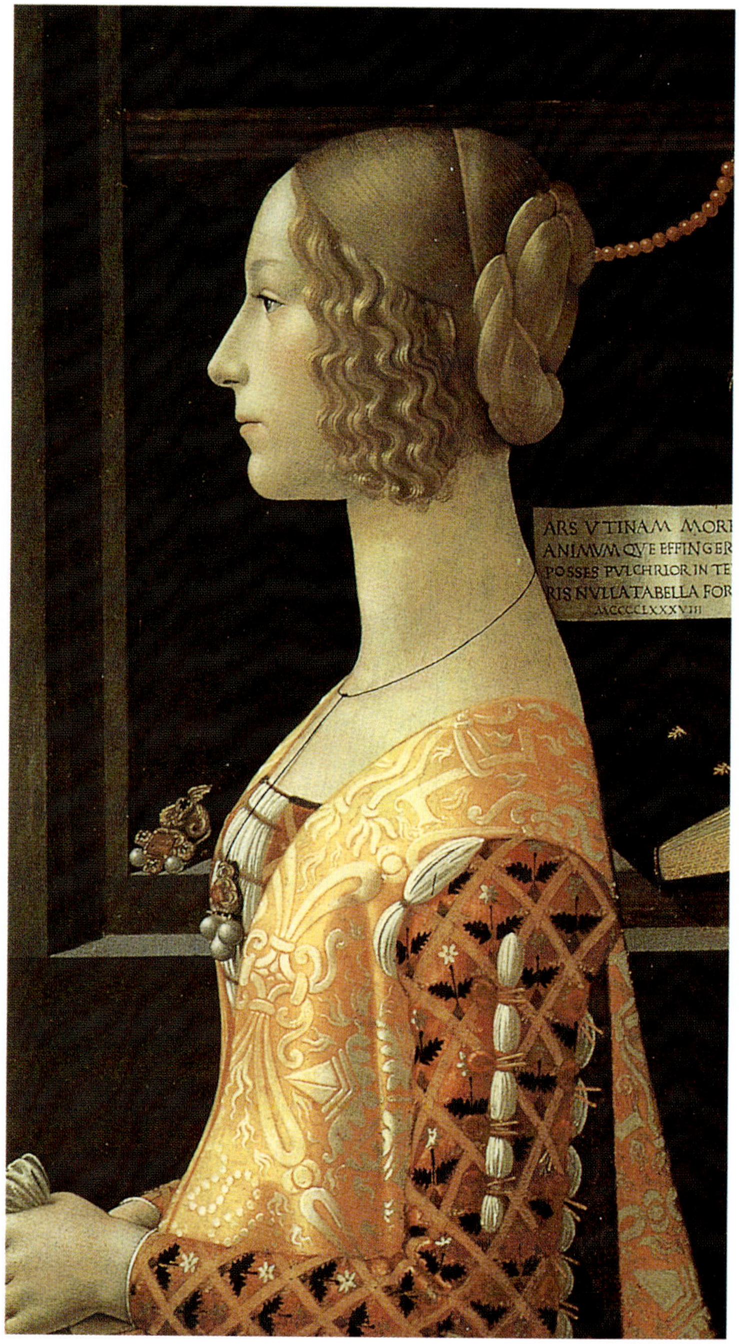

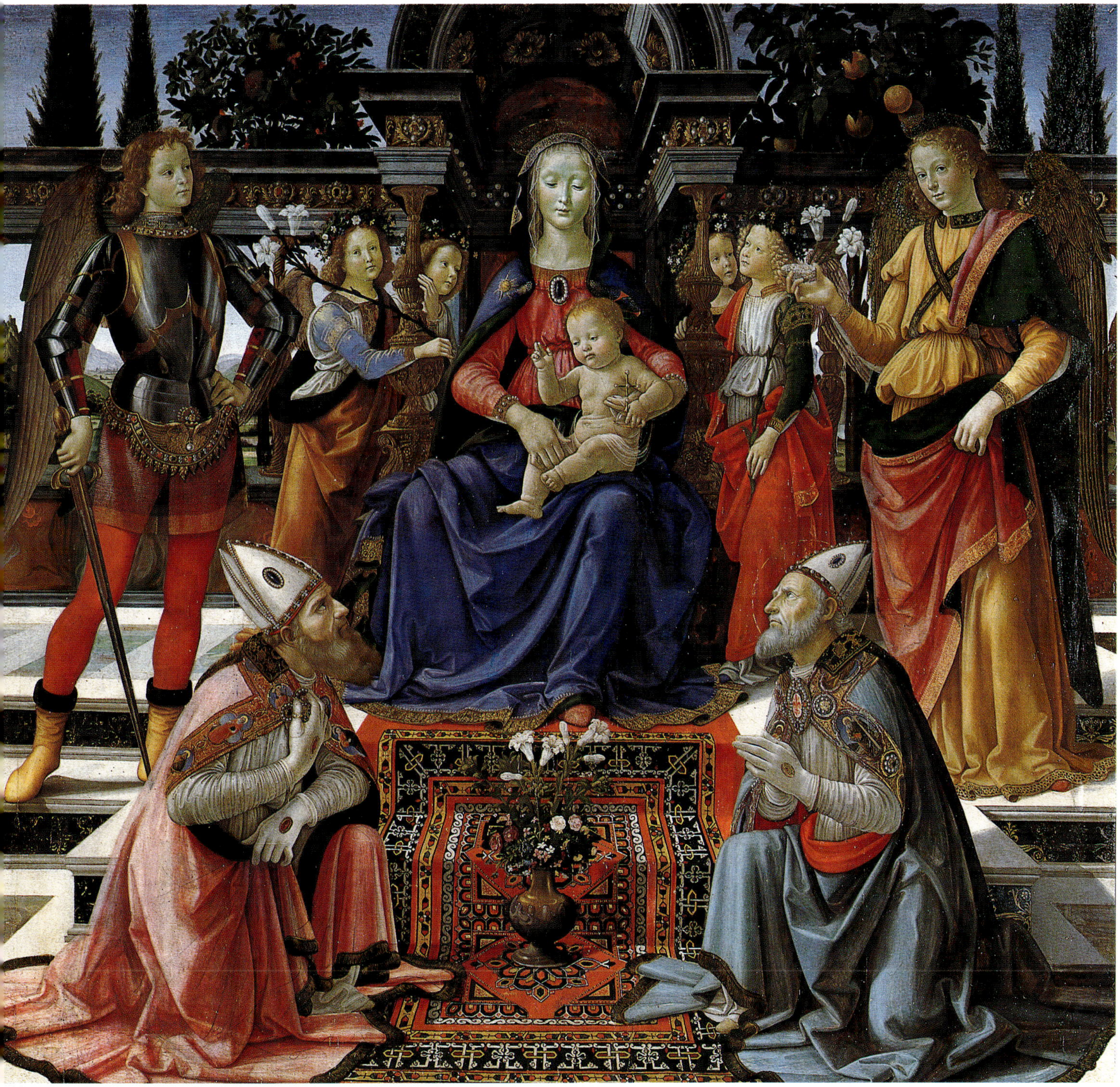

At left:
Domenico Ghirlandaio
Portrait of Giovanna degli Albizzi
c. 1489
panel
Madrid, Thyssen-Bornemisza Foundation.

The Latin epigraph painted in *trompe-l'oeil* in the background of his most famous portrait, a commemorative profile of Lorenzo Tornabuoni's beautiful wife who died in childbirth in 1488, derives from Martial. The wording is ambiguous: perhaps it is the artist's humble admission that he is unable to render the moral qualities of the woman in painting, or it may allude to his skill: "Oh art, if you could only paint the customs and the soul, no picture on earth would be more beautiful".

Domenico Ghirlandaio
Madonna Enthroned with Angels and Saints (Altarpiece of San Giusto degli Ingesuati)
c. 1480
panel
Florence, Uffizi Gallery.

Against the background of a crystal clear sky, in a composition now consolidated in those years in Florence, a balustrade covered in jewels supports the enthroned virgin, surrounded by four garlanded angels. The Child is blessing St Justus, the patron saint of the Florentine church from which the altarpiece comes. Standing out against the serene landscape in the background are cypresses, a hibiscus and an orange tree.

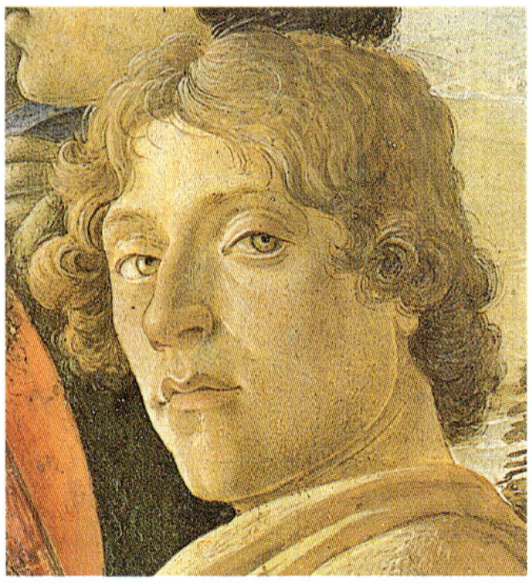

Sandro Botticelli

(Alessandro di Mariano Filipepi, Florence 1445 – 1510)

Various hypotheses have been advanced to explain the pseudonym of Botticelli – son of a leather tanner – who was first apprenticed to a goldsmith, perhaps a certain "Botticello". His brother Antonio was instead a "battigello", or gold-beater, a trade at which Florentine artisans excelled. Sandro, almost twenty, was apprenticed to Filippo Lippi, remaining with him until the painter-monk departed for Spoleto in 1467. The next year he was apprenticed a second time to Verrocchio, and it is then that he produced his first autonomous works such as the *St Ambrose Altarpiece* (Uffizi), still revealing the influence of his two masters. Starting in 1470 Sandro, now independent, worked for private clients and public institutions. In 1475 he began to collaborate with the Medici family, the most powerful family in Florence, for whom he painted his most famous works, now all in the Uffizi, which contains the

Sandro Botticelli, *Self-portrait,* detail of the *Adoration of the Magi*, c. 1475. Florence, Uffizi Gallery.

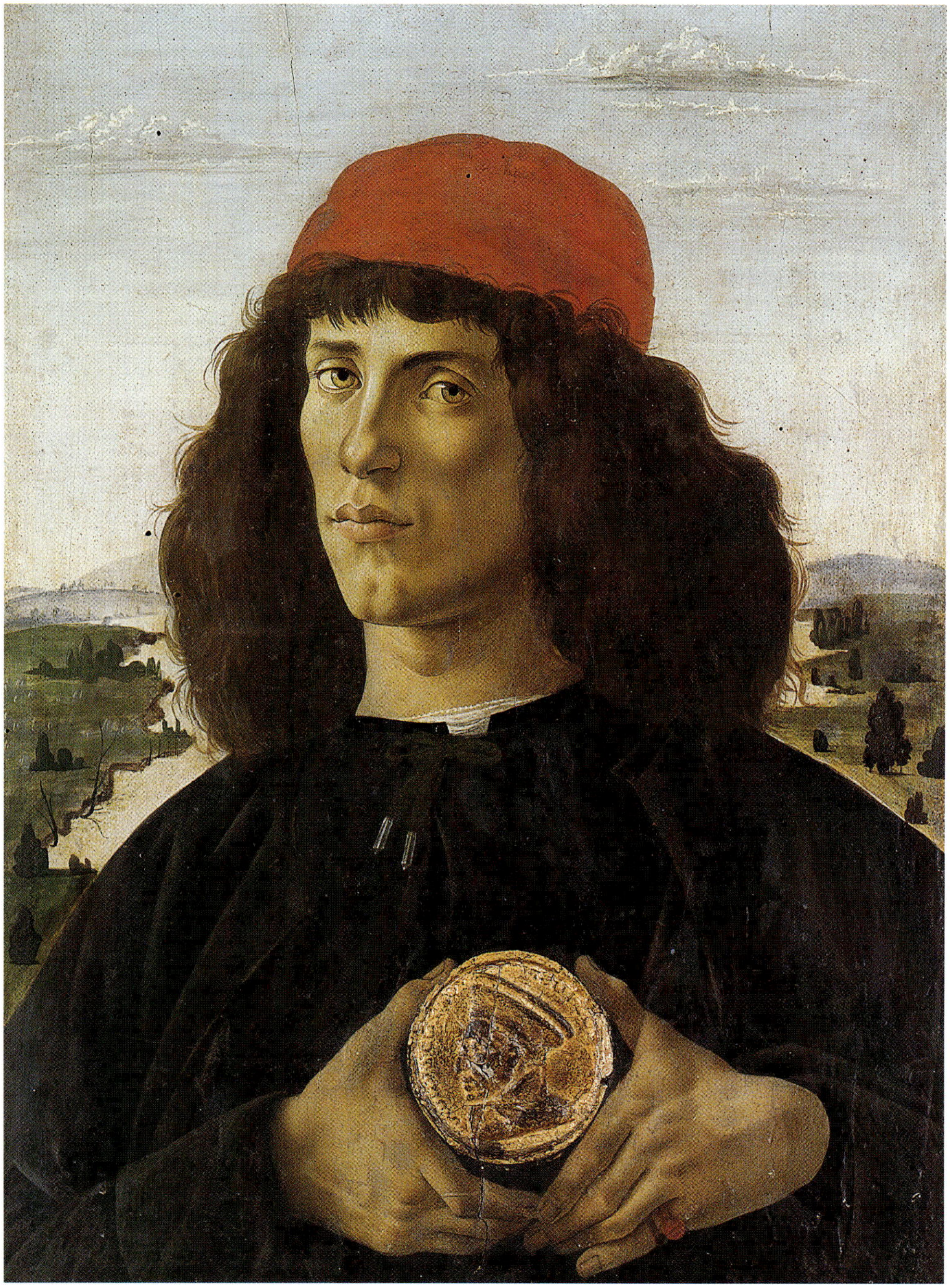

Sandro Botticelli
Portrait of a Youth with a Medal
c. 1470-75
panel
Florence, Uffizi Gallery.

A beautiful youth, who has now entered the collective imagination as one of the most enigmatic models of the Renaissance, fixes the spectator with a vaguely melancholy gaze against the background of a landscape inspired by Flemish painting, much admired by the Florentines. The gilded stucco mould portraying the profile of Cosimo the Elder, *Pater Patriae*, accompanied by the wording MAGNVS COSMVS MEDICES PPP, is that of a medal coined in 1464. Since the young man displays the effigy of the founder of the Medici family, it has been thought that he may be a personage close to Medici circles. Another possibility, suggested by the ring he wears on his little finger, is that he may be Sandro's brother Antonio Filipepi, a goldsmith and medallist.

Sandro Botticelli
Pallas and the Centaur
c. 1482-83
canvas
Florence, Uffizi Gallery.

Lorenzo di Pierfrancesco de' Medici, cousin of Lorenzo the Magnificent, commissioned this canvas, which originally hung above the door of a room in his Florentine palace. The meaning of the painting is highly enigmatic: against the background of an aquatic landscape a centaur stands beside a young woman armed with a lance, who grasps a lock of his mane. Her body is thinly veiled by a light robe adorned with olive wreaths and embroidered with the Medici emblem of interwoven diamonds (from their motto DEO AMANTE, "to God devoted"). Perhaps this is an allegory inspired by the contrast between two natures: Chastity and Lust, or Instinct and Reason, or again, Humility and Pride.

largest core of his paintings and drawings. In addition to allegorical subjects such as the *Primavera*, the *Birth of Venus*, *Pallas and the Centaur* are others of religious nature such as the *Adoration of the Magi*, rich in symbolic allusions and portraits of contemporaries. In 1481 he was summoned to Rome by Pope Sixtus IV, where he painted three frescoes for the Sistine Chapel. Returning to Florence the following year, he was now one of the most prominent artists in the gilded city of Lorenzo the Magnificent. But political upheavals leading to the expulsion of the Medici and a personal spiritual crisis influenced by the preaching of Savonarola, of whom he became a follower, wrought changes in his soul and in his art. Sandro withdrew into a depressive, almost hallucinatory reticence, dedicating himself to mystical works already presaged by the imposing *St Mark's Altarpiece* (1490). Then came the *Calumny* (1495, Uffizi), the *Crucifixion* (c. 1497, Cambridge Fogg Museum), the *Mystic Nativity* (1501, London, National Gallery). With the changing taste of the new century, Sandro was to die almost forgotten and in disgrace. Much later, Romantic criticism was to revive the myth of this great master, some of whose creations, namely the *Primavera* and the *Venus*, now arouse the almost fanatical veneration of visitors from all over the world in the Uffizi.

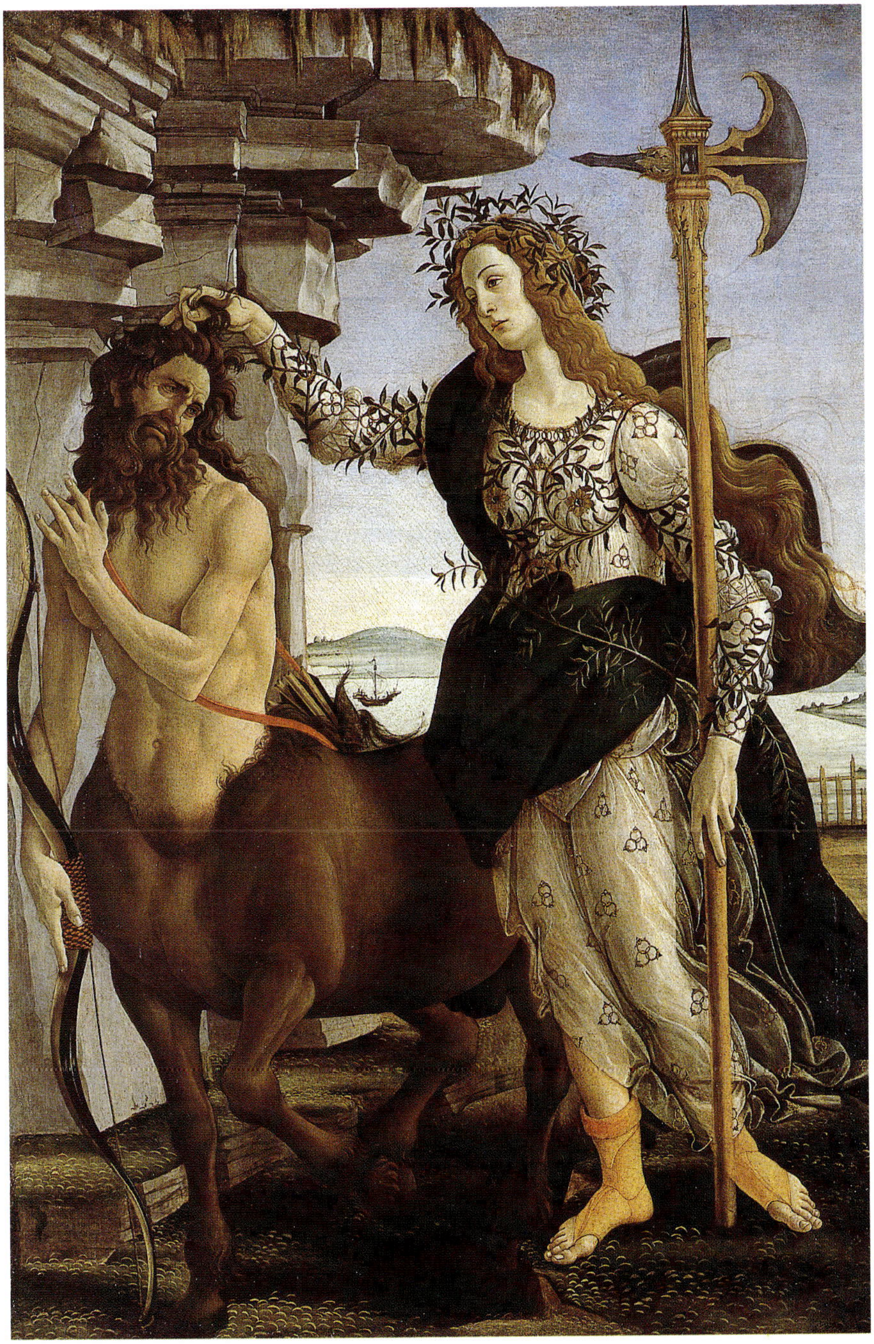

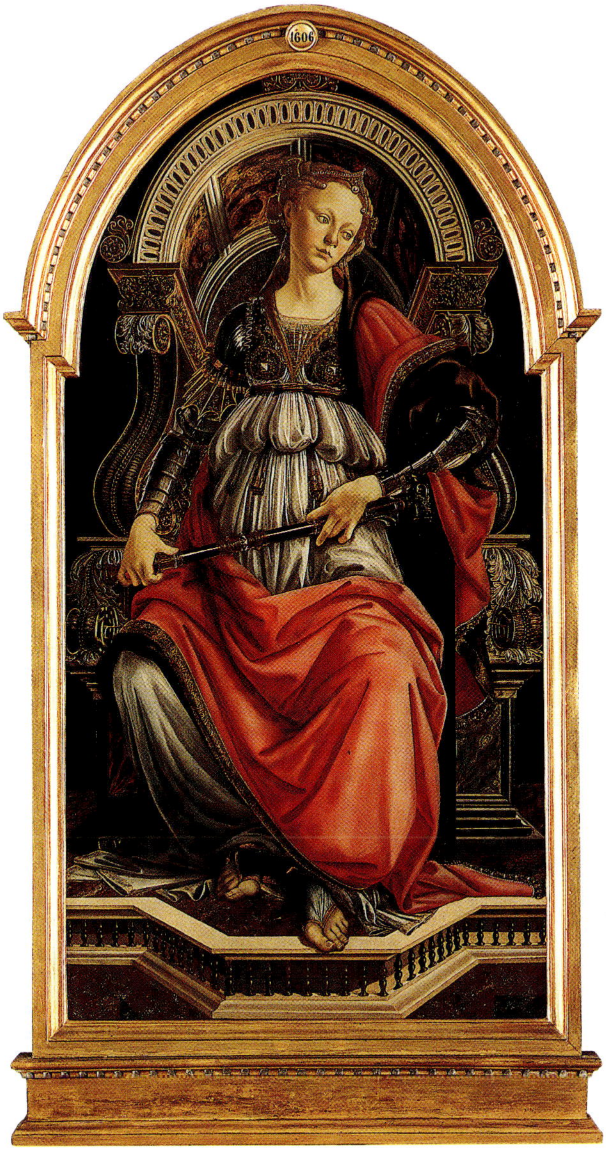

Sandro Botticelli
Fortitude
1470
panel
Florence, Uffizi Gallery.

It was painted to decorate, with another six *Virtues* by Piero del Pollaiolo, the Sala delle Udienze in the palace of the Merchants' Guild.

Sandro Botticelli
Punishment of the Rebels
1482
fresco, detail
Vatican City, Sistine Chapel.

For the walls of the chapel erected for Pope Sixtus IV Della Rovere in 1481, Botticelli frescoed three Biblical episodes: *Moses and the Daughters of Jethro*, the *Trials of Christ* and the *Chastisement of Chore*. At the same time three more famous artists, two of them Florentines, were working on the cycle of frescoes in the chapel – Pietro Perugino, Domenico Ghirlandaio and Cosimo Rosselli. But the ambitious undertaking (which, with obviously self-laudatory intentions, called for the illustration of ten episodes from the Old and the New Testament), could not be finished within the date set, March 15, 1482, also due to the well-known tendency of this Pope to leave his debts unpaid. Sixtus IV, one of the greatest theologians of his time, was particularly drawn to the philosophy of St Augustine, on which he based an esoteric interpretation of the Scriptures with comparison and symbolic links between the Old and the New Testament. The decorative scheme of the frescoes in the chapel is thus based on this theme. Even the architecture of the chapel is conceived according to the proportions of Solomon's Temple, with which the Pope wished to establish an ideal link. The Sistine Chapel, as stated by wording in Perugino's famous fresco of the *Consignment of the Keys*, is less magnificent than Solomon's Temple but is superior to it in religion and spirituality. Botticelli's fresco shown here, which faces Perugino's *Consignment of the Keys*, depicts the Biblical episode of the punishment of Chore, Datan and Abiron, rebels against Moses and Aaron, who had been invested with the authority of God the Father. While in Perugino's painting the prestige of the Pope designated by Christ is symbolized by the Church Triumphant, here instead the buildings are in ruins to signify the inferiority of the Old Testament. The fresco may also allude to the attempt made in 1481 to convene a council against the Pope by the Archbishop of Cranea, a "rebel" like Chore, Datan and Abiron.

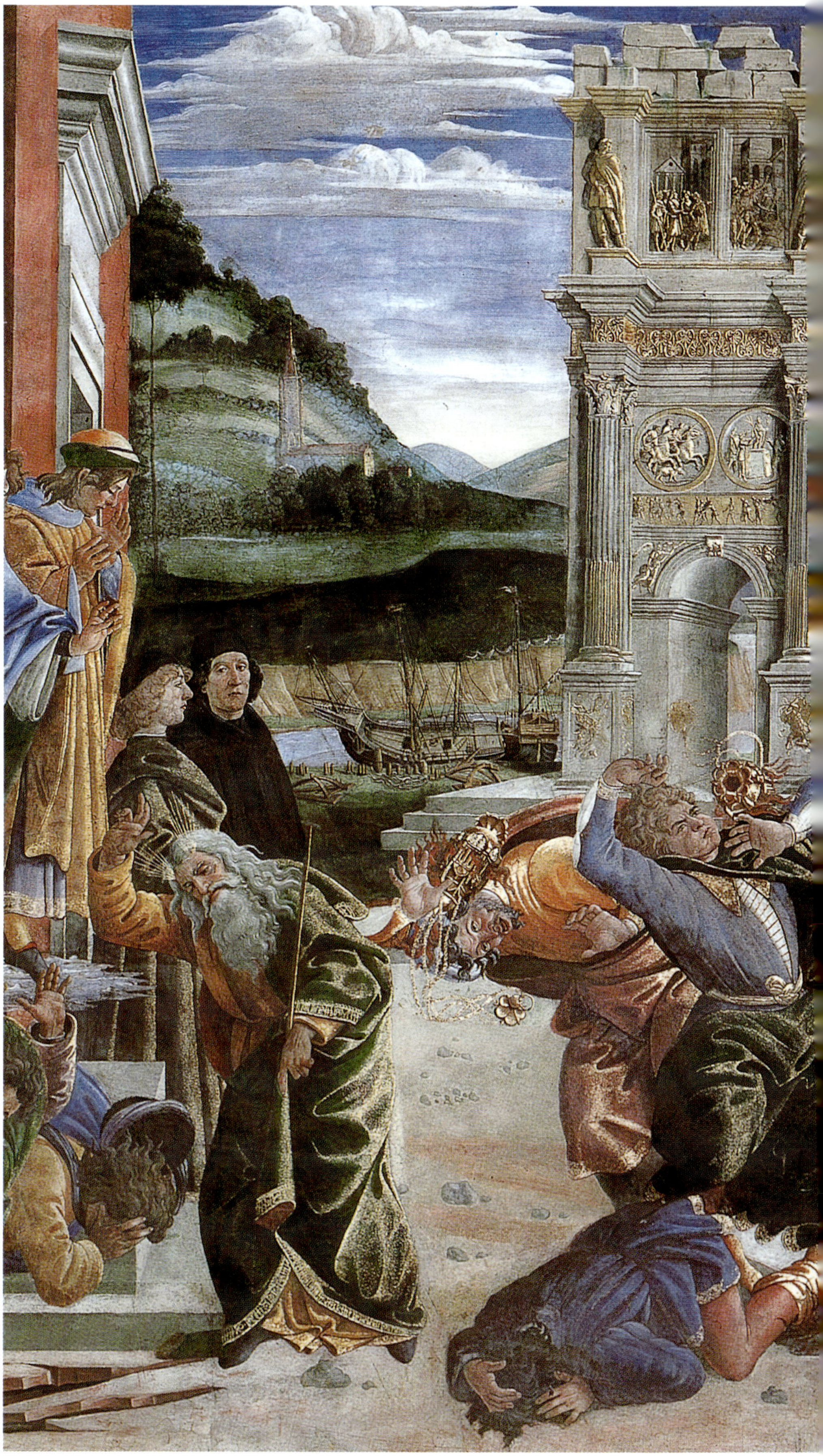

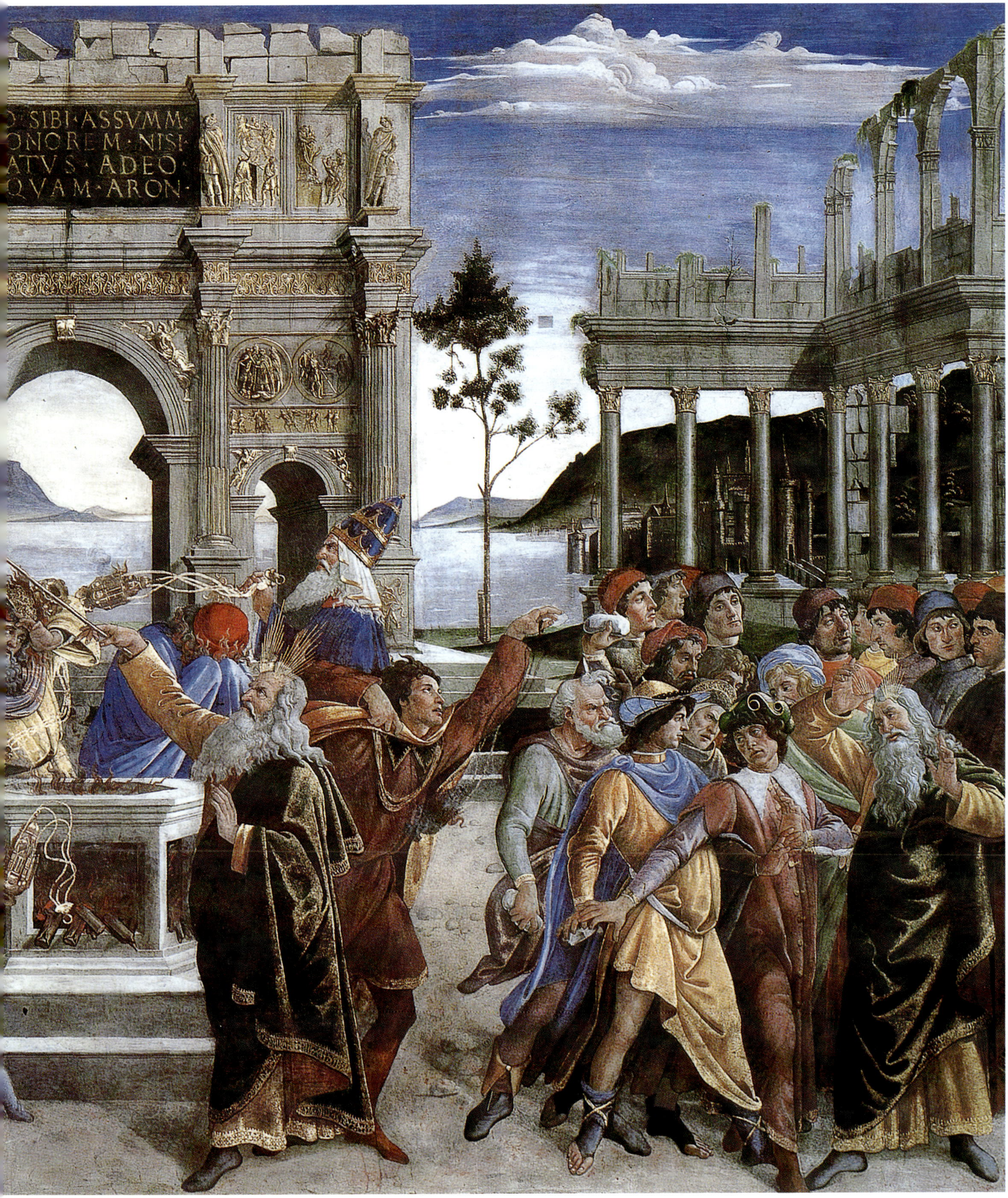
SIBI·ASSVMM
ONOREM·NISI
ATVS·ADEO
QVAM·ARON·

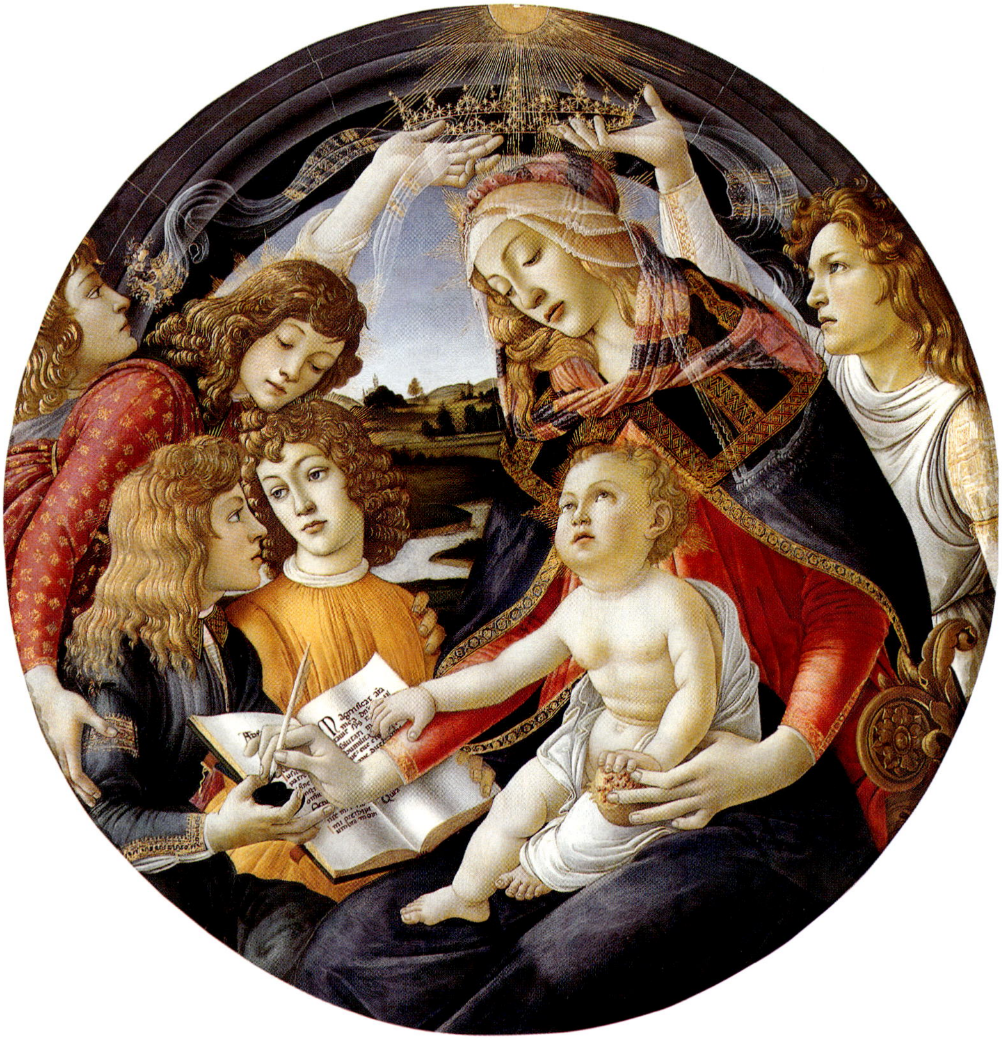

Sandro Botticelli
Madonna of the Magnificat
c. 1485
panel
Florence, Uffizi Gallery.

The subject of this tondo is inspired by the canticle Maria sings in praise of the Lord during her visit to Elisabeth, the wife of Zaccariah, who is expecting a child (the future John the Baptist) as reported in St Luke's Gospel (I, 46). *Magnificat anima mea* can be read on the right-hand page of the book held open by angels, and the child Jesus points to those words while Mary dips her pin in ink to transcribe the page. The pomegranate held in the hands of mother and child, with the ruby red of its seeds, probably presages the Passion of Christ. A distant river gives the sense of a deep, extensive space, while all of the figures in the foreground are harmoniously inserted within the circle of the panel, almost as if reflected in a mirror.

At right:
Sandro Botticelli
Primavera (Spring)
c. 1482
panel
Florence, Uffizi Gallery.

In 1498 this famous painting, among the highest expressions of the ideal return of the golden age to Lorenzo's Florence, hung above a chest in the home of Lorenzo and Giovanni di Pierfrancesco de' Medici, cousins of the Magnificent. The allegory seems to have been inspired by Ovid and Lucretius, and by certain verses of Agnolo Poliziano (1475), friend of the Medici and of the artist, who describes a garden with the three Graces garlanded with flowers and the springtime breeze Zephyrus, recognizable here in the winged genie on the right who pursues and possesses the nymph Chloris, bestowing on her the power to germinate flowers (blossoms are falling from her mouth). The smiling figure clothed in flowered robes probably represents the transformation of Chloris into Flora, the Latin goddess of Spring, while the woman at the center is possibly Venus, and this is her garden. The three women weaving a dance around her, derived from the ancient image of the Three Graces, may be the symbol of Liberality. Above is Cupid, the blindfolded god of Love, and at the left Mercury, the herald of Jove, scattering the clouds with his stick. The allegory of Spring, the season in which the invisible world of Forms descends to shape matter, may allude to the marriage between the erudite Lorenzo di Pierfrancesco, friend of Botticelli, and Sermaide Appiani, a relative of Simonetta Vespucci, legendary for her beauty and for her presumed liaison with Giuliano de' Medici. A more recent interpretation sees the painting as a metaphorical celebration of the Liberal Arts, to be read in a nuptial key.

Sandro Botticelli
The Birth of Venus
c. 1484
linen
Florence, Uffizi Gallery.

While roses drop from the sky, in an idealized seascape the nude Venus, standing on a seashell, lands – rather than being born, as indicated by the 19th century title – on the shore of the Island of Cyprus (or perhaps Kythera), borne over the waves by the breath of the winds Zephyrus and Auras. A young girl, perhaps one of the Graces or the Hora of Spring, welcomes her with a richly embroidered mantle. While the figures on the left may be taken from the *Tazza Farnese*, then in Lorenzo the Magnificent's gem collection (Naples, Archaeological Museum), the pose of Venus is inspired by the ancient sculpture of the *Chaste Venus*, copied in the past by Giovanni Pisano. Like the *Primavera*, the canvas bears witness to the most serene and graceful phase of Botticelli's art. The neo-Platonic atmosphere of Lorenzo's age is reflected here in the probable allusion to the fusion of Spirit and Matter, of Idea and Nature.

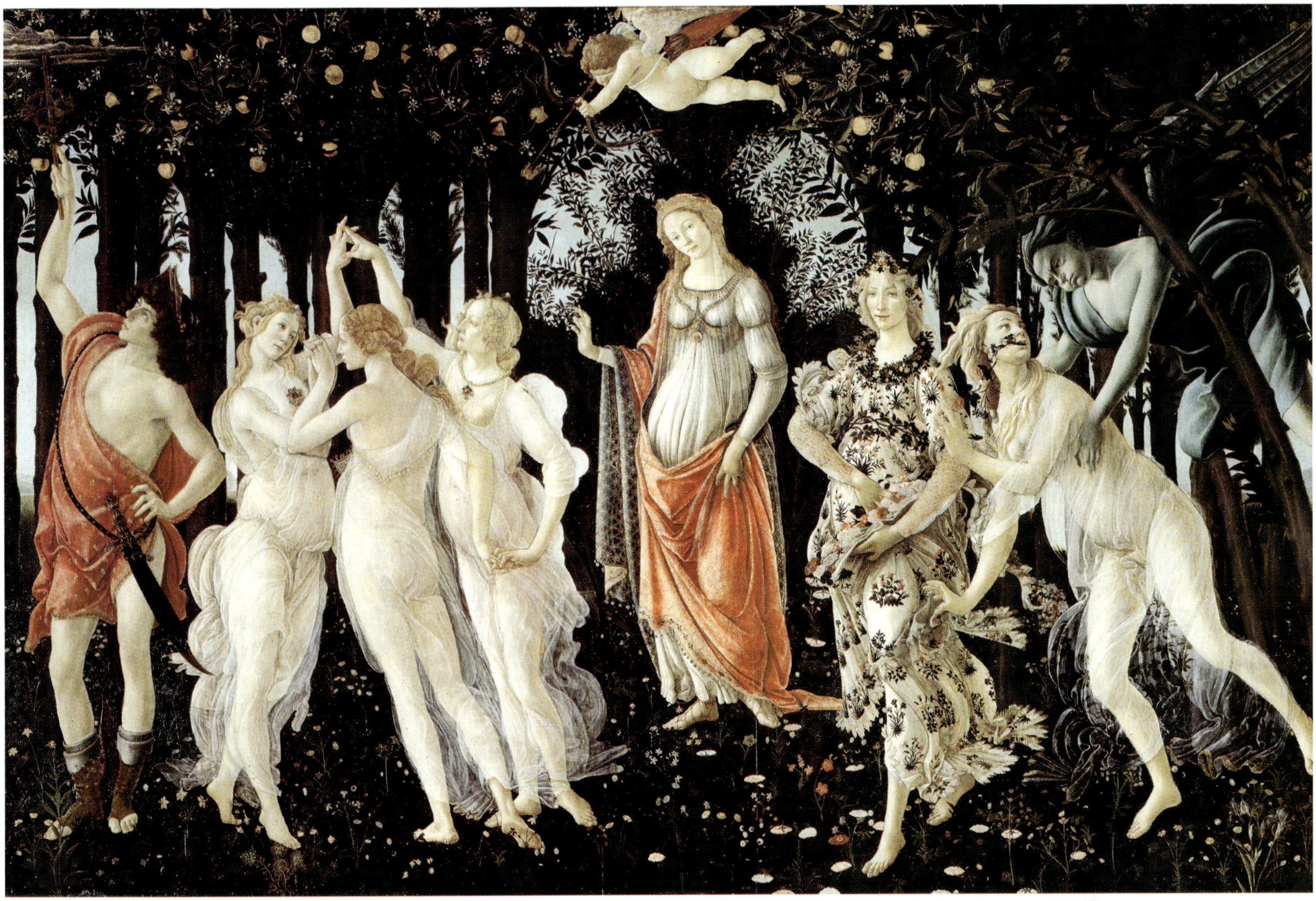

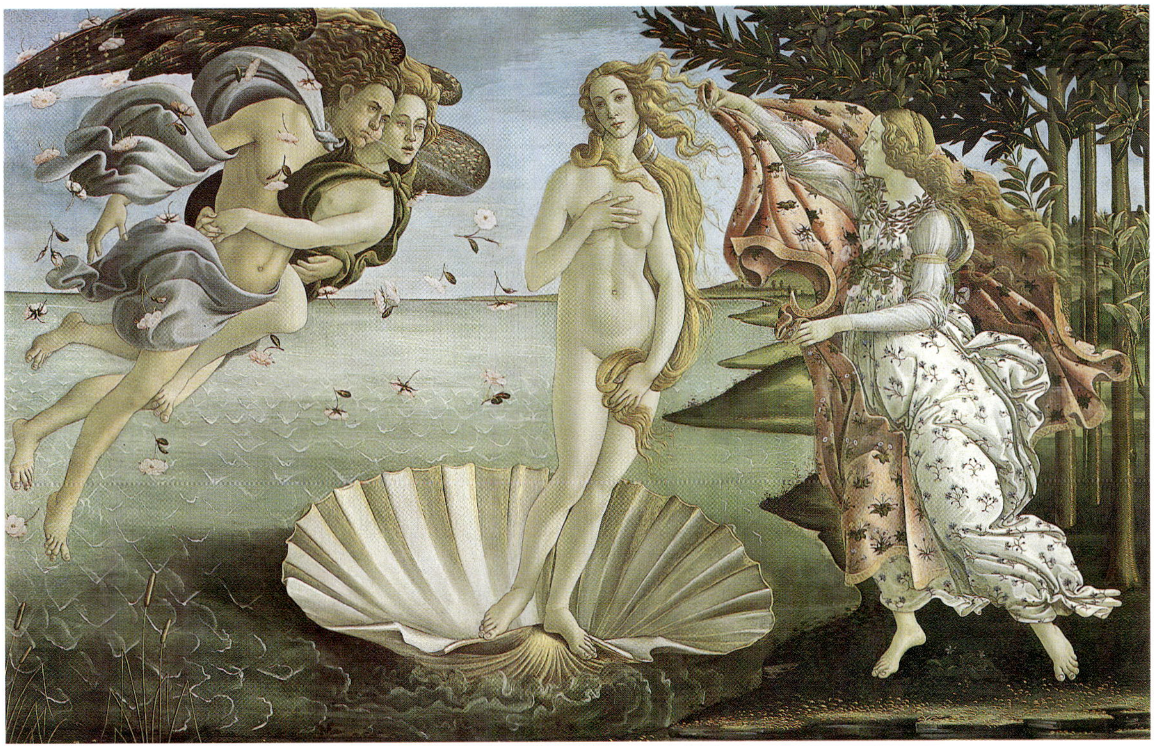

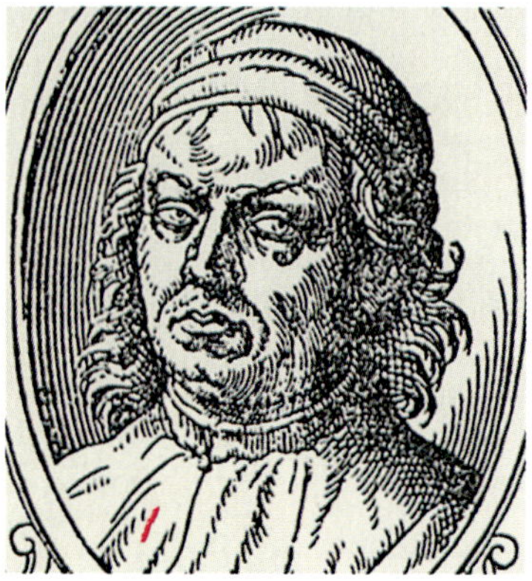

Pietro Perugino

(Pietro Vannucci,
Città della Pieve 1450 – Perugia 1523)

Perugia, near which the artist was born, gave him his pseudonym. His art was soon copied, "so popular in its time that many came from France, Spain, England and other provinces to learn it", reports Vasari, noting that "many traded in his paintings... before the appearance of Michelangelo's style". But Vasari's comments are harsh: the artist was venial, "of little religion", skeptical and stubborn, with a "rock-hard brain". His painting, after having inspired neo-classics and romantics, has been recognized only in the early 20th century as innovative, harmonious and monumental. After training at Florence, where he returned to work several times, he ran two shops contemporaneously, in Florence and Perugia, working also in Venice, Milan, Rome, where in 1481-83 his fine frescoes on the walls of the Sistine Chapel included the famous *Consignment of the Keys.*

Giorgio Vasari, *Portrait of Pietro Perugino*, from the *Lives*, Florence, Giunti, 1568.

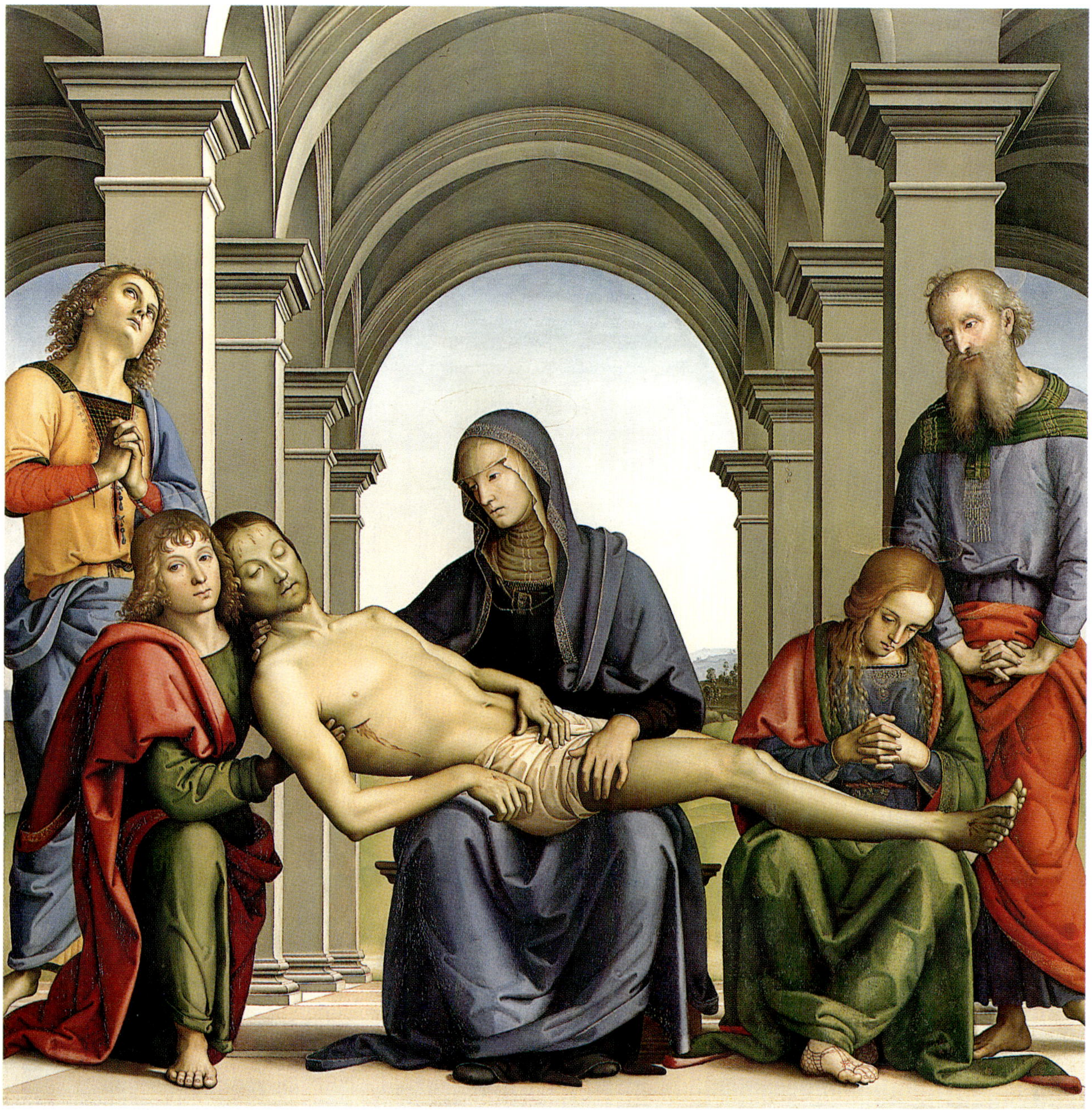

Pietro Perugino
Pietà
c. 1490
panel
Florence, Uffizi Gallery.

The altarpiece of the Florentine church of the Ingesuati is imbued with intense spirituality, perhaps inspired by the sermons of Gerolamo Savonarola, who arrived in Florence in 1489. Framed by a harmonious portico with arches degrading toward the almost infinite space of a landscape barely visible in the distance, the Madonna holds on her lap the rigid, ashen body of Christ, supported by John the Evangelist: "a dead Christ all stiffened as if He had been hanging on a cross so long that time and cold had reduced Him to such a state", notes Vasari.

Pietro Perugino
Last Supper
c. 1485-90
fresco, detail
Florence, Cenacolo di Foligno.

Painted for the Florentine monastery of an erudite, aristocratic group of Franciscan Tertiaries whose mother house was the Monastery of Sant'Anna di Foligno, the frescoes of the *Last Supper* are exemplary of Perugino's balanced composition, combining a monumental conception of the whole with great delicacy in each part. It is understandable that he continued to use these figures, so well conceived and painted, a fact Giorgio Vasari was not to pardon him in the 16th century: "he had such an abundance of paintings to complete that he often placed the same details in his figures, and reduced the theory of his craft to such a fixed style that he gave them all the same expression".

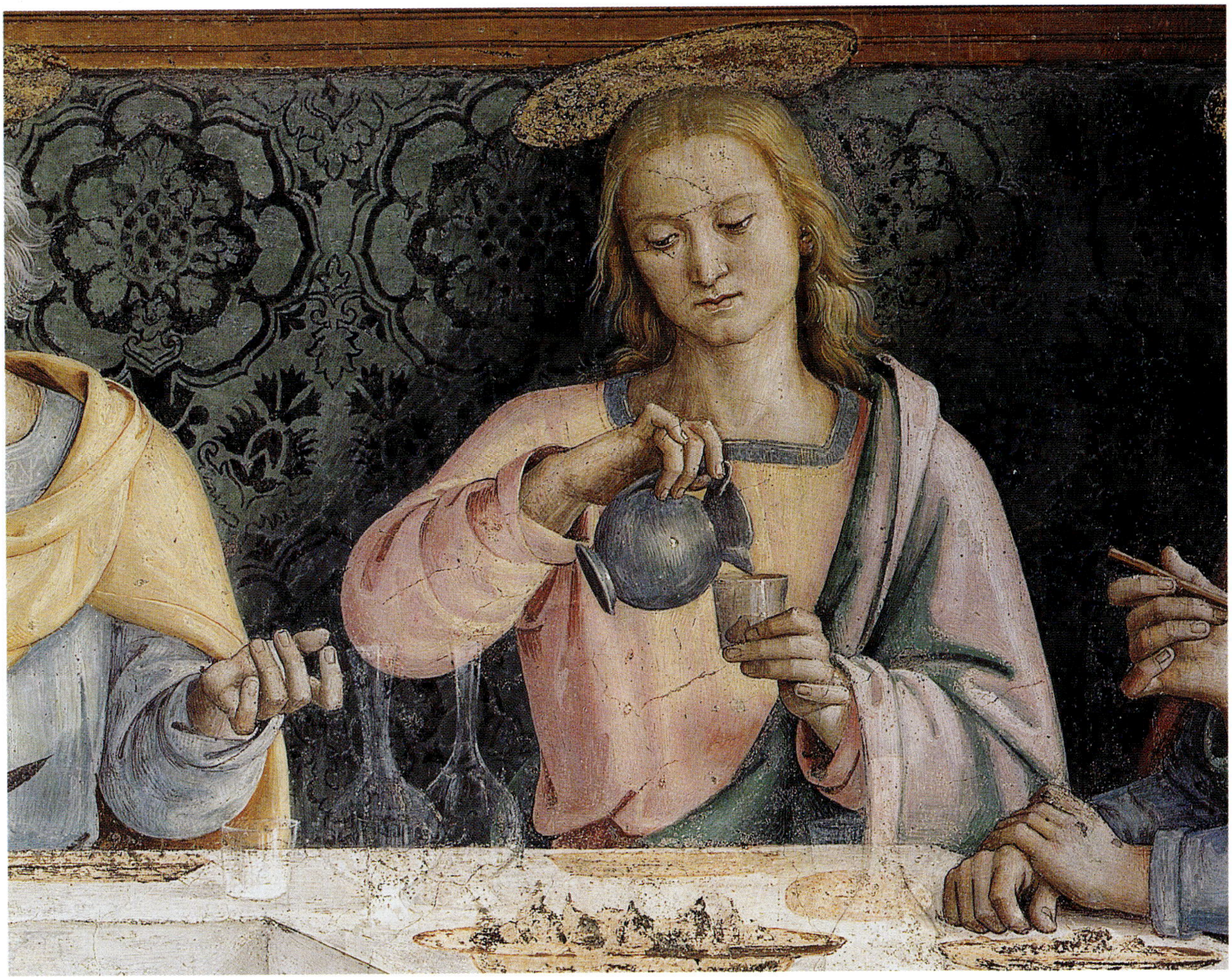

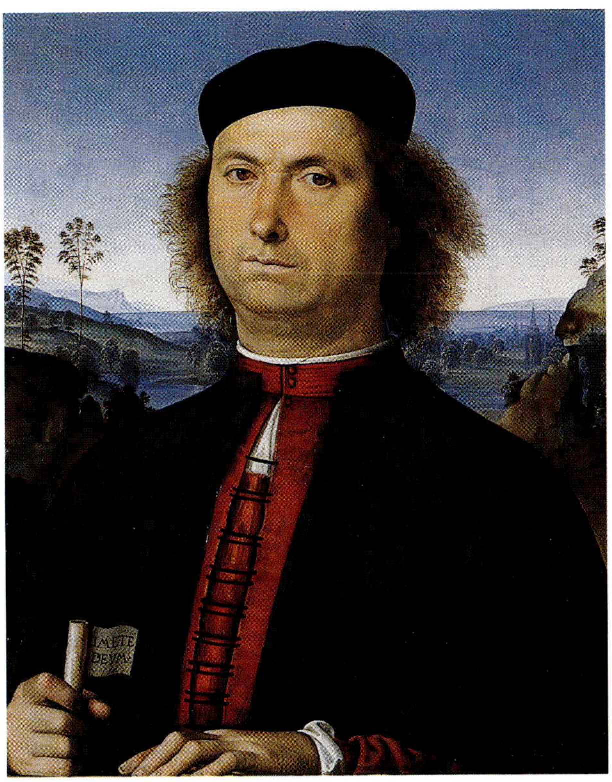

Pietro Perugino
Portrait of Francesco delle Opere
signed and dated on the back, 1494
panel
Florence, Uffizi Gallery.

The subject of the portrait, Francesco delle Opere, whose name is written on the back of the panel, was a Florentine artisan who died in Venice in 1496, the brother of a friend of the painter, Giovanni delle Corniole, like him a master gem cutter and a friend of Perugino. The scroll which the man holds in his hand, bearing the words TIMETE DEVM, alludes to the *incipit* of a prayer by Savonarola. The "photographic" precision of the features, the position of the figure with its hand leaning on the balustrade, and the landscape in the background are clearly inspired by Flemish art, particularly by Memling's portraits which were already known in Florence.

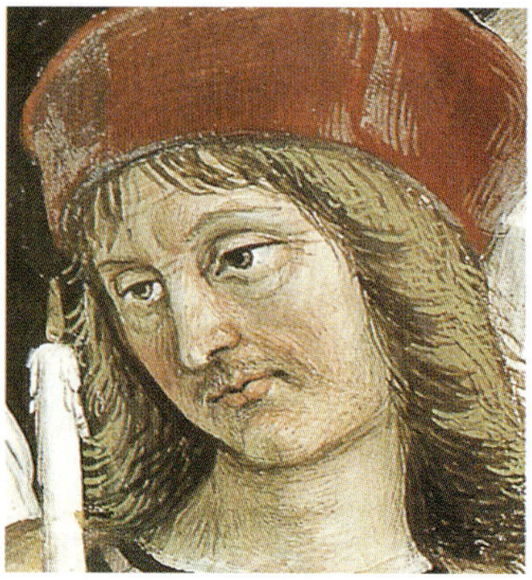

Pinturicchio

(Bernardino di Betto, Perugia c. 1454 – Siena 1513)

A pupil of his fellow citizen Bartolomeo Caporali (1420-1506), Pinturicchio then assisted Perugino, with whom he worked on the *Stories of San Bernardino* (1473, Perugia, Galleria Nazionale) and the Sistine Chapel in Rome. He is famous for the frescoes in the Piccolomini Library in Siena, a profane cycle among the most important of the times, where among magnificent vedutas he displays his talent as pleasant narrator. The frescoes depict stories of Pope Pius II, a Humanist and accomplished diplomat. Pinturicchio also worked, with many assistants, on other important projects: in Rome, on Ara Coeli and Santa Maria del Popolo, as well as the Della Rovere palace and the Borgia Apartments (1492-94); in Spoleto on the Eroli Chapel in the Duomo.

Pinturicchio, *Presumed Self-portrait*, detail of the *Canonization of St Catherine*, 1505. Siena, Duomo, Piccolomini Library.

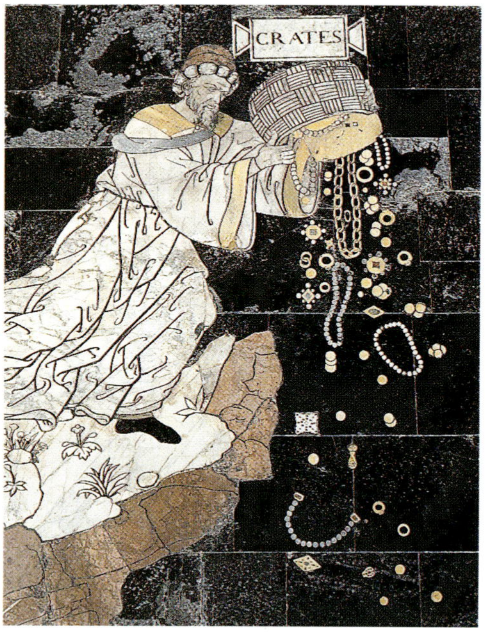

Pinturicchio
Crates
colored marble, detail of the *Hill of Virtue*
1505
Siena, Duomo, floor of the central nave.

On the Hill of Virtue Crates, a Greek grammarian from the 2nd century AD, throws into the sea his jewels, symbol of human wealth. Here he is joined by the sages who, having landed on the island of Fortune, abandon it, preferring Wisdom. The splendid inlaid marble forms part of the flooring of the Duomo on which various artists worked.

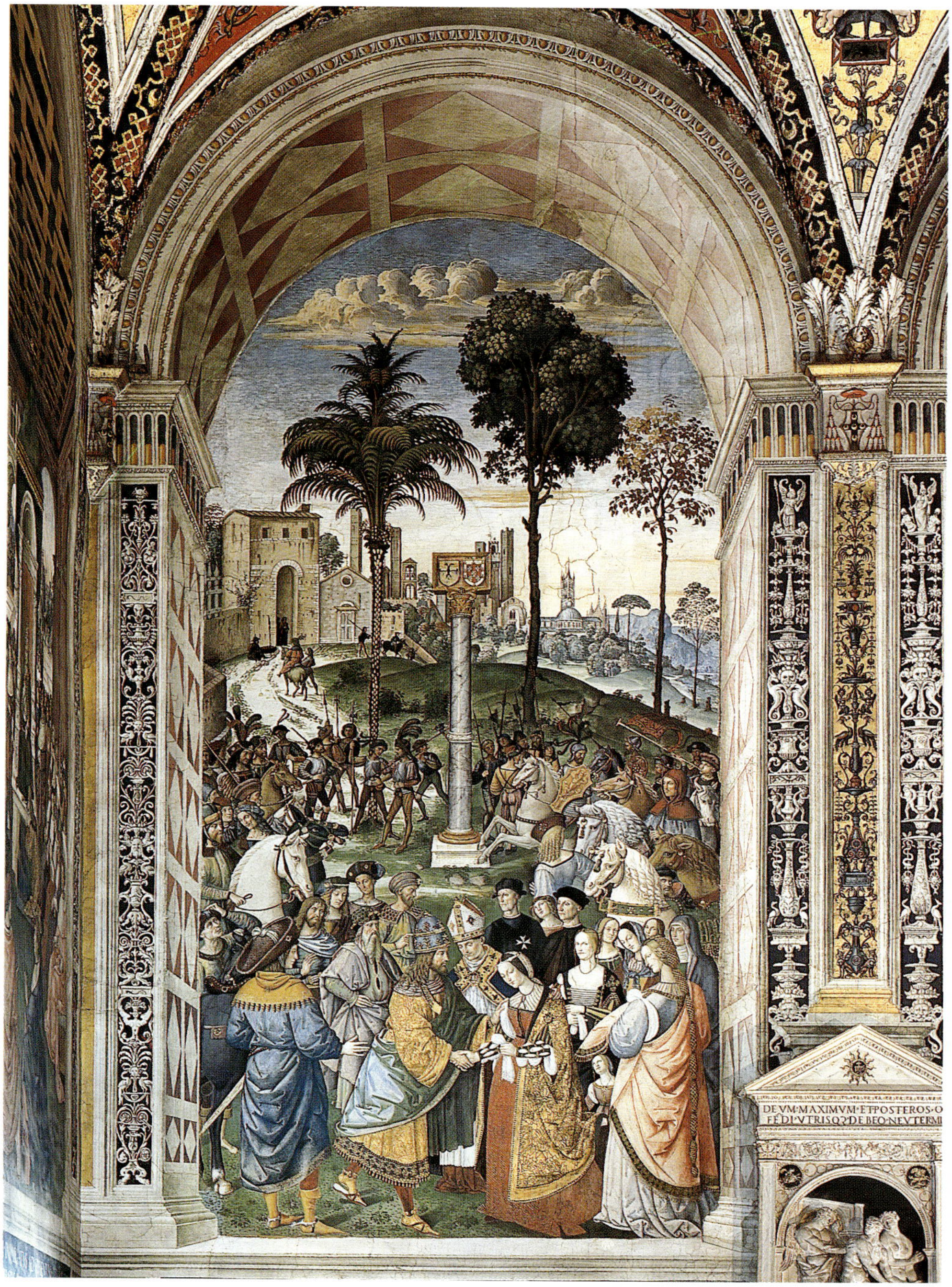

Pinturicchio
Enea Silvio Piccolomini presents Eleonora of Portugal to Frederich III
fresco
1505
Siena, Duomo, Piccolomini Library.

In 1492 Cardinal Francesco Todeschini Piccolomini, later Pope Pius III, decided to honor his maternal uncle Enea Silvio with a library that would house the exceptional collection of the great Humanist Pope. In the old presbytery annexed to the Duomo the frescoes were painted by Pinturrichio alone starting in 1505.

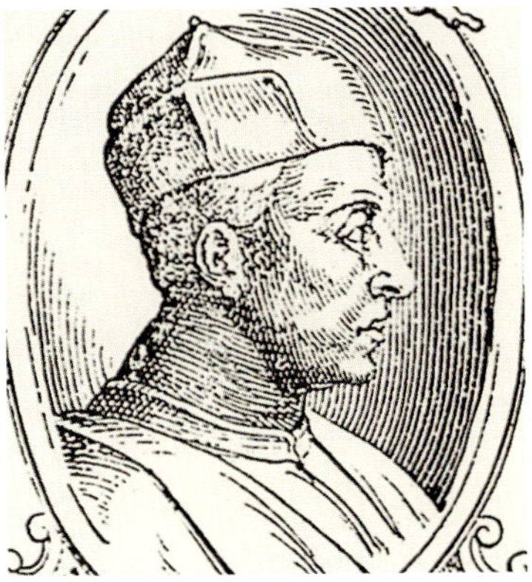

Luca Signorelli

(Cortona c. 1445 – 1523)

A painter endowed with "ingenuity and a pilgrim spirit", according to the *Chronicles* (1470-80) of Santi, Raphael's father, he was one of the finest artists of the whole century (not by chance, his figures were copied by Raphael himself). In the evolutionist theory of Vasari, who saw Michelangelo as the peak of artistic perfection, Signorelli's style was deemed a crucially important precedent, a judgement that was to favor the critical fortunes of the master from Cortona. His works, painted during a long career in central Italy, show a skillful blending of different elements: the linear drawing of Florence, the luminist effects of Piero della Francesca, and the dynamism of bodies, always depicted with great mathematical precision.

Giorgio Vasari, *Portrait of Luca Signorelli*, from the *Lives*, Florence, Giunti, 1568.

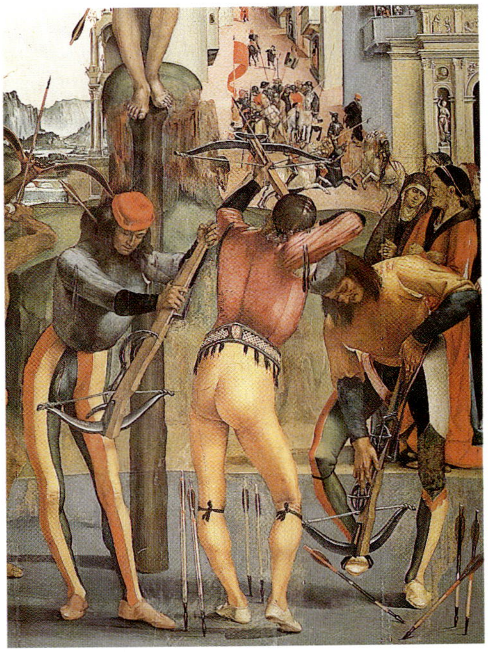

Luca Signorelli
Martyrdom of St Sebastian
1498
panel, detail
Città di Castello,
Pinacoteca Nazionale.

Painted for the Church of San Domenico in Città di Castello, in 1832 the panel still bore the date and names, later lost, of the patrons, Tommaso and Francesca de' Brozzi. The dynamic poses of the two archers standing at the feet of the martyred saint were admired and copied by Raphael (drawings at Lille and Oxford).

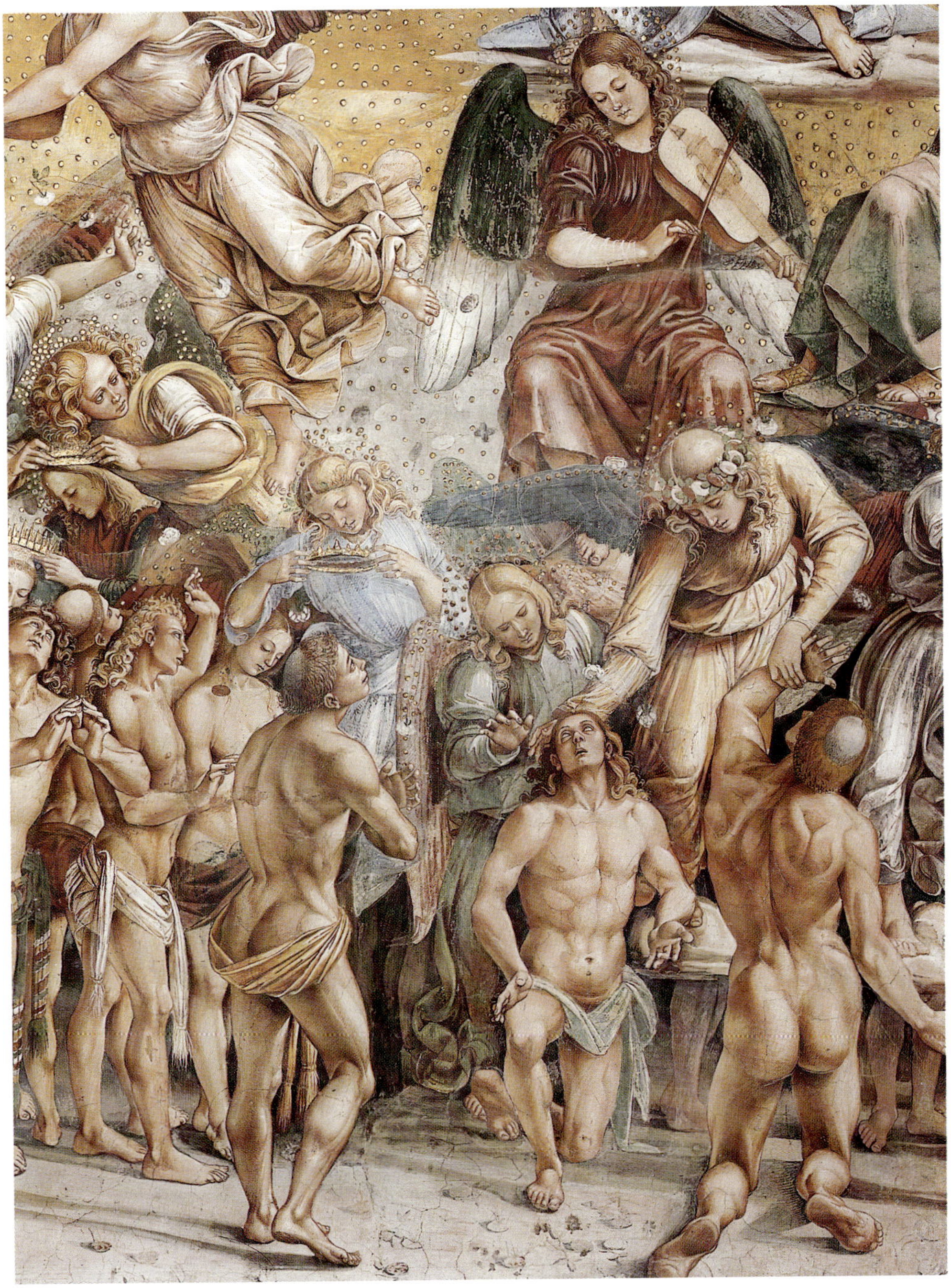

Luca Signorelli
The Blessed
1499-1502
fresco, detail
Orvieto, Duomo,
San Brizio Chapel.

Signorelli's masterpiece in fresco, the famous cycle of Orvieto, with *Stories of the Anti-Christ*, *Resurrection of the Flesh*, *The Damned*, *The Blessed*, *Paradise* and *Inferno*, reveals in its numerous nudes masterful studies from life.

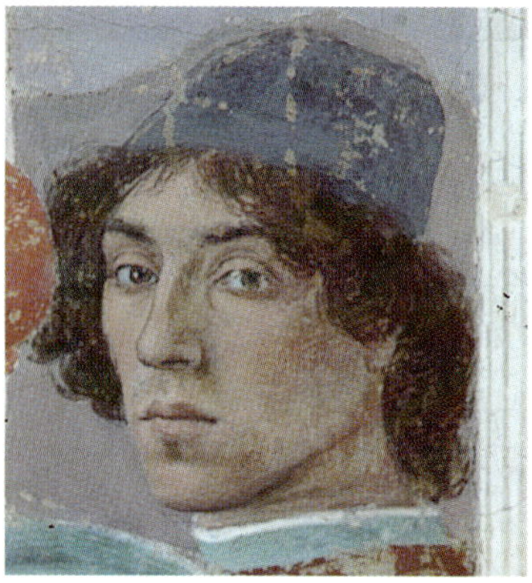

Filippino Lippi

(Prato c. 1457 – Florence 1504)

The son of Fra Filippo and the nun Lucrezia Buti, in Spoleto as a boy with his father, at the latter's death he assisted Fra Diamante in finishing the frescoes in the Duomo. From 1472 in Florence he was "dipintore with Sandro Botticello", a former pupil of Filippo's, in a fruitful alliance lasting ten years. Becoming independent, he was assigned important projects such as the frescoes in the Brancacci Chapel. For powerful patrons he painted works of capital importance for the art of the times, such as the *Vision of St Bernard* for Francesco del Pugliese (now in the Badia Fiorentina) and the great altarpiece for the Council Hall in Palazzo Vecchio (Uffizi), paid 1,200 lire at the decree of the Magnificent. Thanks to Lorenzo, he frescoed the Carafa Chapel in Rome, dense in classical allusions. In 1502 he completed for the Strozzi the frescoes in Santa Maria Novella, now displaying the symptoms of the new century's disquiet.

Filippino Lippi,
Self-portrait, detail of the *Crucifixion of St Peter*, c. 1485. Florence, Santa Maria del Carmine, Brancacci Chapel.

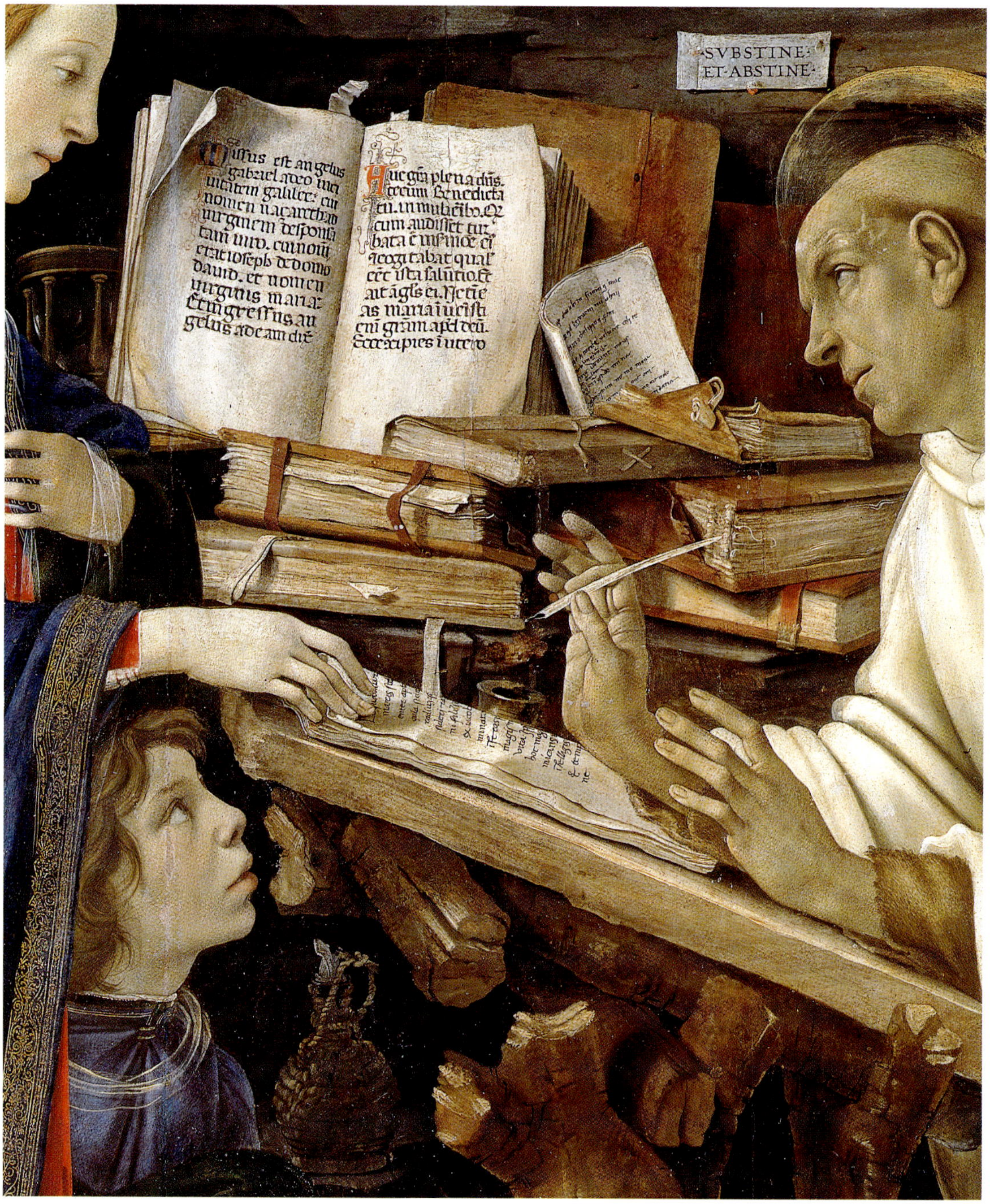

Filippino Lippi
Vision of St Bernard
c. 1485
panel, detail
Florence, Badia Fiorentina.

In one of his intense religious paintings, Filippino left the finest example of the analytic taste, derived from Flemish art, characteristic of Florentine painting in those years. Many artists were strongly influenced by the arrival in Florence in 1483 of the grandiose Flemish triptych *The Adoration of the Shepherds* (Florence, Uffizi), painted at Bruges in about 1478 by Hugo van der Goes. The work was placed above the high altar of the Church of Sant'Egidio, and Filippino must have studied it attentively.

Filippino Lippi
Triumph of St Thomas of Aquinas
c. 1492
fresco, detail
Rome, Santa Maria sopra Minerva, Carafa Chapel.

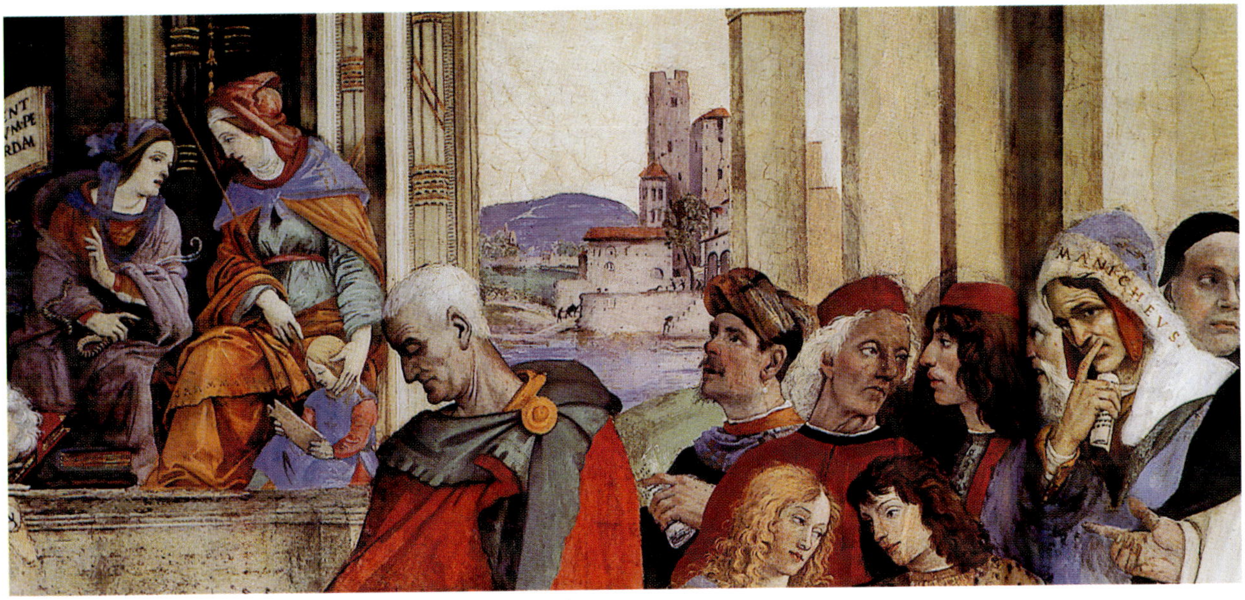

Requested for the chapel of the Neapolitan Cardinal Olivieri Carafa, friend of the Magnificent, the frescoes cost 2,000 gold ducats "without counting the blues and the shop boys". Filippino decorated the ceiling with *Sibyls*, and the walls with the *Triumph and Calling of Thomas*, *Assumption of the Virgin* and *Annunciation*. There are many contemporary portraits and views of a vanished Rome, such as the Dogana of Ripa Grande, landing place of pilgrims and merchants.

Filippino Lippi
Nerli Altarpiece
c. 1494
panel
Florence, Santo Spirito.

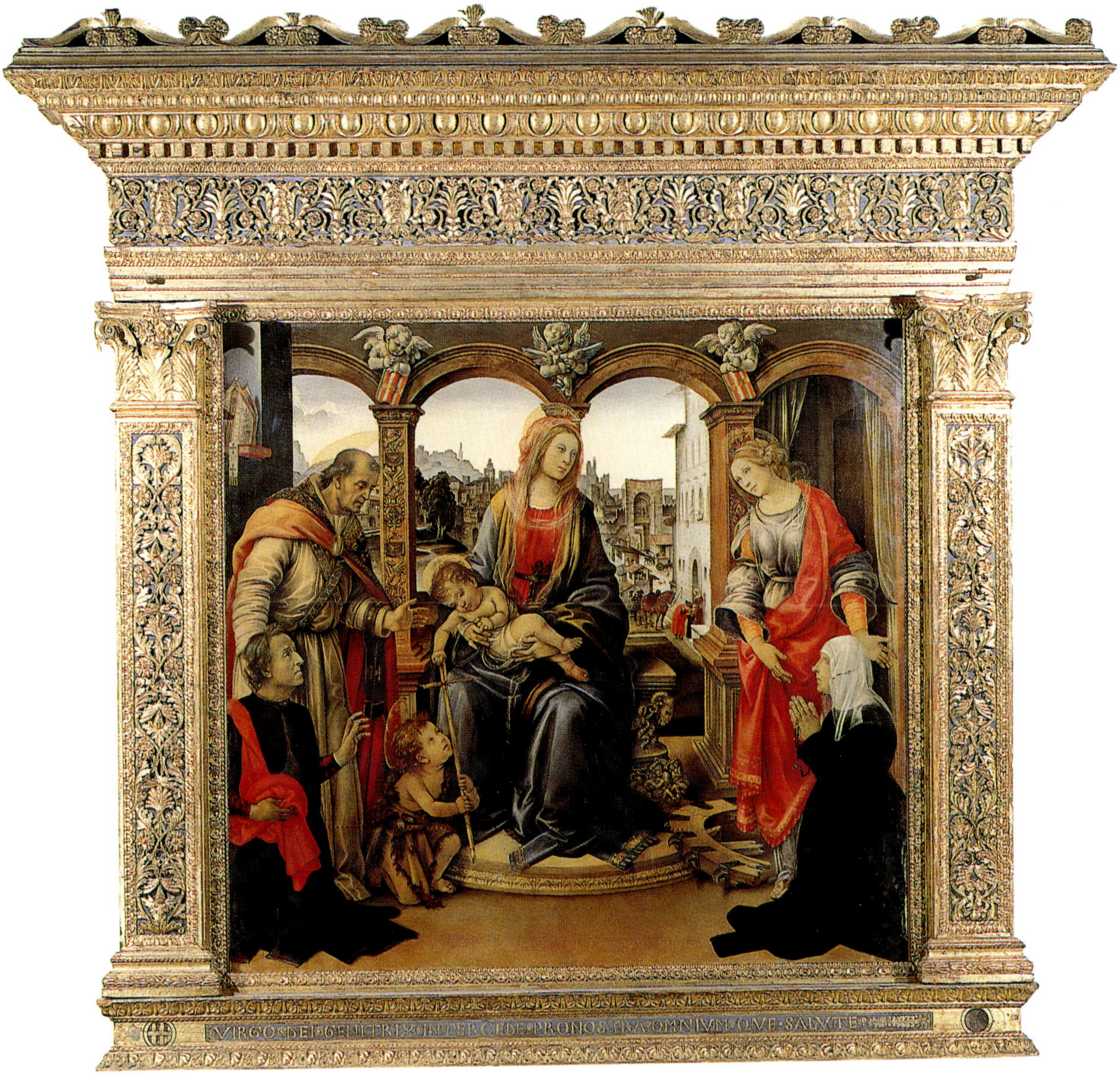

The wealthy politician Tanai Nerli appears in the foreground at the feet of St Martin, facing his wife who kneels below St Catherine of Alexandria. In the background, in the lively neighborhood of San Frediano, Tanai can be seen beside his horse, on the threshold of his palace in Borgo San Jacopo, embracing his daughter Caterina (alluded to by the saint in the foreground). The rich frame, inlaid and gilded, is now attributed to the woodworker Chimenti del Tasso, who collaborated in those years with the Da Maiano shop.

The Rossellino Brothers

Bernardo
(Settignano 1409 – Florence 1464)
Antonio
(Settignano 1427 – Florence c. 1478/81)

Both trained as sculptors, they were born on the Florentine hillside near the Maiano quarries from which came another great sculptor of the times, Desiderio da Settignano (c. 1430-1464). The brothers accomplished works of clear humanistic imprint in various Italian cities. In addition to Florence, Empoli and Prato, Antonio the sculptor worked in Ferrara, Rome and Naples. Bernardo, who as architect collaborated with Alberti, worked in Rome and Pienza for Popes Nicholas V and Pius II.

The Da Maiano Brothers

Giuliano
(Maiano 1432 – Naples 1490)
Benedetto
(Maiano 1442 – Florence 1497)

Heading a shop in Florence that produced frames, inlay work and portals, later taken over by the Del Tasso, the brothers were also architects, assuming a role similar to that of the other "great" Florentine brothers, Antonio (1455-1434) and Giuliano da Sangallo (1445-1516). In addition to woodworking (Sacristy of the Messe, door of the Sala dell'Udienza in Palazzo Vecchio), they carried out major architectural projects in Florence, Siena, Arezzo, Loreto, Rome, Perugia, Faenza, Naples.

Bernardo Rossellino
Façade of the Duomo and Palazzo Piccolomini
1459-62
Pienza, Piazza Pio II.

Pienza, the ancient Corsignano near Siena, was given its new name in 1459 by Pope Pius II, Enea Silvio Piccolomini, poet, humanist, politician, born here in 1405 of one the oldest Sienese patrician families, owner of vast lands in Maremma. Elected pope in 1458, Piccolomini immediately decided to transform his birthplace into a city expressing all of the humanistic ideals of harmony and rationality. Today Pienza can boast of having preserved intact, alone among Italian cities, the urban and architectural aspect desired by the pope and commissioned of Bernardo Rossellino, who like himself was to die in 1464 without entirely finishing the project. The ideal fulcrum of the city is the square with the Bishop's palace to the west, the town hall to the south, the Duomo to the north (reminiscent of Alberti's Tempio Malatestiano at Rimini), and the family palace to the east, inspired by Palazzo Rucellai, built in Florence by Alberti in collaboration with Bernardo.

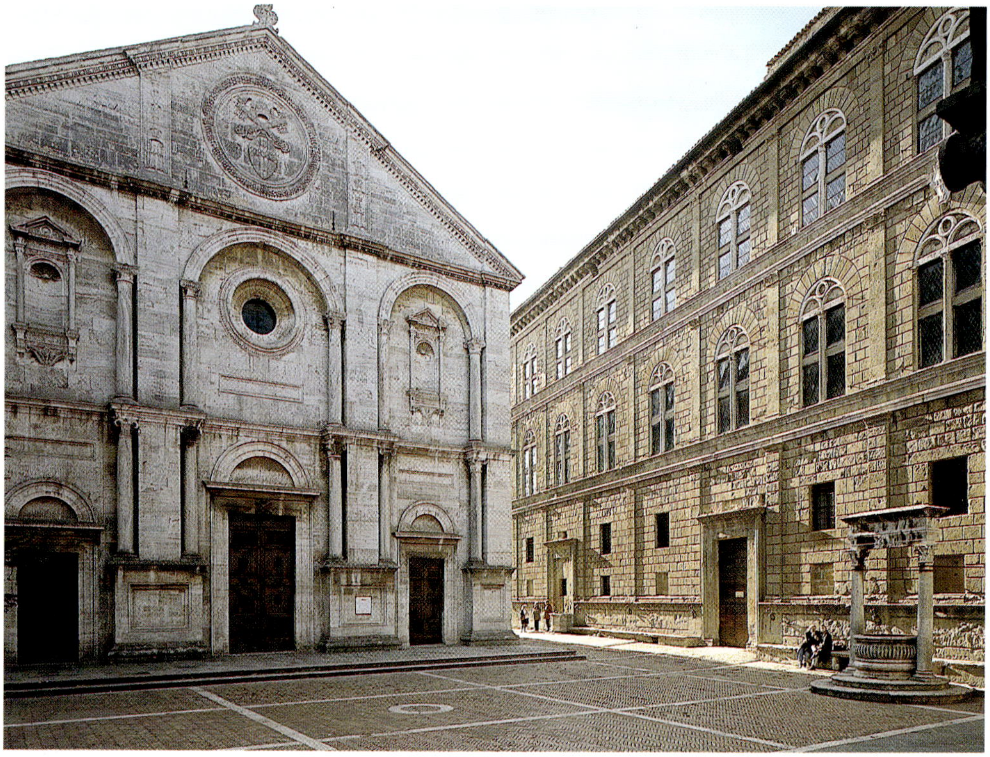

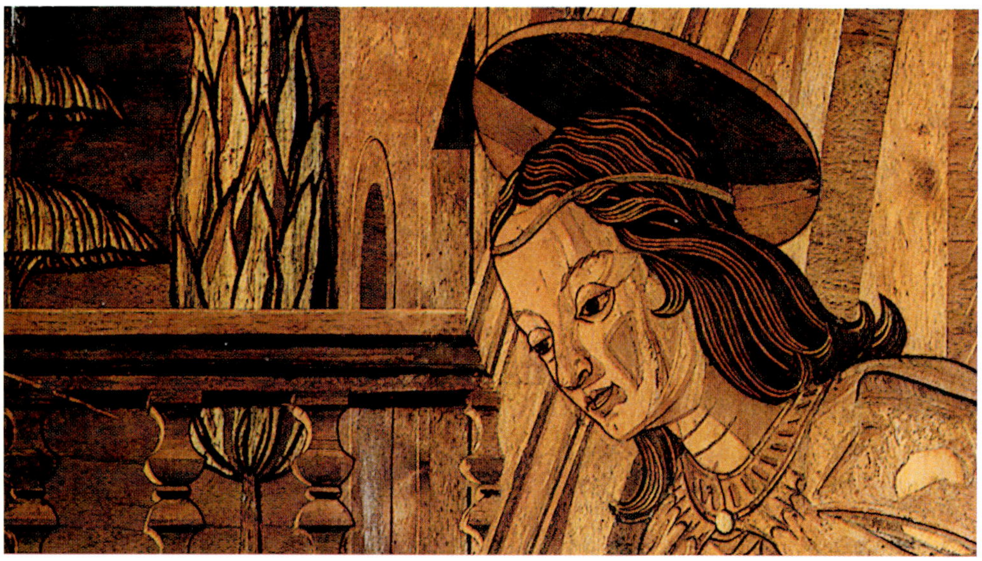

Giuliano da Maiano
Annunciation
1463-68
inlaid wood, detail of the east wall
Florence, Duomo, Sacristy of the Messe.

Executed to the design of Maso Finiguerra, skillful goldsmith and niello-worker (1426-64), at the time when the Florentine shops flourished at their highest, the panel forms part of the splendid ambiance of the Sacristy of the Messe in the Cathedral of Santa Maria del Fiore, whose four walls are lined with inlaid-wood cabinets. Begun by Antonio Manetti (1432-97), architect, man of letters, mathematician and astronomer, as well as friend and biographer of Brunelleschi, the tarsia work was continued by Giuliano with the assistance of several artisans. It was here, in 1478, that Lorenzo the Magnificent took refuge, escaping from death in the Pazzi conspiracy.

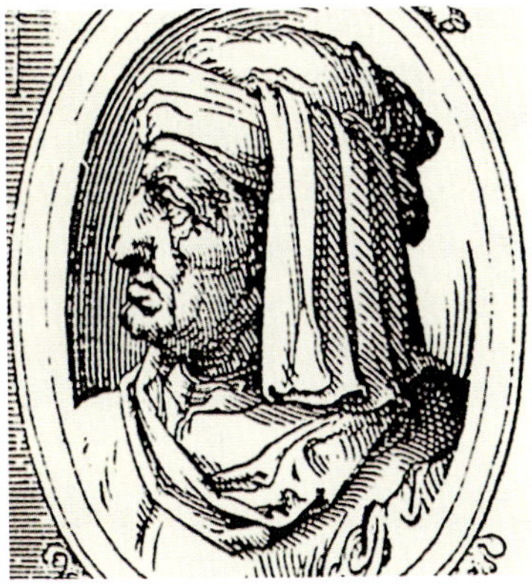

The Della Robbias

Luca di Simone
(Florence c. 1399 – 1482)
Andrea di Marco
(Florence 1435 – 1525)

The fame of Luca, deemed one of the century's greatest artists by Alberti, is linked to the invention of glazed terra-cotta: "a new art", says Vasari, "useful and beautiful", which could be used for the decoration "with beauty and without great expense of any damp, aquatic place" and which in sculpture rendered figures glossy and resistant. Trained also as goldsmith, Luca collaborated with Donatello on Ghiberti's *Doors of Paradise*. His classicizing style, already apparent in the marble *Choir*, developed through friendship with Brunelleschi, Nanni di Banco and the learned Humanist Niccolò Niccoli. In the early 1420s Luca abandoned marble for his new technique, launching a prolific shop continued by his grandson Andrea, Giovanni's third child, and then by other members of the family.

Giorgio Vasari, *Portrait of Luca della Robbia*, from the *Lives*, Florence, Giunti, 1568.

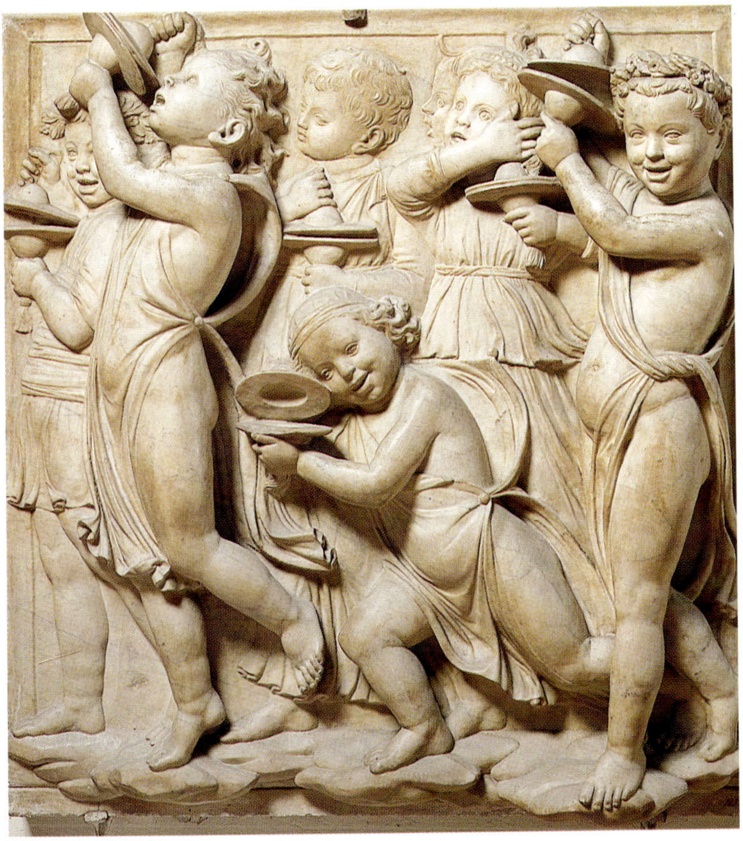

Luca della Robbia
Choir
1431-38
marble, detail
Florence, Museo dell'Opera del Duomo.

The two great "masters of carving" of the times, Luca and Donatello, found themselves almost competing in the important choirs commissioned by the Opera del Duomo of Florence. The two works, now displayed in the same room in the museum, clearly reveal the different styles of their makers. Luca chose a classicizing model with panels framed by architectural elements, while Donatello conceived a single scene as if set within a portico. The wild dance, the panic throng of Donatello's children, although "rough-hewn and not finished" as noted by Antonio Billi in about 1530, is "more striking" when seen from below, "than the figures of Luca". Today Luca's revival of classicism is acknowledged to be more homogeneous and typical than the innovative, transgressive vision of Donatello.

Andrea della Robbia
Ideal Effigy of a Youth
c. 1500
glazed terra-cotta
Fiesole, Bandini Museum.

From a dark shell-shaped background, colored purple-black in imitation of marble, forcefully emerge the regular, classical features of a young man with a vaguely melancholy gaze. Framing the medallion is the typical Della Robbia garland with pine cones, flowers and leaves, brightly colored in contrasting yellows, browns and greens. This is one of the most intense examples of the glazed terra-cotta production of Andrea della Robbia, expert in softly modeling his reliefs, marked by a strong classical tendency. Medallions of this type, of both profane and religious nature, were generally used in decorating exteriors.

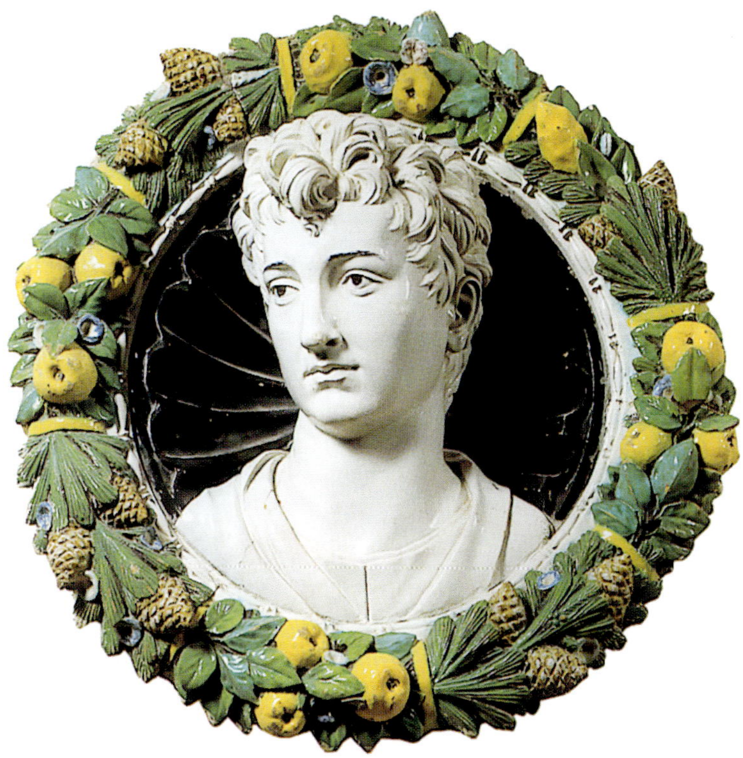

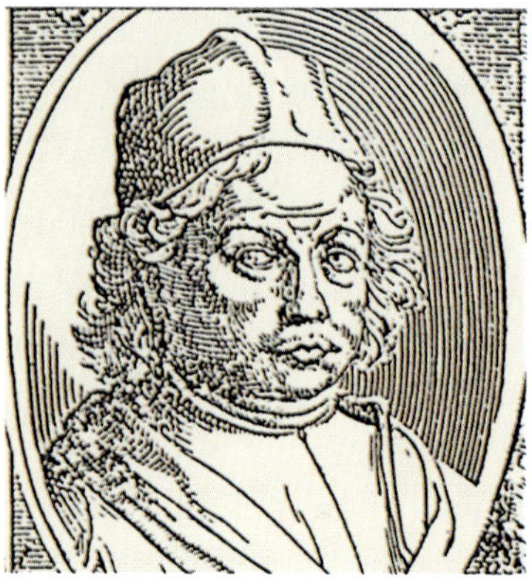

Verrocchio

(Andrea di Francesco di Cione, Florence 1435 – Venice 1488)

Andrea, who took his pseudonym from the goldsmith Giuliano Verrocchi to whom he was apprenticed, often infringed the law. As a youth he killed a worker in the street with a stone, perhaps by accident, and later was accused of illicit relations with his shop boys, among them Leonardo (whose delicate 13-year-old features he may have incarnated in the Bargello's bronze *David*, 1465), and the beloved Lorenzo di Credi, named his heir. "Goldsmith, perspective artist, sculptor, engraver, painter and musician", as Vasari reports, he headed an eclectic shop rivaled only by that of the Pollaiolos. Many youths who were to become famous, not Florentines alone, trained with him at the turn of the century – Perugino as well as Leonardo and Lorenzo di Credi. In addition to his works in Florence and Pistoia is the monument to Colleoni in Venice, left unfinished in 1488.

Giorgio Vasari, *Portrait of Verrocchio*, from the *Lives*, Florence, Giunti, 1568.

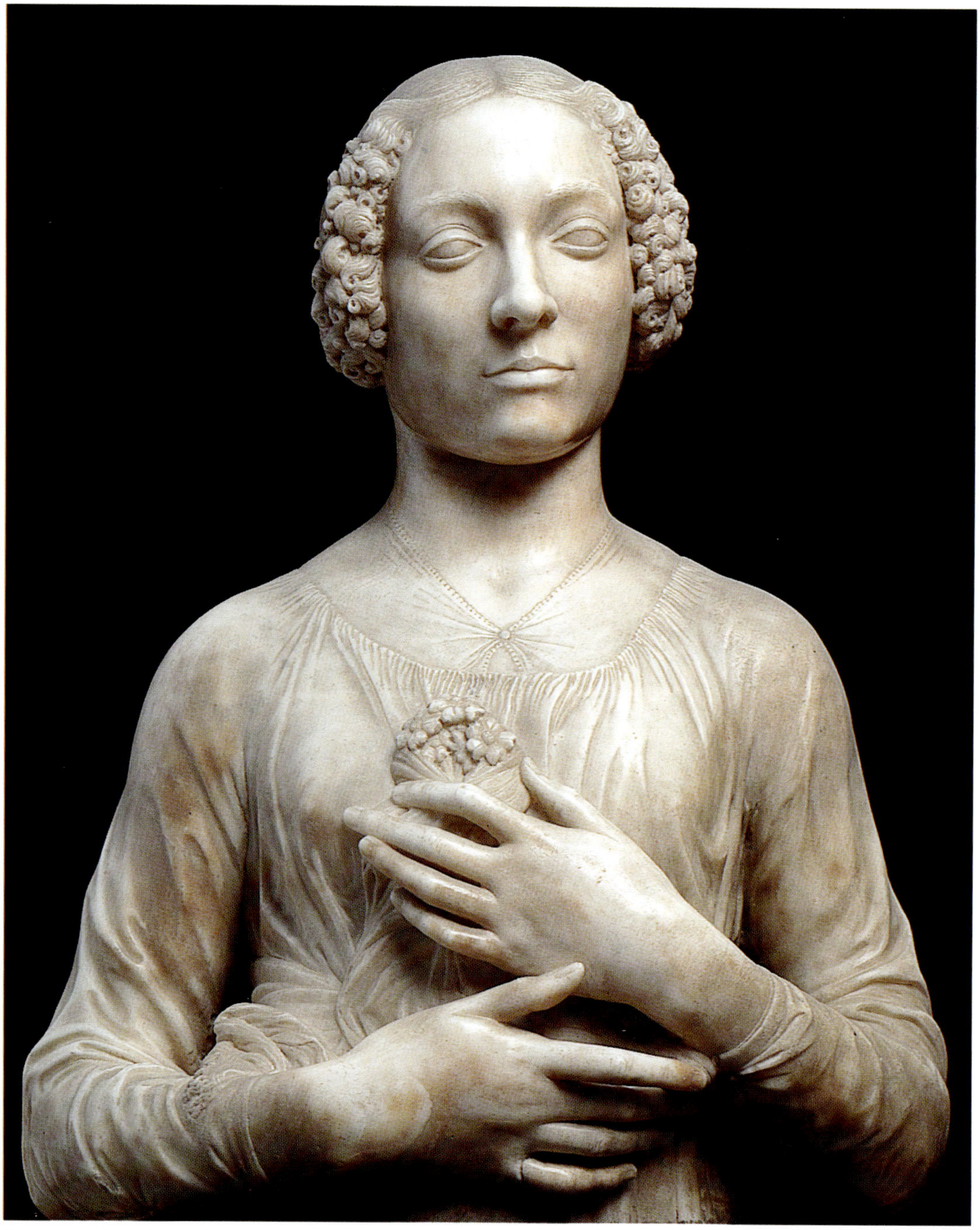

Verrocchio
Lady with a Bouquet
c. 1475
marble
Florence, Bargello Museum.

The identification of the smooth, polished sculpture of a lady, one of the most highly admired marble busts, is still today mysterious. It has been hypothesized that the subject is Lucrezia Donati, the legendary Platonic love of Lorenzo the Magnificent, who kept a portrait of her in his bedchamber; and even that she is Ginevra de' Benci, also portrayed by Leonardo in about 1475. It may really be the young Leonardo, as is still sometimes suggested, who carved the delicate hands with their long tapering fingers holding the bouquet of wild roses, or perhaps primulas.

Verrocchio
Cherub with a Dolphin
c. 1476
bronze
Florence, Palazzo Vecchio, Terrace of Juno.

Destined by Lorenzo the Magnificent to the fountain of the Medicean villa of Careggi, the famous bronze was placed by Cosimo I in about 1556 above Vasari's fountain in Palazzo Vecchio, where it is still today the object of admiration. Apparently similar in subject and size to the *Cupid-Atys* sculpted for the Doni family by Donatello (c. 1440, Bargello), it is in reality inspired by a combination of different types of cherubs and cupids from antiquity. The statue is hollow to let water spew from the dolphin's mouth.

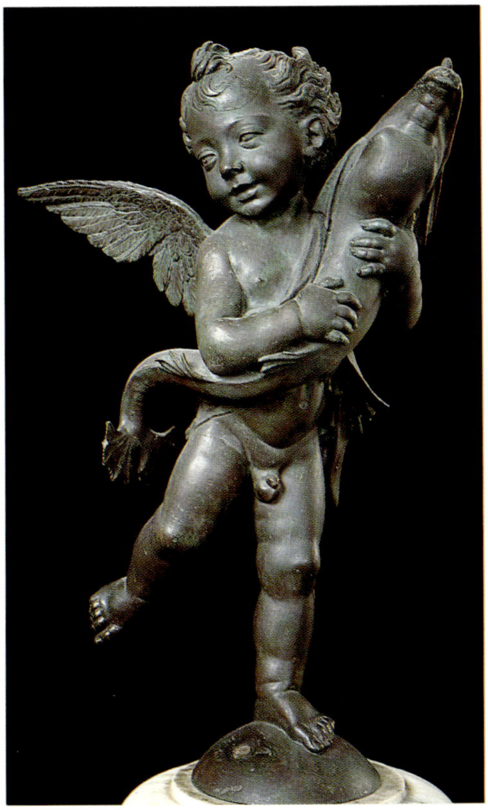

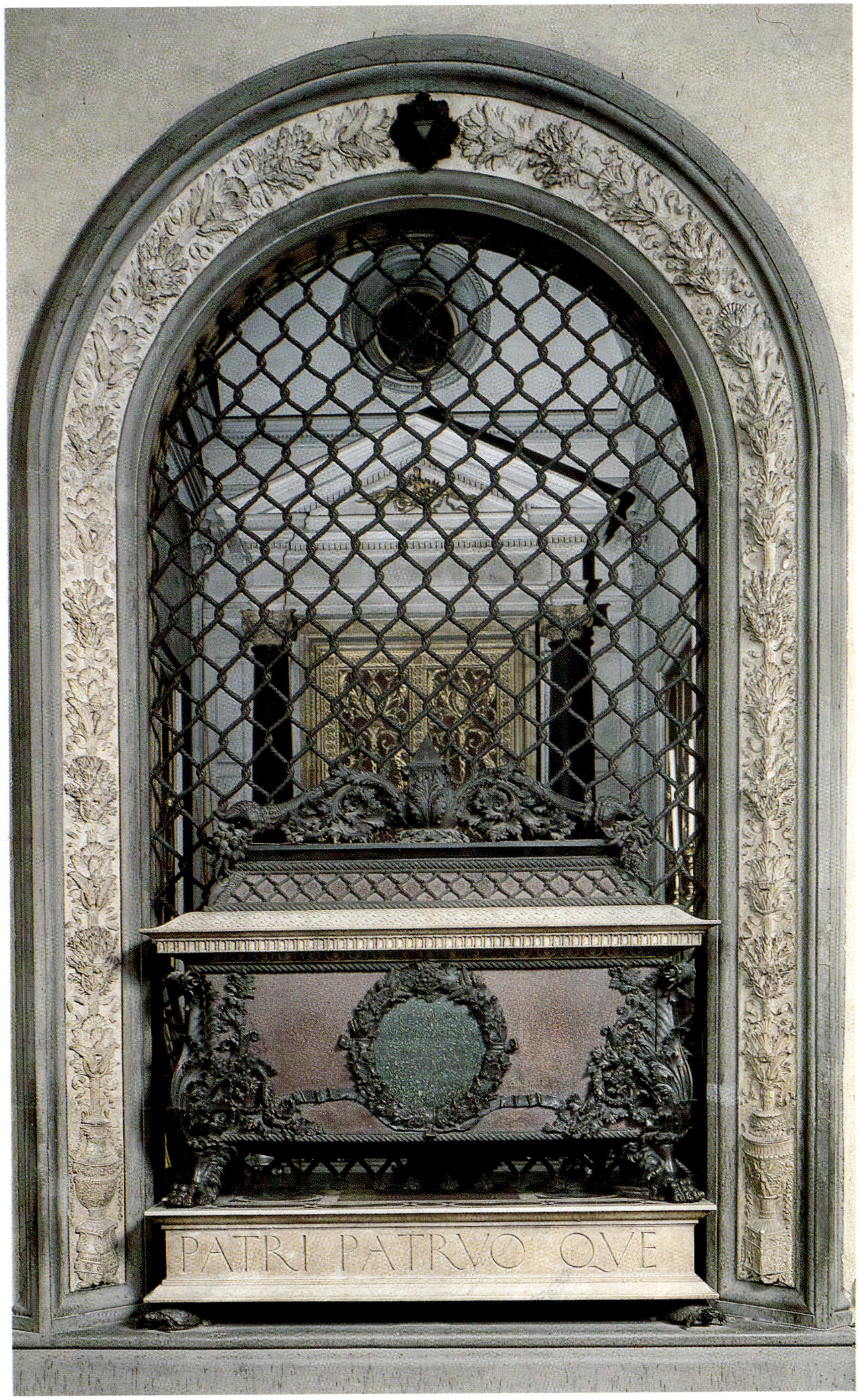

Verrocchio
Sepulcher of Piero and Giovanni de' Medici
1469-72
marble, porphyry and bronze
Florence, Basilica of San Lorenzo, Old Sacristy.

Soon called "one of the marvels of the world" was the work commissioned by Lorenzo and Giuliano de' Medici to commemorate their father Piero (died in 1469) and their uncle Giovanni (died in 1463): a splendid porphyry sarcophagus with bronze decorations inspired by nature and "scientifically exact" (Zeri), behind which, framed by a marble frieze of garlands, is a grating "of bronze ropes in an almond-shaped pattern, perfectly natural in appearance", admiringly reports Vasari, who however judged Verrocchio's art in general to be "very hard and crude".

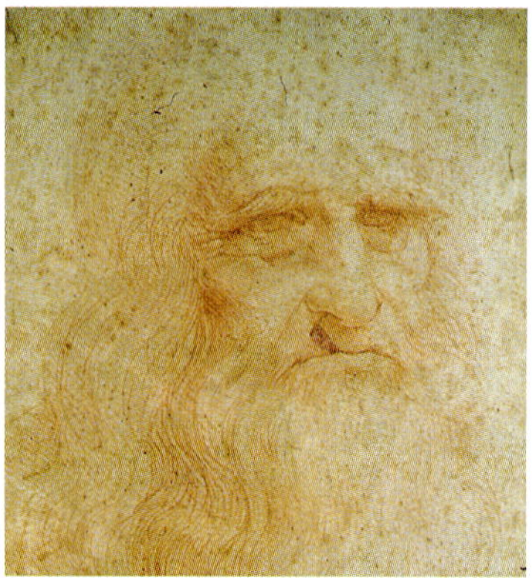

Leonardo da Vinci

(Vinci 1452 – Amboise 1519)

For the most famous, fascinating artist/scientist of all time it is impossible to avoid the cliché of "universal genius": tireless investigator of nature, anatomy, science and technology, philosopher and poet, although calling himself a "man without letters", Leonardo incarnates the highest ideals of Renaissance man. A free spirit, he was seemingly indifferent to the political situations around him but sensitive to the horrors of violence, despite his studies of war machines, and more interested in planning revolutionary projects than in carrying them out. For this reason he has left an impressive number of drawings but few finished works, as noted already by his contemporaries. His life was spent between Florence, Laurentian and then Republican, and the Milan of the Sforza lords; then Venice, Emilia (with Cesare Borgia), Pavia and Rome, and lastly the France of Francis I.

Leonardo da Vinci,
Self-portrait, after 1515.
Turin, Biblioteca Reale.

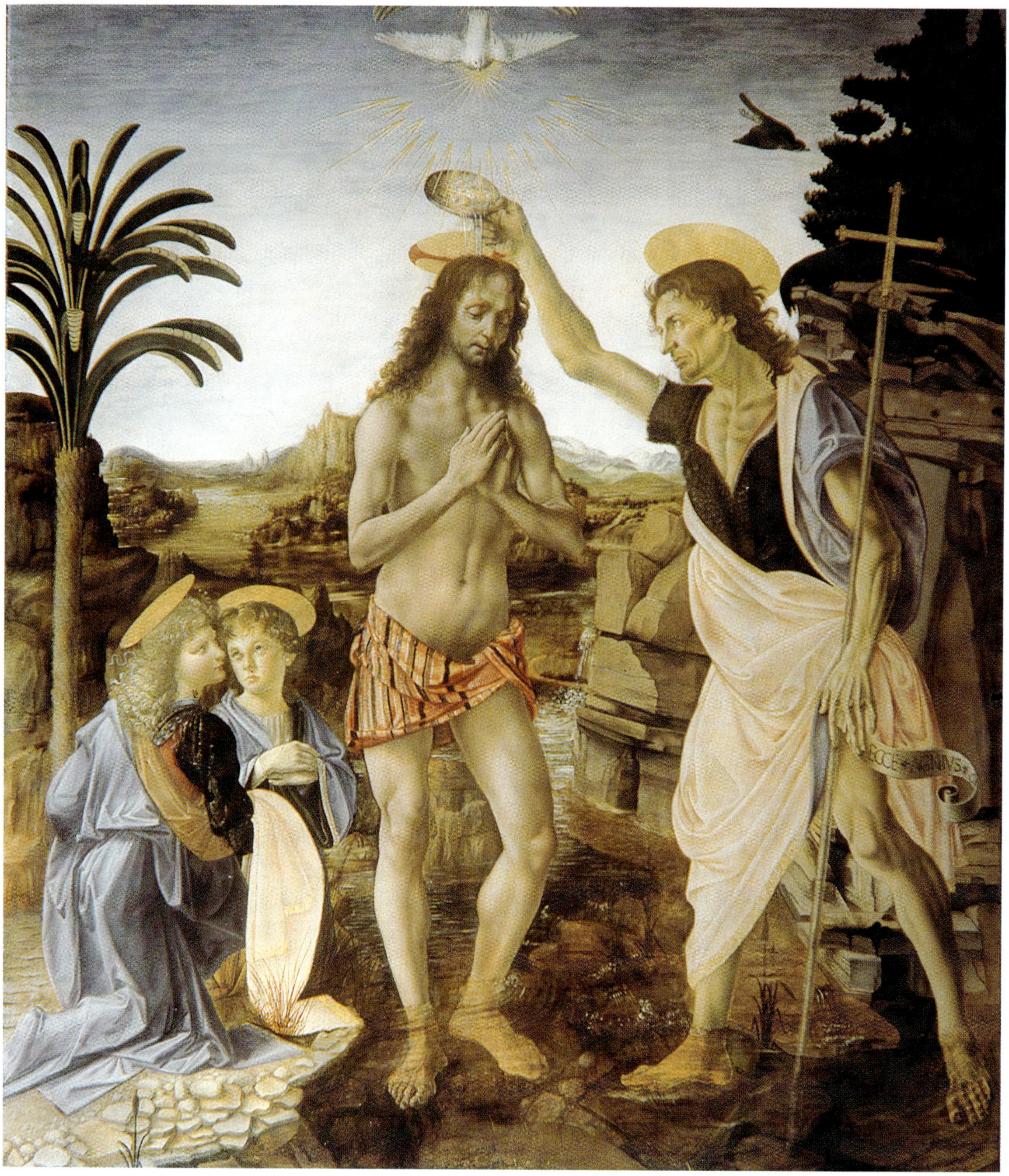

Verrocchio, Leonardo and other artists
The Baptism of Christ
variously dated between 1473 and 1478
panel
Florence, Uffizi Gallery.

This is the most telling example of the vitality of Verrocchio's shop. According to Vasari the artist gave up painting "offended that a young boy [Leonardo] knew more than he". The angel on the left and the background have been traditionally attributed to Leonardo, but stylistic differences are even more evident since the restoration of 1998, which has also revealed the detail of the ducks in the water behind the Baptist's elbow. Now it is clear that the dry style of the palm tree and the rocky outcrop behind the Baptist, as well as his own figure, can be attributed neither to Verrocchio nor to Leonardo, whose mountains fade softly into the distance. It now seems that not only apprentices but at least one other great artist, perhaps Botticelli for the angel on the right, must have worked on the painting.

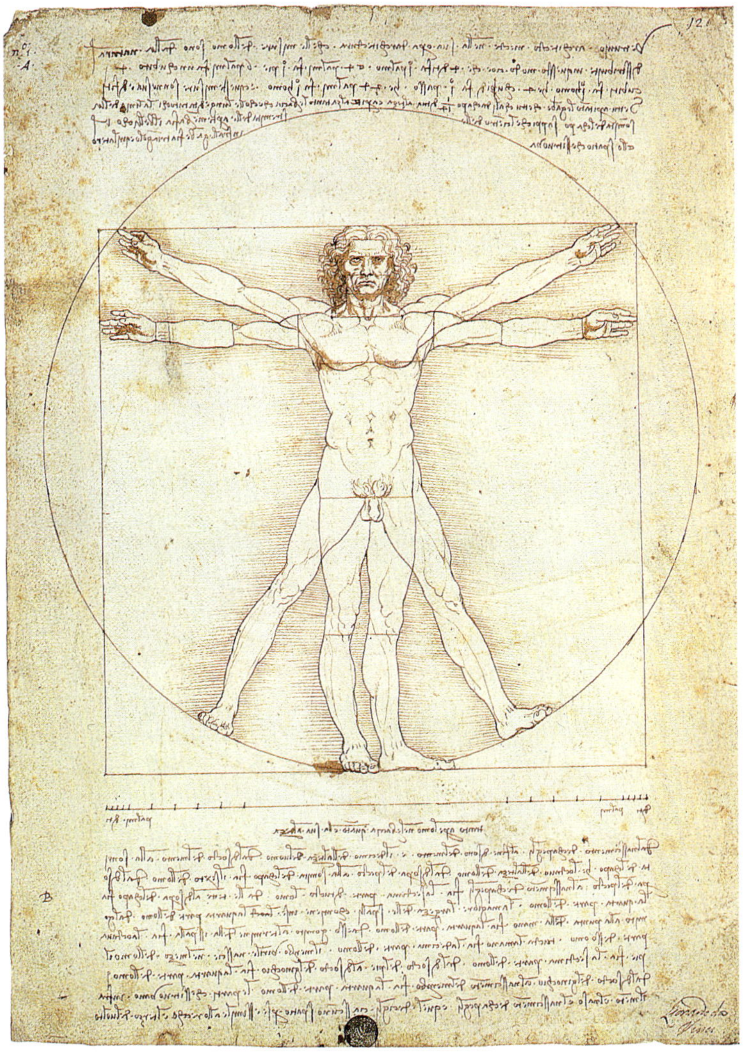

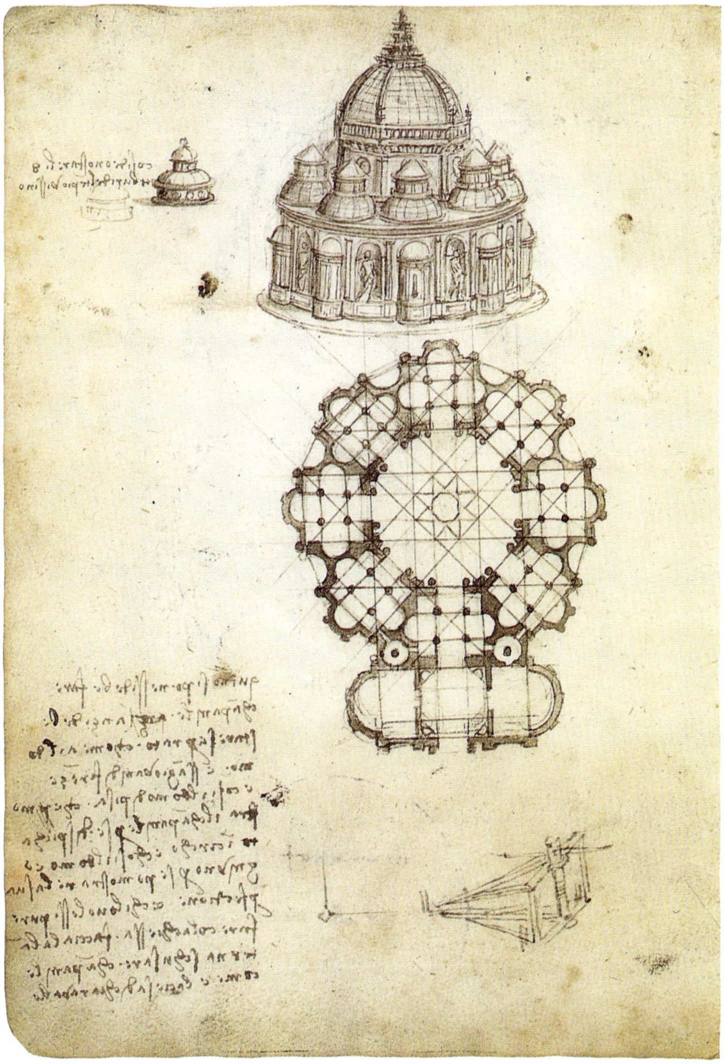

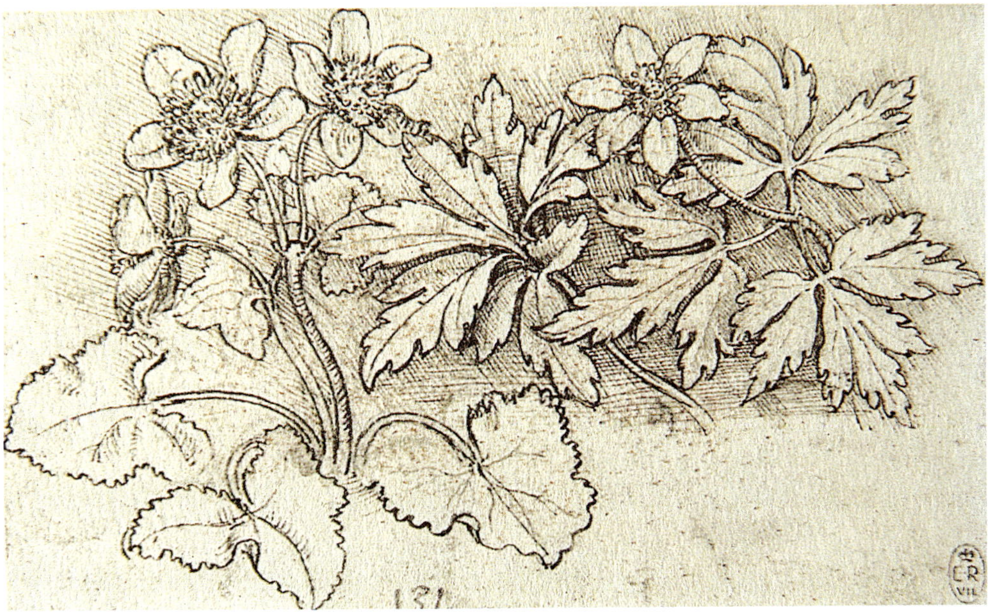

Leonardo da Vinci

Homo Vitruvianus
c. 1490
paper
Venice, Gallerie dell'Accademia.

Study of church with circular plan
1487-90
paper
Paris, Library of the Institut de France, Manuscript B, c. 95 r.

Study of two plants for the Leda
c. 1508-10
paper
Windsor, Royal Library, c. 23 r.

Three examples of Leonardo's enormous graphic production: the famous study of proportions with the human figure inscribed in a circle and in a square; a testimony to the many architectural projects never carried out, and a study from life for the *Leda* painting, lost but known through copies by various artists, among them the Lombard Cesare da Sesto (1477-1523) and the Sienese Sodoma (1477-1529).

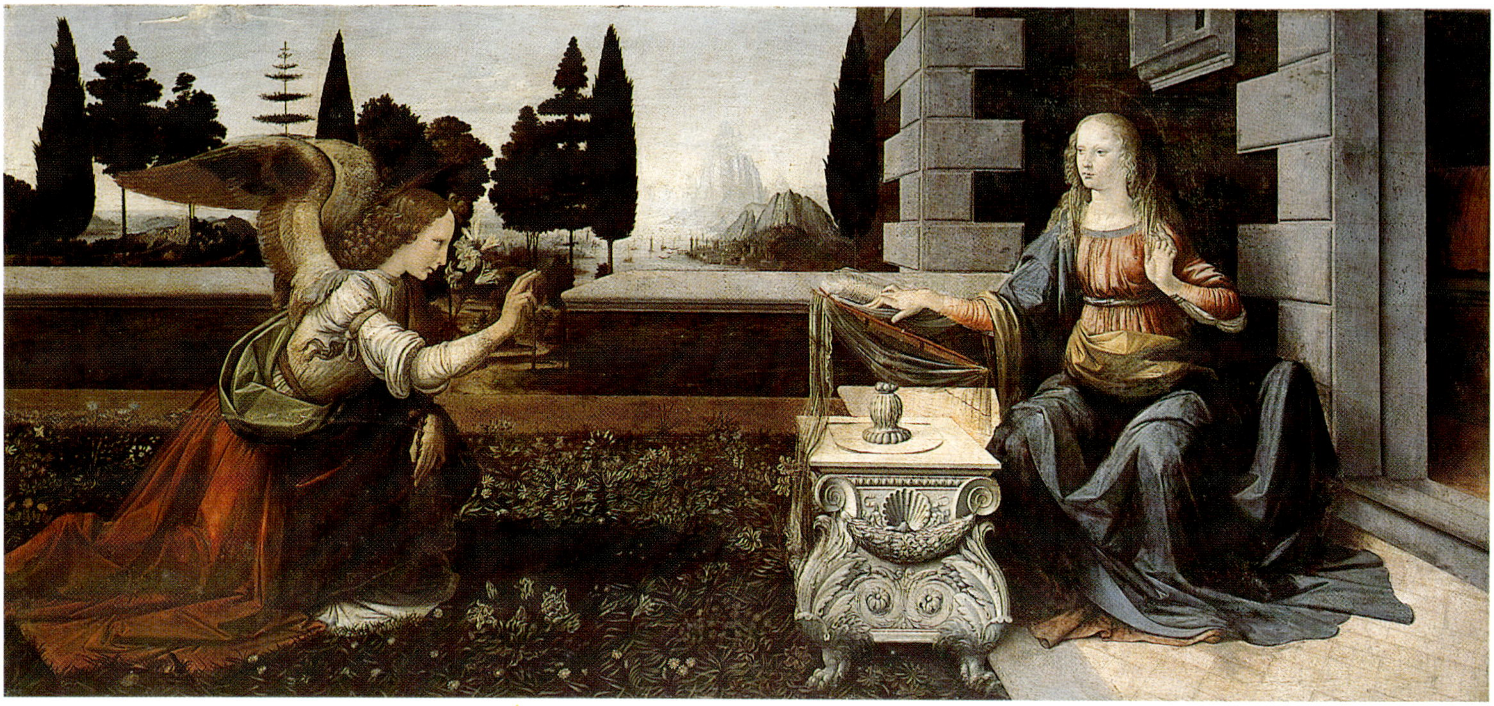

Leonardo
Annunciation
c. 1475-80
panel
Florence, Uffizi Gallery.

New hypotheses for the reading of this painting have been stimulated by its restoration, completed in March 2000, which has revealed not only its luminosity and clarity of detail but a stronger sense of perspective in the architectural foreshortening on the right (the door, of which both doorjambs can now be seen, gives a clearer glimpse of the baldachin in the room). Still controversial is the dating of the work painted in Florence for the Church of San Bartolomeo a Oliveto. Hypotheses range from the early 1460s, when the artist was only a little over twenty, almost up to the beginning of the next decade. In some details the influence of Verrocchio, or perhaps Leonardo's homage to his master, can be recognized (especially in the base supporting the lectern, reminiscent of the Sepulcher of Giovanni and Piero de' Medici in San Lorenzo). The Virgin's arm seems disproportionately elongated, unable to reach the book on the lectern, and the angel's shadow is too dark for the light of dawn, which restoration has shown to be the hour chosen by Leonardo as the setting, perhaps with symbolic overtones, for the Annunciation. The meadow is sprinkled with a myriad of flowers studied from life; in the beautiful landscape, typical Tuscan cypresses trail off into the distance where the minute details of a lake-side city blend into the bluish tones of the bare mountains in the background.

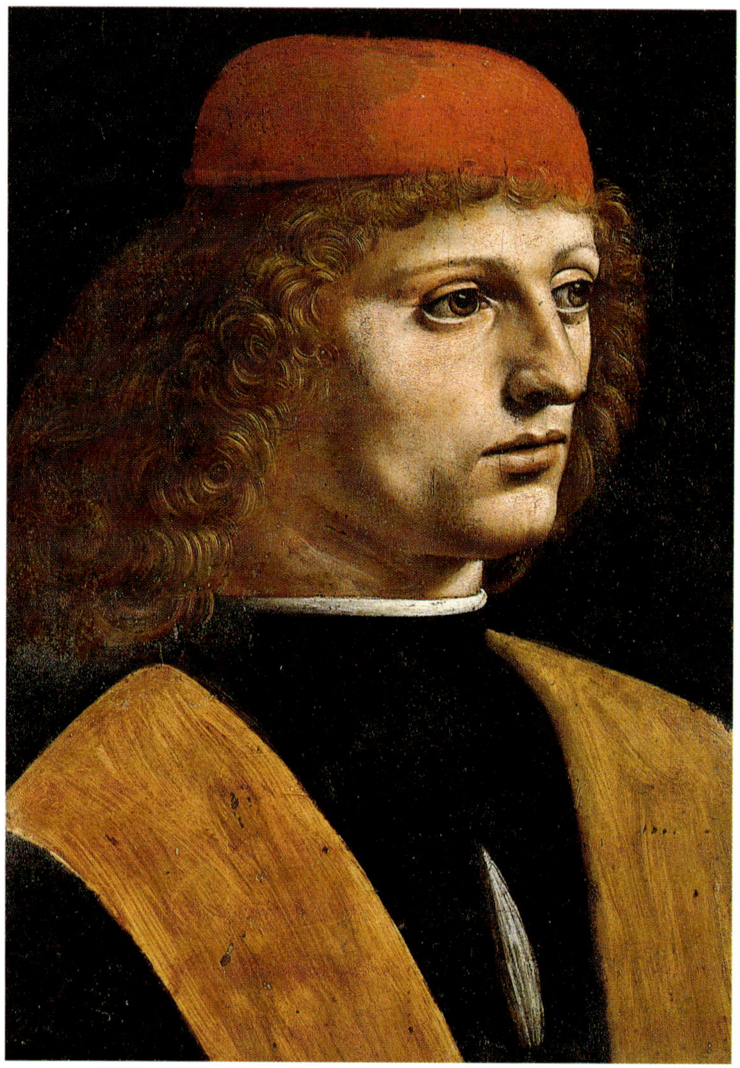

Leonardo
Portrait of a Musician
c. 1484
panel
Milan, Pinacoteca Ambrosiana.

The model could be Franchino Gaffurio, in 1483 chapel master of Santa Maria Maggiore in Bergamo, and the next year occupying the same position in the Milan Duomo. The painting is typical of Leonardo's Milan period (1482-1499), marked by strong psychological introspection in spite of the uncertainty of the hands, an aspect which links it to the Crakow *Lady with an Ermine*. The influence of northern painting is also probable, and may have been mediated through the artist's knowledge of Flemish-style works such as the Louvre's *Condottiero* by Antonello da Messina, who journeyed to Milan in 1475.

Leonardo da Vinci
The Last Supper
1495-98
fresco
Milan, refectory
of Santa Maria delle Grazie.

Completed by 1498, as shown by the dedicatory letter to Ludovico il Moro, Duke of Milan, in the *De divina proportione* by the mathematician Luca Pacioli, nothing is known of the commissioner of the fresco, for which Leonardo adopted such an unsuitable technique that he himself was obliged to restore it soon afterward. Retouched many times over the centuries, it was now almost illegible when the American writer Henry James visited it in 1869, describing it as "the shadow of a shadow", "the saddest and the greatest masterpiece". Restoration having been completed in 1999 after decades of work, *The Last Supper*, although difficult to read, shows in the apostles' faces a careful, specific study of physiognomy, aimed at defining on the one hand the "permanent" and scientific traits based on the artist's incessant anatomical research, and on the other the temporary passions, the so-called "mental motions". It has recently been observed by Carlo Pedretti that Christ's shadow resembles that of Leonardo himself, as it appears in one of his drawings.

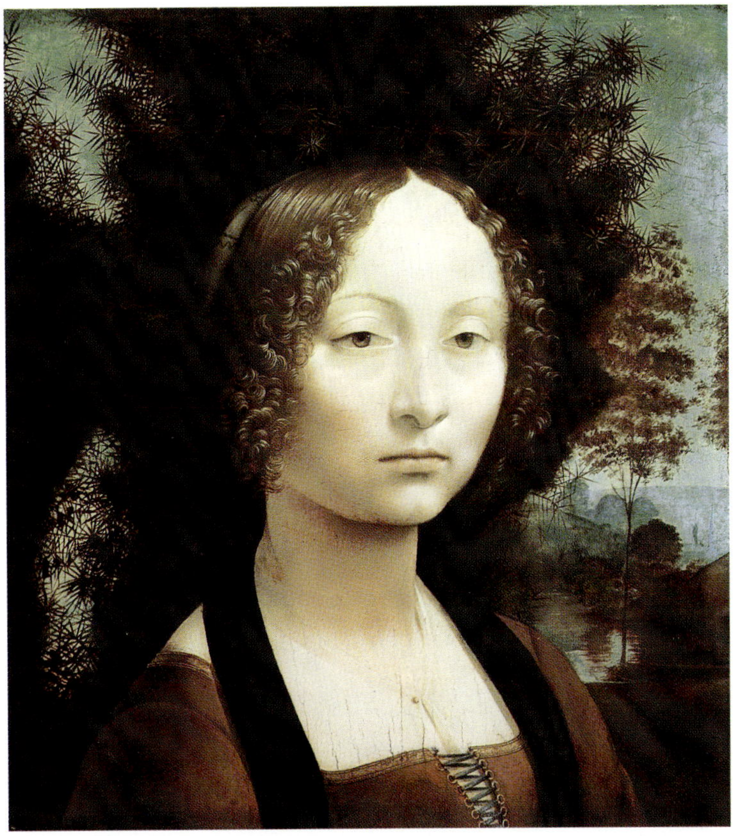

Leonardo da Vinci
Ginevra de' Benci
c. 1475
panel
Washington, National Gallery.

"Beauty adorns virtue" declare the words in Latin accompanying the emblem on the back of the panel, cut off at the bottom (originally the hands were visible in the painting, allowing a comparison with Verrocchio's *Lady with a Bouquet*). The beautiful Florentine girl (admired, it seems, by Bernardo Bembo, Venetian ambassador to Florence in 1475) was born in 1457 and was the sister of a certain Giovanni d'Amerigo de' Benci mentioned several times by Leonardo.

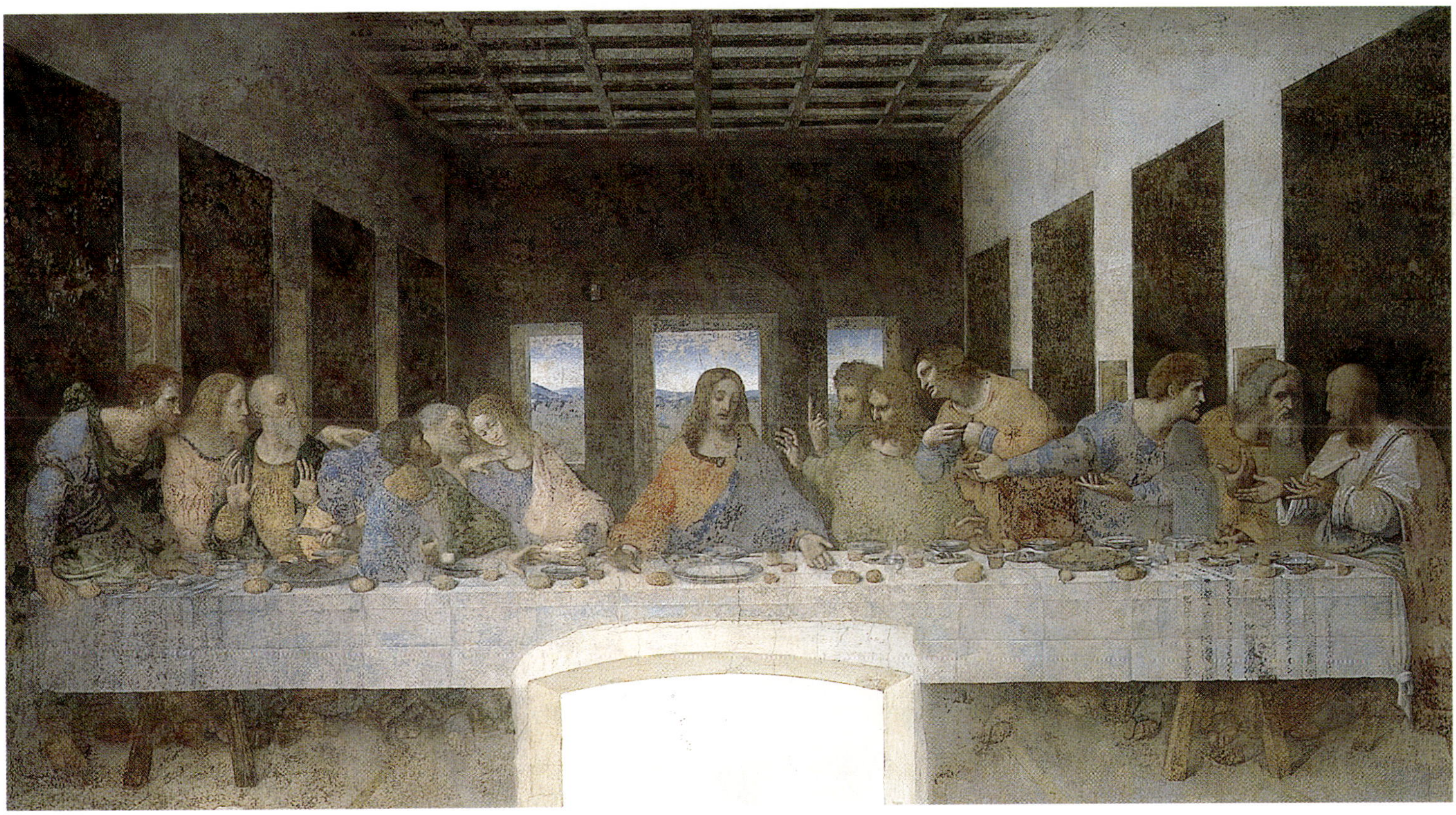

Leonardo da Vinci
The Lady with an Ermine
c. 1488-90
panel
Crakow, Czartoryski Muzeum.

This is probably a painting of Cecilia Gallerani, the favorite of Ludovico Sforza, later married to Count Bergamini. The ermine, in Greek *galè*, may allude to her name. If so, this would be the portrait of Cecilia painted "at such an imperfect age", sent to Isabella d'Este Duchess of Mantua in 1498 to allow her to compare it with portraits by the Venetian artist Giovanni Bellini. The dating of this famous "shoulder portrait", a type adopted by Leonardo subsequent to his studies on the dynamics of the human body in around 1487, can be deduced also from a sonnet describing it by the Florentine poet Bernardo Bellincioni, a friend of Leonardo, who was at the court of Ludovico il Moro in 1485 (and died there in 1492).

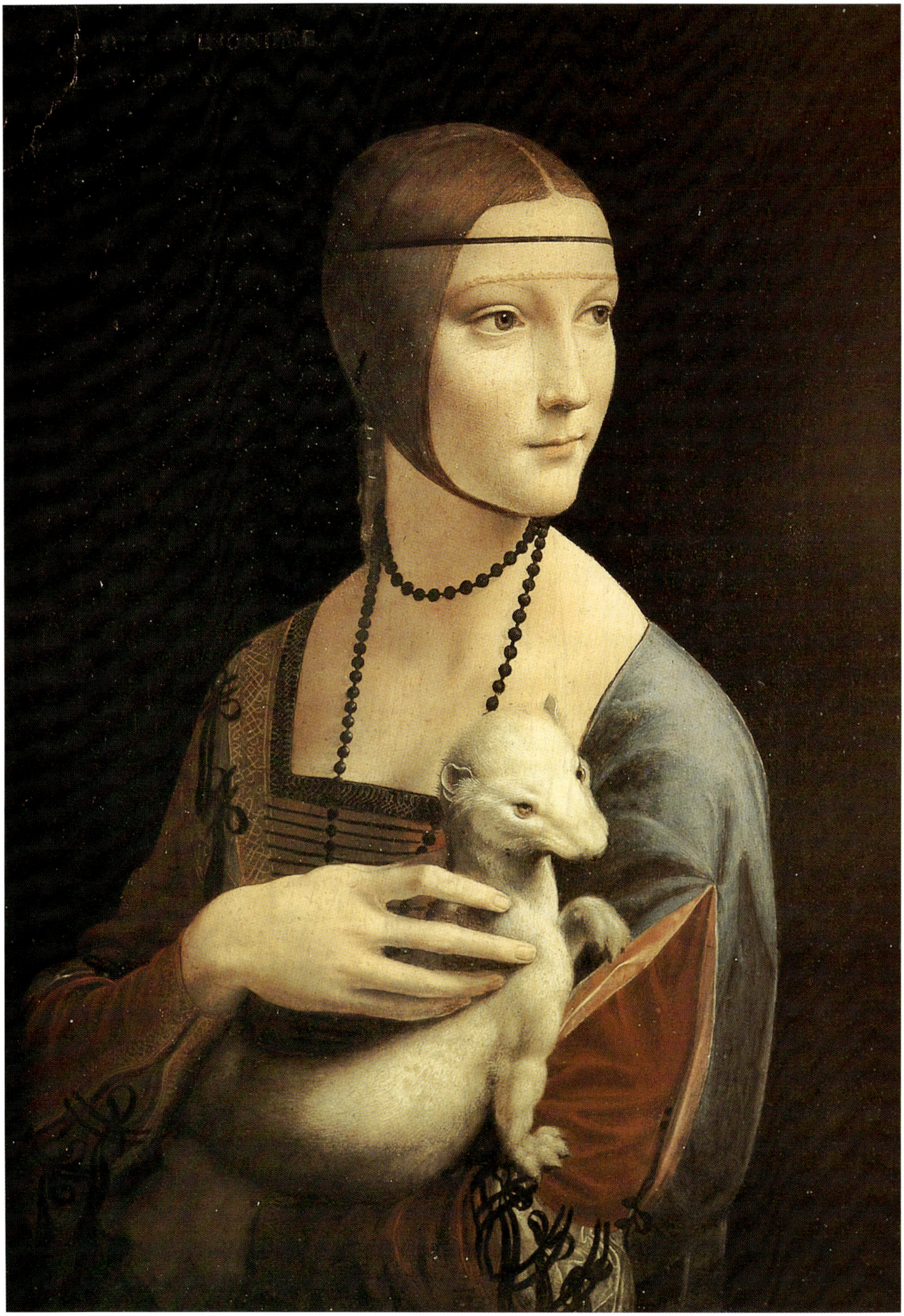

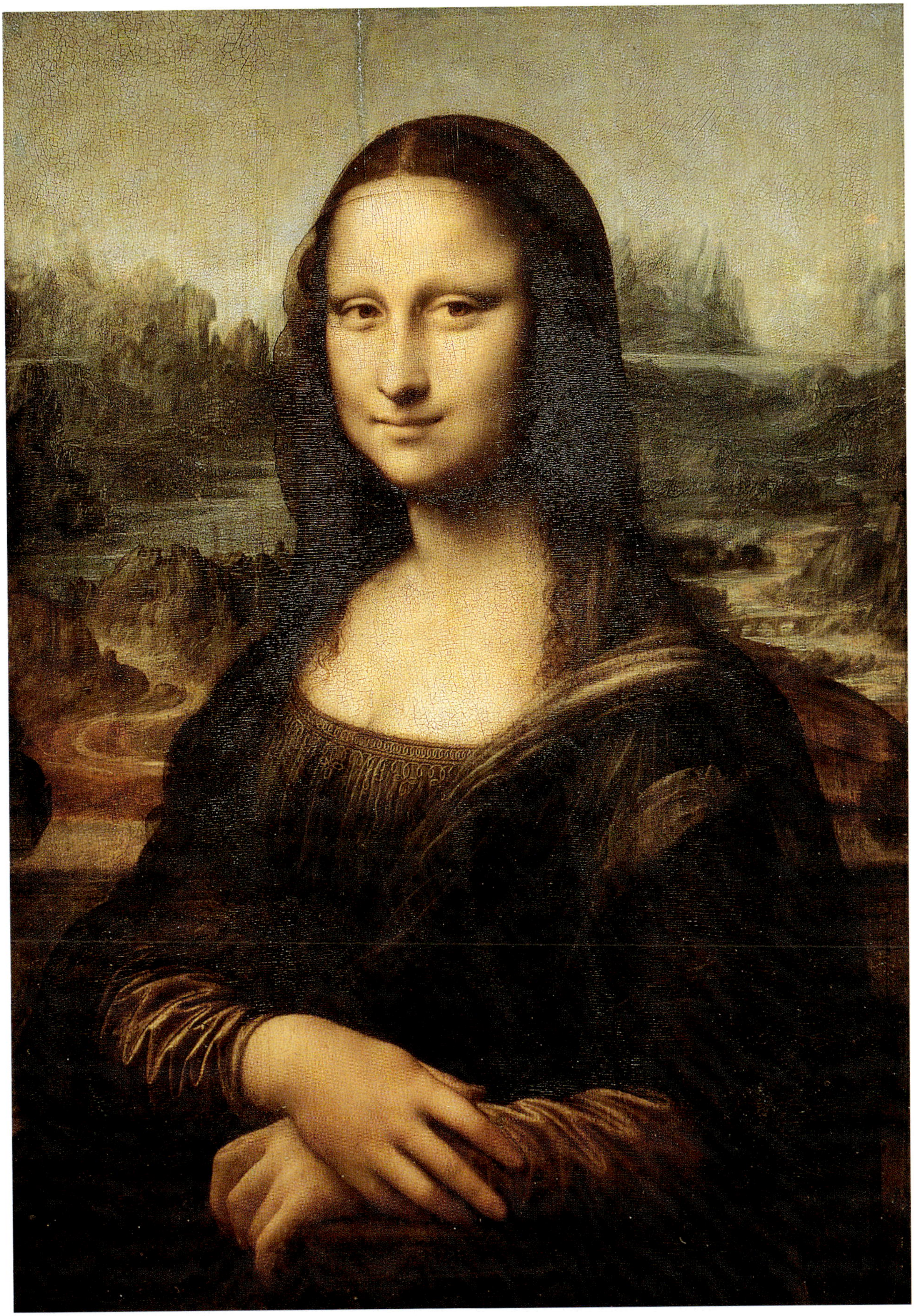

Leonardo da Vinci
Portrait of a Lady
(*La Gioconda*
or *Mona Lisa*)
1506/10 or 1513/16
panel
Paris, Louvre.

"The literature on the *Mona Lisa* is boundless, like her fame. For a century now she has offered only two elements easy to grasp: the exaltation of sentiment or sarcasm, effusion or derision. Under the name of the 'Gioconda myth' the strange situation of 'the most famous painting in the world' has led to various attempts to classify the fantasies, fables, and derision of which the painting has never ceased – and will never cease – to be the subject". Thus Chastel comments on the "illustrious unknown", as he calls her, in the book dedicated to the fortunes (or misfortunes) of Mona Lisa, who from Corot's re-evocation to Duchamp's ready-made has arrived at our own times drinking through a straw, slyly winking and running away naked to kiss the nearest portrait. Such is the fascination of this masterpiece, whose many unsolved mysteries add to its enchantment.

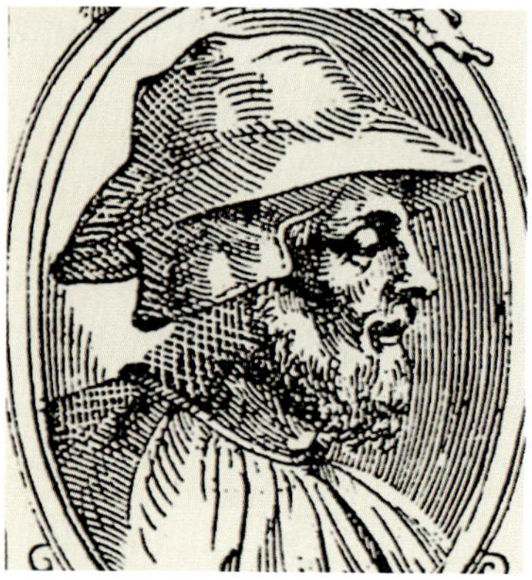

Piero di Cosimo

(Piero di Lorenzo di Chimenti, Florence c. 1461 – 1522)

In 1480 apprenticed to the shop of Cosimo Rosselli (1439-1507) from whom he took his nickname, Piero was called by Vasari "distracted and deformed intellect", perhaps for his indifference to official spheres and circles. Today he has been reevaluated as "highest example of that line which carried down to the early 16th century the authentic spirit of the Founding Fathers [of the Renaissance], renewing it with touches of vivacious, profound lyricism", as noted by Federico Zeri. He collaborated with Cosimo Rosselli in frescoing the walls of the Sistine Chapel, but soon left his master, more attracted, like Filippino Lippi, to northern influences. Although he approached the new language of Leonardo and Raphael in his last stage, his style remained autonomous, marked by a fantastic re-elaboration of landscapes and physiognomies.

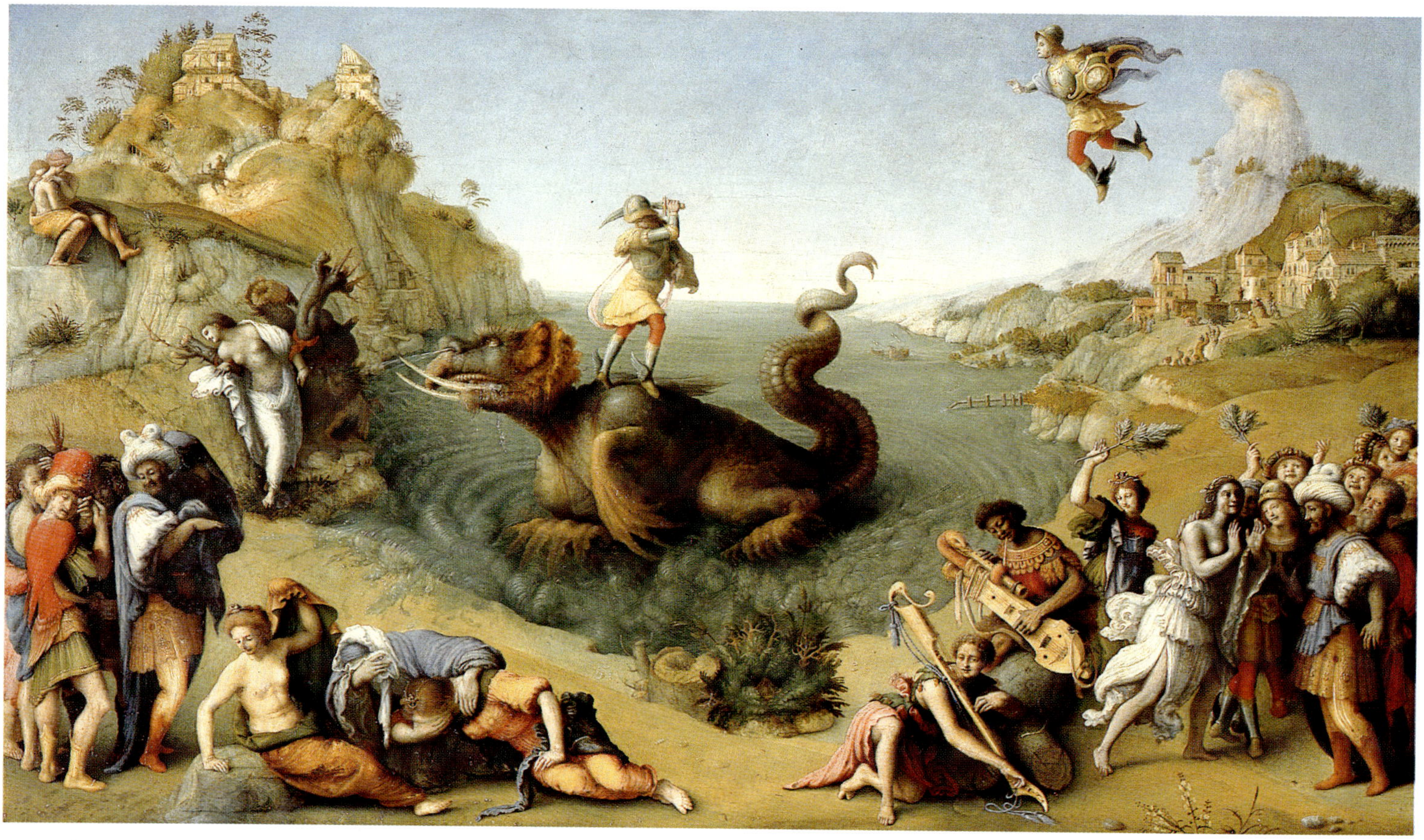

Giorgio Vasari, *Portrait of Piero di Cosimo*, from the *Lives*, Florence, Giunti, 1568.

Piero di Cosimo
Liberation of Andromeda
1510 or 1513
panel
Florence, Uffizi Gallery.

Piero narrates in highly original manner the myth of Perseus who frees Andromeda by slaying the sea monster. The central scene is dominated by the dragon in its death-throes, but the eye is also drawn to the anthropomorphic landscape, the exotic figures and the fairy-tale houses on the unlikely-looking hilltops. It has been suggested that the theatrical composition may have been inspired by the Florentine carnival of 1513 when the Medici returned to the city – symbolized by the dried branch with its new shoot, the Medici "broncone" emblem. Alternatively, it has recently been suggested that the work which, according to Vasari, was painted for a member the Strozzi family, belonged to Filippo the Younger, who it seems paid Piero in that year for a painting to hang in his bedchamber.

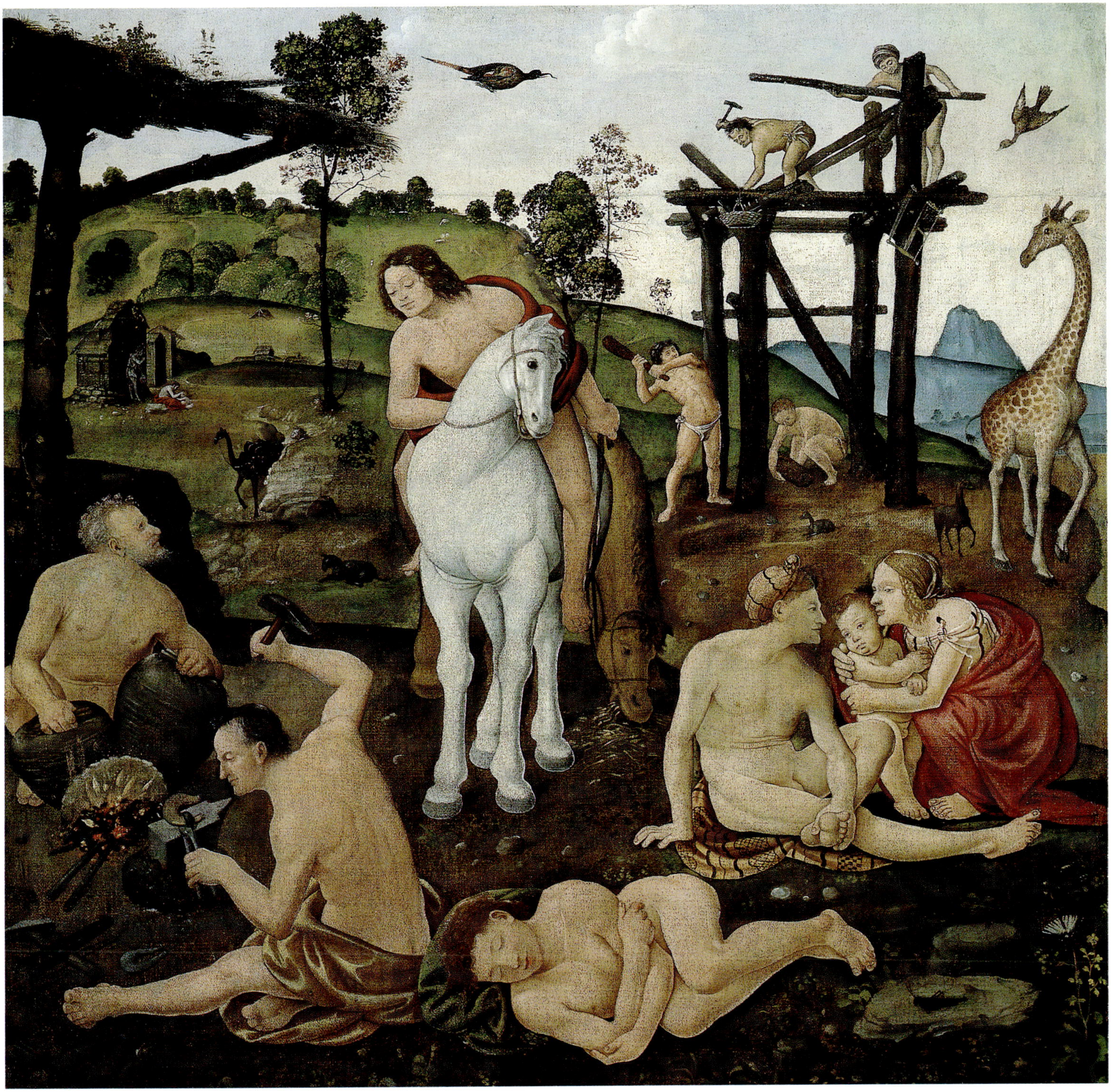

Piero di Cosimo
Vulcan and Aeolus
c. 1485-90
canvas
Ottawa, National Gallery of Canada.

The painting probably forms part of the cycle dedicated to the *Stories of Vulcan*, requested for his bedchamber by the Florentine Francesco del Pugliese, who also commissioned works from Filippino Lippi in those years. An eccentric politician, Francesco had a magnificent home adorned with works of art. A passage from Vitruvius describing the birth of human civilization seems to have inspired the cycle: "Men, like wild animals, were born in the forest, in the woods and in caves, and fed on wild foods" (*De architectura*, II, 1).

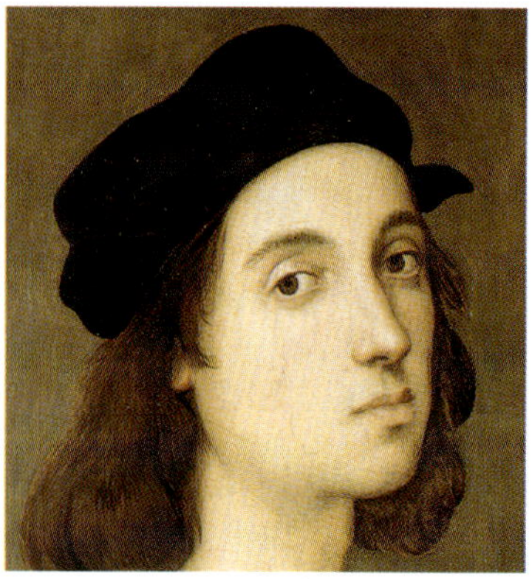

Raphael

(Raffaello Sanzio, Urbino 1483 – Rome 1520)

The personality of Raphael, more famous as painter than as architect although equally important in the latter field, seems in many aspects an antithesis to that of Michelangelo, only slightly older but active much longer: the one extroverted and friend of the powerful, lover of company, surrounded by a flock of followers and admirers; the other solitary and disdainful of power, reluctant to have pupils around him. Raphael exemplified the Renaissance figure of court artist at its highest, while Michelangelo rarely allowed any interference in his projects. The careers of both, however, broke the boundaries of the traditional 15th century workshop system. Raphael, son of the painter Giovanni Santi, was already working independently in Urbino while still very young. In about 1500 he collaborated with Perugino and four years later, with a letter of presentation to the Gonfaloniere of the

Raphael, *Self-portrait*, c. 1506. Florence, Uffizi Gallery.

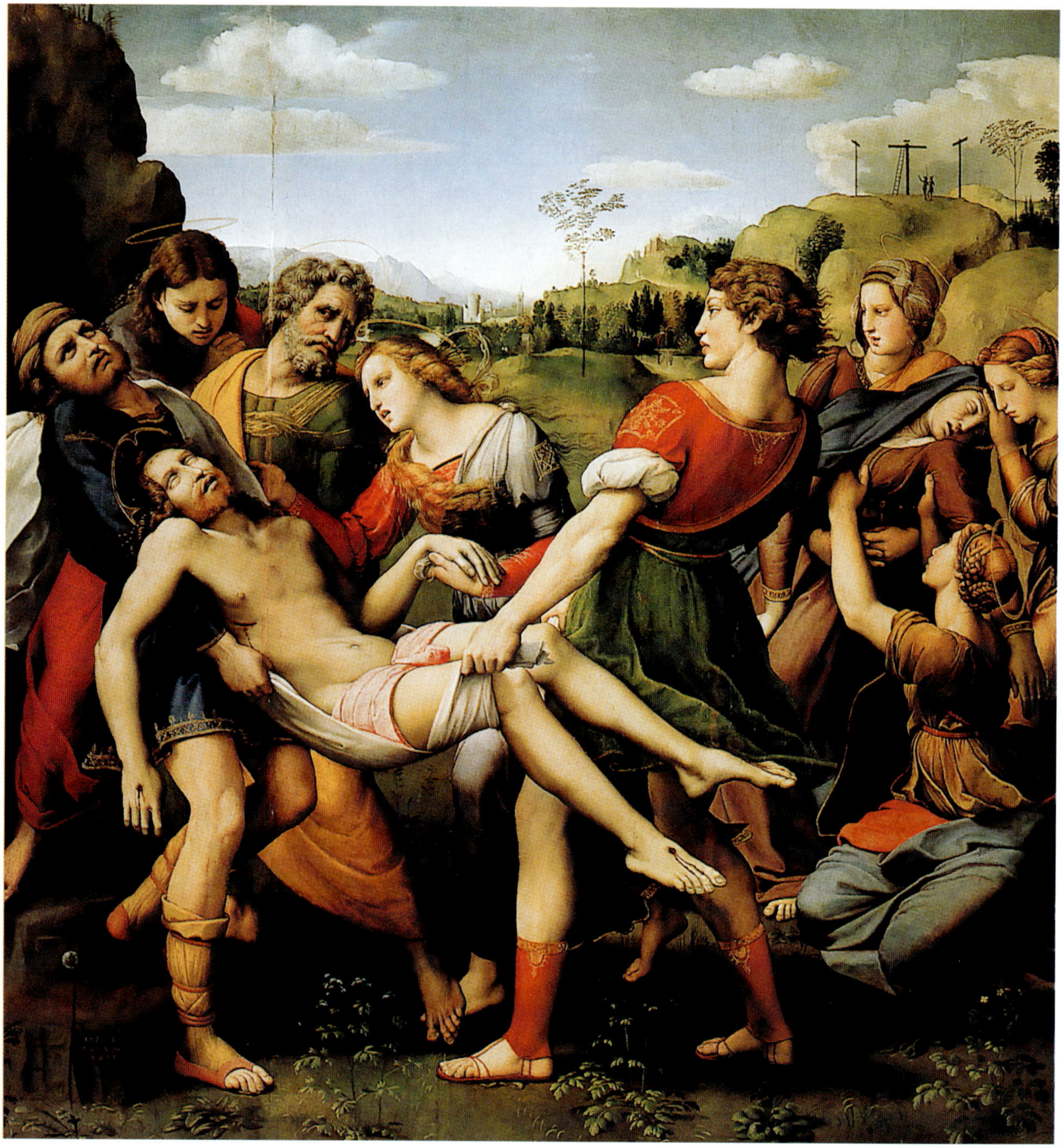

Raphael
Transport of Christ (The Borghese Deposition)
signed and dated 1507
panel
Rome, Galleria Borghese.

The altarpiece was commissioned for the family chapel in the Church of San Francesco at Perugia by Atalanta Baglioni, the mother of Grifone, assassinated in 1500 in a tragic feud between Perugian families. The sacred subject clearly refers to the dramatic end of the young man, who at death's door had pardoned his assassins at the desire of his mother. While the strongly rhythmic composition derives from an ancient sarcophagus portraying the *Death of Meleager*, one of the women supporting the fainting mother is clearly inspired by the pose of the Madonna in the *Doni Tondo*, just painted by Michelangelo.

Republic Soderini, he arrived in Florence at a crucial moment: for some months Leonardo and Michelangelo had been preparing the cartoons for the frescoes of the Battles of Anghiari and of Cascina that were to be painted in Palazzo Vecchio (Leonardo's was lost before being finished, Michelangelo's was never executed). The young Raphael studied those cartoons, called "the school of the world" by Benvenuto Cellini. He frequented various shops and painters such as Ridolfo del Ghirlandaio (1483-1561); received commissions, although not public ones, from wealthy families such as the Doni, also patrons of Michelangelo, and the Nasi (*Madonna of the Goldfinch*, c. 1506, Uffizi). Called to Rome by Julius II to fresco the rooms of his apartment in the Vatican (originally the Pope's "secret library"), he began in 1508 with the Stanza della Segnatura, continuing with that of Heliodorus (1511-13). During this time Raphael painted numerous portraits, altarpieces and frescoes. Only under Pope Leo X, and especially after the death of his rival Bramante in 1514, did Raphael dedicate himself to architecture, leaving many painting commissions to his pupils and becoming the official architect of the Fabric of St Peter's. He died at the age of only thirty-seven.

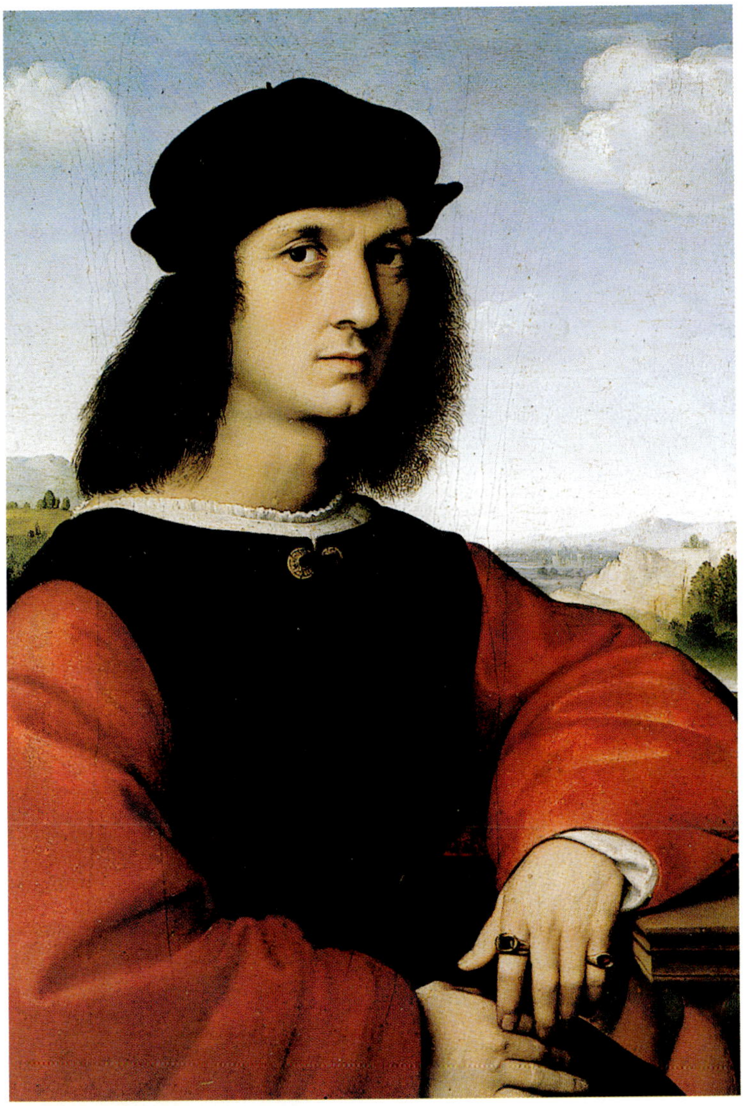

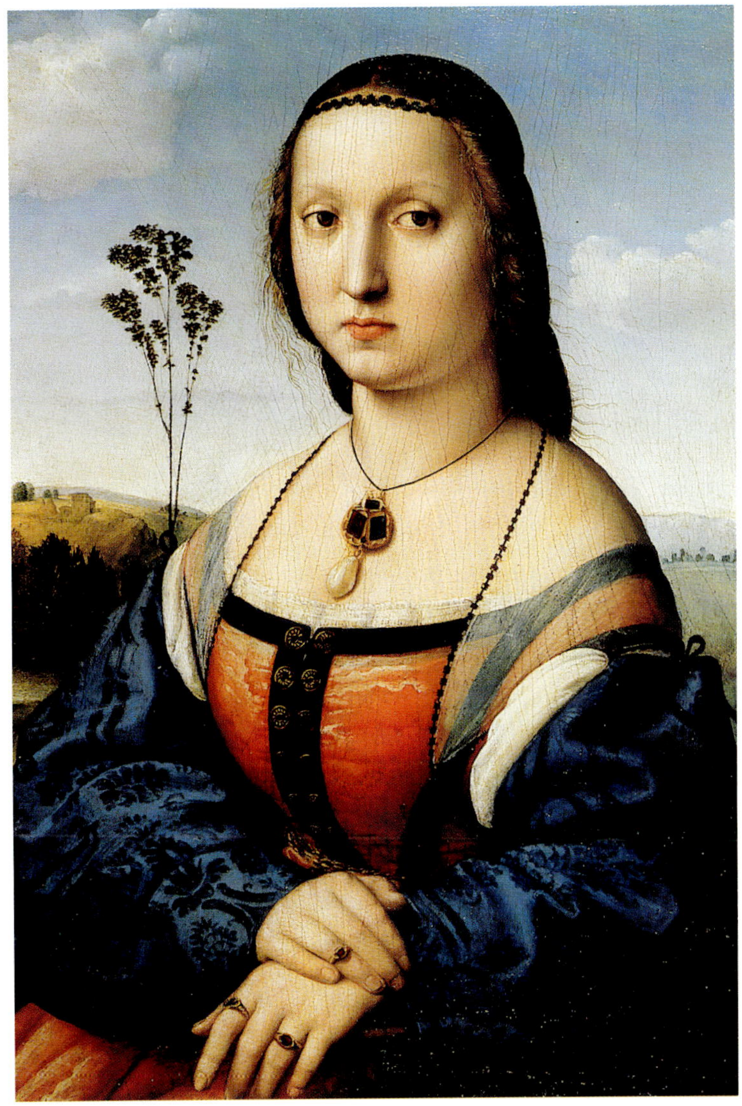

Raphael
Portraits of Agnolo Doni and Maddalena Strozzi
c. 1506-07
panel
Florence, Palatine Gallery.

Agnolo Doni (1474-1539), a rich Florentine merchant, and his wife Maddalena (1489-1540) collected in their home fine works of art. While commissioning their portraits of the young Raphael, they requested of Michelangelo at about the same time the famous tondo of the *Holy Family*. On the backs of the two panels, which already reveal Raphael's knowledge of Leonardo's portraiture, appear two episodes from the myth of Deucalion and Pyrrha, alluding to fertility.

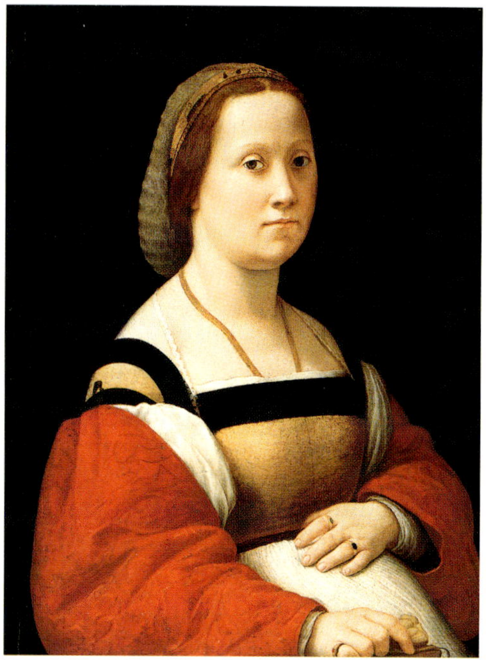

Raphael
The Pregnant Woman
1507
panel
Florence, Palatine Gallery.

Belonging to the Florentine period but painted for an unknown client, the woman expecting a child emerges from a dark background, unlike other paintings of this period set against a landscape.

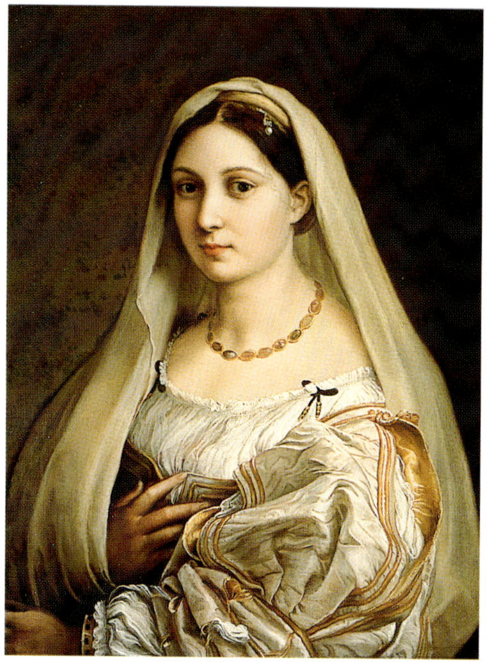

Raphael
The Veiled Lady
c. 1513
panel
Florence, Palatine Gallery.

The virtuoso masterpiece of the mature Raphael, painted after the frescoing of the Vatican Stanze, has gone down in history for the magnificent silk sleeve comparable only to those magically produced by the brush of Titian.

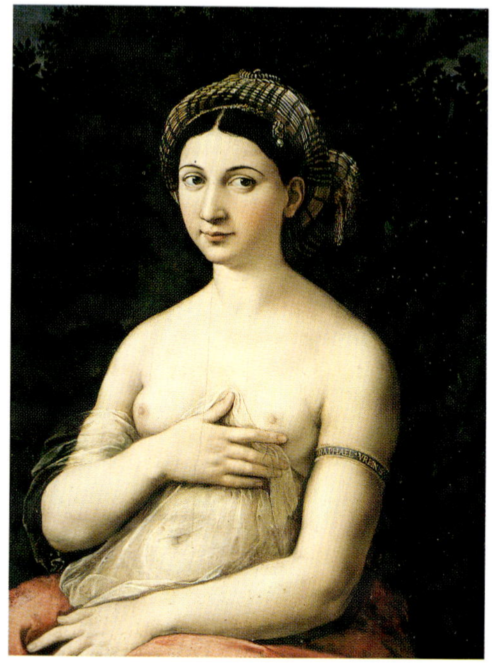

Raphael
La Fornarina
signed, c. 1518-19
panel
Rome, Galleria Nazionale d'Arte Antica, Palazzo Barberini.

The painting, on which Giulio Romano may have collaborated, traditionally represents the mythical woman loved by Raphael in Rome, although this is not confirmed by any documentation. More probably she is a courtesan.

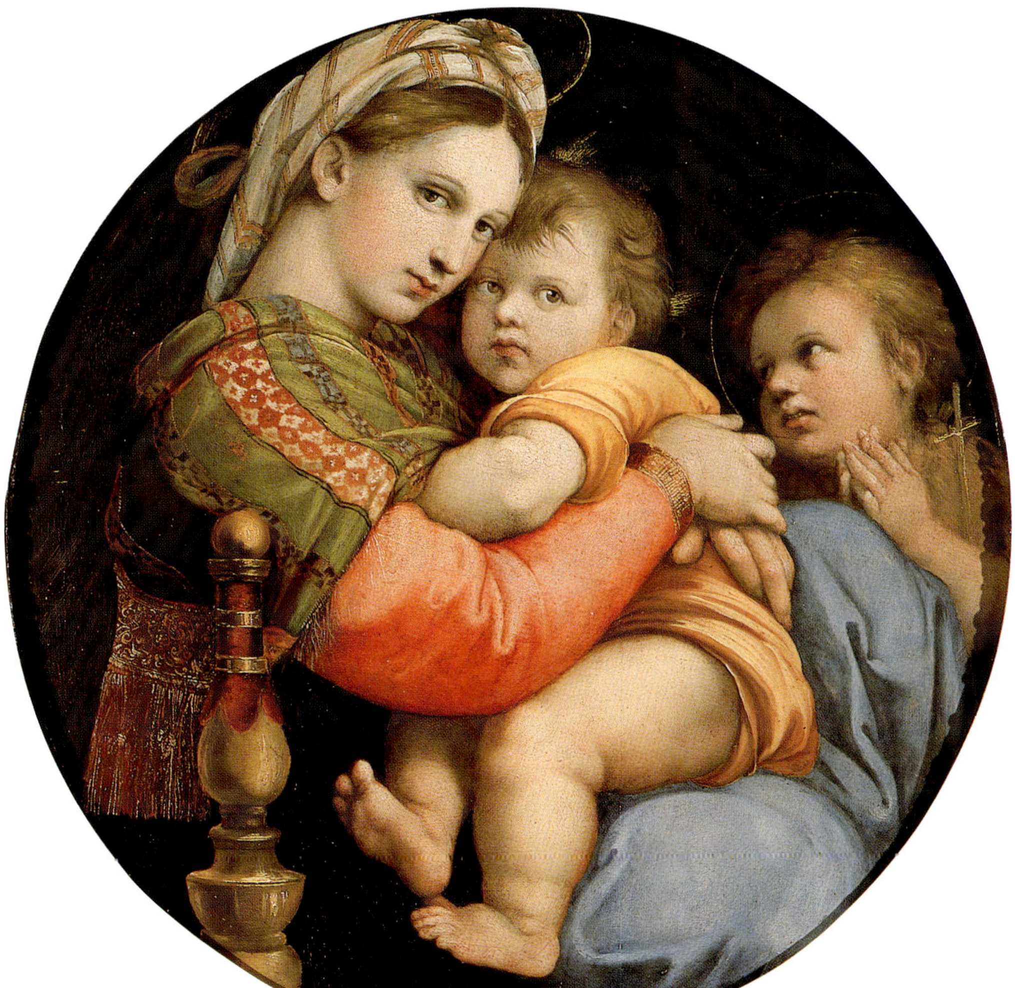

Raphael
The Madonna of the Chair
c. 1513-16
panel
Florence, Palatine Gallery.

The tondo, greatly loved and copied innumerable times by other artists, was painted in Rome, perhaps for Pope Leo X. Within the circular form the three figures are masterfully portrayed in a composition of monumental beauty.

Raphael
Leo X with Cardinals Giulio de' Medici and Luigi de' Rossi
1518
panel
Florence, Uffizi Gallery.

The portrait of Pope Leo X, in the world Giovanni de' Medici (1475-1521), elected Pope in 1513, arrived in Florence from Rome in 1518. The painting was to be exalted by Vasari for the figures "not false, but in rounded relief", for the damask gown "which gleams and shimmers", for the skins of the lining "soft and living", for the glossy knob that reflects "the light from the windows, the Pope's shoulders, and the interiors of the rooms". Restoration in 1996, which has brought out the different tones of red and the extraordinary luminosity of the work, has also led to new hypotheses concerning the two Cardinals, who seem to have been added later by another hand (it has been suggested that they are the work of Sebastiano del Piombo).

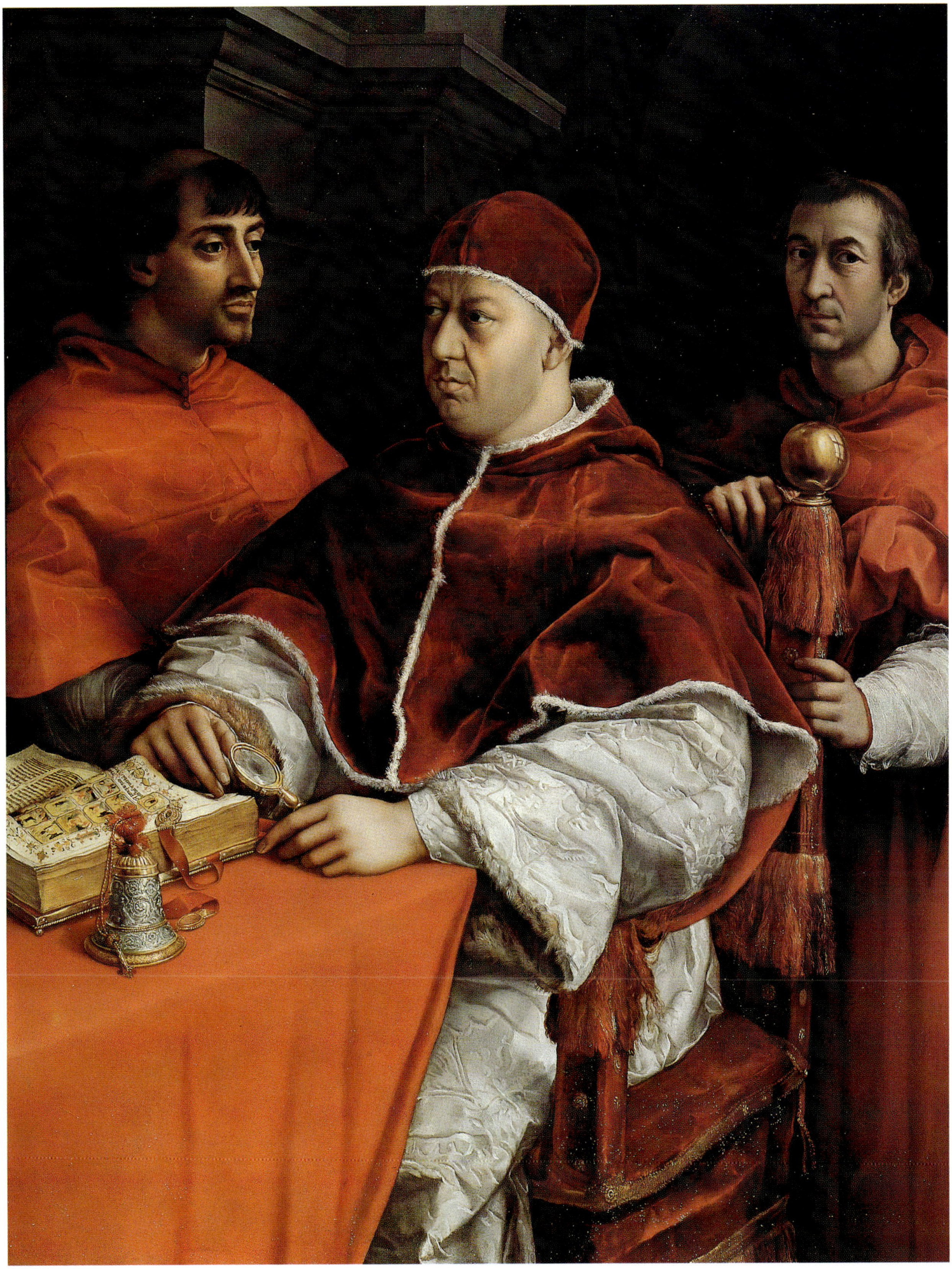

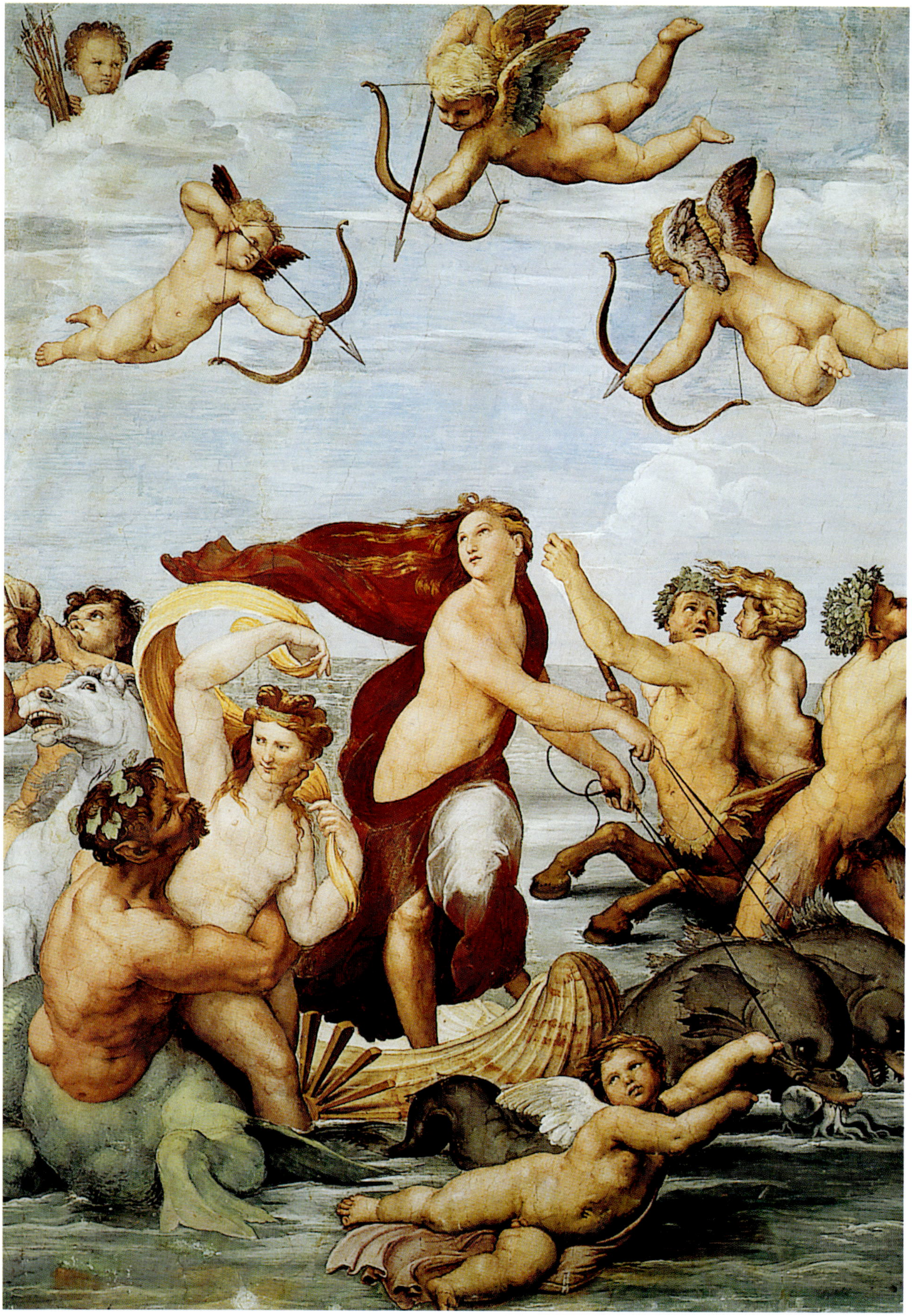

Raphael
The Triumph of Galatea
1512
fresco
Rome, Villa Farnesina.

The fresco, painted for the Sienese banker Agostino Chigi for his Roman villa at Lungara, alludes to verses in Poliziano's *Stanze* (118, I) which describe Galatea and her companions passing before Polyphemus: a Neo-platonic re-elaboration of the myth according to which the young woman is looking toward divine Love and the others, pierced by arrows, toward sensual love.

Raphael
School of Athens
1510
fresco, detail
Rome, Vatican Palaces, Stanza della Segnatura.

In the vast rectangular hall of the Segnatura, entirely decorated by Raphael, including the ceilings (apart from the eight scenes already painted by Sodoma), the great *School of Athens* represents the culminating point of the structural harmony and compositional clarity achieved by the artist.

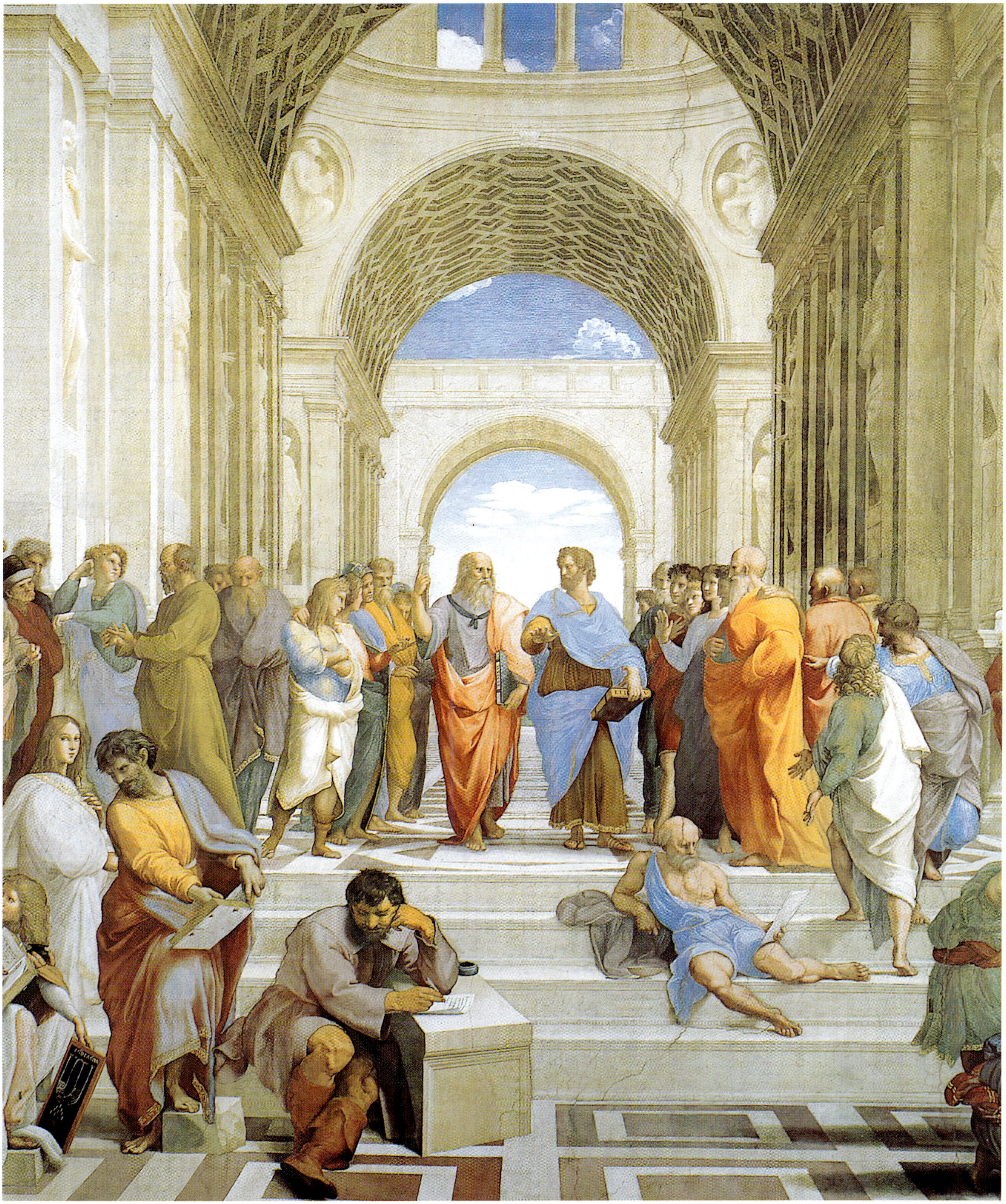

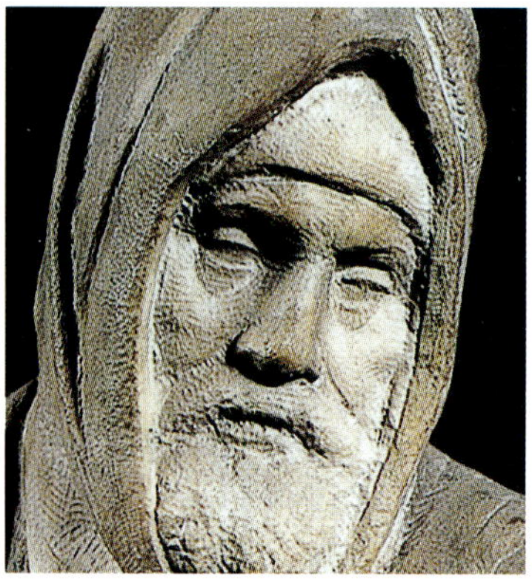

Michelangelo

(Michelangelo Buonarroti, Caprese, Arezzo, 1475 – Rome 1564)

"I say that painting may be considered better the more it approaches relief, and relief may be considered worse the more it approaches painting; and so I used to believe that sculpture is the lamp of painting, and the first related to the second as the sun to the moon", wrote Michelangelo in a letter to Benedetto Varchi, promoter of an academic discussion "on which is the noblest, Sculpture or Painting". These words reveal the intimate essence of a long, laborious career of painter and sculptor (as well as architect, man of letters and poet). It is unusual that, as in his case, an artist's work is linked to a tormented personality, a dramatic, eventful life, as he himself described it to his brother: "I have been traipsing around all Italy, borne all kinds of disgrace, suffered every calamity, lacerated my body with cruel toil". And again, he writes to Martelli: "I see that you have imagined that I am

Michelangelo, *Presumed Self-portrait as Nicodemus,* detail of the *Bandini Pietà*, 1550-55. Florence, Museo dell'Opera del Duomo.

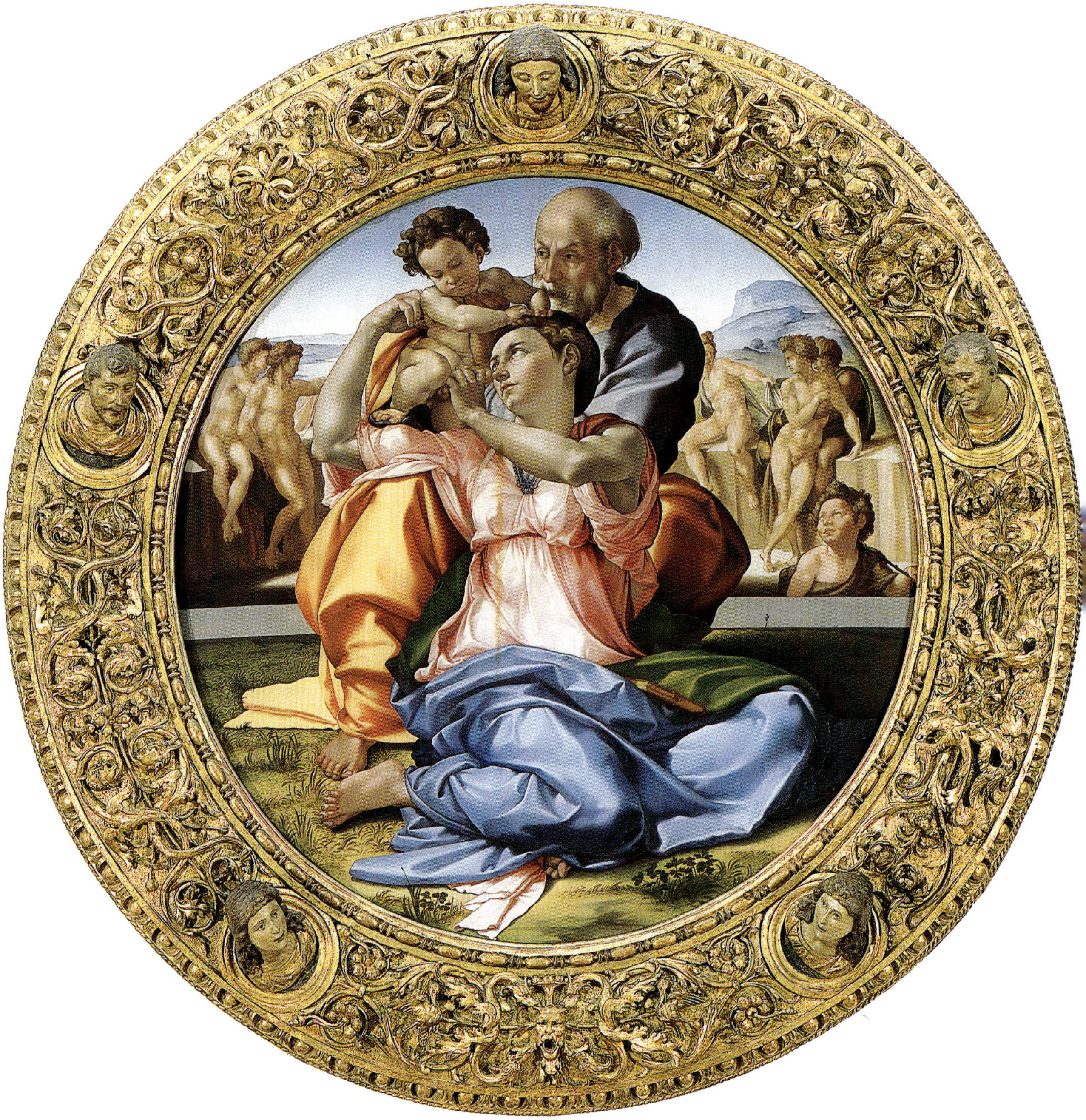

Michelangelo
Holy Family with the Infant St John (Doni Tondo)
c. 1506-1508
panel (inlaid and gilded coeval frame, attr. to Marco and Francesco del Tasso)
Florence, Uffizi Gallery.

The work was painted for the Doni spouses, perhaps at the birth of their daughter Maria (September 8, 1507), and certainly after January 1506, date of the discovery of the *Laocoon* from which derives the pose of the nude behind St Joseph. Michelangelo interpreted the *Holy Family* with gelid colors and a strange serpentine composition. The Virgin offering the Child to St Joseph is counterbalanced by five young nudes behind a low wall, beyond which is a misty landscape. The meaning of the work is obscure, perhaps alluding to the birth of Jesus and to baptism, suggested by the Infant St John and the all-round medallions with Christ, angels and prophets in the splendid frame.

what God wished me to be. I am a poor man of little value, laboring over that art which God has given me, to lengthen my life as much as I can". Working in republican Florence, then for the Medici and in the Rome of many popes, all of whom gave him enormous problems, he nonetheless created one masterpiece after another. Even in his last thirty years spent in Rome in voluntary exile from the Florence of the Medici he produced crucially important works, although Vasari's evolutionary theory, that after him no further progress would have been possible, has proved untrue.

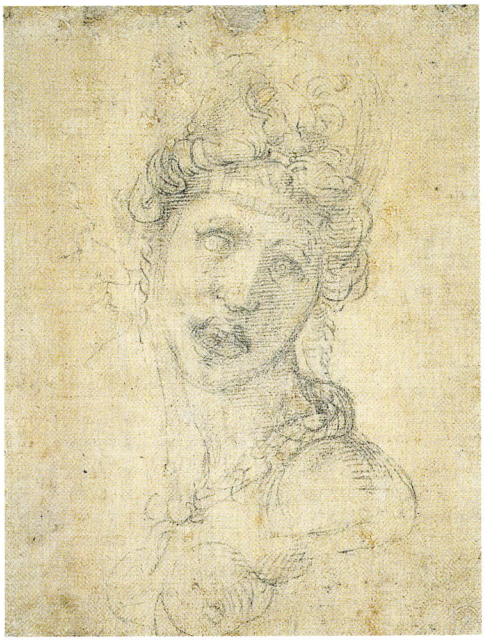

Michelangelo
Head of a God (Cleopatra)
c. 1535
paper
Florence, Casa Buonarroti Museum.

Discovered during recent restoration on the back of another drawing by Michelangelo, it too portraying a woman's head with braided hair and a serpent at her breast, the drawing appears on the sheet donated to Duke Cosimo dei Medici in 1562 by Tommaso dei Cavalieri, the young Roman whom Michelangelo met in 1532. This is one of the so-called *presentation drawings*, according to the term coined by the German scholar Johannes Wilde, that is, designed to be donated as a gift, with compositions that are often complex. This may be one of the "heads of gods" mentioned by Vasari.

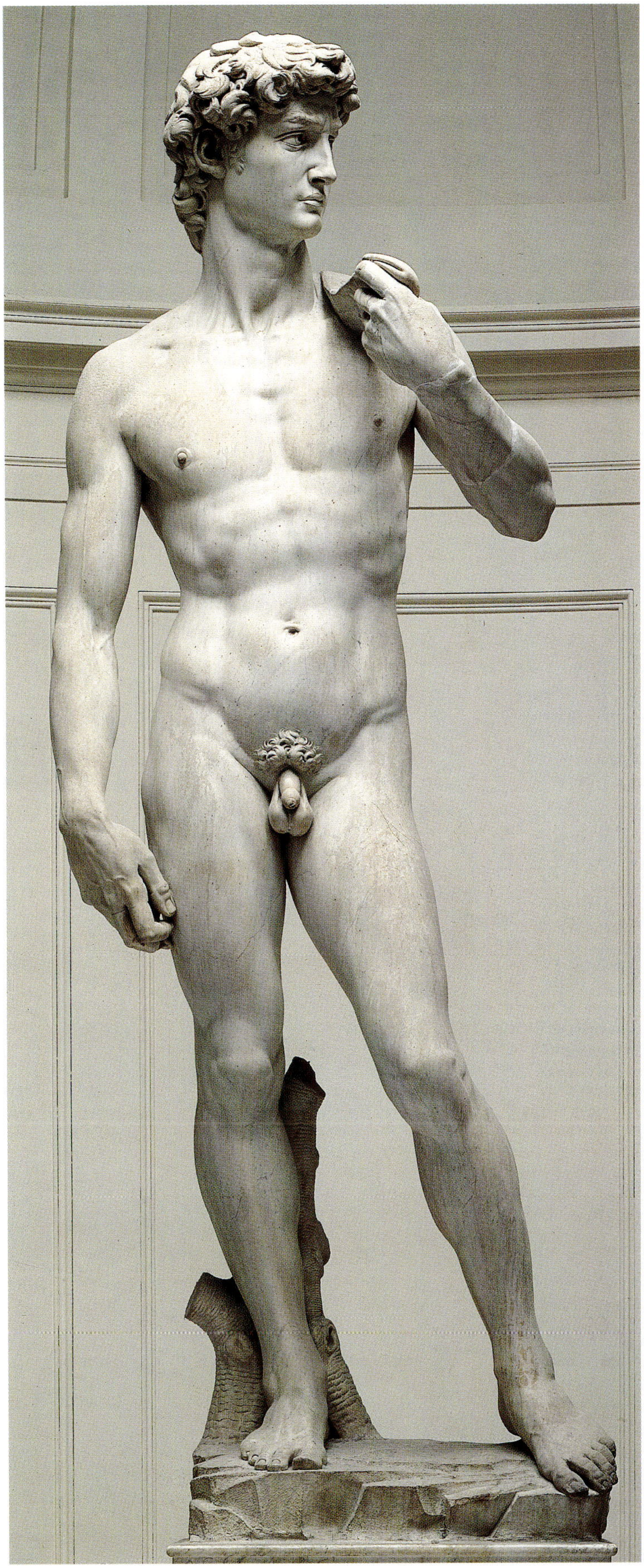

Michelangelo
David
1501-04
marble
Florence, Accademia Gallery.

In the years when Pier Soderini was Gonfaloniere the marble colossus, which confirmed the thirty-year-old Michelangelo as the greatest sculptor of his times, was commissioned by the Opera del Duomo for the Cathedral of Santa Maria del Fiore. But when it was finished, in June 1504, after sharp debate among the greatest artists of the day (Leonardo, Botticelli, Filippino Lippi, Giuliano and Antonio da Sangallo, Andrea della Robbia) the statue was placed before the façade of Palazzo Vecchio, in substitution for Donatello's *Judith*. It thus assumed the values, in republican Florence, of freedom and civic virtue.

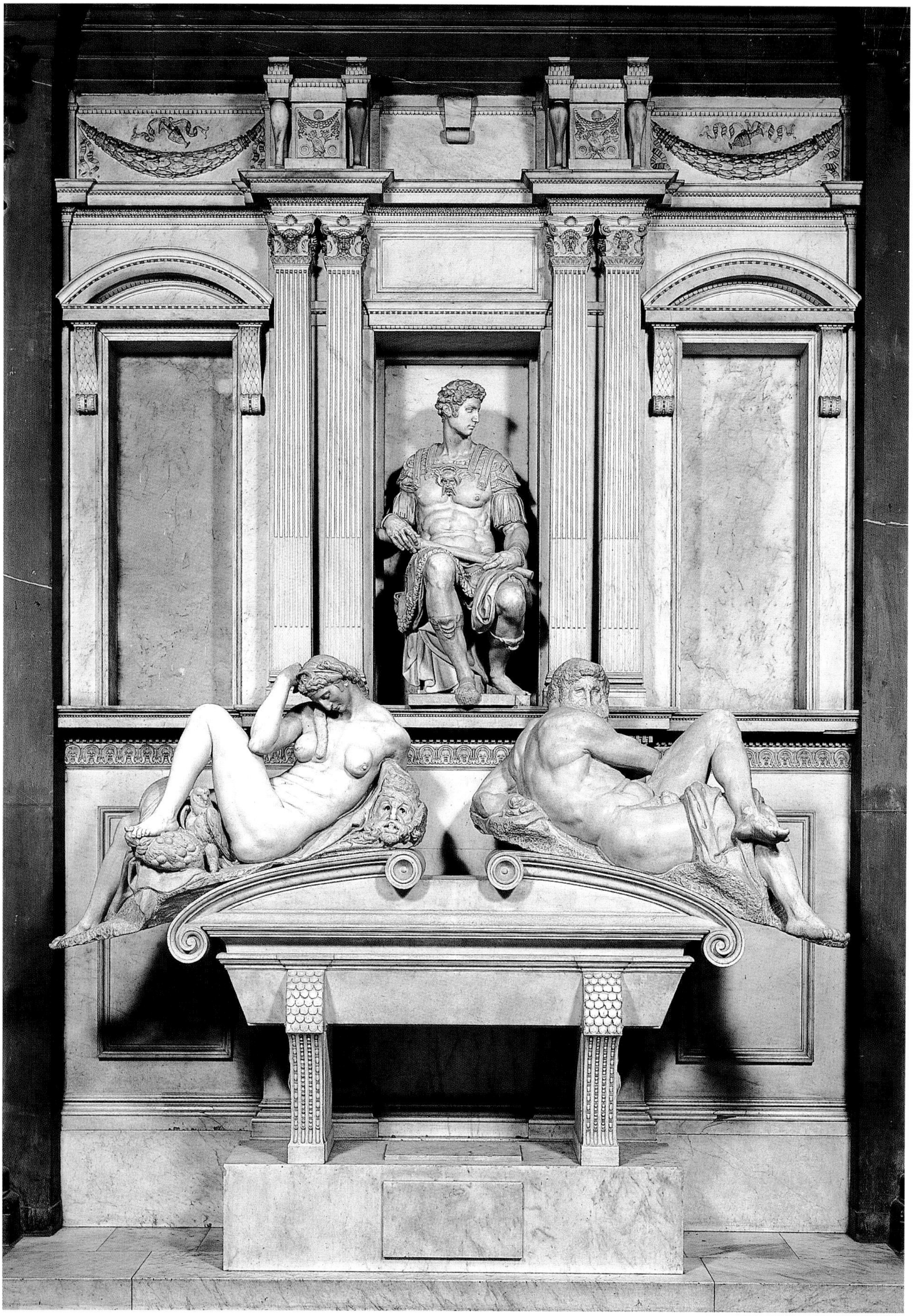

Michelangelo
Tomb of Giuliano de' Medici Duke of Nemours, with the statue of the deceased, Night and Day
1526-34
marble
Florence, San Lorenzo, New Sacristy (Medici Chapels).

"I work as much as I can", wrote Michelangelo in 1526 to Clement VII referring to the sculptures for the New Sacristy. He had been commissioned by Cardinal Giulio de' Medici and by Leo X to build the sacristy designed to house the last Medici tombs in the Laurentian Basilica. After an interruption during the siege of Florence and before he definitively abandoned the city in 1534, the undertaking was completed by him only in part and was finished by other artists. Referring to the *Night* accompanying the personification of *Day* below the statue of the Duke, Michelangelo wrote verses revealing his sorrow at the uncertain situation of his city: "Dear to me is sleep; still more to sleep in stone while harm and shame persist; not to see, not to feel, is bliss; speak softly, do not wake me, do not weep".

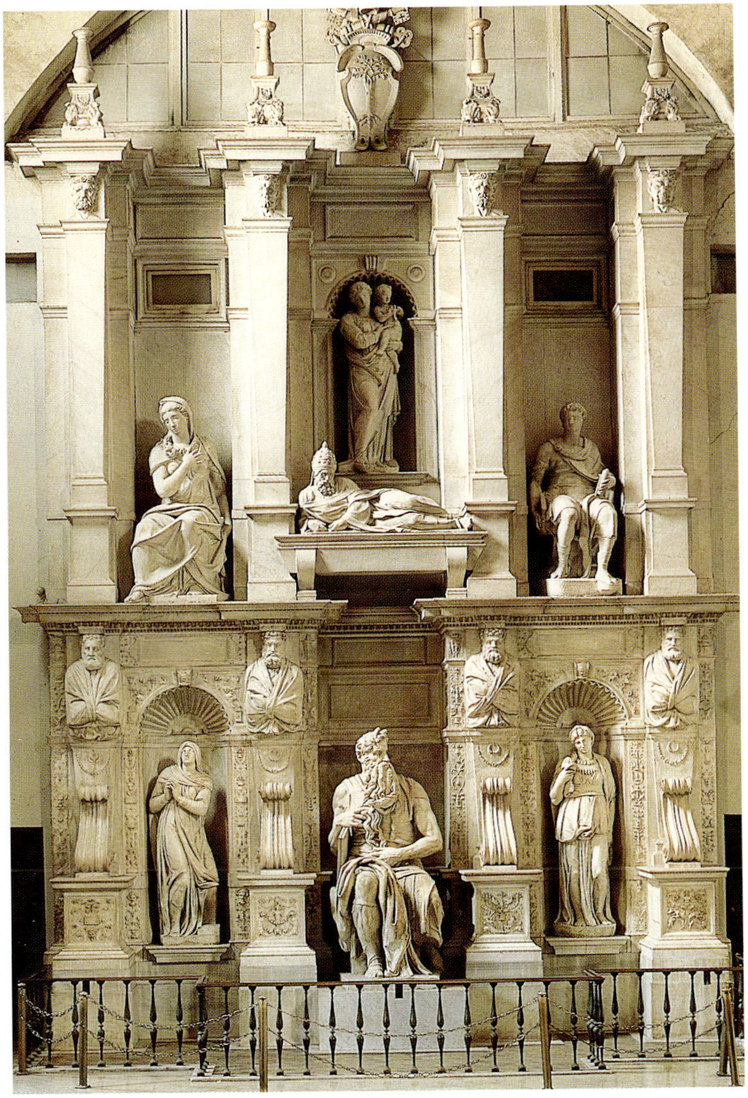

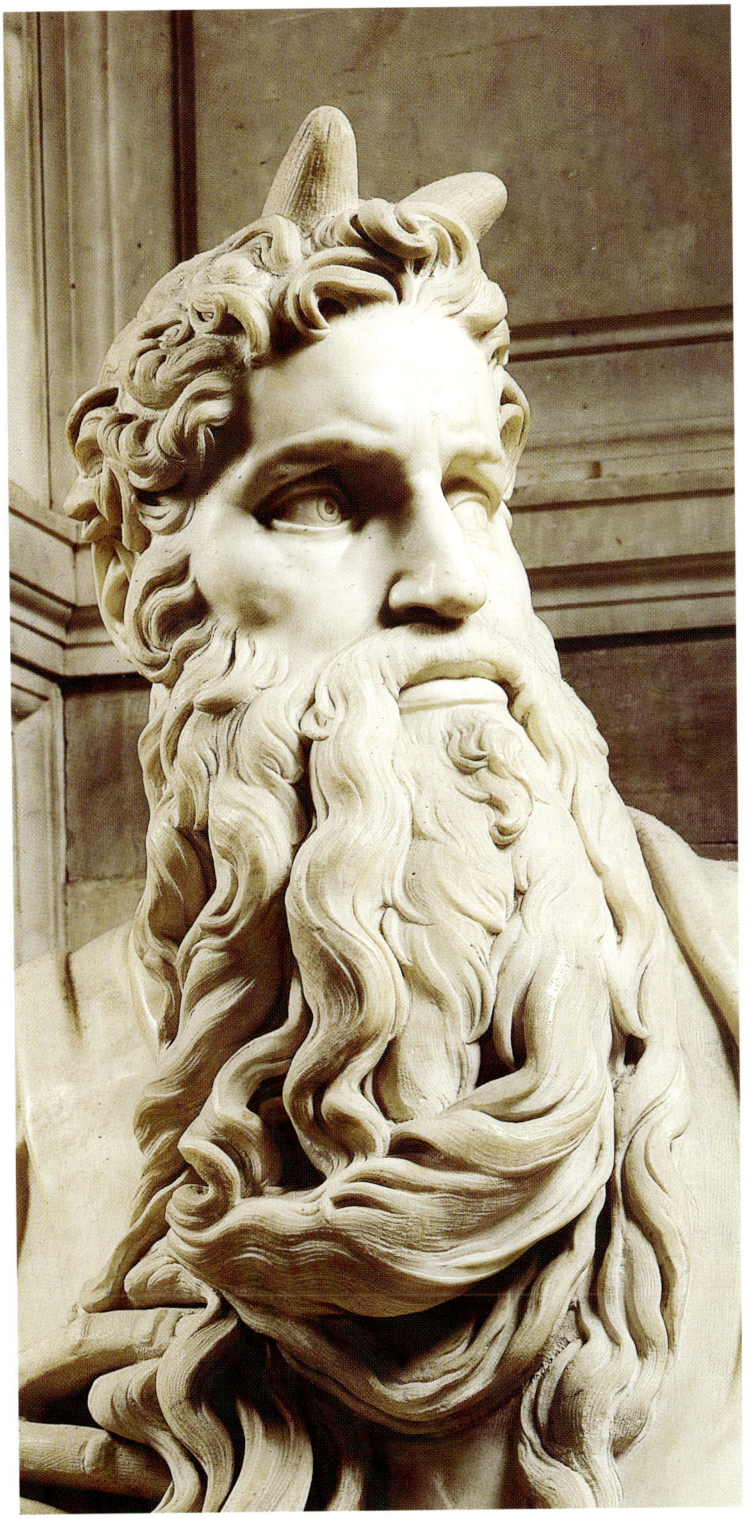

Michelangelo
Tomb of Julius II
1513, completed in 1547
marble, whole and detail of the head of *Moses*
Rome, San Pietro in Vincoli.

In 1505 Pope Julius II Della Rovere summoned Michelangelo to build his funerary monument, originally destined to occupy the choir of St Peter's Basilica. The initial project was designed like an ancient mausoleum free on all sides, and the artist immediately journeyed to Carrara to choose the marble. But in the meantime the Pope was distracted by plans for rebuilding St Peter's Basilica, entrusted to Bramante, and refused even to receive Michelangelo, who left Rome and took refuge in Florence. Work on the monument was repeatedly interrupted and only after the Pope's death in 1513 was the project resumed, severely scaled down, and now including the famous *Moses* as well as the figures of the *Slaves* that were to remain in the artist's Florence workshop until his death.

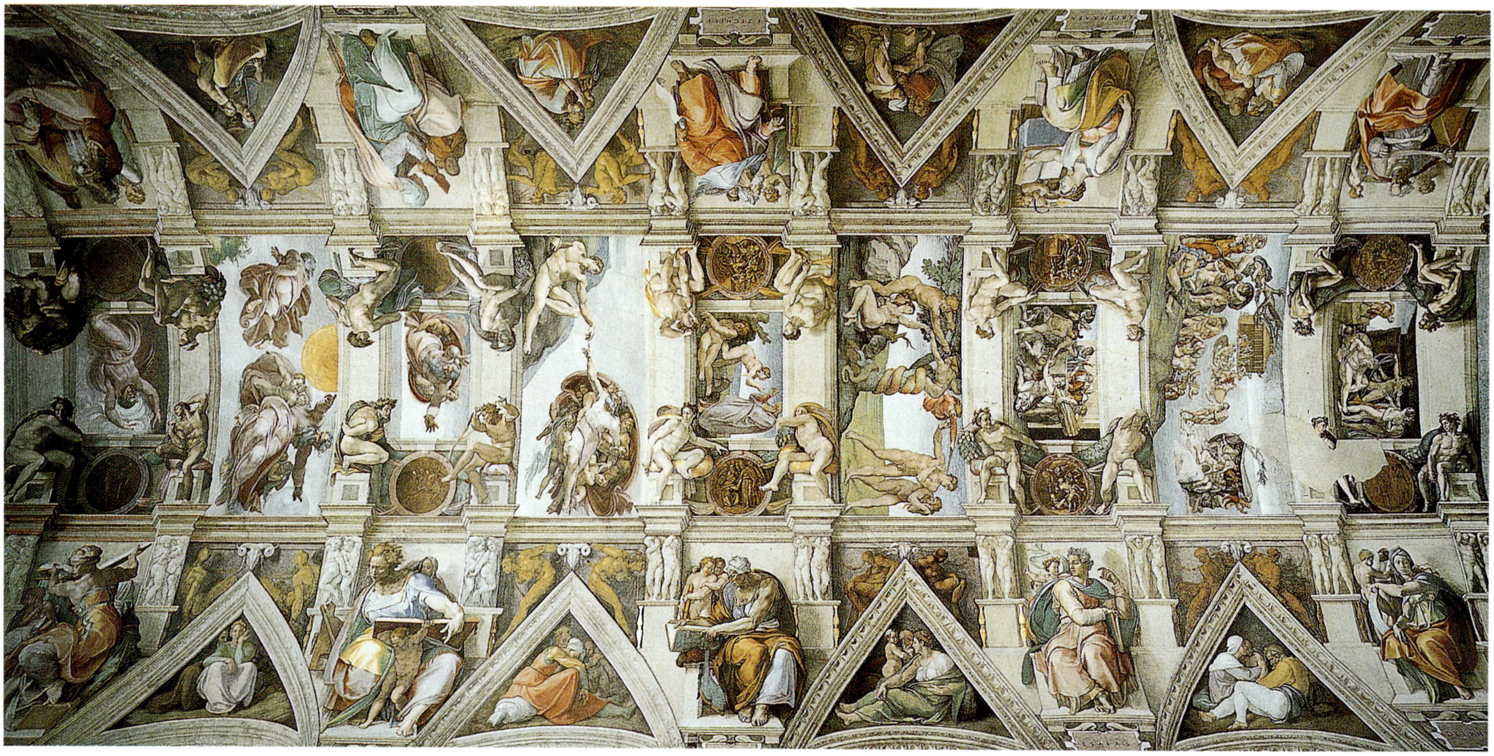

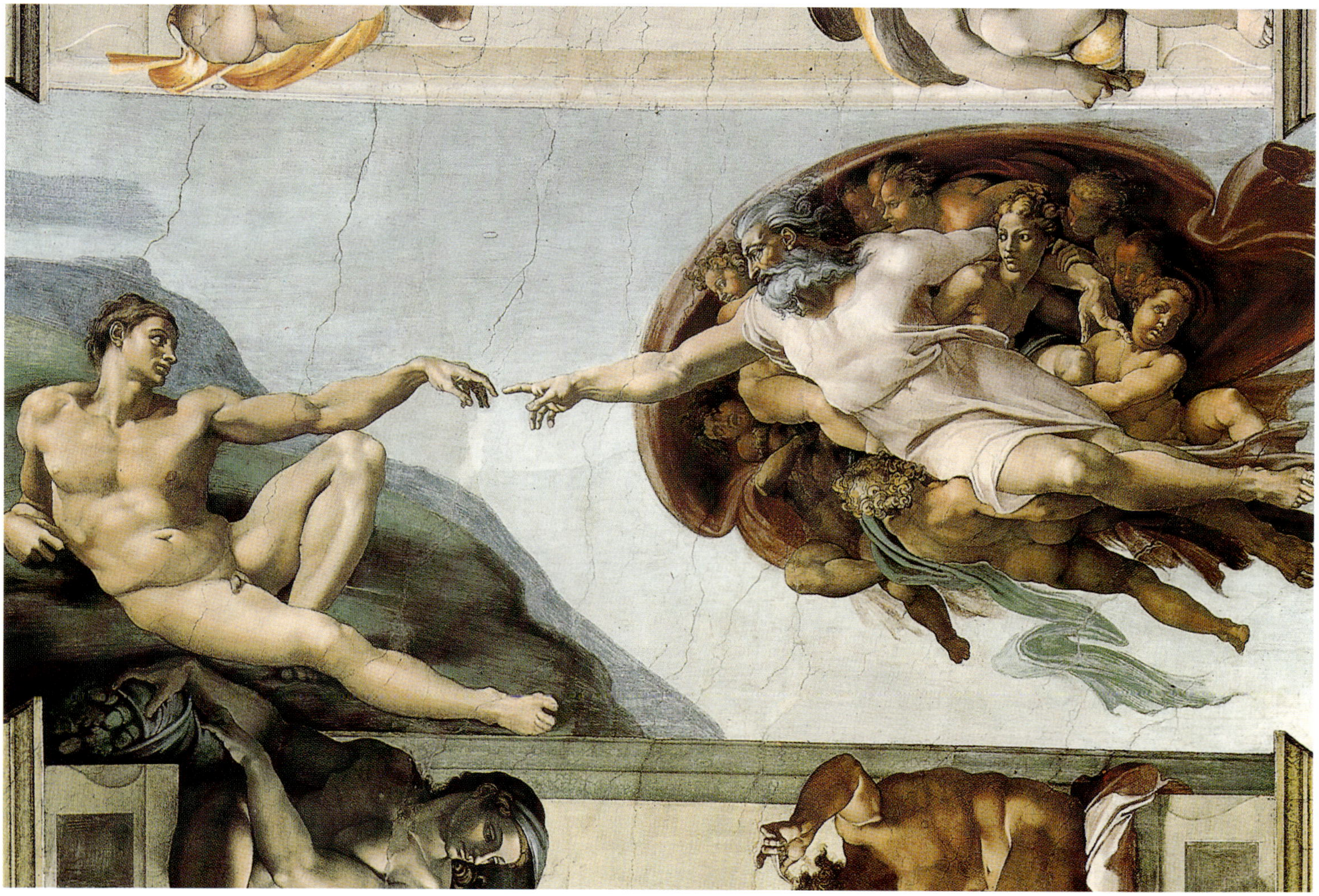

At left and on page 160:
Michelangelo
Ceiling of the Sistine Chapel
1508-12
fresco, whole and details
Vatican City,
Sistine Chapel.

The contract for the immense ceiling having been stipulated in 1508, Michelangelo undertook the titanic project under pressure from Julius II and with enormous difficulty. The first project called for only a few figures as replacement for the gilded stars against a blue background that then decorated the ceiling rising above the frescoes from the time of Sixtus V; but the design was gradually changed to include a scheme of enormous complexity with about three hundred figures. The famous *ignudi* were to inspire generations of artists for centuries, up to Cézanne and beyond.

Michelangelo
Last Judgement
1536-41
fresco, detail
Vatican City, Sistine Chapel.

On the wall originally decorated by Perugino, Michelangelo painted the *Last Judgement*, at the desire of Clement VII and the later urging of Paul III. The gigantic composition centers around the colossal *Christ the Judge*, whose gesture seems to dominate the movement of all of the other figures.

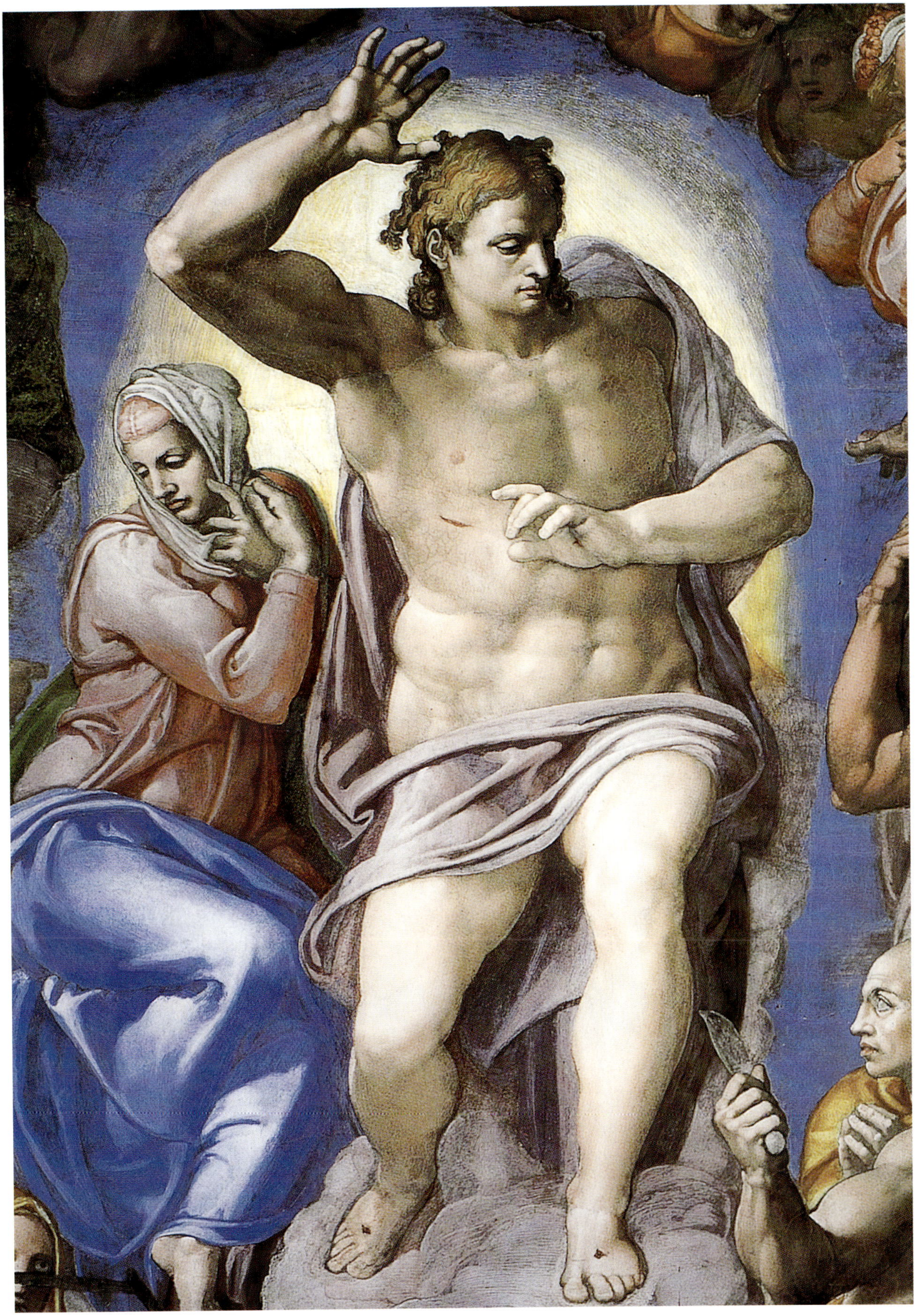

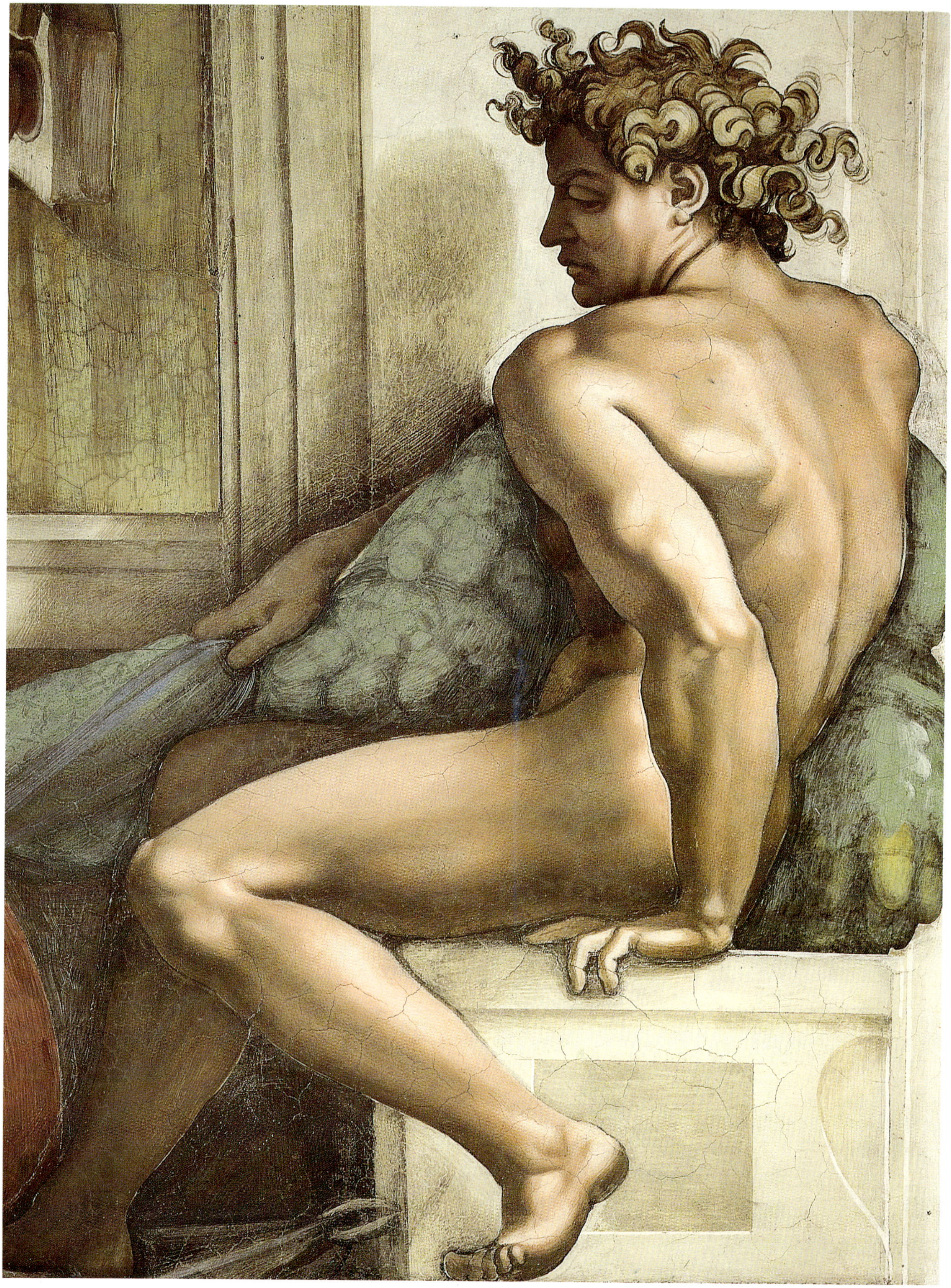

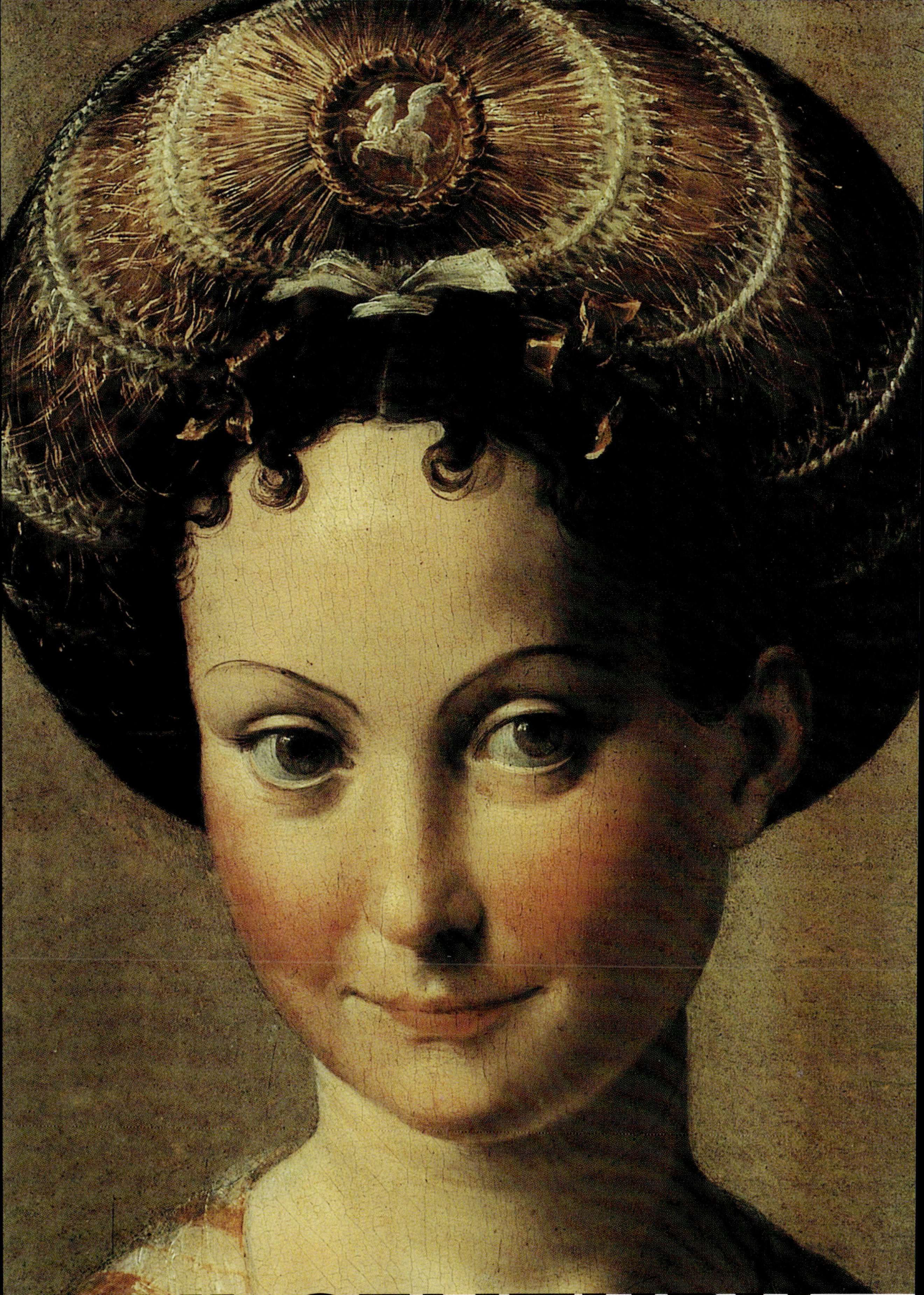

THE XVI CENTURY

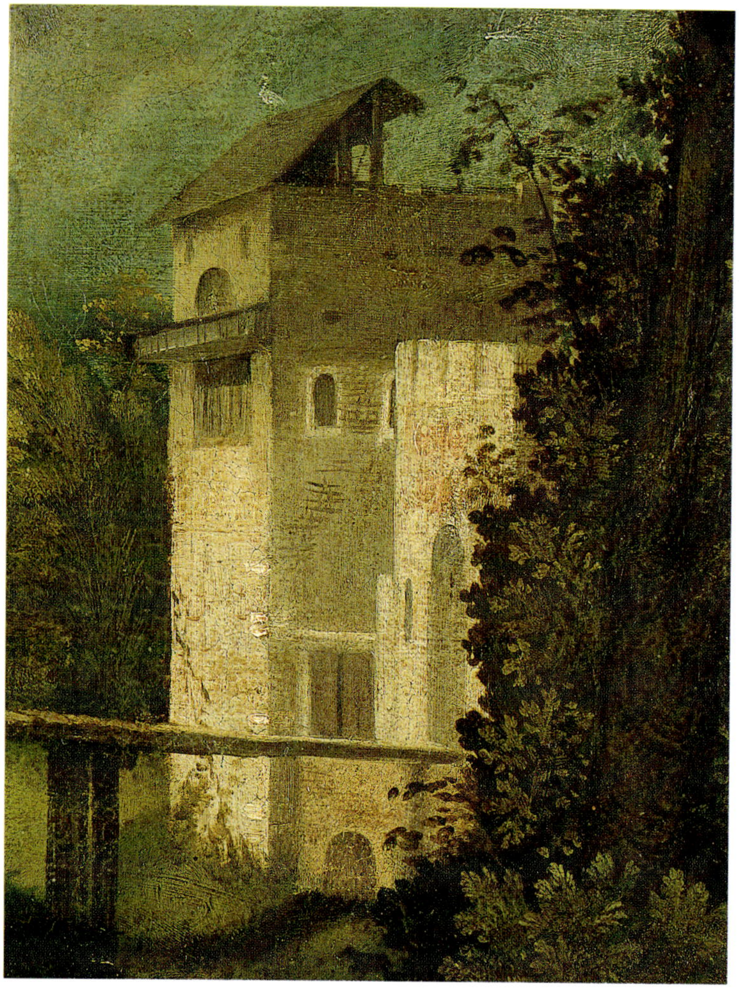

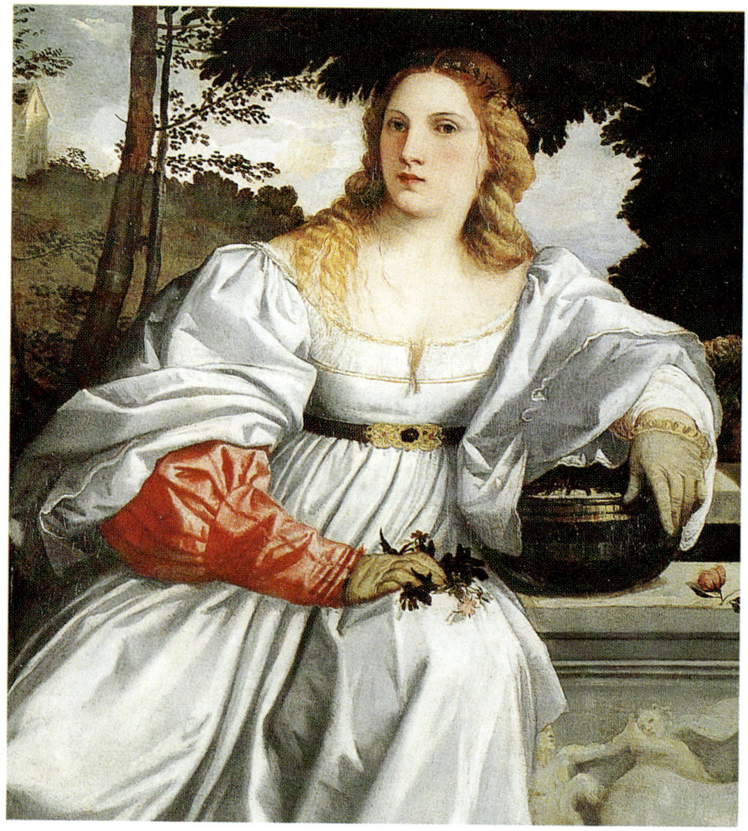

Giorgione, *The Tempest*, detail, 1507-1508. Venice, Gallerie dell'Accademia.

Titian, *Sacred and Profane Love*, 1514. Rome, Borghese Gallery.

Rosso Fiorentino, *Marriage of the Virgin*, detail, 1523. Florence, San Lorenzo Basilica.

Preceding page: **Parmigianino**, *Portrait of a Young Woman (The Turkish Slave)*, detail, c. 1530. Parma, National Gallery.

At the dawn of the new century the world awoke to find itself profoundly transformed, and during the course of the sixteenth century other changes were to occur. With the discovery of those new lands that were called the Americas in honor of Americus Vespucci, the nations bordering on the Mediterranean lost all geographic, and thus political, centrality, leaving the field free to those lapped by the Atlantic Ocean. This could even be called a sign, since in the brief span of a few decades other certainties, taken for granted in the preceding centuries, began to crumble. Even the monolithic image of the Catholic Church started to break up. Biting criticism was addressed to the Roman Curia by Martin Luther, whose ninety-five theses nailed to the door of the church in Wittenberg (site of the university where the Augustinian monk taught) were translated from Latin to German, printed and diffused all over Germany. Modes of communication had changed and the printing press, invented by Gutenberg in 1456, had reaped its first illustrious victim. The year was 1517, and the unity of the Church had been destroyed forever. Even man's view of the universe was to change in the course of the sixteenth century. Nicolaus Copernicus, a Polish physician and canon, published in 1543, the year of his death, the *De revolutionibus orbium coelestium*, in which the Ptolemaic model of the cosmos was abandoned. Copernicus maintained that the center of the universe was not the Earth, as had been thought for centuries after Ptolemy, but the Sun. In other words, the cultural foundation stones that had guided untold generations for hundreds of years were no longer valid. Man's place in the world had to be totally reconsid-

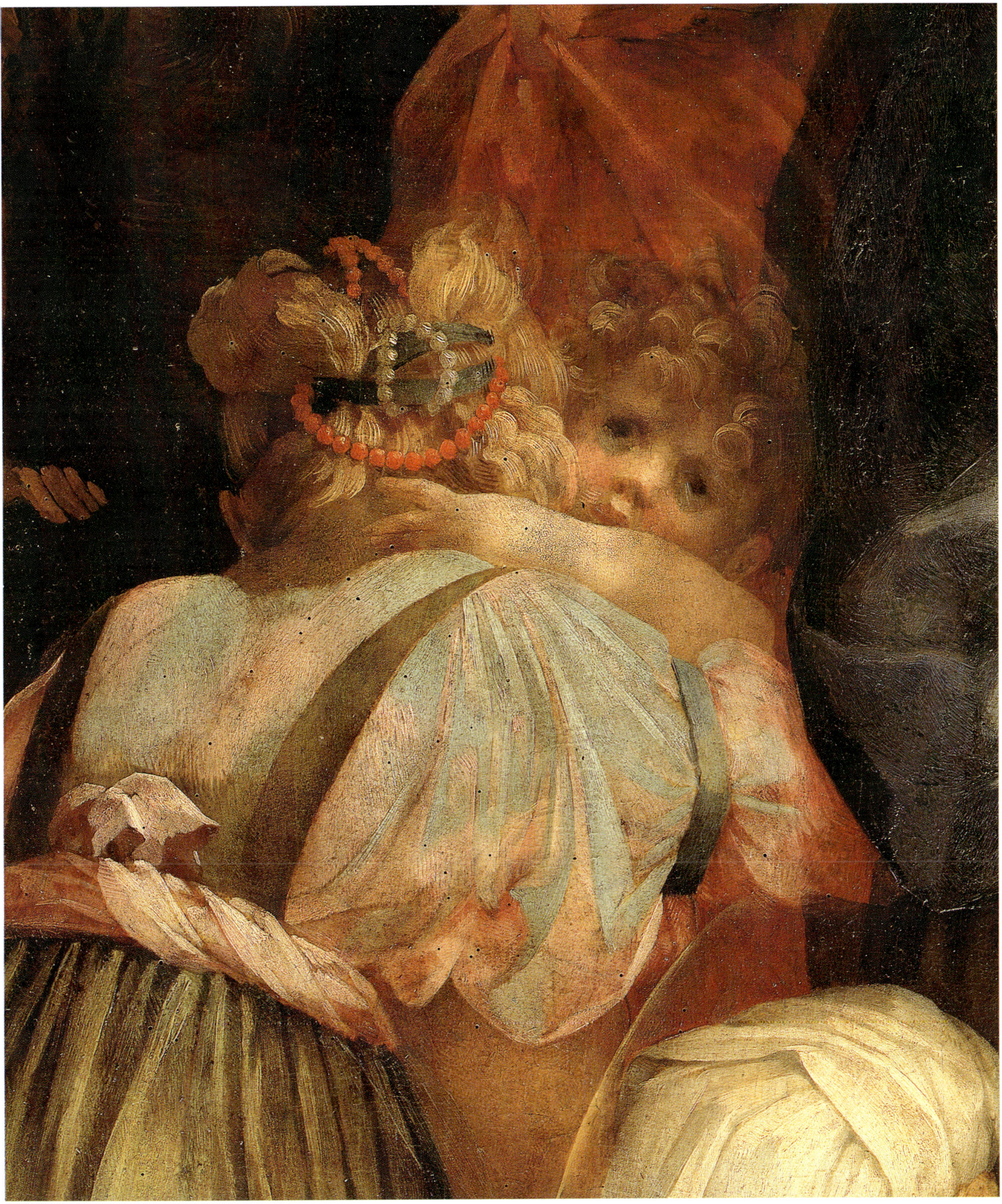

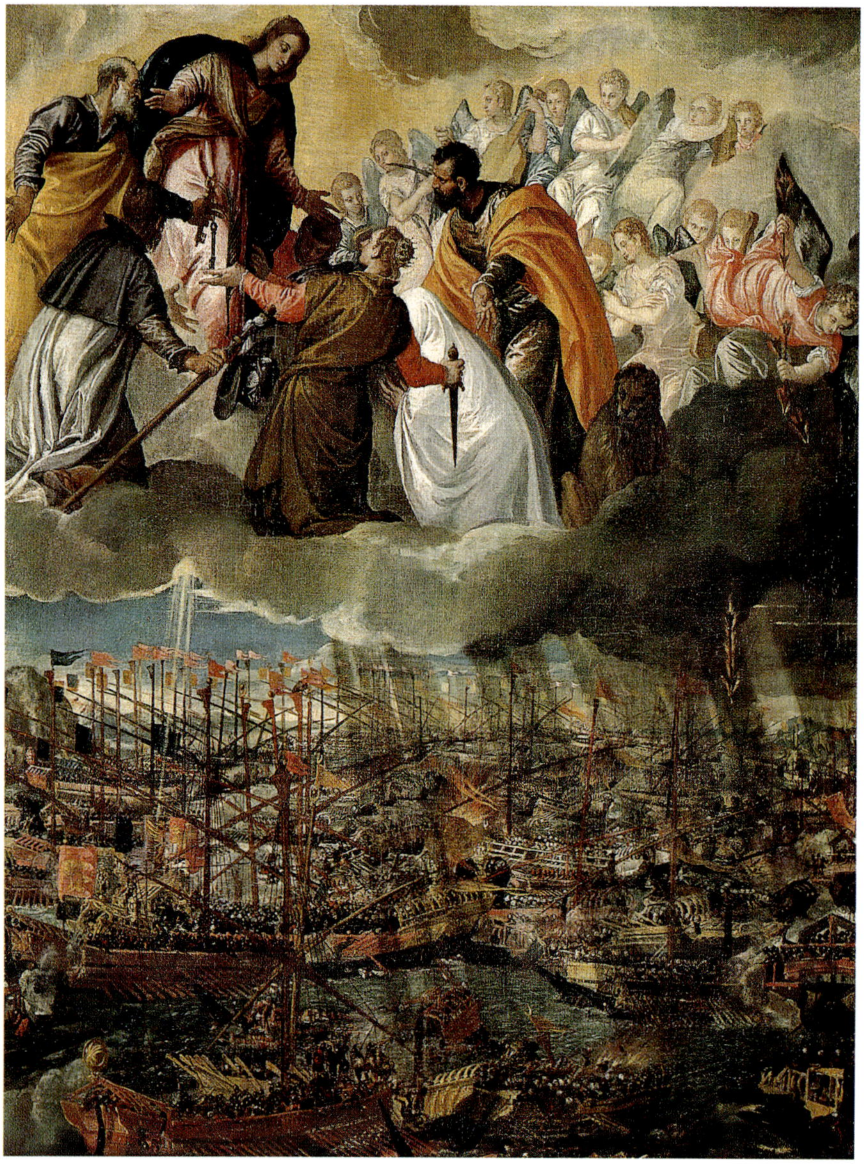

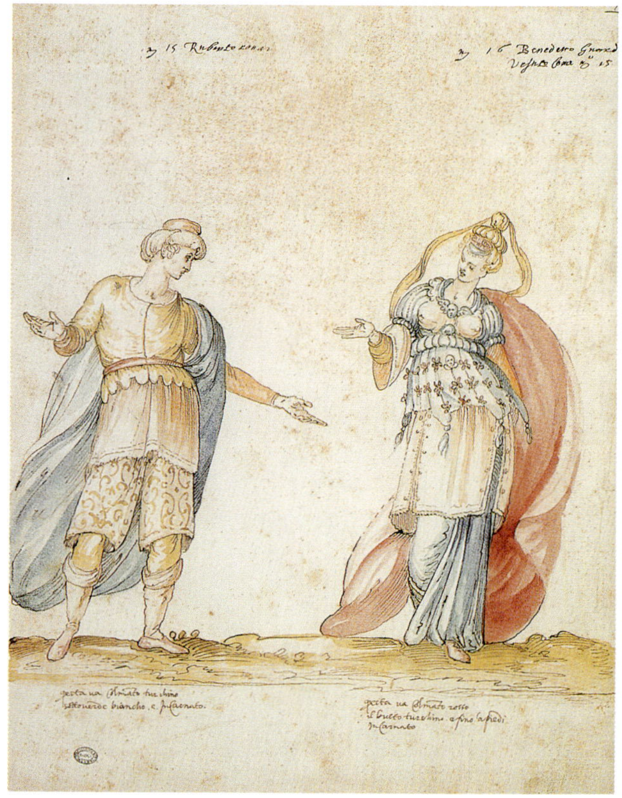

Paolo Veronese, *The Battle of Lepanto*, c. 1573. Venice, Gallerie dell'Accademia.

Bernardo Buontalenti, *Delphic Couple*, drawing for the third intermezzo of the *Pellegrina*, performed at Florence in the Medicean Theatre, c. 1589. Florence, National Central Library, Pal. C.B.3.53/II, c. 17r.

Giambologna, *The Apennines*, c. 1580. Pratolino, Florence, Park of the Medicean Villa.

ered. Reactions to such radical changes were not lacking. The Church questioned itself for eighteen long years, from 1545 to 1563, giving origin to what historians call the Counter Reformation, centered around the city of Trent; but its efforts were not to obtain – due also to its own errors – the desired effect. Nor was the situation improved by the founding of the Company of Jesus by Saint Ignatius of Loyola, in 1540. New political powers were arising instead, such as the Spain of Charles V and Philip II or the England of Elisabeth I, a nation which had already escaped from the spiritual domination of the Roman Church to form an exclusively Anglican clergy. Italy, broken up into small states and potentates, was relegated to a minor role in political affairs, especially after the invasion of Charles VIII in 1498, which inaugurated the period of the so-called Italian wars, with the presence of foreign powers on the peninsula.

The worst crisis came in 1527, with the violation of the Holy City of the West, the "Babylonian whore" of the Protestant peoples – the Sack of Rome. The Lansquenets, Lutheran mercenaries from Frundsberg, laid siege to Pope Clement VII in Castel Sant'Angelo, and history would undoubtedly have taken another path except for an epidemic that broke out among the invading troops, forcing them to retreat. But af-

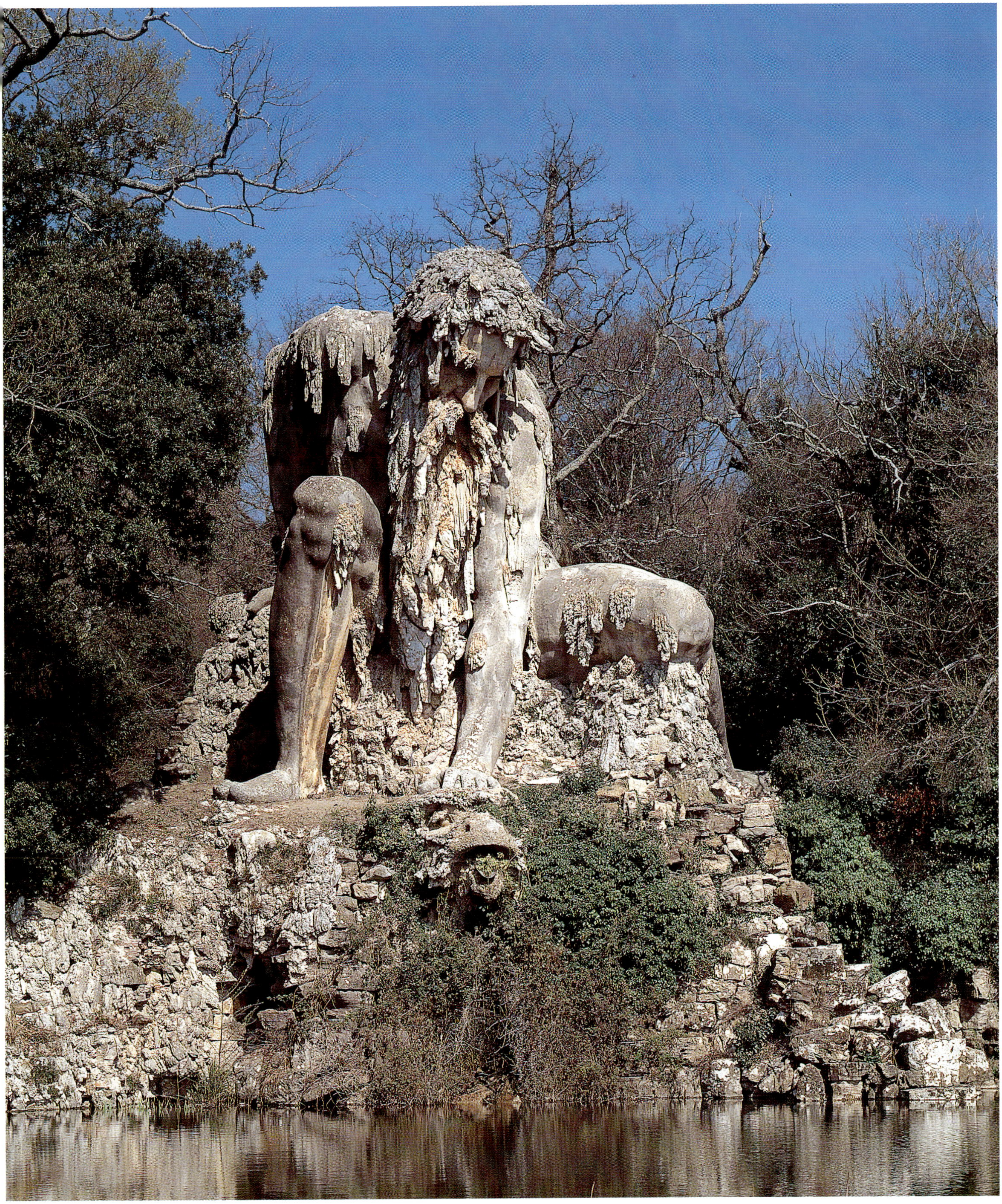

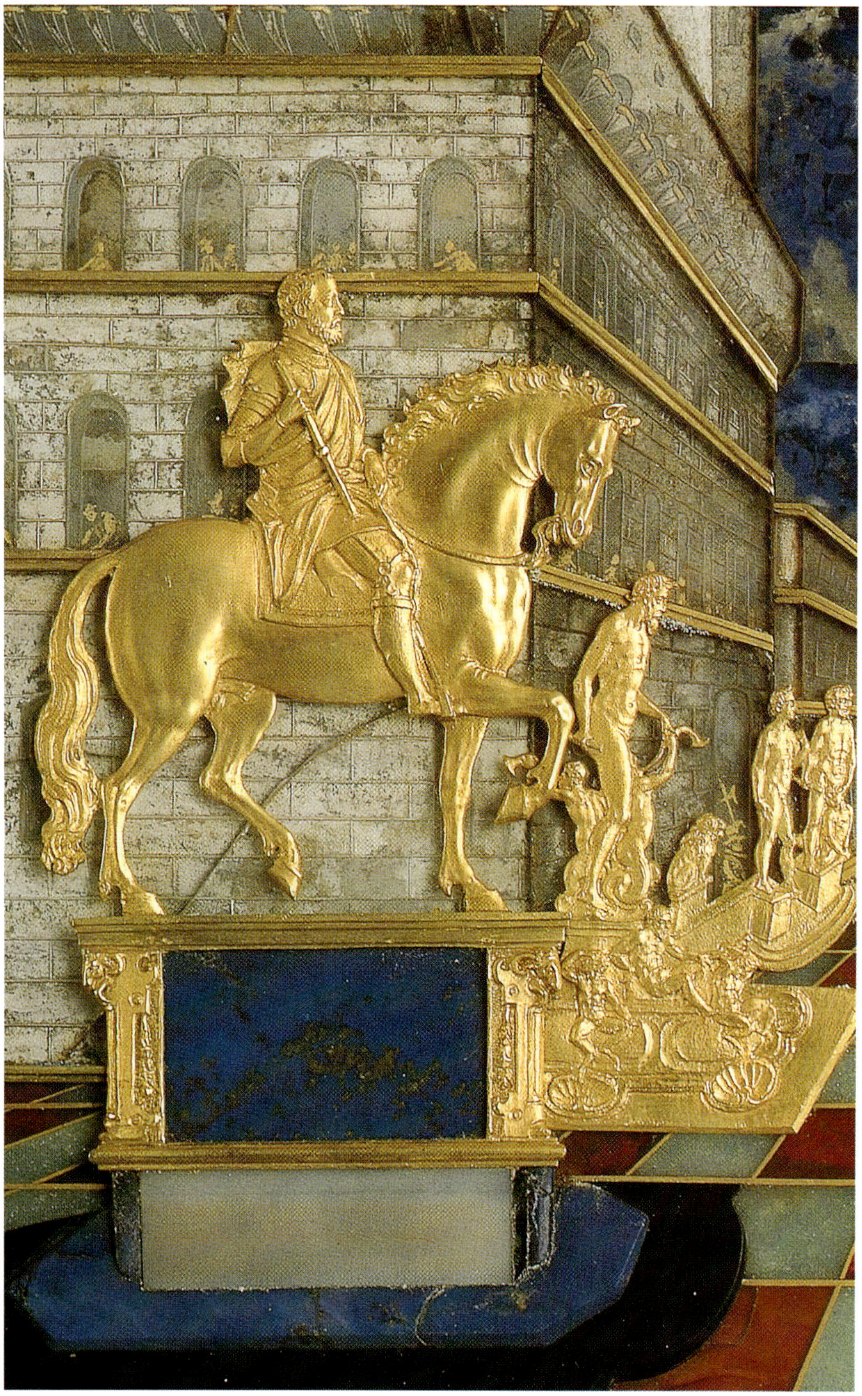

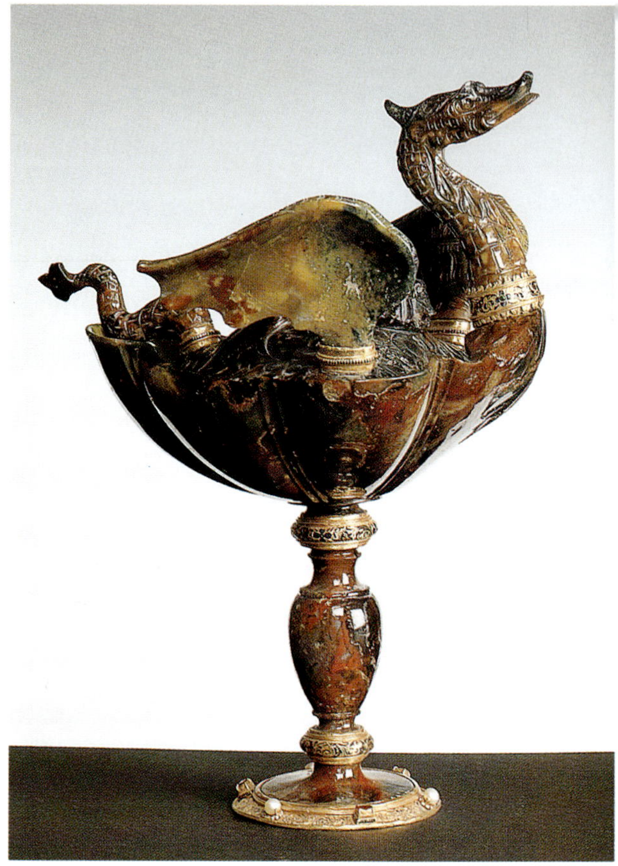

Bernardino Gaffurri and **Jaques Bylivelt**, *Mosaic in semi-precious stones with gold relief*, detail, c. 1599, Florence, Silver Museum.

Saracchi Shop in Milan, *Vase made of diaspore, pearls, rubies and gold with enamel*, second half of the 16th c. Florence, Silver Museum.

ter this date Rome was never to be the same again. Of the supreme artistic triad of the Renaissance, only Michelangelo was still alive. Leonardo had died in France in 1519 and Raphael one year later, leaving to Rome the heritage of his school and his shop headed by Giulio Romano. After the Sack, this immense heritage of art and ideas was dispersed throughout Italy and elsewhere, diffusing the pictorial, architectural and decorative models that had been developed in Rome. Giulio Romano had anticipated this trend, moving to Mantua in 1524. After the Sack, however, the Diaspora of the artists was total: Perin del Vaga moved to Genoa, Rosso Fiorentino went first to Venice, then to Fontainebleau in France, Parmigianino took refuge in Bologna, Giovanni da Udine left for Venice, while Polidoro da Caravaggio stayed first in Naples, then in Sicily. This conferred a national (and ultra-national, considering that Fontainebleau was a point of attraction to which Rosso, Primaticcio and Niccolò dell'Abate were drawn) dimension on that artistic phenomenon known as Mannerism, which involved not only painting but also architecture, sculpture and the decorative arts.

Without pausing to trace the complex critical events that were to lead to the coining of this term in the 20th century, we may note that the first to use it was Giorgio Vasari. "Bella maniera" (beautiful manner) was the term used by the

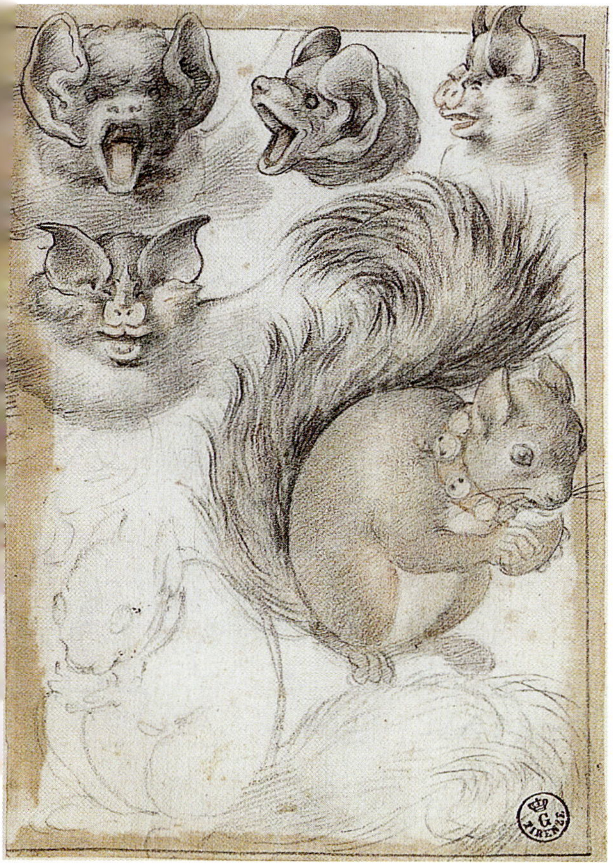

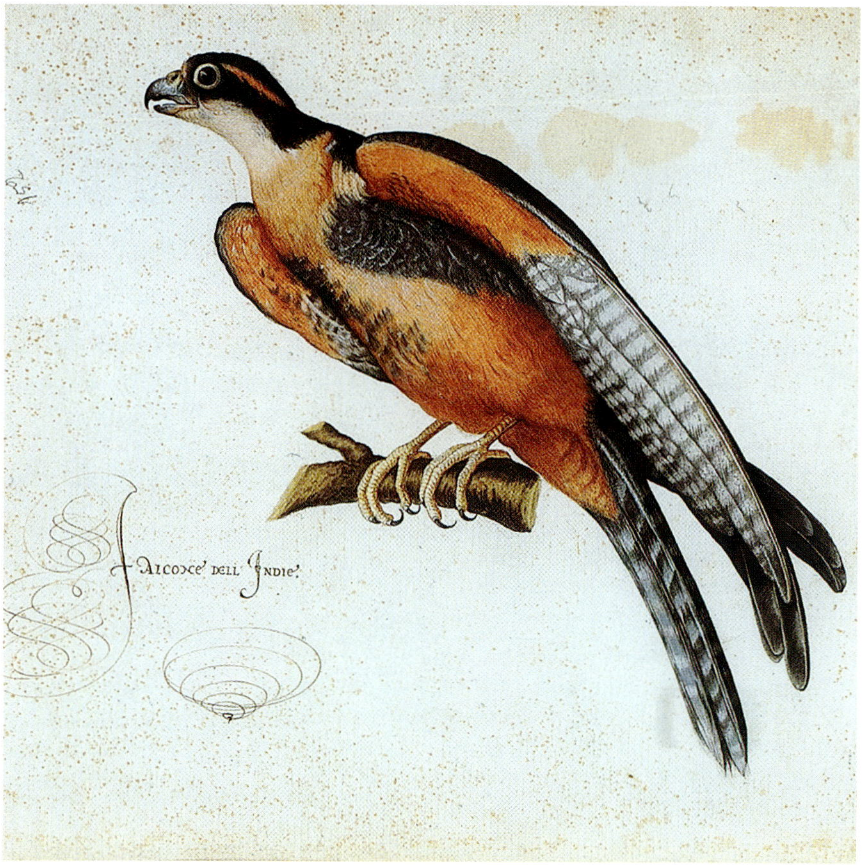

historiographer from Arezzo to indicate that the basic paradigm was no longer nature, but the art of Leonardo, Raphael and above all Michelangelo. The phenomenon, nourished by the fervent activity of Michelangelo, who died in 1564, and by the stylistic evolution of his work, consisted of experimentation in color rich in luministic effects such as those of Domenico Beccafumi and Tintoretto, and in the use of twisting, serpentine forms, considered by the theorist Lomazzo to be the Mannerist canon par excellence. A good example can be seen in the sculptures of Giambologna, where the human figure is elongated and twisted. At the basis of this new aesthetics may be placed the concept expressed by Vasari, who explains: "The most beautiful style comes from constantly copying the most beautiful things, combining the most beautiful hands, heads, bodies or legs together to create from all these beautiful qualities the most perfect figure possible....". Architecture too, while strongly influenced by the heritage of Michelangelo, could not escape the fascination of the "Manner", as confirmed by the flourishing revival of Vitruvian studies. It was not by chance that the architect and treatise writer Vignola published, in 1562, the *Rule of the Five Orders of Architecture*. And in 1570, just one year before the Battle of Lepanto in which the Venetians drove the Turks out of the Mediterranean, Palladio published his *Four Books of Architecture*. It would be erroneous, however, to consider the 16th century as exclusively Mannerist, since along with Salviati and Zuccari we find Giorgione and Titian, Correggio and Lorenzo Lotto, Alessandro Moretto and Veronese in a variety of trends that make this one of the richest centuries in Italian art – an art which achieved superb effects using costly materials such as semi-precious stones, glass and metal and which also, thanks to the new geographical discoveries, renewed interest in naturalist and scientific investigation.

Francesco Morandini known as Il Poppi, *Study of bats and squirrels*, second half of the 16th c. Florence, Cabinet of Prints and Drawings, Uffizi.

Ulisse Aldrovandi, *Falcon from the Indies*, before 1598. Bologna, Biblioteca Universitaria, Corpus Aldrovandino, I, c. 152.

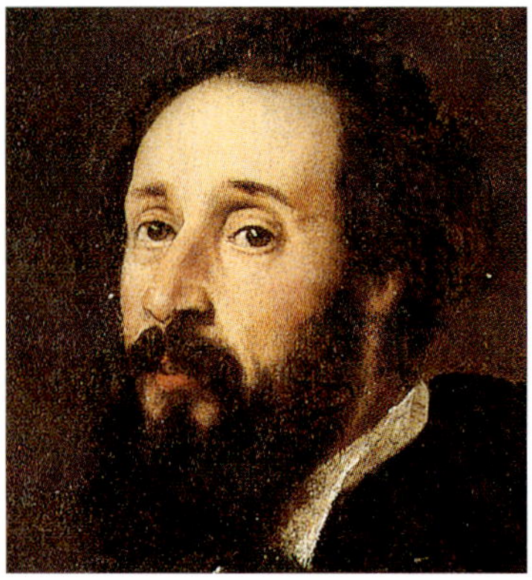

Giulio Romano

(Giulio Pippi,
Rome 1499 – Mantua 1546)

Painter, decorator and architect, Giulio Pippi, known as "Romano" due to the fact that he was born in the Papal city, entered Raphael's shop as a boy, only ten years old. Increasingly involved in the master's major works, he participated with other assistants in frescoing the Stanza of the *Conflagration* and the Logge in the Vatican, as well as in the decoration of the Psyche Loggia in the villa of Agostino Chigi, known today as the Farnesina. With the early death of Raphael in 1521, Giulio remained the unquestionable head of the shop which was to complete the works left unfinished by the master, such as the Hall of Constantine in the Vatican Palaces. In 1524 the artist moved to Mantua where he designed and frescoed Palazzo Te, the Duomo, his own house and the Fish Market.

Titian (Tiziano Vecellio), *Portrait of Giulio Romano*, 1536.

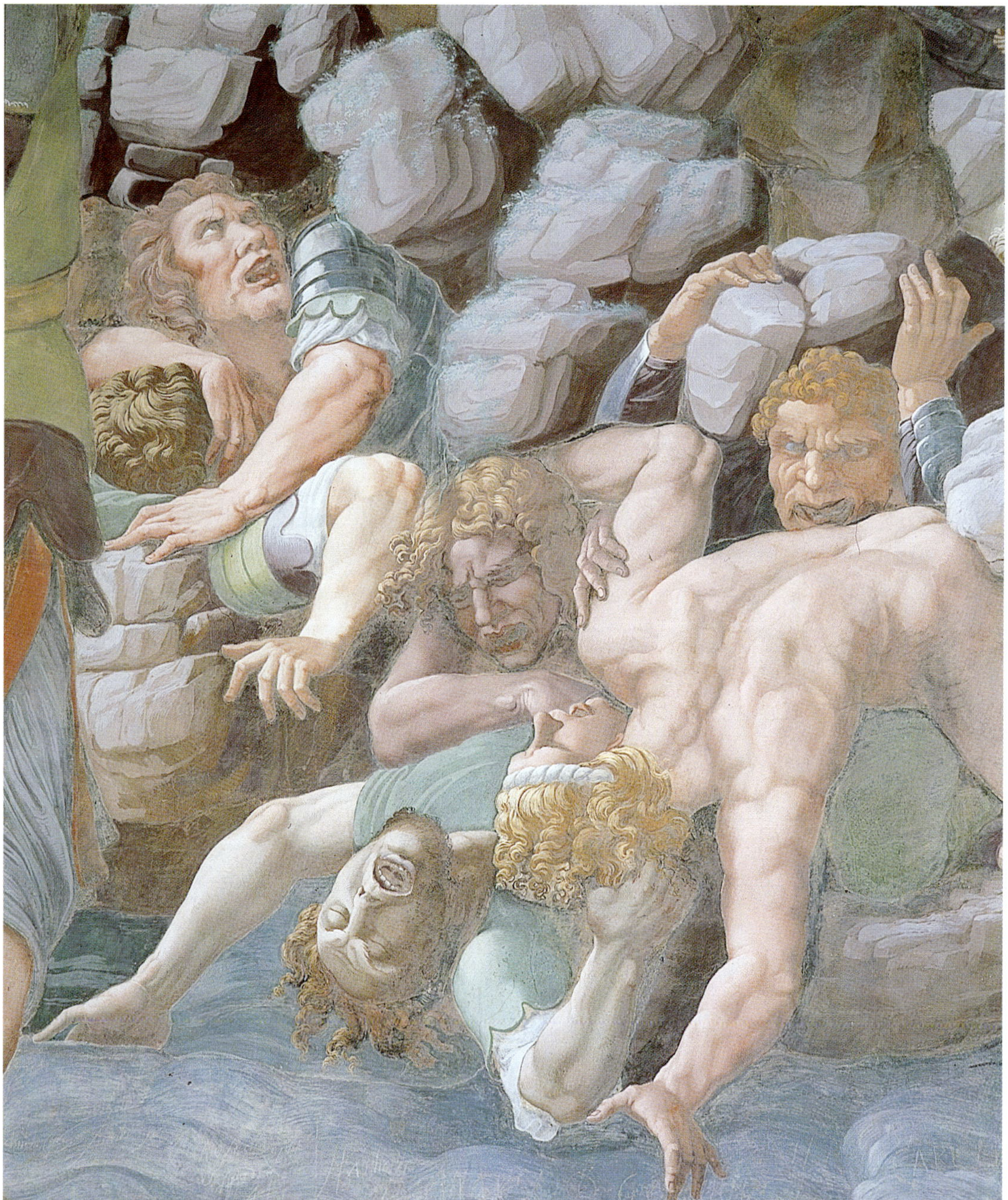

Giulio Romano and Assistance
Hall of the Giants
c. 1531
frescoes, detail
Mantua, Palazzo Te.

The theme, derived from Hesiod's *Teogonia* (vv. 646-734), is interpreted by the artist in spectacular manner. The choice of this subject was probably influenced by the desire of Federico II Gonzaga (1519-40) to reiterate his own fidelity to Charles V, the Emperor-Jove of the times. The myth tells of the father of the gods who drives the race of Giants and Titans back to Tartarus, thus re-establishing order throughout the cosmos. The entire architectural structure of the room seems to collapse under the impetus of the struggle, foreshadowing typically Baroque spectacular effects.

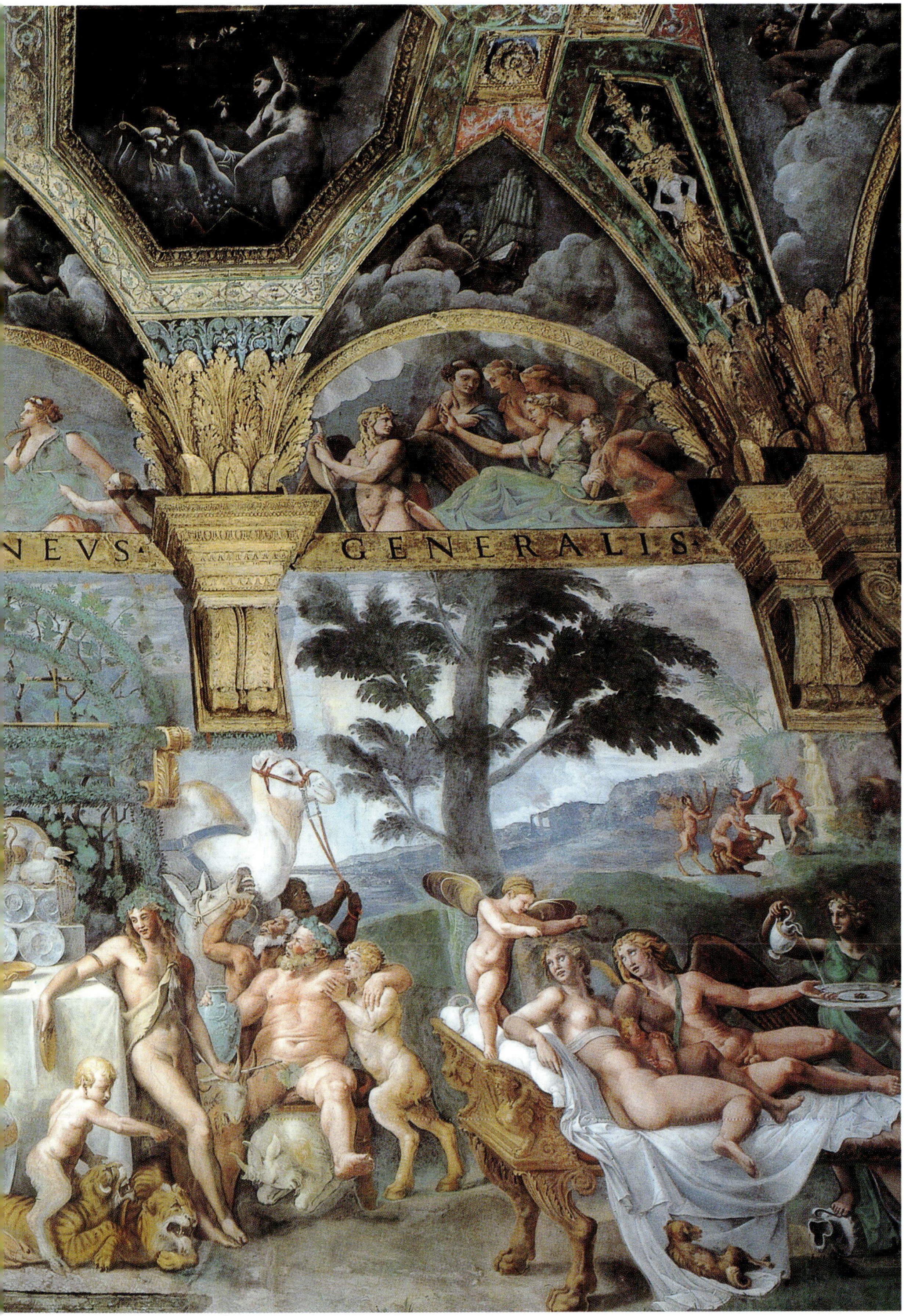

Giulio Romano and Assistance
Hall of Cupid and Psyche
c. 1526-28
frescoes, detail
Mantua, Palazzo Te.

The well-known fable by Apuleius tells of Psyche, the beautiful girl loved by Cupid, who has however forbidden her to look at him. Incapable of obeying, Psyche spies on Cupid while he sleeps, but is left no time to enjoy his beauty, as he disappears immediately. The desperate girl wanders about searching for her love. After endless adventures she manages to find him, and joins him forever when Jove bestows on her the gift of immortality. The artist depicts the salient stages of the story, but dedicates to the nuptial banquet in particular the great frescoes covering the northern and western walls.

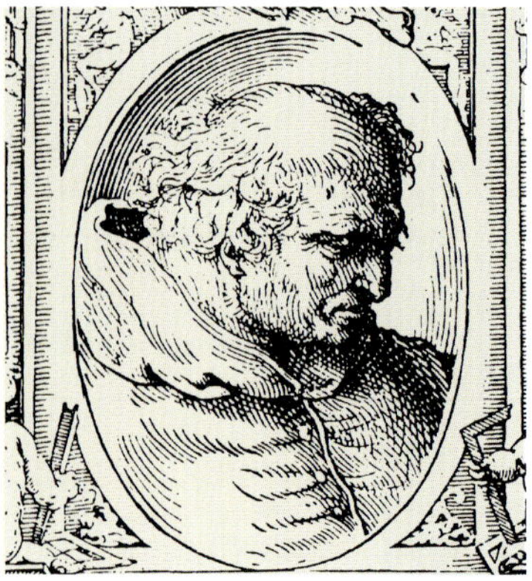

Donato Bramante

(Donato di Pascuccio di Antonio, Monte Asdruvaldo, Pesaro, 1444 – Rome 1514)

Probably a collaborator of Piero della Francesca (he may have painted the background of the *Montefeltro Altarpiece* now at Brera), Donato seems to have trained in the Urbino milieu and worked in Perugia and Ferrara. One of the most important painters and architects of the early Renaissance, he undoubtedly decorated the Palazzo del Podestà in Bergamo in 1477. Of this undertaking, fragments of frescoes with philosophers and architectural perspectives, now in the Bergamo Civic Museum, remain. From 1480 to 1492 he designed notable buildings such as Santa Maria presso San Satiro in Milan and the Duomo of Pavia. At Rome from 1490, he constructed works of fundamental importance such as the courtyard of Santa Maria della Pace (1500) and the Vatican Belvedere (1504-1505). He also designed the new St Peter's, later modified by Michelangelo and others.

Giorgio Vasari, *Portrait of Donato Bramante*, from the *Lives*, Florence, Giunti, 1568.

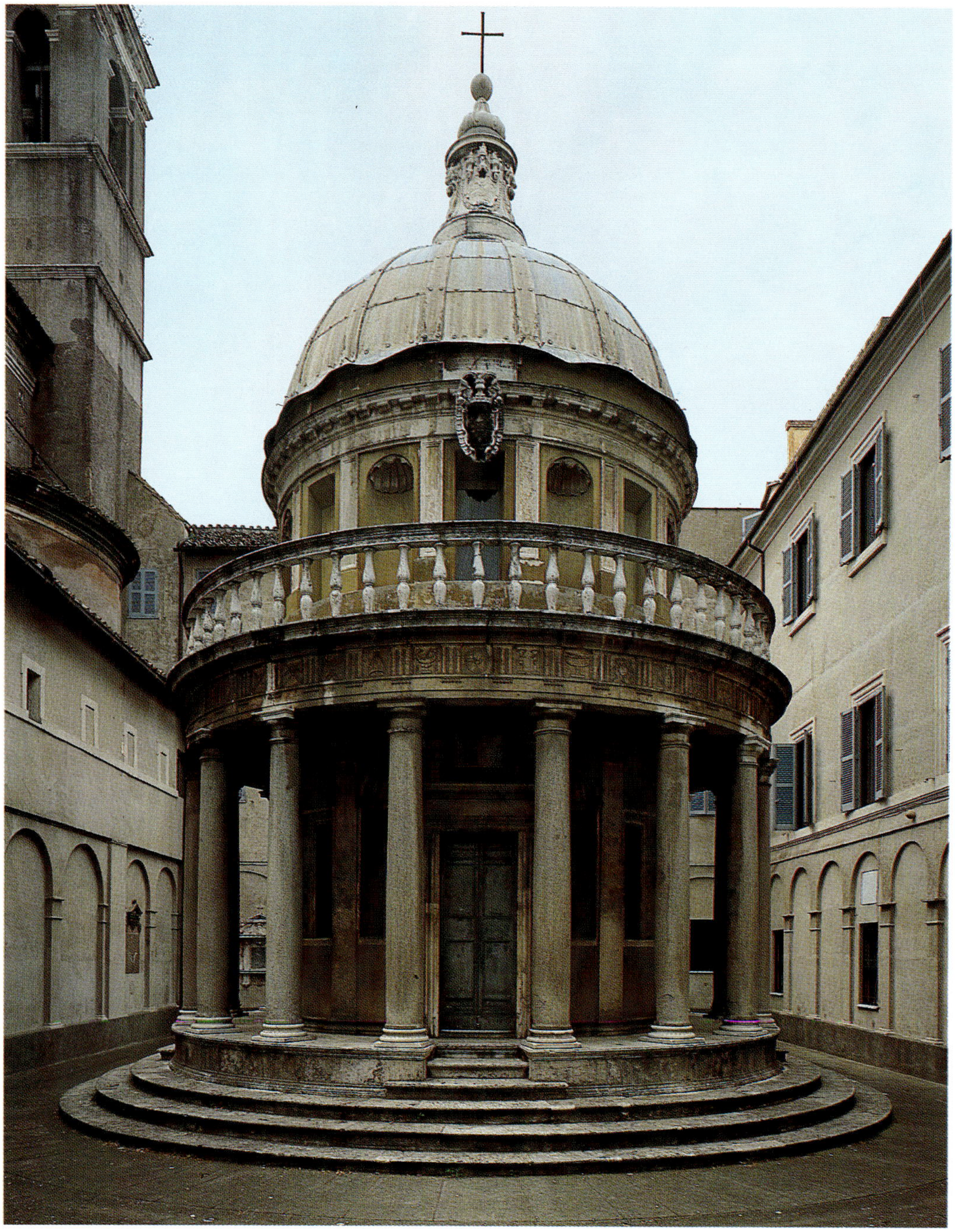

Donato Bramante
Templet of St Peter in Montorio
1502-1506
Rome.

The date of 1502 confirmed by an epigraph should probably be considered as that of the start of the work, while the erection of the church dates from after 1505. With circular plan, the building – which, it seems, served as inspiration to Raphael for the construction appearing in the background of the *Marriage of the Virgin* (1504, Milan, Brera) – reflects the ideals of harmony rediscovered by the Renaissance through its study of Vitruvius. The *ratio* between the diameter and the total height of the temple, for example, is 3 to 4, according to the consonance established between the theory of music and architecture.

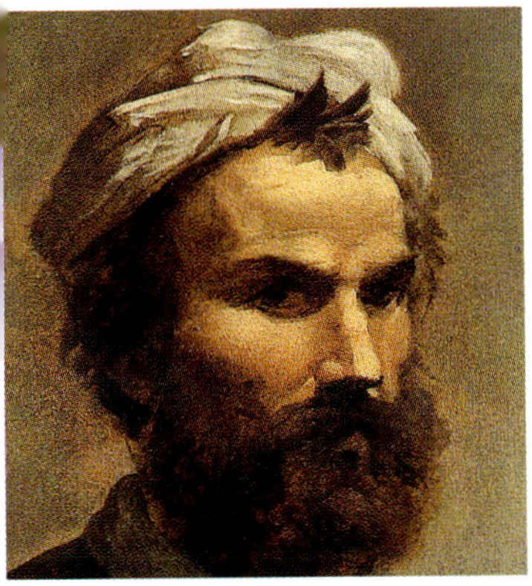

Domenico Beccafumi

(Domenico di Giacomo di Pace, Siena 1486 – 1551)

The primary source for information on the life and works of Beccafumi is the second edition of Vasari's *Lives*. Nicknamed Il Mecherino, perhaps for his short stature, Domenico took the pseudonym of Beccafumi from the name of the landowner for whom his family worked. Attracted by esoteric disciplines such as alchemy, according to Vasari, the painter developed his style through a prolonged stay in Rome (c. 1510-13). Returning to his native city, he became the outstanding figure in sixteenth century Sienese art. He designed the cartoons for the flooring of the Duomo (in the area of the transept and apse, 1518), and frescoed Palazzo Pubblico (1529-35) and the apse of the Duomo (1544). He also worked in Genoa and Pisa.

Domenico Beccafumi, *Self-portrait*, c. 1527. Florence, Uffizi Gallery.

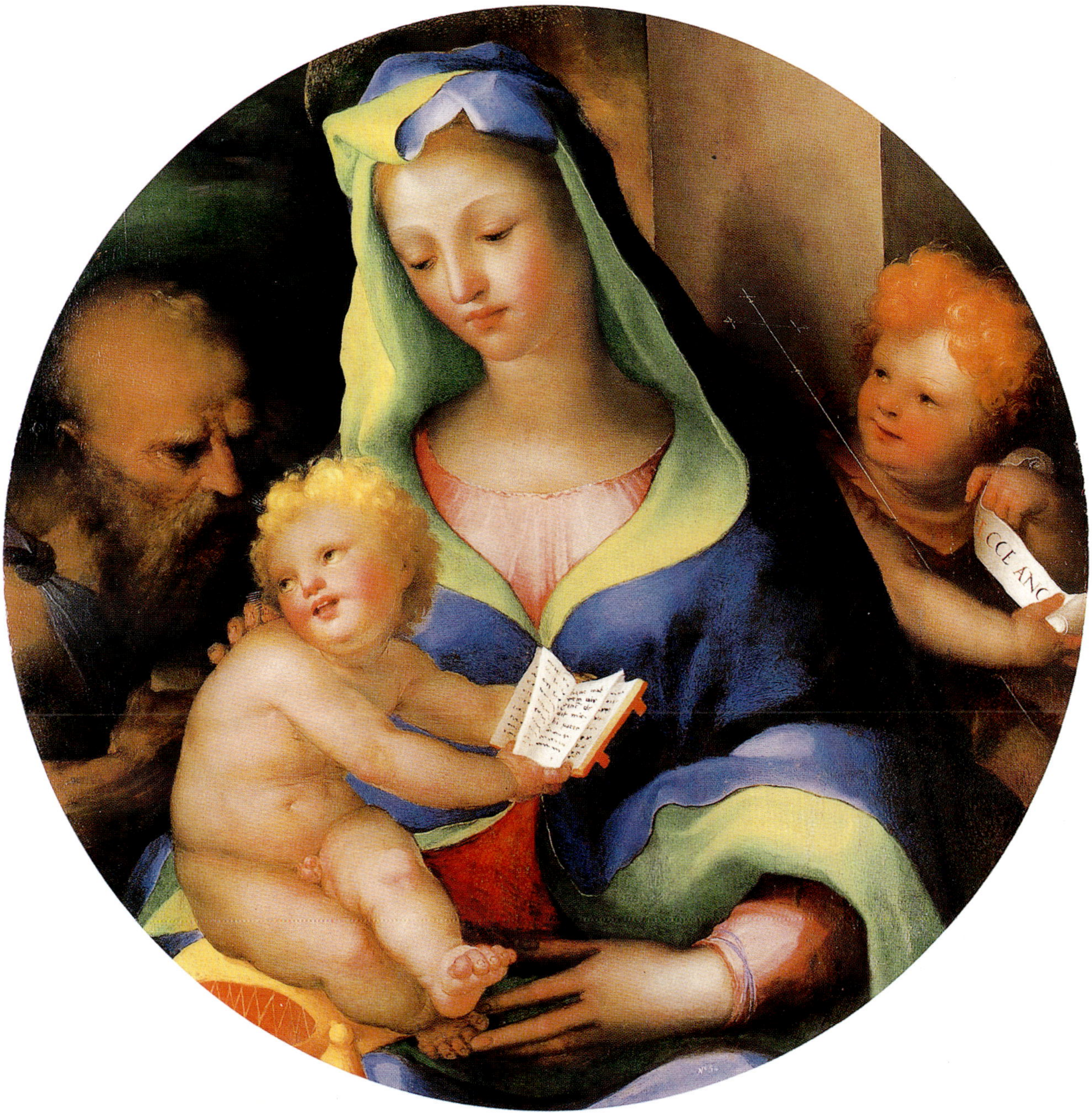

Domenico Beccafumi
Madonna with Child, St Jerome and the Infant St John
c. 1519
panel
Madrid, Thyssen-Bornemisza Collection.

The work, recently discovered (1983), presents a subject frequently reiterated in Beccafumi's production. The little Christ Child gazes at the repentant St Jerome while the Virgin watches over him with maternal care. Behind her, at her left, is the infant St John. The iridescent palette utilized by the artist testifies to his Roman experience, already assimilated, while the iconography is very similar to that of the Uffizi *Holy Family*, of which even the arrangement of the mantle over Mary's head it is reminiscent; a detail which may be traced back to Jacopo della Quercia.

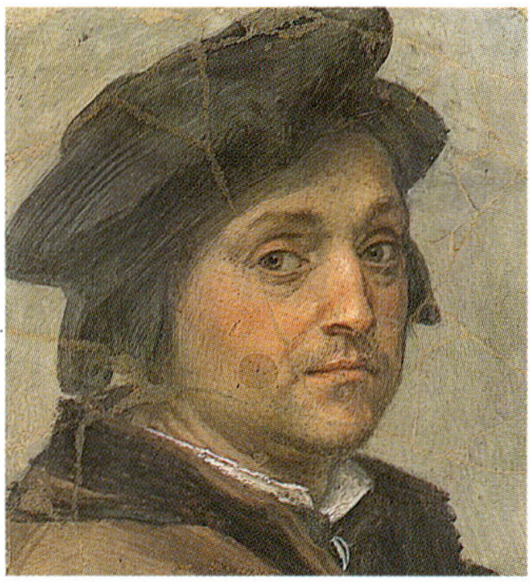

Andrea del Sarto

(Andrea d'Agnolo,
Florence 1486 – 1530)

When Andrea, known as "del Sarto" from the profession of his father Agnolo di Francesco, a tailor, finally opened his own shop in Florence in 1508, Raphael had just left for Rome, leaving him a figurative heritage which he tempered with that of Leonardo and Fra Bartolomeo. A pupil of Piero di Cosimo, Andrea was always attentive to the newest innovations in painting, adopting them without exaggeration. A painter of tranquil, pleasant style, he moved frequently, to Rome (1511 and 1514), to Venice and as far as the court of Francis I of France, although the center of his activity was always to remain Florence, where his projects included the frescoing of the cloisters of the Annunziata and the Scalzi churches. His importance to the development of Italian painting lies also in the artistic heritage received from him by the Mannerist generation, from Pontormo to Vasari.

Andrea del Sarto,
Self-portrait, 1528-30.
Florence, Uffizi Gallery.

Andrea del Sarto
Woman with the "Petrarchino"
c. 1528
panel
Florence, Uffizi Gallery.

A great portrait painter, Andrea del Sarto here confronts the theme of the unofficial portrait, pervaded by a private, domestic atmosphere. Among the various hypotheses as to the identity of the sitter, the most credible seems to be that she is the painter's stepdaughter Maria del Berrettaio, caught at a moment when, almost as if the painter had called her name, she looks up from the book she is reading, Petrarch's sonnets. Although the young woman turns to gaze at the spectator, her index finger holds the pages open, clearly indicating that she is about to resume her reading.

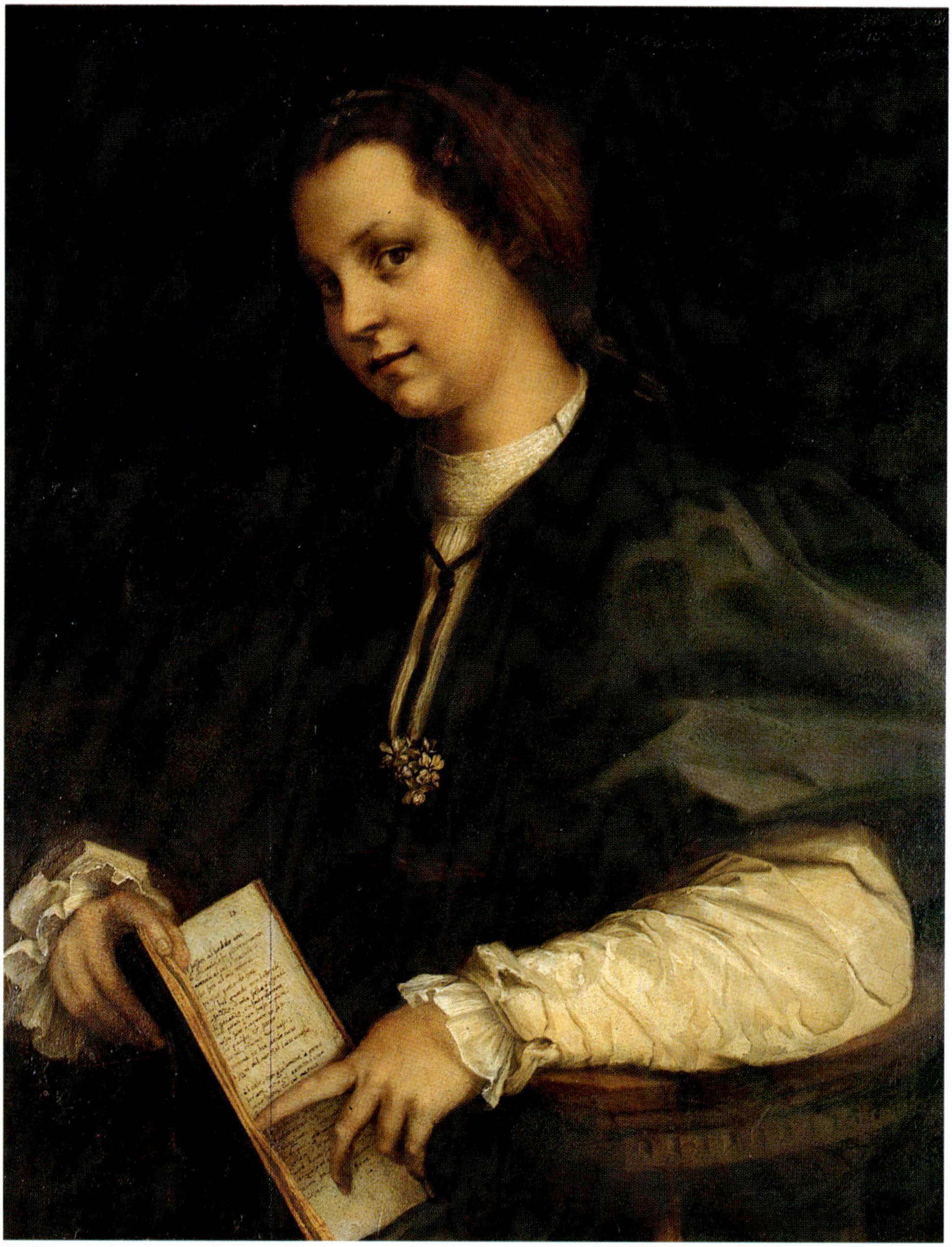

Andrea del Sarto
Madonna of the Harpies
1517
panel
Florence, Uffizi Gallery.

The name of the painting comes from an error made by Vasari, who thought the figures appearing on the pedestal the Virgin stands were harpies. In reality they are, as has been demonstrated by critics, locusts, depicted as they are described in the Apocalypse (IX, 7-10), as having faces "of men" and "hair like that of women". Apart from the complex symbolism, the reference is justified by the presence of St John the Evangelist, traditionally held to be the author of the Apocalypse. The other saint is Francis, rather than the Bonaventura originally requested by the patrons.

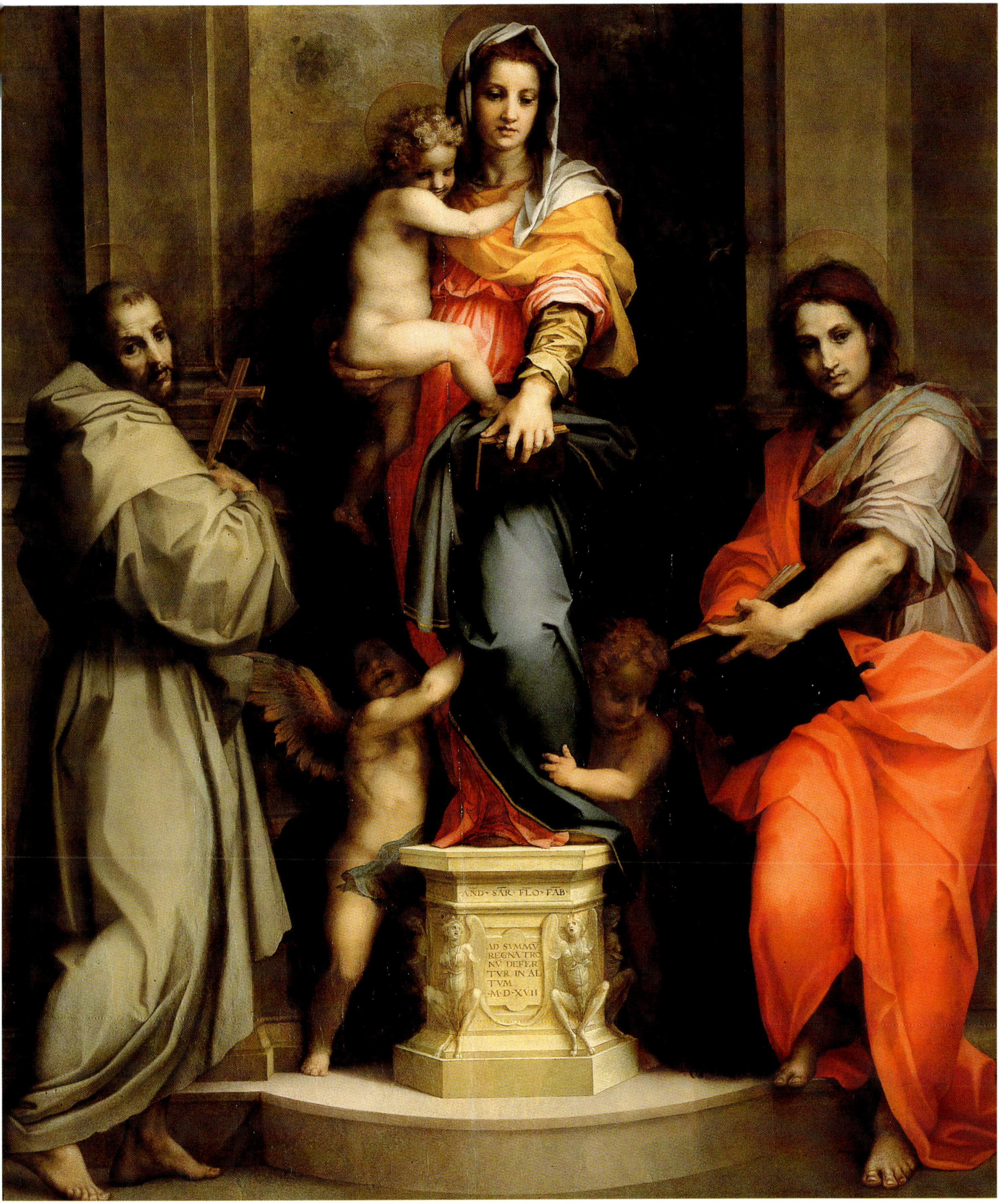
AND · SAR · FLO · FAB
AD SVMMV REGNA TRO NV DEFER TVR IN AL TVM M·D·XVII

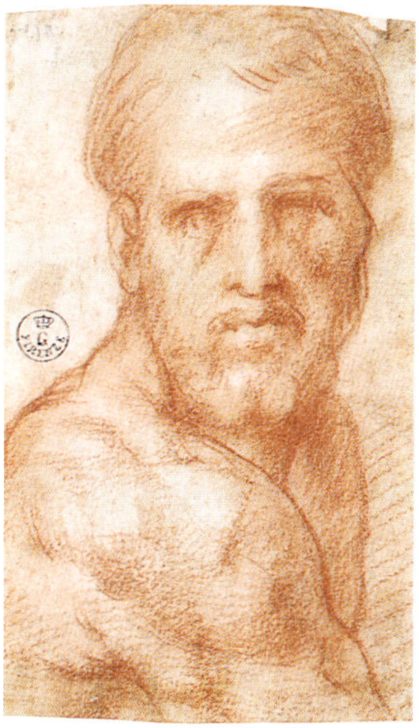

Pontormo

(Jacopo Carucci, Pontormo, Empoli, 1494 – Florence 1550)

A child of art – his father Bartolomeo was a pupil of Ghirlandaio – Jacopo is considered the founder of the Mannerist figurative culture, capable of blending Michelangelo's forceful colors and monumental figures (as in the ceiling of the Sistine Chapel) with the metallic rigidity of the Northern painters, such as Dürer. Trained at Florence, he worked with Rosso Fiorentino (1512) in the shop of Andrea del Sarto, which he soon abandoned consequent to disagreements. Pope Leo X, passing through Florence on a journey (1515), gave him important commissions, including the frescoing of the Pope's Chapel in Santa Maria Novella. He traveled to Rome but worked mainly in Florence, where he participated with the *Stories of Joseph* (London, National Gallery) in the decoration of the nuptial chamber of Pierfrancesco Borgherini (1515-19).

Pontormo
Study for a Self-portrait
1516
paper
Florence, Cabinet of Prints and Drawings, Uffizi.

This red chalk drawing is Michelangelesque not only in the monumental effects, the abrupt turn of the head and the powerful shoulder, but also through the artist's desire to physically resemble the unrivaled master.

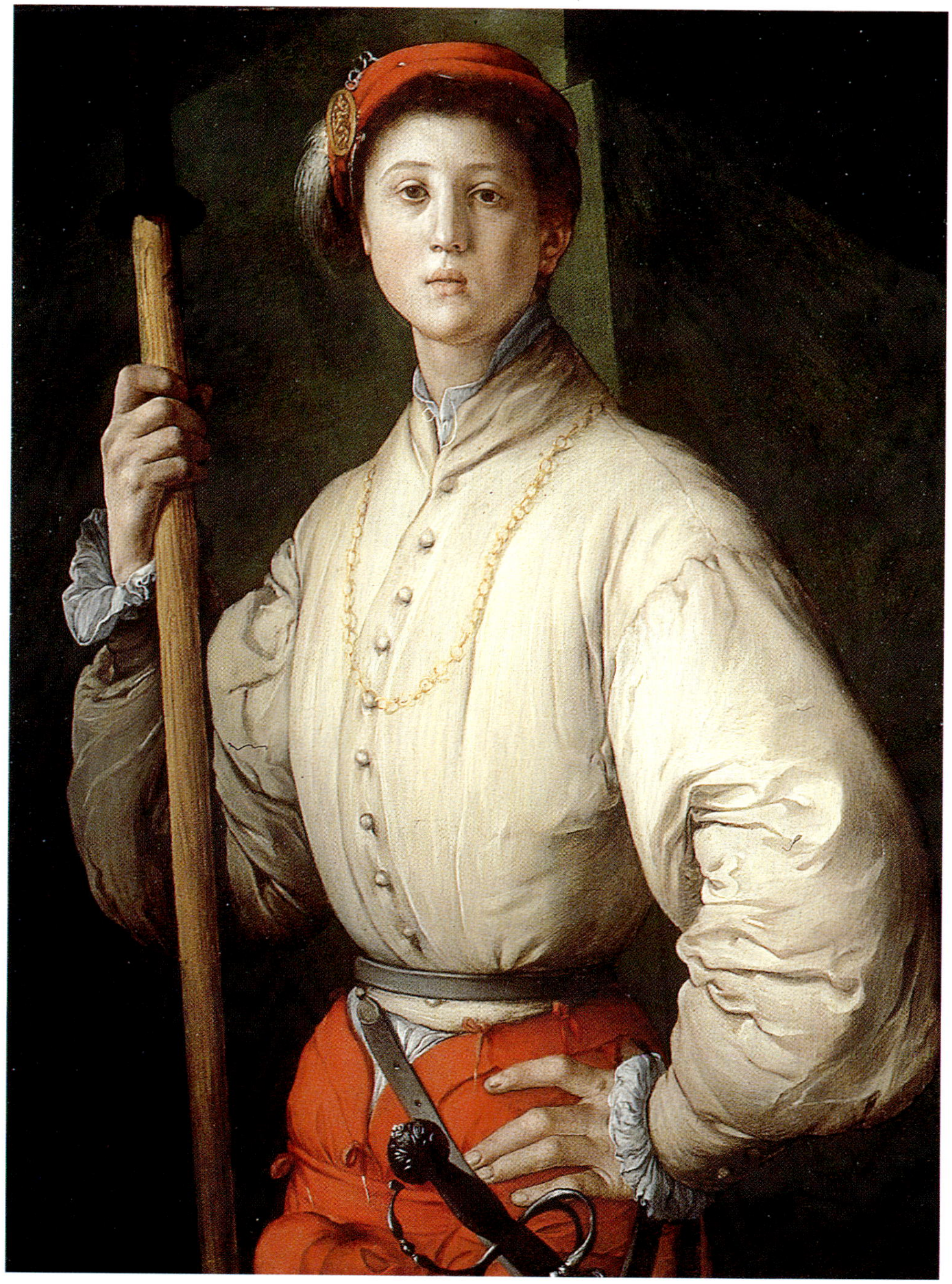

Pontormo
The Halberdier
c. 1529-30
canvas
Malibu, The J. Paul Getty Museum.

"He also painted, during the time of the siege of Florence, Francesco Guardi dressed as a solder, which was a magnificent work; and then on the cover to this painting, Bronzino painted Pygmalion praying to Venus", reports Vasari. Archival documents have identified a certain Francesco Guardi, born in April 1514, who is in all probability the model for the young man portrayed by Pontormo in one of his most fascinating portraits. On the back of the picture, as mentioned by Vasari, there was originally a panel with the myth of Pygmalion and Galatea painted by Bronzino (now in Palazzo Vecchio).

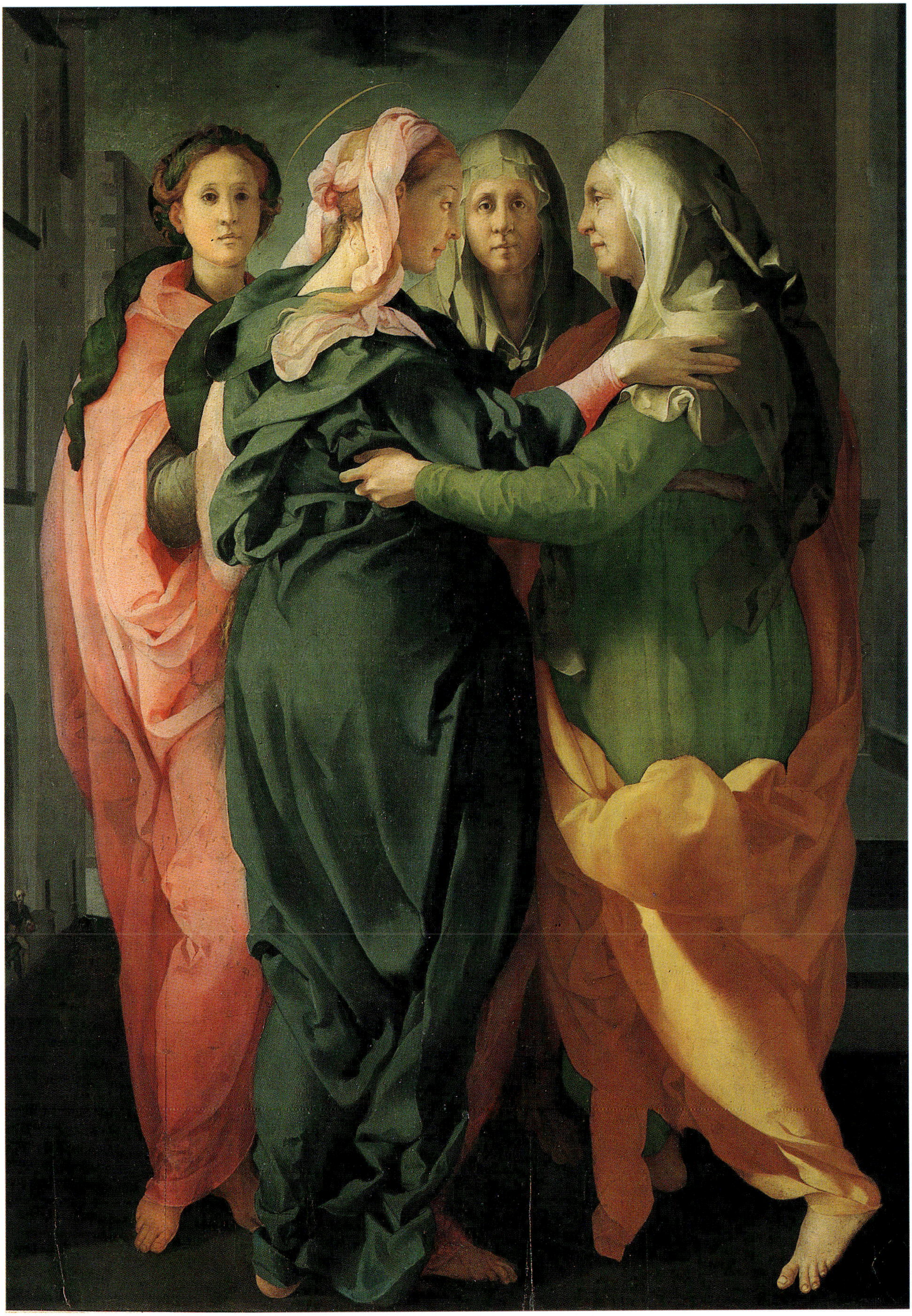

Pontormo
Visitation
c. 1528-29
panel
Carmignano, Prato,
Pieve di San Michele.

The composition, simple but highly effective, was inspired by Dürer's famous print known as *The Four Witches* or *The Four Nude Women*, from 1497. Imitated by Nicoletto da Modena in an engraving from 1500, the German artist's work had in turn been modeled on the traditional group of the three Graces, to which a fourth was added. Pontormo insistently plays on the symmetry and the opposition between the two pairs of women who are presented, coupled, in full-face and in profile. To this the Florentine painter adds a skillful, parsimonious use of color, basically limited to tones of red and green. Furthermore, for the figures in the foreground Pontormo adopts the solution of heraldic nature employed by Piero della Francesca in the *Madonna del Parto*, that of dressing the two women in symmetrically inverted colors.

Pontormo
Deposition
c. 1527
panel, details
Florence, Santa Felicita,
Capponi Chapel.

Unanimously held to be Pontormo's masterpiece, the work belongs to the cycle of paintings decorating the Capponi Chapel in Santa Felicita, on which the artist's friend Bronzino also worked. The panel is a sort of manifesto of Mannerist poetics where the figures, devoid of any architectural or environmental setting (apart form the cloud), come alive through their acidulous color and intensely spiraling forms.

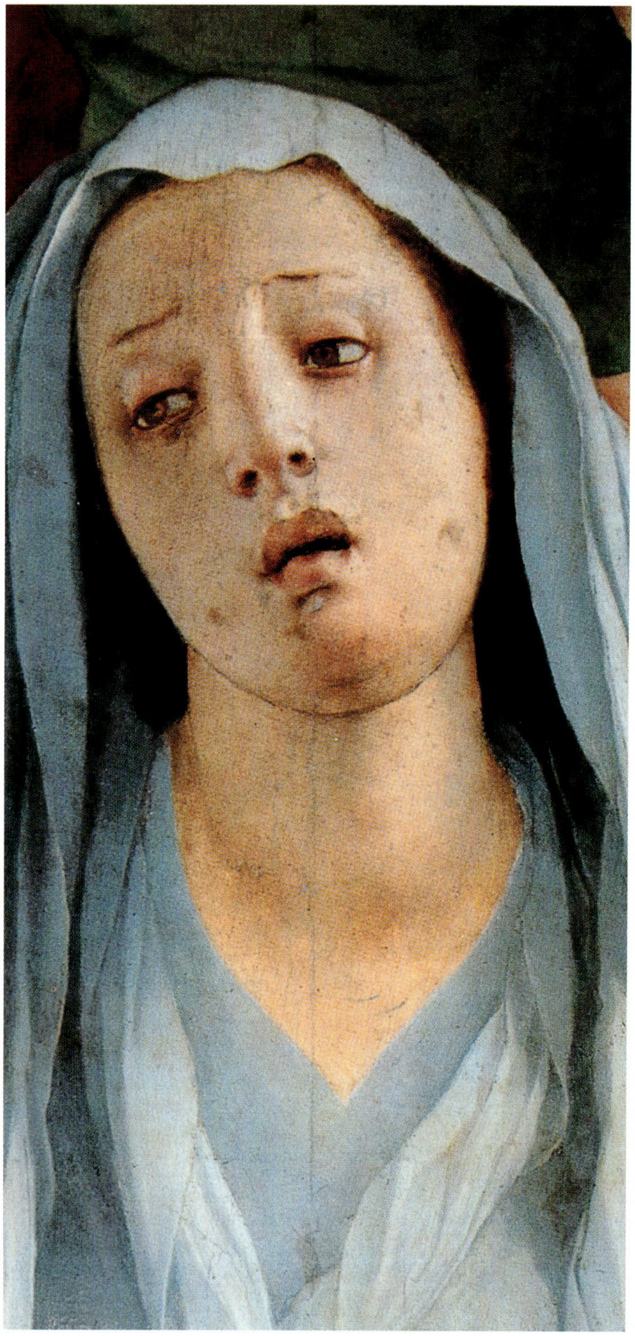

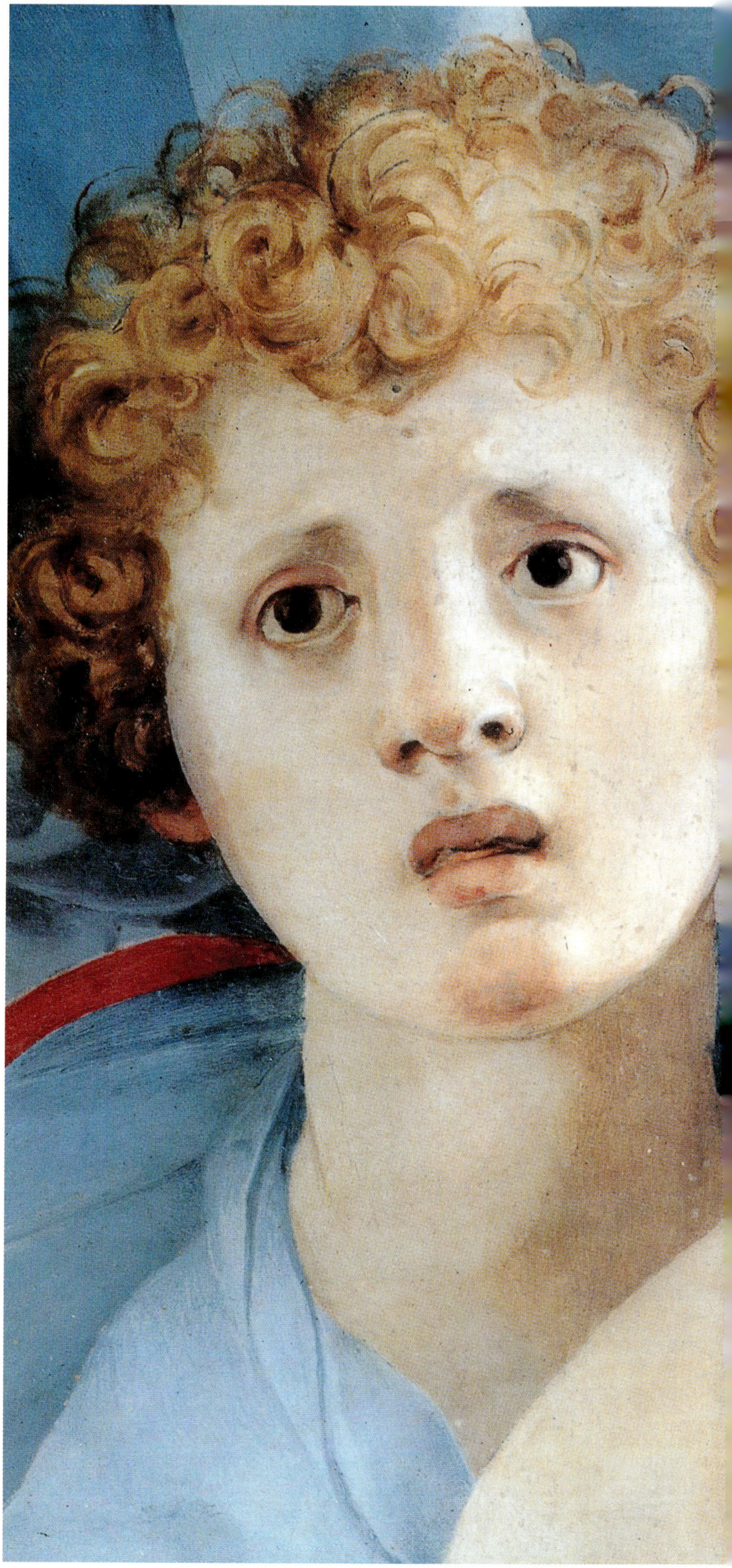

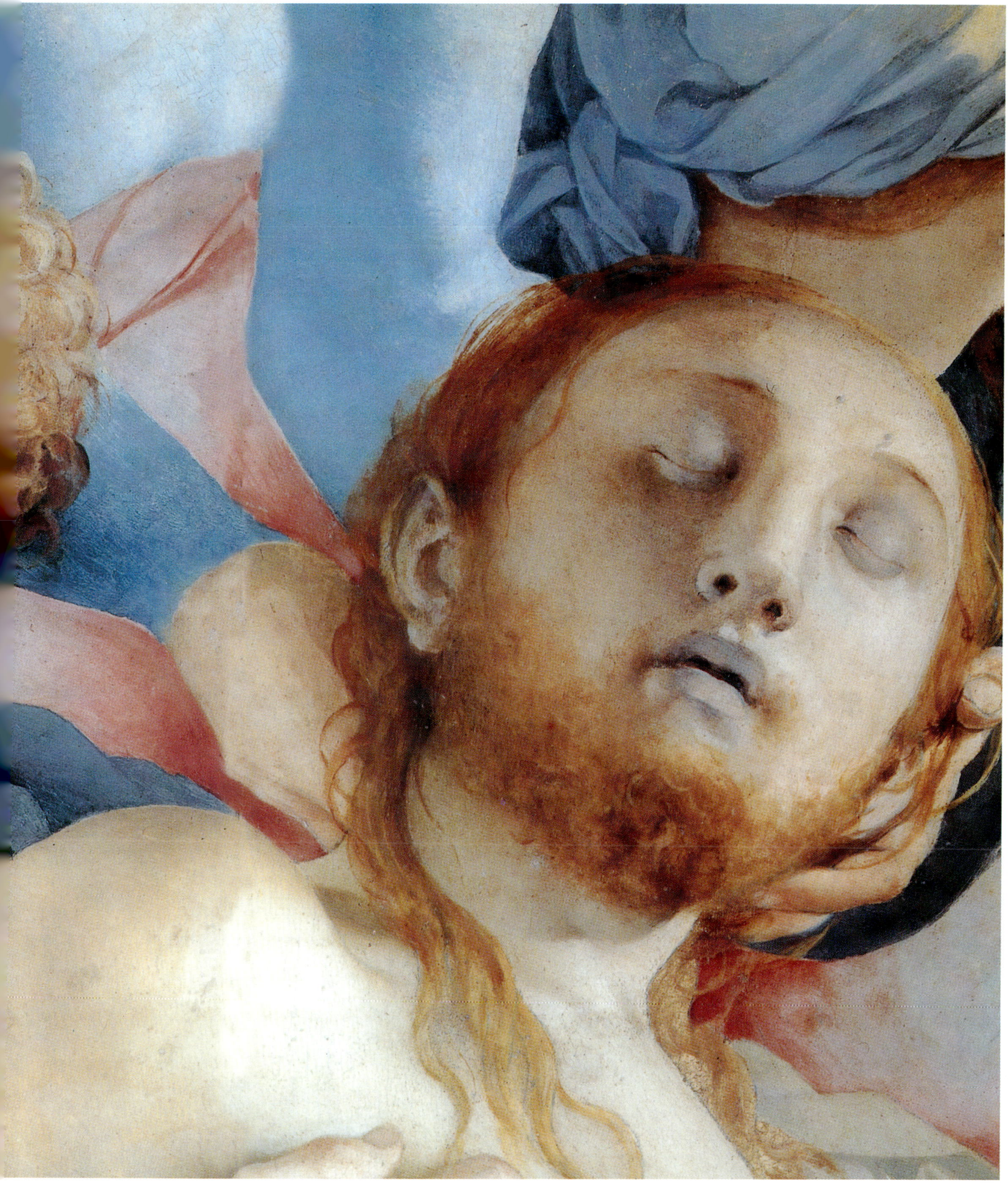

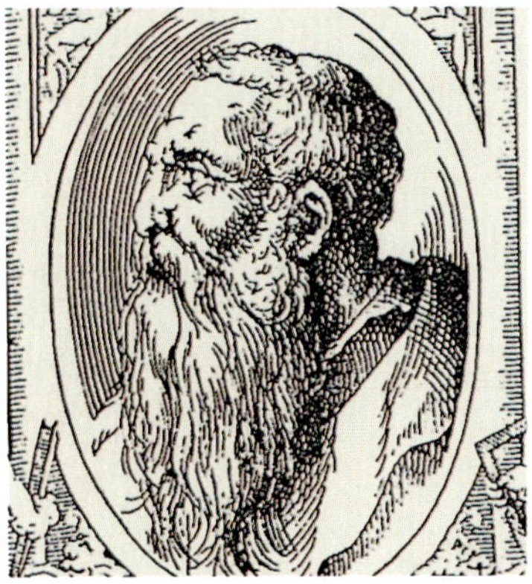

Rosso Fiorentino

(Giovan Battista di Jacopo, Florence 1495 – Fontainebleau 1540)

The human life and artistic career of Rosso Fiorentino can be roughly divided into three stages. The first, that of his training and the period spent in Andrea del Sarto's shop, led to the painting of the frescoes in the cloister of Santissima Annunziata in collaboration with Pontormo. This is the period of the famous *Deposition* of Volterra (Pinacoteca). In 1523 Rosso was in Rome, where he frescoed Santa Maria della Pace and was struck by the impact of Michelangelo's Roman works. A bizarre, obstinate character, he left the city after the Sack of 1527. Following a brief period spent wandering through Northern Italy, he reached the court of France (where Andrea del Sarto had already worked) and became the official painter of Francis I. The gallery he designed in the Castle of Fontainebleau was to serve as cornerstone for diffusion of the Mannerist style throughout Europe.

Giorgio Vasari, *Portrait of Rosso Fiorentino*, from the *Lives*, Florence, Giunti, 1568.

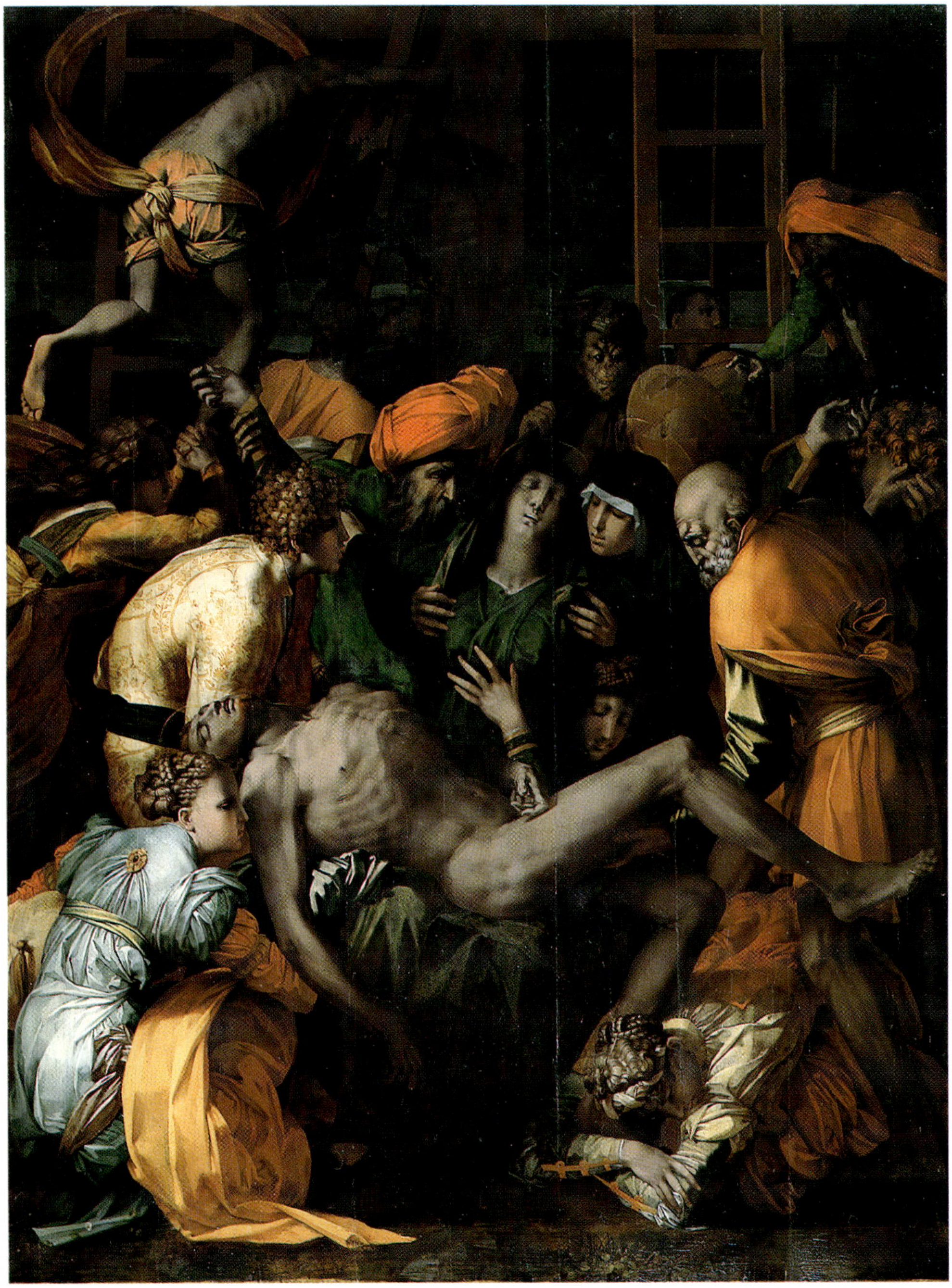

Rosso Fiorentino
Deposition
c. 1529
canvas
Sansepolcro, San Lorenzo alle Orfanelle.

The subject of the *Deposition* or the *Lament for Christ Dead* is a recurrent theme in the history of art, that of the 16th century in particular, as exemplified by Andrea del Sarto's *Pietà* now in the Pitti Palace. However, the work of Rosso Fiorentino takes on highly unusual dramatic connotations. Profoundly struck by the vicissitudes ensuring on the Sack of Rome, the artist invests the painting with all of his anxiety, and Christ's asphyxious chest is the emblem of a civilization that has risked death by suffocation.

Rosso Fiorentino
Marriage of the Virgin
1523
panel
Florence, Basilica of San Lorenzo.

Painted slightly before the artist moved to Rome, the panel shows a solid compositional structure. A theatrical effect is created by the figures, closely ranked at the sides of the bride and groom. Joseph, a young man, holds in his hand the flowering branch that designates him as the chosen bridegroom. Mary instead is wholly concentrated on the act of receiving on her finger the wedding ring offered by her future husband. The solemnity of the moment is emphasized by the light that falls on the Virgin's face.

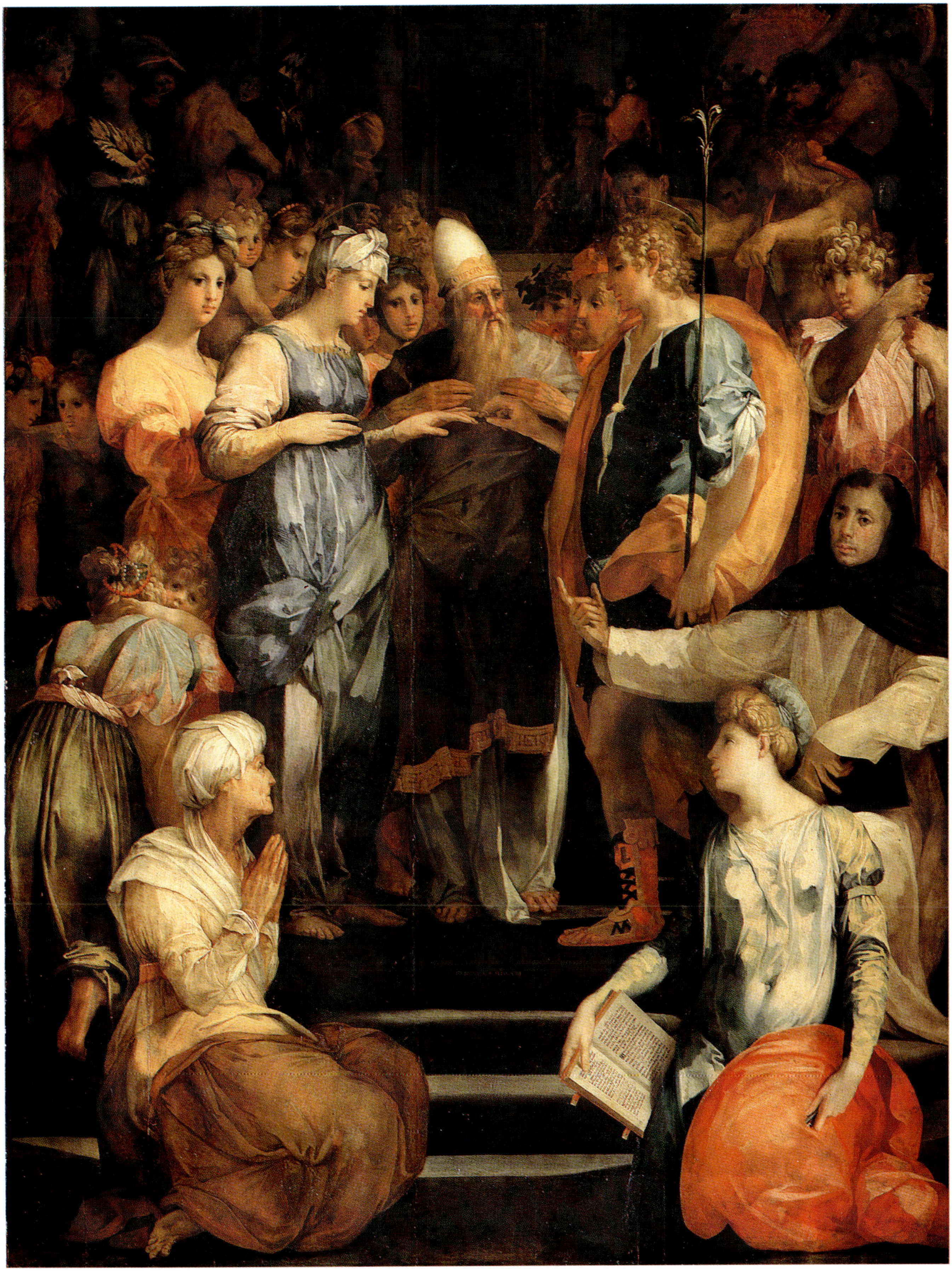

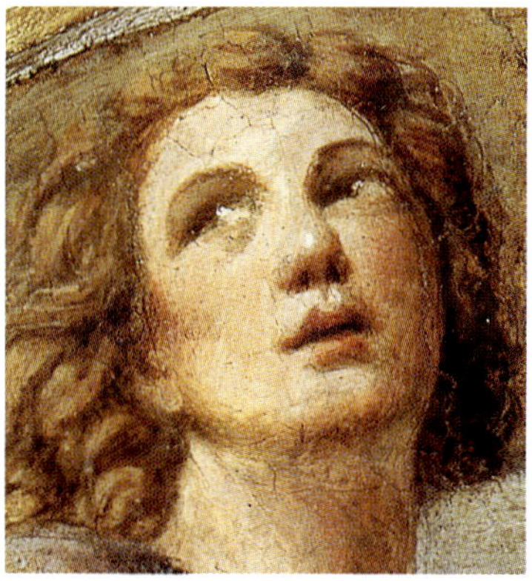

Correggio

(Antonio Allegri,
Correggio, Parma, 1489 – 1534)

Correggio's painting is a demonstration of the great creative potential of the so-called "Italian provinces", and their enormous contribution to the national art. Living almost always between Parma and his home town, from which he took his pseudonym, Antonio trained in the shop of the Modenese painter Francesco Bianchi Ferrari and then in the schools of Mantegna and Lorenzo Costa. His painting, with its soft golden colors, looks however in the direction of Raphael and Leonardo. Critics have assumed that the artist journeyed to Rome in about 1519, or in any case after the election of Pope Leo X. Correggio painted works crucial to the development of the Italian Renaissance, such as the Abbess' Chamber in the Convent of San Paolo at Parma (1519), the frescoes of San Giovanni Evangelista (1520-23) and those of the Duomo (1526-30) in the same Emilian city.

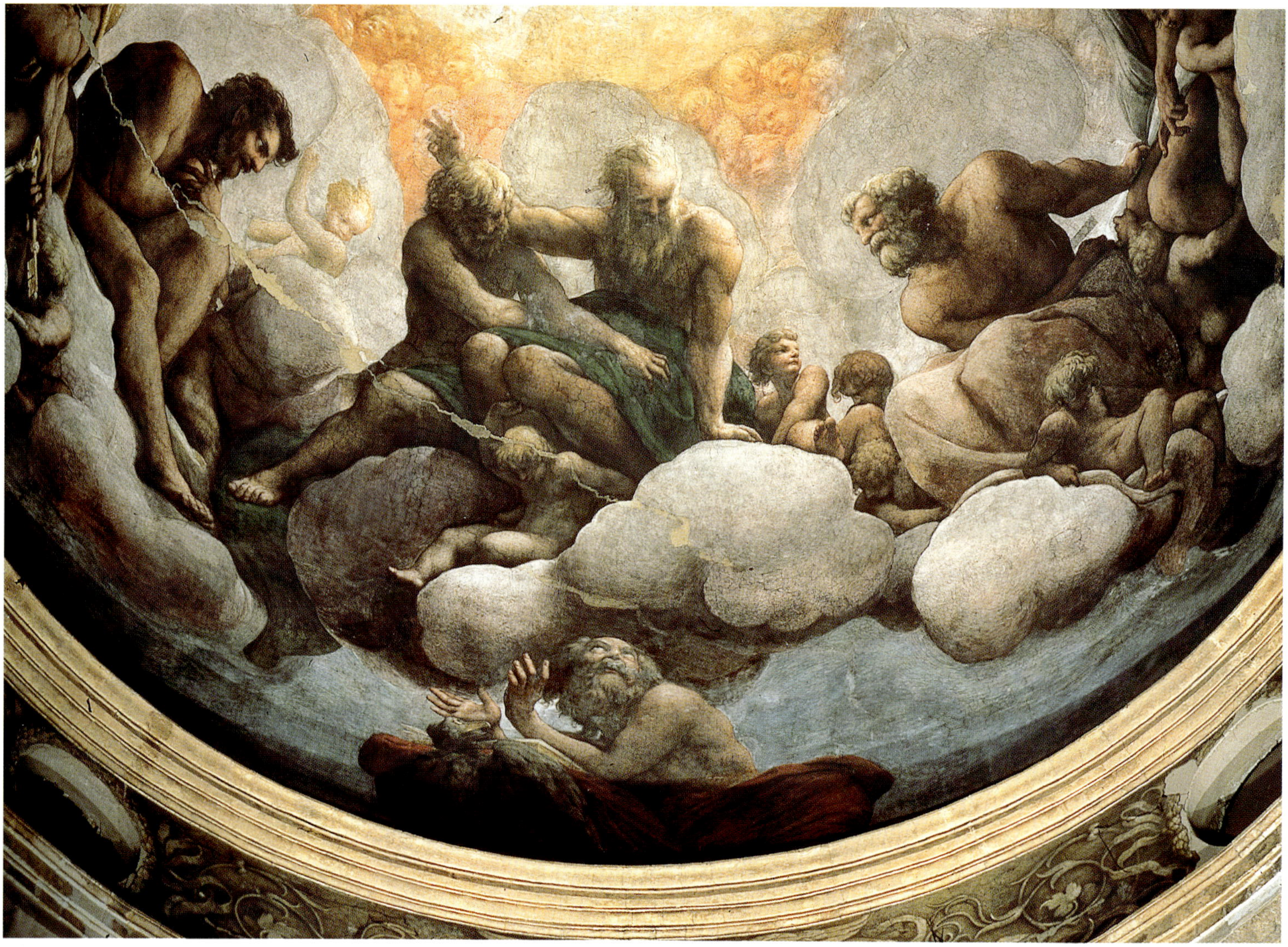

Correggio, *St Anthony of Padua*, presumed self-portrait, detail of the *San Francesco Madonna*, 1514-15. Dresden, Gemäldegalerie.

Correggio
Vision of St John at Patmos
1520-23
fresco, detail
Parma, San Giovanni Evangelista.

Inspired by the passage in the Apocalypse (I, 7) which states: "Behold, he is coming with the clouds and every eye will see him", the decoration of the dome is based on the pictorial models of Mantegna's *Bridal Chamber* and the dome of the Chigi Chapel by Raphael in Santa Maria del Popolo at Rome. The absence of architectural structures in the composition and the exaggeratedly low viewpoint from below anticipate the heavens typical of Baroque painting.

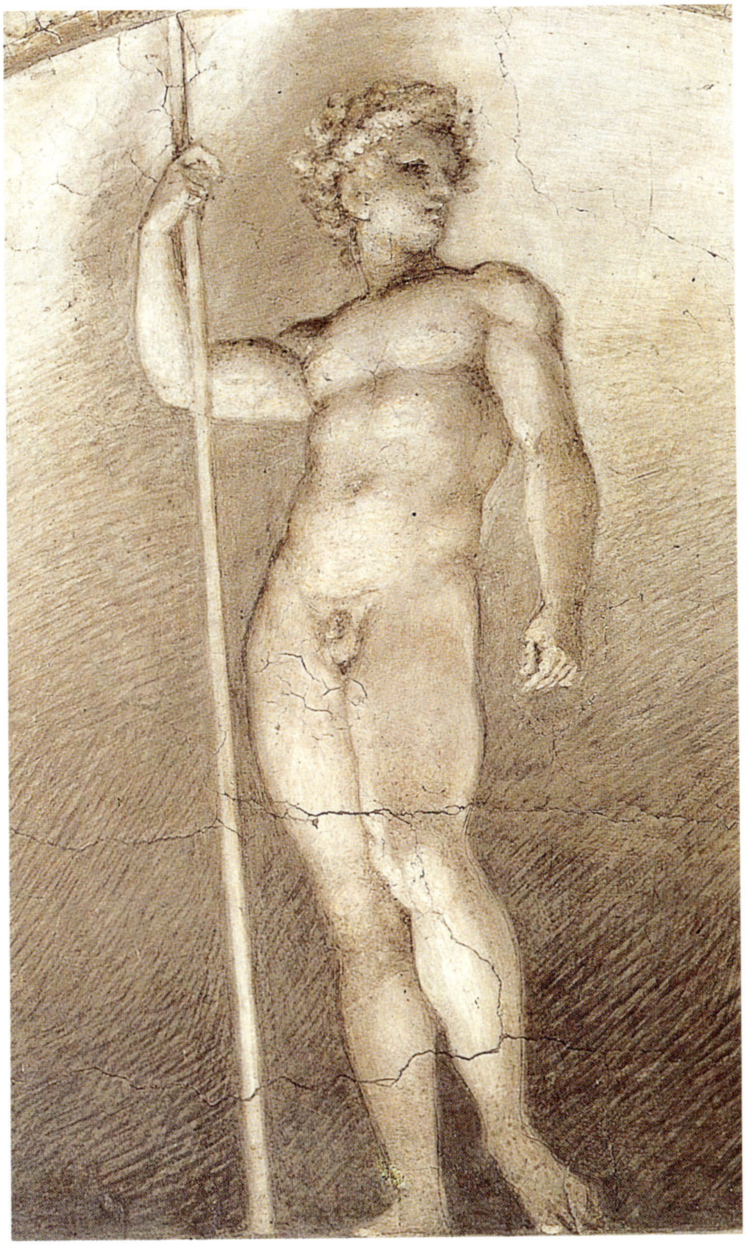

Correggio
A Spirit
1519
fresco, detail of the Abbess Piacenza's Chamber
Parma, Convent of San Paolo.

Perhaps conceived by the Sienese humanist Giorgio Anselmi, this cycle of frescoes – of complex symbolism – decorates the room where the Abbess Giovanna Piacenza held dinners and literary banquets.

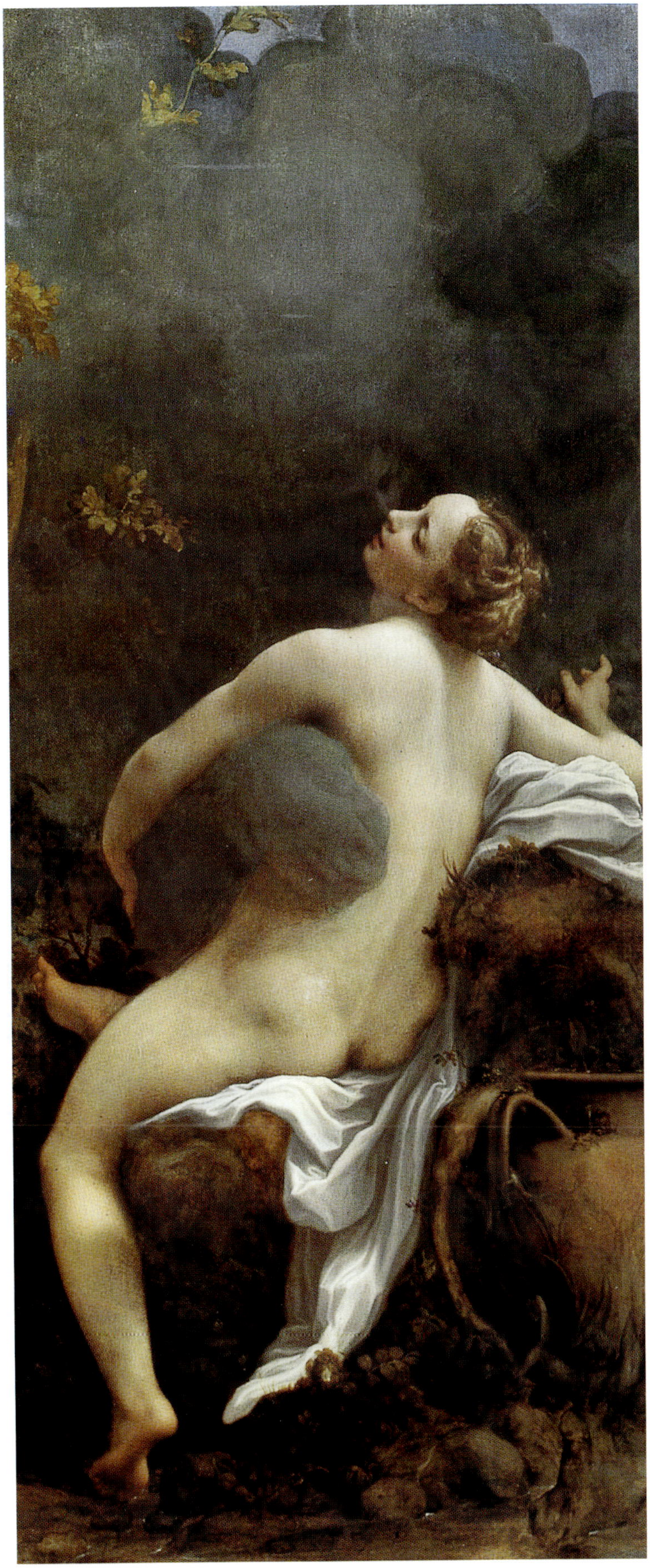

Correggio
Io
1531
canvas
Vienna, Kunsthistorisches Museum.

The work forms part of a series on the loves of Jove, commissioned by Duke Federico II Gonzaga (1519-40) as a gift for the Emperor Charles V on the occasion of his coronation at Bologna in 1530. It seems however that the canvases were never consigned to the illustrious personage for whom they were painted. The subjects, *Danae*, *Leda*, *Ganymede* and *Io*, are taken from Ovid's *Metamorphosis*, which narrates Jove's love for Io, the daughter of the priestess Hera and the King of Argos Inaco. Jove visits the girl under the form of a cloud and Juno, his wife, revengefully transforms her into a cow. The child Epaphus, who was to become the King of Egypt, was born of Jove's love for Io.

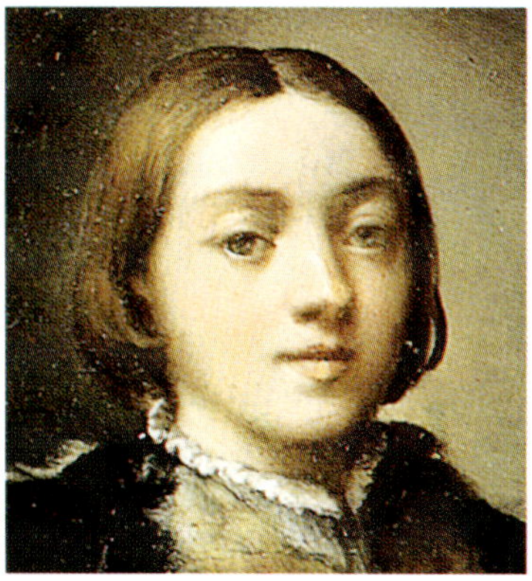

Parmigianino

(Francesco Mazzola, Parma 1503 – Casalmaggiore, Parma, 1540)

When Filippo Mazzola, Francesco's father, died in 1503 the newborn infant was entrusted to his uncles, Michele and Pier Ilario, also painters. Highly precocious, according to Vasari, he received his first important commission at the age of seventeen. In 1520, in fact, he frescoed the private chamber of Paola Gonzaga in the Rocca Sanvitale at Fontanellato, near Parma. Two years later we find him, together with Correggio and others, engaged in decorating the Duomo of his native city. From 1524 to 1527 he was in Rome, where he was admitted to the circle of Pope Clement VII. Here he not only admired the work of Michelangelo and Raphael, but became personally acquainted with Rosso, Perin del Vaga, Giulio Romano, and Giovanni da Udine. After the Sack of Rome he went to Bologna and from 1531 he was in Parma (frescoes, unfinished, for the Church of Santa Maria della Steccata).

Parmigianino, *Self-portrait in a Convex Mirror*, detail, 1523-24. Vienna, Kunsthistorisches Museum.

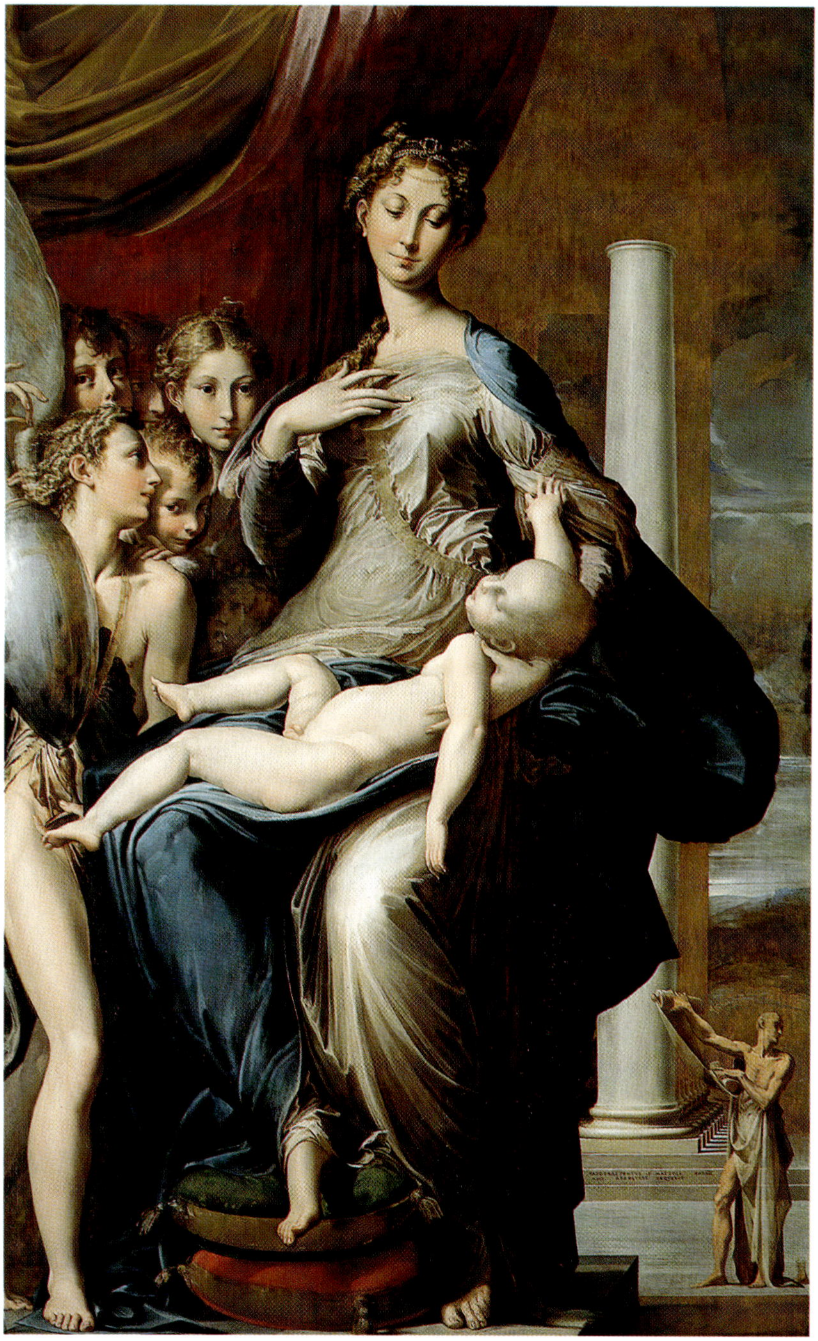

Parmigianino
Madonna of the Long Neck
c. 1534-39
panel
Florence, Uffizi Gallery.

The panel, which takes its name from the unusual length of the Virgin's neck, shows Maria and the Christ Child surrounded by angels. In the background is the figure of St Jerome with his scroll and, behind him, the foot of what was to have been another saint. The columns allude to Solomon's temple, to the Medieval hymn *Collum tuum ut columna* and to the Immaculate Conception. Painted for the Church of the Servi at Parma, but left unfinished (as stated in the inscription on the steps at the bottom), the panel is permeated with alchemist symbolism, where Christ is seen as the philosopher's stone and Mary as the *vas*, the most pure vessel which contains it.

Lorenzo Lotto, *Portrait of Mercurio Bua*, detail, previously thought to be a *Self-portrait of Lorenzo Lotto*, c. 1530. Rome, Borghese Gallery.

Lorenzo Lotto
Venus and Cupid
1513
canvas
New York, The Metropolitan Museum of Art.

This is one of Lotto's rare paintings of mythological subject. The circumstances of its commissioning are however unknown. It may have been requested by the artist's nephew, Mario D'Armano, whose name appears in his uncle's ledger as the purchaser of a "Venus", usually identified as the *Venus Adorned by the Graces*. The unquestionably high quality of the painting is accompanied by a certain complexity in the iconography, typical of the Venetian artist. The goddess, whose body is scattered with rose petals symbolizing love, holds a wreath of myrtle (another symbol of love) through which an impertinent Cupid is urinating. In the simplest reading, this could be an omen of good luck and fertility. Deeper investigation could explain the urinating Eros as mercurial water and Venus as the Alchemist's *athanor*, or crucible in which the *opus* is created.

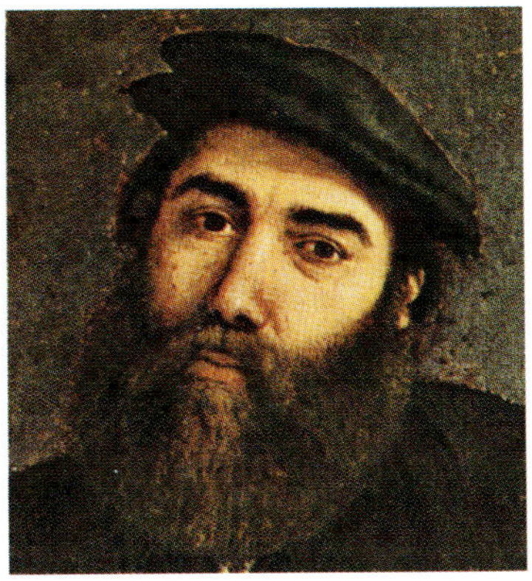

Lorenzo Lotto

(Venice 1480 – Loreto 1556)

Unjustly considered a minor artist up to the 1950s, Lorenzo Lotto is instead one of the most interesting, eclectic and autonomous personalities of the Italian 16th century. After first working at Treviso for Bishop de' Rossi (1503), he came into his element in the Marches. In 1509 he was in Rome for work (now lost) to decorate the apartments of Pope Julius II (1503-13). After another stay in the Marches (1511-12) he went to Bergamo where he received important commissions, among them that of frescoing the Oratory of Battista Suardi at Trescore (1524). Returning to Venice in 1525 he concentrated mainly on portraits for private individuals, while retaining his contacts with Bergamo and the Marches. In 1544, now elderly, poor, and disappointed, he became an Oblate at the Santa Casa di Loreto, where he painted canvases for the basilica.

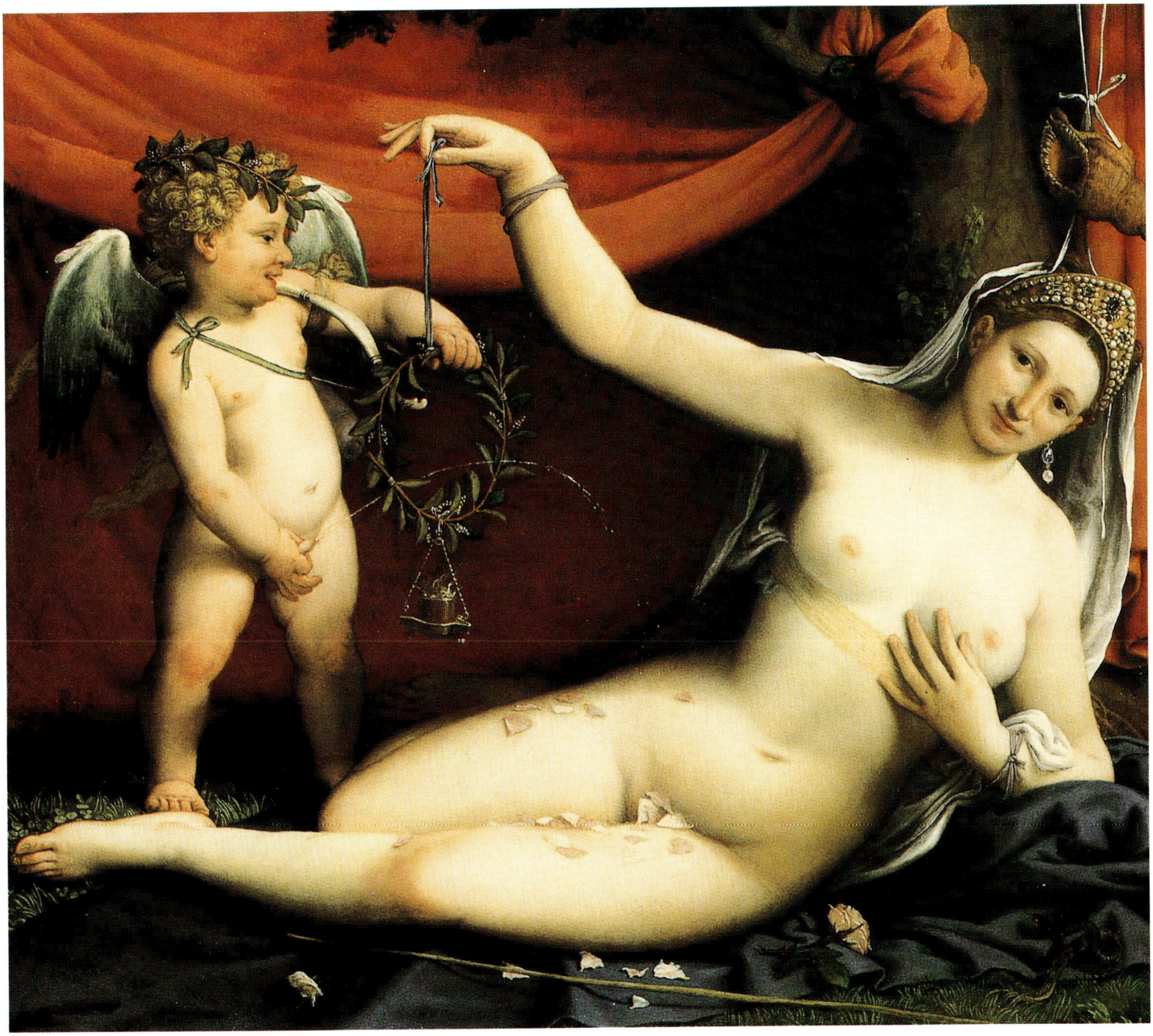

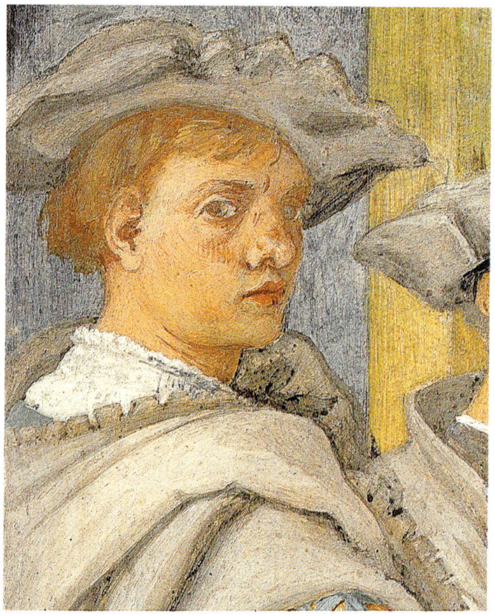

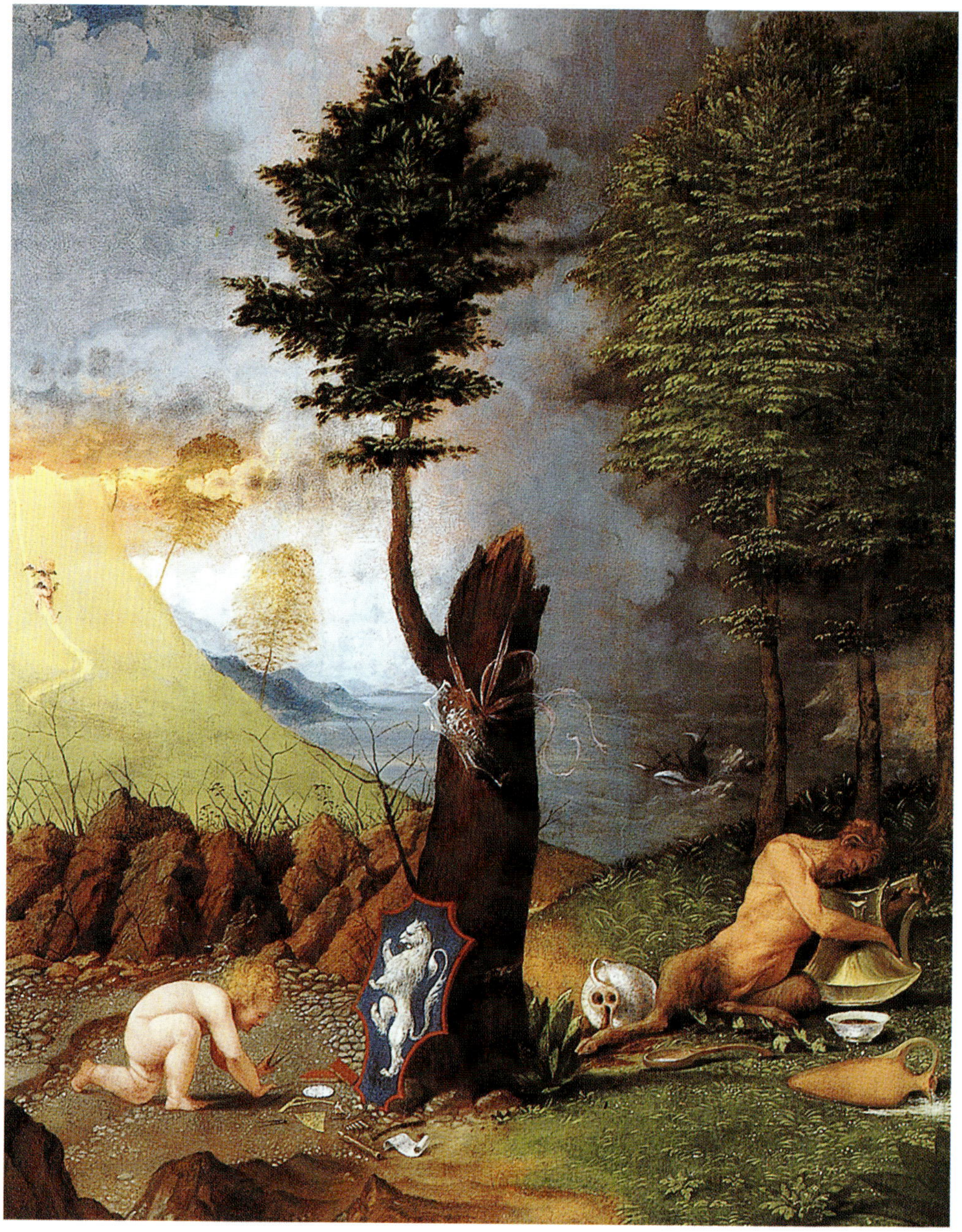

Lorenzo Lotto
Portrait of a Man
c. 1550
canvas.

The work belongs to the artist's last season, when he dedicated himself to portraying persons of various social extraction, earning his living in this way.

Lorenzo Lotto
A Nobleman
1524
fresco, detail of the *Stories of St Bridget*
Trescore (Bergamo), Suardi Oratory.

The detail comes from the painting on the right wall depicting the *Clothing of St Bridget*.

Lorenzo Lotto
The De' Rossi Allegory
1505
panel
Washington, National Gallery, Samuel H. Kress Collection.

The work was to have served as cover to the portrait of Bishop Bernardo de' Rossi, now at Capodimonte. This is demonstrated not only by the compatibility of the dimensions and the style, but also by the Latin inscription (now unfortunately illegible) that appeared on the back of the panel. Thorough iconological studies have revealed the meaning of the composition: a sort of spiritual profile of the bishop and an invitation to chose the path of virtue.

Lorenzo Lotto
The Chastity of Susannah
signed and dated 1517
panel
Florence, Uffizi Gallery.

The Biblical episode narrated in the Book of Daniel (XIII, 1-63) is depicted by Lotto with hearty gusto. To render the scene immediate, the artist adopts the expedient of scrolls bearing the dialogue between the chaste Susannah and the lecherous old men. As in a modern comic strip, the spectator is immediately informed of the intentions of Susannah, who does not want to sin, while the spiteful men accuse her of adultery.

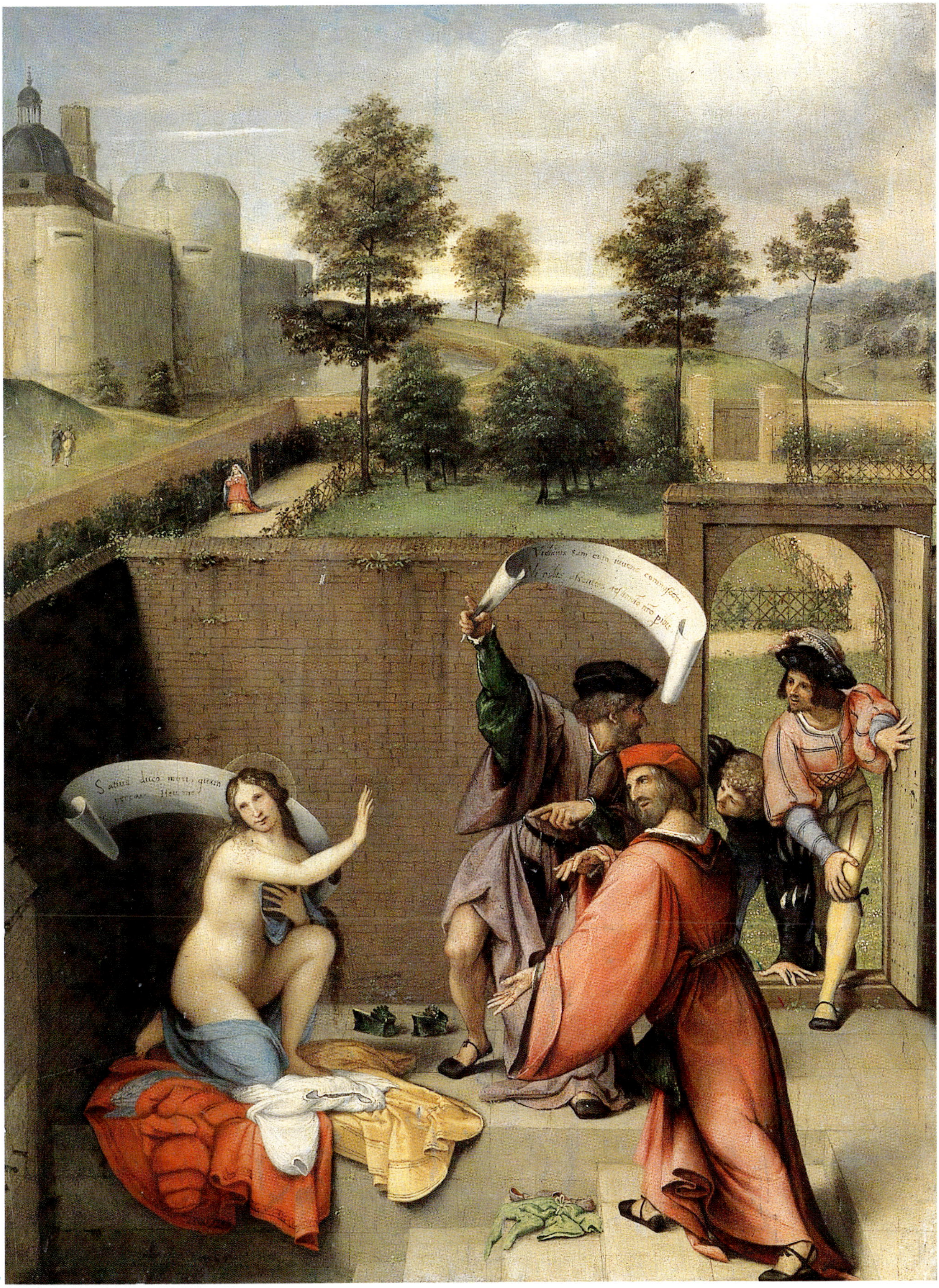
Satius duco mori, quam

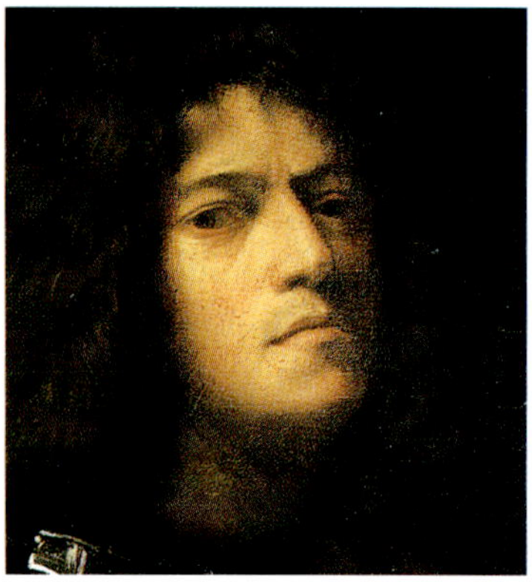

Giorgione

(Giorgio Zorzi, Castelfranco Veneto 1477 – Venice 1510)

Famous already in its time, Giorgione's work is the 16th century root of Venetian painting, which was to unfold in all its splendor with Titian (called by the master to work with him on the frescoes of the Fondaco dei Tedeschi), and then with Tintoretto and Veronese. Despite an almost total lack of documentation, the most recent criticism believes the artist to have been Jewish, also on the basis of the Braunschweig *Self-portrait*, where he is presented as David. A man of vast culture, he decorated Casa Marta at Castelfranco (1502-1503) with a moralizing frieze of astrological subject intended to affirm the supremacy of virtue over fate. This is one of the artist's first works which has survived to our day. The astrological theme was to appear recurrently in his production, as in the *Three Philosophers* (1504-1505) of the Kunsthistorisches Museum in Vienna.

Giorgione, *Self-portrait*, detail, c. 1508. Braunschweig, Herzog Anton Ulrich Museum.

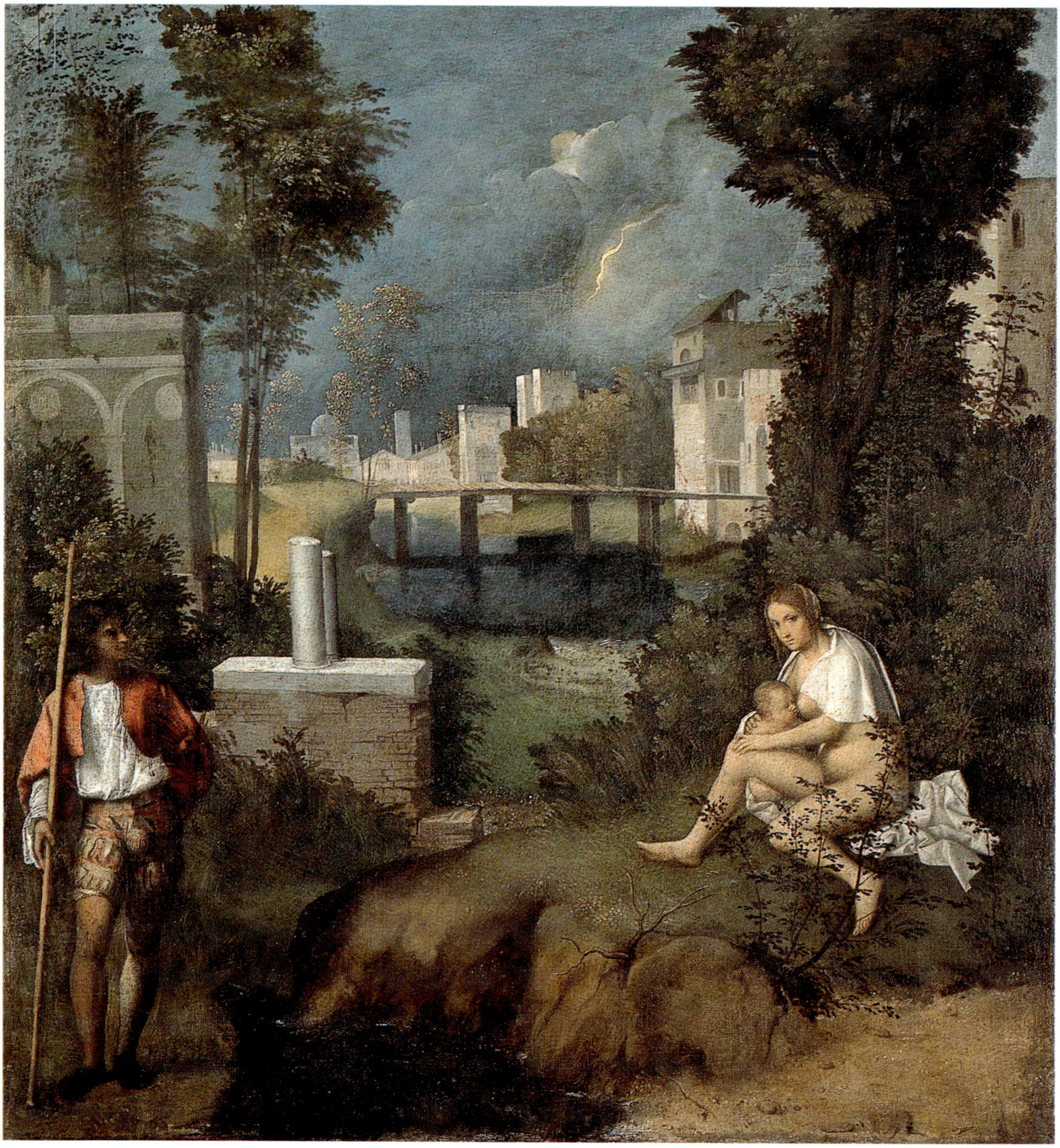

Giorgione
The Tempest
1507-1508
canvas
Venice, Gallerie dell'Accademia.

Over this work the proverbial rivers of ink have flowed. The ambiguity of the subject has triggered the conjectures of iconologists and iconographers. In one of the most convincing hypotheses, the painting represents the condemnation of Adam and Eve after the original sin, a reading which now takes on new light if we accept the Jewish origins of the artist. This also explains the redeeming nature of the bridge and the presence of the bolt of lightening, a sign of divine wrath. From a purely pictorial point of view, however, the painting is a milestone in Venetian art.

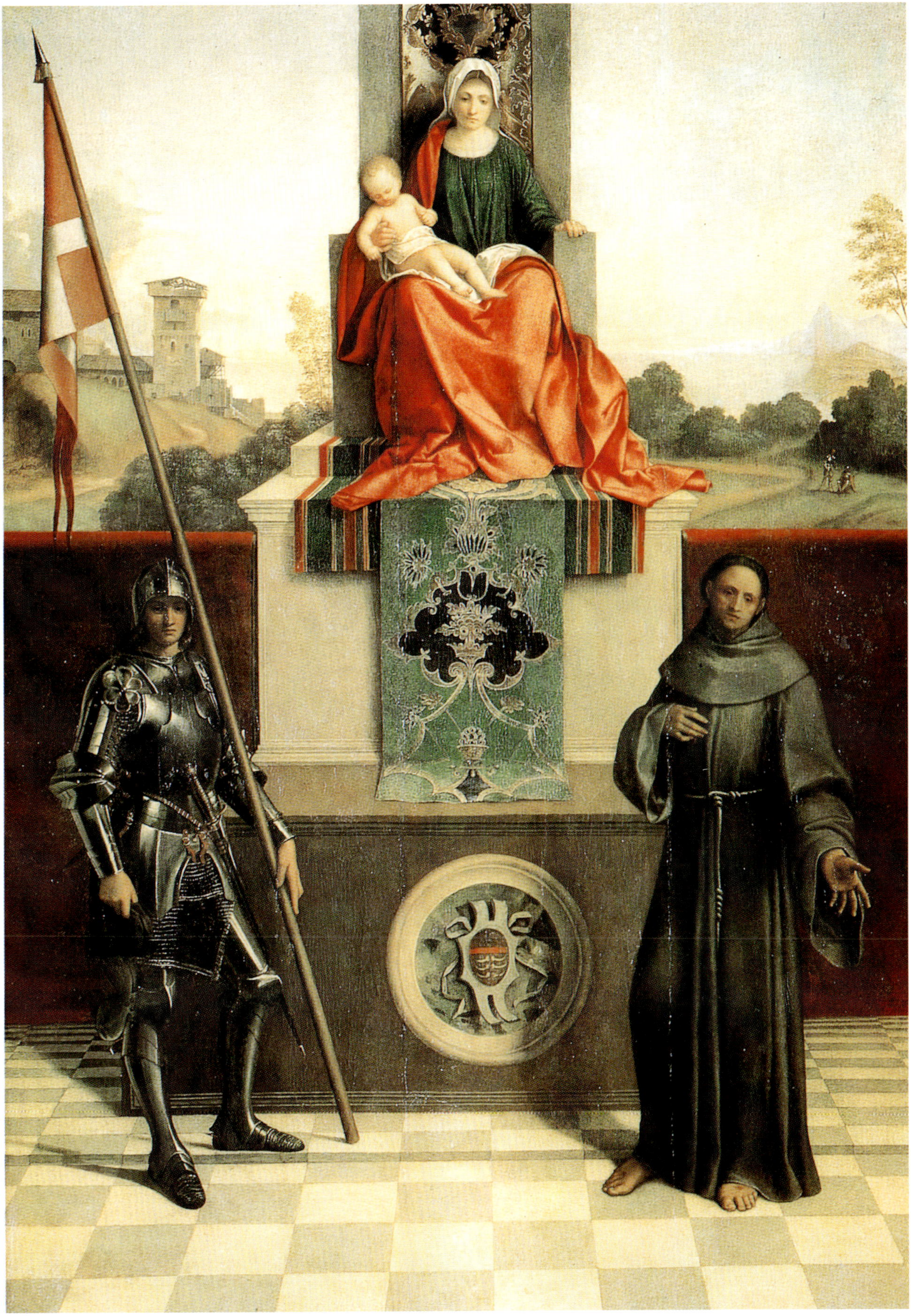

Giorgione
Madonna with Child and Saints Francis and George
1502
panel
Castelfranco Veneto, Duomo.

Better known as the *Castelfranco Altarpiece* for its collocation in the Duomo of the Venetian town, the painting was commissioned, as shown by the coat-of-arms appearing on the upper part of the base on which rests Mary's throne, by Tuzio Costanzo, a Knight of Jerusalem, for his chapel. The Virgin is depicted in a sober back-lit scene, viewed from a slightly lowered perspective. Standing below her, the two saints bring closer to the spectator a Madonna who, in spite of the tenderly sleeping child, seems rather distant. The so-called St. George could be either Liberale, the saint for whom the Duomo is named, or Nicasio, martyr of the Knights of Jerusalem, or again, and this is perhaps the most credible hypothesis, he may personify all three of these personages in a single figure.

Giorgione
Portrait of a Gentleman (Terris Portrait)
1508-10
panel
San Diego, San Diego Museum of Art.

Although much restored, the portrait displays stylistic canons linked to the artist's last period.

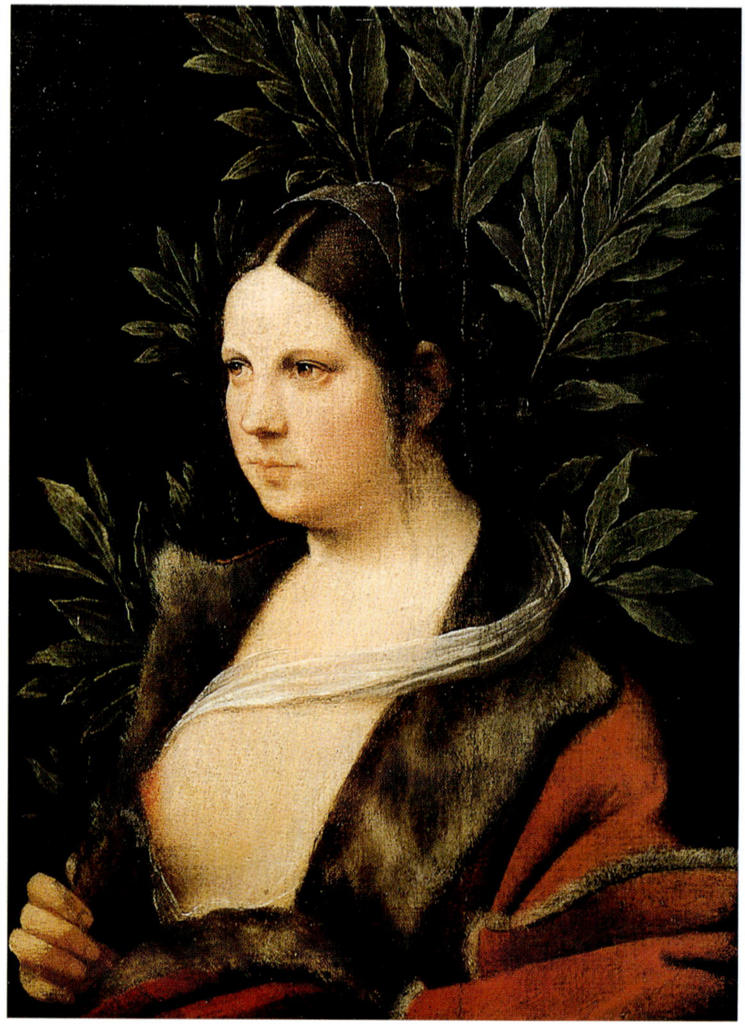

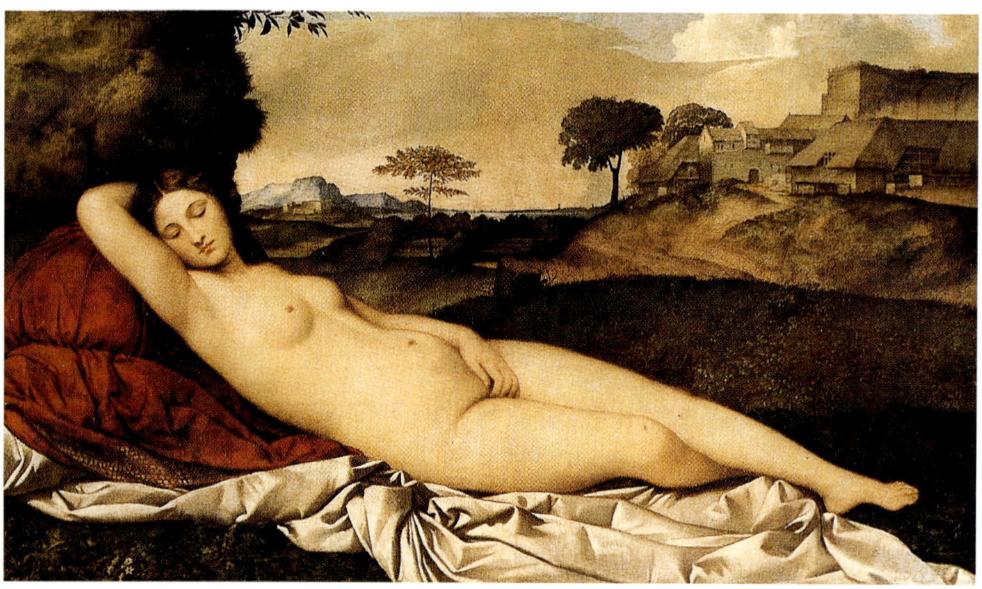

Giorgione and Titian
The Sleeping Venus
1507-12, canvas
Dresden, Gemäldegalerie.

The work testifies to the close collaboration between Giorgione and Titian. Painted by the former in 1507, it was finished by the latter after the master's death. Titian's task was that of accentuating the erotic quality of the Venus commissioned on the occasion of the wedding of Gerolamo Marcello and Morosina Pisani.

Giorgione
Portrait of a Young Bride (Laura)
1506
canvas
Vienna, Kunsthistorisches Museum.

The inscription on the back, which calls Giorgione the "colleague" of the Bellinian painter Vincenzo Catena, is one of the few certain documents allowing us to trace Giorgione's artistic career. From the stylistic point of view, on the contrary, the allegorical portrait of Laura (her head is framed in laurel branches) leaves behind it the 15th century tradition of Bellini to turn in the direction of Leonardo.

Giorgione and Assistance
The Judgement of Solomon
1502-1508
panel
Florence, Uffizi Gallery.

The episode narrated in the First Book of Kings (III, 16-28) is known to all. The scene is rendered in fresh, vivacious manner, immersed in an animated landscape thought to be painted by the master himself (the personages are attributed to his assistants). Solomon is seated on a throne to the right. The true mother is the kneeling woman, while to her left the executioner brandishes his sword.

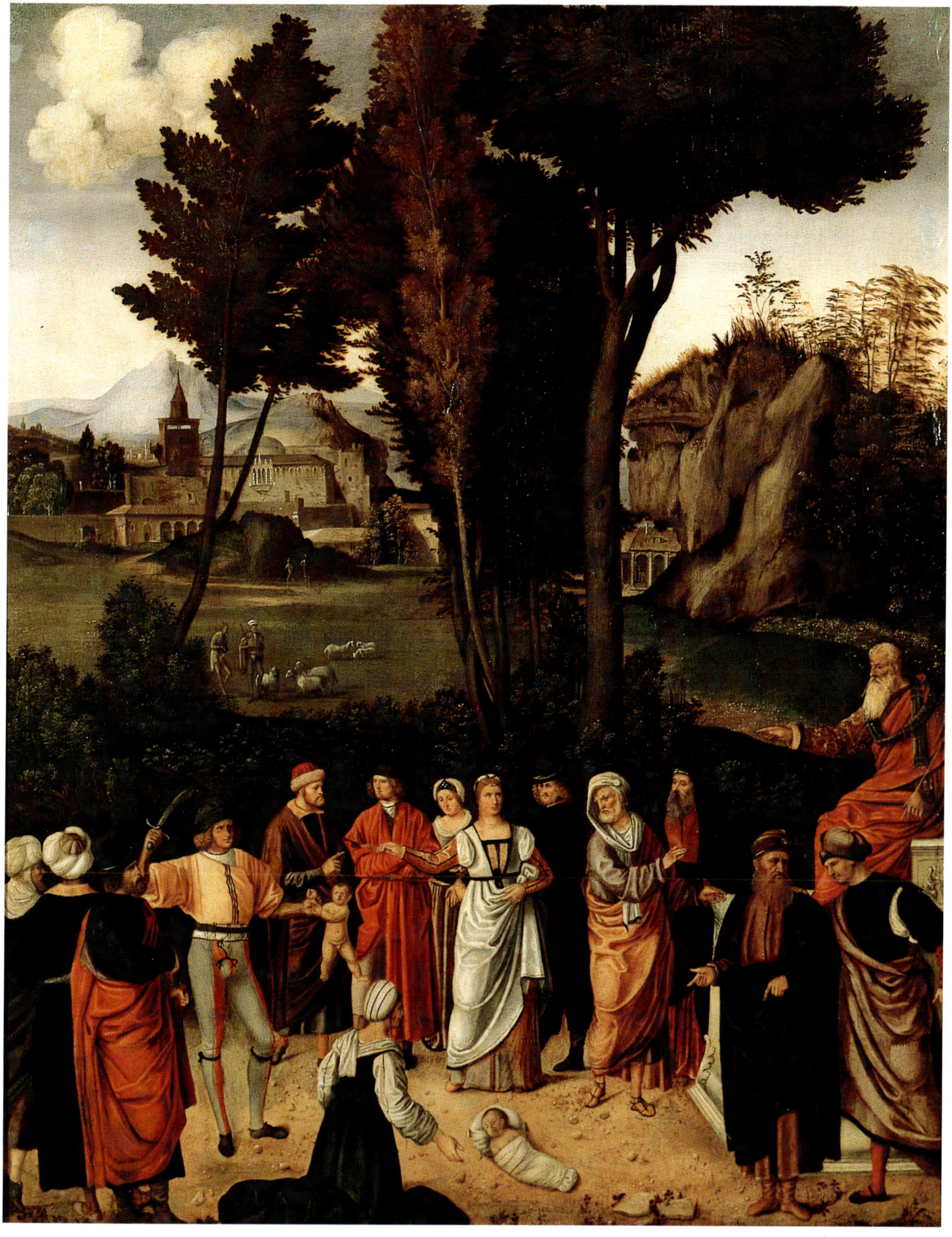

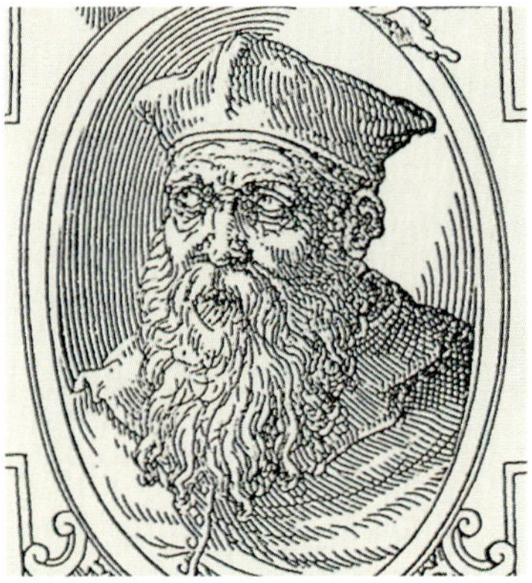

Sebastiano del Piombo

(Sebastiano Luciani, Venice c. 1485 – Rome 1546)

When, in around 1505, Sebastiano entered the shop of Giovanni Bellini, he was about twenty years old and already an accomplished musician who played the lute as soloist. Influenced by the manner of Giorgione, he happened to meet the Sienese banker Agostino Chigi, who in that same 1511 brought him to Rome where he assigned him part of the decoration of his villa on the Tiber, now known as the Farnesina. Here the artist entered the fervent atmosphere of Rome, becoming a friend of Michelangelo, who even gave him some of his drawings (those of the *Resurrection of Lazarus*, 1519). In 1516 he began the frescoes of San Pietro in Montorio. Fleeing from the city during the Sack of Rome, he returned in 1529, to remain for the rest of his life. In 1534 his friendship with Michelangelo waned, but his stylistic dependence remained unchanged.

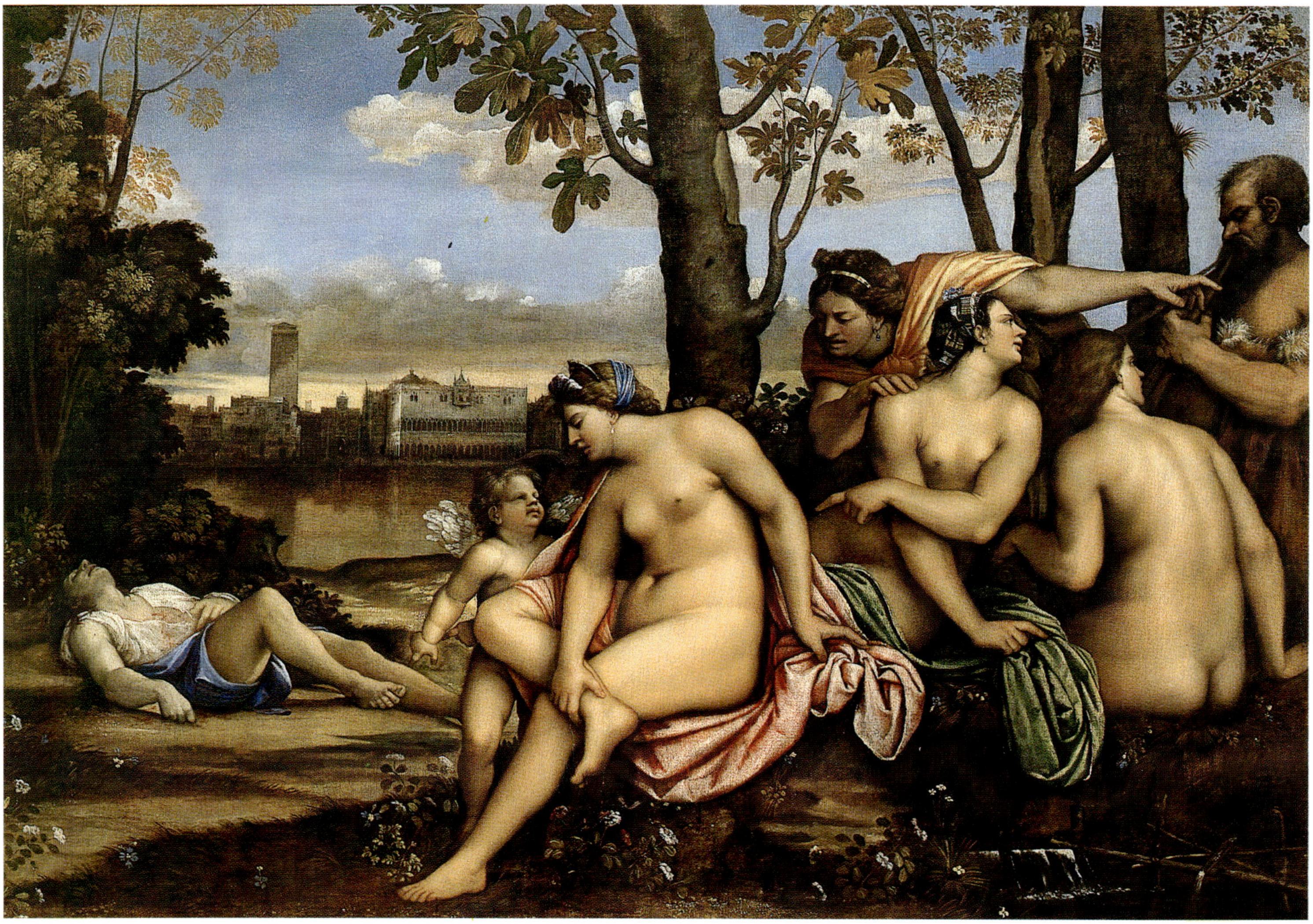

Giorgio Vasari, *Portrait of Sebastiano del Piombo*, from the *Lives*, Florence, Giunti, 1568.

Sebastiano del Piombo
The Death of Adonis
c. 1512
canvas
Florence, Uffizi Gallery.

The work is particularly interesting insofar as it marks, we might say *ad annum*, Sebastiano's abandonment of the Venetian figurative tradition for that of Rome. Critics have noted how the arboreal side-scene framing the figure of the dying young man is practically identical to that of the *Polyphemus* in the Farnesina. The use of color and the golden atmosphere of the landscape are again Venetian. The monumental quality of the drawing, instead, already tends toward the Roman, making it easy enough to detect in the nymph pointing toward Pan a hint of the *Erithrean Sibyl* painted by Michelangelo on the ceiling of the Sistine Chapel and unveiled expressly in 1512. From this same figurative repertoire comes the little Cupid reminiscent of the cherubs/caryatids decorating the Prophets' seats. The pose of Venus is derived from the ancient sculpture of the *Spinario*.

Moretto

(Alessandro Bonvicino, Brescia 1498 – 1554)

The human life and artistic career of the Brescian painter Moretto followed a linear path, marked by the slow rhythms of the provincial Po Valley. Not by chance, after an apprenticeship in Venice or, more probably, Padua, the artist practically never again left his native city where, among other things, he had the good fortune to serve as master to Giovan Battista Moroni, another great portrait painter of the Venetian-Lombard 16th century. A member of the brotherhood of the Most Holy Sacrament, linked to the reformist circles that rotated around Bishop Ugoni and Sister Angela Merici, Moretto is famous not only for his intense portraits but also for having revitalized the Christian message by bringing alive the Evangelical episodes he depicted. Obviously, his unrestricted access to the local ecclesiastical milieu was favorable to commissions. Accordingly, he was chosen to fresco the Chapel of the Most Holy Sacrament in San Giovanni at Brescia and to paint a number of canvases in the sanctuary of Paitone and in the Church of San Francesco di Brescia (1530).

Moretto
Portrait of Count Sciarra-Martinengo Cesaresco
1545-50
canvas
London, National Gallery.

A splendid portrait painter, Moretto was able to render extremely expressive and natural even an official portrait such as this one. Instead of posing haughtily Count Sciarra, the page of Henry II the King of France, appointed by him Knight of St Michael when only 18 years old, is surprised by the painter in a meditative attitude. Gazing indolently away from his personal commitments (traces of which, coins and gloves, appear on the table), he turns toward the spectator with a trace of annoyance. A masterpiece of psychological analysis, the portrait seems to echo the style of Lorenzo Lotto.

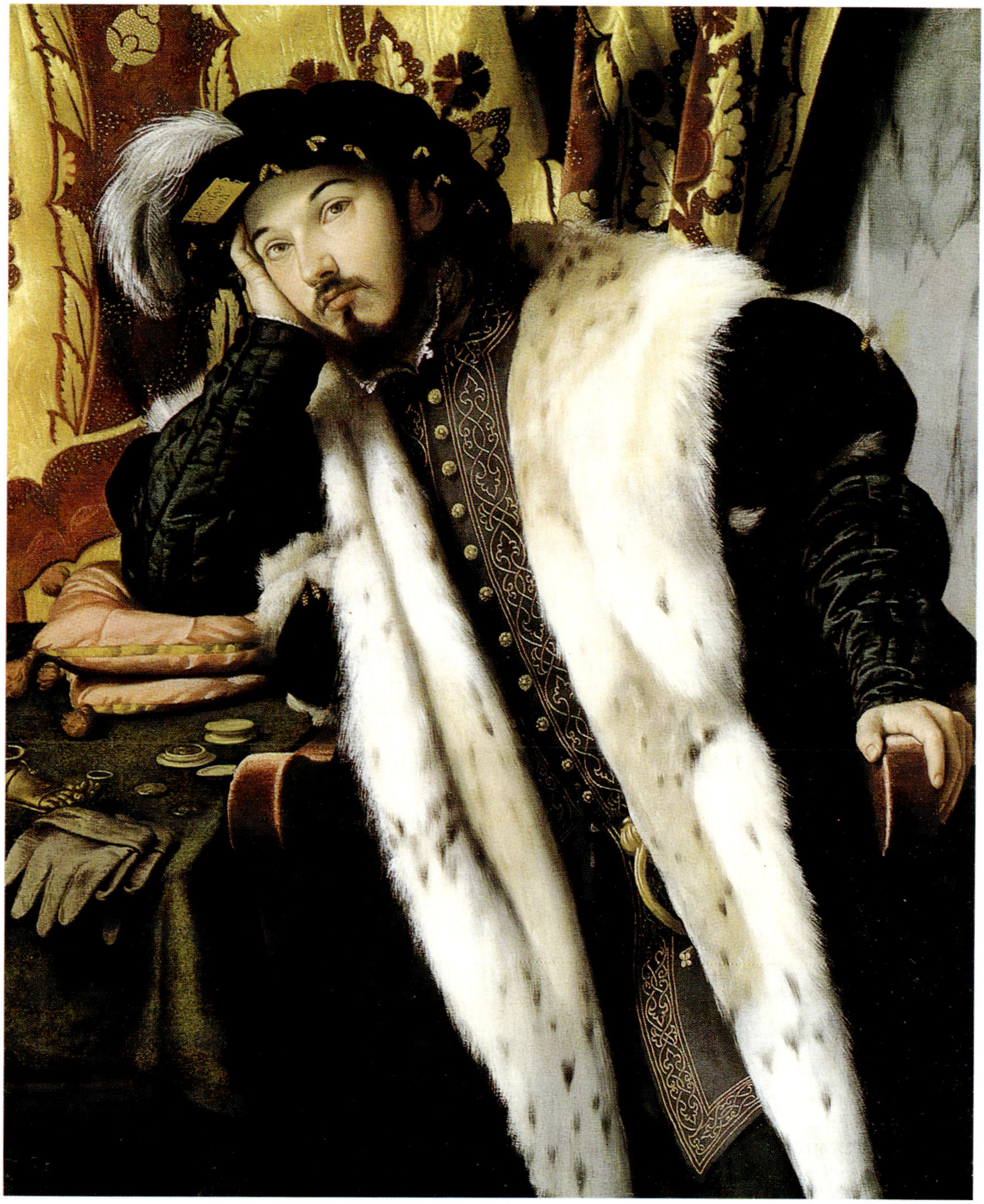

Dosso Dossi

(Giovanni di Niccolò di Lutero, ? c. 1490 – Ferrara 1542)

Unfortunately, most of the works of Dosso Dossi and his brother Battista were lost in the siege and conquest of Ferrara by Papal troops in 1598. The court of Alfonso I (1505-34) and Ercole II d'Este (1534-59) was in fact the stage on which the two artists performed. Probably born in Ferrara, Dosso, the more famous of the two, trained in Mantua and Bologna, while Battista – says tradition – was in Rome working in Raphael's shop. Dosso was clearly influenced by the vivid colors of Giorgione and Titian. His activity extended, however, to Pesaro and Trent, where paintings and cycles of frescoes, also from his youthful period, are preserved (Castello del Buonconsiglio). He was also acquainted with the painting of Rome and Central Italy, as well as that of Florence.

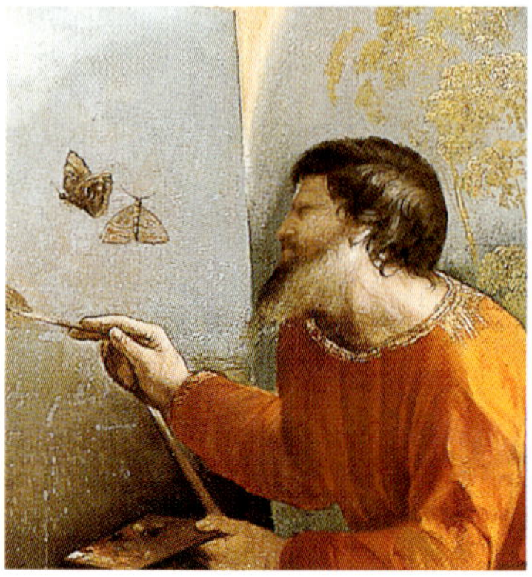

Dosso Dossi, *Jove Painting Butterflies*, detail of *Jove, Mercury and Virtues*, c. 1529. Vienna, Kunsthistorisches Museum.

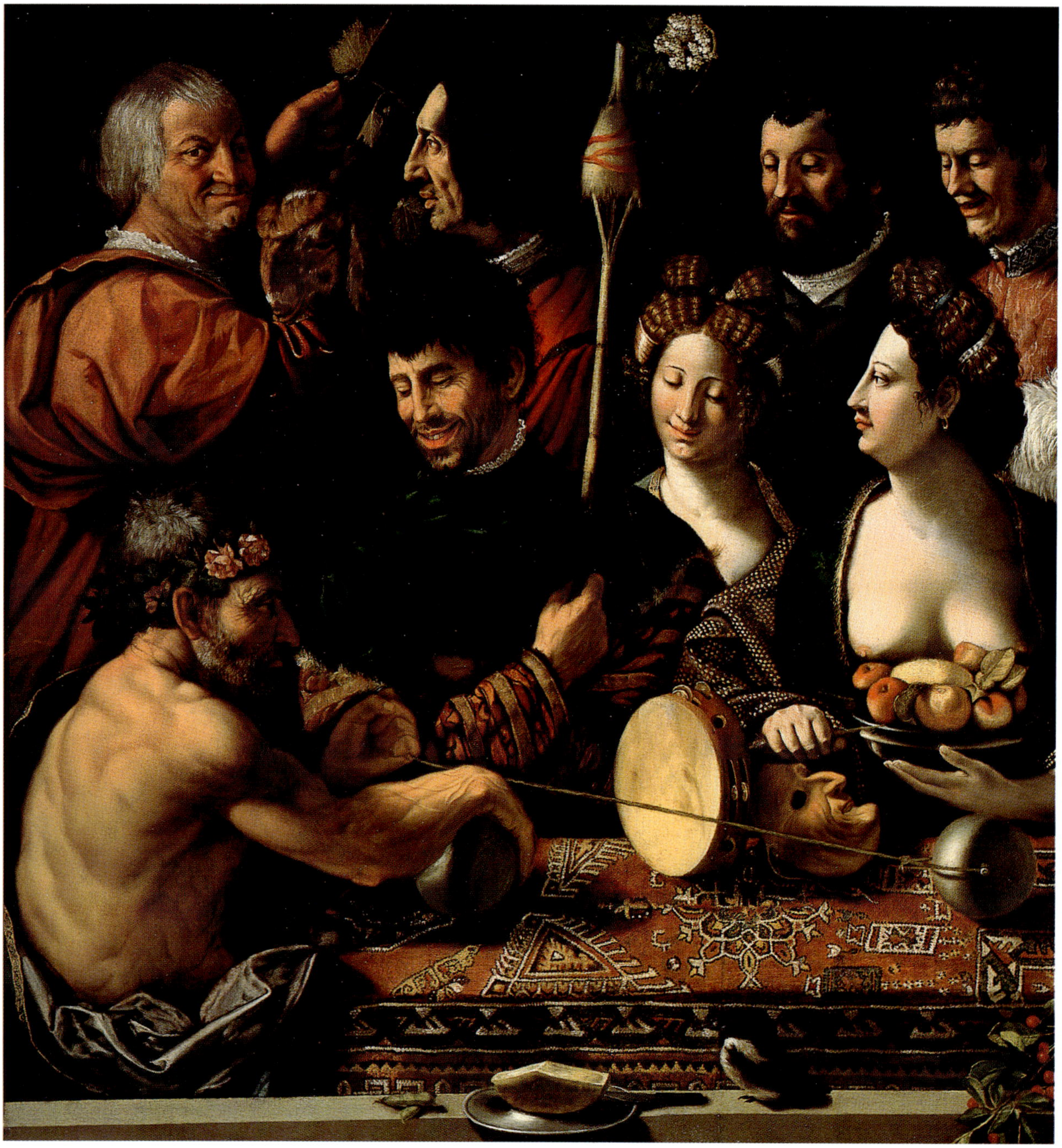

Dosso Dossi
Witchcraft or *Allegory of Hercules*
c. 1535-38
canvas
Florence, Uffizi Gallery.

Listed in the inventory of Cardinal Leopoldo, who had it purchased at Siena in 1665, as a "picture with portraits of the Duke of Ferrara's jesters", the painting should be considered the masterpiece of Dosso's later years. The canvas is distinguished by sharply contrasting light and shadow, but its subject is far from clear. It has been suggested that it is an allegory of Hercules choosing between vice and virtue. This subject, quite common in the Renaissance, becomes even more significant when we consider that in the Ferrara of the times, Hercules was the eponymous hero of Ercole d'Este, the lord of the city.

Giovan Gerolamo Savoldo

(Brescia c. 1480 – Venice, after 1548)

With the pictorial lesson of Savoldo, Venetian-Lombard illuminism was accentuated, with light and shadow assuming sharp contrasts, to the point that critics have seen in him one of the roots of Caravaggio's future distinctive traits. The training of the artist from Brescia was various and complex. He was in Florence at the time when Raphael has just gone to Rome (1508). Later, in 1520, Giovan Gerolamo was in Venice where he became acquainted with Giorgione and Titian, as well as with Flemish culture. Having settled in Venice, he was to remain in contact with his native Brescia, although he was fully accepted in Venetian cultural circles thanks to his friendship with Pietro Contarini, a refined literate of the times and patron of the painter.

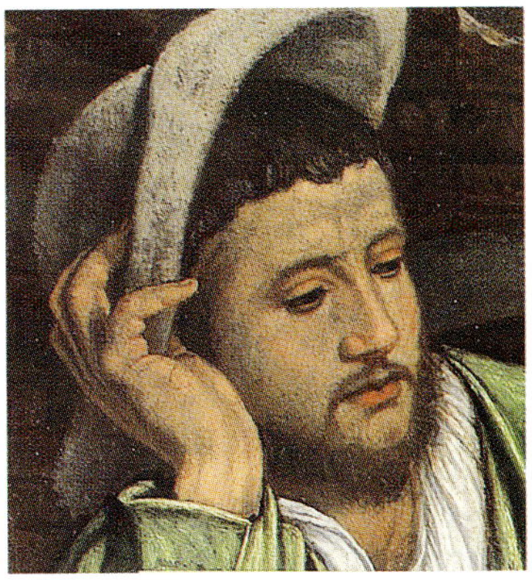

Giovan Gerolamo Savoldo, *Adoration of the Pastors*, detail, c. 1538. Brescia, Civica Pinacoteca Tosio Martinengo.

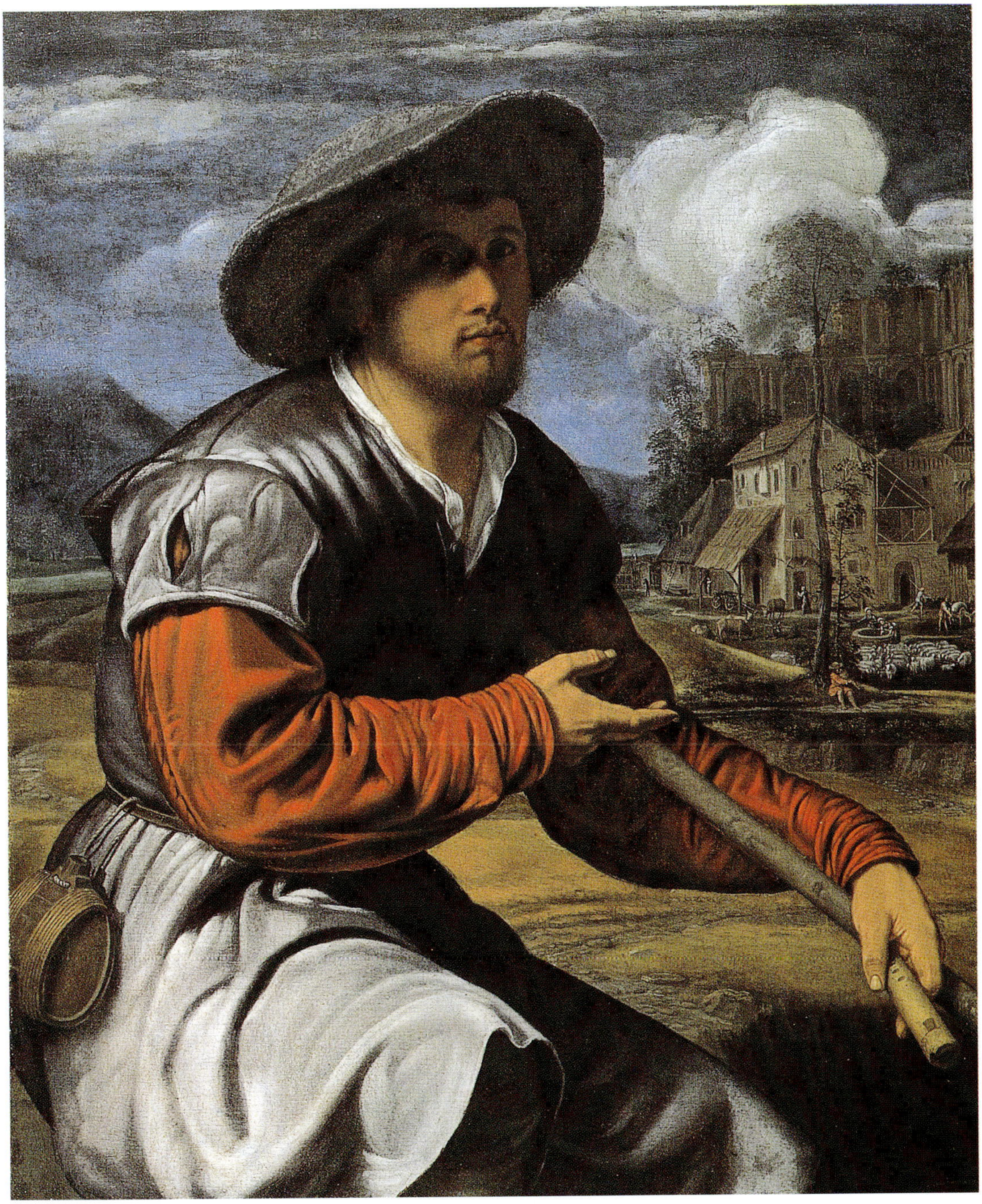

Giovan Gerolamo Savoldo
Shepherd with a Flute
c. 1525-30
canvas
Malibu, The J. Paul Getty Museum.

The painting, presenting complex esoteric and religious aspects which link it to Contarini's literary circle, portrays a shepherd wearing a wide-brimmed hat and holding a flute in his hand. In the background is a landscape darkening into twilight. Identified as the work of Savoldo since the late 19th century (it had formerly been attributed to Sebastiano del Piombo), the painting is one of the highest achievements of the Brescian artist. Its fascinating sense of mystery is accentuated by the back-lighting and the beam of sunlight striking the figure, leaving his face in half-shadow.

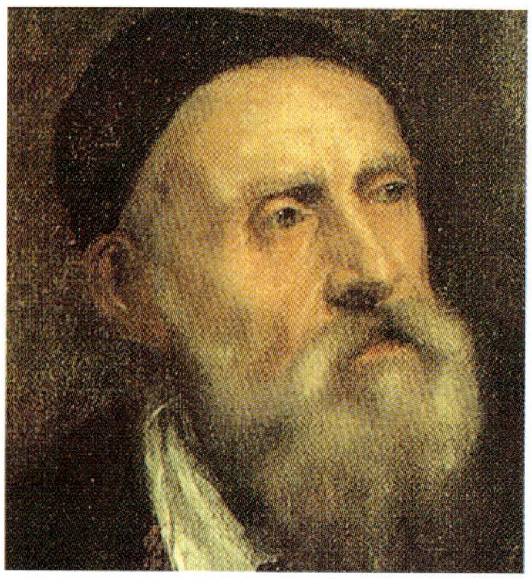

Titian

(Tiziano Vecellio, Pieve di Cadore 1480/85 – Venice 1576)

A pupil of Giovanni Bellini, Titian did not limit himself to "ferrying" Venetian art across the stream from the luminous equilibrium of the fifteenth century to the brilliant splendor of the sixteenth. Ultimately the great artist, thanks also to the gift of a very long life, completely redesigned the panorama of Venetian painting. Moreover, his approach were to have an impact on future generations of artists, not Italian alone, whose ranks include such eminent figures as Velázquez (1599-1660) and Manet (1832-83). It can even be said without fear of contradiction that after Titian the way of applying color to a canvas and the very conception of how color should be used in a painting were never again to be the same. Involved by Giorgione in the undertaking of frescoing the Fondaco dei Tedeschi at Rialto (1508), some detached parts of which have come down to us

Titian, *Self-portrait*, 1562. Berlin, Staatliche Museen.

Titian
The Slave
c. 1511
canvas
London, National Gallery.

Now unanimously attributed to the young Titian (as also proven by the initials T. V. engraved on the end of the parapet), although considered in the past to be the work of Giorgione, this portrait is one of the most original from the 16th century. The artist has amused himself by creating a kind of dialogue between the profile of the head carved in relief on the wall appearing in the foreground and the woman portrayed, who rests her hand on the wall in a gesture of complacent approval. Perhaps the painter wished to contrast the ideal classical features of the relief and the physical carnality of the woman.

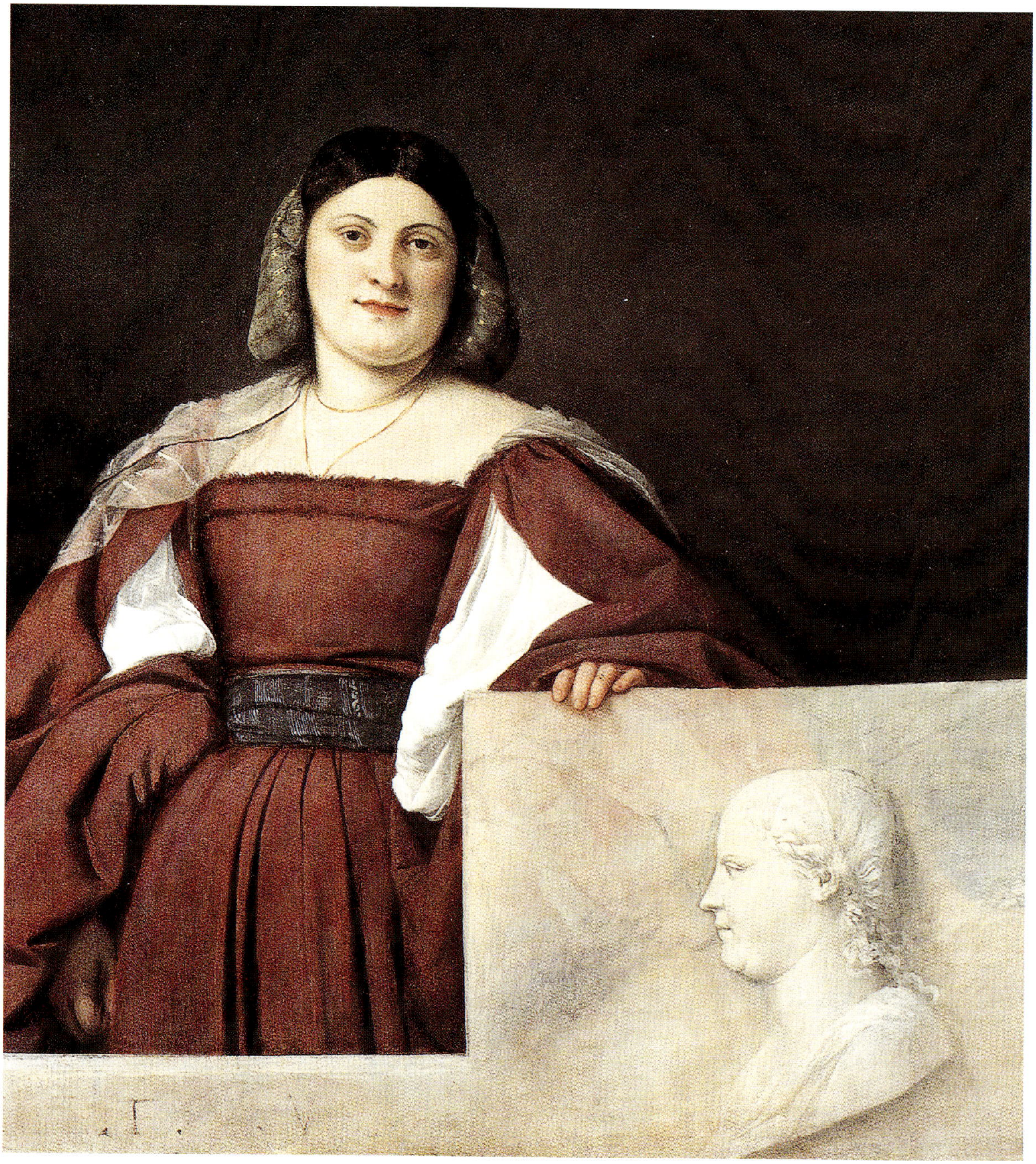

(Venice, Franchetti Gallery), Titian remained for some time linked to the other great Venetian master's pictorial world; and to such an extent that critics have disagreed as to the correct attribution of the famous *Country Concert* in the Louvre (1509-10). Now definitively attributed to Titian, the painting, while retaining a theme (that of musical symbolism, rich in philosophical and literary implications) linked to Giorgione, already shows Titian's splendid mastery of color with the red spot of the man playing the lute sensitively placed against the green background of the landscape. Equally complex from the iconological point of view, the Borghese Gallery's *Sacred and Profane Love* hinges around the same chromatic problem (1514). With the *Assumption* painted for the high altar of the Church of the Frari (1518), Titian's fame exploded. Contacts with the courts of Mantua and Ferrara (for which the artist painted a *Bacchanal*) were established, while even the Doge requested a portrait of him. The artist then entered the favor of the Gonzaga and the Emperor Charles V. While influenced by the seductive power of Mannerism, his painting became increasingly looser and more luminous. In his last years the artist abandoned himself to a solitary, isolated research of great visual impact.

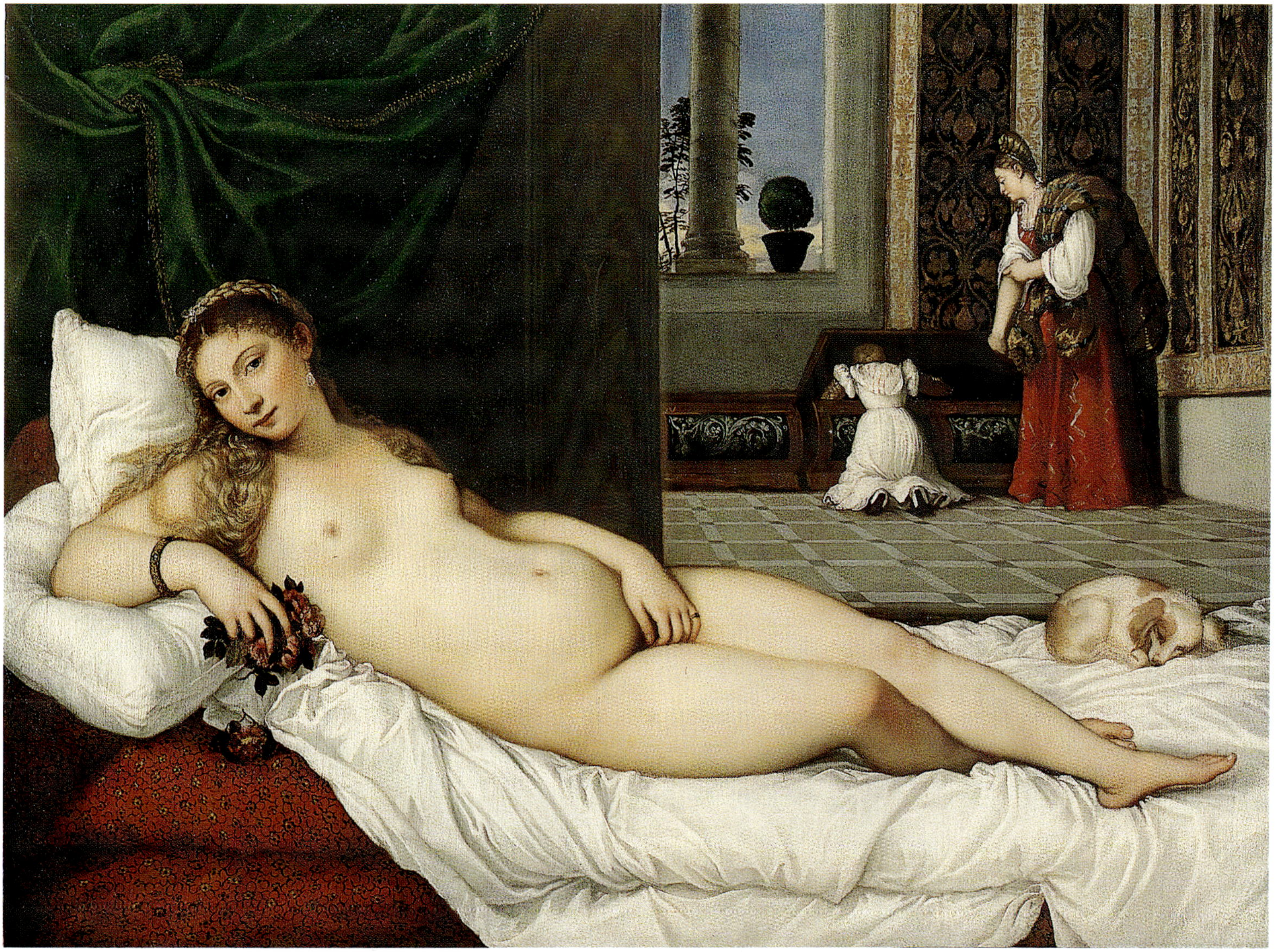

Titian
The Venus of Urbino
1538
canvas
Florence, Uffizi Gallery

Almost an archetype of feminine sensuality (the model for painters such as Ingres, Renoir and, above all, Manet, especially in his *Olympia*), this canvas was commissioned by Tiziano da Guidobaldo della Rovere who had just become Duke of Urbino. The panting was to have served as example for his young bride Giulia Varano; a sort of inspirational source on what conjugal love should be. Not by coincidence, curled up on the side of the bed, is a little dog, an obvious symbol of fidelity. This then is legitimate, but nonetheless ardently passionate love, as reiterated by the roses and the myrtle on the windowsill.

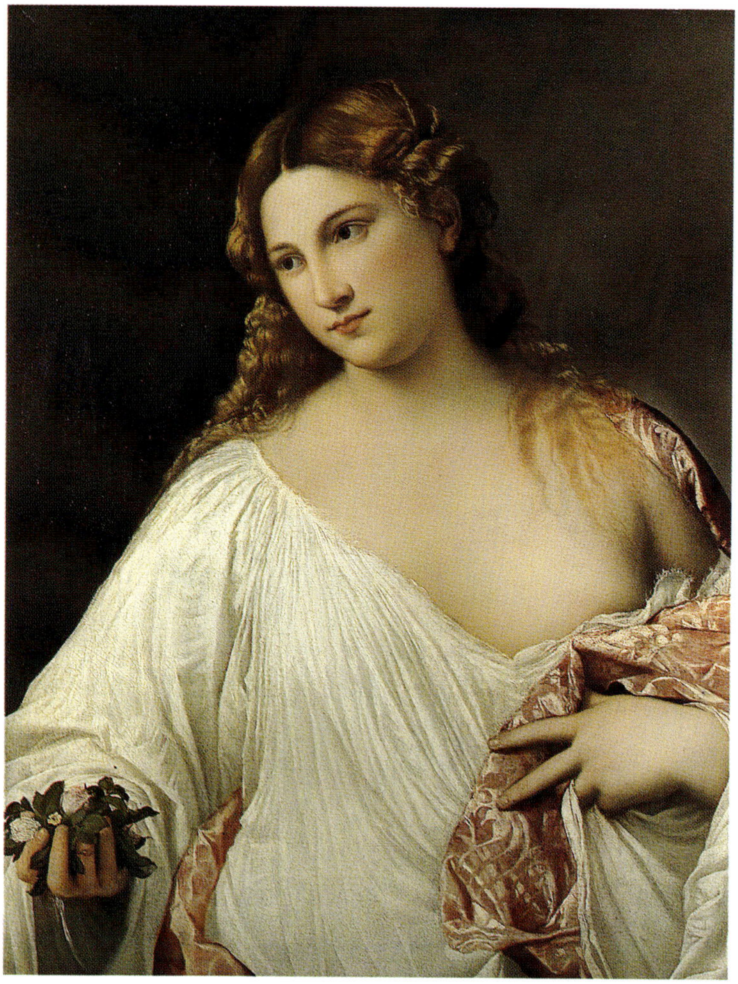

Titian
Eleonora Gonzaga della Rovere
1536-38
canvas
Florence, Uffizi Gallery.

The portrait is a companion piece to the one of Francesco Maria della Rovere, Duke of Urbino, also painted by the master and preserved in the same collection. The little dog on the left alludes to the one quality indispensable for a wife, fidelity. The ornate alarm clock is a status symbol.

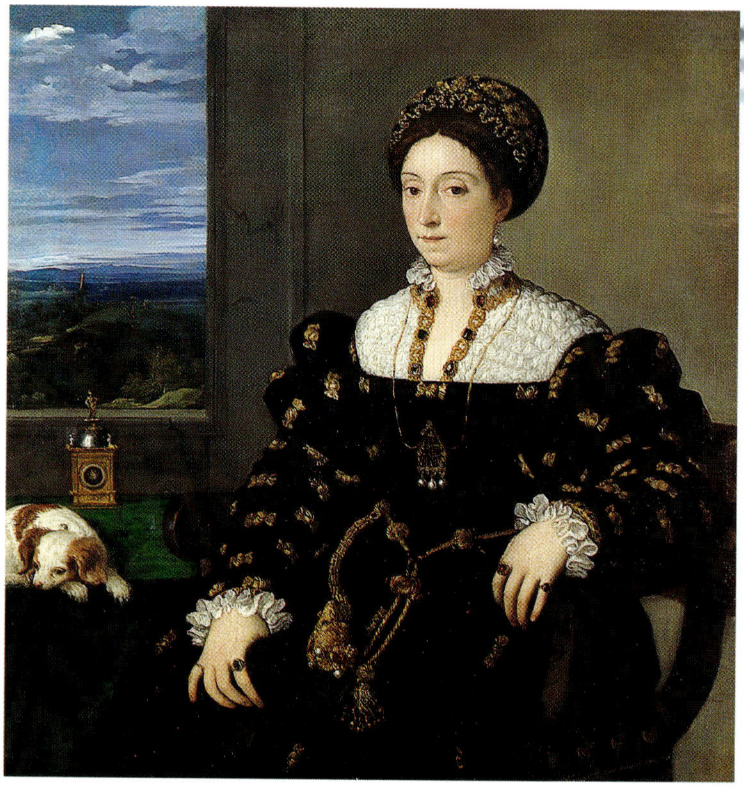

Titian
Flora
c. 1515-17
canvas
Florence, Uffizi Gallery.

In the refined Renaissance culture a special value was attributed to certain mythological figures. Flora, for instance, was the prototype of the bride, and the work is very probably a portrait of a young wife portrayed in the guise of the goddess of springtime. That the subject is conjugal love is demonstrated by the wedding ring displayed on the hand holding the bouquet of flowers which are, significantly, roses.

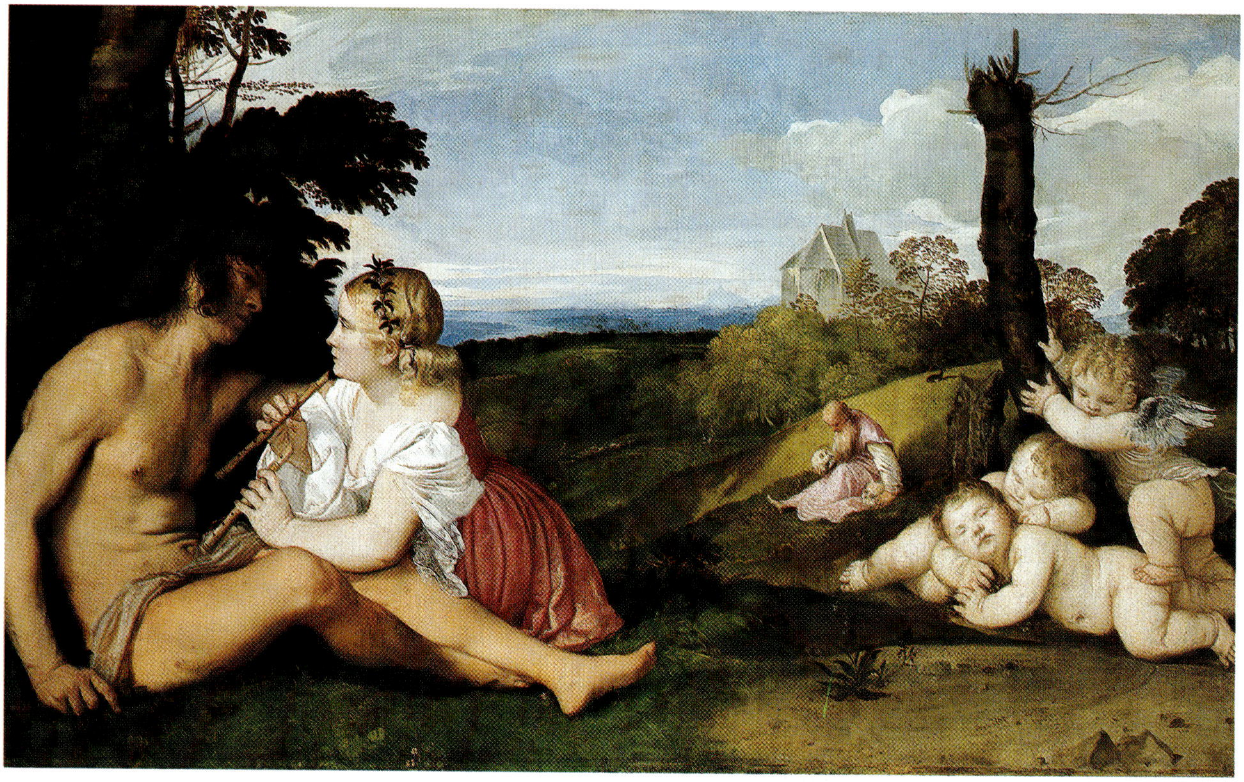

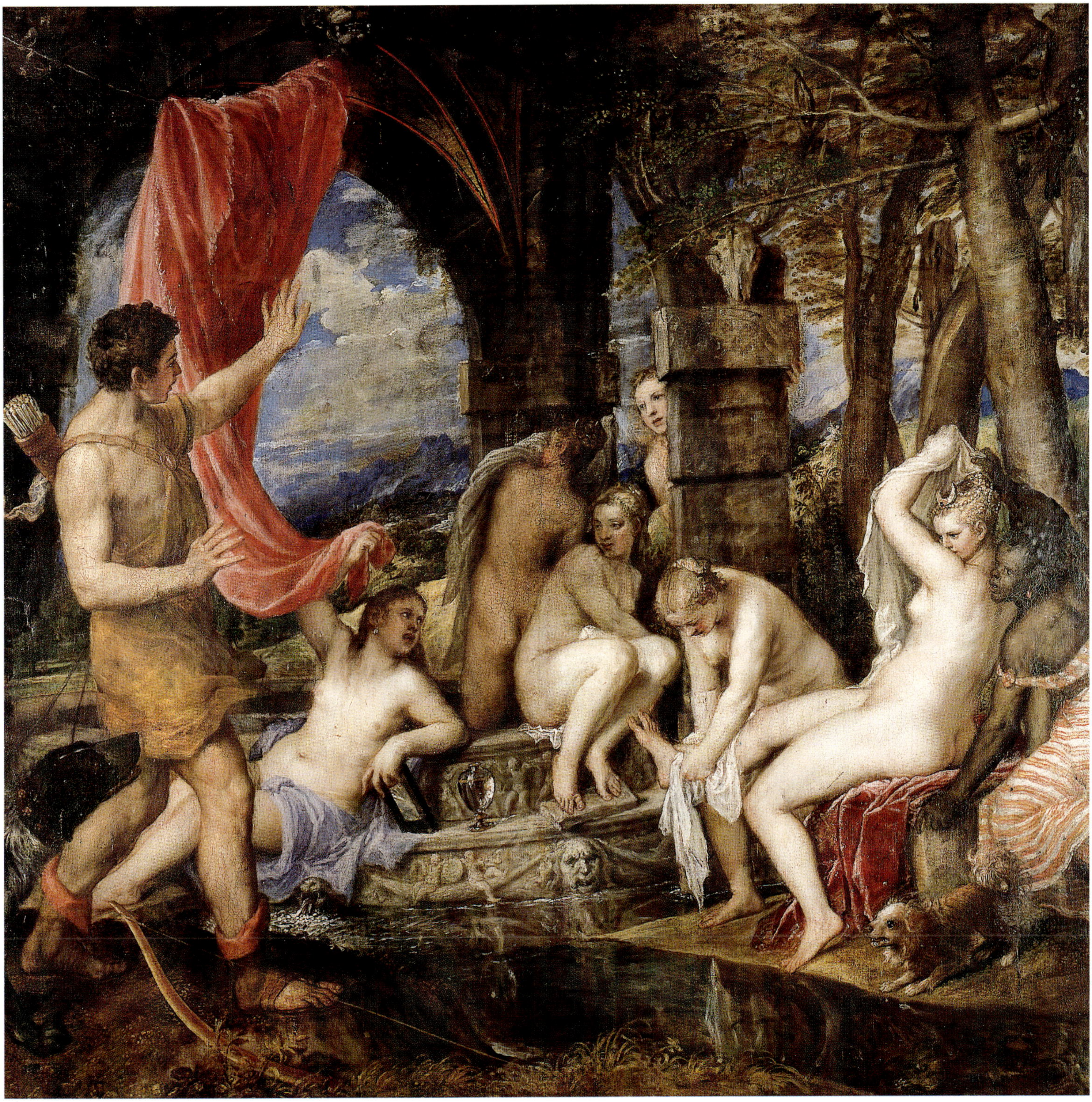

Titian
The Three Ages of Life
1511-12
canvas
Edinburgh, National Gallery of Scotland.

The young man and woman on the left are improvising a musical duet which alludes to an amorous skirmish, while the flute evokes the masculine sex. Love, however, is an ephemeral pleasure, as the old man meditating on the end of existence well knows. The two skulls are in reality those of the two young people. Even infancy appears as a couple, blissfully unaware of the dangers foreshadowed by the withered tree, providentially held up by Eros.

Titian
Diana and Acteon
1556-59
canvas
Edinburgh, National Gallery of Scotland.

Sent to Philip II in late 1559, the painting illustrates an episode poetically narrated by Ovid in his *Metamorphosis*. The mythical hero and Trojan huntsman, educated by the centaur Chiron, chanced to come upon Diana (the Artemis of the Greeks, the virgin goddess par excellence) bathing naked in a pool. This is the moment chosen by Titian. Transformed into a deer by the angry goddess, Acteon was torn to pieces by his own dogs.

Giovan Battista Moroni

(Albino, Bergamo, c. 1520 – Bergamo 1578)

Through Moroni's work the evolution in social status occurring in the territories of Bergamo and Brescia can be traced, at least in part. Up to at 1560 if not later, in fact, Giovan Battista received commissions for portraits not only from noblemen and high-ranking personalities but also from the mercantile middle class that had made this Italian province rich. A pupil of Moretto at Brescia, Giovan Battista also had a production of religious nature which brought him to work at Trento (1548) and then in the churches around Bergamo. After 1560, due to the progressive decline of the great families of clients and protectors, Moroni sought work in the ecclesiastical sphere. Moroni's presence at Trento during the Council probably made him the first artist to absorb the principles of the Reformation.

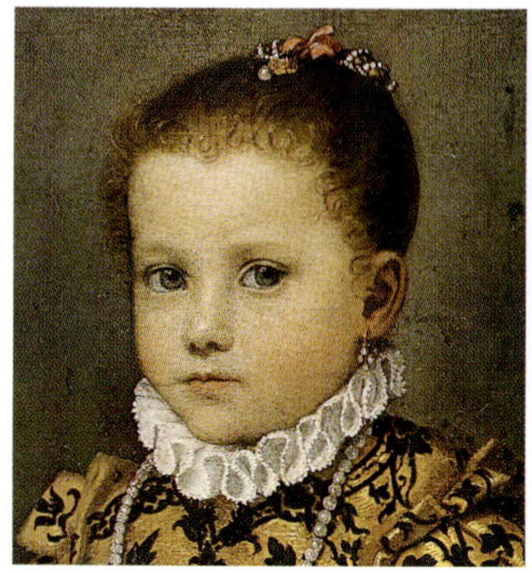

Giovan Battista Moroni, *Portrait of a Little Girl from the Redetti Family*, c. 1570. Bergamo, Accademia Carrara.

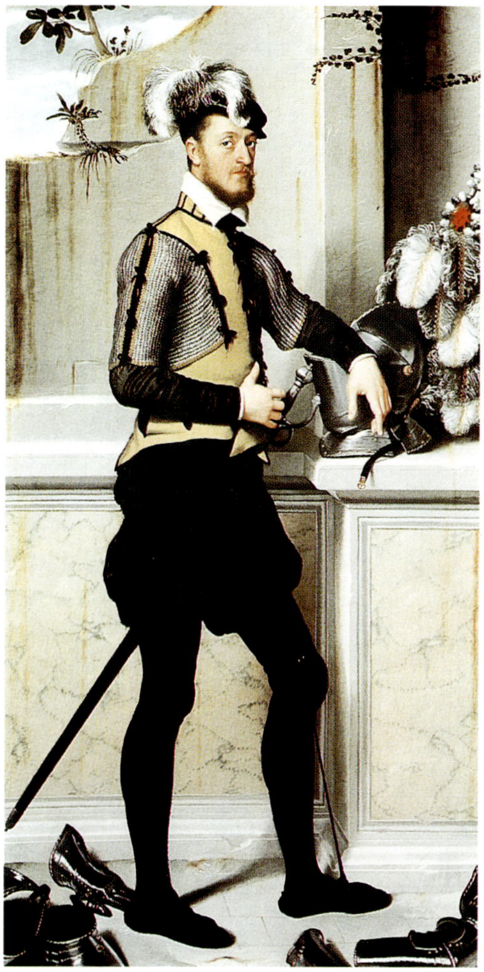

Giovan Battista Moroni
Gentleman of the Avogadro Family (The Knight of the Wounded Foot)
c. 1555
canvas
London, National Gallery.

Coming from the Avogadro Palace at Brescia, the portrait could be that of either Pietro or Faustino Avogadro, men-of-arms and sons of Gerolamo II. Military activity is alluded to by the details of the armor fallen to the floor and the metal binding on the left knee, obviously the sign of a wound.

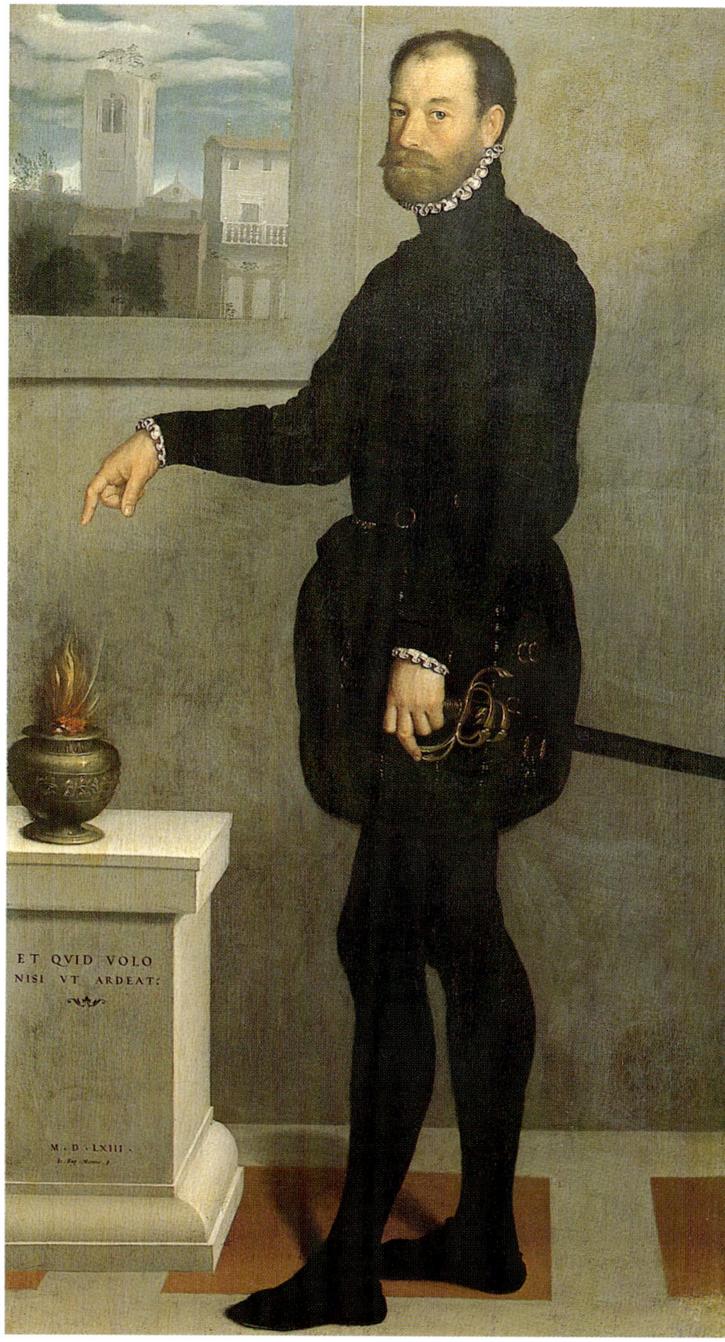

Giovan Battista Moroni
Portrait of Pietro Secco Suardo
signed and dated 1563
canvas
Florence, Uffizi Gallery.

The portrait contains practically all of the elements characteristic of the genre. It is reminiscent of certain works of Titian (the *Portrait of Philip II* in the Prado) and Tintoretto (the *Portrait of a Gentlemen in Fur,* Stuttgart, Staatsgalerie, in which the element of the window appears). This may not be mere coincidence, since Pietro Secco Suardo had been ambassador to Venice since 1545. This is however a "speaking" portrait, with the man pointing to the brazier on which are engraved words from the Gospel of Luke (XII, 49: "How I wish it [the fire] were blazing already"). The Latin words NISI VT ARDEAT conceal in acrostic the nobleman's surname. When the letters NI, I, T, AT are removed, the name SVARDE remains.

Bronzino

(Agnolo di Cosimo di Mariano, Florence 1503 – 1572)

A pupil of Pontormo, apprenticed to him when only fifteen, Bronzino is one of the outstanding figures in second-generation Mannerism, at a time when the political conditions of Florence were changing and the Medici family was taking great steps toward establishing the Grand Duchy of Tuscany (1569). A collaborator of Pontormo from 1526 to 1528 in the Santa Felicita project, Bronzino moved to Urbino after the siege of Florence by Imperial troops. He frescoed the Chapel of Eleonora da Toledo (1540-46) in Palazzo Vecchio and in 1541 entered the Florentine Academy newly founded by Duke Cosimo I. Here he was to remain for seven years. In 1548 he was in Rome, while already for some time he had been working for the Ducal tapestry factory. In 1566 Bronzino, who was also a refined poet, was readmitted to the Academy, and was even appointed Consul shortly before his death.

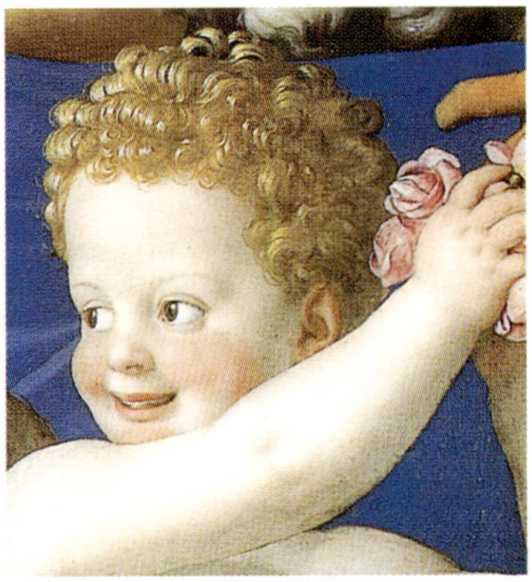

Bronzino, *Lust*, detail, c. 1545. London, National Gallery.

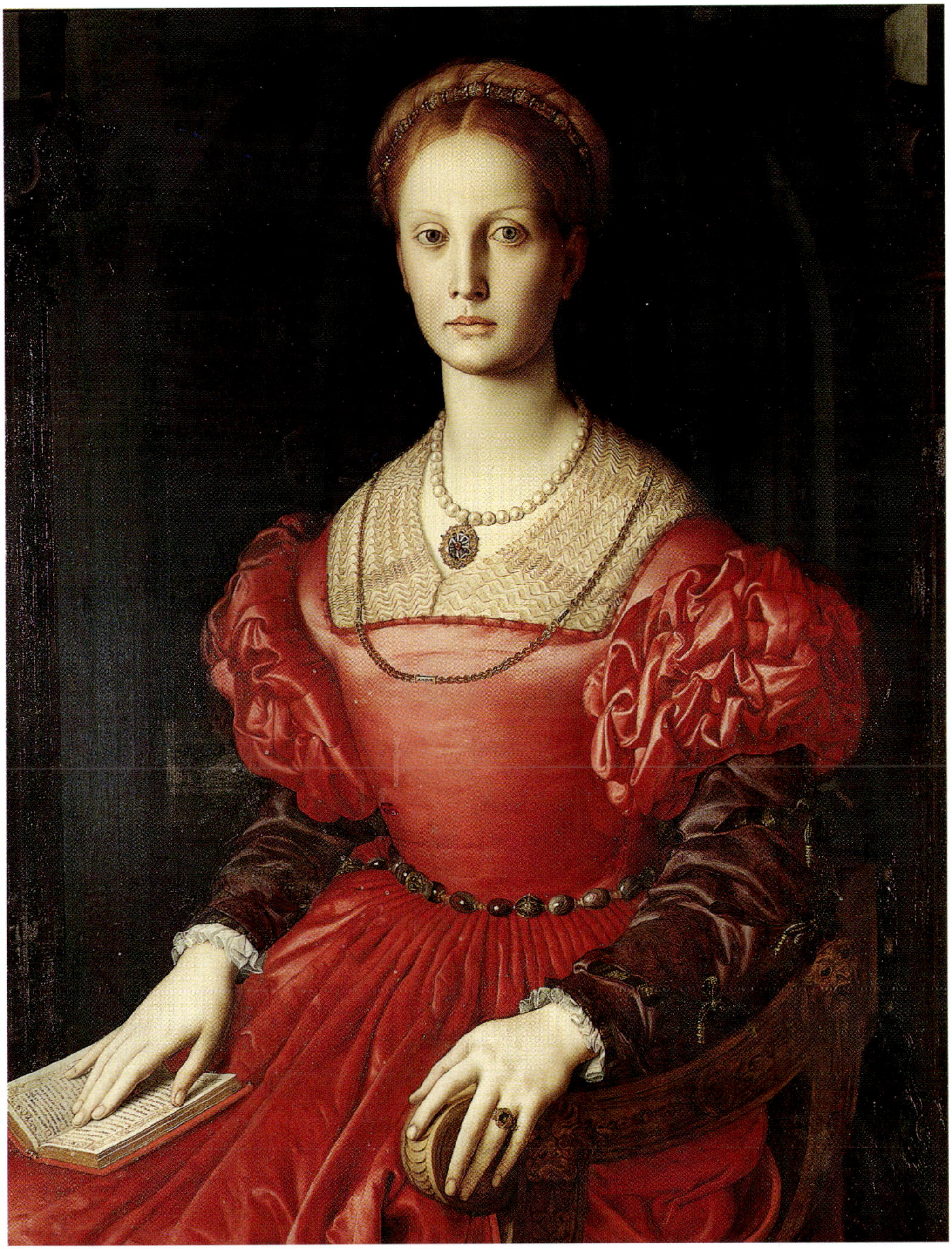

Bronzino
Portrait of Lucrezia Panciatichi
c. 1541
panel
Florence, Uffizi Gallery.

The portrait of Lucrezia di Gismondo Pucci, wife of the wealthy merchant Bartolomeo Panciatichi, whose portrait Bronzino had painted in that same year, is a sort of programmatic manifesto of the artistic ideals of the period. The Mannerist poetics was evolving toward a search for cold formality expressed in smoothest color and an almost metallic surface. A portrait, it was believed, should display above all the decorum of the person portrayed. Accordingly, Lucrezia appears as an effigy incarnating the poised, chaste beauty pursued at the time as an ideal.

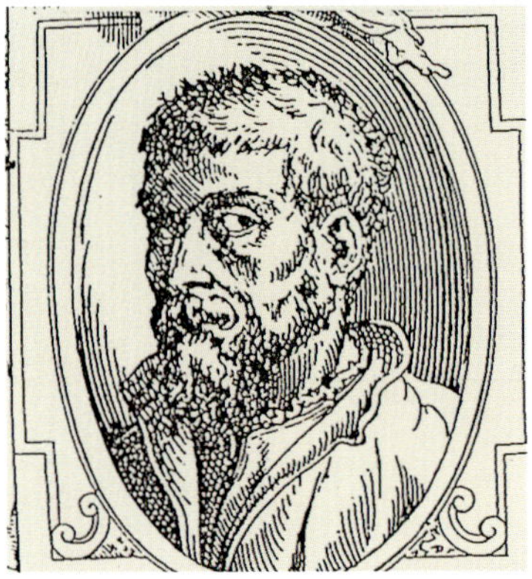

Francesco Salviati

(Francesco de' Rossi,
Florence 1510 – Rome 1563)

Although Vasari describes him as "one of the most talented, acute, proud, and competent artificers of our age", adding that this judgement is based on personal, direct knowledge, the artist's work has been appreciatively re-evaluated only recently. A pupil of Baccio Bandinelli (1493-1560) and Andrea del Sarto, "Checchino" moved to Rome in 1531, where he benefited by the protection of Cardinal Giovanni Salviati, whose name he took. The stay in Rome was significant for his studies of Raphael and his first important commissions. Returning to Florence in 1539, he then moved between Bologna, Mantua and Venice. From 1543 to 1547 he frescoed the Sala dell'Udienza in Palazzo Vecchio and then returned to Rome where he satisfied the requests of the Roman nobility. He is also memorable for his activity as portrait painter, goldsmith and miniaturist.

Giorgio Vasari, *Portrait of Francesco Salviati,* from the *Lives*, Florence, Giunti, 1568.

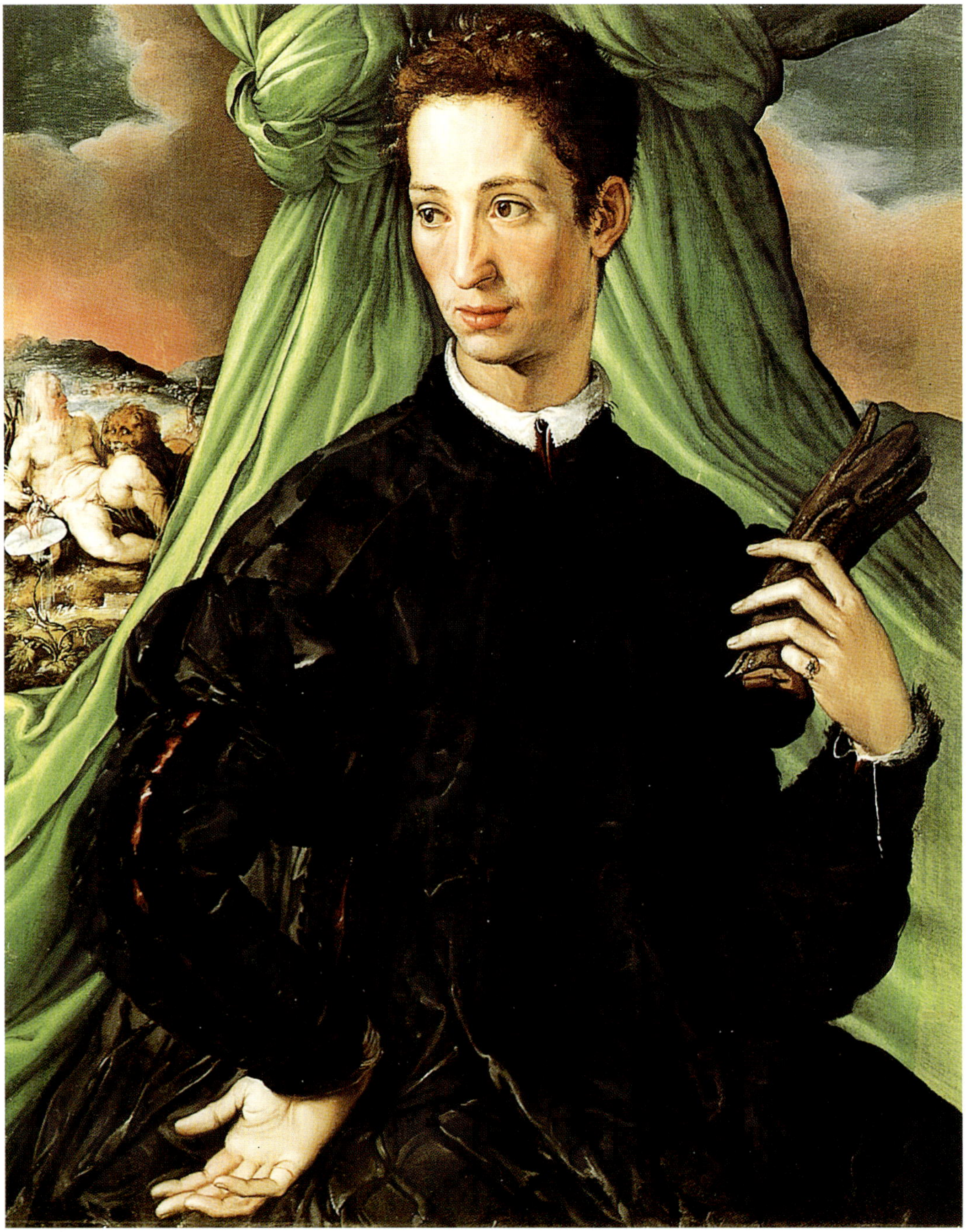

Francesco Salviati
Portrait of a Young Man
1543-47
panel
Saint Louis, The Saint Louis City Art Museum.

Although the identity of the young nobleman is uncertain, a number of indications point to the Florentine sphere and, more precisely, to the academic one. The figure of the old man in the background and the image of the lion refer to the heraldic origin of the Marzocco (symbol of Florence), as stated by Giambullari in his newly published *Gello* (1546). The old man is the personification of the Arno and the lion represents the Florentine Marzocco chosen as emblem for its connection with Hercules, whose name is Mazoc in Aramaic.

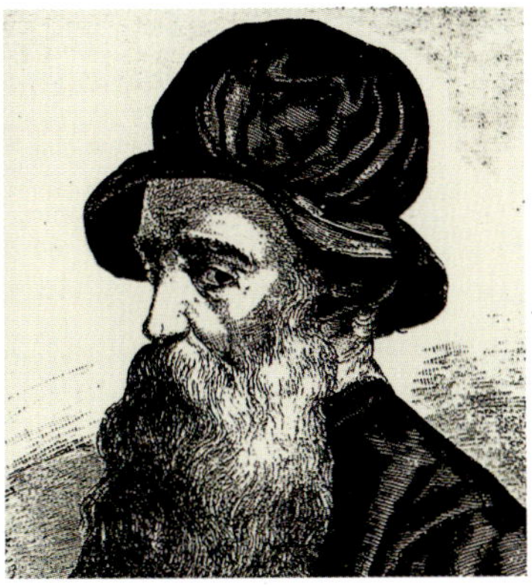

Benvenuto Cellini

(Florence 1500 – 1571)

With his restless, eventful life, Cellini embodies the Renaissance ideal of the artist. A highly versatile personage, he passed effortlessly from the goldsmith's bench to the foundry and from the scalpel to the pen. A brilliant writer, Cellini was the author of his famous autobiography as well as two treatises on gold-working and on sculpture. A child of art – the son of an engraver, Giovanni – he was directed toward the study of music. Gold-working was, however, his passion. From 1519 to 1540 Cellini was in Rome at the service of the popes. The five following years he spent in France at the service of Francis I, between Fontainebleau and Paris. Returning to Florence he worked fervently on the *Perseus*, which occupied him for nine years, during which he created other masterpieces as well. The changing fortunes of his life brought him from the dazzling, ephemeral atmosphere of courts to the squalor of prison.

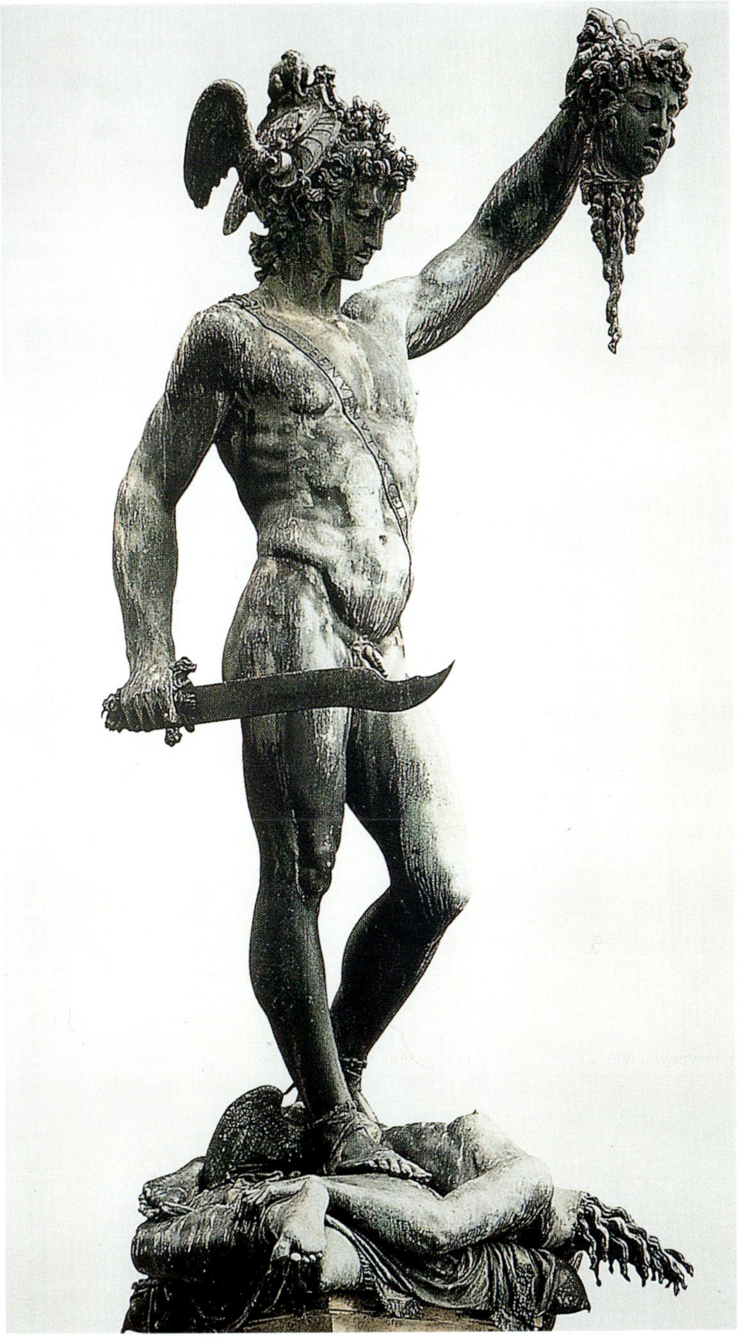

Benvenuto Cellini
Perseus
1545-54
bronze
Florence, Loggia dei Lanzi
(now in restoration).

"Before I die I will leave of myself such a proof to the world, that more than one will remain astounded", states the *Life* (II, 76), begun by Cellini two years after having finished his masterpiece. Commissioned by Cosimo I in May of 1545, when the artist went to visit the future Grand Duke at his villa of Poggio a Caiano, the immense bronze, more than three meters high, was to make life difficult for Benvenuto up to the end. He himself relates the episode in which he was forced to sacrifice all of the pewter table- and kitchenware he owned to make the molten metal flow at the right speed (*idem*, II, 77). Refined in every detail, from the pedestal to the Medusa's snaky hair, the Perseus is a sort of monumental jewel where chiseled perfection sustains an unrivaled inventive synthesis.

Benvenuto Cellini
Salt-cellar of Francis I
1540-43
gold and enamel
Vienna, Kunsthistorisches Museum.

Justly described as a "table monument", the salt-cellar, over thirty centimeters long and twenty-six high, is decorated by the mythological figures of Neptune and Gaea, the Earth, who represent different aspects of salt. On the base are personifications of the seasons and the four stages of the day.

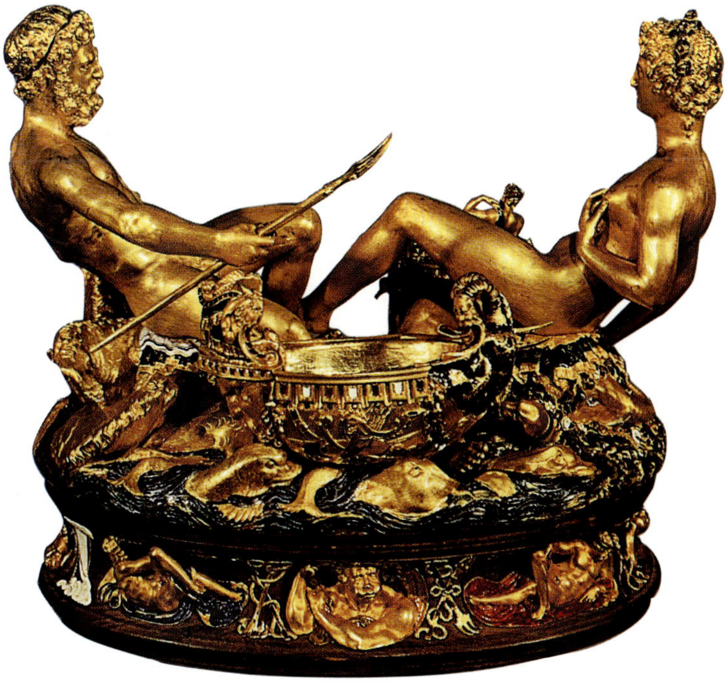

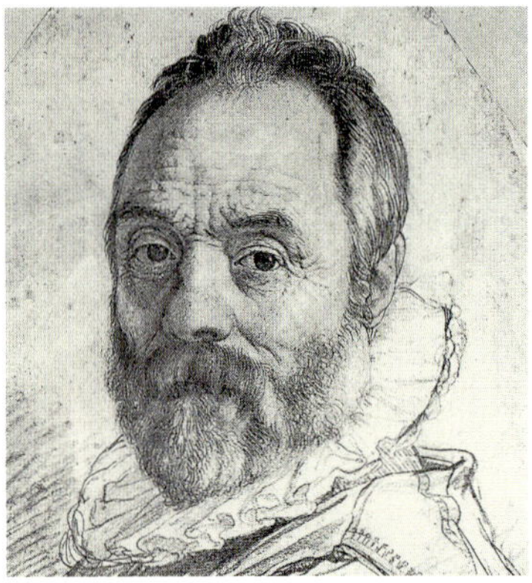

Giambologna

(Jean de Boulogne,
Douai 1529 – Florence 1608)

The artistic career of Giambologna is a tangible sign of the vital cultural exchange that took place, throughout the Renaissance, between the lands of Flanders and Italy. Trained in his homeland, the artist arrived at Rome in 1550 with the precise intention of studying ancient statues and the works of the divine Michelangelo. Passing through Florence on his journey home, he was introduced to the Court of the Medici, who assigned him a salary starting in 1561. In return Jean, who had now been nicknamed Giambologna, produced theatrical scenes and sculptures for festivities, and small, refined decorative marbles and bronzes, including the famous series of "portraits" of animals sculpted from life to adorn the grotto of the Villa Medicea of Castello (now in the Bargello National Museum). He also worked in Lucca, Genoa and Bologna.

Hendrik Goltzius, *Portrait of Giambologna,* 1591. Haarlem, Teylers Museum.

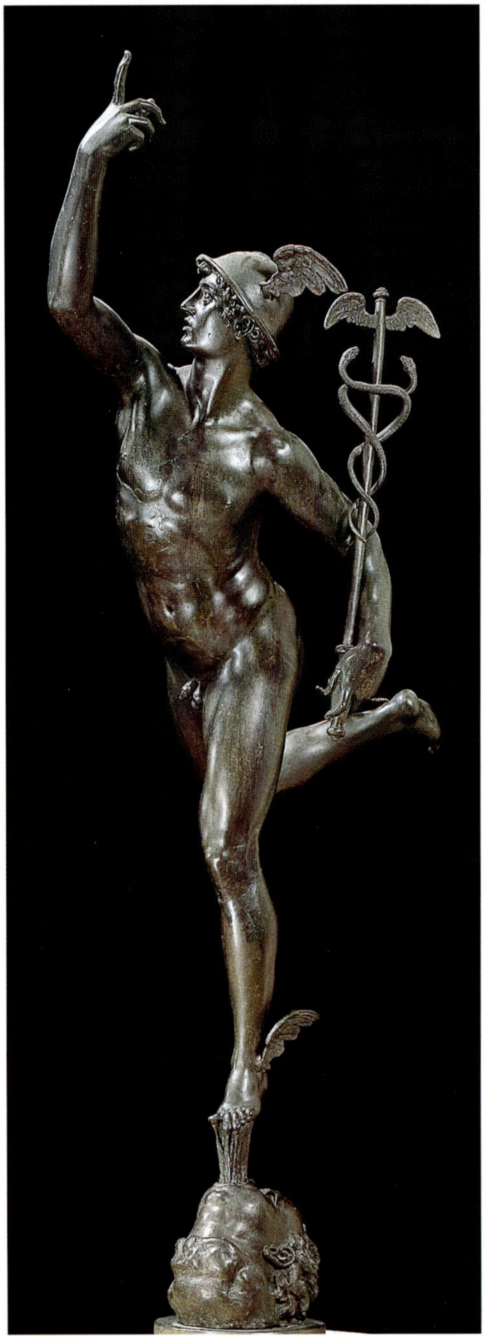

Giambologna
Mercury
c. 1580, bronze
Florence, Bargello Museum.

The winged Mercury resting on the tip of one foot, held up by a powerful gust of wind, is a miracle of equilibrium. His whole body seems in fact absorbed in holding this elegant but arduous pose.

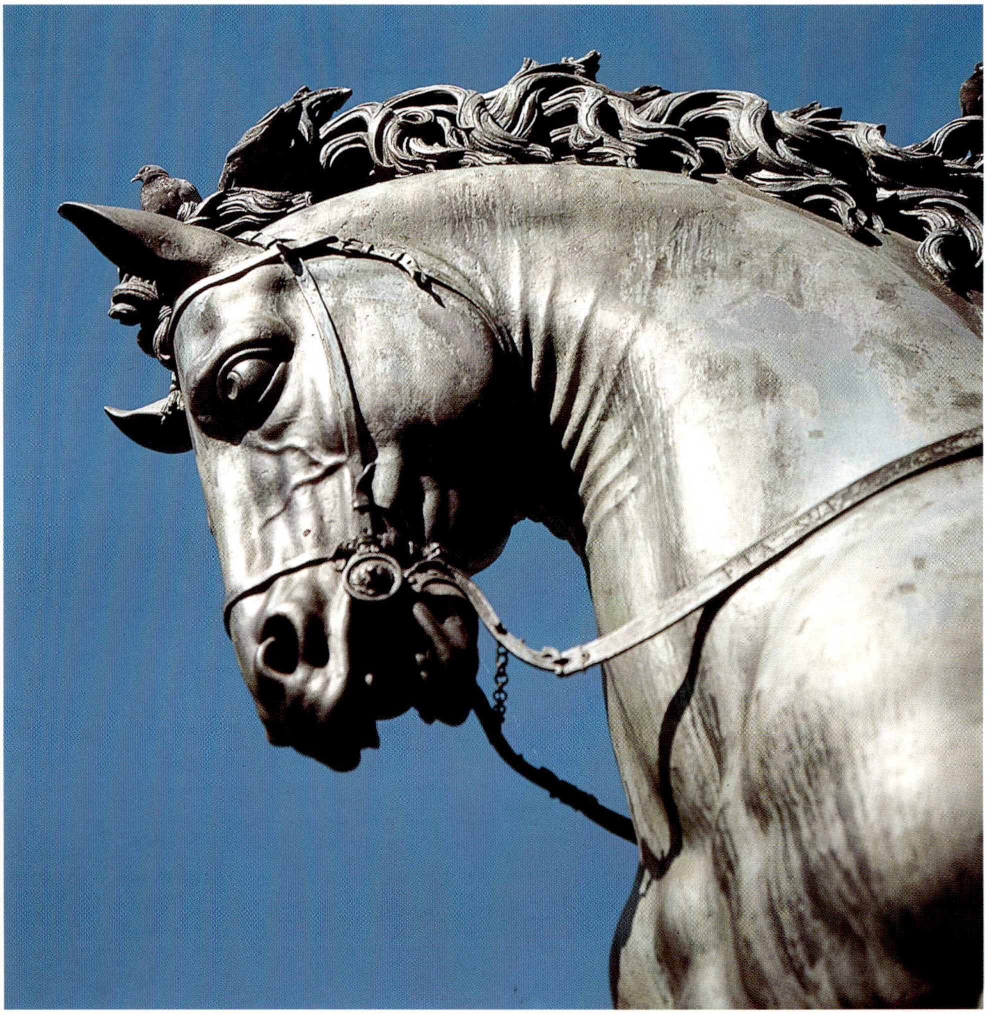

Giambologna
Equestrian Monument to Cosimo I
1594-98
bronze, detail
Florence, Piazza della Signoria.

The basic scheme is that of the statue to *Marcus Aurelius*, which was thought at the time to represent Constantine, the first Christian emperor. The decision to portray Duke Cosimo in this way was thus highly significant.

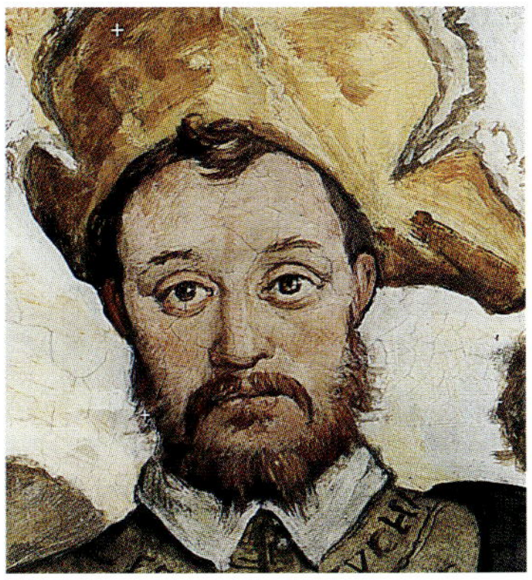

The Zuccari Brothers

Federico
(Sant'Angelo in Vado, Urbino, 1542/43 – Ancona 1609)
Taddeo
(Sant'Angelo in Vado, Urbino, 1529 – Ancona 1566)

A perfect partnership linked the Zuccari brothers. It was never to be broken, not even at the death of Taddeo, since Federico inherited his commissions. The two personalities were complementary to each other. Taddeo, a painter, trained at Rome in the milieu of Mannerism of Raphaelesque stamp. Federico, painter, architect and author, dedicated a good part of his existence to the foundation and improvement of the Academy of Saint Luke in Rome. A pupil of Taddeo (who after his arrival in the Papal city decorated the villas of the Orsini family at Bracciano and the Farnese at Caprarola), Federico codified his own convictions in a treatise (*The Idea of Painters, Sculptors and Architects*, published at Rome in 1607), which championed the primacy of drawing.

Federico Zuccari, *Self-portrait*, detail, 1536. Florence, Duomo, frescoes in the dome.

Federico Zuccari
Federico Zuccari and Vincenzio Borghini discussing the inventions for the frescoes in the dome of Santa Maria del Fiore
paper
Florence, Cabinet of Drawings and Prints, Uffizi.

At a superficial glance, the drawing – which is a sketch for the final work now in the Biblioteca Hertziana at Rome (i.e., Palazzetto Zuccari) – seems a simple exposition of the facts; and this it is, in part. Federico has received a commission to complete the interior decoration of the dome of Sant Maria del Fiore in Florence, and he depicts himself discussing this project with Don Vincenzio Borghini, the spokesman for the Duomo. The painter appears in the foreground on the left, wearing a hat, while he illustrates his projects, holding in his hand a roll of paper, probably more drawings. Don Borghini is in the center, flooded with light, stretching out a hand toward the model of the dome. These are the facts; and now the comments. The girl with the long hair is undoubtedly Fame, while the old man who has fallen asleep is Vasari whom Zuccari disliked and who had painted the first part of the frescoes representing the *Last Judgement*.

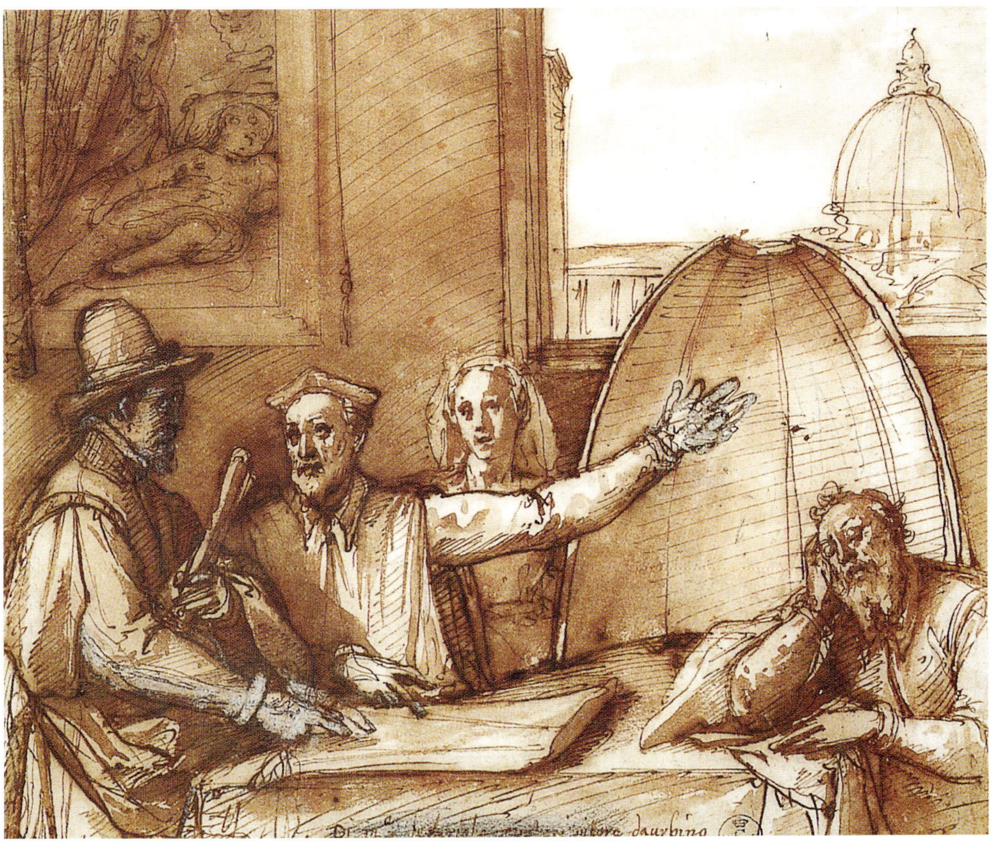

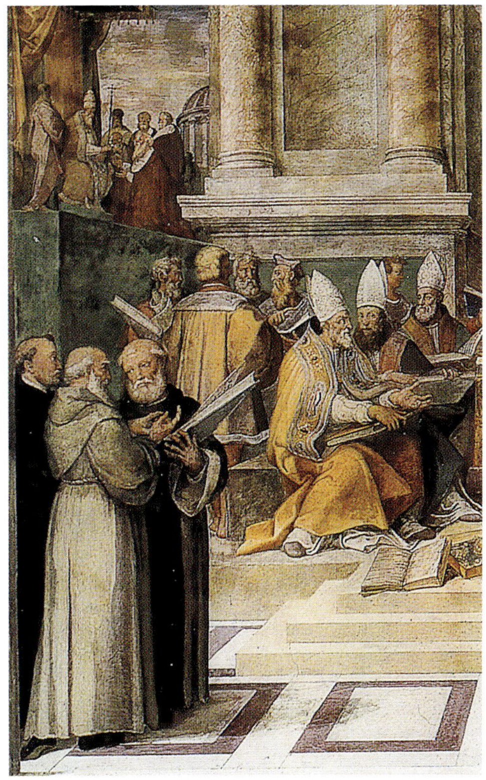

Taddeo Zuccari
Convocation of the Council of Trent
1562-63
fresco, detail
Caprarola, Palazzo Farnese, antechamber of the Council.

The basic scheme is reminiscent of that adopted by Raphael for the *Coronation of Charlemagne*, in the *Stanza of the Conflagration of Borgo* in the Vatican Palaces. The perspective, however, is more clearly articulated, and shows closer attention by the artist to the architectural component of the scene. The atmosphere which Taddeo intends to illustrate is that of great intellectual tension, pending an event which was to change the direction of the Church as well as the society of the times.

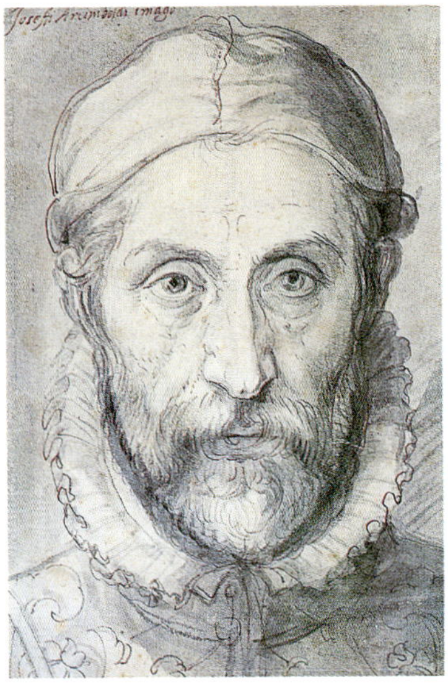

Giuseppe Arcimboldi, *Self-portrait*, c. 1575. Prague, Národní Galerie.

Giuseppe Arcimboldi

(Milan 1527 – 1593)

A unique case in the history of art, Giuseppe Arcimboldi invented a stylistic approach that was to make him immediately recognizable, and to bring him swift success and lasting fame. After beginning to paint, entirely within the canons of the norm, in the Monza Duomo (his is the *Tree of Jesse*), and designing the cartoons for the stained-glass windows in the Milan Duomo, he abruptly changed his style in 1562 when he was called to Prague by Rudolph II of Hapsburg, the erudite alchemist king who immediately appointed him court painter. It was then that Giuseppe began to conceive of human heads (which may also be portraits) composed of fruit, flowers, vegetables, animals or objects suitably chosen in relation to the meaning to be attributed to the image. "Discovered" by Surrealist painters, the work of Archimboldi has become widely known in our time.

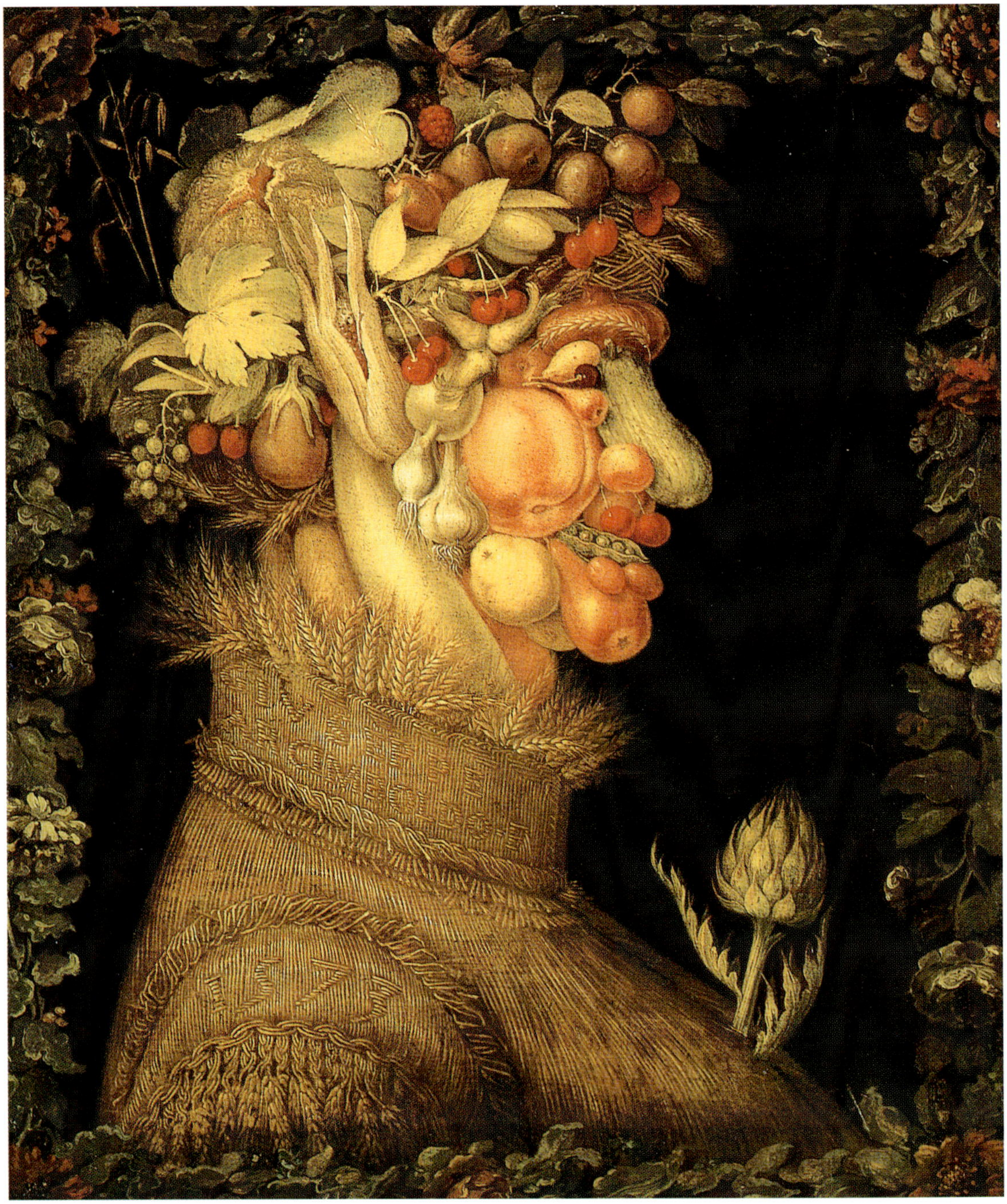

Giuseppe Arcimboldi
Summer
signed and dated 1573
canvas
Paris, Louvre.

This head forms part of the series dedicated to the seasons which was, in turn, to have served as *pendant* to one portraying the four elements and thus creating, between the one and the other, a precise symbolic correspondence. The choice was obviously dictated by the interests of Rudolph II (1552-1612) who dabbled in alchemy. In any case, the female head of *Summer* (whose dress is made of woven straw adorned at the neck with ears of grain) is composed of seasonal fruits and vegetables, ranging from peaches to cucumbers, from pears to cherries, while pinned to the front of her dress, like a rose, is an artichoke.

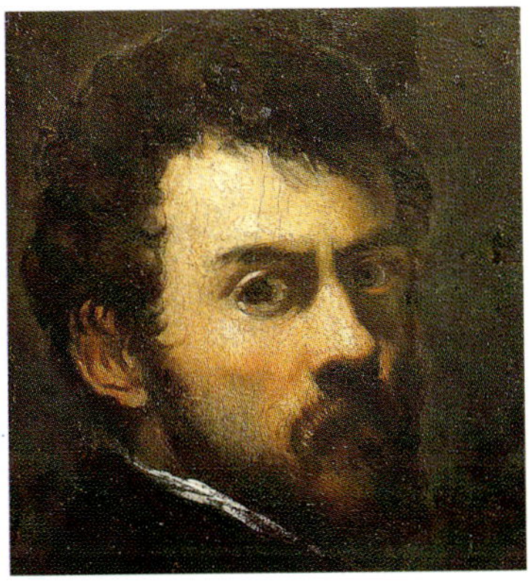

Tintoretto

(Jacopo Robusti, Venice 1518 – 1594)

The son of a silk dyer or *tintore* (the derivation of his pseudonym), Jacopo, one of the greatest artists in the Venetian figurative culture of the 16th century, probably trained in the Pordenone milieu, although 16th century literature on art traditionally considered him to be a pupil of Titian, of whom he was to become the great antagonist. A prolific artist, often working with numerous assistants, he was endowed with abounding energy and a marked capacity for assimilating new trends in art which allowed him to absorb Mannerist modes while Titian was still ignoring or rejecting them. Expert at depicting crowded scenes, mythological compositions and luministic effects, he was able to involve the spectator emotionally. He received a great number of important commissions, such as the paintings for the Scuola Grande di San Marco (1562-66) and for the Scuola di San Rocco.

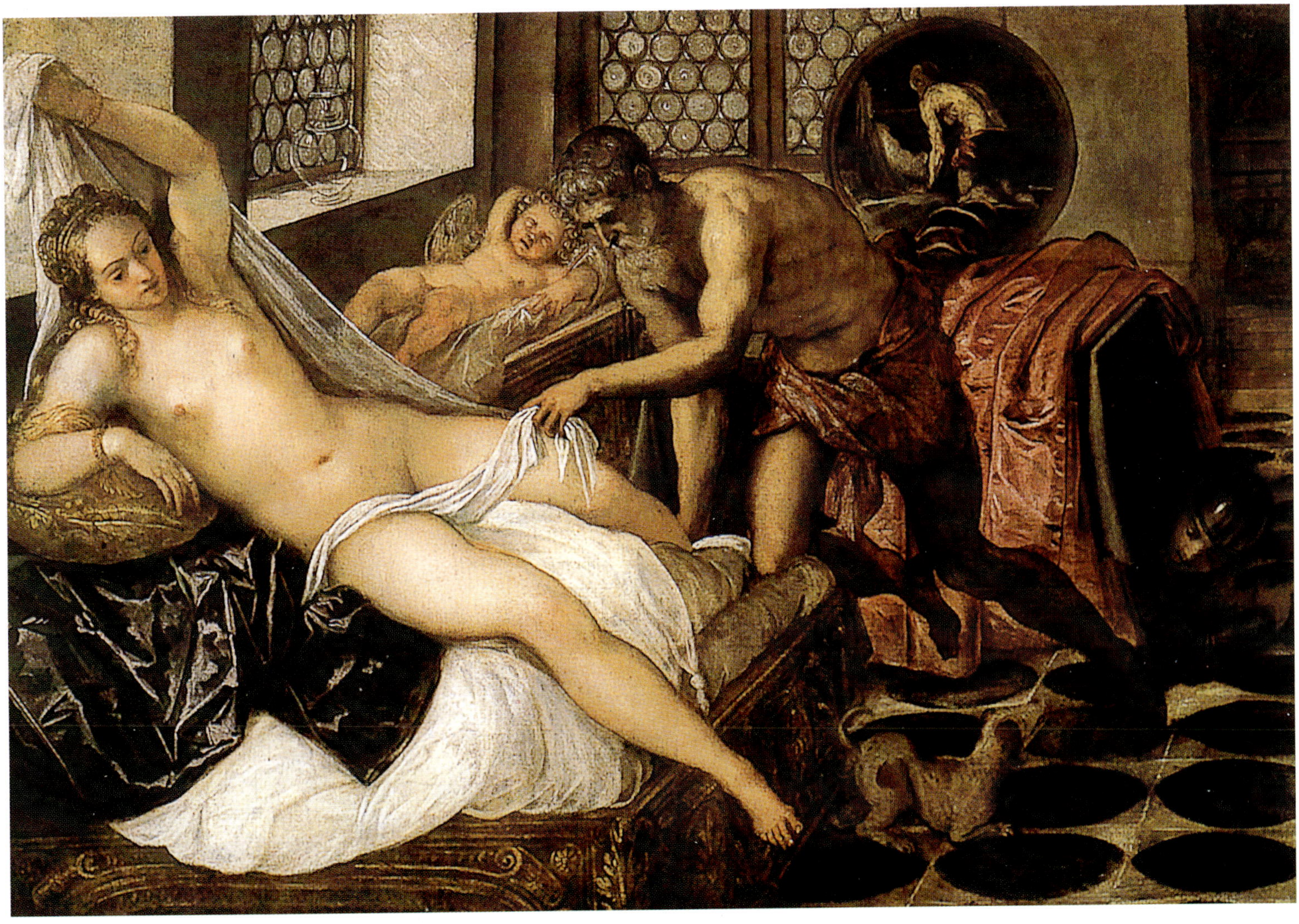

Tintoretto, *Self-portrait*, detail, c. 1548. London, Victoria and Albert Museum.

Tintoretto
Venus, Vulcan and Mars
1545-50
canvas
Munich, Alte Pinakothek.

In fifteenth and sixteenth century symbology, the dog alluded to fidelity. The one in this painting must have tried in vain to defend this value, for it is desperately barking at Mars who, despite the helmet he is wearing, is hiding under a table in the hackneyed style of the lover trying to avoid being caught in the act. But Vulcan must have suspected something, if he leaps suspiciously toward the nuptial bed to examine the linen, still warm, in which his wife Venus is wrapped. Venus, in truth, seems quite unworried, confident as she is of her overpowering fascination. The only personage not involved in the embarrassing incident appears to be Cupid, who is sleeping. But it is an insidious sleep, since it is he who has arranged the rendez-vous.

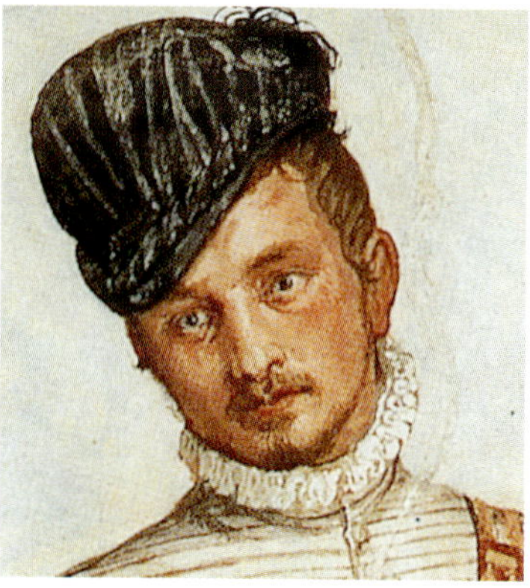

Paolo Veronese

(Paolo Caliari,
Verona 1528 – Venice 1588)

With Titian and Tintoretto, Veronese is the third outstanding personality in the panorama of sixteenth century Venetian painting. The son of a stone-cutter, Paolo took his pseudonym from the name of his native city, where he worked in the shop of Antonio Badile. Trained in the Mannerist style of Parma's figurative culture (Correggio and Parmigianino), he very early abandoned them for a style that was less tormented and more radiant. The effect was undoubtedly heightened by the lowered viewpoint utilized with great skill in the paintings for the Hall of the Council of Ten at Palazzo Ducale (1553-54). This was to be a highly successful stylistic approach, later emulated by Tiepolo. One of the painter's great masterpieces is the *Marriage in Cana*, a work of costume, as well as of religious subject.

Paolo Veronese, *Presumed Self-portrait dressed as a Hunter*, 1561. Maser, Villa Barbaro, last room in the western wing.

Paolo Veronese
Supper in the House of Levi
1573
canvas
Venice, Gallerie dell'Accademia.

For this painting the artist underwent, on July 18, 1573, if not a real trial, a procedure of investigation conducted by the Inquisition. The immense canvas (over 5 meters high and over 12 long) was conceived as a *Last Supper* for the Dominican refectory of Saints John and Paul at Venice. The disapproval of the Inquisition, which judged highly irreverent the presence of jesters, dogs and black servants, forced the artist to change the name of the painting to *Dinner in the House of Levi*, a title less charged with religious implications. The work was created to replace a canvas of similar subject that had been painted by Titian and destroyed in a fire.

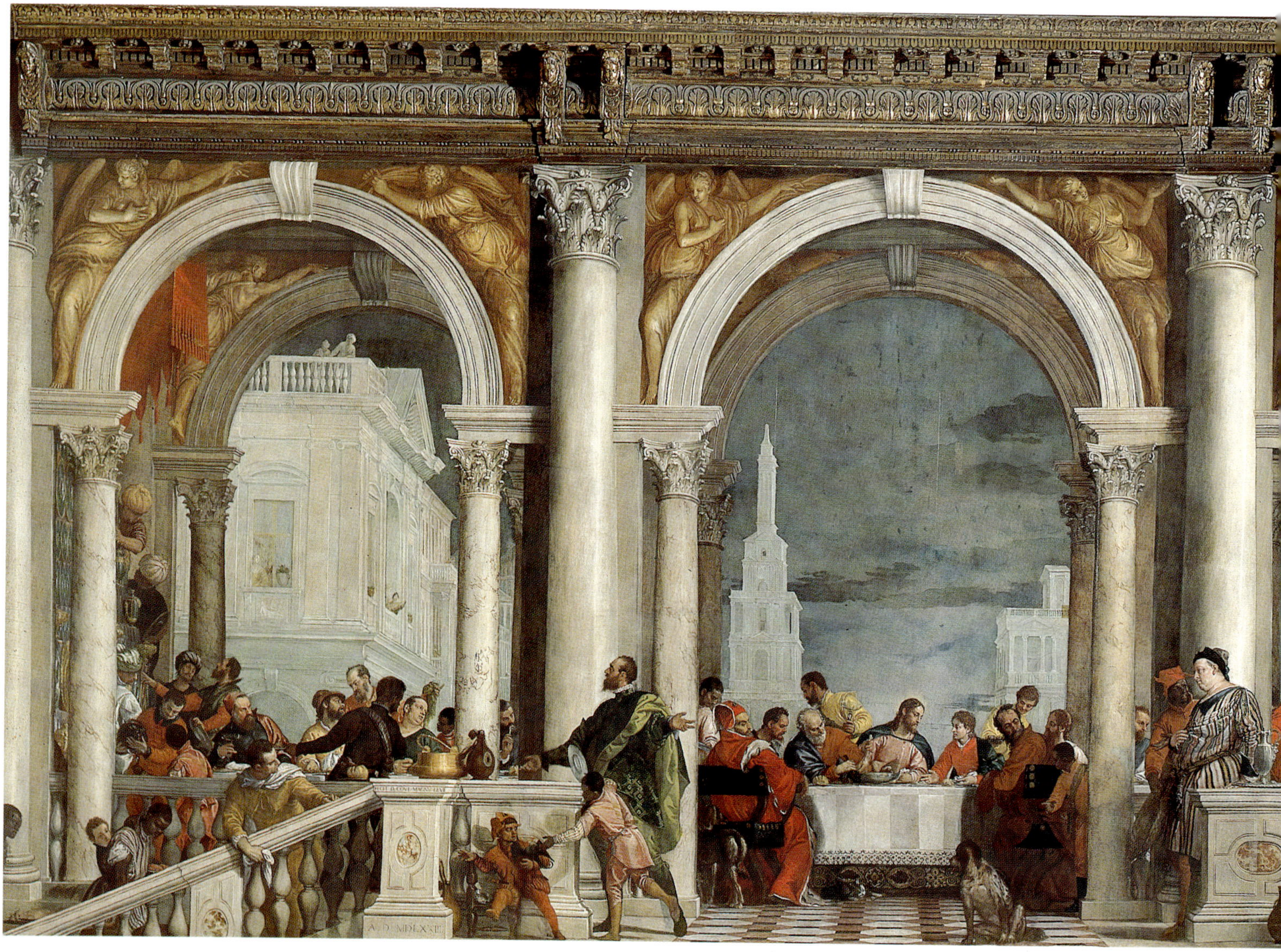

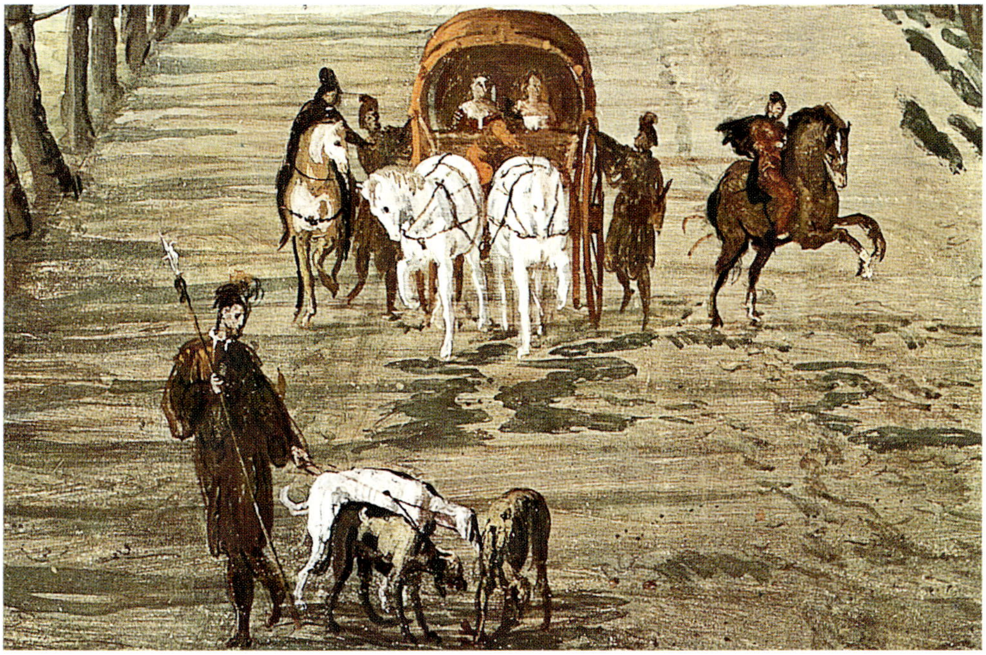

Paolo Veronese
Decorative cycle at Villa Barbaro
1561
fresco, details
Maser, Villa Barbaro.

Villa Barbaro represents one of the highest moments of the encounter between two artists: Palladio the architect of the villa (completed in 1559), and Veronese. The painter's use of perspective and *trompe-l'oeil* provides a pictorial comment to the work of Palladio.

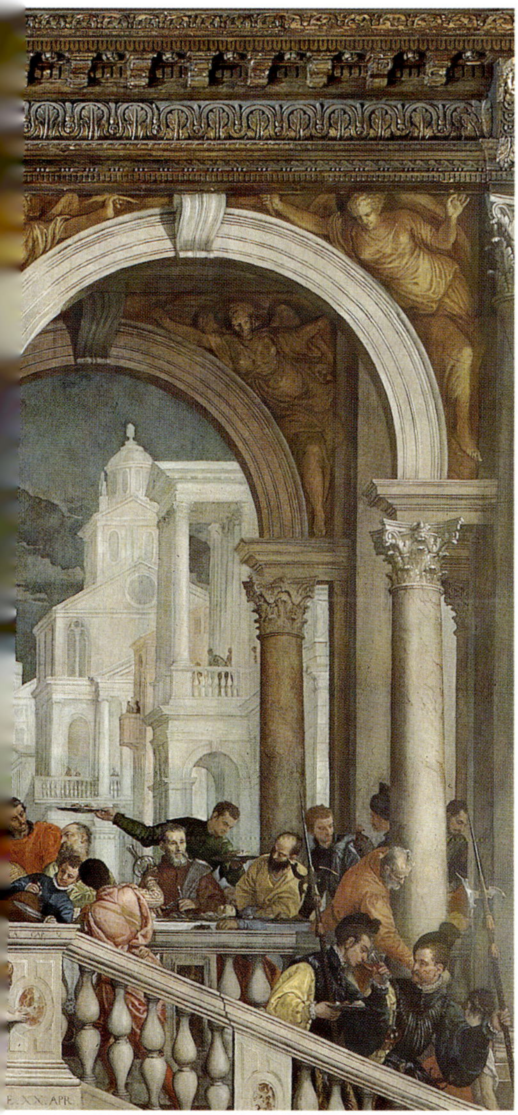

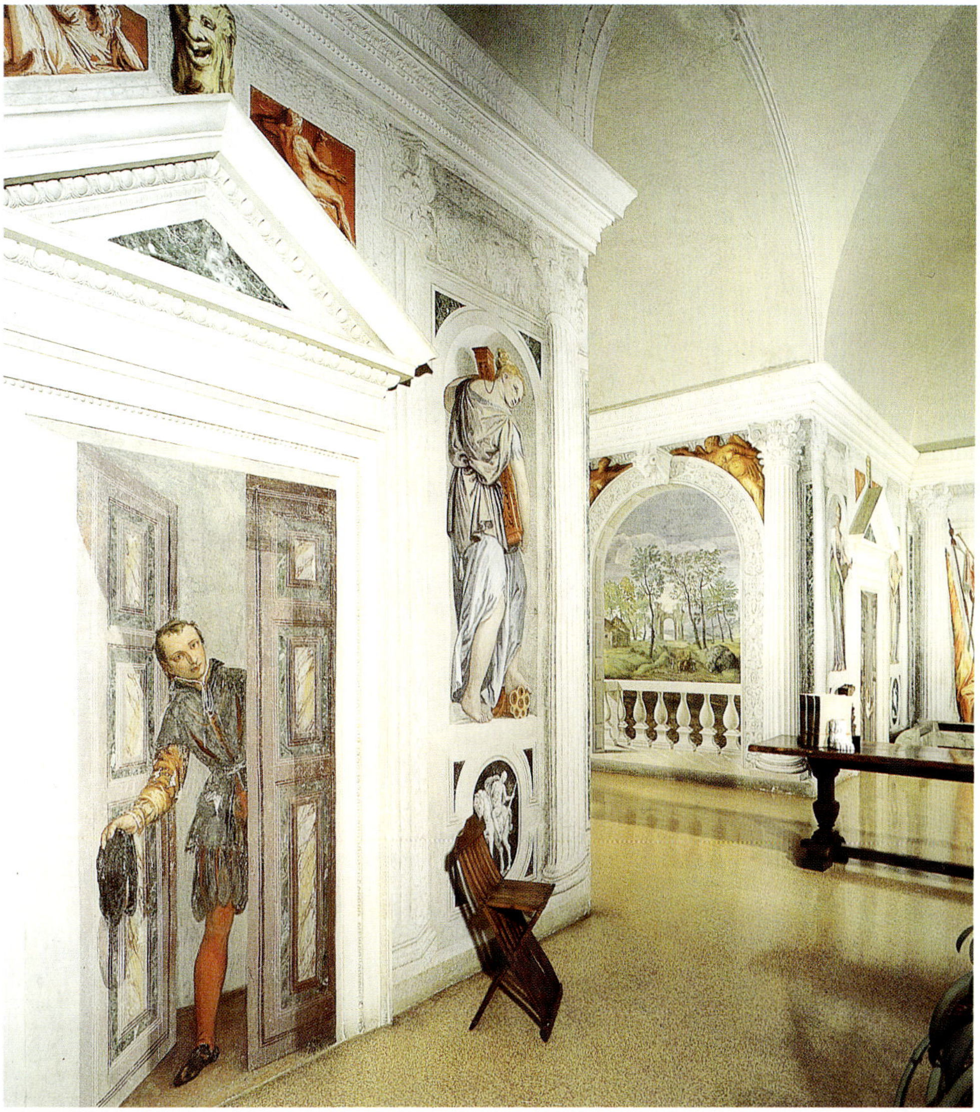

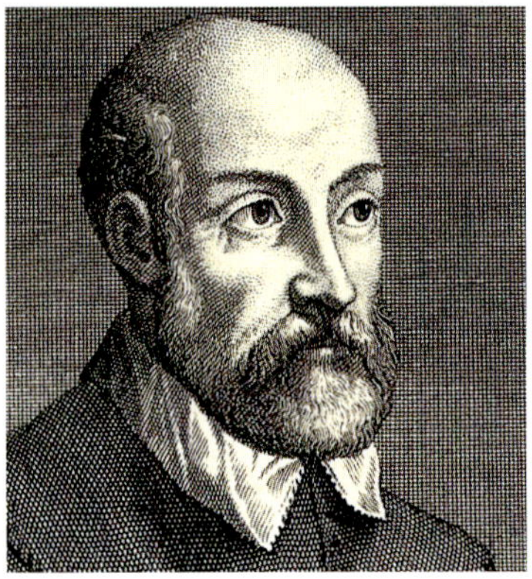

Andrea Palladio

(Andrea di Pietro della Gondola, Padua 1508 – Maser, Treviso, 1580)

"Guided by natural inclination, I turned in youth to the study of Architecture...". With these words Palladio began the Preface to his treatise entitled *The Four Books of Architecture*, published at Venice in 1570. He, the son of a miller, had been passionately interested in architecture since boyhood. Having gone to Vicenza to work as stone-cutter, Andrea found a protector in the man of letters Gian Giorgio Trissino, who allowed him to travel by his side and to visit the great Italian architectural works. The reconstruction of the Palace of Reason at Vicenza (1549) gave Palladio his first important chance to show his talent. Architect of the magnificent country villas around Venice, he designed the churches of San Giorgio Maggiore (1566) and the Redentore (1577-92) in Venice.

Francesco Zucchi, *Portrait of Andrea Palladio*, engraving, perhaps from a lost portrait of Giambattista Maganza.

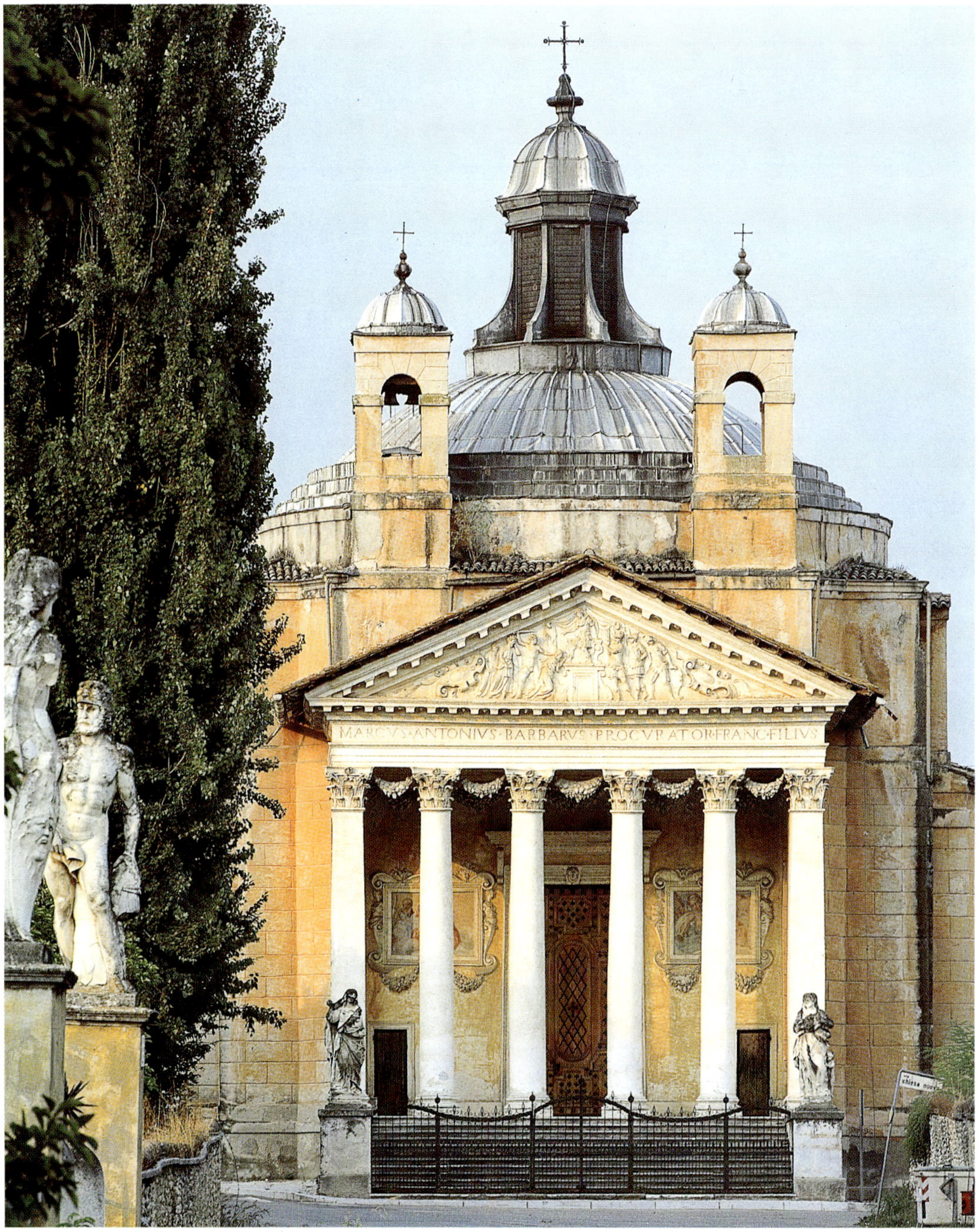

Andrea Palladio
The Maser Templet
1580
Maser, Villa Barbaro.

This is one of the Paduan architect's last works. Palladio returned to Maser at the request of Marcantonio Barbaro, Procurator of Saint Mark's, who planned to embellish his villa with other constructions. One of these, the *Templet*, offered the elderly Palladio a chance to confront the problem of the structure with circular plan according to the aesthetic and proportional canons he had studied in Vitruvius and theorized in the *Five Books*. It is easy enough to see in the *Templet* a sixteenth century version of Agrippa's Pantheon in Rome. Unlike the latter, however, the *Templet* has a lantern on the dome.

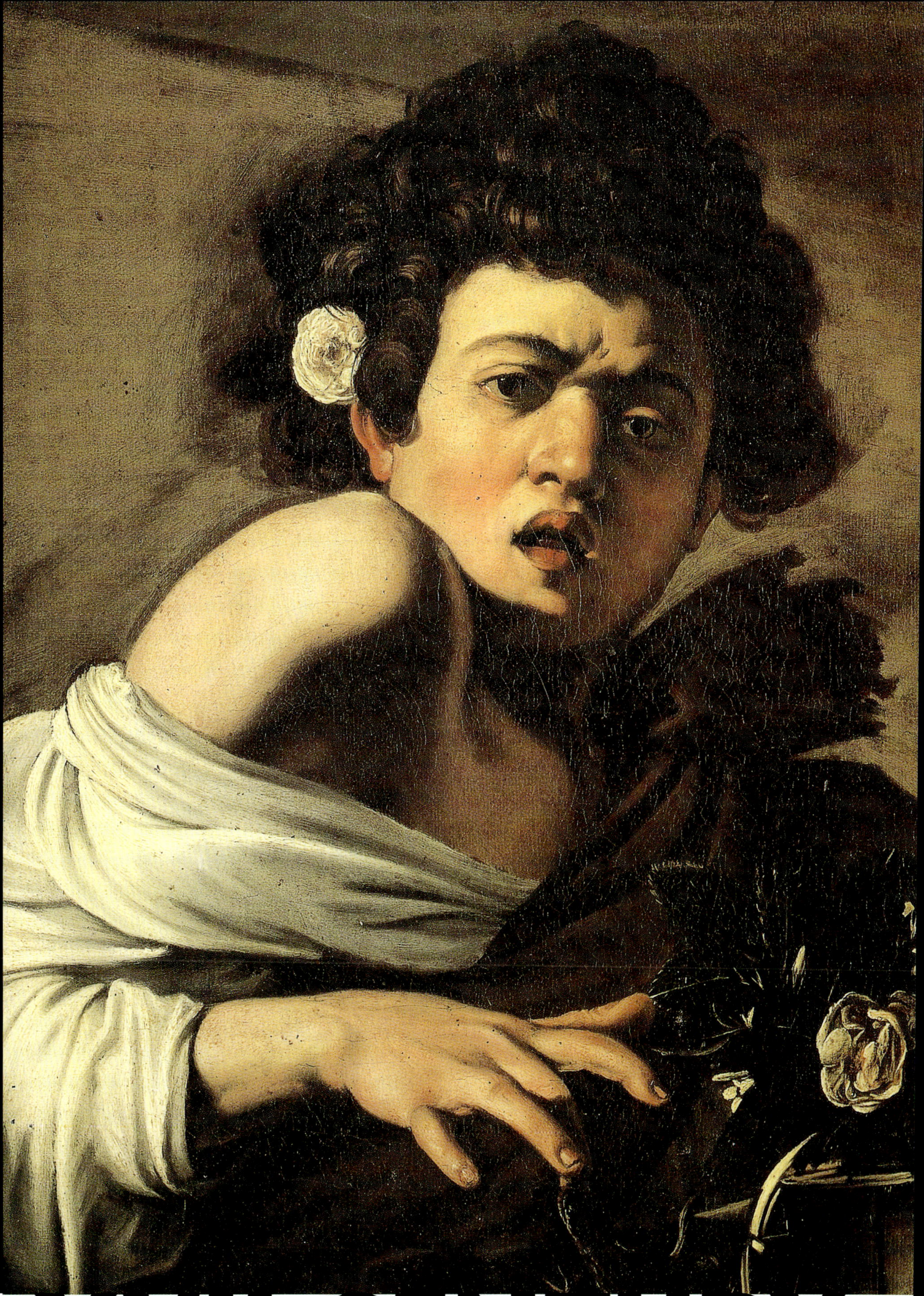

THE XVII CENTURY

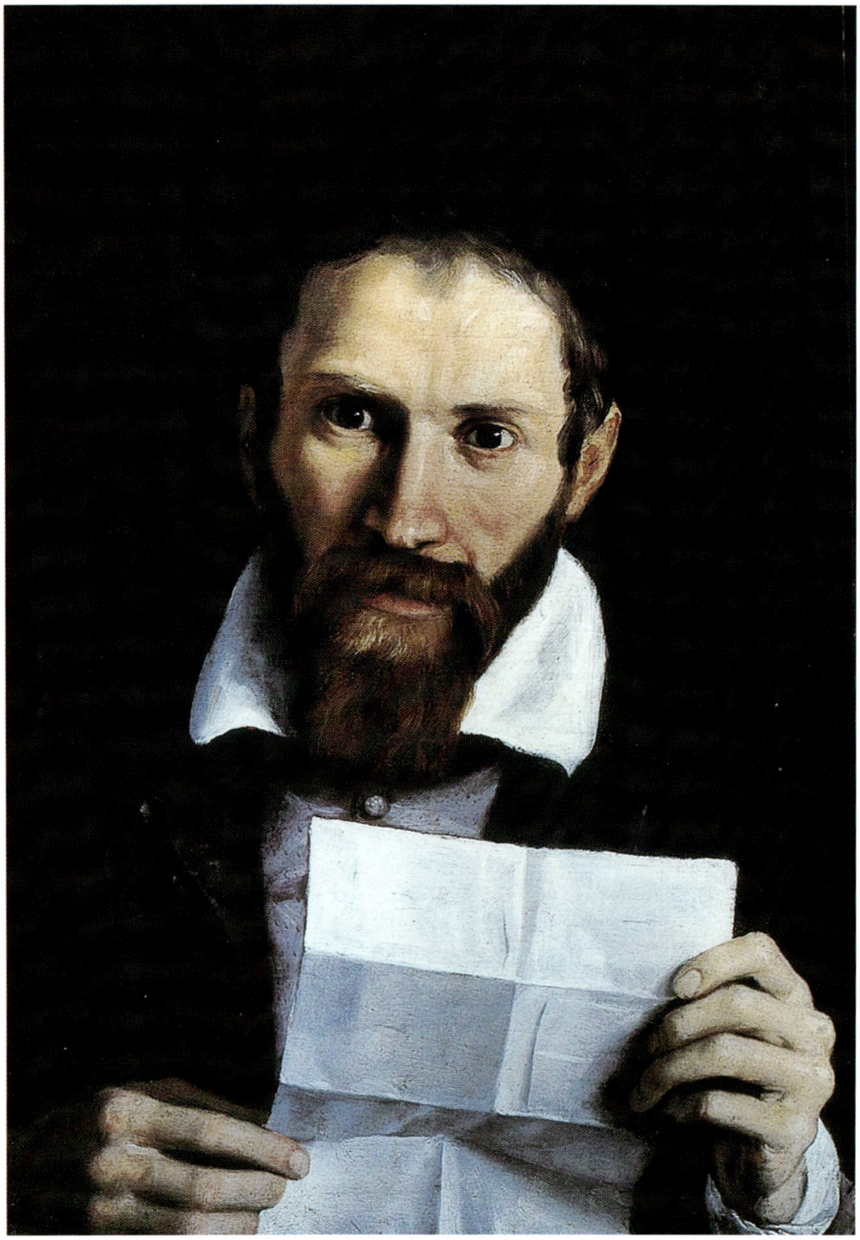

Domenichino (also attr. to Annibale Carracci), *Portrait of Cardinal Giovan Battista Agucchi*, c. 1630. York, City Art Gallery.

Preceding page: **Caravaggio**, *Boy Bitten by a Lizard*, c. 1595. Owned by the Roberto Longhi Foundation for Studies on Art History.

Although relegated to a political role of minor importance (apart from the international presence of the Church), Italy in the 17th century was not torn by the long, extenuating conflicts that were then sweeping through central-northern Europe. On the peninsula the presence of foreign powers was now to some extent taken for granted and, apart from the insurrections of Masaniello (1647) and those of Messina (1674), the small Italian states had come to terms with the great powers of the times, France and Spain, which boasted extensive possessions in Italy. But this substantial political and military subjugation was by no means reflected in the position Italy occupied in the world of art. First of all, our country was famed as a jewel-casket overflowing with artistic and archaeological treasures from a more or less distant past.

Already by the late 16th and early 17th century the "voyage to Italy" was deemed indispensable to the pictorial, sculptural and architectural training, or rather the cultural education of any good artist. Very few indeed were the great artists who did not make their tour of the peninsula, according to a custom that was continue down to the late 19th century. Starting with Bruegel the Elder, Italy was visited by Rubens, Velazquez and Van Dyck, to mention only the most famous. In Rome there was even to emerge an artistic current, that of the Bambochades, composed of foreign painters, headed by Van Laer.

The great fabric of painting had begun to split up into genres – from historical painting deemed the most important (to the point of fascinating the young Rembrandt) to the still life that was to meet with such success in the French-Flemish area. The latter even began to diversify into still further genres: from the still life with fruit culminating in Caravaggio's masterpiece, the *Chest of Fruit*, to the one composed of musical instruments, at which Baschenis excelled. The role of Italy was not, however, that of simple "reservoir" of the European collective imagination, but was much more active. In Rome especially, that international artistic language (exported from Spain as far as South America) which goes

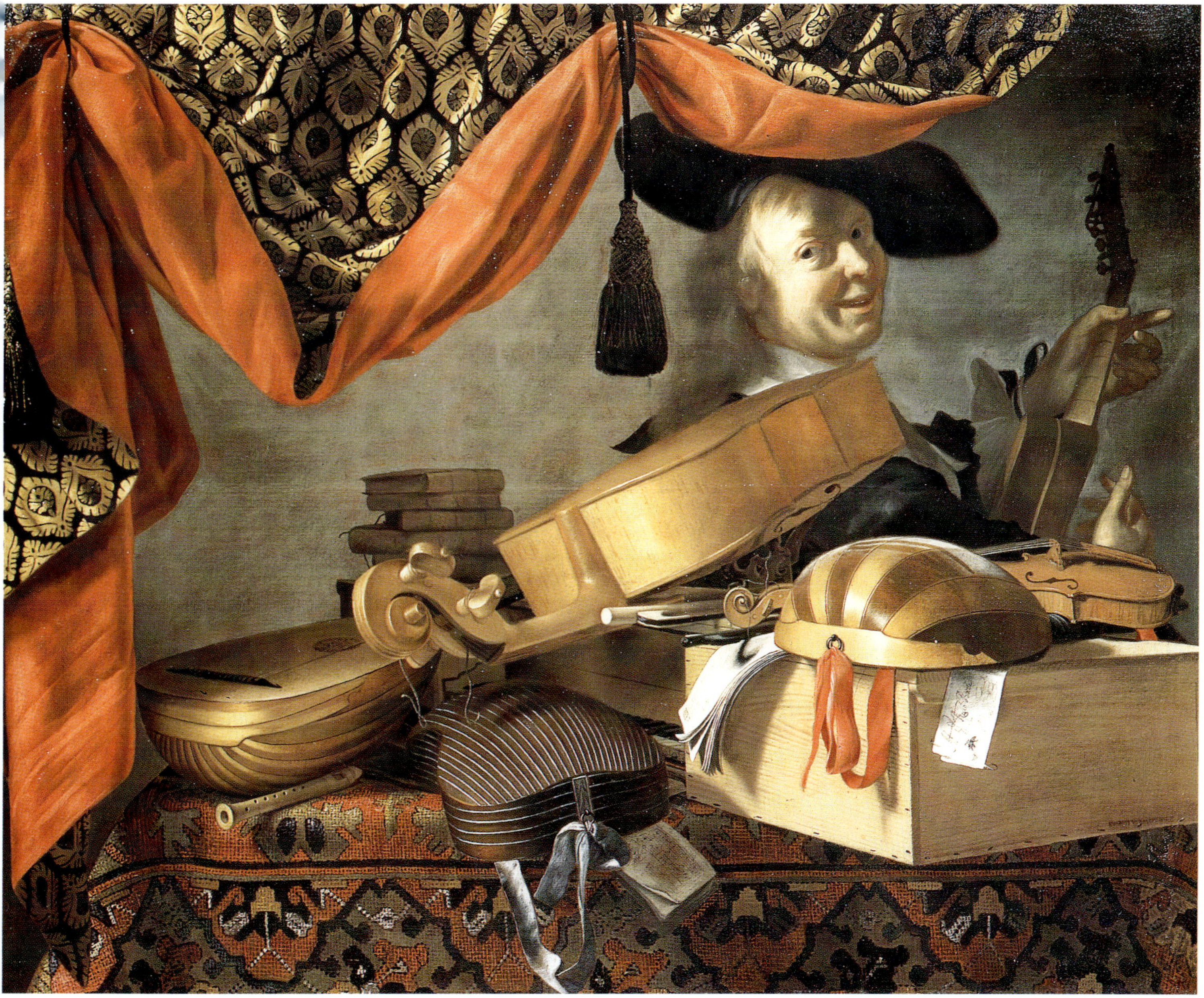

under the name of Baroque was developing rapidly. The term – which originally indicated pearls of irregular form, gibbous pearls, or those ambiguous syllogisms codified by rhetoric, was to be used only at the end of the 18th century, and with a negative significance.

The most recent critics have entirely rehabilitated the Baroque style, even tending to consider it one of the categories of the human spirit. Certainly, the new style did not emerge contemporaneously in all of the arts. On the contrary, its various currents and trends were to interweave continuously throughout the course of the century. In architecture, for instance, the façade of Santa Susanna in Rome, built by Carlo Maderno between 1597 and 1603, can be considered the first manifestation of the Baroque; in sculpture the new trend was well represented by the *St Cecilia* sculpted by Stefano Maderno precisely in the year 1600. The façade of the church, in fact, while inspired by Giacomo della Porta's Church of Gesù, transforms into motion and volumes what had until then been treated as a kind of "curtain", designed and decorated in almost graphic terms. In similar manner, the sculpture of the other Maderno emphasized one of the

Evaristo Baschenis and Salomon Adler, *Musical Instruments with the Portrait of a Man,* painting found in 1996 in the storage deposit of the Brera Academy, c. 1675.

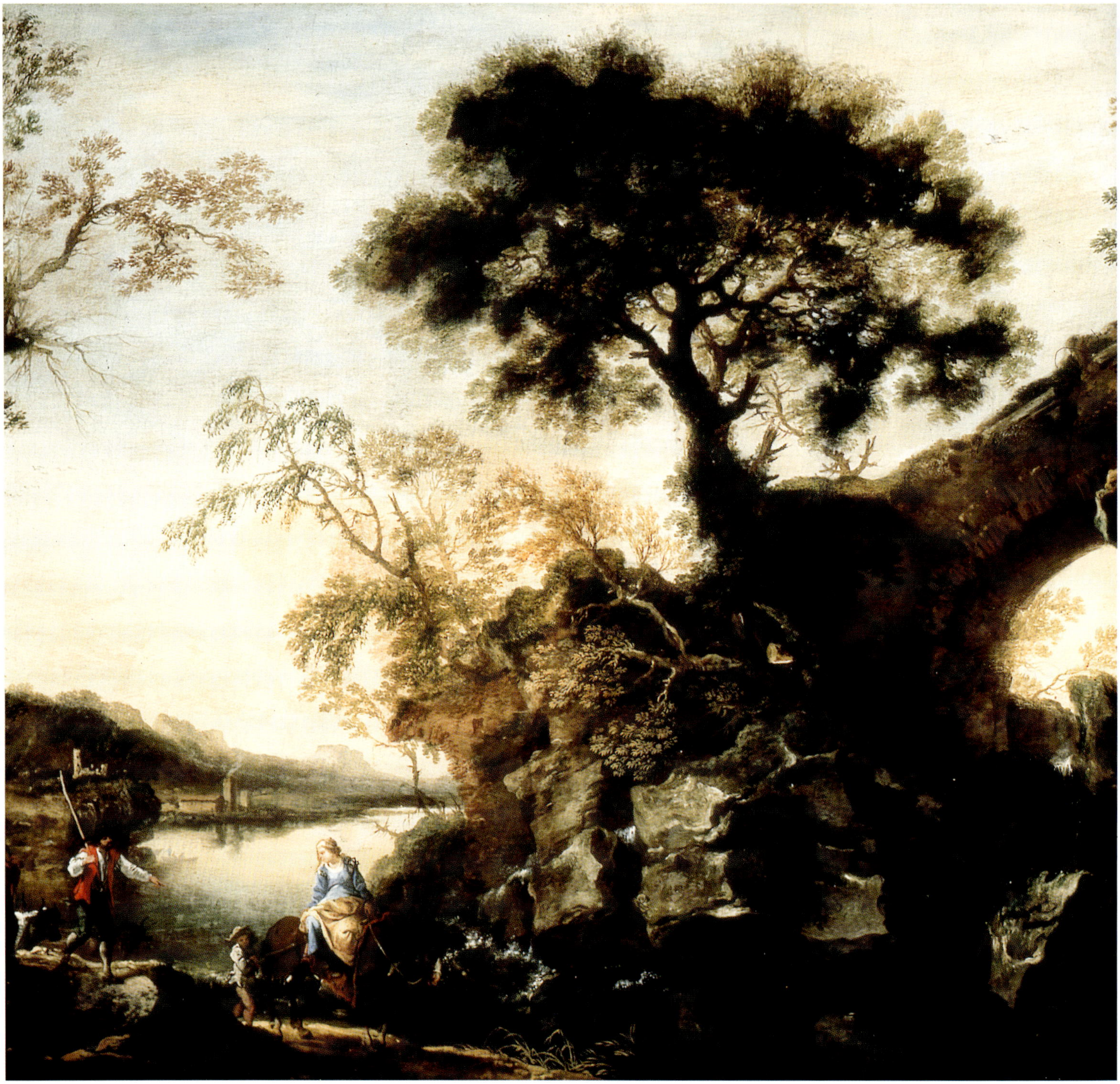

Salvator Rosa, *Rocky Panorama with Waterfall*, c. 1640. Budapest, Szépmüvészeti Múzeum.

themes characteristic of the Baroque poetics, that of the inclinations of the soul, aimed chiefly at involving the spectator emotionally. These trends, briefly summarized here, were developed with enormous intensity through such outstanding figures as Bernini, whose contribution is vitally important in both sculpture and architecture, as exemplified by the Church of Sant'Andrea al Quirinale and the famous sculptural group of *Apollo and Daphne*. No matter how imposing, however, the figure of Bernini represents only one of the multiple facets of the Baroque.

Equally important roles were those of Francesco Borromini, an architect endowed with inexhaustible imagination, and Pietro da Cortona, architect and painter. And along with these were

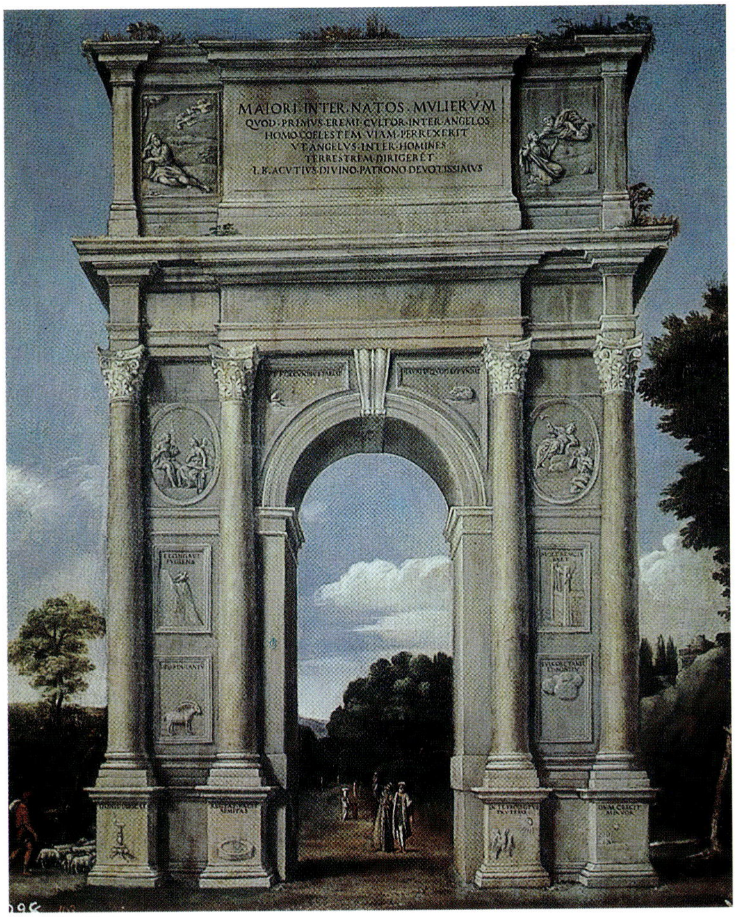

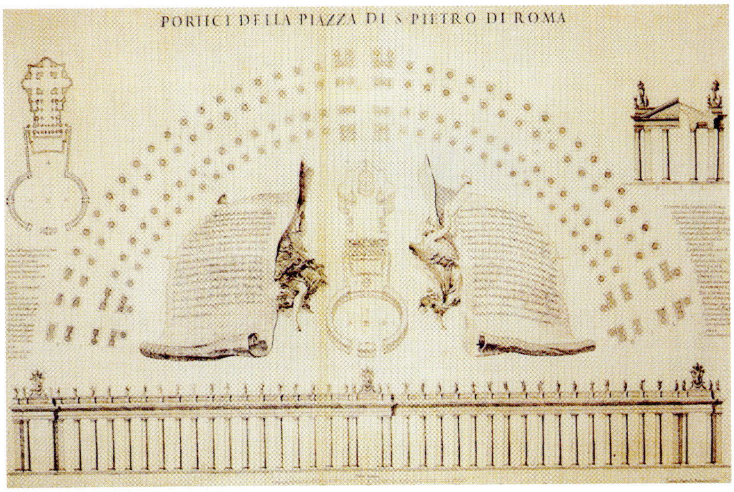

Domenichino, *Triumphal Arch*, 1609. Madrid, Prado Museum.

Giovanni Battista Bonacina, *Section View of St Peter's Square*, 1659. Biblioteca Apostolica Vaticana, Archivi Chigi.

Giovanni Battista Falda, *View of the Pantheon*, with the bell towers erected by Carlo Maderno between 1625 and 1628. Rome, Biblioteca Casanatense.

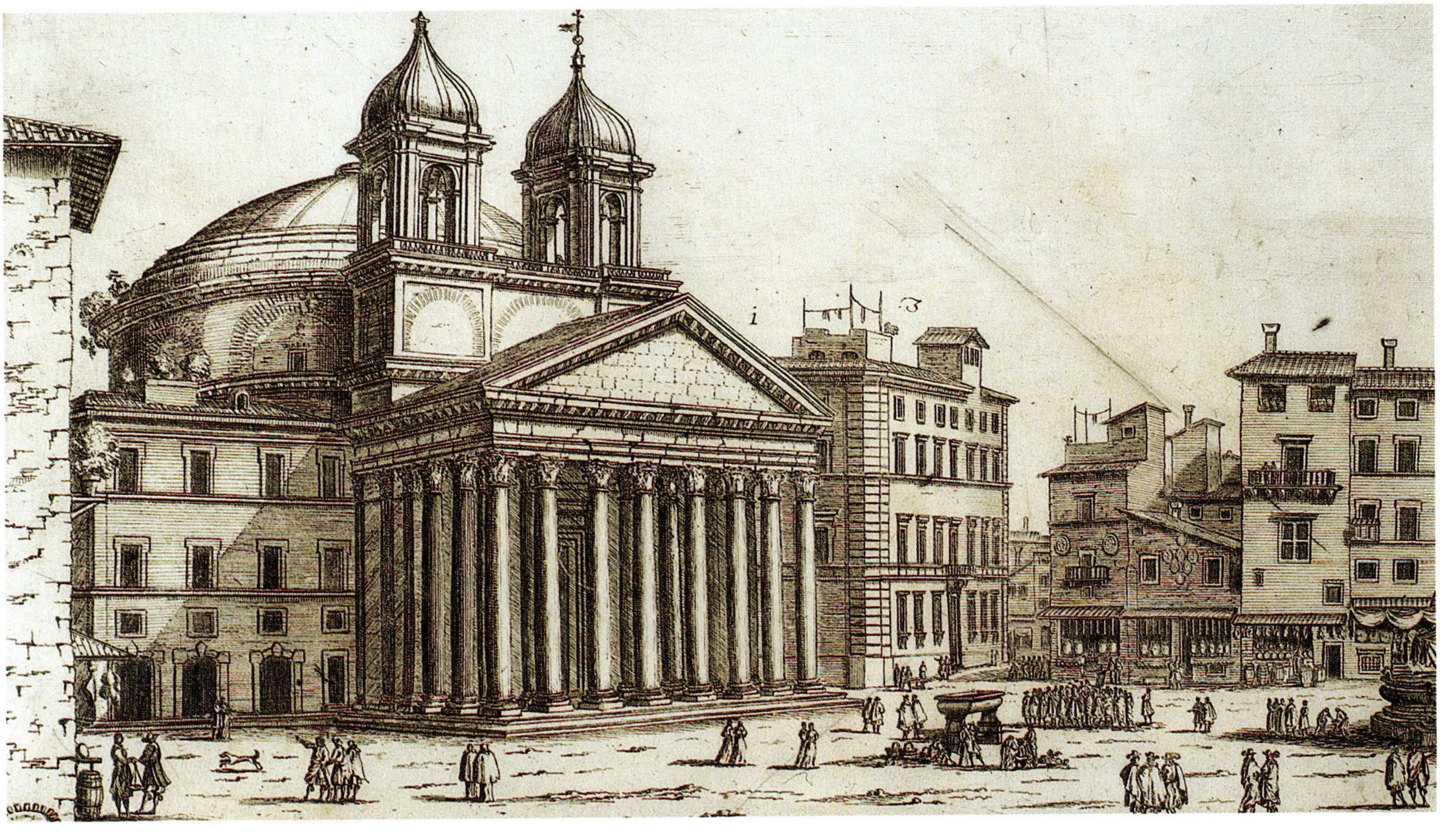

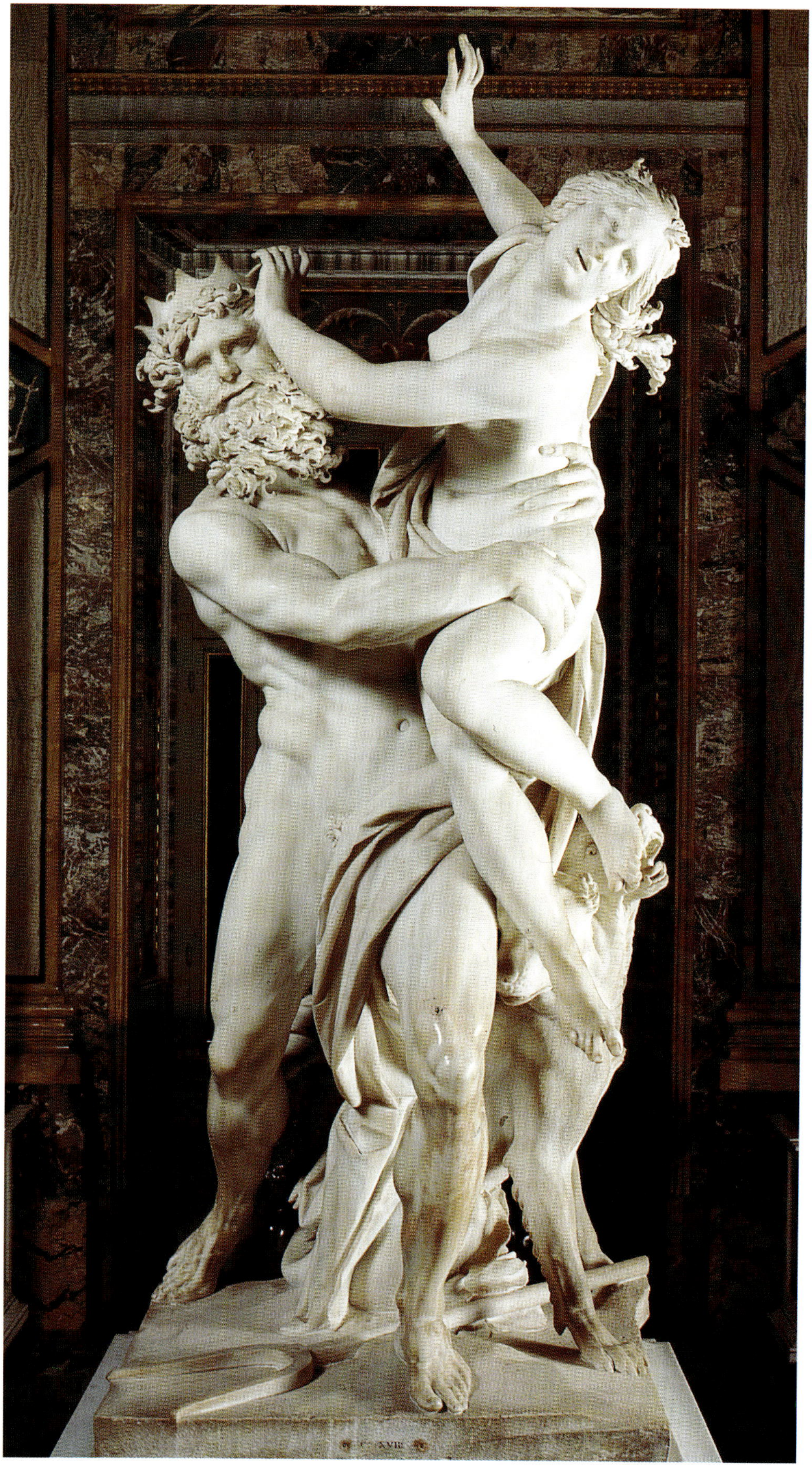

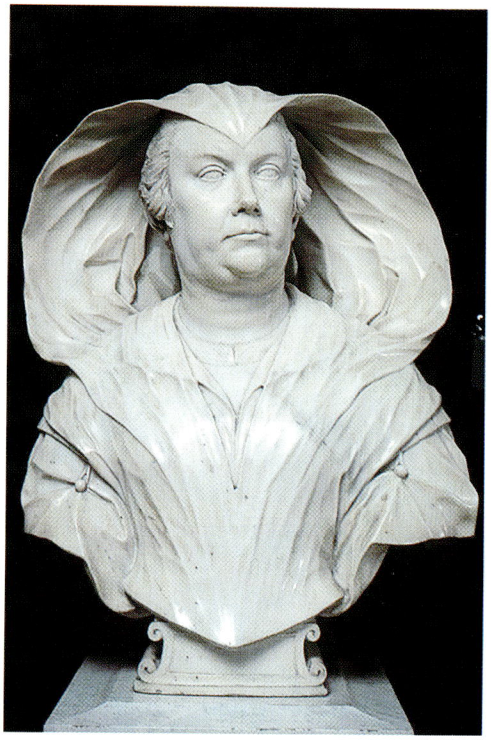

Alessandro Algardi, *Bust of Olimpia Maidalchini*, c. 1646. Rome, Galleria Doria Pamphilj.

Gianlorenzo Bernini, *The Rape of Proserpine*, 1621-22. Rome, Galleria Borghese.

Algardi and Duquesnoy in sculpture, Rainaldi and Maderno in architecture. The 17th century was one of great architectural initiatives: from the completion of St Peter's with its colonnade to the realization of the dramatic Piazza Navona. The great architecture of the 17th century was not, however, confined to Rome alone. We need only recall the names of Baldassarre Longhena and Santa Maria della Salute in Venice, the work of Guarino Guarini in Turin and that of Cosimo Fanzago in Naples. In like manner, great 17th century painting is not Roman alone, although it began in the city of the Popes with the arrival of the Bolognese painters led by Annibale Carracci, Ludovico and Agostino followed by Domenichino and Guido Reni.

It is hard to identify a specific Baroque current of painting. The Bolognese school tended toward a return to Classicism, although the works of Guercino, including the famous frescoes in the Casino Ludovisi, fell wholly within the Baroque sphere, indulging in perspective effects like those which, at the end of the century, were to spread over the ceilings of the Churches of Gesù and of Sant'Ignazio. The entire century was however dominated by the towering figure of Caravaggio, whose luministic approach, although emptied of its original spiritual significance, was to spawn innumerable followers and schools. A broad gulf separates the school of the Carracci from that of Caravaggio. The former emulated the pattern of the Renaissance where pupils were taught directly by the master. Only a few, instead, were the disciples (among them his friend Orazio Gentileschi) working shoulder to shoulder with Merisi, who was to die at the age of only thirty-nine. And yet through artists such as Guido Cagnacci from Forlì, Mattia Preti from Calabria, Bernardo Cavallino from Naples and many others, Caravaggio's style was to spread throughout Italy and beyond the Alps, to Spain and France in particular. The great role of Italian art had been once again renewed.

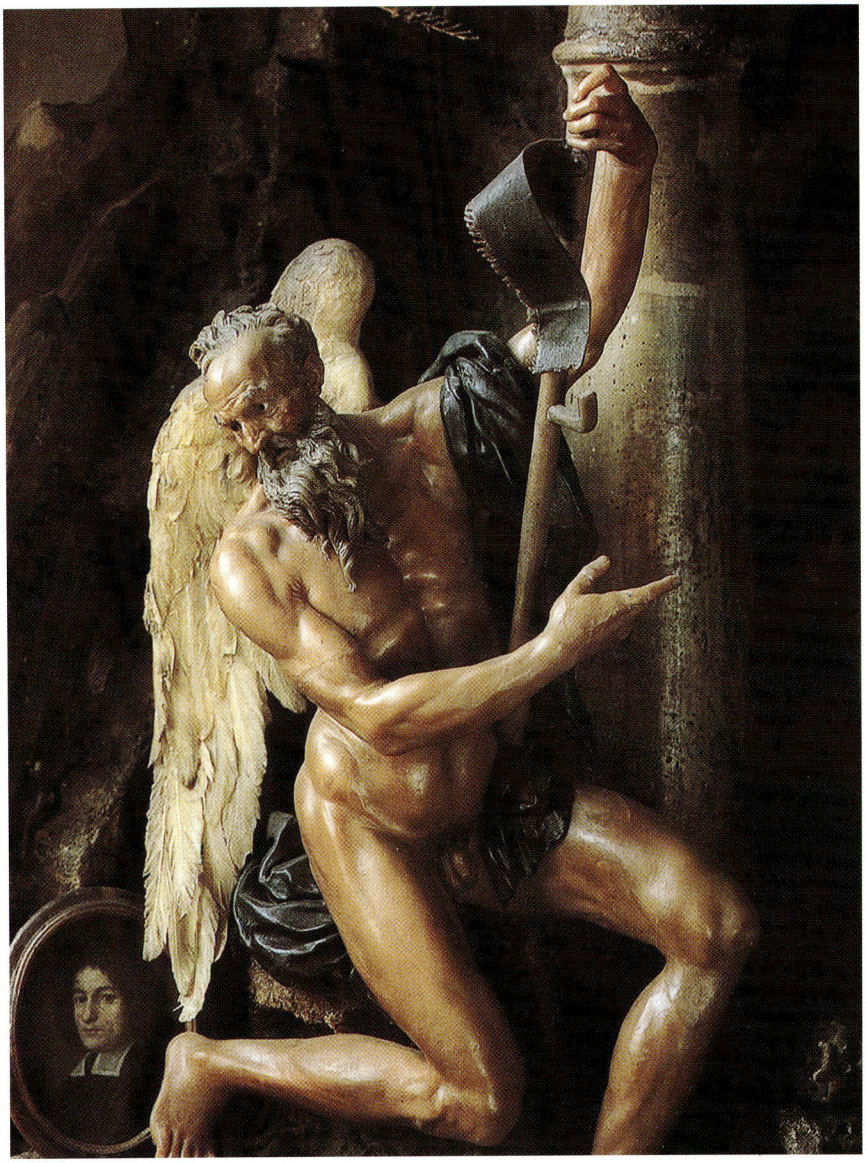

Gaetano Zumbo, *The Triumph of Time*, detail with self-portrait, c. 1694. Florence, Museo della Specola.

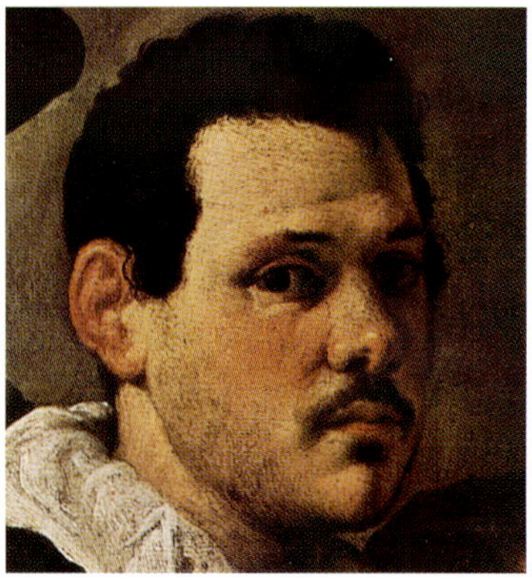

Annibale Carracci, *Self-portrait*, detail c. 1585. Milan, Brera Pinacoteca.

The Carracci Family

Agostino
(Bologna 1557 – Parma 1602)
Annibale
(Bologna 1560 – Rome 1609)
Ludovico
(Bologna 1555 – 1619)

To speak of the Carracci family as a whole is to re-evoke that cultural forum which was the Accademia degli Incamminati (or of Drawing), the lodestone for the artistic life of Bologna, and not for that city alone. Founded in 1582, the Accademia, later re-baptized by the theorist Giovan Pietro Bellori (1613-96) "dei Desiderosi" ... "for the desire they all had to learn", was founded for the express purpose of going beyond that kind of art (painting in particular) which late Mannerism had ultimately congealed into the rules and theoretical precepts of a now vacuous, sophisticated aesthetics. The Carracci school intended to revitalize painting by having theory derive from practice, so that being painting became a committed style of life. Masters, collaborators and pupils were

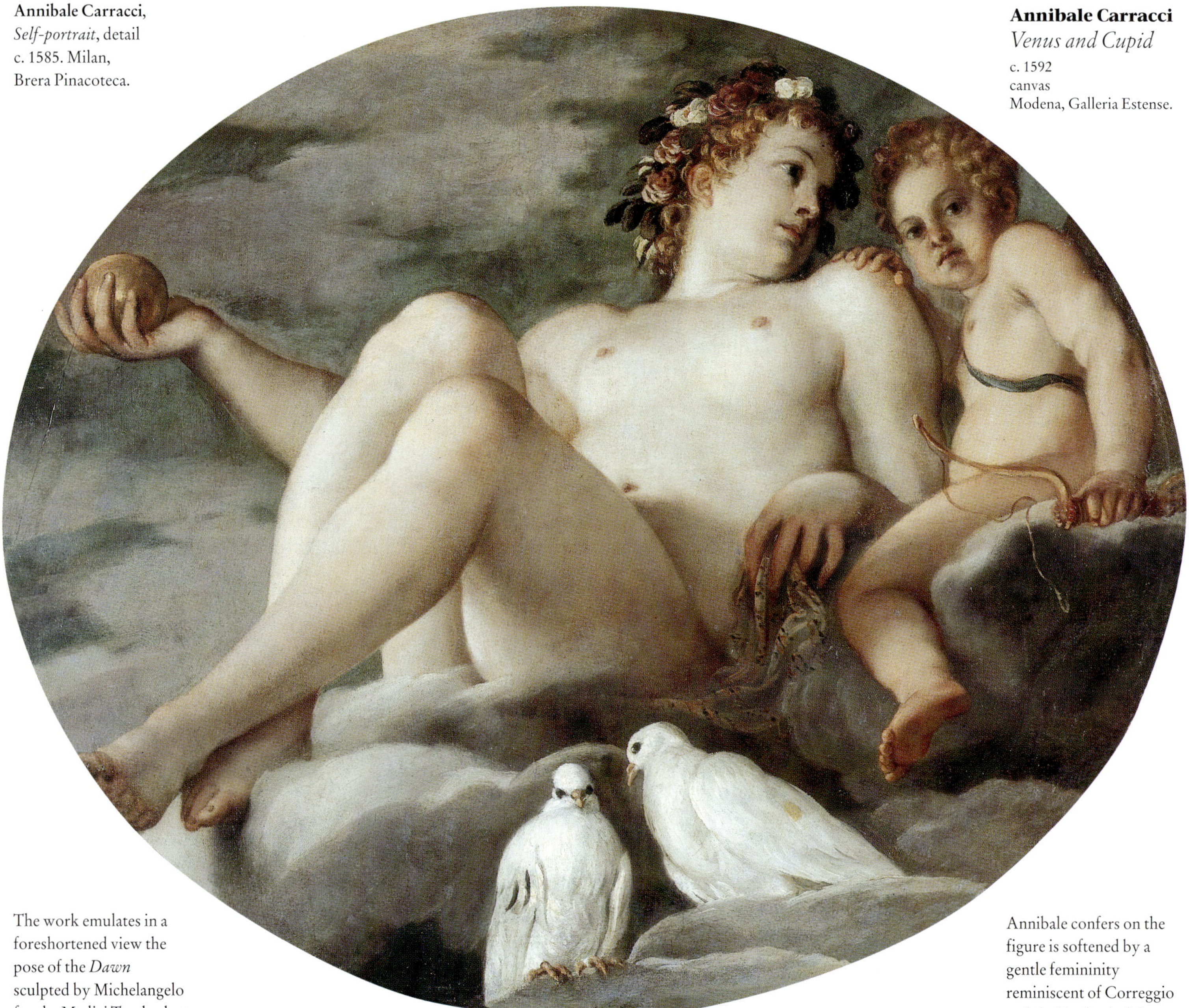

Annibale Carracci
Venus and Cupid
c. 1592
canvas
Modena, Galleria Estense.

The work emulates in a foreshortened view the pose of the *Dawn* sculpted by Michelangelo for the Medici Tombs, but the monumentality which Annibale confers on the figure is softened by a gentle femininity reminiscent of Correggio and the Raphael of the Farnesina.

involved in an adventure that put them all on the same level, driven by a single aim: that of breathing life into painting. What made the difference was drawing from life, along with study of anatomy and, obviously, of perspective. The soul of the institution was Agostino, Annibale's elder brother, an ideal master thanks to his vast culture and talent for teaching. In his style echoes of Tintoretto, Correggio and Raphael were blended. Agostino participated in decorating the Farnese Gallery in Rome and in other joint enterprises of the Carracci family. In 1599 he left Bologna after quarreling with his elder brother and remained at the service of Ranuccio Farnese (1592-1622). Annibale is undoubtedly the family genius, the innovator of Italian pictorial language and the least theoretical of the three: "We painters must speak with our hands" he answered Antonio one day. In addition to the decorations of Palazzo Fava in Bologna (1583-84) and those of the Farnese Gallery (1595-1600), he painted such unrivaled masterpieces as *The Butcher Shop* (1582-83, Oxford, Christ Church) and the *Bean Eater* (1583-84, Rome, Colonna Gallery). Already in their subject matter those paintings renewed the language of art at the end of the century. Ludovico, the cousin of the other two artists, dedicated himself to religious themes in particular.

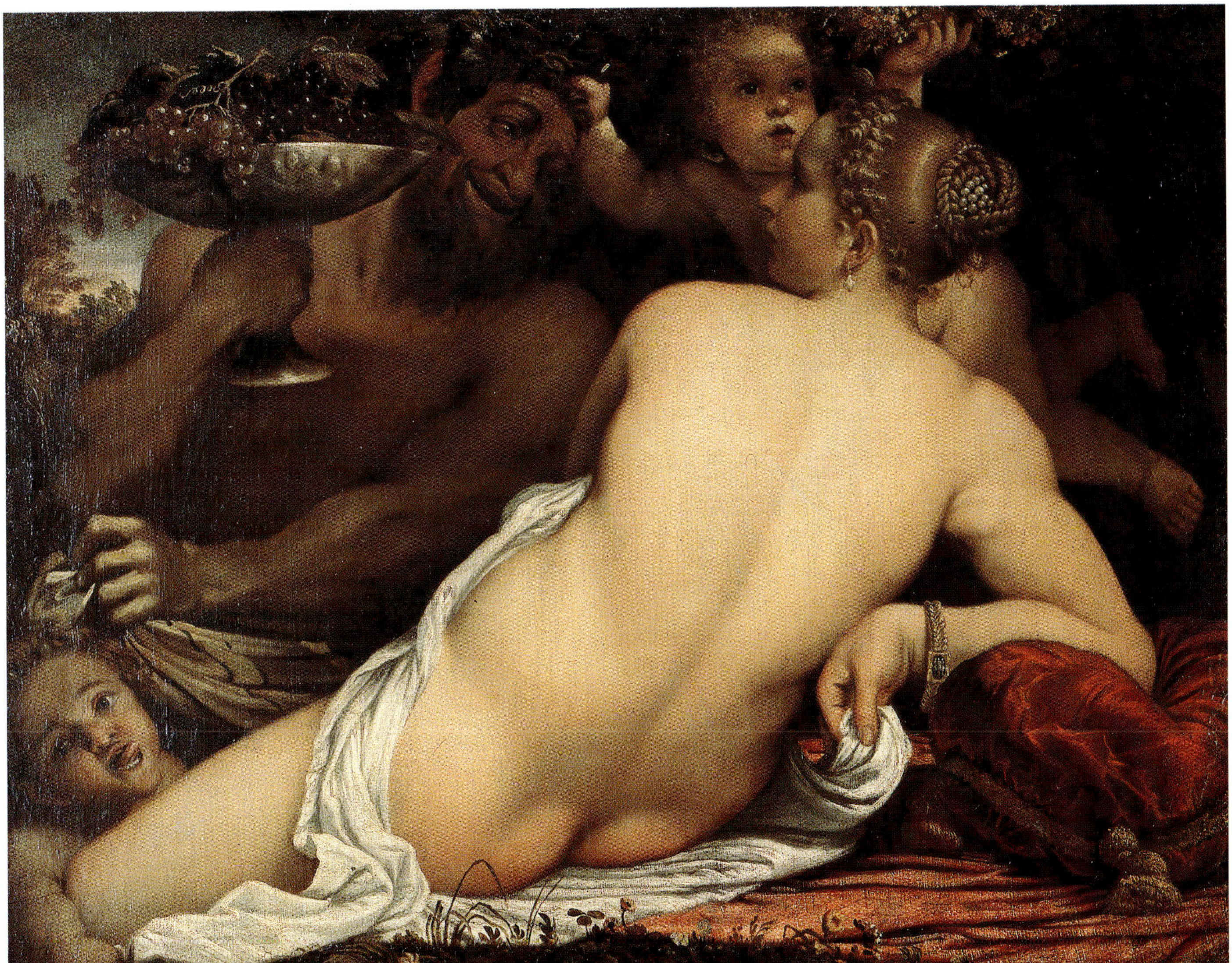

Annibale Carracci
Venus, a Satyr and Two Cherubs
c. 1588
canvas
Florence, Uffizi Gallery.

A curious episode told in relation to this painting clearly illustrates the spirit of the Carracci Academy. According to Malvasia (1616-83), the model who posed for Venus was Ludovico, who did not hesitate to bare his body down to the hips to favor his cousin's work. This was the atmosphere of collaboration that bound the members of the Carracci artistic coalition. In a symbolic reading , the satyr and the littler Eros at the lower left represent vulgar love, Venus and Anteros celestial love.

Ludovico Carracci
Rinaldo and Armida
c. 1602
canvas
Naples, Capodimonte
National Museum.

The work belongs to Ludovico's Roman stage. He was called to Rome by Annibale and by him stimulated to explore the terrain of a rediscovered Classicism. A canvas depicting the same subject, preserved in the same museum, is in fact attributed to Annibale. The one shown here is thus an exception of a kind in Ludovico's production. Apart from collaboration with his cousins in Palazzo Fava at Bologna, where he painted mythological subjects, Ludovico dedicated himself to religious and devout subjects, to some extent anticipating the calm equilibrium of Andrea Sacchi (1599-1661), who was to study his work thoroughly.

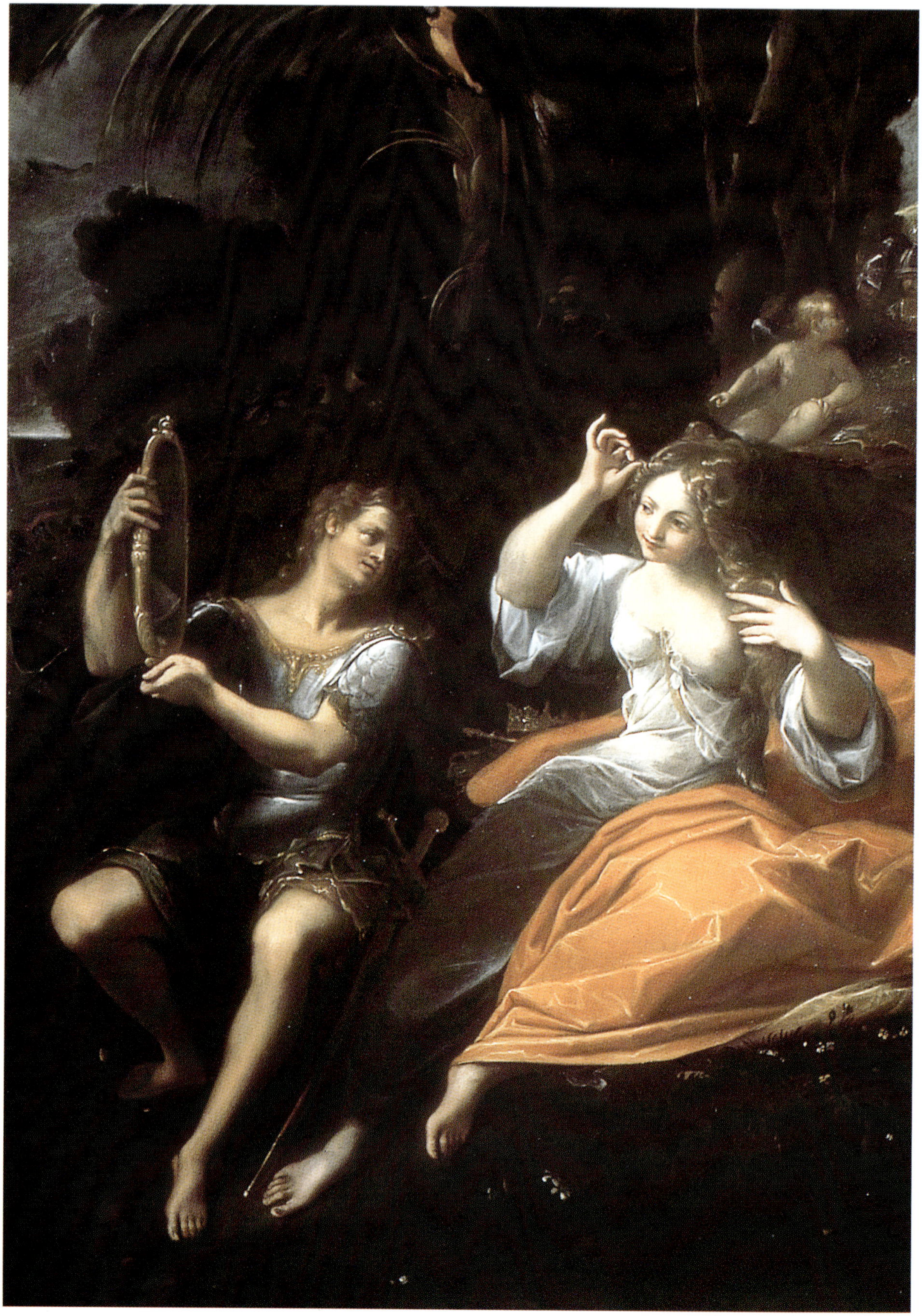

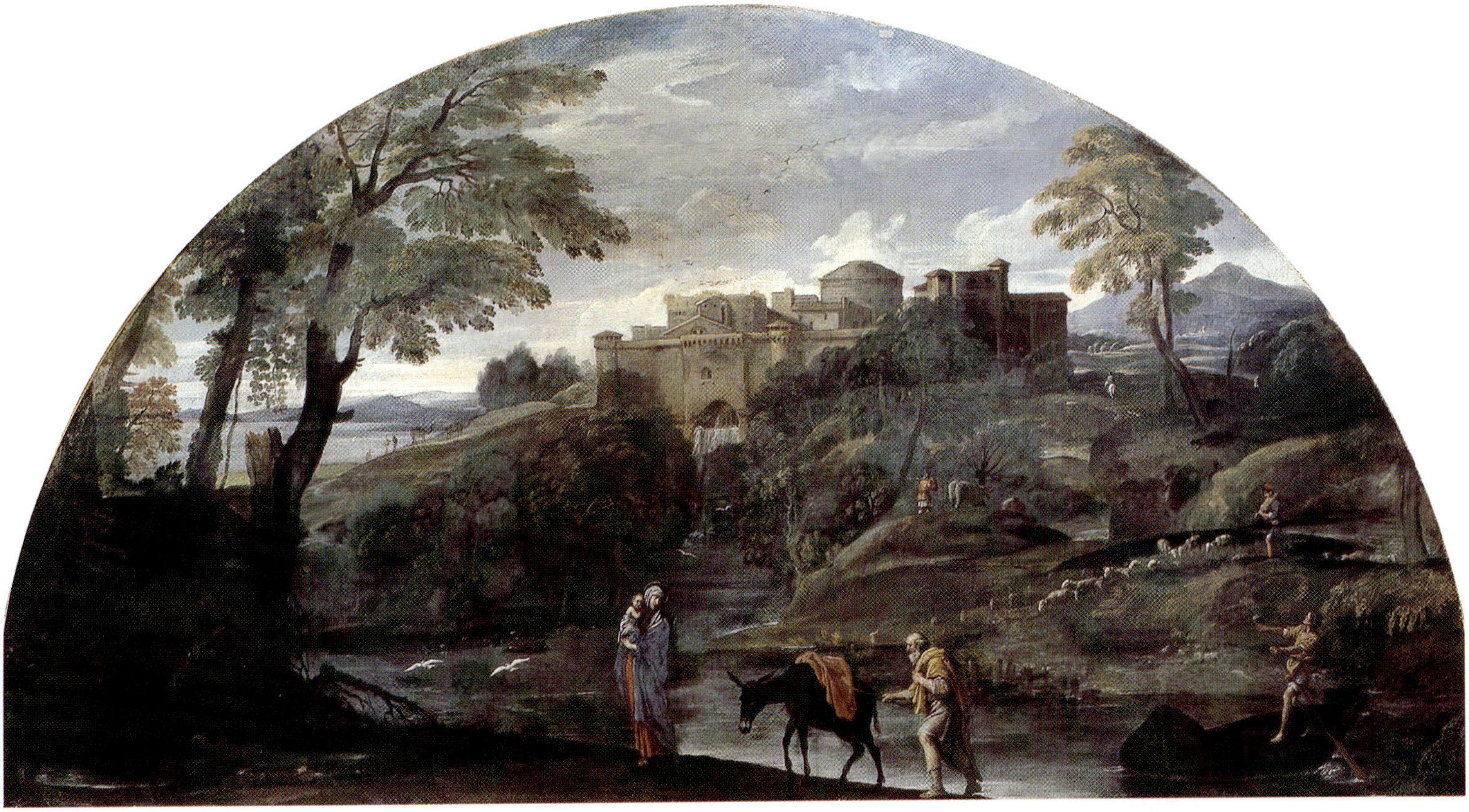

Annibale Carracci
Landscape with the Flight into Egypt
c. 1604
canvas
Rome, Galleria Doria Pamphilj.

The famous lunette is a milestone in the development of 17th century landscape painting in Rome. Even the lesson taught by Poussin (1594-1665) would be incomprehensible without Carracci's masterful precedent. The painting comes from the Chapel of Palazzo Aldobrandini al Corso, where it completed the decoration along with five more paintings of the same form, according to Bellori. Its original collocation is enough in itself to explain the innovatory character of the composition. Instead of concentrating attention on the sacred episode, Carracci sets the Gospel story within a fluvial landscape of gently sloping hills, thus restoring to the event all of the flavor of daily life.

Ludovico Carracci
The Preaching of the Baptist
c. 1589
canvas, detail
Bologna, Pinacoteca Nazionale.

The work shows that turn in the direction of chiaroscuro and vivid highlighting already displayed in the well-known *Conversion of St Paul* in the same Pinacoteca. The lowered viewpoint and the insistence on diagonals, which appear to mark the direction of the light, confer great dynamism on the painting.

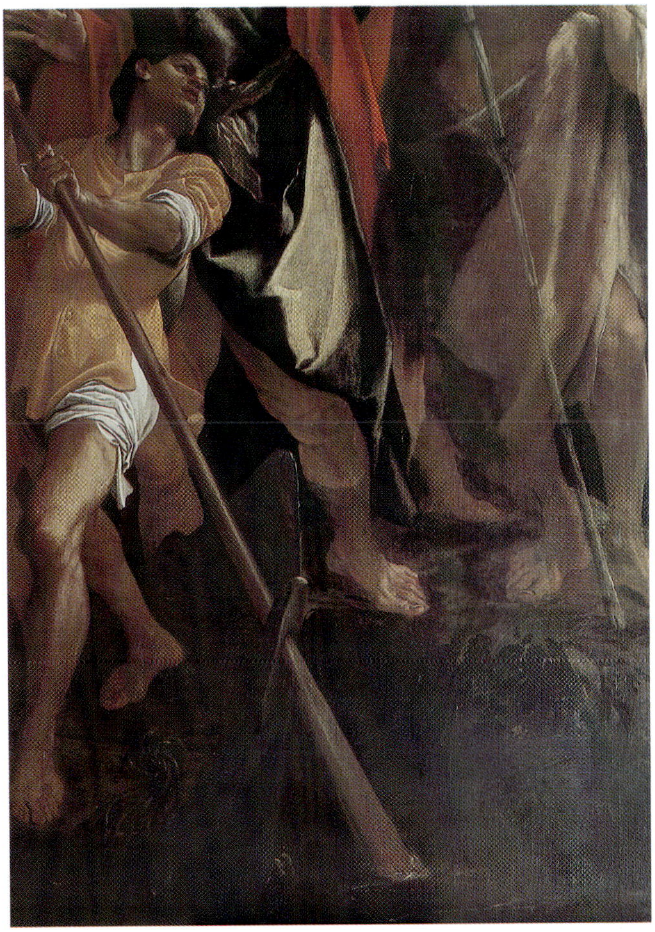

Annibale Carracci
Jove and Juno
c. 1597
fresco, detail
Rome, Palazzo Farnese.

The painting forms part of the frieze that runs along the base of the barrel-vault ceiling in the gallery where the most important scenes are frescoed. The stories of four famous pairs of mythological lovers, designed to illustrate the concept of profane love, appear in the panels on the false cornice. The suggestions of Classicism are evident. Annibale looks in one direction toward Raphael's figures in the Psyche Loggia at the Farnesina, while in the other he is inspired by the famous sculpture group of the *Laocoonte*, discovered at Rome in 1506, and already copied by the Florentine sculptor Baccio Bandinelli in about 1520. The head of Jove shown here is clearly inspired by the Hellenistic statue of the Laocoonte.

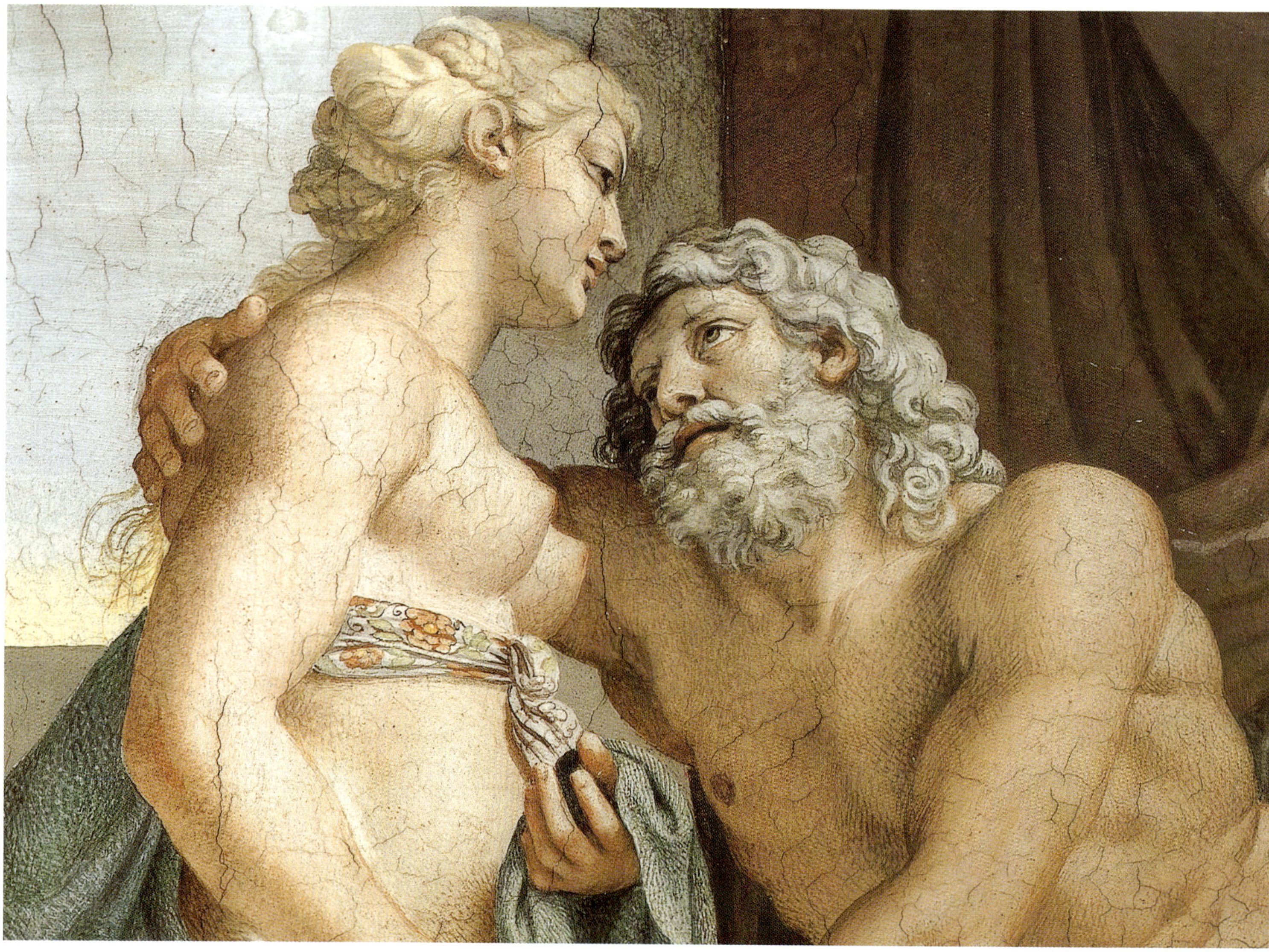

Annibale Carracci
Apollo and Marsyas
c. 1597
fresco
Rome, Palazzo Farnese.

The arrangement of the decoration with the medallion in the center, the atlases in false marble or stucco at the sides and the nudes seated below, clearly reiterates the motifs experimented by Michelangelo in the ceiling of the Sistine Chapel. The mythological episodes represented are taken mainly from Ovid's *Metamorphosis*. The image of Marsyas flayed by Apollo who has defeated him in a musical contest (*Metamorphosis* VI, vv. 382-400) recalls the theme of divine vengeance, already confronted by Raphael in the frescoes on the ceiling of the Stanza della Segnatura.

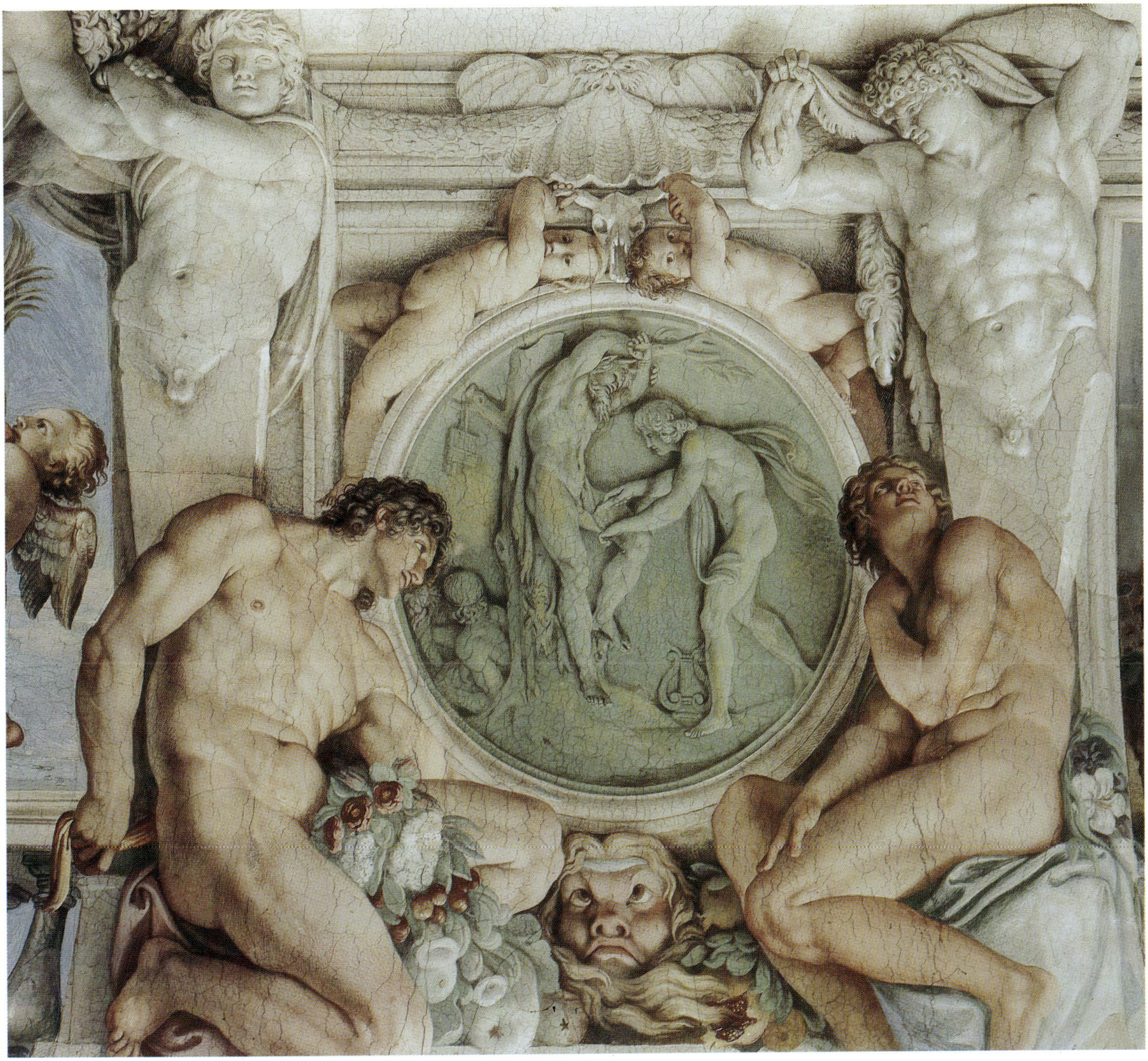

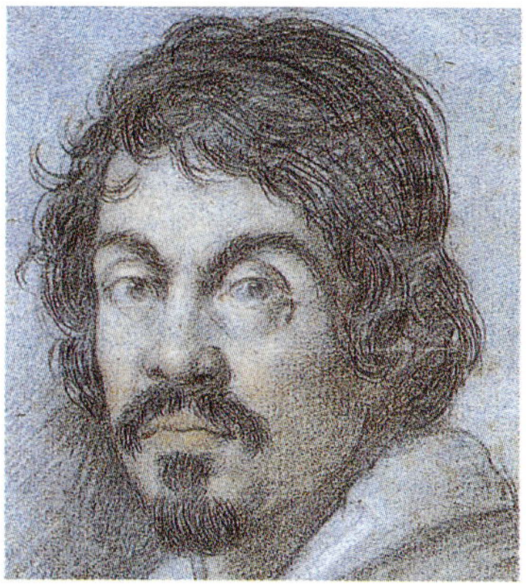

Caravaggio

(Michelangelo Merisi,
Milan 1571 – Porto Ercole 1610)

It is only in the last quarter of a century that the true artistic and human dimension of Michelangelo Merisi, known as Caravaggio from the town where he spent his childhood, has been recognized. Undoubtedly, the intriguing cliché of "peintre maudit", based on the artist's irregular life, has been hard to die ; so much so that still today the artist is sometimes considered a kind of miscreant, born of a family that was poor and totally without means. The artist's father Fermo Merisi was instead "master of the household" of the Marquis Caravaggio and, as such, belonged to the local minor nobility. The family left Milan because of the epidemic of plague in which the painter's father and paternal grandparents died. The child Michelangelo – given this name because he was born on September 29, the feast day of St Michael – spent his boyhood at Caravaggio until 1584, when he was apprenticed

Ottavio Leoni,
Portrait of Caravaggio,
detail, c. 1600.
Florence, Biblioteca Marucelliana.

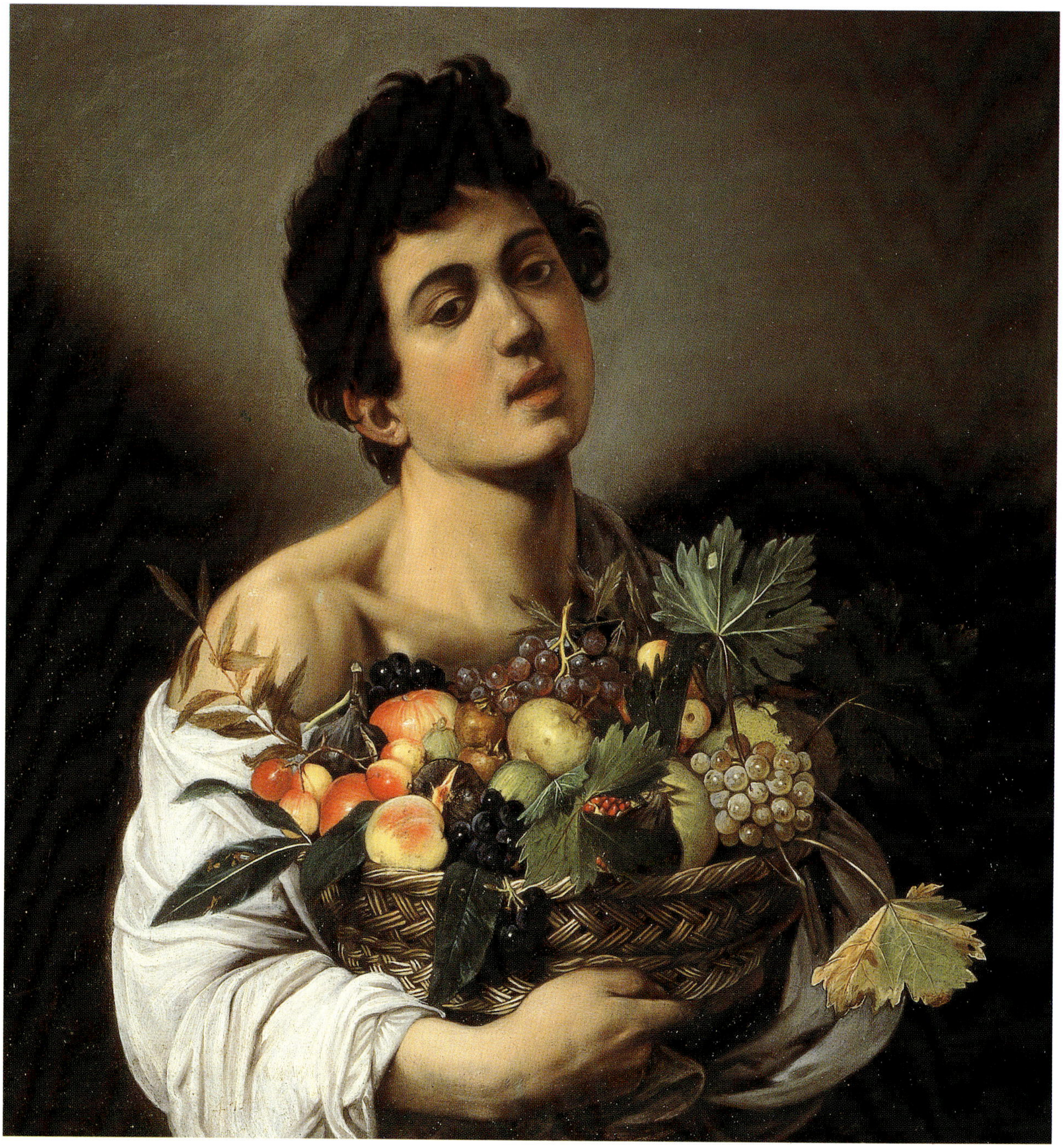

Caravaggio
Boy with a Chest of Fruit
1591
canvas
Rome, Galleria Borghese.

That this is a youthful work can be recognized immediately by the overly tense right shoulder, which however does not spoil the composition. Undoubtedly influenced by the young Merisi's apprenticeship in the Cavalier d'Arpino's workshop, where he dedicated himself to painting motifs of fruit, the basket is the direct ancestor of the *Still Life* now in the Ambrosiana in Milan. Perfectly inscribed within a triangular scheme, the boy, whose features recall those of the young artist, offers to the spectator a triumph of colors that kindle with light the few tints of the composition.

in Milan to the painter Simone Peterzano. Later, after the death of his mother, Michelangelo, then only about twenty years old, went to Rome where he was given hospitality and protection by Cardinal Francesco Maria Del Monte, ambassador of the Grand Duke of Tuscany. The Cardinal not only welcomed the artist to his palace and put him in contact with the erudite prelates of the Roman Curia who were to become his patrons, but also procured him his first public commission, that of the Contarelli Chapel in San Luigi de' Francesi. It was in Rome that Caravaggio's artistic and cultural development was perfected. On the one hand he was fascinated by the sophisticated Christological symbolism known to the cardinals and the Roman theologists he frequented, on the other he often ran into trouble with the law due to his violent, rebellious character. From 1603 to 1606, a series of regrettable incidents occurred, culminating in a brawl during which the artist killed a certain Tommasoni. The last years of Caravaggio's life were thus lived as a fugitive, in Naples, Malta, Messina and Palermo, awaiting the pardon that the Pope was to grant him too late.

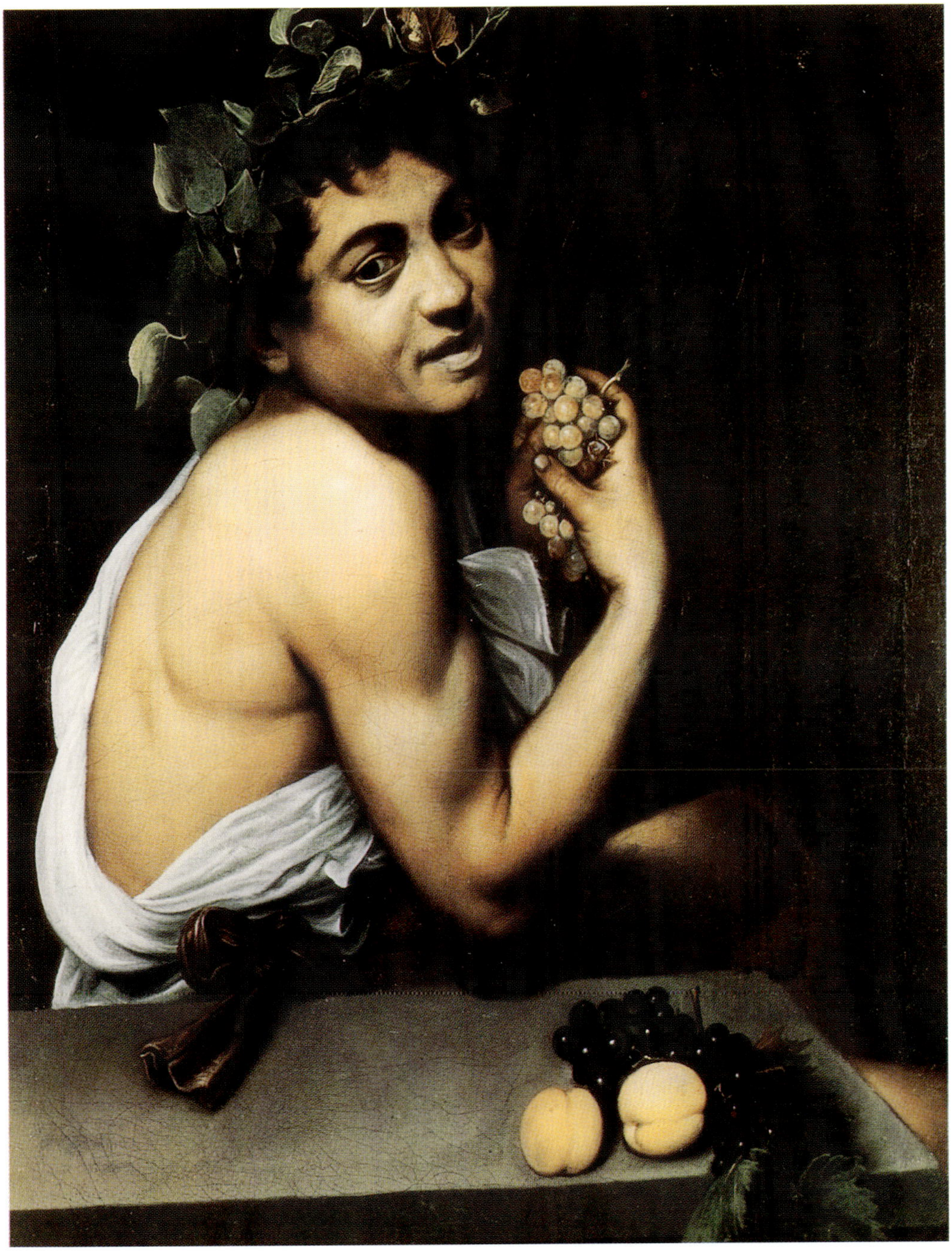

Caravaggio
The Sick Bacchus
c. 1593-94
canvas
Rome, Galleria Borghese.

The painting is a self-portrait showing the painter just recovered from an illness severe enough to require hospitalization in the Hospital of the Consolation in Rome. That the young man portrayed has been ill can be seen from his coloring, his pale face and dry lips. Life in Rome was not easy for Caravaggio at first, before being welcomed to the palace of Cardinal Del Monte. Certainly, eating only salad every evening in Pandolfo Pucci's tavern had not improved his health. But the symbolic decision to present himself as Bacchus, god of life, alludes to a desire for resurrection.

Caravaggio
Judith and Holophernes
1595-96
canvas
Rome, Galleria Nazionale d'Arte Antica, Palazzo Barberini.

According to the story told in the Bible, Judith, by feigning friendliness and compliance, manages to enter the camp of the Philistines, who are about to attack Israel, and the tent of their general Holophernes. Finding him sprawled out on his bed drunk, Judith, the heroine of the Jewish nation, staunchly takes up a saber and beheads him. Caravaggio, like Botticelli and Donatello before him, dramatically portrays the scene as if it were happening in his own day, thus rendering its meaning vitally topical.

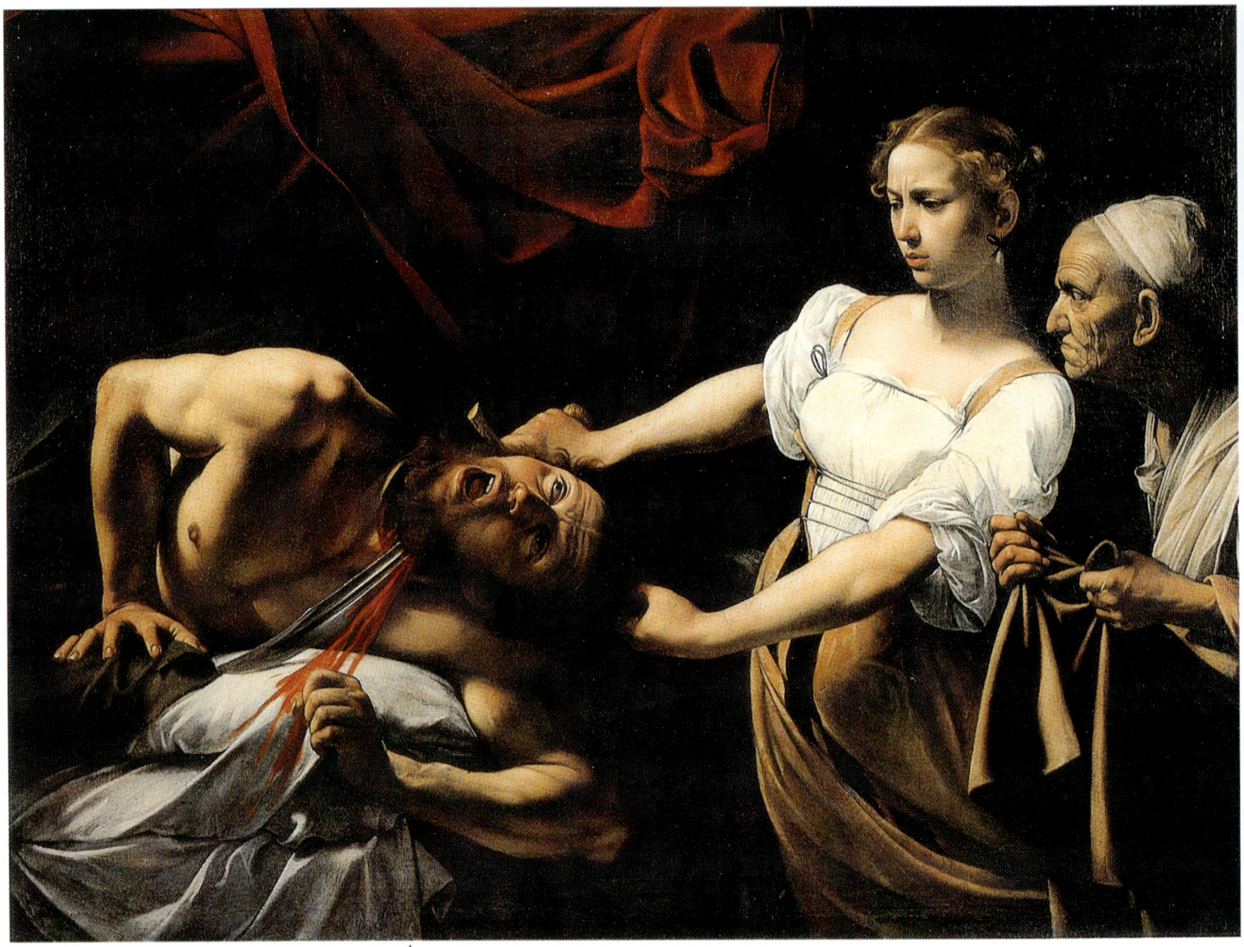

Caravaggio
The Cheats
1594-95
canvas
Forth Worth, Kimbell Art Museum.

The work was painted immediately after Caravaggio left the Cavalier d'Arpino's workshop with no regrets, probably due to some quarrel with the master, already a successful artist although only a few years older than he. An acute reflection on the human condition and the ambiguity of a humanity that is false and unreliable is implied, as in the *Buona Ventura*, a coeval painting also purchased by Cardinal Del Monte.

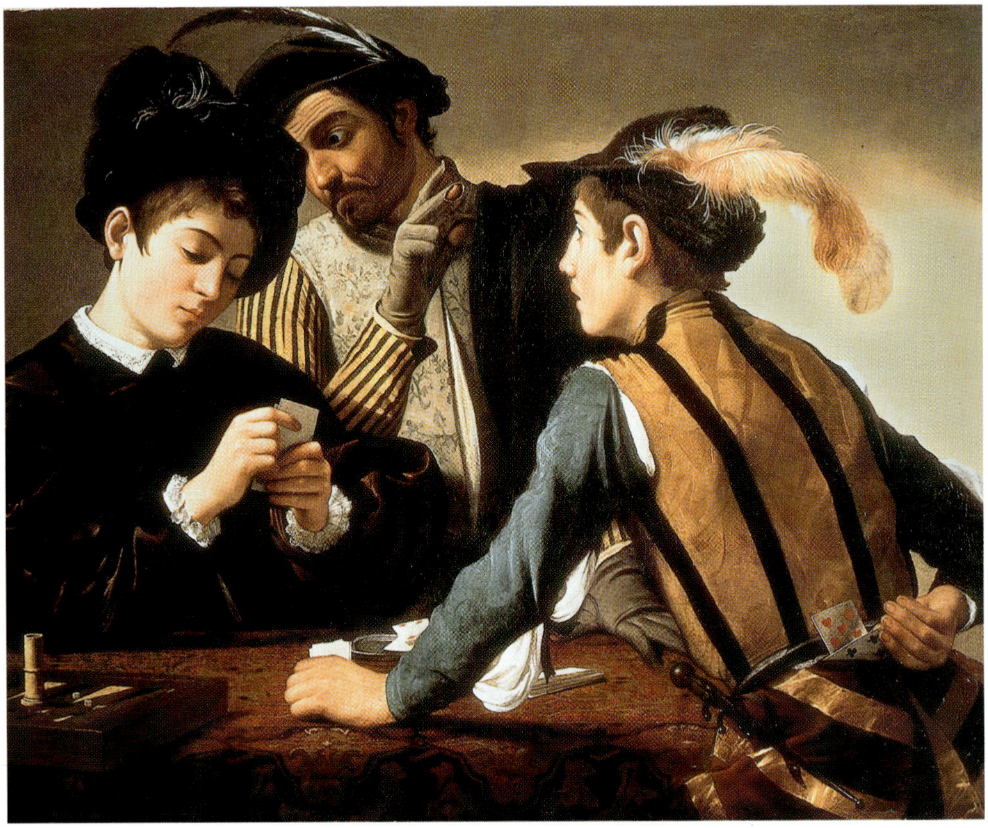

Caravaggio
Bacchus
c. 1596
canvas
Florence, Uffizi Gallery.

As compared to the *Boy with a Chest of Fruit* and the *Sick Bacchus*, the work reveals that the artist is now fully aware of the significance of the symbolism he employs. Bacchus is a paraphrase of Christ, like this one who is offering the cup of salvation. His androgynous appearance is a harmonic image of the union of contraries, male and female. The still life recalls the description in the Song of Songs.

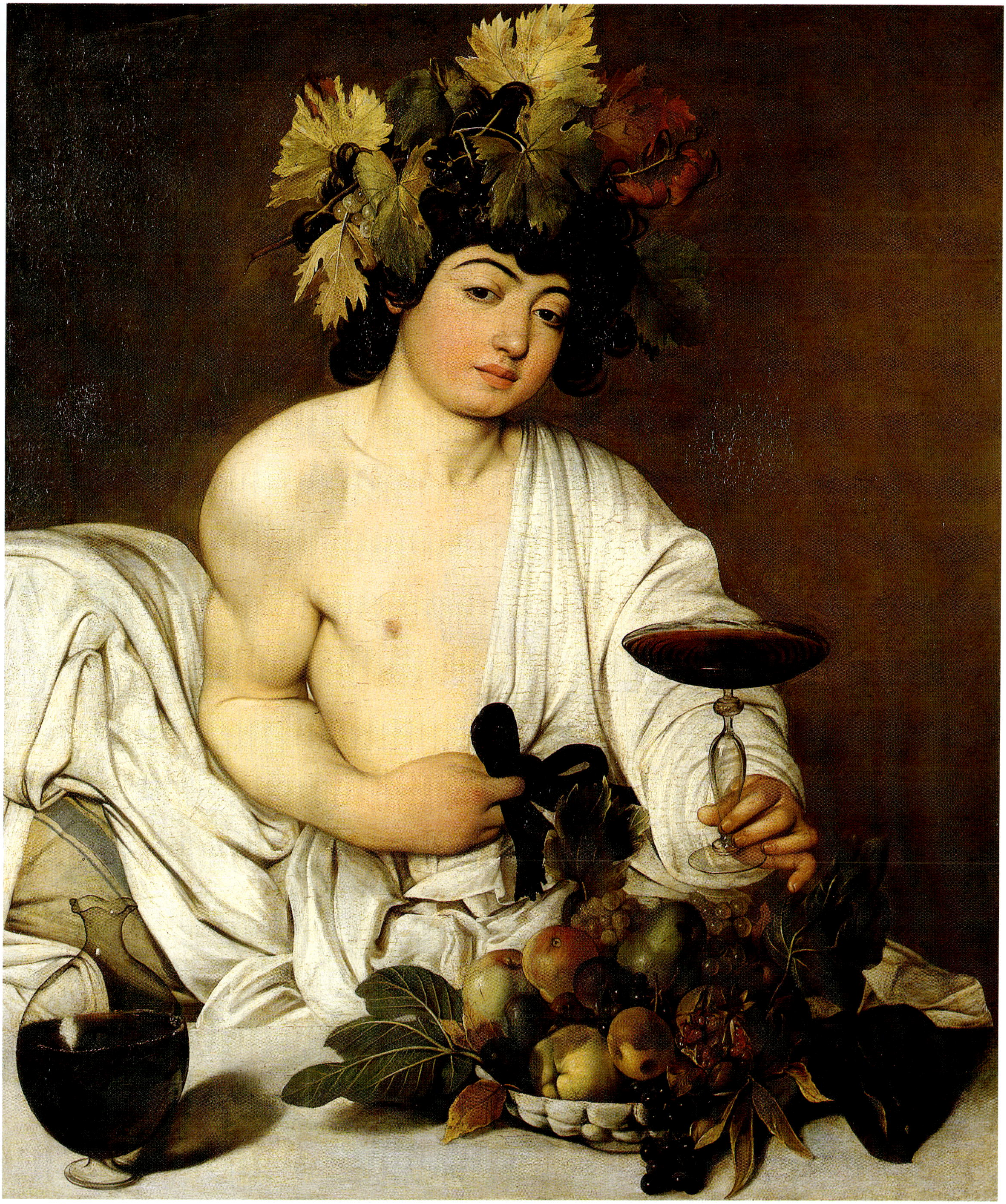

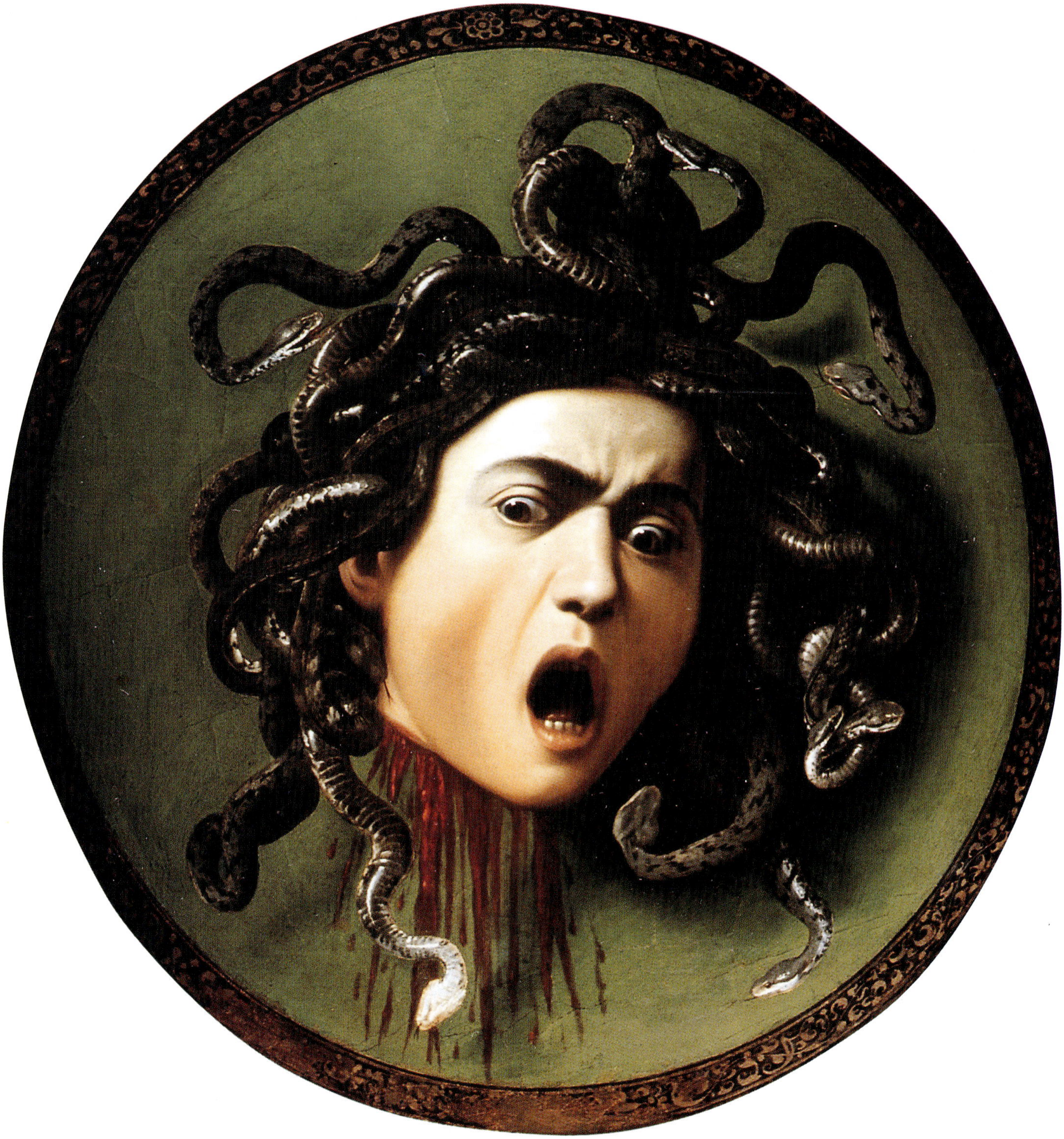

Caravaggio
Medusa
c. 1600
canvas on wood
Florence, Uffizi Gallery.

Painted almost in the style of *trompe-l'oeil*, on a support of canvas-covered wood, the work arrived at the Armoury of Ferdinando de' Medici as a gift from Cardinal Del Monte, the Grand Duke's Ambassador to the Vatican in Rome and Caravaggio's protector. The artist intended primarily to display the horror of Medusa's head only a moment after it has been cut off, spurting bright blood. On closer inspection, the rounded, convex shape of the work is that of a typical tournament shield. The artist is thus alluding to Perseus' shield, on which according to mythology the hero placed the head of the dreadful monster like an ornament.

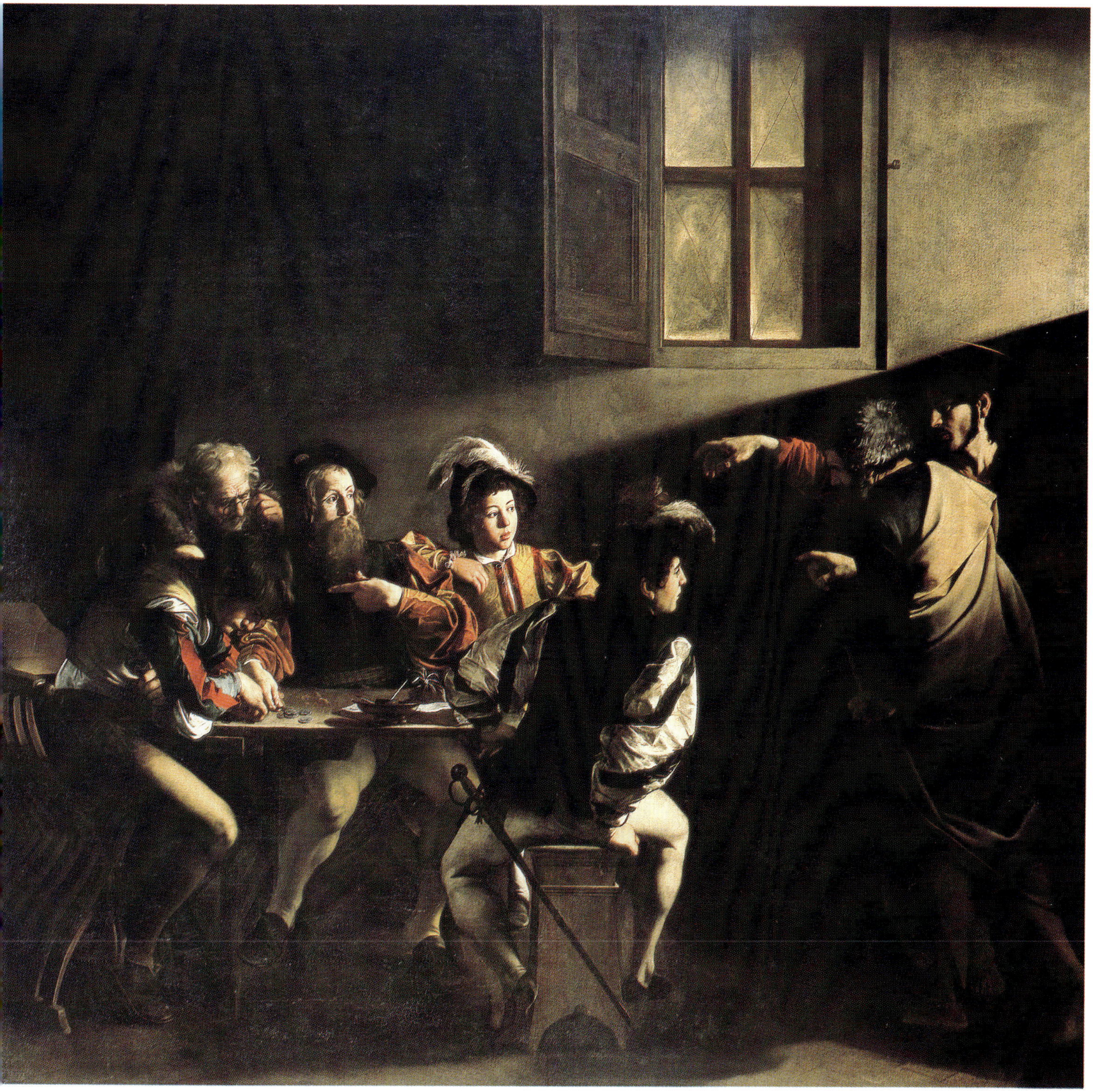

Caravaggio
The Calling of St Matthew
1599-1600
canvas
Rome, San Luigi de' Francesi, Contarelli Chapel.

Matthew, the Apostle who was to become the most learned Evangelist – the only one to narrate the Wise Men's homage to Christ, for instance – was a publican, who collected taxes from the Jews on behalf of the Roman conquerors. As such he was highly unpopular with his fellow citizens, and it was for this very reason that Jesus chose him as a follower. Caravaggio has represented the moment in which Christ summons Matthew the sinner, significantly portrayed at the center of the group, his hands still soiled by the money he is counting. Jesus enters with a beam of light (since he is the light) the dark room (life) where Matthew sits. The publican gazes at him amazed, wondering whether he can really be the chosen one. The subject is that of Grace, so significant at the time in the controversy between Catholics and Huguenots.

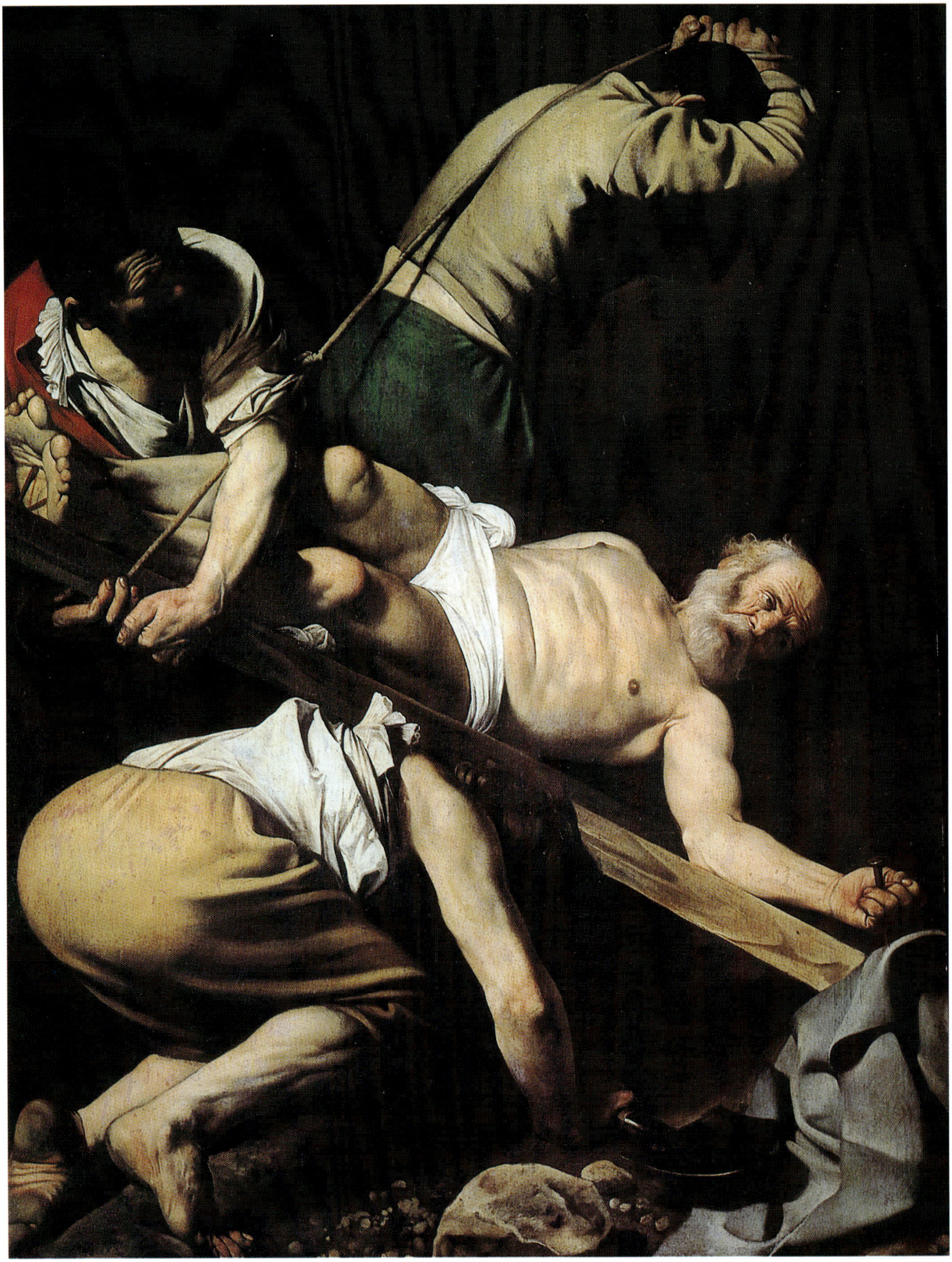

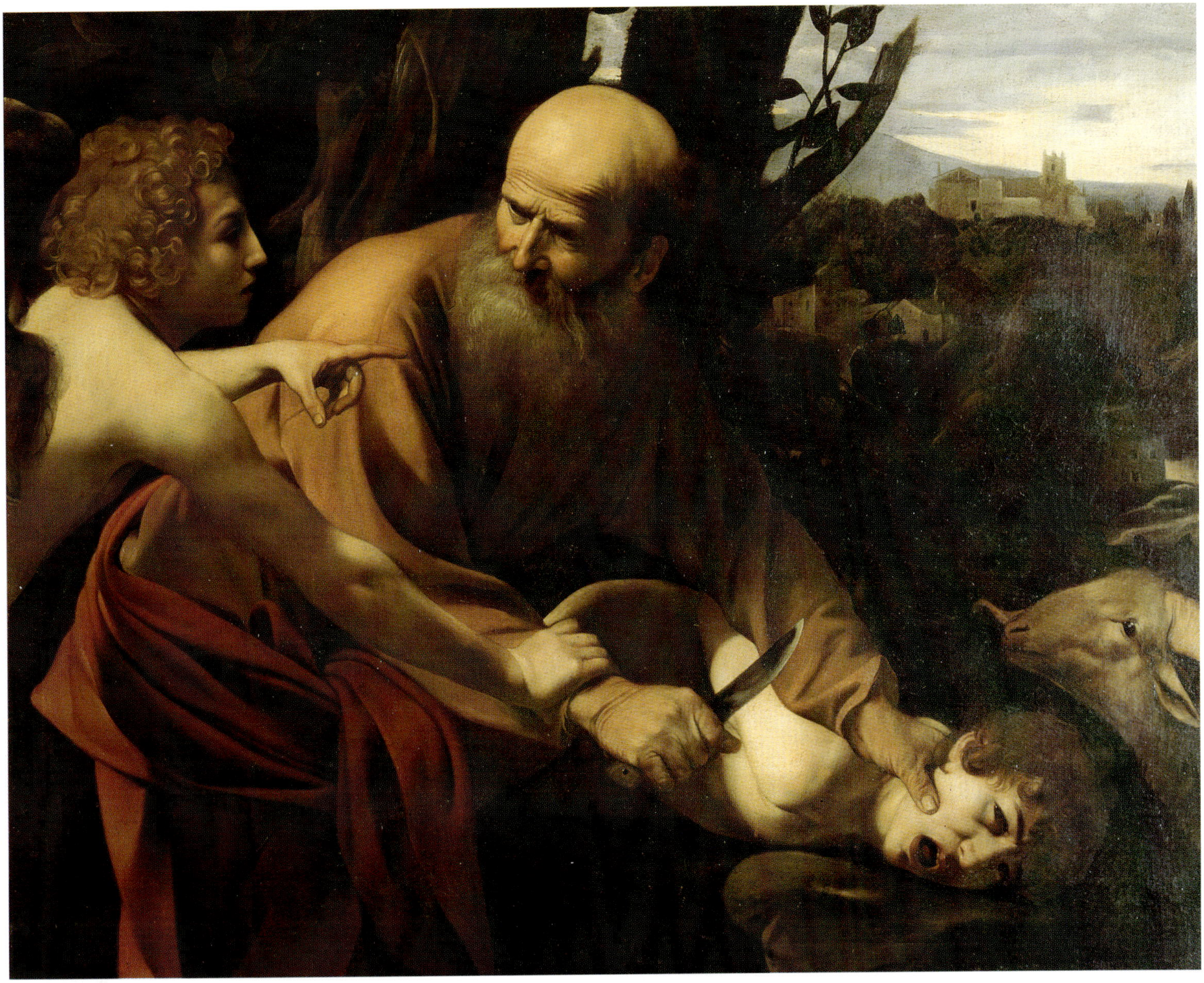

Caravaggio
The Crucifixion of St Peter
1601
canvas
Rome, Santa Maria del Popolo, Cerasi Chapel.

Caravaggio's art proceeds toward a simplification and refinement of the action. As compared to the excitement of the *Martyrdom of St Matthew*, the scene of the *Crucifixion of Peter*, painted slightly later, is marked by its calm, or it might even be said, by the premeditated cynicism with which the saint is being martyred. Slowly and deliberately the executioners ensure that the cross, planted upside down (in respect for the crucifixion of Christ), is raised sturdily, as if it were the pillar of a roof or the mast of a ship. Their indifference seems to intensify the cruelty of the scene whose drama is heightened by the light, the true protagonist of the work, illuminating the only face worthy of being seen: that of Peter. The others are plunged into shadow like the souls of men, prisoners of sin and of their own incapacity to feel.

Caravaggio
The Sacrifice of Isaac
c. 1603
canvas
Florence, Uffizi Gallery.

Caravaggio synthesizes a profound, complex drama in a single scene, concentrating it into a few gestures. Yahweh has asked the elderly Abraham to sacrifice to him his only son Isaac. The patriarch does not hesitate, and is about to fulfill the will of God. But an angel stops him and a goat offers itself in place of Isaac. All of the diagonals in the composition, consisting of the angel's arm and the patriarch's hand grasping his son's head, lead the gaze to converge on a precise point: the hand holding the knife, placed on the mid-line of the canvas, underlined still further by the grazing light. All of the drama is there, in the gesture suspended between action and non-action.

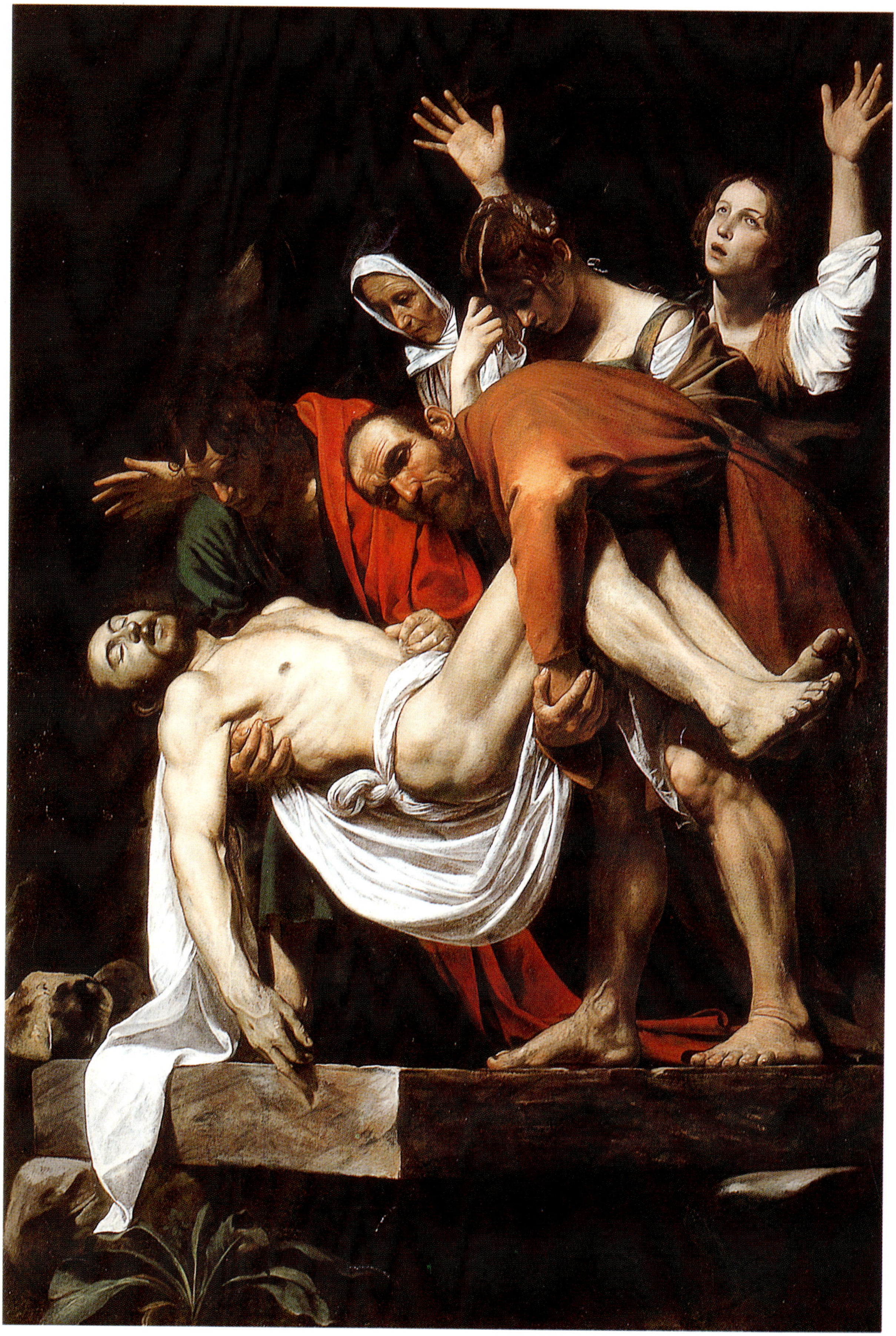

Caravaggio
Deposition
1602-1604
canvas
Rome, Pinacoteca Vaticana.

Conceived within the spiritual climate of the Oratory of San Filippo Neri, this great painting, destined to the Church of Santa Maria in Vallicella in Rome, interprets the feeling of piety that imbues the Apostolic action of the Philippines. The figure of Christ seems a transposition into painting of Michelangelo's sculptural group the *Pietà*, by which the artist was deliberately inspired. The particular viewpoint confers monumentality on the cluster of figures, standing out against an intense dark background. The opens arms of Mary of Cleophas seem the culminating point of a long iconographic itinerary on the theme of the "lamentation for Christ dead" which runs from the Giotto of the Scrovegni Chapel to Niccolò dell'Arca.

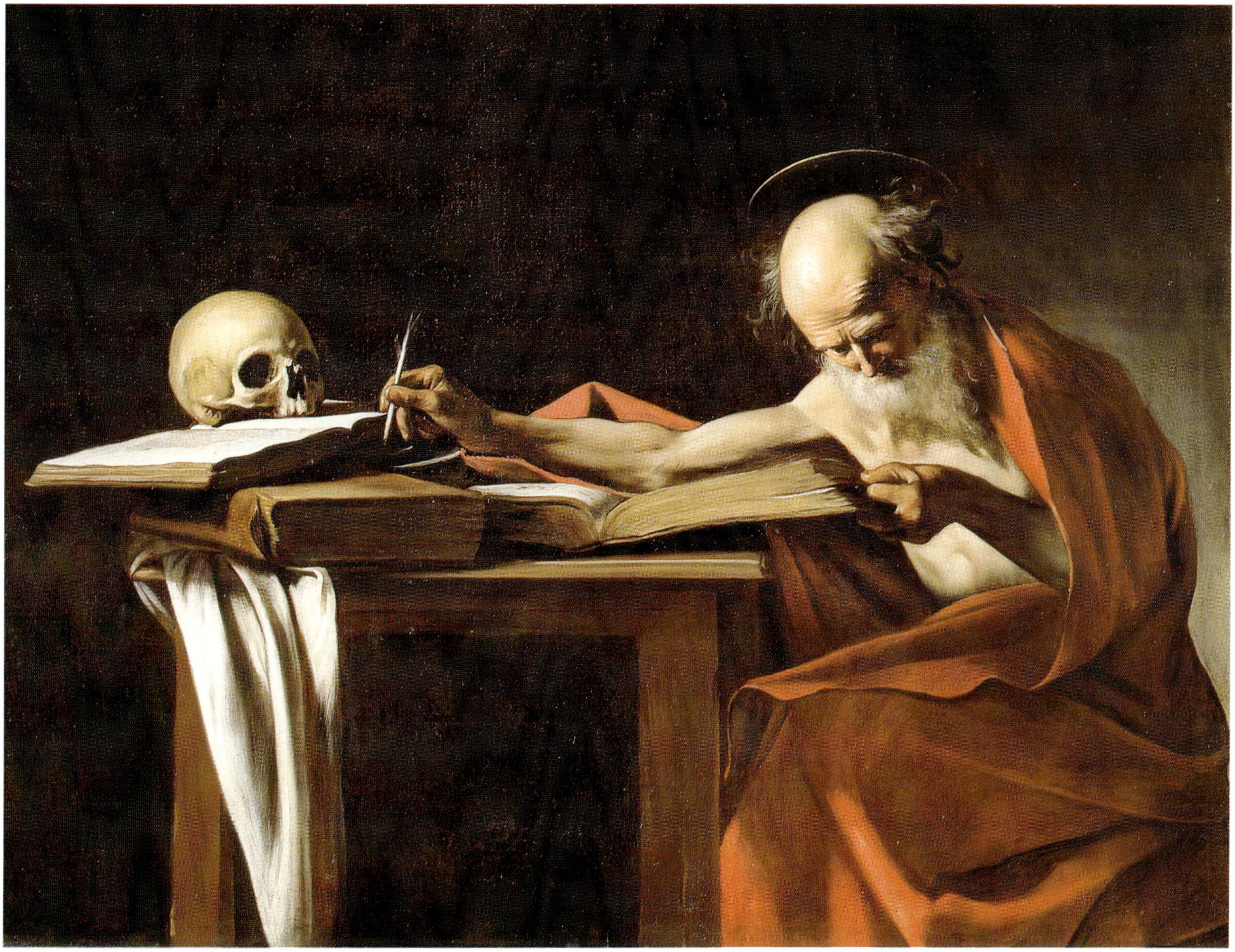

Caravaggio
St Jerome at his Desk
1606
canvas
Rome, Galleria Borghese.

The artist returns here to the theme of a man seated at a desk intent on writing. A precedent for this had been the second version of the *St Matthew and the Angel* in the Contarelli Chapel in San Luigi de' Francesi at Rome. There is, however, an important difference between the two works. In the latter, the saint is seeking a direct relationship with the divine. Gazing upward, he awaits suggestions from the angel, who enumerates the subjects to be discussed with an eloquent gesture of the hands. In the Borghese painting on the contrary, the relationship with God is sought only within the human condition. This is thus an introspection. The saint reflects on himself and doubtless on the divine word of the Holy Scriptures. It is probable, moreover, that Caravaggio wished to show Jerome in the act of writing the Latin version of the Bible, edited by him and known as the Vulgate.

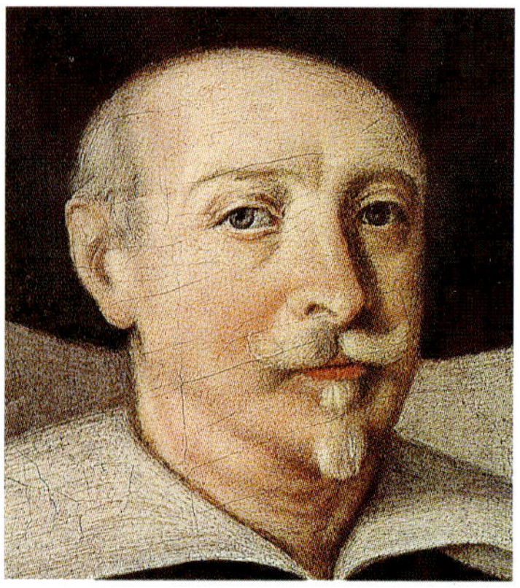

Guido Reni

(Bologna 1575 – 1642)

The young Guido Reni was to have become a musician by profession, since his father Daniele had directed him toward the study of music. His father's choice was justified by the fact that Daniele himself, a musician employed by the city's Signoria, had assured his family a certain well-being and the respect of all. But Guido's passion for painting and art was too strong, and he abandoned his musical studies to enter the shop of the Flemish painter Denijs Calvaert (1540-1619), the head of an important school that was to produce artists such as Domenichino and Francesco Albani. Guido's attention soon focused on the study of Raphael, who was to remain his life-long ideal model. Calvaert's teaching, however; was unable to fully satisfy Guido's aspirations, and at about the age of twenty he entered the Carracci academy. Here he was to remain from 1595 to 1598, tempering with studies from life the classicizing

Guido Reni, *Self-portrait*, detail, c. 1630. Florence, Uffizi Gallery.

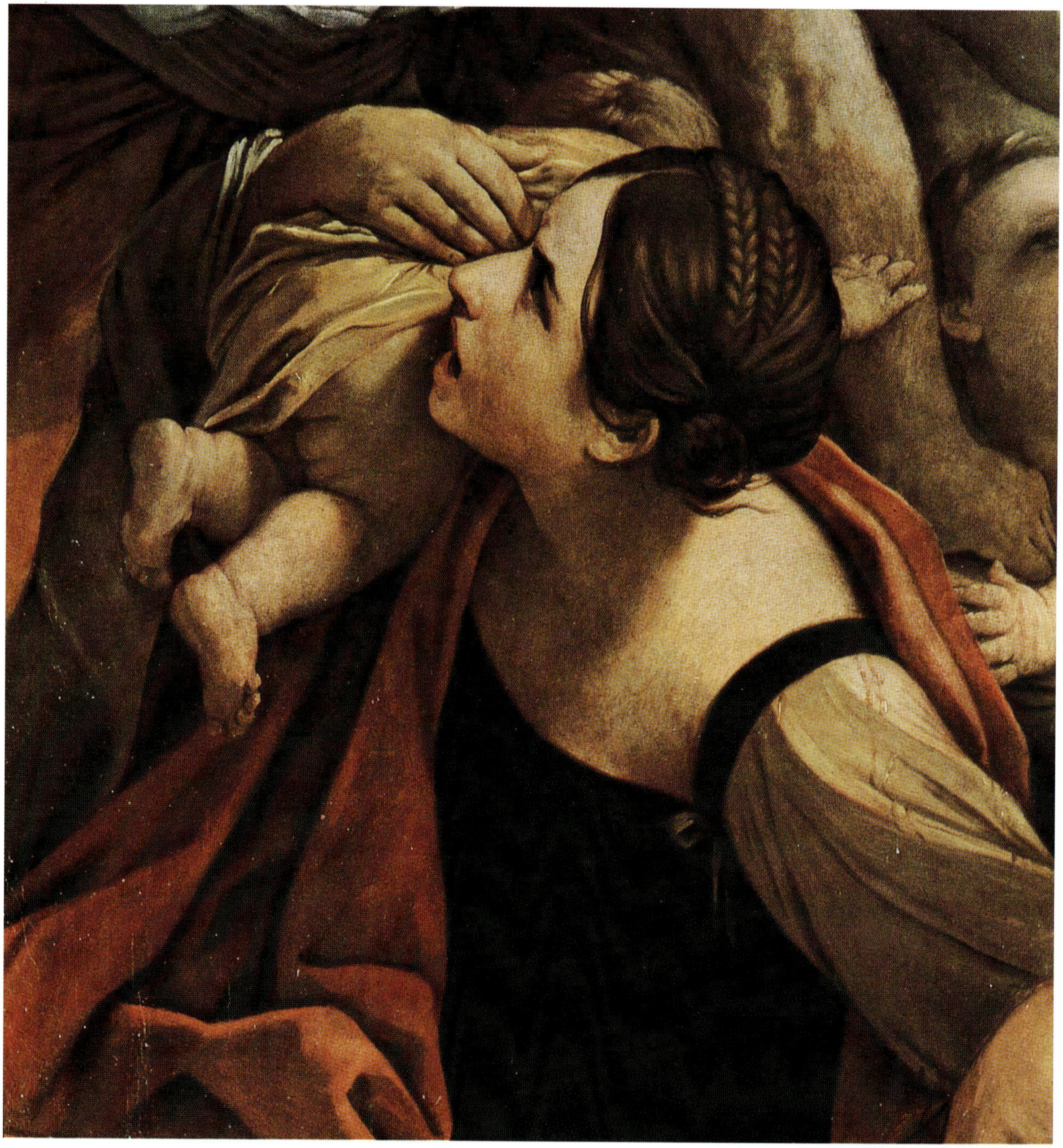

Guido Reni
The Slaughter of the Innocents
1611-12
canvas, detail
Bologna, Pinacoteca Nazionale.

Painted during the artist's brief stay in Bologna, which temporarily interrupted his work on the frescoes in Santa Maria Maggiore (he had left after quarreling with the Pontificial Secretariat), the canvas is unanimously judged to be one of the artist's masterpieces. Originally placed in the Ghisleri Chapel in San Domenico in Bologna, it shows all of Reni's skill at composition. The artist, exploiting the triangular diagonals dovetailed together, manages to communicate simultaneously both convulsed confusion and motionless tragedy, so overwhelming that not even a scream can issue from the woman's mouth.

ideal of Raphael, whose *Ecstasy of Saint Cecilia* he copied several times. His talent, rather than winning him friends, led to conflict within the academy. However, he was admitted to the Congregation of Painters in 1599. It was during this period, up to 1602, that he made frequent trips to Rome, settling there definitively in 1608. His name was now known thanks to the famous *Crucifixion of St Peter*, today in the Pinocoteca Vaticana, painted for Cardinal Aldobrandini between 1604 and 1605. The great altarpiece shows the influence of Caravaggio, which was to become the other basic component of Guido's painting. Important commissions were now given him. The Pope, Paul V Borghese, called for him to decorate the Palace of Montecavallo and the Basilica of Santa Maria Maggiore. Returning definitively to Bologna in 1614, Guido was to leave it only for a journey to Naples in 1622 (frescoes in the Treasury of San Gennaro) and another, in 1627, back to Rome.

Guido Reni
Portrait of an Elderly Woman
c. 1620
canvas
Bologna, Pinacoteca Nazionale.

Traditionally considered to be a portrait of the artist's mother, but without any documentary basis, the painting reveals all of Guido's skill in psychological introspection. The half-bust view and the veil standing out against the dark background lead the spectator's gaze to meet that of the woman, whose face seems to open like a flower between the "petals" of her collar. The austerity of the whole arouses a feeling akin to embarrassment in the spectator observing this face which, though marked by age, shows a hint of past aristocratic beauty.

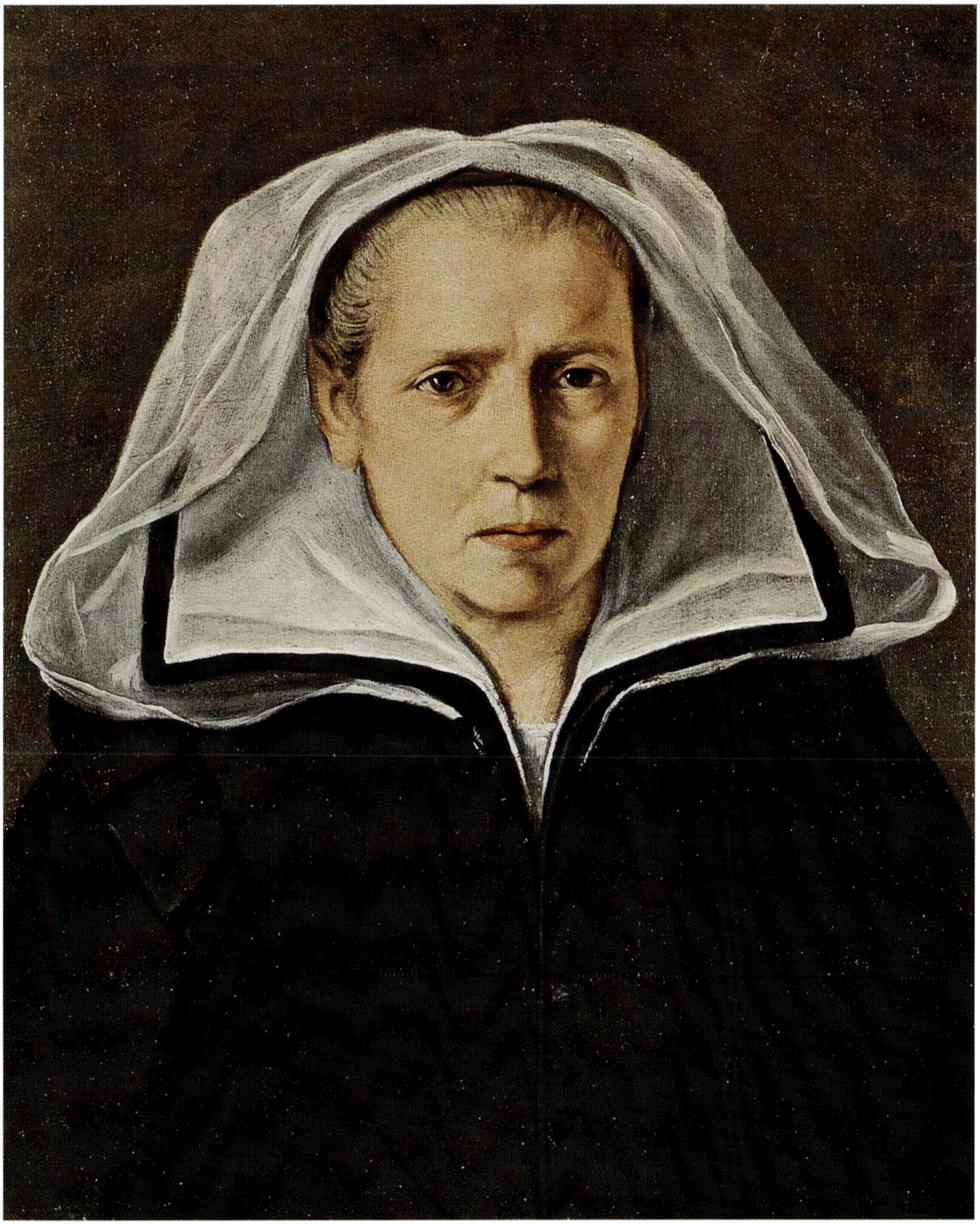

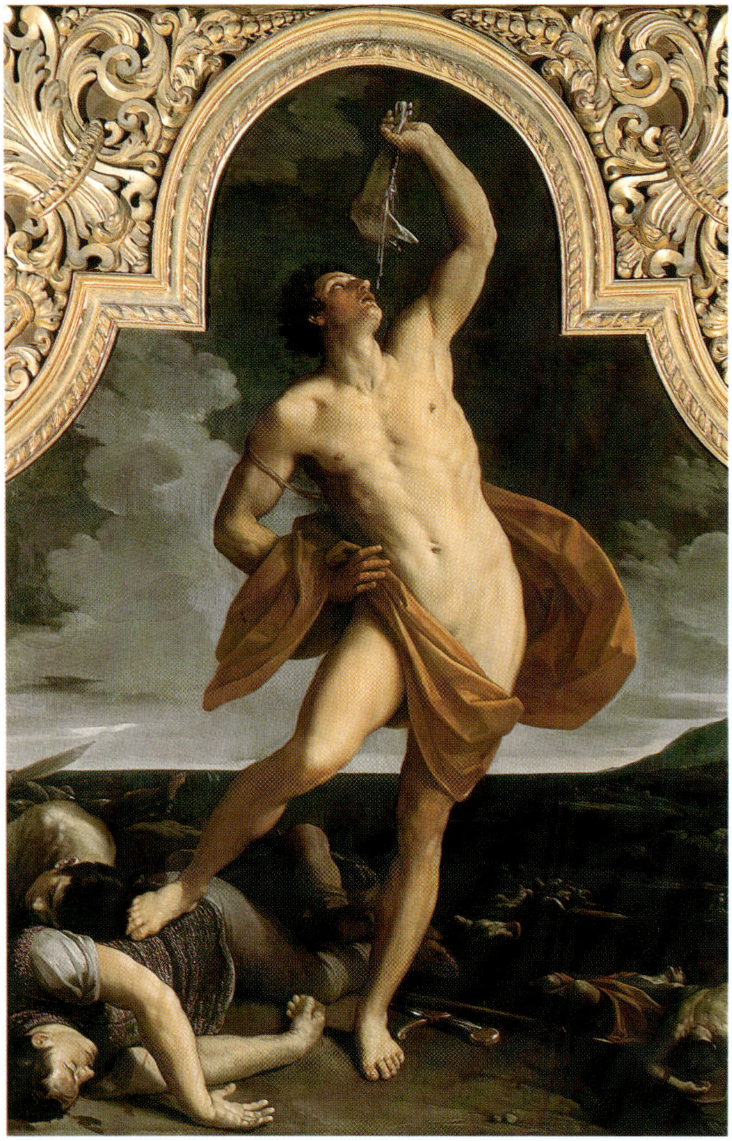

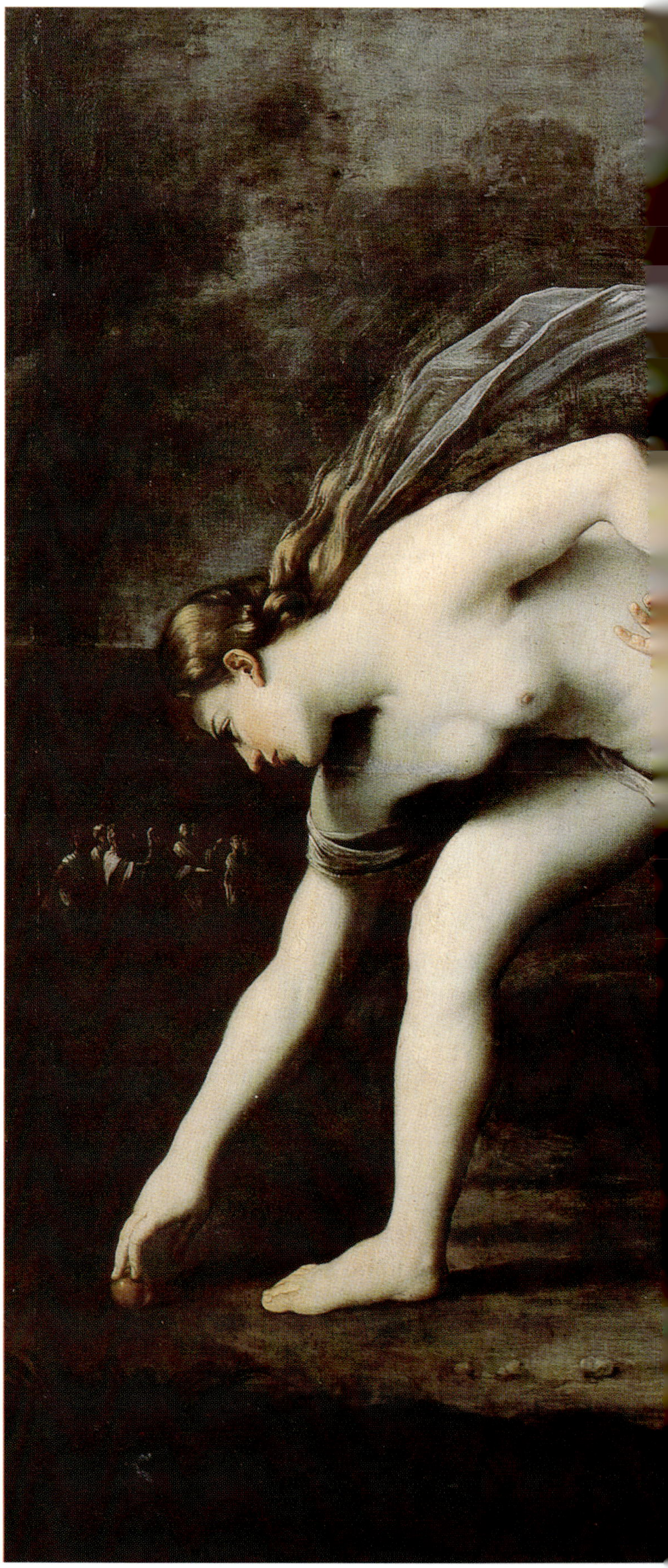

Guido Reni
The Victorious Samson
1611-12
canvas
Bologna, Pinacoteca Nazionale.

Designed to hang over the fireplace in the home of Count Zambeccari in Bologna, the painting is a reinterpretation in modern key of Michelangelo's sculptural group the *Victory*, from which it borrows the particular position of Samson's leg, as he kicks his defeated enemy. The artist's mastery of anatomy appears here at its finest.

Guido Reni
Atalanta and Hippomenes
1615-25
canvas
Madrid, Prado Museum.

The work is a perfect copy by the artist himself of the better known canvas in the Capodimonte Museum in Naples, of which it reproduces even the dimensions. Recorded in the royal inventories of 1666 as the work of Guido Reni, it was instead judged to be a copy in the 19th century and was thus relegated to the storage deposits of the University of Grenada. Only restoration conducted by the Prado in the 1960s has fully confirmed the authenticity of the work as had been indicated by the 17th century inventory. Frequently, moreover, artists replicate a work to satisfy other requests and to fill their own coffers. Certainly this canvas, along with the one in Naples, must be considered one of the masterpieces of the artist who harmoniously blended the heritage of Raphael with that of Caravaggio.

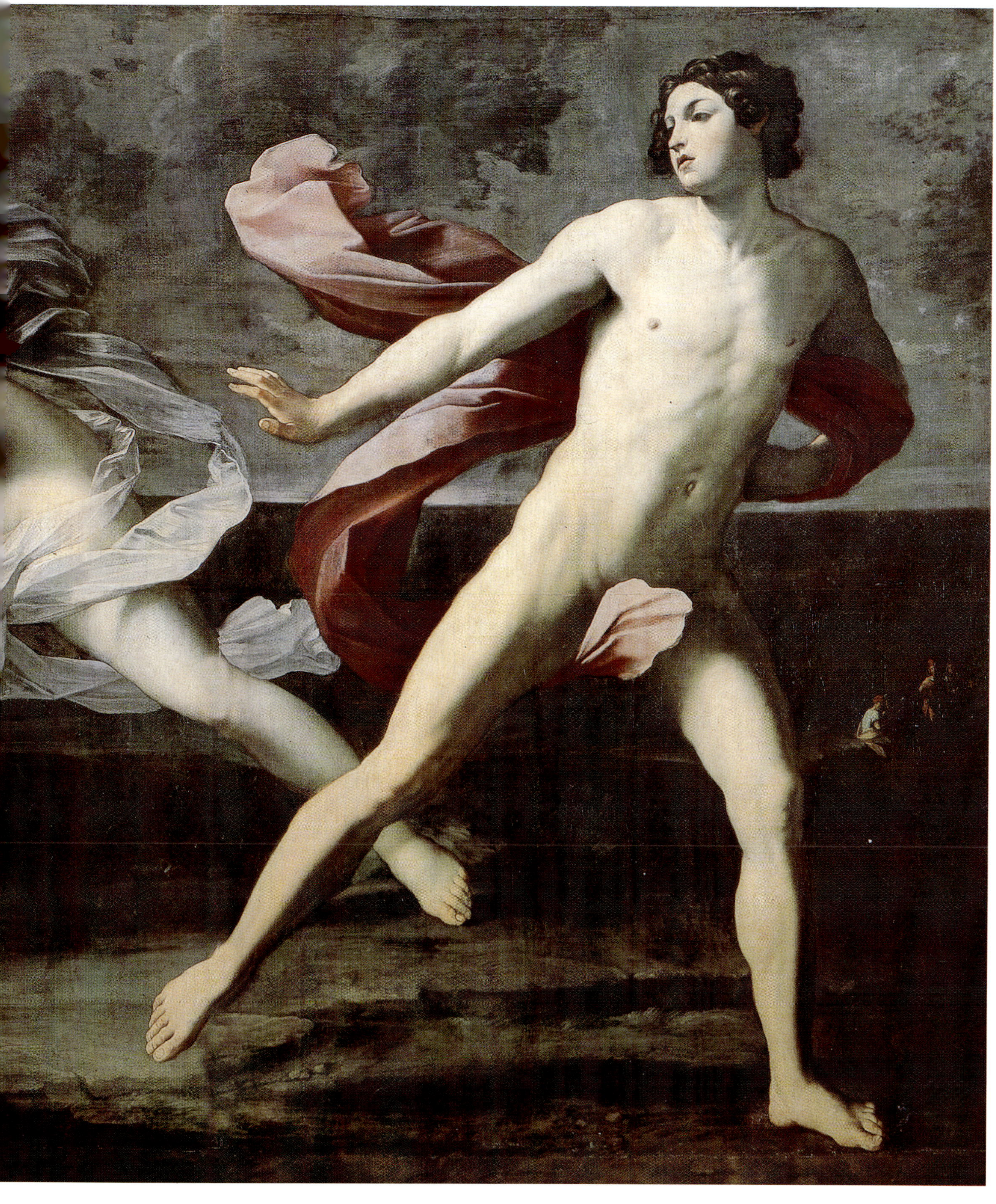

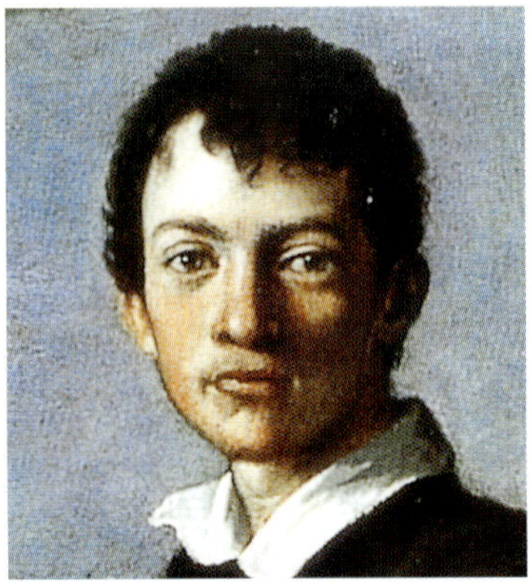

Domenichino

(Domenico Zampieri,
Bologna 1581 – Naples 1641)

Domenichino is the diminutive of Zampieri's Christian name, but his real nickname was "the Ox", as he was called by his companions for his stubbornness and constancy. The artist trained in Bologna first with Denijs Calvaert and then at the school of Ludovico Carracci. In Rome, where he went in 1602, he collaborated with Annibale in the Farnese Gallery. His first independent undertaking consisted of frescoes painting in Grottaferrata, where he decorated between 1608 and 1610 the Chapel of the Founding Saints. His career in art was marked by confrontation and conflict with Lanfranco, who went so far as to slander him, and with whom he competed directly in the frescoes of Sant'Andrea della Valle. Disheartened and discouraged, he left Rome for Naples in 1630.

Domenichino, *Portrait of a Young Man* (presumed self-portrait), detail, 1603. Darmstadt, Hessisches Landesmuseum.

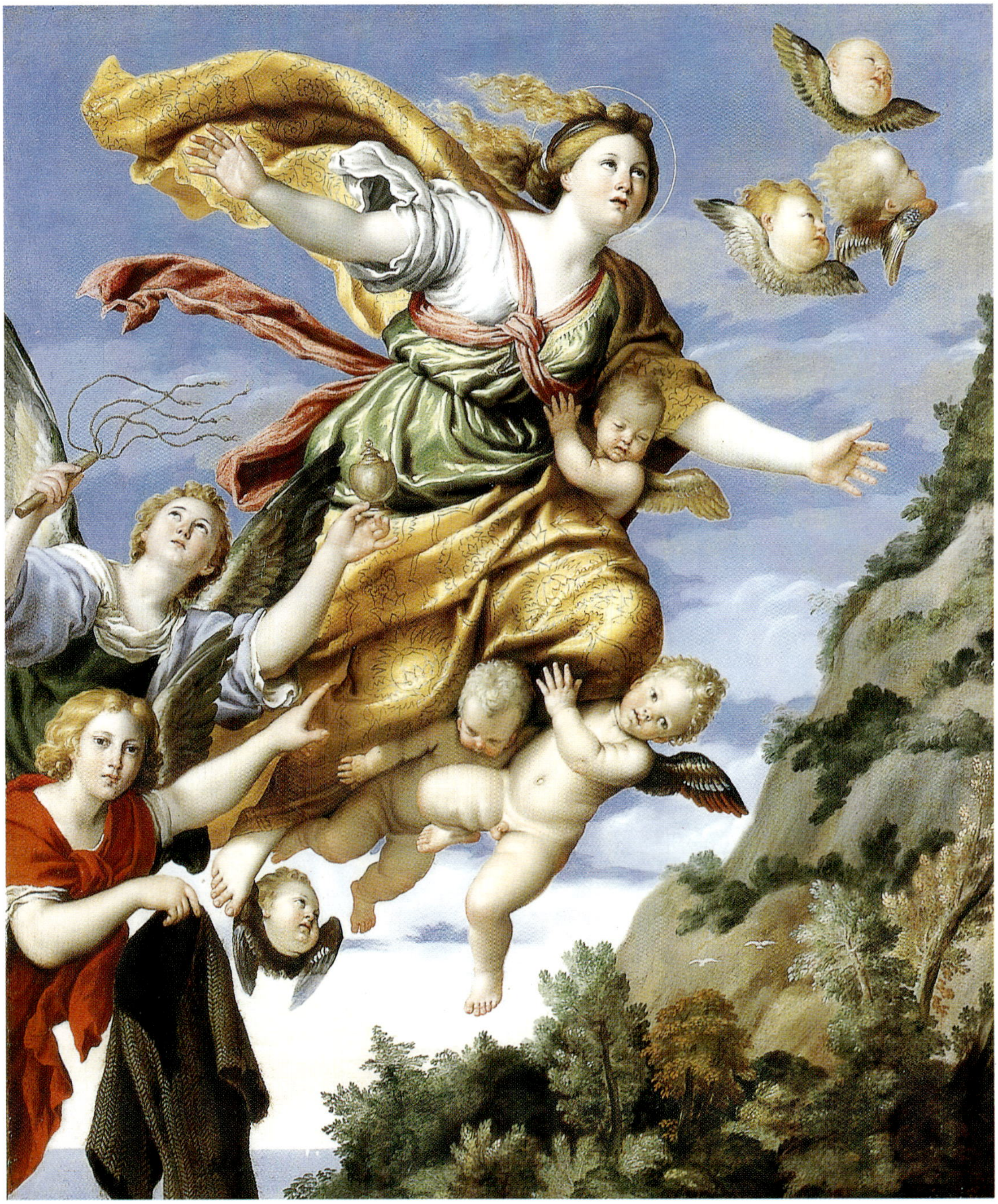

Domenichino
Saint Mary Magdalene in Glory
c. 1620
canvas
St Petersburg, Hermitage.

That the subject is Mary Magdalene is shown by the scourge and the vase carried by the angel. The former alludes to penitence, the latter to the Magdalene's going to the Sepulcher to anoint the body of Christ, accompanied by the other two Marys. The worn garment held up by the angel in the foreground alludes to the hermit's life. The scene in question is substantially described in the *Golden Legend* of Jacopo da Varagine (13th century): "Every day at the hour of precisely seven she was borne aloft by angels and with her earthly ears heard the glorious songs of the celestial armies". The colors are fresh and enameled, while the contrast between the white blouse and the golden robe seems to refer to the liturgical colors of the saint.

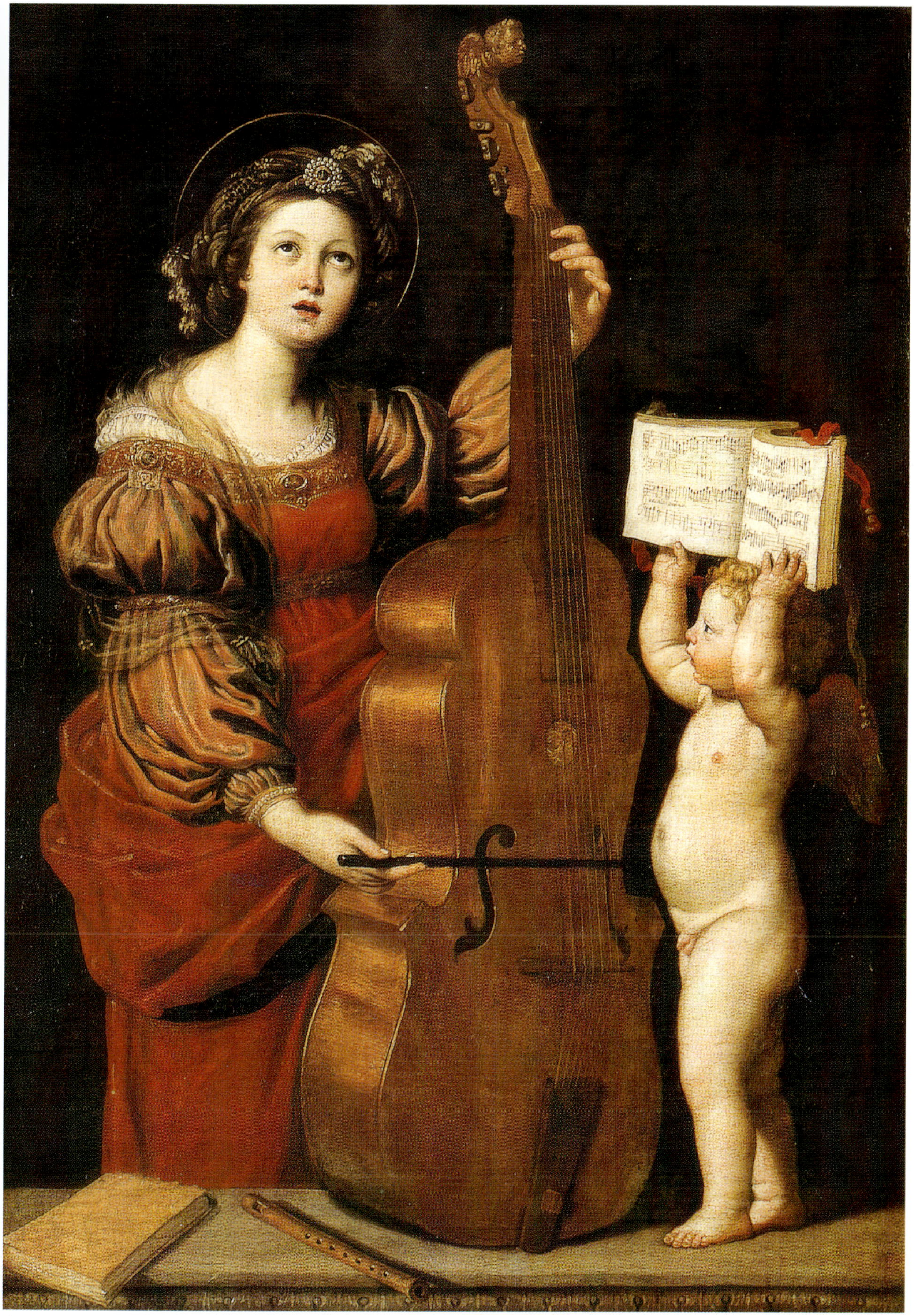

Domenichino
Saint Cecilia
c. 1617-18
canvas
Paris, Louvre.

The painting, coming from the Ludovisi collection, portrays Saint Cecilia, patron saint of music, in the act of playing a "psallenda" on a seven-chord "viola bastarda". The subject is justified not only by the interests of the patron (which were, moreover, shared by the artist), but also by the wave of emotion aroused by the finding of Saint Cecilia's body at the end of the preceding century. Domenichino's knowledge of music is revealed by the accuracy with which the instrument is depicted, but also by the fact that the score held up by the angel is a real one.

Giovanni Lanfranco

(Terenzo, Parma, 1582 – Rome 1647)

It can be stated without exaggeration that the art of Giovanni Lanfranco represents a synthesis of the finest painting tradition of the Po region. A pupil of Agostino Carracci, Lanfranco took from him a love for the Raphaelesque ideal, while from Annibale he draw a firm sense of monumentality, tempered by the softness of Correggio. His closeness to the style of Annibale is demonstrated in particular by a series of drawings, among them an *Apparition of Jove* (Paris, Louvre) which for many years was attributed to the Bolognese artist. After training with Agostino, who involved him in the decoration of the Palazzo del Giardino in Parma, Giovanni then went to work for Annibale, engaged in the undertaking of the Farnese Gallery. His first important commission was for the decoration of the Chamber of the Hermits in the same Palazzo Farnese (c. 1604). In Rome he also worked in collaboration with Guido Reni (frescoes of San Gregorio al Celio, 1608-10) and alone in San Carlo ai Catinari and Sant'Andrea della Valle. From 1634 to 1646 he was in Naples.

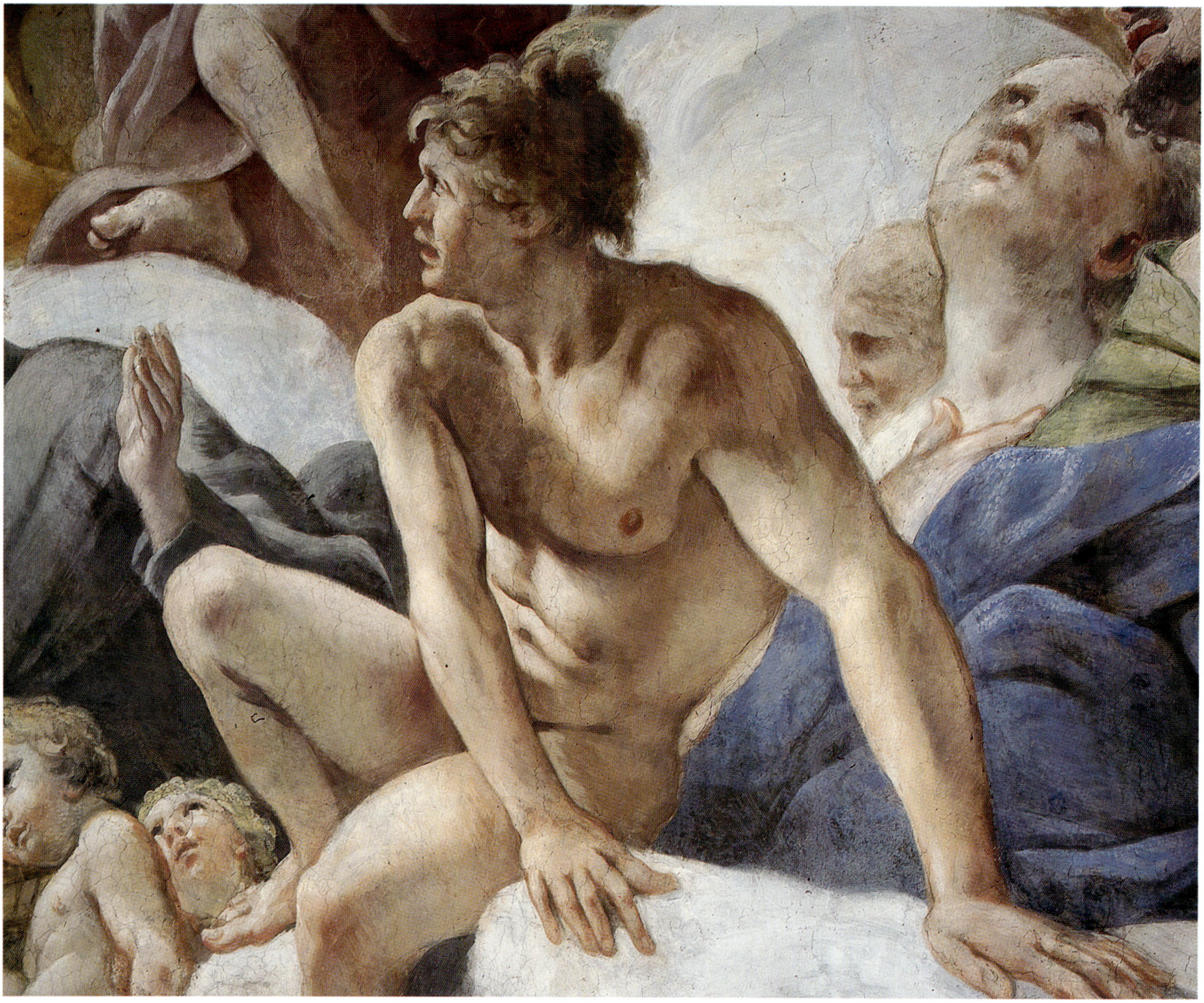

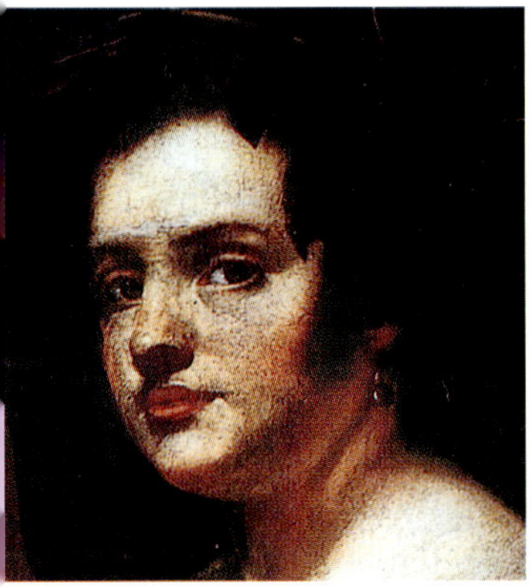

Artemisia Gentileschi

(Rome 1597 – Naples c. 1652)

Only in the last few years have the human vicissitudes of Artemisia Gentileschi been known to the public, through novels and films that have made her a figure of great topical interest, a woman capable of courageously taking in hand her own existence, without stooping to compromise with meanness and hypocrisy. Her life was marked by the scandal of the lawsuit for rape brought against Agostino Tassi Buonamici (1566-1644), a painter from Perugia. A child of art, the daughter of the painter Orazio Gentileschi (1563-1639), Artemisia absorbed from her father the lesson of Caravaggio which Orazio had been among the first to assimilate in the early 17th century, accentuating its realistic components without sparing the spectator any detail. Artemisia worked in the major cities of Italy (Florence, Rome and Naples) and journeyed to England for a brief stay from 1638 to 1639.

Artemisia Gentileschi, *Self-portrait*, detail of the *Allegory of Painting*, c. 1630. Rome, Galleria Nazionale d'Arte Antica, Palazzo Barberini.

Giovanni Lanfranco
Glory of the Virgin
1625-27
fresco, detail
Rome, Sant'Andrea della Valle.

This work, Lanfranco's masterpiece, shows the influence of his stay in Parma (1610-12), where he had been able to admire the frescoes of Correggio, of identical subject, in the Duomo. The dome of Sant'Andrea della Valle opens onto a vortex of clouds which seem to draw the spectator up toward the light, here and there broken by spots of color, as in the Virgin's mantle and gown and some of the saint's robes. The viewpoint from which the composition is seen is exaggeratedly lowered.

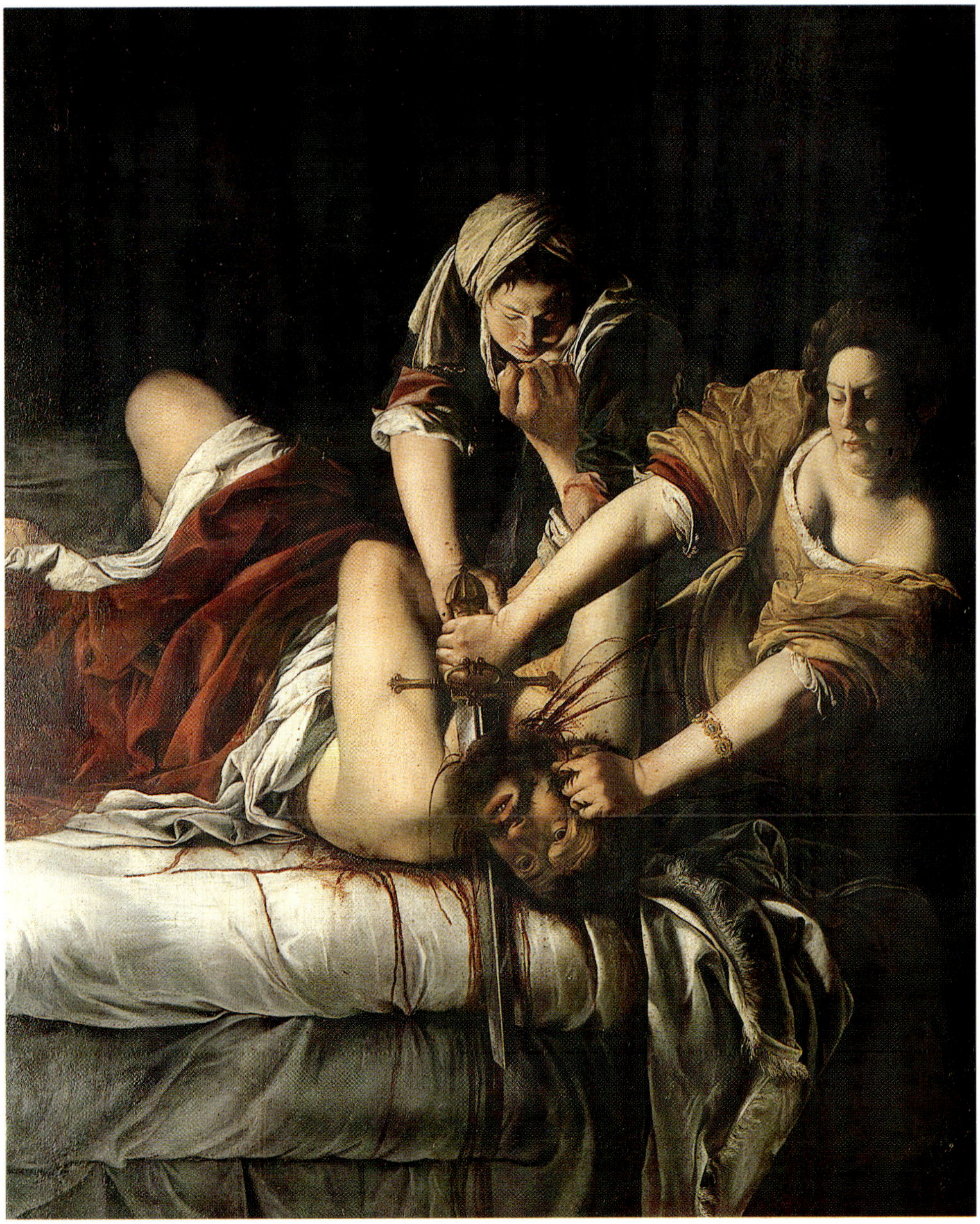

Artemisia Gentileschi
Judith and Holophernes
c. 1620
canvas
Florence, Uffizi Gallery.

The canvas was painted during the artist's stay in Florence. In the Tuscan city where she had taken refuge with her father, a native of Pisa, when the scandal of Agostino Tassi's trial for rape first broke, the painter remained for six years, from 1614 to 1620. Here she was given important commissions, working also for the Medici family, as in the *Magdalene* now in the Pitti Palace. Artemisia arrived in Florence preceded by substantial fame. Her works, known for their fierce brutality, marked a critical change in the Caravaggio style.

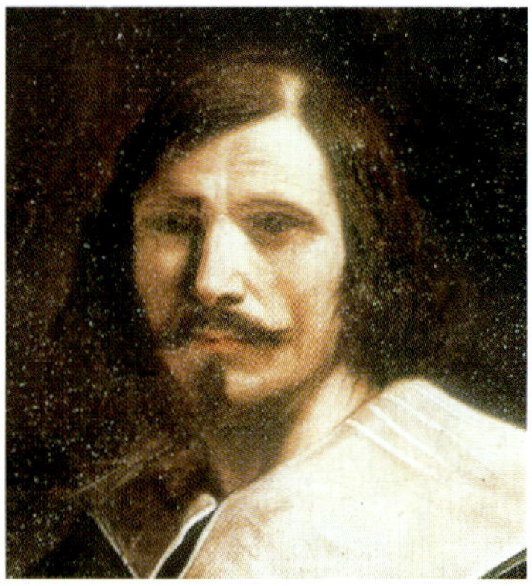

Guercino

(Giovan Francesco Barbieri, Cento, Ferrara, 1591 – Bologna 1666)

After beginning as a self-taught artist Guercino worked in the workshop of Benedetto Gennari. He also worked for Alessandro Ludovisi, Archbishop of Bologna and later Cardinal, painting four large canvases now in different museums. The artist's great occasion arose when Cardinal Ludovisi was elected Pope under the name of Gregory XV in 1621. Called to Rome to decorate the palaces of the Roman nobility, Guercino frescoed Palazzo Costaguti, Palazzo Lancellotti and, most important of all, Casino Ludovisi, where works such as *Dawn* and *Fame* made his name famous. In 1623 he left Rome to return to his home town, the little Cento, where he soon became a reference point for Emilian painting of the 17th century.

Guercino, *Self-portrait*, c. 1630.

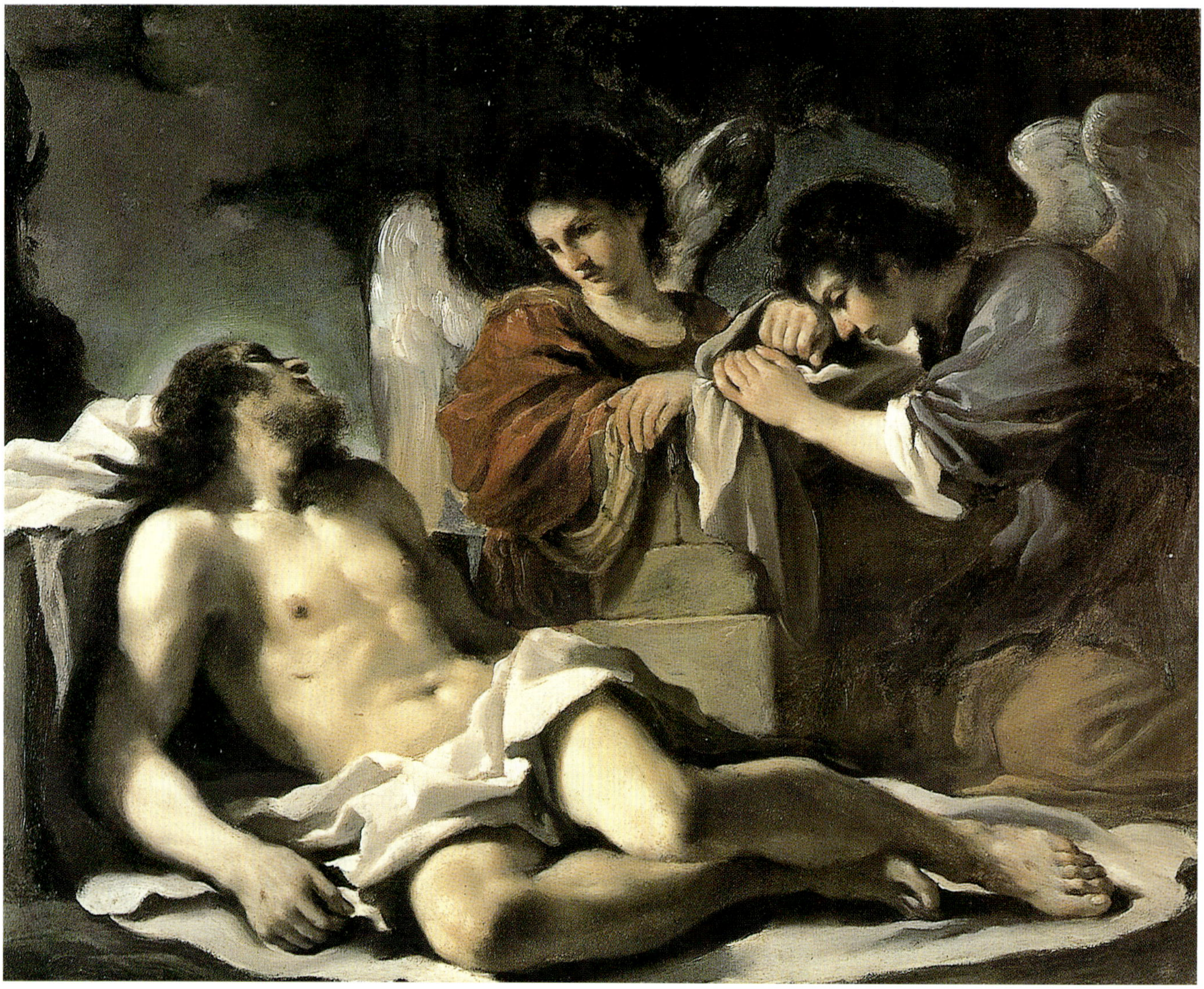

Guercino
Lament for Christ Dead
c. 1617-18
copper
London, National Gallery.

Coming from the Borghese collection, this is another of the endless reinterpretations of Annibale Carracci's canvas known as the *Pietà* or the *Three Marys*, datable between 1604 and 1606 and now too in London (The Trustees of the National Gallery). Annibale's work, which in turn was inspired by Correggio's *Deposition* in Parma, was a model for many painters, and Giovanni Lanfranco gave a livid interpretation of it which calls to mind the other *Pietà* by Annibale, the one in the Louvre. Guercino, instead, avoids any contaminating influence and the oblique body of Christ shows a precise lineage. Obviously, there are significant variations: in place of the Marys are two angels, and the accentuation of the shadows and lights is reminiscent of Caravaggio, another inevitable source of inspiration for the artist.

Guercino
Christ and the Samaritan Woman
1647
canvas
Modena, Banco di San Geminiano.

The subject, indubitably one of the most widely popular in the 17th century, relates to the later stage of the artist's career, after the 1630s. The convulsed excitement of his youthful works, including the famous fresco of the Casino Ludovisi, had now been replaced by serenity and equilibrium. The colors too play a major role in the composition. Both Christ and the Samaritan woman, in fact, wear soft, flowing robes that balance each other like the weights on a scale. Christ's azure mantle is echoed by the lapis lazuli of the sky arching above the Emilian countryside in the background. The reddish cloud, on the contrary, reflects the tones of the well and the copper pail held by the Samaritan woman. The formal equilibrium is like that of a chessboard, where everything has been calculated.

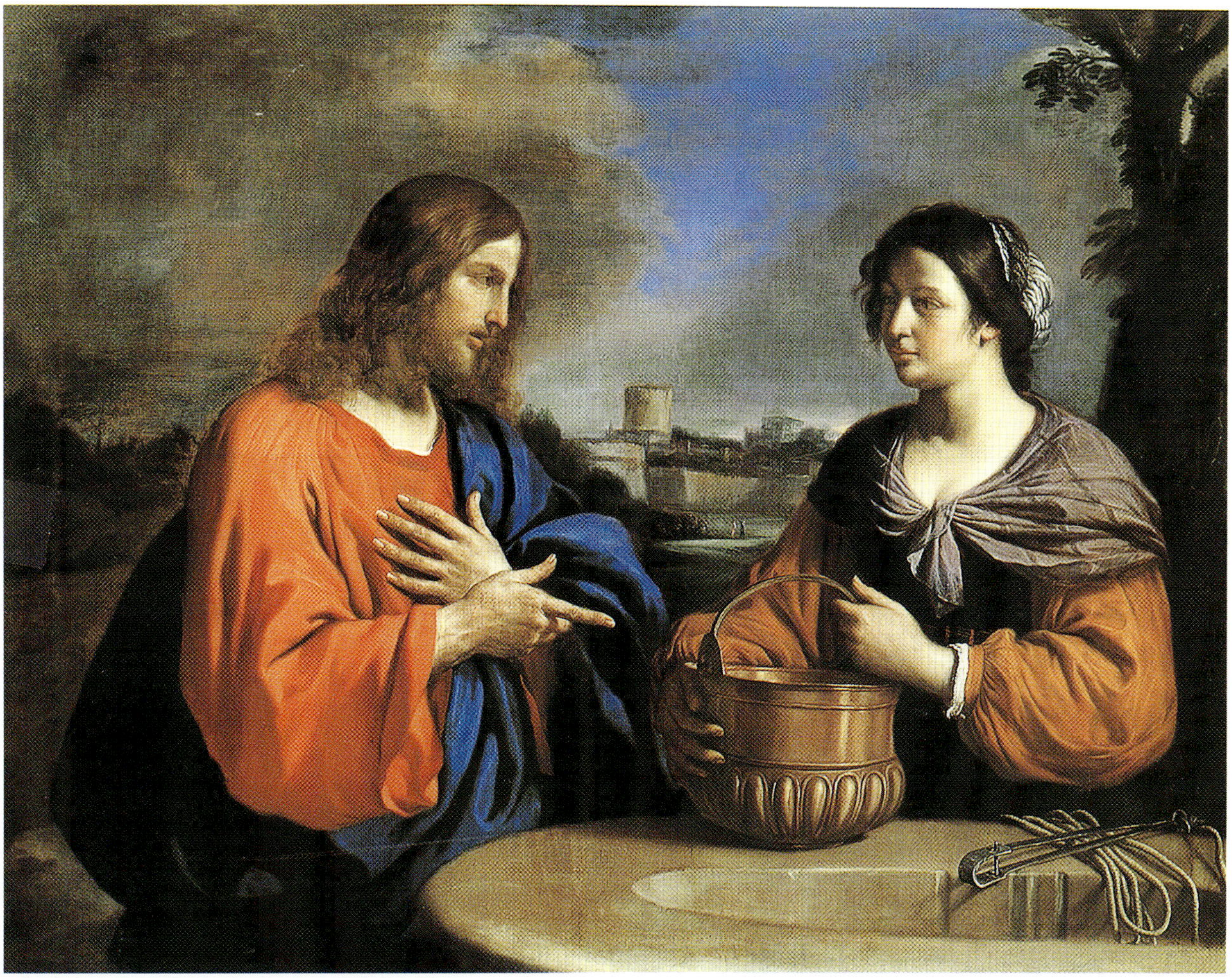

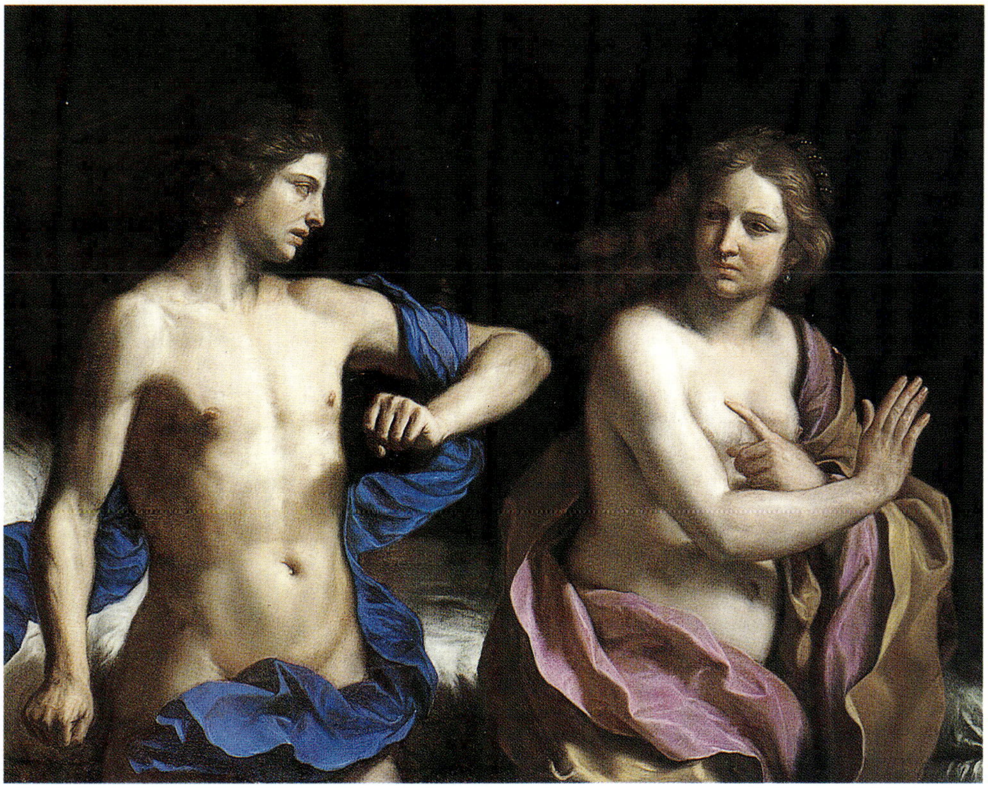

Guercino
Ammon Driving Away Tamar
1649
canvas
Washington, National Gallery.

Commissioned by Messer Aurelio Zanoletti, this painting of moralizing subject, like the lost *Apollo and Daphne*, is inspired by the theme of chastity. Painted by the artist in his maturity, it shows those gifts of composure and balance characteristic of the second stage of his career, when even the influence of Caravaggio had been attenuated.

Bartolomeo Schedoni

(Formigone, Modena, c. 1578 – Parma 1615)

As was the case with many other artists of the times, the life of Bartolomeo Schedoni unfolded within the shadow of a noble family. The Duke of Parma and Piacenza, Ranuccio Farnese (1592-1622) invited him to Rome toward the end of the century, and then called him to his service in Parma starting from 1607. Probably trained on the basis of the Mannerism of Niccolò dell'Abate (1509-1571), whom he may have known through the trials for Palazzo Poggi in Bologna, Bartolemeo renewed his style in the light of the Carracci lesson. To this he added the intense luminosity of Caravaggio, which lights up the acidulous tints taken from Mannerism. The result is a style of great personality which can be justly considered one of the interpretations of Baroque that mingles and blends the drama of Caravaggio, the monumentality of Carracci and the soft tones of Correggio, but also the stiffness of Mannerism. Unfortunately the troubled life of the artist, whose violent, quarrelsome nature frequently led him into trouble with the law, prevented any further development of his painting. It is suspected that he died a suicide.

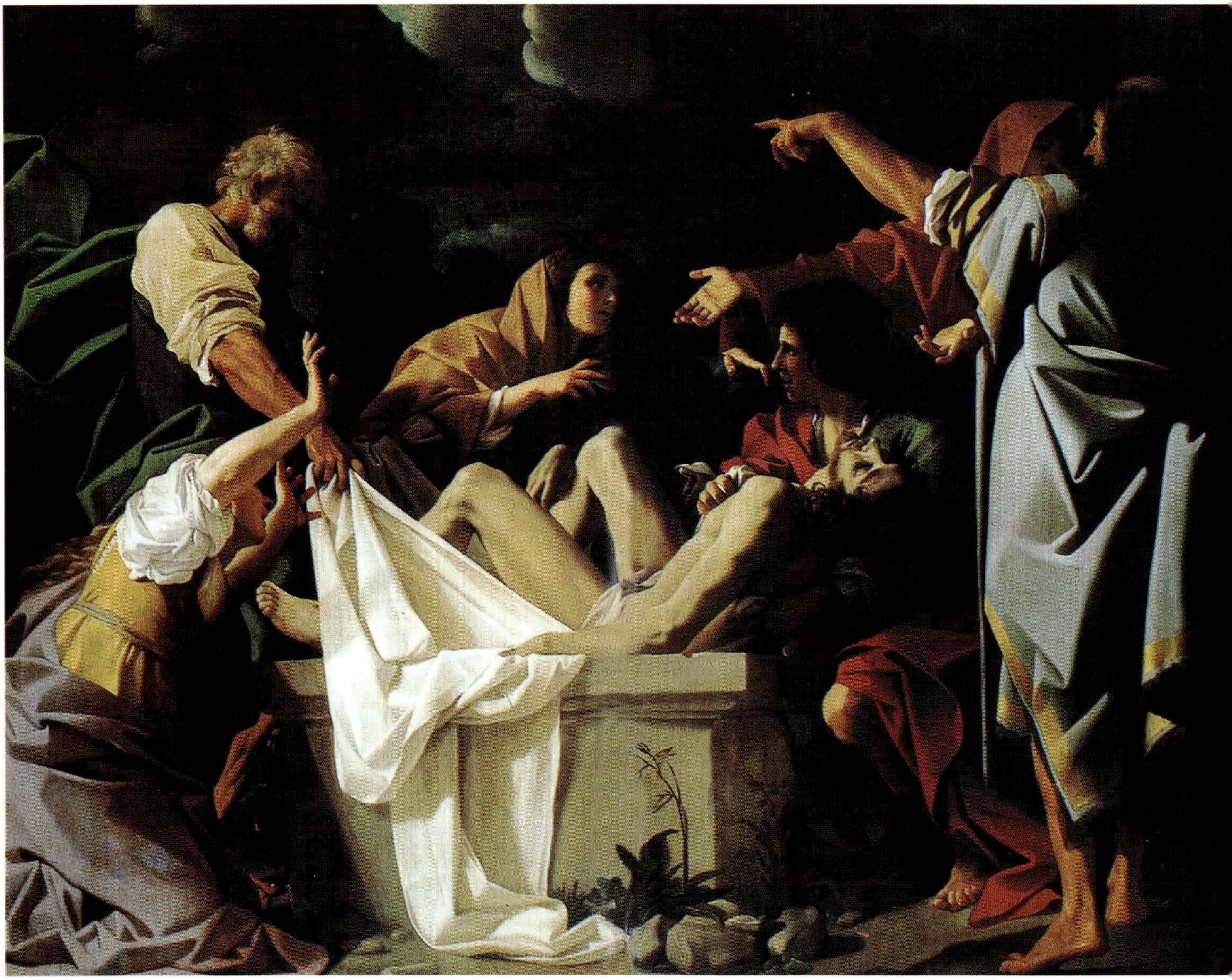

Bartolomeo Schedoni
Deposition
1613, canvas
Parma, National Gallery.

Coming from the Capuchin Monastery of Fontevivo, not far from Parma, the painting, along with the *Marys at the Sepulcher* now in the same museum, forms part of the decorative program of the building carried out for Ranuccio Farnese in 1605. The extraordinary grazing light emphasizes the volumes and the plastic forms of the personages while simultaneously conferring metallic consistency on the fabrics tormented by folds. All of the great colorist's skill can be seen here in the blinding white of the shroud and the blouses contrasting with the greens and reds of the gowns.

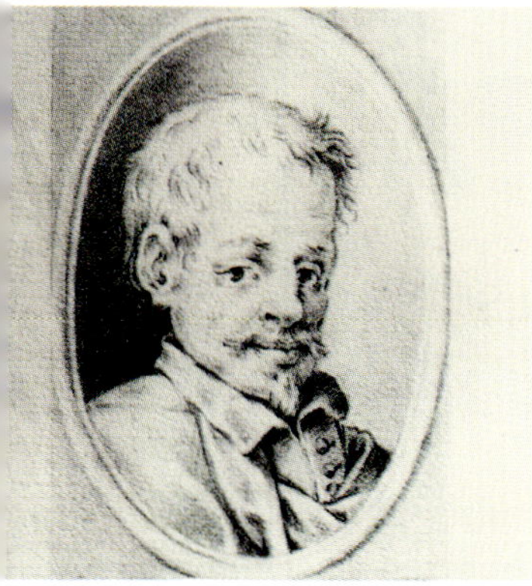

Guido Cagnacci

(Sant'Arcangelo di Romagna, Forlì, 1601 – Vienna 1663)

Only recently have critics justly reassessed the work of Guido Cagnacci, which was entirely unappreciated by his contemporaries. Cesare Malvasia in fact (1616-83) wrote in his *Lives of the Bolognese Painters* on the subject of Guido Reni: "[...] he worked hard [...] with certain pale and bluish tints mixed among the half tones and the flesh tones; as was later done perhaps too boldly by Cagnacci his pupil". Cagnacci's painting, instead, is warm with the heightened tones of grazing light, rich in the play of shadows and colors. First linked to his native city (where he worked in the Duomo), he went to Venice in 1650, where he assimilated the heritage of Venetian art. Called to Vienna by Leopold I eight years later, he was to remain there for the rest of his life, exerting a major influence on painting beyond the borders of Italy.

Marino Medici, *Portrait of Guido Cagnacci*, c. 1752. Rimini, Biblioteca Gambalunghiana.

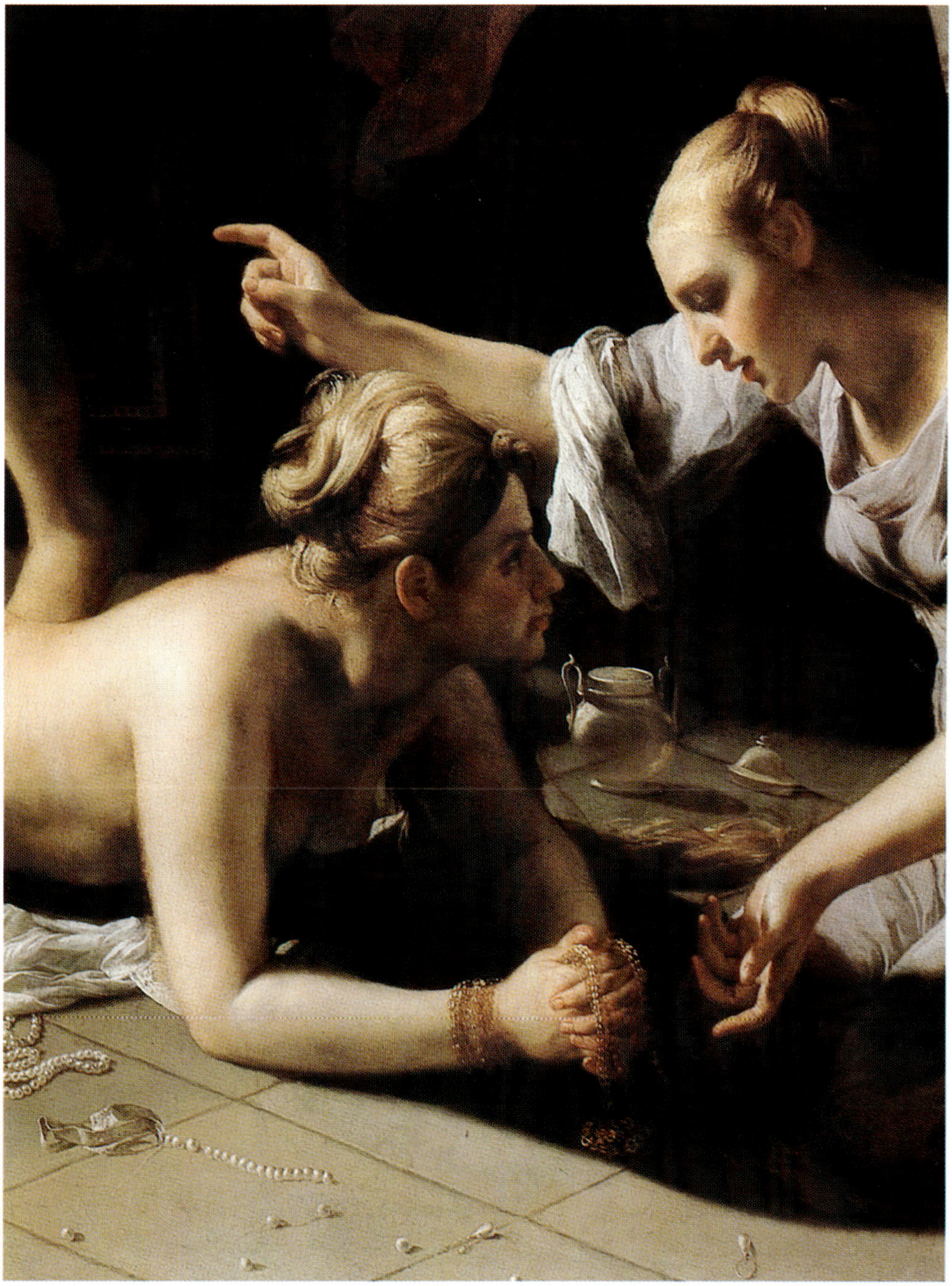

Guido Cagnacci
The Conversion of the Magdalene
between 1650 and 1658
canvas, detail
Pasadena, Museum of Art, Norton Simon Foundation.

The crucial point of the scene lies in the two faces in confrontation, which express two different ways of life. Mary Magdalene, entirely devoted to earthly pleasures, lies stretched out on the floor, her face in shadow like her soul. The other woman, her face flooded with light, is her sister Martha who is endeavoring to convert her. Guido exploits the lighting of Caravaggio with his customary skill, imbuing it with further significance. The pearl necklace lying broken on the floor and the other abandoned ornaments are a sign that Martha's words are having an effect.

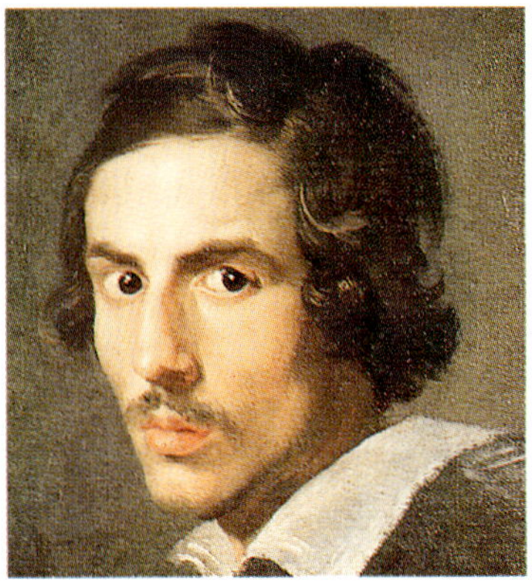

Gianlorenzo Bernini

(Naples 1598 – Rome 1680)

Painter, sculptor, architect, set designer and playwright, Bernini was considered by his contemporaries the Michelangelo of his time. Pope Urban VIII Barberini (1623-44) even saw in the artist's very existence the sign of a divine project: "A rare man, of sublime intellect, and born by divine disposition, and for the glory of Rome to bring light to the century...", he is reported to have stated. In any case, Gianlorenzo was the most important artificer of the renovation in style of 17th century Italian art, as well as the unwitting founder of the Baroque poetics. The son of Pietro Bernini (1562-1629), a sculptor of a certain talent, Gianlorenzo took his first steps as artist, apart from the wondrous anecdotes related by his biographers, beside his father who, with his acquaintances, could introduce him to the gilded, exclusive world of patrons who were cardinals and popes. At the age of only twenty he be-

Gianlorenzo Bernini, *Self-portrait of the Artist as a Young Man*, c. 1623. Rome, Galleria Borghese.

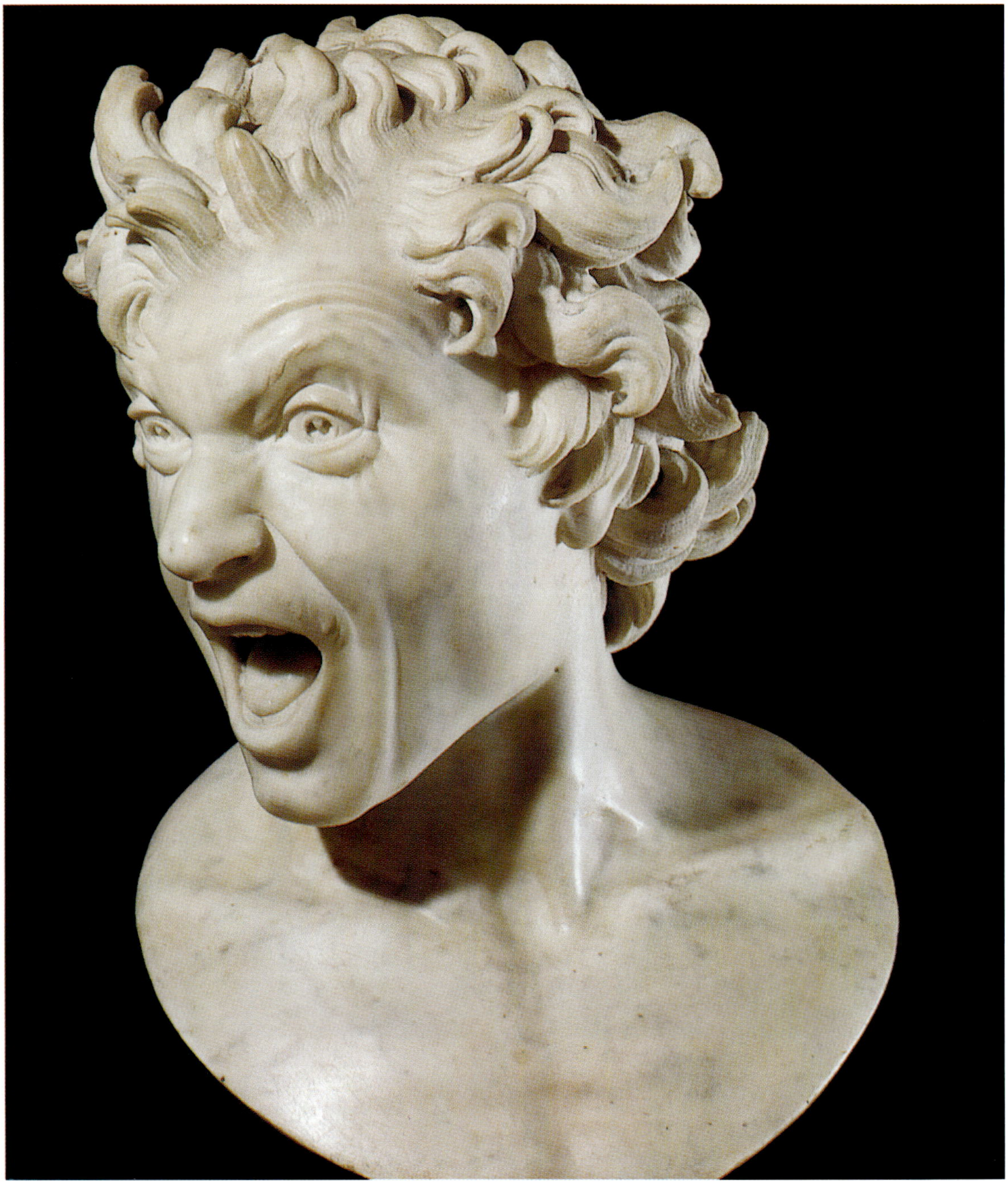

Gianlorenzo Bernini
Damned Soul
1619
white marble
Rome, Spanish Embassy to the Vatican.

Sculpted for the Spanish priest Pedro de Foix Montoya (1556-1630) who worked in the Curia, the marble bust of the *Damned Soul* is a companion piece to the one called the *Blessed Soul*, conserved in the same place. The latter portrays a girl, her head adorned with a garland of roses, who is looking on high with an inspired gaze. The *Damned Soul* could be a self-portrait with exaggerated features contorted in a scream. Of indubitable moralizing intention, the two busts are a modern elaboration of the concept of "a good death" advocated by Catholic doctrine.

gan to work for Cardinal Scipione Borghese, for whom he was to sculpt some of the most important groups in Baroque art: the *Aeneas, Anchise and Ascanius* (1618-19), the *Rape of Proserpine* (1621-22), the *David* (1623-24) and the *Apollo and Daphne* (1622-25), all now in the Borghese Gallery. At the court of the Cardinal, Gianlorenzo had the chance to meet the future Urban VIII, who commissioned from him in 1624 that Baldachin placed at the center of the transept in St Peter's Cathedral, justly considered the monumental transposition of the ephemeral machines for religious ceremonies which characterized Roman life in those days. From this time on Bernini's career was one success after another. He was appointed master of the Pontificial foundries, superintendent of the Acqua Felice aqueduct and "Architect of St Peter's". A moment of crisis occurred when the bell tower on the façade of the Vatican Basilica collapsed, and only the project for the *Fountain of the Rivers* managed to restore the artist to the favor of Innocent X (1644-55). Under the papacy of Alexander VII (1655-67), Bernini was to create grandiose works such as the colonnade of St Peter's square.

Gianlorenzo Bernini
St Lawrence
1617
white marble
Florence, Uffizi Gallery, Contini Bonacossi Collection.

Sculpted for Cardinal Maffeo Barberini (the future Urban VIII), the statue, which measures a little over sixty centimeters in length, is a product of the artist's youthful stage. Although small in size the work displays all of the monumentality that was to emerge later in the marble groups sculpted for Cardinal Borghese. Closely linked to the *St Sebastian* in the Thyssen-Bornemisza Collection (sculpted for the same patron), the *St Lawrence* re-elaborates in its pose traditional and 14th century themes associated with the art of Michelangelo (as in the *Adam* of the Sistine Chapel).

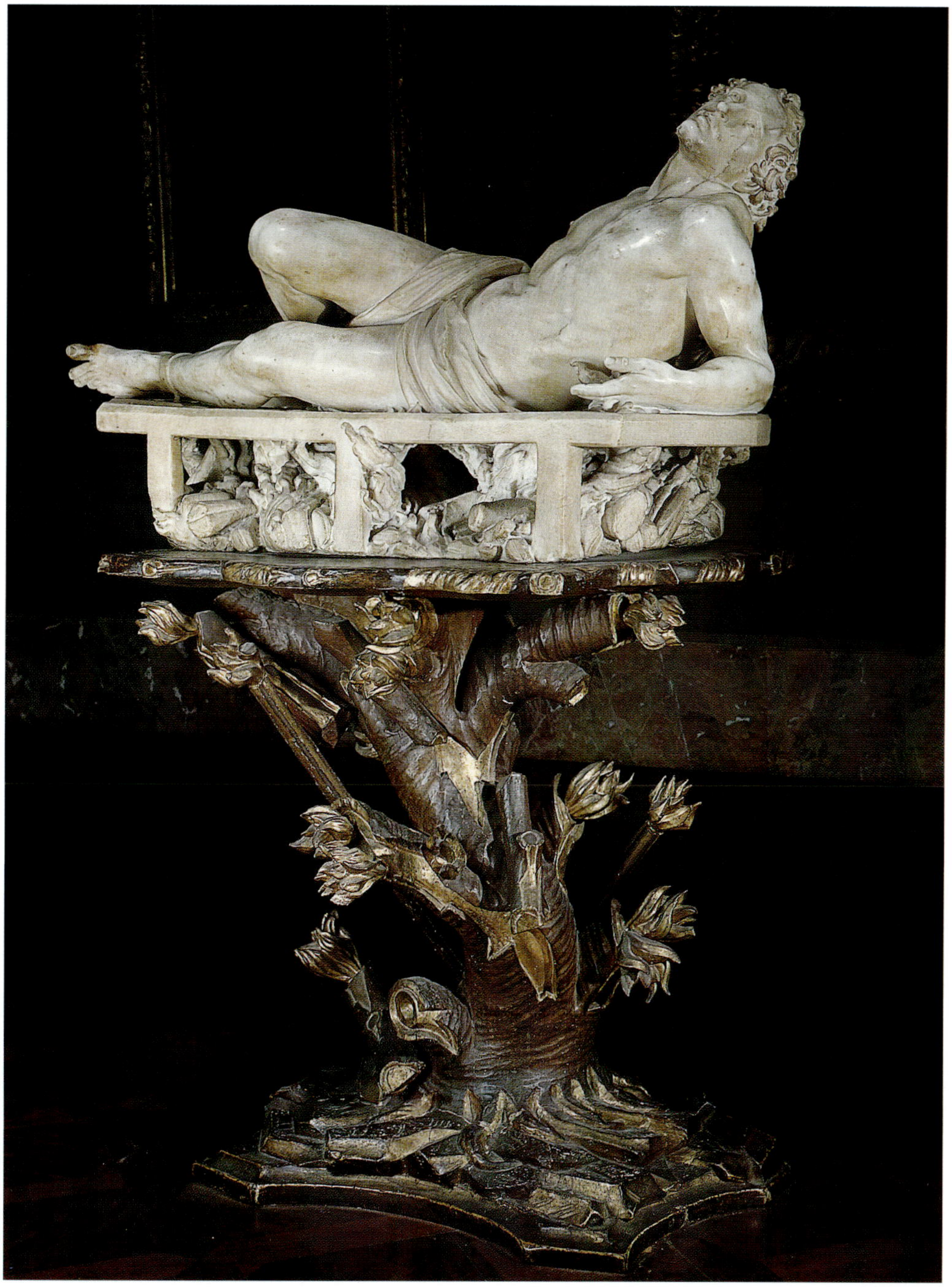

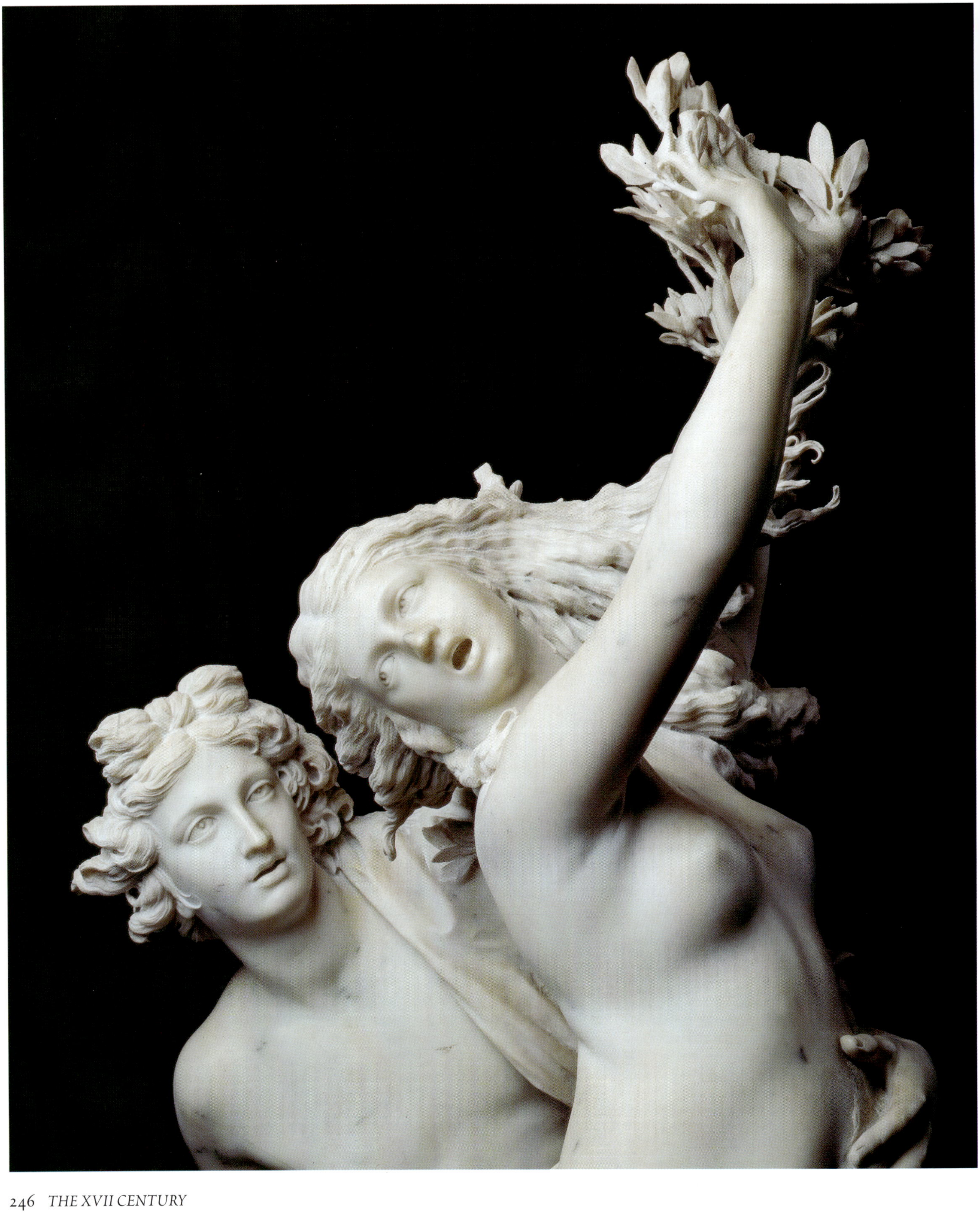

Gianlorenzo Bernini
Apollo and Daphne
1622-25
white marble, detail
Rome, Galleria Borghese.

The dating covers a long period due to the fact that Cardinal Borghese decided to commission of the artist, who had already begun the work, a *David* as well. The *Apollo and Daphne* group draws inspiration from Ovid's *Metamorphosis*, where the poet sings of the impossible love of the god for the nymph who, as revealed by her name, preferred to be transformed into a laurel tree rather than yield to his desire. The figure of Apollo echoes that of the *Belvedere Apollo*.

Gianlorenzo Bernini
The Ecstasy of Saint Teresa
1647-51
white marble
Rome, Santa Maria della Vittoria, Cornaro Chapel.

Built for Federico Cornaro, the family funeral chapel is designed like a mystic stage at the center of which, in the tabernacle, is represented the ecstasy of the saint, compared at the time to that of St Francis. The marble group, one of the masterpieces of Baroque art, is inspired by the words of Teresa: "I saw beside me [...] an angel in human form [...] low and most beautiful [...].
In his hands I saw a long golden lance [...] with which he seemed to piece by heart [...].

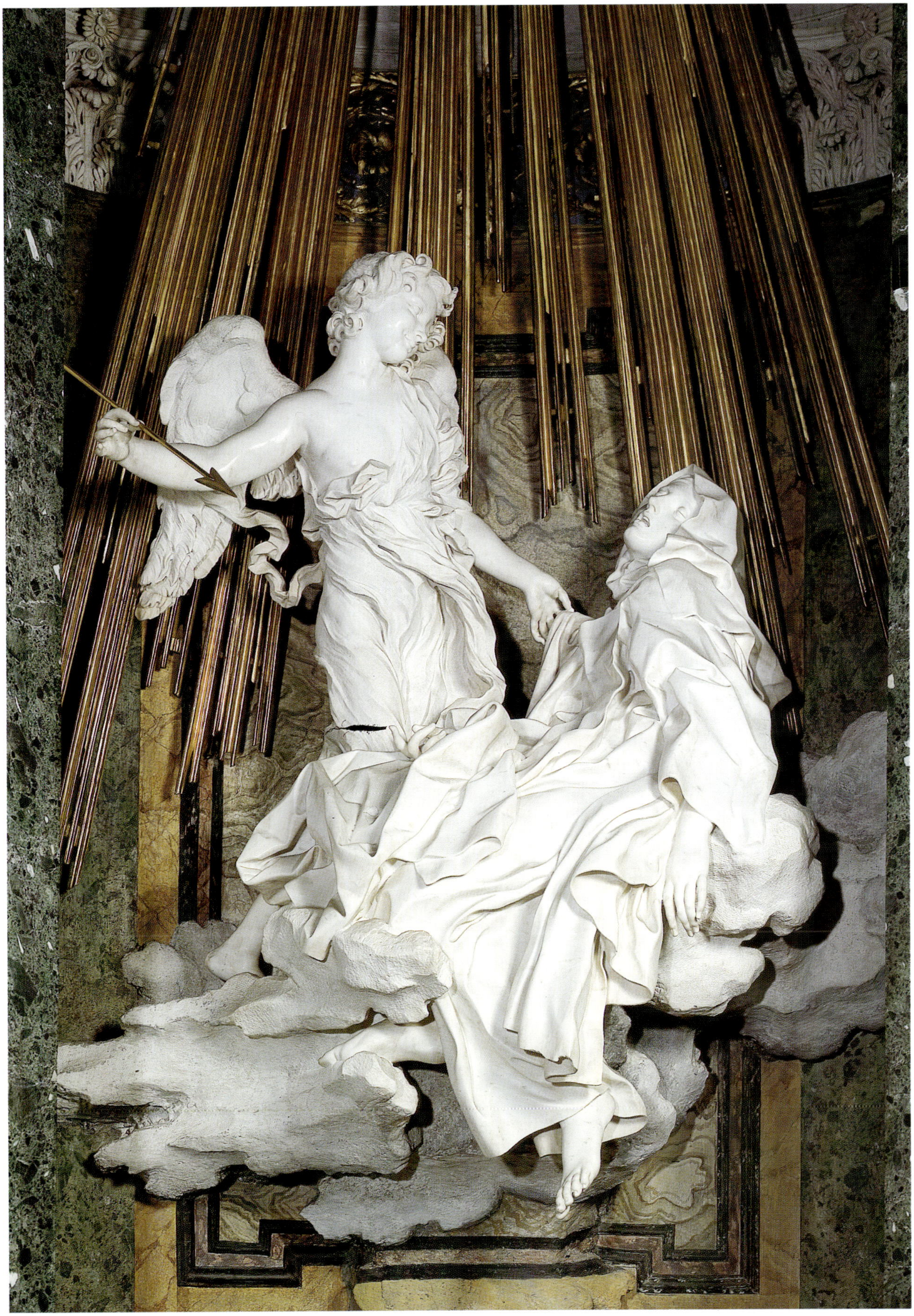

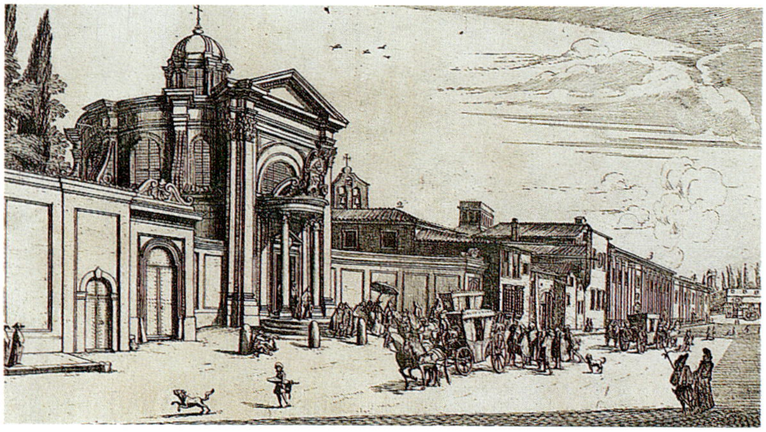

Gianlorenzo Bernini
Sant'Andrea al Quirinale
1658-71
engraving by Giovanni Battista Falda
Rome, Biblioteca Casanatense.

Built at the desire of Cardinal Camillo Pamphilj, the nephew of Innocent X, the church was one of the projects commissioned of Bernini by private clients. Distinguished by a strongly projecting prothyreum which vivaciously animates the façade, the building has an ovoid plan. The interior, with its rich marble inlays, is inspired by the Pantheon, of which its coffered dome is a re-interpretation.

Gianlorenzo Bernini
Fountain of the Rivers
1648-51
travertine and porphyry, detail
Rome, Piazza Navona.

The object most highly appreciated by Donna Olympia Maidalchini, the power behind the throne of Pope Innocent X, seems to have been the solid silver model of the fountain given her by the artist. The Pope, for his part, said that he would be able to refuse a project by Bernini only if he had not yet seen it. The occasion for the fountain was created by the discovery of the obelisk, which Bernini then placed above a great open rock surrounded by figures representing the rivers of the four continents known at the time: the *Danube* (illustrated here), the *Nile*, the *Ganges* and the *Rio della Plata*.

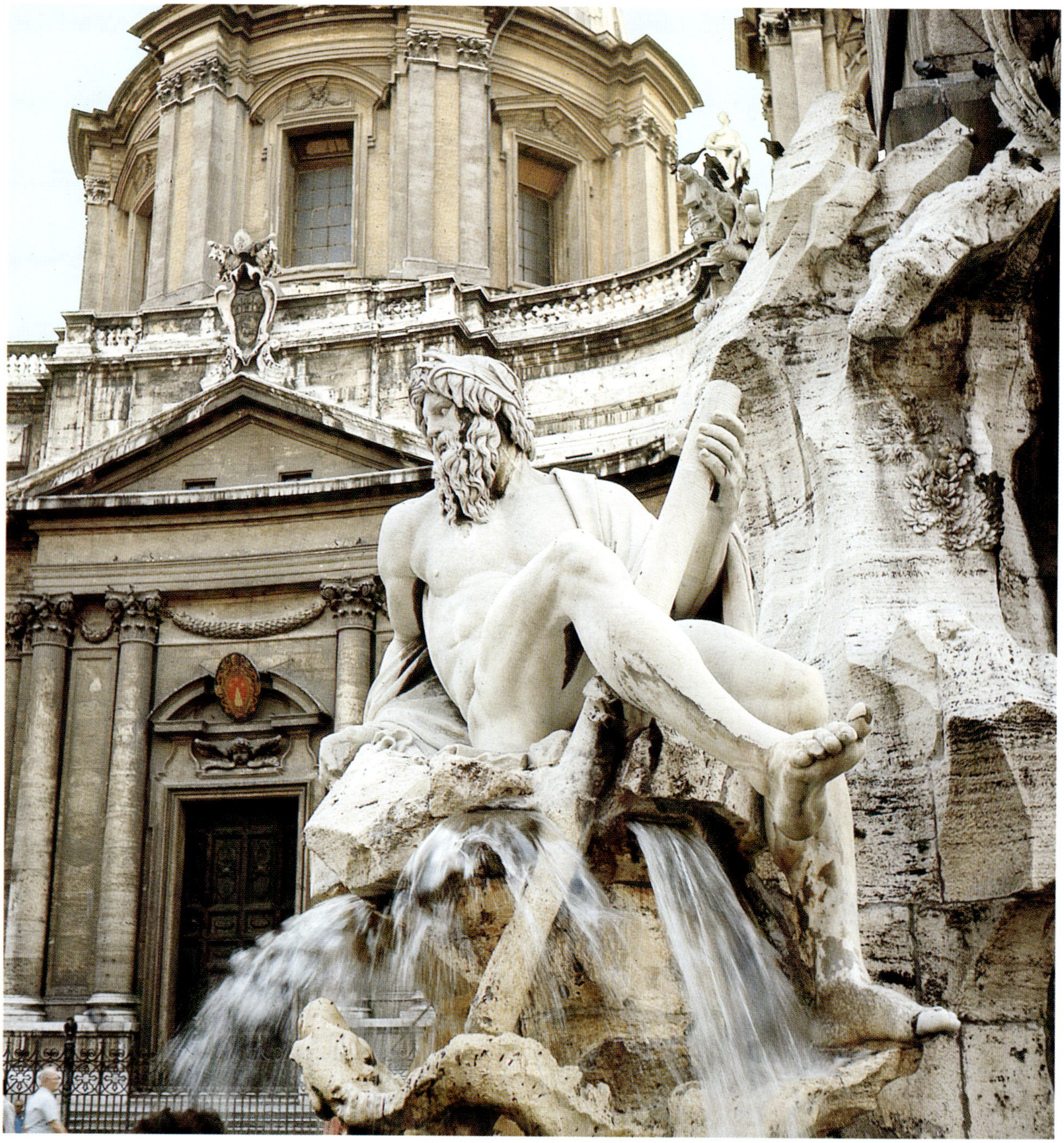

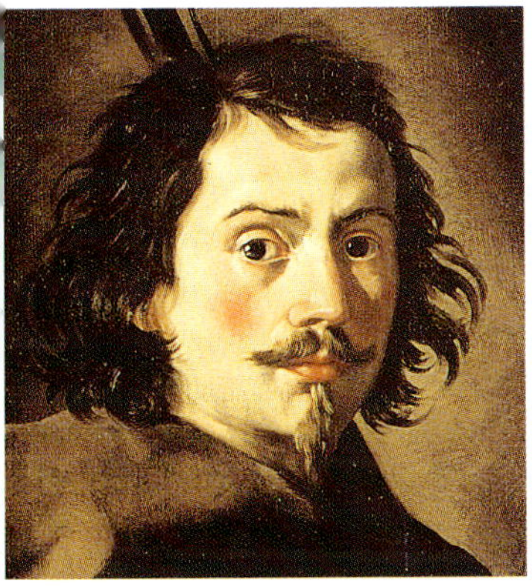

Francesco Borromini

(Francesco Castelli, Bisone, Canton Ticino, 1599 – Rome 1667)

The architect Francesco Borromini indubitably represents the other soul of Italian Baroque art: apparently capricious and far from the balanced artifice of a Bernini. It is no coincidence that the two were fierce rivals. Borromini had worked under Bernini on the Baldachin of St Peter's and both had been assistants to Carlo Maderno (1556-1629) in the construction of Palazzo Barberini. A restless spirit – he was to die a suicide – Borromini designed some of the masterpieces of Baroque architecture. Working almost always in Rome (apart from the Filomarino altar in the Santi Apostoli Church in Naples), he constructed San Carlo alle Quattro Fontane, the façade of the Filippini Oratory, the Church of Sant'Agnese in Agone, the Propaganda Fide Collegiate, and restored the interior of San Giovanni in Laterano.

Anonymous, *Portrait of Francesco Borromini*, detail, c. 1630.

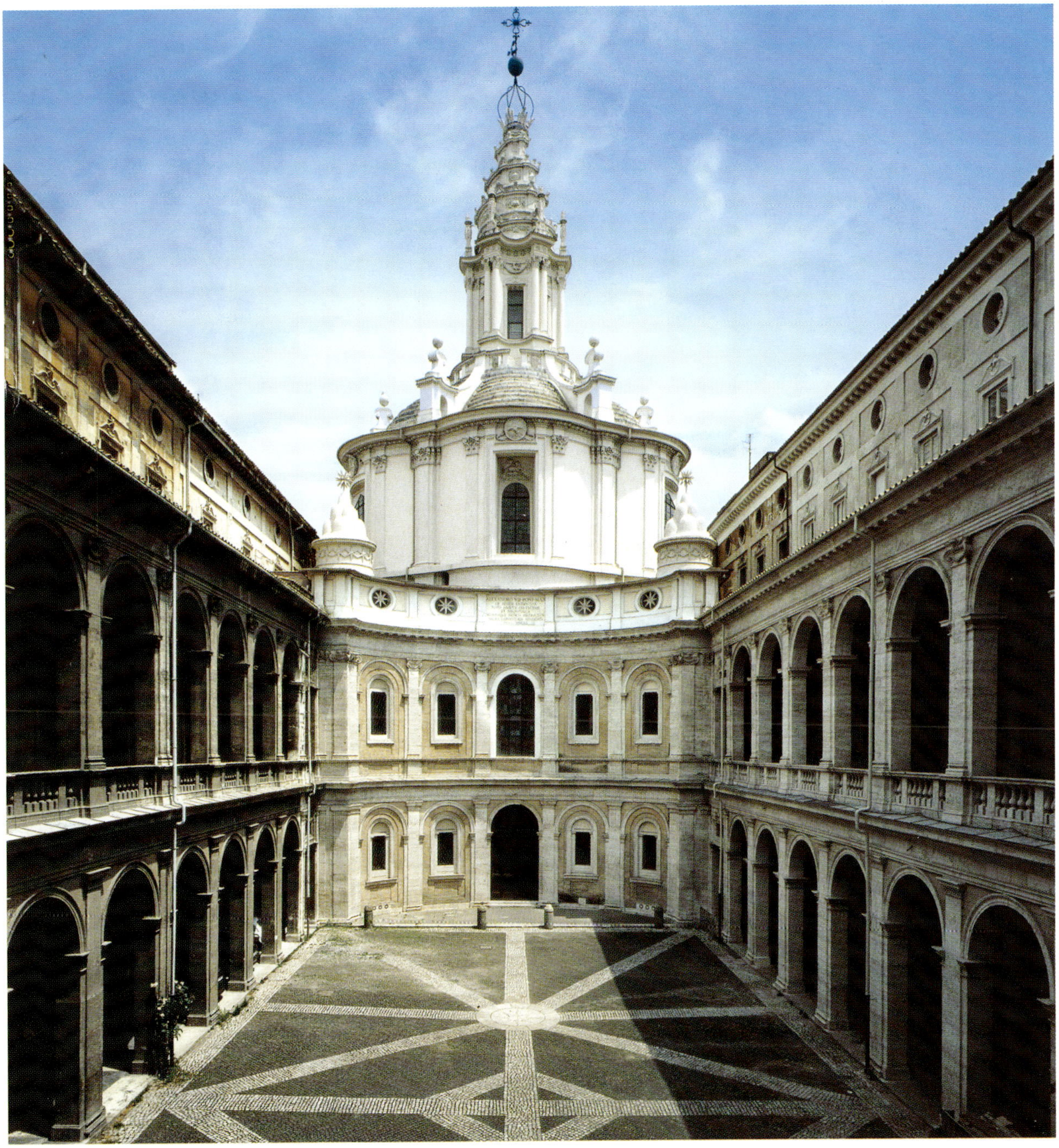

Francesco Borromini
Sant'Ivo alla Sapienza
1642-62
Rome.

Originally a chapel annexed to the Papal Archiginnasio (that is, the university, and known for this reason as "alla Sapienza", or Wisdom), the Church of Sant'Ivo was constructed within an established space, the one left by Giacomo Della Porta (1553-1602), the architect of the courtyard and the Palazzo della Sapienza. The plan of Borromini's building is inspired by the Salomonic seal of the six-pointed star, a design appropriate to the concept of Wisdom. The phantasmagoric dome is decorated with the visual allegories of Cesare Ripa (1560-1625) which refer to the same sphere: that of the representation of divine Wisdom.

Baldassarre Longhena

(Venice 1597 – 1682)

Defined by critics as "the only high class alternative to Roman Baroque", the architecture of Longhena renewed the Venetian tradition without betraying it. A pupil of Vincenzo Scamozzi (1552-1616), the architect brought with him the sensitivity acquired in his apprenticeship as sculptor. His first work was that of completing his master's Procuratie Vecchie. He then designed the Church of the Scalzi (1660) and the civic buildings of Ca' Pesaro (1660) and Ca' Rezzonico (1667).

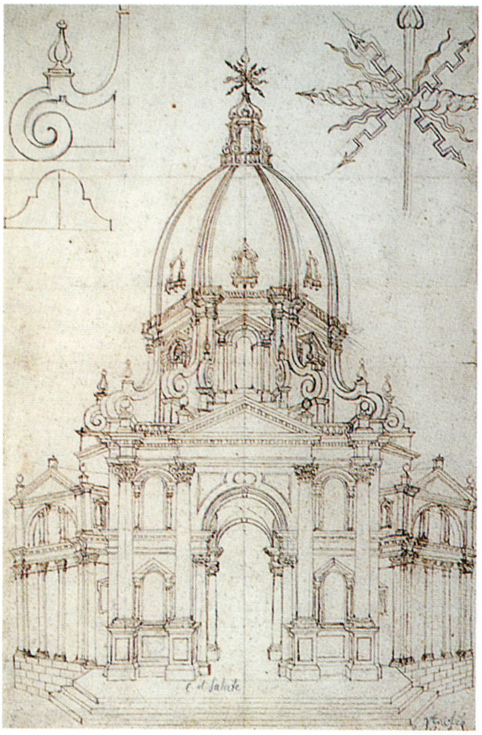

Baldassarre Longhena (attr.), *Façade of the Church of Santa Maria della Salute in Venice*, c. 1631. Vienna, Graphische Sammlung Albertina.

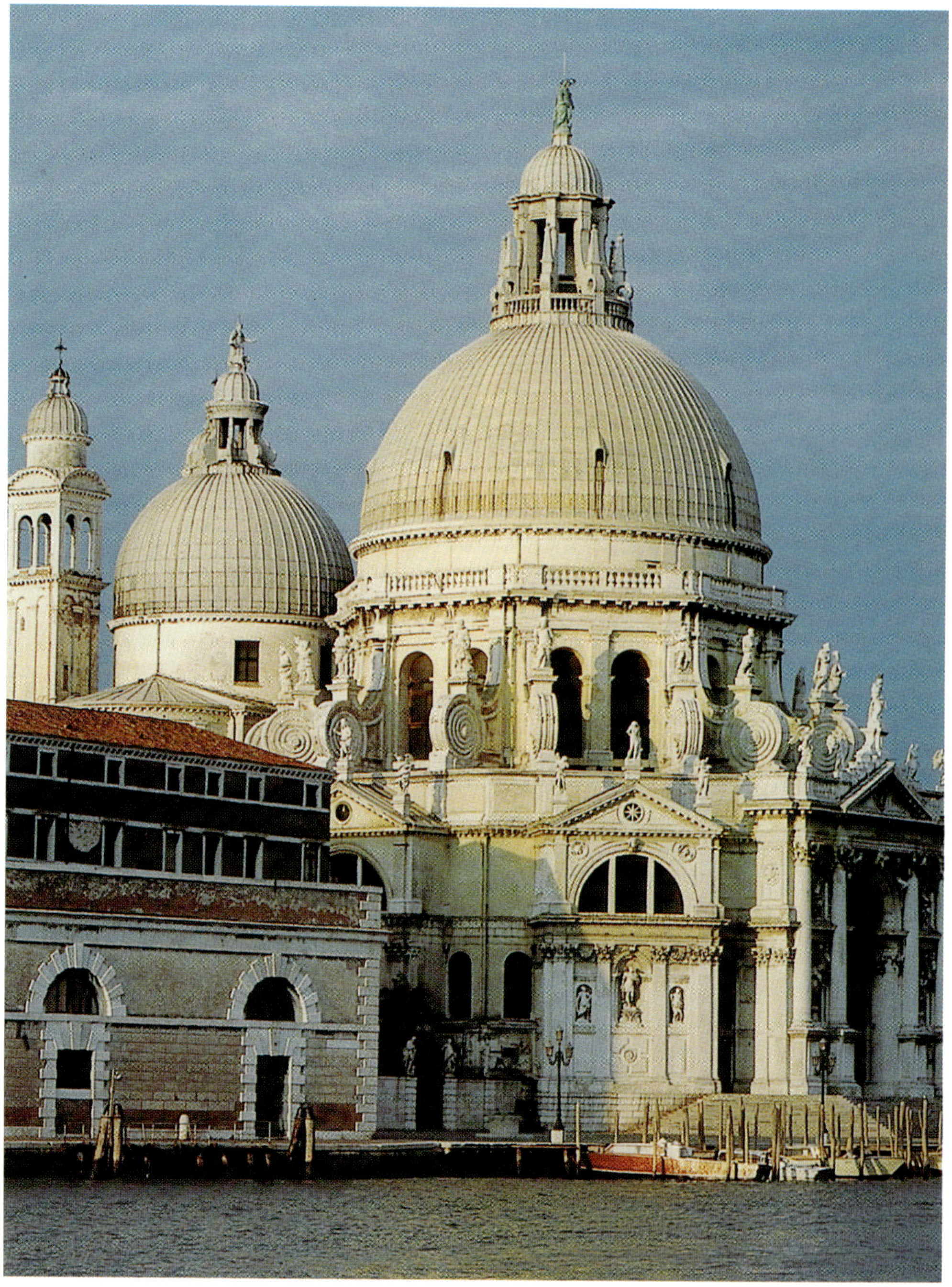

Baldassarre Longhena
Santa Maria della Salute
1631-87
Venice.

Considered by art historians to be the absolute masterpiece of Baldassarre Longhena, the Church of Santa Maria della Salute was erected as a votive temple dedicated to the Virgin to implore the end of the plague of 1630, later recalled by Manzoni in his famous "Promessi Sposi". Completed by Antonio Gaspari in 1687, the building is situated on the point of the Dogana reconstructed between 1677 and 1683 by the architect Giuseppe Benoni. Justly described as a prayer in marble which unites religious devotion and civic piety the church, with octagonal plan and transverse apse, shows a return to Palladio's architectural synthesis, but transposed to Baroque sensitivity. This is apparent in the vitality and imaginative fantasy of original solutions such as the double dome, the connecting volutes between the body of the building and the lantern, and in the swarming proliferation of statues.

Bernardo Strozzi

(known as Il Cappuccino
and Il Prete Genovese,
Genoa 1581 – Venice 1644)

The artist is one of the outstanding figures in the great 17th century art of Genoa, distinguished by international contacts and by the presence of eminent artists such as Rubens (1577-1640) and above all Van Dyck (1599-1641), who lived there from 1621 to 1626, the year in which he also visited many other Italian cities. Trained in the school of the Sienese Pietro Sorri, a late Mannerist painter, Strozzi later assimilated the lesson taught by foreign artists, as well as by Morazzone (1573-1626) and Cerano (1567/8-1632), to breathe life into a personal, mature, easily enjoyable style of his own. Moreover, Bernardo never banished from his work the traits of Caravaggio, probably assimilated during a hypothetical journey to Rome. Living a rather turbulent life, the artist entered the order of the Capuchin monks and then left it to help his family overcome a moment marked by financial difficulties. In 1630 he left Genoa for Venice, where he was widely successful. He is also known as a painter of still lifes.

Bernardo Strozzi
Joseph Explaining Dreams
c. 1633
canvas

The work belongs to the artist's first Venetian period, when he now possessed full mastery of his pictorial means. In it we find the monumentality of Rubens, the skillful luminosity of Caravaggio and the facile drawing ability of Cerano. The painting illustrates, and gives topical significance to, the well-known Biblical episode in which Joseph, the son of Jacob, explains the meaning of the dream of Pharaoh's head steward (Genesis, XL, 9-12). The grapevine that Bernardo has painted in the background of the canvas is itself the subject of the steward's dream.

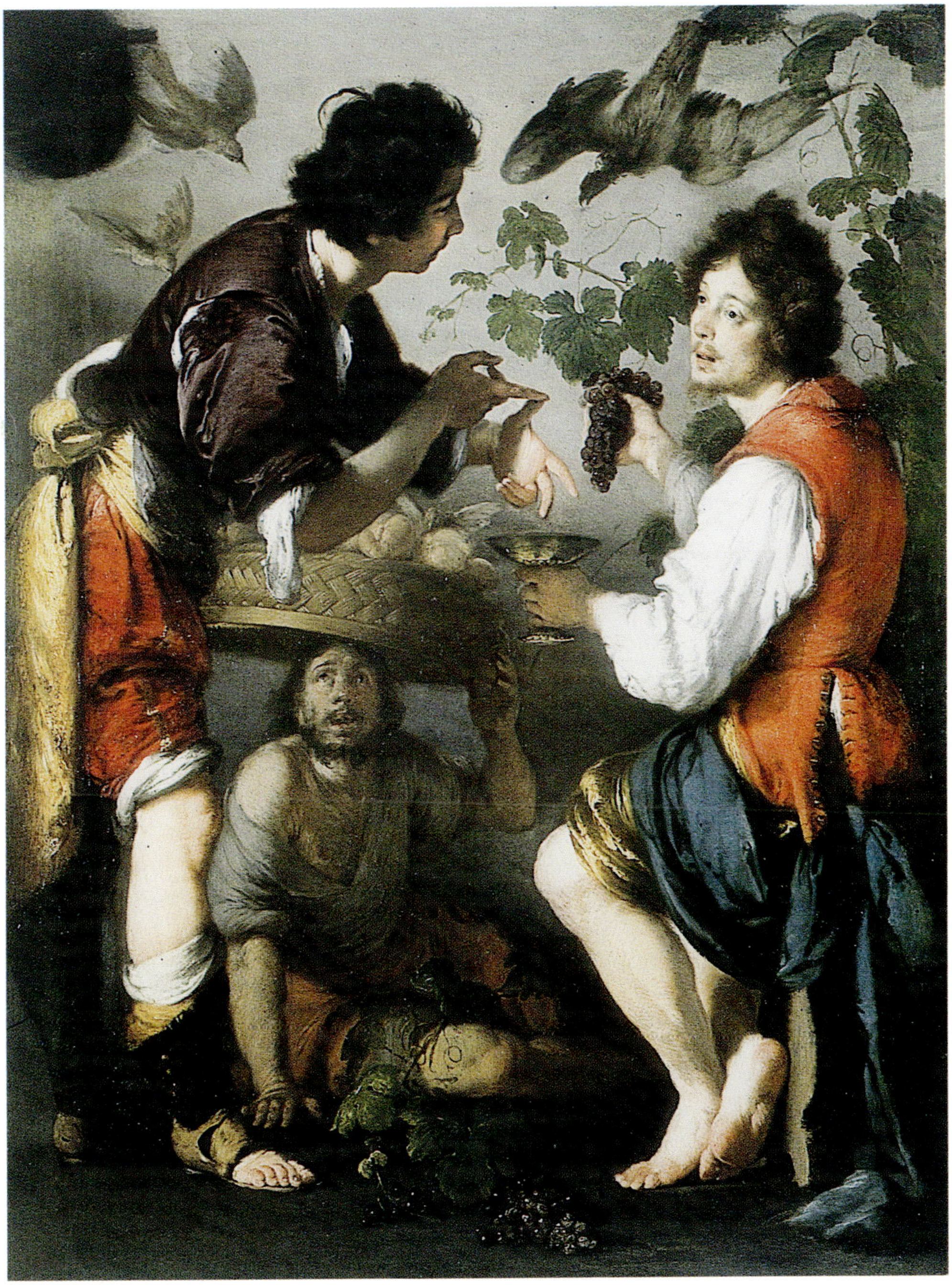

Battistello Caracciolo

(Giovan Battista Caracciolo, Naples c. 1570 – 1635)

The artistic career of Giovan Battista Caracciolo, known as "il Battistello", is a clear demonstration of the driving force and suggestive influence of Caravaggio's painting. Probably trained in the late Mannerist school of Corenzio and certainly his assistant in painting the frescoes at Monte di Pietà, Battistello radically changed his style after Caravaggio's stay in Naples (1606). Attracted by the lesson to be learned from the *Seven Works of Charity* (Naples, Pio Monte della Misericordia Chapel) and the *Madonna of the Rosary* (now in the Kunsthistorisches Museum in Vienna) painted by the Milanese artist in Naples between 1606 and 1607, Caracciolo painted for Santa Maria della Stella the *Immaculate Conception with St Dominic and St Francis of Paola*. Journeys to Rome and to Genoa starting in 1618 rendered the stylistic characteristics of the Neapolitan painter even more articulate, through confrontation with the heritage of the Carracci family and of Guido Reni. He returned to Naples to find himself the unrivaled master in the field.

Battistello Caracciolo
Tobias and the Angel
c. 1622
canvas
London, Walpole Gallery.

The painting illustrates the Biblical episode of the angel who advises Tobias to take the fish lying on the banks of the Tigris, advice which will be crucially important to the life of the young man and to God's will. The grazing light employed by Battistello in the scene confers an air of mystery to the episode. The artist shows himself attentive to the Biblical text, and the size of the fish is justified by the fact that the beast is reported to have tried to devour Tobias.

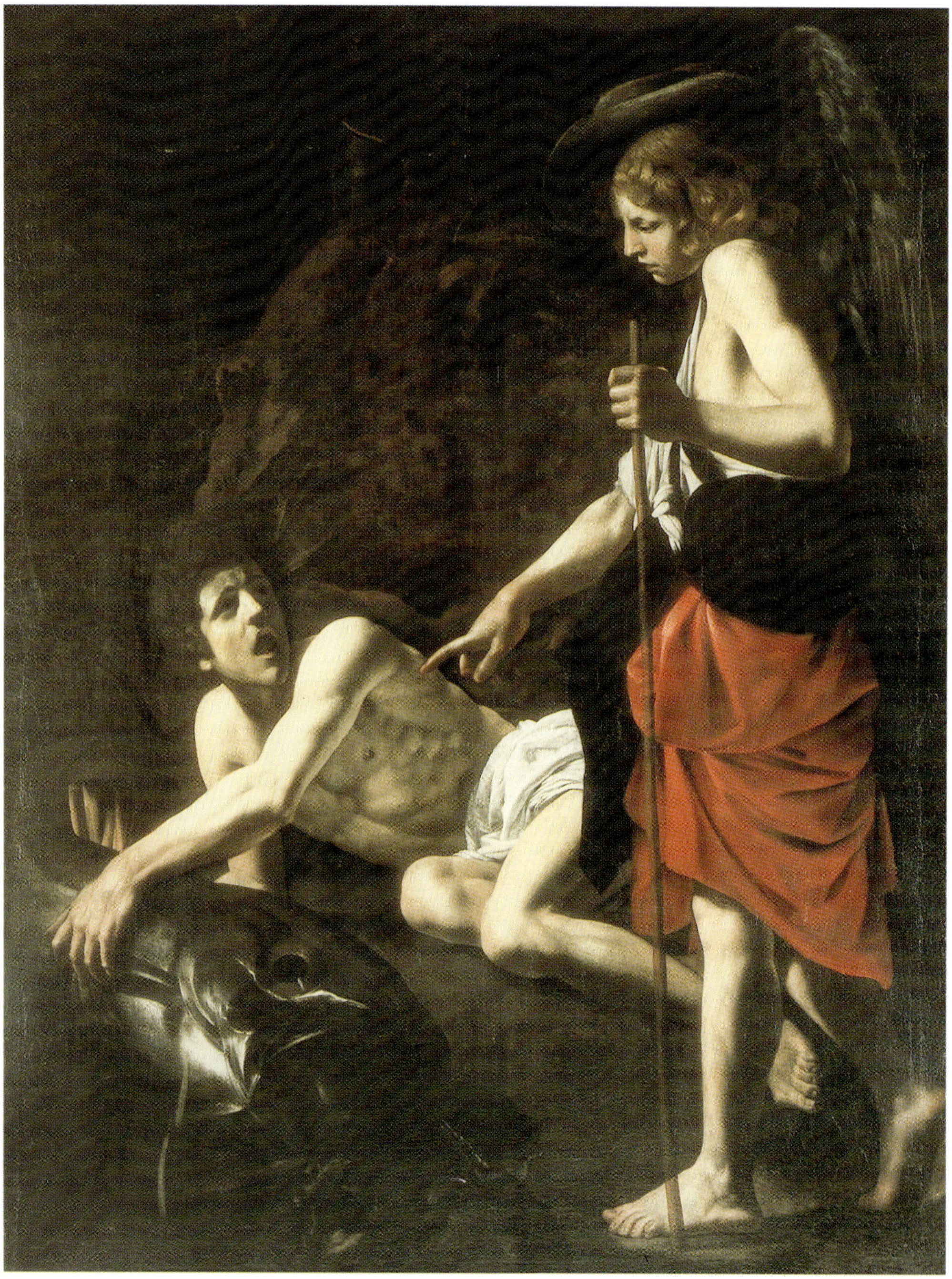

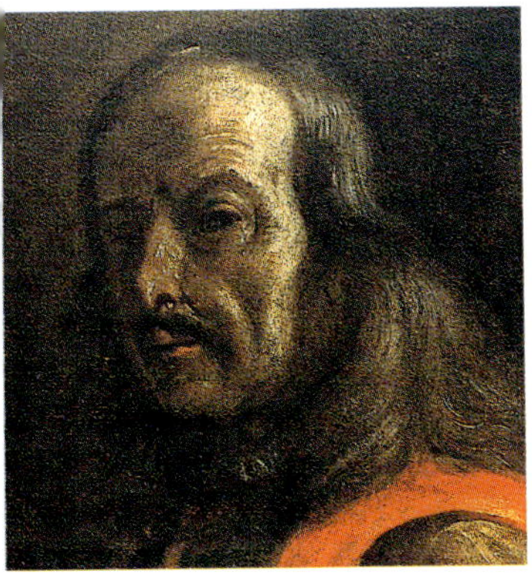

Mattia Preti

(Cavalier Calabrese, Taverna, Catanzaro, 1613 – La Valletta 1699)

The fact that Mattia was named Knight of Malta when only twenty-nine (1642) caused a sensation, so that he was given the nickname of "Cavalier Calabrese", a name that united his regional origins and the new honor he had received. This recognition was however justified. At that age Mattia had already won a name for himself as painter, journeying to Naples (1630), where he immediately embraced the "Manfredi genre", as Caravaggism was then called, and then to Rome, where he was elected among the Virtuosi of the Pantheon and where he painted frescoes in San Carlo ai Catinari (1642) and Sant'Andrea della Valle. Travelling between Modena and Naples, he moved to Valletta in 1661, where he was to remain, apart from occasional journeys, for the rest of his life.

Mattia Preti,
Self-portrait, detail, 1660. Florence, Uffizi Gallery.

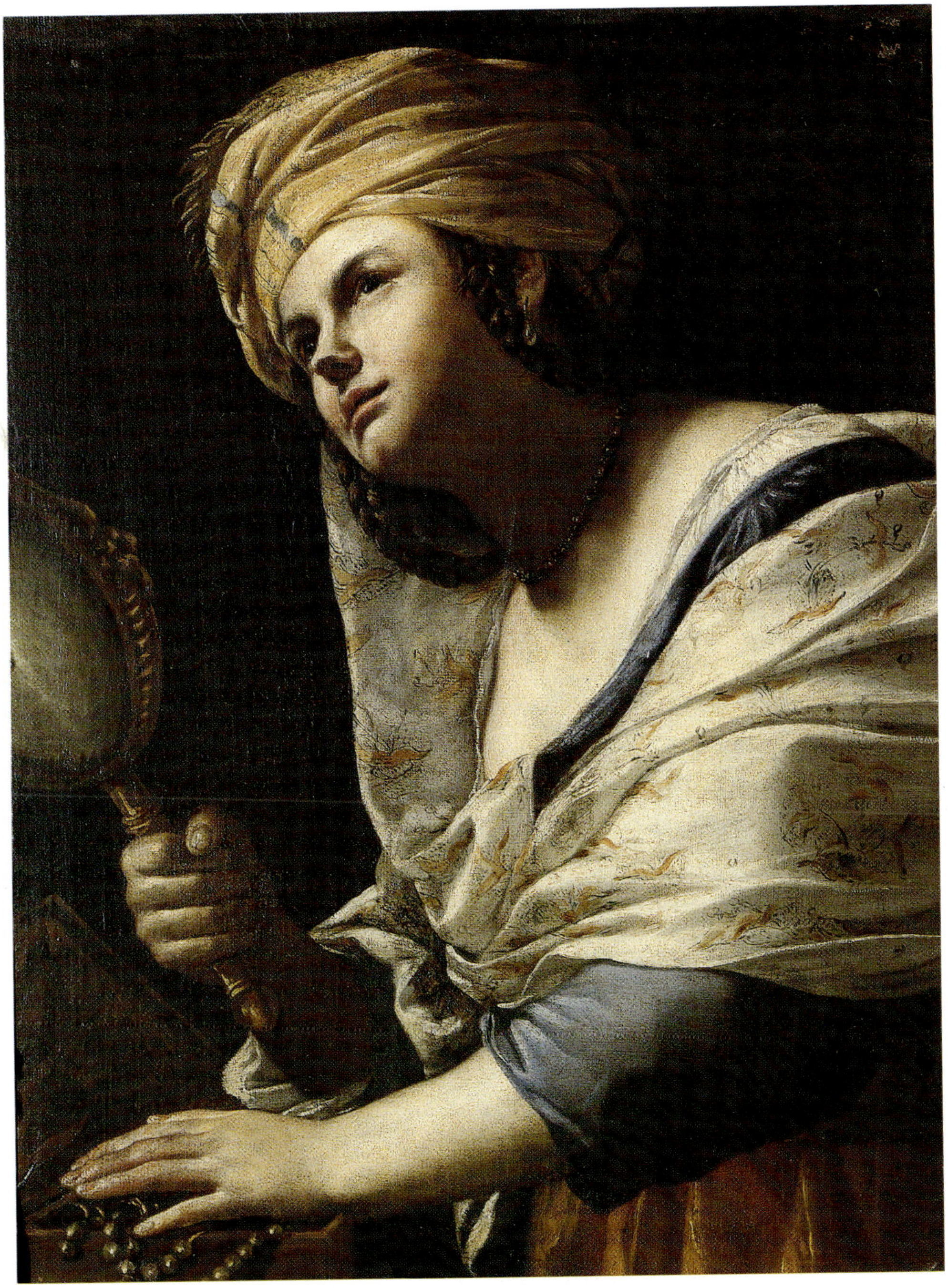

Mattia Preti
Vanity
canvas
c. 1650-70
Florence, Uffizi Gallery.

Purchased in 1951 from a private collection, this canvas may have formed part of a larger composition that has been cut down. The gesture of rejecting riches is accentuated by the inspired gaze and attitude of the subject. The warm natural light that falls from the upper left-hand corner of the painting thus takes on mystic, religious values. The pose and clothing of the figure testify to Mattia Preti's interest in other artists, such as Domenichino whose work he had undoubtedly studied during the periods spent in Rome.

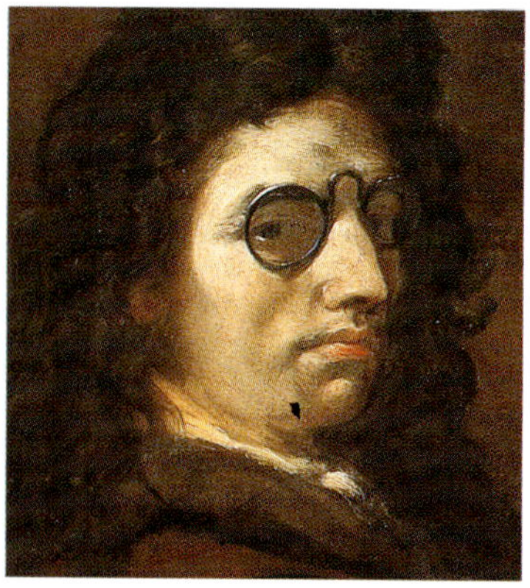

Luca Giordano

(Naples 1634 – 1705)

He was the most versatile and prolific figure in Neapolitan 17th century painting of the second generation, which now took Caravaggism for granted and was turning toward other styles. Son of the copyist Antonio Giordano, Luca worked in the shop of the now elderly Juan Jusepe de Ribera (1591-1652) and assimilated the dramatic intensity of Caravaggio's luminism. Starting in 1652 he traveled through Italy, meeting other painters and viewing their work. In this manner he discovered Correggio and Venetian art, but also Lanfranco and the painters of Emilian tradition; and again, Pietro da Cortona and the Roman figurative sphere. Between 1682 and 1686 he was in Florence, where he frescoed the *Apotheosis of the Medici Dynasty* in Palazzo Medici Riccardi. He stayed for ten years (1692-1702) in Spain, but his last years were spent in his own Naples, where he frescoed the Chapel of the Treasury of San Martino.

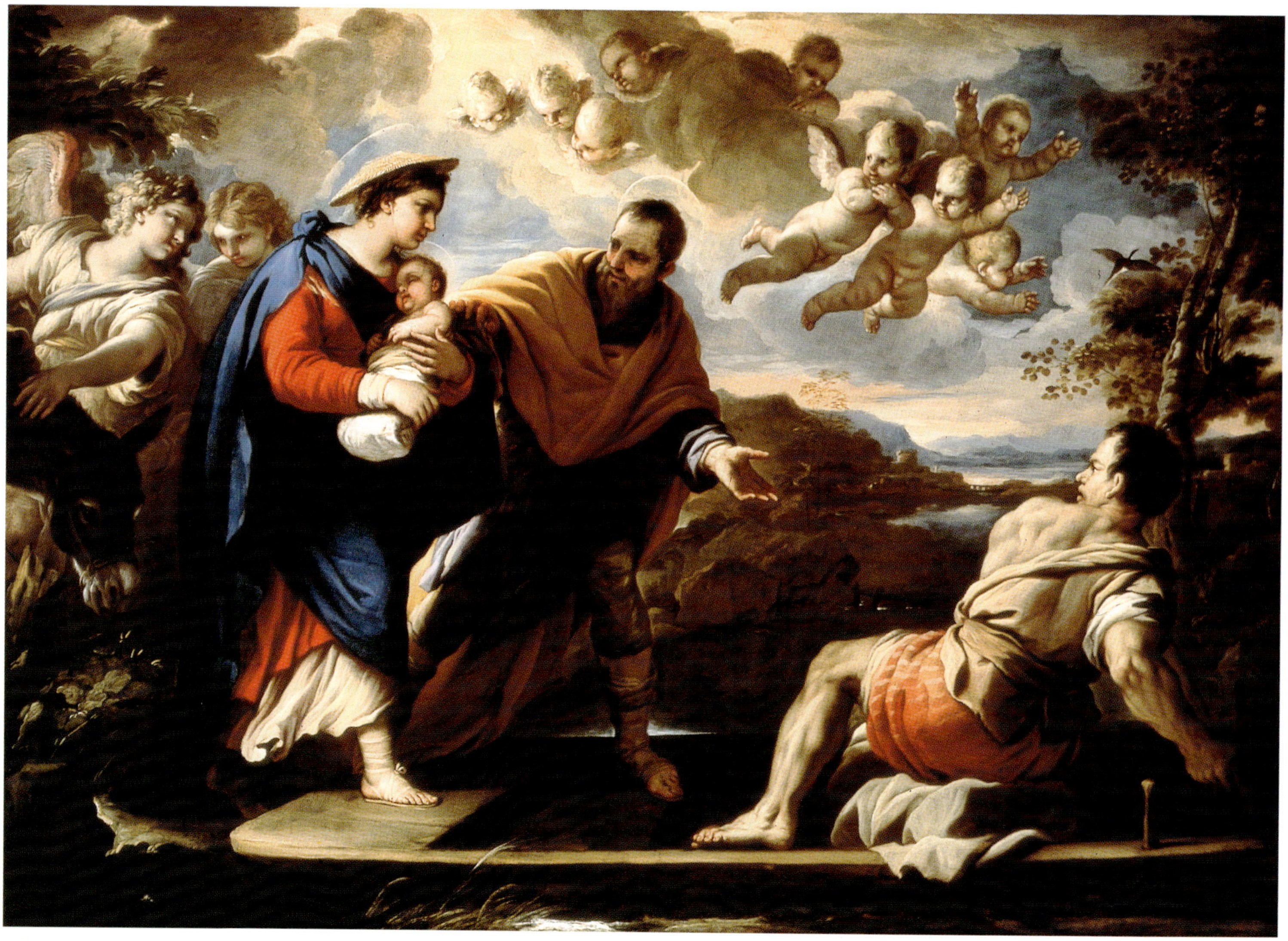

Luca Giordano,
Self-portrait, c. 1629.
Naples, Pio Monte della Misericordia.

Luca Giordano
Flight into Egypt
1684-85
canvas
Madrid, Santa Marca Collection.

The particular iconography of this subject (The Flight into Egypt is usually represented as taking place on land) indicates that the Neapolitan artist was inspired by important works from Roman 16th century art such as Raphael's *Miraculous Catch*, whose cartoon for a tapestry is now in the Victoria and Albert Museum in London. Even the choice of colors seems to indicate this direction. Accordingly, we find the return of formal and chromatic elements that, while also common to artists such as Poussin (1594-1665), can be seen as anticipating the airy gracefulness that was to typify Rococo.

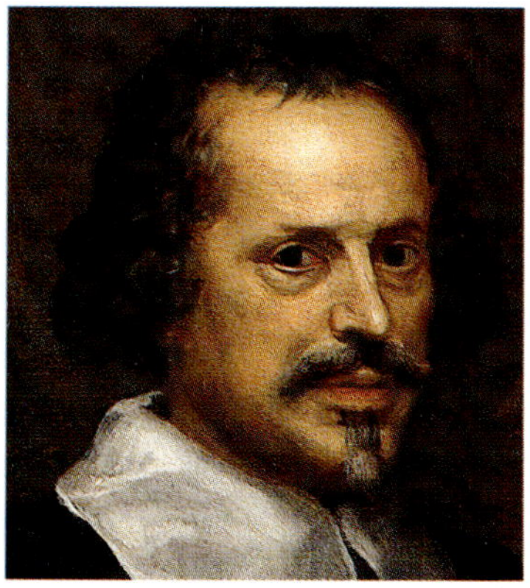

Pietro da Cortona

(Pietro Berrettini, Cortona 1596 – Rome 1669)

Painter and architect, Pietro represents in both fields the "third way" as compared to Bernini and Borromini or Caravaggio and Carracci, which was to give rise to the phenomenon of "Cortonism". Arriving in Rome in 1612 following his master, the Florentine Andrea Commodi, Pietro owed his fortune to contact with the Barberini family, who commissioned of him major works such as the *Triumph of Divine Providence* (1633-39), frescoed on the ceiling of the family palace, which had just been built in what were then the outskirts of the city. Elected Prince of the Academy of San Luca, the artist designed the headquarters of the Academy, then situated in the Church of Santi Luca e Martina. The Roman churches of Santa Maria in Via Lata (1658-62) and Santa Maria della Pace (1656-57) are also his work.

Pietro da Cortona, *Self-portrait*, detail, c. 1630. Florence, Uffizi Gallery.

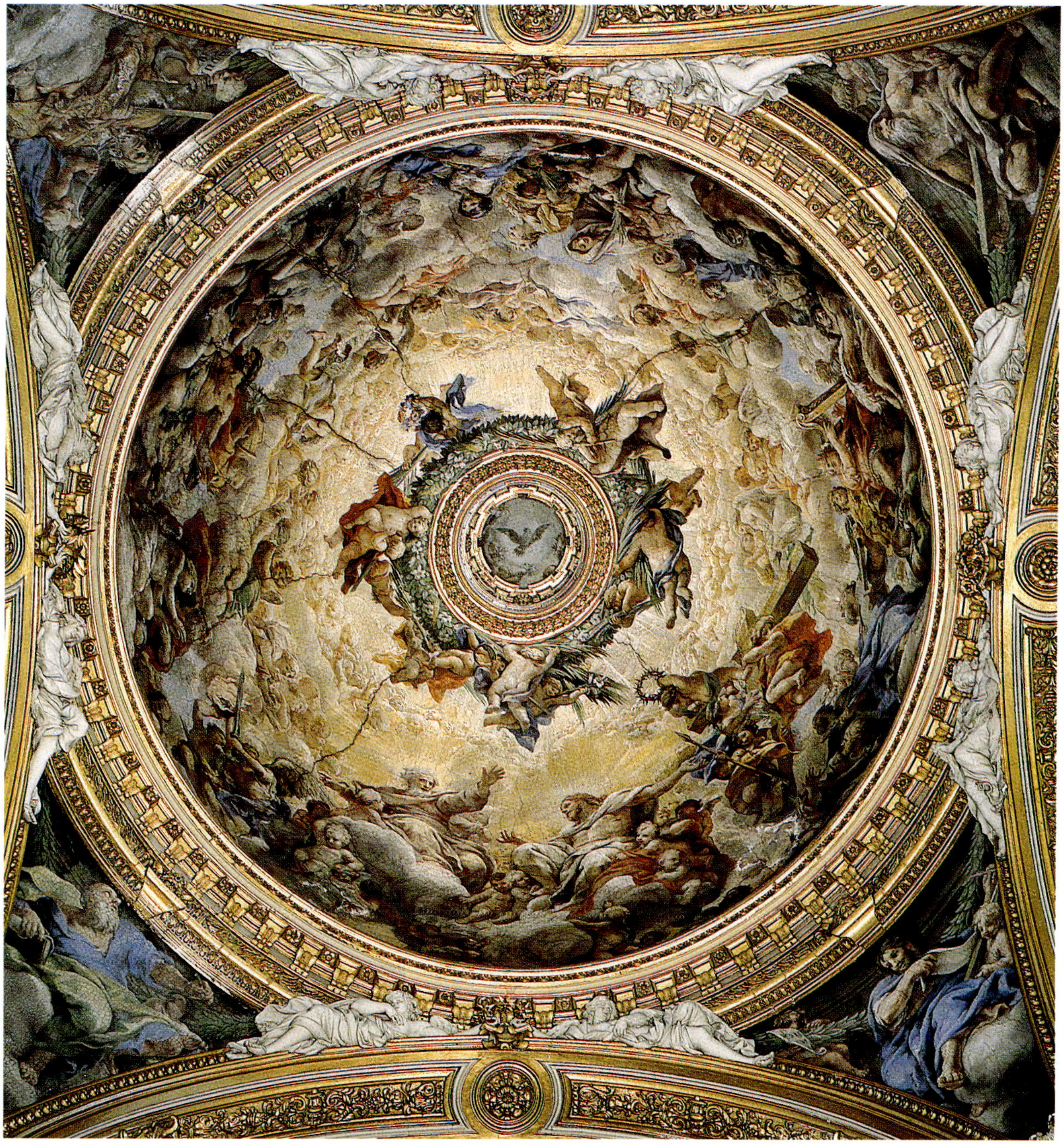

Pietro da Cortona
Trinity in Glory among the Saints and Exaltation of the Instruments of the Passion
1648-51
fresco
Rome, Santa Maria in Vallicella.

The church is situated at a short distance from Sant'Andrea della Valle, and the interior decoration of its dome is modeled on that of the church frescoed by Giovanni Lanfranco. Cortona chose, in fact, the solution of concentric circles of figures already experimented by Correggio. But in his version the vortex is accentuated even further. At the center is a garland of cherubs surrounding the Holy Spirit represented in the form of a dove. In spite of its spectacular, theatrical solutions, the painting is distinguished by balance and composure.

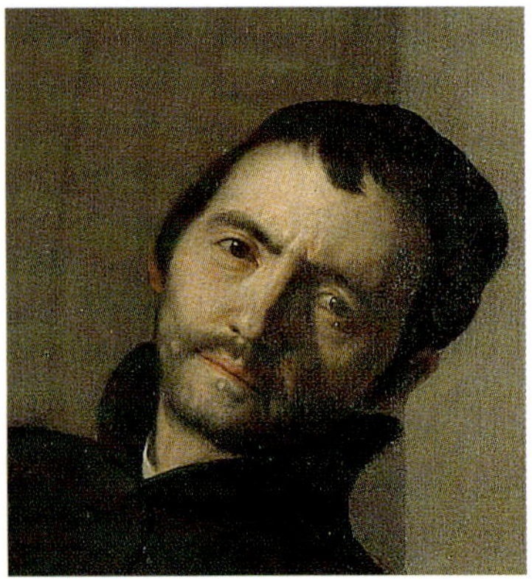

Andrea Pozzo

(Trento 1642 – Vienna 1709)

Architect, set designer and theorist of perspective, Andrea Pozzo is one of those Baroque artists who, through the force of their brushes and their imagination, broke open the ceilings and vaults of churches to let paradise descend. Not by coincidence, his most famous work is the *Glory of St Ignazio*, in the Roman church of the same name where, if the viewer stands in a certain place and raises his eyes, he will have a marvelous vision of the saints in glory. In 1703 he was called to Vienna where he became a reference point for the German painters of the 18th century. An excellent mathematician, he wrote a treatise on perspective, the *Perspectiva pictorum et architectorum*.

Andrea Pozzo, *Self-portrait*, detail, c. 1680. Florence, Uffizi Gallery.

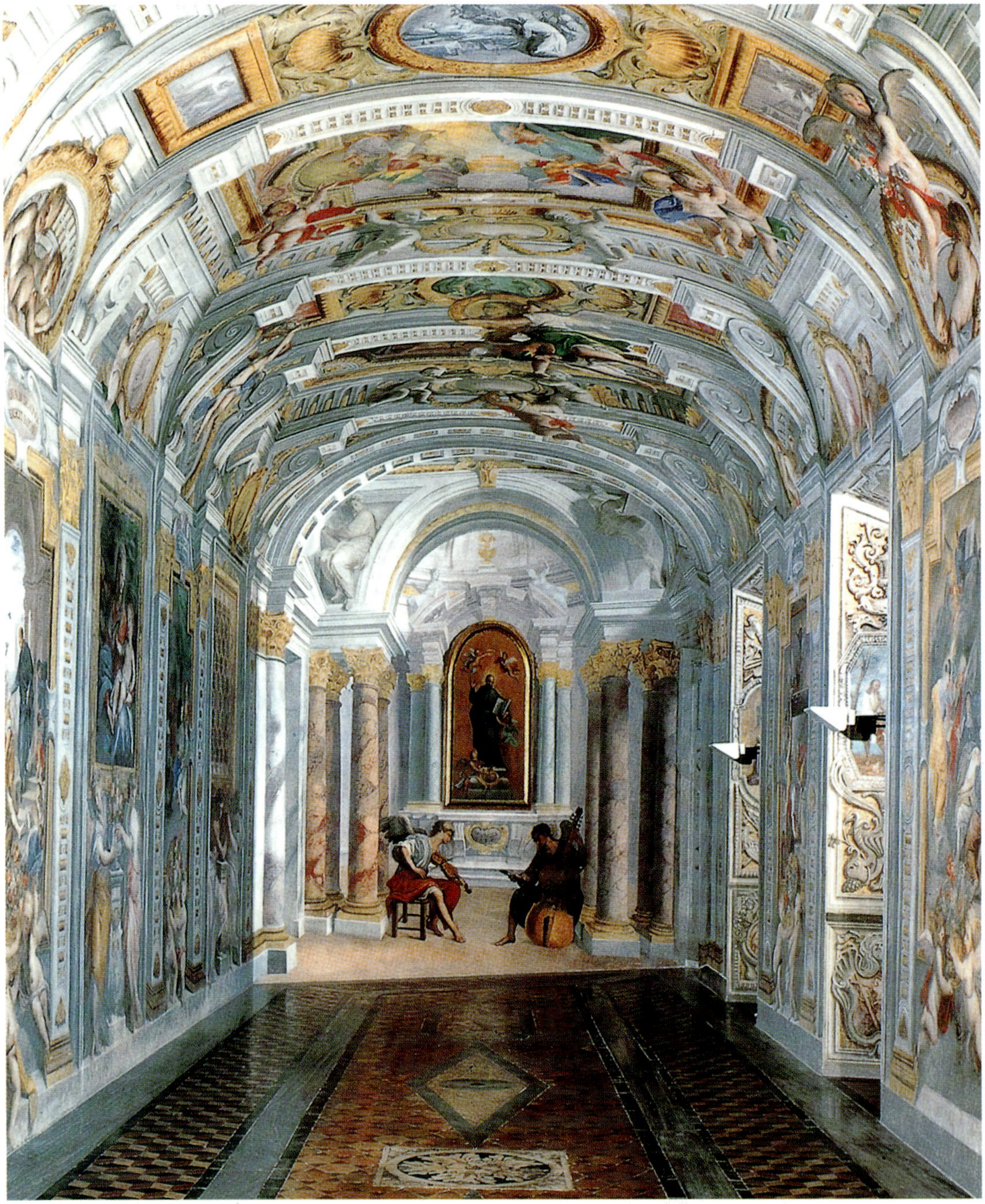

Andrea Pozzo
Perspective Gallery
1681-82
fresco
Rome, Church of Gesù, St Ignazio's Chambers.

The problem was both simple and complex: how to render a narrow, irregular space beautiful, ample and attractive. To resolve this problem Giovanni Paolo Oliva, Father General of the Jesuits, called Father Pozzo to fresco the rooms in St Ignazio's house, still open to visitors in Piazza del Gesù. Under the magic of Father Andrea's brush the dark barrel-vaulted ceiling is animated with arches resting on corbels separating scenes from the life of the saint, while on the back wall there even opens out a false chapel with an altar to St Ignazio.

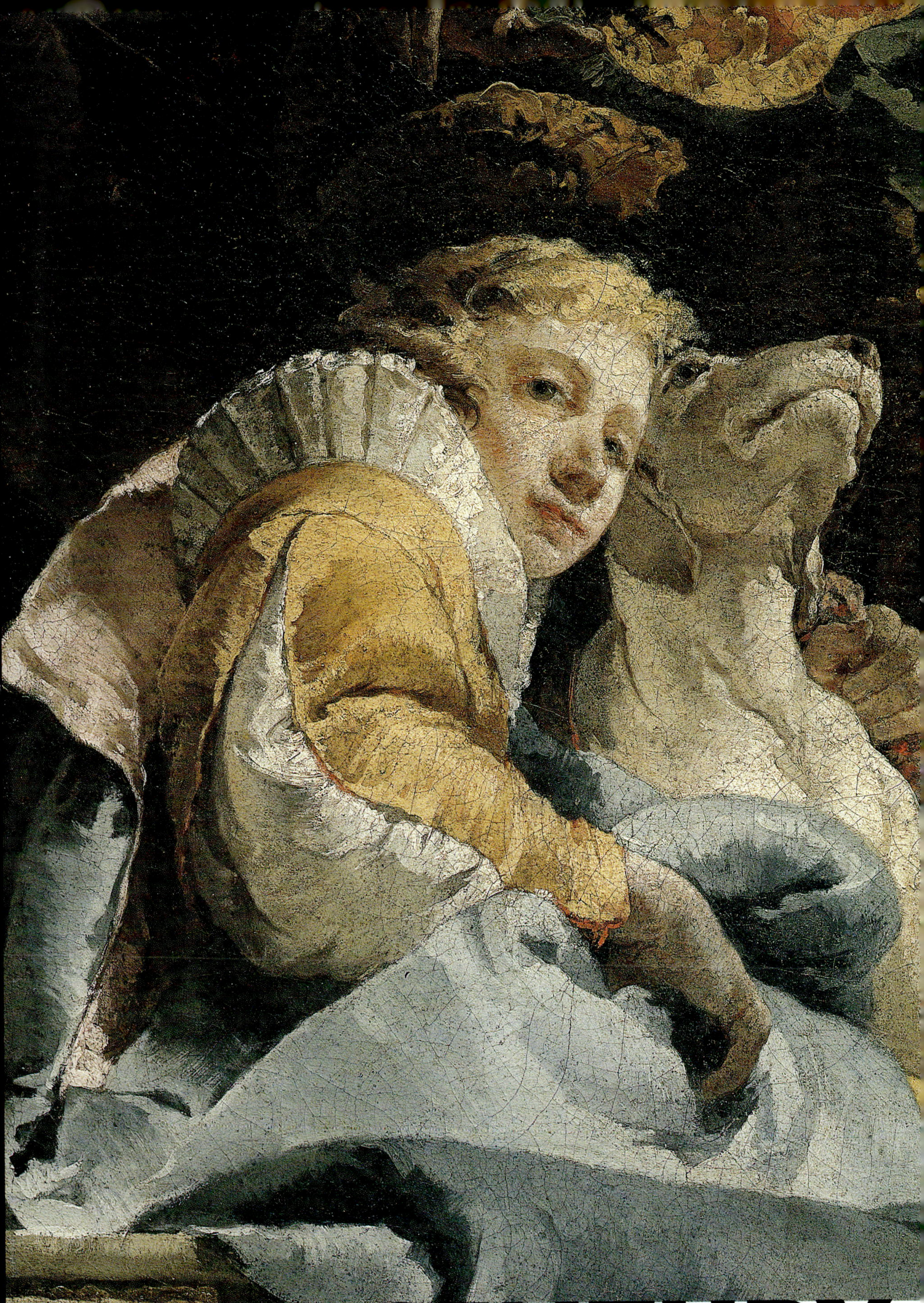

THE XVIII CENTURY

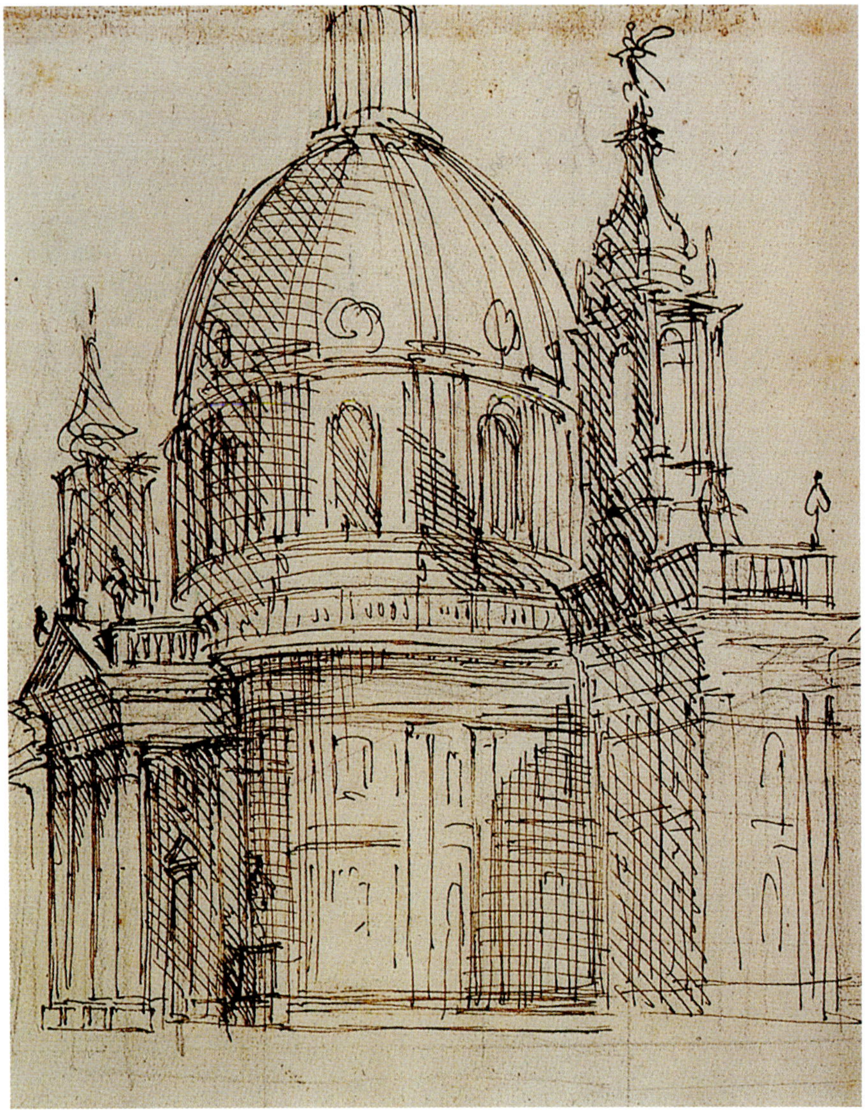

Filippo Juvarra, *Perspective Study of the Basilica of Superga*, 1719-21, from the *Album of Drawings*, II, c. 82. Turin, Civic Museum of Antique Art, Palazzo Madama.

Previous page: **Giambattista Tiepolo**, *Erection of a Statue to an Emperor*, detail, c. 1735-36. Florence, Uffizi Gallery.

In the 18th century Italy, invaded by foreign armies contending its possession, underwent dramatic political/military turmoil and intervals of great poverty. Almost entirely Spanish at the beginning of the century, it was divided between Austria and France in 1763, a date which marks the end of the hostilities. While Venice retained its independence – but only for a brief time: it was to lose it in 1797, when Napoleon granted the city to Austria – Lombardy and Tuscany found themselves directly or indirectly under Austrian control, the Duchy of Parma and the Kingdom of Naples under that of France.

Subjugated by military force and reduced to the rank of diplomatic pawn, Italy nonetheless showed extraordinary artistic and cultural vitality. Never as in the 18th century did Italian artists enjoy international prestige and reputation, being called to this or that court, to this or that sovereign aspiring to make use of their services as painters, decorators, sculptors, and architects. The history of 18th century Italian art is still a history of cities and urban contexts, with a wealth and variety of schools unrivaled throughout Europe. At Bologna the Carracci naturalist tradition still prevailed, renewing itself. In Milan, Bergamo and Brescia, often thanks to the support given the arts by an "enlightened" aristocracy, the premises for a painting of historical and civic nature were laid. In Florence artists from all over Italy, called to court by Ferdinando, the last great patron of the Medici family, were able in the early years of the century to admire Dutch and Flemish art in the Granducal collections, drawing from it lasting inspiration. In Turin expert architects at the service of the reigning family – such as Filippo Juvarra (1678-1736) – were building churches, palaces and splendid country homes modeled on Versailles. In Rome, at about mid-century, new modes of approaching and comprehending antiquity were emerging. In Naples, a city which underwent extensive urban renovation under Charles of Bourbon, the royal manufacturies and the porcelain works of Capodimonte were established, at the initiative of this sovereign; for some decades they rivaled those of Sèvres and Meissen. Among the Italian cities Venice was remarkable for its many resident artists and its prosperous art market. It was

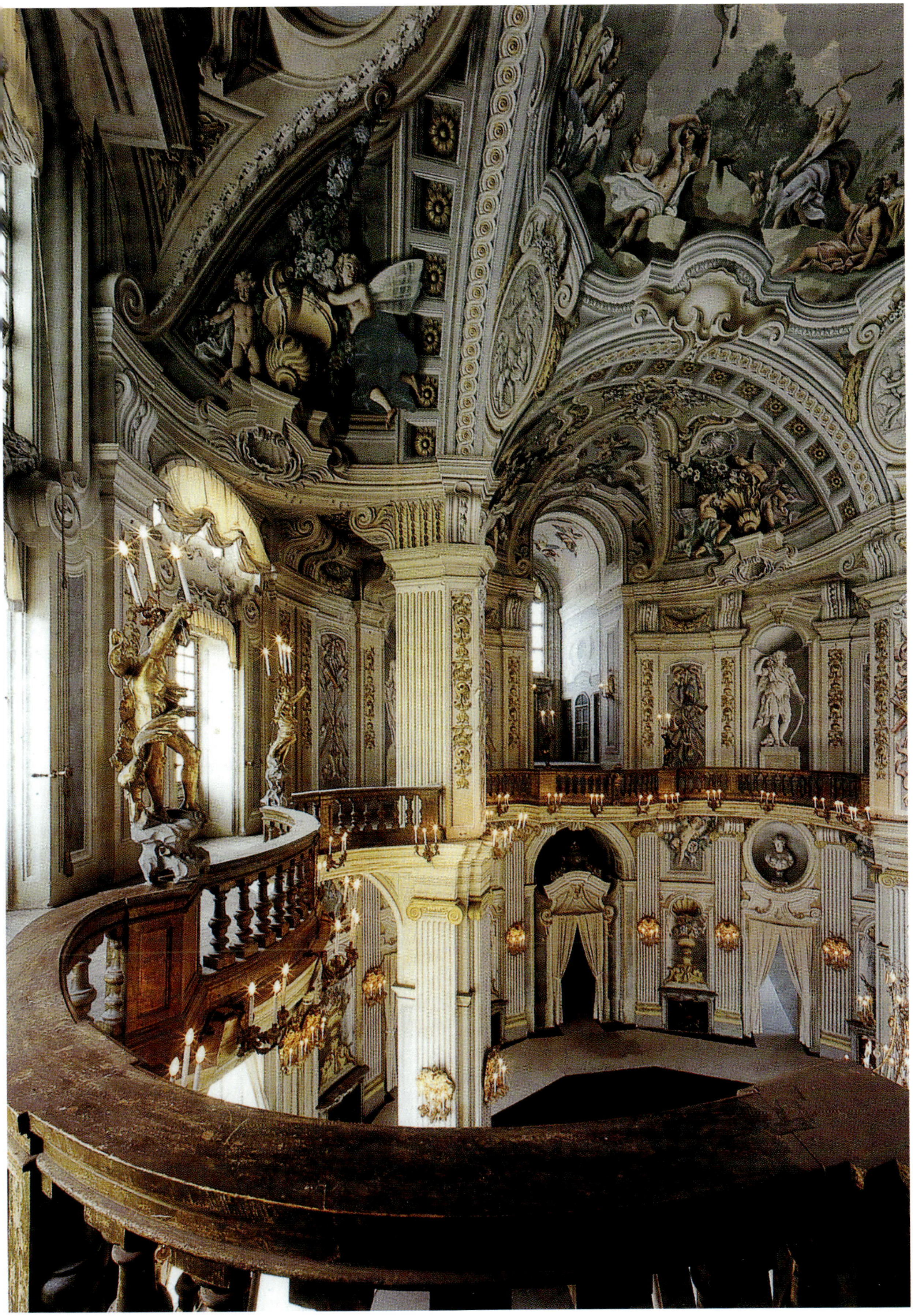

Filippo Juvarra, The great hall in the hunting lodge of Stupinigi (Turin), 1729-31.

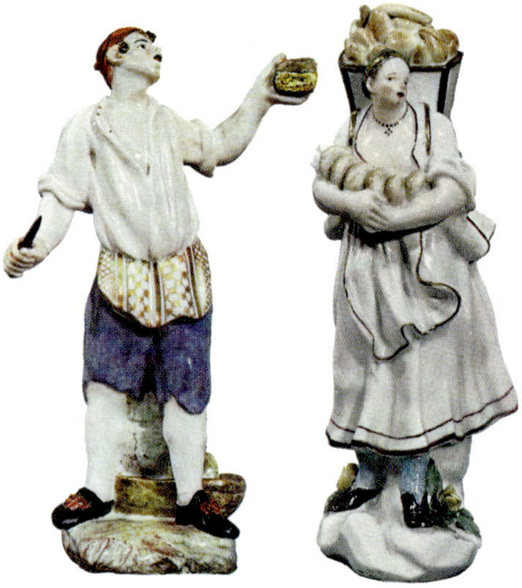

Giuseppe Gricci,
Statuettes, c. 1750.
Naples, Capodimonte National Museum.

in this city surrounded by its lagoon that the veduta genre definitively emerged. Accompanied by their consultants, wealthy tourists visited the locales of art, taking home with them souvenirs: images or, more precisely, vedutas. Many painters began to specialize in depicting archaeological sites and architectural complexes, picturesque corners, local characters and costumes. The 18th century was marked by curiosity for what was considered "typical" no less than by

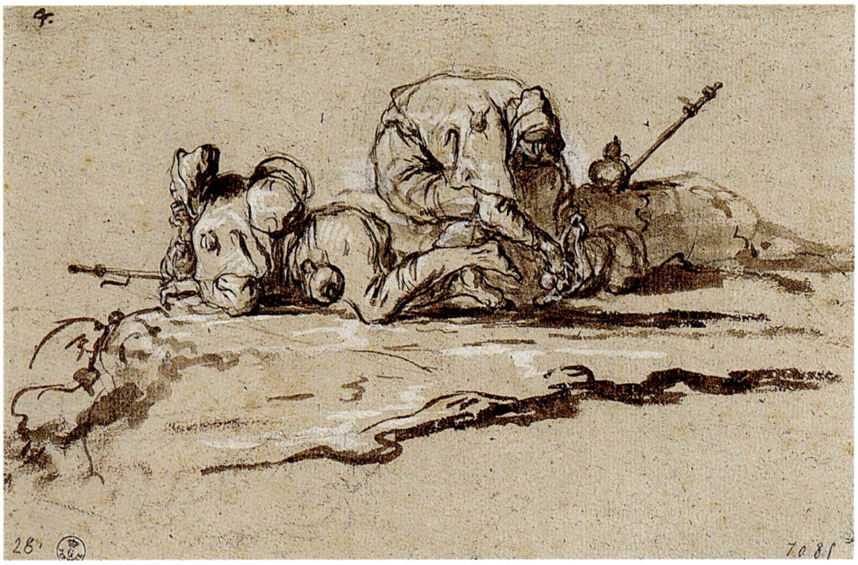

Alessandro Magnasco,
Pilgrims at Rest, first decade of the 18th century.
Florence, Cabinet of Drawings and Prints Uffizi Gallery, inv. no. 7085.

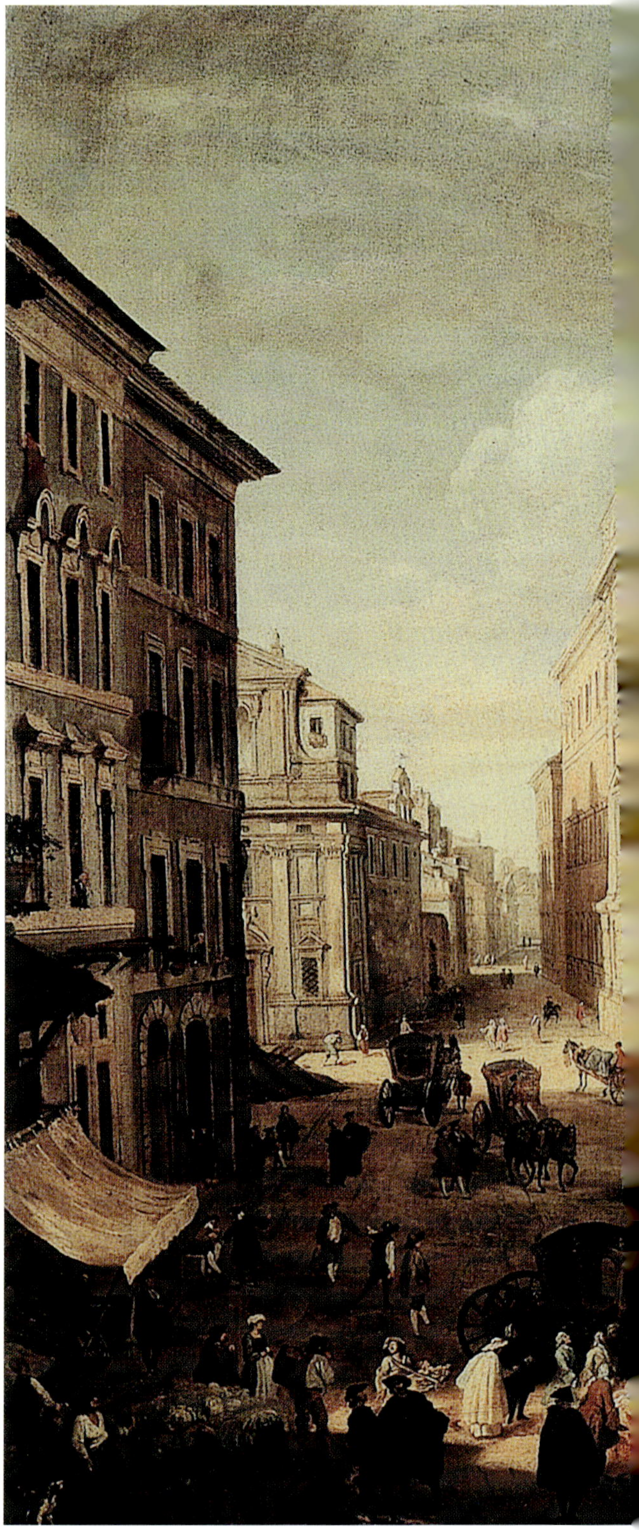

interest in fashion and novelty in general, particularly of the technical or alimentary kind – from the colonies of the "new world" coffee and chocolate had begun to arrive. The custom of the cultural journey, the Grand Tour, stimulated the demand for Italian art, both contemporary and from the Renaissance, already considered sublime, especially by the wealthy, cosmopolitan English. The first real international merchants and antiquarians appeared, often collectors themselves. Artists began to present themselves as refined connoisseurs of local tradition, virtu-

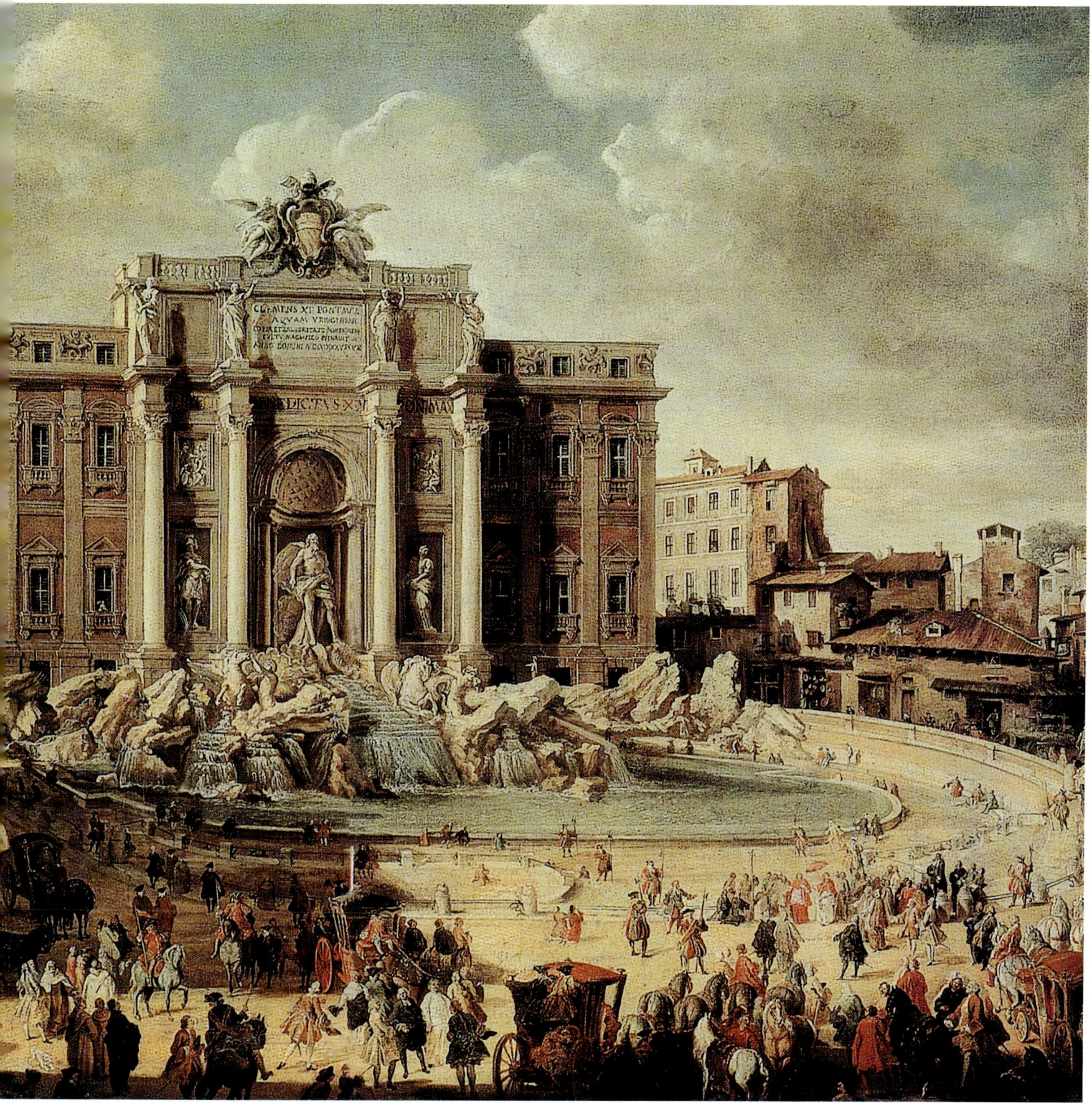

oso interpreters of an elect repertoire (without hesitating to indulge in plagiarism and pastiches: Sebastiano Ricci, a Venetian artist of the generation preceding that of Tiepolo, won fame and success by painting in the "Paolesque manner", that is, by imitating Veronese). The most successful workshops took on large, well-organized dimensions. Several persons could participate in a painting, sharing in the work by depicting a background of landscape or architecture or by adding figures. Existing motifs taken either from tradition and or from a project previously signed

Giovanni Paolo Panini, *Benedict XIV Visits the Just Completed Fountain of Trevi*, c. 1744-Moscow, Puškin Museum.

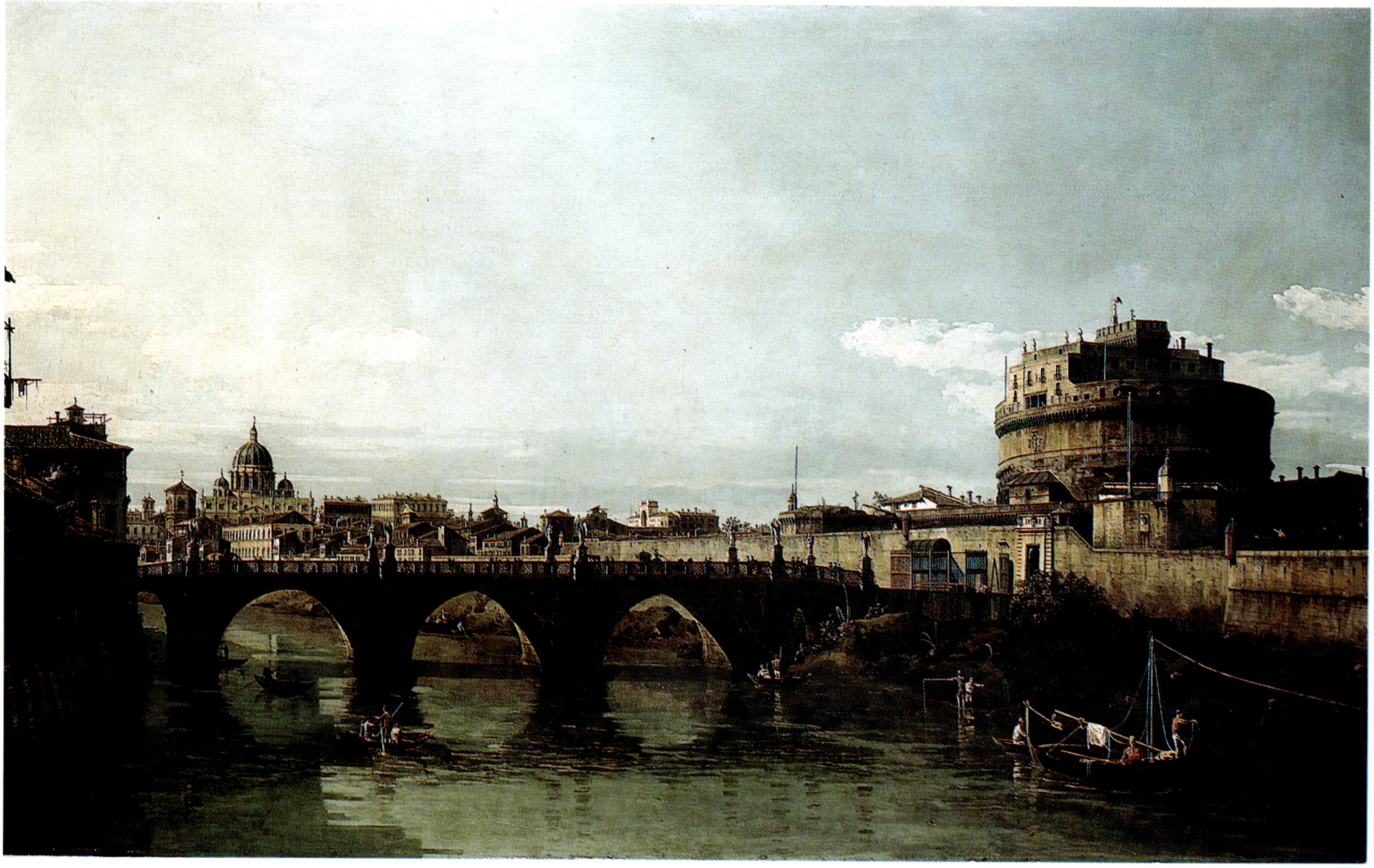

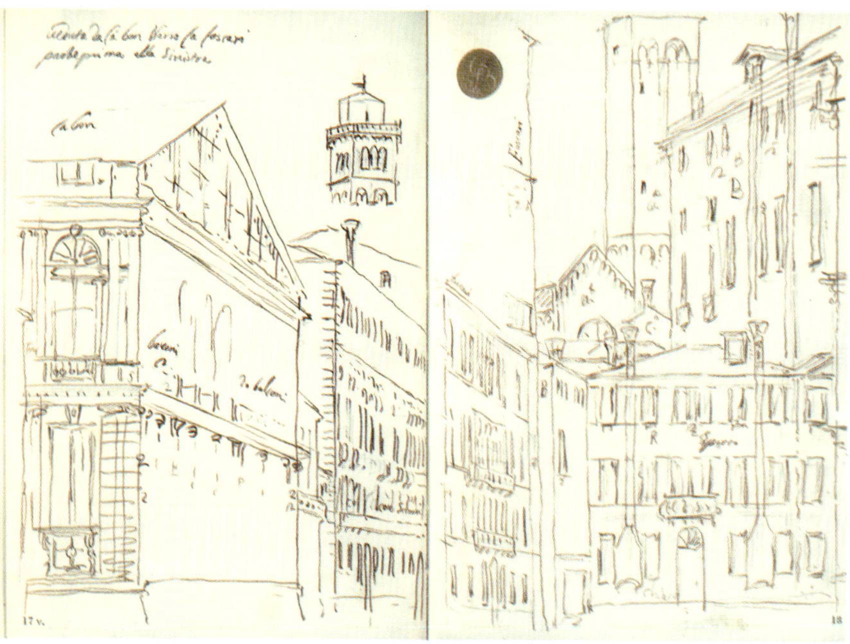

by the head artist in the shop were utilized. Optical instruments were sometimes used, in the attempt to learn more about natural phenomena. Full mastery of the art of *chiaroscuro* and perspective was the artists' goal. It is known that, already before Canaletto, Carlevarijs and Crespi were using the *camera ottica*, a device that gave the artist greater control over his subject, making it easier to represent it in precise detail. Interestingly enough, the study of nature was conducted at times with a subtle taste for the deformed image, the visual caprice, in a word, for magic: "the lens having been reversed", wrote Roberto Longhi in regard to Crespi, "[we wait for] some bizarre, extreme 'luministic' effect to appear on the screen, leaping about on the little

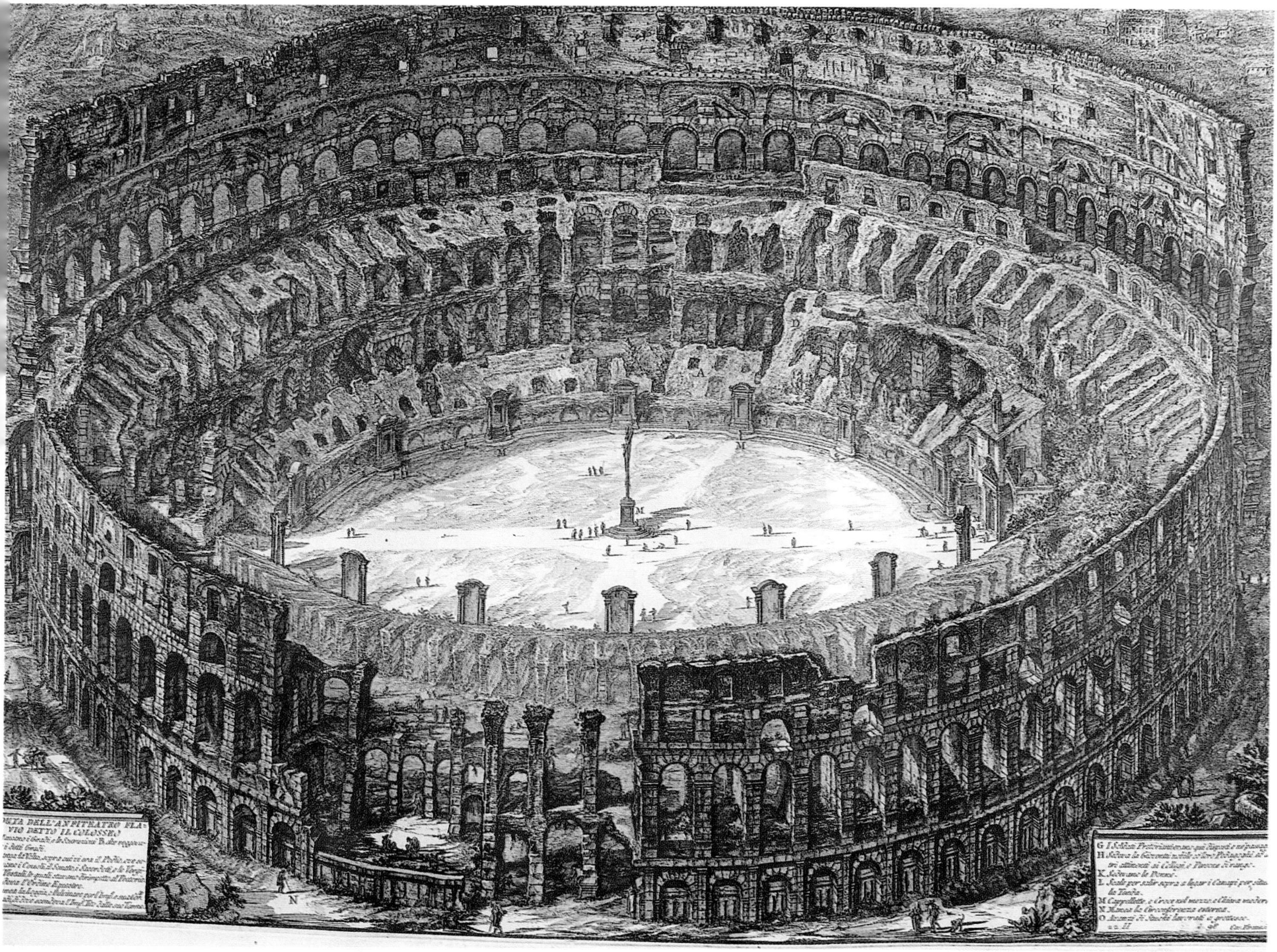

stage of already prepared gestures". Any succession of images and figures, such as the one presented in this chapter, clearly shows how 18th century Italian art possesses traits less limpid and rational than the luminous views of Canaletto and his nephew Bernardo Bellotto would seem to indicate. Elusive touches, even sinister at times, appear in compositions of often disturbing beauty. The prevailing approach however is inquisitive and caustic, and a glimpse of this can be seen even in the highly respectful society chronicles of Pietro Longhi.

There is an air of kinship in fact, between the *pittori pitocchi* of Magnasco; the beggars, the lame, the poor peasants of Ceruti; and the "entertainment for boys" of Giandomenico Tiepolo, drawings illustrating the life of Pulcinella done while the Napoleonic armies were already conquering Italy, shooting their adversaries (a circumstance to which Tiepolo alludes in a drawing where Pulcinella is executed by a firing squad); an air of kinship and a kind of fluctuation between farcical laughter and a sense of civil, human desolation.

Giovanni Battista Piranesi, *Interior of the Coliseum with Aedicules for the Via Crucis*, 1746-50. Rome, Casanatense Biblioteca.

At left:
Bernardo Bellotto, *View of the Tiber at Castel Sant'Angelo*, c. 1742. Detroit, The Detroit Institute of Arts, Gift of Mr. and Mrs. Edgar B. Withcomb.

Canaletto, *View from Ca' Bon Looking Toward Ca' Foscari*, from the *Notebook of Drawings*, 1730 c. Venice, Gallerie dell'Accademia, c. 17 v-18.

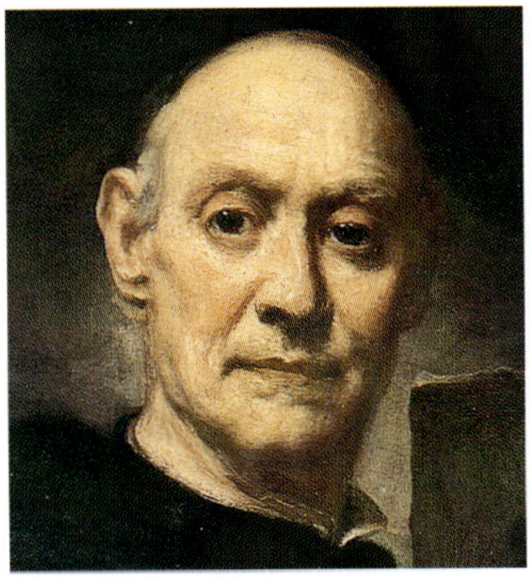

Fra Galgario

(Vittore Ghislandi,
Bergamo 1655 – 1743)

His father's pupil, a quadraturist and veduta painter, Fra Galgario was apprenticed first at Bergamo, then at Venice, where he arrived in 1675 to don the habit of a Minimite lay brother. After a return to Bergamo, he was in Milan with the German painter Salomon Adler; then in Bergamo definitively as Minorite friar in the monastery of Sal Galgario – the saint whose name he took. Particularly appreciated, along with Cerruti, by 20th century historians and critics – he is considered one of the "Lombard painters of reality" – Fra Galgario renewed the tradition of great 16th century Bergamo portrait painting (his model was above all Moroni), revealing fine psychological and moralistic gifts. His portraits compose a gallery of characters: the gentlemen, the priest, the courtier, all portrayed with a keen, sober spirit of observation.

Fra Galgario,
Self-portrait, 1732.
Bergamo, Carrara Academy.

Fra Galgario
Young Man in Red
c. 1719
canvas
Cambridge, Fitzwilliam Museum.

Painted in the colors of red and blue, the canvas, not a portrait but a "character head" alludes, in its slight asymmetry, to the qualities of spontaneity and freshness of the round-faced young model, who turns his head slightly to meet our gaze, sustaining it vivaciously. The same young man posed for the artist on two other occasions, for the so-called *Young Man* and in a pleasantly allegorical composition entitled *Gaiety*.

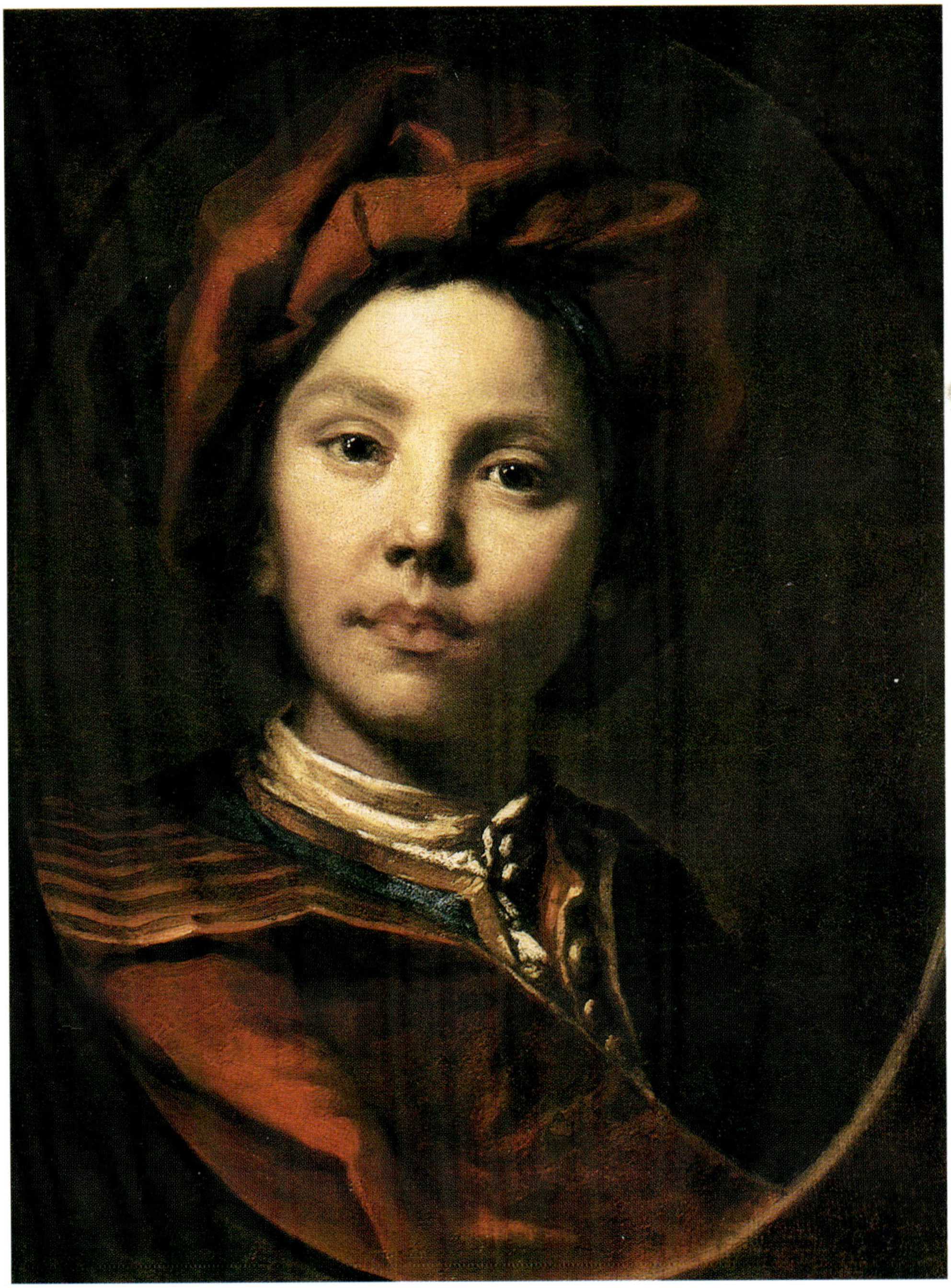

Fra Galgario
Gentleman with a Cocked Hat
c. 1737
canvas
Milan, Poldi Pezzoli Museum.

The portrait of a knight of the Constantinian order – as shown by the emblem appearing on the metal corselet – this is perhaps Fra Galgario's most famous work, admired for a number of reasons: the elegant play of tonal variations on the dominating blue-green color scheme; the execution of the lace-like silver braiding adorning the gentlemen's hat and justicoat; the pungent irony with which the artist, almost anticipating Goya's satirical genius, has caught the arrogant vacuity of the unknown knight.
Certainly in the *Gentleman* Fra Galgario displays his own ability for "mellow painting without those borders that make the paintings of many seem dry and harsh", as already acknowledged by his contemporaries.

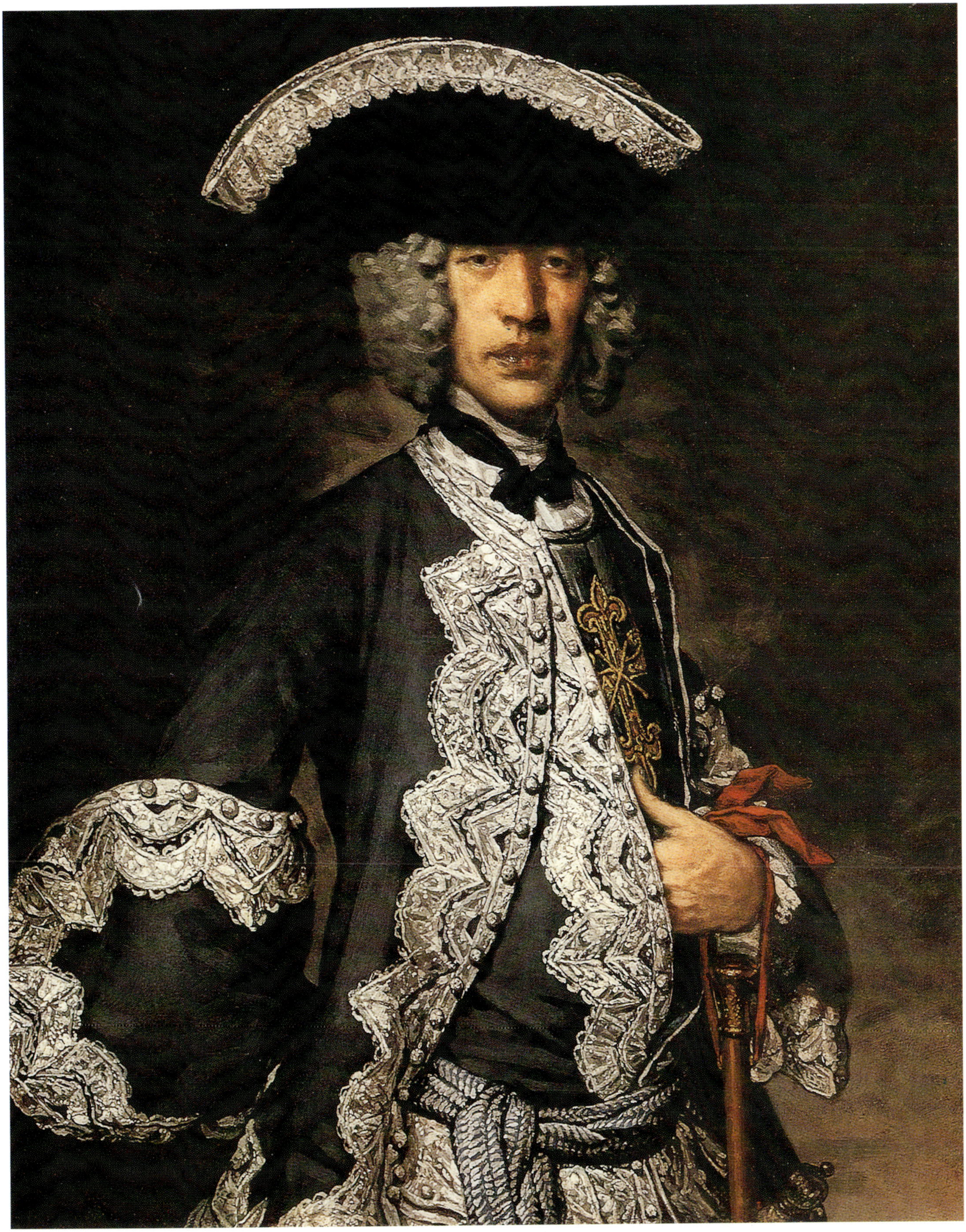

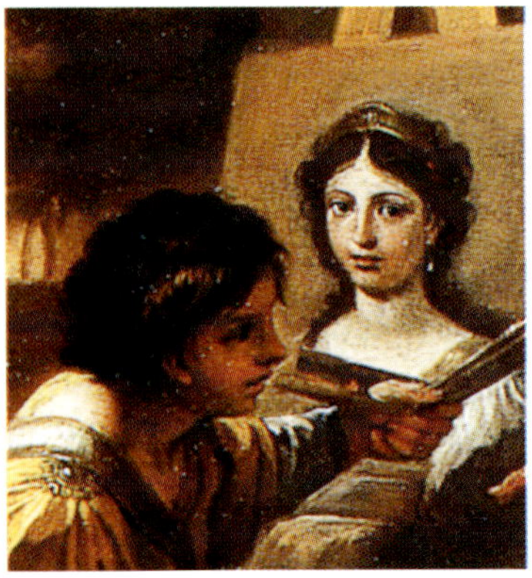

Francesco Solimena

(known as Abbot Ciccio, Canale di Serino, Avellino, 1657 – Barra, Naples, 1747)

Solimena's career began in his father's shop. The artist's first models, in addition to his father Angelo, were Stanzione and Lanfranco. In Naples between 1689 and 1690, engaged in decorating the Sacristy of San Paolo Maggiore, Solimena had the chance to see the innovations introduced in painting by Luca Giordano. In his compositions from this period a radiant light envelops and dissolves the bodies. In dealing with sacred subjects he did not hesitate to arouse profane affections. Near the end of the century he was in Rome, where he met Maratta and the classicists linked to the Academy of France. The artist's Baroque approach underwent an abrupt change. Returning to Naples, he established a successful academy of painting which taught, strictly according to the classical tradition, that "painting is nothing other than drawing".

Francesco Solimena, *Apelles painting Pancaspe*, detail, c. 1685. Detroit, The Detroit Institute of Arts.

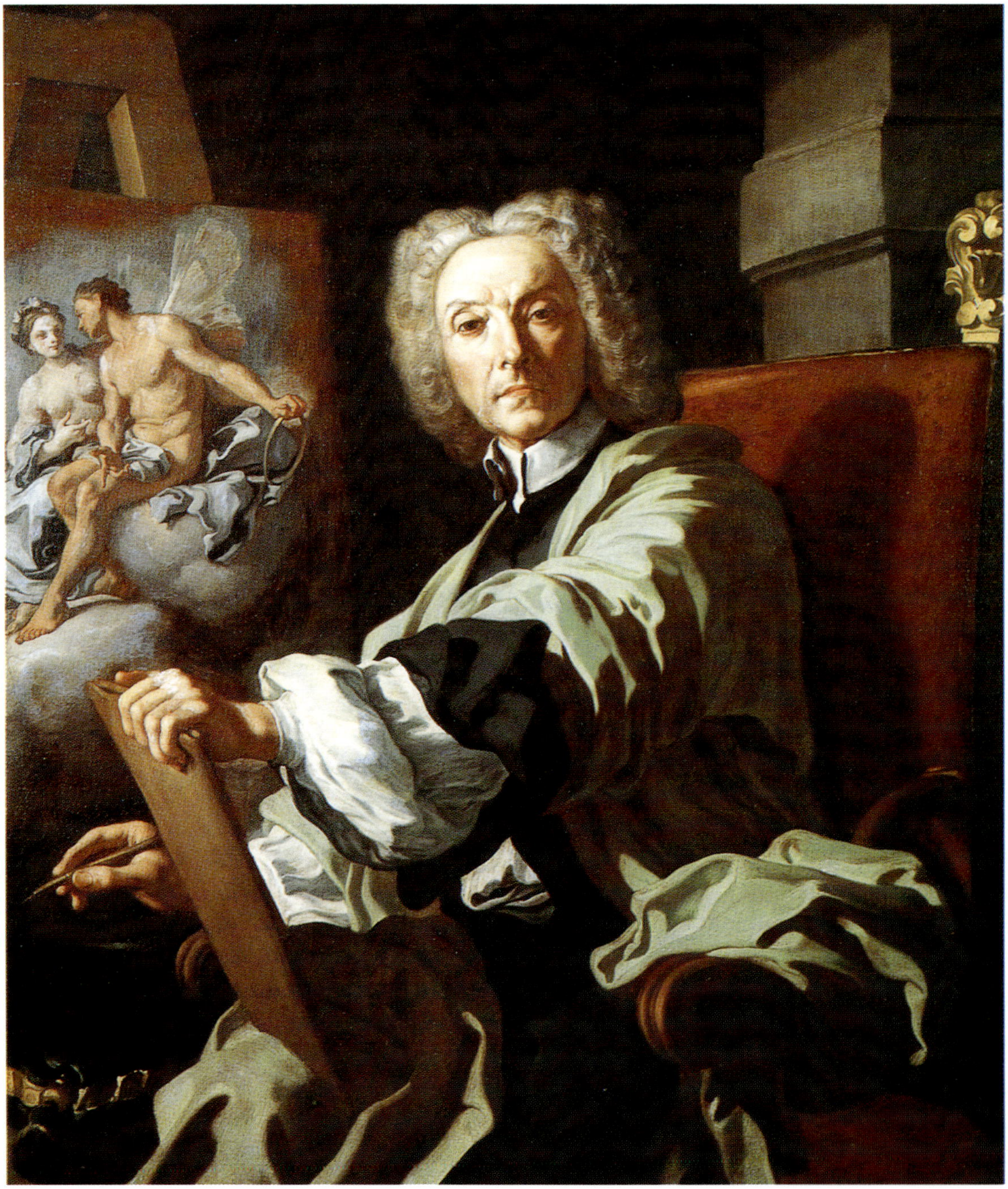

Francesco Solimena
Self-portrait
c. 1715-20
canvas
Naples, San Martino Museum.

Austere and inspired, Solimena portrays himself in the guise of an abbot as well as, recognizably, that of a painter. Piety and moral scruples, he seems to saw, must be accompanied by the search for beauty: "studying the natural", states one of the principles dear to the artist, "one must reproduce what he sees; but in transferring it to paintings, it must be softened and made courteous, noble and select". The artist's left hand grasps a folder for drawings, his right a stylus; in the background is a still uncompleted canvas. A female figure, soave and chaste, seems to exhort an oddly winged male figure to seek the ideal.

Francesco Solimena
Vision of St Gregory Thaumaturge
c. 1680
canvas
Solofra (Avellino),
San Domenico.

Commissioned by the artist's first patron, Cardinal Orsini, the canvas reflects admiration for Lanfranco, Solimena's youthful model, along with growing interest in a light blonder and clearer than in nature, softly enveloping clothing and flesh. Solimena creates multiple sources of light and a complex play of reflections: a delicate amber-hued luminosity spreads softly over the Virgin's face echoing the filtered light of the background, while a warmer, more intense beam glances off the shoulder of St John and the page in the great book, then goes on to strike the habit of Gregory in adoration.

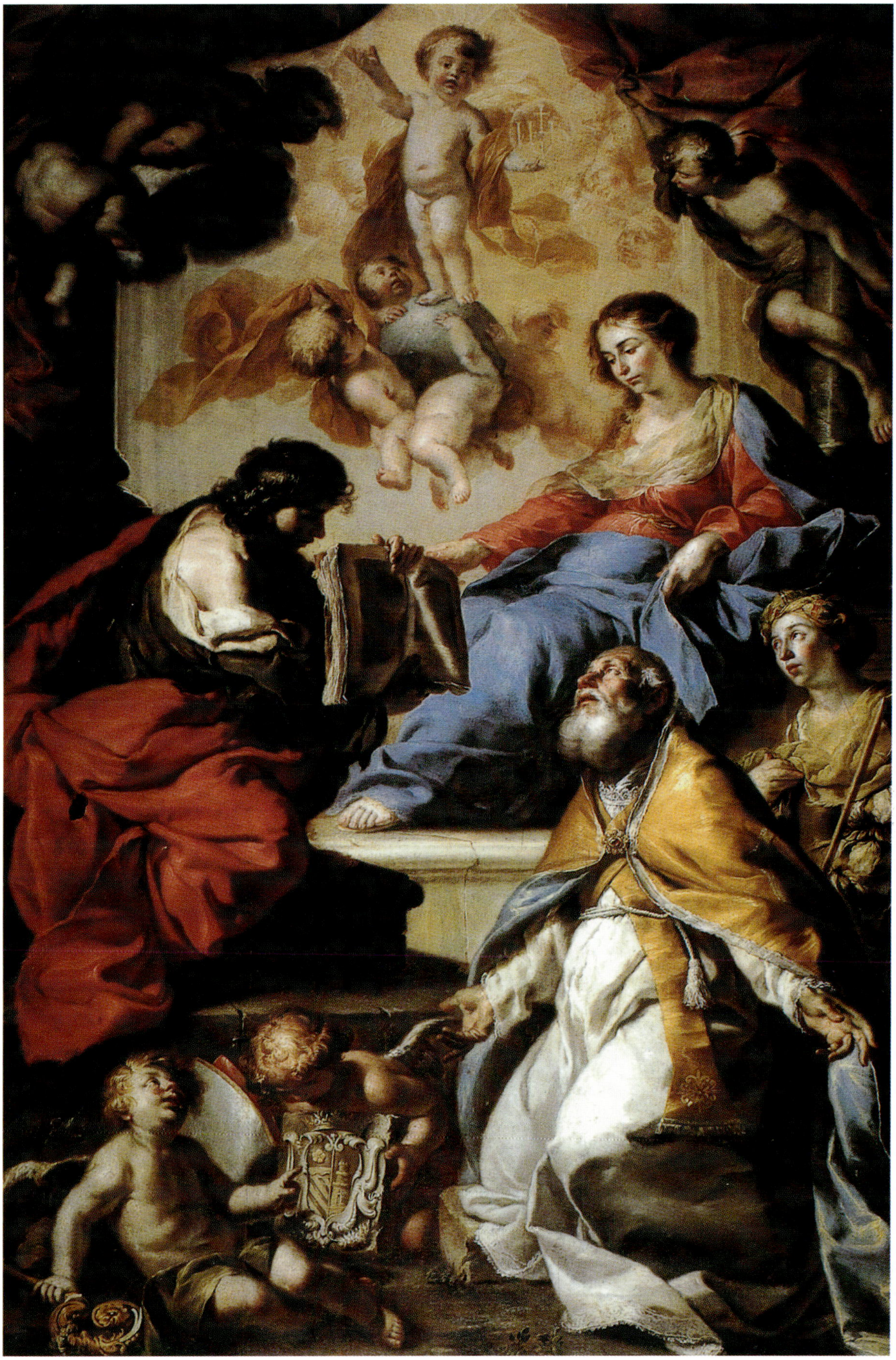

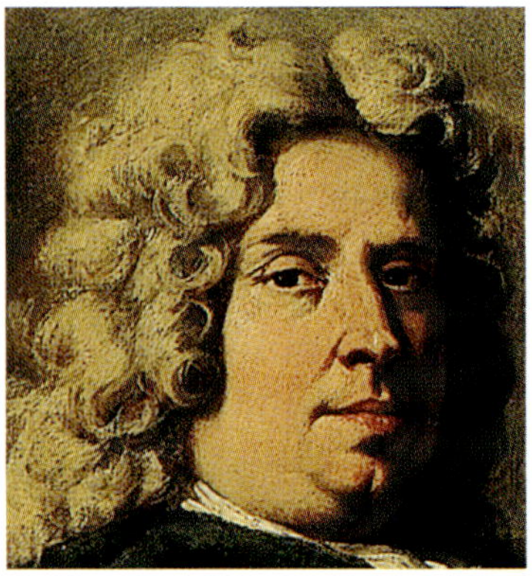

Sebastiano Ricci

(Belluno 1659 – Venice 1734)

At the age of fourteen Sebastiano was already an apprentice in Venice. Active at Bologna and Parma in the 1680s, he was in Rome in 1691; back in Venice in 1696, at Vienna in 1702 and immediately afterward in Florence. Returning once more to Venice, he stayed there until his departure for England where, between 1708 and 1712, he painted a series of mythological works for illustrious patrons. After a brief stay in Paris he returned definitely to Venice. A successful artist, Ricci was the eminent interpreter of the new "chiarista" tendency characteristic of Venetian painting in the late 17th and early 18th centuries, an approach favorable to clear and luminous painting, reminiscent of Veronese in the lighter ranges of color, the refined architectural or Arcadian/pastoral settings, and the scenographic compositions.

Sebastiano Ricci, *Self-portrait*, detail, c. 1706, Florence, Uffizi Gallery.

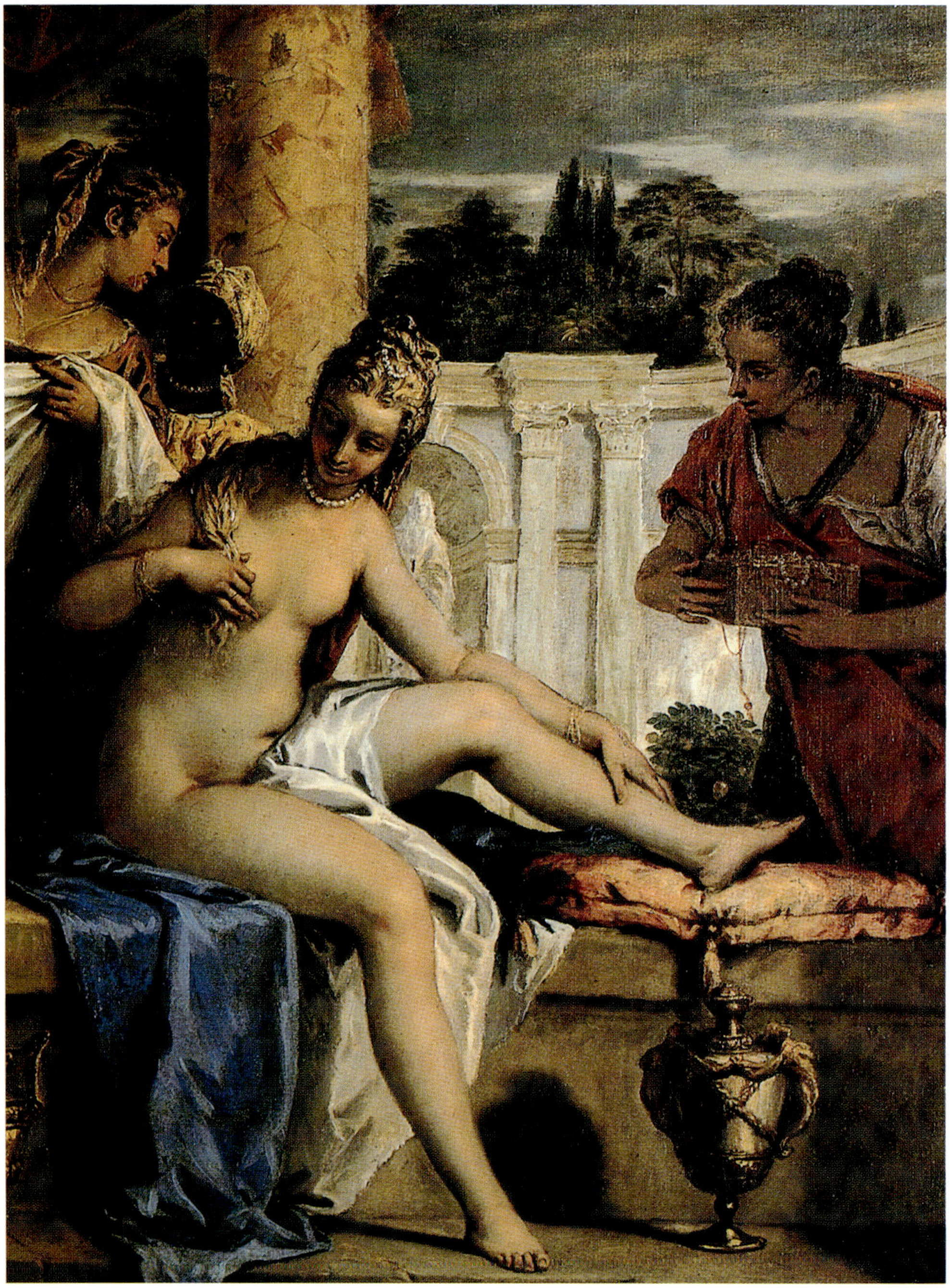

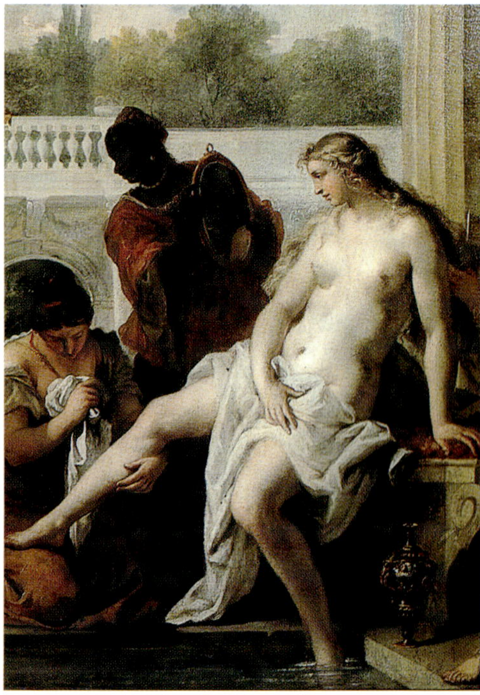

Sebastiano Ricci

The Toilette of Venus
w.d.
canvas
Berlin, Staatliche Museen.

Batheshba at her Bath
c. 1724
canvas, detail
Budapest, Szépmüvészeti Múzeum.

In his paintings of the female nude Ricci shows himself to be a virtuoso of painting and a brilliant connoisseur of the Venetian Renaissance tradition, of which he imitates, casually and self-confidently, the sensual, pleasantly mythological repertoire. The figures are placed in magnificent architectural and natural settings, among opulent gowns, patrician furnishings and decorations. The painter works with rapid, sure brushstrokes. His use of pearly white and yellow-brown tonalities confers a particular luminosity on his canvases. For the drapery the artist employs pure colors in the manner of the great 16th century painters, Titian and Paolo Veronese in particular.

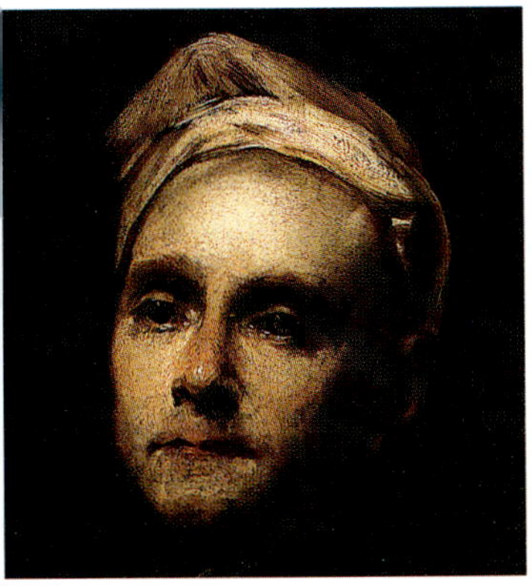

Giuseppe Maria Crespi

(known as Lo Spagnolo, Bologna 1665 – 1747)

A highly cultivated artist whose training was complex and prolonged – he visited Parma, Urbino, and Venice in voyages of study; was in Florence between 1708 and 1709, called there by the Grand Duke Ferdinand – the artist owes his curious nickname to the style in which he dressed as a youth. Among the greatest Italian painters of the times, Crespi is appreciated for his genre scenes, which variously reflect his knowledge of 16th century Venetian tradition, of Carracci, Guercino, and the Northern painters. Unusual angles, a wealth of bizarre details, refined tonal harmonies and convincing effects of *chiaroscuro* are combined in compositions surprising for their sophistication masked by an apparent simplicity. Active also as painter of history and mythology, he was the father of painters and the head of a successful school of painting.

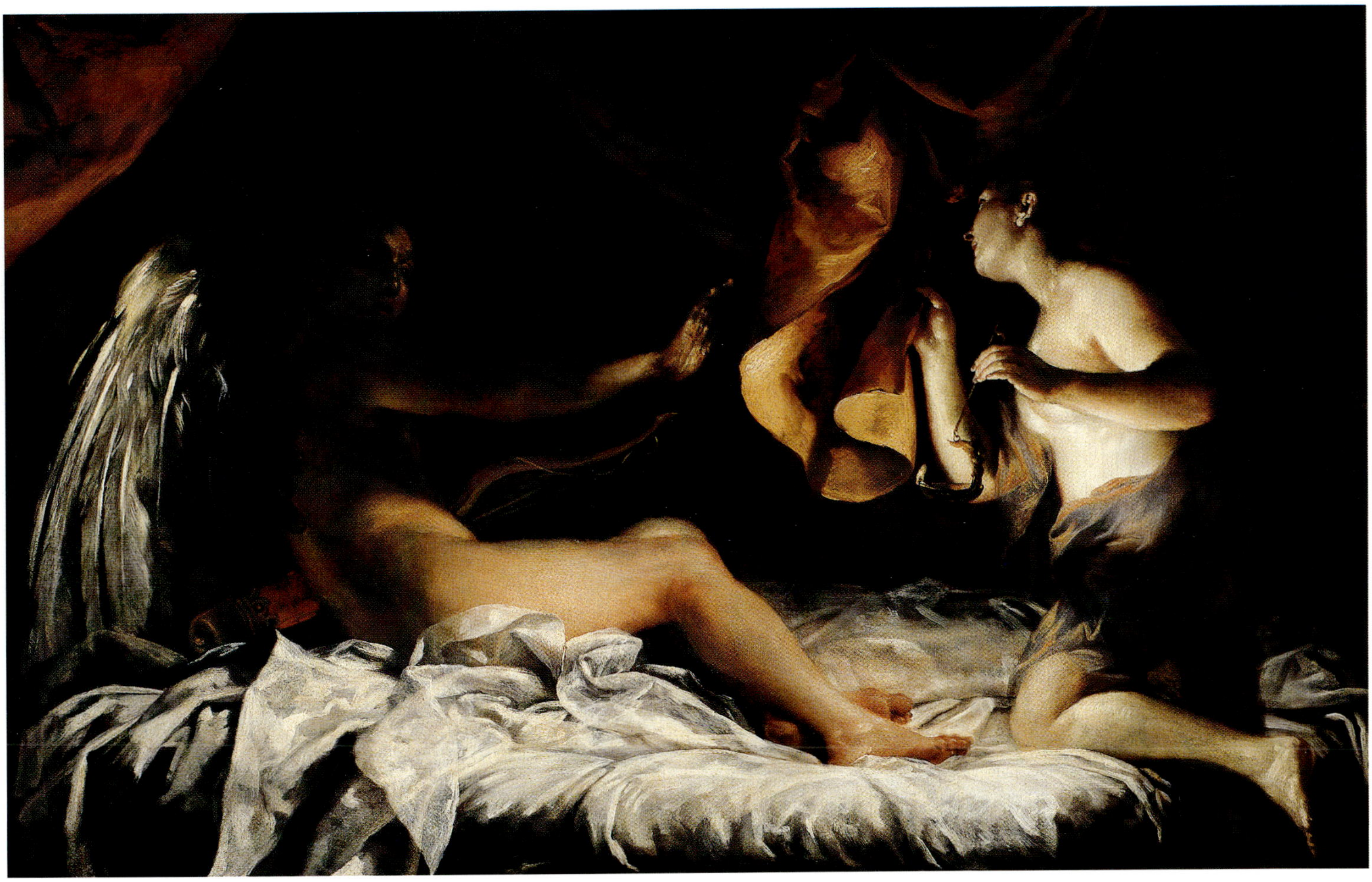

Giuseppe Maria Crespi, *Self-portrait*, detail, 1708. Florence, Uffizi Gallery.

Giuseppe Maria Crespi
Cupid and Psyche
1707-09
canvas
Florence, Uffizi Gallery.

The theme is taken from Apuleius: Psyche, overcome by curiosity, holds a lamp to the face of her mysterious lover, Cupid, to know what he looks like at last. In doing so she violates a precept: and will lose her love. Crespi's nocturnal scene can be seen as an excellent neo-Mannerist exercise: long-limbed adolescent nudes caught in a twisting movement, lost profiles, golden hair, blond complexions. An extreme looseness of execution gives fabrics the softness and volatile nature of feathers. Cupid's wing, half in full light, becomes almost the emblem of a mode of painting in which a careful study of natural appearances is resolved on the level of magic and of style.

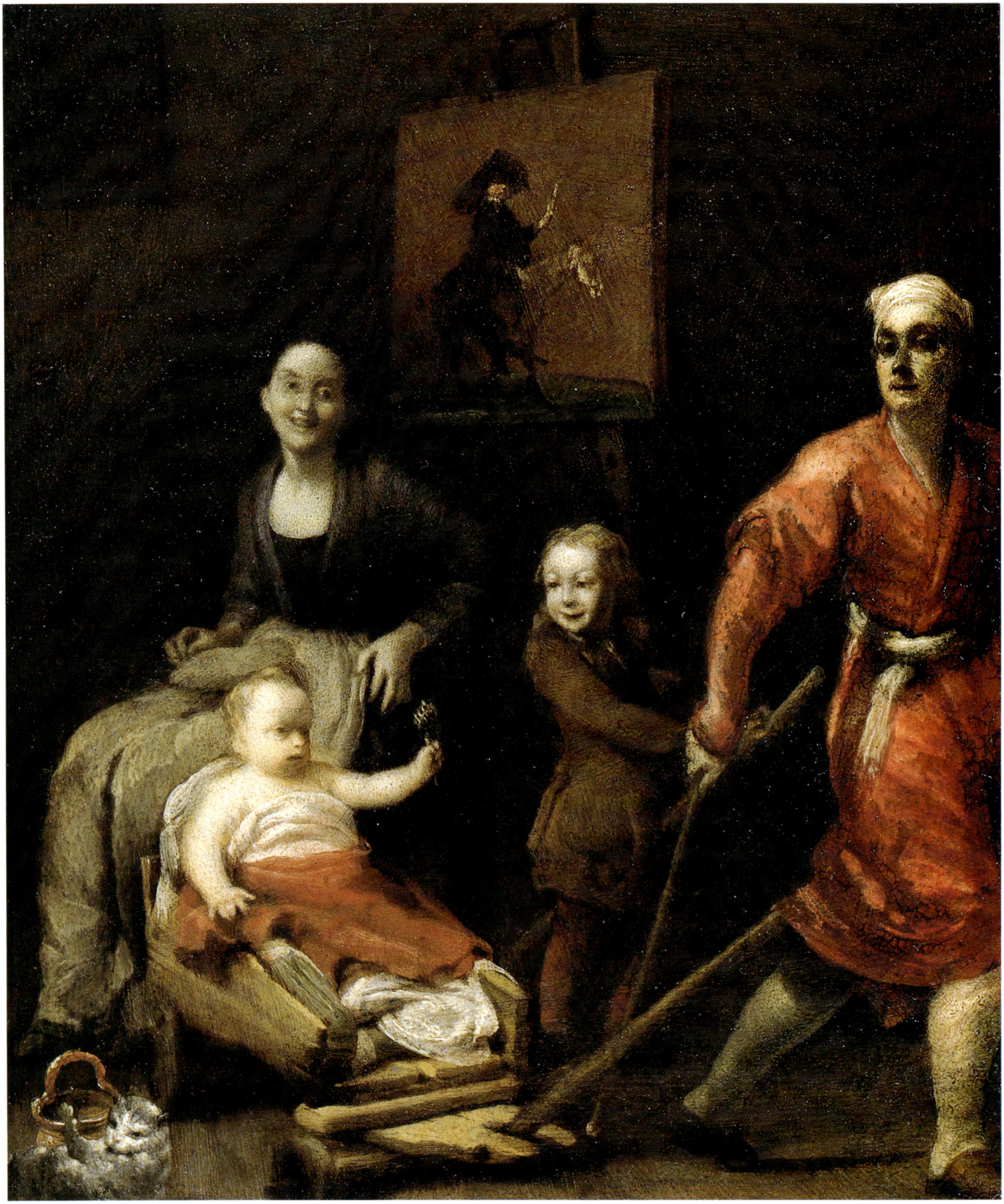

Giuseppe Maria Crespi
The Painter's Family
1708
copper
Florence, Uffizi Gallery.

The composition is astute and subtly diplomatic: Crespi's homage to the Grand Duke Ferdinand de' Medici portrays the painter pulling his son Luigi, a future painter and biographer, on a little cart. While he ironically reminds the Grand Duke (and wealthy patron of the arts) of his responsibilities as a family man, the artist entertains him by making fun of a mutual acquaintance. Behind the painter, his wife and their two children can be seen a canvas, a sort of picture within a picture. It portrays an ecclesiastic riding a mule. This is Don Carlo Silva, a Bolognese priest who, having appropriated a picture painted by Crespi and promised to the Grand Duke, has here become the subject of a caricature.

Giuseppe Maria Crespi
The Flea
c. 1715
copper
Florence, Uffizi Gallery.

We do not know whether this small painting on copper depicts an episode from the "life of a singer" which the artist painted for an English client, or "the miserable life of a woman of ill repute", as his son Luigi was to write. In either case, the taste for scenes of "vulgar" nature which Crespi shared with Northern artists of bambocciade tradition is clearly evident.

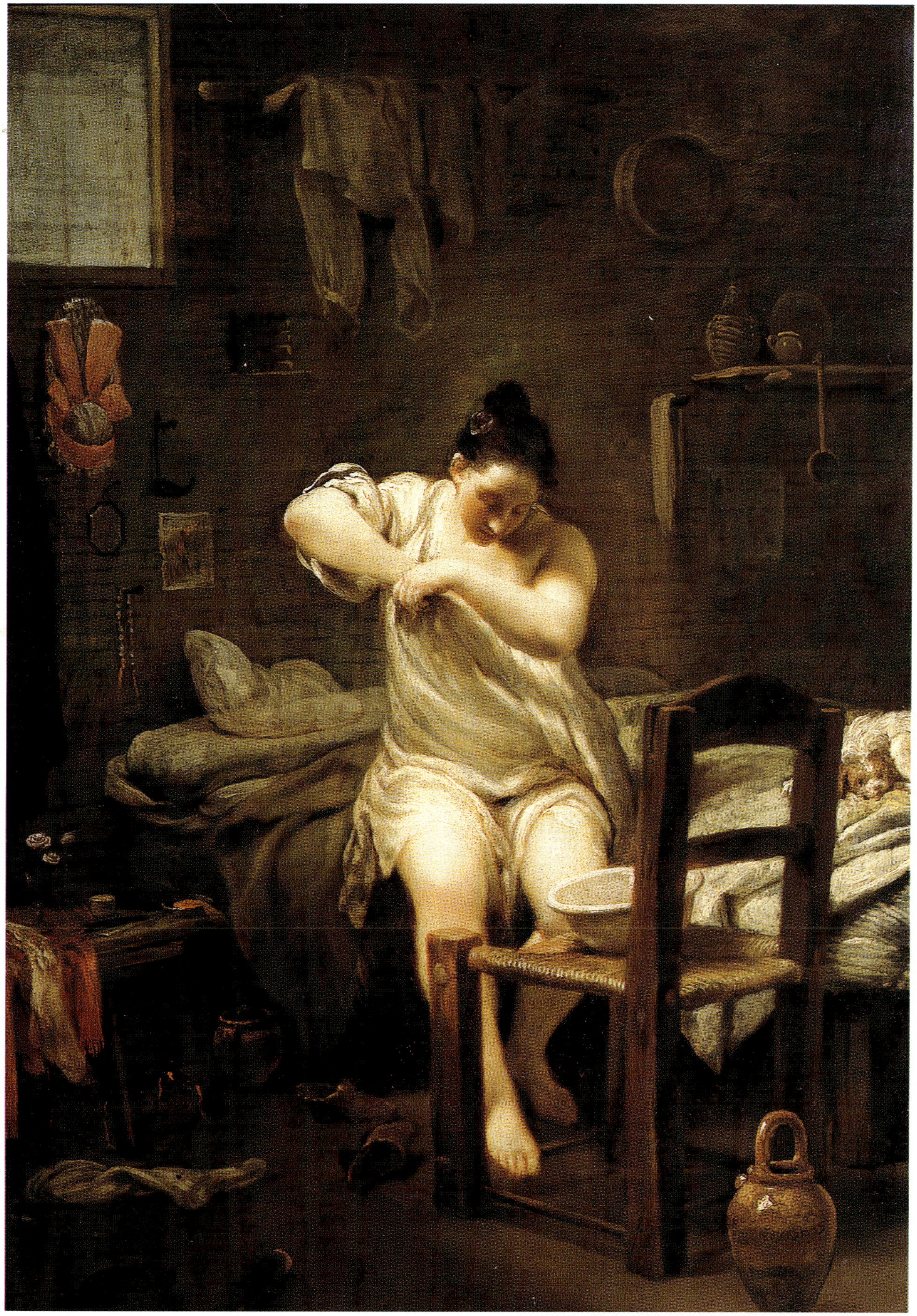

Alessandro Magnasco

(known as Il Lissandrino, Genoa 1667 – 1749)

Training while still a boy with his father Stefano, he was in Milan by 1677, collaborating with Filippo Abbiati. He launched a production of genre scenes, which were to make him famous as painter of figures, with imaginary veduta and landscape artists (among others Antonio Francesco Peruzzini, Clemente Spera and Marco Ricci). At Florence for long periods between 1703 and 1711, he viewed attentively Callot and the Dutch and Flemish painters of the Grand Ducal collections. He painted episodes from the lives of the poor and of courtiers. He lived in Milan up to 1735. In contact with the families of the "enlightened aristocracy", he concealed satirical intentions – satire against ignorance, lack of reflection, prejudice, greed – in images that are striking for their pictorial motifs. His last period of activity, according to 18th century biographers, was spent in Genoa.

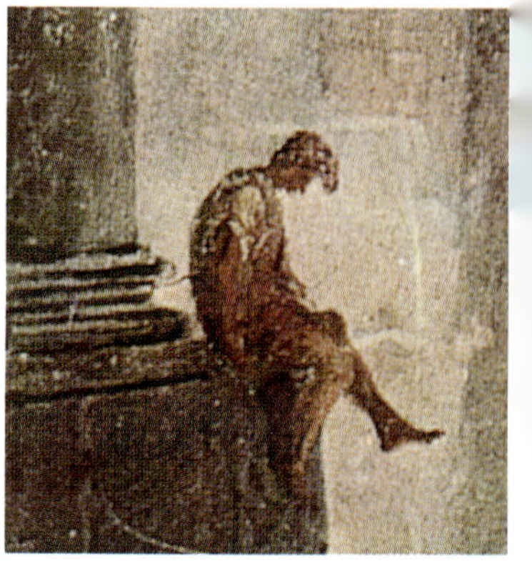

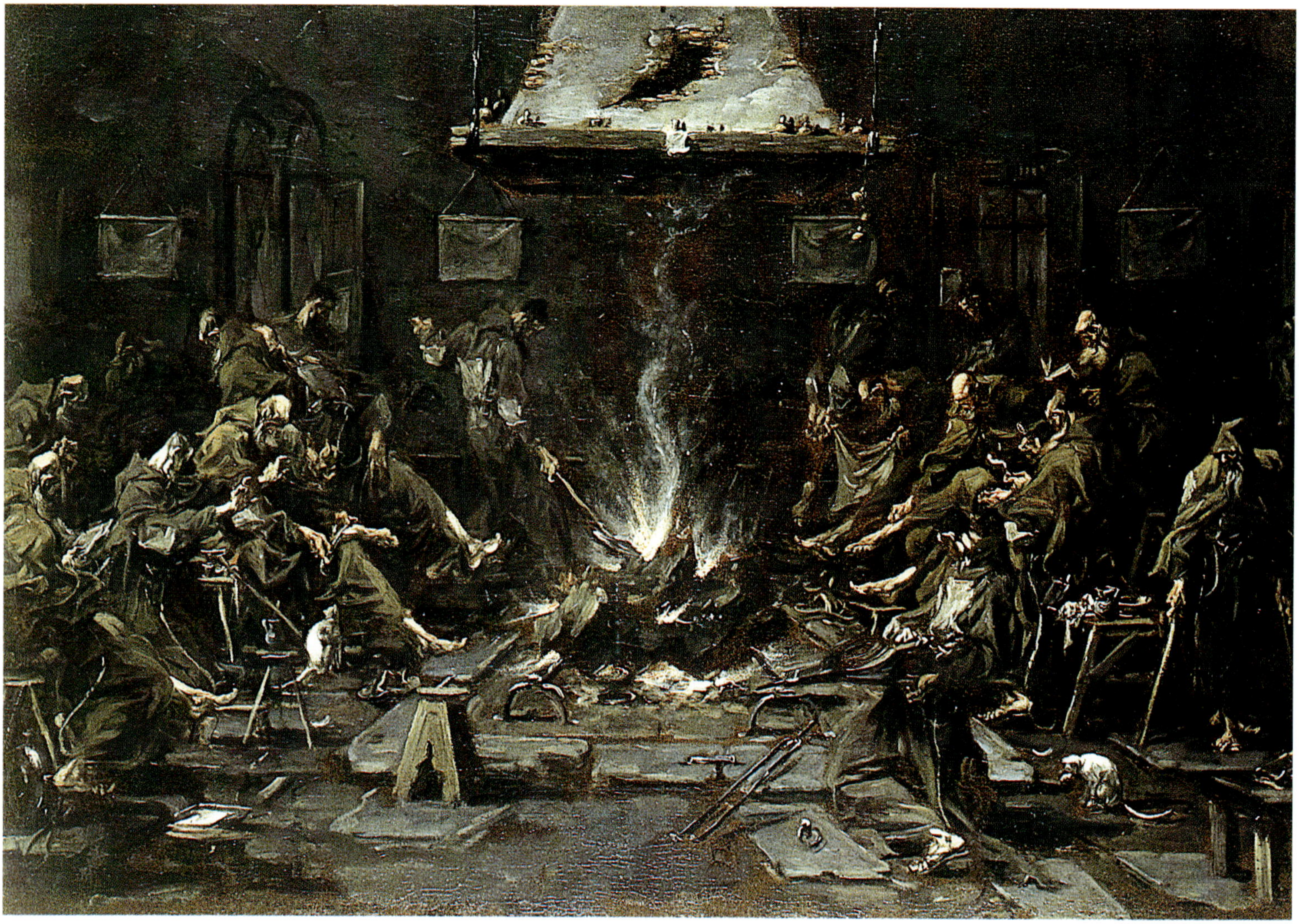

Alessandro Magnasco
Capuchins around the Hearth
w.d.
canvas

These "friars" scenes appear recurrently in Magnasco's work, almost as if to satisfy his bizarre, discerning taste. Painted with quick, virtuoso brushstrokes, the friars are shown in the quiet industriousness of their days or as they pause to rest, at the refectory perhaps or, as in the case of the *Capuchins around the Hearth*, around a fire lit in a dark, dank room. In contrast to the paintings of monastic life, crowded and often grotesque, are those of solitary hermits. Should the ascetic monk, emaciated and led into temptation, be seen as the artist's *alter ego*?

Alessandro Magnasco, *The Shore*, detail, 1716. Brignano Gera d'Adda (Treviglio), Castello.

Alessandro Magnasco
The Gypsies' Meal
c. 1710
canvas
Florence, Uffizi Gallery.

Magnasco's genre scenes are for the most part images of crowds, with a great number of personages appearing as if called onto the stage. A reference to the *commedia dell'arte*, although indirect, seems appropriate: brilliant improvisers, *capocomici* it might be said, tread the boards exhibiting their repertoires. Almost invariably, we have the melancholic, the braggart, the fellow guests, the hostess, the old monk, the waiter, the beggar, the zealot and the soldier. But each of these recites for himself: the action is fragmentary and disassociated, as in the *Gypsies' Meal*, where the personages are eating, ordering wine from the waiter, feeding animals. At the center of the composition a parrot on its perch turns to gaze at the spectator.

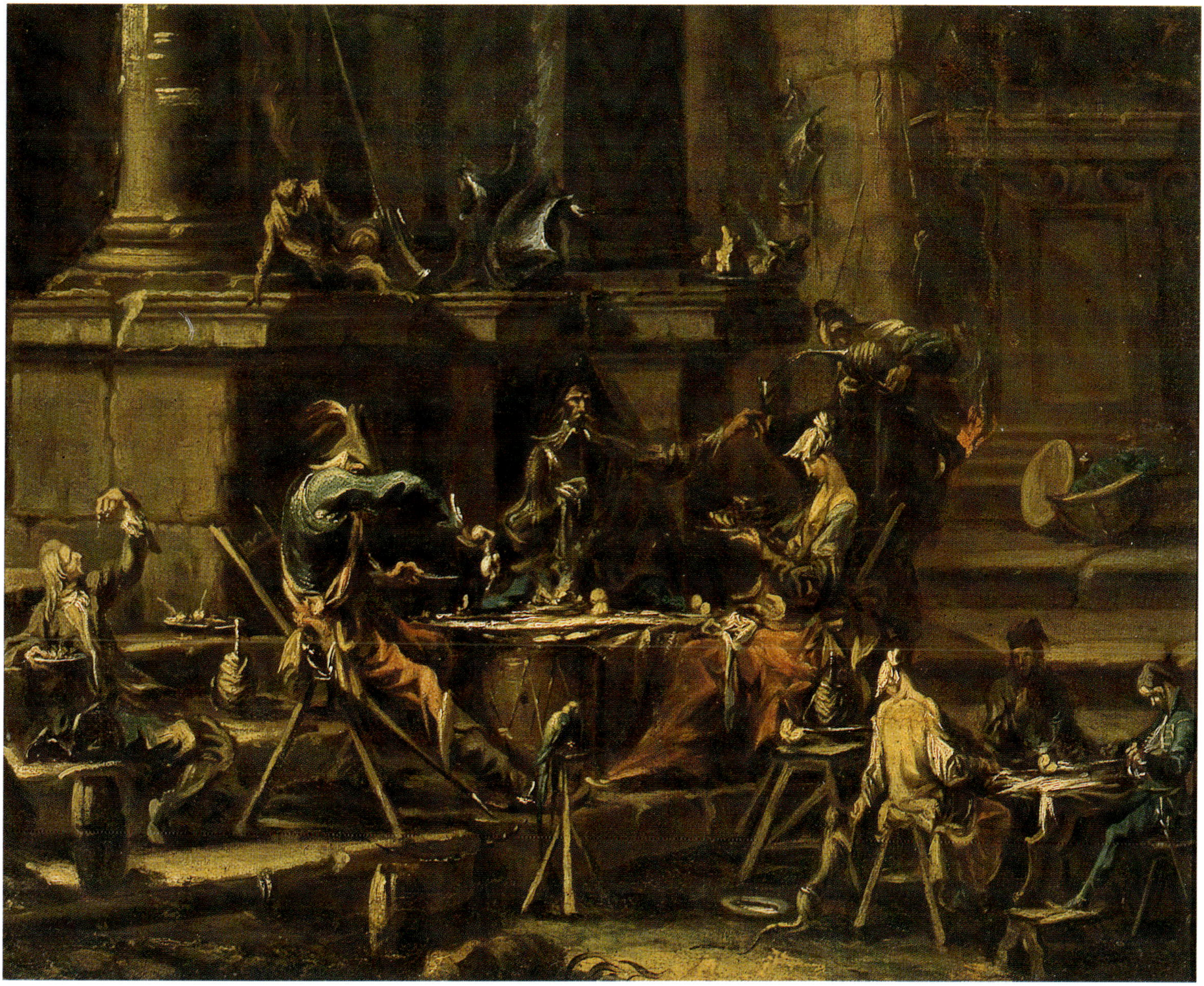

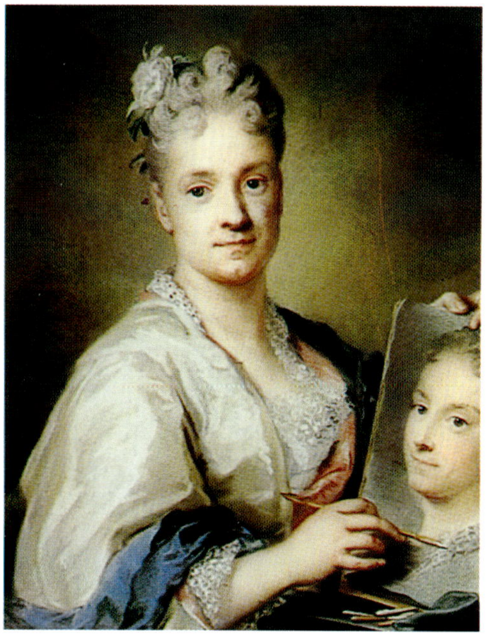

Rosalba Carriera

(Venice 1675 – 1757)

The artist's early training may have consisted of preparing embroidery patterns for her mother. Portraits painted in pastels gave her widespread renown. Commissioned by the aristocracy and by foreigners visiting Venice, she was an interpreter of the new orientation in Venetian painting. Skillful at small formats (also portraits for tobacco boxes, or on ivory) she conferred grace, courtesy and delicacy on her models. In Paris around 1720, she met Watteau and became member of the Académie Royal de Peinture. She left an important collection of letters.

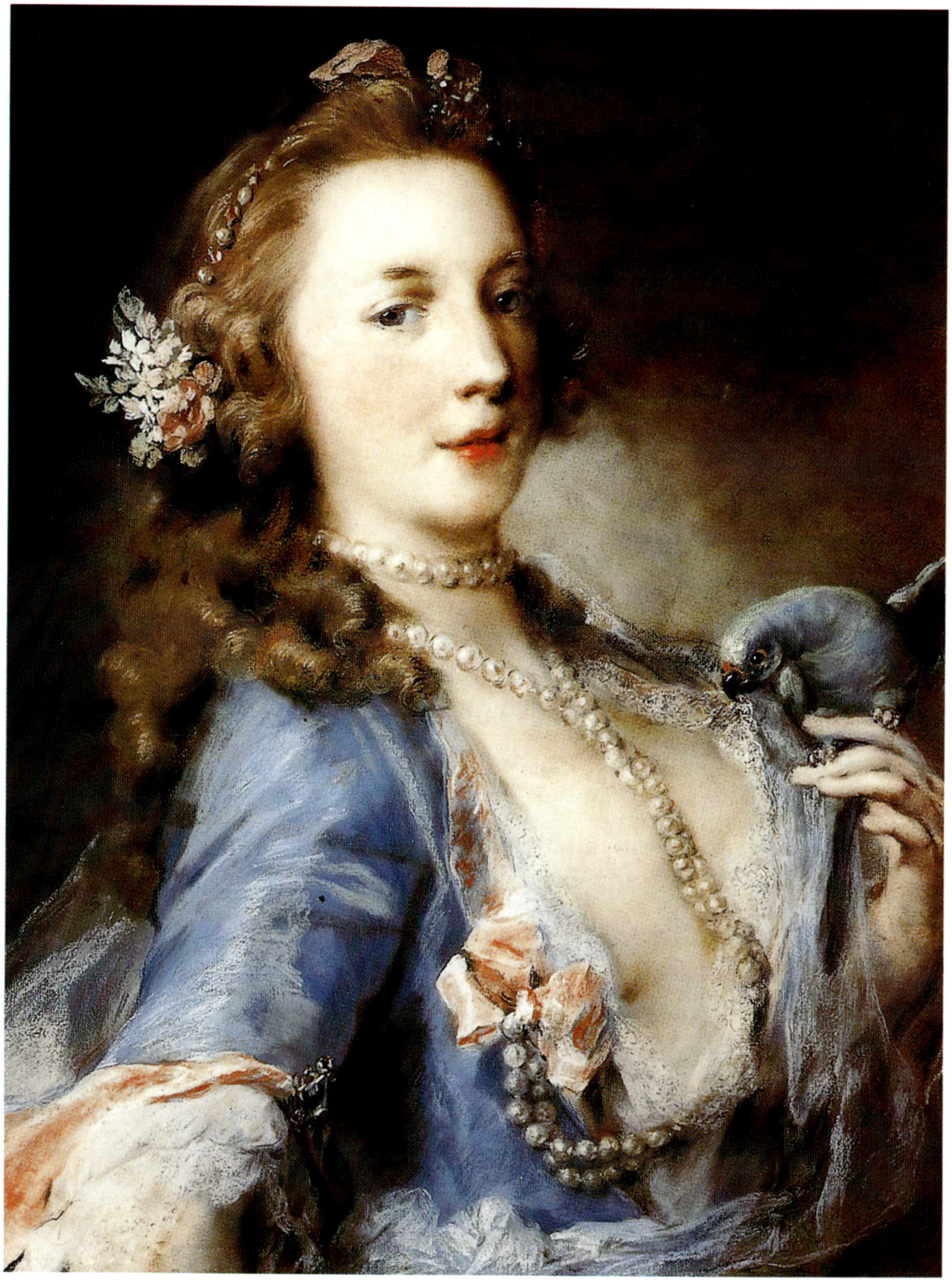

Rosalba Carriera
Self-portrait
1709
pastel on paper
Florence, Uffizi Gallery.

Rosalba portrays herself in professional stance, holding up to the observer a portrait she has painted of her sister Giovanna. She also indicates a special skill of her own: the pastel rests on the paper precisely at the complex embroidery adorning the collar of her sister's dress. Lightness and mobility of touch, extreme attention to the changing light, subtle psychology: these, Carriera seems to say, are the requisites of the excellent portrait painter.

Rosalba Carriera
Girl with a Parrot
c. 1720
canvas
Chicago, Art Institute.

Female figures with small animals are not rare in Rosalba's work. While the presence of cats or parrots may be seen as a sly homage to woman's sensuality, it also provides an expedient. In the *Girl with a Parrot* the bird has managed to bare the girl's breast, daring to do what she herself would never have dared. The candor of the skin, the shapely bosom, are thus exposed to admiration without violating the rules of modesty.

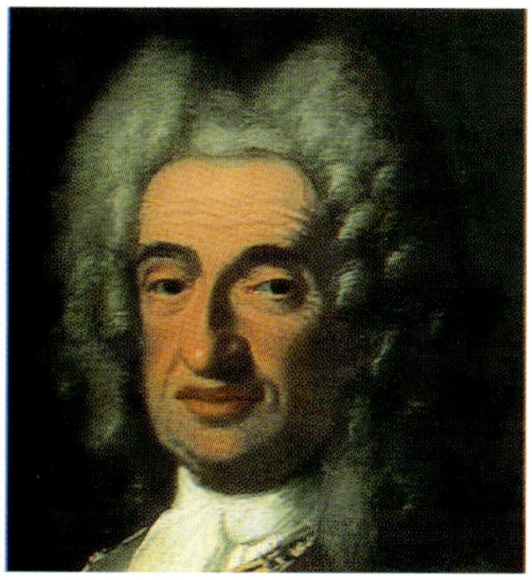

Luca Carlevarijs

(Udine 1663 – Venice 1730)

The artist was in Venice, orphaned of both parents, already by 1679. A journey to Rome first mentioned by his 19th century biographers probably took place around 1690. The impact of viewing Gaspard van Wittel's oriented his style in a new and lasting manner. In contact with Northern veduta artists active in Venice, such as Eismann, probably his master, and Stom, Carlevarijs was one of the first in Venice to abandon the tradition of the imaginary veduta. In 1703 he published his first collection of etchings, signed and dated. It contained 104 "buildings and scenes of Venice drawn, placed in perspective and engraved". Striking for his topographical objectivity, Carlevarijs shows himself equally skillful in the distribution of light and shadow. The evocative *chiaroscuro* effects of his compositions often reveal a careful study of Claude Lorrain.

Bartolomeo Nazzari,
Portrait of Luca Carlevarijs, detail,
w.d. Oxford, Ashmolean Museum.

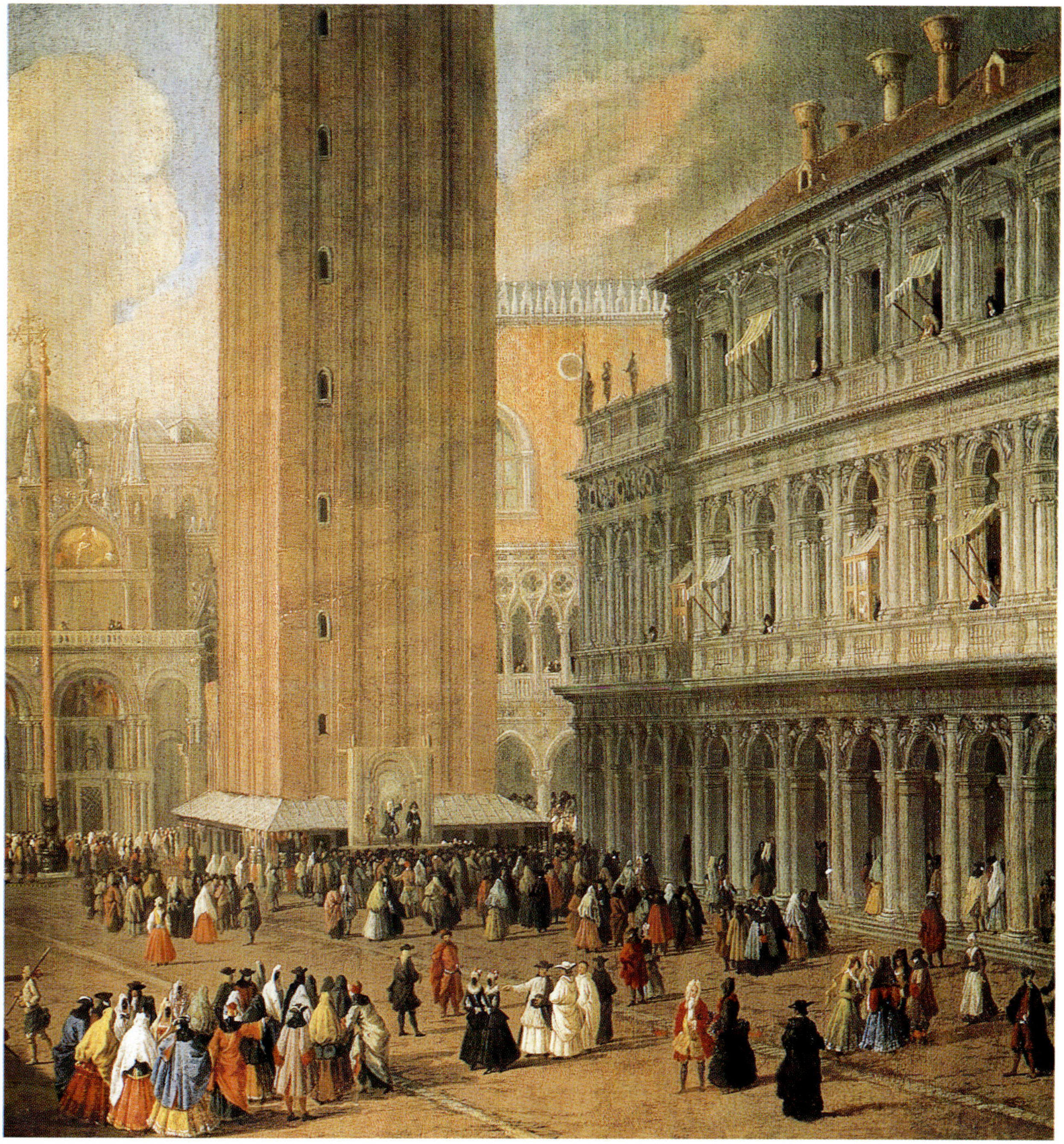

Luca Carlevarijs
St Mark's Square
c. 1720
canvas
Madrid, Thyssen-Bornemisza Collection.

Painted at times with the aid of the *camera ottica*, Carlevarijs' vedutas are distinguished by the scrupulous precision of his rendering of buildings and the great quantity of human types and caricatures depicted.
In *St Mark's Square* the foreground is crowed with splendidly dressed ladies and gentlemen and masked figures.
A gentlemen turns toward us – dressed in red and beige, he wears a great wig – while a poor woman enters the scene from the right. The light falls abruptly and unevenly, as if passing between one cloud and another after a storm. In the background a *commedia dell'arte* performance is being held.

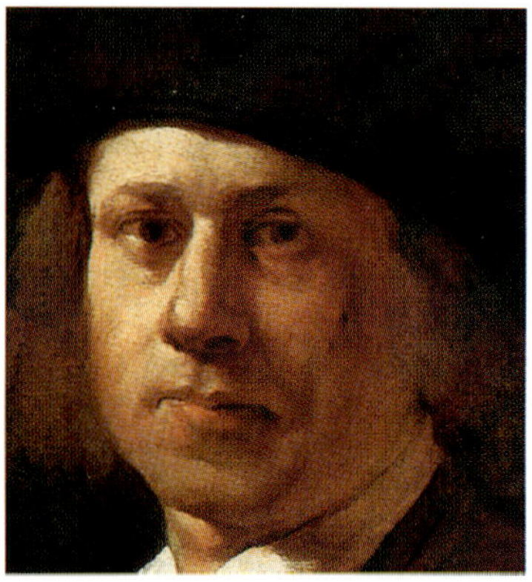

Giovan Battista Piazzetta, *Self-portrait*, c. 1720

Giovan Battista Piazzetta

(Venice 1683 – 1754)

Son of a modest sculptor, Piazzetta was at Bologna in the early years of the century, where he met Crespi. Settled in Venice starting from 1711, he was first the proprietor of a successful workshop and later, starting in 1750, the head of the school of painting that was to become the Venetian Academy. Renowned for his large religious compositions, he also painted pictures of medium-sized format, portraying mythological subjects or genre scenes. The "great genius of *chiaroscuro*", as he was called, in 1733, by Antonio Maria Zanetti, was not however indiffer ent to the new trends emerging on the Venetian scene. The attention with which Piazzetta viewed Sebastiano Ricci and the young Giambattista Tiepolo is revealed especially in works from the third and fourth decades of the 18th century, more strongly marked by clear tonalities and great luminosity.

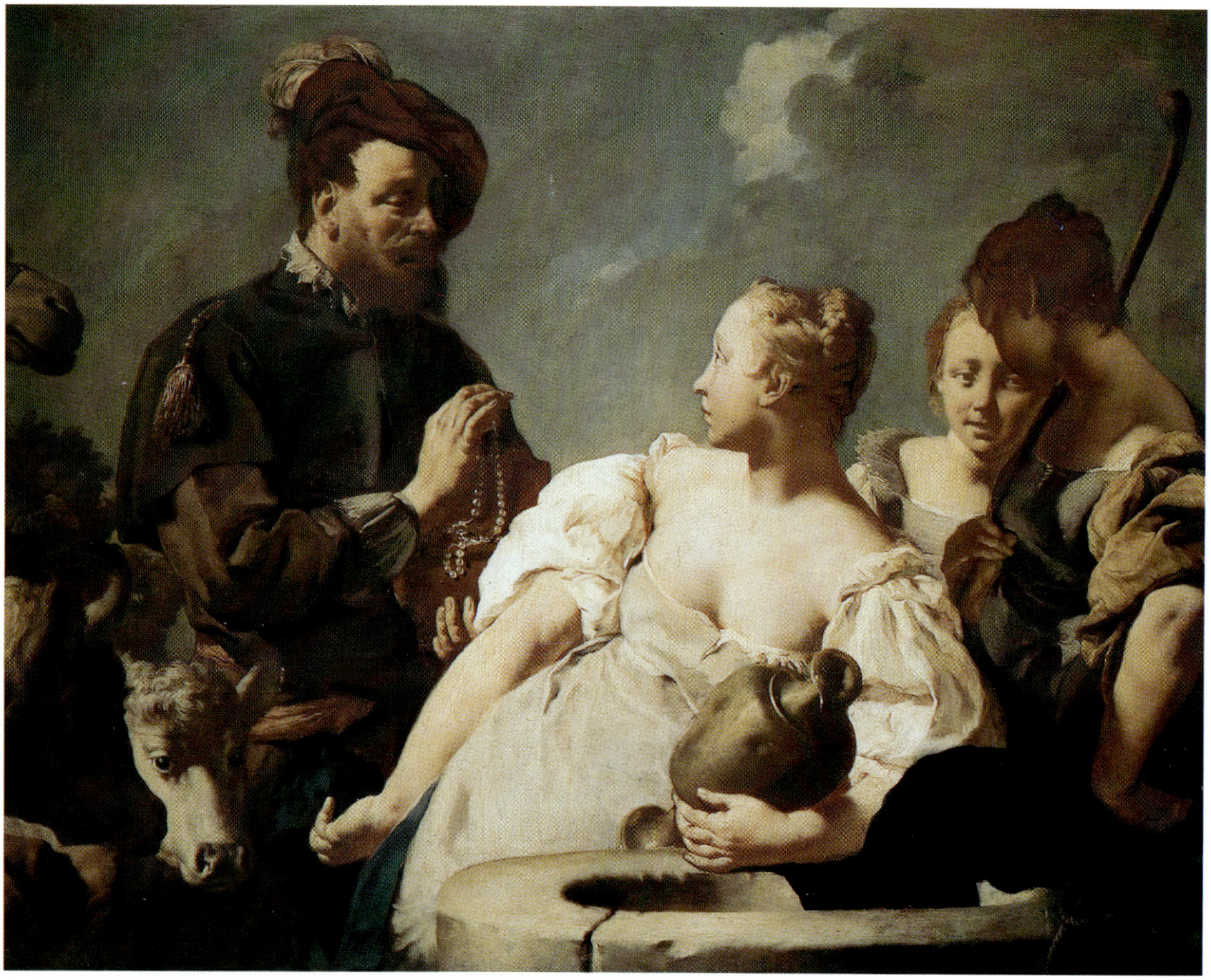

Giovan Battista Piazzetta
Rebecca at the Well
c. 1738
canvas
Milan, Brera Pinacoteca.

The Biblical episode becomes, for Piazzetta, a pretext for depicting a pastoral scene in the warm, radiant light of a last Spring or Summer morning. The oblong shape of the composition is typically neo-Veronesian, as are the twisted, serpentine postures of the figures and their sinuous attitudes; and neo-Veronesian is even the feminine type chosen by Piazzetta for the personage of Rebecca, blond, sensual, of whitest, almost alabaster complexion. The heads of animals and some objects placed in evidence – the vase, the cord, the well, the shepherd's stick – create a lively rustic frame for the main scene.

Giovan Battista Piazzetta
Young Sculptor
w.d.
canvas
Springfield, Museum of Fine Arts.

Skilled at presenting his figures enveloped in an intense, shadowy *chiaroscuro*, in portraits Piazzetta chooses for his models attitudes that are either boldly arrogant (as in his self-portraits) or introspective. The lowered viewpoint adopted by the artist for the *Young Sculptor* confers on the youth, who wears an ostentatious fur hat, reserved elegance and an unexpectedly solemn air.

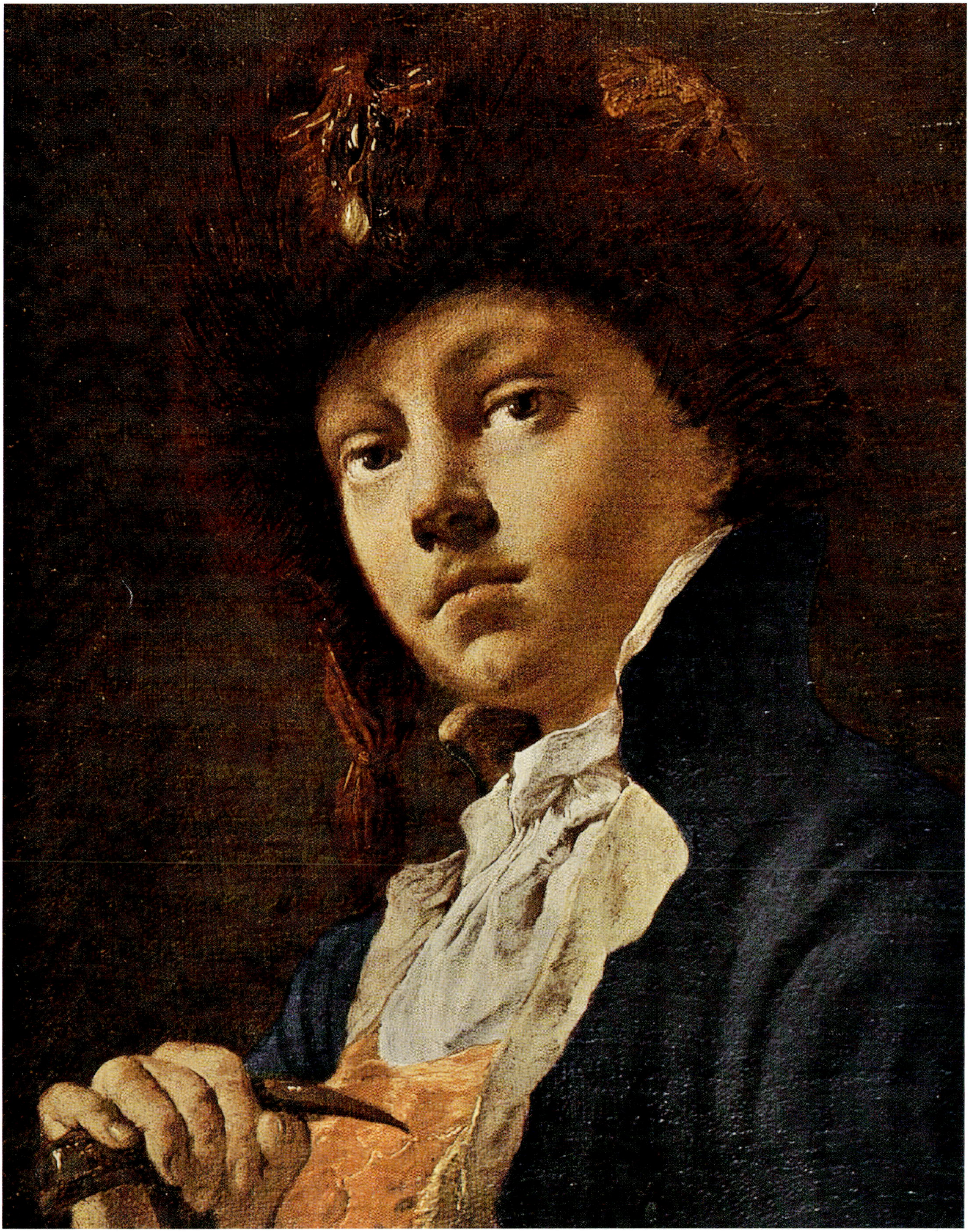

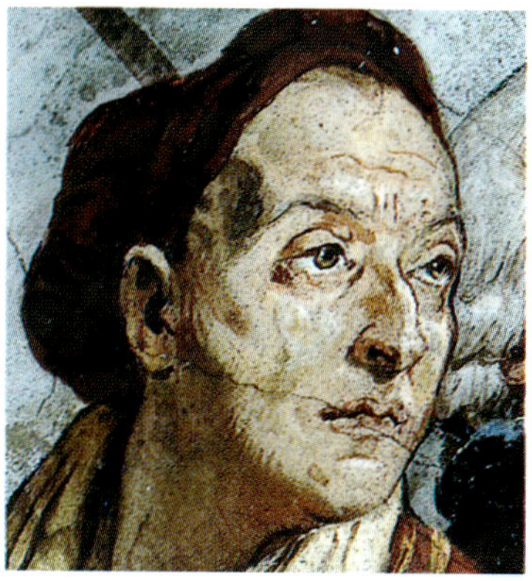

Giambattista Tiepolo

(Venice 1696 – Madrid 1770)

The son of Orsetta and Domenico Tiepolo, "merchant of naval supply shops", Tiepolo was both artist and adept, sophisticated entrepreneur, the owner of a large workshop engaged in important projects. Two of his seven children, Giovanni Domenico (Giandomenico) and Lorenzo worked with him. Active in Venice, Udine and Milan, Tiepolo preferred the *a fresco* execution of large figurative programs to the individual painting. He painted neither portraits nor vedutas, genres that were particularly in vogue at the time, remaining faithful to the great Venetian decorative tradition – his knowledge of Veronese was profound. At Würzburg between 1750 and 1753, he worked on the Residence of the local Bishop-Prince. In 1762 he went to Madrid, called there by Carlo III, where he was to die after having experienced the insidious rivalry of the younger neo-classical generation.

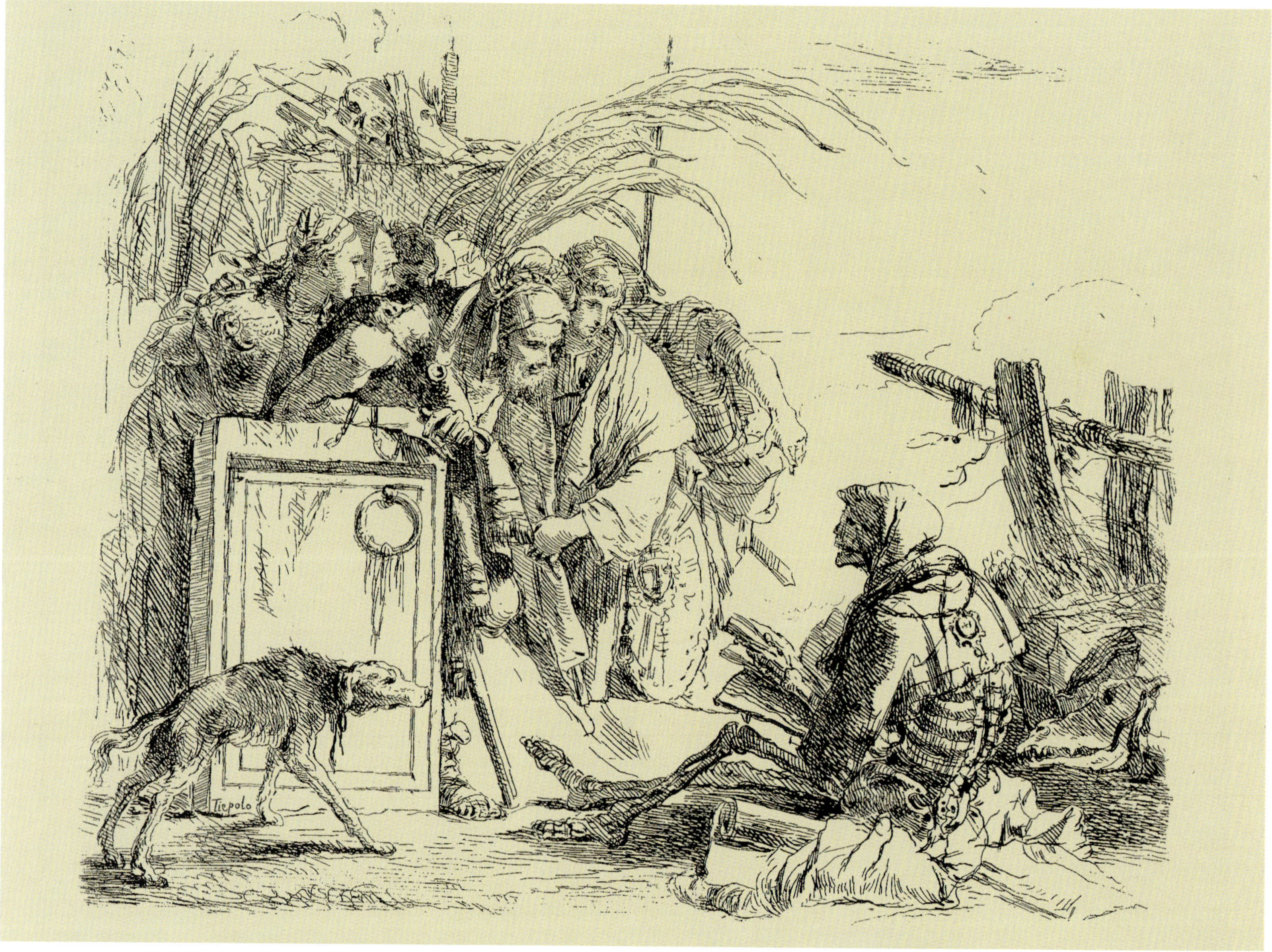

Giambattista Tiepolo, *Europe*, detail of frieze with self-portrait, 1753. Würzburg, Residence.

Giambattista Tiepolo
Death holds a Hearing
c. 1735
etching
Padua, Civic Museum.

Completed within the span of a few years and appearing probably in 1743 in a limited edition for Antonio Maria Zanetti, Venetian bibliophile and man of culture, the *Capricci* contained, along with the subsequent *Scherzi di fantasia*, the entire body of Giambattista's etchings: bizarre, enigmatic in theme, rich in physiognomies and attitudes, the *Capricci* and the *Scherzi* were immediately sought after by collectors all over Europe, such as the Grand Dukes of Saxony at Dresden, Pierre-Jean Mariette at Paris, and the British Consul Joseph Smith at Venice.

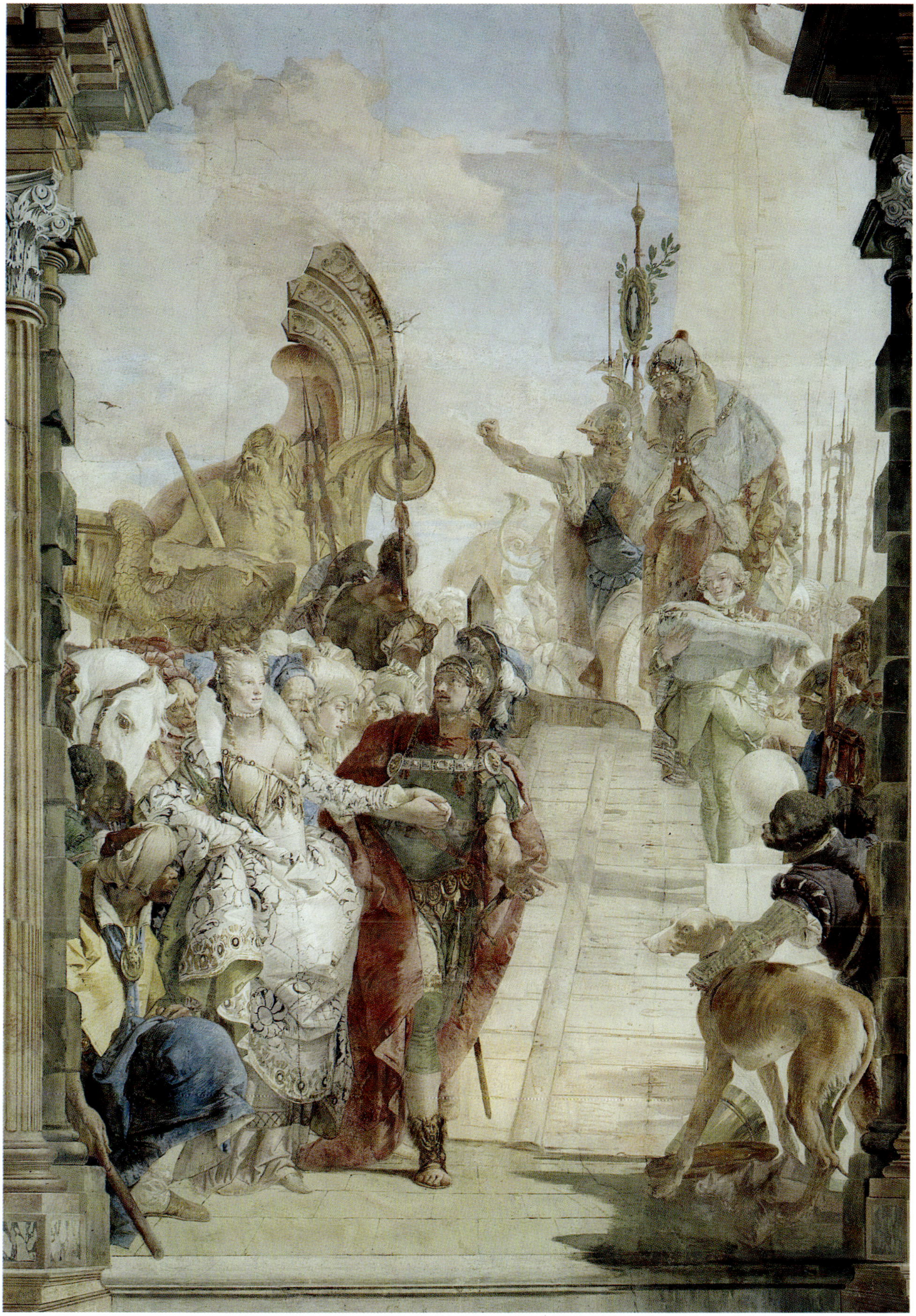

Giambattista Tiepolo
The Meeting of Antonio and Cleopatra
c. 1745-48
fresco
Venice, Palazzo Labia.

Commissioned to paint the walls of the Labia family's Venetian palace, Tiepolo collaborated on this occasion with Girolamo Mengozzi Colonna, a painter specialized in depicting complex architecture in *trompe-l'oeil* or, in the terminology of the times, an expert "quadraturist". The two most famous lovers in Roman history advance in the foreground amid a colorful crowd of pages, elders of the court and servants. They are seen through a stately arch held up by columns and pillows – arch, columns and pillars painted by Mengozzi Colonna. At the upper right, visible only in part, are sails blowing in the wind, rigging, and masts of ships with young sailors climbing aloft.

Giambattista Tiepolo
Africa
1752-53
fresco, detail
Würzburg, Residence.

In July of 1752 Tiepolo submitted to the Bishop-Prince a project for the ceiling of the Residence: a fresco representing the four continents along the sides surrounding Apollo, the sun god, in glory above them. It was an extremely arduous undertaking due to the immense surface to be frescoed – over 600 square meters; but the theme, relatively rare, left the artist great freedom of imagination. The fresco was completed in November of 1753. In the friezes of the continents Tiepolo lavished all of the elements – costumes, flora, fauna, archaeology – most vividly characteristic of the lands known at the time.

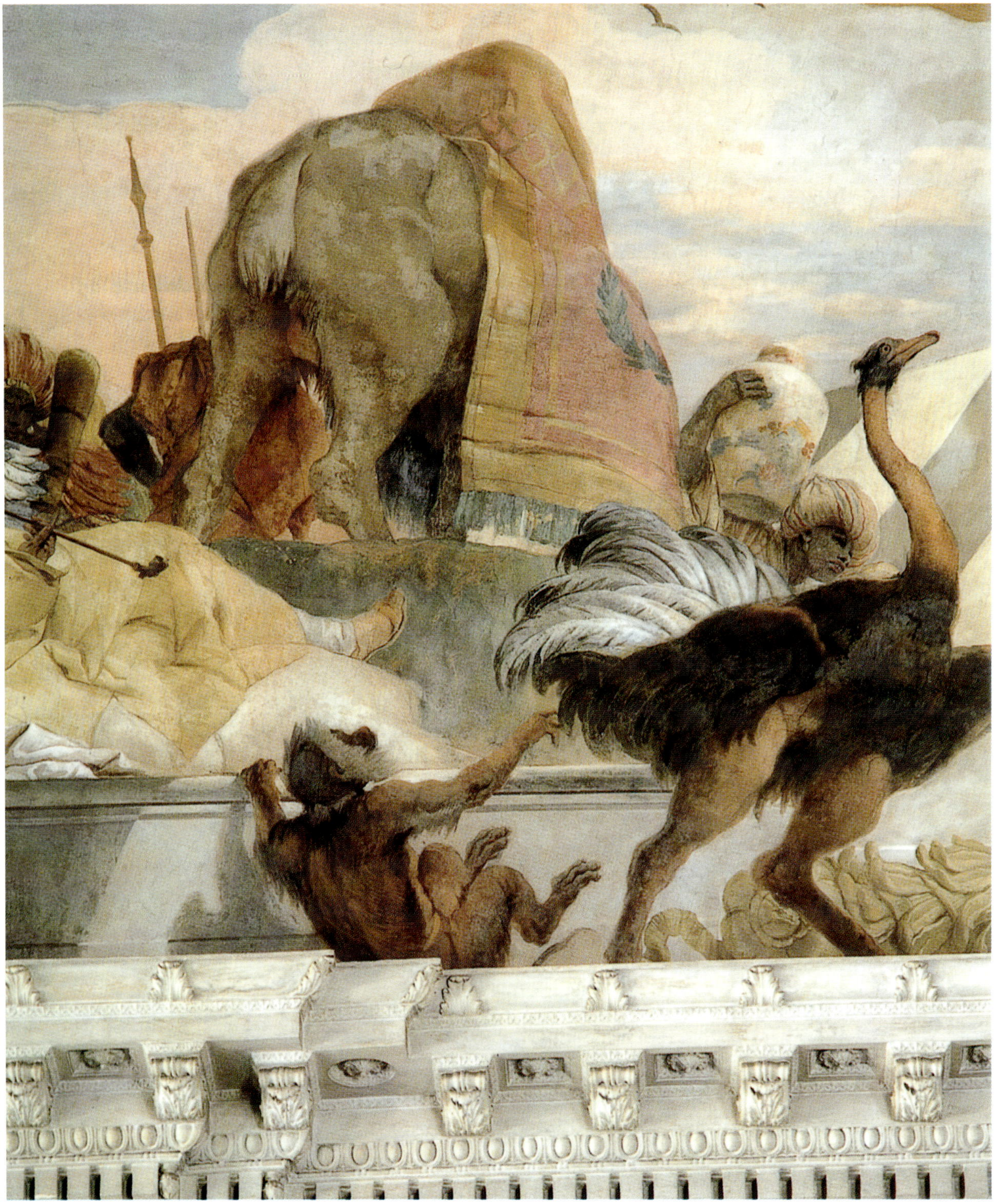

Giambattista Tiepolo
Africa
1752-53
fresco, detail
Würzburg, Residence.

The allegorical personification of Africa rides on camel-back, regal and imposing; behind her appears the face of a servant. In the foreground a black page, viewed from the back, seems to genuflect before Africa. He holds a parasol, burns incense, and carries a quiver. A great azure vase rests on the ground beside two half-hidden elephant tusks. The edge of a precious fabric hangs from the *trompe-l'oeil* cornice. The attributes of Africa are goods: spices, arms, silk and ivory. In the friezes of the continents the lively commerce between distant peoples is reflected.

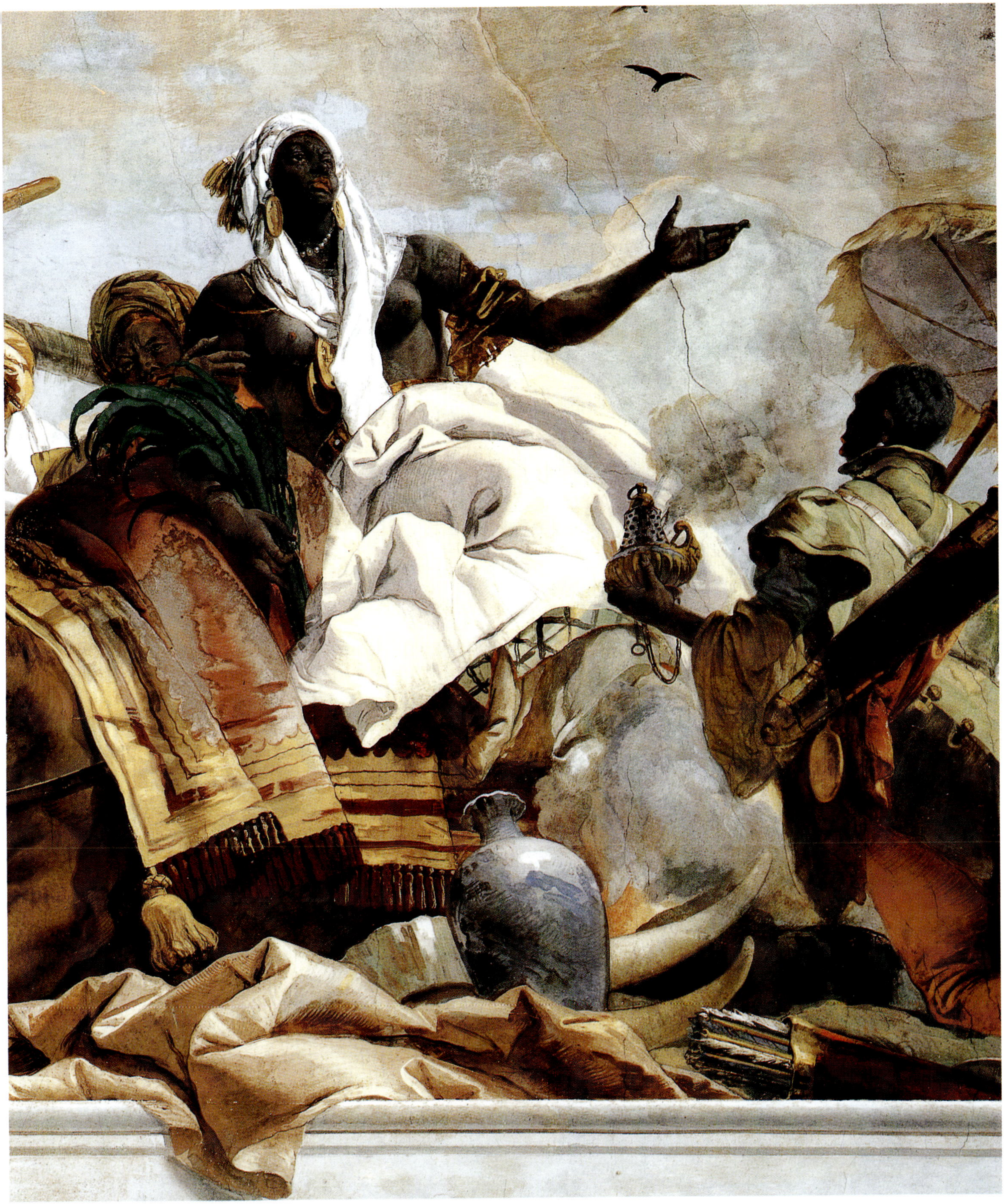

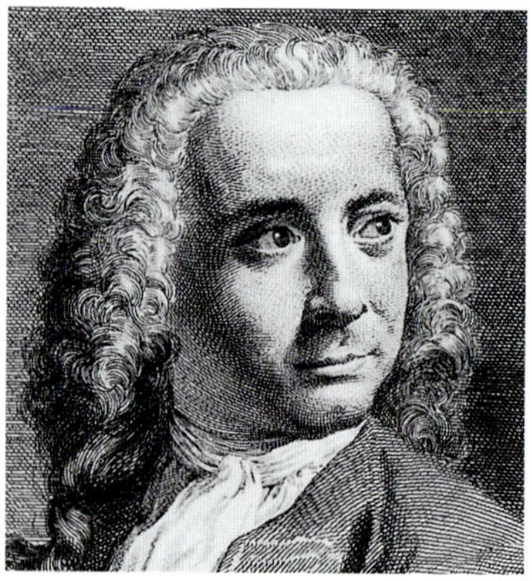

Canaletto

(Giovanni Antonio Canal, Venice 1697 – 1768)

An internationally famous artist, Canaletto was eminently responsible for the success of the veduta. A child of art – his father, Bernardo, was a theatrical painter – he himself began as set designer. In 1719, however "annoyed by the indiscretion of the dramatic poets", writes Antonio Maria Zanetti, a contemporary historian, "he solemnly excommunicated the theater and left for Rome", where he was to live for one or two years. Having viewed the work of the Flemish veduta artists, he was back in Venice again just after 1720, now a "painter of vedutas", choosing for his subjects famous monumental sites such as St Mark's Square or the Grand Canal, but not neglecting to document the daily life of the city. In great demand by English collectors, he was in London in 1746 where, apart from periodic returns to Venice, he was to live for almost a decade.

Antonio Visentini,
Portrait of Canaletto, engraving by Giovan Battista Piazzetta for the frontispiece of the *Prospectus Magni Canalis Venetarium*, containing engravings by Canaletto, prior to 1735.

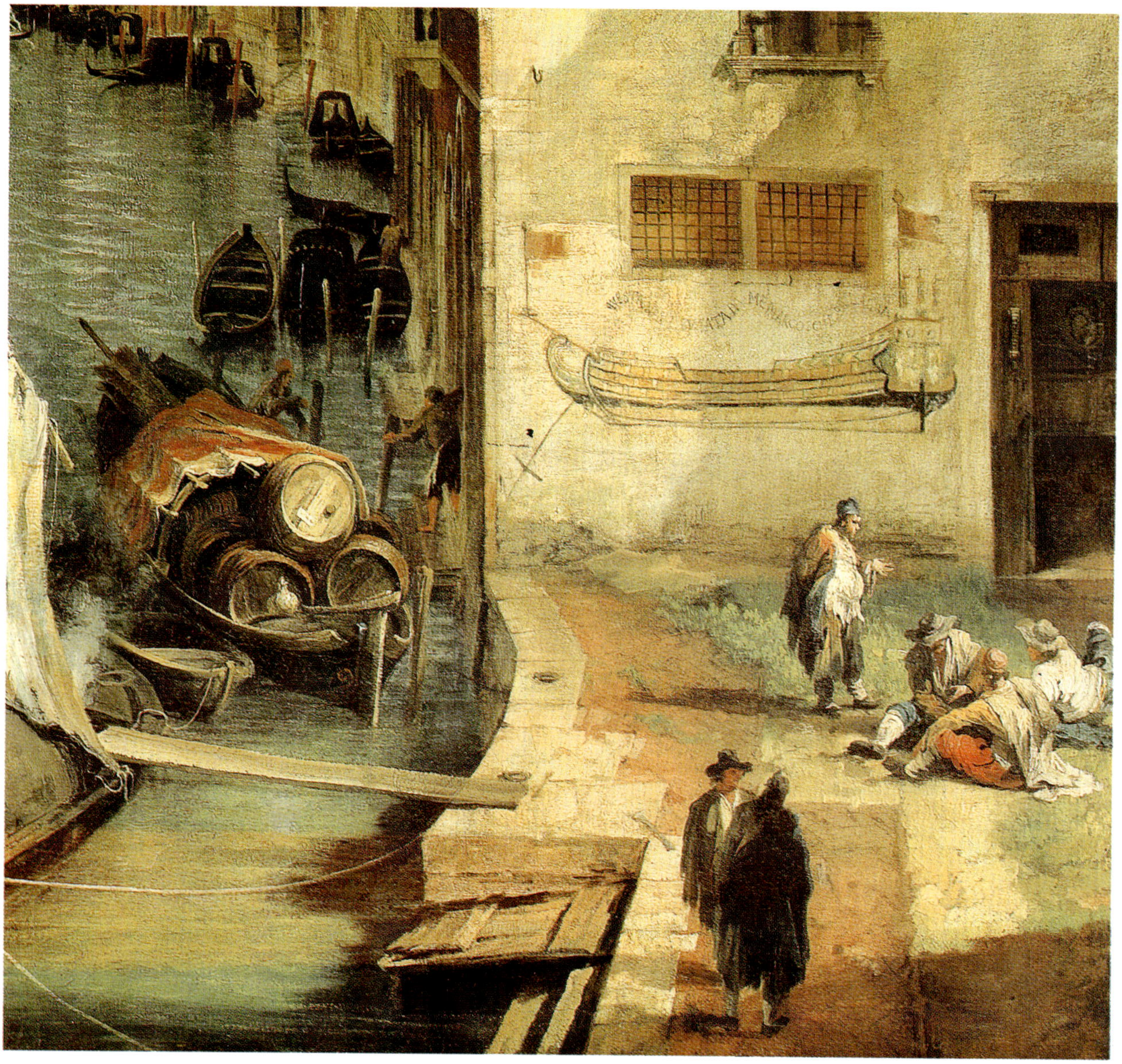

Canaletto
View of the Grand Canal from Campo San Vio
after 1719
canvas, detail
Madrid, Thyssen-Bornemisza Collection.

The young Canaletto frequently painted caprices and vedutas of his own invention. Even the first vedutas faithful to the subject retain traces of his taste for the bizarre, the curious, and the picturesque. Common people, beggars and idlers seated on the ground, are here engaged in heated discussion. Behind them appears an elegant ship, its flags flying in the wind.

Canaletto
Interior of St Mark's with Choir-Singers
1766
pencil, pen, water colors on paper
Hamburg, Kunsthalle.

The drawing, executed with extreme precision by Canaletto – and, moreover, "without glasses", as the elderly artist specified on a note – is a partial view of the interior of St Mark's Cathedral, showing the mixed crowd that gathers in the basilica: the choir of ecclesiastics, the faithful in prayer, an old beggar-woman whose heart is gladdened by the hymn of devotion. The Byzantine mosaics, the 16th century altars, and the great chandeliers are all fully entitled to be included in the composition; the Christian temple holds memories and vestiges of every age.

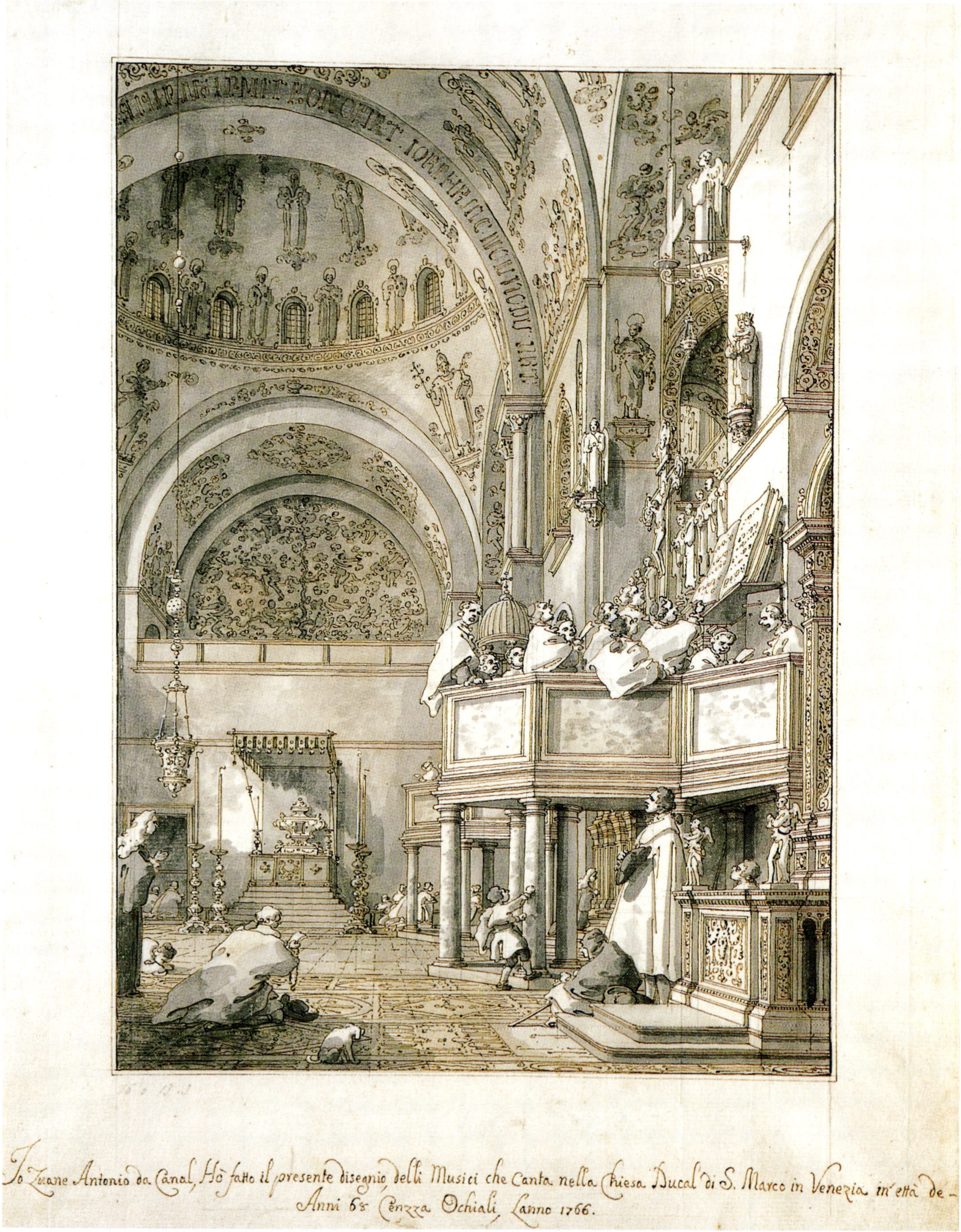
Io Zuane Antonio da Canal, Hò fatto il presente disegnio delli Musici che Canta nella Chiesa Ducal di S. Marco in Venezia in età de
Anni 68 Cenzza Ochiali, Lanno 1766.

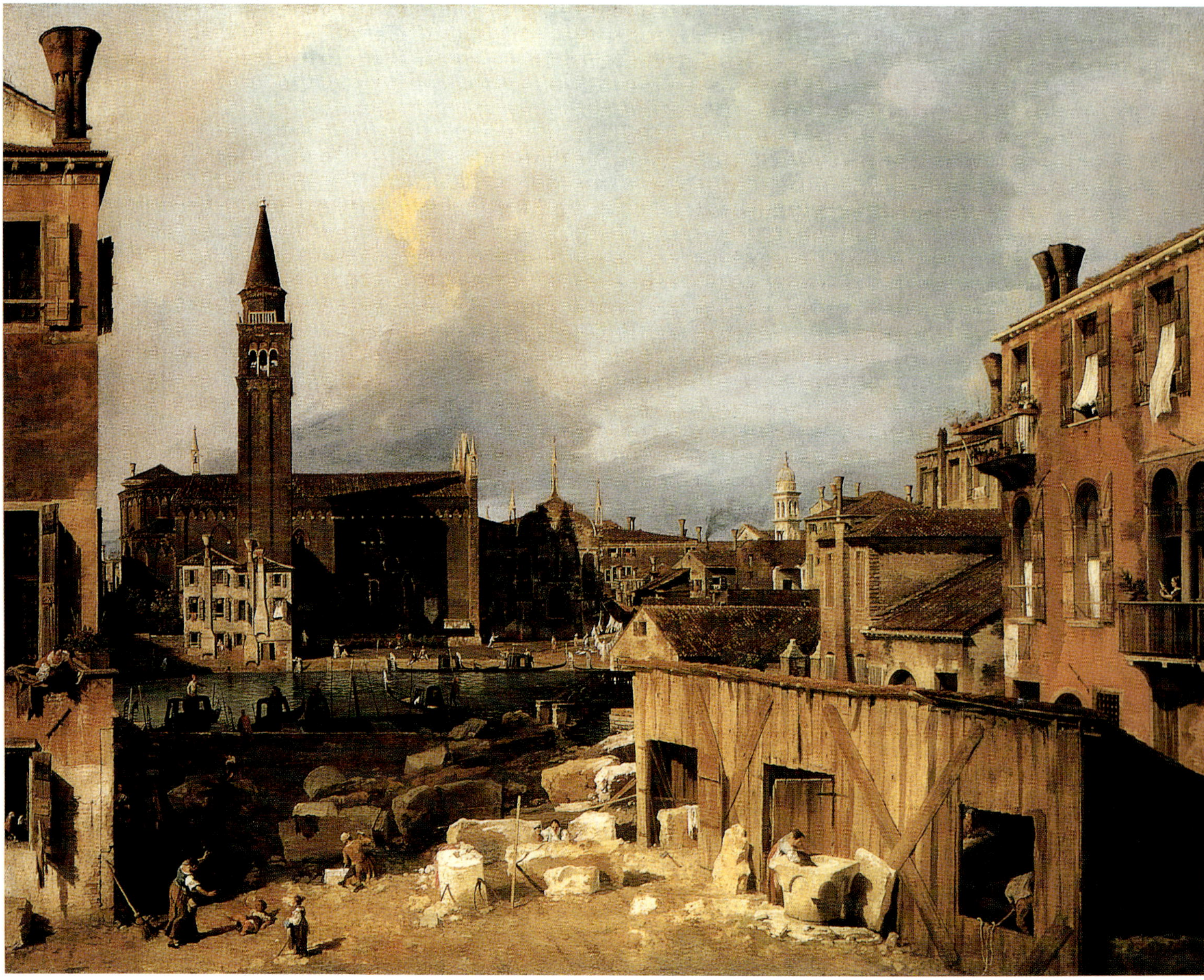

Canaletto
The Marble Workers' Square
c. 1730
canvas
London, National Gallery.

In the veduta known as the *Marble Workers' Square* Canaletto chose not to depict one of the city's elegant sites but rather a small, obscure square, surrounded by the modest dwellings of artisans and the shops of marble workers, most of whom were probably engaged in the reconstruction of the Church of San Vitale. The clear light of early morning on the lagoon touches the fronts of the houses, the wooden beams of the artisans' shops, the laundry hung out to dry, the bell towers and the marble. The genre scenes are strikingly vivacious. Gondoliers are awaiting passengers, women are spinning on their balconies or looking out of windows, children are playing in the courtyard below, stone-workers are surprised in the act of cutting and rough-hewing great blocks of marble. In the background idlers are resting, seated or half-lying on the steps leading down to the wharf.

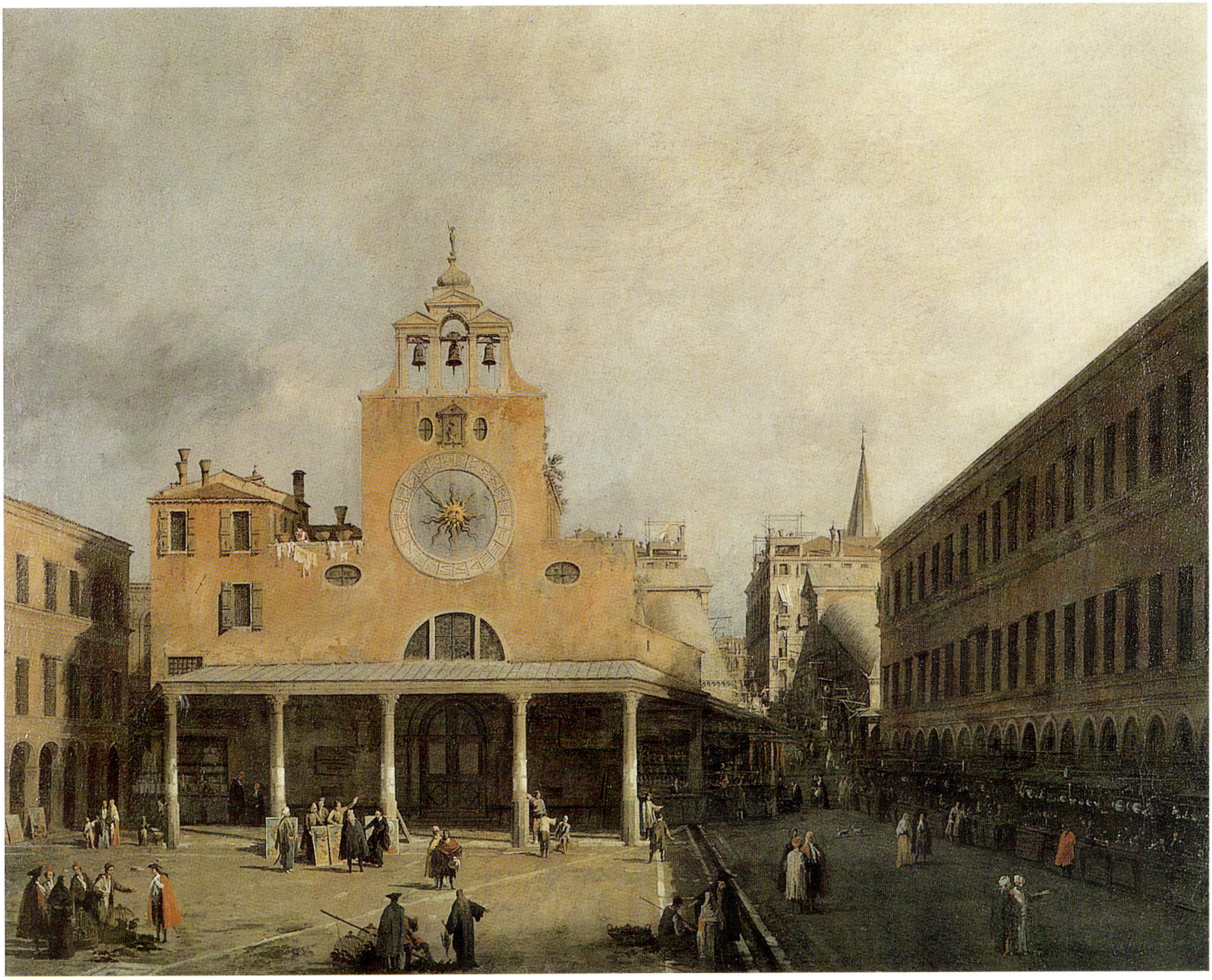

Canaletto
San Giacomo di Rialto
c. 1730
canvas
Dresden, Gemäldegalerie.

In painting his vedutas Canaletto utilized the *camera ottica*. A precursor of the camera, it was a box with mirrors which projected the subject, through a series of reflections, onto a sheet of paper, allowing the artist to "copy" directly from the real image. It is surprising how the use of a simple optical device yields images pervaded by an intense, radiant light, clearer than that of nature. Canaletto, wrote a contemporary admirer, "universally amazes everyone in this country who sees his works, which are similar to Carlevari's but in which the shining of the sun can be seen".

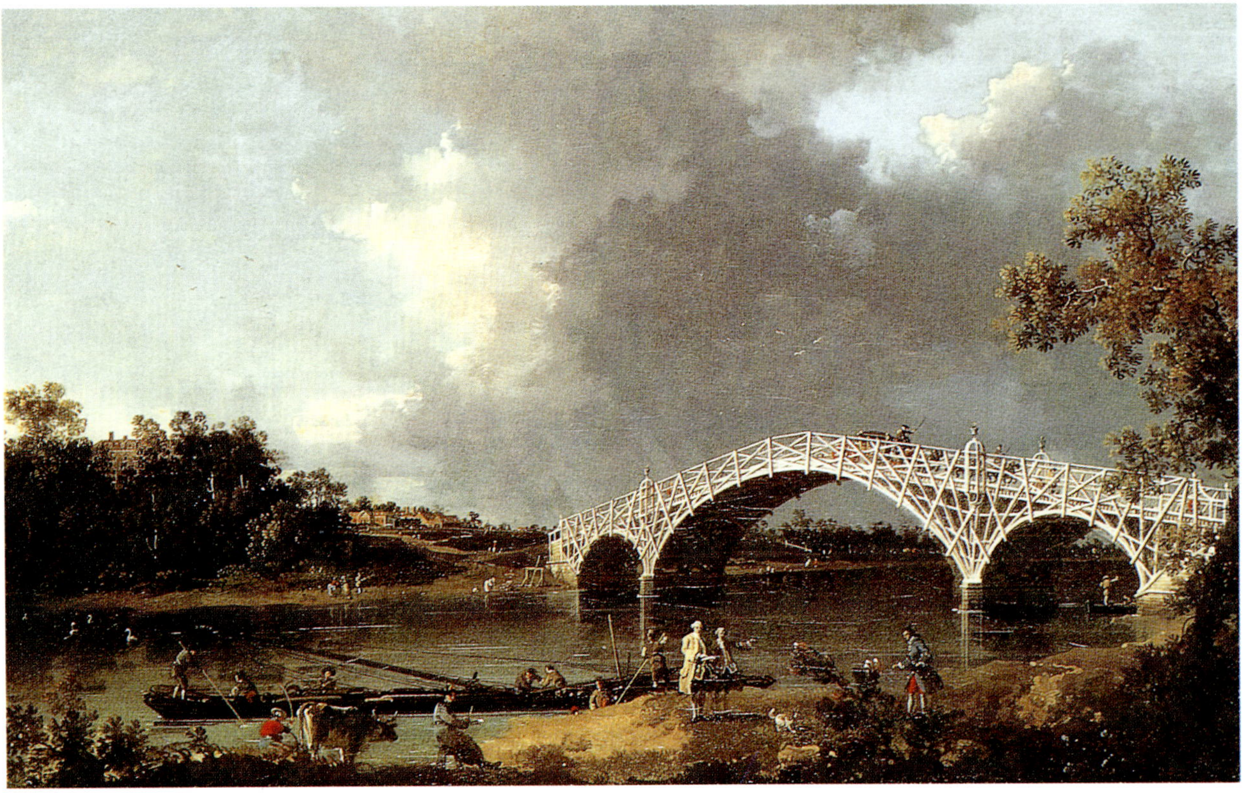

Canaletto
The Grand Canal with the Church of San Simeone Piccolo looking toward the Fondamenta della Croce
c. 1729-34
canvas
London, National Gallery.

Daily traffic, the movement of objects and persons, commerce, all take place on the crowded waters of the Grand Canal. Along the banks rise majestic Christian churches and patrician palaces. Canaletto's Venice is not exclusively antiquarian. The city lives its present-day life, vivacious and laborious, rich in initiative.
A multiplicity of minor episodes enhances the fascination of the artist's vedutas. Strollers meet, mothers are talking from the thresholds of their houses while children play, church-goers distribute alms to the beggars waiting on the stairway, and little flower-vases decorate the balconies as they had in the past, in the paintings of Carpaccio and Antonello da Messina.

Canaletto
Old Walton Bridge
1754
canvas
London, Dulwich Picture Gallery.

"Done in 1754 for the first and last time with all greatest attention" – wrote Canaletto on the back of the canvas – the picture, owned by a friend of the Consul Joseph Smith, depicts a wooden bridge over the Thames about twenty-five miles from Westminster, which no longer exists today. Supported by three arches, the Old Walton Bridge has a light structure made of painted wood. It seems to vibrate in the luminous country landscape extending all around, bathed in the light falling from above.

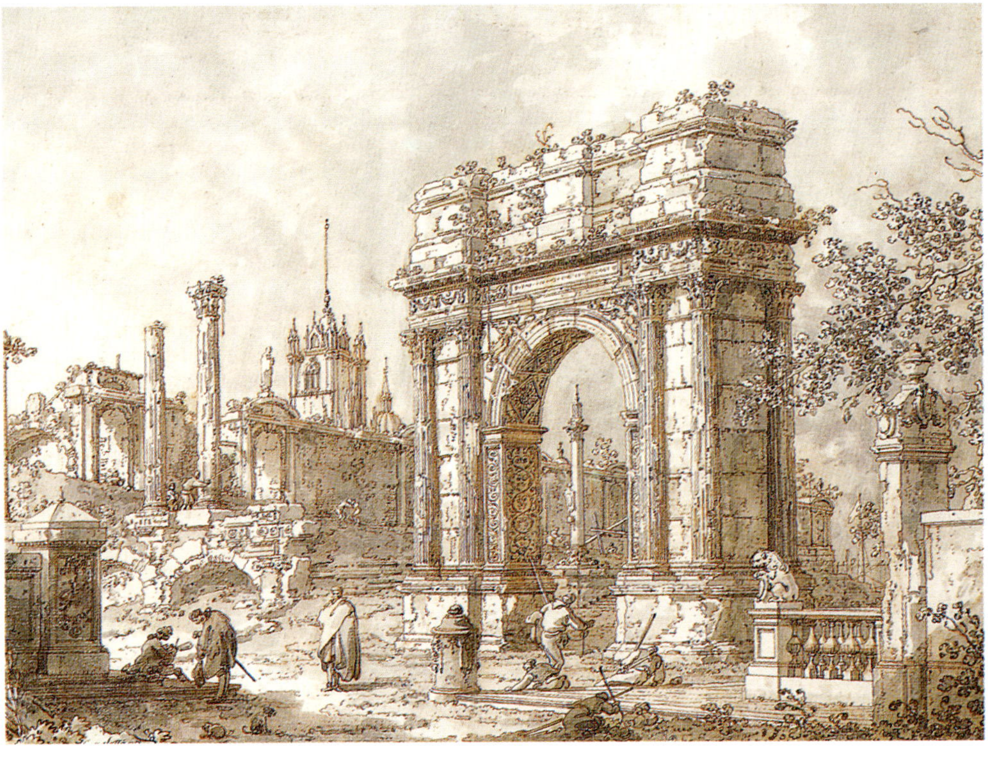

Canaletto
Caprice with Roman Triumphal Arch and Ruins
after 1748
pencil, pen, ink and water color on paper
New York, The Metropolitan Museum of Art.

The triumphal arch is that of Pola, an archaeological site on the Istrian peninsula. Canaletto had never been there; perhaps he took the motif of the arch from an engraving by Piranesi. Finely executed in every detail, the drawing shows columns and ruins of other arches around the main one. An artist sits intent on his drawing while in the background, at the lower right, appears a glimpse of the sea and the mast of a ship.

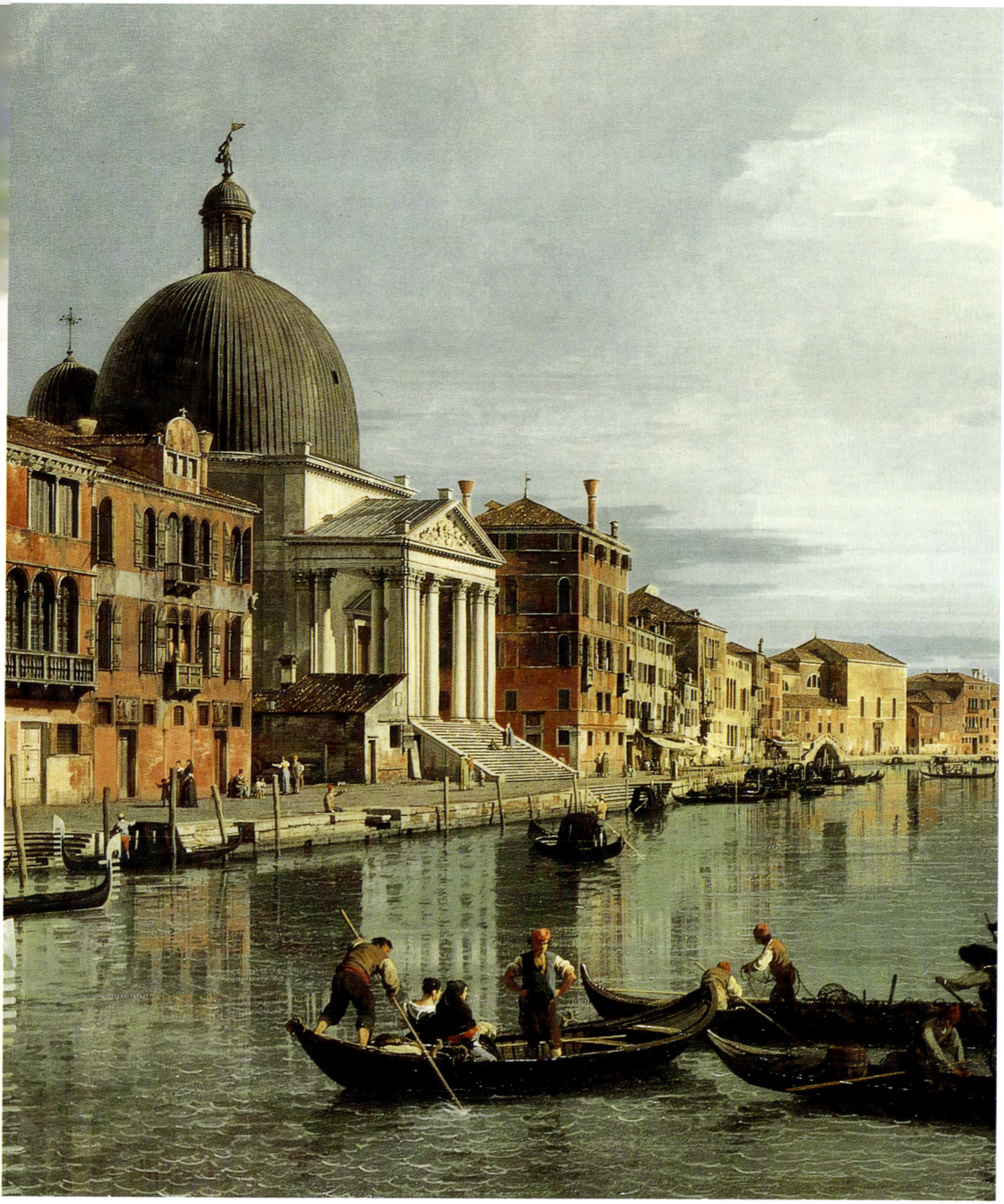

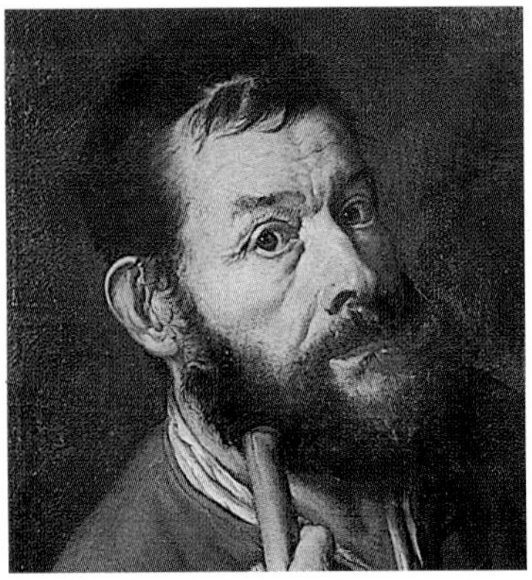

Giacomo Ceruti

(known as Il Pitocchetto, Milan 1698 – 1767)

Active at Brescia in his youth, Ceruti was at Venice in 1736; later at Piacenza, then again at Brescia and Milan. A successful potrait painter, he also painted works of religious subject and still lifes. He owes his fame, however, to images of the poor – beggars, pilgrims, peasants, minor artisans – engaged in their modest activities or glimpsed during moments of rest. Near to 17th century painters such as Le Nain and Murillo, Ceruti was a refined stylist – his compositions invariably tend toward the monochrome – and a keen observer of social reality. The extreme poverty shown by many of his personages was in fact common to the peasants and urban poor during the decades in which the artist was painting. Ceruti's clientele was aristocratic. The images of poverty were edifying, a proof of philanthropy, and occasionally evocative of laughter (in accordance with the Carracci tradition).

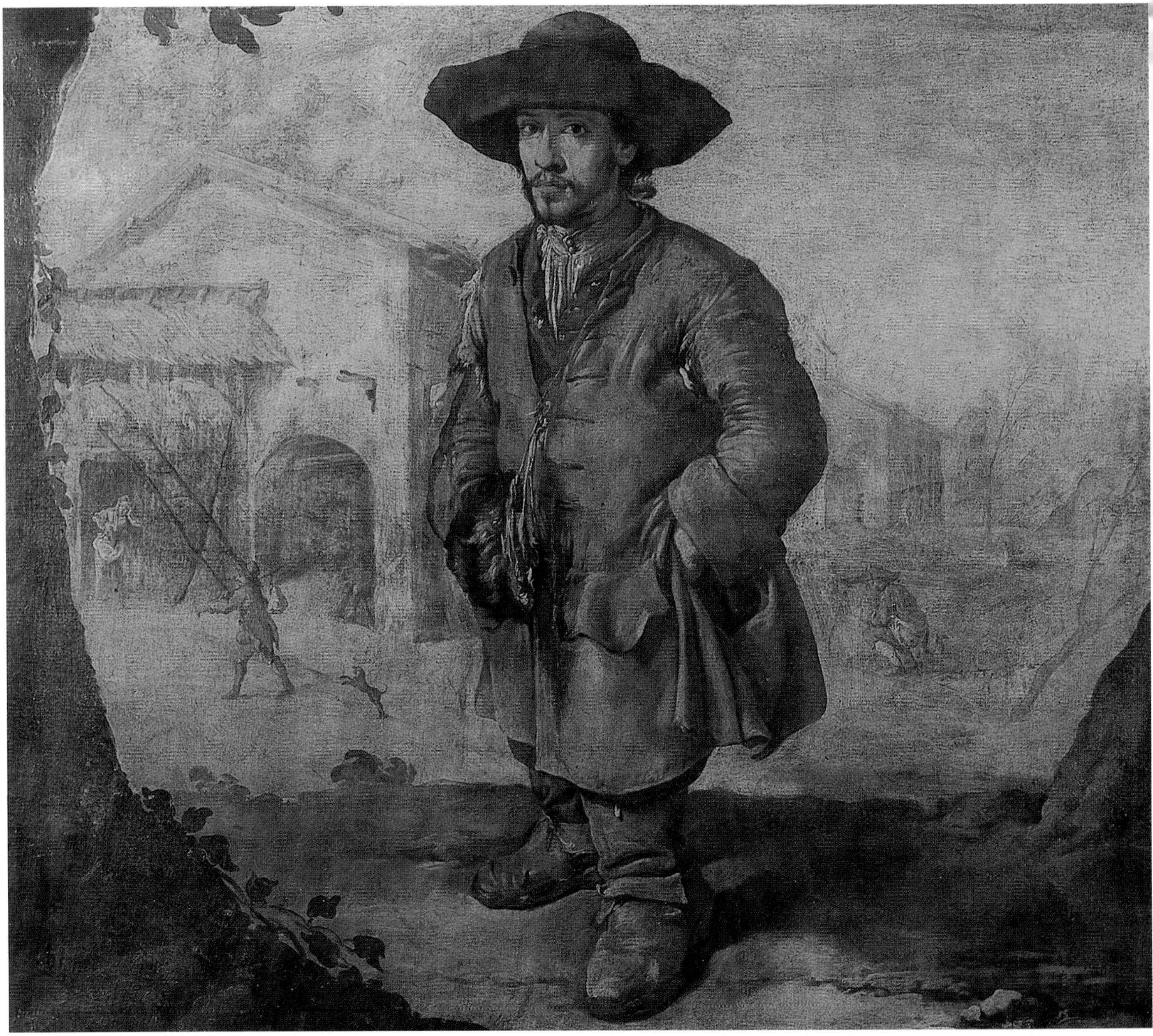

At left:
Giacomo Ceruti,
Self-portrait as a Pilgrim, 1737. Abano Terme, Comune.

Giacomo Ceruti
The Dwarf
w.d.
canvas

Although indulging in a representation of deformity, the painting is not devoid of human intensity. Unquestionably belonging to the comic genre – to satisfy the expectations of the clients – it nonetheless raises the genre scene to the level of portraiture, depicting an individual psychology. The dwarf's gaze awaits that of the observer; on his fine face, fear and resolution alternate. The background, sketched in with faint hues, is carelessly crude. The farm on the left is taken from an engraving by Callot. The man on the right is defecating, placidly certain that here in the countryside no will can see him.

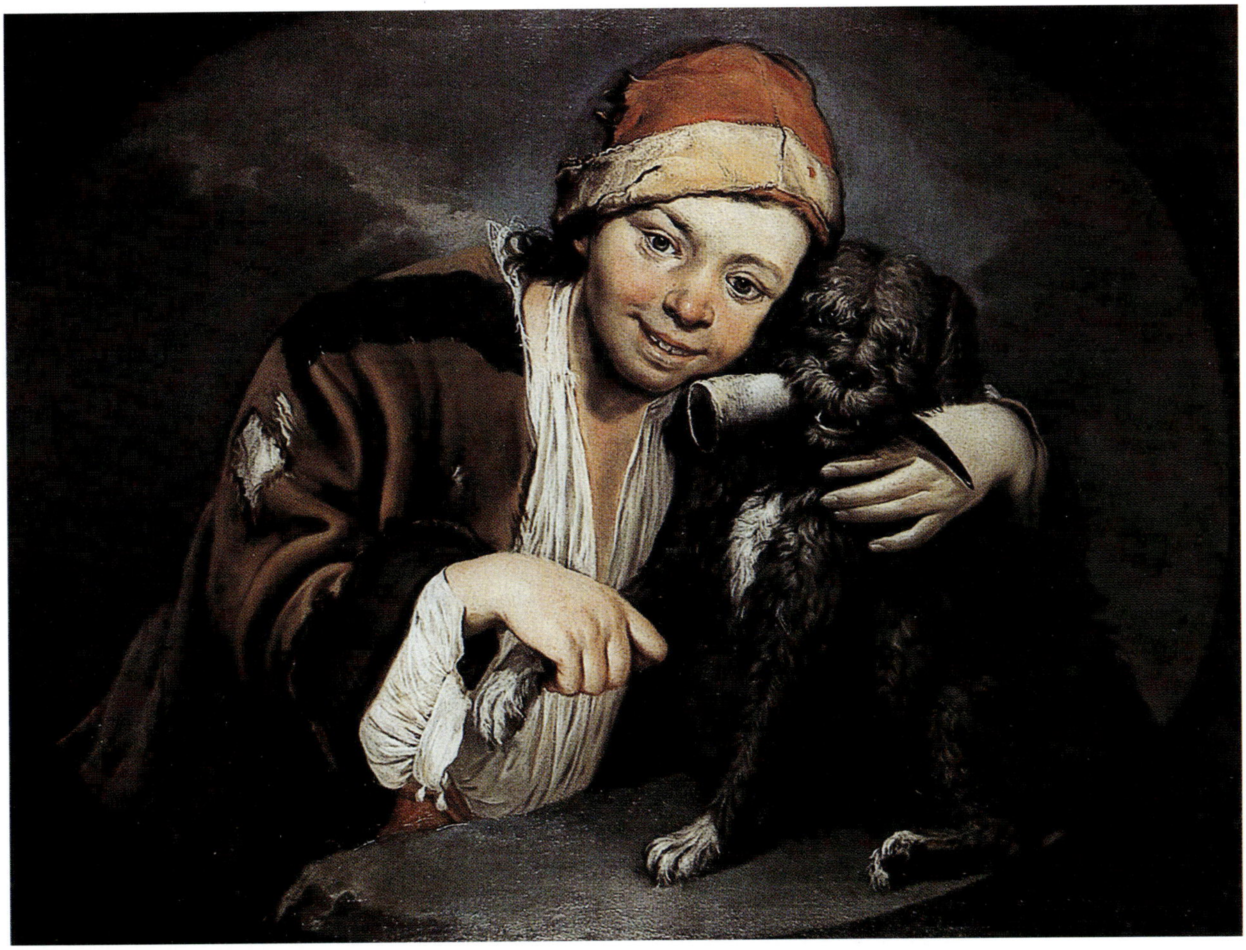

Giacomo Ceruti
Boy with a Dog
w.d.
canvas
Belfast, Ulster Museum.

An allegorical composition rather than a portrait, as might be suggested by the search for verisimilitude in the portrayal of the face, the hands and the clothing, the subject of the *Boy with a Dog* is that of hunting, to which the horn held in the dog's mouth, appearing as an attribute, alludes.

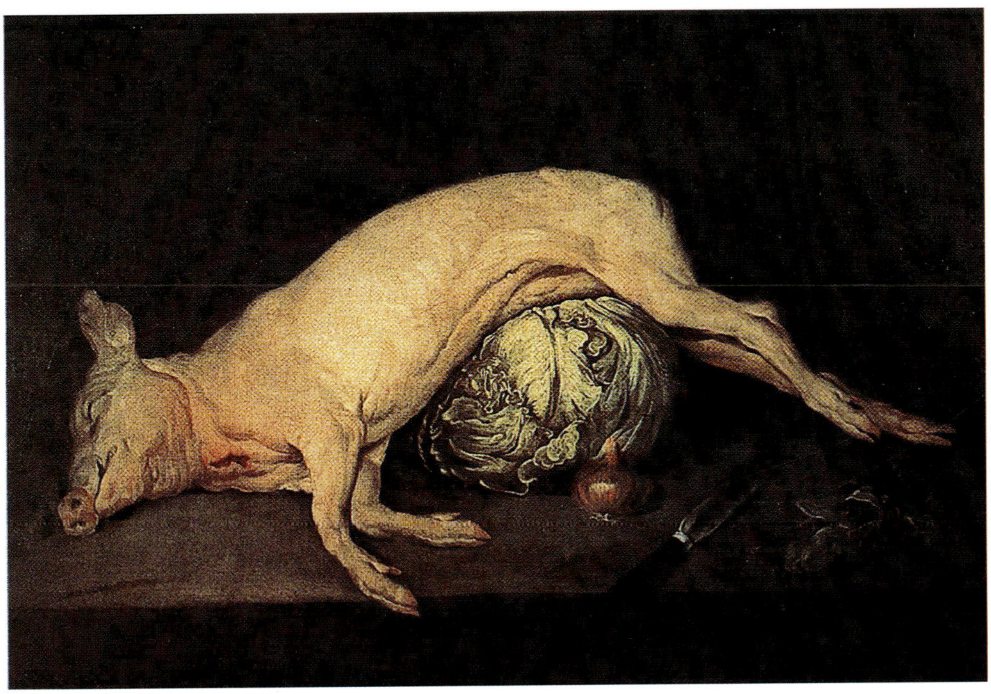

Giacomo Ceruti
Still life with Piglet
w.d.
canvas

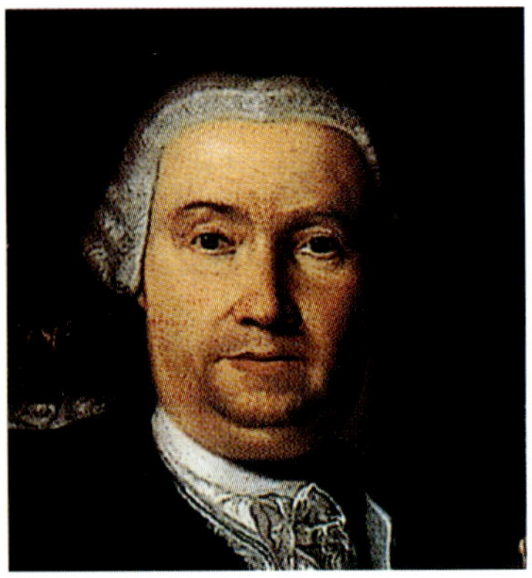

Luigi Vanvitelli

(Naples 1700 – Caserta 1773)

The son of Gaspard van Wittle, the renowned Dutch veduta artist residing in Rome, Vanvitelli studied with his father in preparation for a career as painter. Emerging as architect only after 1730, he was active in Rome and in numerous cities of central Italy – Perugia, Siena, Loreto, Ancona. He was called to Naples in 1751 by Charles III of Bourbon. The king, who intended to renovate the city by financing large-scale urban projects, commissioned Vanvitelli to build the new Royal Palace (Reggia) at Caserta. A highly versatile architect, he interpreted with refined sobriety each task assigned him, conducting restoration, acting as civil engineer, erecting military barracks, building villas (such as Villa Campolieto at Resina, 1766) and churches (among them the Church of the Santissima Annunziata at Naples, 1761).

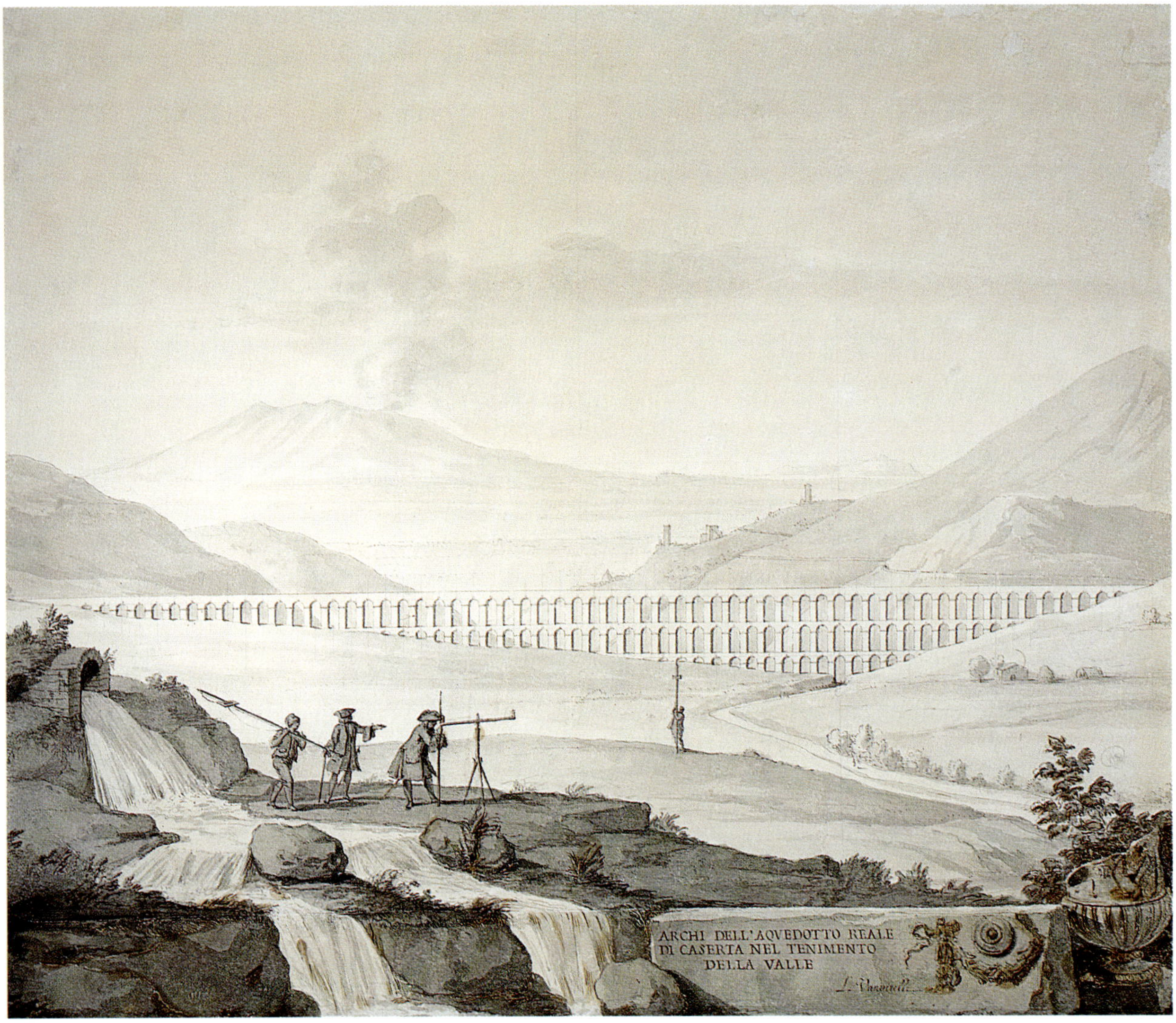

Luigi Vanvitelli
View of the Royal Palace from the Fountain of Venus and Adonis
1752-74
Caserta.

The Royal Palace, with its elegant, restrained exterior and its ostentatious, pretentious interior, its 1200 rooms, its perspectives, its octagonal central vestibule and its immense monumental stairway, rivals the great royal residences of Europe, first among them Versailles. The building, rectangular in shape, measures 247 meters on the longer sides, 184 meters on the shorter ones. The four courtyards designed as parade grounds are not visible from the exterior. Around the palace extends a park of over 120 hectares. Scattered among the woods, fountains and water games are statues of gods and heroes from classical mythology, placed there by Vanvitelli to surprise visitors. Most of the sculptures in the park celebrate hunting, an activity particularly beloved by the Bourbons.

Giacinto Diano, *Portrait of Luigi Vanvitelli*, c. 1762.
Caserta, Royal Palace.

Luigi Vanvitelli
The Carolingian Aqueduct
1752
pen, gray ink, water color on paper
Caserta, Royal Palace.

The Carolingian aqueduct was conceived for the dual purpose of feeding the splendid fountains in the park of the Caserta Palace and providing water for the city of Naples; but it was never to fulfill the latter function. The foundations were laid in 1753 and the entire aqueduct was completed in 1759. Vanvitelli's picture, conceived as a veduta, shows the Valle bridge, the aesthetic high point of the project, against a pleasant, picturesque background. The bridge, with its three orders of arches, is reminiscent of the Roman Pont du Gard in Provence.

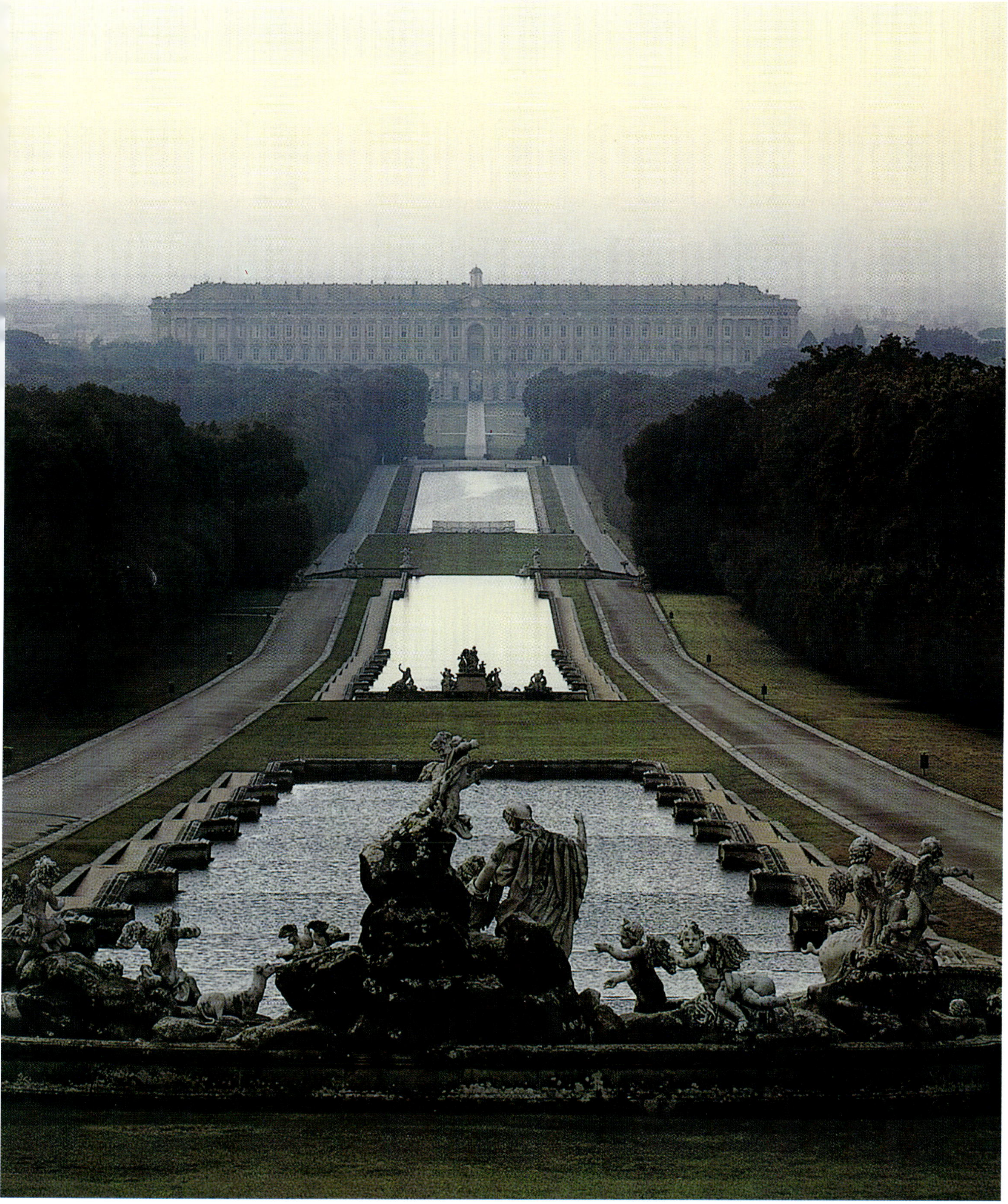

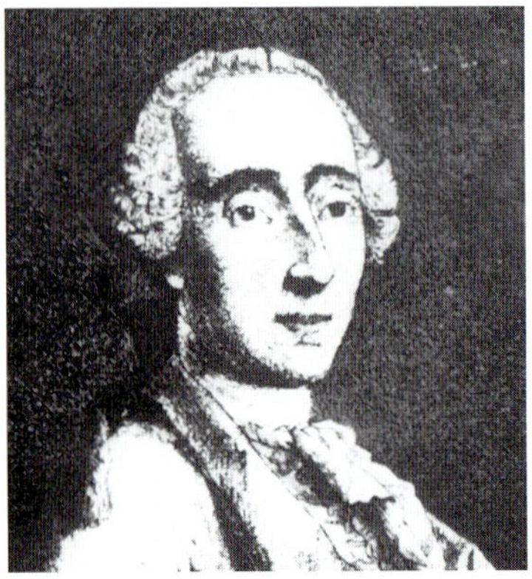

Pietro Longhi

(Pietro Falca, Venice 1702 – 1785)

Beginning his career as a painter of history and religion, Longhi changed his approach subsequent to a stay in Bologna and an encounter with Crespi's work. His abandonment of the "grand manner" dates from 1732. His son Alessandro relates: "he changed his thought, and having a brilliant and bizarre spirit, began to paint [...] conversations, with jests of love [and] jealousy". Acclaimed as a brilliant figurative chronicler of the city's life – the Venetian aristocracy and middle class are portrayed in his paintings with keen observation and vivid irony – Longhi dedicated extreme care to painting the scenes of contemporary subject which were to make him famous. He made numerous drawings and preparatory studies, reproducing a multitude of atmospheric effects (he was familiar with the work of Watteau, perhaps through Rosalba Carriera).

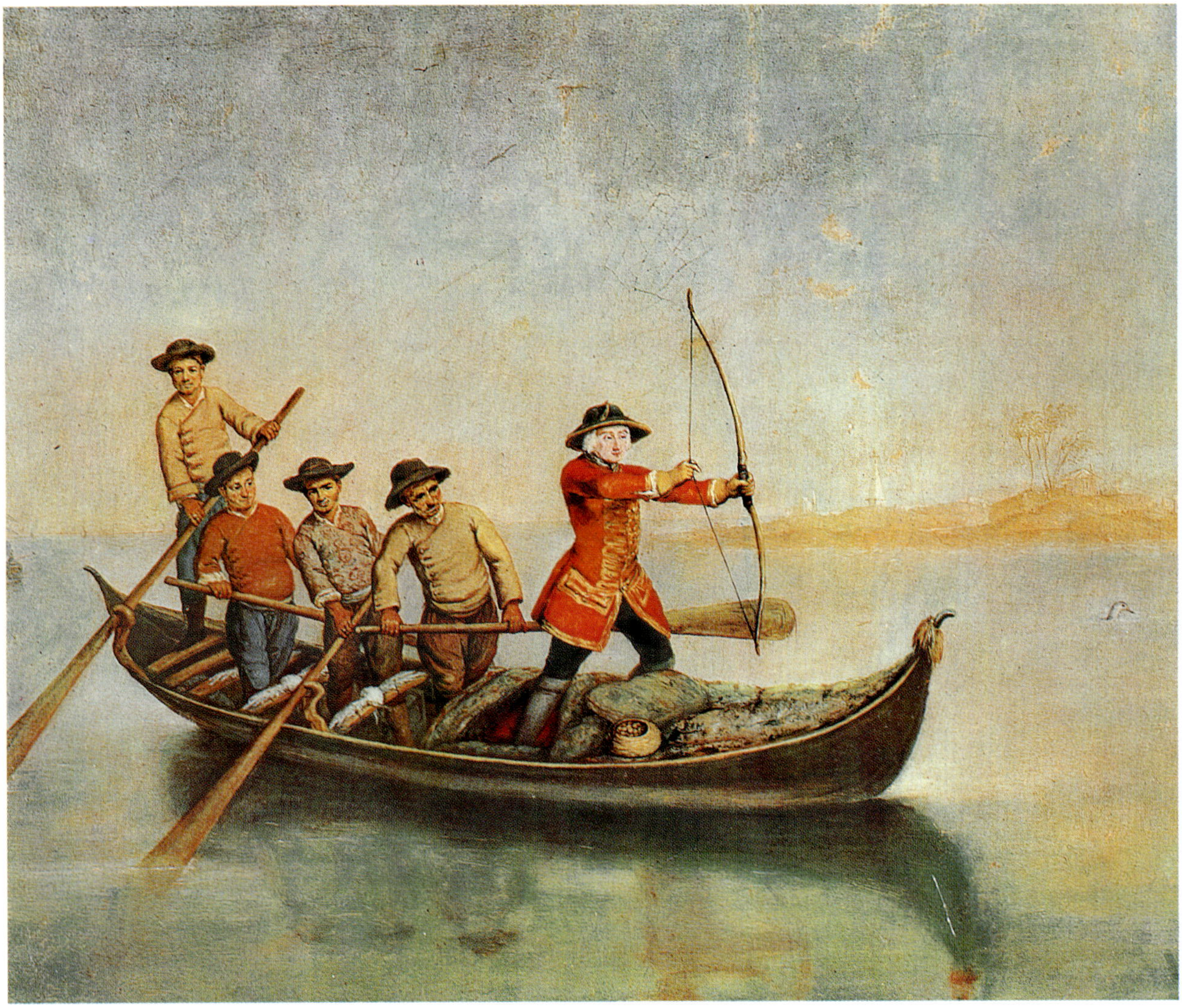

Pietro Longhi
The Hairdresser and the Lady
c. 1755-60
canvas
Venice, Correr Museum.

Playing on refined variations in the tones of blue-green, blue and red, the composition shows a Venetian *nobildonna* engaged in the ritual of hairdressing. Seated at her toilette, she receives the attentions of the hairdresser while a companion, or more probably a nurse, brings her a little girl. The faces are cool, composed, and somewhat conventional; the poses are stiff. Longhi's attention is not focused on individual psychology, but rather on details of costume. He faithfully and acutely describes the clothing which reveals, in its greater or lesser opulence, the rank of the person wearing it. His gaze pauses on the objects scattered over the top of the dresser, each of them depicted with extreme precision. On the floor, particularly evident, lies a spool of thread.

Anonymous engraving,
Portrait of Pietro Longhi.

Pietro Longhi
The Duck Hunt
c. 1755
canvas
Venice, Pinacoteca Querini Stampalia.

The painting has the grace and humor of a brief account of customs: a minor episode, a duck hunt, serves as pretext for subtle social and moral observations. In the silence of the lagoon, veiled by an early-morning fog, the archer, elegantly dressed, his hair well-powdered, is about to shoot his arrow. Behind him the rowers, wearing their everyday working clothes, are waiting to judge the hunter's skill. Among the participants in the common undertaking, a secret rivalry exists for a moment. Admirable details include the cushions in the bottom of the boat and the dead fowl lying on the crossboards.

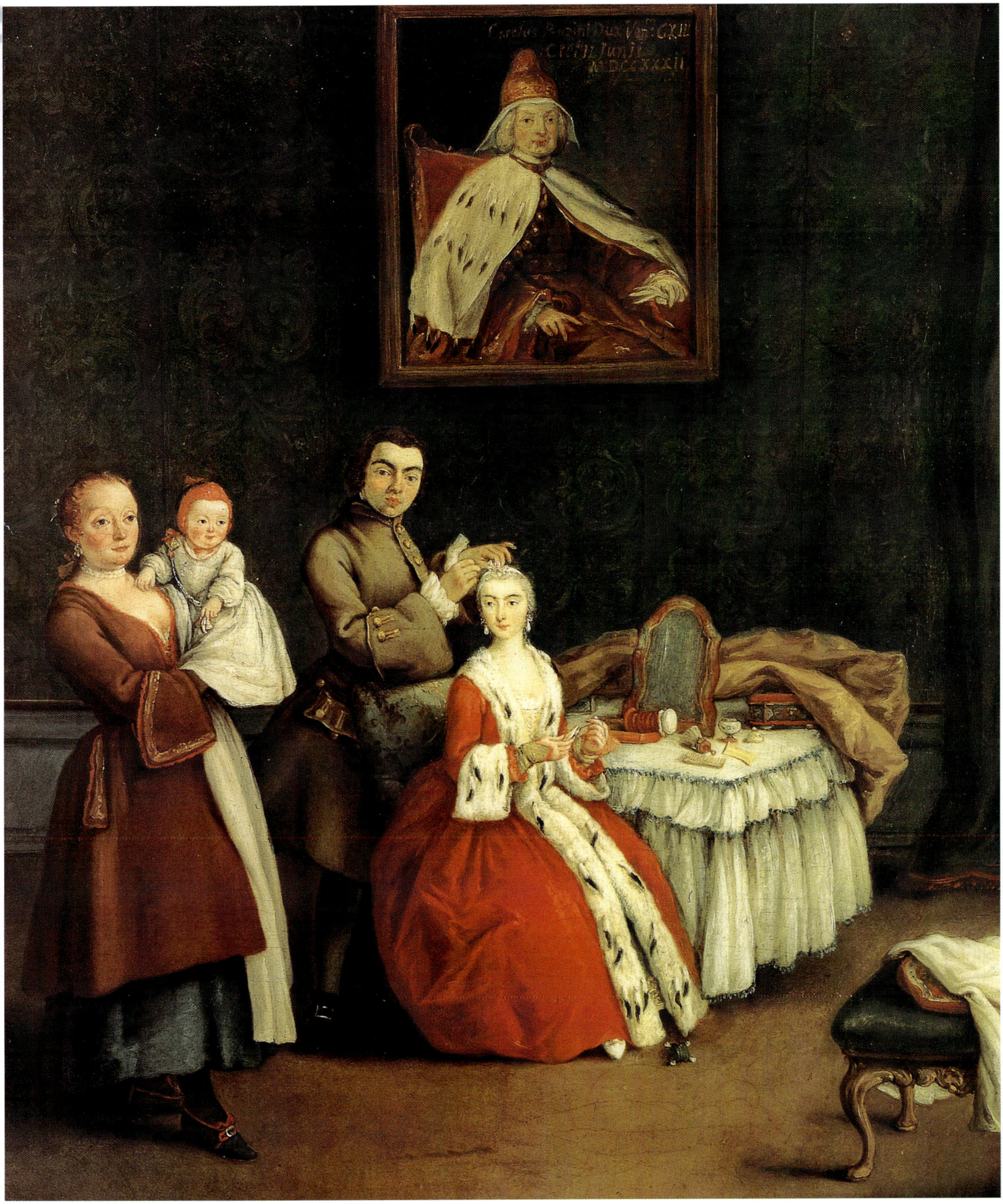

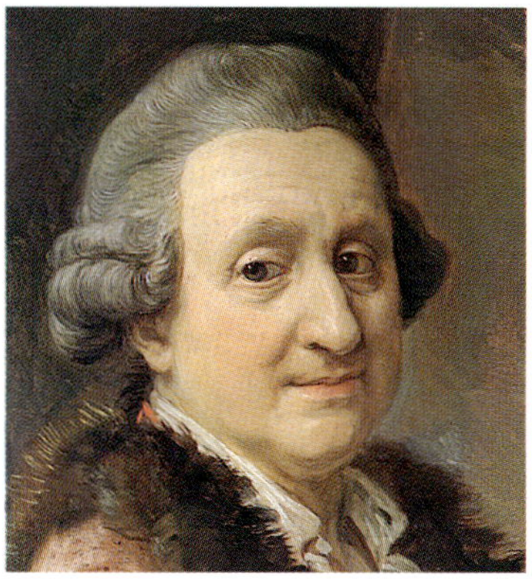

Pompeo Batoni

(Lucca 1708 – Rome 1787)

After early training in drawing with his father, a goldsmith, Batoni was at Rome in 1727, where he was assisted financially by patrons of the arts from Lucca. He made drawings of ancient statues which he sold to foreigners. He studied Raphael and the great 17th century Classicists, from whom he learned balanced naturalness. Starting as collaborator of successful landscape artists, specializing in painting figures, by the middle of the century Batoni had become one of the most successful artists in Rome. He was ranked on the same level as Mengs, with whom he contended the title of first painter of the neo-classical school. Active in religious and mythological painting, a portrait painter of international fame, in great demand by foreigners visiting Rome, he was a highly cultivated but never programmatic artist. He combines sensual irony with a search for easy elegance.

Pompeo Batoni,
Self-portrait, detail,
c. 1773-87.
Florence, Uffizi
Gallery.

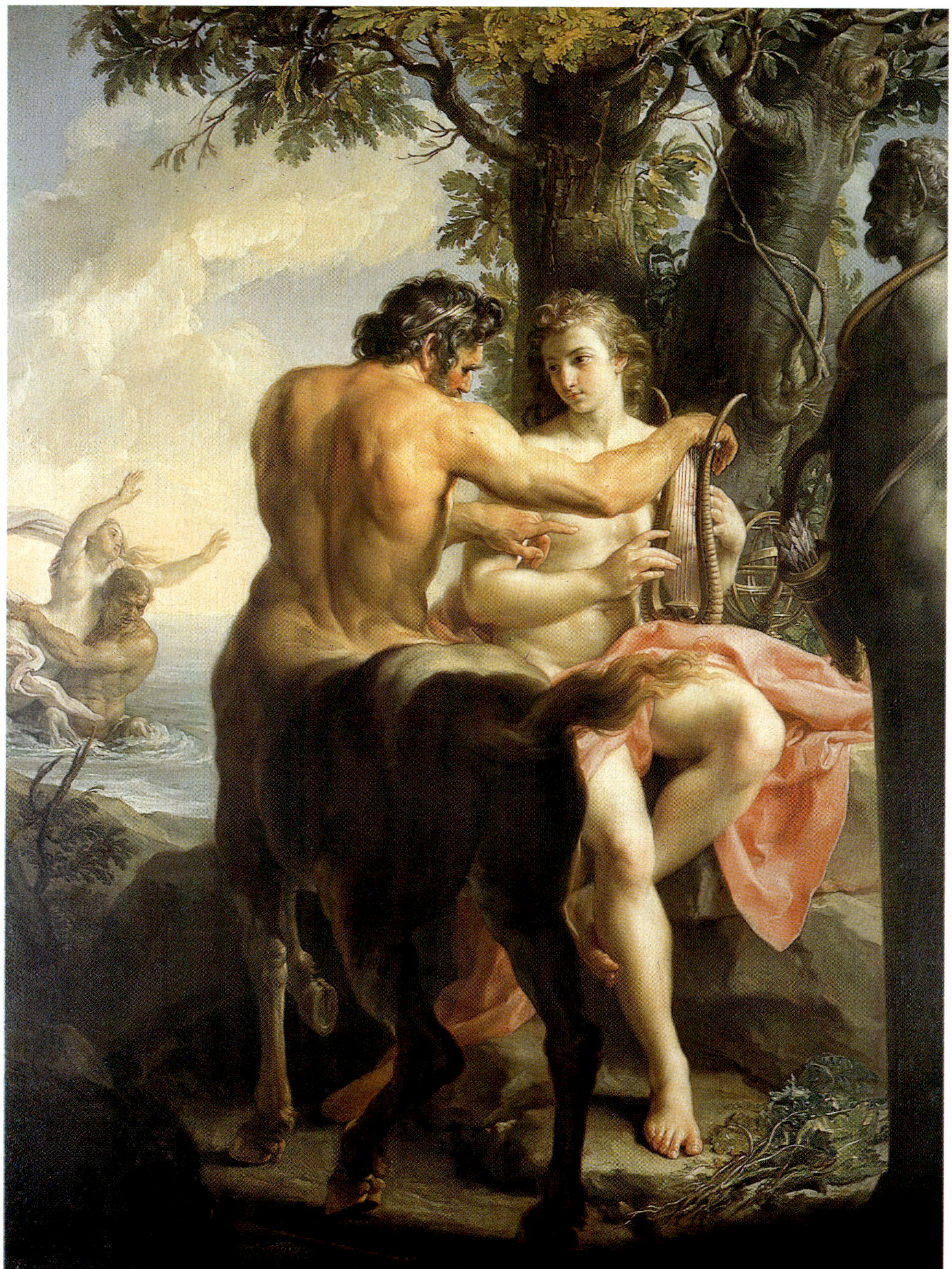

Pompeo Batoni
Achilles and Chiron the Centaur
1746
canvas
Florence, Uffizi
Gallery.

The painting reflects a very attentive, even zealous knowledge of the great 16th-17th century mythological tradition. For every detail a source could be indicated, a citation mentioned – the Veronesian herma, Gaspard Dughet's great leafy oaks, Domenichino's pale flesh, Reni's scenes of abduction. But such a catalogue of historical references would have no particular importance. Batoni choose to lean on a repertoire and to re-interpret it substantially, conferring on it new life. In confrontation with the great Classical-Renaissance tradition, he shows the delicate touch of the archaeologist/restorer.

Pompeo Batoni
Achilles at the Court of Lycomedes
1746
canvas
Florence, Uffizi
Gallery.

According to mythology Achilles, at the wish of his mother the goddess Thetis, agrees to disguise himself as a woman and take refuge at the court of King Lycomedes, to escape the call to arms that has summoned the Acheian princes to move against Troy. But Ulysses, arriving at the same court, employs a shrewd expedient to expose the young warrior. Invited to chose a gift Achilles, alone among the young girls, prefers a sword to precious stones and jewelry. His fate is decided: he will leave for Troy. In depicting the episode Batoni shows the culminating moment – Achilles' choice – and arranges the figures within a rigorous architectural frame.

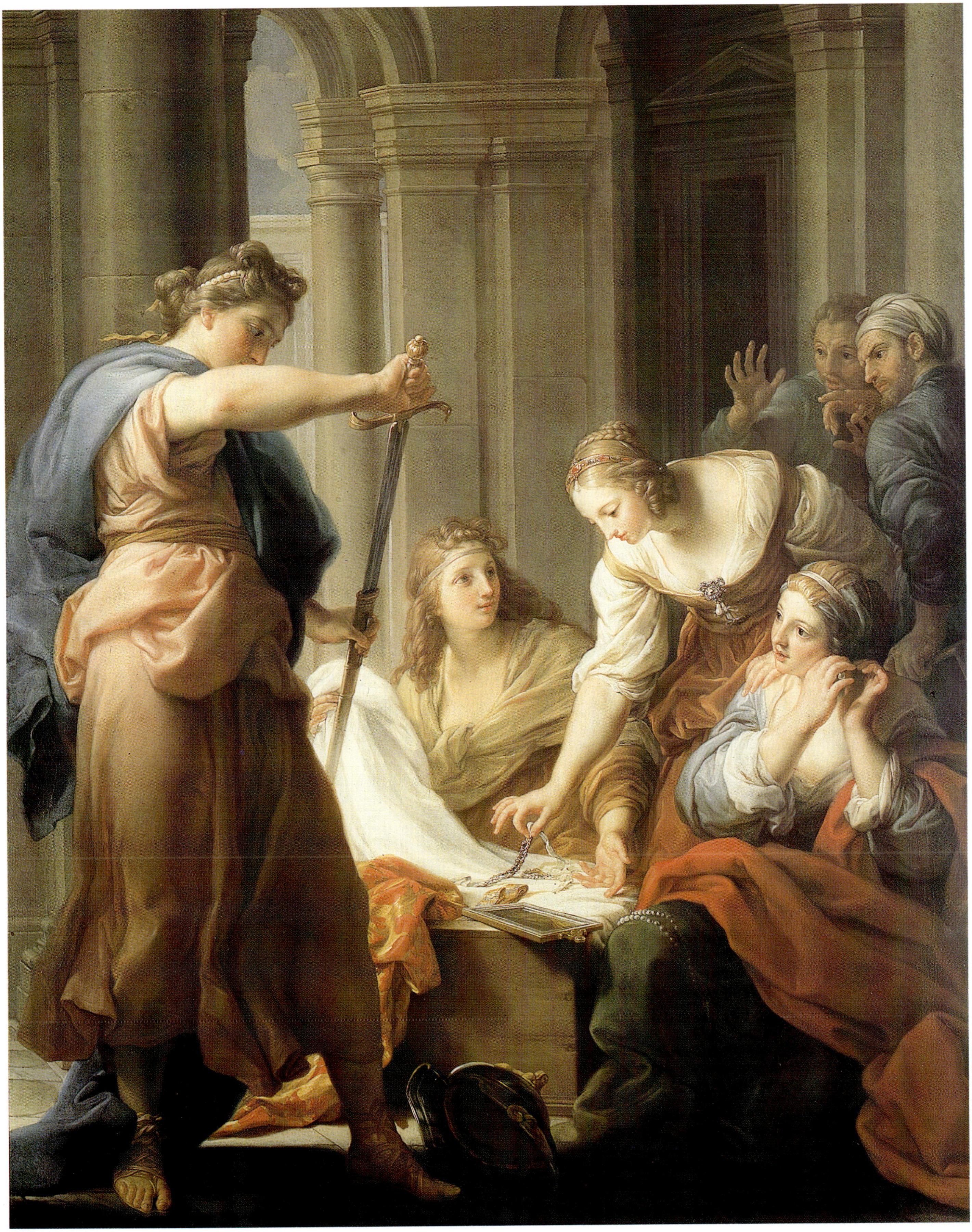

Francesco Guardi

(Venice 1712 – 1793)

Specialized in painting figures for the compositions of his brother Gianantonio, head of the family shop, Francesco had a career as lengthy as it was relatively obscure. It is uncertain whether his activity as veduta artist developed already before or only after the death of his brother in 1760, and whether or not he was apprenticed for some time to Canaletto (Guardi's contemporaries called him the "good scholar of the renowned Canaletto"). It is however probable that his most terse and luminous vedutas, painted with the goal of precision, are also his first; and that only subsequently did the artist free himself from the Canaletto model. His name is linked to capricious vedutas in which figures and buildings, arranged in imaginary or entirely invented combinations, seem to dissolve in the atmosphere. Great scenes of crowds, festivals, regattas and concerts were his most famous motifs.

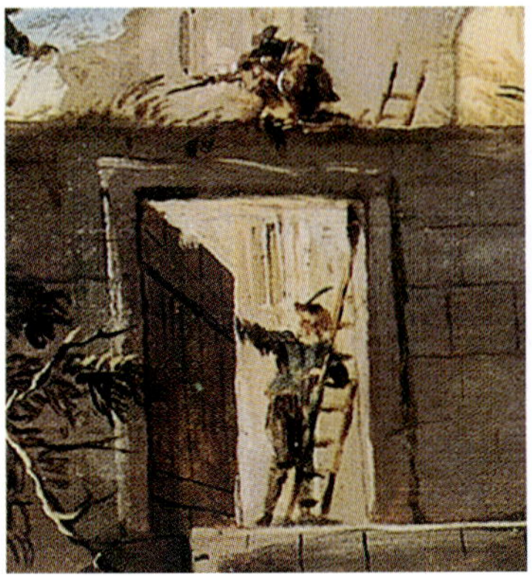

Francesco Guardi, *Caprice*, detail, c. 1730-35.

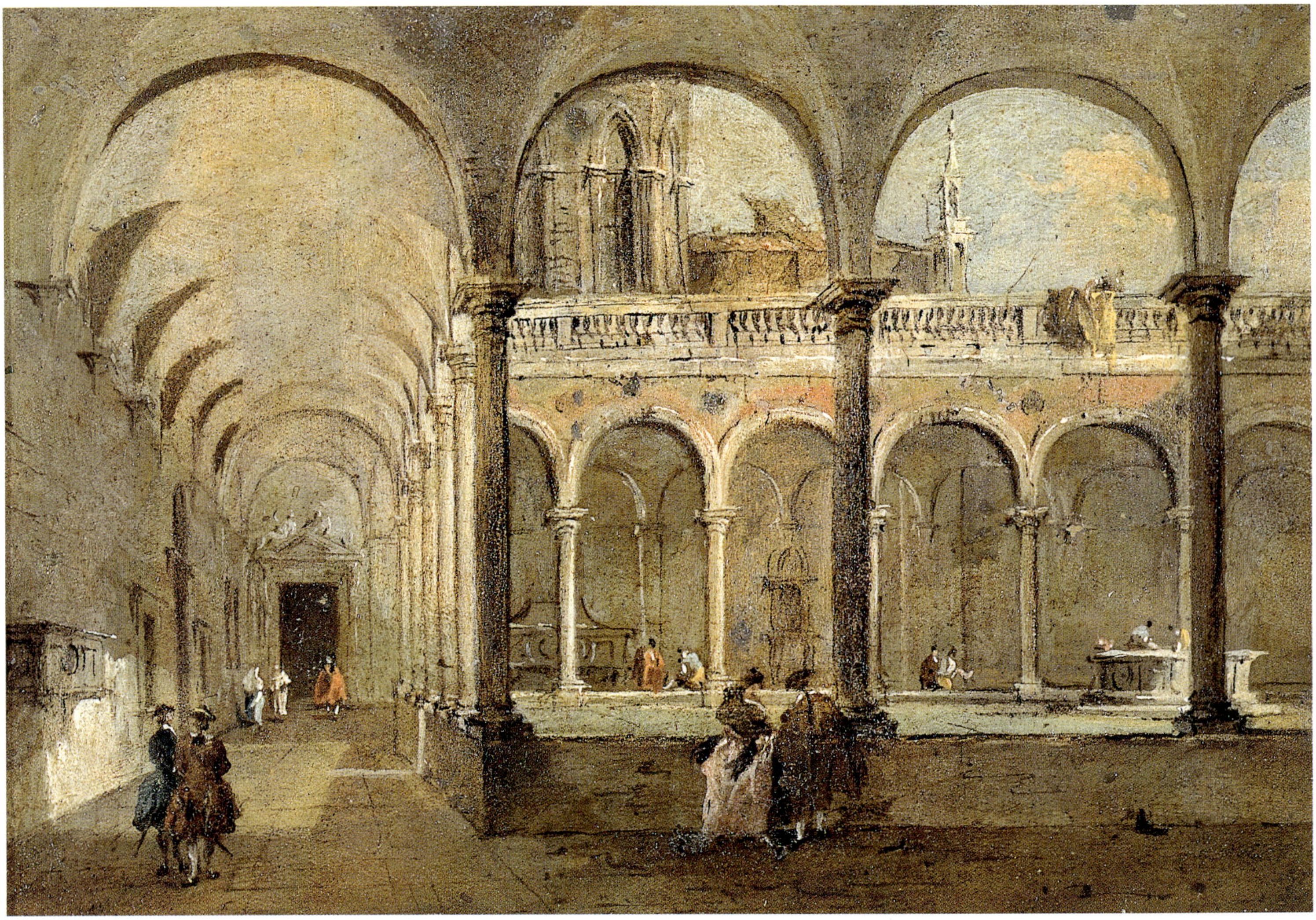

Francesco Guardi
The Friars' Cloister in Venice
w.d.
canvas
Bergamo, Carrara Academy.

Often interpreted as a melancholy presentiment of dissolution, Guardi's vedutas contain no psychological or literary considerations. They reflect instead the contemporary taste for picturesque motifs and Italian "macchiette" – figurines in typical costume appearing against a background of ancient ruins, painted with virtuoso technique in rapid touches of color and frequently vibrating in the clear light of day.

Bernardo Bellotto

(Venice 1721 – Warsaw 1780)

A pupil and nephew of Canaletto (his mother was Fiorenza Canal, the famous artist's sister), Bellotto was in Rome between 1741 and 1742, at Dresden in 1747. The latter city, admired throughout Europe for its light, fantastic Baroque architecture (it was known as the "Florence of the Elbe") was then at the peak of its splendor. Bellotto, who painted numerous views of Dresden applying the conventions of the Canaletto veduta, was appointed court painter by Augustus III. During the Seven Years' War the artist was in Vienna, at the court of the Empress Maria Teresa of Austria, and in Munich. He painted much admired views of both of these cities showing, at the request of the clients, the abundance of churches and palaces built in recent years. Starting in 1764 he taught painting at the newly established Dresden Academy of Fine Arts. In 1767 he was court painter at Warsaw.

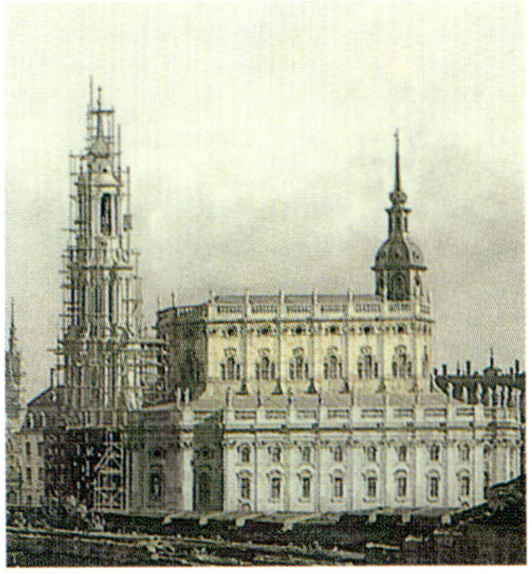

Bernardo Bellotto, *Dresden from the Right Bank of the Elbe downstream of the Augustus Bridge*, detail, 1748-50. Dublin, National Gallery of Ireland.

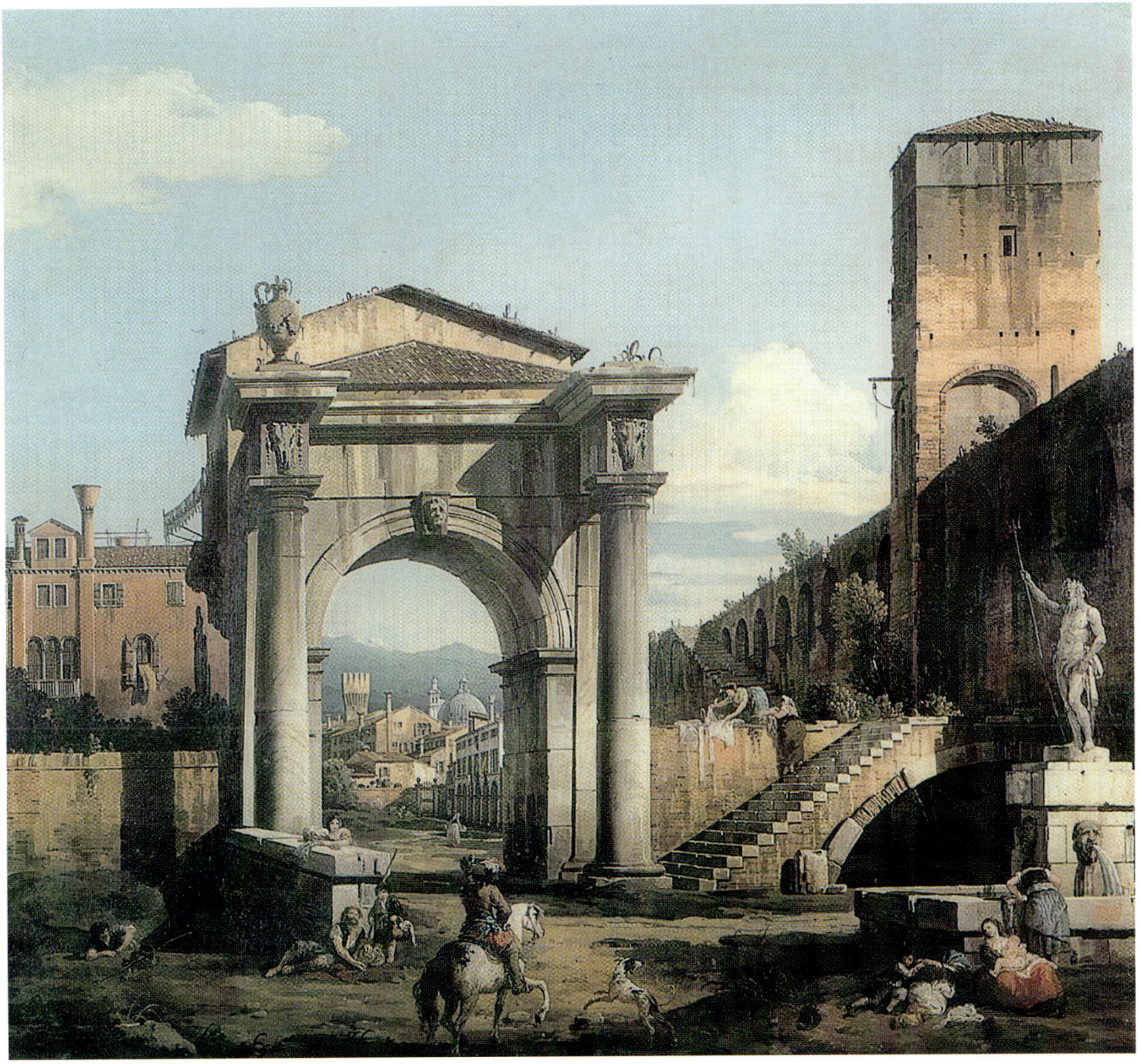

Bernardo Bellotto
Caprice with Gate and a City in Veneto
c. 1746
canvas
Parma, National Gallery.

Painted in collaboration with Francesco Zuccarelli, author of the "machiette" in the foreground, the *Caprice* mimics precise topographical sites while actually presenting an imaginary veduta. The tower seen through the arch recalls the Ezzelino Tower in Padua; the dome, white as the snowy peaks in the background, is instead reminiscent of St Mark's Basilica in Venice. The house on the left recalls Venetian buildings painted by Canaletto while the statue on the right, the sculptural friezes, and the arch in the foreground are the fruit of pure invention. Bellotto utilizes a repertoire in composing his caprice, combining figurative parts of various provenance in a variety of different combinations.

Giandomenico Tiepolo

(Venice 1727 – 1804)

His father's pupil, and soon collaborator, Giandomenico was a versatile and discerning artist. Resembling Giambattista in his taste for the bizarre and for loose brushstrokes, he reveals in the frescoes of Villa Valmarana and those painted for his father's villa of Zianigo (now at Ca' Rezzonico), as well as in his surprising drawings of "pulcinellas" a full and admirably autonomous artistic individuality. Attentive observer of the phenomena of light, fascinated by the radiant beams of early morning, he confers on his masked figures, even when ugly and deformed, an inexplicable beauty. At Würzberg with his father between 1750 and 1753, he followed the latter to Madrid as well. Returning to Venice at the death of Giambattista, he was appointed president of the Academy of Painting.

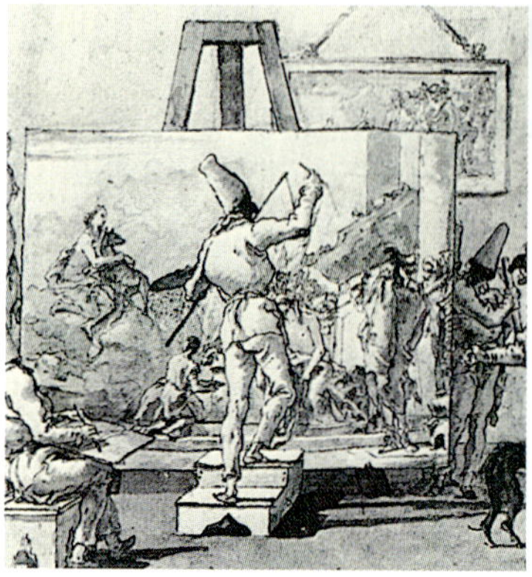

Giandomenico Tiepolo, *Pulcinella Painting a Tiepolo* (*Pulcinella Painter of Historical Subjects*), 1797-1804.

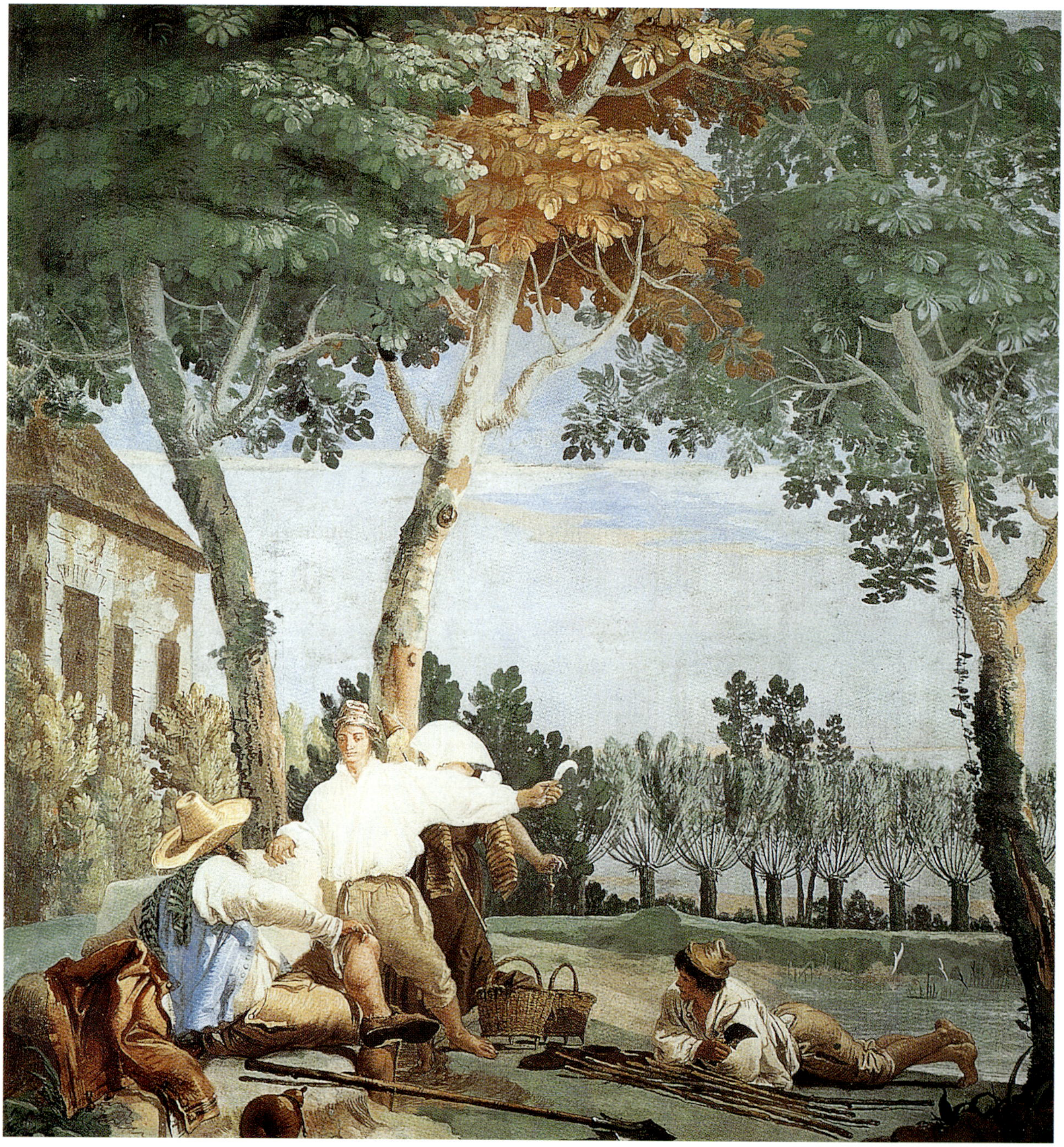

Giandomenico Tiepolo
Peasants at Rest
1757
fresco
Vicenza, Villa Valmarana.

While Giambattista was engaged in frescoing heroic subjects at Villa Valmarana, his son Giandomenico preferred genre scenes, drawing inspiration from the life of peasants and aristocrats to present again in large format the rustic idylls of Veronesian tradition. In the shade of leafy trees, seated or stretched out on the grass in *dolce far niente*, peasants are resting and talking on a Summer afternoon. Behind them a woman is spinning. The front of the house reflects the clear light of day that already bathes the clothing and headgear of the figures in the foreground. Tiepolo is a painter of light and of details: not of psychology. The clear, almost pearly tones of the composition foreshadow the *plein air* luminosity of the late 19th century.

Giandomenico Tiepolo
Frontispiece
1797-1804
pencil, charcoal, ink on paper
Kansas City, Nelson Gallery-Atkins Museum (Nelson Fund).

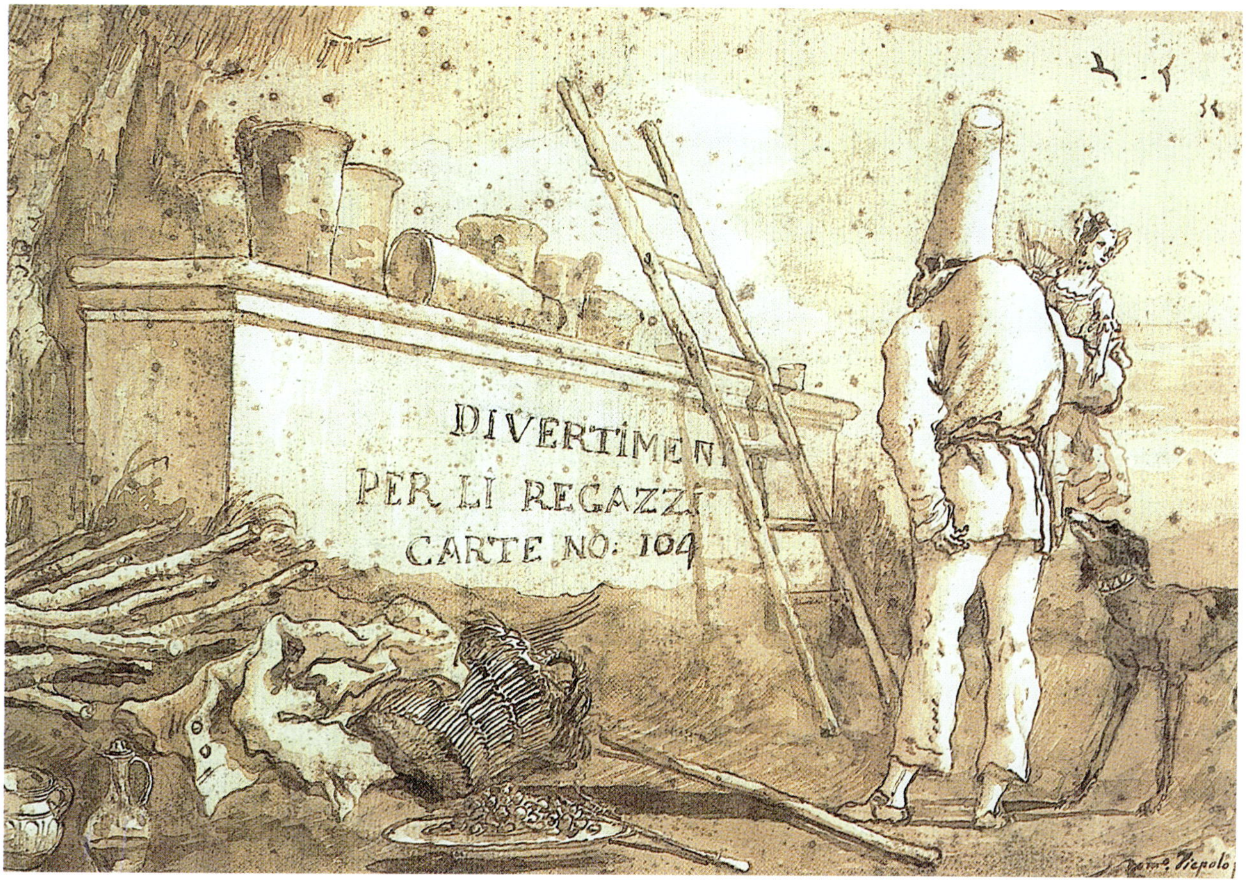

The Firing Squad
1797-1804
ink on paper
pencil, charcoal

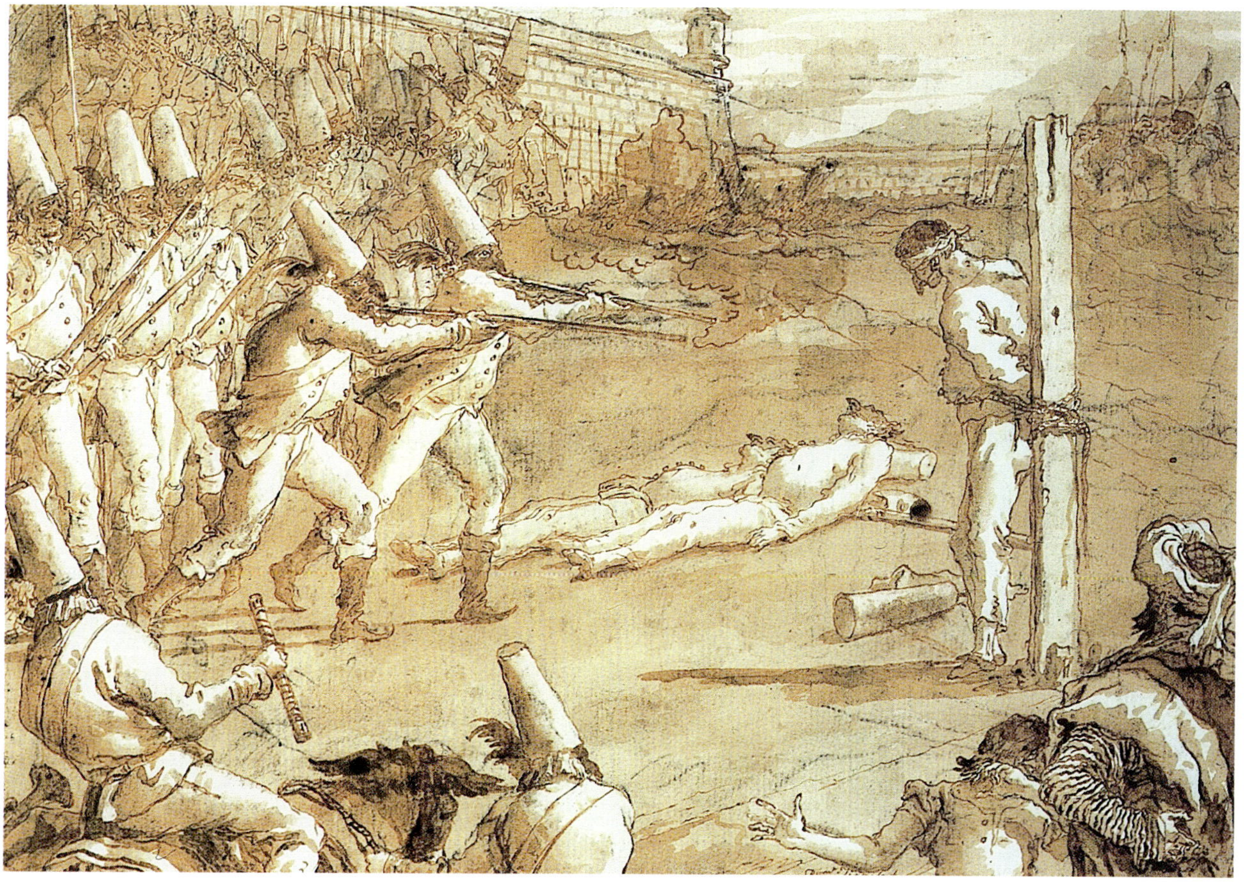

Dispersed in 1921 during a Paris sale, the collection of drawings illustrating the life of Pulcinella is a late work of Giandomenico, pervaded by a subtle *nostalgia*. The artist began this series of 104 folios when he was seventy years old, and it concluded with his death in 1804. It is hard to detect a linear narrative sequence, and perhaps it did not exist in the artist's mind. Tiepolo confers on a masked character from the *commedia dell'arte*, Pulcinella, attitudes which are fully human. He reinterprets the character outside of the Carnival tradition, where its features are immutable – Pulcinella is a braggart, greedy, violent, treacherous – to show him in everyday situations. Born from an egg, Pulcinella grows up, marries, has children, gets into trouble with the law, tries different professions, and lastly sickens and dies, surrounded by the affection of friends and family. His parallel world mirrors our own, where joy and pain, gratification and distress alternate according to inexplicable laws.

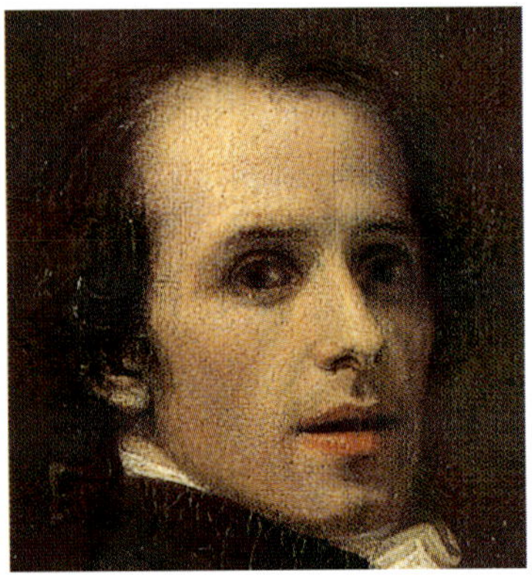

Antonio Canova

(Possagno, Treviso, 1757 – Venice 1822)

After an apprenticeship in the Venetian workshop of Giuseppe Bernardi, Canova was in Rome in 1799. A young artist who frequented distinguished intellectual circles – Quatremère de Quincy and Gavin Hamilton, archaeologists and art critics, were his friends- he met with success already in 1787, when his *Funerary Monument to Clement XIV* was inaugurated in the Basilica dei Santi Apostoli in Rome. From this time on, the production of works of mythological subject was interwoven, in the artist's career, with that of funerary monuments. The hint of sensuality in the former won him the admiration of his contemporaries, while the latter provided occasions for civic commemoration or solemn elegy. At the peak of his fame in the Napoleonic era, Canova was assigned discreet diplomatic and cultural functions at the downfall of Napoleon. In 1815 he journeyed to London to see the marbles from the Parthenon.

Antonio Canova,
Self-portrait, 1792.
Florence, Uffizi Gallery.

Antonio Canova
Cupid and Psyche
terra-cotta
c. 1787
Venice, Museo Correr.

This small terra-cotta sculpture depicts a youth lying on the ground who seems to push away the female figure above him, almost as if she were trying to seduce him. In obvious formal relationship with the artist's more famous sculptural group, the *Cupid and Psyche Embracing*, now in the Louvre, this sketch portrays not a mythological idyll but more probably a licentious love scene. In sculpting it Canova seems to take heed of Winckelmann's exhortation to "sketch with fire". When a work is transposed to marble, the intensity of the draft version is sometimes lost.

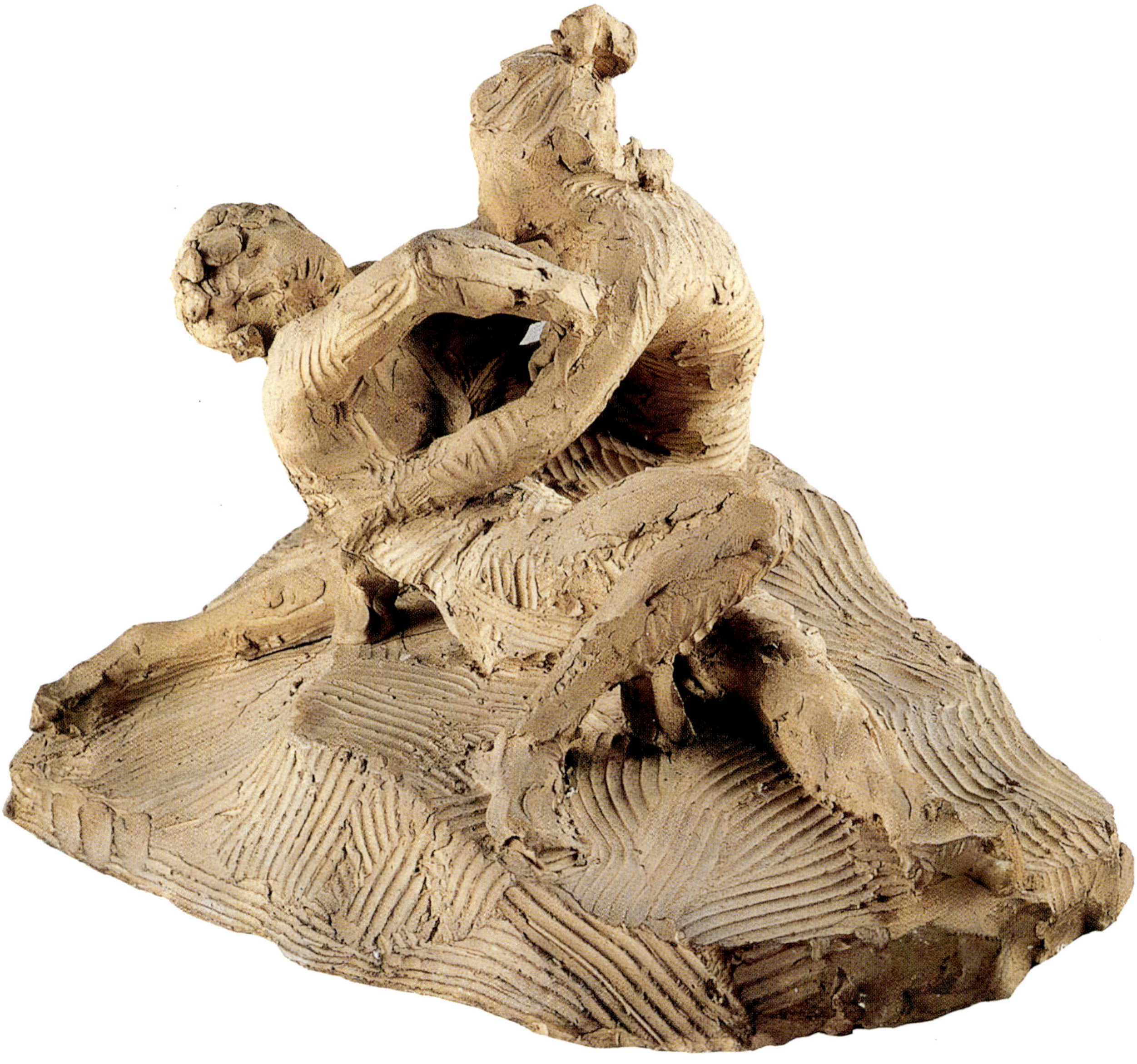

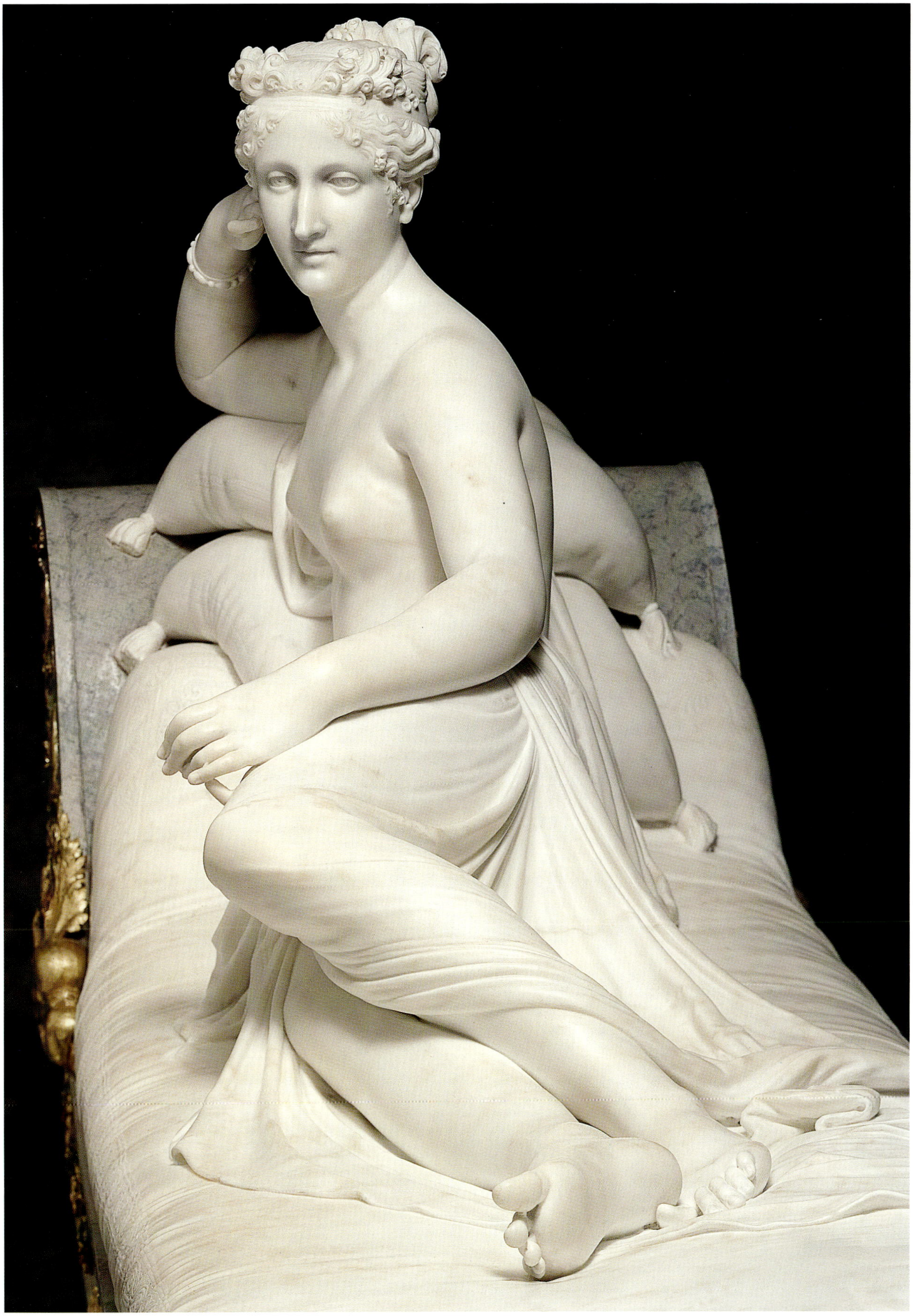

Antonio Canova
Paolina Borghese Bonaparte as Venus the Vanquisher
1804-08
marble
Rome, Galleria Borghese.

After having sculpted, between 1803 and 1806, the portrait of Napoleon as *Mars the Peace- maker* (the statue is now in London), Canova was commissioned to portray Paolina Borghese Bonaparte, the Emperor's sister, in 1804. Here he employed a new and flattering mythological comparison: the woman is represented as *Venus the Vanquisher*. Dressed in ancient fashion and resting on soft cushions, Paolina appears in her sensuous beauty within the context of a work of great elegance, distinguished not only by the soft modeling of the semi-nude body but also by the care with which the artist confers a lustrous glow, consistency, and singular tactile feel to the various objects sculpted – wood, fabrics.

Antonio Canova
The Graces
1813
terra-cotta
Lyon, Musée
des Beaux-Arts.

Canova was fascinated for years by the motif of the three female figures, nude and dancing, who appear recurrently in his drawings and paintings. Here the "idea" - it is Canova himself, in the inscription appearing on the base, to use this term - is modeled in a burst of inspiration. Admired by his contemporaries, the *Graces* were particularly beloved by writers and poets. Stendhal went to Rome purposely to see them, and Ugo Foscolo dedicated an entire poem to them.a

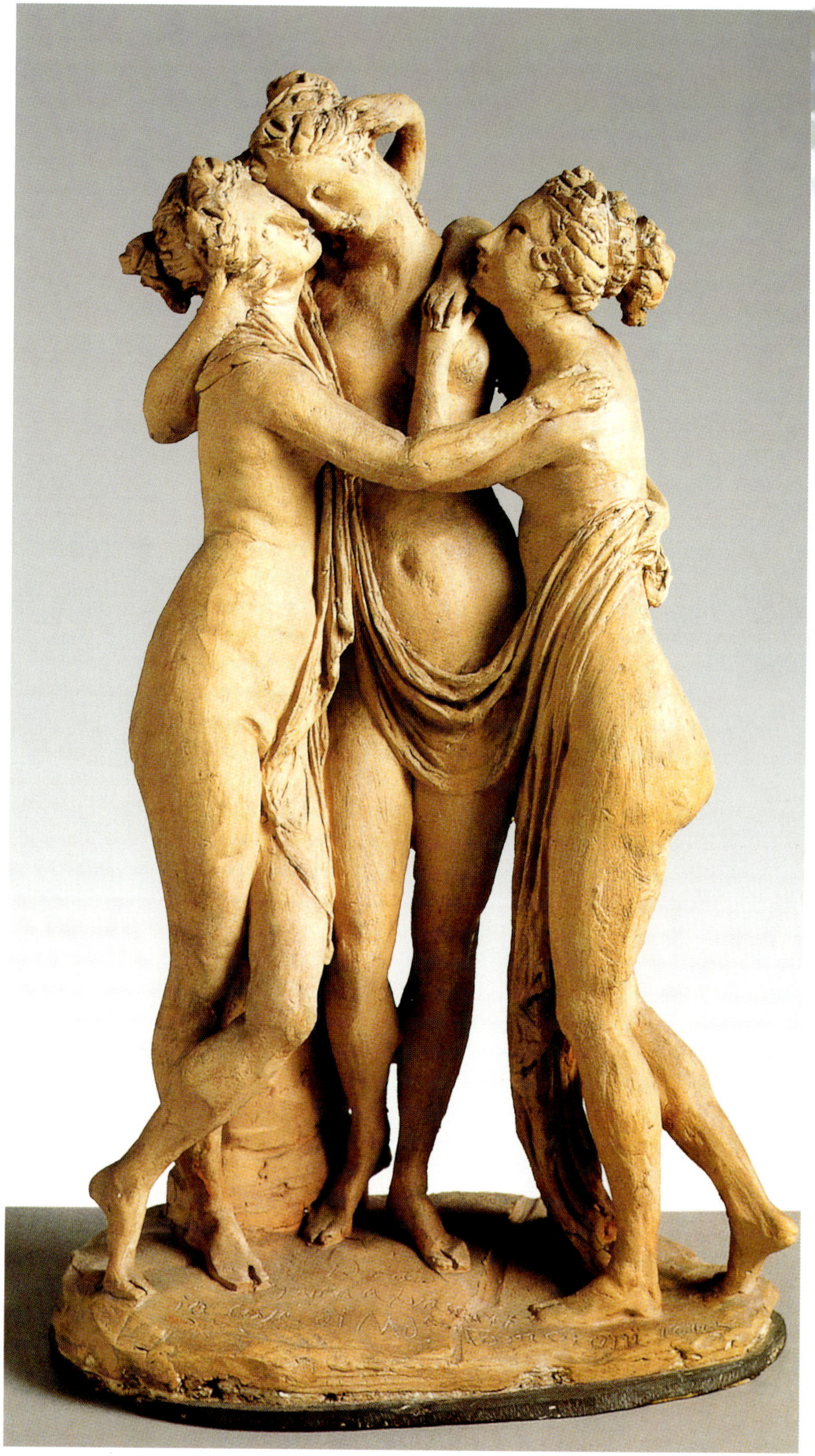

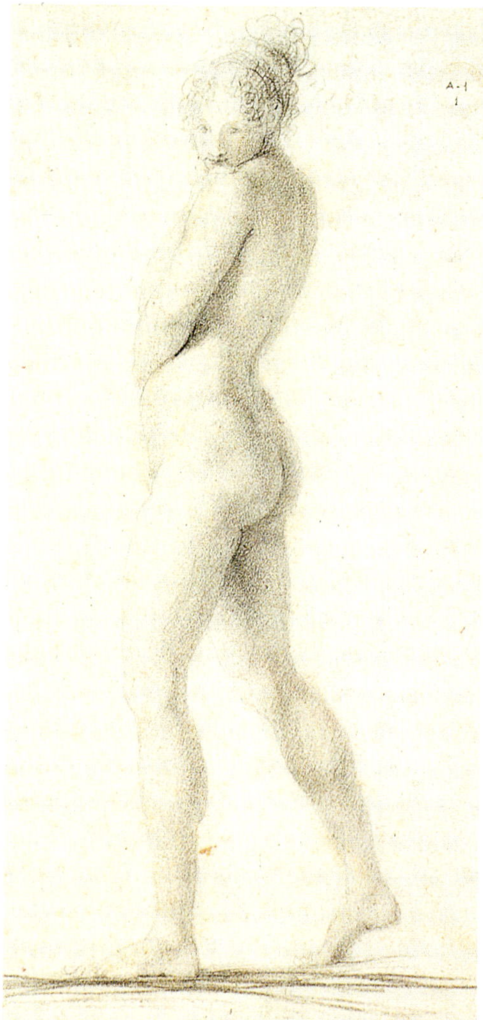

Antonio Canova
Female Nude
c. 1790
pencil and charcoal on paper
Bassano, Civic Museum.

The drawing belongs to an album entirely composed of studies of the female nude figure. Since it was not executed in preparation for a sculpture, it must be considered an autonomous work. Woman's beauty, considered as grace, was for Canova the manifestation of natural perfection: in it the "idea" and the "truth" were marvelously intermingled.

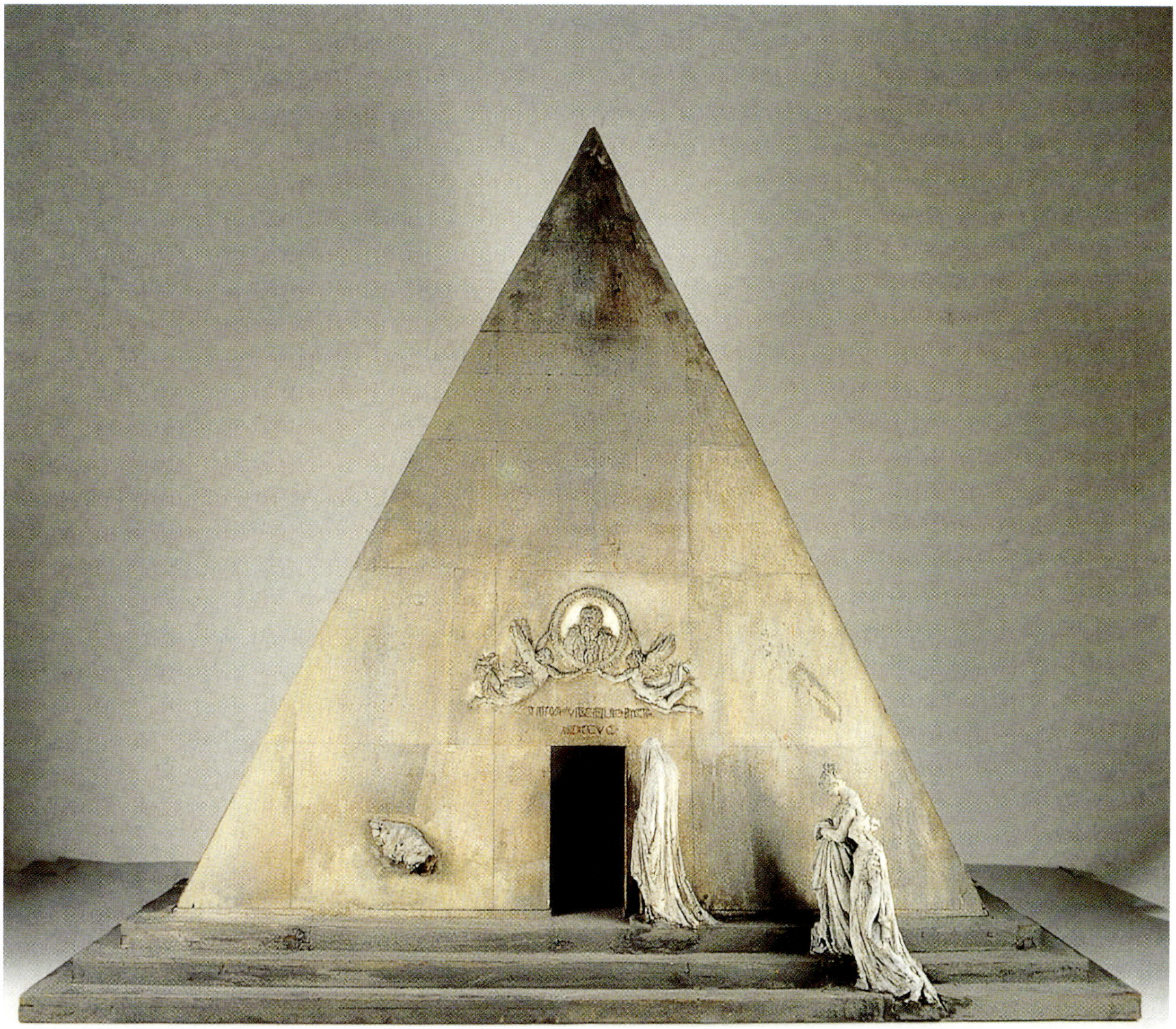

Antonio Canova
Monument to Titian
1791-95
terra-cotta and wood
Venice, Correr Museum.

In the various models Canova made for the monument to Titian, to be erected in the Venetian Church of the Frari, the unifying motif is that of the pyramid of Caius Cestius at Rome. Another source of inspiration may have been the grandiose temporary architecture once erected in Rome for the funerals of illustrious personages, the popes for example. In formulating the project the artist introduced profound innovations in the tradition of the funerary monument: no longer a glorification of the deceased, Canova's pyramid is instead a meditation on death and the darkness that awaits beyond the threshold. The pyramid, however, was not to be used in the monument to Titian, planned but never executed. Canova was instead to adopt it for the *Monument to Maria Cristina of Austria* (1798-1805), in the Augustinerkirche at Vienna.

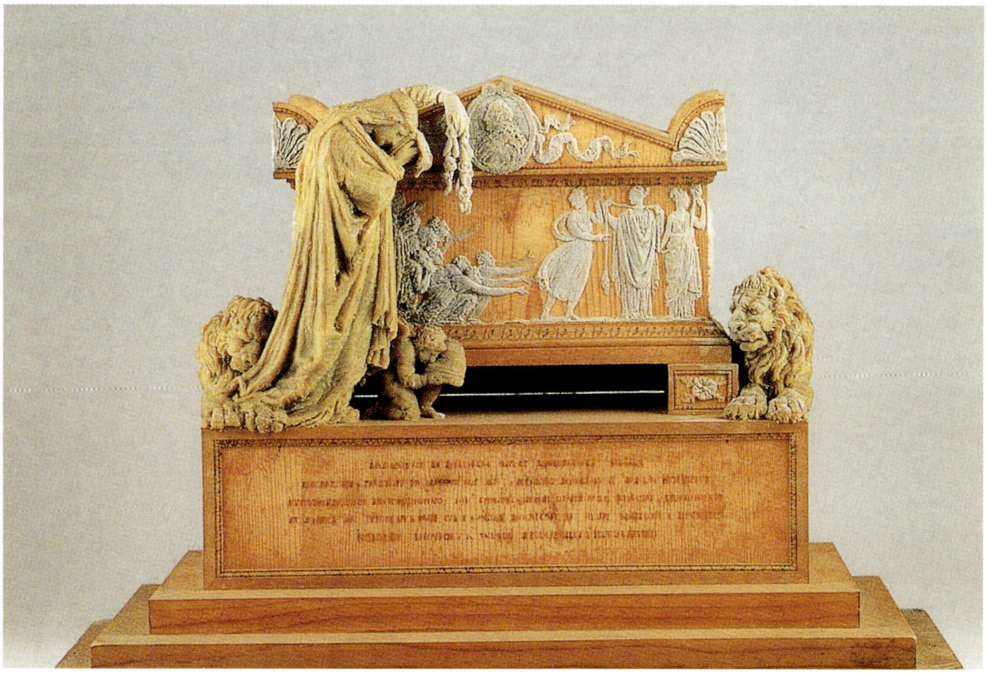

Antonio Canova
Funerary Monument to Francesco Pesaro
1799
wax and wood
Venice, Correr Museum.

A Venetian patrician opposed to Napoleon and the French, the last librarian of the Republic, Francesco Pesaro is portrayed in profile on the medallion appearing on the tympanum. He is mourned by a standing figure, the allegorical personification of Venice; by the *venete genti*, the people of Venice, in the bass-relief on the front of the sarcophagus; and by the lions, emblems of the Venetian Republic. The funerary monument to Pesaro was to have been erected in St Mark's Basilica. This project having failed, Canova became the owner of the model, which was to remain unknown to his contemporaries until in the third decade of the 19th century, long after the artist's death.

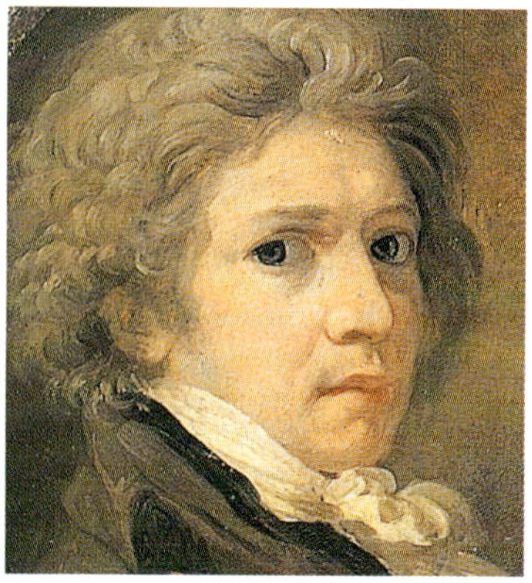

Andrea Appiani

(Milan 1754 – 1817)

A cultured artist who moved in intellectual circles – he was a friend of Parini, who starting in 1776 held lessons on history and mythology at the Brera Academy; and of Giuseppe Bossi – Appiani experimented in his youth with the fresco technique, perfected through his study of Leonardo and Raphael. Precociously approaching neo-classical modes, he conceived his images as sculptural friezes. In his best work the principles of neo-classical "good taste" are tempered by soothing recollections of the Lombard naturalistic tradition. In 1791 the artist visited Parma, Bologna, Florence and Rome to observe the works of the great 16th and 17th century masters. Upon Napoleon's entry into Milan in May 1796, Appiani was one of the most fervent advocates of the Cisalpine Republic, of which he became the official painter. He was to paint a series of Napoleonic portraits widely admired even in France.

Andrea Appiani, *Self-portrait*, c. 1795. Milan, Brera Pinacoteca.

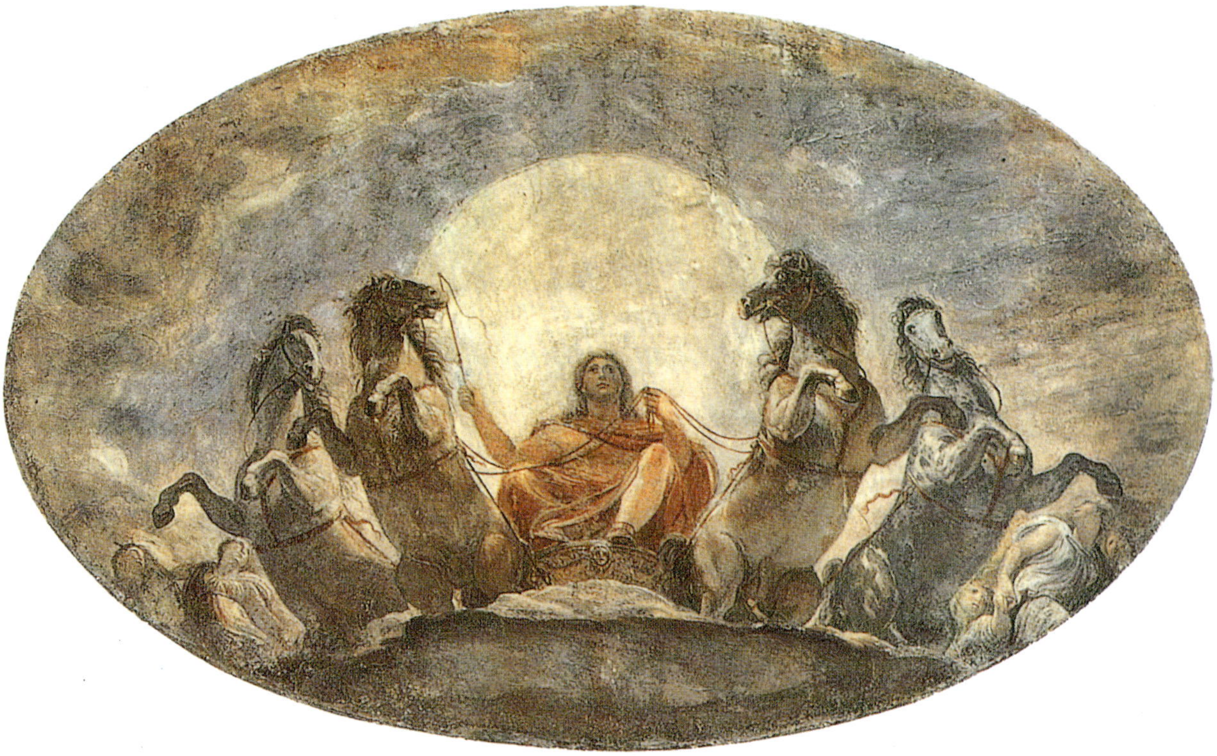

Andrea Appiani
Apollo's Chariot
c. 1799
fresco transferred to canvas
Milan, Brera Pinacoteca.

In 1799, at the time when Appiani was frescoing *Apollo's Chariot* in Casa Sannazzaro, Austrian troops returned to Milan, and the artist's public commission was suspended. It is easy enough, however, to see in the blond and radiant god who drives the chariot an allusion to Napoleon, in the eyes of the artist the bearer of a new civilization, rather than a neutral re-evocation of the classical myth. Stylistically the fresco is striking for the almost archaic majesty of Apollo, whose head is a perfect oval placed at the center of the solar disk. The image, conceived according to strict rules of symmetry – note also how the chariot opens exactly in half, divided by a vertical axis – reveals attentive study of Early Renaissance masters, Piero della Francesca in particular.

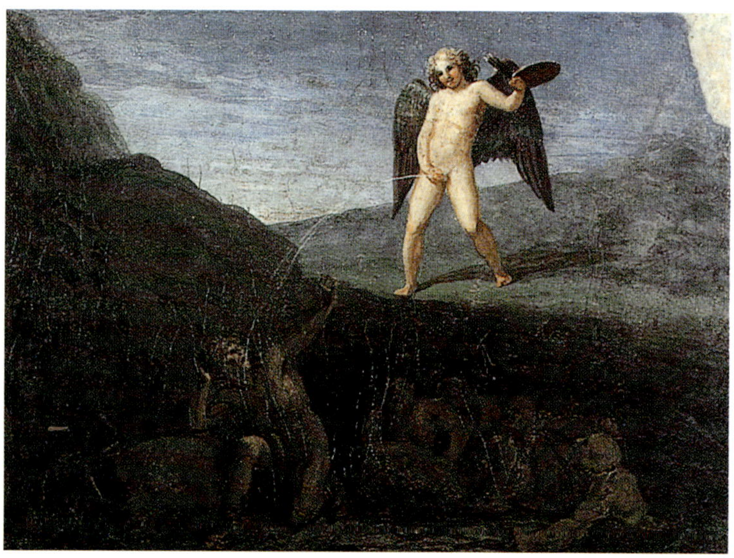

Andrea Appiani
The Genius of Art and the Envious Ones
c. 1805
fresco transferred to canvas
Milan, Civic Gallery of Modern Art.

The image possesses the lightness of a comic episode studied on Hellenistic vases, appearing in the two-dimensional, softly tonal manner of a Pompeian fresco. The urinating cupid who ridicules the "envious ones" has a palette and paintbrushes. Himself a painter, he jokingly adapts classical mythology to the purposes of a contemporary dispute on art.

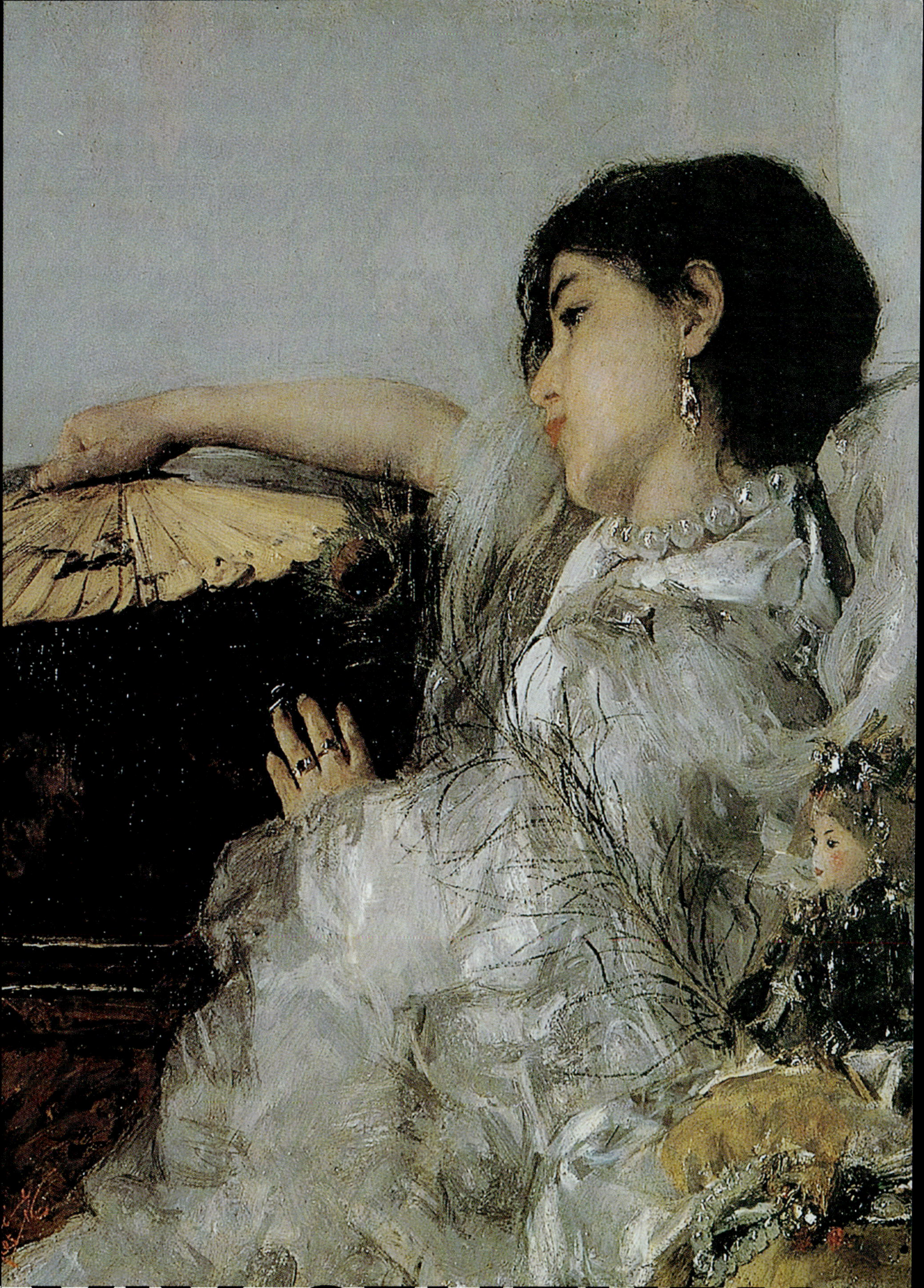

THE XIX CENTURY

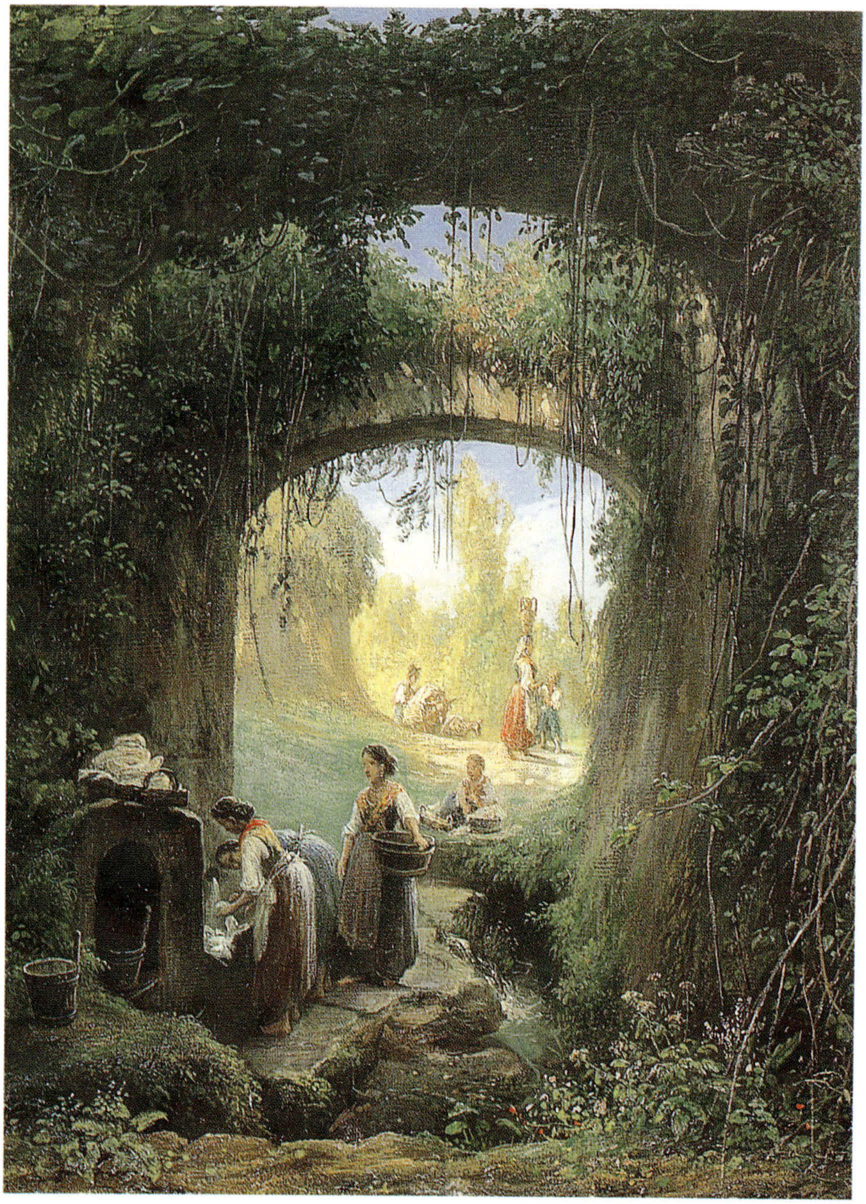

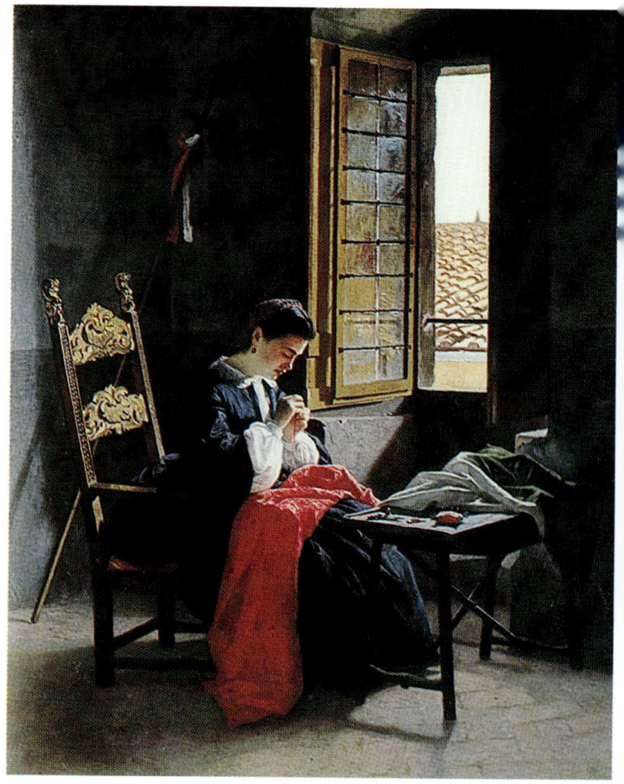

Giuseppe Palizzi,
Landscape with Figures,
1863. Milan, Gallery
of Modern Art.

Odoardo Borrani,
April 26, 1859, 1861.

Preceding page:
Antonio Mancini,
The Two Dolls, 1876.

Either disparaged as pathetic and provincial or defended with stubborn passion, Italian art of the nineteenth century was long the center of heated debate. If avant-garde art history and the critics allied to it, such as Roberto Longhi and Lionello Venturi, have felt little appreciation for artists intimately linked to contemporary historical events, connoisseurs and collectors have shown a preference for paintings and sculpture not always motivated on the level of international confrontation. Today these works and events can be viewed more objectively. We possess enough knowledge to begin to evaluate our 19th century within the broader context of contemporary European art. We can document the circulation of artists and works – the "trips to Paris", the participation in great international exhibitions, the artists' relations with Italian or foreign gallery owners, the opportunities for exhibition and sale – and make pertinent comparisons, wasting no time over futile questions of national artistic supremacy.

Italian art was discussed, during the 19th century, years before Italy as a sovereign state came into existence. The dramatic process of national unification had inevitable reflections on artistic production, and even on the biographies of the artists themselves. Many among them, we

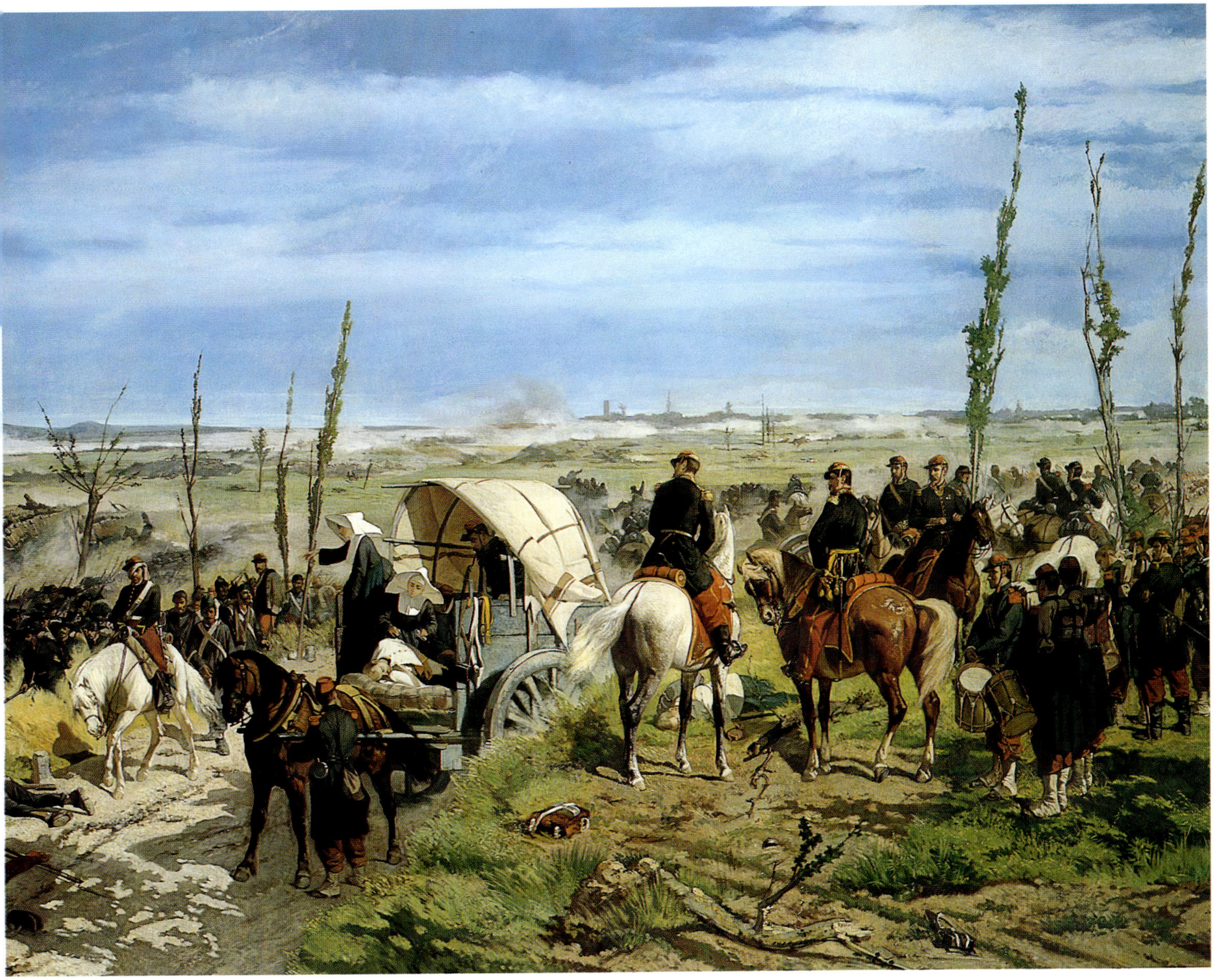

find, fought as volunteers, engaged in politics, held diplomatic positions. The alternating vicissitudes of the Risorgimento first, the decades of monarchy and national unification later – the expectations, the disappointments – conferred significance and urgency on debates, on the stances assumed, on stylistic changes, on consecration or censure.

Geographic and regional components still prevailed. Rome in the first decades of the century, then Milan, Florence and Naples could at various times aspire to the role of capital of Italian art, although none of them was to hold this place definitively. While a common Italian language now existed, albeit only on the literary level, the same cannot be said of the visual arts. In Milan the most confirmed Romantic tradition was to re-emerge, in the latter half of the century, in a naturalism marked by strong social accents. In Florence a common traditionalist orientation advocating a return to the origins of Italian art linked, at times unpredictably, Purists and Macchiaioli. In Rome, alongside cultural and archeological tendencies a vivacious popular art was fast emerging. In Naples a local circle of painter/artisans, the Posillipo School, evolved in the direction of modern landscape painting *en plein air*. Dialects, accents, and in-

Giovanni Fattori, *The Italian Camp at the Battle of Magenta*, 1862. Florence, Pitti Palace Gallery of Modern Art.

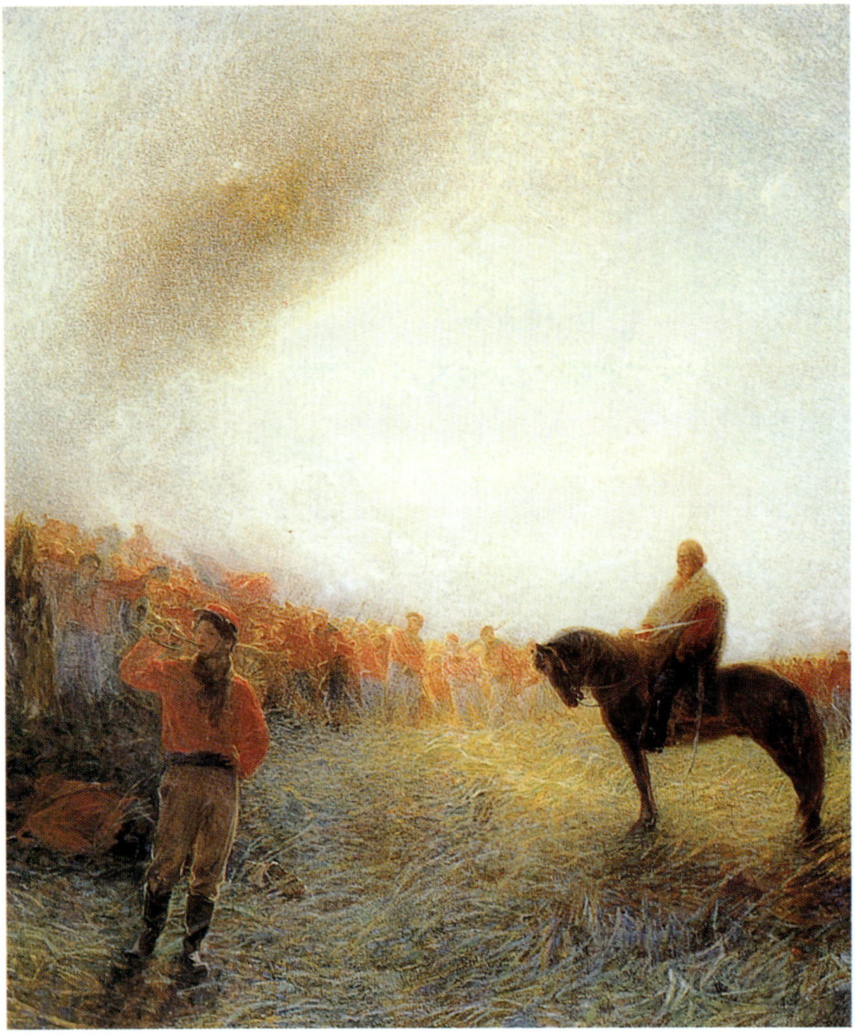

Plinio Nomellini,
Garibaldi, c. 1907.
Livorno, Giovanni Fattori Civic Museum.

flections predominated, considering the interest of the romantic/naturalistic generation in local and native elements (Cecioni, for example, wrote in praise of Lega: "this artist has the great merit of producing a local art that belongs to Florence. His works show not only his own individuality, but the individuality of the country"). Market trends also encouraged this tendency. The production of art for foreign tourists, English and American in particular, grew at the same fast pace as the number of wealthy travelers who visited Italy. Tourists created a constant demand for souvenir paintings, stimulated a kind of specialization, and encouraged the production of stereotypes. Their taste, no less than that of the local artists, is reflected in genre scenes and vedutas. Along with the flourishing market for the "picturesque" there remained, at times unheeded, at times like a statement of principle, the appeal to an art that was recognizably national, dealing with current events in the terms of the great historical painting, transforming genre painting into popular art, marked by no connotations of locale or school. Among the most fervent advocates of this appeal was Gabriele D'Annunzio and later, in the twentieth century, Filippo Tommaso Marinetti. "Born to a poor family in 1791 at Venice, [Hayez] is neither pagan nor Catholic, nor eclectic nor materialist. He is a great Italian idealist painter of the 19th century", wrote Giuseppe Mazzini from exile in London in 1841, in presenting the Romantic artist to the British public. "He is the head of the School of Historic Painting, which National thought proclaimed in Italy; the artist most deeply immersed in the sentiment of the ideal which is called upon to govern all of the works of the Epoch. His inspiration emanates directly from the People; his power directly from Genius". And Pasquale Villari, illustrious Meridionalist and historian, was to add a few decades later, al-

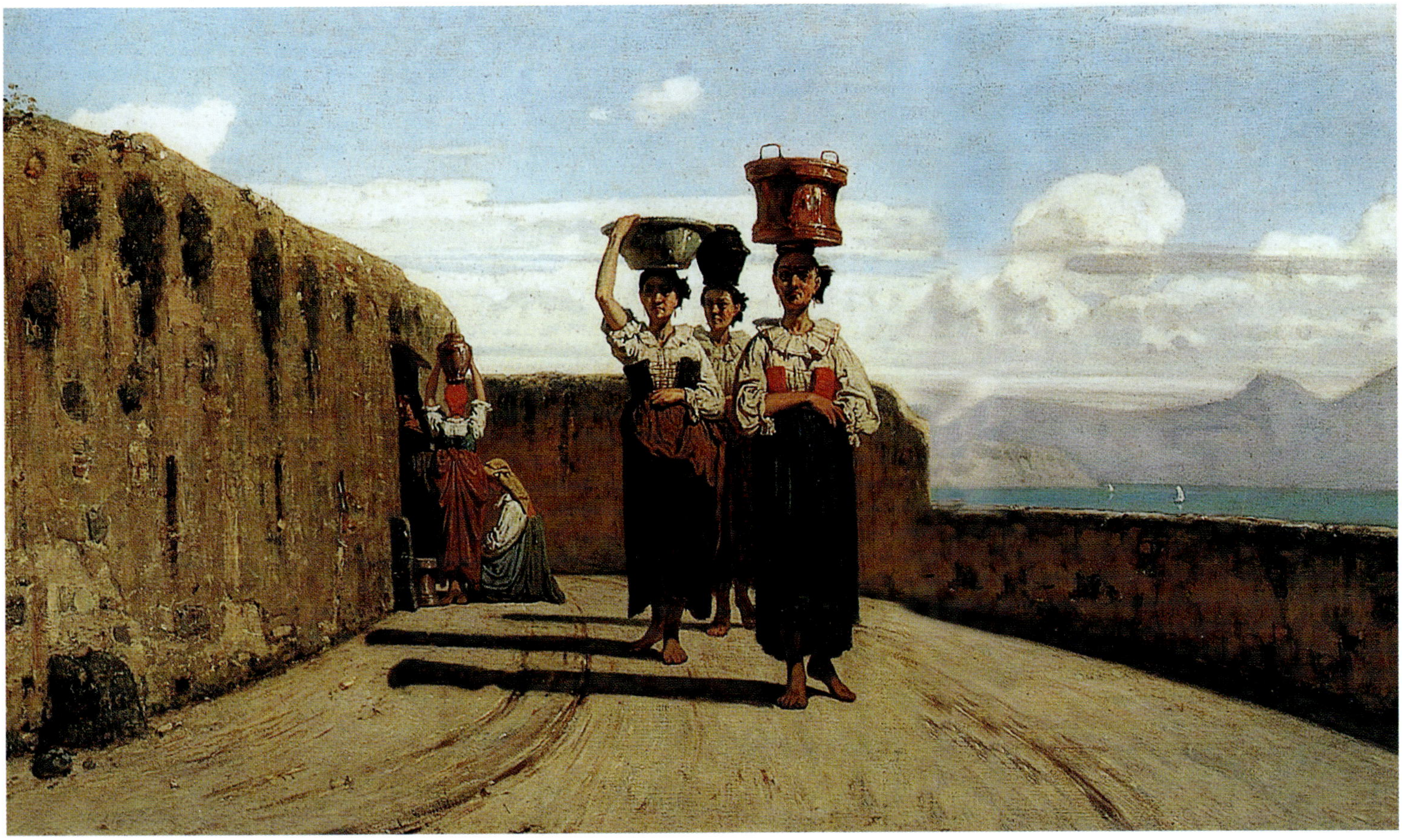

Vincenzo Cabianca,
Water Bearers at La Spezia, 1864.

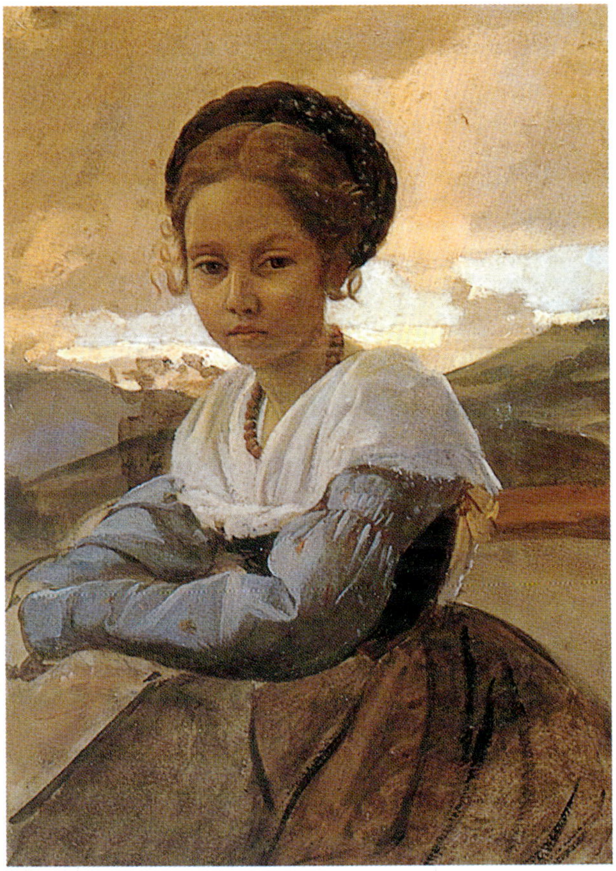

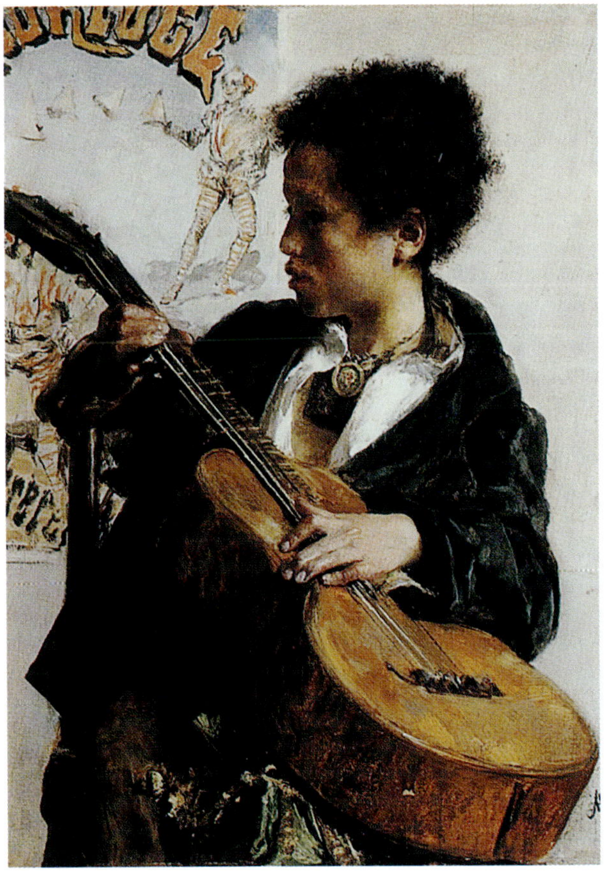

Nino Costa, *Girl from Lazio*, c. 1863.

Antonio Mancini,
Street-Boy with Guitar, 1877.

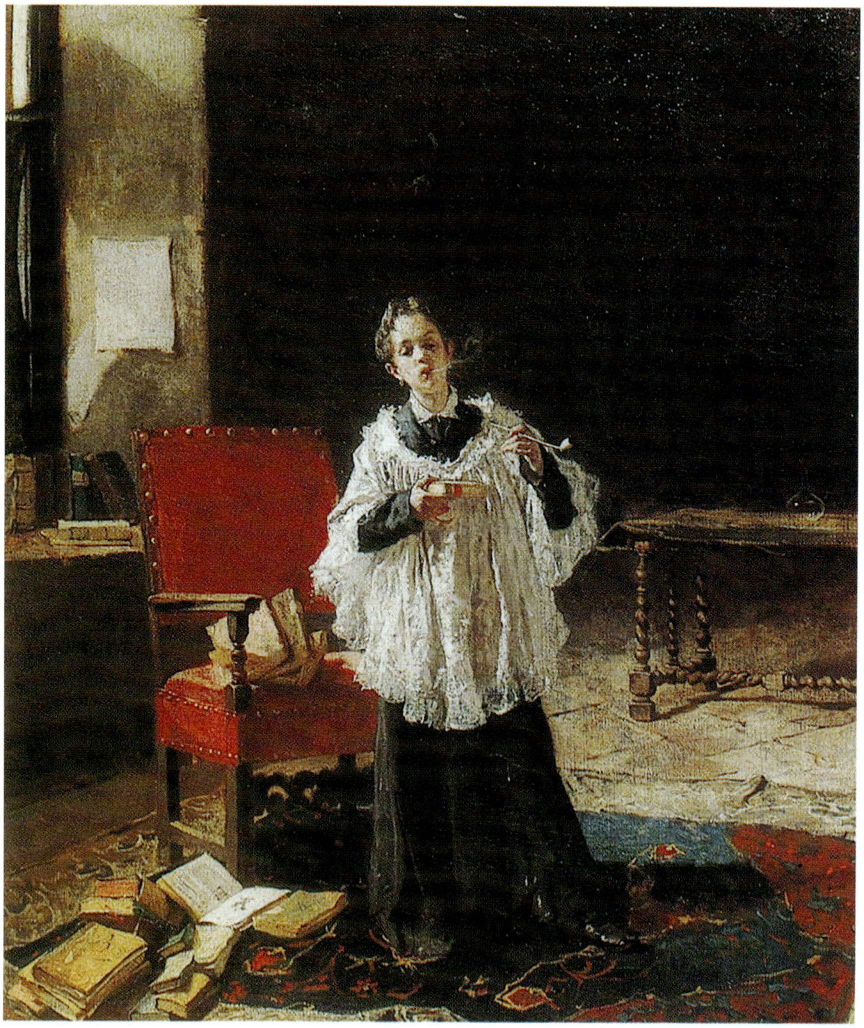

most as if to outline a Verist program (and having first traced the artistic/literary parallels Alfieri-Canova, Manzoni-Hayez): "[we must] be modern without being foreigners; be Italian without being of another century; approach the spoken language of the people; seek simplicity, naturalness and truth".

The post-unification decades saw the decline of historical painting of the romantic/literary tradition, and the progressive emerging of naturalistic approaches, accompanied by increasing cultural exchange and commerce in art among the major European nations. A number of Italian artists were to benefit by the establishment, primarily in Paris, of privately owned

Mosè Bianchi, *Love of Study. A Good Smoke*, 1870.

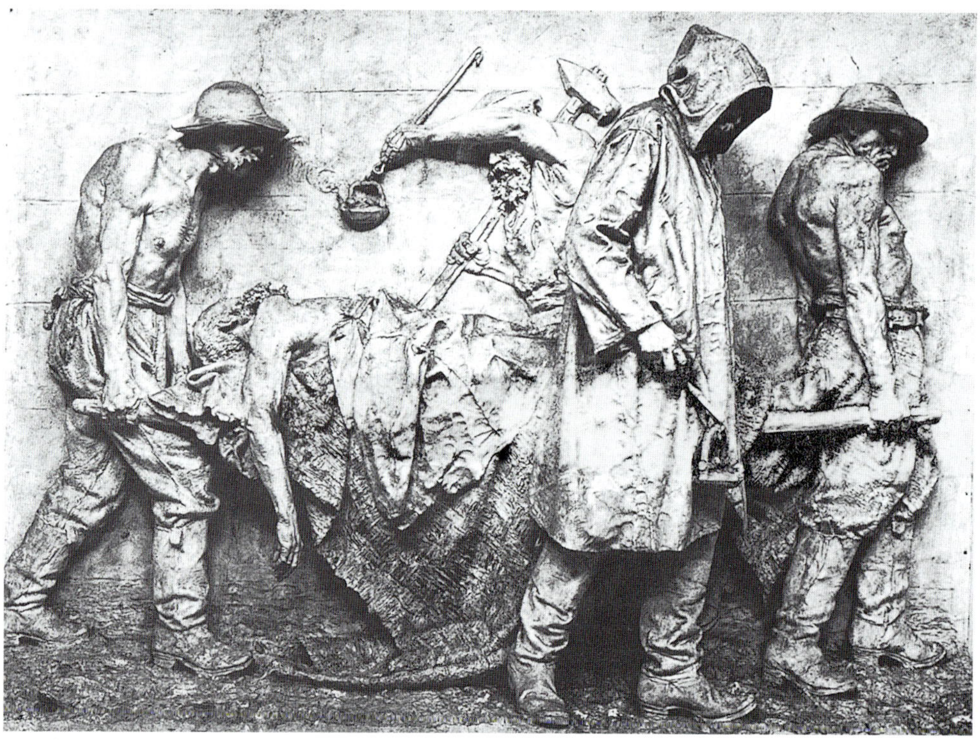

Vincenzo Vela, *Victims of Work*, 1882. Rome, National Gallery of Modern Art.

Facing page:
Tranquillo Cremona, *Curiosity*, 1876 77.

and managed art galleries, and by the growing phenomenon of active, cosmopolitan collectors. The career of a painter and sculptor could now develop entirely independent of public institutions such as the academies – as demonstrated by the relations between De Nittis and Michetti and the Maison Goupil; and between Zandomeneghi and Paul Durand-Ruel, the art dealer of the Impressionists. Often it was the artists themselves who decided to join forces in order to face a dual competition: the one among ideas and the other, more concrete, among works. While the significance of Lega's opening an art gallery in Piazza Santa Trinita in Florence in 1873, with Odoardo Borrani as partner, is mainly anecdotal, and while Morbelli failed in his attempt to bring the divisionists together in an association, Vittore Grubicy de Dragon, gallery owner, critic and painter himself, provides the first example in Italy of an artistic and cultural entrepreneur. Skillful strategist and refined man of culture, Grubicy, with his brother Albert, introduced the divisionist *vague* to Italy, promoted artists through publications and exhibitions in Italy and abroad – such as the Italian Exhibition, organized in 1888 at London – and stipulated contracts, interpreting his own role as that of urging artists to take immediate action on the level of communication, of address.

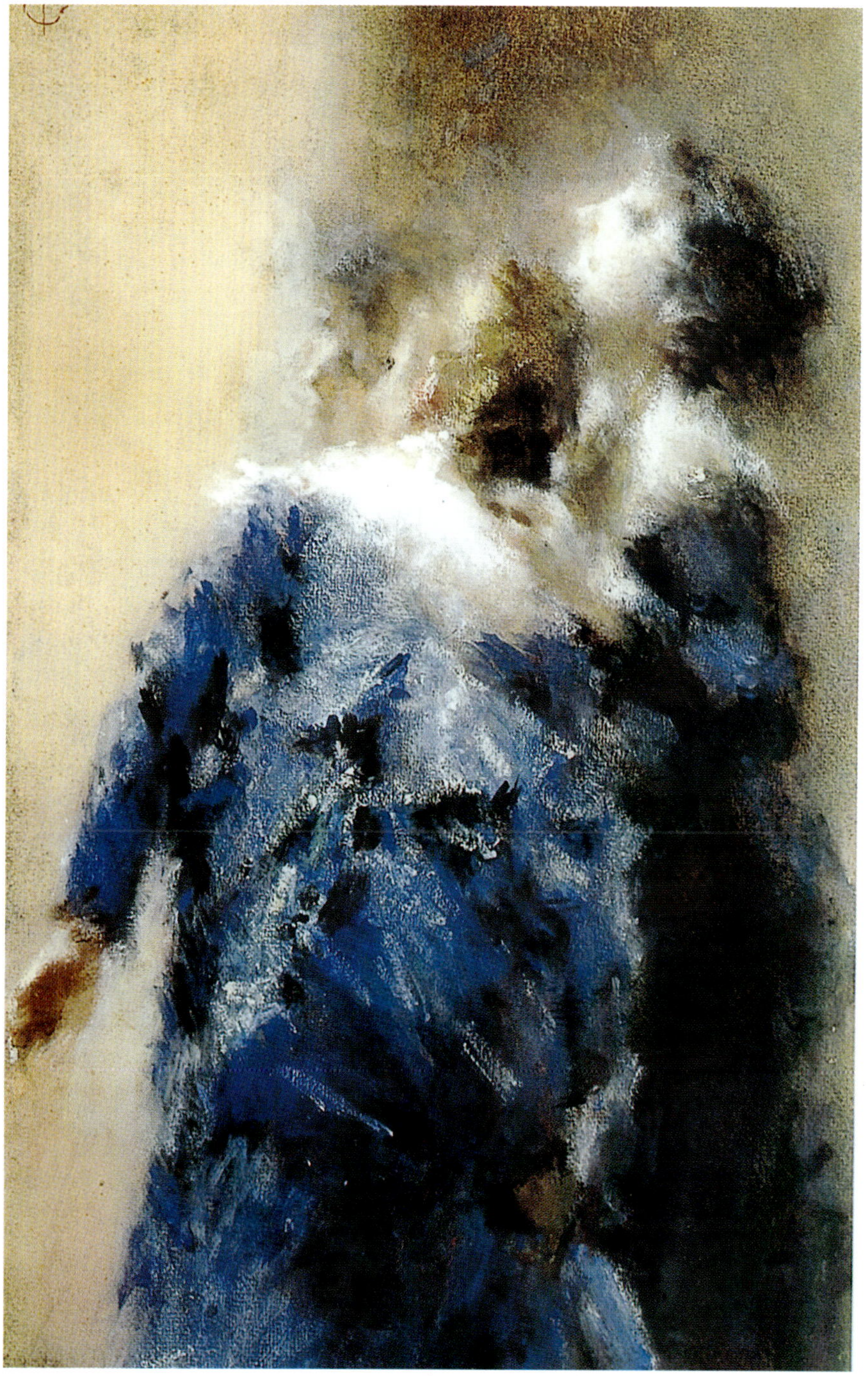

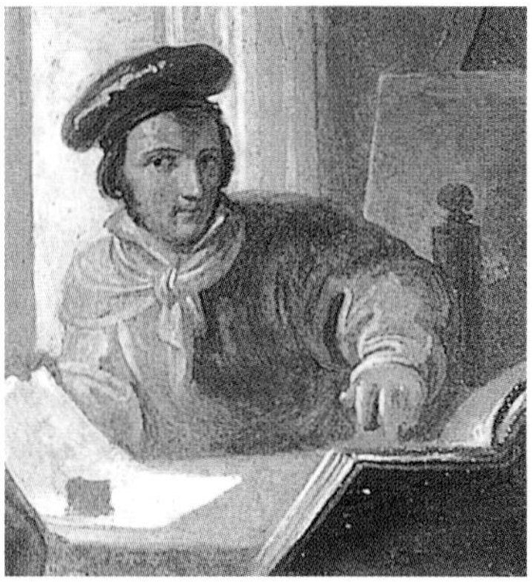

Tommaso Minardi

(Faenza 1787 – Rome 1871)

Born in Faenza but trained in Rome, where he attended first the Academy of the Italic Kingdom, then the Academy of San Luca, Minardi was among the most inventive interpreters of the archaicizing tendency that spread through Italy and Europe as a whole in the early years of the 19th century. His models were eclectic: Perugino and the young Raphael for the precision and linear softness of the drawing, the Flemish primitives for the use of local colors, and the Venetians. Minardi's relationships with contemporary artists were extensive. In contact with the Milanese circle of Appiani and Bossi, Minardi was also close to the Nazarenes, a group of German artists living in Rome who favored a return to the modes and techniques of religious art in the early Renaissance. In 1842 Minardi signed with Overbeck, Bianchini and Tenerani, the manifesto of Purism.

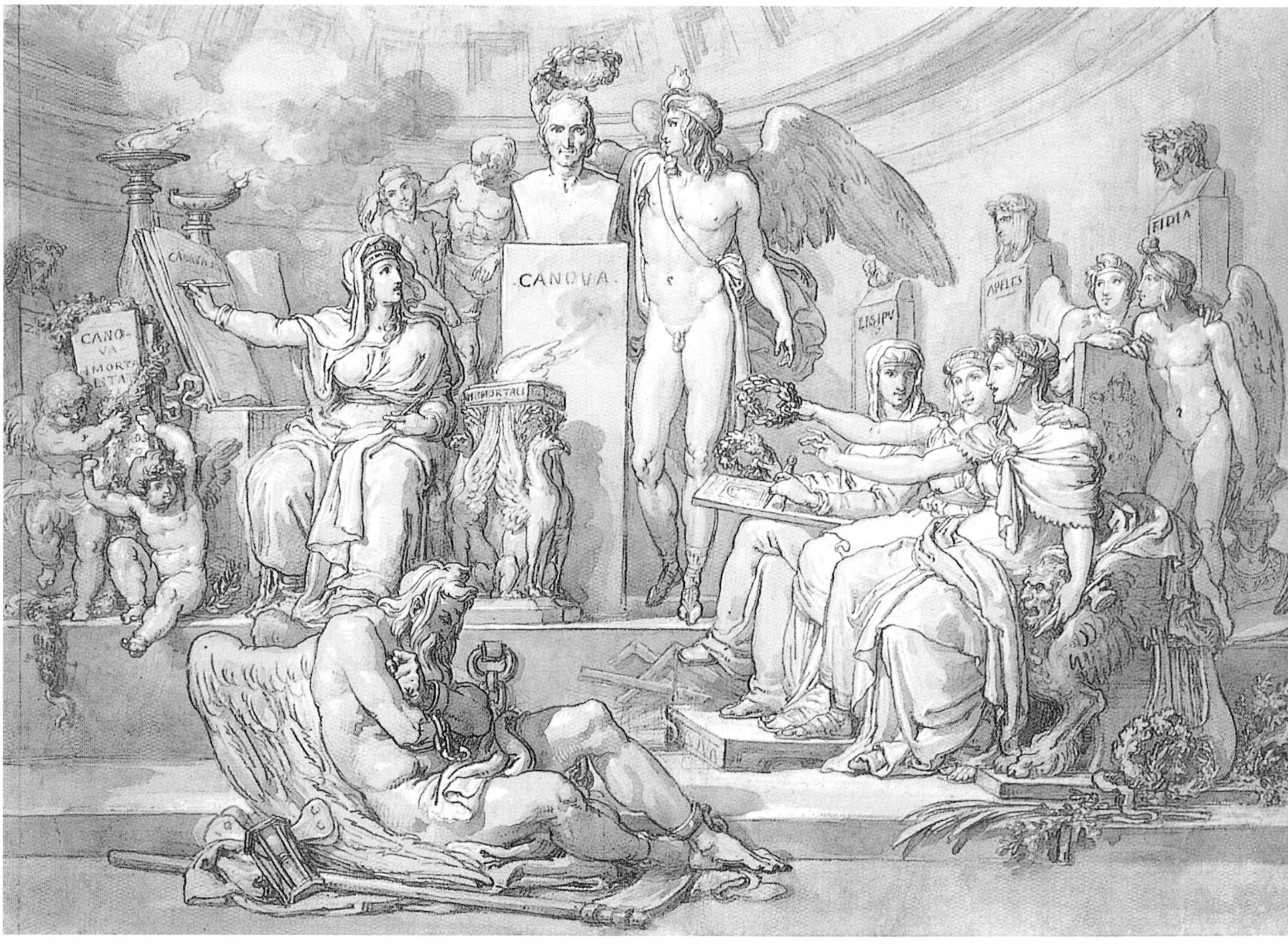

Tommaso Minardi, *Self-portrait*, c. 1805. Faenza, Pinacoteca Comunale.

Tommaso Minardi
Canova Crowned by the Genius of the Fine Arts
1812
pencil, ink, white lead on paper

The composition, a kind of figurative eulogy, pays homage to the most famous Italian neo-classical sculptor in a work that seems more relief than painting. Eliminating color, Minardi models the bodies utilizing a three-tone scale: full light, half light, shadow. The busts of the greatest sculptors of antiquity – the names of Lysippus, Apelles and Phidias can be read – watch over the coronation. The allegorical personifications of Architecture, Painting and Sculpture are exultant. At the foot of the podium, in chains, is the figure of Time with his attribute of the hourglass. His action, in the presence of genius, loses all power. Fame – this is the meaning of the picture – is perennial.

Tommaso Minardi
Socrates Surprises Alcibiades in a Brothel
1807
paper
Faenza, Pinacoteca Comunale.

Curio Dentato Refuses the Gifts of the Sannites
1807
paper
Rome, National Gallery of Modern Art.

Struggle between Argante and Tancredi
c. 1819
paper
Rome, National Gallery of Modern Art.

First attracted by ancient history, by the life of Socrates and the Homeric epics, by the 1820s Minardi was drawing inspiration mainly from Dante and from the chivalric poetry of Ariosto and Tasso. A didactic approach, at times excessively dry, began to yield to more emotionally appealing religious and imaginative dimensions. Heavily shaded, the *Struggle* reveals an artist who is highly cultivated, inspired by a multitude of cultural references, and at the same time light, surprising.

Tommaso Minardi
Madonna of the Rosary
1840
canvas
Rome, National Gallery of Modern Art.

Minardi, appointed director of the Perugia Academy in 1819 and professor of drawing at the Rome Academy of San Luca in 1822, spent the second and third decade of the century in study and travel, mainly through Central Italy. His cult of the origins brought him naturally to Florence and to Assisi, Spoleto, Bologna and Ravenna, on the traces of the old masters. In the meantime he was maturing his Purist approach, favorable to the wedding of art and religion and a return to the Renaissance Umbro-Tuscan tradition. The *Madonna of the Rosary*, with its mingled recollections of Perugino and Raphael, clearly exemplifies the artist's position.

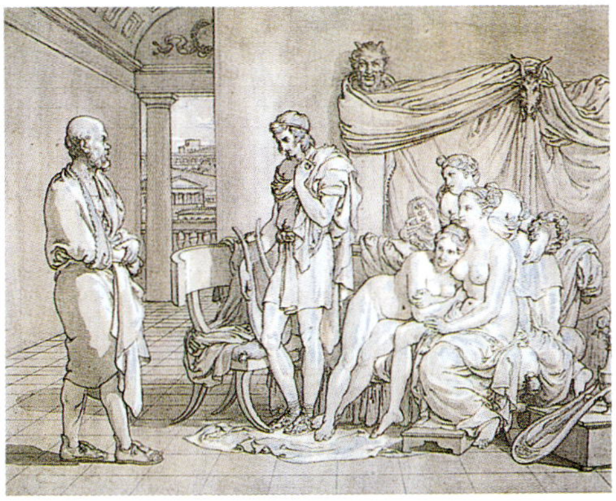

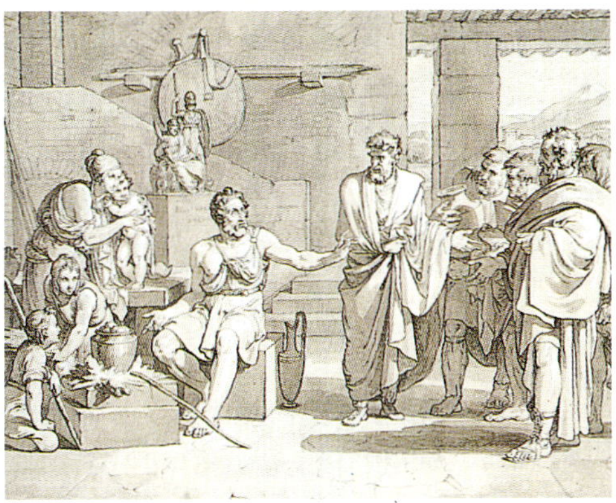

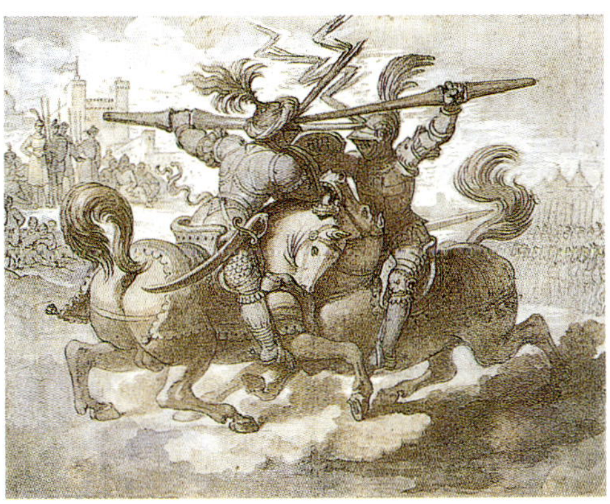

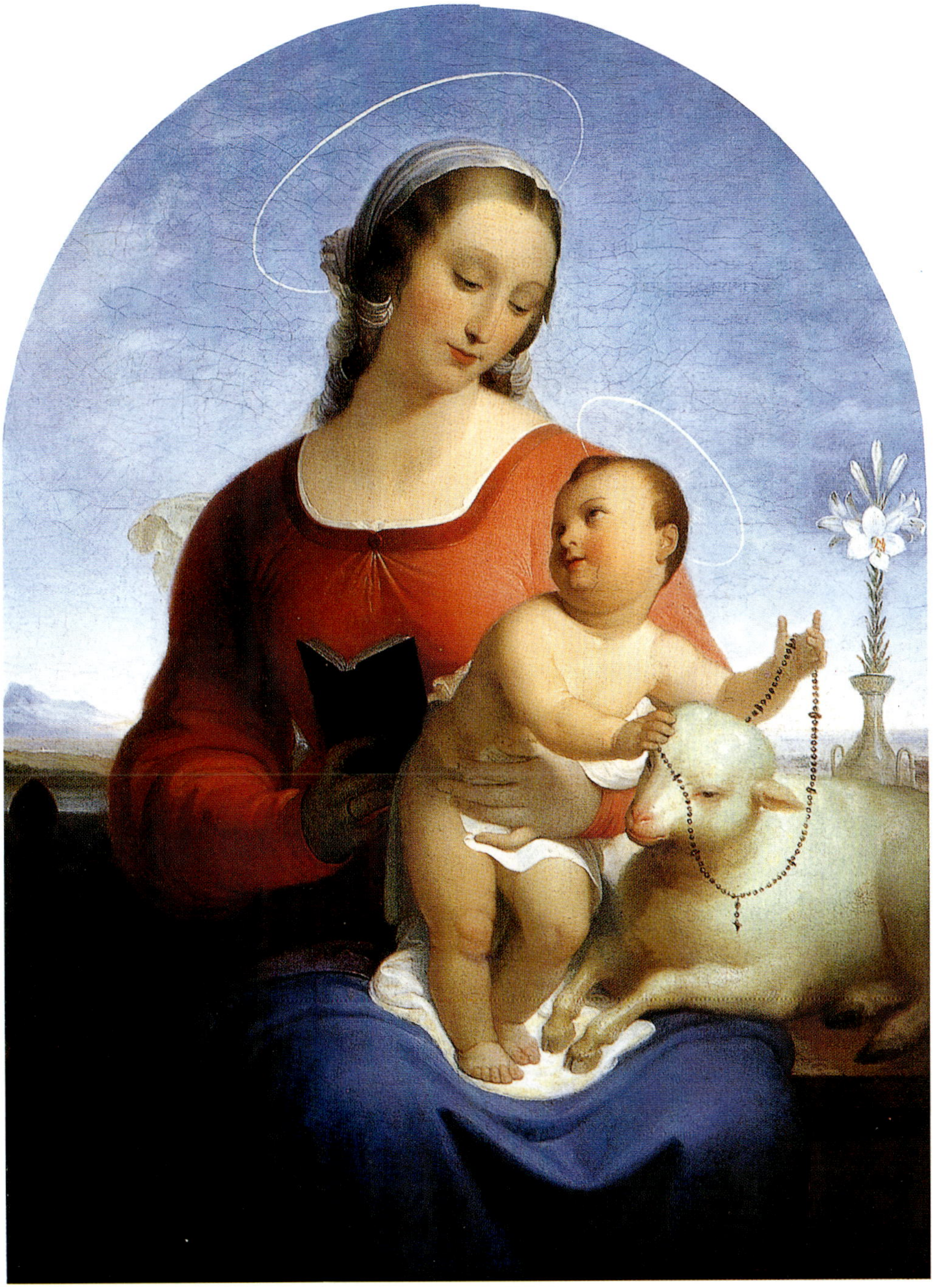

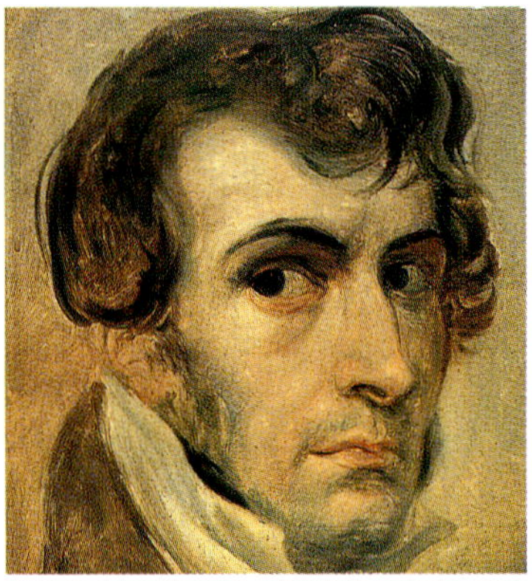

Giuseppe Bossi

(Busto Arsizio 1777 – Milan 1815)

A passionate and versatile artist, refined man of culture, historian and art critic, Giuseppe Bossi was both artist and cultural organizer, an Enlightenment intellectual who firmly believed in the morality of the arts, the civil function of images and words. After a strict neo-classical apprenticeship – the artist was in Rome in 1795, where he met Canova and established a friendship with him that was to last a lifetime – he went in 1802 to Paris, where he met David and encountered the first archaicizing trends. Concepts of "energetic language", of figurative eloquence, alternate in his work with soft evasion into the erotic and fantastic genre. Starting in 1807 he was engaged in copying Leonardo's *Last Supper* and in intense philological research on the great master. In 1810 he published a volume entitled *On the Last Supper of Leonardo da Vinci.*

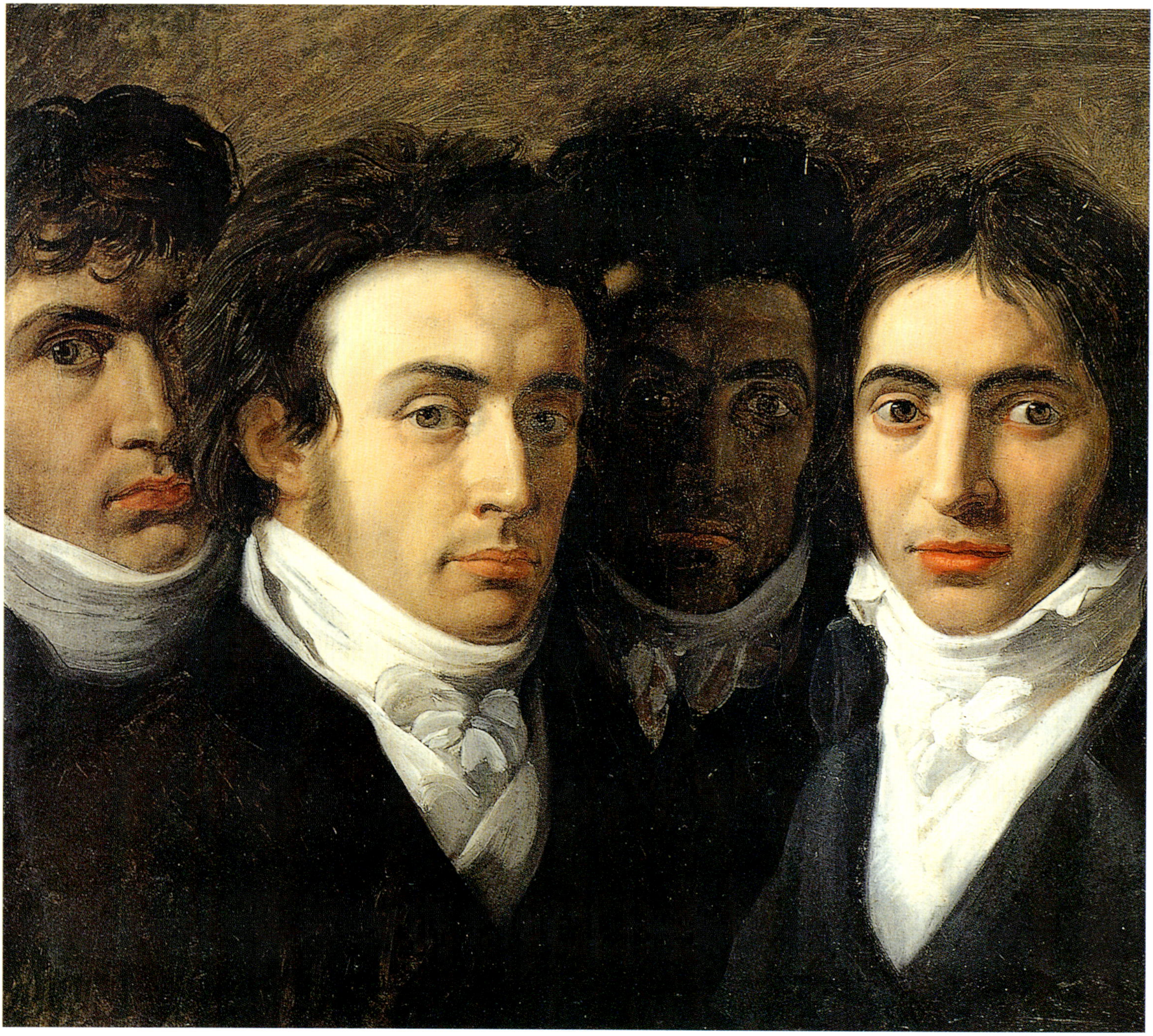

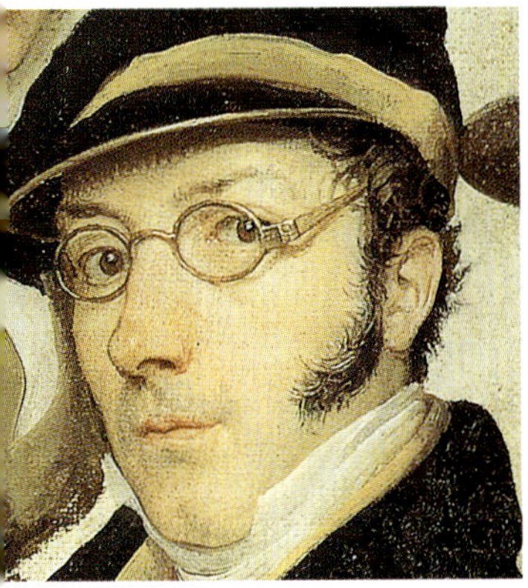

Francesco Hayez

(Venice 1791 – Milan 1882)

Venetian by birth, Hayez owed his early training to the years spent in Rome (1809-17) as protégé of Canova and Leopoldo Cicognara, living on a grant from the Venice Academy. It was in Rome that the young artist emerged, through strategic participation in important competitions, as a talent able to restore to Italian art its past glory. Skilled at interpreting historical subjects, imbuing them with current interest; a brilliant portrait painter and creator of sensual nudes, Hayez was acclaimed already in his lifetime as the most important Italian Romantic painter, hailed as national glory in years of foreign domination only to be deprecated as taste changed. His merits are recognized today: a refined stylist, Hayez conferred on painting of the historical genre, through his choice of subjects and execution, gripping epic-popular dimensions comparable to those of the historical romance and melodrama of the same period.

At left:
Giuseppe Bossi,
Self-portrait, detail,
c. 1805. Milan,
Brera Pinacoteca.

Giuseppe Bossi
Self-portrait with Gaetano Cattaneo, Giuseppe Traversa and Carlo Porta (The Portian Chamber)
1809
canvas
Milan, Treccani degli Alfieri Collection.

Self-portraits recur rather frequently in Bossi's work. The artist, portrayed either alone or with others, presents himself to the public involved in some urgent endeavor, and acutely aware of the importance of his role. The *Self-portrait* of 1809 shows him with Gaetano Cattaneo, his first biographer, and the poet Carlo Porta, which whom he shared an interest in dialect literature (Bossi also wrote poetry in dialect). The four, who pose standing close together, all facing the viewer, seem almost to be boasting of their union in an association.

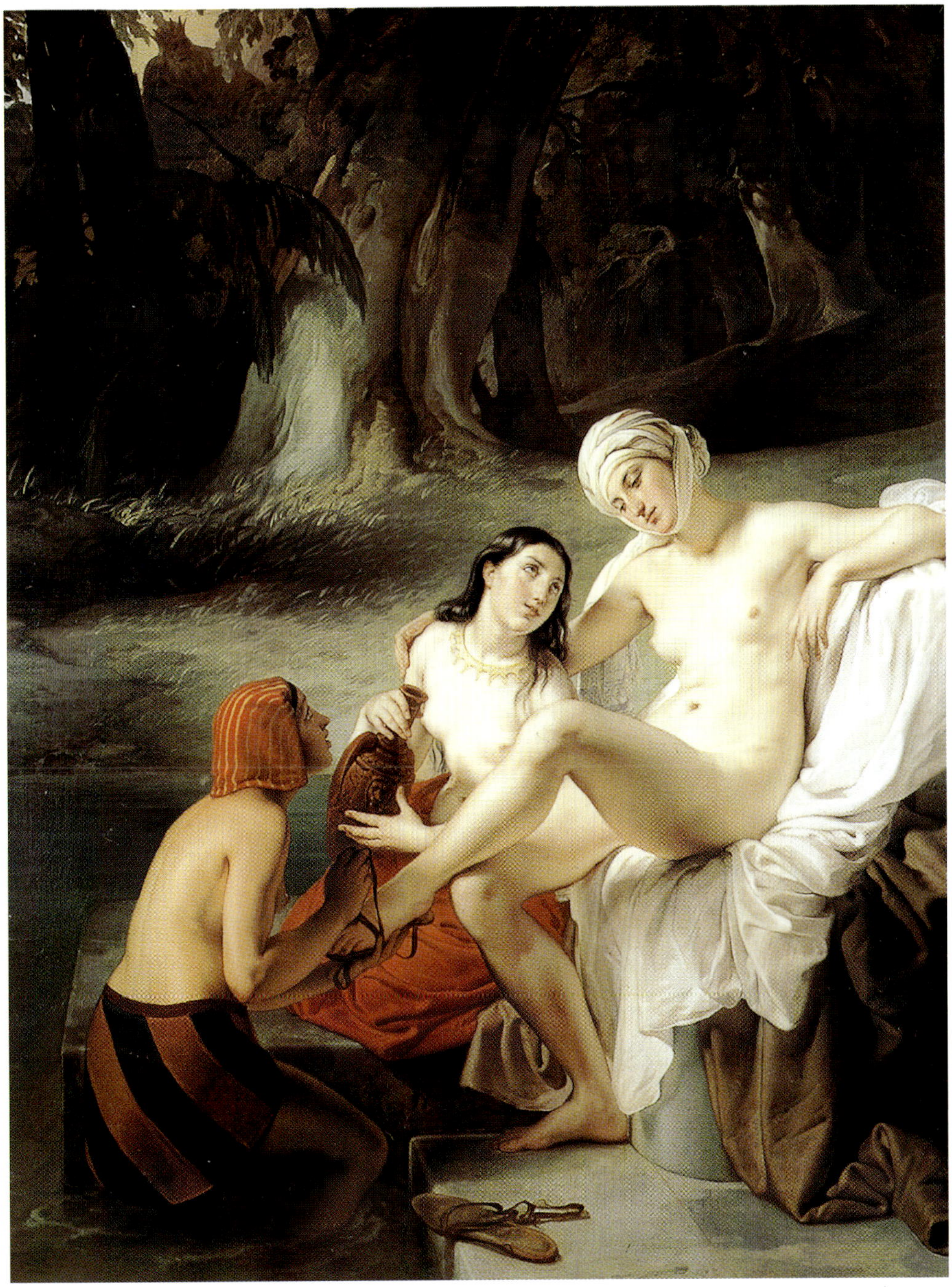

Francesco Hayez,
Self-portrait with Friends,
detail, 1827. Milan,
Poldi Pezzoli Museum.

Francesco Hayez
Bathsheba at her Bath
1834
canvas

This painting clearly exemplifies Hayez' fantastic/narrative tendencies, shared by the Romantic movement as a whole. The historical subject of the composition, King David who falls in love with Bathsheba upon surprising her nude, accompanied by her handmaidens and intent on her bath, serves as little more than a pretext. What really interests the artist are the possibilities of fairy-tale magic, enchantment and erotic development of the Biblical episode. The two halves of the composition, lower and upper, are entirely filled with the images of the nude figure and the forest, so thick and interwoven as to give no glimpse of the sky (King David appears at the upper left). The handmaiden on the left is dressed in Egyptian style and Hayez willingly lingers on exotic details of costume.

Francesco Hayez
Lion and Tiger in a Cage with a Portrait of the Painter
1831
canvas
Milan, Poldi Pezzoli Museum.

A self-portrait of the artist as a young man, the painting shows him posing before a cage where a lion and a tiger are kept in captivity. A homage to the artist's talent viewed as instinct, imbued with animal furor and elegance, the self-portrait concretely displays traits of the artist that might be called predatory: the eye that devours the image as it is born, the hand that grasps the borders with the motion of an acrobat. Hayez' gaze appears firmly fixed on the observer, emblematical. In the concrete of the wall, cracks and fissures testify to the "energetic" qualities of the sign.

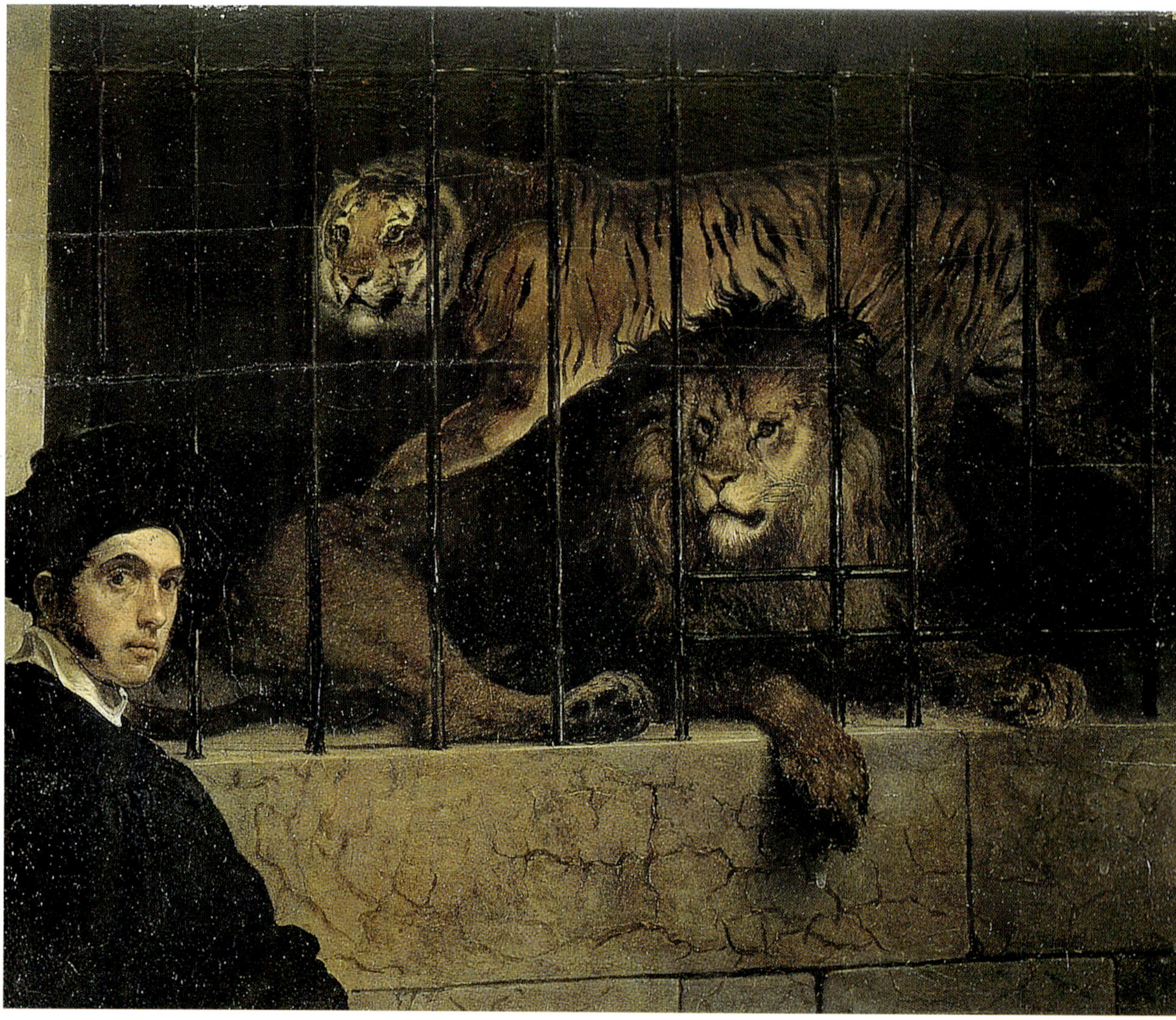

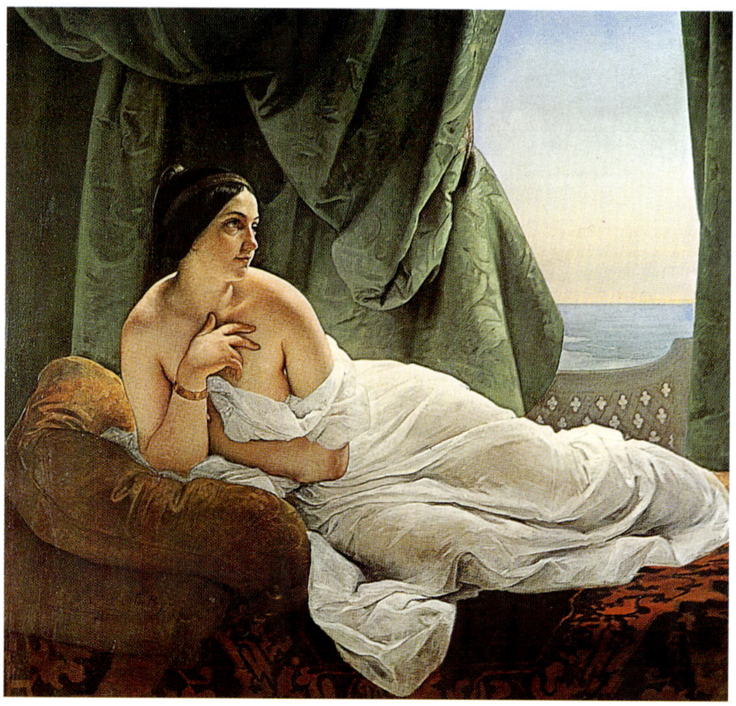

Francesco Hayez
Reclining Odalisque
1839
canvas

Hayez painted a series of odalisques. This motif offered the painter a chance to confront images of ideal beauty, in the absence of additional narrative elements, while simultaneously gratifying the taste for the exotic so marked in the Romantic generation. The model poses half reclining against the background of a great velvet curtain and a tranquil seaside view. Her bust is nude; the lower half of the body, wrapped in a veil, emerges through its transparency. In the *Reclining Odalisque*, homage and citations abound; from Raphael to Titian, from Canova to Ingres, whose *Great Odalisque*, painted at Rome in 1814, had perhaps been seen by Hayez.

Francesco Hayez
The Kiss.
A Youthful Episode.
Customs of the XIV
Century
1859
canvas
Milan, Brera Pinacoteca.

This picture, of which a second version exists, is among the most popular in Italian painting. Plain and appealing at first glance – the sugar-sweet motif of the kiss, a "youthful episode", is sufficient in itself to arouse sympathy – the painting reveals, upon closer consideration, complex historical and political implications. The colors in which the garments of the two young lovers are painted are, more or less explicitly in the two different versions, those of the flags of Italy and France, two nations whose history, at the time when the picture was painted, was closely interwoven. It was in fact thanks to the alliance with France procured by Cavour's skillful foreign policy that Italy won its independence, precisely in 1859. The lining of the man's hood is green, his trousers are red; the lining of the sleeves in the girl's dress is white; and the dress itself is blue.

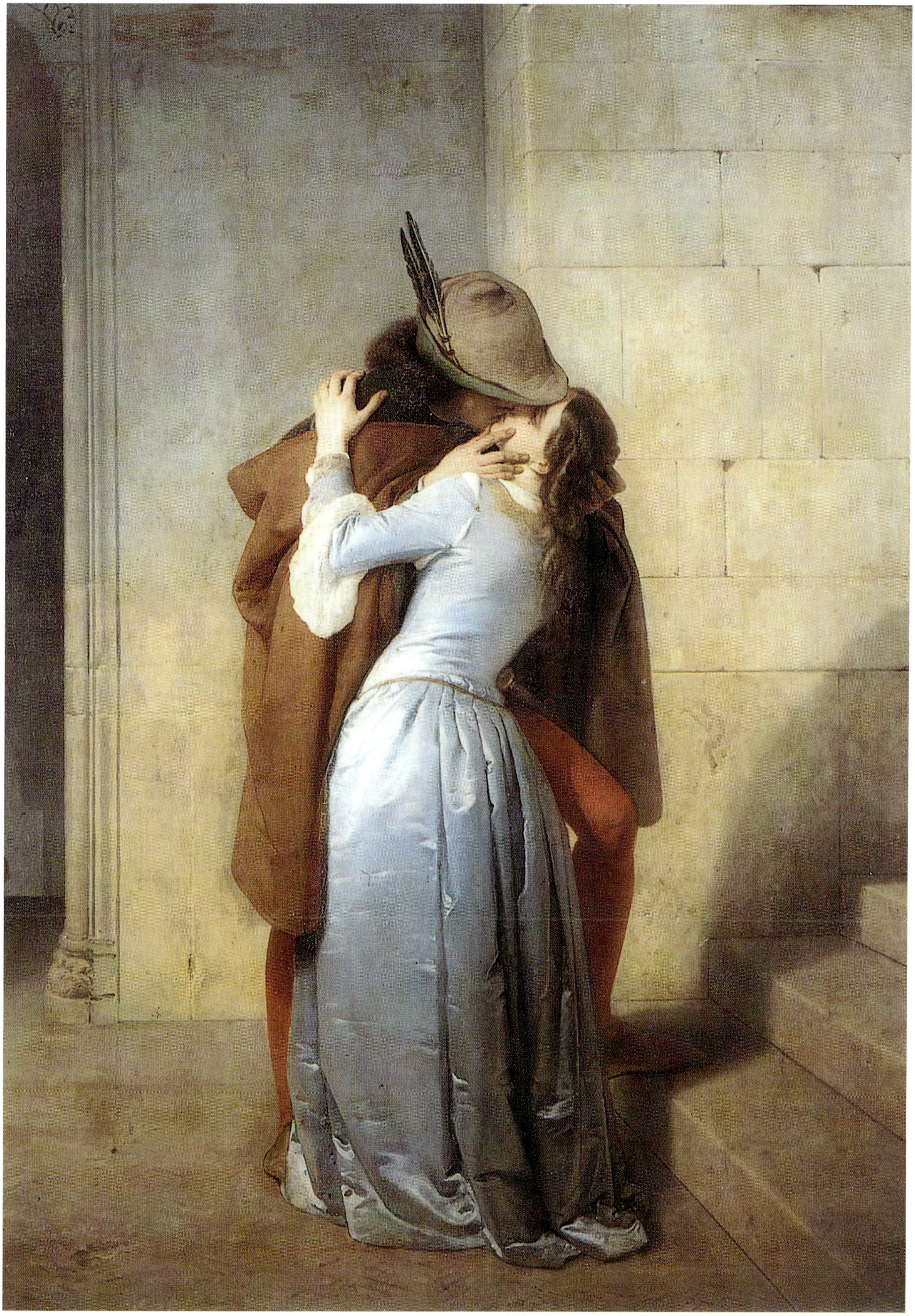

Luigi Mussini

(Berlin 1813 – Siena 1888)

Son of a chapel master at the Prussian court, Mussini trained at the Florence Academy and went on to become a highly cultured, cosmopolitan artist. Starting in 1840 he spent three years in Rome, where he adhered to strict Nazarene positions. In Florence he contributed to orienting in the Purist direction the city's figurative Romanticism, opposing its popular patriotic dimension as well as the other trend, naturalistic and sensual, of Giuseppe Bezzuoli, although the latter had been his master. In 1849 he participated as volunteer in insurrections. Between 1849 and 1851 he was in France, at Paris, where he met Ingres, Flandrin, Chassériau, and Gérôme. His youthful approach, dryly concentrated on drawing, took on a new softness. The goal of a kind of stylistic chastity did not, however, cause Mussini to banish grace and sweetness from his painting.

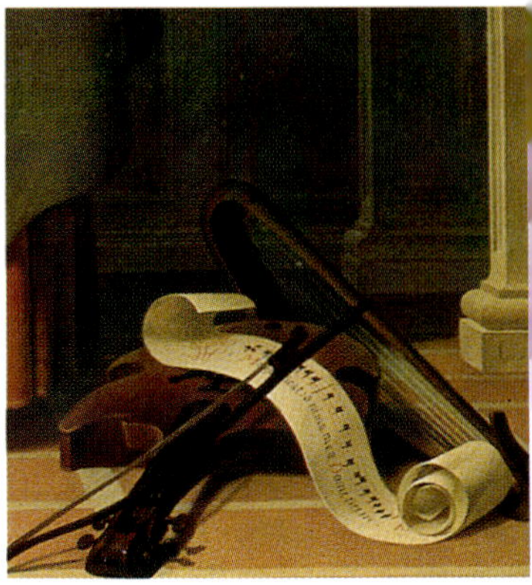

Luigi Mussini
Sacred Music
1841
canvas, whole and detail
Florence, Accademia Gallery.

The composition shows how, for Mussini and in accordance with Purist principles, the first Romantic experiences tended to be reconfigured in a more devotional and formal sense. The clearly recognizable homage to Umbro-Tuscan tradition is combined with a refined use of chiaroscuro in the painting, and a heightening of tones which cannot be called neo-Quattrocentesco. In chanting a sacred hymn the angel seems to comment on the edifying, eulogistic function of the arts, which do not flourish in a fully natural environment but rather in the shelter of a simple, typical religious building. The artist's predilection for drawing with pure borders appears emblematic where the image becomes simple notation: in the detail of the score, carefully transcribed on the scroll held up by the angel and the one resting on the floor.

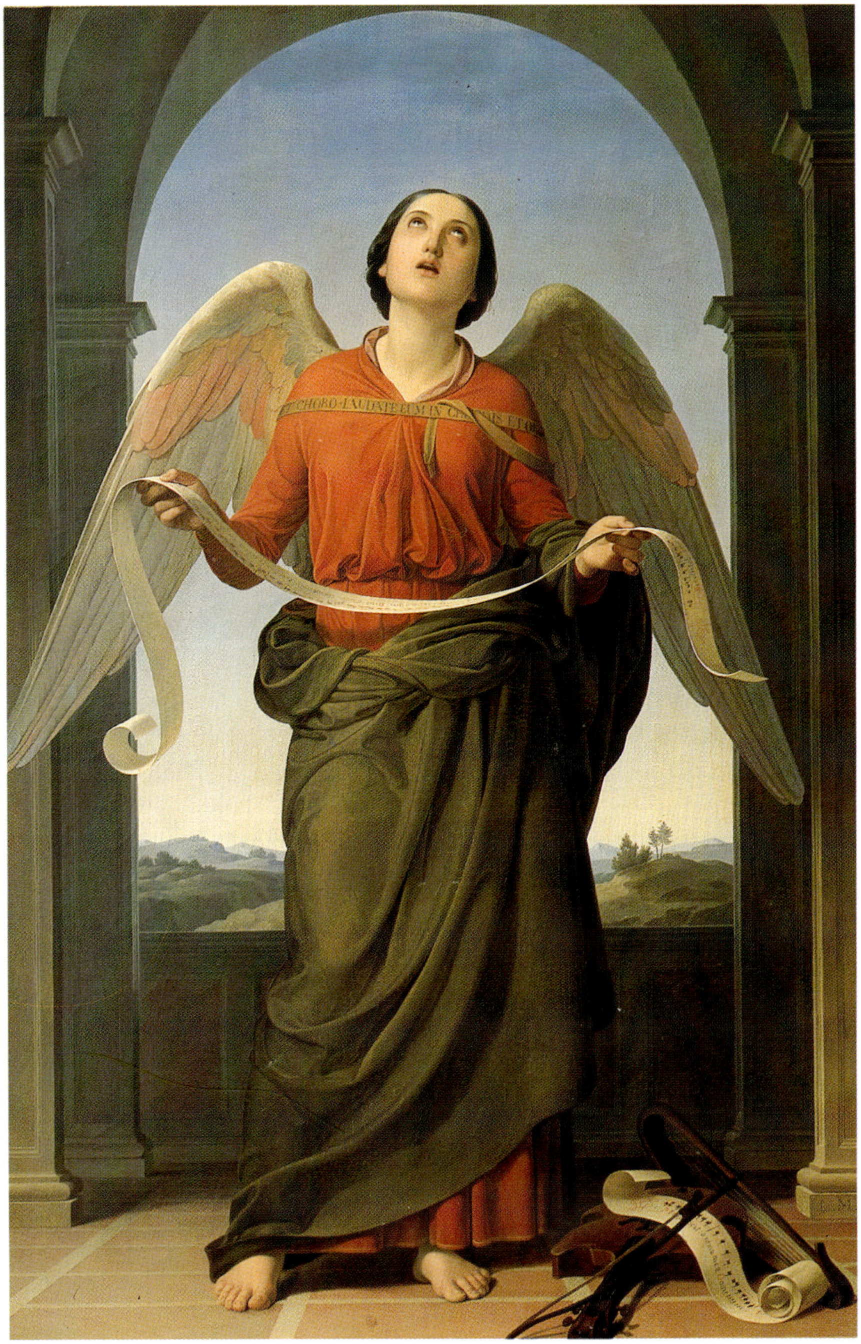

Lorenzo Bartolini

(Prato 1777 – Florence 1850)

In Paris between 1799 and 1808, Bartolini was a pupil of Jacques-Louis David. In the studio of the great neo-classical artist, the meeting place of all the young talents on the Parisian scene, he met Ingres, with whom he shared a predilection for pure forms, for a classic, barely archaicizing manner, and for a highly refined combination of Renaissance elements in which the severity of the ideal was tempered by the use of soft chiaroscuro. His objective, he wrote, was that of "approaching unattainable nature". Having settled in Florence, Bartolini soon emerged as interpreter of the Purist approach imposed on sculpture already by the late Canova. Among his most famous works are the tomb of Countess Sophia Zamojska, in Santa Croce, and the *Faith in God*, now at the Poldi Pezzoli Museum in Milan.

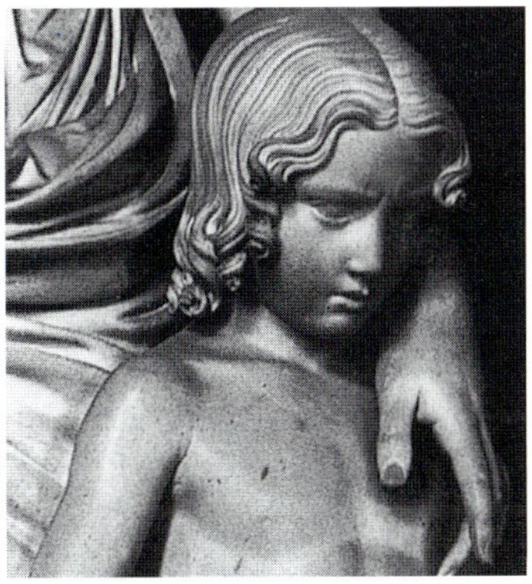

Lorenzo Bartolini, *Charity as Educator*, detail, 1824-36. Florence, Palatine Gallery.

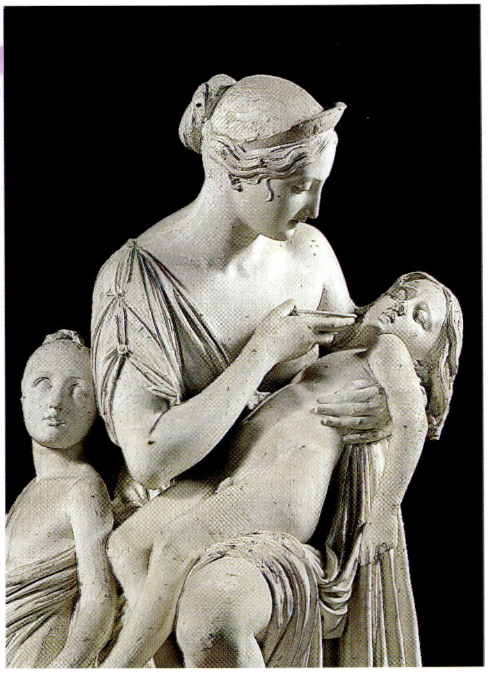

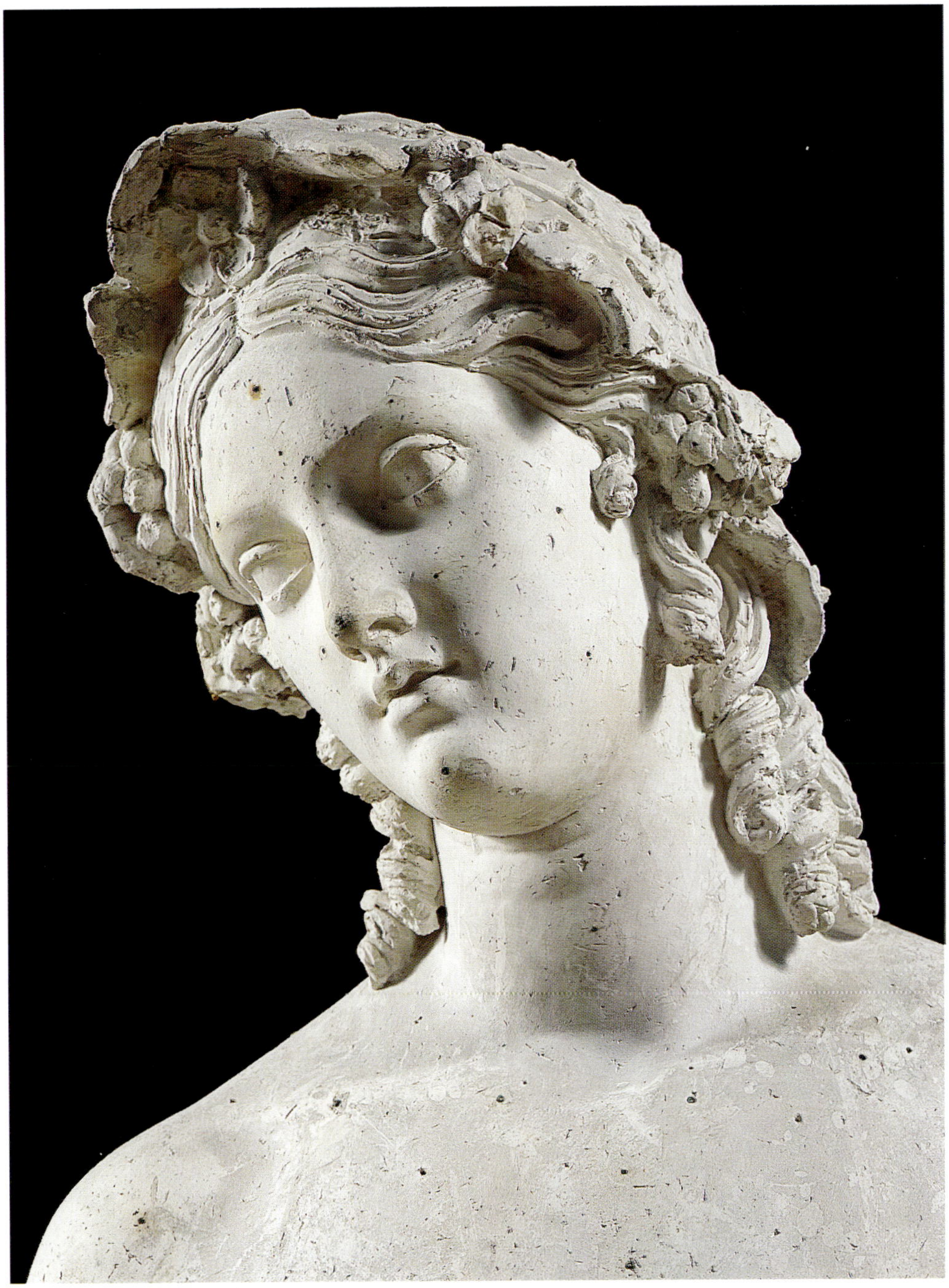

Lorenzo Bartolini
Demidoff Monument
1828-50
plaster cast, details
Florence, Accademia Gallery.

Commissioned by his sons Paolo and Anatolio at the death of their father Niccolò, a Russian aristocrat who owned mines in Siberia and was the husband of Princess Matilde Bonaparte, the monument had a long and complicated history. Bartolini worked on it in several stages. It was executed in marble, after the artist's death, by Romanelli, his pupil. Its installation on the left bank of the Arno dates from 1871. The work is composed of a central group with Niccolò and Anatolio accompanied by a number of allegorical figures larger than life-size, among them *Recognition*, *Charity*, *Siberia*, the *Muse of Festivals* and *Nature Reveals Herself to Art*.

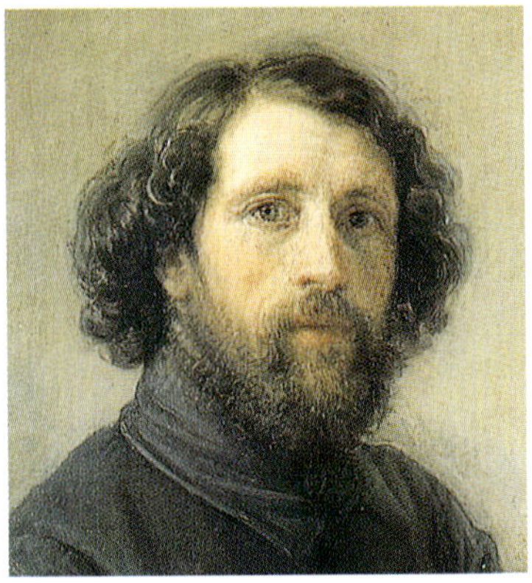

Il Piccio

(Giovanni Carnovali, Montegrino, Varese, 1804 – Caltaro sul Po, Cremona, 1873)

Son of a builder expert in constructing water games for fountains, Il Piccio trained at the Carrara Academy of Bergamo, to which he was admitted very young. A passionate admirer of the Venetian and Lombard masters of the 15th-16th centuries, he drew inspiration from them for his naturalistic effects and soft sfumato, predilections that were to be definitively confirmed by his study of Correggio's work at Parma. A legendary walker, he made his first voyages of study on foot: to Rome and to Parma in 1831, perhaps to Paris in 1845, to view the work of Delacroix and the Barbizon landscape artists, then back to Rome in 1848 and 1855. With his sentimental, imaginative talent, Il Piccio excelled in portraits, highly acute, and in great nature scenes, often suggested by literary episodes, where slender, sensual figures appear enveloped in mysterious shadows.

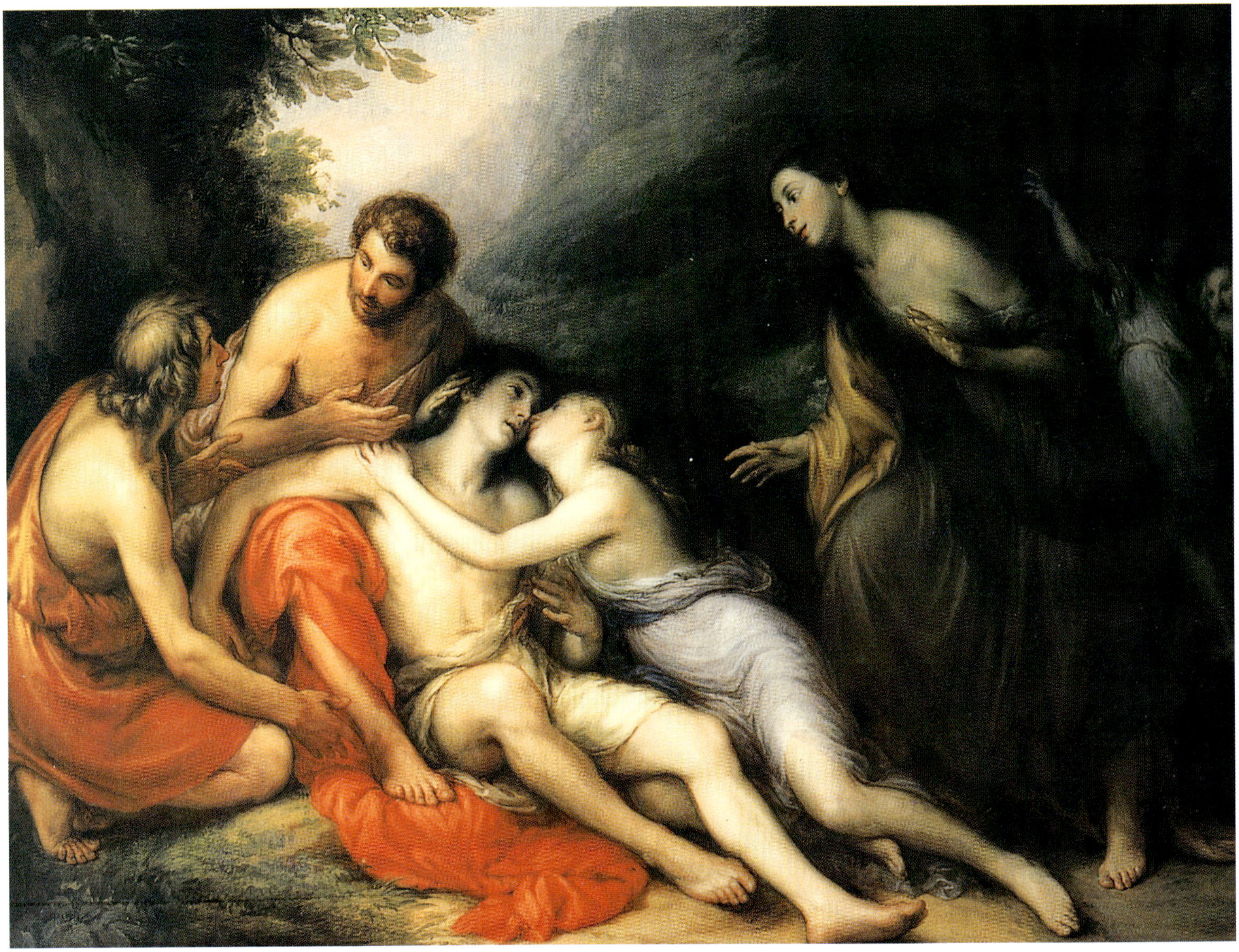

Il Piccio
The Death of Aminta
c. 1835
canvas
Piacenza, Banca Popolare.

The story of Aminta, narrated by Torquato Tasso when only thirty, has a happy ending. The shepherd Aminta, enamored of the nymph Silvia, wins her favors through various and occasionally dramatic vicissitudes. Believing Silvia dead, Aminta even arrives at the point of throwing himself off a cliff, but is saved when a tree breaks his fall. For Il Piccio, Tasso's "bucolic fable" is instead a variation on the theme of love and death. He portrays Aminta dying, with Silvia weeping at having denied her love to such a devoted lover.

Il Piccio, *Self-portrait with Palette*, detail, 1846-50. Bergamo, Carrara Academy.

Il Piccio
Salmace and Hermaphrodite
signed and dated 1856
canvas

The poets sing of the nymph Salmace, inhabitant of "a pond of water crystal clear down to the bottom", who fell in love with the youth Hermaphrodite; and who, rejected by him, asked the gods to be joined forever to his body, in an indissoluble embrace. Attracted by the soft, elegant nature of the mythological fable, Il Piccio creates a leafy natural dell, with only a hint of crystalline waters and distant hills, in which to portray the struggle for love. The nymph with her flowing blonde hair, slender and clinging in Mannerist style, draws to herself the reluctant youth, his face reddening in a blush, "holds him close as he struggles to escape, kisses his unwilling lips, caresses him below the belly", in the words of the poet Ovid.

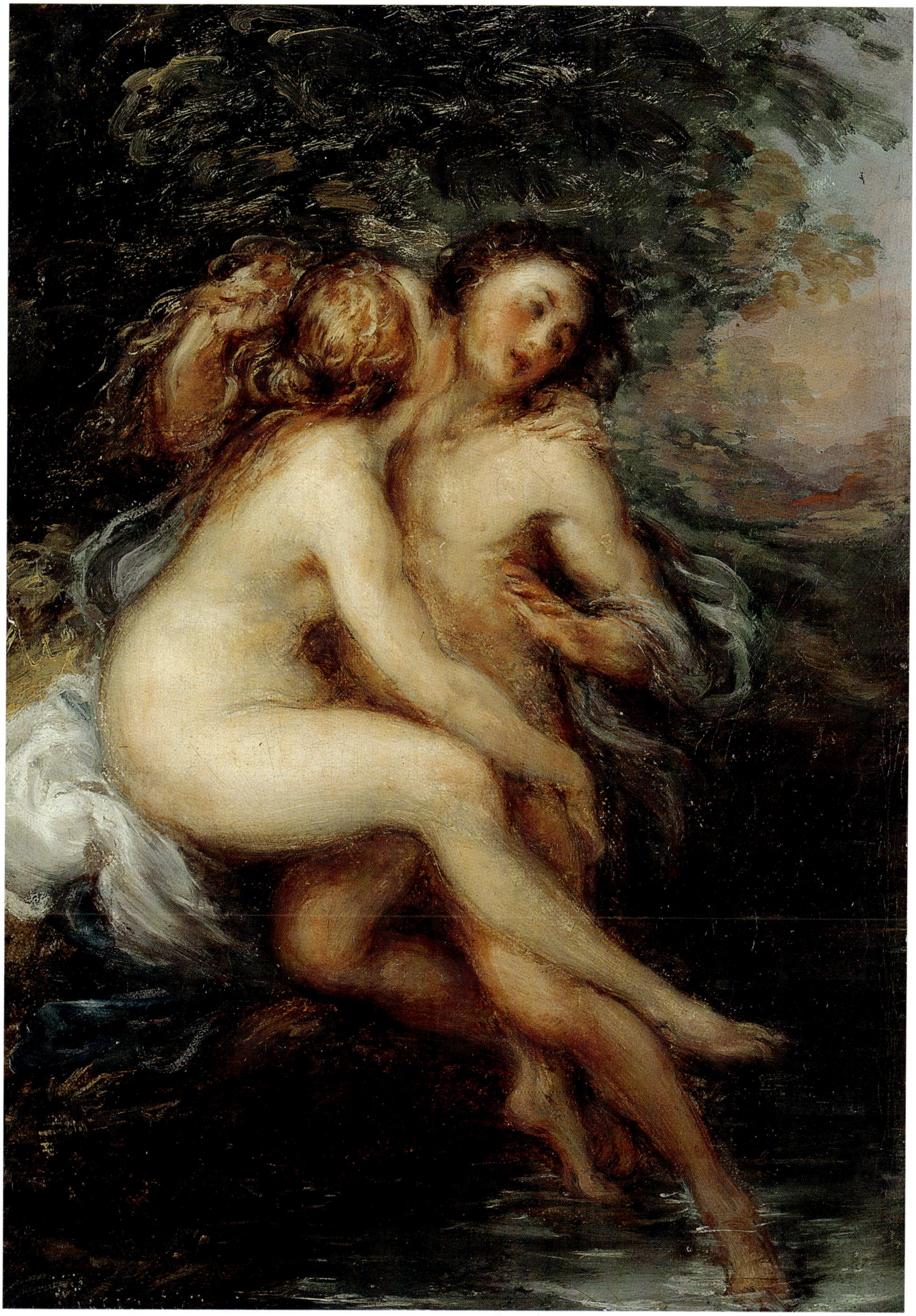

Bartolomeo Pinelli

(Rome 1781 – 1835)

A child of art – his father sculpted small ornamental bas-reliefs and devotional terracottas – Pinelli began to sculpt and draw while still a boy before regularly attending any school of art. Trained according to neo-classical principles of composition, he preferred clear forms decidedly delineated by boundaries. His fame is linked to engravings with "picturesque" themes – particularly appreciated by cultured tourists and lovers of Rome as well as by foreign artists residing in the city, such as Bertel Thorvaldsen – and to illustrations for popular literary works in the Romanesque dialect, such as *Meo Patacca* by Giuseppe Bernieri and *Il maggio romanesco ovvero il palio conquistato* by Giovanni Camillo Peresio. Among the subjects of the engravings are ancient and popular customs, episodes from Roman history and the lives of the brigands.

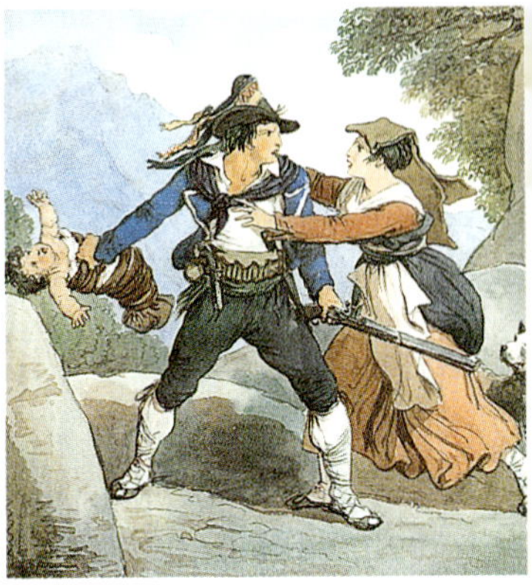

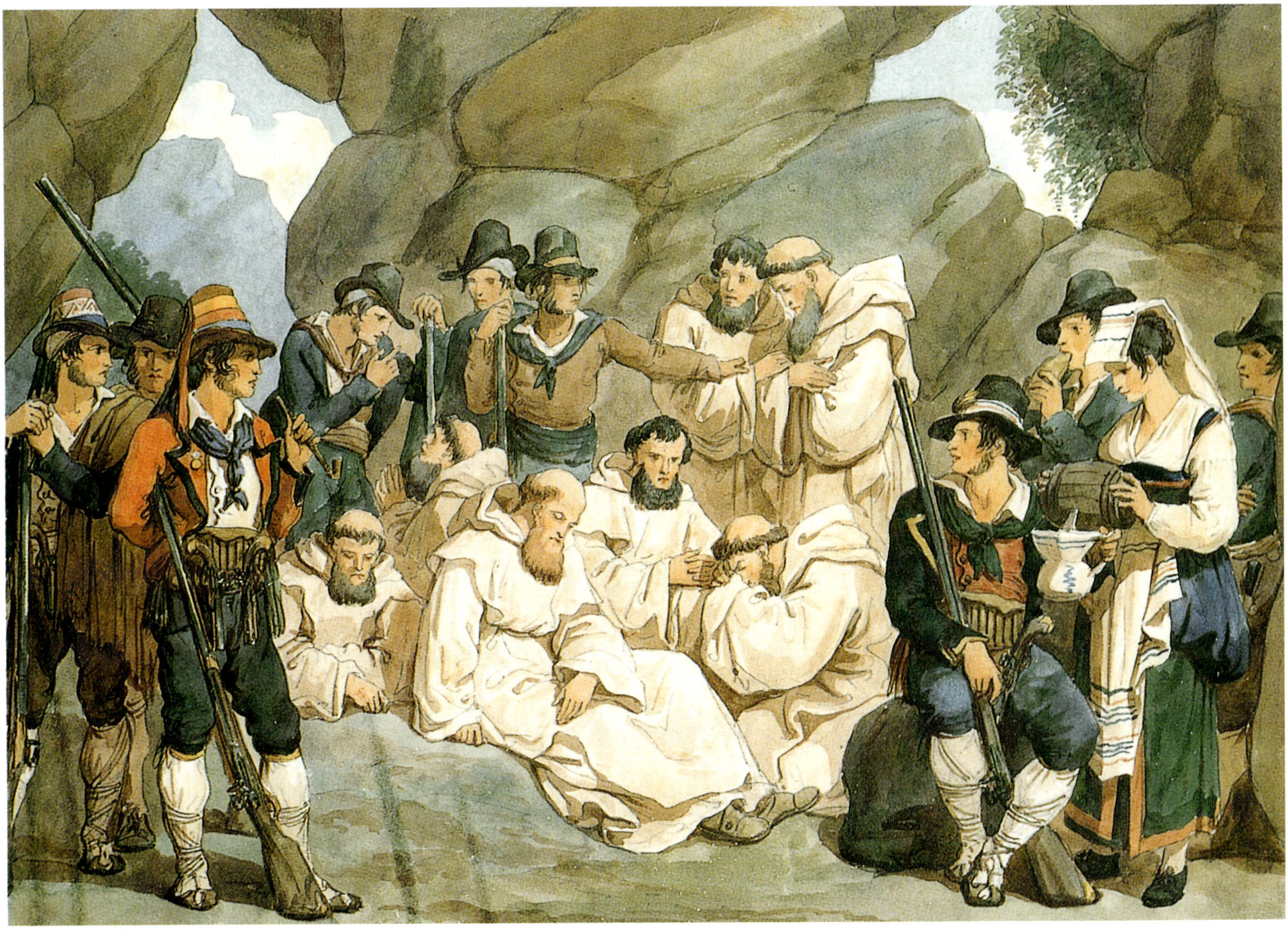

Bartolomeo Pinelli
The Frascati Camaldolensian Friars prisoners of the Brigand Massaroni's band

1821
water color on paper
Rome, Museum of Rome.

Against the background of an impervious Latium landscape, as rocky, rough and wild as the Alps, a band of well-armed brigands poses in picturesque costume along with seven Camaldolensian friars held prisoner. Among the friars, some are supplicating the brigands, some are praying and others are calmly waiting in faith. A pretty young water-seller is pouring water for a thirsty brigand. The spacious blue sky with its scattered summer clouds, glimpsed above, is no less splendid for the crime that is being committed. The episode, in itself dramatic, offers the artist a pretext for displaying local curiosities and natural beauty.

Bartolomeo Pinelli,
A Brigand having strangled her son, his wife kills him as he sleeps
detail, 1823. Rome, Museum of Rome.

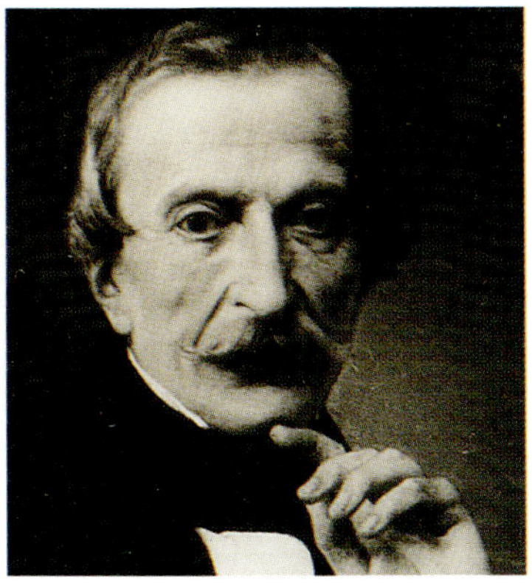

Massimo d'Azeglio

(Turin 1798 – 1866)

Politician and man of letters, D'Azeglio approached painting for the first time in 1814, at Rome, where he was then living since his father was a minister of the Vatican. He was later to dedicate himself assiduously to this art. In Rome a second time in 1820, he began to work from life as the Northern artists did. He studied nature in every minimum detail, spending hours outdoors, in direct contact with his subject, walking and riding for miles over the Roman countryside. Success was to smile on him early, thanks also to his relations with important, influential clients (among his admirers were Carlo Alberto and King Carlo Felice). While his contemporaries appreciated in particular the small landscapes composed without literary concerns, his own preference was always for compositions which, as he wrote in his memoirs *Miei ricordi*, "leave ample range to fantasy and to higher concepts".

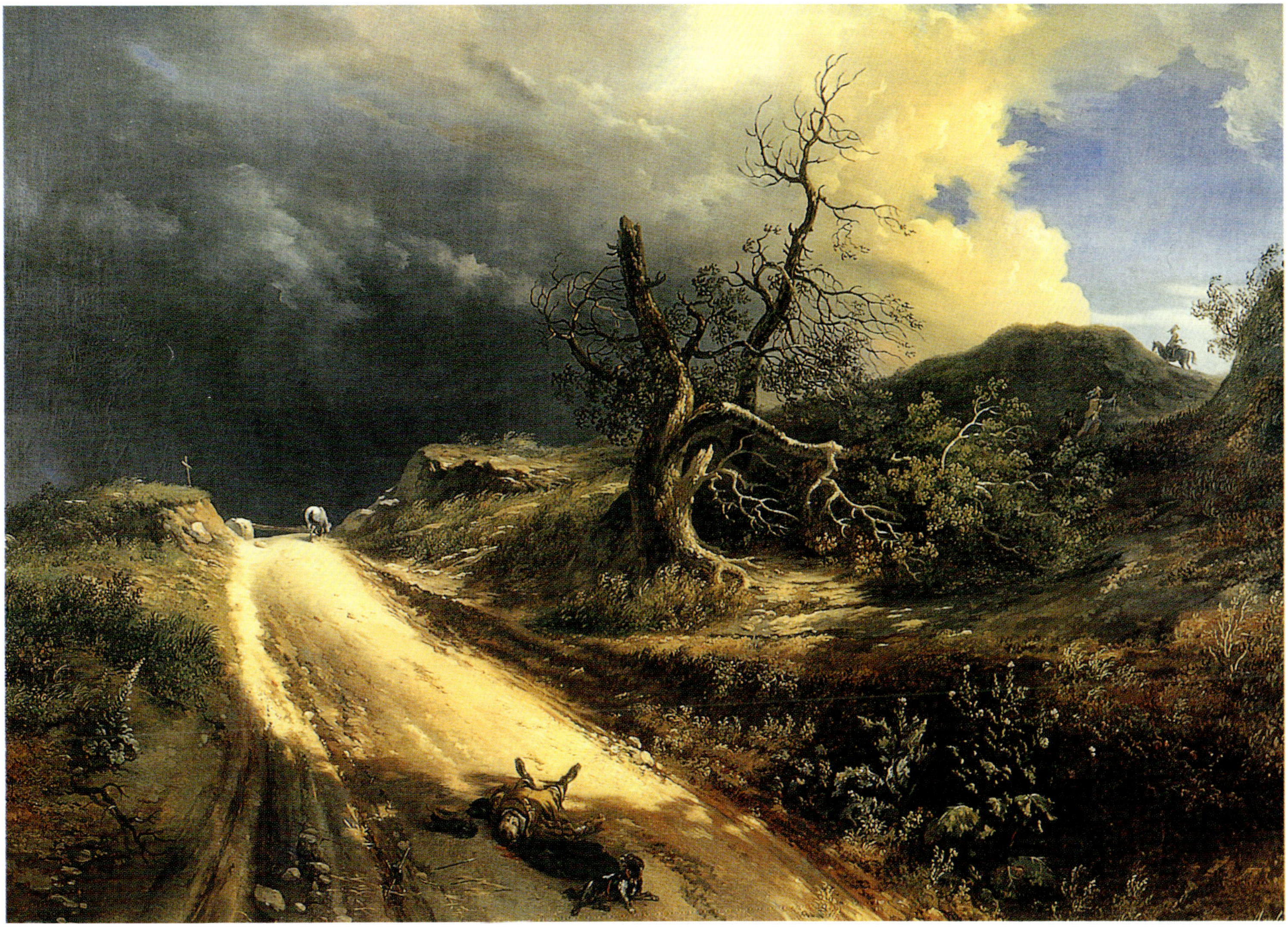

Francesco Hayez, *Portrait of Massimo d'Azeglio*, detail, 1864. Milan, Brera Academy (in storage at the Modern Civic Art Gallery).

Massimo d'Azeglio
Vendetta
1835
canvas
Milan, Brera Pinacoteca (in storage at the Gallery of Modern Art).

D'Azeglio's reputation as painter is linked to "historical landscapes", in which famous episodes taken from historical novels are depicted against the background of landscapes painted with extreme accuracy. His works reveal a Romantic taste for re-evocation of the national past along with a surprising familiarity with the picturesque tradition. "The Dutch-Flemish school", he stated, "populated its paintings only with shepherds and animals. I have called to my aid paladins, errant knights and damsels. In literature this was no novelty; in landscape painting it was".

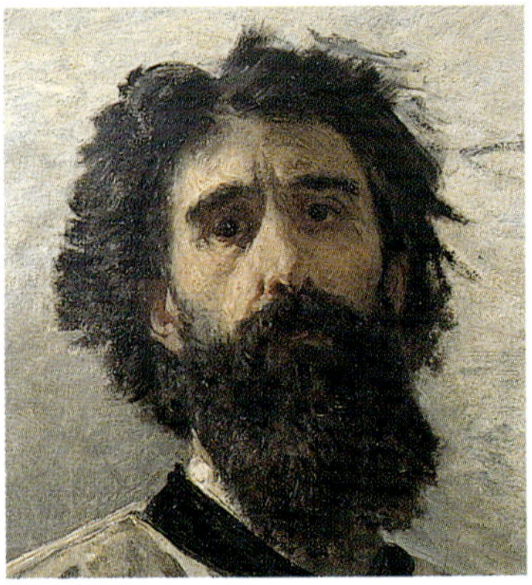

Domenico Morelli

(Naples 1823 – 1901)

A brilliant, cultured artist, Morelli had a particularly significant and well-articulated development. After training at the Naples Academy he soon came into contact with the Florentine artists of the Caffè Michelangelo. In the early 1850s Morelli became the outstanding representative of the romantic Neapolitan school, with paintings of historical subjects conceived in the manner of Hayez. At Paris in 1855 to visit the great International Exposition, he was struck by the surprisingly imitative attitudes displayed by the painters then in vogue. This was followed by a period in which, while still faithful to the historical theme, the artist placed special emphasis on detail. Morelli's last stage was marked by the increasingly forceful emergence of symbolic attitudes and themes, and the painter came to occupy a place not far from pre-Raphaelite and German-Roman tendencies.

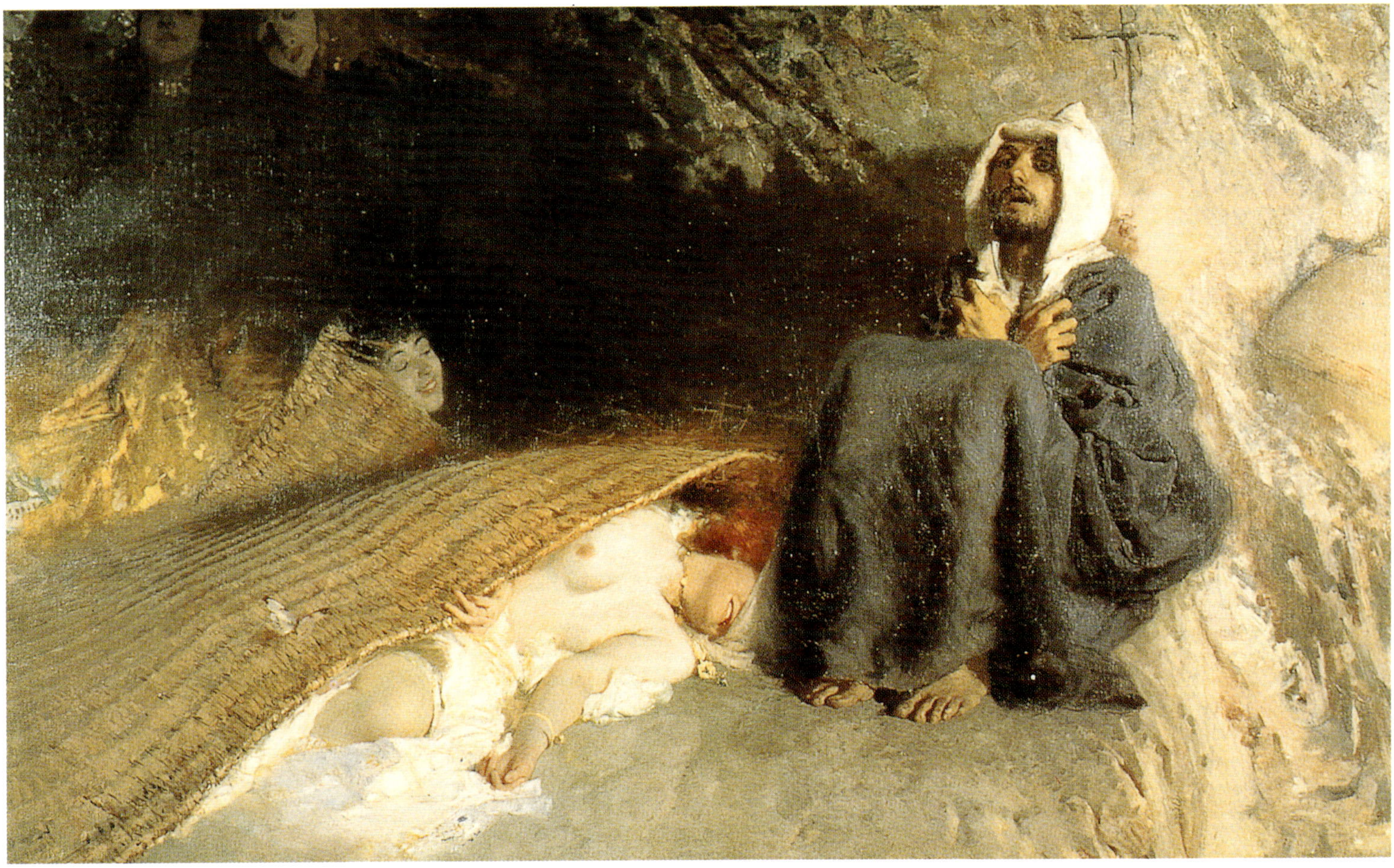

Domenico Morelli, *Self-portrait*, detail, 1860 c. Florence, Uffizi Gallery.

Domenico Morelli
The Temptation of St Anthony
1878
canvas
Rome, National Gallery of Modern Art.

In the final stage of his career Morelli was increasingly interested in mystical/religious themes on the one hand, ethnographic ones on the other. To broaden his knowledge of monotheist religions in the Mediterranean area he assiduously studied the Old and New Testaments and the Koran. With his background as painter of ideas, he executed paintings with the objective of extreme verisimilitude. The historical episode takes place in the most normal daily circumstances, provoking effects of alienation. The *Temptation of St Anthony* can be broken down into the various studies at its origin: studies of Arab or Middle Eastern costume in the figure of the saint, studies of rocks in the surrounding landscape, studies of the nude and of gold-work in the figure of the first temptress, lying on the ground half-concealed by a mat, and studies of fabrics. Morelli varies his brushstrokes – in frequency, breadth, width – depending on the nature of the surface to be painted, whether tactile or relevant to the phenomena of reflected light. He performs as virtuoso of the brush, displaying the vast range of mimetic effects of which he is a master.

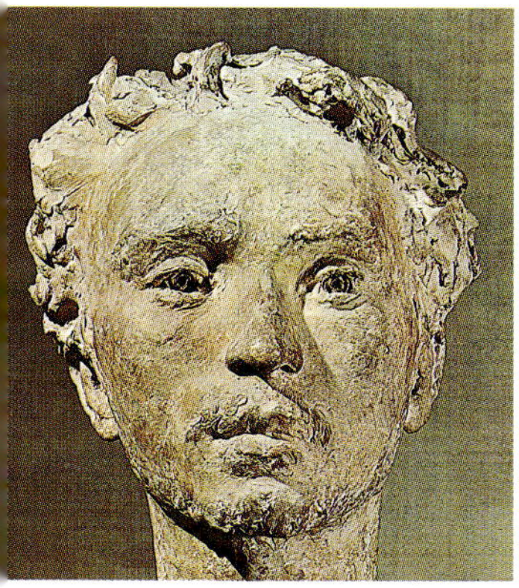

Francesco Paolo Michetti

(Tocco Casauria, Pescara, 1851 – Francavilla al Mare, Chieti, 1929)

A pupil of Domenico Morelli at the Royal Institute of Fine Arts in Naples, Michetti came into contact with the Parisian artistic scene and with major galleries starting from 1871 – it was De Nittis to introduce him first to Reutlinger, then to the Maison Goupil. He painted in the manner of Fortuny, displaying an abbreviated, sure technique and surprising illusionist effects, with motifs that were anecdotal and emotionally appealing. As professor at the same Naples Royal Institute of Fine Arts starting in 1878, he was extremely attentive to what was happening around him, visiting and participating in exhibitions held in the major cities of Europe – Paris, Munich, Vienna and Berlin. His paintings were exhibited at the first Venice Biennale, held in 1895, and the four following ones. Starting from the 1880s Michetti dedicated himself mainly to photography.

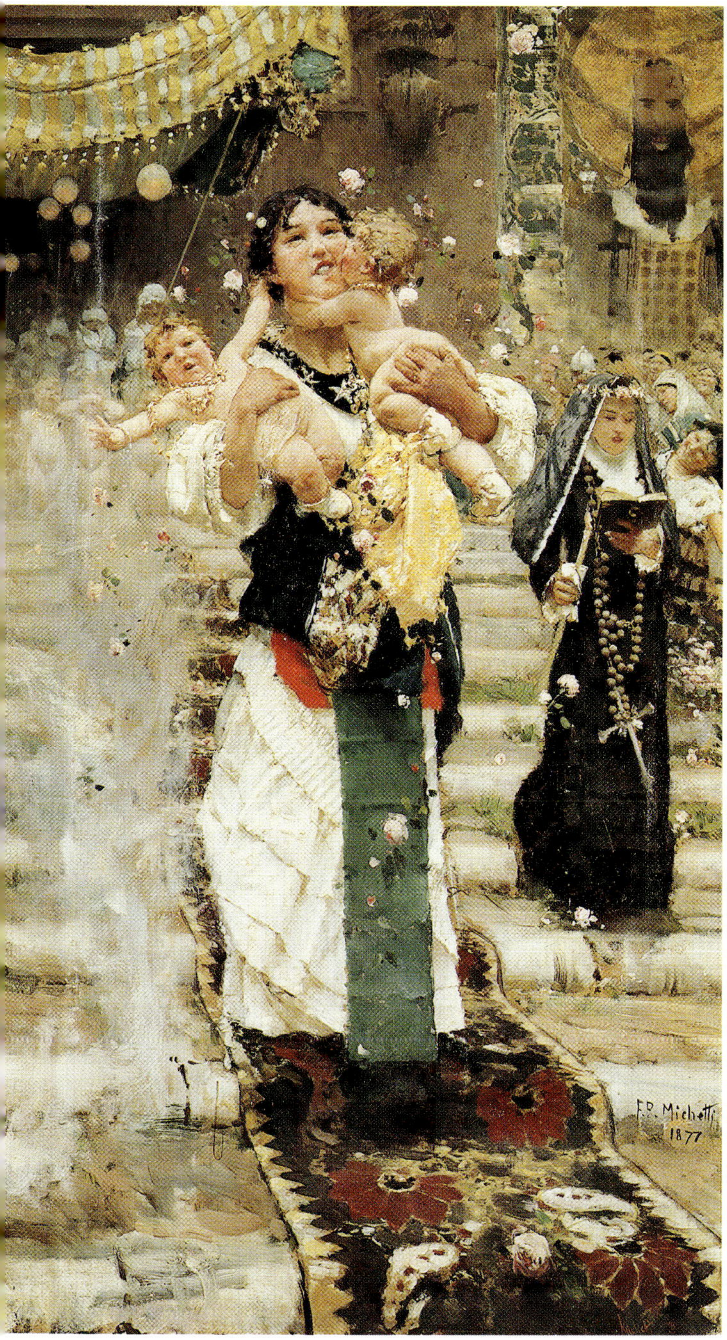

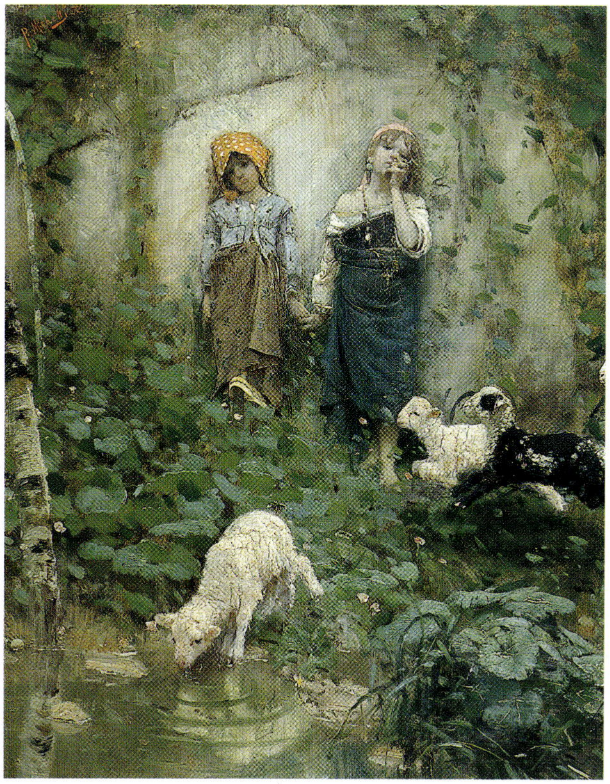

Vincenzo Gemito,
Portrait of Michetti,
detail, 1873.

Francesco Paolo Michetti
The Corpus Domini Procession at Chieti
signed and dated 1877
canvas
Piacenza, Civic Museum.

Exposed to cosmopolitan modes and tendencies, the artist remained closely linked to the land of his birth, whose popular customs and religious traditions he studied with the attention of an ethnographer. The Abruzzi was for him what the rural regions of France had been for the previous generation of French painters. Religious rites and trappings, objects of popular craftsmanship, even the regional features of faces and bodies attracted the artist's attention. The painting brings together and puts on scene a multiplicity of observations – of "snapshots", it might even be said.

Francesco Paolo Michetti
Shepherdesses
signed and dated 1872
panel
Florence, Pitti Palace, Gallery of Modern Art.

Two shepherdesses pose on the banks of stream, where lambs come down to drink. The light is opaque, artificial. The image seems to have been assembled in the studio from various fragments observed from life.

Giuseppe Valadier

(Rome 1762 – 1839)

Son of a goldsmith and bronze smelter, Valadier was to emancipate the profession of architect from its customary task of constructing individual buildings. With him the architect became urban planner. Laying aside the guise of exquisite master of elegance, he began to design not only façades and balconies, capitals and gardens, but modes of communication, patterns of collective behavior. Well-versed in the traditions of classical architecture and of Palladio – he was for many years director of important archaeological works, responsible among other things for restoring the Arch of Titus – and simultaneously open to French experience, Valadier directed the most important neoclassical projects carried out in Rome, from the façade of San Pantaleo to the Casina Valadier, from the rearrangement of Piazza del Popolo to the reconstruction of the Valle Theater, and to the façade of San Rocco.

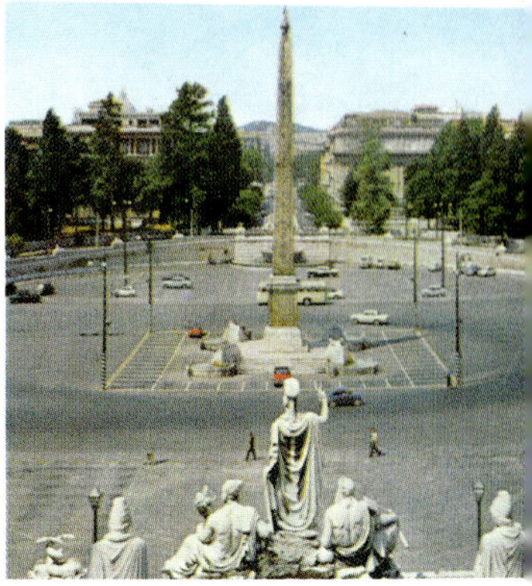

Giuseppe Valadier, *Piazza del Popolo* in Rome, 1816-22.

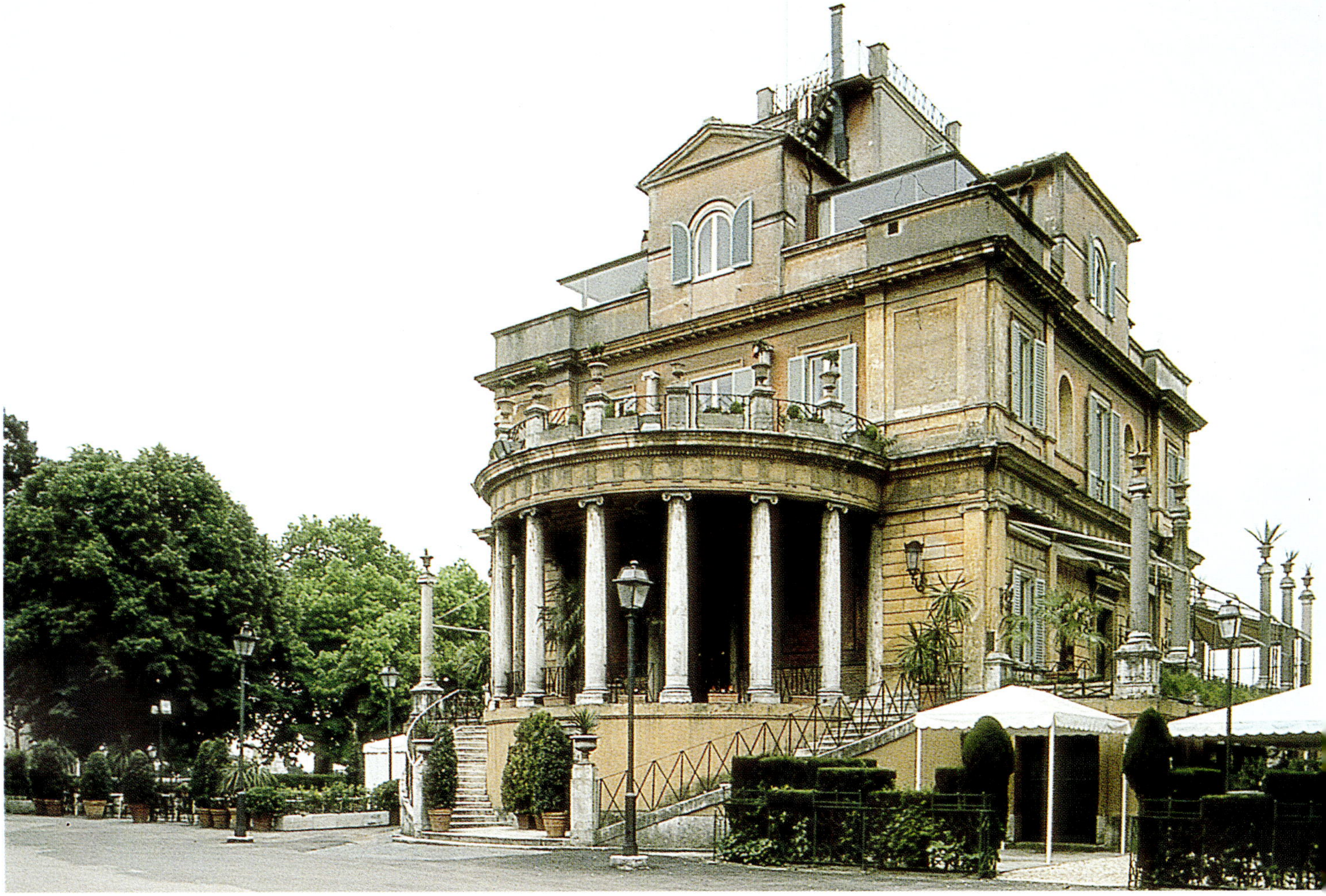

Giuseppe Valadier
Casina Valadier
c. 1830
Rome.

In designing Piazza del Popolo as we see it today, Valadier revealed to the utmost his talent as urban planner, skillfully arranging symmetries and vanishing points in perspective to confer on the square a vastness more apparent than real. He terraced the Pincio hill to blend the work of nature and that of man in a magnificent scenic effect. In the Casina Valadier his role was more traditional, although he gave the building a semi-circular colonnade that superbly overlooks the open area below. The body of the building, with its dynamic volumes, refrains from any tendency toward the monumental.

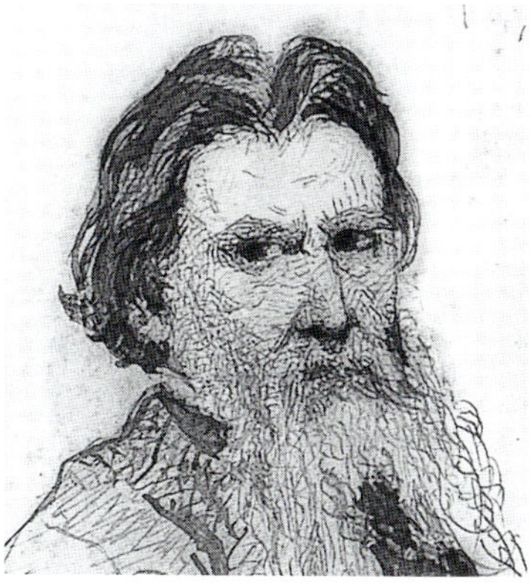

Giovanni Dupré

(Siena 1817 – Florence 1882)

Trained at the Siena Academy, Dupré emerged as an artist in the 1840s, carrying the cultured, tempered naturalism of Bartolini toward cruder effects. An eclectic artist of wide renown, capable of conceiving and accomplishing works very different in nature, clientele, and function – the historical monument, the devotional statue, the female nude – Dupré was, in the eyes of his contemporaries, the heir to the great Italian plastic tradition. A member of important international juries, he visited the exhibitions held in Paris and Vienna, presenting his own sculptures although declaring his disappointment with the "monstrous agglomerations of products, machines, raw materials, edible materials, drinkable liquids, religious utensils, war machines" among which the few figurative works seemed lost, in an age distinguished by the triumph of industry.

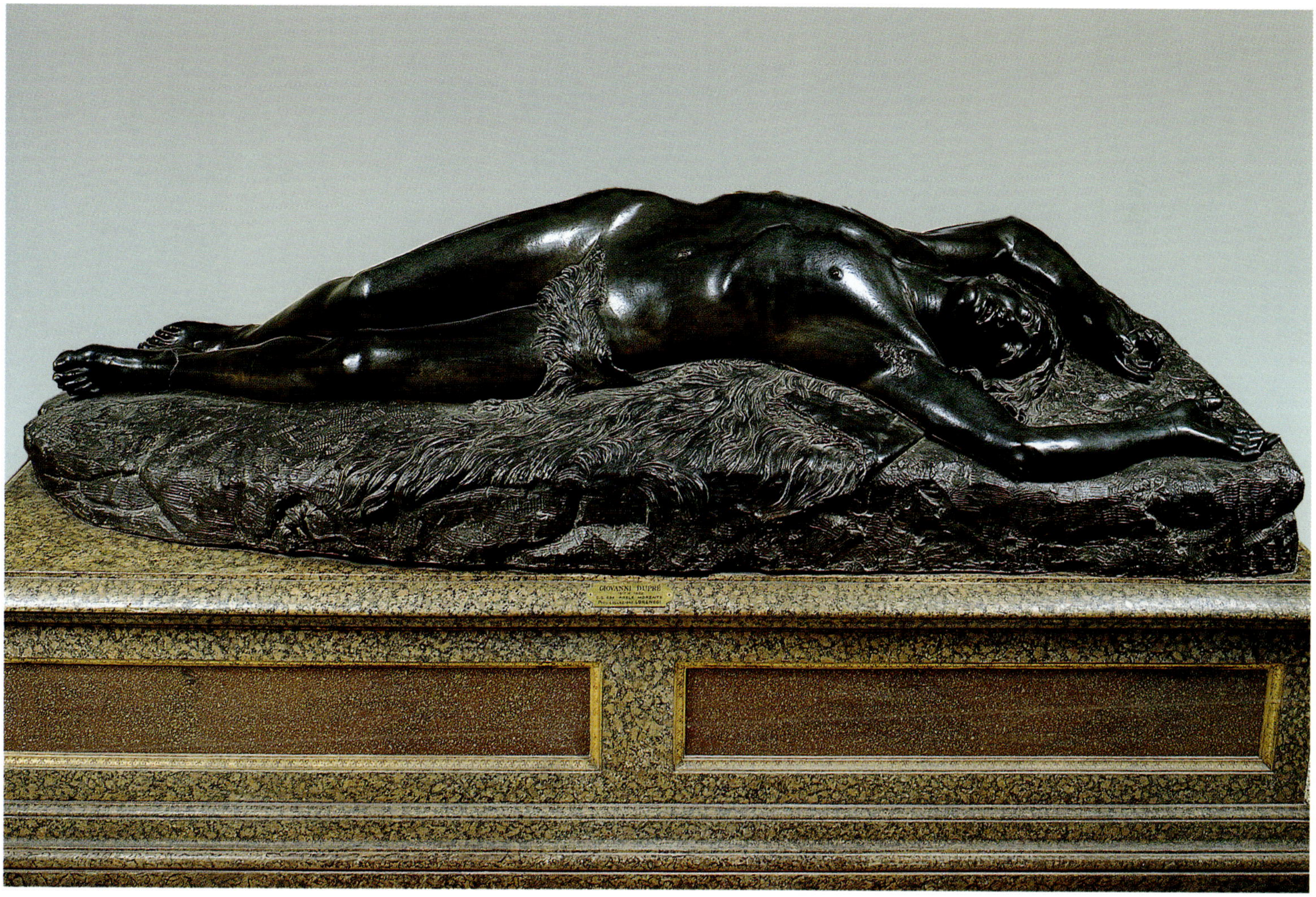

Giovanni Dupré,
Self-portrait in half-bust, detail, w.d.
Fiesole, Dupré Museum.

Giovanni Dupré
Death of Abel
1842
Florence, Pitti Palace
Gallery of Modern Art.

Dupré himself, in his *Writings on Art and Autobiographical Memoirs*, relates how, disappointed at not being granted "a pension for sculpture" with a ten-year duration, he conceived of *Abel*, his first *succès de scandale*. Determined to win success, "I tried to think of a new, serious, appealing subject in which to put my whole heart, my strength, my will, my hopes, everything; and I found it". With it he also found "good movement and correct expression". Presented to the public, *Abel* was severely criticized as resembling too closely the "real", and was actually thought by the professors of the Academy to be cast from a mould.

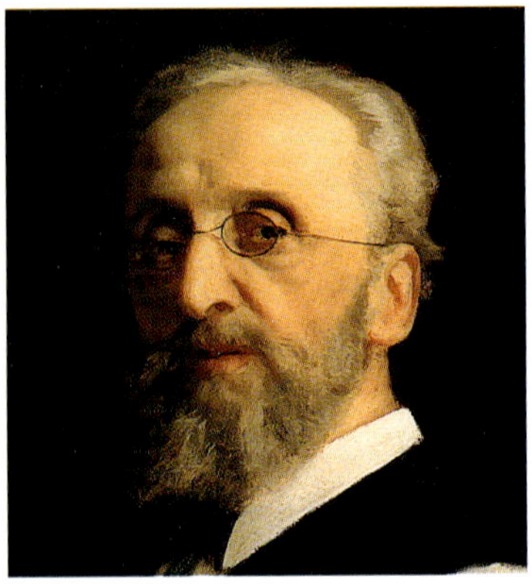

Antonio Ciseri

(Ronco, Canton Ticino, 1821 – Florence 1891)

Trained at the Florence Academy of Fine Arts and first close to the positions of Bezzuoli, Ciseri later evolved in the direction of a refined Purism. A cultured artist with a wealth of acquaintances among artists – in 1867 he met the pre-Raphaelite William Holman Hunt, and in 1870 Alexandre Cabanel, one of the French painters most in vogue at the time – Ciseri showed himself well aware of the research then being carried out in the international academic world. His most ambitious compositions, mainly of devotional nature, were scrupulously prepared, reflecting the goal of exactness in depicting furnishings, costumes, and architecture. The painter, in his case, was also an archaeologist. An acclaimed portrait painter – even Cavour and Umberto I posed for him – Ciseri had a career starred with victories, such as the gold medal awarded him the Universal Exposition of Vienna in 1873.

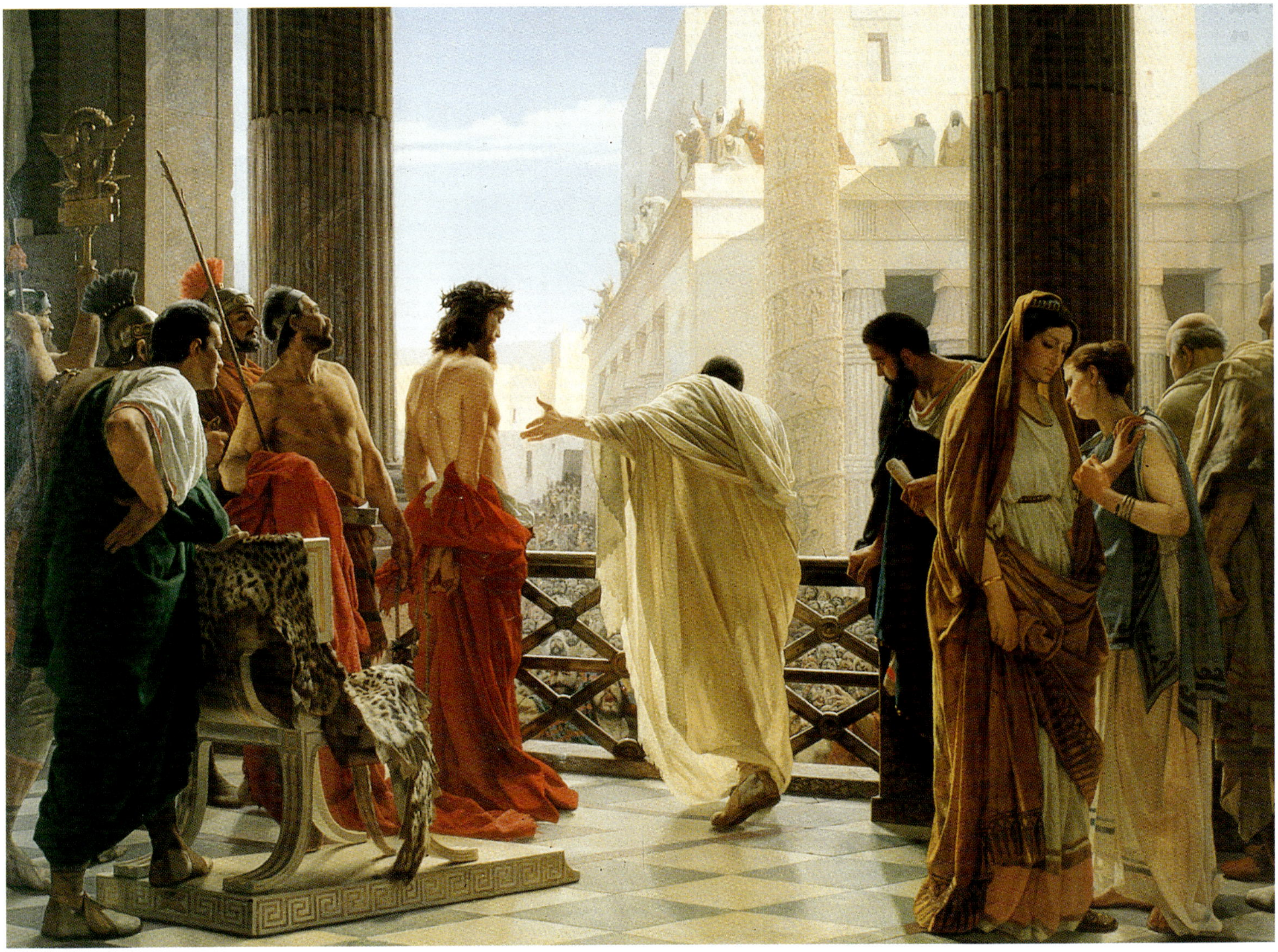

Antonio Ciseri,
Self-portrait, detail,
c. 1885-90, Florence,
Uffizi Gallery.

Antonio Ciseri
Ecce Homo
1880-91
canvas
Florence, Pitti Palace,
Gallery of Modern Art.

Commissioned in 1870 and preceded by preparatory studies and sketches, the *Ecce Homo* is clearly the masterpiece desired and planned for years. Ciseri worked on it up to his death, expectant of the success that the painting, exhibited posthumously, would in fact attain. In accomplishing this work the artist placed painting in explicit competition with photography. The foreground of the picture, showing Pilate in the act of offering the crowd to exchange Barabbas for Jesus, is strikingly realistic.

Alberto Pasini

(Busseto, Parma, 1826 – Cavoretto, Turin, 1899)

Lithographer and owner of a private atelier of painting in Parma, Pasini moved to Paris in 1851. Having seen the works of Eugène Fromentin and the Barbizon landscape artists, he painted landscapes according to a romantic/naturalistic taste. He shared a studio with Théodore Chassériau, who, called upon to participate in a diplomatic mission to Persia, asked Pasini to take his place. Between 1855 and 1856 the young artist thus had the chance to visit Turkey, Egypt, Syria, and the Arabian peninsula. In his travel notebooks Pasini revealed his gifts as keen observer of costumes, architecture and landscapes. An artist of acknowledged fame and a great traveler, Pasini participated in the change in orientalism that took place around mid-century and was consolidated in the following decades: the romantic evocation of a fantastic Orient was superseded by a taste for ethnographic reporting.

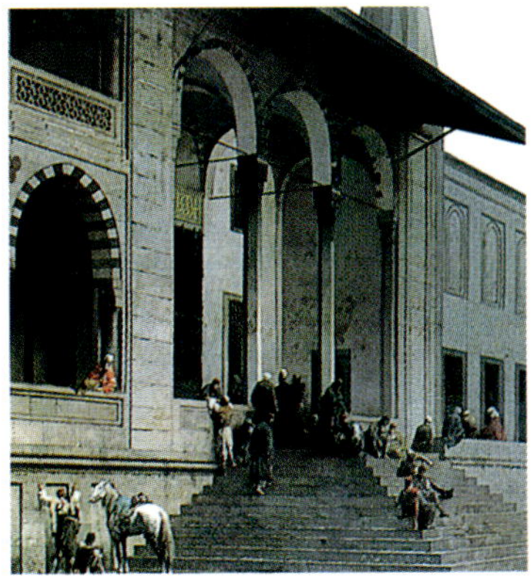

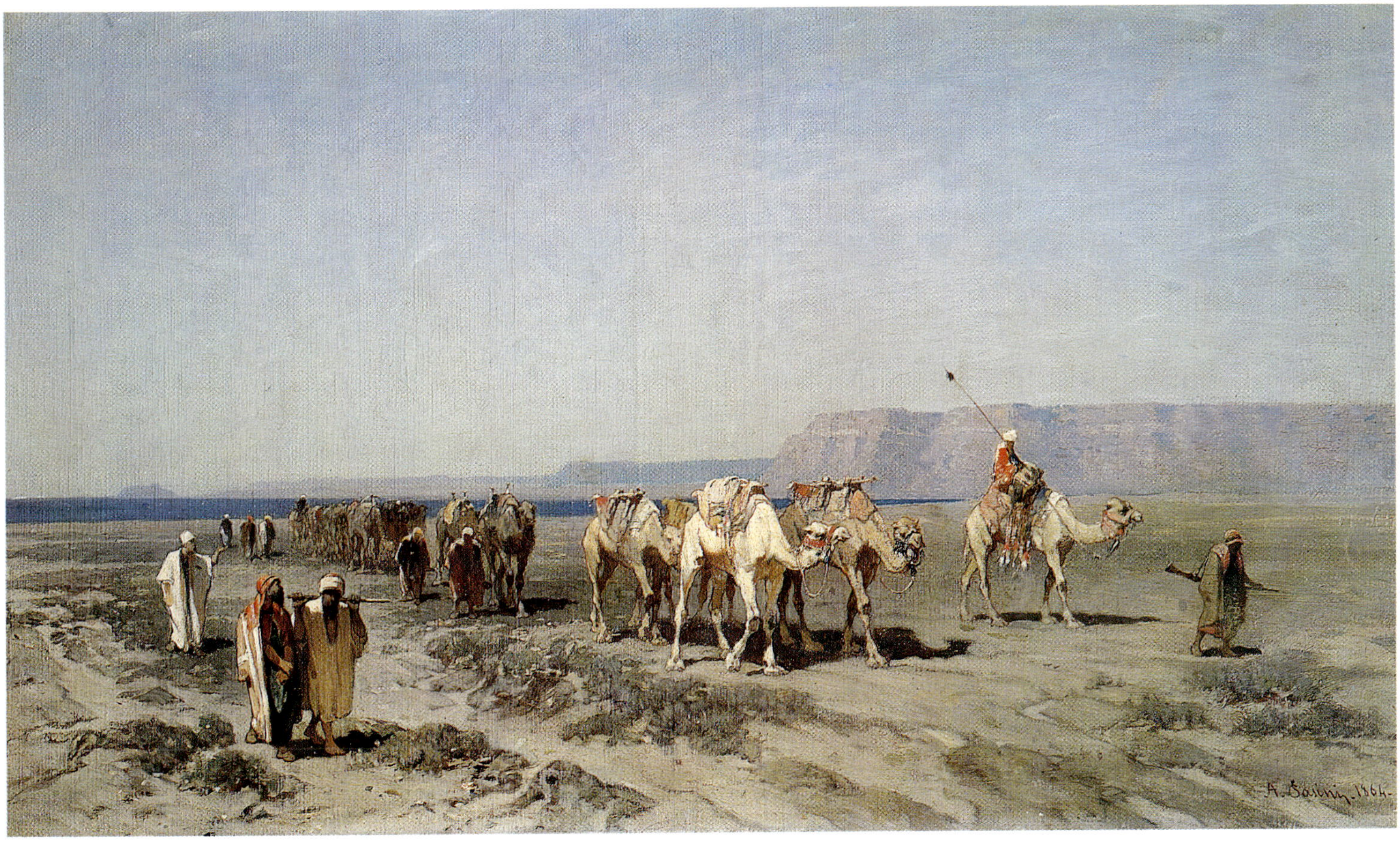

Alberto Pasini
Caravan to the Red Sea
signed and dated 1864
canvas
Florence, Pitti Palace, Gallery of Modern Art.

Pasini was in Egypt in 1860, Turkey and Greece in 1867, Constantinople from 1867 to 1869, Spain and Syria in 1869, and Asia Minor in 1873. His reputation as expert on the Southern Mediterranean and the Middle East was solidly established. One of the most popular motifs of the orientalist genre was the caravan, open to various elements of exotic fascination: the desert landscape, the costumes of the nomads, archaic and adventurous trade, often consisting of barter (blocks of salt, extremely useful to the sub-Sahara populations, were sometimes exchanged for precious stones and ivory).
A comparison between Orient and Occident is implicit. The apparent immobility of the former is contrasted, in the eyes of the "painter-travelers" and their contemporary public, with the industriousness of the

Alberto Pasini, *Door of the Yeni Djami Mosque at Constantinople*, detail, 1870.

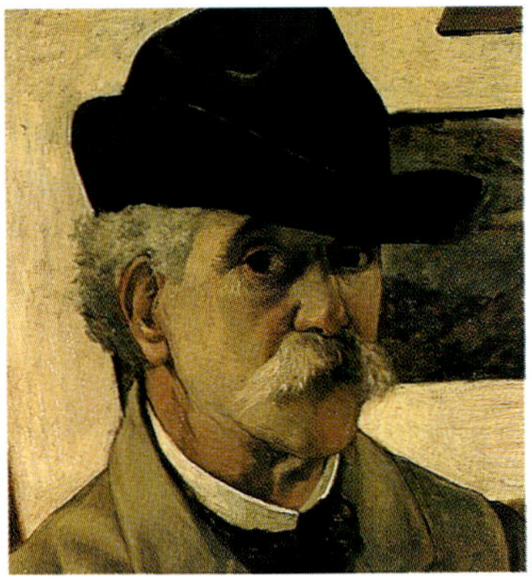

Giovanni Fattori

(Livorno 1825 – Florence 1908)

In Florence to study painting, Fattori was torn between the practice of art and patriotic activism. In 1859 he began a series of scenes of military life that won him his first acclaim, and he was always to remain interested in Risorgimental motifs. An habitué of the Caffè Michelangelo, he was among those who recognized the innovations of contemporary French painting – his chief reference point, at this date, was undoubtedly Degas. "In 1854 or '56", Fattori relates, "upon returning from Paris Serafino Tivoli [...] brought to us young artists an art that was entirely new [...], the first attempts of the *macchia*. Our program was, and is: reality as we see it and love it. Returning to the Quattrocento only with a new address". Professor at the Florence Academy in 1869, Fattori was in Paris in 1875. His fame grew with success in the technique of etching and engraving.

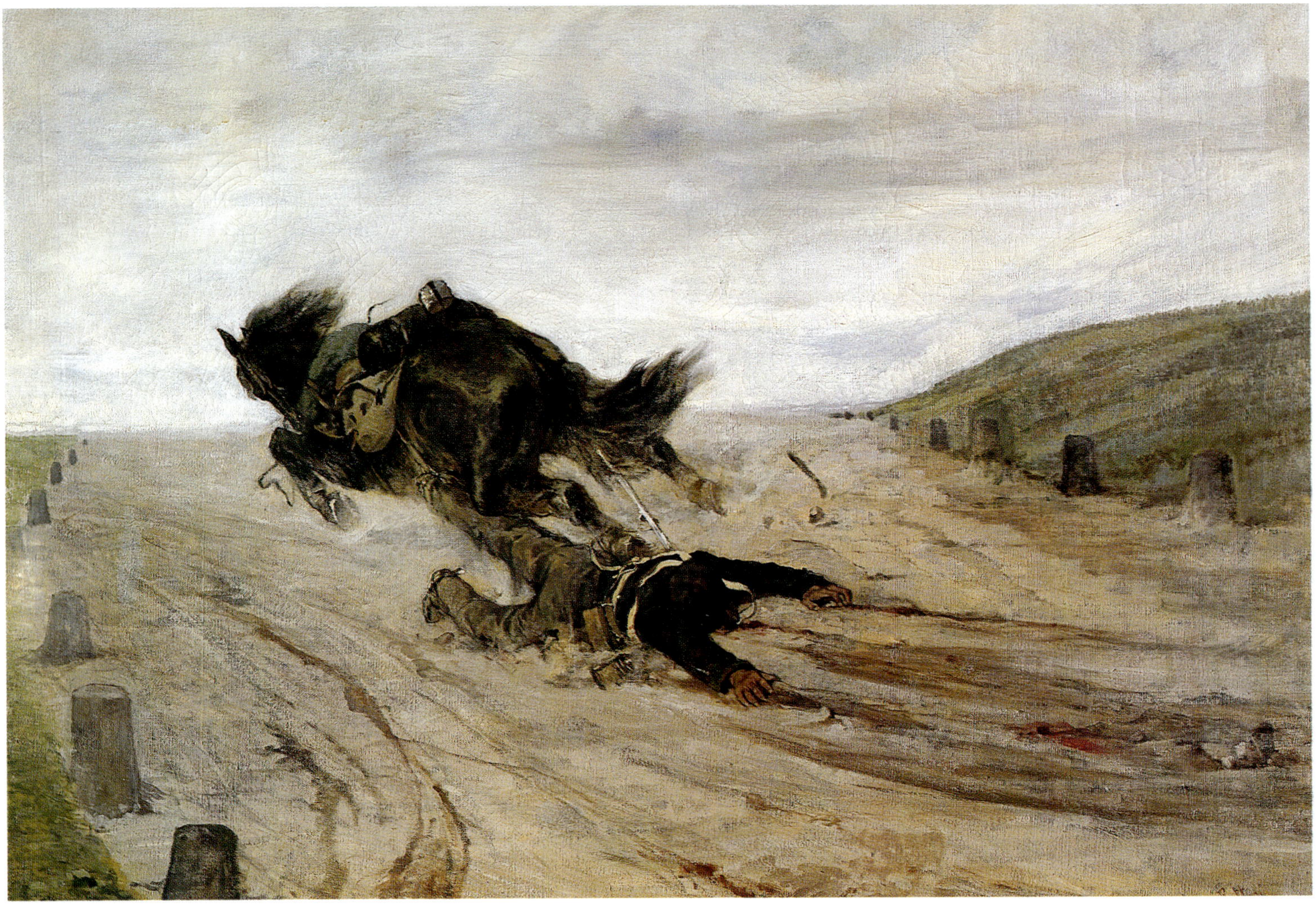

Giovanni Fattori,
Self-portrait, 1894.

Giovanni Fattori
Caught in the Stirrup
1880
canvas
Florence, Pitti Palace, Gallery of Modern Art.

This painting, as famous as it was controversial – already on the occasion of its first presentation to the public, in 1880, Fattori had been criticized for the soft and simultaneously sinister nature of the image – appears somehow detached from the production of Fattori the painter of battles. An image of death both dismal and heroic, it celebrates the force of the horse while portraying with pathetic but macabre touches the horrifying fate of the soldier. Decades after the Risorgimental mobilization the artist considers the event in terms that are in some way fatal. The elements of the drama are biological rather than historical/social: the survival instinct, flight and escape, fear; the quiet landscape with its low horizon, desolate and almost primordial.

Giovanni Fattori
Cousin Argia
1861
cardboard
Florence, Pitti Palace, Gallery of Modern Art.

A study of harmony in gray-green and ochre, the portrait approaches the model according to the canons of intimism that pervaded French painting of the mid-19th century. Not by coincidence have the names of Corot and Nino Costa, a refined follower of Corot, friend and admirer of Fattori, frequently been mentioned in connection with it. Intensely aware of the artist's presence, the woman gazes toward us with a decided, almost piqued attitude. The painting, rather than dwelling on the unique traits of an individual existence, fixes the image of a type, a feminine character with strongly regional features.

Giovanni Fattori
Mending the Nets
c. 1872
canvas

The artist aims here at the apparently facile execution and skill of the narrator of sketches – a skill which, when resolved on the compositional level (as in the case of the strange cap worn by the net-mender standing on the right: a simple biomorphic silhouette; or the "eye" with which the nets regard us, at the lower center of the composition; and more generally the drawing of the figures) is reminiscent of Mannerist grotesques and Japanese linear caprices. The format is that of a woodcut rather than a veduta, a loose two-dimensional manner that heightens the emphasis on borders, *aplats* of color; here and there, appearing more as expedients than as convincingly integrated elements, are concessions to the third dimension – the stick tilted to suggest depth, the terracotta.

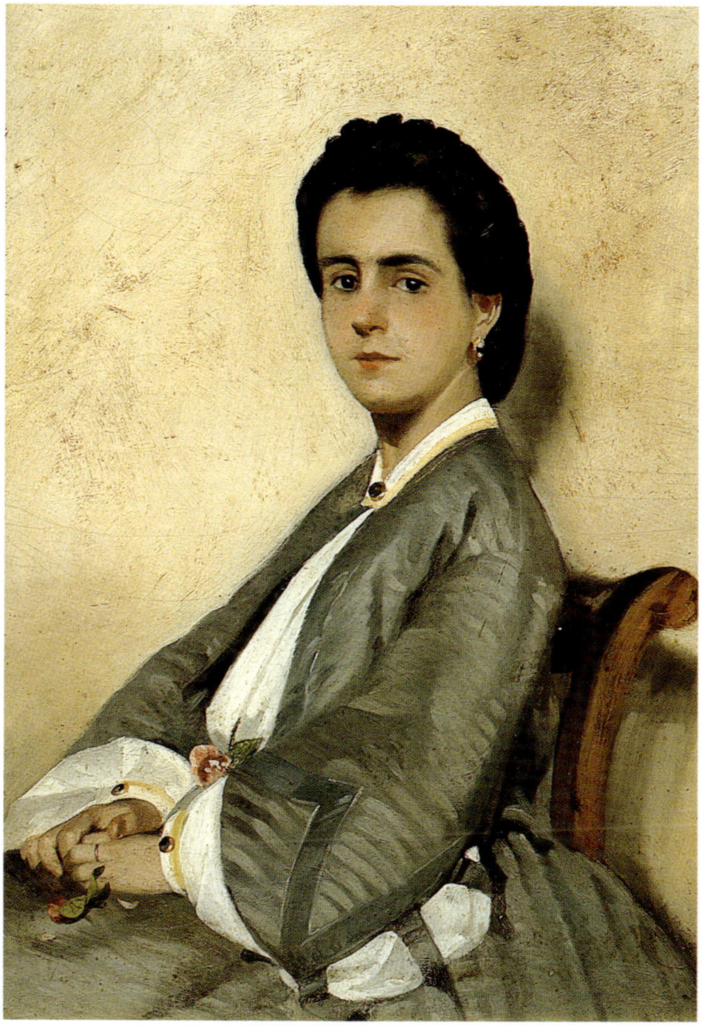

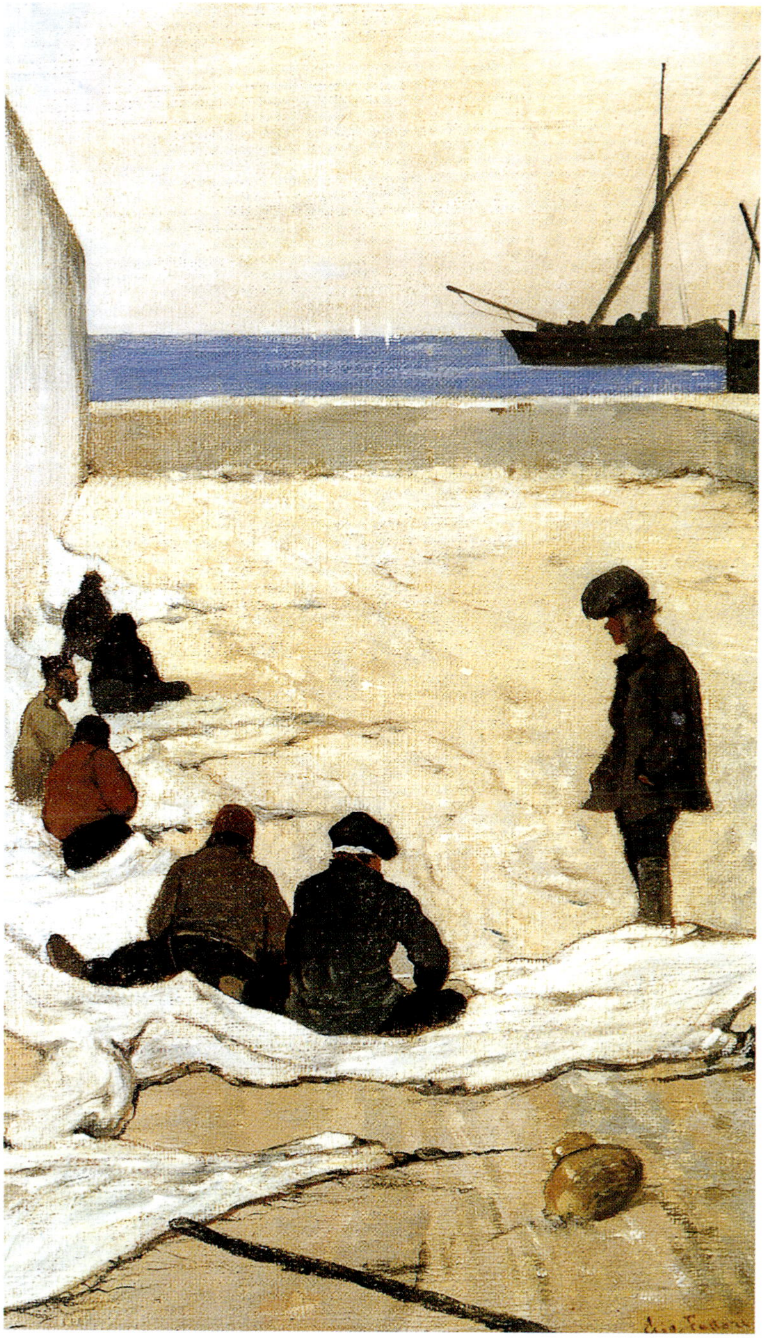

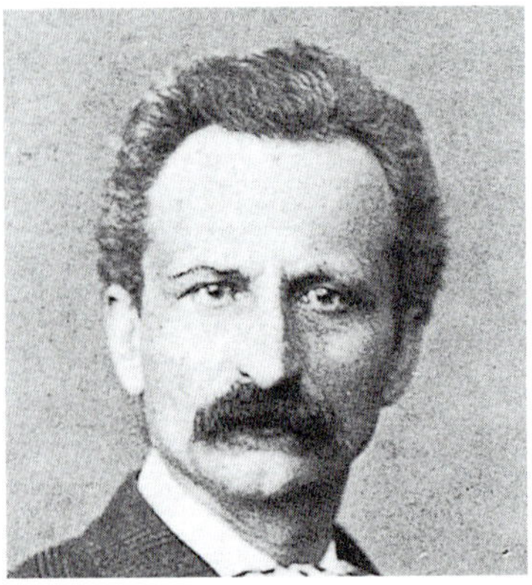

Silvestro Lega

(Modigliana, Forlì, 1826 – Florence 1895)

A pupil first of Bezzuoli at the Florence Academy of Fine Arts and then, still at Florence, of Mussini, he served his apprenticeship under the sign of romantic historical painting. A republican, he fought in 1848 as volunteer at Curtatone and Montanara. He then began a series of compositions having as subject the Bersaglieri. The war for Italian independence was for him a war of the people. A frequenter of the Caffè Michelangelo, he gradually turned in the direction of the Macchiaioli. Dating from the 1860s are many of Lega's most famous paintings, characterized by intimist themes and a refined, harmonious palette. His predilection for soft borders and light colours reflects his Purist apprenticeship. Starting from the 1880s he painted landscapes of the countryside around Livorno and portraits of peasants, acknowledging a greater importance to colour.

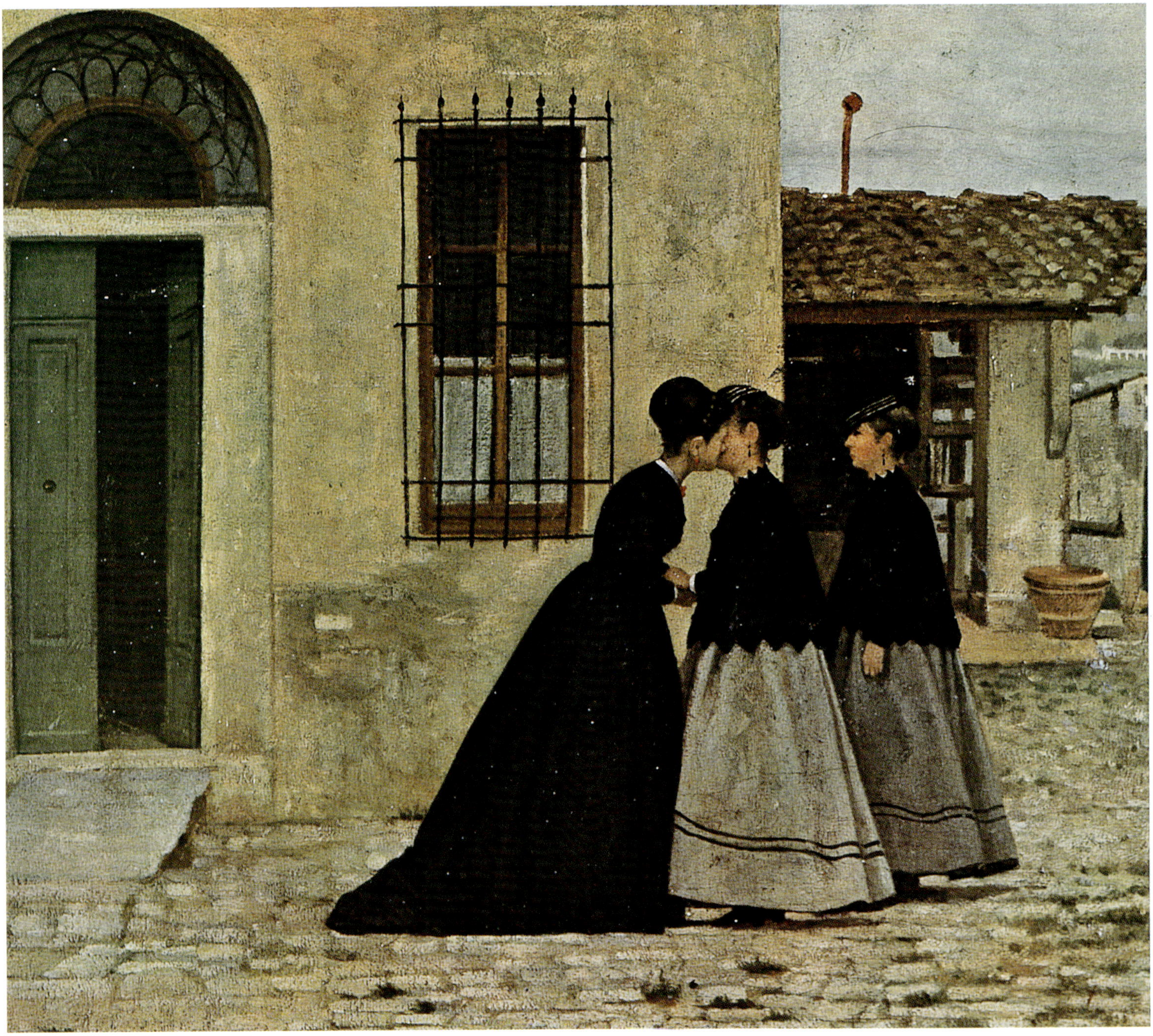

Silvestro Lega
A Visit
1868
canvas, detail
Rome, National Gallery of Modern Art.

A barely disguised variation on the theme of the *Visitation*, the painting, so discrete in appearance, has the clarity of a manifesto. For the artist it is a question of returning to the origins of the Italian artistic tradition, interpreting them in the light of contemporary landscapes and costumes. When simultaneously viewed reductively as a "Verist" painting, *A Visit* is remarkable for its deliberate ingenuousness. "It has a touch of the puerile", wrote Camillo Boito in 1877, "there is a cottage with an arched door and certain windows that seem to have been produced after much study by the hand of an ingenious child; [...], the manner has a certain primitive simplicity which at first glance seems clumsy but which little by little persuades and pleases".

Silvestro Lega
An Afternoon
1868
canvas
Milan, Brera Pinacoteca.

The subject of the painting is a pause, a glimpse of a quiet familiar moment within a women's community: a minor rite, it could be said, considering how Lega attempts to reveal, hour by hour, the natural religious sentiment that pervades existence in conditions of simplicity. Painted with apparent looseness in the parts depicting vegetation and landscape, *An Afternoon* is subtly allegorical. If the three central figures, the girl, the young woman, and the lady with the fan refer to the ages of life, the lady herself, who turns toward the maidservant, seems to invite us to considerations that are both religious and social.

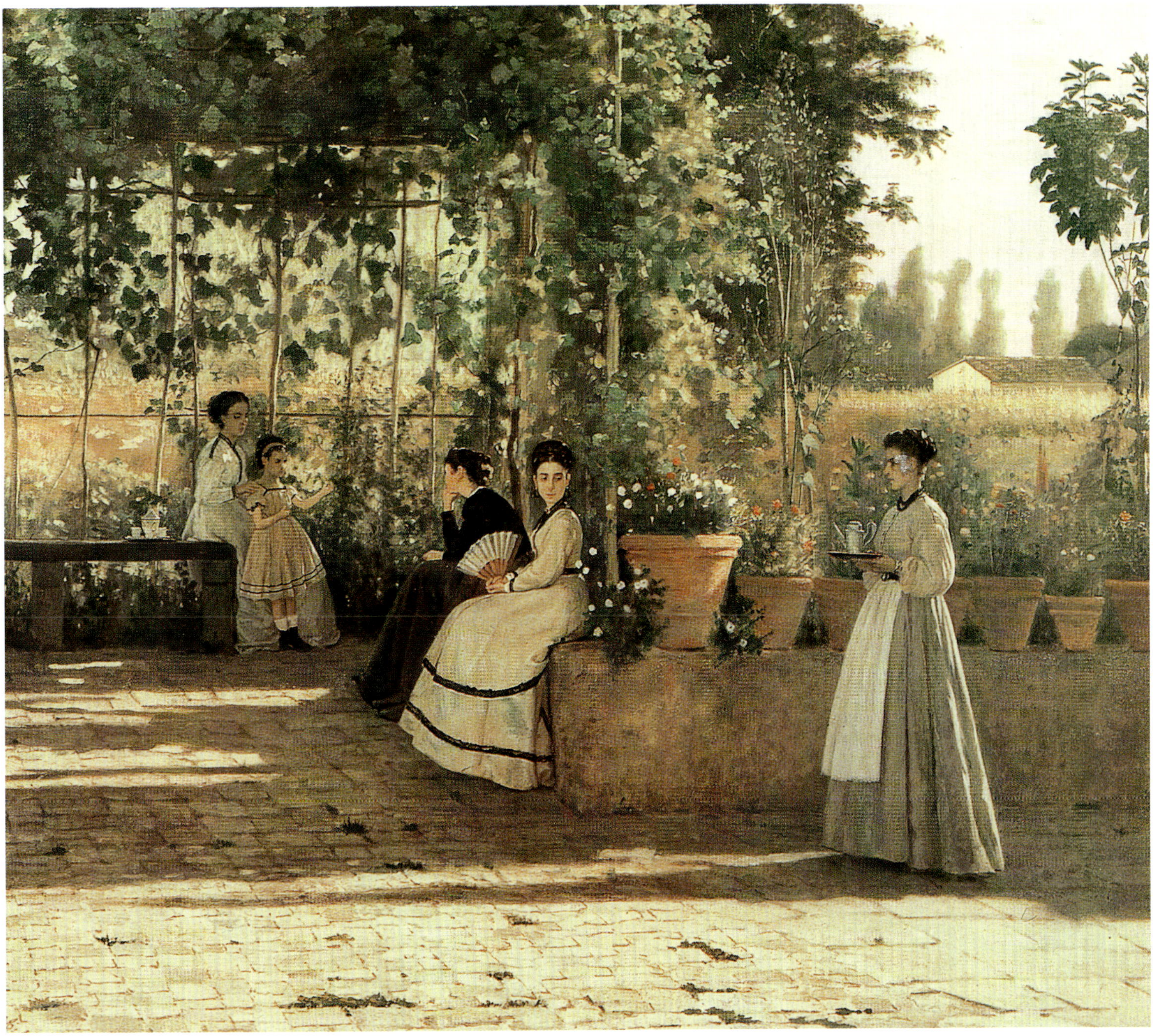

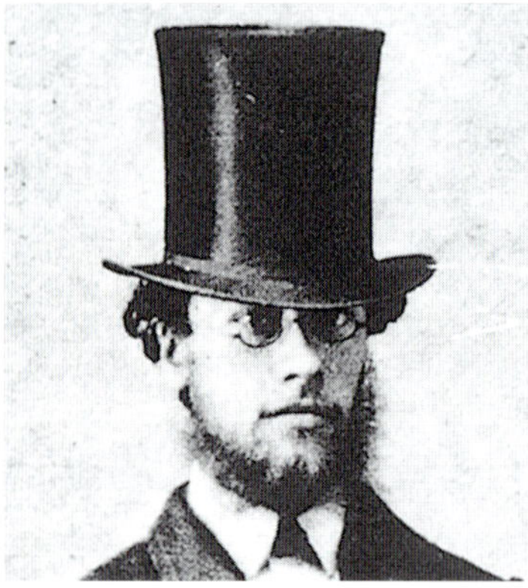

Telemaco Signorini

(Florence 1835 – 1901)

The son of a refined veduta painter in Granducal Florence, Signorini painted and drew even as a child. He copied Dutch and Flemish landscapes in Florentine collections, inspired by them with a lasting predilection for the typical and the local. His apprenticeship was Romantic; painting landscapes and views of the Tuscan countryside, he experimented with the historical genre. An assiduous frequenter of the Caffè Michelangelo, he turned increasingly strongly in the naturalistic direction and adopted the technique of the *macchia*. Representation was entrusted to an assembly of tones, in the absence of any chiaroscuro elaboration. A volunteer with Garibaldi in 1859, Signorini was in Paris in 1861, when national unification had now been achieved. His passionate homage to regional landscapes, costumes and populations is similar to that of the Barbizon landscape artists.

Telemaco Signorini
Leith
1881
canvas
Florence, Pitti Palace, Gallery of Modern Art.

Signorini visited Edinburgh in the summer of 1881 – Leith is one of the two ports of the Scottish city – and during his visit drew some sketches which were to provide a basis for the painting. Far from being a simple snapshot, *Leith* is a sort of catalogue or repertoire of social types and costumes. We see a policeman, a young nurse, a man wearing a kilt, a water-seller, a vivandier. The large advertising poster completes a narrative related under the sign of the picturesque. An eye-catching invitation to consumerism plastered onto the wall of an old, decaying house, it serves as optimistic emblem of the intense and frequently dramatic transformations undergone by Great Britain in the Victorian age.

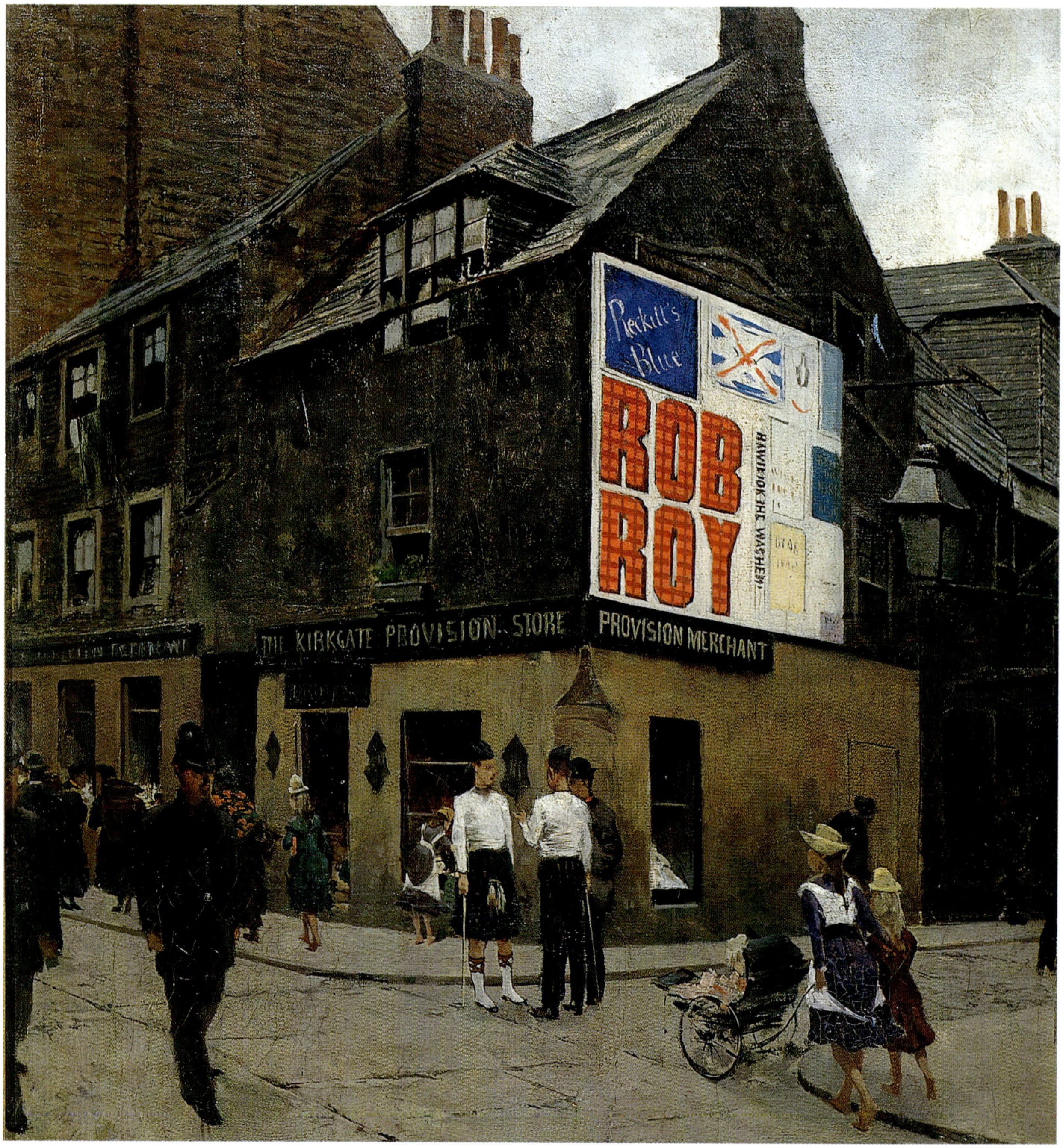

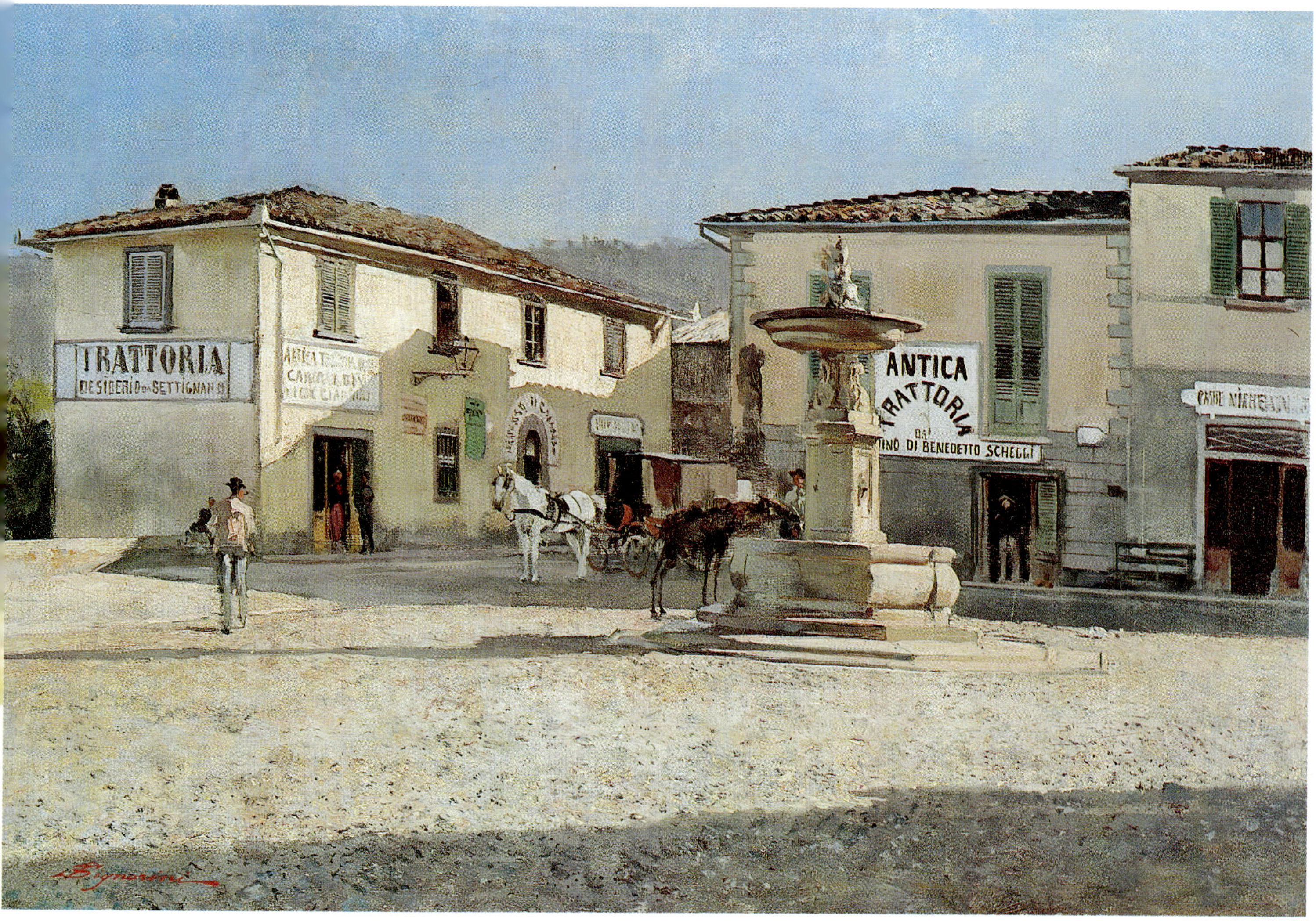

Telemaco Signorini
The Square in Settignano
c. 1881
canvas

The signs establish places and customs; they take the place of narration, it might be said. The village scene is painted almost like a still life. The individual elements have no mutual relationship, recalling the kit of an assembly set, or rather a sample collection of nostalgic goods, of old memories.

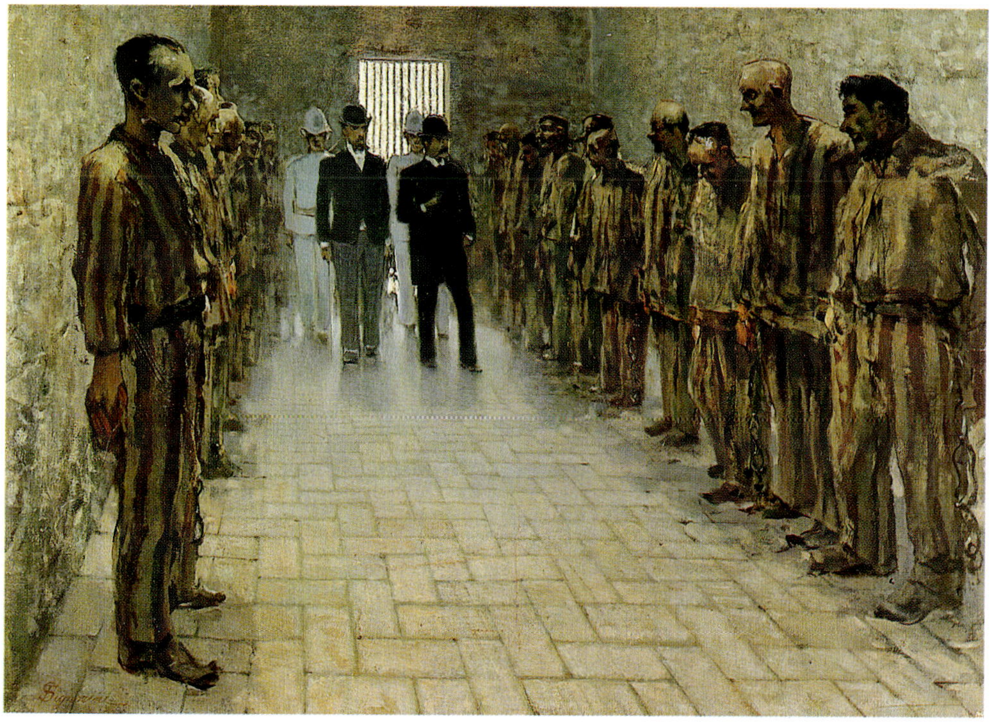

Telemaco Signorini
The Prison at Portoferraio
1894
canvas
Florence, Pitti Palace, Gallery of Modern Art.

Keen observer of the historical reality around him, as well as artist sensitive to social issues, Signorini visited the penitentiary at Portoferraio in 1888. Struck by the conditions of the prisoners, he painted the picture some years later, endowing it with a touch of humanitarian denouncement.

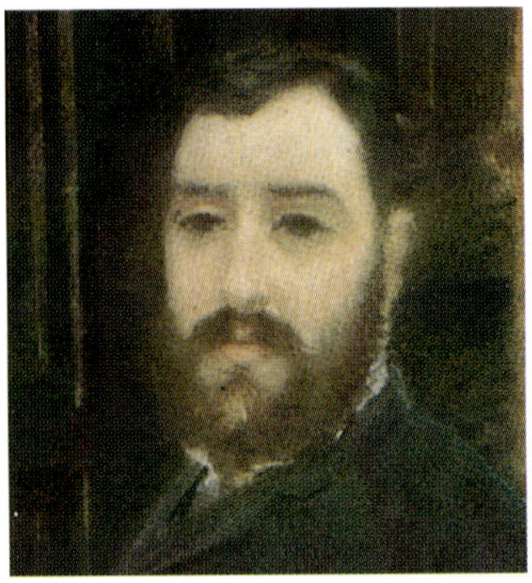

Giuseppe De Nittis

(Barletta 1846 – Saint-German-en-Laye 1884)

After training at the Naples Institute of Fine Arts, De Nittis painted landscapes *en plein air* which were appreciated by the Macchiaioli, encountered at Florence in 1867. Moving to Paris in 1868, the ambitious, talented painter made his home a meeting place for artists, intellectuals and collectors, and signed a contract with the Maison Goupil. Although his first Parisian success arrived thanks to costume paintings, De Nittis did not neglect landscapes or contemporary genre scenes. In 1874 he exhibited, although without strong conviction, with the Impressionists. His first pastels date from 1875. De Nittis won definitive recognition at the Exposition Universelle (1878). He was among the most acclaimed "painters of the elegant life" skilled at unusual angles and brilliant society chronicles. In perception and narrative power his paintings rivaled the contemporary novel.

Giuseppe De Nittis, *Self-portrait*, detail, autograph of Léontine De Nittis, dated 1884.

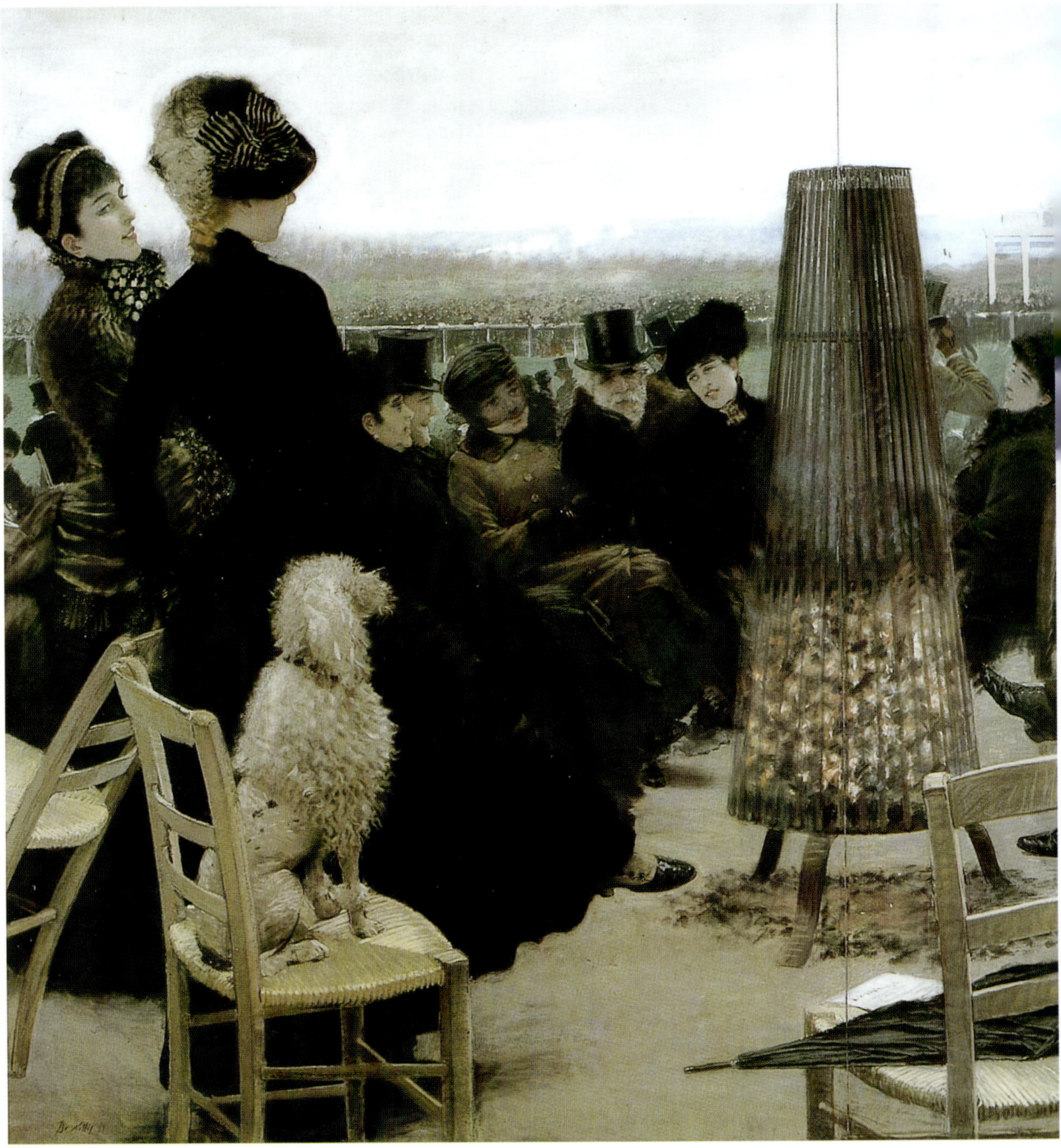

Giuseppe De Nittis
The Racetrack at Auteuil
1881
pastel, central panel of triptych
Rome, National Gallery of Modern Art.

In adopting the triptych form for his *Racetrack at Auteuil*, De Nittis effected a sort of consecration of the contemporary motif. Complimentary and refined, the composition boldly asks for the admiration of the public to which it is addressed. The great variety of types, situations and contexts portrayed reflects the objective of attaining a certain completeness. The artist plastically portrays a set of states of mind, sketches erotic-pathetic plots, displays a sample collection of high fashion clothing, alternates severity and frivolity – as demonstrated by the image of the brazier and the young woman warming her foot, with the poodle sitting near her. On the whole, the artist seems to offer himself in the dual role of *arbiter elegantarium* and confidant of high society.

Giuseppe De Nittis
The Racetrack at Auteuil
1881
pastel, side panels of triptych
Rome, National Gallery of Modern Art.

De Nittis' first compositions in pastel date from 1875. In abandoning oil painting for pastels, the artist attempted to resolve a problem felt by many of the painters who were his contemporaries, such as Caillebotte and Degas, Tissot and Gervex . The problem, which appeared even more urgent to De Nittis in view of his Italian origin, was that of keeping the drawing component intact while satisfying the modern taste for paintings of light, touch, and color.

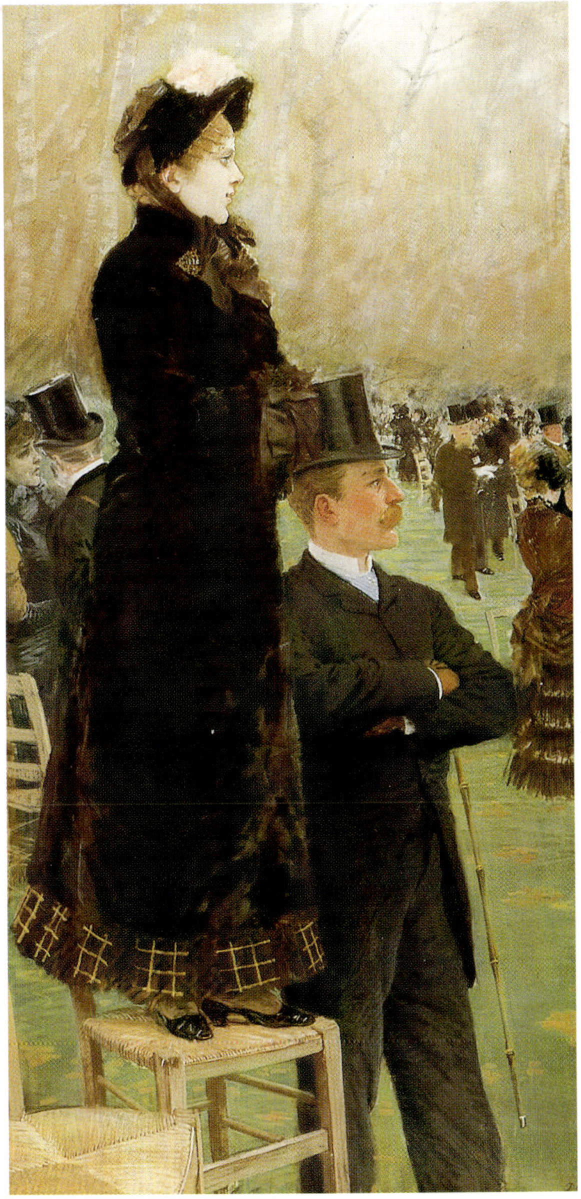

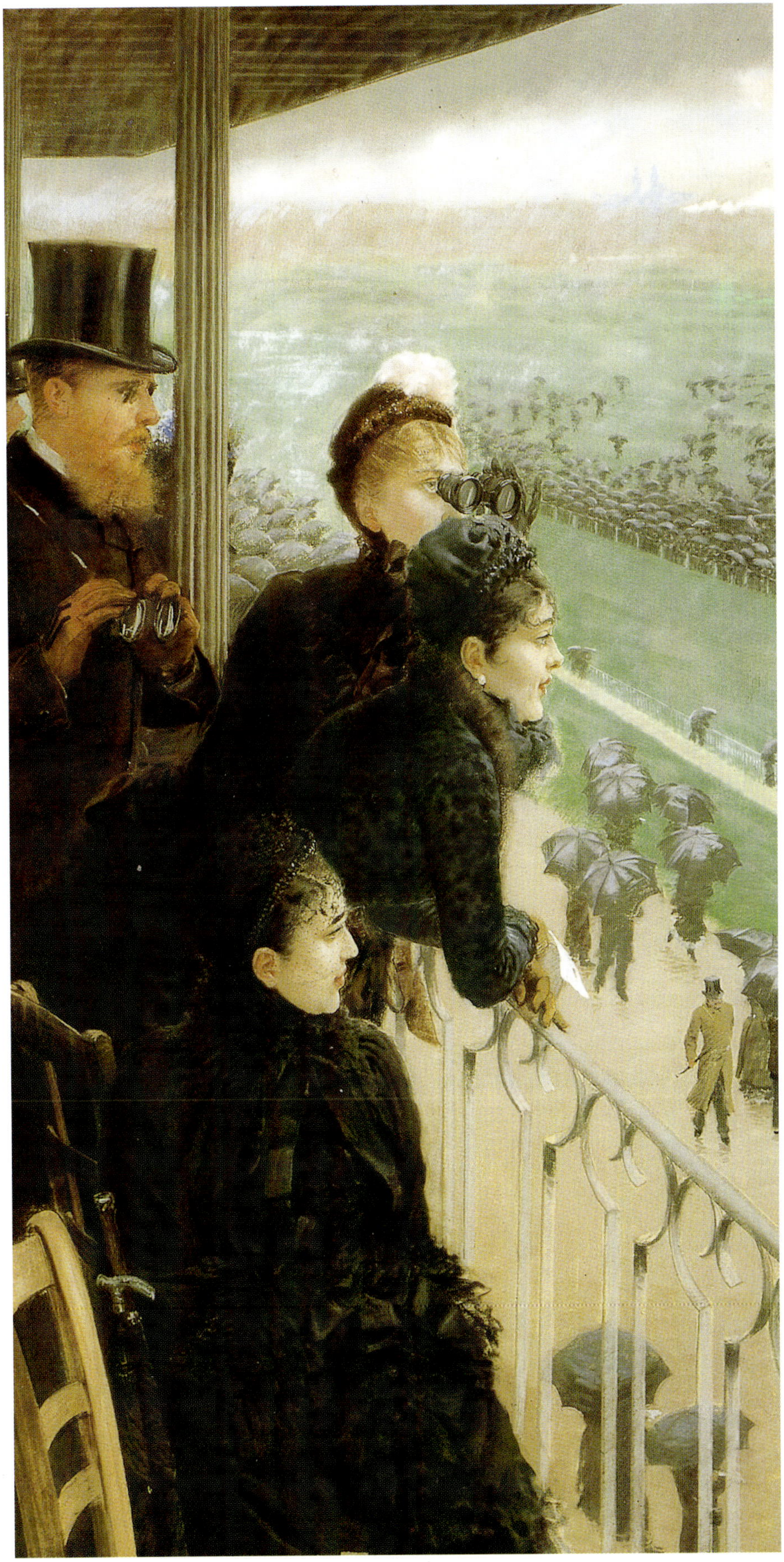

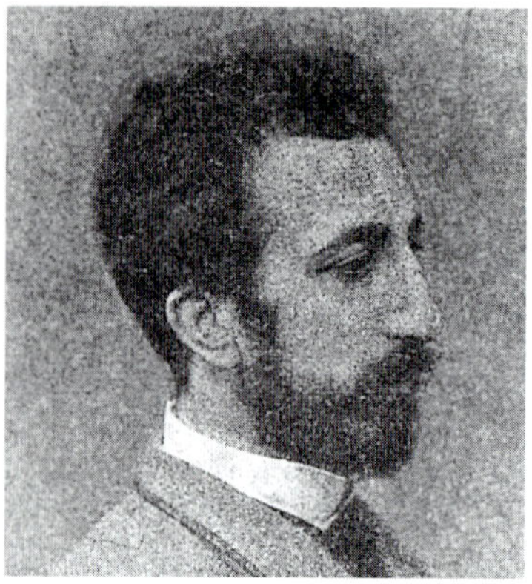

Federico Zandomeneghi

(Venice 1841 – Paris 1917)

After training at the Venice Academy Zandomeneghi, only 18 at the time, took part in the Expedition of the Thousand. In Florence in 1862 he met the Macchiaioli. In 1874, at the conclusion of a "Verist" period, the artist moved to Paris. The support of Paul Durand-Ruel, gallery owner, collector and patron of the arts, ensured him moderate financial well-being. Initially opposed to the most innovative painters, whom he judged excessively formal, he gradually moved closer to Pissarro and Degas. Starting from 1879 he exhibited regularly with the Impressionists and in 1888 experimented with the divisionist technique for the first time. "Looking, listening, discussing", he recalled, "I transformed myself [...]; my artistic life was a succession of infinite evolutions". His first one-man show at Durand-Ruel, with whom he signed a contract for exclusive rights, was held in 1893.

Federico Zandomeneghi
Mother and Daughter
1879
canvas

The study seems to render homage to Degas, to whom the artist was particularly close in this year of 1879. This is suggested by the subject of a woman's toilette, the compositional elements, the singular immobility and absence of relationship that distinguishes the figures, totally unaware of the artist's presence. The mother is dressing her daughter's hair; the daughter is looking at herself in a mirror. Should this episode be viewed as an allusion to feminine vanity or rather as an allegory of painting intended as the fixing of an image and the reduction to two dimensions of three-dimensional reality?

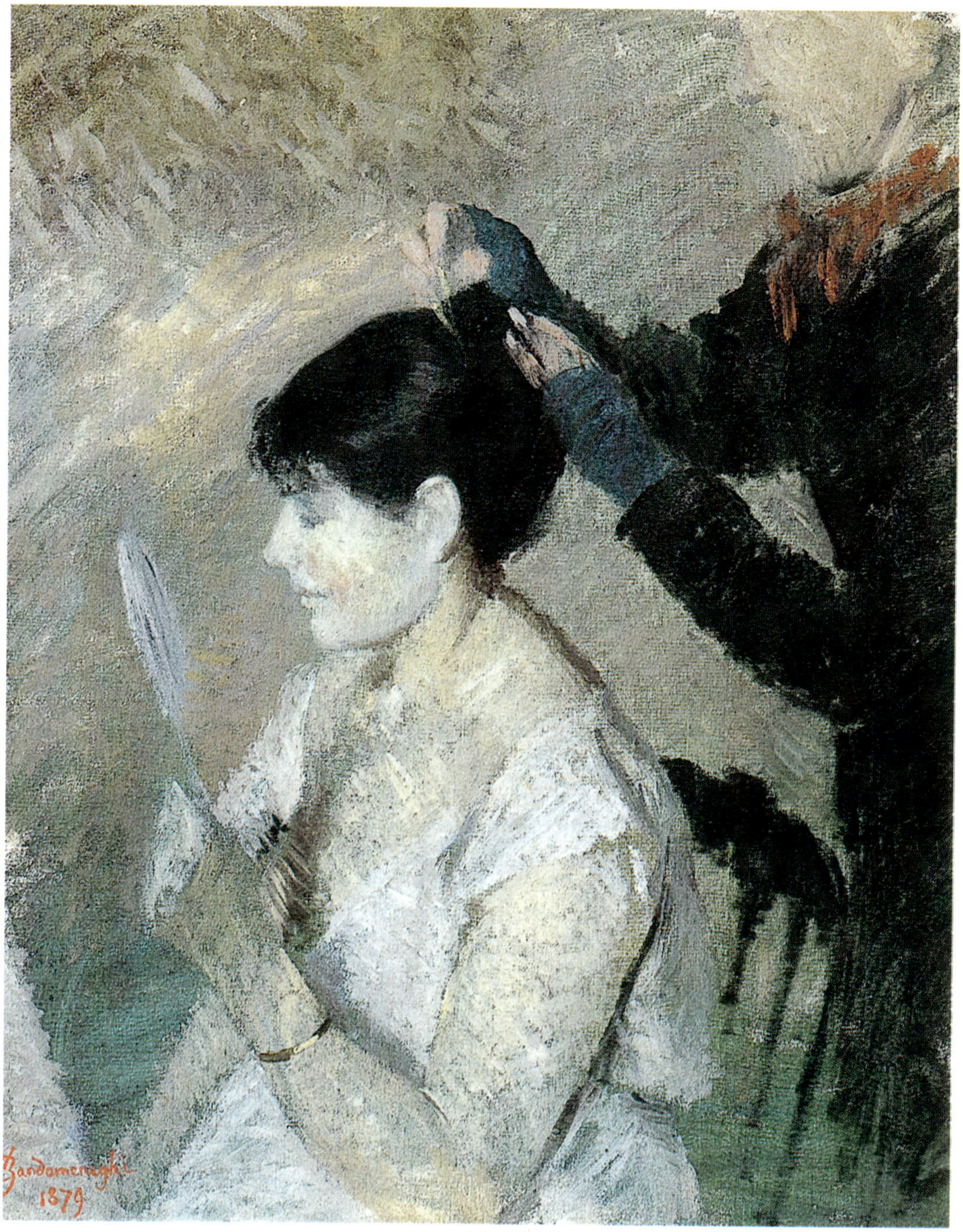

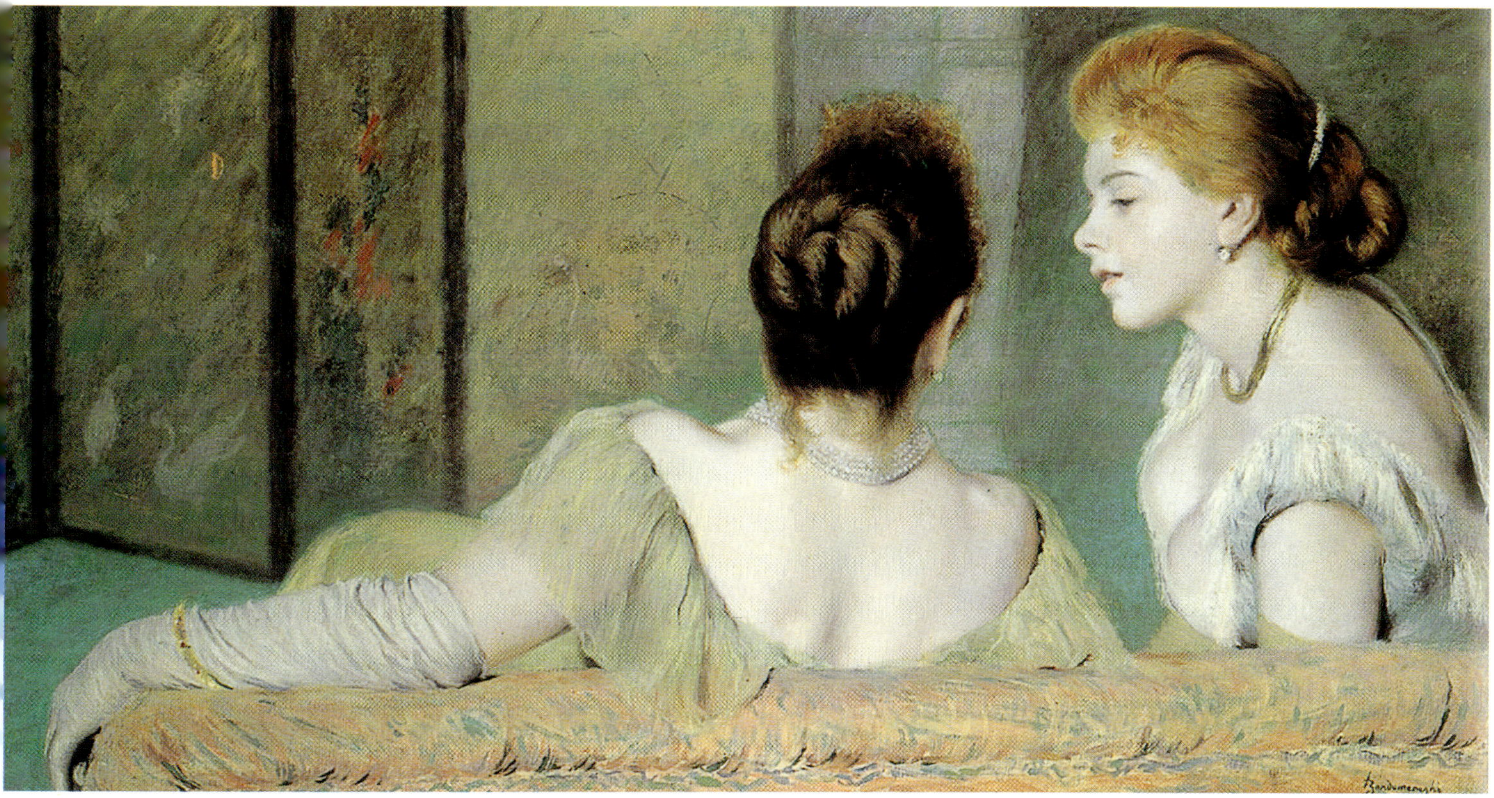

Federico Zandomeneghi
On the Divan (Causerie)
c. 1885-90
canvas

The French critics of the times, at least the most severe among them, were unable to accept Zandomeneghi's naive, stubborn fidelity to his subject: a fidelity on the whole naturalistic or "veristic" in decades of decided autonomy of the work – of "art for art's sake", laments the Venetian painter. And so it happens that his female figures, distinguished by an "elegance devoid of anything spontaneous and an aspect similar to that of soap", were found "vulgar", as Félix Fénéon, a critic close to Degas and even more to Seurat, was to write with a touch of venom in his pen.

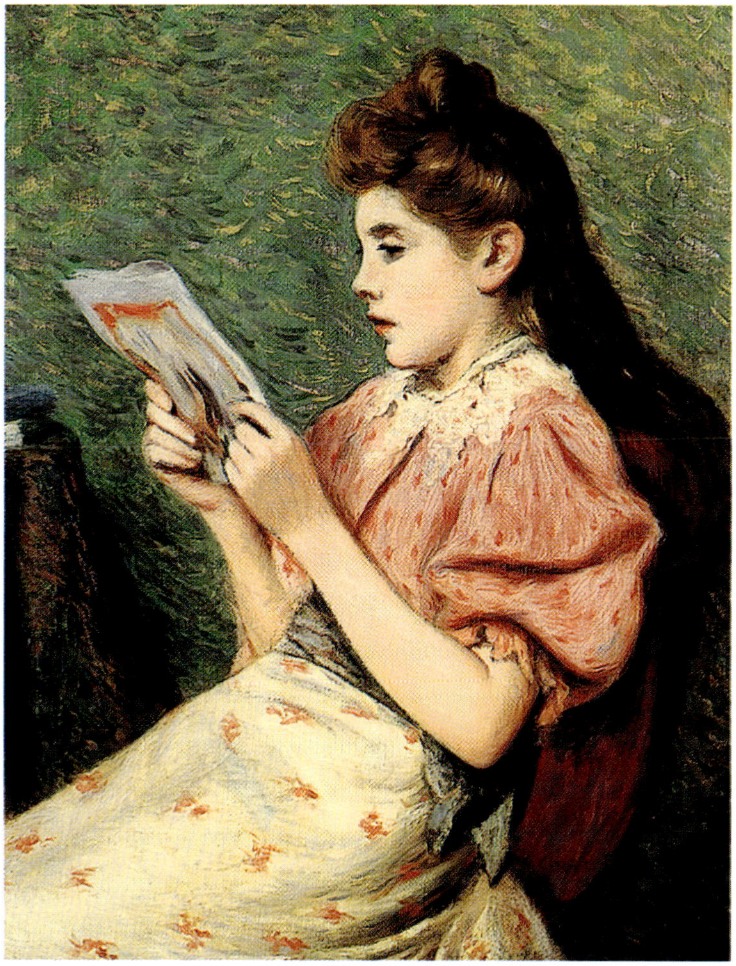

Federico Zandomeneghi
The Reading Girl
c. 1885-90
canvas

The motif of a girl reading was dear to those, in the French painting of intimist tradition, who insisted on particular requisites of calm, precision, and absence of ostentation in the painting itself. This emerged from a prolonged practice of observation – it could even be said, of deciphering.
In this painting Zandomeneghi is especially attentive to the play of reflections. These, and not the volumes, become the principles of form and composition.

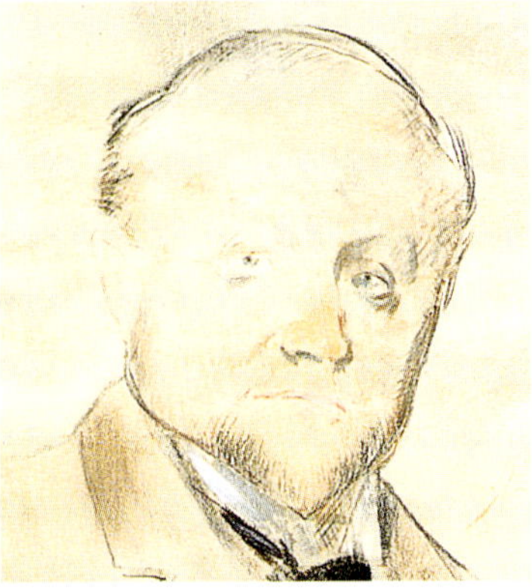

Giovanni Boldini

(Ferrara 1842 – Paris 1931)

Boldini, who trained with his painter father, was in Florence in 1862. Enrolled in the Academy, he greatly benefited by frequenting the Caffè Michelangelo. At Paris in 1867 to visit the Universal Exhibition, he traveled to London in 1870 to study the aristocratic portraiture of the 18th century. Boldini settled in Paris in 1871, where he was appreciated for his genre paintings and commemorative portraits. A master of the virtuoso brushstroke, of loose, fast execution, and of the international Velázquez style in vogue during the last decades of the century, he traveled frequently and could boast of numerous friendships among artists. He was in Germany in 1876, where he met Menzel; later stayed in Venice, sharing a studio with Sargent; and traveled to Morocco with Degas in 1889. Participating in international salons and exhibitions, he also exhibited at New York in 1897.

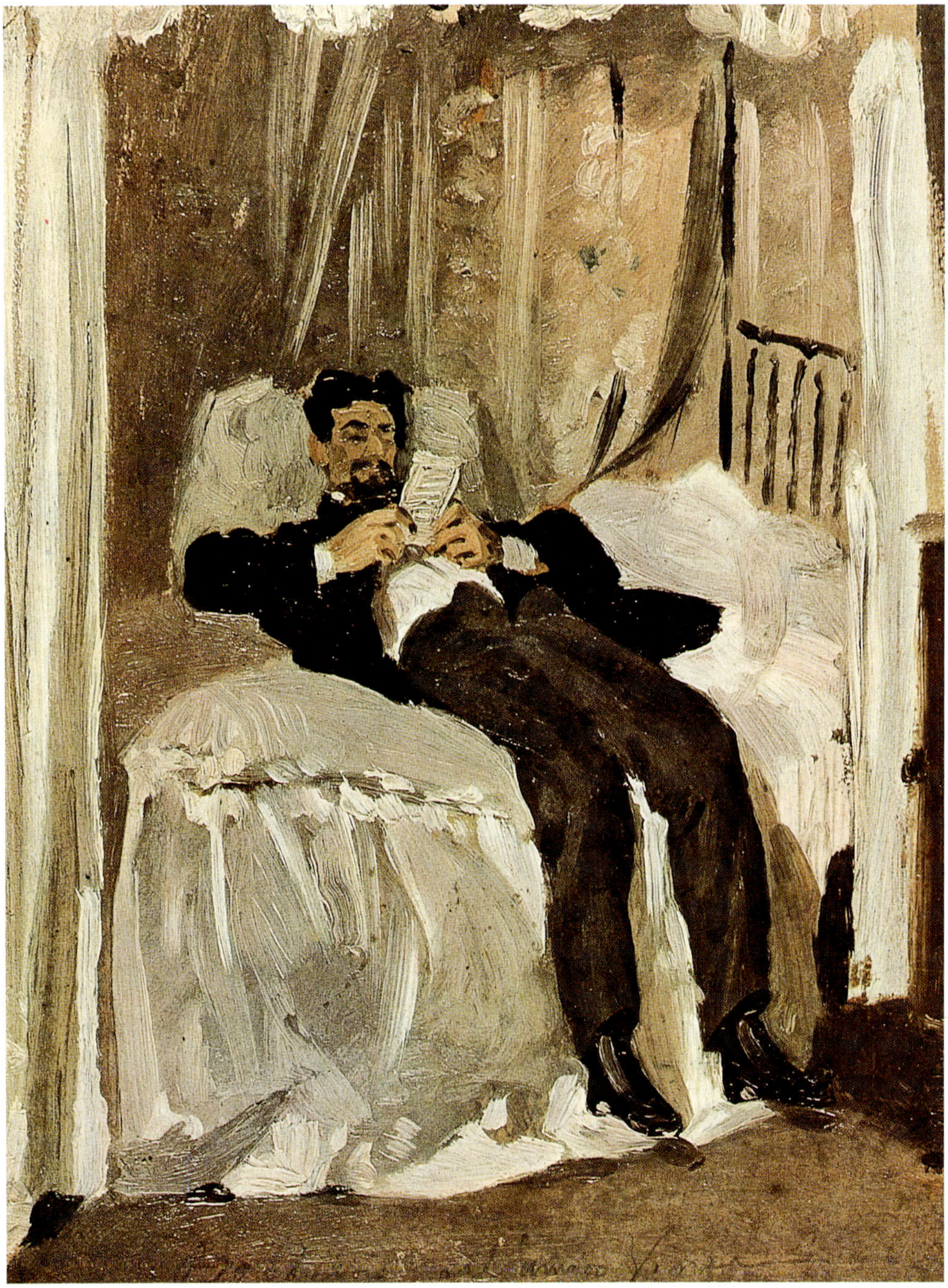

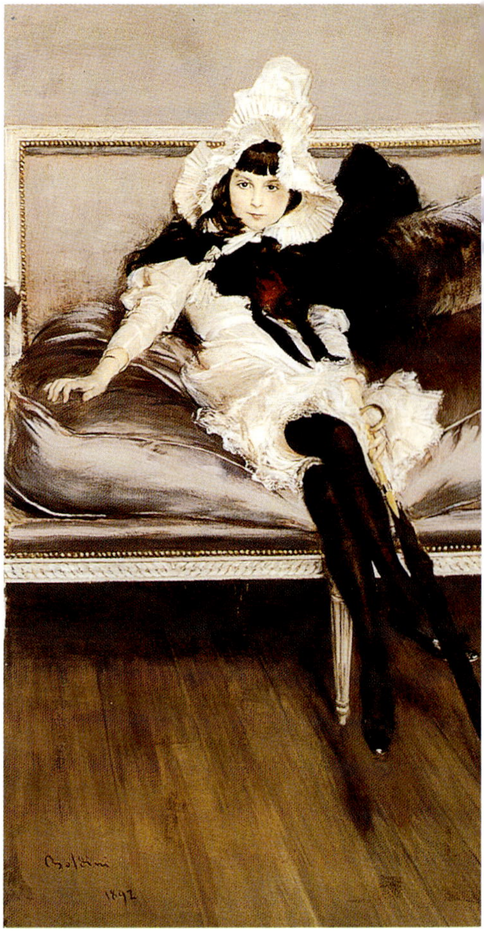

Giovanni Boldini
Portrait of the Painter Cabianca (?)
1863
oil on cardboard

It is probable that Vincenzo Cabianca, in Florence between 1853 and 1863, was the subject painted by Boldini in an elegantly Bohemian attitude.

Giovanni Boldini
Portrait of the Young Errazuriz
signed and dated 1892
canvas

The composition is insistently vertical. The parquet escapes downward while the woman's legs, umbrella and hat combine to render her figure slender and long-limbed.

At left:
Edgar Degas, *Half-Bust Portrait of Boldini*, detail, c. 1889.

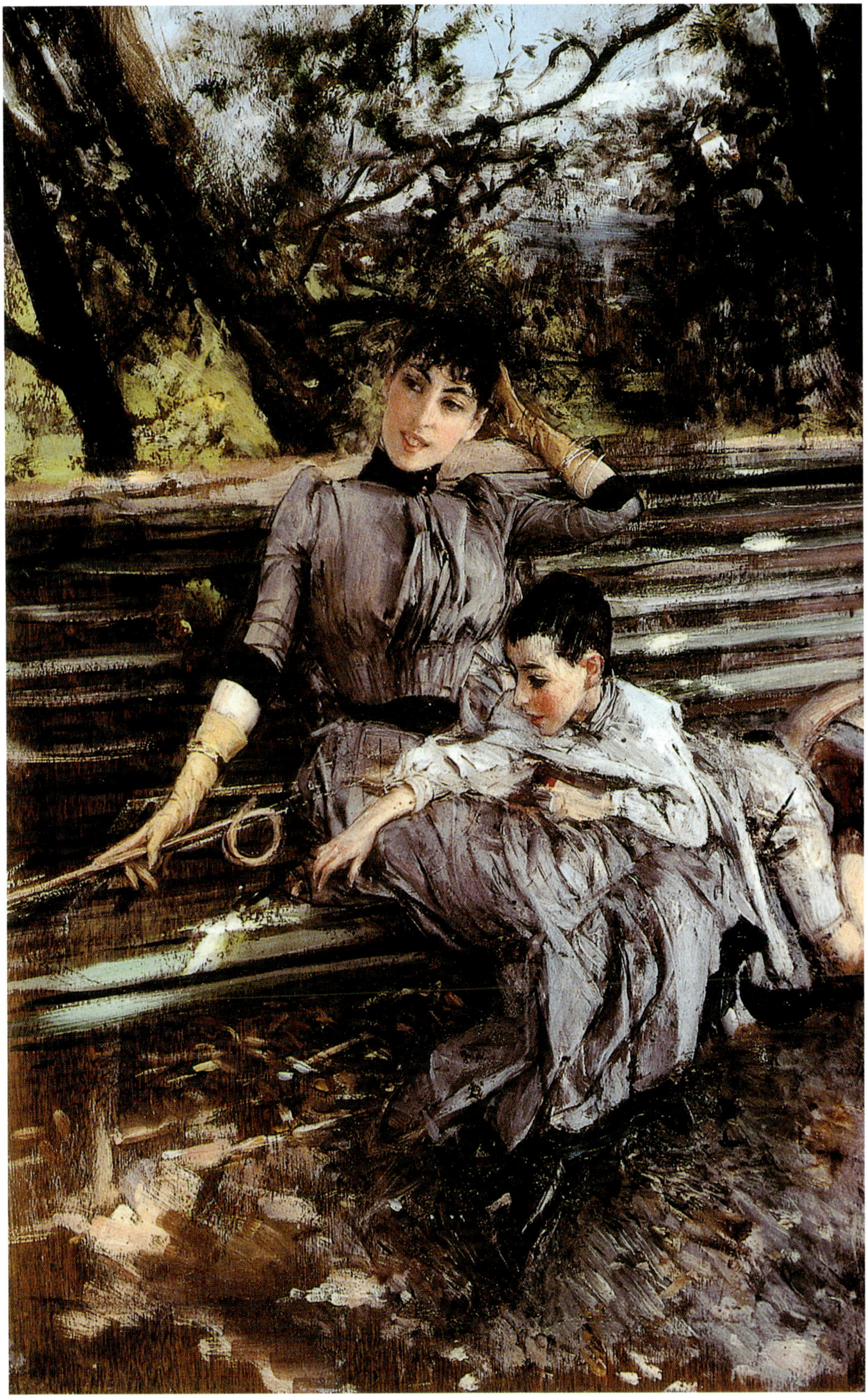

Giovanni Boldini
In the Garden
1885
panel

Fascinated by elegance, wealth and nobility, Boldini did not often experiment with intimist portraiture. Alaide Banti, portrayed here, was the daughter of Cristiano, a Macchiaiolo painter which whom Boldini had established a long-lasting friendship. After having met Banti in 1862, Boldini painted several portraits of him. Banti was Boldini's guest at Versailles, and Boldini stayed with the Banti family a number of times in Florence. Boldini was linked to Alaide by an intense emotional relationship. He always considered her his "Italian fiancée", asking her to marry him in 1903, only to withdraw immediately afterward from the ceremony he had always feared.

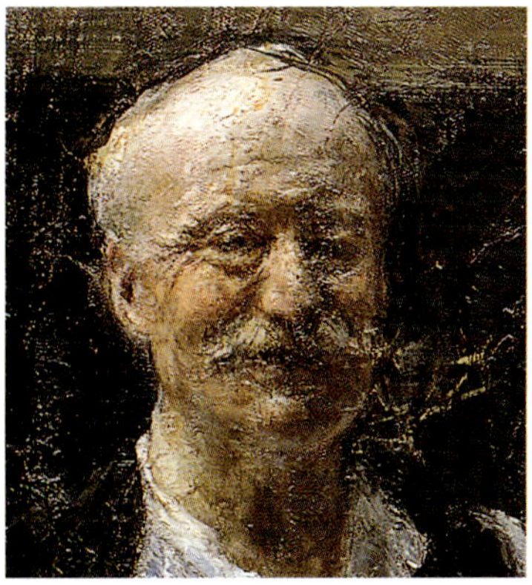

Antonio Mancini

(Rome 1852 – 1930)

A pupil of Morelli at the Naples Institute of Fine Arts, Mancini drew from his master's teaching a strong interest in the 17th century Neapolitan tradition. A studio companion of Vincenzo Gemito, he turned to observation of the popular world of Naples, painting types taken from life. Mancini made his debut at Paris when only twenty years old, in 1872, and established contact with the Maison Goupil in the same year. His first two periods spent in Paris were in 1875 and 1877-78. Awareness of what was happening on the scene in the French capital confirmed the artist in his stylistic approach: loose, rapid execution, pasta painting, effects of light and color. In the attempt to confer greater brilliance on the figurative surface, Mancini added fabrics, sequins, and bits of colored glass. Success came late: after presenting a one-man show at the XII Biennial, he was appointed to the Italian Academy in 1927.

Antonio Mancini,
Self-portrait, detail,
c. 1929, Florence,
Uffizi Gallery.

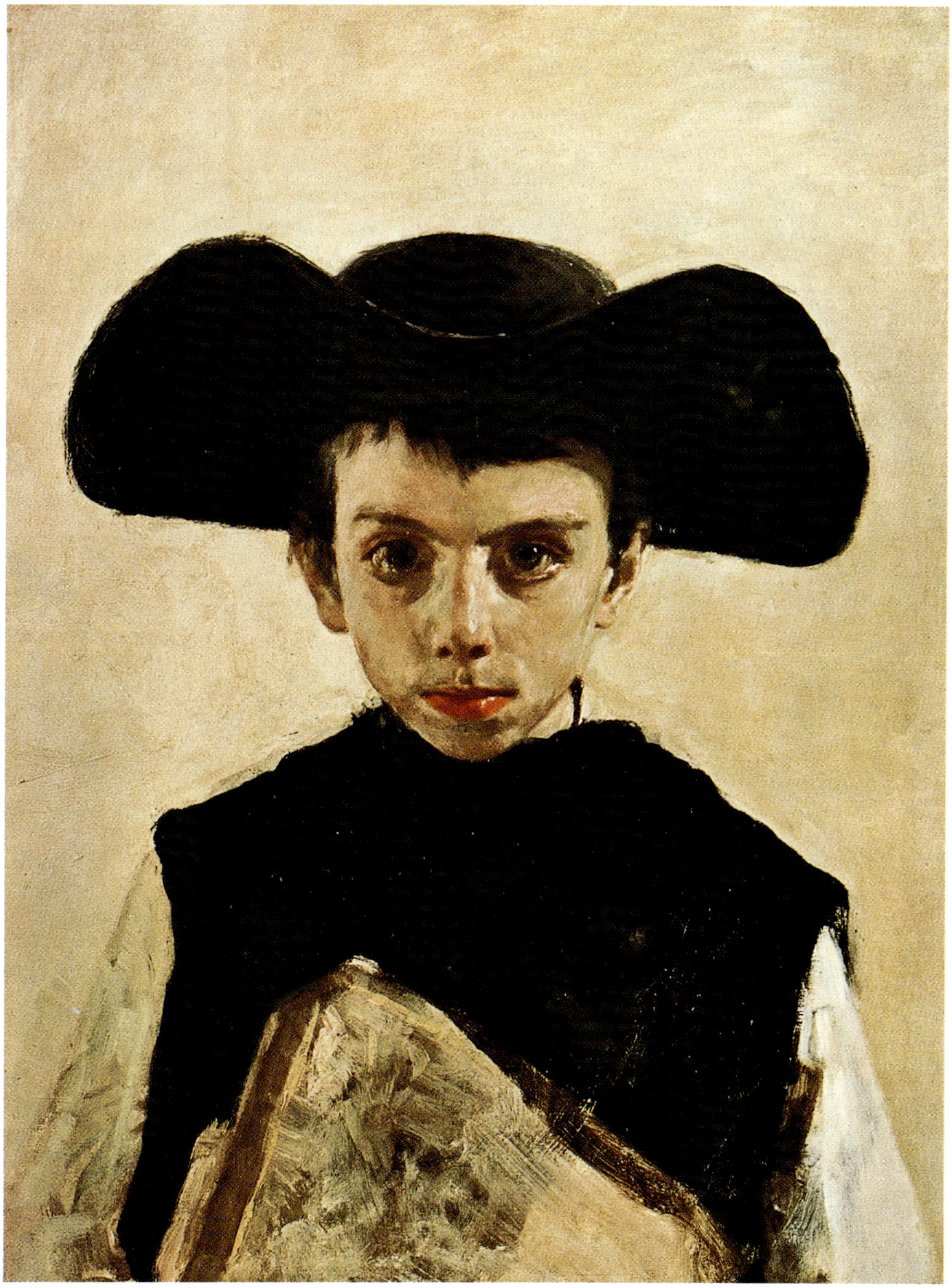

Antonio Mancini
'O prevetariello
1870
canvas
Naples, San Martino
Museum.

Among the favorite subjects of the young Mancini were boys and "scugnizzi", or street urchins, in demand by foreign collectors and artists in search of "souvenirs d'Italie". Among the first to appreciate Mancini was Hendrik Mesdag, a naturalist painter of The Hague school. Little seminarians and coral-vendors, street children and fragile water-sellers easily satisfied the contemporary taste for pathetic/picturesque images with decidedly local traits.

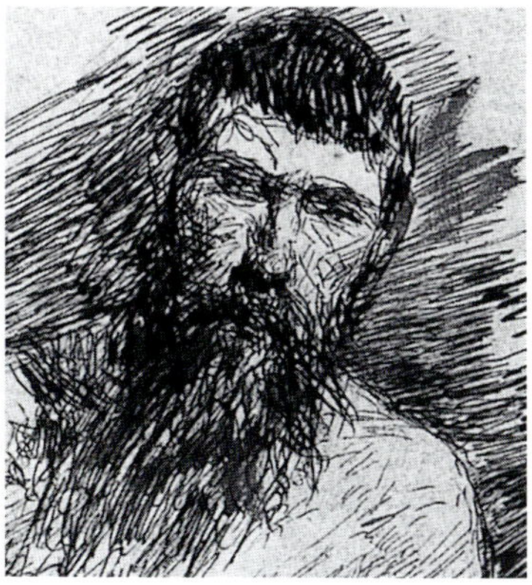

Vincenzo Gemito

(Naples 1852 – 1929)

A friend of Mancini, with whom he shared a studio, Gemiti owed his first notoriety to a series of small typical figures, mostly beggars, sculpted in clay. As a portrait painter he was highly appreciated also in Paris, where he exhibited for the first time in 1876 – posing for him, along with Morelli, were Verdi, Fortuny, Michetti, Boldini and Meissonier. For the latter, master of costume painting, the artist expressed open admiration. Gemito lived for some time in the French capital, then returned to Naples in 1880 to open a fine-arts foundry that met with growing success. Rather suddenly, however, he went into total isolation, from which he was to emerge only in 1905. Dressed in a redingote, he lay on the floor and stubbornly refused to wash or to leave his home. In his last period of activity, between 1917 and 1925, Gemito dedicated himself to small, refined sculptures in silver and bronze.

Vincenzo Gemito, *Self-portrait with Nude Torso*, detail, c. 1881.

Vincenzo Gemito
Fisher Boy
1877
bronze
Florence, Bargello Museum.

Exhibited at the Paris Salon in 1877, a first version of the *Fisher Boy* was enthusiastically acclaimed. Gemito was induced to remain in Paris, the guest of Meissonier. Barely dissimulated beneath the facile "Verist" narrative quality of the motif are cultured, even archaeological elements reflecting the artist's interest in Hellenistic statuary, particularly as regards aspects of daily life and humoristic hunting and fishing scenes associated with figures of children. The result is a gentle, nostalgic re-evocation of the Mediterranean myth. Humanity and nature live side-by-side in happy equilibrium, an equilibrium untouched by the vicissitudes of history or by technical/industrial evolution. The world of antiquity has never really come to an end. Rich in citations and carefully attentive to naturalistic detail – the cane fishing rod; the net bag; the boy's wet, salty hair; his eyelashes – the statue shows carefully modeled surfaces and particular linear elegance attained on the level of silhouette.

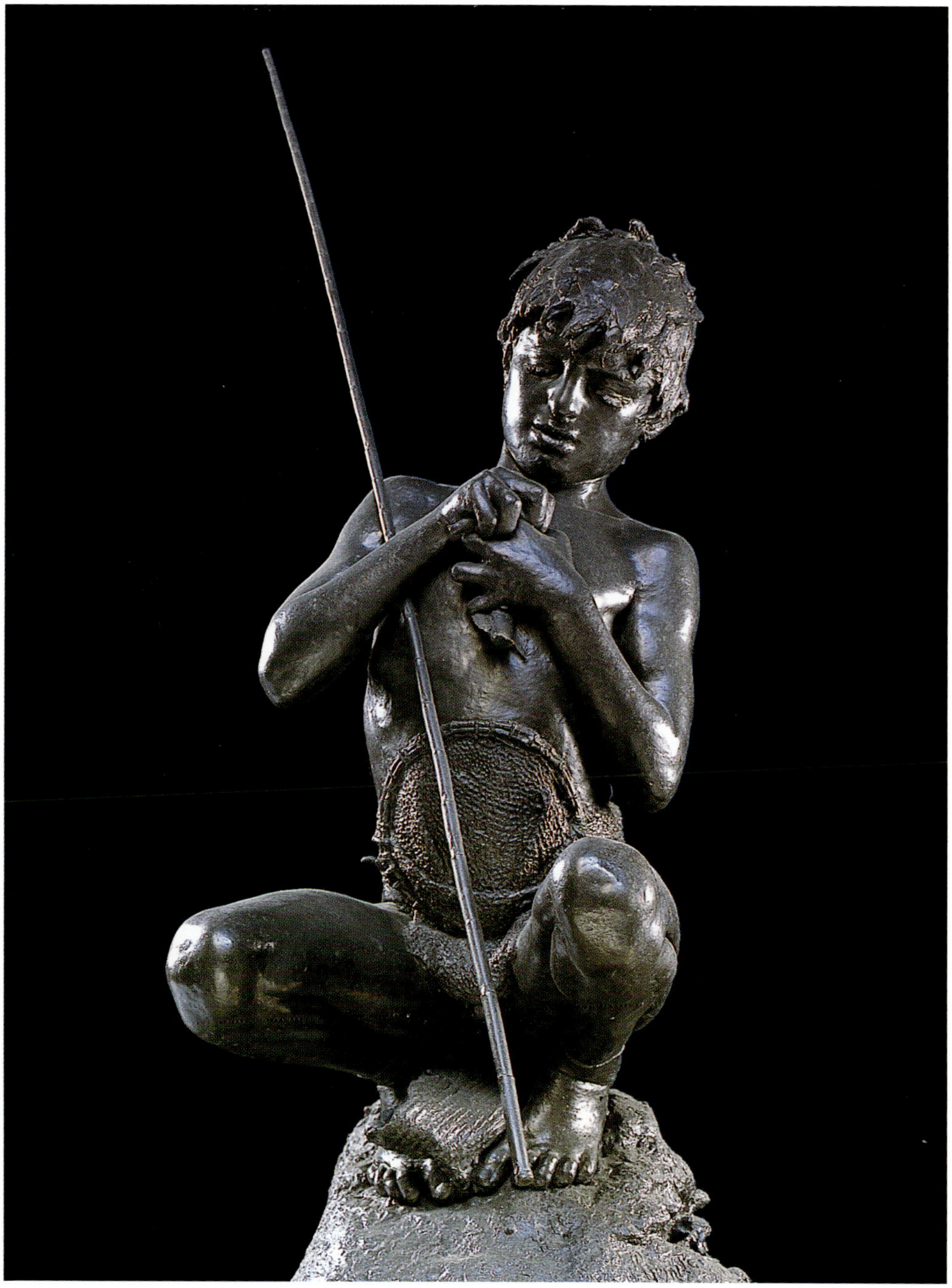

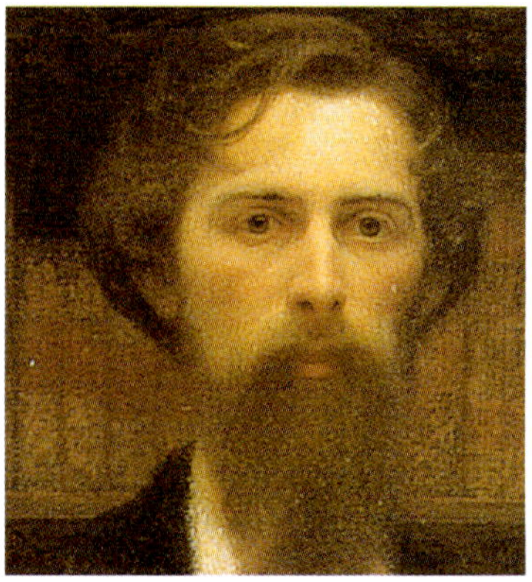

Giuseppe Pellizza da Volpedo

(Volpedo, Alessandria, 1868 – 1907)

Training first at the Brera Academy, then at the Rome and Florence Academies, the artist went to Paris in 1889 to visit the Universal Exposition. Upon returning to Volpedo, where his family owned land, he painting scenes from life: landscapes and views, still lifes and portraits. In the early Nineties he experimented with the divisionist technique. With Morelli, a very close friend, he shared an interest in social issues. Close to spiritualist circles in Florence, he was in Rome in 1896, where he studied the Raphael of the *Stanze* in the search for a model of historical painting. He aimed at images that could fix present events, transposing them, through formal elements, to the level of pure beauty. Contemporary history and standard canons are intermingled in compositions meditated at length. Still in Rome in 1906, Pellizza met Balla, Boccioni and Severini. In 1907 he was to die a suicide.

Giuseppe Pellizza da Volpedo, *Self-portrait*, detail, 1897-99. Florence, Uffizi Gallery.

Giuseppe Pellizza da Volpedo
The Fourth Estate
signed and dated 1901
canvas
Milan, Civic Gallery of Modern Art.

Already in 1890 and 1891 Pellizza has been attracted by the subject of a crowd of workers advancing. The artist, who for years held roles of responsibility in agricultural/labour mutual aid societies, wished to show his solidarity with the socialist cause. But the reasons behind the painting are only in part "Veristic"; in it are interwoven stylistic and symbolic aspects. This is apparent in the figures of the workers, studied in large cartoons and conceived according to principles of sculptural fullness, and in the absence of emphatic gestures.

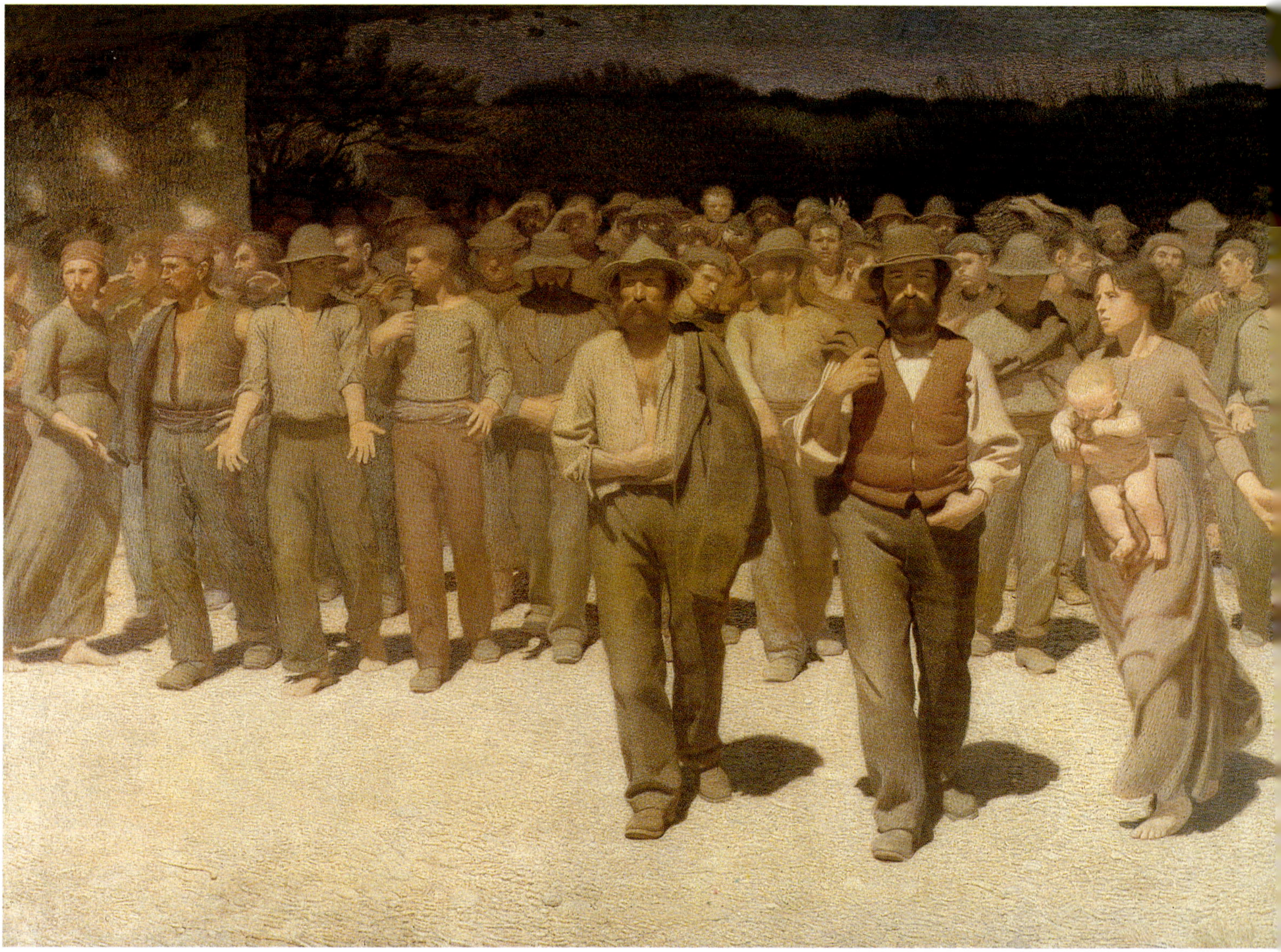

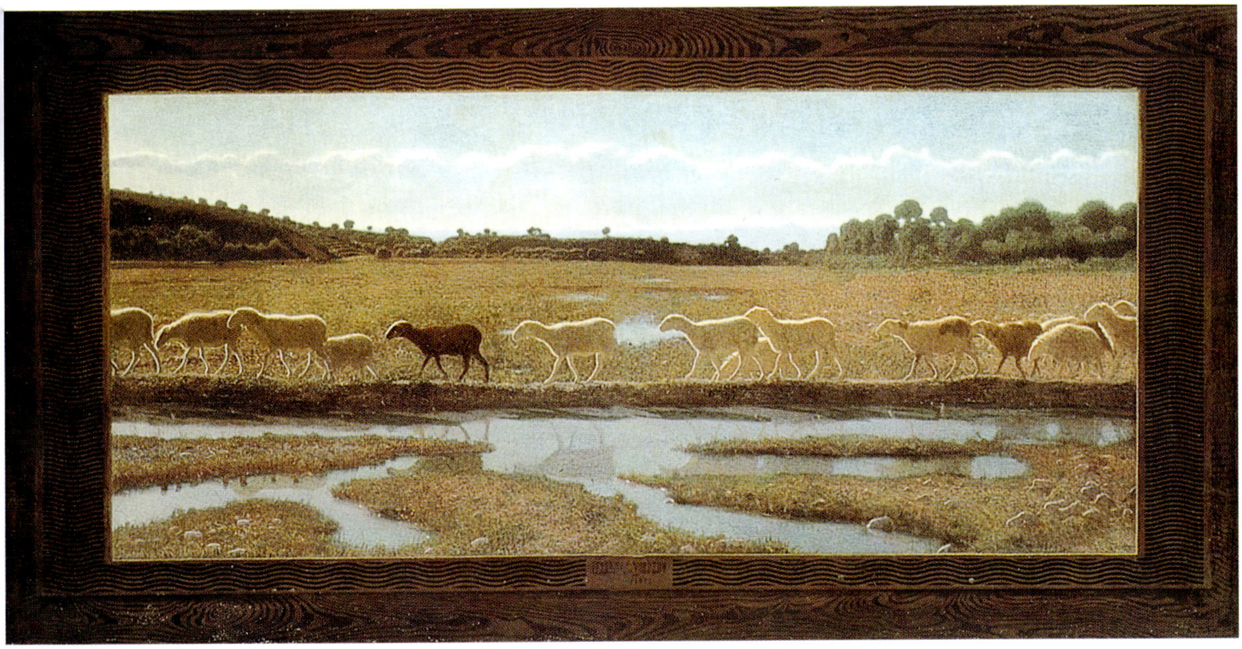

Giuseppe Pellizza da Volpedo
The Mirror of Life
1895-98
canvas
Turin, Civic Gallery of Modern and Contemporary Art.

The subtitle to this painting quotes a verse by Dante from the third canto of the Purgatory: "And what one does, the others do" (or: "And what the first does, the others also do"). Painting, for Pellizza, cannot be reduced to the practice of a refined profession. It is intellectual activity, akin to poetry, music, philosophy. The *Mirror of Life* is presented, in fact, as a reflection on humanity, or rather a meditation, not simply as a painted image. In the arabesque motifs of the frame and the curvilinear profiles of the herd shown in silhouette, it insists on the cyclic nature and recurrence of life, on the perennial alternation of birth and death, on good and evil – among the sheep, one is black – on youth and old age.

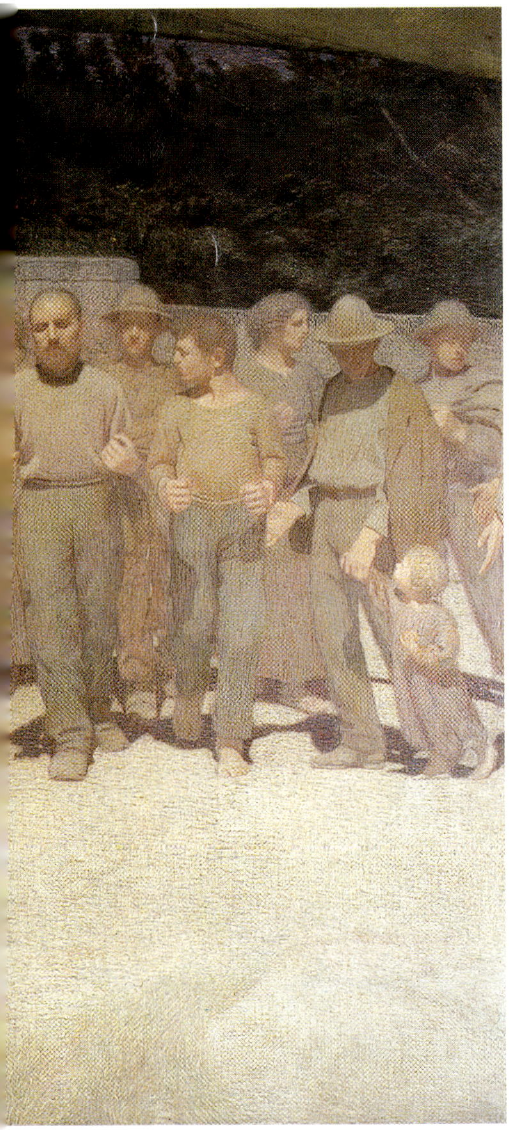

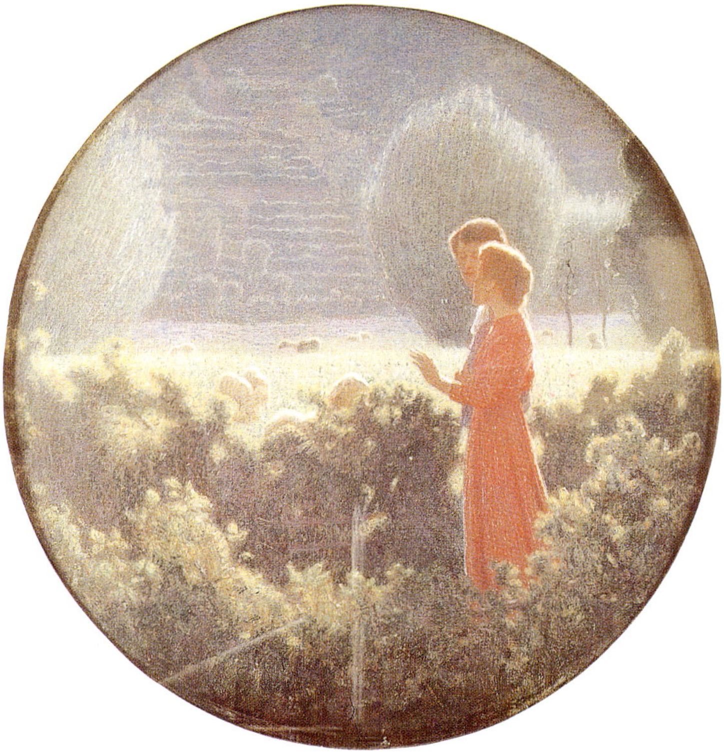

Giuseppe Pellizza da Volpedo
An Amorous Walk
1901-1902
canvas
Ascoli Piceno, Civic Pinacoteca.

Between 1896 and 1903 Pellizza dedicated himself to a series of works on the theme of love, to which he gave the name *Idylls*. In painting by cycles, the artist reveals his objective of attaining narrative completeness, of moving beyond the taste for the fragmentary, for the landscape or figure taken from life typical of the naturalist generation.

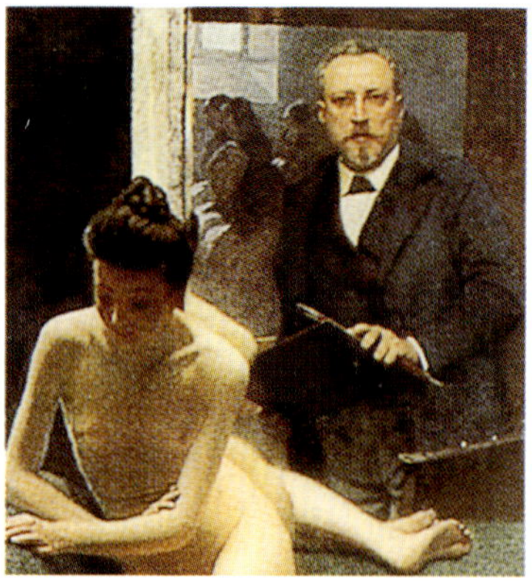

Angelo Morbelli

(Alessandria 1853 – Milan 1919)

After training at the Brera Academy, Morbelli moved toward Lombard naturalist tendencies. In his first paintings he combined atmospheric observation, freedom of touch and social analysis. Starting from 1890 he experimented with the divisionist technique, soon becoming its strictest interpreter in Italy. His predilection for "Verist" subjects was not however contradicted by the adoption of a more refined pictorial style. Morbelli drew inspiration from observing the world of work and poverty, urban isolation and emotional solitude encountered in the modern industrial metropolis, especially by the elderly – especially touching are his representations of the "old men" in the Pio Albergo Trivulzio hospice. His last years of activity saw a progressive detachment from the civil tension of his most famous compositions and a turn toward landscape painting, for which he made photographic studies.

Angelo Morbelli, *Self-portrait in a Mirror with the Model*, detail, 1901.

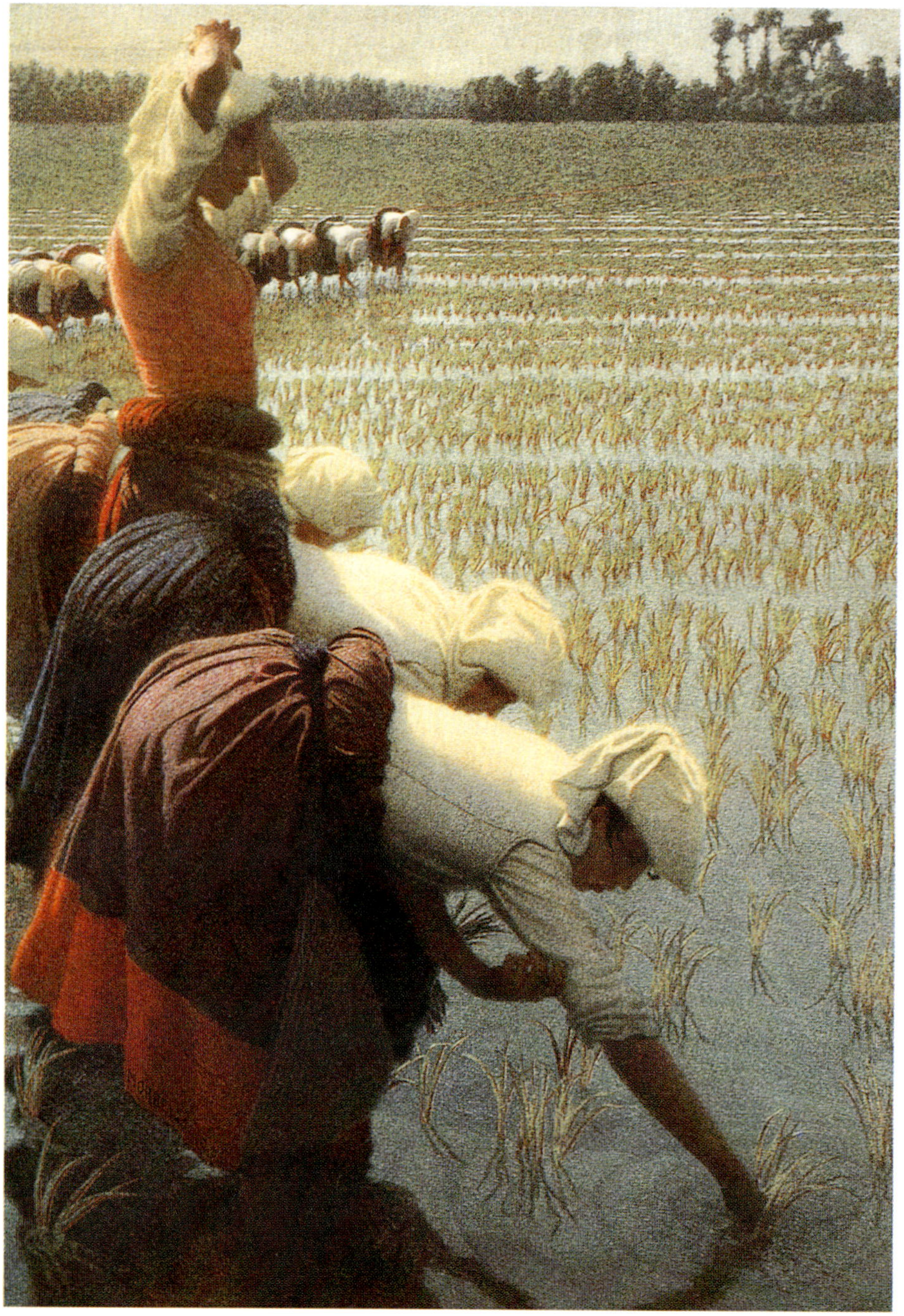

Angelo Morbelli
The Rice Paddy
signed and dated 1901
canvas

The painting reveals the artist's dual interests. Sober and forthright in its guise of "social" documentation – we see the harsh conditions under which the rice-gatherers work, bent over the water for hours and hours; their youth; the ardour and the silence that follow fatigue – it is nonetheless vibrant with cultured archaeological references employed to render the subject as beautiful as possible. Ancient Egyptian reliefs and Impressionist landscapes are no less important, for Morbelli, that a scrupulous study of light, of landscape and of local flora.

Medardo Rosso

(Turin 1858 – Milan 1928)

A pupil at the Brera Academy in 1882 and '83, Rosso approached the artists of the Scapigliatura, drawing from them a lasting preference for barely suggested forms and insistent effects of light and shadow. Between 1885 and 1886 he was in Paris, at the time when the painting of touch and color generically known as Impressionism was most in vogue. He chose subjects of pathetic/sentimental nature almost as if in flight from any attempt at fashion and affected elegance. He combined an interest in new materials and new painting techniques with his previous "Verist" attitudes. His sculptures rival paintings and illustrations in the unusual angles of the image and the suggestive effects of atmosphere – the border lines tend to dissolve, the figures to blend into their surroundings. If the *Impression d'omnibus* (1884-85) and the *Impression de boulevard. Paris la nuit* (1895-96) have now been lost – only photographs remain – the *Conversation en Plein Air* (1896) remains as witness to the artist's intentions. He breaks out of the limitations of sculpture, experimenting with the urban landscape, the contemporary genre scene. In 1889 Rosso settled permanently in Paris. Expressive busts and portraits characterized his last years as artist.

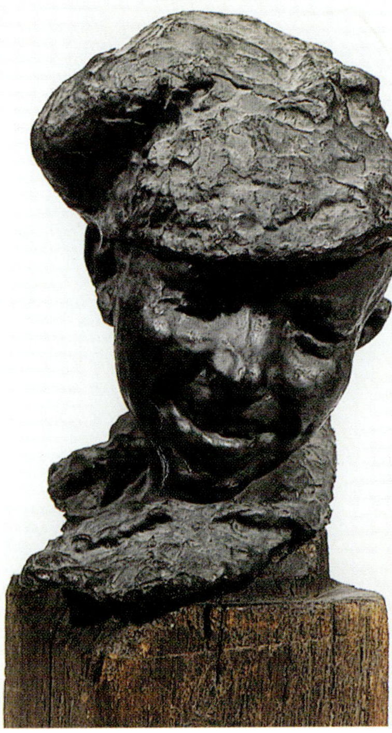

Medardo Rosso
Gavroche
1882
bronze
Milan, Civic Gallery of Modern Art.

The original title of the sculpture, more consonant to the verist taste of the young Rosso, was that of *Street Urchin* – the present title, which superseded it, dates to the time of the artist's first stay in France.

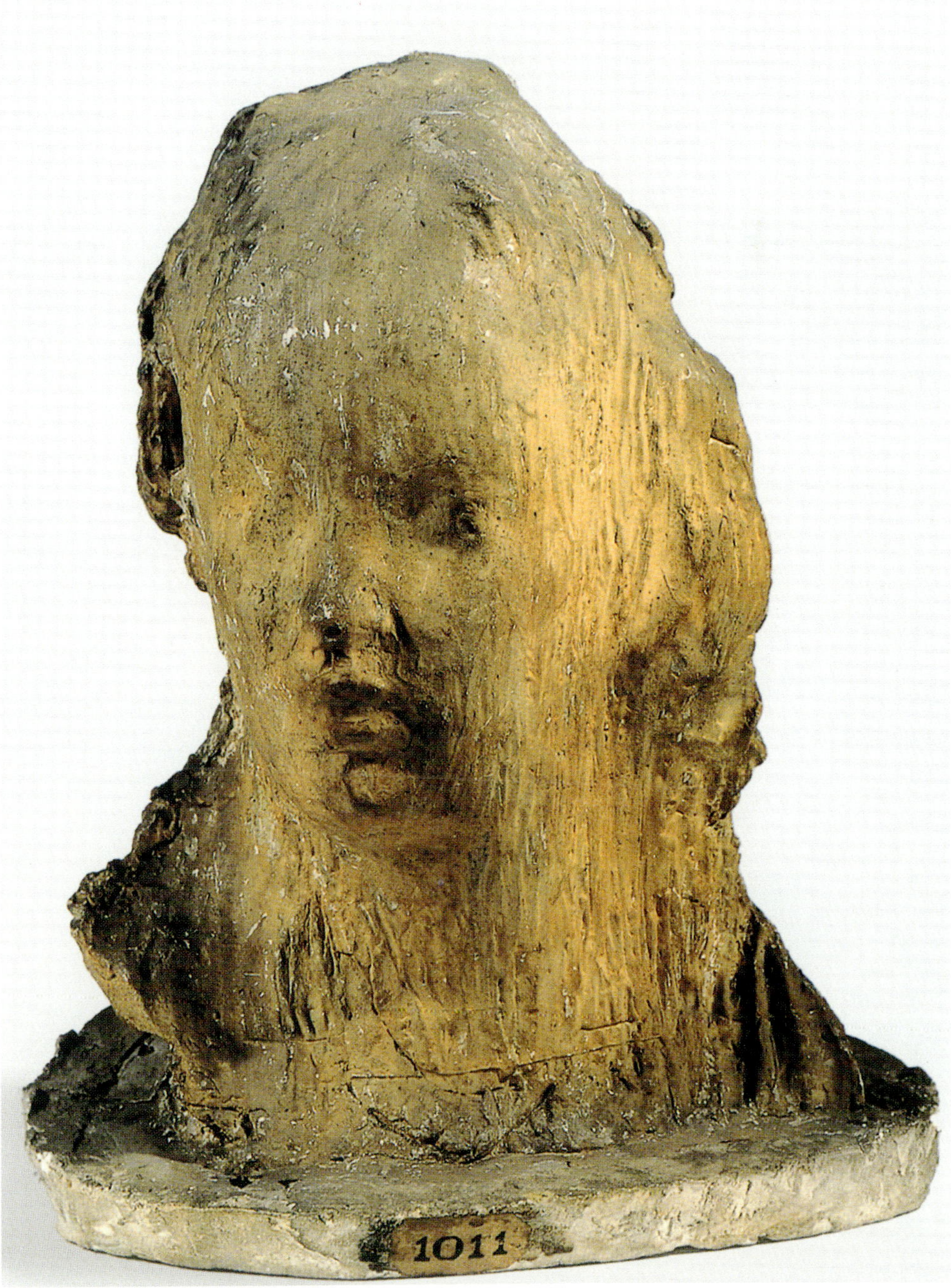

Medardo Rosso
Ecce Puer
1906
plaster cast
Milan, Civic Gallery of Modern Art.

The *Ecce Puer* marks, with other late sculptures, the point of greatest confluence between Rosso's research and the figurative tendencies of the Symbolist movement. The concrete form is almost made to disappear in favour of pure figurative elements, such as lines, which appear to reveal a state of mind.

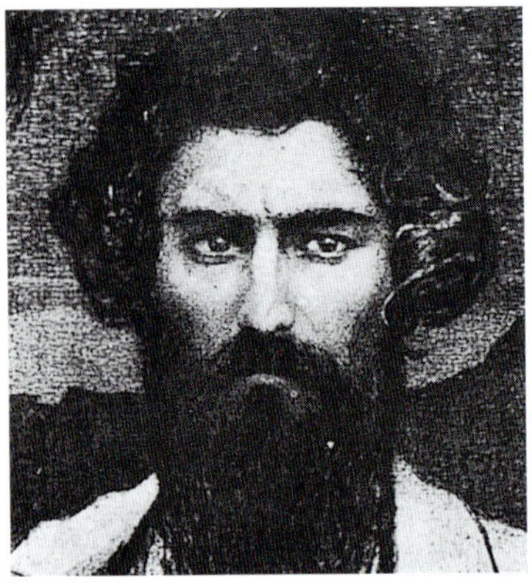

Giovanni Segantini

(Arco, Trento, 1858 – Schafberg sul Maloja, Engadina, 1899)

Trained at the Brera Academy, Segantini was close to the naturalists and the Scapigliati. In contact with Vittore Grubicy de Dragon, owner of a gallery in Milan, artist, critic, art theoretician, and the first to introduce into Italy the divisionist technique, Segantini painted his first works with a pure palette and divisionist brush strokes in the latter half of the 1880s. Starting from 1891 he abandoned his naturalistic approach in favor of allegorical/religious themes. Invited to exhibit in important international events, he enjoyed dual fame: appreciated in Italy as a regionalist painter, and in Europe, especially in the nations of Germanic language and figurative culture, as a refined and mystical painter. Dating from his last period are large cosmic/nature compositions: the Alpine landscape becomes a motive, for the artist, for reflection on the great cycle of life and death.

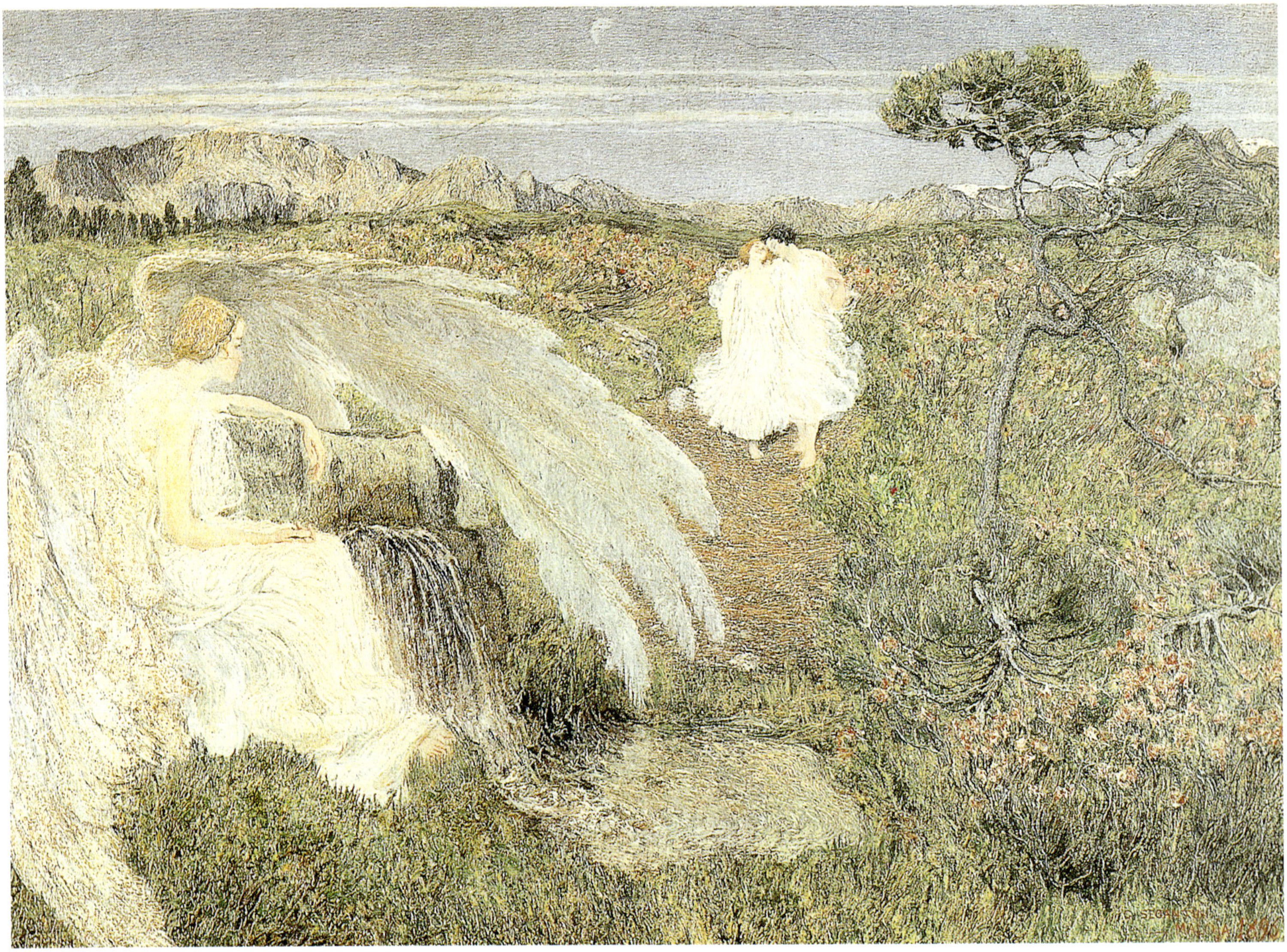

Photograph of *Self-portrait* retouched by the painter, 1895.

Giovanni Segantini
Love at the Sources of Life
1896
canvas
Milan, Civic Gallery of Modern Art.

A joint representation, according to Segnatini, of woman's love, light and joyful, and virile love, sterner and more serious, the painting portrays two young lovers dressed in white advancing along a narrow path bordered by flowering rhododendrons. An androgynous angel extends his wing to protect and simultaneously conceal the source of life. In the eyes of the artist, water and bare rock, over which the water flows, are symbols of eternity. In the background is a great Alpine landscape, limpid and benevolently primordial, with its snow-capped peaks, light flowing into shadow, the sun, the moon.

Giovanni Segantini
Return from the Woods
1890
canvas

The snowy landscape, dear to the Impressionists, offers the artist an occasion for painting without concern for depth and perspective. In such a setting the motif is naturally reduced to the two-dimensional quality so admired in Japanese prints. A few flat, horizontal touches of color are enough to represent the village toward which the woman turns with her sled. Some windows are lighted by fires burning on the hearths. Shown from the back, the figure of the woman may conceal an allegorical intent; and the great trunk lying on the sled confers on the image the quality of an Alpine *Pietà*.

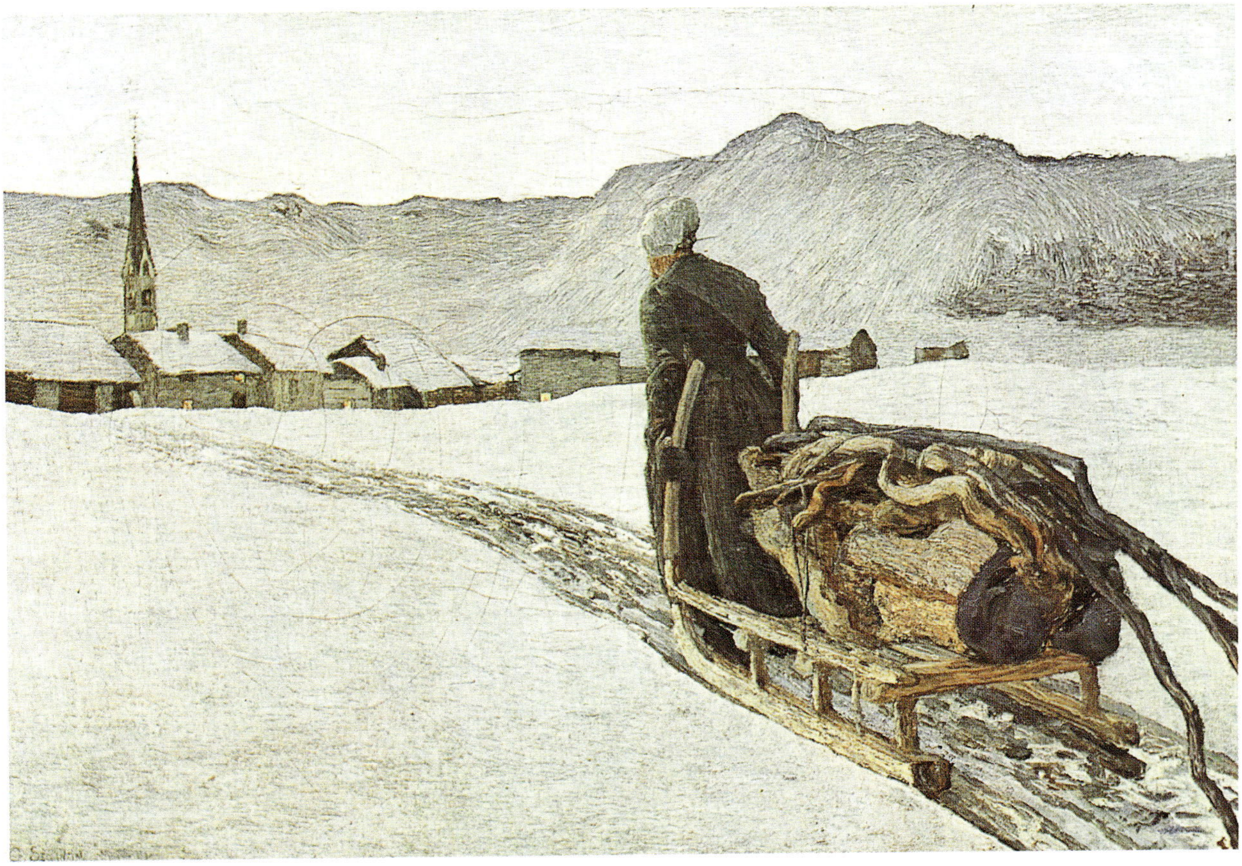

Giovanni Segantini
The Two Mothers
1889
canvas

Effects of light, gently pathetic action, a study of nature – note the figure of the cow with her new-born calf at her feet; the chiaroscuro modeling of the infant's face; the large hands of the young woman. In the *Two Women*, a sort of consecration of a humble peasant maternity, Segantini re-interprets the theme of the nativity in terms of prosaic daily life.

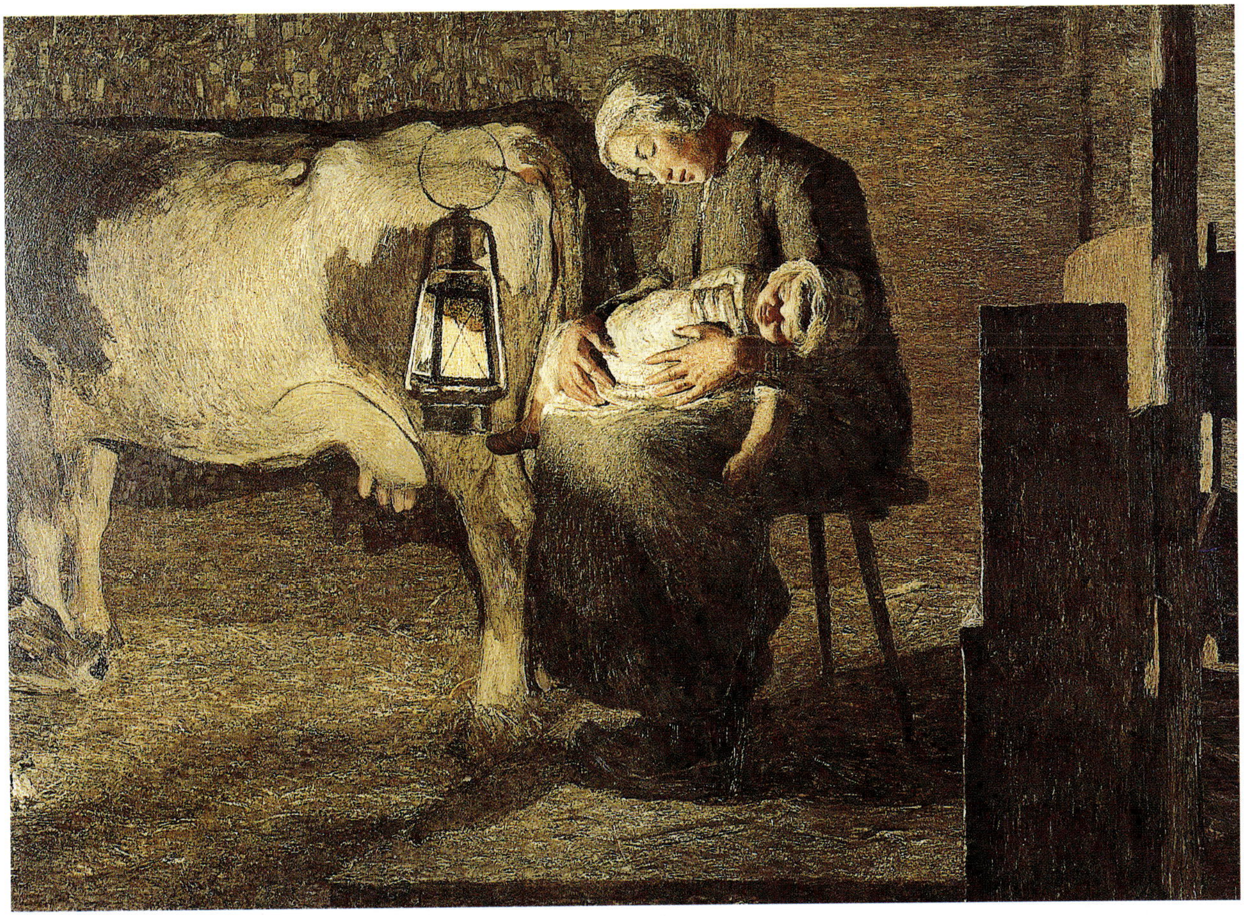

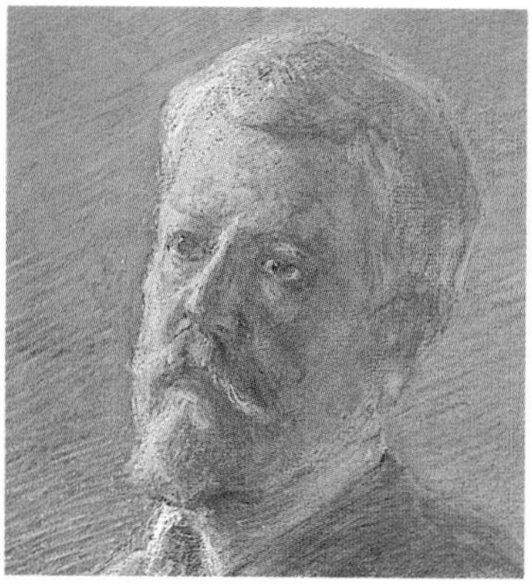

Gaetano Previati

(Ferrara 1852 – Lavagna, Genoa, 1920)

Close to the Scapigliati, the young Previati became known for great canvases of patriotic and literary subjects. He later adopted the divisionist technique and emerged as painter of ideas (his first illustrations for Poe's *Tales* date from 1887). His study of lighting effects became increasingly intense. He experimented with painting using ample, long filaments of color and a variety of back-lighting effects, narrowed his range of colours to heighten contrasts, sought for his images supra-sensitive dimensions, either obscurely stormy or paradisiacal: "gales", he wrote, "snowstorms, dawns, sunsets. Tenuous harmonies of pallid lights, iridescence, bonfires of purple and gold". Invited to exhibit at the Salon de la Rose-Croix in 1892, he was among the most admired artists of European symbolism – audacious in his choice of subjects, at his ease in complex techniques, adept at theorizing.

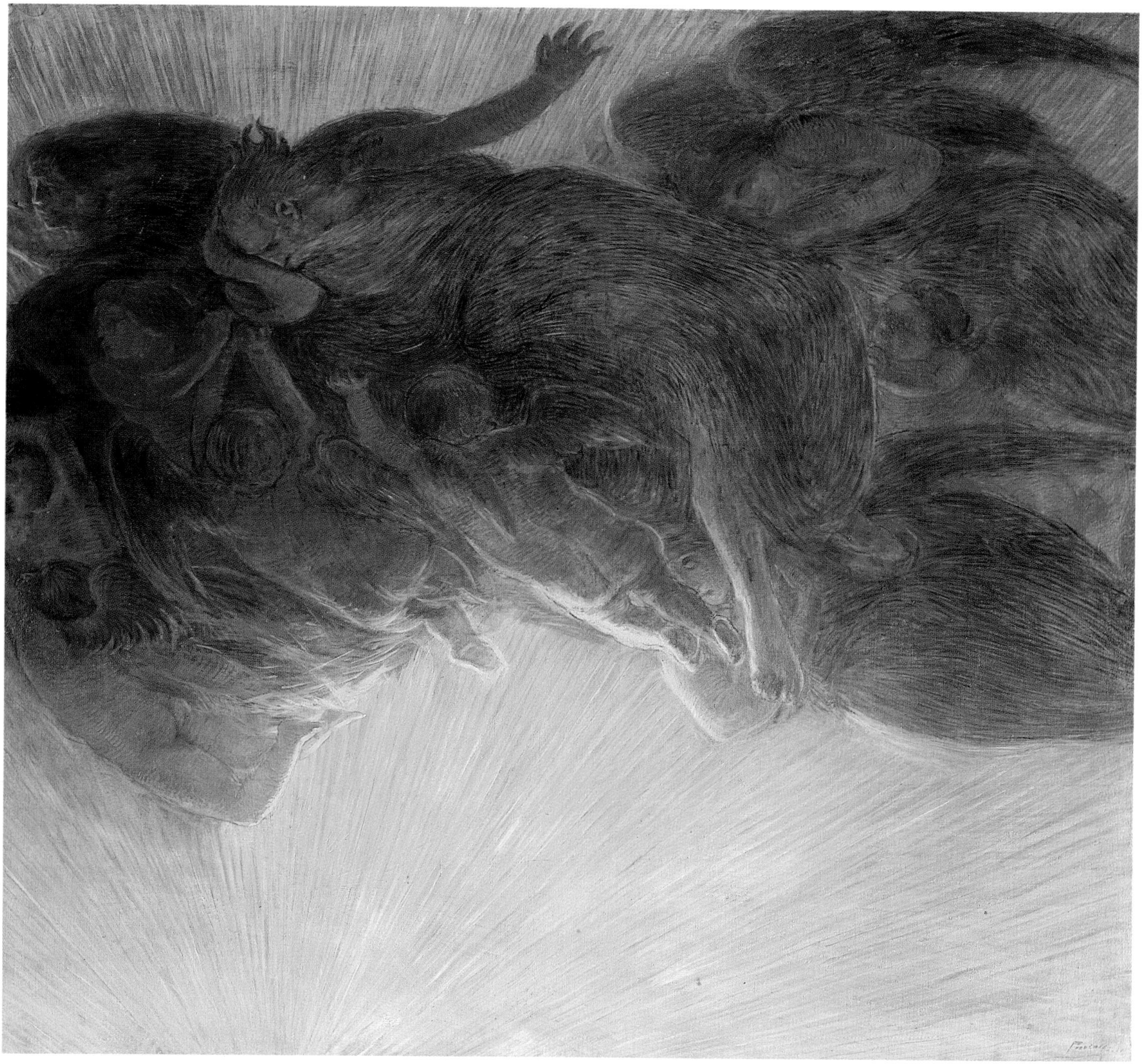

At left:
Gaetano Previati,
Self-portrait, detail,
c. 1910, Florence, Uffizi
Gallery.

Gaetano Previati
The Creation of Light
1913
canvas
Rome, National Gallery
of Modern Art.

Painting, for Previati, meant portraying high concepts, conferring perceptible form on the "ideal [that] wafts through the dreams of the artist". In testing himself with such an immensely difficult theme as God's dividing the light from the dark, a subject certainly not to be observed while strolling through the streets, the artist reveals his desire to compete with the great Italian tradition of the 16th century, with the Michelangelo of the Sistine Chapel for instance. His activity was now accompanied by complex figurative programs.

Gaetano Previati
Quiet
1896
canvas
Milan, Civic Gallery
of Modern Art.

The painting has a dual nature, being both a homage and a challenge to Monet. Although the motif of the young woman with the parasol renders explicit homage to the Impressionist painter, Previati did not share Monet's taste for the naturalistic fragment, for the fleeting moment of pure beauty devoid of any stern morality. *Quiet* seems to have been born as a rustic idyll, to transform itself immediately afterward into a gentle allegory.

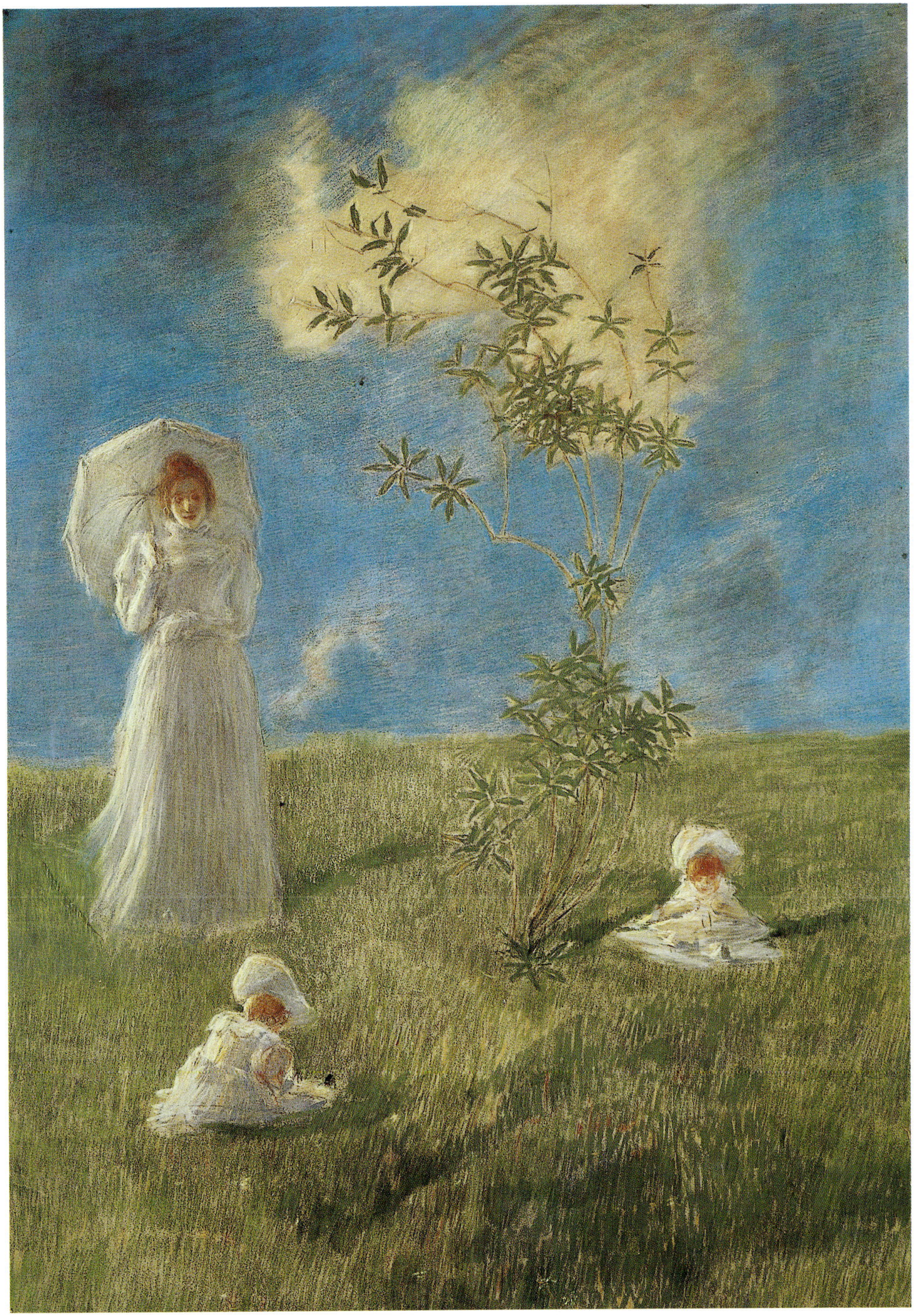

Alessandro Antonelli

(Ghemme, Novara, 1798 – Turin 1888)

Trained as architect and engineer at Milan and Turin, Alessandro Antonelli went on to further studies in Rome between 1828 and 1831. Respectful of the structural elements of the classical tradition such as the arch, the dome and the column, he combined his faithfulness to the antique with a surprising tendency toward experimentation, which urged him to try new techniques and unusual materials. Eclectic like the finest Piedmont architects of the previous century, he conceived bold projects showing a special propensity for vertical constructions. The utilization of iron allowed him to achieve greater structural solidity. Responsible for major civil and religious projects, he was active also as urban planner, devising a plan for transforming the center of Turin which was never to be carried out, and regulatory plans for Novara and Ferrara.

Alessandro Antonelli
The Antonellian Mole
1863-80
Turin.

The construction of the Antonellian Mole began in 1863. The building, designed as a Jewish temple, was purchased by the City of Turin for use as a museum and conference hall. The construction work was finished by the City itself. The Mole, 167 meters high and elegantly composed in its architectural style and structural elements, was the tallest building designed by Antonelli. The dome of San Gaudenzio in Novara, built in 1841, measures instead 125 meters.

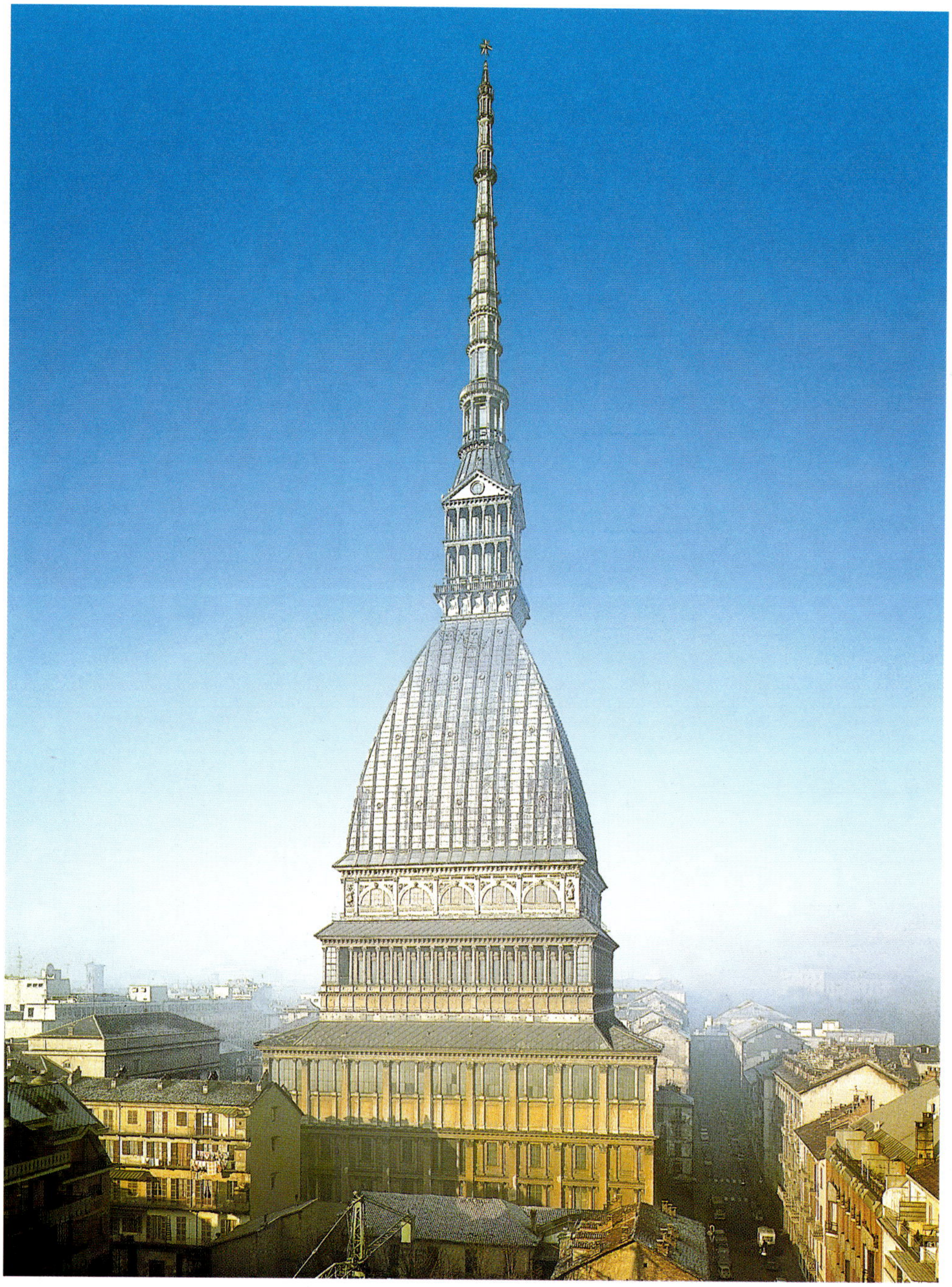

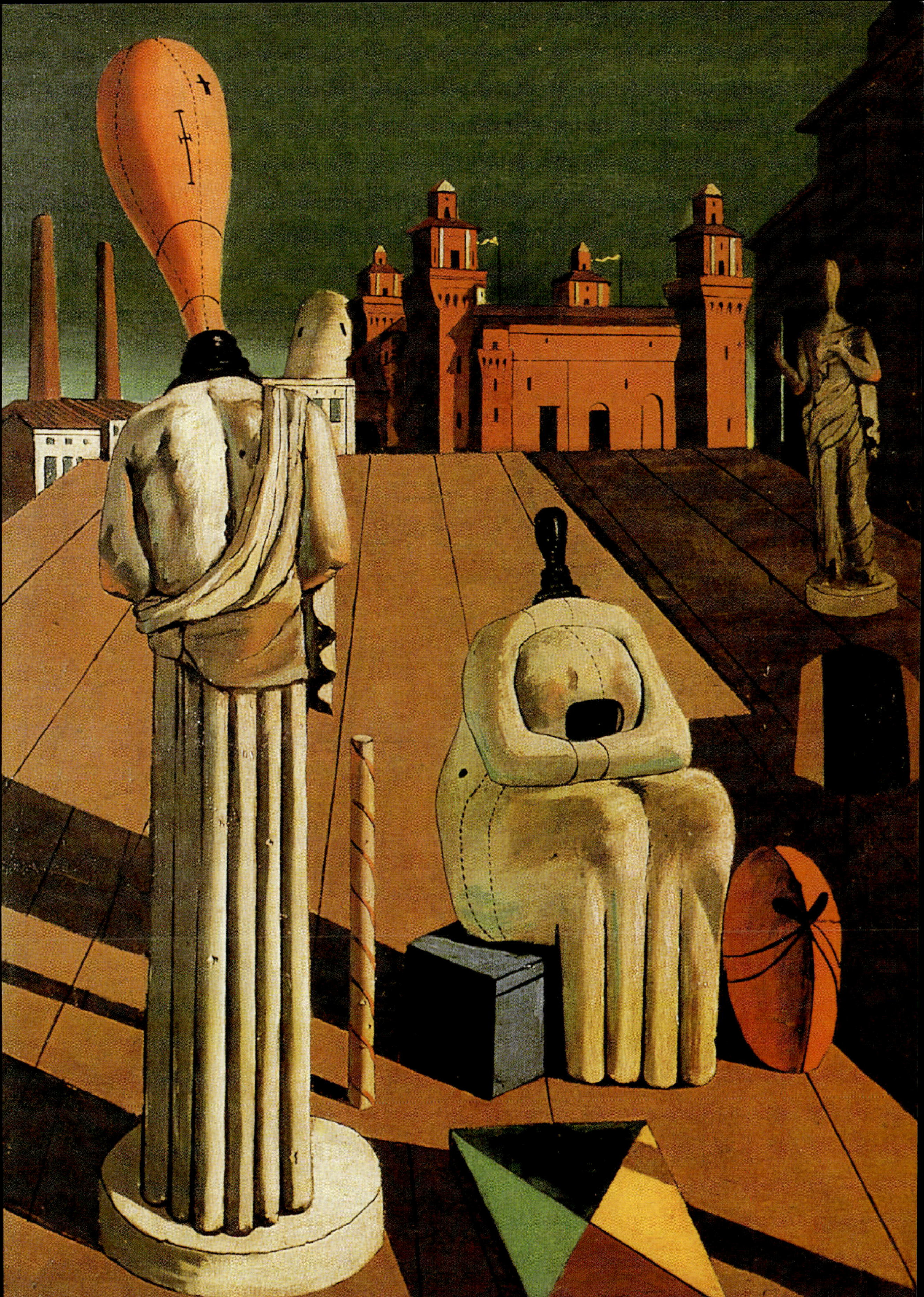

THE XX CENTURY

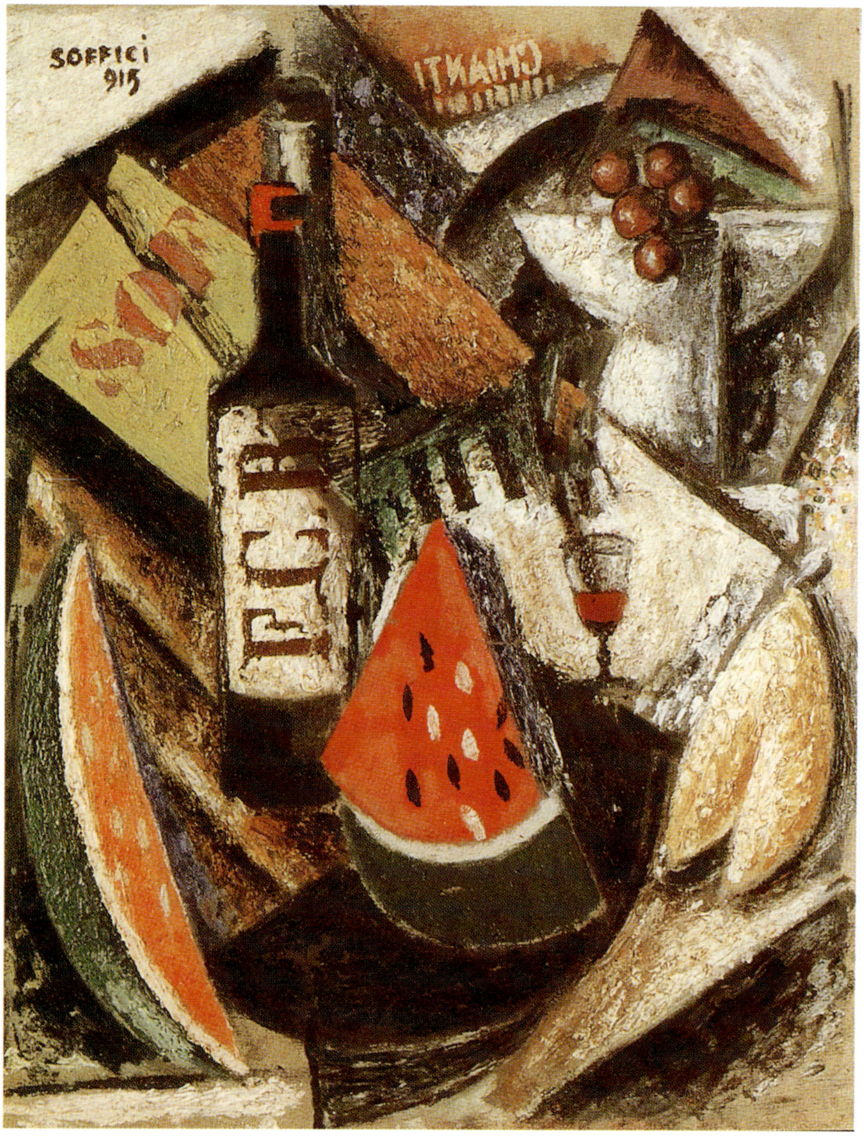

Ardengo Soffici,
Fruit and Liqueurs, 1915.

Previous page:
Giorgio de Chirico,
The Disquieting Muses,
1918.

In the early years of the twentieth century a strong tendency toward the international diffusion of common artistic trends began to emerge. This was clearly linked to the development and growth, particularly in Paris, of an art system in the modern sense, with private galleries, critics and collectors, free from any central governmental control. A successful career in art now depended on the support of a private entrepreneur, the gallery owner, and the favor of the public rather than on winning prizes in academic competitions or being appointed to a university chair of painting and sculpture. France, upheld by liberal institutions after its defeat in the Franco-Prussian War, was the leading nation in art also from the economic and social viewpoint, although in the first decade of the century Germany was to become the world's richest market for works of art.

Within the context of evolution in taste and in public and private cultural institutions, the persistent importance of geography in art can still be seen. Italy's first 20th century avant garde, the Futurist movement, proclaimed for itself in fact aggressively nationalistic/cultural traits, and aimed to produce an art that was recognizably Italian. Artists and writers, as was reiterated in the manifestos and journals of this movement such as "Lacerba", proposed to operate within a precise cultural context, the national one, promoting an overall renewal imbued with political and social implications. An imaginary catalogue of works of art from the Italian twentieth century can easily be compiled. In its pages will be found unambiguous geographical indications that make a clear statement, or at least an admission, of territoriality. Both Boccioni's *Rising City* and Balla's *Flags on the Altar to the Fatherland* are, obviously, Italian urban landscapes. The former is an allegorical portrayal of expectations of collective cultural and industrial growth. In the latter a patriotic demonstration surprises a crowd unanimously ranked in favor of entering the war. In both cases the artist is the interpreter of a renewed national unity and grandeur, based on the work ethic in the case of Boccioni, on patriotic interventionism in that of Balla (Carrà as well painted an *Interventionist Demonstration*, in 1914). The artist, in other words, is a prophet, or at least a herald. A vein of continuity, at times surprising, emerged in the first half of the century between artists and movements that were stylistically very different.

The *Italian Piazzas* through which De Chirico wanders, albeit with a troubled air, are still places, and specifically Italian places; but for him this is not the time for new myths nor patriotic fervour. Italian locales are again the industrial districts depicted by Sironi, still in the role of artist/intellectual, artist/prophet, although doubt-ridden and insecure. Strangely enough, Sironi occasionally inserts in his *Urban Landscapes* figures of horsemen resembling Giuseppe Garibaldi – almost as if the "hero of two worlds", the artist's alter ego, had returned to the sites of the nation so recently restored to unity to ponder its destiny, to question himself as to a Risorgimento still to be completed, since it has been interrupted.

The viewpoint from which the present is seen might vary, tending more or less toward involvement or bitterness, toward consensus or ironic reserve – particularly after 1922, the date of the March on Rome. But what remains immutable is the role of the artist, who exemplifies in himself a strongly public image, a kind of oracle, and whose work touches on the sphere of political activity in its broadest sense – as a construction project of national character. Excluded from all this are the eccentrics, the artists who neither desire nor seek institutional responsibilities and mandates, who do not even feel called upon to keep faith with the Italian tradition: De Pisis, for instance, and Scipione, Licini, Fontana, Carolrama.

Burri too will be considered, thus outlining a history of Italian art by themes, attitudes, tendencies and not by styles; a history of art in draft form, traversing the vicissitudes of politics, institutions and war. This brings us up 1949 or 1950, the time of Burri's first experience with *Sacks*. Significantly, some of the sacks he used were those, bearing wording in English, that

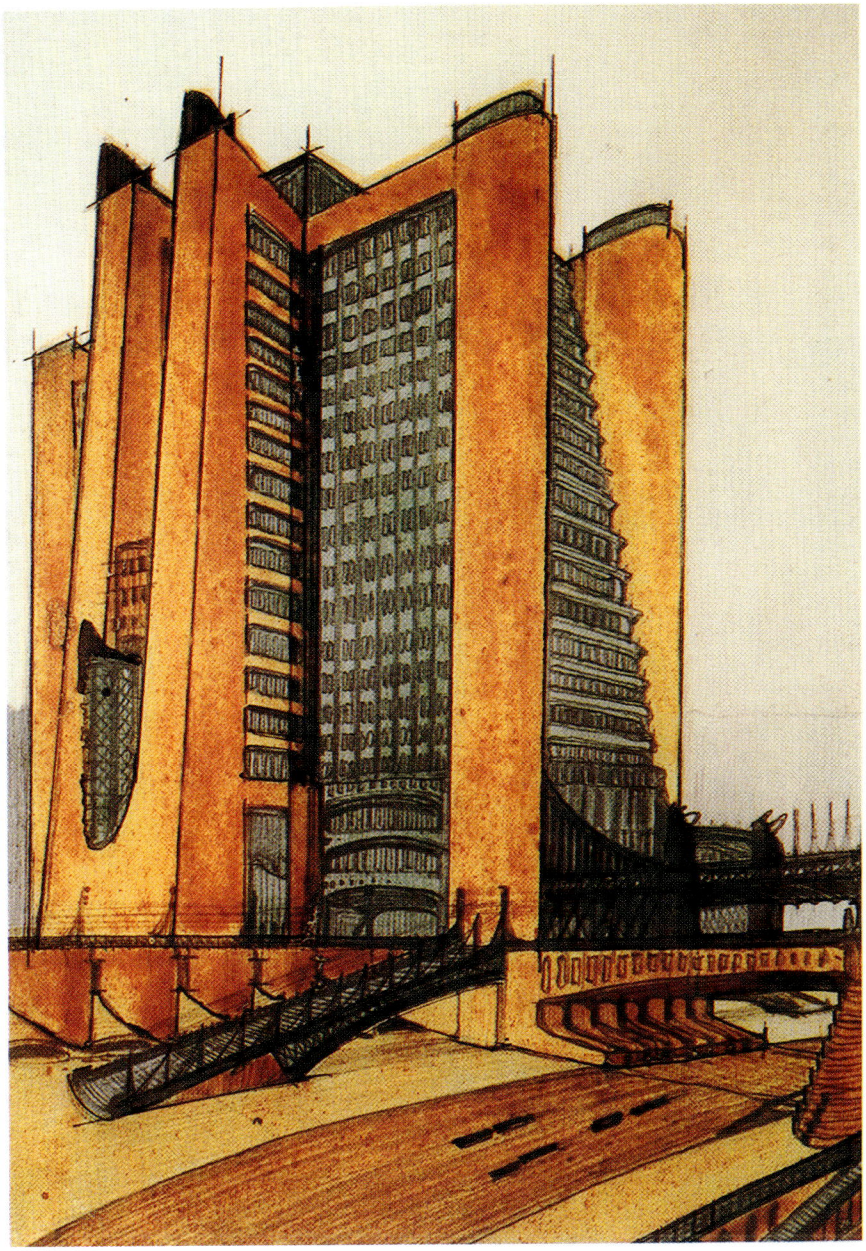

Antonio Sant'Elia,
The New City, 1914.

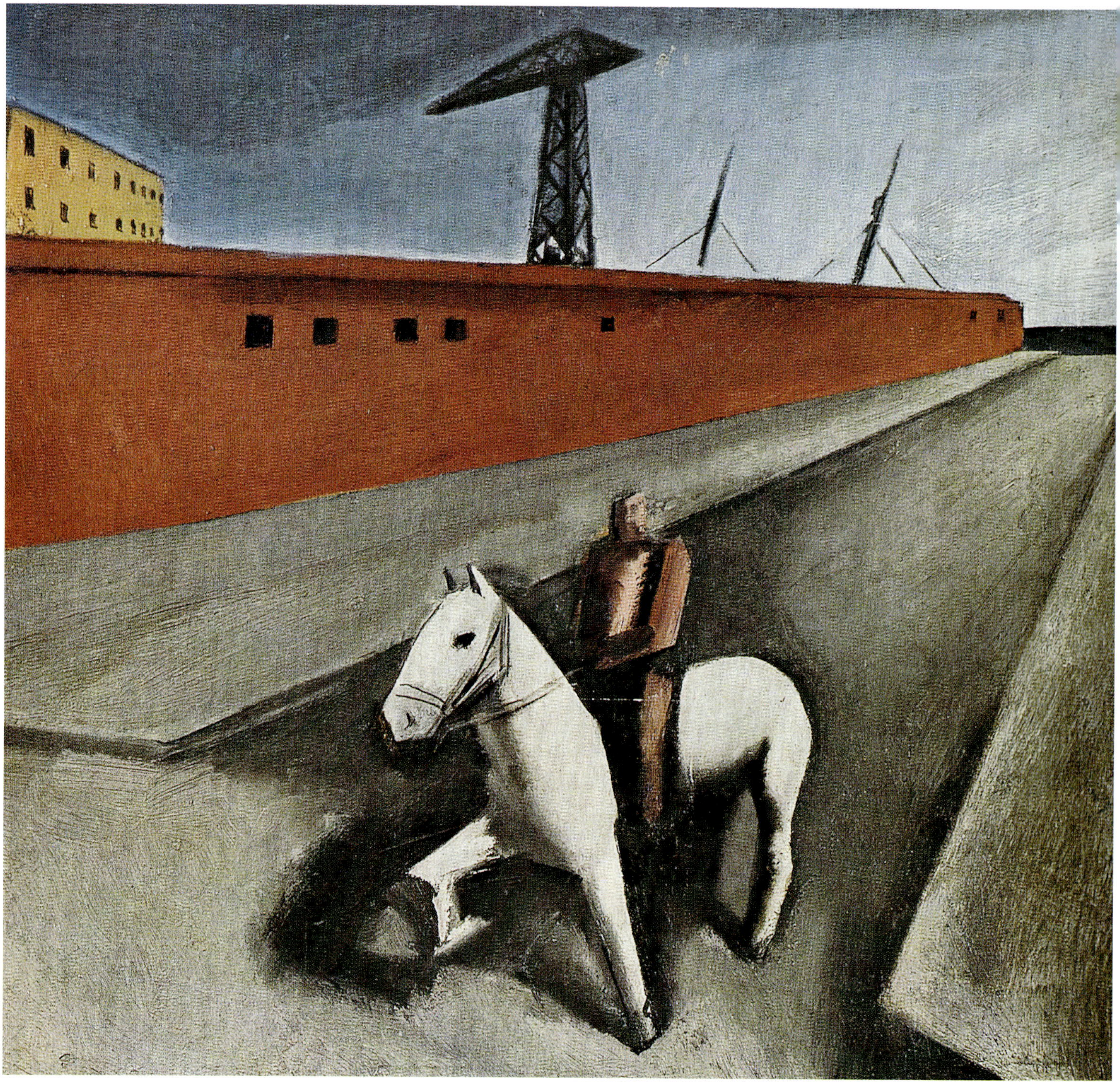

Mario Sironi, *Outskirts of City with Horseman*, 1924.

had contained food distributed by American soldiers to the famished population of Italy just after the war.

Not by chance, perhaps, these sacks appear in elusive metaphysical compositions, where heads recline like those of ancient statues, painfully afflicted by the state of the nation. Is this a caustic reference to the post-war period, perhaps even to the allied aid policy? It may be; but it is also possible that the historical starting point rapidly dwindles to a mere expedient for attracting attention. In the late Forties and early Fifties the activity of artists took on a specific autonomy, a haste to decline responsibility, to bury memories, resentment, social duties; to leave behind the artistic and cultural orientation of the years between the two wars. What interests Burri (and what others surely learned from him) is not an evocation of the horrors of war nor the open wounds in the body of a nation divided and defeated; nor even Italy's state of restricted independence under the Marshall Plan. He is much more concerned with focusing attention on the construction of the canvas, on the bare laborious work that precedes the image, and lastly on the private and voluntary nature of the artist's activity.

It is on this level, finely balanced between rhetoric of (and responsibility for) the construction and free play of composition, that the artists of the younger generations encounter Burri – with a decided predilection for playfulness; and the obligation to refer to any historical or social context fades away or vanishes entirely. Proof of this is offered by the two artists who more than all the others – for biography, catalogue of works and sphere of acceptance – exemplified the new artistic and social scenario of the Sixties.

This decade was to see the affirmation of new painting techniques, the establishing of new relations between artists and the public, the mildly authoritarian emerging of a new condition of interest and even of aesthetic evaluation, the demographic age. Starting in the Sixties, self-portraits of artists were to benefit essentially by the fact of being self-portraits of the artist as a young man. Both Piero Manzoni and Pino Pascali seem to personify the *enfant prodige*, even on the level of concrete existence. They were both to die young, either for secret vulnerability or for fragile, insouciant recklessness. Their work, abundant and produced with no apparent difficulty, effort or premeditation, in a state of light-hearted ease, pleasure and superior incompetence, shows none of the painful fatigue, the tragic sublimity of the traditional artist, struggling against a hostile society and the great

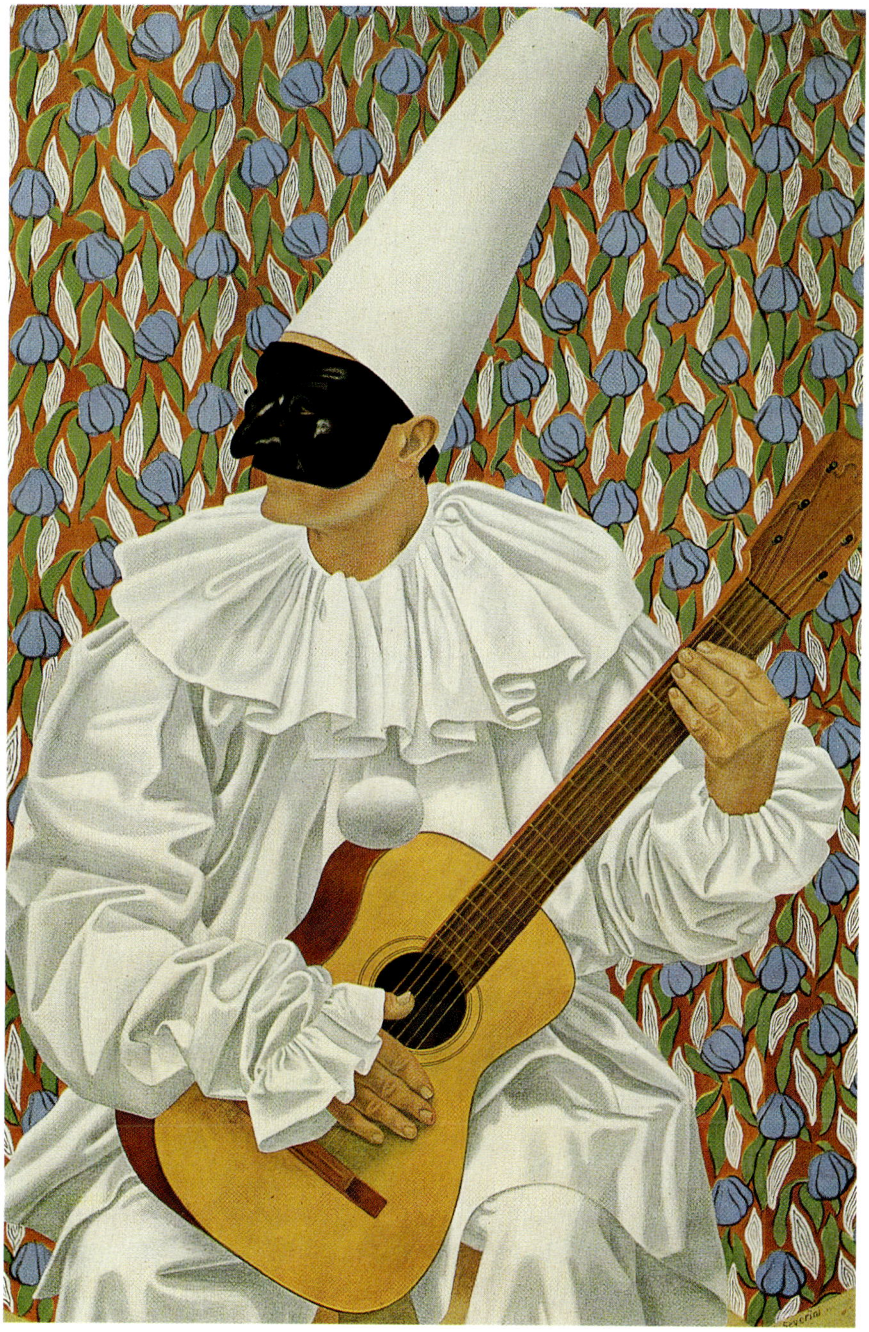

Gino Severini, *Pulcinella*, 1924. Rotterdam, Boymans-van Beuningen Museum.

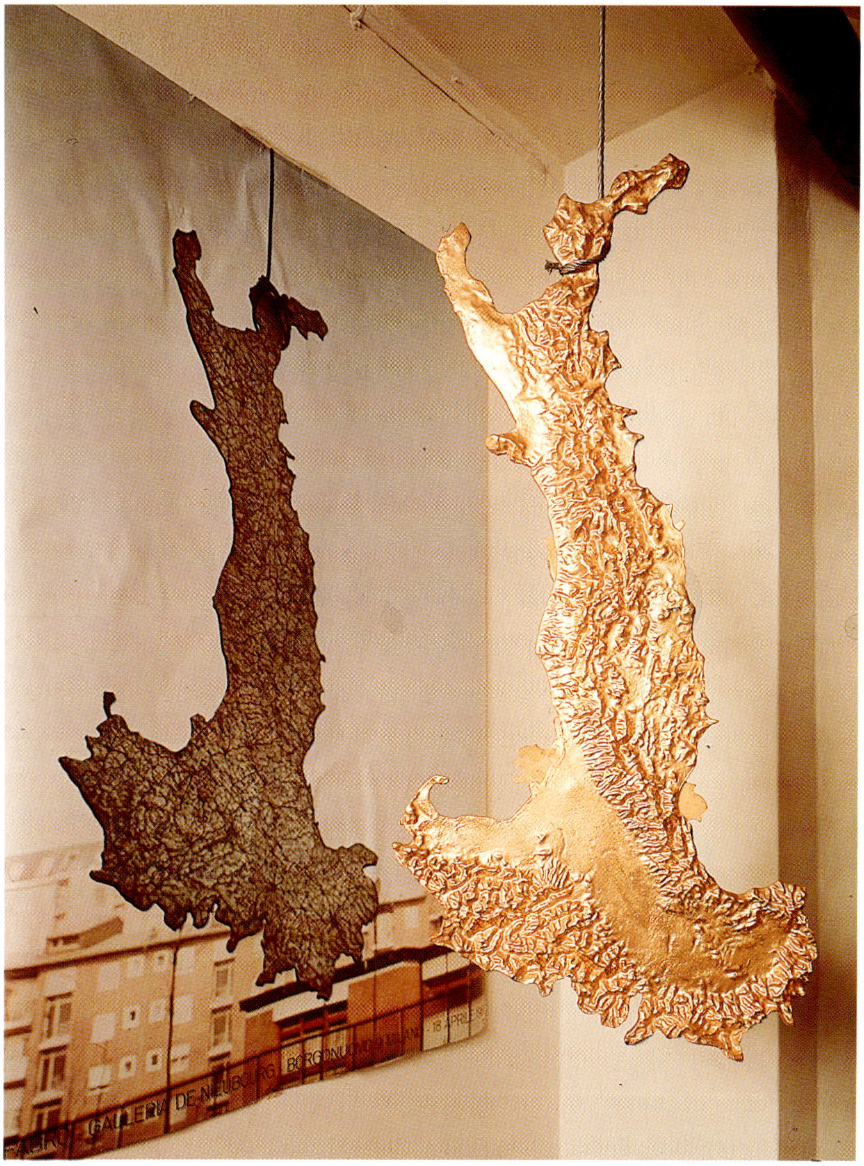

Luciano Fabro,
Golden Italy, 1971.

masters of the past. With seductive skill they move within the shadow of illustrious tutors, artists, art historians, collectors, suddenly grasping, like adolescent demigods to whom nothing is denied, marvellous opportunities – taking from art history whatever they want and making it their own, reinventing it with no concern for the boring, archaic laws of ownership.

As noted by Alberto Arbasino, the early Sixties saw the start of the "youthful tendency to utilize no more tradition and the past to construct new ensembles (according to literary images and figurative emblems: modern dwarfs on the shoulders of classical giants, the plant of new life on the ruins of the ancient world...), but rather to exploit existing elements: institutes, buildings, vehicles, apartments, household furnishings, cultural channels established by others, of which to ask hospitality, complicity and passage (while in older, more restricted epochs, each generation constructed by itself its own institutions and its own structures)...".

Art is neither torment nor genius nor social and intellectual representation, nor even profession. Rejected as such – as the earning of merit through the patriarchal social rules of labour and fatigue – it is rather an attitude permeating existence as a whole, it is irony, exploration and journey, time reduced to pure motion, paradisiacal physiology.

A final comment on the following pages remains to be made. We have attempted to present the individual artists, especially those of the most recent decades, without excessive reference to movements, tendencies, "group poetics". These, with the passage of time, tend to become more remote. In retrospect they no longer seem so influential, as least not such as to allow us to classify artistic activity collectively.

Obviously, consensus has at times reigned between certain critics and certain artists in regard to an artistic/cultural agenda, an issue, a viewpoint; more or less intense, significant relationships have existed; and these have had consequences, at least on the level in which the work (and the discussion of the work) becomes communication.

Here we should recall at least the "poor art" movements that emerged in the late Sixties and

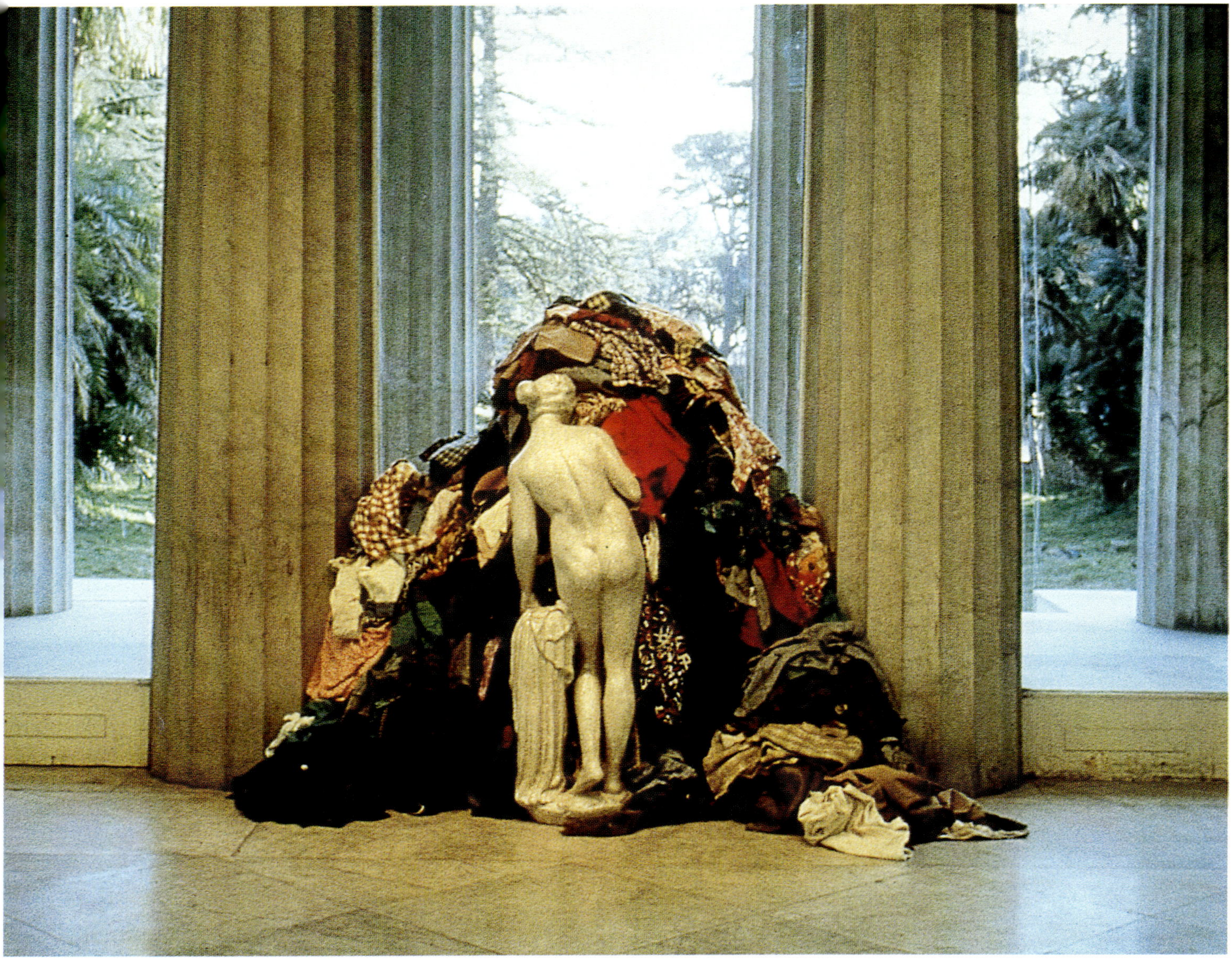

early Seventies around conceptual tendencies; and the "Transavanguardia" movement that heralded, in the very early Eighties, the striking return of painting and sculpture to public and critical favor. In the Nineties the panorama of Italian art reflected the neo-conceptual orientation predominant on the international scene: photography, installations, and video became once more the figurative genres most congenial to artists.

Michelangelo Pistoletto, *Venus of the Rags*, 1968.

Gino Rossi

(Venice 1884 – Sant'Artemio di Treviso 1947)

The apprenticeship of the intense, cosmopolitan artist Gino Rossi was predominantly French. In Brittany in 1907, then in Paris, Belgium and Holland, he was close to the Nabis and Symbolist trends. His painting shows characteristics of elegant *cloisonné*, like a lacquer, a Medieval enamel that encompasses within a single plane of representation figures, landscape elements, and details of costume and furnishing. In 1912 Rossi exhibited his works at the Salon d'Automne in Paris along with Modigliani and Arturo Martini. With both of these artists he shared a search for models of strongly synthetic image, where the motion of the lines expresses, without departing from the plane or simulating depth through the traditional techniques of chiaroscuro, the fullness of forms. In the post-war period Rossi moved closer to generically cubist or neo-cubist principles of composition, but without abandoning his basic predilections. In 1926 he was admitted to a psychiatric hospital, and his activity as artist came to an end.

Gino Rossi
Girl with a Flower
1909
canvas

Presented against the background of a wall painted in deep Marian blue, flanked by two niches holding floral compositions, a girl, probably Breton, meets the observer's gaze with the unflinching steadiness and remoteness of a statue. She has been compared with figurines of Far Eastern idols, and with the Breton and Provençal adolescents painted by Gaugin and Cézanne. Certainly the heraldic maiden of Rossi displays traits of allegorical personification, as she sits at the center of the painting – it might even be said, of the tapestry – almost as if to testify to the archaic, regal composure of a life that is both intensely religious and natural.

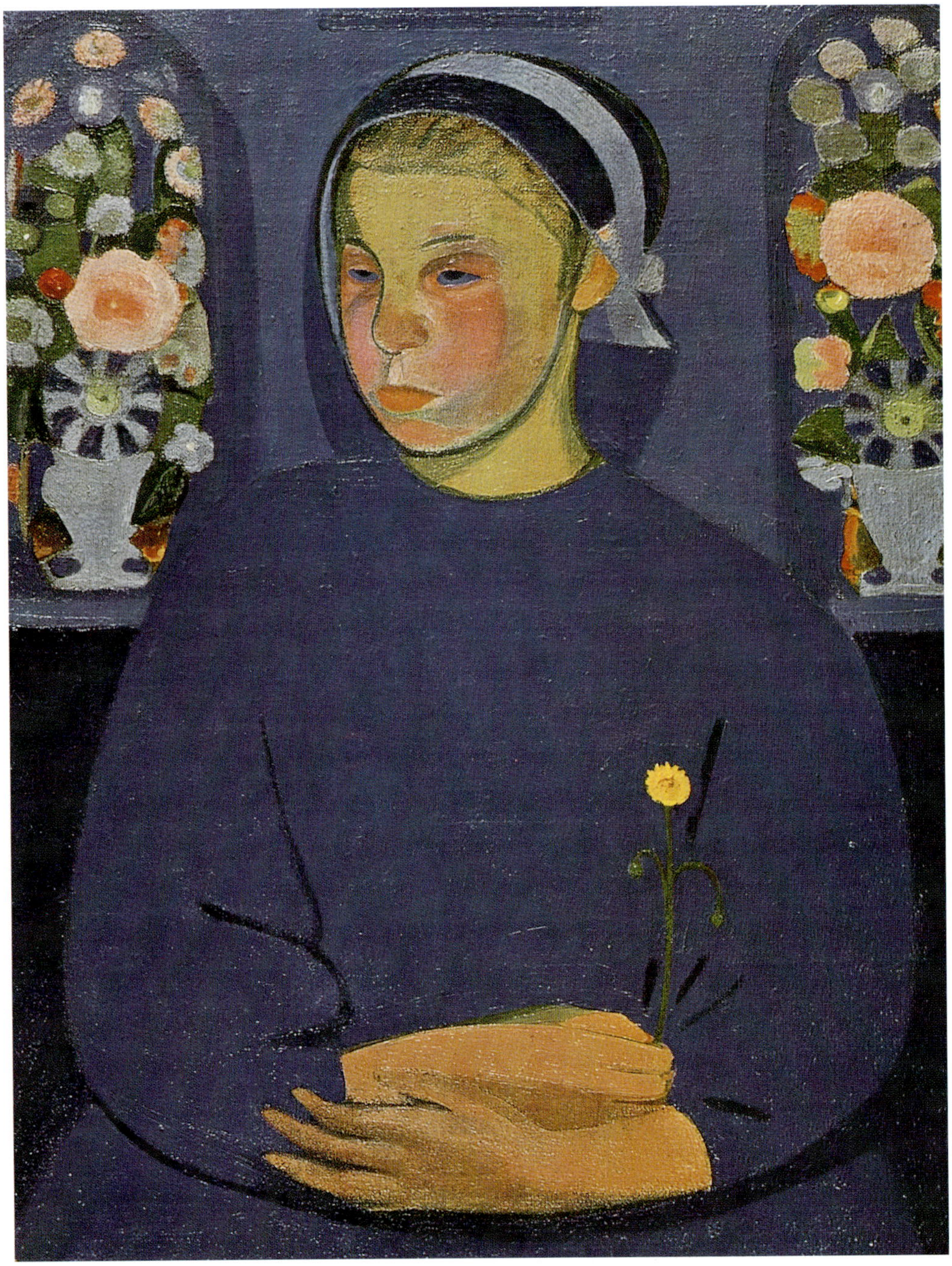

Arturo Martini
The Prostitute
1913
polychrome terracotta
Venice, Ca' Pesaro
Modern Art Gallery.

Dedicated to Nino Barbantini, organiser of exhibitions of young artists' work at Ca' Pesaro in Venice, the *Prostitute* reflects the young Martini's caustic, unprejudiced assimilation of generically primitive tendencies in contemporary painting and sculpture, as found in Minne, the Picasso of the blue period, Matisse, and even Kirchner. The female figure, her posture a parody of that of Rodin's *Penseur*, has a decidedly two-dimensional orientation. Like the bow of a ship fending the waves, she seems decorated with elements in high relief.

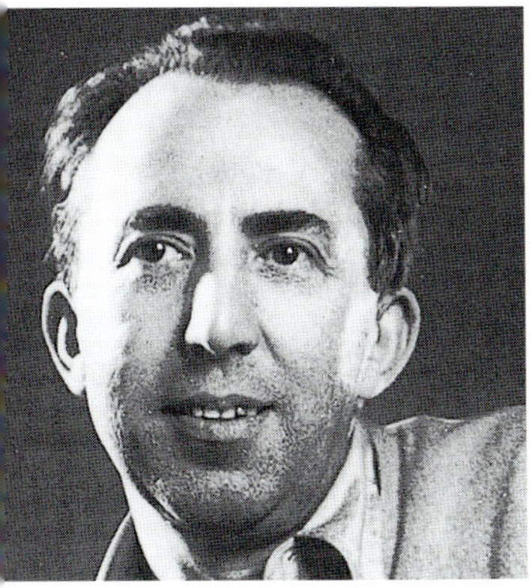

Arturo Martini

(Treviso 1889 – Milan 1947)

After training in Munich at the school of the German sculptor Adolf Hildebrand, Martini soon came into contact with the young Italian artists who were promoting a renewal in national art in the years prior to World War I. A temperamental artist, extremely sensitive to materials, Martini was a friend of Gino Rossi, with whom he traveled in 1912 to Paris, where he met Modigliani and Boccioni. His first sculptures show a provocatory archaicizing plastic orientation: severely two-dimensional, they frequently recur to polychrome effects. In the Twenties Martini joined the general trend toward a return to tradition, distinguishing himself, however, for irony, agility and eclectic capacity to combine or reinterpret sources within a context, the Italian art world of the time, dominated by the hyperstylistic attitude of sculptors purposely dedicated to imitating classic archeological models.

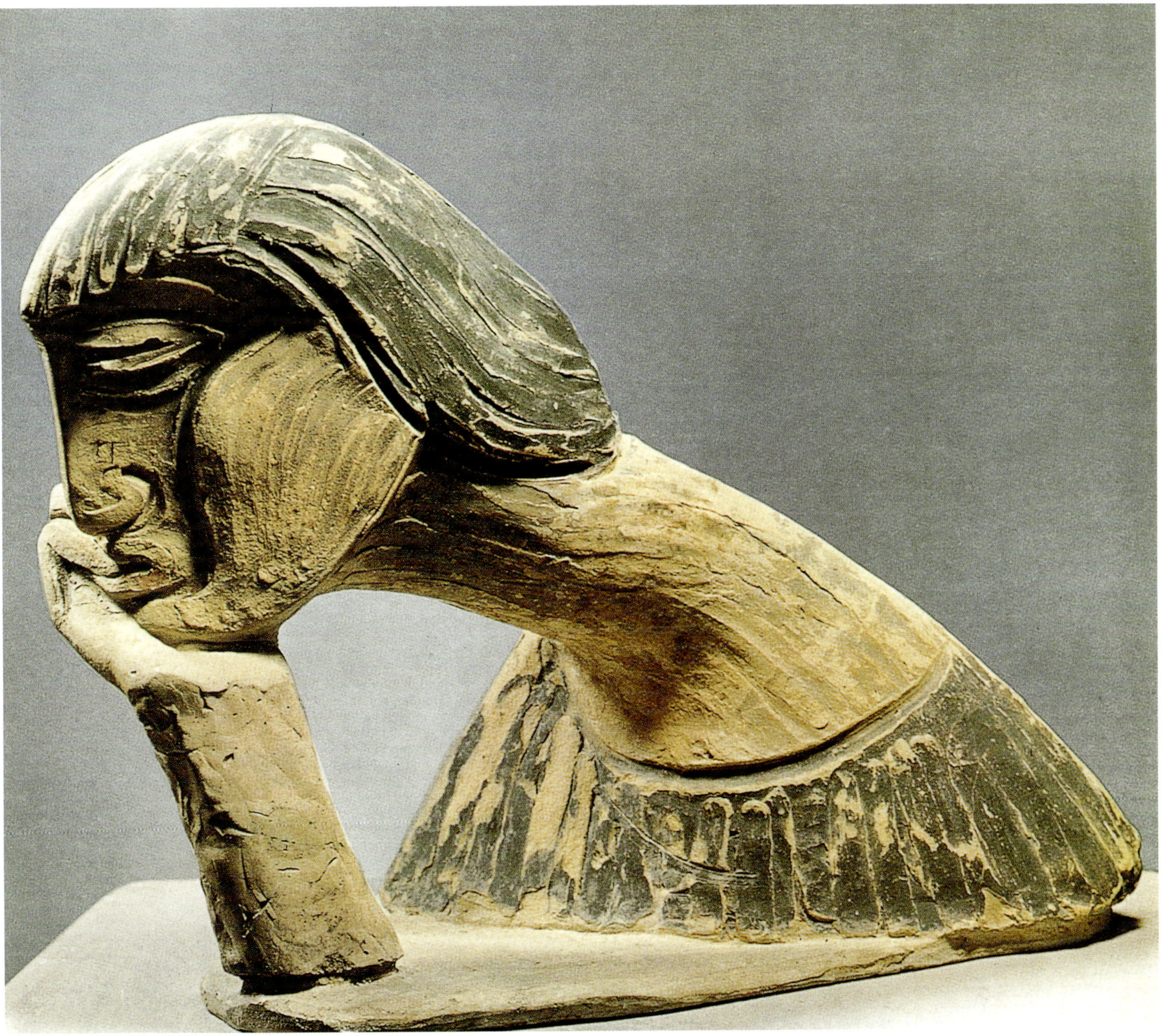

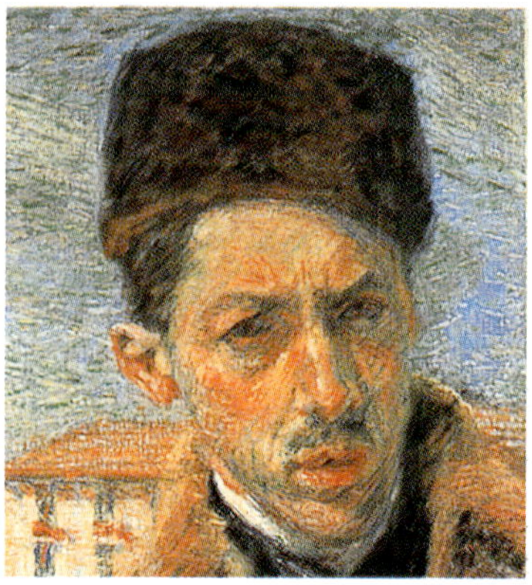

Umberto Boccioni

(Reggio Calabria 1882 – Verona 1916)

Boccioni, like Severini and Sironi a friend and admirer of Balla, underwent a divisionist apprenticeship at Rome and after several trips to Paris settled in Milan. An acute observer of the contemporary world, he exemplified from youth the typical Italian avant garde artist, torn between his own high, urgent expectations and disillusionment with the cultural and social situation of his nation. Immediately joining the Futurist movement, he became, with Marinetti, its most prominent member in the pre-war years. Active as painter and sculptor, he signed many manifestoes participated in the debate on the avant garde, arguing fiercely with French Cubists and German Expressionists. As cultural organizer, he promoted the new tendencies. As volunteer in the war he changed his approach returning to a more balanced plastic and chromatic composition reflecting the art of Cézanne.

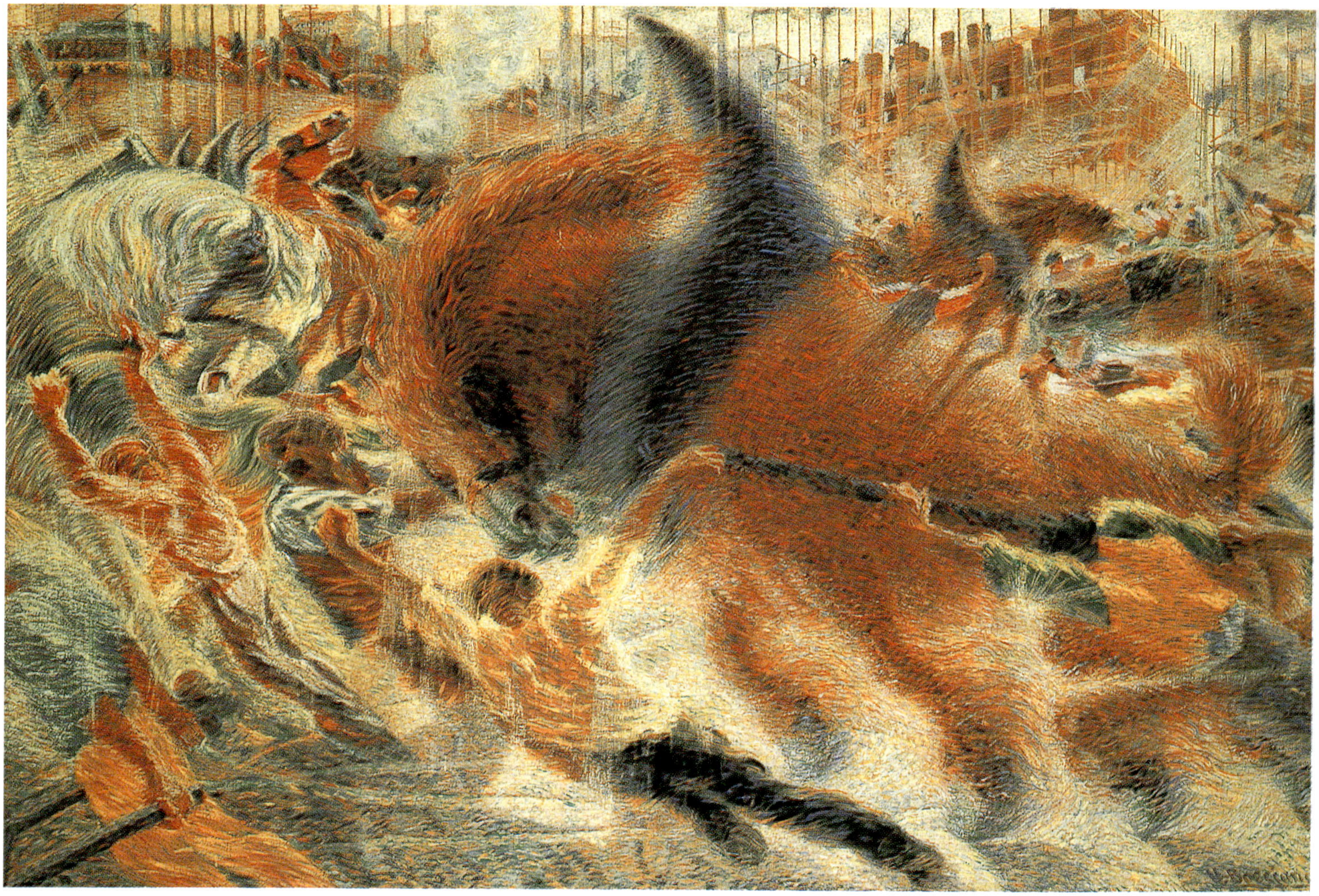

Umberto Boccioni, *Self-portrait*, detail, 1908. Milan, Brera Pinacoteca.

Umberto Boccioni
The Rising City
1910-11
canvas
New York, Museum of Modern Art.

The painting, which describes and simultaneously commemorates construction work as the model for great collective action, shows a crowd of workers struggling to control the fiery horses used at the worksite. In the background of the composition, still divisionist in technique, appears the great future city, goal and emblem of a conflictual, dramatic modernity. A young nation with unevenly populated regions, upheld by fragile institutions and a poorly representative monarchy, Italy occupied a position among Western European nations, in the opinion of contemporary commentators, that was economically and politically backward. In Boccioni's "rising city" can be recognized Milan at the turn of the century, a place that, in the eyes of the artist, is half utopia, half reality.

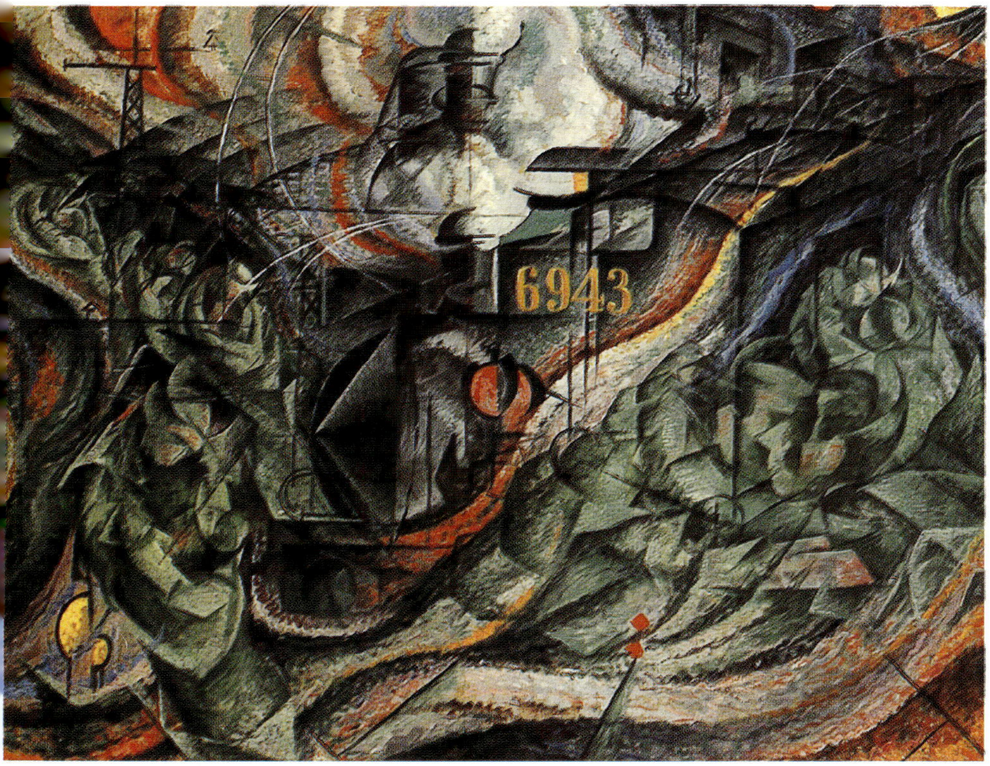

Umberto Boccioni
States of Mind II: Farewells
1911
canvas
New York, Museum of Modern Art.

This painting, in reality a second version of the *Farewells* theme, is part of a triptych conceived to illustrate the key locales and emotional dimensions of modernity. The scene portrayed is that of a railway station. A crowd falls back in a double wing before an advancing locomotive; its sharp, menacing profile, coated with hard metal, is puffing steam into a gray, lowering sky. In the background are glimpses of a semi-urban landscape: electrified hills, railway stations. The entire composition can be viewed as an ensemble of independent narrative elements. The image is not a unitary whole, but springs to life through the associations established first by the artist, then by the observer, between landscapes, figures, and circumstances that may be concurrent but are presented as multiple, listed as within a series – in Boccioni's words, "simultaneous". At the center of the composition stands out a number vividly painted in yellow-orange, almost like a semaphore, a device to attract attention. The "simultaneous" image – this is the meaning of the curious insertion – precludes the traditional requisite of Albertian window to form, as in a code, a conventional aggregate of signs, an inscription.

Umberto Boccioni
Single Forms in the Continuity of Space
1913
bronze
Milan, Civic Gallery of Modern Art.

Boccioni turned to sculpture after Cubist experimentation had deprived painting, in his opinion, of any reality or contact with reality. The level of abstraction reached in the *Triptych of States of Mind* represented, for the artist, an extreme limit from which he was prepared to withdraw. The statue portrays a vigorous male figure striding boldly forward – it may be a titan, a hero or more probably an athlete. Surprisingly, Boccioni interprets the space around the figure as a part of it, and the figure as a part of the space, according to principles of fluid continuity, and thus, so to say, baroque. The motion possesses body and unfolds in ample, consistent volutes, in lateral curls arranged on closely placed parallel planes, conceived as in relief.

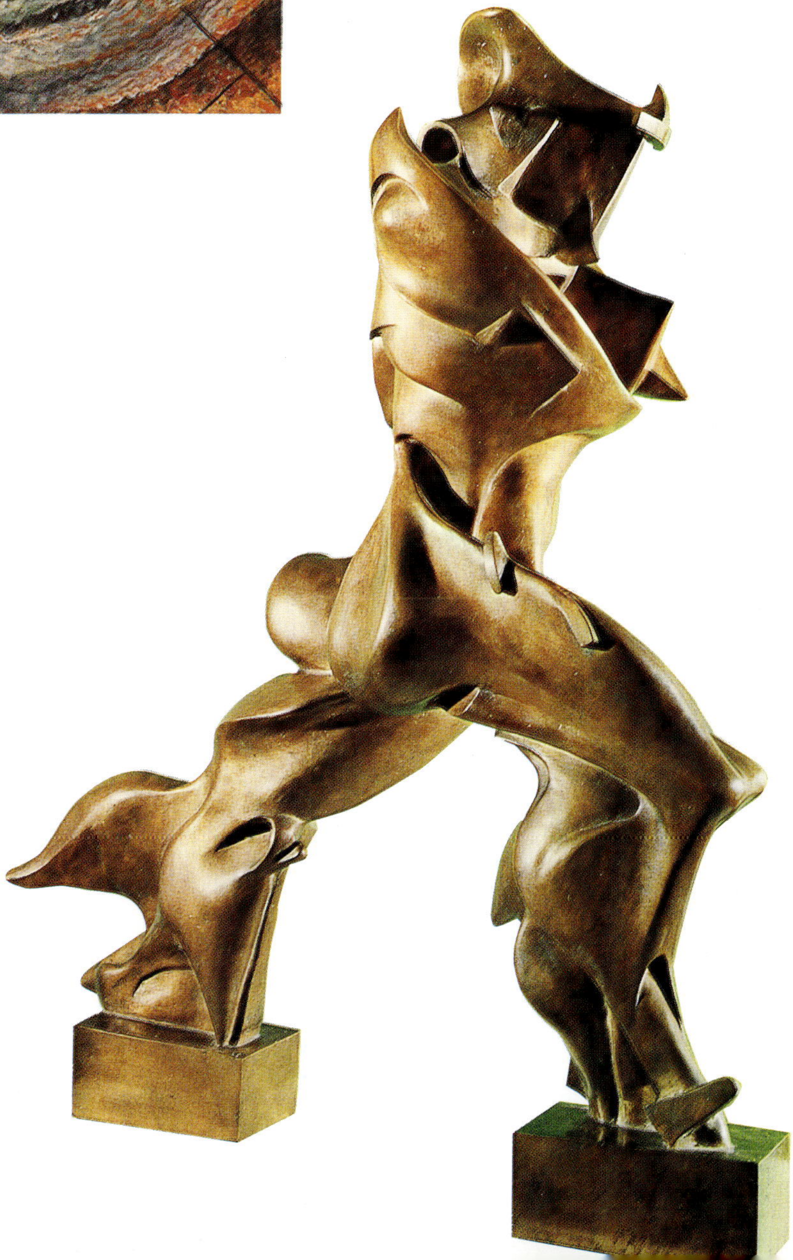

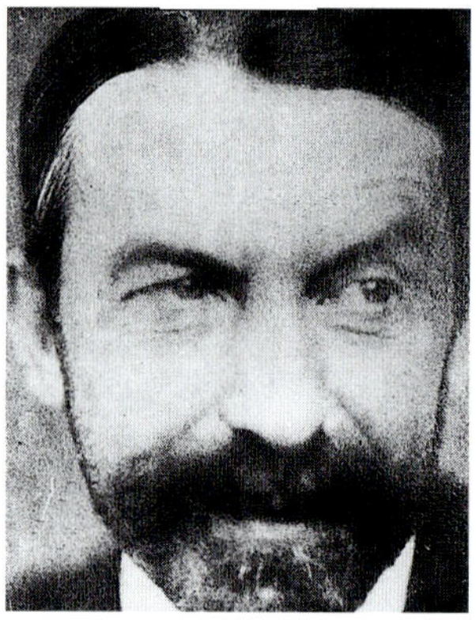

Giacomo Balla

(Turin 1871 – Rome 1958)

In Rome since 1895, Balla was a precursor whose importance as such has only recently been recognized. Imaginative experimenter, unconventional but not drastic, he first transferred to the Futurist avant garde the research and sensitivity matured in a divisionist apprenticeship: eminently formal problems such as that of the pictorial representation of light or its processes of propagation. Although long absorbed in the *Iridescent Compenetrations* (1912-14), among the first entirely abstract works of the European avant garde, he never forget his interest in current historical and social issues. The *Futurist Reconstruction of the Universe* manifesto, signed with Depero in 1915, marked a break with the most acute, destructive stage of Futurism, in favor of a joyfully figurative or neo-figurative art, akin to play and even to the elementary plastic activities of childhood, open to design, to fashion, and to the visual arts.

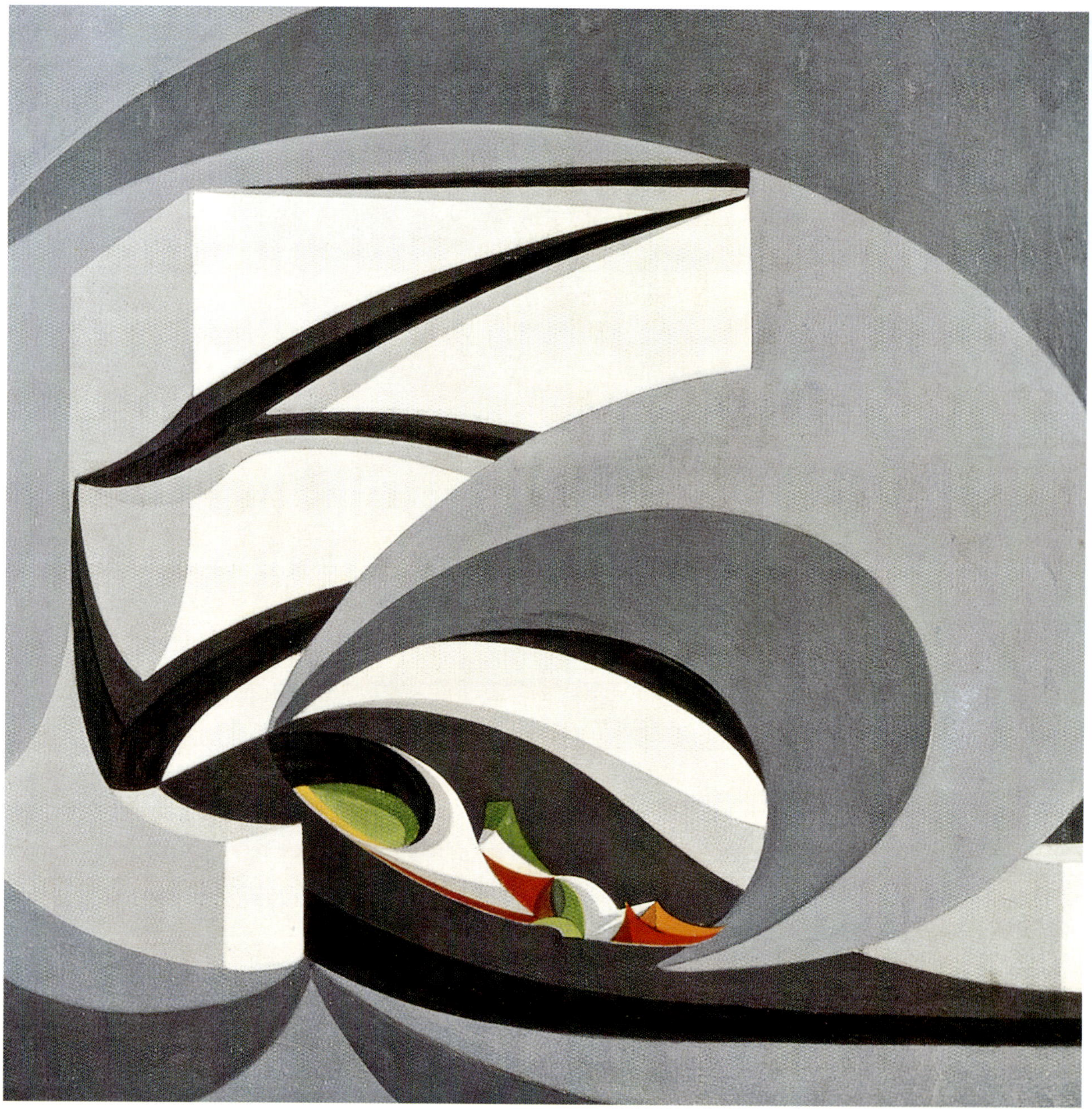

Giacomo Balla
Flags on the Altar to the Fatherland
1915
canvas

Balla's orientation around 1915, destined to exert a lasting influence on Futurism between the two wars, is clearly evident in this painting. The fragmented, deliberately convulsive images of the first period have now been replaced by a search for more composed, relaxing figurative dimensions, for a plastic world similar to that of construction toys. A bright polychrome palette confers on the images, regardless of the subject, the nature of toys. In *Flags on the Altar to the Fatherland* the patriotic theme, in itself solemn and charged with allusions to war, is presented without detriment to the limpid formal autonomy of the composition. The waving tri-colour flags occupy the centre of the painting. Around the crowd, portrayed not directly but through the flags, blue-grey plastic elements rise wave-like toward the sky, transmuting into plastic terms the unanimous voice that rises from the procession.

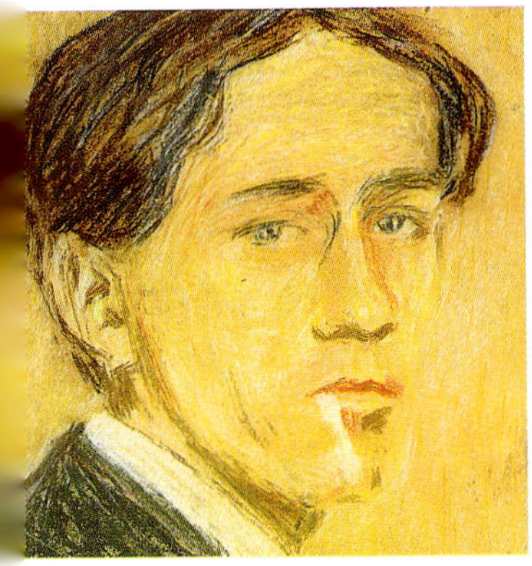

Gino Severini

(Cortona 1883 – Paris 1966)

Already a divisionist painter in Rome, a friend of Balla and Boccioni, Severini moved to Paris in 1906, resolved to become a versatile, refined *peintre de la vie moderne*. He adhered to Futurism at the very start of the movement, participating in the group's first exhibitions; lingering, in his paintings, on the places and customs that characterized the modernity of the metropolis; fervently exploring bold new painting techniques. He experimented with collages, multi-materials, and compositions of words. In the World War I years his attitude changed even more drastically than that of the other Futurists. The return to an art reminiscent of tradition and traditional techniques signified for him, having declared the avant garde experience concluded, a kind of religious issue, a conversion. The profession of artist had become both popular and consecrated.

Gino Severini, *Self-portrait*, detail, 1907-1908. Gina Severini-Franchina Collection.

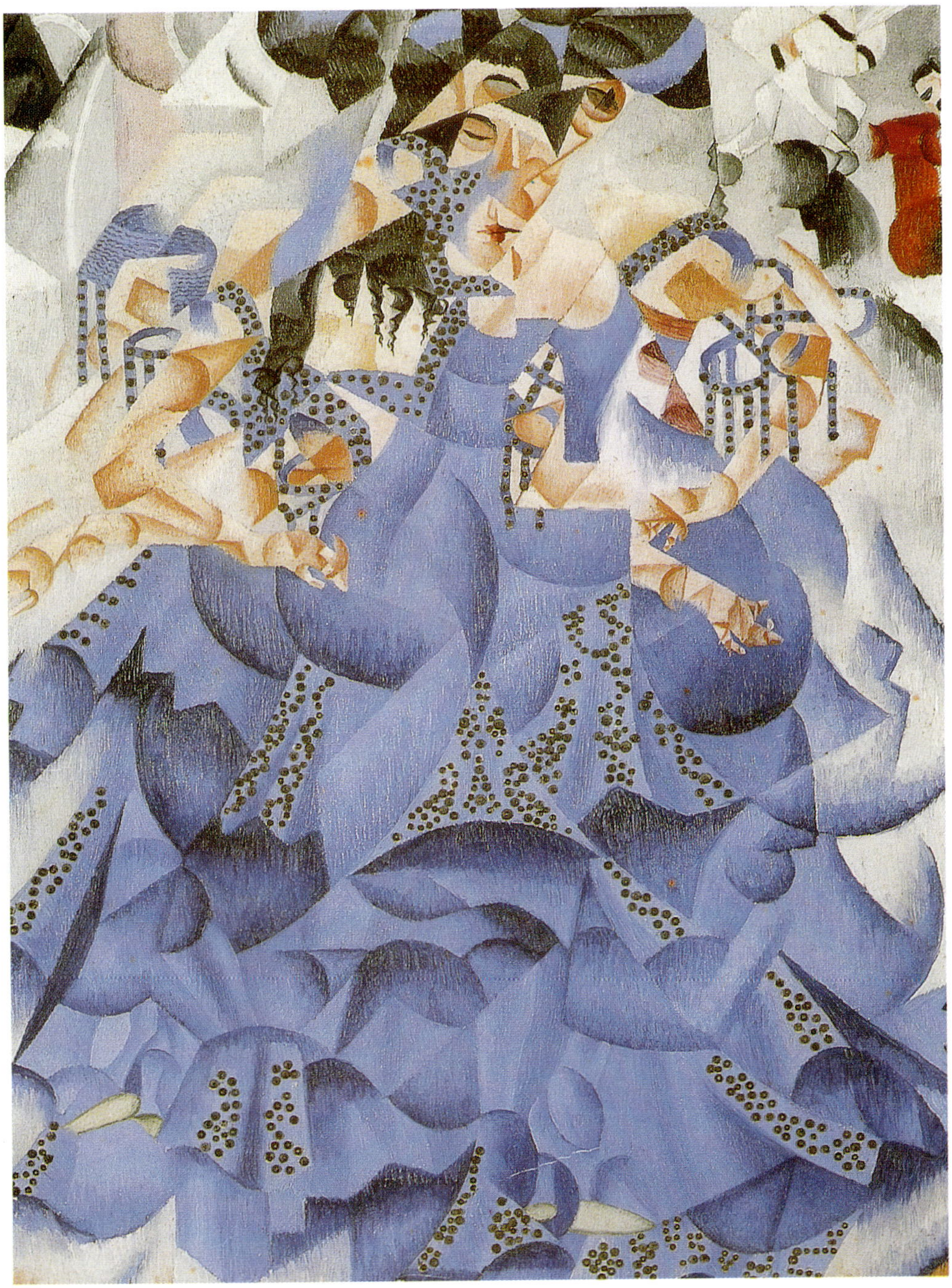

Gino Severini
The Blue Dancer
1912
canvas

The composition is painted in the colours of the French flag, blue, red and white, as if in homage to the leading nation in the artistic and cultural world of the times. It portrays an exotic dancer, probably Spanish, wrapped in a mantilla – on the whole, a Manet-like theme. The figure of the dancer is fragmented as if seen through a kaleidoscope, a crystal prism. Minute refractions cause the image to move, impose movement on the eyes of the observer.

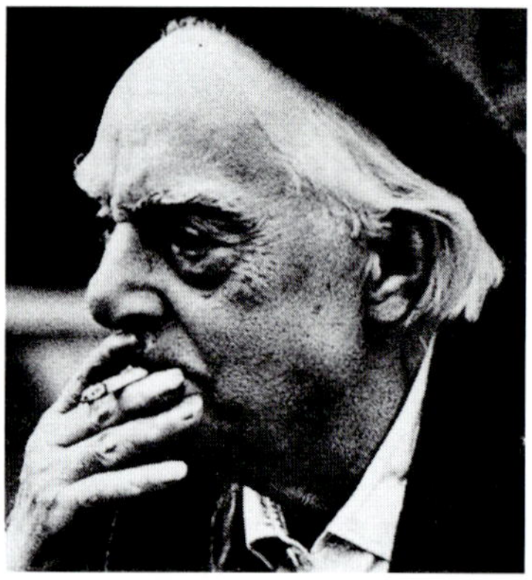

Carlo Carrà

(Quargnento 1881 – Milan 1966)

Born in Quargnento, near Alessandria, of a humble family perhaps of Provençal origin, Carrà arrived late at painting, enrolling in the Milan Academy of Brera in 1906. His participation in avant garde movements was tempestuous, gradually becoming more purposeful. Already by 1910 he was a member of the first Futurist movement. His metaphysical period, starting in 1917, brought him into close contact with De Chirico, Savinio, and De Pisis. In the decades between the two wars the artist was committed to a tradition-based approach of severe ethical and civil implications. Predominating in Carrà's work is a strong desire for solidity and order of composition interwoven with interest in current historical and social themes. Never yielding to the temptation to display a prodigious technique, nor any bizarre attitude or doctrine, he explained that his attention was focused on the mystery of "ordinary things".

Carlo Carrà
The Daughters of Lot
1919
canvas
Cologne, Ludwig Museum.

This composition, generally considered to mark the beginning of the painter's "Giottesque" stage, seems a version in code of the Christian theme of the Annunciation. The two figures, which the title tells us are the daughters of Lot, the ancient Biblical patriarch, pose like the Announcing Angel and the Virgin Mary in a 14th or 15th century panel. The standing woman places a hand over her belly as if to welcome or to reveal her incipient maternity. Painting – this is the meaning of the picture – makes of itself the womb of purest tradition, welcoming revelation in an attitude of humility.

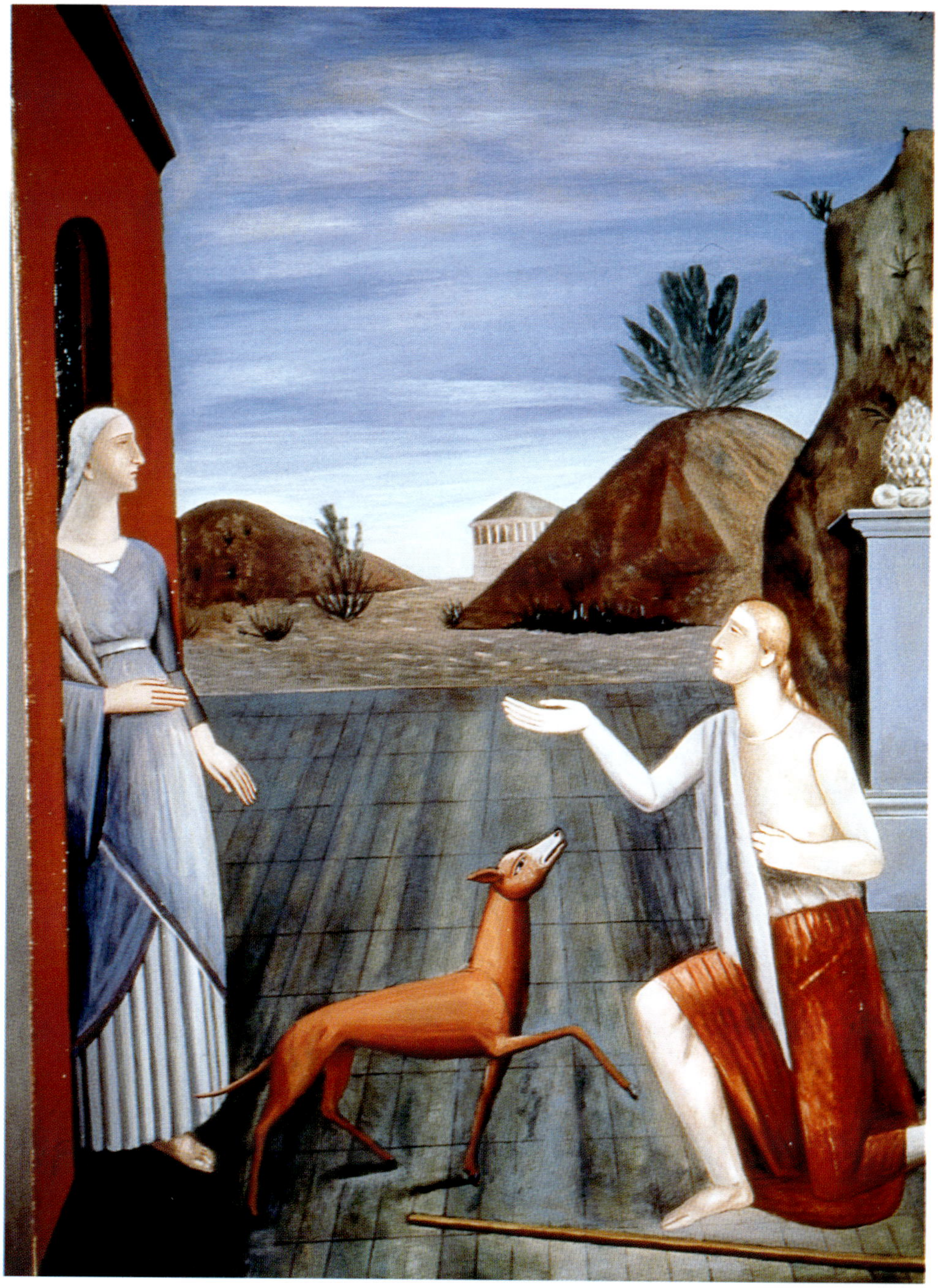

Carlo Carrà
The Hermaphrodite Idol
1917
canvas

Carra's "metaphysical" period began in 1917, at Ferrara. The Futurist fragmentation of images was superseded by a desire for well-ordered figuration. The ancient theme of the human figure reappears here, albeit in the ironical form of a mannequin. The idol's room presents an elementary perspective arrangement. The colours are the resplendent local ones of early Renaissance frescoes. Carrà himself was to recall how, in 1917, he conceived of the first compositions with mannequins: "My thoughts about art had arrived at the point in which the soul finds peace in the tranquil contemplation of reality [...]. Finding myself one night [...] wandering through the streets of Ferrara, I happened to see some mannequins abandoned against an old house lit up by a romantic moon. An apparition...".

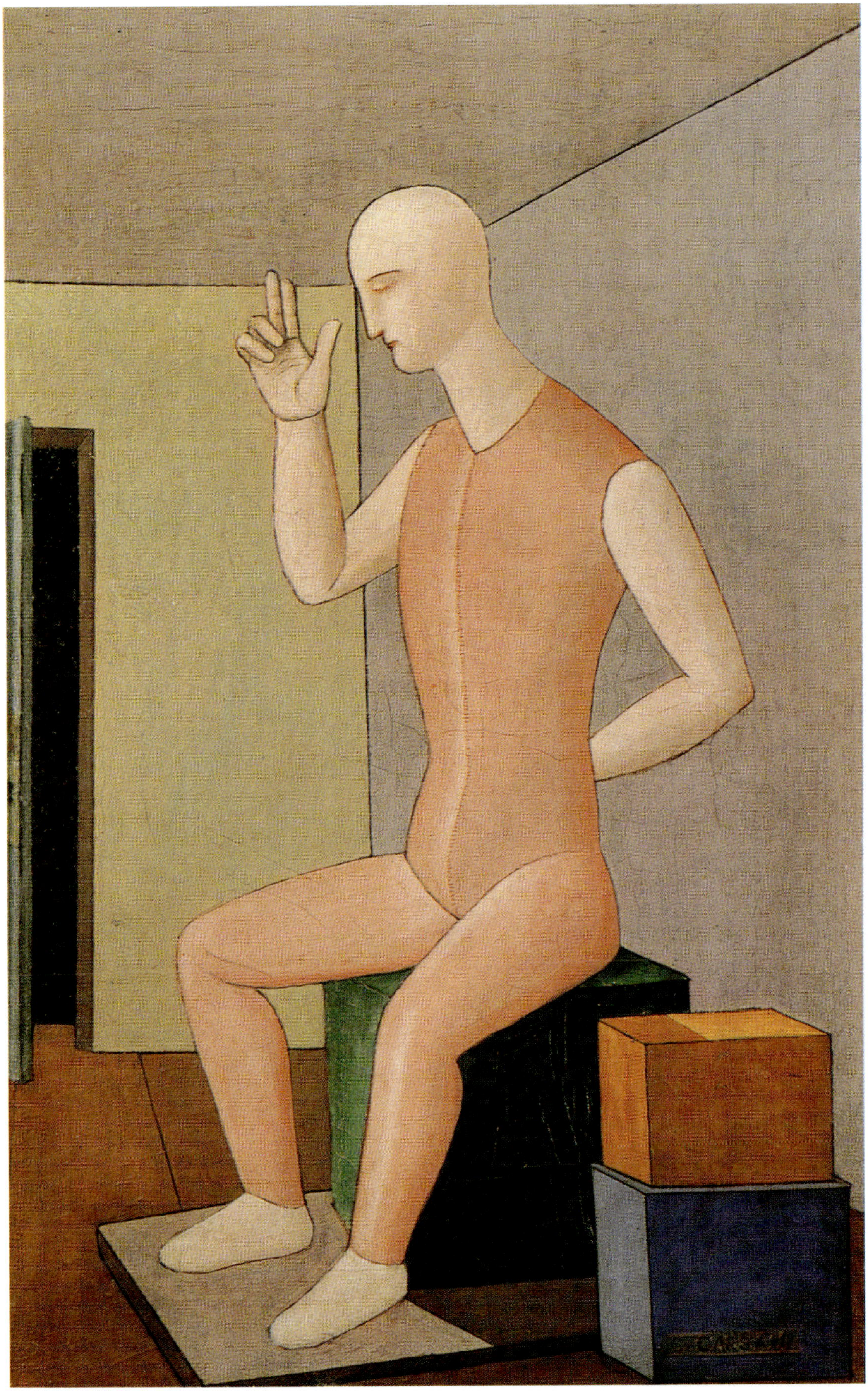

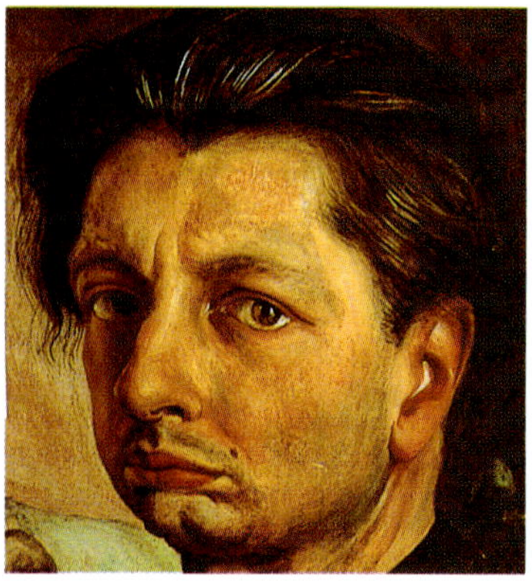

Giorgio de Chirico

(Vólos, Greece 1888 – Rome 1978)

Born in Greece of Italian parents – his father was a railway engineer, his mother a Genoese aristocrat – De Chirico, with his brother Alberto Savinio, constitutes an exception in the Italian artistic and cultural scenario of the first half of the century. He was a cosmopolitan who studied at Munich in 1906 and lived at different times and for many years in Paris; a polyglot, a connoisseur of music and literature as well as of the figurative arts, and author of literary and theatrical texts. With his complex experience and wide-ranging curiosity De Chirico fails to fit the *cliché* of the painter dedicated only to his art, devoted to his profession. His career included numerous periods marked by changes, at times radical. In conflict with the Cubist avant garde, De Chirico first conceived his "metaphysical" compositions as an ironic response to the experimentation of Picasso and Braque. Between 1917 and 1919-20 he was closely linked to

Giorgio de Chirico, *Self-portrait with Bust of Euripides*, detail, 1923.

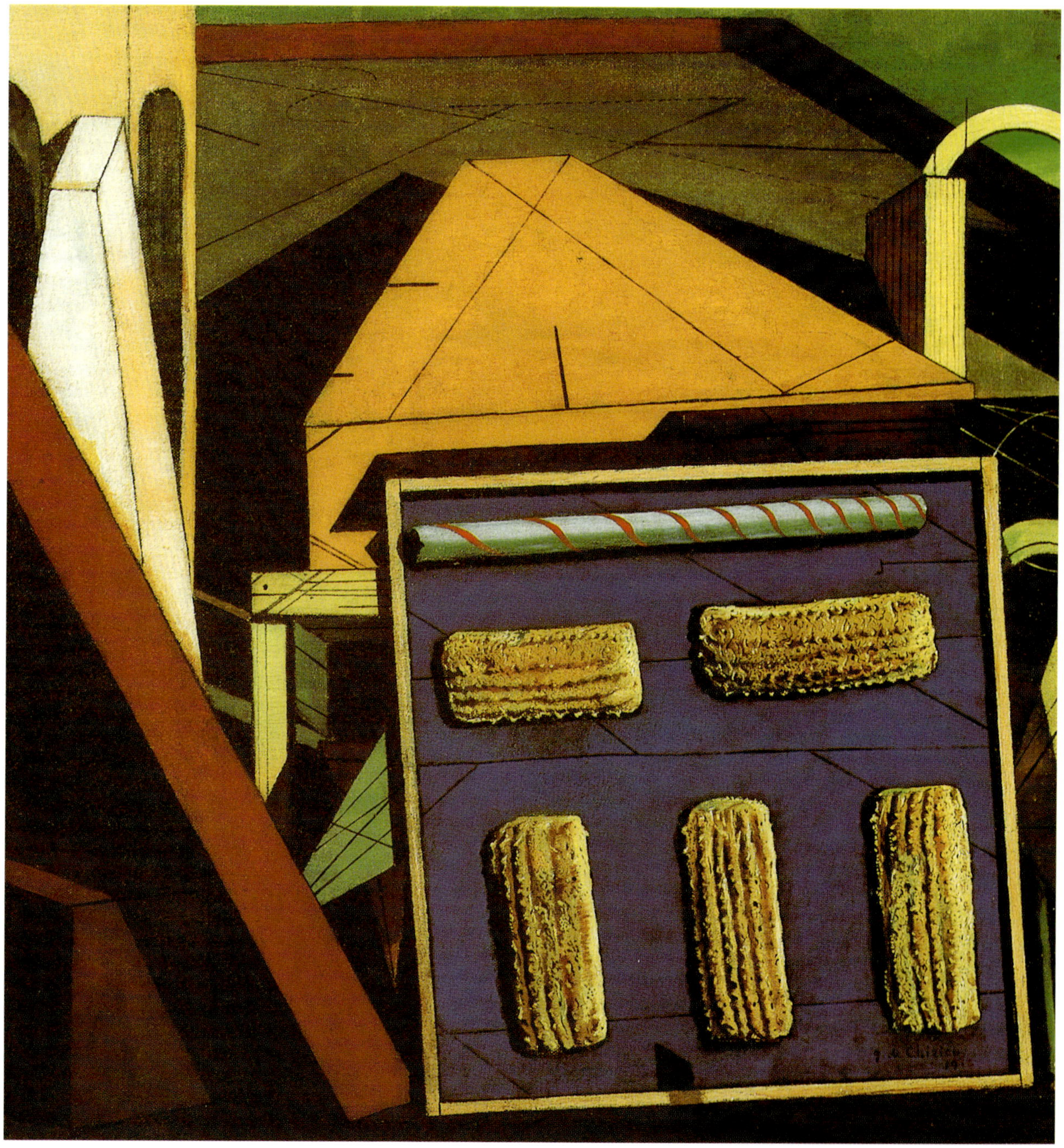

Carrà. In the early postwar period, having moved to Rome, he became the champion of a specifically Italian art, capable of re-establishing a dialogue with the grand tradition. But his classicism was always of abnormal stamp, with elements of mild parody and true kitsch cropping up as if in denial of his declared faithfulness to the canons.

Giorgio de Chirico
The Gentle Afternoon
1916
canvas
Venice, Peggy Guggenheim Foundation.

In 1916 De Chirico was in Ferrara, enlisted in the army. Practically unknown in Italy, he was still sending his works to Paul Guillaume, his Paris merchant. But it was Italy that the artist thought of as his homeland, Italian culture as his true sphere of action. He alternated compositions depicting mannequins and "metaphysical architecture" with others containing biscuits, loaves of Ferrara bread, match-boxes, spools of yarn, gloves, rulers and squares. He conceived his images as letters, elements in a ciphered correspondence, enigmatic riddles the key to which would be held only by an elect few. Here De Chirico seems to depict, in his usual hermetic way, the objects linked to his present reflections, his current existence. Proposals for action are mingled with melancholy comments on the nation, and nostalgic recollections of the family "interiors" of his childhood.

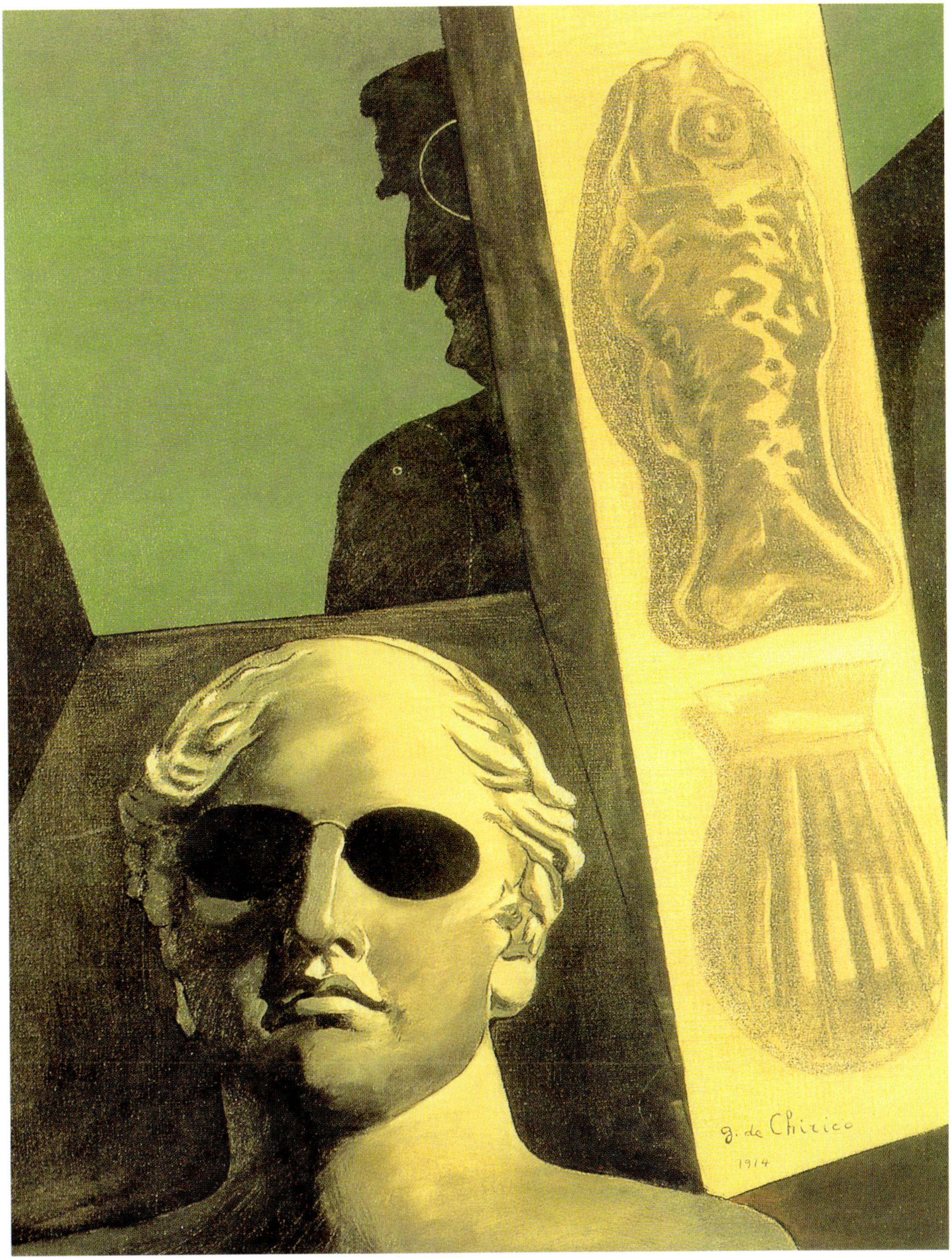

Giorgio de Chirico
Guillaume Apollinaire
1914
canvas
Paris, National Museum of Modern Art, Pompidou Centre.

A plaster cast portrait bust wears dark sunglasses and poses in place of the poet, a friend and supporter of the Cubists. The shadow of Apollinaire, with his distinctive profile, appears in the background. The model is curiously absent from the painting, which portrays instead two of his doubles – the bust and the shadow. Beside the plaster case is a fish, inhabitant of the depths and symbol of the Eucharist. Apollinaire, blind and clairvoyant, unites opposites and conciliates the human and the divine as Christ had done before him.

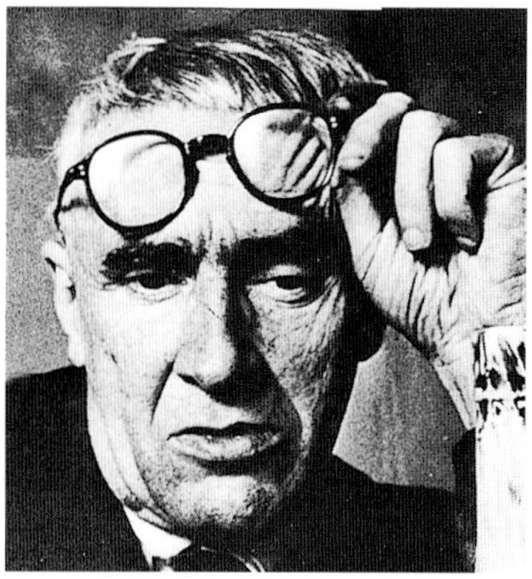

Giorgio Morandi

(Bologna 1890 – 1964)

Despite Morandi's provocatively Futurist debut, his career is exemplary for reserve and apparent detachment from contemporary culture and the loudly proclaimed politics of the times. Disinclined to involvement in the organisational and promotional aspects of the avant garde, he led a solitary, aloof existence, intolerant and caustic with the artists of his own age or younger who aimed to introduce into art more strongly historical and social aspects, even to the detriment of technique. His entire work reveals the attempt to take his place within an honored historical/ artistic genealogy, that of the modern French masters of still life and landscape. Following a brief "metaphysical" period Morandi became increasingly concerned with problems of light, of the local magic of forms, of a pictorial rendering of surfaces reminiscent of Cézanne and Chardin.

Giorgio Morandi
Bottles and Fruit Bowl
1916
canvas

Three pieces of household glass are placed against a polychrome blue-brown background, painted in horizontal bands almost in the manner of the most ancient illuminated manuscripts. The space is divided by the different bands of color. The dark brown band in the foreground stands for the thickness of the table on which rest the bottles and the fruit bowl, the light brown band for the table itself, shadowed toward the inside; and the ash-blue band for the back wall. The slight asymmetry conferred by the artist on the two most distinctly characterized objects in the still life – the bottle on the left, the fruit bowl on the right – and the vivid rotatory movement of the fruit bowl animate the forms as if to suggest that they possess an inner, secret existence; as if to mysteriously re-evoke before our eyes ancient battles.

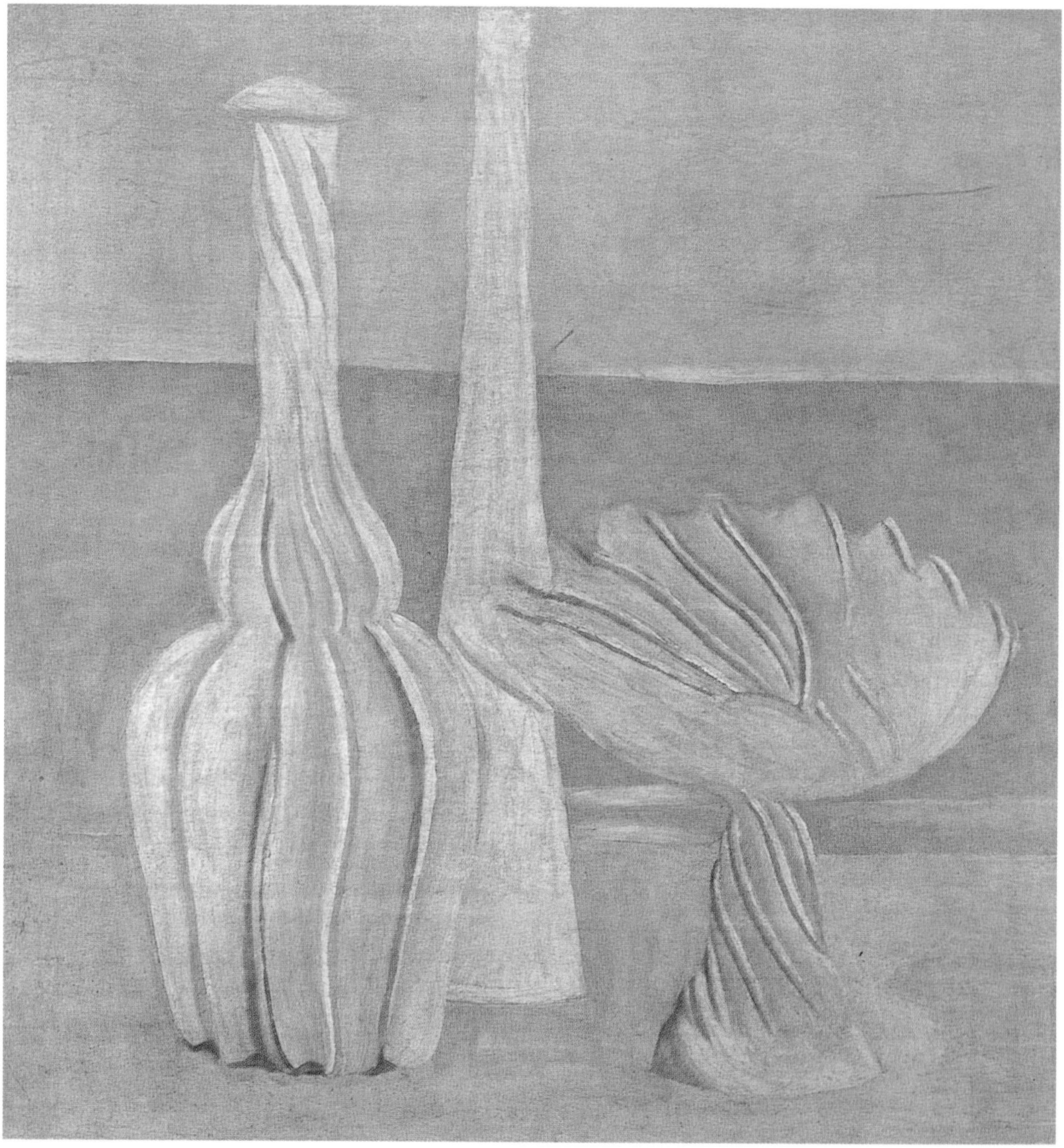

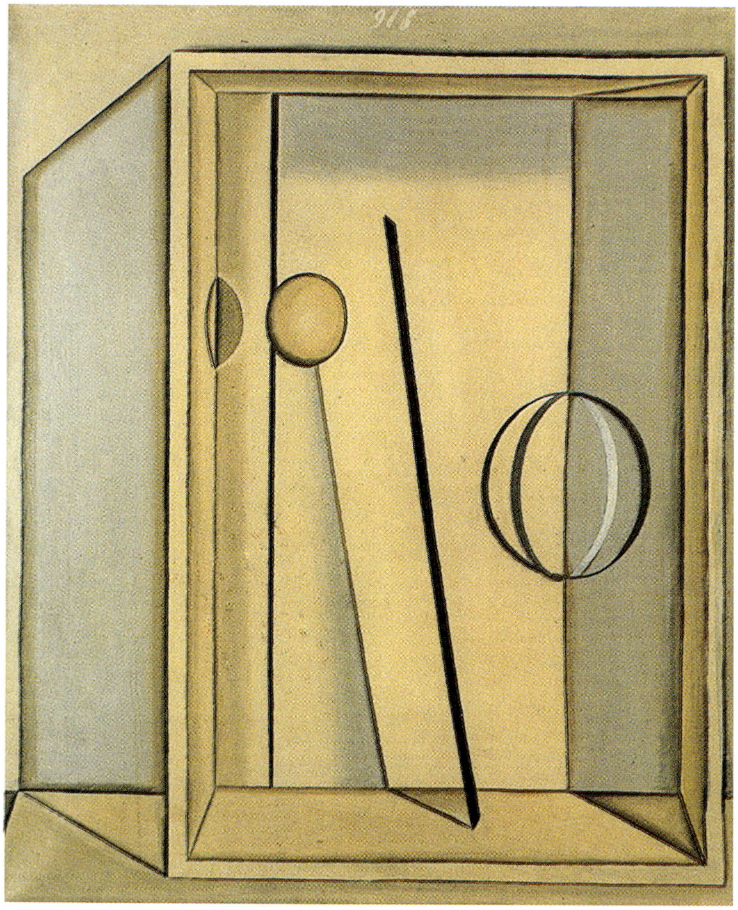

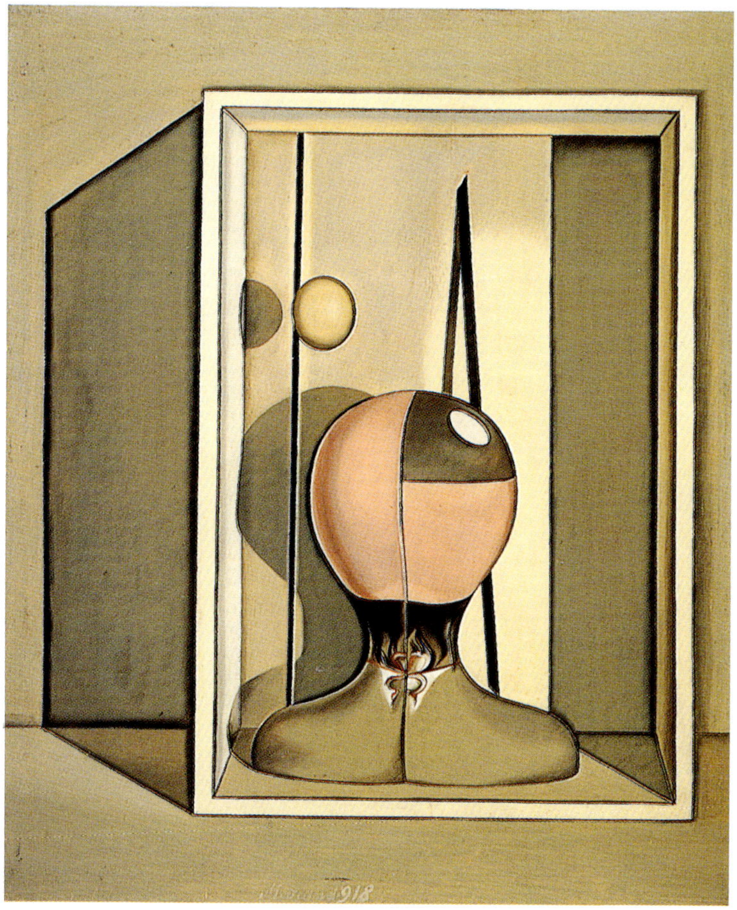

Giorgio Morandi
Still Life with Ball
1918
canvas
Milan, Civic Museum of Contemporary Art.

Still Life with Mannequin
1918
Canvas
St Petersburg, Hermitage.

Morandi's two most famous metaphysical still lifes are companion pieces to each other. Within the cases are the painter's tools of the trade. Rulers, spheres, bizarre mannequins, arranged according to magic rules of balance, almost suspended in the void, and accompanied by an evocative shadow, seem to await one who will make use of them, while simultaneously hinting at a revelation.

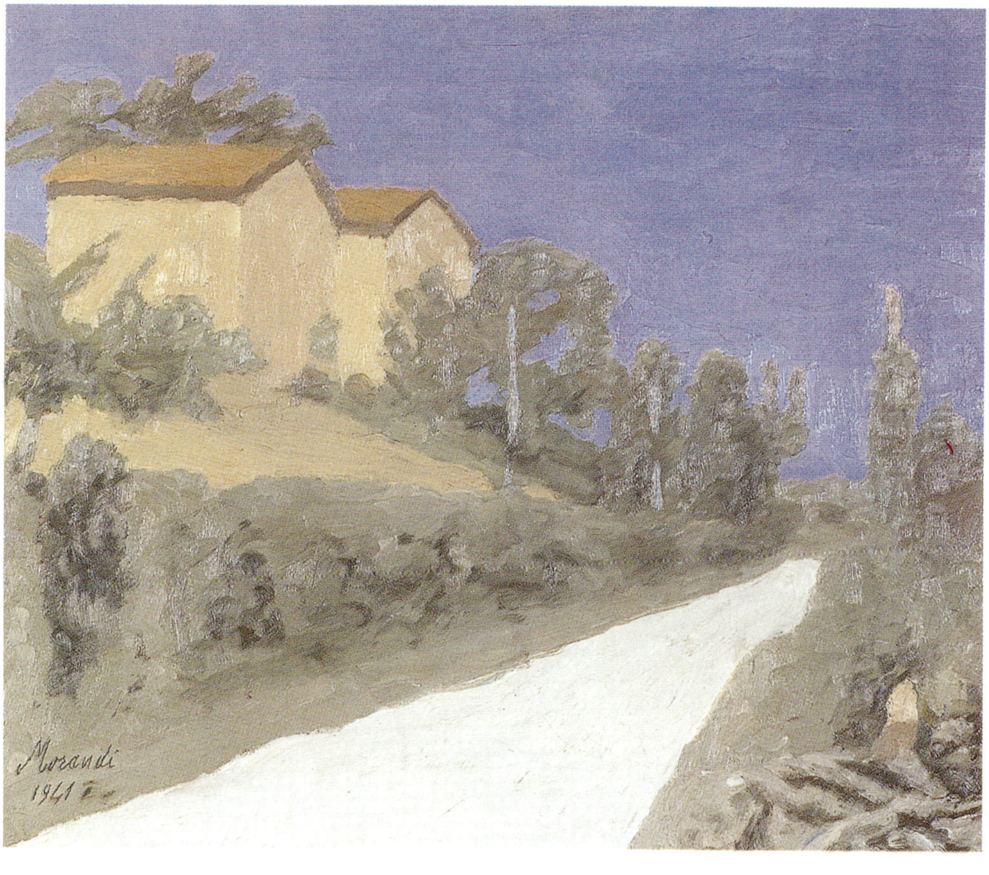

Giorgio Morandi
White Road
1941
canvas

Starting from 1927 Morandi spent his summers at Grizzana, a little town in the Apennines above Bologna. Here he walked, painted, and met with a few intimate friends. He worked on landscapes, fascinated by the possibility of transferring to canvas, and thus to a two-dimensional support, a reality made up of three dimensions. His landscapes present the features, both liquid and cohesive, of enamels and lacquers. The stylizing is not dissimulated: the artist's aim is expressly that of inducing appearance – trees, hills, paths, houses – to show itself as artifice.

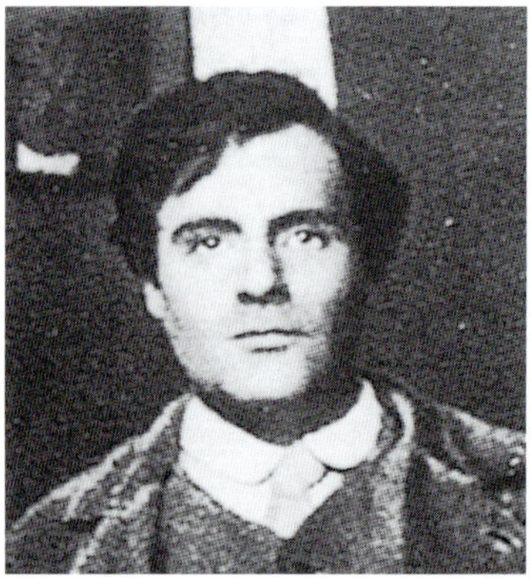

Amedeo Modigliani

(Livorno 1884 – Paris 1920)

Modigliani's biography seems to possess all the requisites that a *fin de siècle* novelist might ask of an artist: born in Livorno, after apprenticeship with a late Macchiaiolo painter he moved to Paris for a brief fiery career. Beautiful and passionate, unlucky and destructive, his real life soon became practically indistinguishable from legend. Attracted by African and aboriginal sculpture he turned, like his friend the Rumanian sculptor Constantin Brancusi, in the direction explored by André Derain, toward a synthesis between European art, particularly that of 14th century Central Italy, and non-European art. The muted palette distinctive of his compositions, his preference for complementary tonalities, blue-purple and red-orange or ochre, and the slightly caricatured inclination of his figures reveal his unceasing admiration for Cézanne.

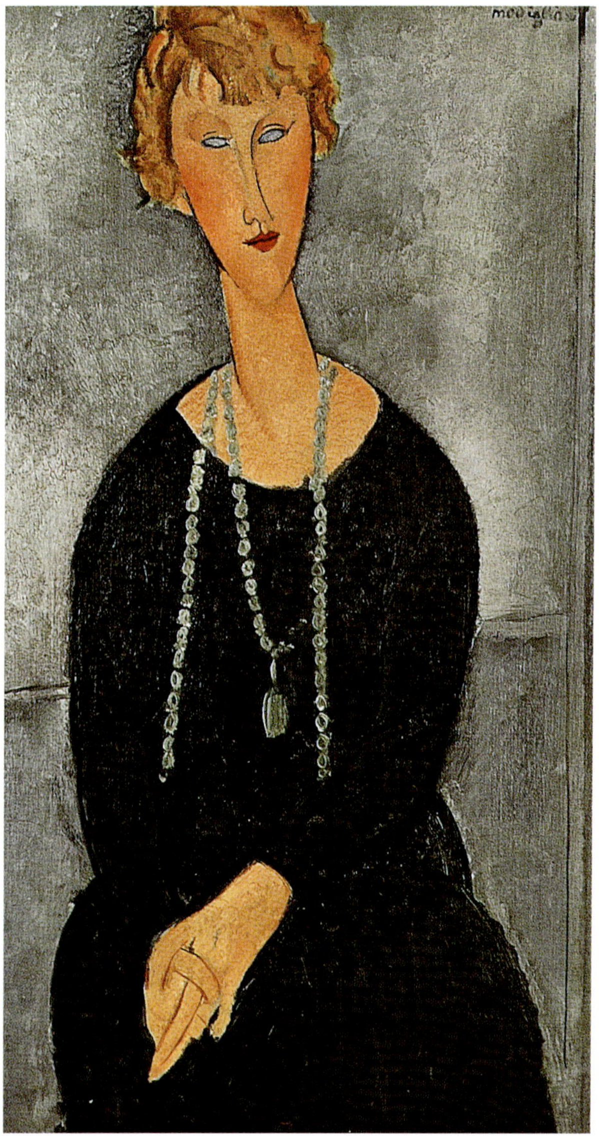

Amedeo Modigliani
Portrait of Madame Menier
1917
canvas

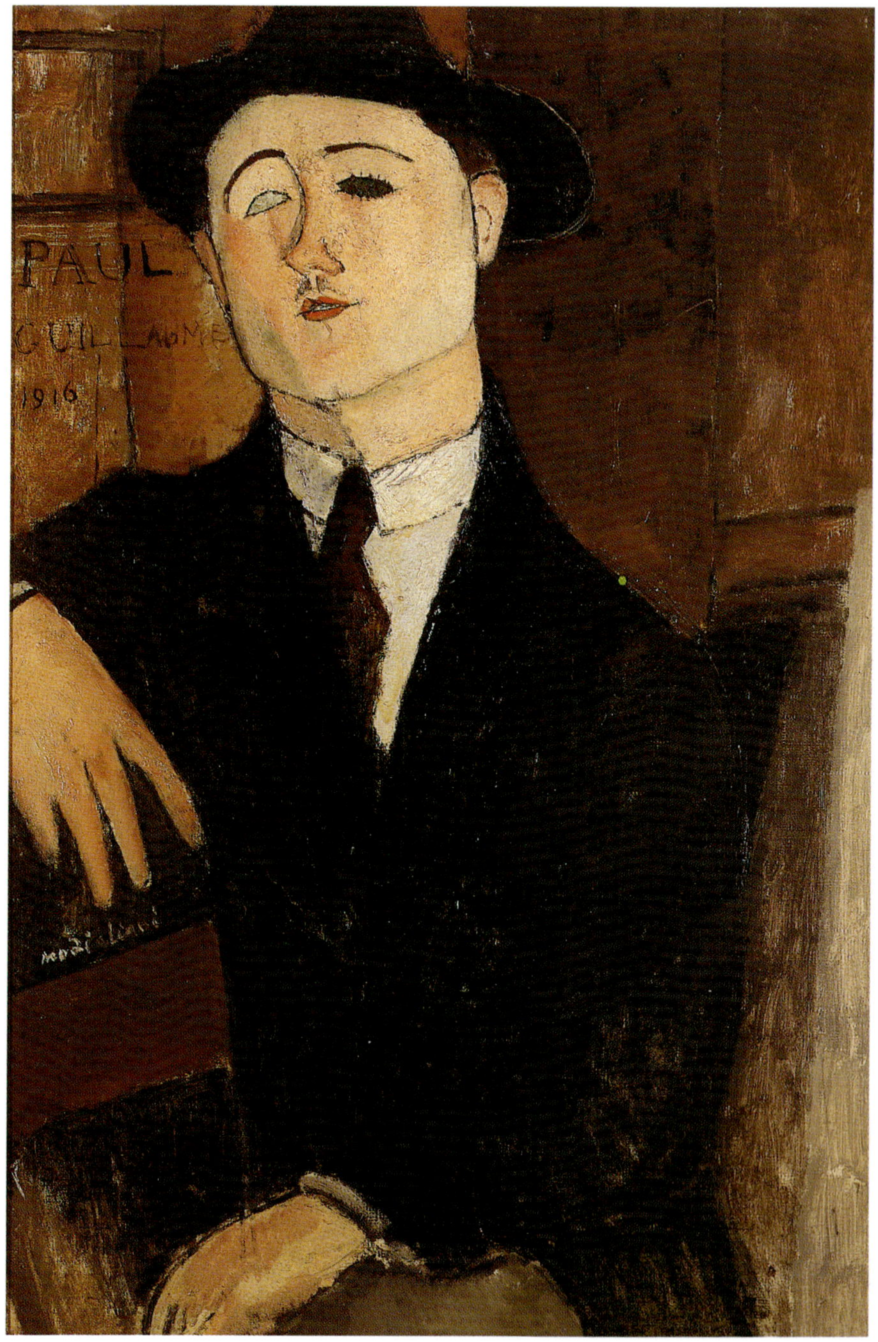

Amedeo Modigliani
Portrait of Paul Guillaume
1916
canvas
Milan, Civic Museum of Contemporary Art.

Guillaume was a well-known personage in the Paris of the times, and in the years between the two wars: art dealer and editor, he collected contemporary as well as African and aboriginal art, which had been little studied at the time. Guillaume supported Modigliani during his Montparnasse years. Here he is portrayed in the dual dimension of aesthete with delicate feminine lips and man of the world, casually elegant.

Amedeo Modigliani
Red Nude
1917
canvas

In Italy Modigliani's reputation spread fast after the artist's death, first of all among the young Turin painters who gathered around the art historian Lionello Venturi. An extensive exhibition of his works at the Biennale in 1930 placed Modigliani, within the contemporary canon, somewhere between the isolated figures or eccentrics and the "erotics" – such as Osvaldo Licini, another painter who undoubtedly drew inspiration from Modigliani.

Compositions such as the *Red Nude* fully justify the interest in Modigliani, particularly in the years when the pressure for an art of historical and political significance – "fascist art" was strongest in Italy. With no desire to confront the issues of current events or assume official poses, Modigliani chose to deal with the theme of the female nude, intimately conjoining painting, freedom of expression and desire.

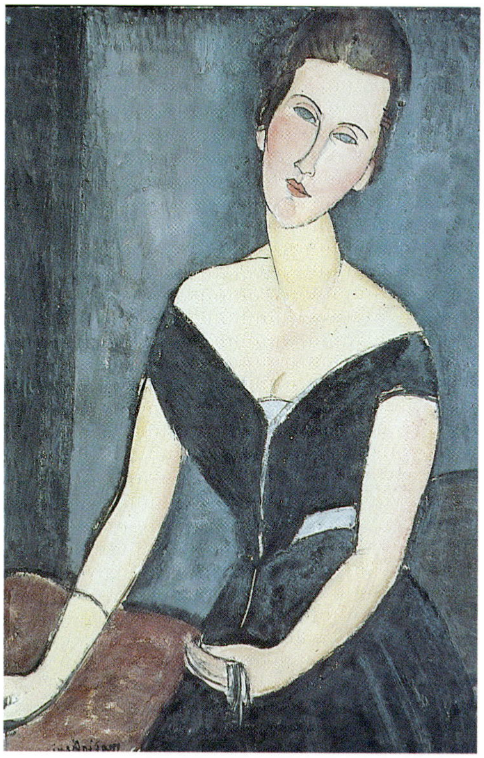

Amedeo Modigliani
Portrait of Madame G. van Muyden
1917
canvas
Sao Paolo, Brazil, Art Museum.

Something of a courtly routine – this is the aspect of the artist's activity communicated to us by this portrait, painted in tones of blue and typical, in its plastic simplification, of Modigliani's style. The neck appears elongated and cylindrical. The face, thin and pathetically turned, is reduced to an oval. The arms hang soft and inert, almost invertebrate, in the classic tradition of the aristocratic portrait.

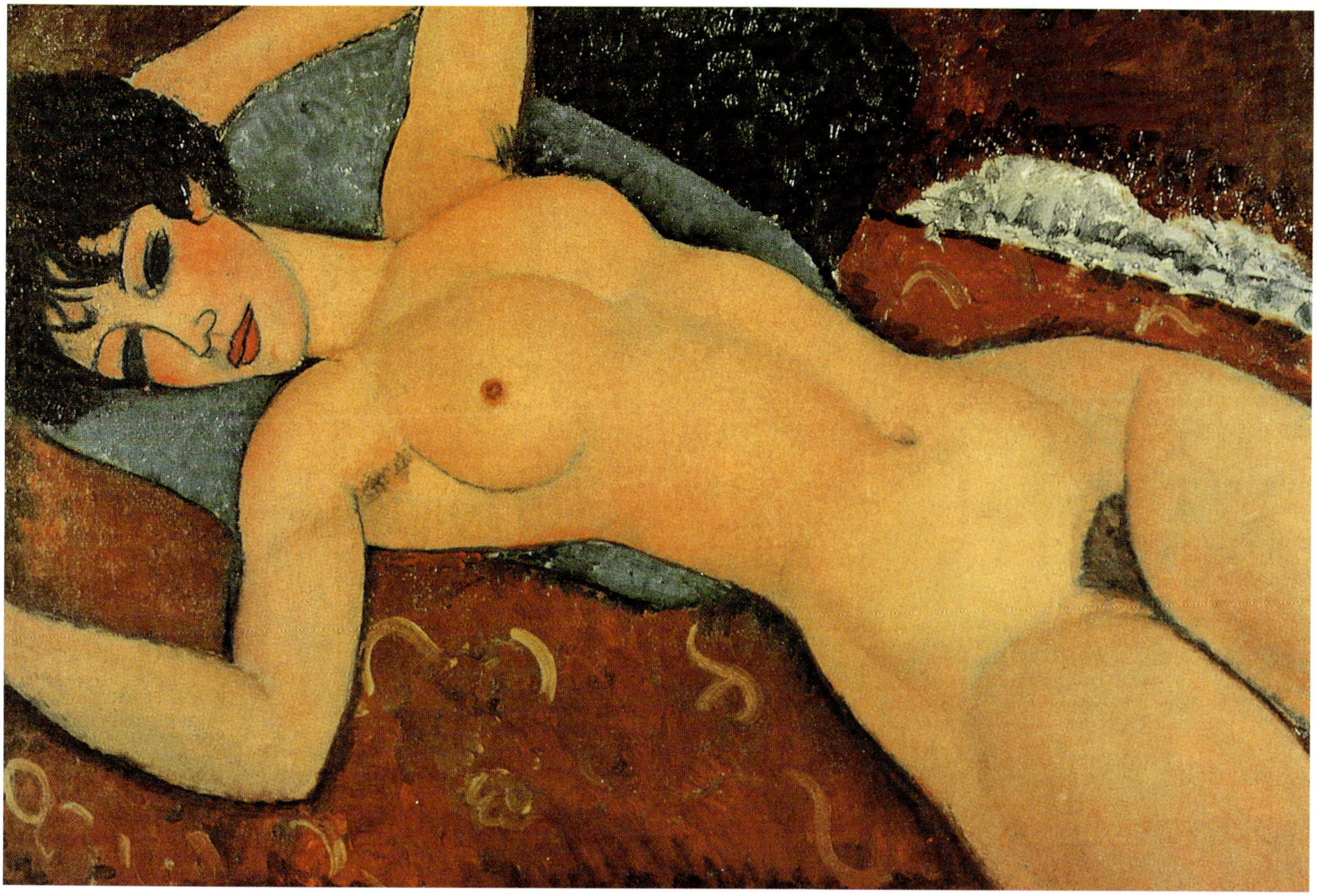

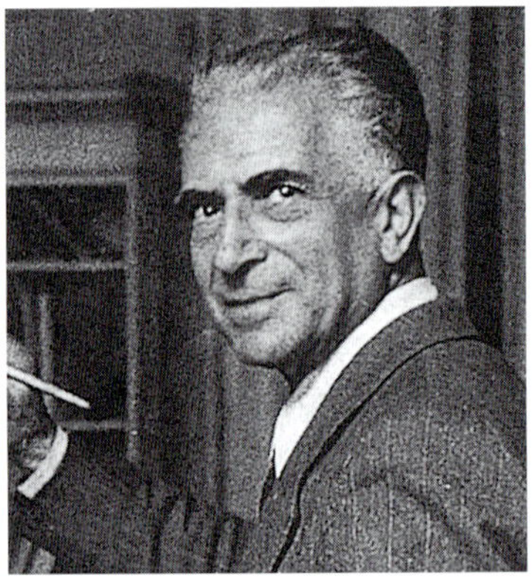

Felice Casorati

(Novara 1886 – Turin 1963)

Already present at the Venice Biennale of 1907, the young Casorati showed himself attentive to Central European, and specifically Austrian, figurative tendencies: an extreme care for detail, a preference for sharp, incisive drawing, a moderate inclination for enigma combined with a search for two-dimensional simplification of the image and a polychrome palette as refined as it was strident. Upon moving to Turin at the war's end he participated in the progressive, liberal environment of the Piedmont capital (Piero Gobetti was to write an article on him in 1923). His work evolved first in the direction of metaphysical painting, while his ambition to become a "painter of ideas" and not to operate simply on the level of profession brought him closer to De Chirico. Subsequently he moved toward a moderately archaizing classicism, with ample, soft expanses of colour and forms that are composed and solemn.

Felice Casorati
The Marionettes
1914
canvas

Four marionettes appear against the dark background of a puppet theatre. Painted like profiles or silhouettes, with no concern for any effect of depth, they are in fact reduced to their costumes and their gaudily made-up faces. A play room, here a puppet theatre, is waiting for someone to come to play, to animate otherwise inert toys. It is awaiting the director of the performance, the Puppet Master, a simple child. Between painting and puppet theatre Casorati constructs, in this painting, a subtle network of analogies and comparisons.

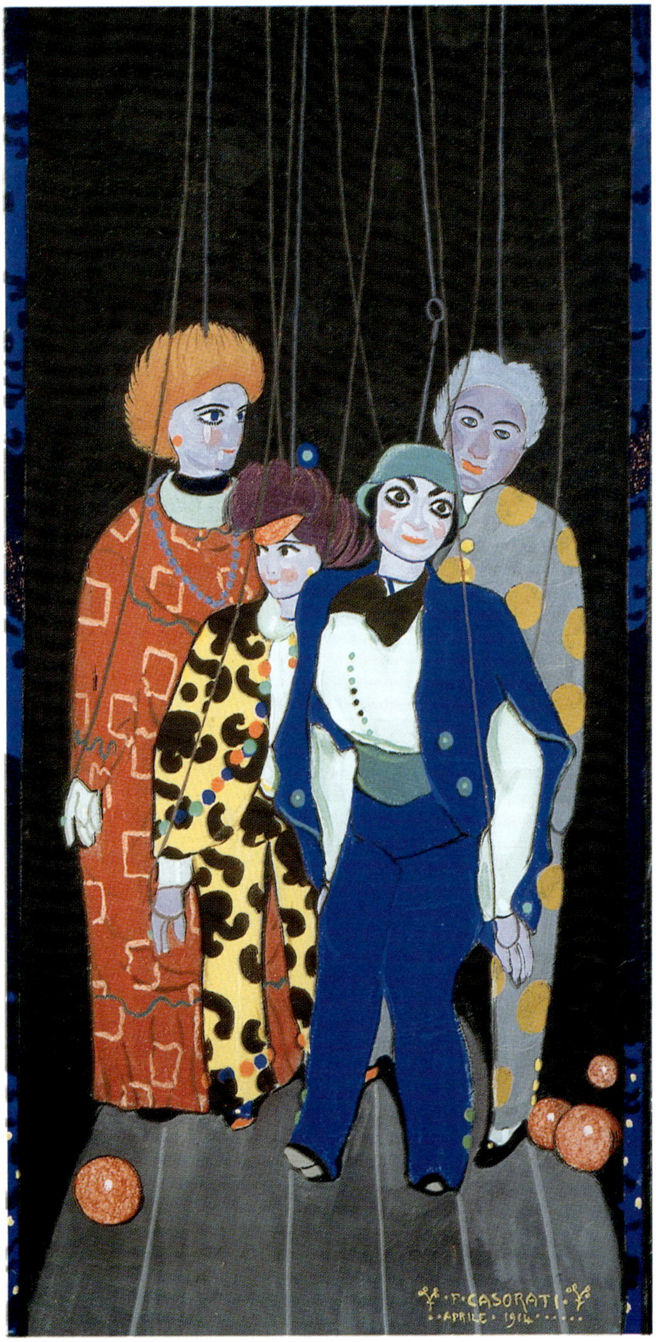

Felice Casorati
Daphne at Pavarolo
1934
plywood

Against the background of a gentle, cultivated Piedmont countryside the figure of a woman, an occasional model, lends itself to the painter's complex compositional activity. The painter transforms the real landscape into the simulation of a surface, conferring a strictly two-dimensional nature on what really exists in three dimensions – more or less as is done by the mirroring window panes, painted not by chance to the right and the left of the model. He transforms a woman into a statue, aesthetically pure in form; lengthens her neck, conferring on it a cylindrical form, brings her arms together in an almond shape, and visibly inscribes her person in an elementary solid, either cube or parallelepiped.

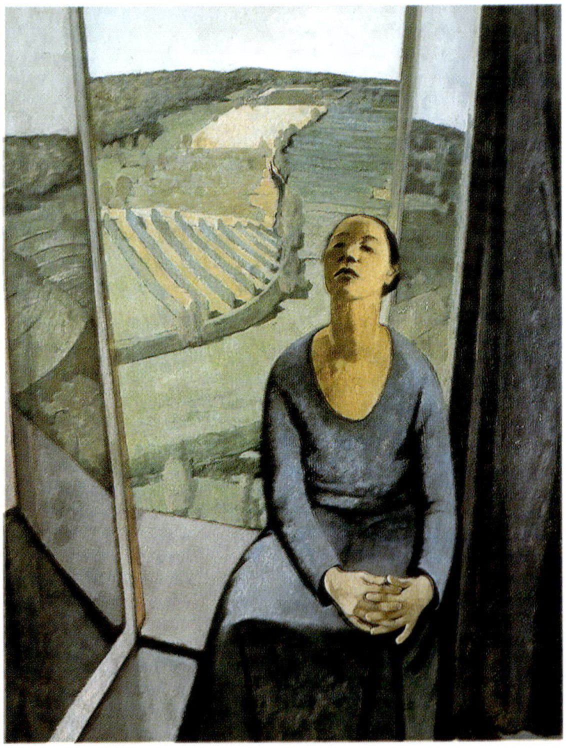

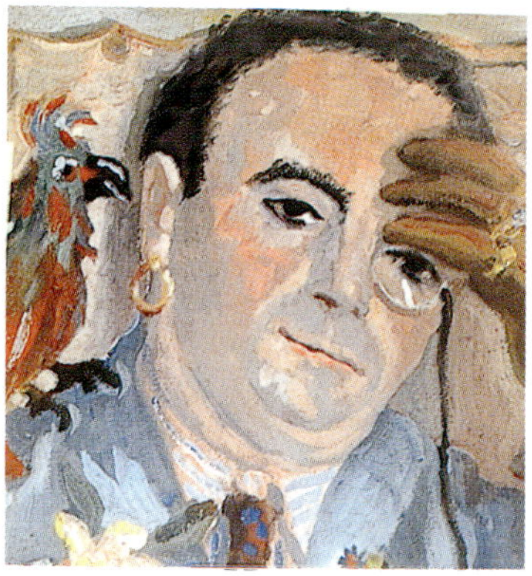

Filippo De Pisis

(Filippo Tibertelli,
Ferrara 1869 – Milan 1956)

Within the context of Italian art between the two wars the figure of De Pisis is in many ways eccentric: highly cultivated, cosmopolitan, versatile, he showed neither the ambitious extremism nor the scornful, embittered reserve of many of his contemporaries. He was a painter, poet and narrator who shrank from serious, official poses. An acute observer, gently ironic and languidly sentimental, he was singularly unconventional and self-confident. Much is known of his daily life: his vivacity, his urgent and unorthodox loves. His first compositions retain the characteristics of painted collages, of metaphysical puzzles – his meeting with De Chirico and Savinio dates from 1916, at Ferrara. In the latter half of the Twenties he participated in the general return to the painting of touch and colour then characteristic of the Parisian scene (the artist lived in Paris from 1925).

Carlo Levi, *Portrait of De Pisis with a Parrot* detail, c. 1933.
Rome, Carlo Levi Foundation.

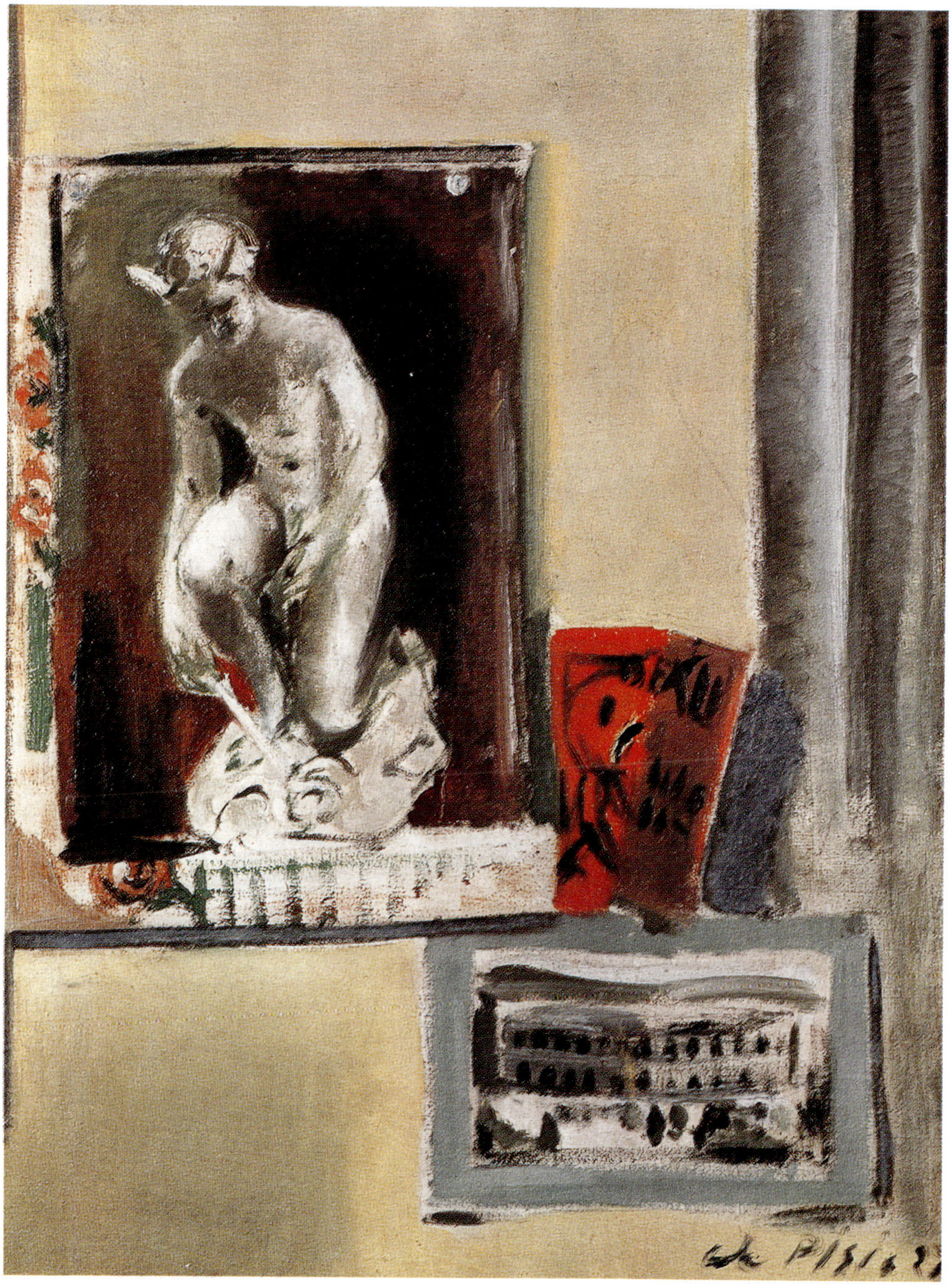

Filippo De Pisis
Still Life with Sculpture
1927
canvas
Rome, National Gallery of Modern Art.

The composition draws an analogy, as brilliant as it is dissimulated, between painting and literature. We find ourselves in a domestic interior, within a private space. On the wall is the painting or coloured print of a classical kneeling faun; a curious scarlet ex libris, resembling the scribbling of a child; a view of an ancient monument, probably an amphitheatre (the Coliseum? – another "souvenir d'Italie", like the faun, for the Parisian De Pisis). The three elements in the composition are not figures, but figures of figures. Differing in scale, in context, in type, they are contiguous and independent like parts of a collage, linked to each other like episodes in a narrative that centers around a central figure, a nude adolescent male appearing in the predominating position. But this narrative is not immediately comprehensible. The task of reconstructing the plot, recognizing the allusions, formulating links and conjectures, is left to our perspicacity as observers.

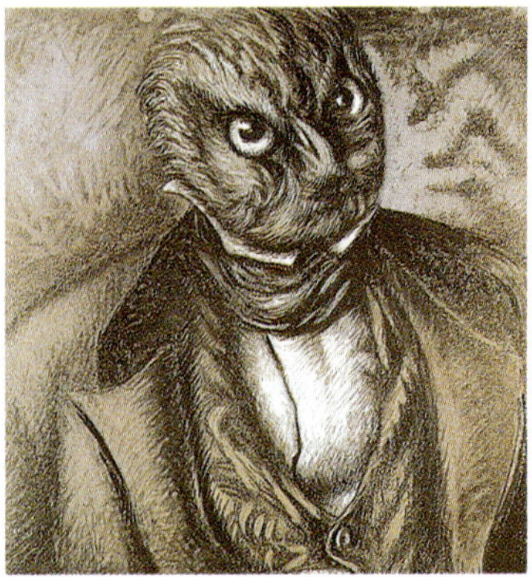

Alberto Savinio

(Andrea de Chirico,
Athens 1891 – Rome 1952)

Brother of Giorgio de Chirico, he began his career as musician and writer. After a classical education in Greece he lived first in Munich and then, in 1910, in Paris. Here he participated in avant garde figurative, literary and musical circles, displaying his bizarre talent in singular musical performances. In 1916 he was at Ferrara with his brother, engaged in weaving a complex fabric of historical, biographical and cultural references around metaphysical compositions. In the post-war period he was a critic for the most important art review of the times, "Valori Plastici" (for which De Chirico, Carrà and Savinio himself were the most deeply committed and authoritative voices). Savinio's first one-man show in 1927 at Paris, where he was then living, aroused immediate attention for an artist whom the classicists of "Mediterranean" inspiration and the surrealists contended from opposing positions.

Alberto Savinio,
Self-portrait, detail,
1936. Turin, Civic Gallery of Modern Art.

Alberto Savinio
Sodom
1929
canvas

The Bible tells of the ancient city of Sodom and its legendary fornicators. It also tells of the divine ire that struck the voluptuous city, and of how only Lot, a virtuous man, was saved from its destruction. The archetypal name for all future invective against contemporary forms of decadence, Sodom was frequently to re-emerge in the art and literature of the Twenties. It has been seen how Carrà also referred to it indirectly in a painting entitled *The Daughters of Lot*. Savinio portrays Sodom enveloped in high flames, while a bizarre nimbus of toys intermingled with ideographic stelae and a black banner flies through the sky like a destroying deity (or a horseman of the Apocalypse). Will the new art – either the "ideographic" one of Picasso's emulators or that of his brother De Chirico – save the Western World from its dread "twilight"? Savinio seems both to ask and to parody this question.

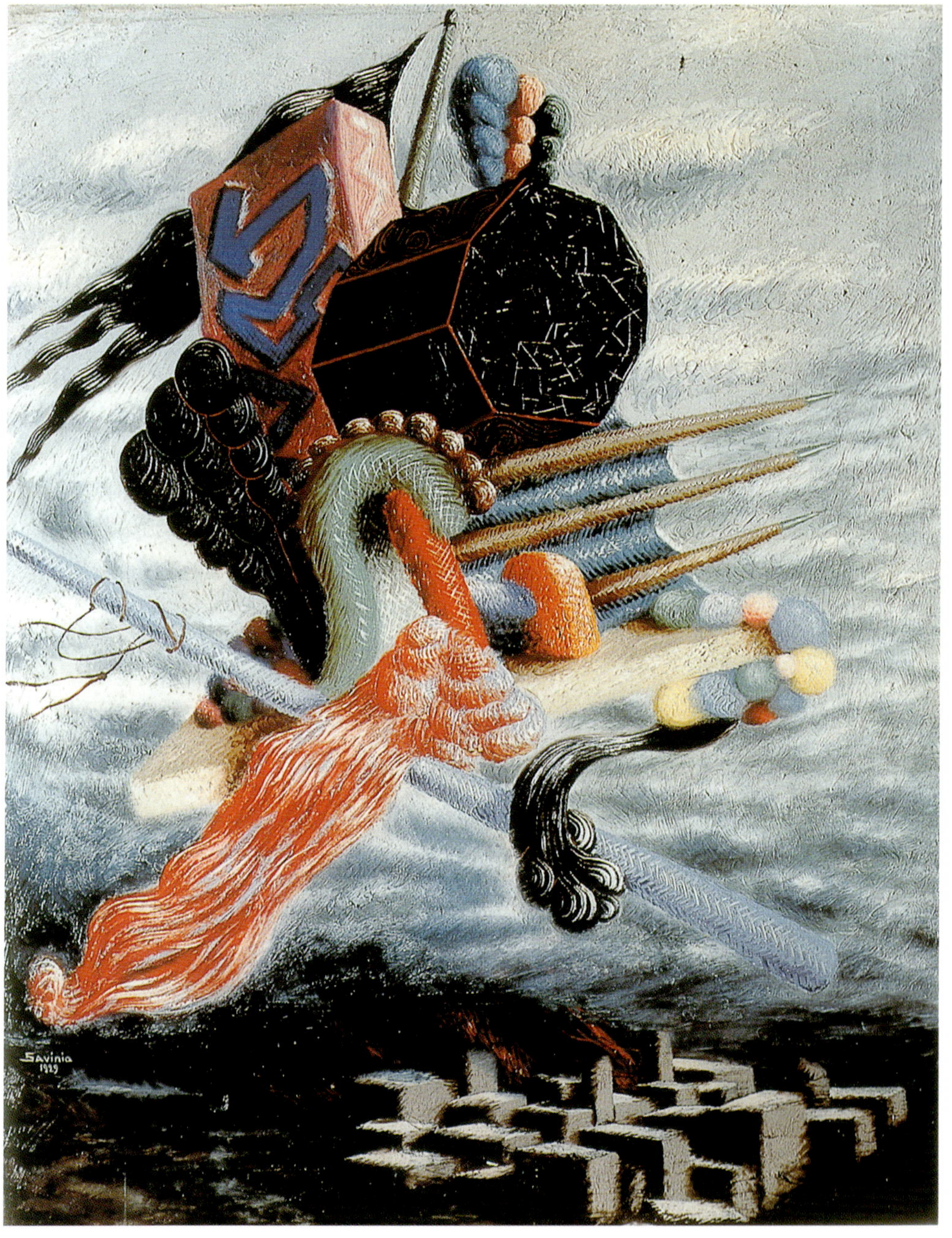

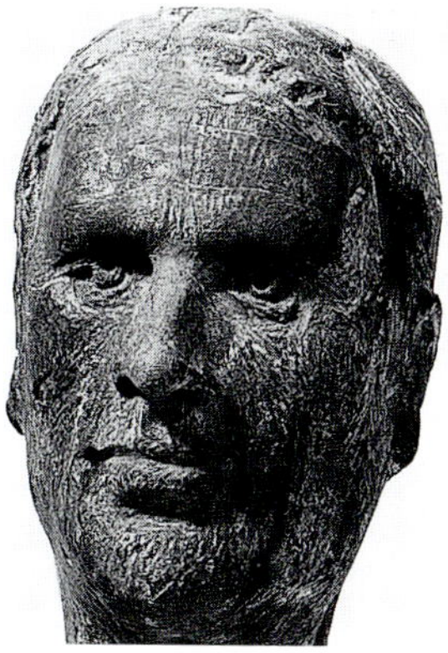

Marino Marini

(Pistoia 1901 – Forte dei Marmi 1980)

Developing during the years when archeological trends were in vogue in Italian art, Marini managed to avoid the most extenuating elegance, the most calculated eclecticism, combining his study of classical/archaic models, those of Central Italy in particular (and thus Etruscan and Roman) with a decided aptitude for "colour" in sculpture, obtained if not by adding pigment, by a painstaking cold-working of the surface, scratched and engraved. The themes of his sculpture are evocative of a mythical Mediterranean world untouched by time or history. In the post-war period the artist moved in the direction of greater abstraction, generically neo-Cubist, purposely omitting the precise historical and geographical references that had marked his earlier work. His multifarious activity now seemed to render homage to international taste.

Marino Marini, *Self-portrait*, 1942. Florence, Marino Marini Museum.

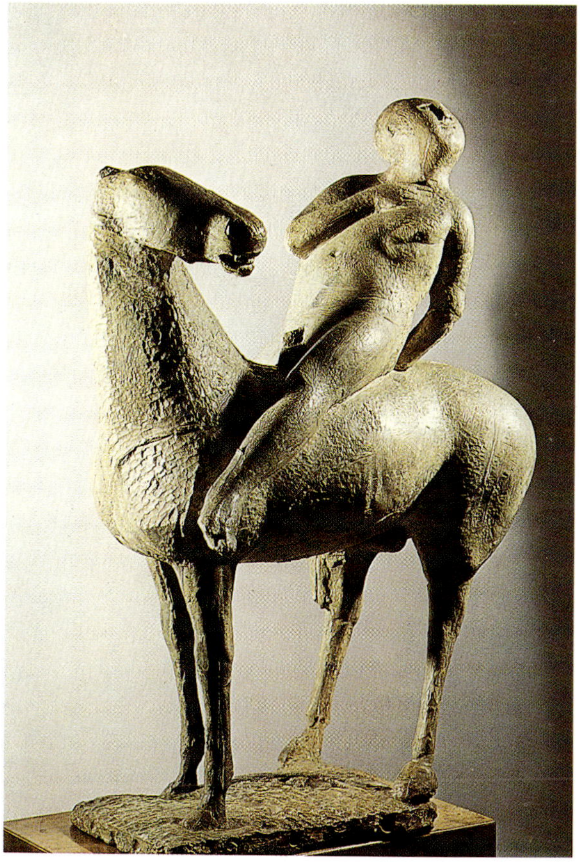

Marino Marini
Rider
1947
bronze
Amsterdam, Stedelijk Museum.

The *Horse and Rider* series occupied the artist for over two decades, starting in 1935. The numerous works bearing this title differ significantly from each other. For Marino the equestrian group possesses no impassive public traits; it is not a monument. What the artist intended to express plastically was a kind of state of mind: horse and rider appear now harmoniously detached, now disoriented, disturbed, even convulsed.

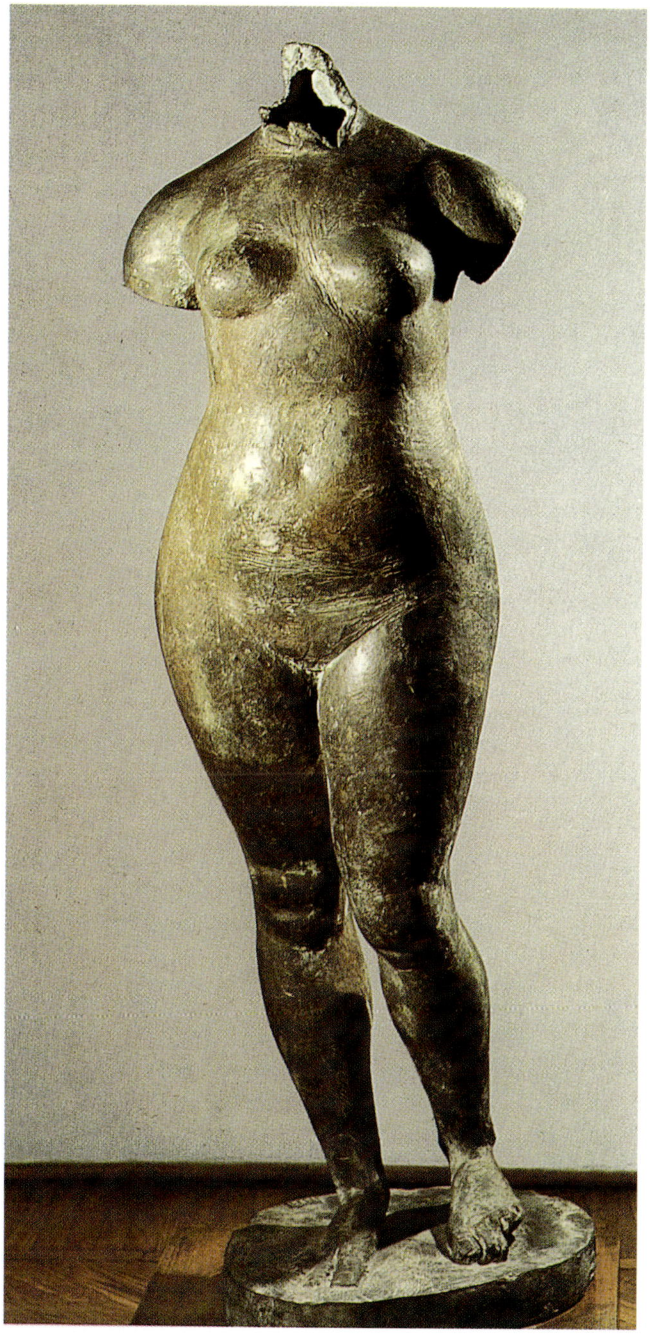

Marino Marini
Pomona
1941
bronze
Brussels, Royal Museum of Fine Arts.

Pomona is a rustic deity, more precisely the goddess of gardens and fruit trees venerated by the ancient Italic populations (her name derives from *pomum*, meaning "fruit").

Marino's interest lies in presenting a mythological subject and simultaneously sculpting a frankly erotic female nude.

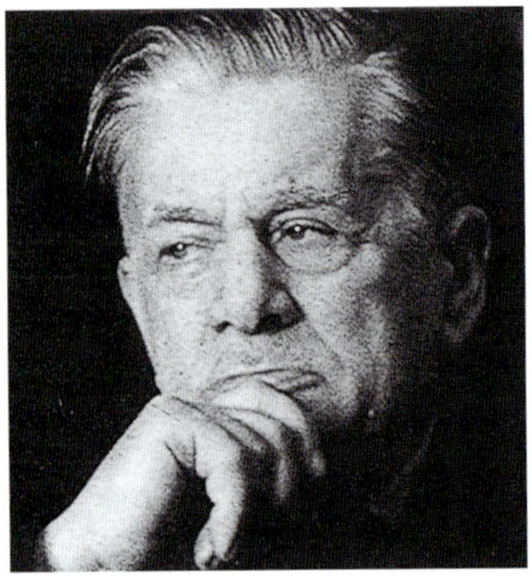

Mario Sironi

(Sassari 1885 – Milan 1961)

Sironi, student of engineering at the University of Rome and pupil of the Academy, was a frequent visitor, with Boccioni and Severini, to Balla's studio. His divisionist and futurist apprenticeship was marked by a caustic, pungent talent that distinguished and sustained him, first in the war years, then in the postwar period, in his activity as illustrator. Still in the postwar period Sironi, with the "Novecento" movement, championed a traditionalist and strictly constructive plastic orientation, banishing from his painting any light narrative dimension or exercise in visual seduction. His compositions are imbued with civic gravity and didactic/allegorical aspects. They are a continuation, in more demanding and openly institutional form, of De Chirico's reflections on the "Italian piazzas", on the historical and social condition of the nation within which the painter carries out his activity, not a merely private one.

Mario Sironi
Solitude
1926
canvas
Rome, National Gallery of Modern Art.

Sironi's work in the period between the two wars can be roughly divided into three classes of image: female nudes, compositions on labour themes, and urban landscapes. The female nudes, such as the one in *Solitude*, cannot be considered merely erotic figures. They are instead exercises in an eminent genre of painting, that of the nude, conceived less as the unveiling of a body than as the occasion for a figurative discourse on the goal of any aesthetic activity (on what Sironi considered to be the goal of all aesthetic activity): beauty united to morality, "chaste beauty".

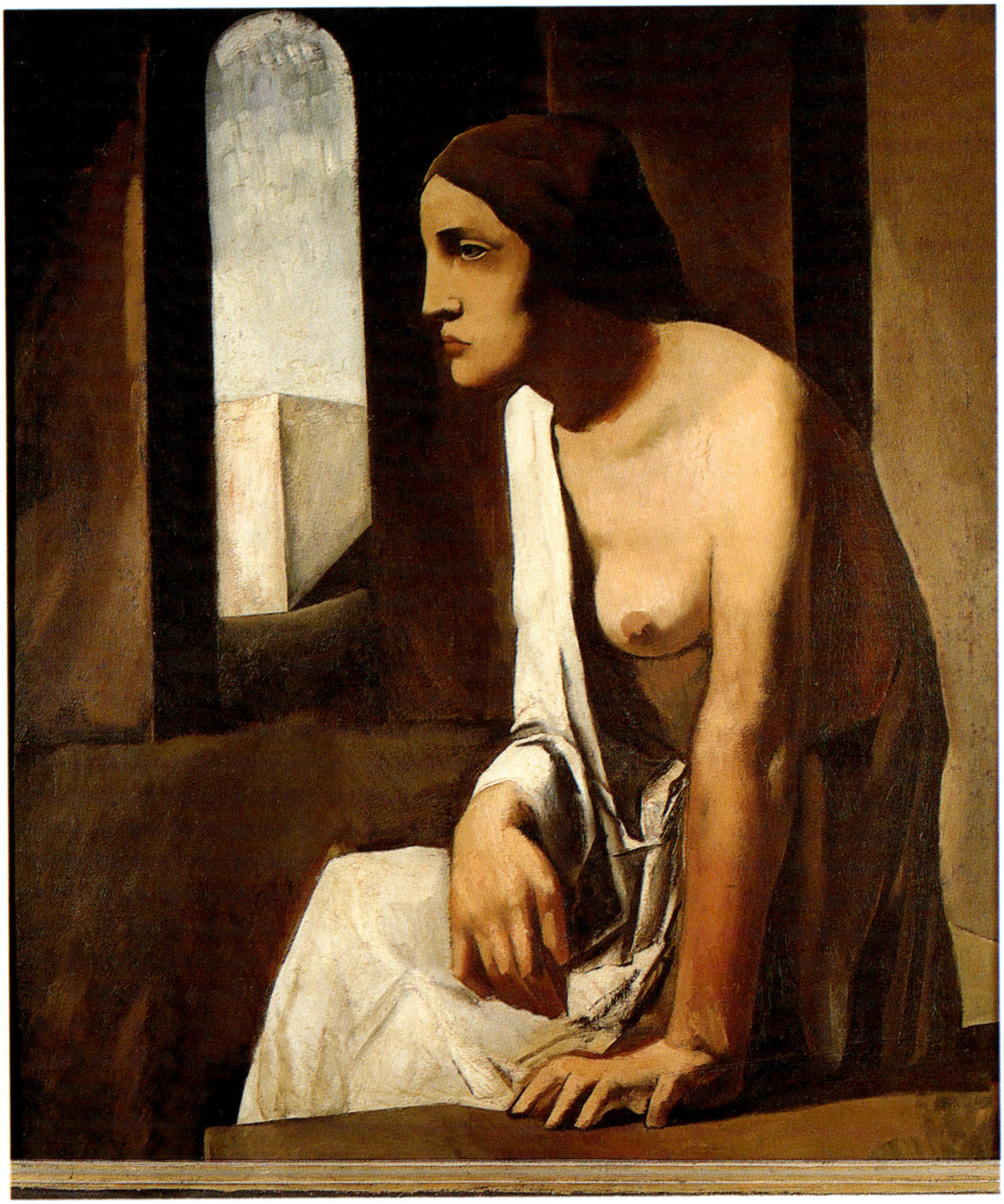

Marcello Piacentini

(Rome 1881 – 1960)

Architect and urban planner, Marcello Piacentini was as highly influential in the field of architecture between the two wars as he was later to be harshly criticized. Only recently has his work been approached in more objective terms. It has been possible to extricate the vicissitudes of the architect from those of the academic and polemicist, and to consider his projects and achievements more serenely, acknowledging, within the proper limits, even the motivations for his classicism.

Giuseppe Terragni

(Meda 1904 – Como 1943)

Terragni is, with Antonio Sant'Elia, a milestone in the Italian modern movement. A leading figure in the rationalist movement, which he joined at a very young age, he conceived of the new architecture as a severe, heroic correlative of the national character, reawakened – as was first hoped – by the Fascist movement. His need for rigorous design soon put him out of favour with the regime. Drafted into the military service in 1939 and sent to the Russian front, he was to return psychologically and physically destroyed.

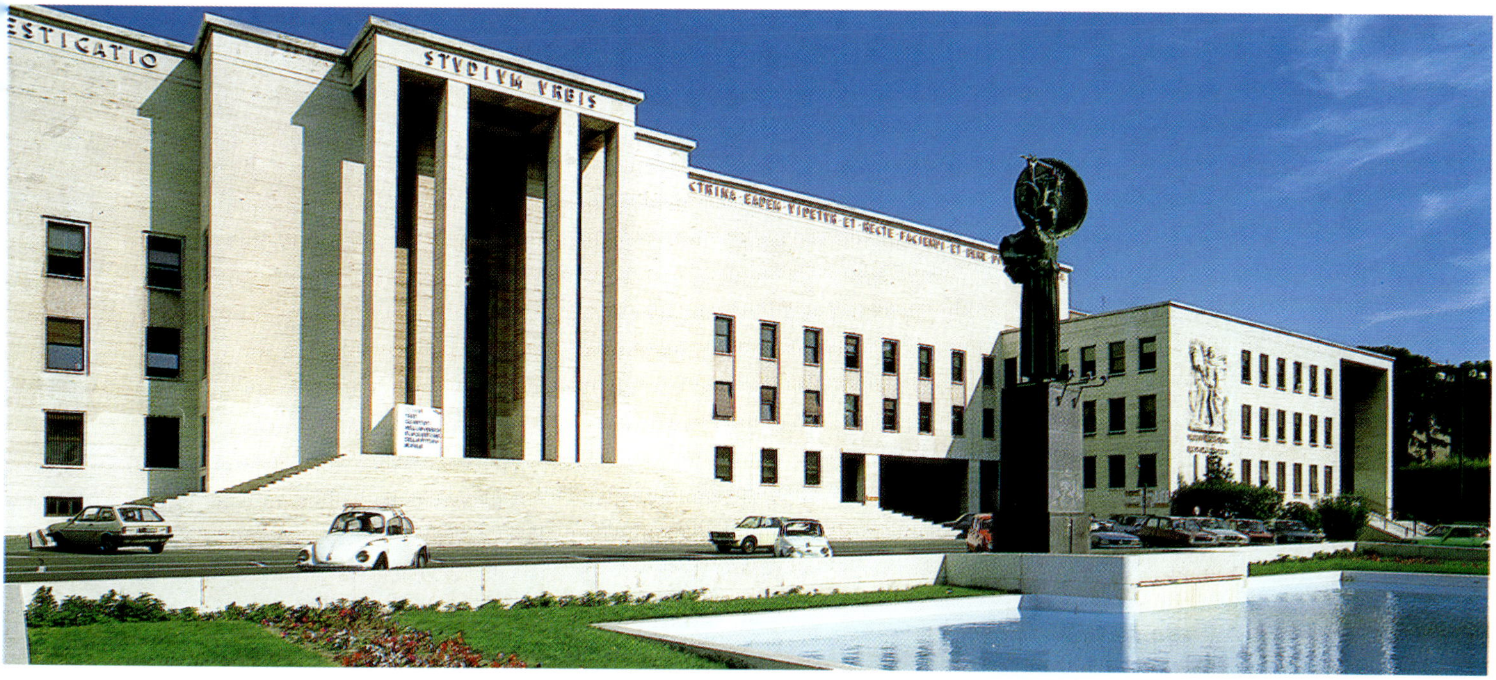

Marcello Piacentini
The Rectorate
1932-35
Rome, La Sapienza University City.

Attracted by models of bare secessionist monumentality, Piacentini accepted, of the simplifications introduced by rationalism, only what could be combined with ornamental elements of Graeco-Roman tradition. Architecture could not be reduced, in his opinion, to sober functionality.

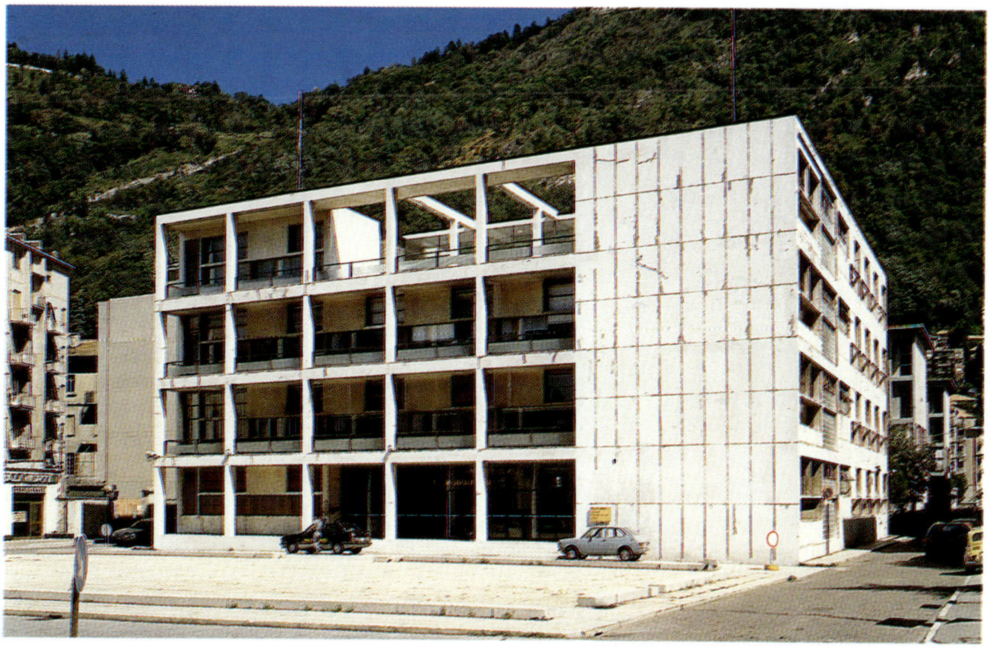

Giuseppe Terragni
House of the Fasces
1932-36
Como.

In designing the Como seat of the party he at first ardently supported, Terragni showed himself amply familiar with the techniques and methods of European rationalism. The solutions he adopted stem from Le Corbusier and Gropius. Elementary in form and distinguished by the absence of any façade in the traditional sense, the building is not designed to yield to any commemorative temptation.

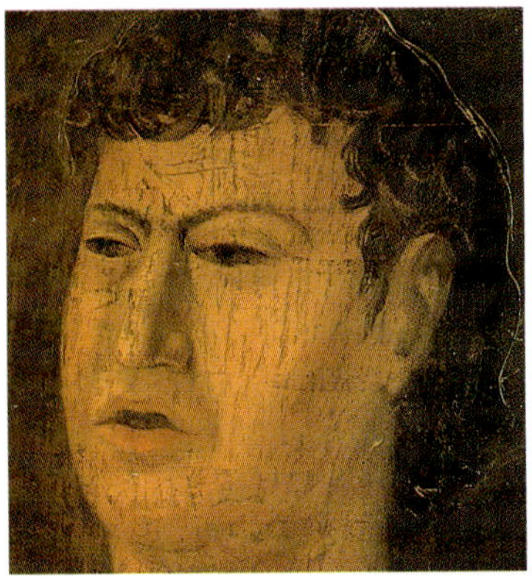

Scipione

(Gino Bonichi,
Macerata 1904 – Arco, Trento, 1933)

Surprising, in Scipione, is a singular conjunction of local and cosmopolitan elements. Rome is not only the background of many paintings but also an electively Baroque locale, as if the artist wished it were his own painting – and is archetypal. Nothing of the artistically contemporary Rome, moreover, except for "magic/realistic" touches, appears in compositions distinguished by a palette restricted to yellow-orange tonalities and forms brought to the threshold of disintegration. While the forms seem to dissolve, the compositions reflect instead a knowledge of the European Expressionist tradition (Ensor, Kokoschka, Pascin, Soutine were Scipone's favorite artists, although known to him only through reproductions). With Mafai and Antonietta Raphael, Scipione formed a close-knit group, christened the "Via Cavour School" by the critic Roberto Longhi.

Scipione, *Self-portrait*, detail, 1928. Prato, Giuliano Gori Collection.

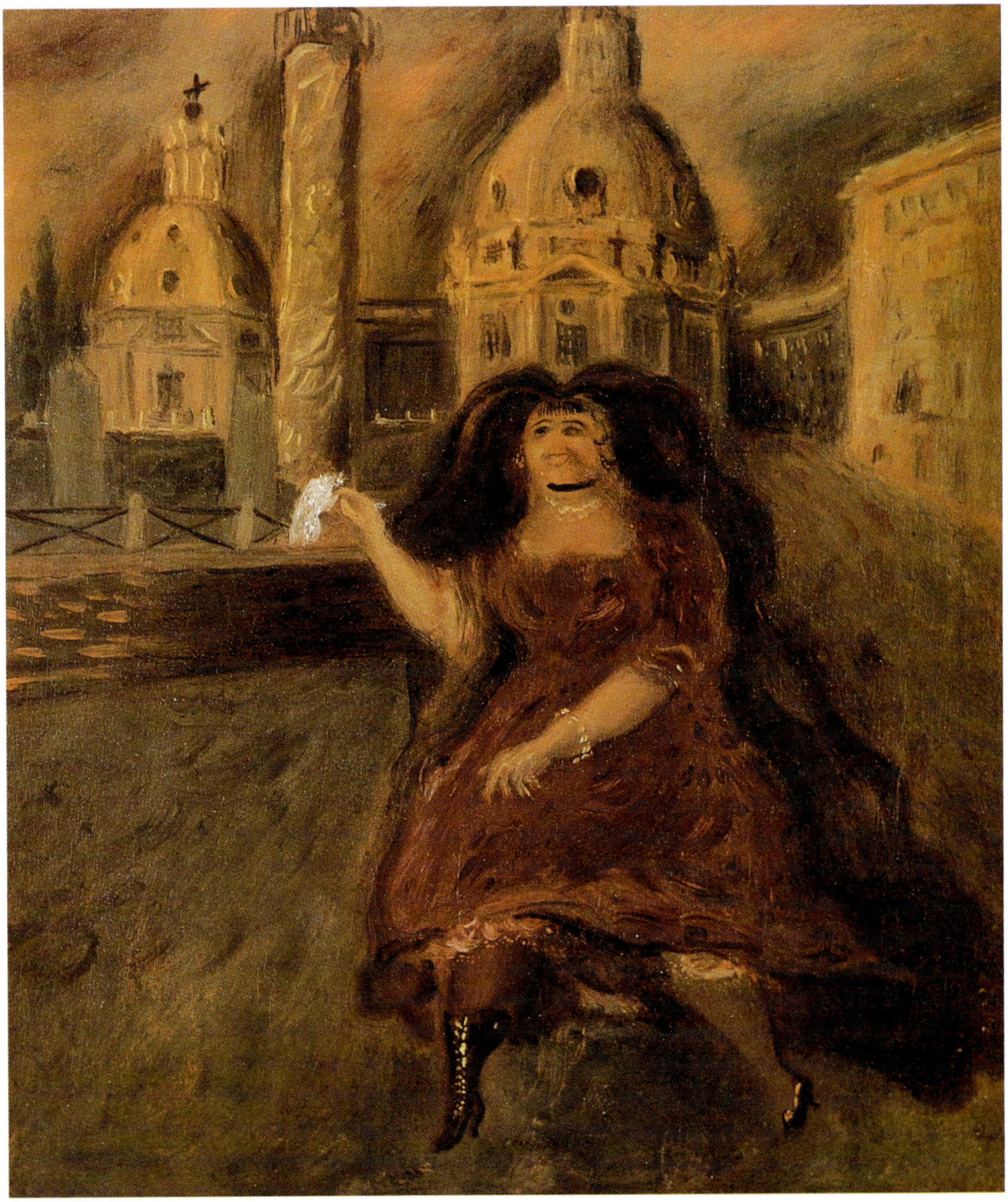

Scipione
Roman Courtesan
1930
canvas

Scipione's painting provides a real catalogue of types and personalities: the *Catholic Prince*, the *Cardinal Dean*, and this *Roman Courtesan* exist apart from time and history, exist in a state of immutability against the background of a Rome that is both clerical and pagan, entirely given over to sorcery and magic.

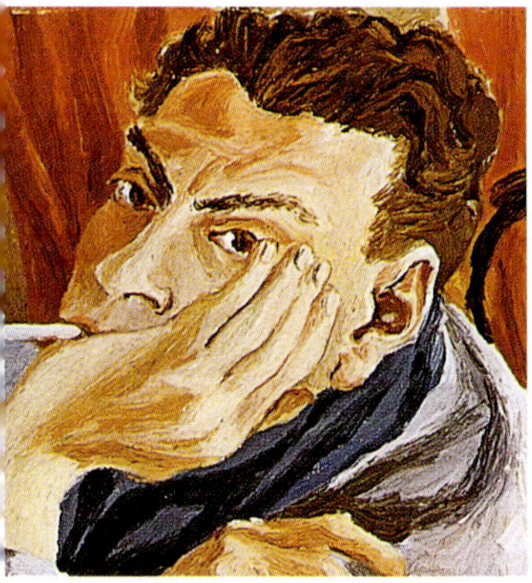

Renato Guttuso

(Bagheria, Palermo, 1912 – Rome 1987)

One of the most controversial personalities in Italian twentieth century art, Guttuso was as flattered and admired in life as neglected in the *post-mortem* decade. Today his work and cultural heritage seem to be undergoing a more balanced historical and artistic evaluation. Beginning his career in Sicily and Rome, the artist lived in Milan in 1935-37. In 1940 he participated in the founding of the anti-twentieth century movement *Corrente di vita giovanile*. Meanwhile the artistic and civic star of the Picasso of *Guernica* (1937) was blazing for him, urging him to turn toward a style that "can live as an expressive cry and manifestation of wrath, love, justice on the street corners and in the city squares". In Rome in the post war period his outlook grew increasingly more political. Accepting a now institutional role, he became the outstanding representative of partisan orthodoxy in art.

Renato Guttuso, *Self-portrait*, detail, 1936. Palermo, Modern Art Gallery.

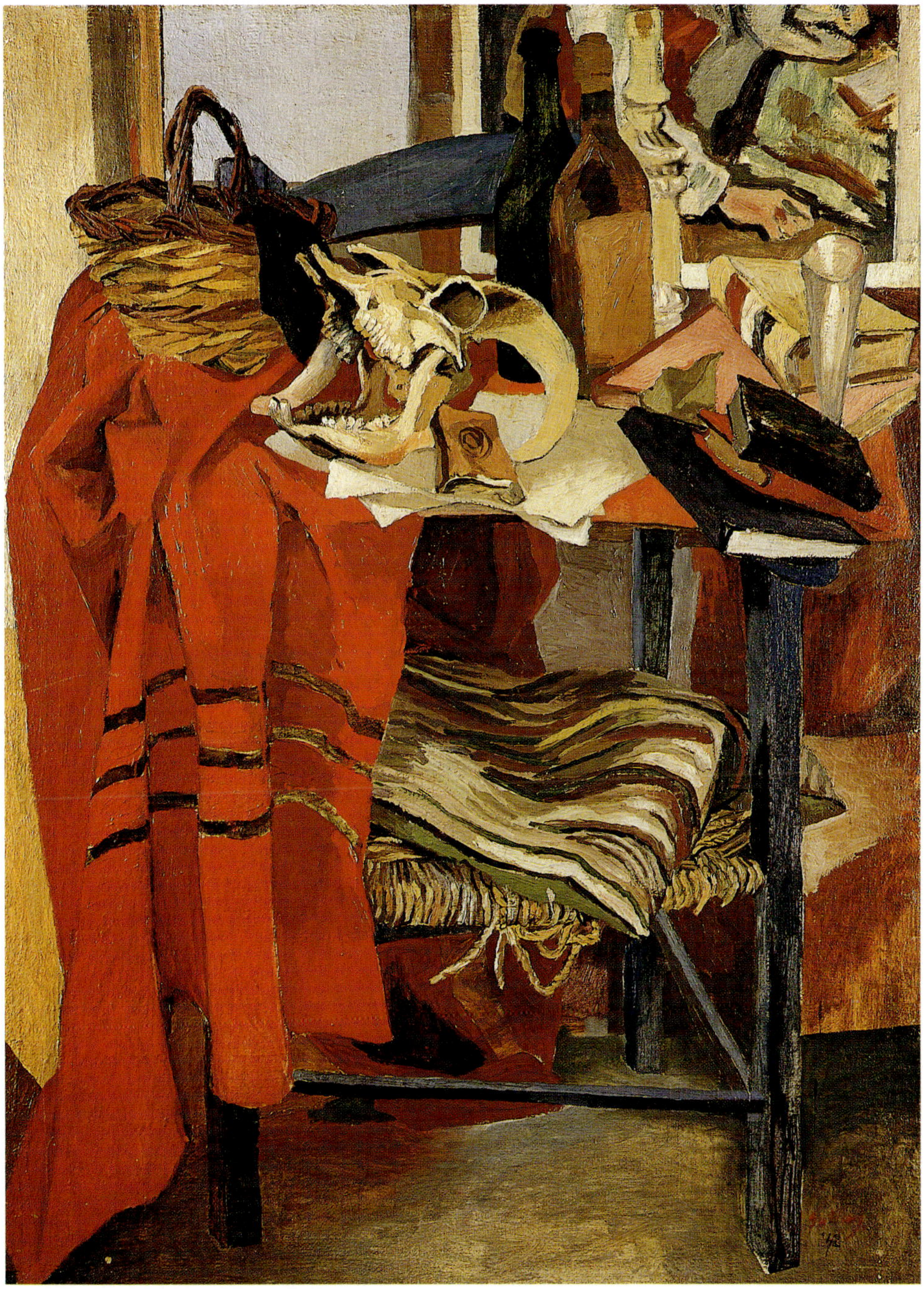

Renato Guttuso
Still Life with Red Flag
1942
canvas

The composition, apparently sober and detached, could even be erroneously thought to belong to the intimate genre. In spite of this, it reveals the political dimension of Guttuso's art, already evident by this date. The painting is a sort of self-portrait *in absentia* with the red flag, a skull and books scattered about – a self-portrait of the angry artist who refuses to accept censure, who rebels. In the background is what seems to be a detail from a painting by Cézanne, in the foreground a straw-bottomed chair, a simple object of popular craftsmanship. Contemporary art, the artist seems to say, is constitutionally poor, extreme, in a word, protestant.

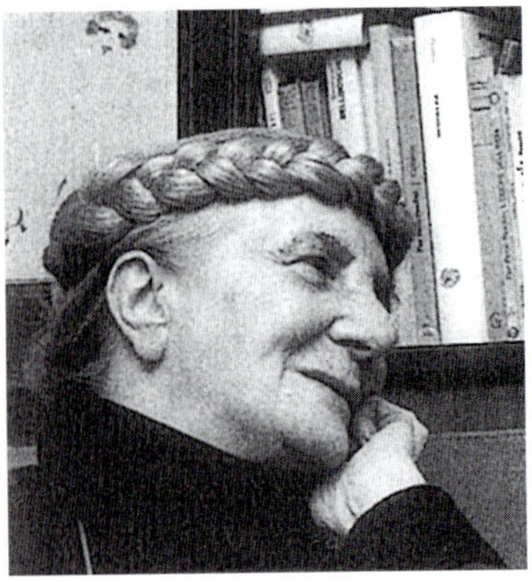

Carolrama

(Olga Carol Rama, Turin 1918)

As a young artist in the Rome of the late Thirties Carolrama was appreciated by many, Casorati among others, but was frequently considered more an eccentric coming from a difficult adolescence than an elusive, refined artist. In 1945 her first show of water colours, portraying with perverse innocence an entire instrumentarium of erotics, was closed by the censors. Near to the abstract-constructionist orientation of the Concrete Art Movement in the Fifties, she later explored the technique of *assemblage*. Her works began to be populated by children's' eyes, fingernails, teeth, needles, syringes, rubbers – materials in some way metaphorical. In the late Fifties Carolrama returned to drawing and to colour. On architect's boards she elaborated "projects designed by friends of mine, so that they can help me invent an image that is erotic, sentimental, private but that is not so closely linked to me".

Carolrama
Appassionata
1940
paper

The composition has the light touch of an erotic water-colour and the brilliant causticity of an image of crime. Although not devoid of cultural and current references – drawings of the nude from the French *fin de siècle* tradition, *Neue Sachlichkeit* social satires with perverts and persecutors, fetishists and robbers, prostitutes and transsexuals – it possesses a whimsical and singular insouciance, as if of something born of itself. The erotic obsession – enacted? submitted to? – is portrayed with irony and nonchalant license. Everything, in the body of the young woman and even in her scanty clothing, becomes breast, genital zone, orifice – like the leafy fronds that adorn her head or the flagrantly displayed slippers that turn into fur.

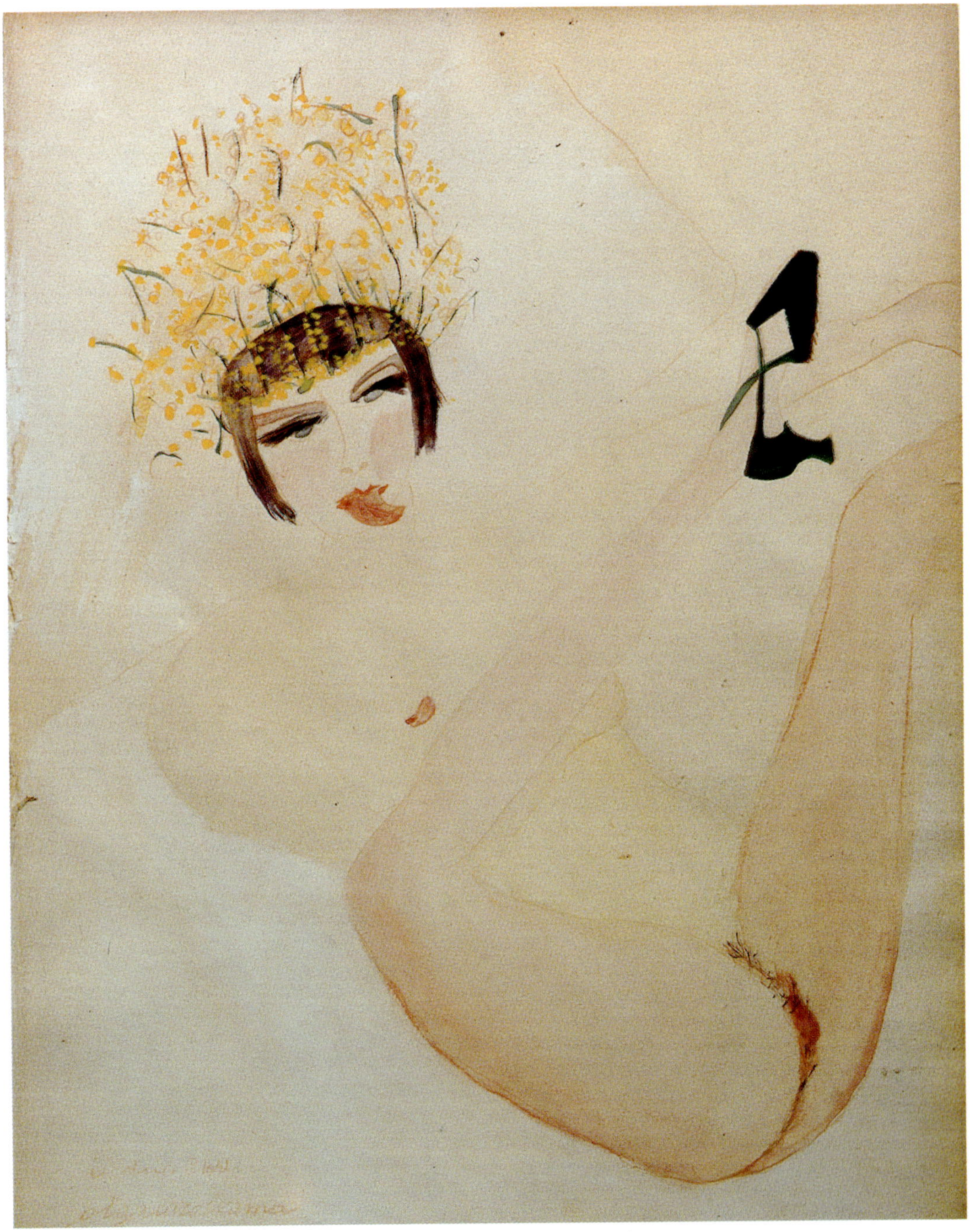

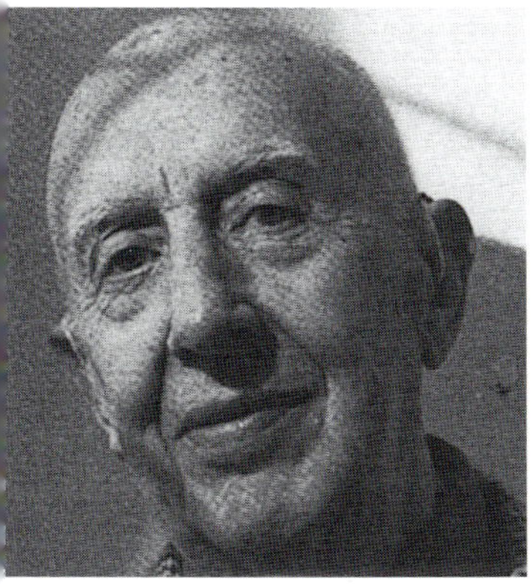

Fausto Melotti

(Rovereto 1901 – Milan 1986)

A pupil of Adolfo Wildt at the Brera Academy, Melotti held his first one-man show in 1935 at the "Milione", the Milanese gallery around which the abstract movement revolved in the years between the two wars. The public and critical success of the show was null. Attracted by the controlled execution and the poetic sophistication of Wildt's works while simultaneously desirous of exploring new paths and rejecting monumental, commemorative aims, Melotti brought the practice of linear drawing to interact with sculpture. Fine lines engrave pure forms or create relief on them, perfect ovals create wombs or projecting forms, line in general begins to exist as plastic element. For this to happen, it was sufficient to create sculptures in the form of harps or tetrachords, consisting of a void and simple stretched wires of stainless steel. In the postwar period he turned to ceramics, confronting the problems of polychrome sculpture.

Fausto Melotti at Milan in 1976 in a photograph by Antonia Mulas.

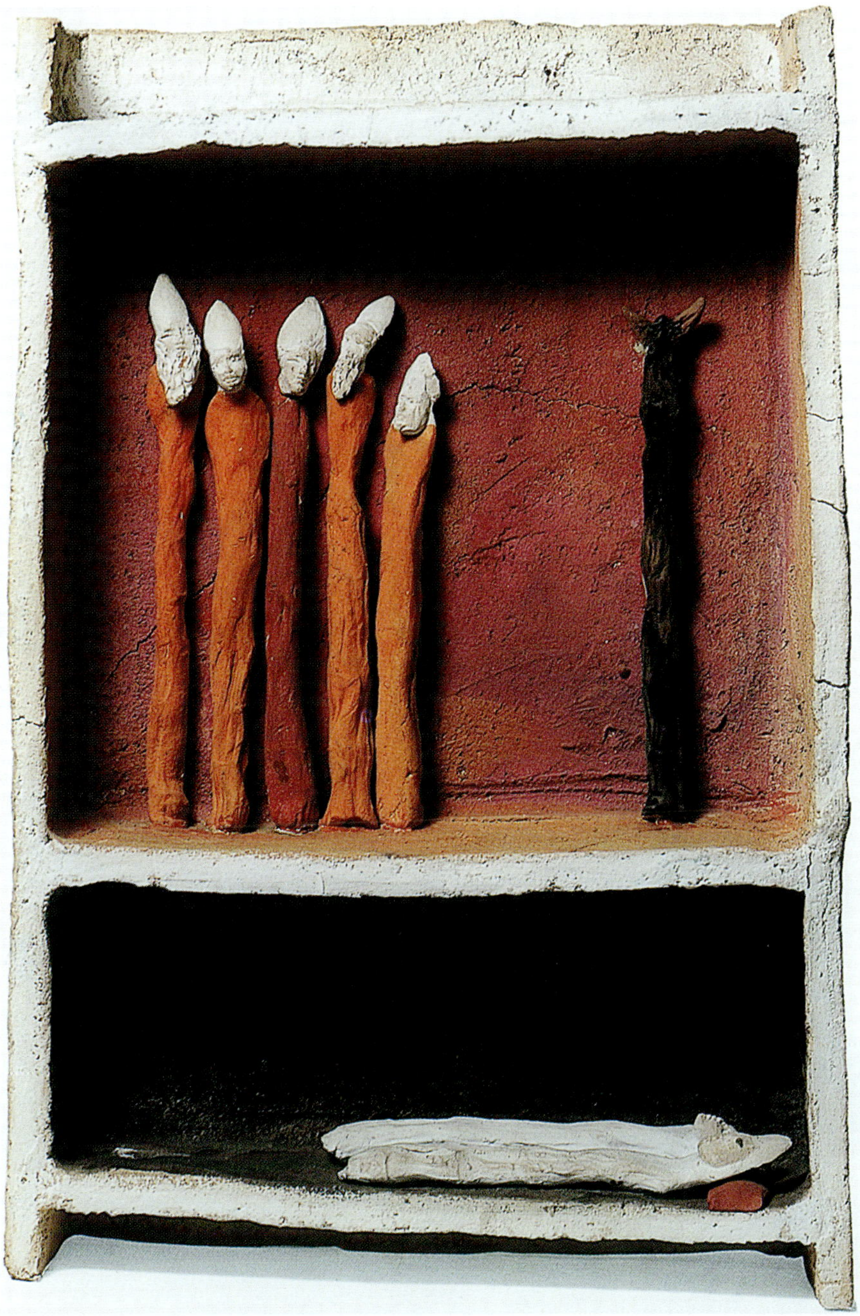

Fausto Melotti
The Heresiarchs and the Holy Bishops
1952
terracotta
Milan, collection of the Melotti heirs.

The figurative objectives of this composition are not disguised by its whimsical subject. While sculpture is traditionally a weighty art, linked to a difficult, heavy material – marble, for example, or another stone – Melotti moves, with terracotta, with the light touch more consonant to the painter's art. He neither breaks nor hammers, but models in small touches, then adds color. Within the ambiance that surrounds the "heresiarchs and the holy bishops" the empty areas predominate over the full ones. The individual figures exist as words, as parts of a visual or even musical notation.

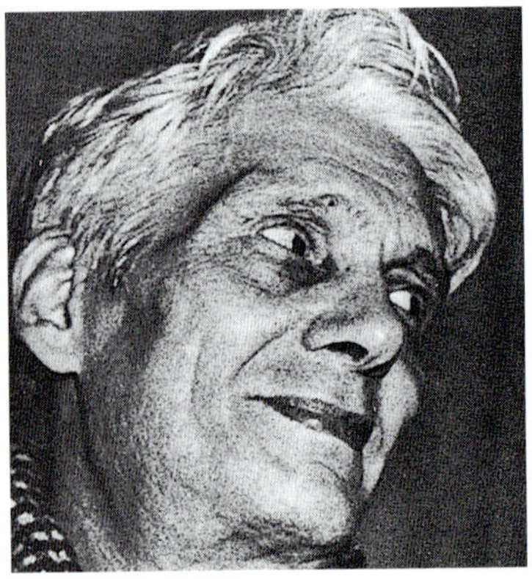

Osvaldo Licini

(Monte Vidon Corrado, Ascoli Piceno, 1894 – 1958)

The great eccentric, along with De Pisis, of Italian art in the first half of the twentieth century – well described, in the title of one of his youthful books, as *errant, erotic, heretical* – Licini cannot be fit into any current art-history scheme. In Paris between 1919 and 1925; with Melotti and Fontana, close to the Milanese abstract painters throughout the Thirties, he was irritated by orthodox positions. He aimed at a painting that would be the "art of colors and of signs", at a "geometry" as "sentiment", but with no intention of abandoning the imaginative. In the early Forties, having exhausted any reason for adhering to the abstract movement, he began to compose by cycles, creating the *Amalasunte*, the *Rebellious Angels*, and the *Flying Dutchmen*, heroes of a personal world of fantasy. Remaining unchanged was his caustic attitude: his compositions were to become pages in a captious diary.

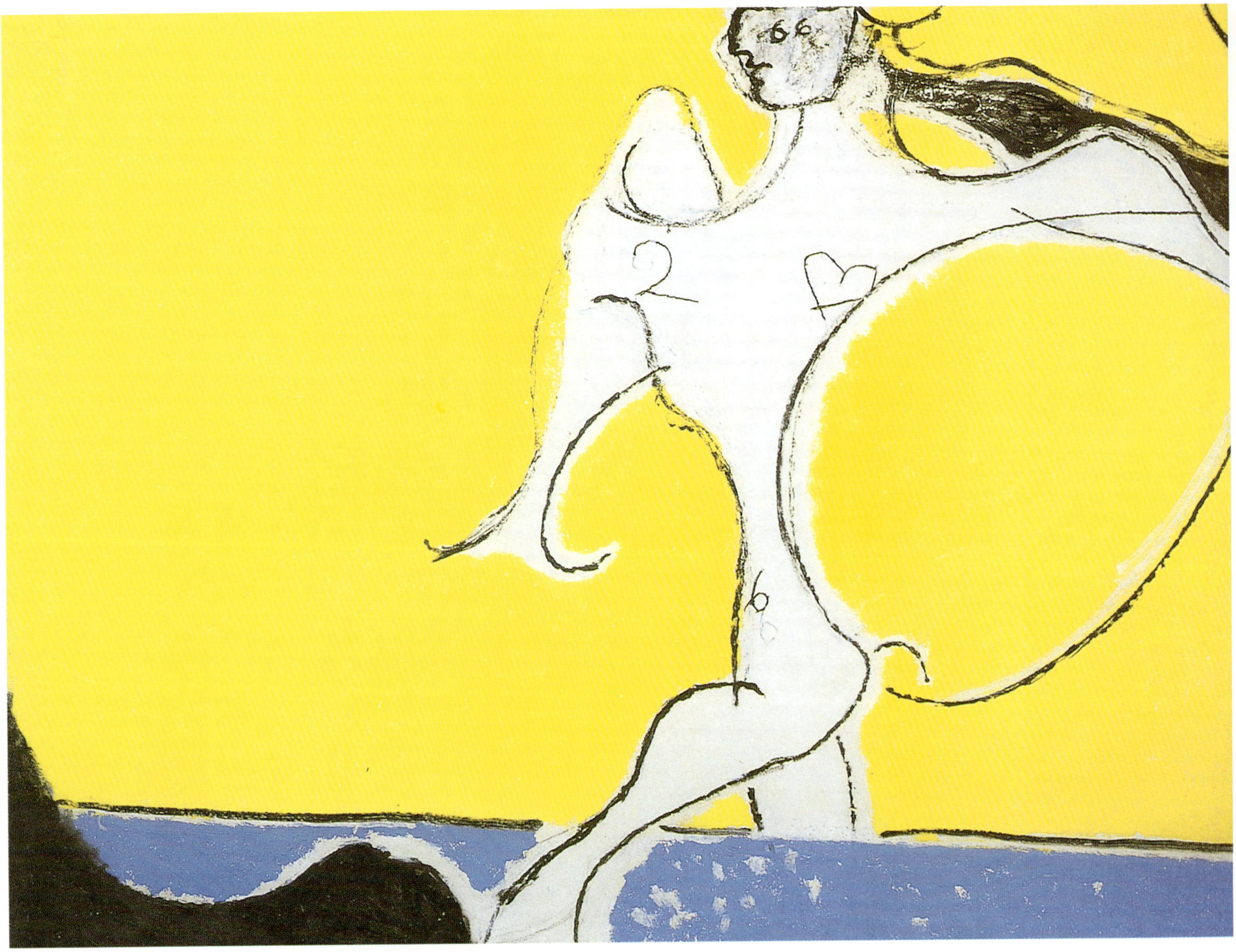

Osvaldo Licini
Rebellious Angel
1950-52
masonite
Milan, Civic Museum of Contemporary Art.

A majestic and terribly angry angel strides from the right side of the picture over seas and skies. A dark wing of hair follows him waving in the wind; a promontory at the lower left seems to await him. Strangely enough, he displays digits in place of anatomical details. The number 6 appears twice in place of the eyes, 2 where the right shoulder joins the wing, and 6 again at the naval. The heart, instead, beats steadily on the left side.

Afro

(Oreste Basaldella,
Udine 1912 – Zurich 1976)

The third of three artist brothers – the other two are Dino and Mirko – Afro very early aligned himself with the most innovative trends in Italian art. His neo-cubist apprenticeship took place in the early Forties, while his affiliation with the New Frontier in Art dates from 1947. Afro was a painter both skillful and refined, whose ingenuousness masked a keen awareness. Immediately after the war he was among the first artists to journey to the United States. He went there in 1950, just before exhibiting at the Venice Biennale, and drew long-lasting suggestions from his stay in America. The New York scene encountered by Afro was that of the action painting of Pollock, De Kooning, and Rothko, but it was Gorky above all to whom the artist looked in the attempt to conjoin relaxed, subtle linear exercises and simple expanses of colour. He aimed to reproduce, in his compositions, that loose interference of drawing and colour found in the work of the artists he looked to as masters – Matisse, Klee and Morandi.

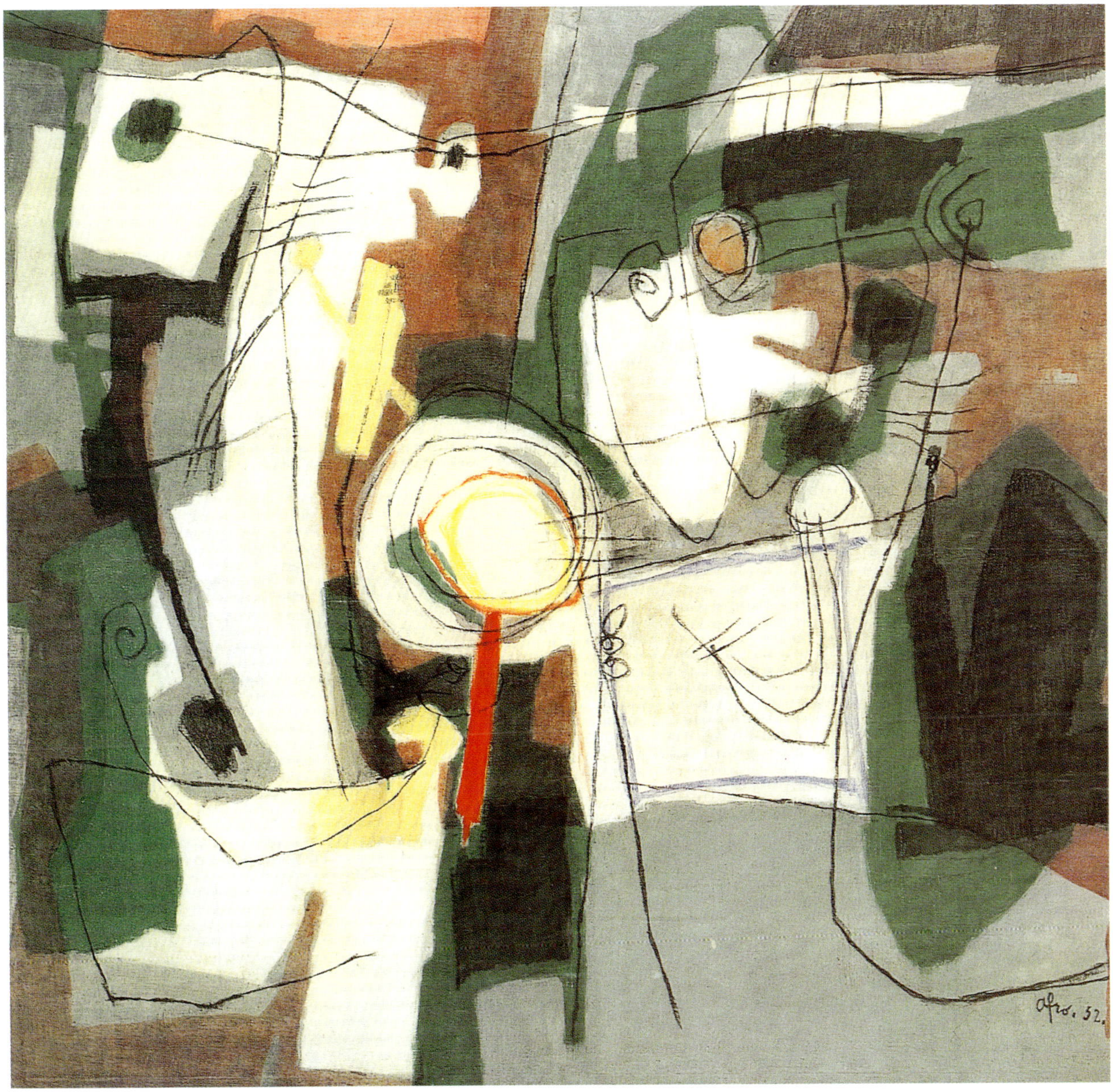

Afro
Villa Fleurante
1952
canvas
Venice, Ca' Pesaro
Gallery of Modern Art.

The painting is a fine example of Afro's interests and compositional tendencies. Fields of color, variously and irregularly polygonal in shape, occupy the entire surface. Terse, concise linear paths are superimposed on the expanses of colour with no apparent relationship to them and almost as if to produce skillful effects of depth and transparency.

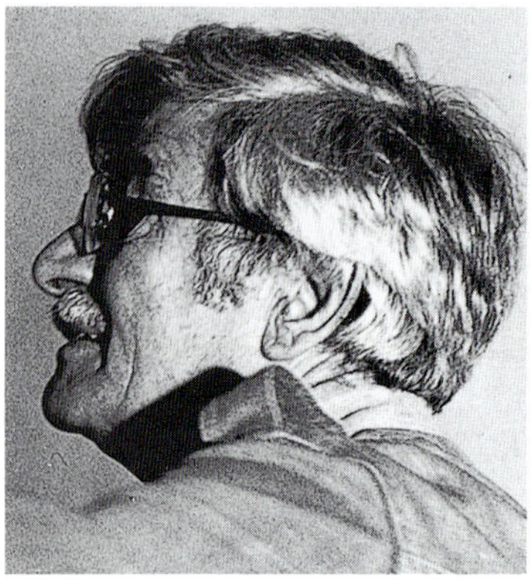

Alberto Burri

(Città di Castello 1915 – Beaulieu 1995)

A military physician, he was captured by the Americans during World War II. He began to paint in a prison camp in Texas, using whatever supports he could find. Returning to Italy, he settled in Rome, abandoning the medical profession to dedicate himself to painting. His first sack-cloth compositions date from 1952. Laying aside his brushes, Burri began to work as a fortuitous tailor, surgeon, patcher and mender. His compositions won international acclaim. Subsequently he worked with wood, burned plastic, iron bars; and then added the cycle of the *Cracks*. Figurative illusions are not lacking in his compositions. Burri seems to have amused himself by evoking pictorial images just while refusing to paint. It may be more useful, however, to view the artist's work in the light of the activity involved, the fervor of construction, than to seek in it recollections of tradition and the museum.

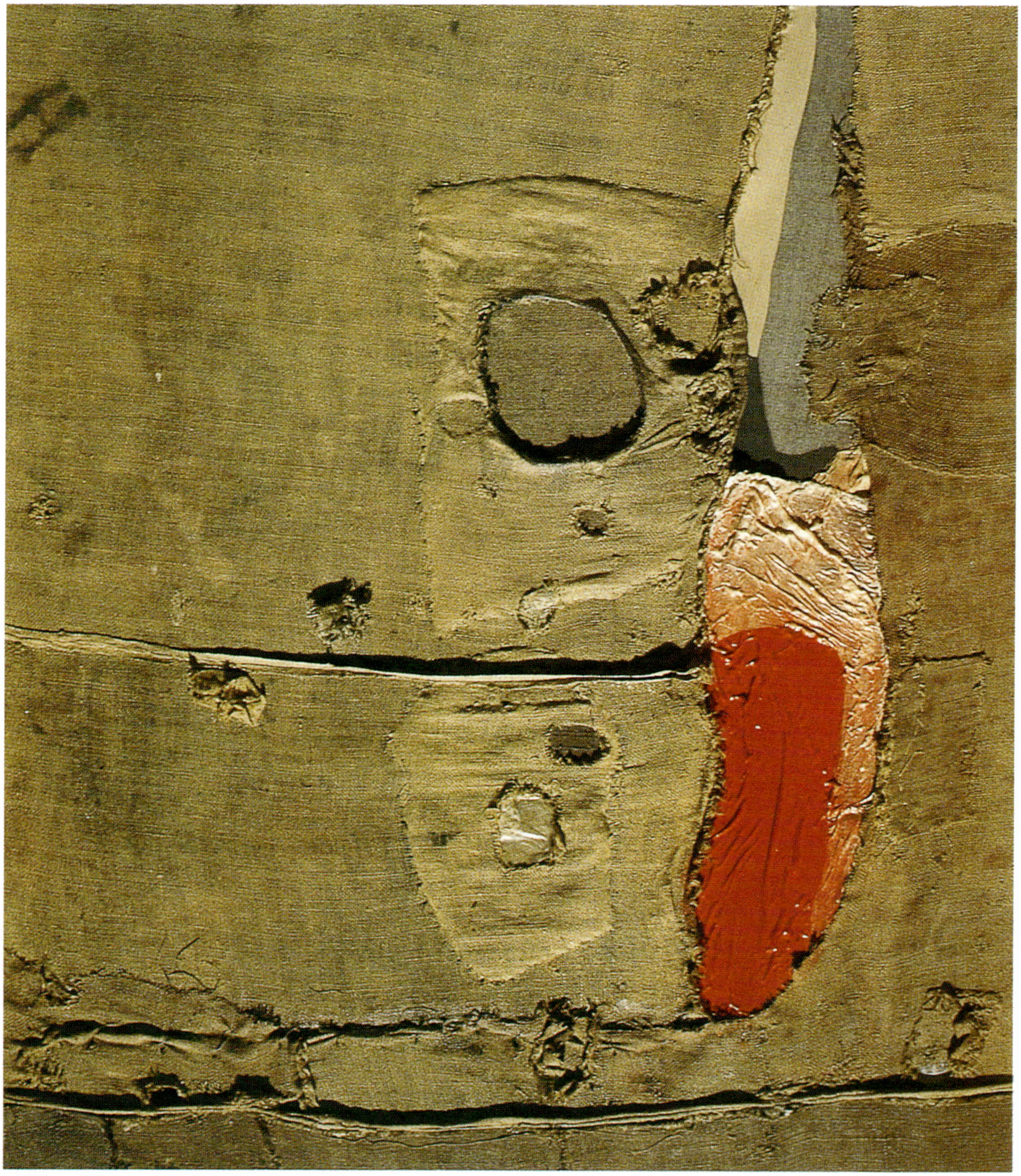

Alberto Burri
Sack 5 P
1953
sack, acrylic, vinavil, fabric on canvas
Città di Castello, Palazzo Albizzini Foundation.

Burri's work, the *Sacks* in particular, never cease to evoke aesthetic emotions, to arouse admiration for what is considered to be specific beauty. Burri was skillful at preserving, in compositions that are non-figurative and non-pictorial, the narrative seeds and memories of painting: in *Sack 5 P* we note some holes, and our attention is immediately captured by them. The holes are looking, the holes are eyes; the holes are asking for penetration, the holes are orifices – and a pendulous strip of colour, a kind of exercise in monochrome.

Alberto Burri
Big Red
1956
sack, oil and acrylic on canvas
Città di Castello, Palazzo Albizzini Foundation.

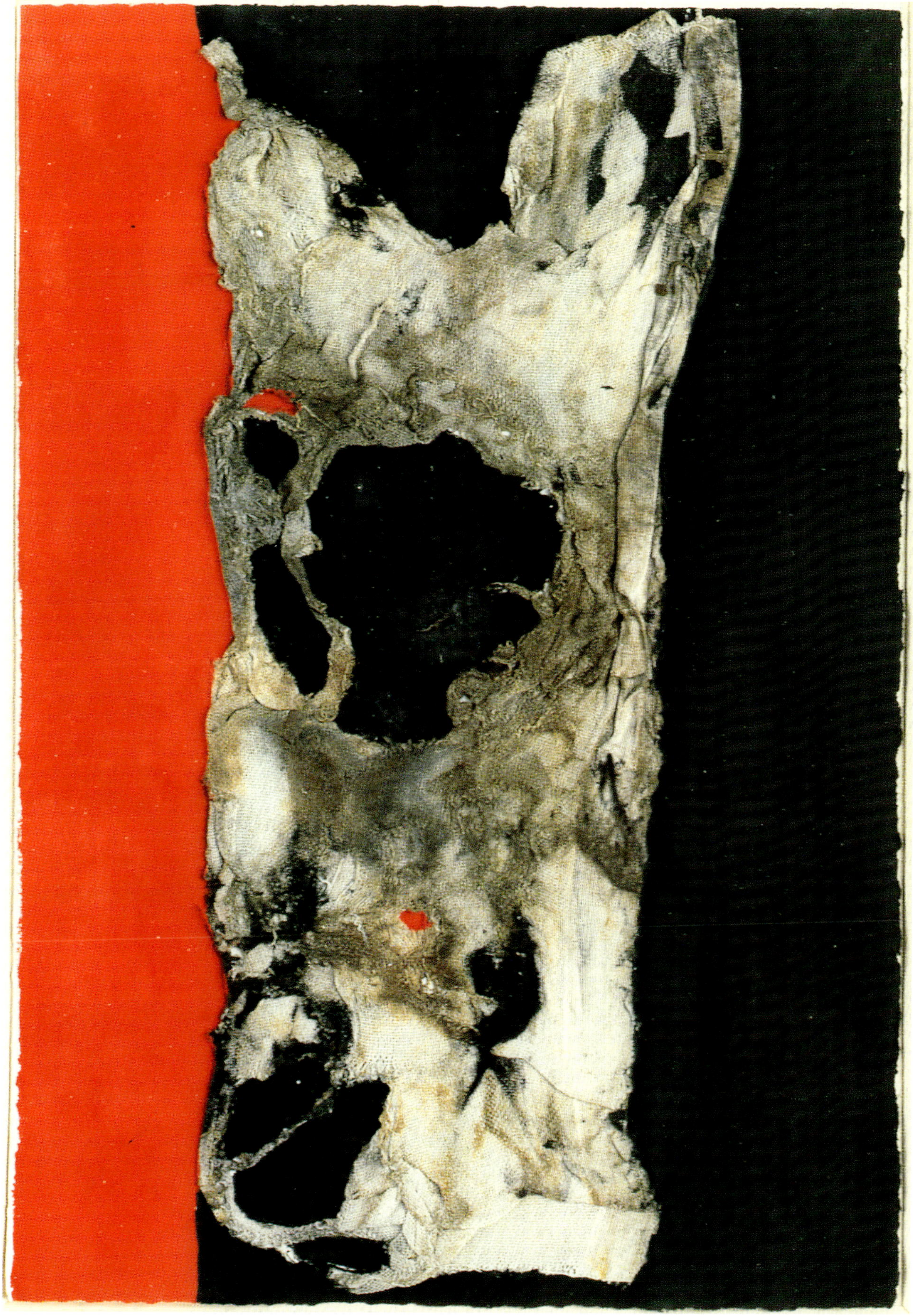

From the morphological viewpoint the composition recalls still life paintings with game: the hanging beef carcasses of Rembrandtian tradition, the hares and fowl of Ensor and Soutine. But Burri states, almost as if to admit a strategy of ambiguity: "in my work there are neither signs nor symbols [...]. Certainly those who look at it always find references, but if I myself wanted to establish references, I would see different ones".

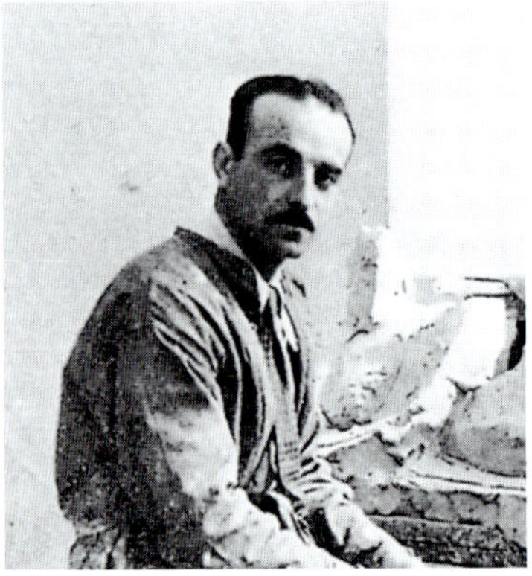

Lucio Fontana

(Rosario di Santa Fé 1899 – Comabbio, Varese, 1968)

A pupil of Wildt at the Brera Academy, Fontana was immediately recognized by the master as an artist of great talent. Attentive to what was happening in France, he was also curious about prehistoric art – his first terracottas reveal a knowledge of the Altamira graffiti – and interested in collaboration between the figurative arts and architecture. In the post-war years Fontana became the most authoritative figure, along with Burri, for young Italian artists, with his *Manifesto* (1946) and *Technical Manifesto of Spatialism* (1951), the movement named by him; his *Environments* are installations of lights, colours, and shapes within three-dimensional spaces. *Spatial Concepts*, a series of monochrome canvases pierced by one or more cuts, began in 1951. At the origin of many of the post-informal tendencies of the late Fifties, they also heralded the conceptual trends immediately to follow.

Lucio Fontana
Spatial Concept, Awaiting
canvas
1960
Milan, Civic Museum of Contemporary Art.

The *Concepts* undoubtedly express irritation, annoyance. They manifest what Fontana himself called a "transformation", or better the "end of the painting" considered as a furnishing object finely executed with the skill of the artisan/artist. In contrast to a futile, naively ornamental art, Fontana presents monochrome canvases violated by a cut. What interests him lies beyond the canvas, beyond the representative make-believe, in the direction of artistic experience, of the "nothing...: and man reduced to nothing does not mean that he is destroyed. He becomes a man as simple as a plant, a flower, and when he is this pure, man will be perfect".

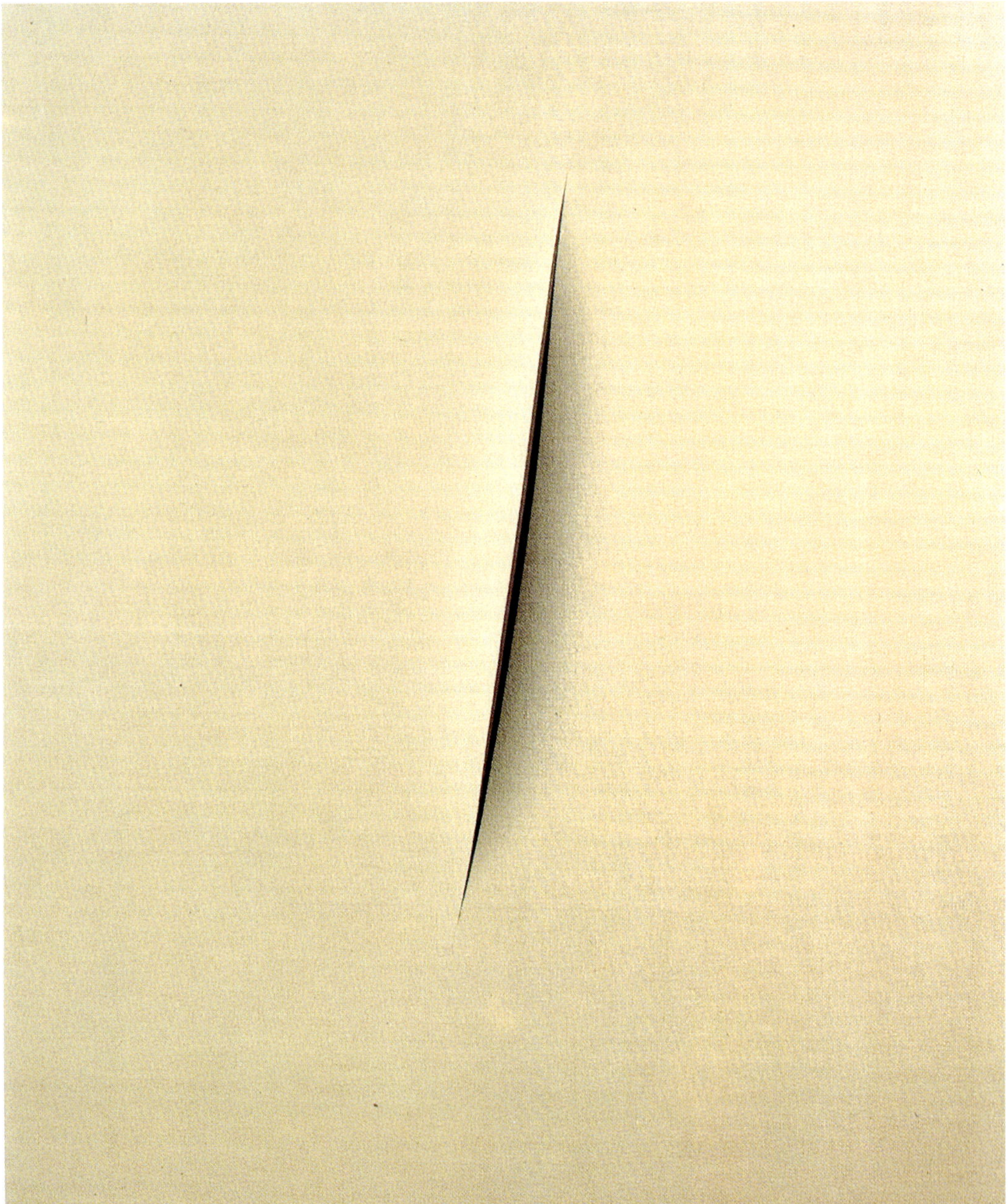

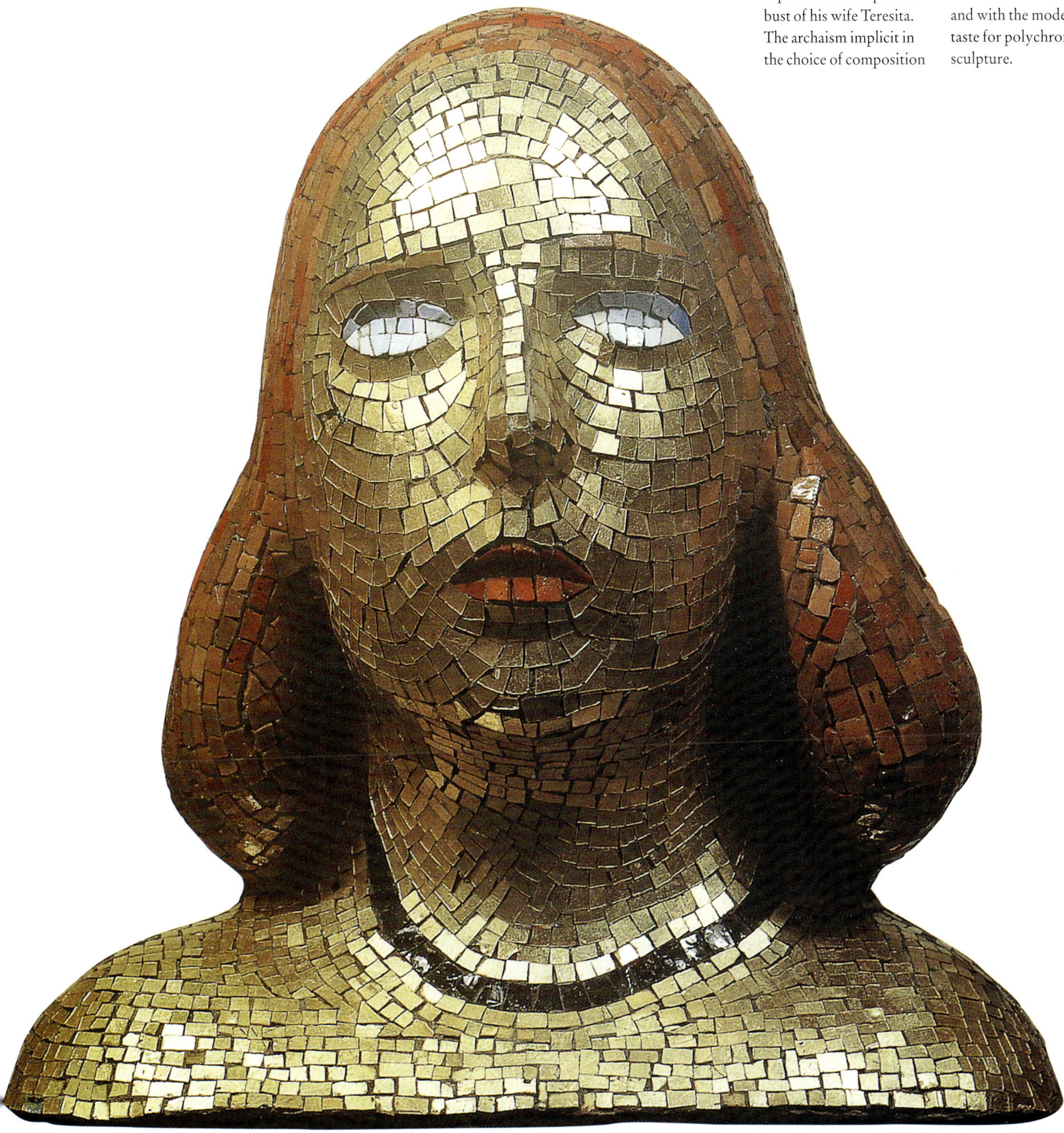

Lucio Fontana
Portrait of Teresita
1938
mosaic
Milan, Lucio Fontana Foundation.

Testifying to Fontana's vivacious propensity for experiment is the portrait bust of his wife Teresita. The archaism implicit in the choice of composition – the bust is the typical genre of fifteenth century Florentine sculptural portraiture – and in the mosaic-work technique imposes no restrictive severity; on the contrary, it merges fittingly with the soft curvilinear forms, and with the modernistic taste for polychrome sculpture.

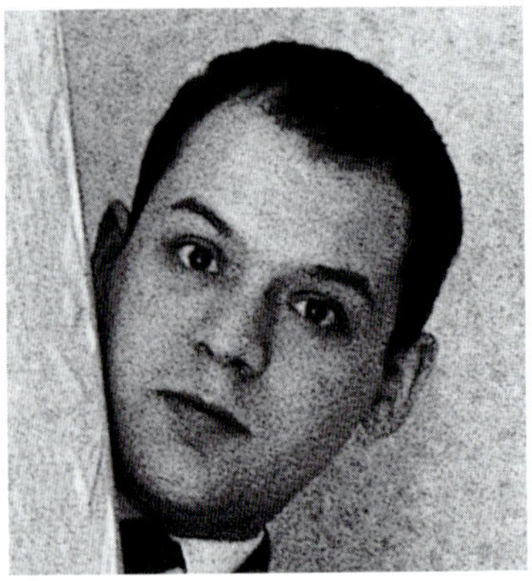

Piero Manzoni

(Soncino 1934 – Milan 1963)

Enfant prodige of Italian art in the late Fifties and early Sixties, Manzoni was one of the first to grasp the importance of Fontana's work and to interpret his heritage; but he was to go even further than his friend and master in attempting to move beyond any logic of recognizable shapes and formal consistency. He experimented with different techniques, materials and even styles to establish the supremacy of creativity as aptitude, versatility, resource, over art degraded as profession. Emphasising the importance of the peculiar and expressly physiological element in art, he refused to disassociate the dimension of the work from the most concrete experiences of the artist. His monochrome canvases and *assemblages*, performances and installations are always imbued with a keen comic and theatrical sense; but in the pauses between cabaret acts can be felt delicate suspensions, subtly pathetic attitudes.

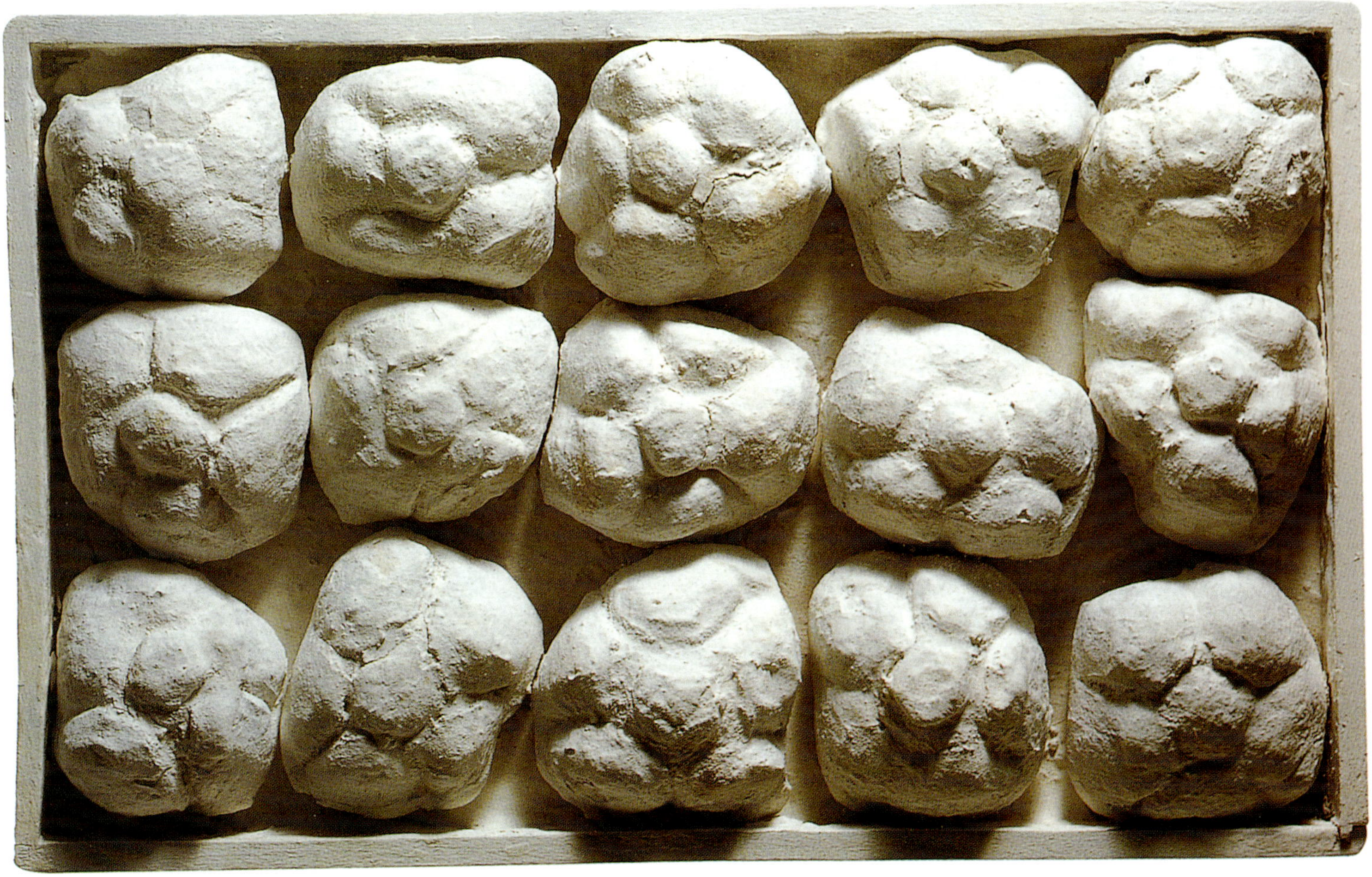

Piero Manzoni
Achrome
1961-62
canvas

The composition possesses both the irreverence of fast food and the candid geometric rigour of neo-plastic compositions. Aligned in three horizontal rows of five, fifteen buns in a pure white box seem caught within a dimension of awaiting. Are they waiting to be consumed in a mysterious lunch? We do not know; but the *Achrome* – according to Manzoni inspired by pure chance, on the occasion of a visit to the neighborhood bakery – has a kind of light, white crumbling air, something between the pharmacological and the funereal.

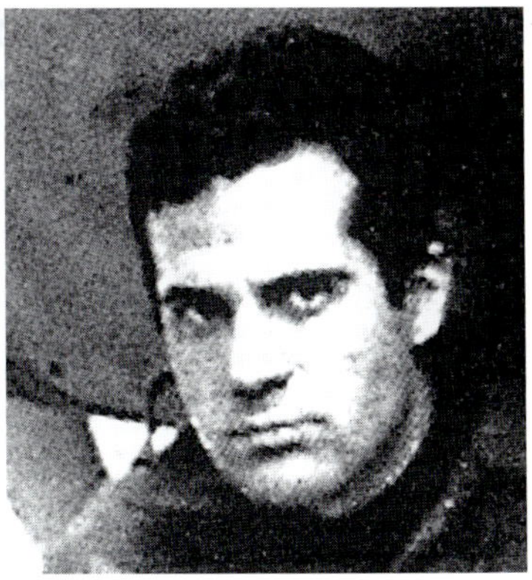

Pino Pascali

(Polignano a Mare 1935 – Rome 1968)

A pupil of Toti Scialoja at the Rome Academy, already by the early Sixties Pascal had grasped the sense of what was happening in young American art, which seemed to point in the direction of an ironic, disillusioned, brilliant, detachment from action painting. His first works alternate between *assemblages* and playful, showy pop aesthetics: ships in scale weigh anchor on the canvas to which they are glued, great protruding red lips bring to Italy some of the seduction and the mercenary quality of the "American dream". Beginning in 1965, Pascali produced installations, building toy weapons as if for the joy of construction itself, creating portable "seas", exotic landscapes and fantastic animals – spiders, giraffes, whales and worms. Animals interest him insofar as they are "intruders"; to them the complex rituals of recognition that reign within the space of an art gallery are wholly extraneous.

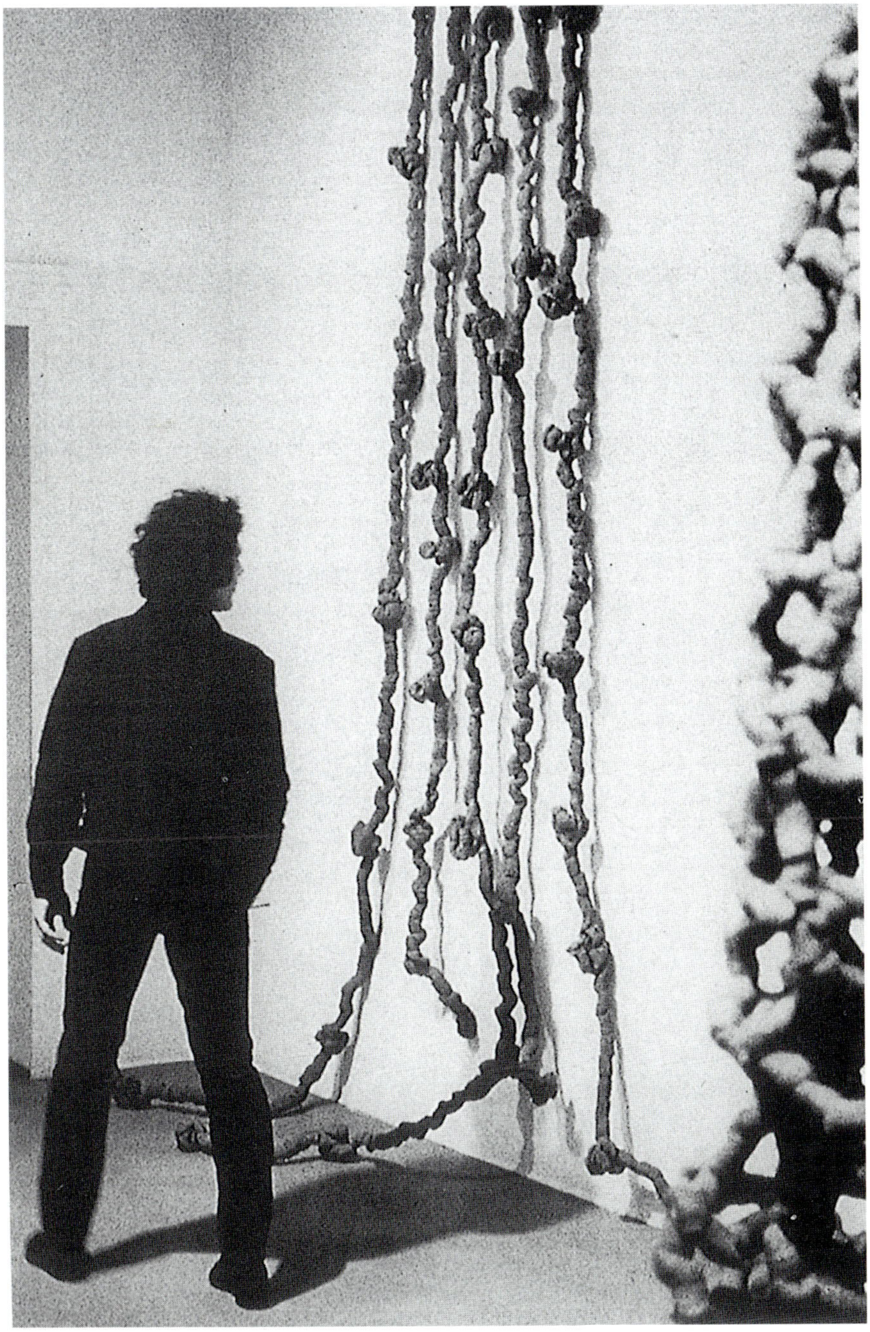

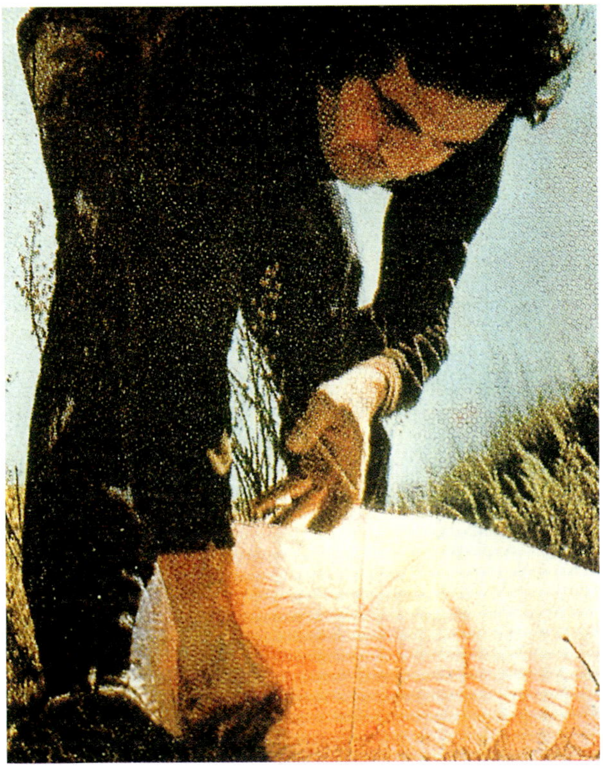

Pino Pascali
Lianas
1968
steel wool

Pascal displayed a singular ethnographic propensity in an exploration of Mediterranean myths, costumes, and beliefs that was more than a homage to his own origins. The artist, a native of the Apulia region, attempted to express in plastic form the differences existing between his own activity, situated in a certain geographical context, and that of an American artist. The theme of travel is, moreover, implicit in many of his installations – travel as adventure, invitation to lay aside rigidly established roles and cultural identities; in a word, discovery.

Pino Pascali
in a performance of the Sixties.

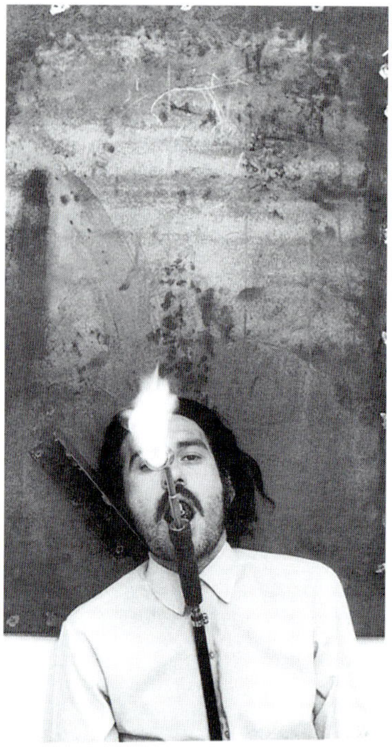

Jannis Kounellis

(Peraeus, Athens, 1936)

Born in Athens in 1936, he moved to Rome in 1956, enrolling in the Academy. His first compositions, oils on canvas, consisted of numbers and simple alphabetical characters. Starting from 1966 he produced installations of great complexity and visual seduction, utilizing inorganic and organic materials, approaching a kind of poetics of the element – iron, cotton, wool, wood, fire, stone, earth, coffee, cactus and parrots. Poised at the threshold of the picture, of the great painting, he created three-dimensional works that, for their choice of composition, rich colours and allegorical or metalinguistic aspects, often concealed a reflection on rejected technique. Among the most renowned and influential artists on the international level, he owes his first notoriety to an installation dated 1969 and presented at "L'attico" Gallery in Rome. There the spectators found awaiting them, in place of inanimate objects, twelve pawing horses.

Jannis Kounellis
Without title
1960
canvas

A digit and two letters appear in the white space of the canvas; a fourth letter, deleted, is barely visible. The colored surface and the individual signs are accomplished through a technique in some way reminiscent of Pollock's dripping. The signs seem to carry out the functions of toys that are both linguistic and figurative: macroscopic and devoid of reciprocal links, they stand on the canvas as if waiting to be spelled aloud by the voice of a child, or recited by a phonetic poet, half futurist, half hermetic.

Jannis Kounellis
Without title
1973
photograph of performance
Naples, Lucio Amelio Gallery.

Kounellis, a young man with long hair and a steady, hostile gaze, poses as both dreamy jazz saxophonist and destroying angel. His instrument emits flames, not sounds, and the concert is being held against the background of a gray iron plate rather than in a brightly lit night-club. The iron plate, a metallurgical product, places the artist's activity within the context of a precise industrial landscape – that of Italy in 1973. Contemporary historical and social conflicts are accompanied by this fire music.

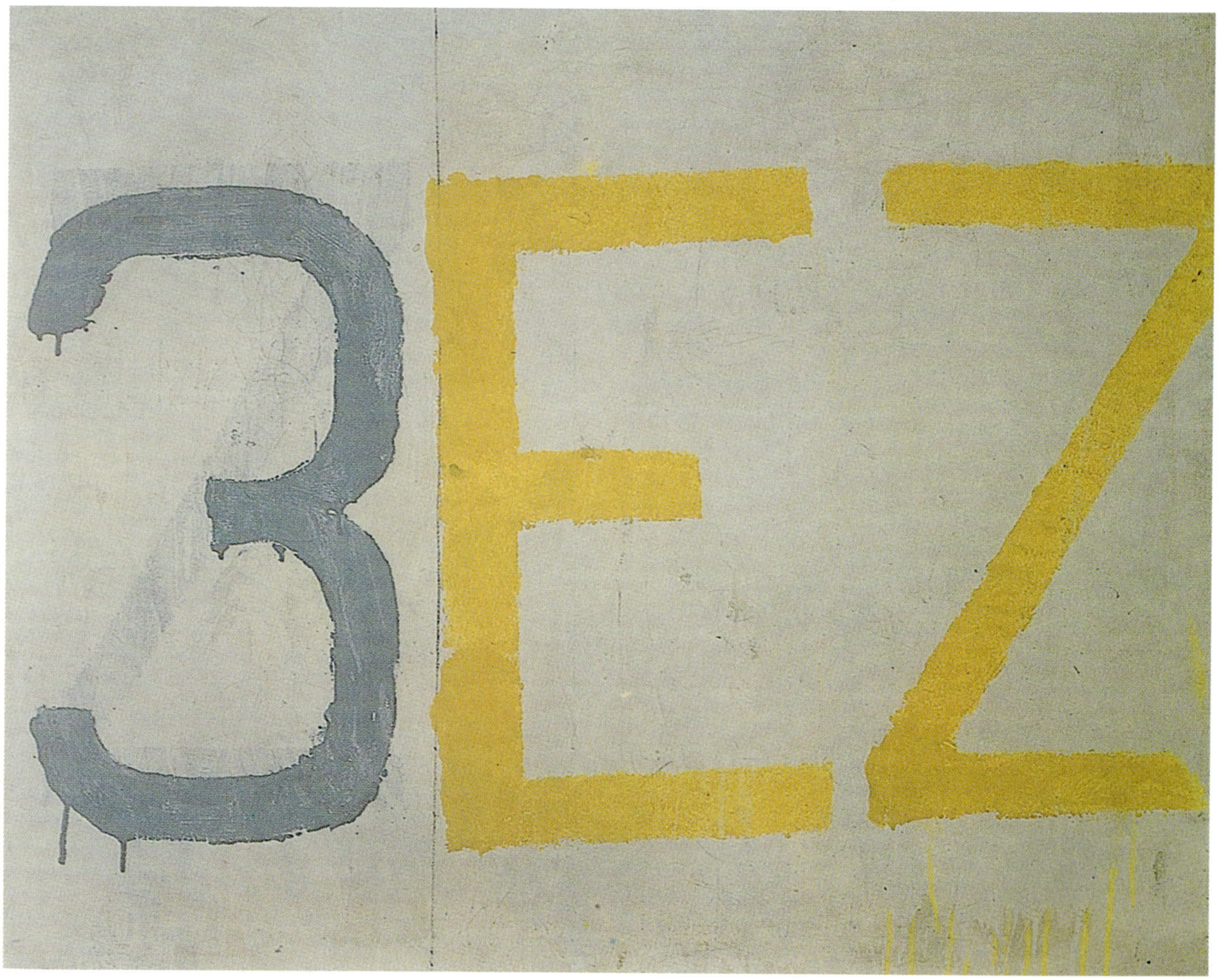

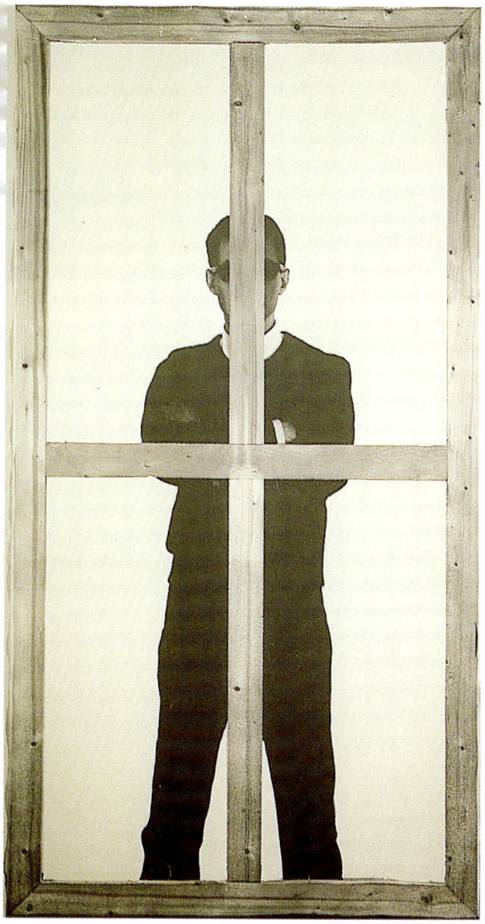

Giulio Paolini
Delphi
1965
canvas

The artist poses with folded arms. Although his gaze is turned toward us, we do not know whether it reflects on us, his spectators, or on the canvas which he has not begun to paint; certainly he hides his face. With its rough weave and simple frame of boards the canvas is, along with the artist, the theme of the composition. It seems turned toward the wall, as if refusing to lend itself to the usual purposes of pictorial figuration, deception and seduction: it is bare, nude, unaccomplished. "What should I do?" seems to be the question asked by the artist.

Giulio Paolini
Mimesis
1975
plaster casts
Turin, Brandolini collection.

In *Mimesis* we find a different Paolini, more supple and figurative. At a distance of exactly one decade from *Delphi*, no fear is felt before beauty. On the contrary, duplication is employed in the effort to reawaken the enchantment of an ancient statue.

Giulio Paolini

(Genoa 1940)

His art is distinguished by rigour and restrained, modernistic elegance. Apparently discerning and consistent, not devoid of self-citation and thematic reiteration, it reveals a kind of natural, relaxed inner discourse. His first works are dominated by a meta-linguistic dimension, by reflection on the techniques, materials, and social significance of art. Paolini himself indicated De Chirico and the Fontana of the "cuts" as his primary reference points within recent Italian tradition. Subsequently the need for control persists, but a freer visual and imaginative attitude emerges.

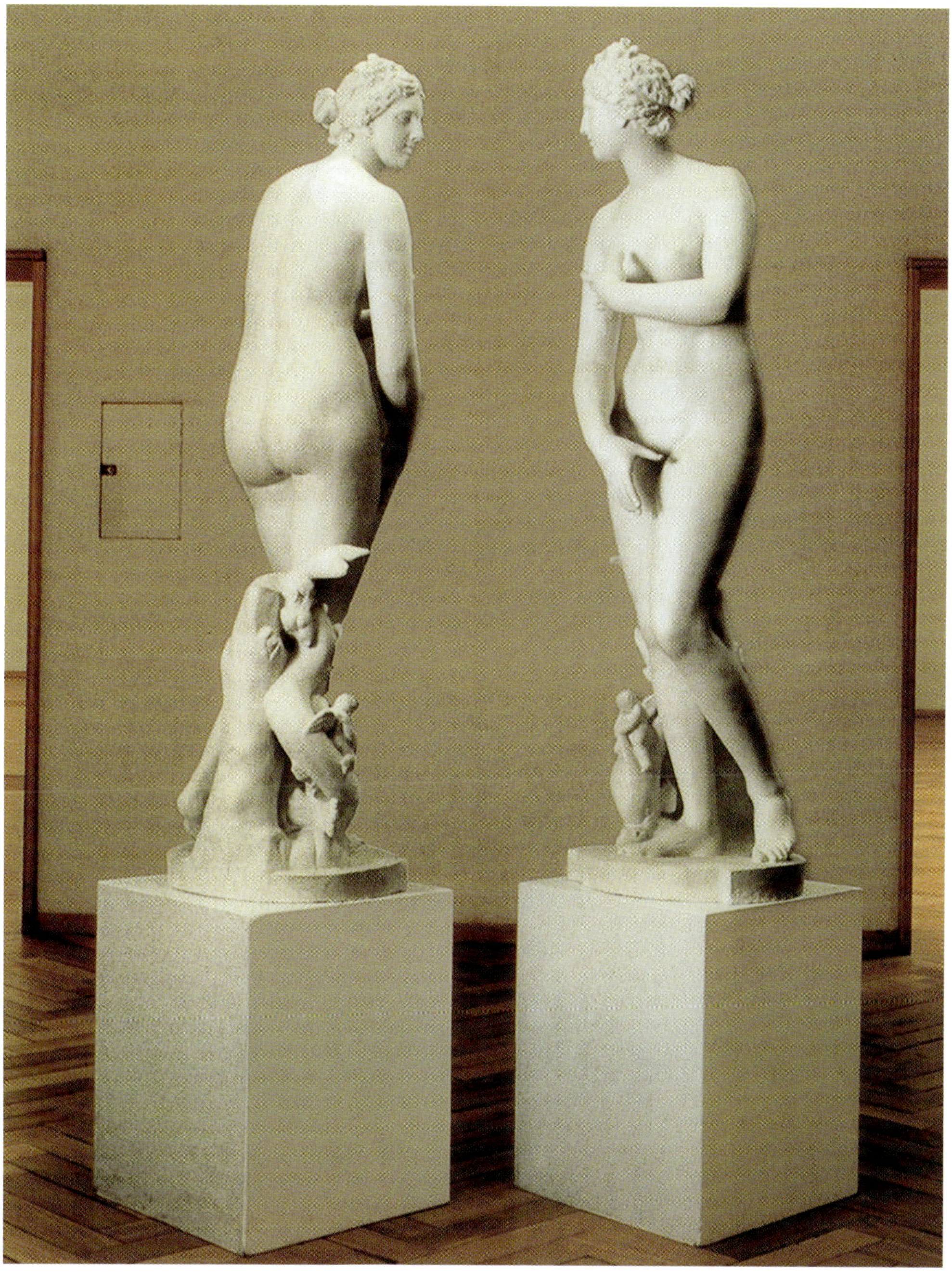

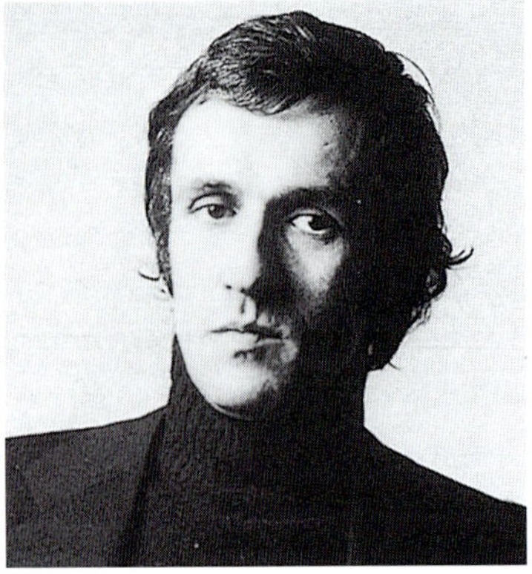

Alighiero Boetti

(Turin 1940 – Rome 1994)

Born and trained in Turin before moving to Rome in the early Seventies – in flight from the artistic and cultural milieu of the Piedmont capital, rejecting control and excessive strategy – Boetti was an elusive, complex artist. He experimented with numerous artistic or artistic/industrial techniques (drawing, weaving, printing, photocopying, photography) and extended the sphere of the visual arts to the point of including letters and telegrams. Interested in the collaborative aspect of art – as shown in the compositions with stamped envelopes and postcards, or the carpets woven, for example, at Kabul in Afghanistan – he rejected the emphasis placed on the concepts of author and authorship. To the figure of the cultural hero he preferred that of the traveler, the enthusiastic, many-sided observer, or perhaps the gentle madman who splits his own personality (his works were signed Alighiero & Boetti).

Alighiero Boetti
Musical Instrument,
detail, 1970.

Alighiero Boetti
Addition
1984
embroidery on canvas
Rome, Boetti Archives.

Fascinated by systems of classification, by catalogues, by arbitrary, conventional systematics, Boetti conceived his works as marvelous, but secretly obsessive devices. Virtually interminable, they develop through inner mechanics and processes of serial growth (that is, by "addition"), with the apparent simplicity of a child's game, a singsong melody, a repetitive chant.

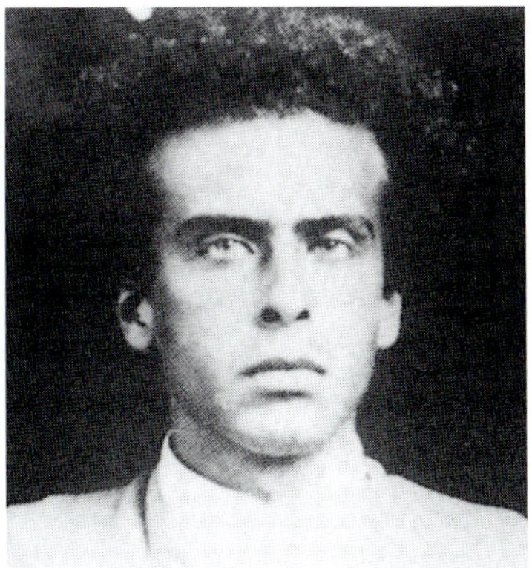

Francesco Clemente

(Naples 1952)

"In '68 I was 16 years old. In the evening I fell asleep before Luca Giordano, in the morning I looked at the sleeves of records by Jimi Hendrix, Bob Dylan and the Pink Floyd". Clemente himself, a Neapolitan who now lives in New York, recalls his first figurative experiences. Arriving at Rome in 1970, he met Cy Twombly and Boetti; took photographs; and convinced himself of the plausibility of an artistic approach that inventively explores techniques and images, that unites the cultural and the popular, the community and the individual. Starting in the latter half of the Seventies he made frequent trips to India. In approaching the local art and myths he added a sensual world of images from his own repertoire. Among the first to acclaim the new-found interest in painting – he was in the movement called Transavanguardia – he won international recognition at a relatively early age.

Francesco Clemente
Seeds
1978
tempera on fabric-covered paper
Milan, Alessandro Grassi collection.

Recollections of Neapolitan painting are interwoven, in the artist's compositions, with folklore or ethnographic curiosities; with a vivid interest in religious symbols, variously composed; with a predilection for the human figure caught in its specifically promiscuous and erotic dimension – the self-portraits are many. But these compositions are always marked by enigmatic traits. The individual figures are not composed within a unitary setting such as a landscape, but give rise, states the artist, to an "ideogram".

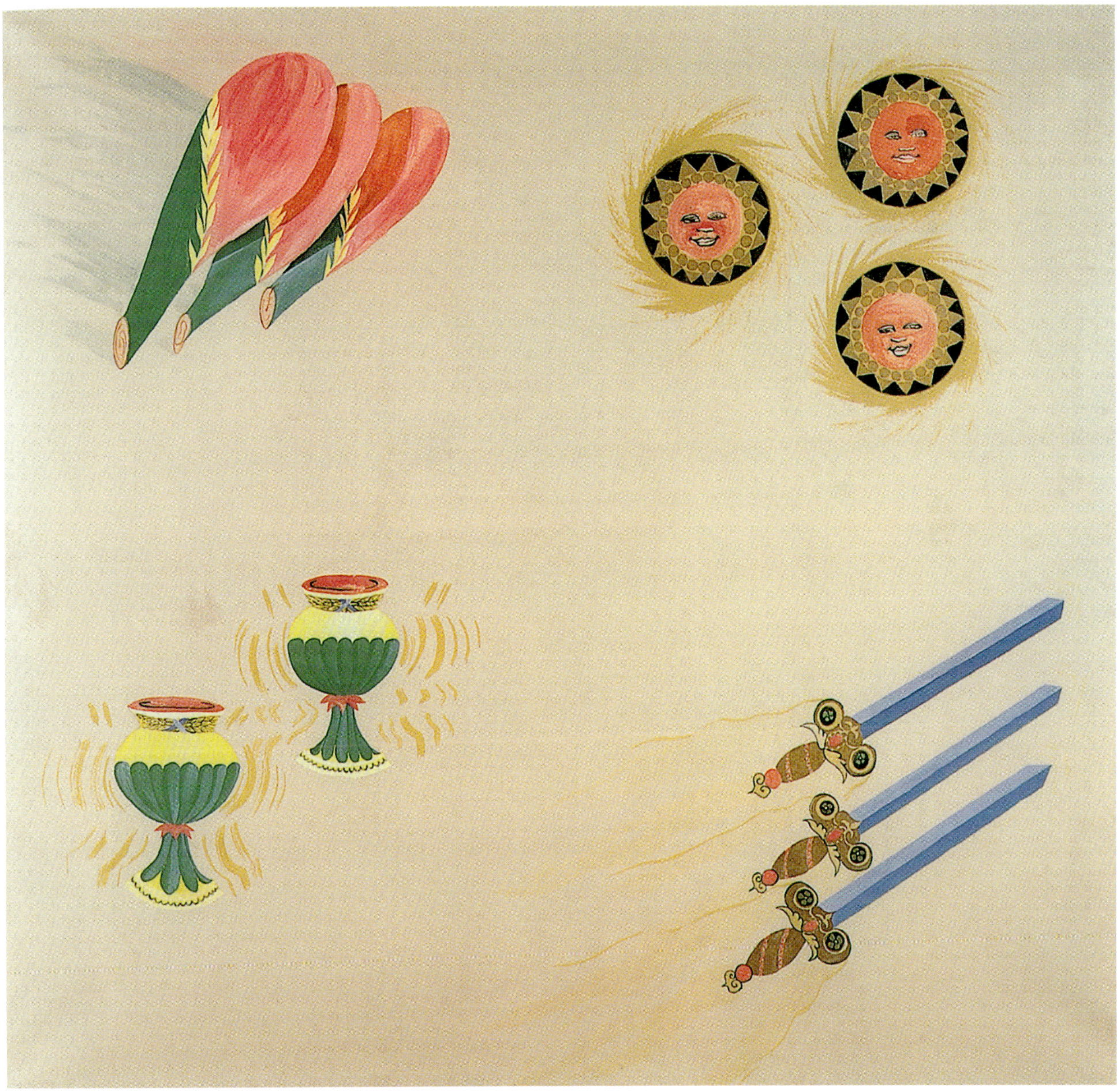

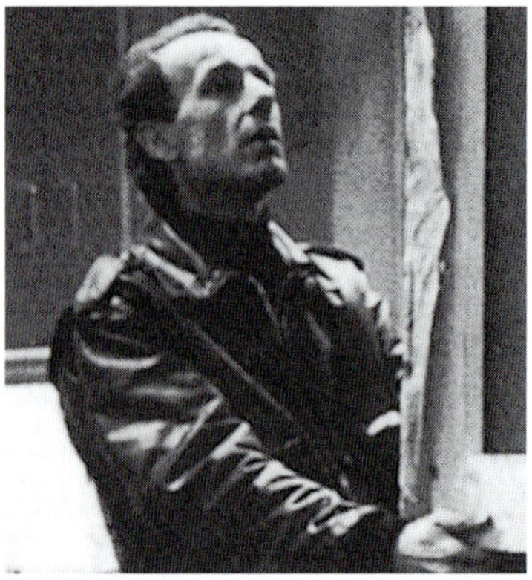

Enzo Cucchi

(Morro d'Alba, Ancona, 1949)

Gifted with great talent and inventiveness, he was active in the Seventies as poet and figurative artist. Still very young he gave performances riding a bicycle with inked tires. Great sheets of paper spread over the floor recorded the movement, proffering lines as paths. The artist's interest in art viewed as travel, adventure, emotion, remained vivid when he returned, among the first, to painting near the end of the decade. From then on his best-known compositions presented large formats, traces of feet – as if the artist had walked on them – scenes of desert regions, of navigation and shipwreck painted in the dark, stormy manner of a Romantic artist, with a black and brown-red palette. Citation became the fertile principle of the painting, his compositional machine. Art always repeats the "infinite mass of signs" of which its museum is made up. But its destiny to repeat produces no conflict: the history of art is a plaything.

Enzo Cucchi
Mediterranean Hunt
1979
canvas
Zurich, Bruno Bischofberger Gallery.

Predominating among the artists of Cucchi's generation was the desire to divorce the practice of art from any reflections on history, art history in particular. Competitive attitudes were to be avoided, entering into competition with past epochs was to be shunned, the aggressiveness of the avantgarde and its myth of "originality" was to be left behind. "And so dear artists, you who stand among the flames and signs of art at the risk of being crushed", wrote Cucchi in his customary panegyric tones, almost as if to comment on the *Mediterranean Hunt*, "what is it that you marvel at? It is art that, to let herself be tamed, demands that the artist emancipate himself from her and from her evolution".

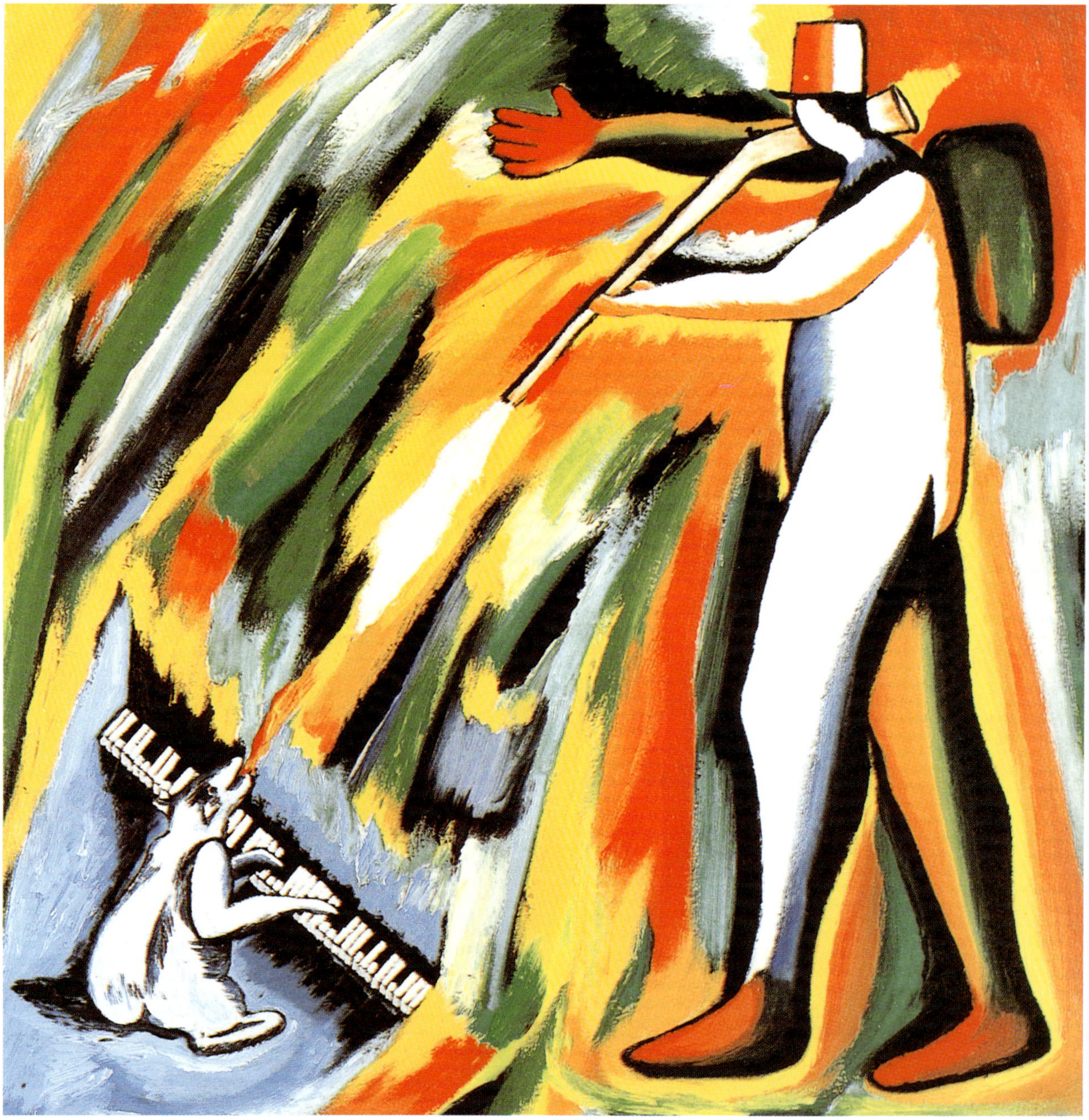

Maurizio Cattelan

(Padova 1960)

Involved first in the sphere of anti-functional design, in the late Eighties Cattelan transferred his tendency toward provocation to a specifically artistic/figurative activity. His initiatives aim to bring to light concealed secrets, unwritten rules, the subtly discriminatory attitudes of the art system, based on principles of industrial marketing; or refer to dramatic collective episodes in the historical/cultural context surrounding them. Dating from 1994 is an installation with rubble taken from the Milan Contemporary Art Pavilion, severely damaged by Mafia bombs; and from 1995 is an installation in neon with the star of the Red Brigades. Cattelan alternates the role of artist with that of cultural promoter. Co-editor of a review – "Permanent Foods" – he is at present one of the curators of the First Biennale of the Tropics.

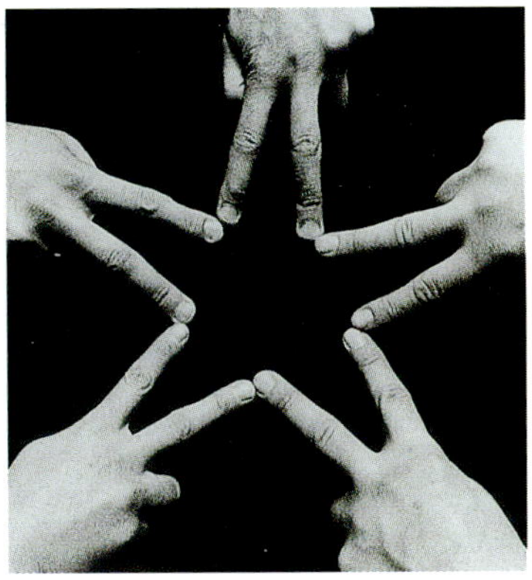

Maurizio Cattelan
Errotin, le Vrai Lapin
1994
performance
Paris, Emmanuel Perrotin.

Cattelan rents his own exhibition spaces to advertising agencies; calls on gallery owners to carry out performances in their own galleries – as in the case of Emmanuele Perrotin, director of the Parisian Ma Galery; brings into the art gallery live animals or more frequently stuffed ones as a stimulus to reflection on the limited nature of what is meant by art and collecting, and on a specific form of necrophilia. "We live in the empire of marketing, ostentation and seduction", explains the artist, always finely balanced between critical intuition and skillful self-promotion, "and thus [the task] of artists and critics is that of deconstructing strategies, resisting their logic, using them and/or finding new ways of acting against them".

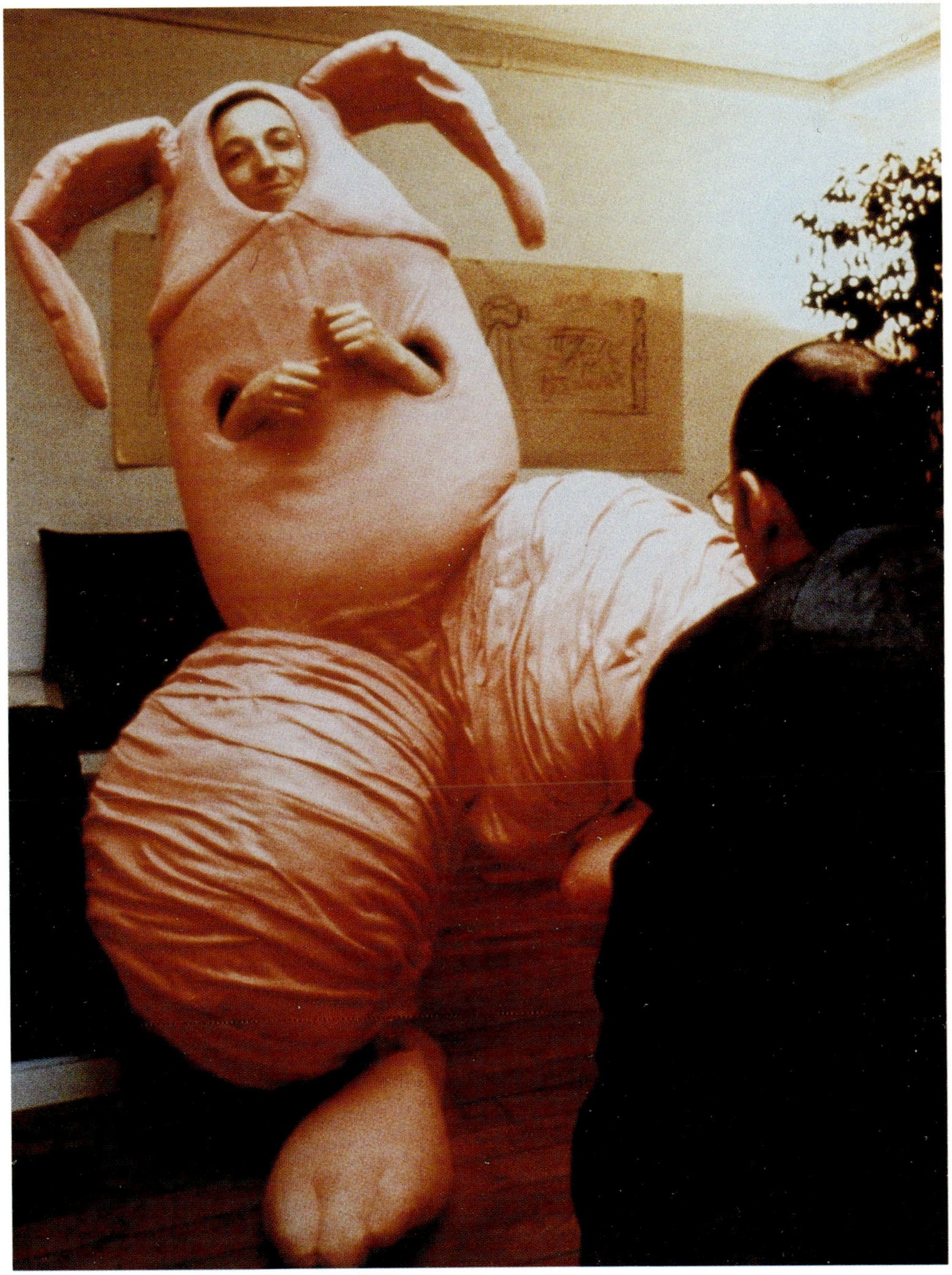

Maurizio Cattelan,
Without title, 1996.

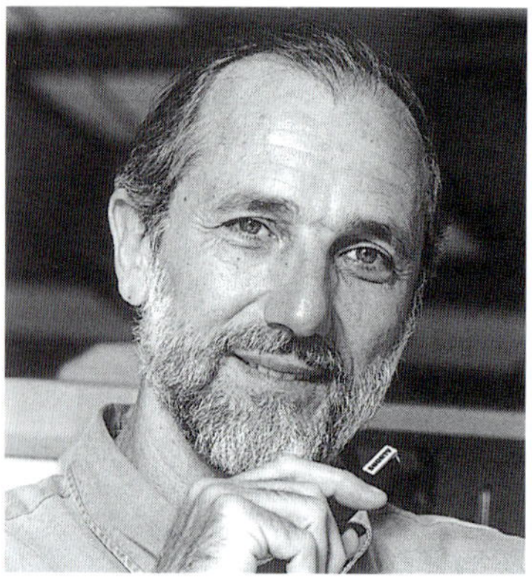

Renzo Piano

(Genoa 1937)

Piano, who graduated in 1964 from the Milan Polytechnic Institute and trained in Philadelphia and London from 1965 to 1970, is especially attentive to the way in which research and technology can harmoniously meet with the needs of the habitat to provide welcoming, concretely human spaces. In 1971 Piano & Rogers was founded. The two architects were to design together the Beaubourg. This was followed by projects for important cultural institutions and museums. The construction of the headquarters of IRCAM, the French institute for musical research, dates from 1977; the Museum built to house the de Menil collection in Houston from 1986; and the new Paul Klee Museum at Berne is now in an advanced stage of study. Particularly famous is the project for the Osaka Airport, completed in 1994. The construction, which rises from the sea like a great flower, called for the building of an artificial island.

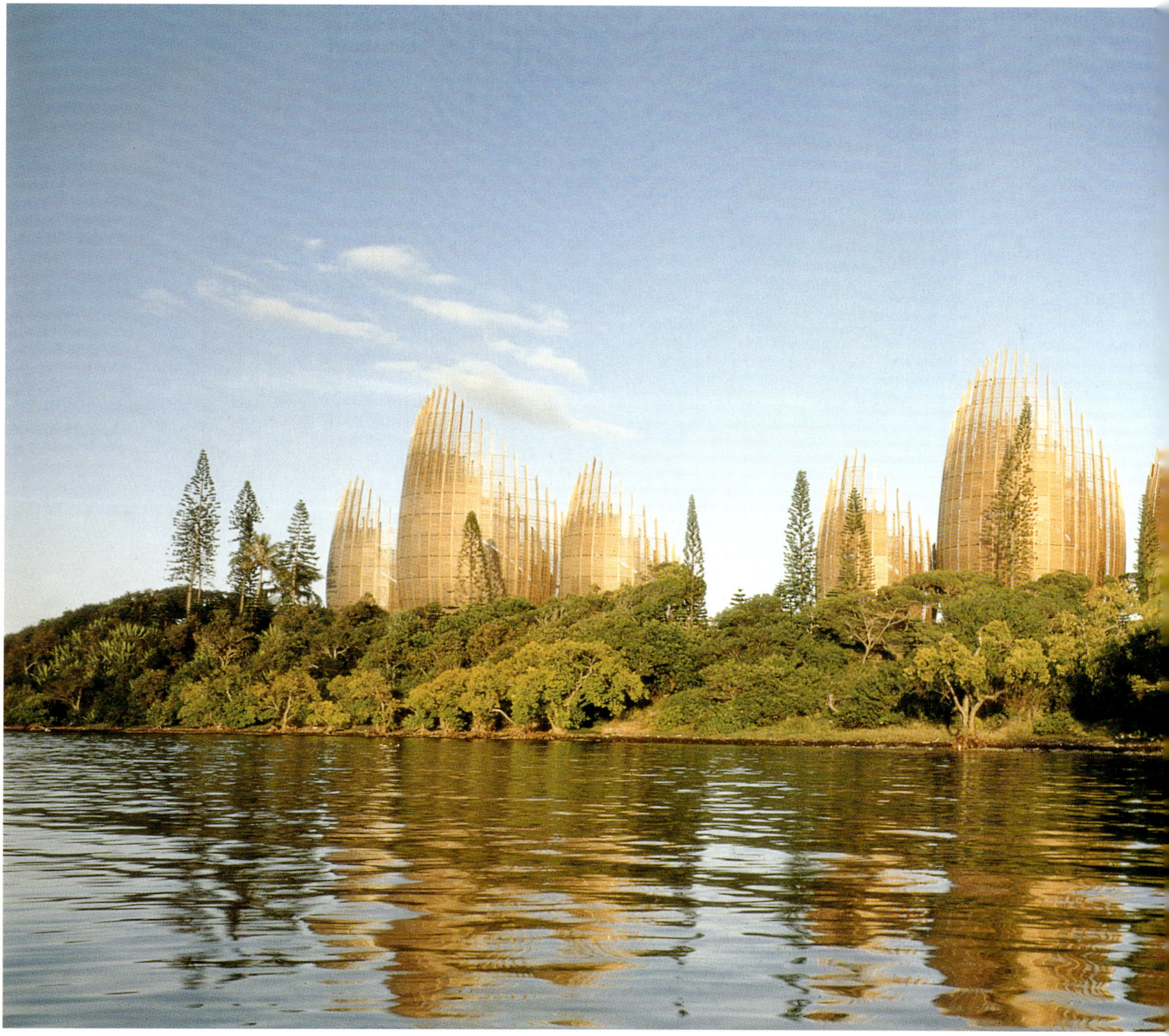

Renzo Piano
Kanak Cultural Center "Jean Marie Tjibaou"
1991-98
Nouméa, New Caledonia.

New Caledonia, a former French colony which achieved peaceful independence, is the land of the Kanak, an ethnic group spread over the Pacific area. The Cultural Center built at Nouméa, in a natural scenario of great natural beauty, bears the name of a Kanak leader who died in 1989. Piano, who consulted with ethnographers for this project, has designed the Center not as a single building but as a complex surrounded on three sides by the sea. The individual parts, reminiscent of the huts in Kanak villages, are immersed in green and connected by walkways.

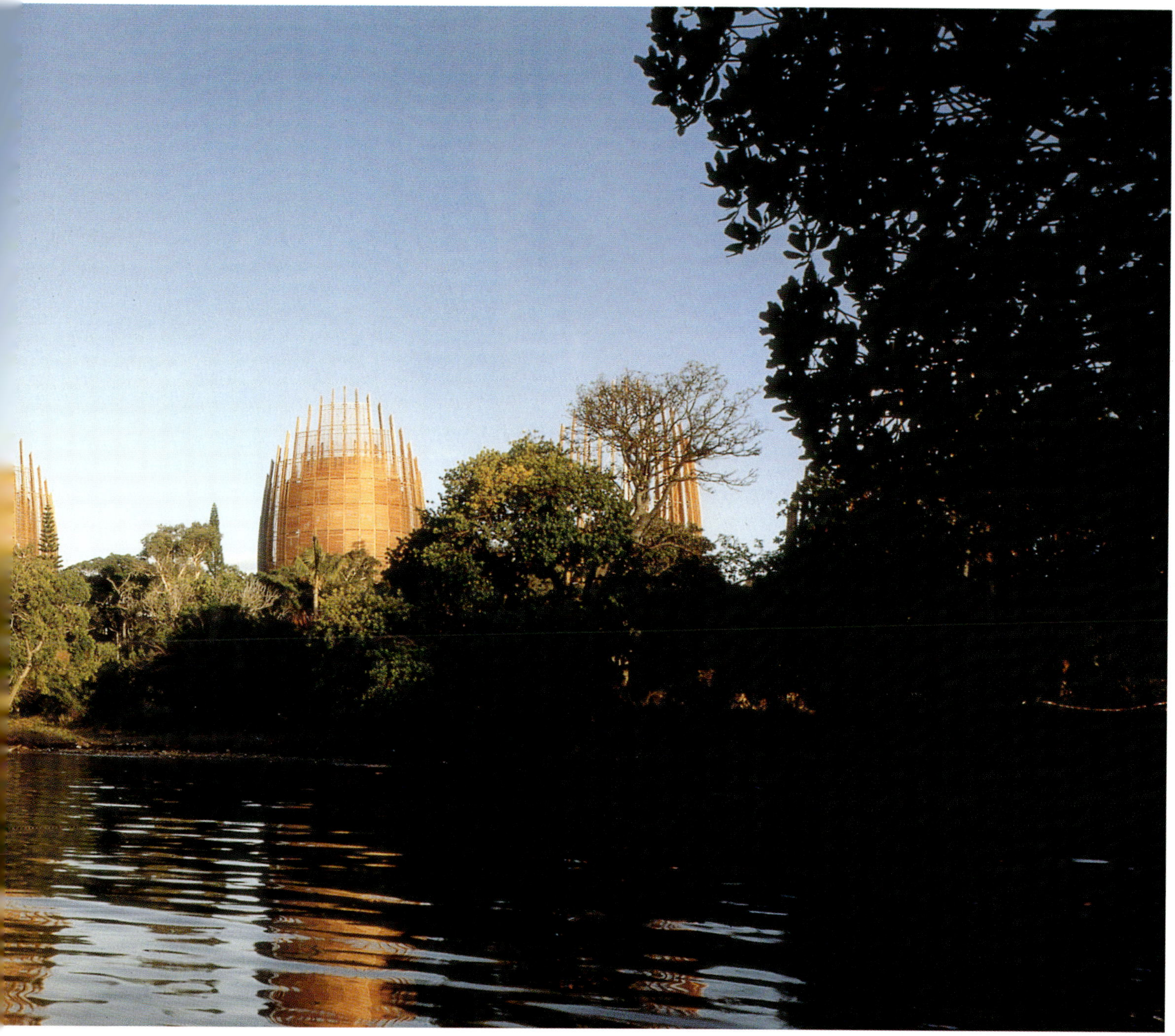

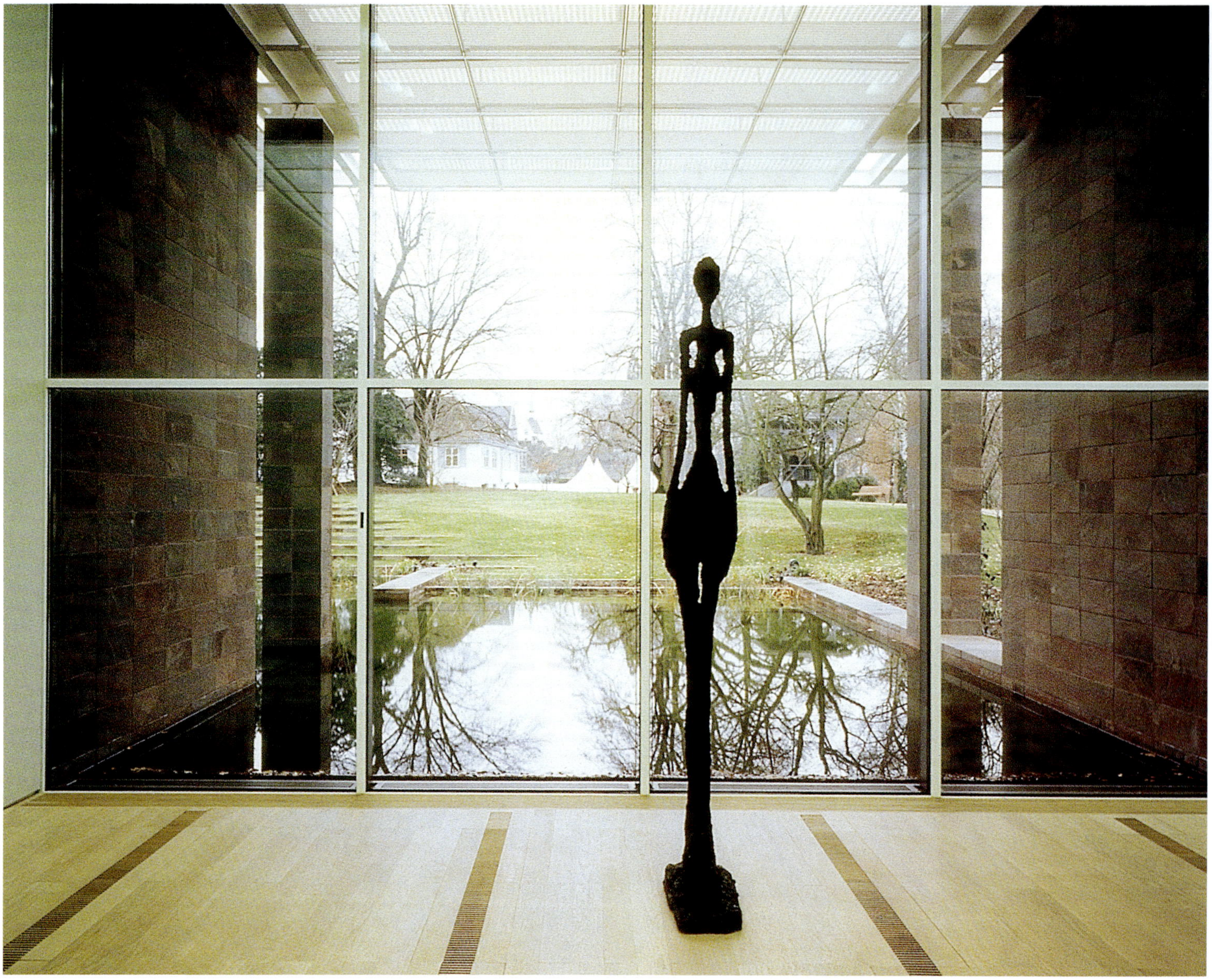

Renzo Piano
Beyeler Foundation Museum
1991-97
Riehen, Basil.

The Beyeler Foundation Museum, inaugurated at Riehen, near Basil, in the Autumn of 1997, houses the collection of contemporary art of the gallery owners Hildy and Ernst Beyeler. For Piano "a building to be used as a museum must try to reflect the character of the collection it houses and its relationship with the landscape. Accordingly, it must play a role that is active but not aggressive". Large glass panels, placed at strategic points, offer the visitor a view over the park. White walls and glass ceilings provide the best conditions of visibility for viewing the works.

Chronological Tables

Glossary

Index of Names and Works

Index of Places

CHRONOLOGICAL TABLES

THE MIDDLE AGES	ITALY		EUROPE AND OTHER COUNTRIES	
1000	1046-1115	Matilde di Canossa; Basilica of San Miniato al Monte in Florence	1050	Sainte-Foi in Conques
	1059	Consecration of the Baptistery in Florence	1066	Battle of Hastings: the Norman King William in England
	1060	Campo dei Miracoli in Pisa	1075	Santiago de Compostela
	1063	Victory of the Pisans over the Saracens; Buscheto begins work on the Pisa Cathedral	1078	Tower of London
	1071	Consecration of Monte Cassino	1080	Start of work on Saint-Sernin in Toulouse
	1075	Frescoes of Sant'Angelo in Formis	1085	Liberation of Toledo from the Moors
	1077	Henry IV in Canossa	1086	Compiling of the *Domesday Book*
	1093	St Mark's Basilica in Venice	1088	Abbey of Cluny III
	1096-99	First Crusade	1090	Norwich Cathedral
	1099-1110	Lanfranco and Wiligelmo: Duomo of Modena	1093	Durham Cathedral
			1098	Foundation of the Cistercian Order
1100	1100	Frescoes in the Basilica of San Piero a Grado (Pisa)	1104	La Madeleine in Vézelay
	1106	Consecration of the Duomo of Modena	1120	Wells Cathedral; Saint-Front in Périgueux, Saint-Lazare in Autun
	1131-1200	Duomo of Cefalù (Palermo)	1122	Suger becomes Abbot of Saint-Denis
	1132-89	Palatine Chapel in Palermo	1137-80	Rebuilding of Saint-Denis Abbey
	1138	San Zeno in Verona	1145-70	Chartres Cathedral
	1157	Magistri Antelami in Genoa	1163	Notre-Dame in Paris
	1159-62	Guglielmo: Pulpit of the Duomo of Pisa	1165	Laon Cathedral
	1176	Abbot Leonate begins construction of San Clemente a Casauria (Pescara)	1170	Murder of Thomas Becket
	1178	Benedetto Antelami: *Deposition* (Parma)	1170-80	Saint-Trophime in Arles
	1180-86	Bonanno Pisano: bronze doors (Pisa, Monreale)	1174-78	Canterbury Cathedral
	1196	Commencement of work on the Baptistery of Parma	1183	Treaty of Constance
1200	1200	Mosaics at Torcello (Venice)	1202	Rebuilding of Rouen Cathedral
	1205-1314	Papal Court in Avignon	1204	Constantinople conquered by the Crusaders
	1208	Abbey church of Fossanova	1211	Reims Cathedral
	1210	Mosaics in the St Mark's Basilica in Venice	1215	Magna Carta
	1215	Fourth Lateran Council	1216-72	Henry III of England
	1216	Palazzo del Capitano in Orvieto	1220	Amiens Cathedral
	1218	Palazzo della Ragione in Padua; Abbey of Casamari	1226-70	Louis IX of France, canonised as St. Louis
	1226	Duomo of Siena	1240-50	Lincoln Cathedral
	1235	Bonaventura Berlinghieri: *Pescia Altarpiece*; work of Giunta Pisano (Pisa, Assisi, Bologna)	1235	Villard de Honnecourt: *Livre de portraiture*
	1253	Basilica of San Francesco in Assisi	1238	Beginning of the construction of the Alhambra in Granada
	1260	Basilica of Sant'Antonio in Padua; Franciscan Statutes; Nicola Pisano: Pulpit of the Baptistery of Pisa	1245	Westminster Abbey
	1266	Birth of Giotto	1245-48	Sainte-Chapelle in Paris
	1272	Cimabue in Rome	1272-1307	Edward I of England
	1277	Arnolfo di Cambio in Naples at the court of Charles of Anjou	1273	Building of Uppsala Cathedral (Sweden)
			1275	Ratisbon Cathedral

1278	Nicola and Giovanni Pisano: Fontana maggiore in Perugia	1277	Toledo Cathedral
1279	Santa Maria Novella in Florence		
1280-90	Cimabue: *Maestà di Santa Trinita*	1281	Decoration of the Portail des Libraires of Rouen Cathedral
1285	Duccio di Boninsegna: *Maestà dei Laudesi*		
1290	Duomo of Orvieto	1285-1314	Philip IV of France, known as Philip the Fair
1290-1348	Andrea Pisano	1287	Jean Deschamps: Cathedral of Clermont-Ferrand
1293	Palazzo dei Priori in Perugia	1291	Royal tombs in Westminster abbey (Torel: tomb of Eleonora of Castile)
1293	Arnolfo di Cambio and Pietro Cavallini in Rome		
1296	Arnolfo di Cambio: *Madonna with Child*	1295	Michele Astrapas and Eutipio: frescos in San Clemente at Ochrida in Macedonia
1296-1304	Giotto in Assisi		
1298	Palazzo Pubblico in Siena		
1299	Duomo and Palazzo della Signoria in Florence		

1300

1300	Boniface VIII calls the first Jubilee	1300-34	Jean Pucelle in Paris
1301-1302	Cimabue in Pisa	1304	Philip the Fair decides to place his equestrian portrait in Notre-Dame in Paris
1305	Giotto finishes frescoes in the Scrovegni Chapel in Padua	1305-77	Popes resident in Avignon
1310	Giotto: *Ognissanti Madonna*; Giovanni Pisano: Pulpit of the Duomo of Pisa Lorenzo Maitani begins the facade of the Duomo of Orvieto; the Visconti family in Milan	1308-11	Alcobaça Abbey in Portugal
		1317	Cloister of Pamplona Cathedral
1319	Ambrogio Lorenzetti: *Madonna di Vico l'Abate*	1327-1377	Edward III of England
1320-30	Giotto: frescoes for the Bardi and Peruzzi Chapels in Santa Croce	1330	Gloucester Cathedral
1326-79	Tommaso da Modena	1337-1453	Hundred Years War
1333	Simone Martini and Lippo Memmi: *Annunciation*	1340	Simone Martini in Avignon
1334	Giotto: Bell Tower in Florence	1347-1378	Charles IV Emperor of Prague
1337-40	Ambrogio Lorenzetti: *Allegory of Good Government*, Siena	1350	Palace of the Popes in Avignon
		1356	Tommaso da Modena goes to Karlstein in Bohemia
1340	Master of the Triumph of Death: Camposanto of Pisa	1368-1644	Ming dynasty in China
1340	Palazzo Ducale in Venice	1377-1399	Richard II of England
1342	Ambrogio Lorenzetti: *Presentation in the Temple*	1379	Rebuilding of Durham Cathedral
1345	Collapse of the Bardi and Peruzzi banks	1390	Claus Sluter: sculptures in the Carthusian monastery of Champmol
1348	Black Death		
1360	Bonino da Campione: Monument to Bernabò Visconti in Milan	1392-1399	Melchior Broederlam: *Annunciation*
1367	Frescoes in the Spanish Chapel in Florence		
1386	Duomo of Milan		

THE XV CENTURY

ITALY		EUROPE AND OTHER COUNTRIES	

1400

1401	Competition for the second set of doors for the Baptistry of Florence	1401	Seville Cathedral
		1405	Santa Maria la Bianca in Toledo
1401-66	Francesco Sforza in Milan	1410 ca.	Limbourg brothers: miniatures of the *Très riches heures* of the Duke of Berry
1404-25	Lorenzo Ghiberti: Doors of the Baptistery		
1419-23	Brunelleschi: Spedale degli Innocenti, dome of the Duomo and the Old Sacristy of San Lorenzo in Florence	1419-67	Philip the Good of Burgundy

1420

1422-78	Ludovico Gonzaga in Mantua	1430	Master of Flémalle: *Marriage of the Virgin*
1422-82	Federico da Montefeltro in Urbino		
1423	Gentile da Fabriano: *Adoration of the Magi*		
1425	Donatello: baptismal font in Siena		
1427	Masaccio: frescoes in Santa Maria del Carmine	1434	Jan van Eyck: *Man in a Red Turban*; *Portrait of Giovanni Arnolfini and his Bride*
1431-38	Luca della Robbia: Choir in the Duomo of Florence	1435	Jan van Eyck: *Virgin of Chancellor Rolin*; Rogier van der Weyden: *Deposition*
1433-39	Donatello: Choir in the Duomo of Florence		
1434	Cosimo de' Medici ('il Vecchio') returns from exile	1438	Master of Flémalle: *Saint Barbara*

1440

1440	Platonic Academy in Florence	**1441**	*On the Imitation of Christ* by Thomas à Kempis
	Beato Angelico: frescoes in San Marco in Florence	**1443**	Hôtel Jacques Coeur in Bourges
1443	Donatello: *Gattamelata* in Padua		
1445-47	Paolo Uccello: frescoes in Santa Maria Novella		
1446	Michelozzo: Palazzo Medici in Florence	**1446**	King's College Chapel in Cambridge
1447-50	Beato Angelico: Niccolina Chapel in Rome	**1447**	Jean Fouquet: *Charles VII*
1450	Leon Battista Alberti: Palazzo Rucellai; Church of San Francesco in Rimini	**1450**	Rogier van der Weyden comes to Italy
1450-60	Donatello: bronze *David*		
1451-1508	Ludovico Sforza, known as the Moor		
1452	*Arch of Alfonso of Aragon* in Naples; L.B. Alberti: *Treatise on Architecture*	**1452**	Jaime Huguet: *Polyptych of Saints Cosmas and Damian* (Barcelona Cathedral)
1453-64	Piero della Francesca: frescoes in San Francesco in Arezzo	**1453**	Enguerrand Charonton: *Coronation of the Virgin* (Villeneuve-Les-Avignon, Hospice)
1455	Paolo Uccello: *Battle of San Romano*	**1455-56**	Gutenberg prints the *42-line Bible*
1456	Andrea del Castagno: *Niccolò da Tolentino*		
1458-1564	Duomo and Palazzo Piccolomini in Pienza	**1458**	Burgos Cathedral
1459	Benozzo Gozzoli: frescoes of Palazzo Medici		

1460

1464	Palazzo Ducale in Urbino	**1460**	Petrus Christus: *Portrait of a Young Girl* (Berlin)
1464-192	Lorenzo the Magnficent	**1463**	Town Hall in Leuven
1465-74	Mantegna: frescoes in Mantua		
1470	Basilica of Sant'Andrea in Mantua	**1470-73**	Dieric Bouts: *The Justice of Otto*
1470-80	Francesco del Cossa: frescoes in Ferrara	**1473**	Martin Schongauer: *Virgin and Child in a Rose Garden* in Colmar (Germany)
1470-80	Verrocchio: bronze *David*		
1474	Piero della Francesca in Urbino	**1476**	Nicolas Froment: *The Burning Bush* (Aix-en-Provence)
1478	Bramante: Santa Maria Choir in San Satiro in Milan; failure of the Pazzi Conspiracy	**1477**	Hugo van der Goes: *Portinari Triptych*; St. George's Chapel,Windsor

1480

1480	Discovery of the Domus Aurea in Rome: spread of the taste for the grotesque; Crivelli: *Polyptych of Monte San Martino*		
1481-82	Botticelli and Perugino: frescoes in the Sistine Chapel	**1483-95**	Pedro Berruguete: frescoes in Toledo Cathedral
1483-90	Ghirlandaio: frescoes in Santa Trinita and Santa Maria Novella	**1483-98**	Charles VIII
1485	Leonardo: *Virgin of the Rocks* (Paris, Louvre)	**1485-1509**	Henry VII of England
1487	Andrea della Robbia: tondi for the Spedale degli Innocenti		
1488-93	Filippino Lippi: frescoes in Santa Maria Novella		
1492	Death of Lorenzo the Magnificent; death of Piero della Francesca; Botticelli: *Primavera*; Certosa of Pavia	**1492**	Discovery of America
1494-95	Dürer's first period in Venice	**1493**	Dürer: *Self-portrait* (Paris, Louvre)
1497-99	Michelangelo: *Pietà* in St. Peter's in the Vatican	**1494**	Fall of Constantinople
1498	Leonardo: *The Last Supper*; invasion of Charles IV: beginning of the "Italian Wars"	**1498-1515**	Louis XII

THE XVI CENTURY — ITALY — EUROPE AND OTHER COUNTRIES

1500

1500-1504	Bramante: Cloister in Santa Maria della Pace in Rome	**1500**	Dürer: *Self-portrait in Furs* (Berlin Museums)
1501-1504	Michelangelo sculpts *David*	**1502**	Lucas Cranach the Elder: *Portraits of Johannes and Anna Cuspinian* (Winterthur)
1502	Giorgione: *Altarpiece of Castelfranco*		
1502-1506	Bramante: San Pietro in Montorio Templet	**1503**	Grünewald: *Lindenhardt Altarpiece*
1503	Julius II Pope	**1503-1504**	Bosch paints the *Earthly Paradise Triptych* (Madrid, Prado)
1504	Leonardo, Michelangelo, and Raphael in Florence		
1505-1506	First design by Michelangelo for the *Tomb of Julius II*	**1503-1506**	Hans Baldung Grien in Nuremberg with Dürer
1505-1507	Dürer's second period in Venice	**1506**	Dürer: *Madonna of the Siskin* (Berlin Museums); the *Madonna* sculpted by Michelangelo arrives in Bruges
1506-1508	Lorenzo Lotto: *Polyptych of San Domenico*		
1507-1508	Giorgione: *The Tempest*		

1507-12	Giorgione and Titian: *Sleeping Venus*		
1508	Giorgione: *The Three Philosophers*	1509	Quentin Metsys: Triptych for the chapel of the Brotherhood of Sant'Anna in St. Peter's in Leuven (Brussels)
1508-12	Michelangelo: frescoes in the Sistine Chapel		
1509	The League of Cambrai defeats Venice at Agnadello	1509-11	Hans Baldung Grien: *The Three Ages of Woman* (Vienna)
1509-13	Raphael in the Vatican		
1510	Bramante: Palazzo Caprini in Rome	1510	Hans Baldung Grien: *The Witches* (etchings)
1510-13	Beccafumi in Rome	1510-15	Grünewald: *Isenheim Altarpiece*
1512	Defeat of the Holy League; the French abandon Italy; the Medici return to power in Florence; Machiavelli retires from public life and writes *The Prince*	1511	Erasmus of Rotterdam: *Praise of Madness*
		1513-14	Dürer: *The Knight, Death and the Devil*
1514-15	Titian: *Sacred and Profane Love*	1515	Dürer: *Portrait of Emperor Maximilian I*
1515-19	*Joseph in Egypt* by Pontormo	1515-47	Francis I, King of France
1516	Death of Giovanni Bellini; Sebastiano del Piombo begins the frescoes in San Pietro in Montorio	1517	Martin Luther exhibits the 95 theses at Wittenberg
1517	Raphael: Loggia of Psyche in the Farnesina	1517-18	Leonardo and Andrea del Sarto in France
1519	Leonardo dies in France; Correggio frescoes the Badessa Chamber in Parma; Cellini in Rome; Raphael's letter to Leo X outlines a conservation and restoration program for art works	1519	Charles V of Hapsburg

1520

1520-22	Frescoes by Pordenone in the Duomo of Cremona; Gaudenzio Ferrari begins work on Sacro Monte di Varallo	1520	Excommunication of Martin Luther
1521	Rosso Fiorentino: *Deposition of Volterra*; death of Raphael	1521	Diet of Worms; Hans Holbein the Younger: *Christ in the Tomb* (Basle)
1522	Duchy of Milan invaded by the troops of Charles V		
1523	Clement VII Pope; Rosso Fiorentino: *The Marriage of the Virgin*; Parmigianino: *Self-portrait in a Convex Mirror*		
1524	Giulio Romano begins to fresco Palazzo Te in Mantua; Lotto in Trescore (Oratorio Suardi)	1525	Cortés' army defeats the Aztecs
1526-30	Correggio: frescoes in the dome of the Duomo of Parma	1525-28	Lucas van Leyden: *Adoration of the Golden Calf* (Amsterdam)
1527	Sack of Rome: artists begin to move to other cities in Italy; Pontormo: *Deposition*; Lorenzo Lotto: *Annunciation of Recanati*	1527	Palace of Charles V in Granada
1528	Andrea del Sarto: *Woman with the petrarchino*		
1529	Dosso Dossi: *Jove painting Butterflies*		
1530	Charles V crowned Emperor by the Pope at Bologna		
1531	Salviati in Rome	1532	Francesco Pizzarro conquers the Inca empire
1533	Savoldo: *Saint Matthew and the Angel*	1533	Hans Holbein the Younger: *The Ambassadors*
1534	Romanino: *Crucifixion* in Santa Maria della Neve	1534	Anglican schism; Rosso Fiorentino becomes official painter at the court of Francis I at Fontainebleau
1534	Michelangelo leaves Florence, never to return		
1534-39	Parmigianino: *Madonna with the Long Neck*	1535	Jean Clouet: *Portrait of Guillame Boudé* (New York)
1536	Federico Zuccari frescoes the dome of the Florence Cathedral	1536	Girolamo da Treviso: *The Four Evangelists stone the Pope* (Windsor, Royal Collection)
1536-41	Michelangelo: *Last Judgement*		
1537	Cosimo I de' Medici becomes Duke of Florence		
1538	Salviati: frescoes in Rome; Titian: *Venus of Urbino*		
1538-64	Michelangelo: Capitoline Hill in Rome		

1540

1540	Ignazio di Loyola establishes the Company of Jesus	1540	Francesco I invites the architect Sebastiano Serlio to his court
1541 ca.	Bronzino: *Lucrezia Panciatichi*		
1543	Titian: *Portrait of Paul III*	1540	Production of tapestries in the court of Francis I at Fontainebleau; at Antwerp the corporation of artists organises the first sales exhibition of art objects and paintings of the epoch
1544	First edition of the *Index of Prohibited Books*		
1545-54	Cellini: *Perseus*		
1545-63	Council of Trent		
1546-64	Michelangelo: dome of St. Peter's in the Vatican	1540-43	Benvenuto Cellini: *The Salt-cellar of Francis I*
1548	Moroni in Trento is the first artist to embrace the principles of the Counter-Reformation	1543	Cranach: *Portrait of Martin Luther*; Copernicus: *De revolutionibus orbium coelestium*

	1549	Palazzo della Ragione in Vicenza	1545	Berruguete, painter and sculptor for Charles V in Spain
	1550	First edition of *Lives of the Most Excellent Painters, Sculptors, and Architects* by Vasari	1546	Cour Carrée of the Louvre in Paris
	1552	Parco dei Mostri in Bomarzo		
	1553-54	Veronese: paintings for the Sala del Consiglio dei Dieci in the Palazzo Ducale	1551-71	Works by Titian reach Spain
	1554-1600	Aldrovandi teaches at the University of Bologna	1555	Treaty of Augusta : *Cuius regio, eius religio*
	1559-70	Villa Barbaro in Maser, built by Palladio, is decorated by Veronese	1556-98	Philip II of Spain
			1559	Treaty of Cateau-Cambrésis
1560				
	1562	Arcimboldi called to the court of Rudolf II of Hapsburg	1560	Catherine de' Medici Regent to the throne of France
	1563	Dictates of artistic practice issued by the Council of Trent: orthodoxy of sacred images, allegories to be easily interpretable	1562-98	Wars of Religion in France
			1563	Pieter Bruegel the Elder: *Tower of Babel*
			1563-84	Escorial in Madrid
	1566	Palladio: San Giorgio Maggiore in Venice	1565	Pieter Bruegel the Elder: *Wedding Banquet*
	1568	Vignola: Church of Jesus	1566-67	Protestant iconoclasm in Antwerp
	1570	Palladio: *Four books of Architecture*; final work by Titian: *Punishment of Marsia*	1567	Treatise on architecture by De l'Orme
			1568-1648	War of Independence in the Netherlands
	1570-73	Studiolo of Francesco I in Palazzo Vecchio		
	1571	Battle of Lepanto	1572	Night of Saint Bartholomew in France
	1573	Veronese summoned by the Inquisition for his *Supper in the House of Levi*		
	1573-75	Federico Zuccari frescoes the Oratory of the Gonfalone in Rome		
	1574-80	*Rape of the Sabines* by Giambologna	1576	Rudolf II Emperor of Germany
	1575	Tintoretto: *Discovery of the Body of St. Mark*	1577	El Greco settles in Toledo
1580				
	1580	*The Appenines* and *Mercury* by Giambologna	1580-1666	Frans Hals
	1582	Accademia della Crusca in Florence	1589-1610	Henry IV of France
	1582-83	*The Butcher's Shop* by Annibale Carracci	1590	School of Fontainebleau
	1585-90	Under Sixtus V, urban renewal in Rome	1593-1652	Georges La Tour
	1586	Domenico Fontana erects the Egyptian obelisk in St. Peter's Square in Rome	1594	Conversion of Henry IV
			1588	England defeats Spain
	1587	Ferdinando de' Medici	1598	Edict of Nantes
	1593-94	Caravaggio: *The sick Bacchus*	1598-1621	Philip III of Spain
	1595	Caravaggio: *Boy bitten by a Lizard*	1598-1664	Francisco de Zurbarán

THE XVII CENTURY	ITALY		EUROPE AND OTHER COUNTRIES	
1600				
	1600	Giordano Bruno burnt at the stake; Annibale Carracci frescoes the Galleria Farnese; Stefano Maderno sculpts *Santa Cecilia*; Caravaggio: *Medusa*		
	1600-1608	Rubens in Italy	1602	East India Company in Holland
	1602-1604	Caravaggio: *Deposition*	1603-16	Royal square complex at Isfahan in Persia
	1602-10	Cycle of pictures in memory of San Carlo Borromeo	1603-25	James I of England, Stuart king
	1603	Maderno completes the Church of Santa Susanna in Rome; Caravaggio, tried for defamation, sustains the importance of drawing from life		
	1604	Annibale Carracci: *Landscape with the Flight into Egypt*; Reni: *Crucifixion of St. Peter*	1606-69	Rembrandt
	1605-21	Paul V Pope		
	1607	Caravaggio: *The Seven Acts of Mercy*	1609	Rubens in the service of Albert of Hapsburg; Kepler: *New Astronomy*
	1607-12	Maderno: facade of St. Peter's		
	1610	Death of Caravaggio; Galileo publishes his *Sidereus nuncius*	1609-17	Blue Mosque in Istanbul
			1610	Murder of Henry IV of France; Regency of Maria de' Medici
	1611-12	*Samson Victorious* and *The Slaughter of the Innocents* by Reni	1610-43	Louis XIII

	1613	Schedoni: *Deposition*; Domenichino begins frescoing his *Scenes from the life of Santa Cecilia* in San Luigi de' Francesi	**1618**	Defenestration of Prague: beginning of the Thirty Years War
	1615-25	*Atalanta and Ippomene* by Reni		
	1616	Jusepe de Ribera in Naples	**1619-22**	Jones: *Banqueting House* in London
1620				
	1620	Artemisia Gentileschi: *Judith and Holophernes*	**1620**	The Mayflower sets sail for America
	1621	Guercino: frescoes in the Casino Ludovisi	**1621-25**	Rubens: *Triumphs of Maria de' Medici*
	1621-22	Bernini: *Rape of Proserpine*	**1621-65**	Philip IV of Spain
	1622	Domenichino frescoes Santa Maria della Valle		
	1623	Urban VIII Barberini Pope	**1623**	Velázquez court painter in Spain
	1624-33	Bernini:*The Baldacchino* in St. Peter's	**1624**	Start of the planning of Versailles
	1624-40	Poussin in Rome	**1624-42**	Richelieu
	1625	Van Laer in Rome; Serodine: *The Calling of the Sons of Zebedee*	**1625-49**	Charles I of England
	1625-27	Lanfranco frescoes Santa Maria della Valle		
	1626	Consecration of the new Basilica of St. Peter's; Orazio Gentileschi court painter to Charles I of England	**1627**	Simon Vouet called to Paris by Louis XIII; Caravaggio's style spreads through France
	1629-31	Velázquez' journey in Italy		
	1629-32	Maderno and Bernini: Palazzo Barberini	**1632**	Rembrandt: *Anatomy Lesson*
	1630	Galileo: *Dialogo sui massimi sistemi*	**1635**	Start of work on the Sorbonne; Van Dyck: *Portrait of Charles I Hunting* (Paris, Louvre)
	1630-82	Claude Lorrain in Rome		
	1633-39	Pietro da Cortona: frescoes in Palazzo Barberini	**1636**	*A Discourse on Method* by Descartes
	1637-43	Borromini: Oratory of St. Philip Neri	**1638**	Rubens: *Consequences of War*
1640				
	1640	Salvator Rosa: *Rocky Panorama with Waterfall*	**1642**	Poussin leaves Paris definitively; Rembrandt: *The Night Watch*; Mazarin succeeds Richelieu
	1642	Borromini: beginning of the work on Sant'Ivo alla Sapienza, consecrated in 1660	**1642-61**	Mazarin comes to power
	1644	Innocent X Pope	**1643-1715**	Louis XIV of France
	1646	Ribera: *San Gennaro Emerges Unharmed from the Furnace*		
	1647	Uprising of Masaniello in Naples	**1648**	End of the Thirty Years War and Treaty of Westphalia
	1647-51	Bernini: *Ecstasy of St.Teresa*		
	1649-51	Journey by Velázquez in Italy	**1649**	Charles I beheaded; dictatorship of Cromwell
	1650 ca.	Giordano, Ricci, and Crespi in Florence		
	1655-67	Alexander VII Pope	**1655**	Velázquez: *Venus in the Mirror*
	1656	Bernini begins the Colonnades of St. Peter's Square	**1656**	Velázquez: *Las Meninas*
1660				
	1660	Longhena: *Ca' Pesaro*; Baschenis: *Musical Instruments*	**1660-85**	Charles II of England
			1661	Vermeer: *View of Delft*, *L'atelier*
	1665-67	Borromini: San Carlo alle Quattro Fontane	**1665-1700**	Charles II of Spain
	1672	Bellori publishes the *Lives of Modern Painters, Sculptors, and Architects*	**1666**	Newton: theory of gravitation
			1668-1711	Rebuilding of St. Paul's Cathedral in London
	1674	Uprising of Messina; Bernini: *La beata Ludovica Albertoni*	**1669**	Louis XIV at Versailles
			1670	Mansarde and Bruant: *Les Invalides*
1680				
			1685	Louis XIV revokes the Edict of Nantes
	1680	Death of Bernini	**1685-88**	James II of England
	1682-86	Luca Giordano in Florence	**1690**	José Churriguera in Madrid
			1690-96	Palace of Hampton Court
	1691-94	Andrea Pozzo frescoes Sant'Ignazio in Roma	**1694**	Royal Naval Hospital at Greenwich
	1692	Luca Giordano called to the Spanish court	**1696**	Castle of Schönbrunn (Fischer von Erlach)

THE XVIII CENTURY	ITALY		EUROPE AND OTHER COUNTRIES	
1700				
	1703	Etchings of *"Buildings and views of Venice"* by Carlevarijs; Luca Giordano: *Triumph of Judith* at the Certosa of San Martino in Naples	**1701**	Spanish War of Succession
			1702	Building work commences in Prague on the Church of sv Mikulás a Mala Strana

–	1706	Ferdinando III de' Medici exhibits the works of his Florentine collection and prints a catalogue of the exhibition	1710	Manufacture of porcelain in the Saxon city of Meissen
	1708	Crespi: *The Painter's Family*	1711-12	Addison and the concept of the "sublime"
	1714	War between Venice and the Turks	1714-15	Grand Tour of Lord Burlington
	1717-31	Juvarra builds the Basilica of Superga and renews the facade of Palazzo Madama in Turin	1714-27	George I of England
			1715-25	Vitruvius Britannicus
			1715-74	Louis XV of France
1720	1720	Canaletto painter of vedutas	1726	Swift: *Gulliver's Travels*
	1723-26	Steps of Piazza di Spagna in Rome	1727	Kent develops the concept of the "English garden"
	1725	Solimena: *Cacciata di Eliodoro dal tempio*; Crespi: *La sguattera*	1733	Invention of the automatic spinning machine
	1729-31	Stupinigi: Hunting Palace	1733-54	Works of William Hogarth
	1732	Longhi chronicler of everyday life in Venice; Piazzetta: *Ecstasy of San Francesco*		
	1732-62	Trevi Fountain		
	1734	Capitoline Museum opens to the public		
	1737	Fra Galgario: *Gentleman with a Cocked Hat*		
	1738	First excavations at Ercolano		
1740	1740	Ceruti: *The Washerwoman*	1743-72	Sanctuary of the Fourteen Saints at Bamberg
	1745	Piranesi: *Capricci* e *Carceri d'invenzione*	1744	Hogarth: *Marriage à la Mode*
	1746	Canaletto in London; beginning of work on the Villa Albani in Rome (Marchionni); Batoni: *Achilles and the Centaur* and *Achilles at the Court of Lycomedes*	1748	Treaty of Aquisgrana
	1747	Bellotto in Dresden	1751	The first volume of *Encyclopédie* published; Linneo publishes *Sistema Naturae*
	1748	First excavations in Pompei	1753	London: British Museum
	1750-53	Gianbattista and Giandomenico Tiepolo: frescoes of Würzburg	1755	Winckelmann: *Thoughts on the imitation of Greek works in painting and sculpture*
	1752-74	Vanvitelli: Reggia di Caserta	1756	Institution of the National Porcelain Manufacturers in Sèvres
	1755-68	Winckelmann in Rome; in 1768 Milizia publishes *Lives of the Most Celebrated Architects*	1757-92	Sainte-Geneviève in Paris
	1758-67	Condillac in Parma	1758	Leroy: *Les Ruines de la Grèce*
	1759	Ferdinand of Bourbon becomes King of Naples	1759	Voltaire: *Candide*
1760	1763	Treaty of Paris: Italy divided between Austrian and French influence; Winckelmann Director General of Roman Antiquities	1760	Birth of Hokusai in Japan
	1764	Beccaria: *Dei delitti e delle pene*	1761-62	*Treatise on Athens* by Stuart and Revelt
	1768	Troops of the King of Naples invade the Papal States	1761-80	Library of Osterley Park
	1769	Pietro Leopoldo opens the Uffizi Gallery to the public	1762	Tiepolo in Madrid; much of the collection of Joseph Smith (Venetian veduta painters) purchased by George III of England
	1771-78	In Milan, Palazzo Reale and Teatro alla Scala (Piermarini)	1762-96	Catherine II of Russia, known as Catherine the Great
	1771-93	Vatican, Museo Pio-Clementino	1763	Kassel Gallery in Germany
	1775-80	First stay of David in Rome	1764-75	Small Hermitage in St. Petersburg
	1776	Appiani holds lessons at the Accademia di Brera	1769	Gallery of the Winter Palace in St. Petersburg
	1778	Piranesi: *Views of Rome*	1771	*Encyclopedia Britannica*
	1778 ca.	Zoffany: *The Tribuna of the Uffizi*	1773	Goethe: *Faust*
	1779	Canova in Rome	1774-93	Louis XVI of France
			1776	Declaration of Independence of the United States
			1776-83	American War of Independence
1780	1780	Count Carrara opens his art collection in Bergamo to scholars	1781	La Méridienne at Versailles
	1787	Canova: *Tomb of Clement XIV* (Rome, Santi Apostoli)	1785	David: *Oath of the Horatii*
	1791-95	Canova: *Monument to Titian*	1789	French Revolution
			1789-93	Brandenburg Gate in Berlin (Langhans)
			1792	Capitol Hill in Washington
			1793	Louis XVI goes to the guillotine; foundation of the Louvre; David: *Marat murdered*
	1796	Napoleon's Italian campaign; the Danish sculptor Thorvaldsen in Rome	1794	Robespierre guillotined
			1796-1806	Jefferson: House of Monticello in Virginia

	1797-1804	Giandomenico Tiepolo: drawings for the Life of Pulcinella	1797	Kaiser Friedrich Museum in Berlin
			1799	Napoleon becomes First Consul
THE XIX CENTURY	ITALY		EUROPE AND OTHER COUNTRIES	
1800				
	1801	Bossi institutes the Pinacoteca di Brera, which would then open to the public in 1809	1803	Arc de Triomphe in Paris
	1802	Republic of Italy with Milan as capital	1803-15	Napoleonic Wars
	1804-08	Canova: *Paolina Borghese*	1804	Napoleon becomes emperor
	1806	Ingres in Rome	1806	La Madéleine in Paris
	1807-38	Cagnola: Arch of Peace in Milan	1810-20	Goya: *The Disasters of War*
	1808	Napoleon defeats the Austrians at Marengo	1812	Napoleon's campaign in Russia
	1813	Minardi: *Self-portrait*	1815	Battle of Waterloo and the fall of Napoleon
	1816-22	Valadier: building of Piazza del Popolo	1819	Friedrich: *Two Men contemplating the Moon;* Géricault: *The Raft of the Medusa*
	1819	Turner in Italy		
1820				
	1820	Success of Hayez' paintings at the exhibition of Brera; Romantic painting with historical subject matter	1820 ca.	Goya: the "Quinta del Sordo"
			1820-30	George IV of England
	1823	Reactionary cultural shift under Pope Leo XII; Ingres in Florence	1823	British Museum in London: Constable paints *Salisbury Cathedral*
			1823-30	Altes Museum in Berlin
	1825	Rebuilding of St. Paul's-Outside-the-Walls in Rome	1825	First passenger train
	1828-33	Valadier publishes *Practical Architecture*	1826	Cumberland Terrace in London
	1831	D'Azeglio theorizes the concept of "historical landscape"	1830	Delacroix: *Liberty guides the People on the 28 July*; the Restoration in France, Louis Philip comes to the throne
			1832	Parliamentary reform in England
	1835	Piccio: *The Death of Aminta*; Bartolini: *Faith in God*	1835	Rebuilding of the centre of London; the Barbizon School
			1836-65	Houses of Parliament in London
1840				
	1840-41	Hayez: *Portrait of Alessandro Manzoni*	1840	Viollet-le-Duc: restoration of La Madeleine in Vézelay, Sainte Chapelle and Notre-Dame in Paris
	1841	Mussini: *Sacred Music*	1848	Marx and Engels: Communist Party Manifesto Pre-Raphaelite Brotherhood
	1842	Minardi, Bianchini, Tenerani and Overbeck sign the Manifesto of Purism; definitive edition of *Promessi Sposi*; Dupré: *Death of Abel*	1849	Courbet: *Funeral at Ornans*
	1850	"Five Days" in Milan; proclamation of the Republic of Venice	1851	Great Exhibition of London: Crystal Palace
			1852	Napoleon III of France
	1855-66	The Macchiaioli at the Caffè Michelangelo in Firenze	1853-69	Haussmann: urban renewal of Paris
	1859	Hayez: *The Kiss*	1859	Darwin: *On the Origin of Species*
			1859-63	Ingres: *Turkish Bath*
1860				
	1860	The Expedition of the Thousand; Scapigliatura in Milan; Abbati: *Cloister*; beginning of the rebuilding of the façades of many churches	1861-74	Opéra in Paris
	1861	Proclamation of the Kingdom of Italy		
	1862	Diego Martelli in Paris	1862	Daumier: *Third-Class Carriage*
	1863-80	*Antonellian Mole*	1863	Manet: *Luncheon on the Grass;* Dante Gabriel Rossetti: *Beata Beatrix* (Tate Gallery, London)
	1864	Lega: *Il passaggio del viatico*		
	1866	Fattori: *The Palmieri Rotunda*	1863-72	Albert Memorial in London
	1865	Florence capital of Italy	1865	*Olympia* by Manet at the Salon of Paris
	1868	Lega: *A Visit*; De Nittis in Paris; Cecioni: *Child with a Cock*		
	1870	Breaching of Porta Pia, Annexation of Rome and Lazio to the Kingdom of Italy; Mancini: *'O prevetariello*	1870	Monet and Pissarro get to know the paintings of Turner and Constable; foundation of the Metropolitan Museum of New York and the Museum of Fine Arts in Boston
	1871	Rome capital of Italy	1872	Monet: *Impression: Sunrise*
	1877	Gemito: *Fisher Boy* at the Salon of Paris; Tranquillo Cremona: *High Life*	1874	First Impressionist exhibition
	1878	Morelli: *Temptation of St. Antony*	1876	Renoir: *Le Moulin de la Galette*; *Statue of Liberty* in New York

1880				
	1880	Fattori: *Caught in the Stirrup*; early works by Medardo Rosso	1880	First electric elevator
			1884 ca.	Gaudí: Sagrada Familia in Barcelona
	1881	Signorini: *Leith*	1886-88	Van Gogh in Paris
	1882	Triple Alliance between Italy, Austria, and Germany; Vela: *Victims of work*	1888	Arts and Crafts Exhibition Society
			1889	Great Exhibition of Paris: *Eiffel Tower*
	1883	Modern Art Gallery in Rome: Michetti: *The Vow*	1890	Death of Van Gogh
	1888	Italian Exhibition in London	1890-91	Sullivan: Wainwright Building in Saint Louis
	1889	Segantini: *The Two Mothers*; Boldini exhibits in Paris the *White Pastel*; D'Annunzio writes *Il piacere*	1892 ca.	Cézanne: *Card Players*
			1892	Development of reinforced concrete
	1890-91	Previati: *Maternity*	1893	Munch: *The Scream*
	1892	First Giolitti government; Böcklin moves to Fiesole	1894	Monet: *Rouen Cathedral*
	1893	First individual show by Zandomeneghi in Paris	1894-95	Sullivan: Guarantee Building in Buffalo
	1894	Repression of revolts in Sicily and in the Lunigiana	1896	Kandinsky in Munich. Sullivan: *The Tall Office Building Artistically Considered*
	1895	Morbelli: *For Eighty Cents!*		
			1898	Madame Curie isolates radium
	1899	Marconi invents the wireless telegraph	1899	Guimard: *Métro Station in Paris*
THE XX CENTURY	ITALY		EUROPE AND OTHER COUNTRIES	
1900				
	1900	Umberto I assassinated by the anarchist Bresci	1900	Universal Exhibition in Paris; *Interpretation of Dreams* by Freud
	1901	Pellizza da Volpedo: *The Fourth Estate*	1901	Marconi achieves the first radiotelegraphic connection between Europe and Canada
	1902	First International Exhibition of Decorative Arts in Turin; inauguration of the Modern Art Gallery of Ca'Pesaro	1903	Flight of the Wright brothers in an engine-powered plane; first colour photographs in the *Daily Illustrated Mirror*
	1903-14	Giolitti era	1904	Matisse: *Luxe, Calme et Volupté*
			1905	"Blood Sunday" in St. Petersburg; Die Brucke in Germany and the Fauves at the Salon d'Automne
			1906	Women gain the right to vote in Finland; Picasso: *Portrait of Gertrude Stein*
	1909	Marinetti publishes the Manifesto of Futurism	1907	Picasso: *Demoiselles d'Avignon*
	1910	Modigliani in Paris; Previati, Boccioni and Carrà exhibit at the Palazzo della Società per le Belle Arti in Milan	1908-09	Matisse: *The Red Room*
			1911	Die Blaue Reiter in Germany; Franz Marc: *The Dream*; Mondrian: *The Silver coated Tree*
	1912	Carrà: *The Galleria in Milan*; Balla: *Dynamism of a Dog on the Leash*; Boccioni: *Technical Manifesto of Futurist Sculpture*	1912	Balkan Wars; sinking of the Titanic; *The Spiritual in Art* by Kandinsky
			1913	Apollinaire: *Méditations esthetiques. Les peintres cubistes*
	1914	Antonio Sant'Elia: *Manifesto of Futurist Architecture*	1914-18	First World War
	1915	Italy enters the war; public assemblies by D'Annunzio	1917	October Revolution; Duchamp: *Pissoir*
	1918	End of the war; De Chirico: *The Disquieting Muses*	1919	Bauhaus in Weimar; First Salzburg Music Festival
1920				
	1921	Italian Communist Party founded in Livorno; Mussolini founds the Italian Fascist Party	1921	Hitler becomes president of the National Socialist Party
			1922	Murals by Siqueiros and Rivera in Mexico
	1922	March on Rome	1924	Manifesto of Surrealism by André Breton
	1925	Croce promotes the Manifesto of Antifascist Intellectuals in response to Gentile; Casorati: *Platonic Conversation*	1925	First surrealist exhibition at the Galerie Pierre
			1929	Wall Street crash; Dix begins the *War* triptych
			1931	Dalì: *The Persistence of Memory*
	1926	"Leggi fascistissime"	1933	Hitler becomes Chancellor of the Reich; Roosevelt and the New Deal
	1929	Lateran Treaty		
	1932	First Venice Film Festival	1935	Racial laws passed in Nuremberg
			1936	Spanish Civil War, murder of García Lorca
			1937	Picasso: *Guernica*
			1939	Beginning of the Second World War; 5000 "degenerate" works of art burnt in Berlin
1940				
			1940	Frida Kahlo: *Self-portrait with hair cut*
	1945	Mussolini captured and executed by the partisans in Piazzale Loreto	1944	Inauguration of the Konkrete Kunst exhibition in Basle

1946 New Front for the Arts in Italy; Vittorini: "Il Politecnico"
1948 Introduction of the new constitution
1949 First television transmissions
1950 Beginning of the centrist era; Longhi founds the arts and literary magazine "Paragone"
1950-1957 Torre Velasca in Milan (BBPR)
1952 Burri: *Sacks*
1955 Admission to the UN
1955-1959 Nervi and Ponti: Pirelli Skyscraper in Milan

1945 Atomic bomb on Hiroshima and Nagasaki; end of the war and Noremberg trials
1946 Jackson Pollock begins painting using the dripping technique
1947 Robert Capa, Henri Cartier-Bresson and other photographers found the Magnum agency; Escher: *Other World*
1948 Start of the European Recovery Program (Marshall Plan); Universal Declaration of the Rights of Man
1949 Division of Germany
1953 Bacon: Study from Velázquez' *Innocent X*
1954 Rauschenberg: first combine-paintings
1955 *Lolita* by Nabokov
1956 *Mobile* by Calder
1957 *On the Road* by Kerouac
1958 French Nouvelle Vague
1959 Tinguely: *Méta-Matic*

1960

1960 Fontana: *Spatial Concept, Awaiting*; Informal movement
1961 Manzoni: *Artist's Shit*
1962-1965 Second Vatican Council
1964 Pop Art on exhibition in Venice
1966 Modern languages replace Latin in Catholic liturgy
1967 Exhibition of Poor Art in Genoa
1968 Beginning of the students protest movement in Trento; Pistoletto: *Venus of the Rags*
1969 Terrorist attack in Piazza Fontana in Milan
1971 Start of the Centre Georges Pompidou by Renzo Piano and Richard Rogers
1973 Gina Pane: *Sentimental Action*; Alighiero Boetti opens a hotel in Kabul
1978 Assassination of Aldo Moro

1961 Start of the building of the Berlin Wall
1962 Andy Warhol: *Can of Campbell's Soup*; Marshall McLuhan coins the term " global village"
1963 Kennedy assassinated in Dallas
1964-75 War in Vietnam
1965 Birth of op art marked by the exhibition"The Responsive Eye" at the MOMA in New York
1966 Minimal Art; Louise Bougeois: *Le regard*
1968 Youth and workers' revolt
1969 Neil Armstrong is the first man to set foot on the moon; Land Art
1978 Louise Brown is the first "test tube baby" ; Karol Wojtyla elected Pope with the name of John Paul II

1980

1980 Bologna terrorist massacre
1981 Clemente: *Rudo*
1982 Transavanguardia movement
1992 "Tangentopoli" and the "Clean Hands" judicial investigations; *Videoambienti 1982-1992*, individual show by Studio Azzurro in Milan; Judges Falcone and Borsellino murdered by the Mafia
1993 Mafia bombs at the Uffizi and the Contemporary Art Pavilion in Milan
1997 Earthquake in Umbria, which also included serious damage to art works; Costa: *Agglomerato n. 9* Cattelan: *Little Sperms*
1998 Vanessa Beecroft: *Show*
1999 48th Venice Biennial: Pipilotti Rist, Grazia Toderi, Franz Gertsch, Zhen Chen, Jorge Molder
2000 Jubilee in Rome

1980 Beginning of the war between Iran and Iraq; inauguration in France of the first high-speed train; Bill Gates produces the operational language MS/DOS for IBM; spread of cellular phones and faxes; electronic art
1983 First music videos
1985 First works by Cindy Sherman
1986 Nuclear disarmament summit in Reykjavik between Reagan and Gorbachev
1988 *Glass Pyramid* by the Chinese-American architect Pei in the courtyard of the Louvre
1989 Collapse of the Berlin Wall
1991 Gulf War; birth of the World Wide Web
1993 Establishment of the European Union; opening of the Grand Louvre
1994 Mariko Mori: *Tea Ceremony*
1998 Success of animal cloning experiments
1999 Conclusion of the armed intervention in Kosovo; Mattew Barney: *Cremaster 4*

GLOSSARY

A

ABBEY (*abbazia*) Group of buildings housing a religious community (courtyard, cloister, porch, *basilica*, baptistery, cells, refectory, stables, *scriptorium*, abbot's house, guest lodgings).

ALLEGORY Representation of concepts or ideas by means of people, animals, or objects which possess a separate autonomous meaning of their own.

ALTARPIECE (*pala*) Also known as an ancon if it is part of the architecture.
A rectangular panel, which is sometimes cuspidate, placed above the altar. The altarpiece is depicted with a sacred subject and is usually painted. It may also be realized in embossed or enamelled metal or, more frequently, in the shape of carved wood or marble bas-reliefs.

AMBO (*ambone*) Pulpit closed in on three sides by a parapet, while the fourth one opens onto steps. Originally used for the reading of holy texts.

AMBULATORY (*deambulatorio*) In Romanesque and Gothic churches, this is the aisle around the choir, which often opens onto outward-radiating chapels.

APSE (*abside*) Constructed according to a semicircular, polygonal, or lobed *plan*, it is the final section of the central *nave* and is covered by a semicupola. It lies behind the altar and houses the *choir*.

ARCH (*arcata*) Each individual element of an architectural series of arched and vaulted structures.

ARCHITRAVE Horizontal architectural beam connecting two upright elements (columns, *pillars*). Constitutes the lower part of the trabeation that rests on the abacus.

ASHLAR (*bugnato*) The facing on the external walls of a building obtained by using ashlars, square-cut masonry stones which protrude uniformly from the surface of the wall. It may be smooth (with a minimum relief), rustic (with roughly-cut, highly-protruding ashlars), or diamond-shaped (stones with pyramidal protrusions).

B

BAPTISTERY (*battistero*) Central-plan building erected next to early Christian and Romanesque basilicas. Houses the baptismal font.

BASILICA Title connected with historically and religiously important churches upon which privileges had been conferred by the Holy See. The early Christian basilica derived from the Roman buildings of three or five naves which were used for public functions; the naves of these basilicas ended at three quarters the length of the building, where a transept divided the area reserved for the congregation from the area for the clergy, thus producing a plan in the form of a cross. In front of the basilica were four porticos, sometimes reduced to one (known as the narthex) that ran along the whole front of the facade.

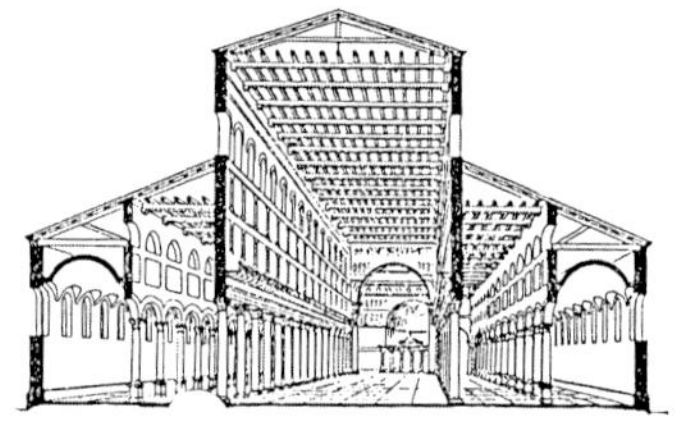

BISCUIT White chalk-coloured porcelain which has been fired twice but not glazed.

BUTTRESS (*contrafforte*) Architectural stone or brick structure which reinforces a building, counter-balancing from the exterior the thrust of an arch.

C

CANVAS (*tela*) Linen or cotton cloth mounted and stretched on a frame, which after preliminary treatment with glue-based substances is then ready for the application of colour.

CAPITAL (*capitello*) Final section at the head of a column. According to architectural norms, the classical capital may be one of three types: Doric, Ionic, or Corinthian. Unlike classical capitals, those found in ancient Eastern civilisations and Byzantine, Romanesque, and Gothic constructions are often typologically simpler (such as the Romanesque dado capitals), and often have figurative or scenic decorations which may sometimes be stylized vegetal elements.

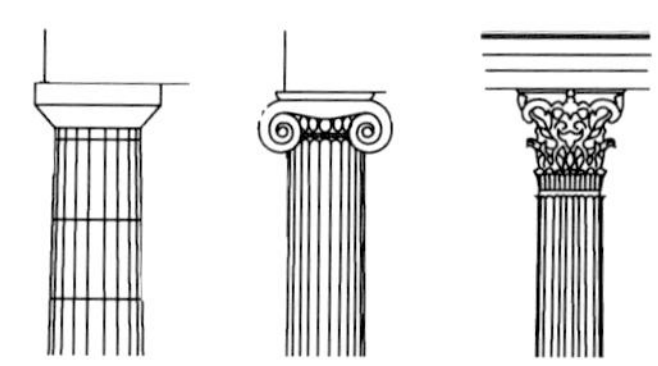

DORIC IONIC CORINTHIAN

CARTOON (*cartone*) Preparatory, full-size drawing carried out on heavy paper, which is then transferred onto a wall, panel, or glass. It is generally squared to make the transfer, or pouncing, easier. The outline of the design is riddled with holes and then powdered charcoal is dusted over it so that a trace comes through on the surface underneath.

CARVING, ENGRAVING (*intaglio*) Decoration obtained by incision onto a particular material.

CARYATID Sculpted female figure used to support brackets or architraves.

CATHEDRAL Ecclesiastical building which is the seat of the bishop.

CERAMICS From the Greek *kéramos* (clay), it refers to any product obtained from clay which has been kneaded and moulded, either mechanically or by hand, and then fired in a high-temperature oven. Usually decorated or covered with an enamel or glaze.

CHIAROSCURO Technique in painting which gives plastic relief to images through the progressive shift from darker to lighter shades, creating an effect of diffuse luminosity.

CHOIR (*coro*) Part of the *apse* behind the altar, with stalls for the *schola cantorum*. By extension, it can be used to refer to the apse itself.

CODEX (*codice*) This Latin word refers to a wooden writing block covered with wax; a set of parchment (made of dried and bleached sheepskin) or paper sheets tied together to form a manuscript book.

CRYPT In Greek and Roman times it indicated a hidden subterranean place which had a sacred or burial purpose. In Christian basilicas it was the underground space with a vaulted ceiling where the remains of the martyr to whom the church was dedicated were preserved. The columns of the crypt support the floor of the presbytery, the area of the church reserved for the officiating clergy, which is raised above the central nave.

CUPOLA Rounded covering of a building, situated on a circular or polygonal base and revolving around its own central axis. It can either be perfectly hemispherical or with an ellipsoidal or extended curve.

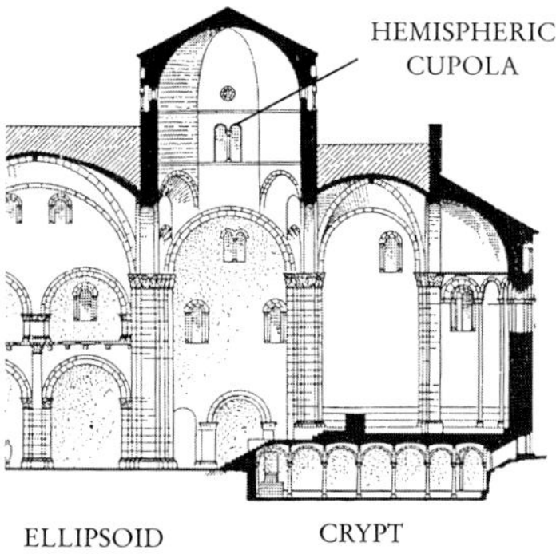

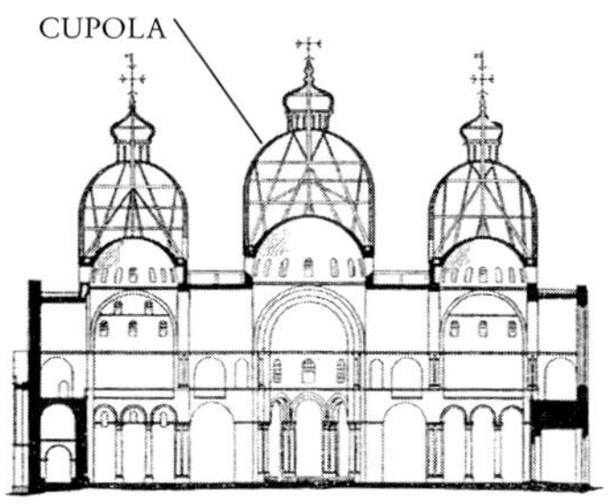

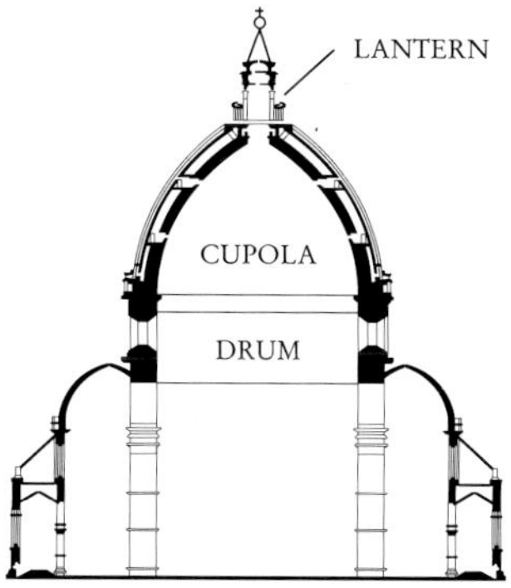

D

DIPTYCH (*dittico*) In ancient times, it was a writing tablet that was generally made of carved ivory and had waxed inner sides; diptychs were often presented as gifts on occasions marking remembrances or happy events. More commonly, the term is used to name a painting of a sacred subject consisting of two hinged and painted panels.

E

ENCRUSTATION Decoration of a smooth surface with materials of different colour and quality.

ENGRAVING (*incisione*) Technique which involves cutting out the lines of a pattern on metal, stone, or some other material; by extension, it is also used to refer to the depiction itself.

ETCHING (*acquaforte*) Engraving technique on metal, which is obtained by covering a sheet of copper or zinc with a greasy acid-resistant varnish, and then cutting the desired pattern in the protective layer with a metal needle. The sheet is then immersed in a corrosive bath of diluted nitric acid which etches the drawn lines into the metal. When the varnish has been removed, the sheet is inked and then cleaned in such a way that the ink only remains in the channels that have been cut by the metal point. The next step is printing: the pressure of a press imprints the pattern onto paper that has been dampened and placed in contact with the sheet.

F

FORESHORTENING (*scorcio*) A trick of perspective which makes it possible to obtain three-dimensional effects. It consists in the distortion or shortening of figures or bodies parallel to the plane of the image.

FRESCO (*affresco*) Wall painting technique which consists of painting rapidly onto damp mortar with coloured pigments dissolved in water; the paint filters into the plaster and is absorbed by the wall, and can only subsequently be retouched with distemper.

FUSION Technique of casting bronze in a closed form so as to produce sculptural works from a plaster cast. In *lost wax* casting, a wax negative of the model was made, inside of which there was a core of refractory material. The model was then covered with more refractory material; when heated, the wax melted and came out through special holes in the external covering, known as the *manto*. To give the sides of this covering maximum resistance, it was placed underground, and then the cast was made from molten bronze. The 'sand' or 'flask' system involved applying a layer of refractory earth and sand to the plaster model, then surrounding the whole thing (the matrix) with metal flasks. When the plaster cast was destroyed and a refractory core had been positioned inside, the molten bronze was then poured in.

G

GENRE-PAINTING A pictorial work that depicts everyday or anecdotal scenes of life, marked by a certain vivacity and with an abundance of detail.

GLAZE (*smalto*) Mixture of vitreous substances of varying colours, used for covering walls and for many different kinds of decoration. In Italian, the term *smalto* is also used in a more general sense to refer to all objects decorated with such material.

I

ICONOGRAPHY Broadly speaking, this is the discipline that studies the meaning of images from historical, cultural, allegorical, mythological, and religious points of view. Recently, a distinction has been made between *iconography* and *iconology*. The former is specifically concerned with the recognition and identification of the subject, while the latter is more concerned with the intrinsic meaning of the work.

INLAY Common in cabinet-making, this inlay work involves the composing of designs or patterns from woods of various different colours and qualities; it may also include the use of metals, mother-of-pearl, or ivory fixed onto an underlying surface.

L

LACQUER Coloured varnish with a resin base, applied in coats onto everyday objects, furniture, statues, and finished off with painted or engraved motifs; the decoration sometimes included silver or mother-of-pearl encrustations.

LAPIS LAZULI Hard, semi-precious stone, dark-blue in colour and with some golden veining.

LITHOGRAPHY Printing technique developed at the end of the eighteenth century and still used nowadays for important prints. It involves tracing a pattern with a greasy pencil onto a special kind of stone. The mark left by the pencil holds the ink, while the acid-treated stone repels it. The ink of the pattern is printed onto damp sheets with a press.

LOGGIA A structure which has at least one of its sides open to the exterior and has columns, *pillars*, or a balustrade. Often used as a place where people could meet.

LUMINISM Pictorial rendering of light on body surfaces by means of strong contrasts of light and shade, or through touches of light that stand out from a darker background.

M

MAIOLICA A form of earthenware covered by a layer of glaze; the name originates from the island of Majorca which sold it on a large scale.

METOPE Square panel, almost always decorated; metopes alternate with triglyphs in a Doric frieze.

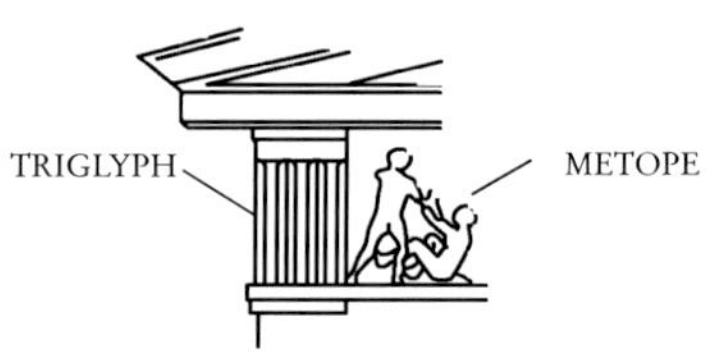

MINIATURE Pictorial technique of Eastern origin carried out on parchment, paper, or ivory. The term, in use since the tenth century A.D., derives from *minium*, an orange-red pigment used by scribes to trace rubrics or the decorated initial letters of manuscripts. Also used to refer to each individual illustration in a *codex*.

MOSAIC Figurative technique based on the arrangement and juxtaposition of small pieces of stone, marble, or coloured glass called tesserae, which are applied onto a bed of lime. The procedure originated in the East, and although the Chaldeans only used it to a limited degree, the Egyptians did so widely and with great skill. The Greeks also used mosaic widely as a floor decoration, and it was much favoured by the Romans, who gave the name *opus sectile* to works made with rectangular pieces of stone, and *opus tassellatum* to those with cubic pieces. The wall mosaics made from glass tesserae date back to the Alexandrine era and were the most typically representative technique used in Byzantine art: the small brightly-coloured tesserae which were sometimes laid out in an undulating manner (*opus vermiculatum*) were made particularly shiny by the skilful use of gold leaf (metallic tesserae) which were carefully positioned with varying degrees of inclination in relation to the surface level.

MOTHER-OF-PEARL Inner part of pearl-oysters used in cabinet-making and in the decoration of objects such as fans, snuffboxes, caskets, etc.

MYTHOLOGY The myths and legends of a people.

N

NAVE (*navata*) Longitudinal area of a church, divided by rows of columns or *pillars*. There may be one or more of such naves; the central one is called the main nave, while the flanking ones are called side naves.

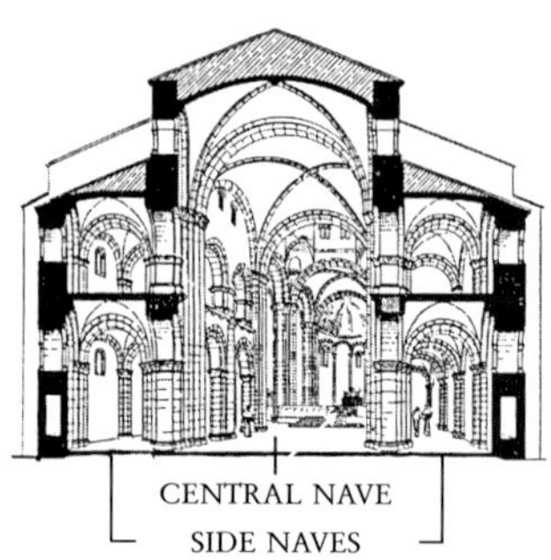

O

OBELISK Very long monolithic pillar, with a pyramidal-shaped end, and often decorated with numerous hieroglyphic inscriptions. They are of Eastern origin and are characteristic of Egyptian art, often being positioned for celebratory or ornamental purposes on a square base.

P

PALETTE Object on which the painter mixes oil colours, temperas, or watercolours; it is a simple piece of wood, enamelled metal, or porcelain which has a hole into which one's fingers can be inserted so as to provide support along with the forearm. By extension, it has also come to mean the characteristic chromatic range of a particular painter.

PANEL

1. Term generally used to indicate a wooden support on which the artist paints.
2. (*pannello* or *formella*) Flat surface of a structure, generally framed by a cornice, which may be important for the construction but is more often ornamental. In such a case it is painted or carved. The term can also be used to indicate each of the painted boards forming a polyptych.

PANTHEON Originally it was the temple dedicated to all the Gods, but subsequently the name was used for the sacred monumental building erected to the memory of illustrious men. The term also indicates the panoply of divinities of a polytheistic religious system.

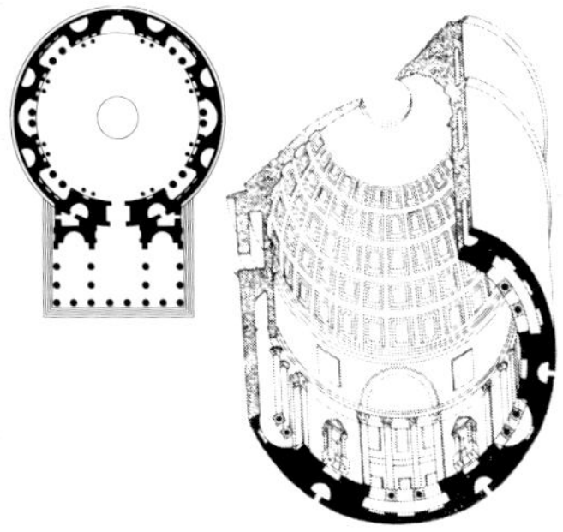

Pantheon of Rome

PARTITION (*tramezzo*) Thin wall in wood or masonry, which was erected in medieval churches to divide the section of the building reserved for the clergy from that for the congregation.

PENDENTIVE (*pennacchio*) A curved triangle forming the intersection between the square or polygonal section of a building and the curve of a dome. The term may also indicate the wall surfaces between two adjoining arches.

PERSPECTIVE A branch of descriptive geometry dealing with the representation of three-dimensional bodies on a surface from a specific point of view. In the field of art, the term is used more generally to refer to the way particular artists or historical periods represent space; as a consequence, there are as many forms of perspective as there are conceptions of space in the various different epochs and cultures.

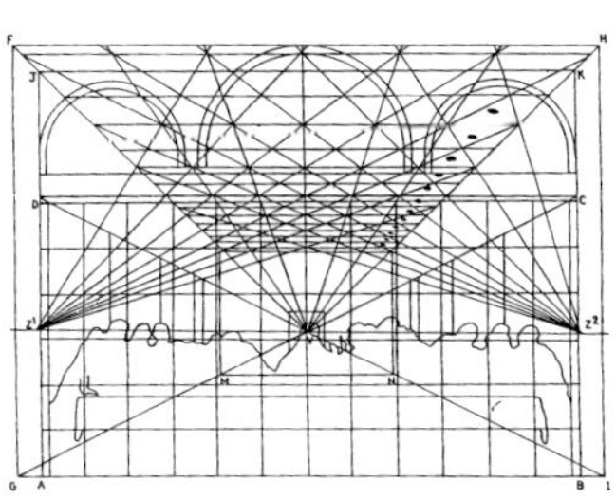

PERSPECTIVE DIAGRAM OF LEONARDO'S LAST SUPPER

PILLAR (*pilastro*) An architectural structure which is generally quadrangular but may also be polygonal or of a compound form. It has the same function as a column and may be smooth or decorated, with or without a base or capital, and either on its own, in a corner, or up against a wall.

PLAN (*pianta*) The design of a construction, a part thereof, or of an architectural element represented in a horizontal section at a given level. The Greek cross plan has the structure of a cross with four arms of equal length; the Latin cross plan has the form of a cross whose cross arm is significantly shorter than the longitudinal one. The radial plan is typical of Romanesque churches and is characterized by a series of small *apses*, which can be reached by an aisle called the *ambulatory*, arranged in a radial pattern around the main apse.

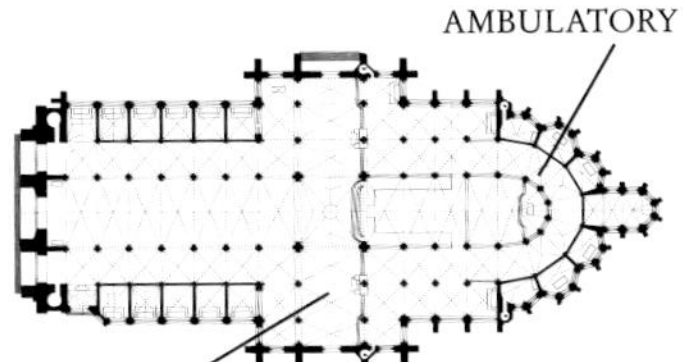

PLANIMETRIC PLAN A further way of describing a *plan* in technical design; it is generally used to refer to a group consisting of more than one building.

PLASTER (*intonaco*) The smoothed and levelled mortar which is the preliminary surface for mural pictures.

PLASTICITY The impression given by a figurative work of being three-dimensional.

POLYCHROMATIC Something with various different colours, usually creating a pleasing decorative effect.

PORCELAIN A very hard-paste ceramic obtained from kaolin mixed with quartz and feldspar and fired at an extremely high temperature. Produced in ancient times in China, it spread to Europe in the eighteenth century.

PORTAL Monumental entrance to civic and cathedral buildings, where elaborate reliefs or full-blown architectural compositions flank and crown the entrance.

PULPIT (*pulpito* or *pergamo*) The raised, independent platforms which in Christian churches are used by the officiant to preach to the congregation.

Q

QUADRATURA The backdrop scene painted onto vaults, cupolas, walls, and ceilings in the seventeenth and eighteenth centuries, which gave an effect of real architectural perspective. This particular form of frescoed decoration was practised by the so-called *quadraturisti*.

R

ROSE WINDOW (*rosone*) Large circular window with splays and radial sections, with a mainly ornamental function, found on the facade of a church above the *portal* or sometimes at the end of the *transept*.
It is characteristic of Romanesque and Gothic cathedrals. When there are small radiating columns it takes the name of wheel window.

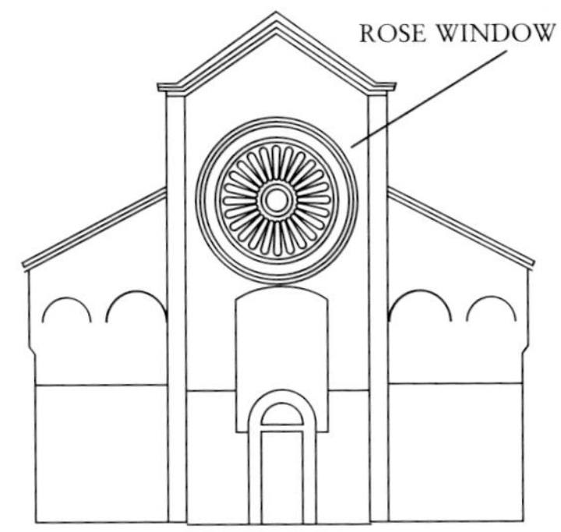

S

SACRISTY A room adjoining the church where the vestments, altar cloths, and holy vessels are kept in cupboards; these are often carved or inlaid.

SANGUINE (*sanguigna*) Ochre red pastel, and by extension also the picture produced with it.

SARCOPHAGUS Ancient stone or marble funerary urn of particular solemnity. The term comes from the Greek *sarkophàgos*, which literally means 'that which consumes flesh', and is the name of a calcareous stone which was attributed with the property of rapidly consuming corpses.

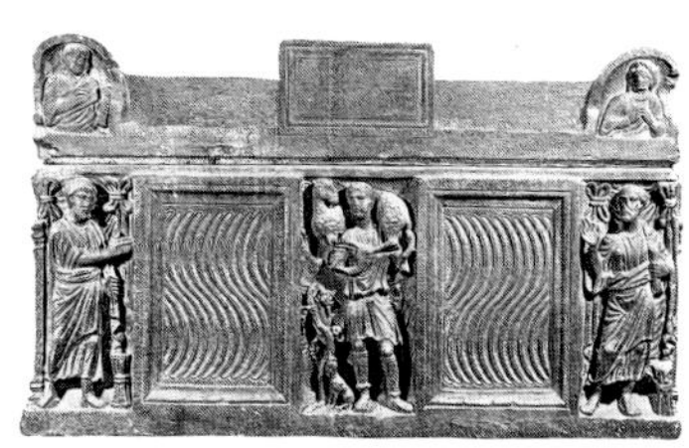

SCRIPTORIUM Room in a monastery, cathedral, or bishop's school reserved for the transcription and illustration of ancient texts.

SCROLL (*rotolo*) Ancient manuscript consisting of strips of papyrus wrapped around a small wooden or bone cylinder. By extension, the word is also used to refer to medieval paper documents wrapped in a similar way, such as the 'liturgical scrolls', used in southern Italy from the tenth to the fourteenth centuries, which bore the text of prayers interspersed with *miniatures*.

SFUMATO Similar pictorial technique to that of *chiaroscuro*, it is based on the delicate grading of light and shade, and is used in particular in reference to the work of Leonardo da Vinci and his pupils.

SKETCH (*schizzo*) Rapidly executed drawing or painting done to capture the essential features of an idea or the preliminary image to be used in the definitive work.

STAINED GLASS (*vetrata*) Consists of a set of variously coloured glass pieces, held in a lead framework, forming figurative compositions or ornamental designs. In order to avoid an excessive reduction in the size of the tesserae of glass used for complex depictions, *grisaille* was used. This was a vitreous mixture which covered to varying degrees, enabling the delineation and creation of shades in the composition, thus making the outlines of the figures more evident.

STIACCIATO Relief or very slight protuberance, typical of the early Renaissance, which evokes the depth of space; the illusion of the degradation of planes is due to the skilful use of perspective.

STILL LIFE (*natura morta*) The painting of flowers, fruit, game, and various objects. Already present in Flemish fifteenth century art, it spread through Europe as an independent genre above all in the seventeenth century.

STONE AND WOOD INLAY (tarsia) Consists of wooden or marble pieces which are cut and arranged according to a pre-established design. Synonymous with 'intarsia'.

STUCCO Modelling material which solidifies slowly and consists of lime, fired chalk, pozzolana, clay, and marble dust. Used above all in interiors to cover ceilings and such like with relief decorations. It may be coloured or adorned with gold leaf.

T

TAPESTRY (*arazzo*) Hand-woven drape made by arranging weft threads so as to form a picture or design. Used as a sumptuous wall-hanging decoration.

TESSERAE (*tessere* or *tasselle*) The small pieces of stone or vitreous material which are used for *mosaics*.

TONDO Circular painting or bas-relief, produced particularly in the Renaissance.

TRANSEPT (*transetto*) Cross *nave* of churches with a Latin cross-shaped plan.

TROMPE-L'OEIL In French this means 'deceives the eye'. A kind of painting characterized by an accentuated naturalism where the use of tricks of perspective and composition give illusionistic effects and suggest surprisingly concrete images and spaces.

TYMPANUM Triangular-shaped architectural form, either carved or smooth, lying between the *trabeation* and the oblique *cornices* of the *pediment*.

V

VAULT (*volta*) Curved covering of a building formed by stone *arches* which rest on imposts and are mutually-supporting. They have different names according to their characteristics: the *circular* vault is formed by curved arches forming a semicircumference; the *barrel* vault has a semicylindrical profile; the *cross* vault is formed by the perpendicular intersection of two barrel vaults; the *Gothic cross* vault consists of two load-bearing arches (or *vaulting ribs*) which discharge the weight of the entire vault onto the four corner pillars of the *bay*.

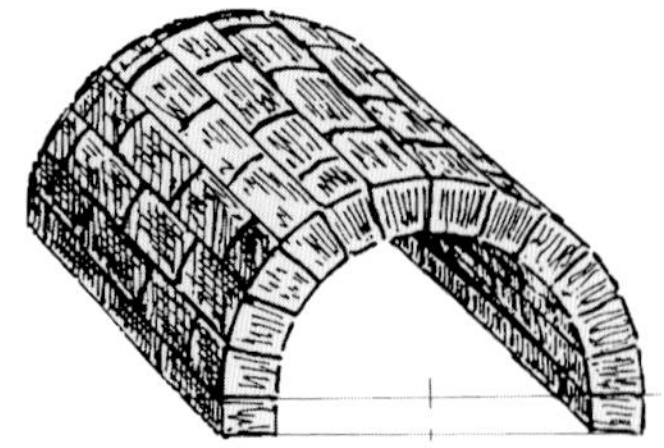

BARREL VAULT

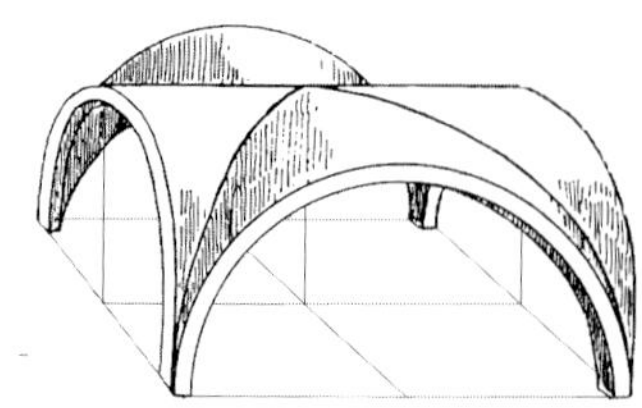

CROSS VAULT

W

WALL-PAINTING A picture painted on the walls of a building. Also known as a *mural*.

WATERCOLOUR (*acquerello*) Painting technique whereby coloured pigments, mixed with gum arabic and diluted in water at the moment of use, are applied with a brush onto paper or silk. Watercolour painting does not allow for 'second-thoughts' or retouching, and paler colours are obtained not by adding white, but by diluting with water.

INDEX OF NAMES AND WORKS

The numbers in italics refer to the biographical pages dedicated to each artist; the titles of the illustrated works are listed below.

INDEX OF PLACES

PHOTOGRAPHIC ACKNOWLEDGEMENTS

Apart from those included in the other acknowledgements, all of the photos are from the Giunti Archives (in particular those of the following photographers are listed: Cameraphoto, Venice: 64b, 70b. Claudio Carretta, Pontedera: 44c, 45. Pino dell'Aquila, Turin: 382b. Stefano Giraldi, Florence: 24, 102b, 103a, 122a, 134a, 135b, 139b. Nicola Grifoni, Antella: 8a, 9, 25, 29, 34a, 34b, 35a, 35b, 66b, 91b, 103b, 110-11, 122b, 131a, 132b, 132c, 133c, 134b, 139b, 150c, 163, 178b, 179, 222b, 224a, 231. Marco Rabatti-Serge Domingie, Florence: 6, 8b, 14, 55, 58, 59a, 59b, 61a, 67, 71, 72a, 74b, 74c, 85b, 88b, 89a, 89b, 91a, 92c, 94b, 101, 105b, 118a, 118b, 118c, 119a, 119b, 119c, 120b, 121a, 124a, 124b, 125a, 125b, 128, 129a, 129b, 130b, 131b, 138b, 142a, 146b, 150a, 154b, 155b, 156, 173, 182b, 185, 190b, 192b, 195, 196a, 196b, 198c, 255a, 257, 260c, 269, 270, 271, 273, 294a, 307, 318a, 318b, 319b, 319c, 324a, 327b, 328a, 328b, 329b, 330b, 331a, 334b, 335b, 342a, 343b, 350a. Foto Saporetti, Milan: 344-45. Humberto Serra, Rome: 13, 213a, 247, 248a, 263).

Other acknowledgements: Archivio Marco Rabatti-Serge Domingie, Florence: 10, 42b, 50a, 52b, 65, 66a, 68a, 69, 70a, 72b, 95c, 113b, 114, 116b, 117a, 117b, 136a, 137b, 139a, 157a, 157b, 164-65, 170b, 175, 186b, 206-207, 219a, 227, 296, 325c. Archivio Scala, Florence: 52a, 90a, 94a, 234a, 276b, 324b, 325b, 326b, 350b, 352b, 379a, 379b. Archivio Vasari, Rome: 249. Courtesy Biblioteca Apostolica Vaticana: 41a, 41b. Courtesy Cassa di Risparmio di Firenze: 201b. Zeno Colantoni, Rome: 302. Courtesy Fondazione di Studi di Storia dell'Arte Roberto Longhi: 209. Courtesy Massimo Listri, Florence: 19, 37a, 37b. Courtesy Monte de' Paschi di Siena/Foto 3 Lensini, Siena: 60b. Franco Cosimo Panini Editore, Modena-foto Ghigo Roli: 30, 31, 33. Museumsfoto B.P. Keiser, Braunschweig, Herzog Anton Ulrich Museum: 186a. Renzo Piano Building Workshop, Genoa: photo M. Denancé, 400; photo S. Goldberg, 398a; photo J. Gollings, 398-99.